MW00825073

A Hunter Must Hunt

When we made the official guide to Dark Souls we didn't really know what we were getting into. We hadn't worked with Fromsoft before, and though we'd played and loved Demon's Souls we hadn't got a real look behind the systems that make their games work so well. You might think that by now, with Bloodborne, we would know what to expect from Mr. Miyazaki and his team. But Bloodborne refuses to keep things simple or follow a pattern; we had to completely rethink how to structure the guide, and even then it often defied our attempts at order.

We care a great deal about Bloodborne, and want this book to be accurate and useful long after the game's release, so we've continued testing and writing long past our initial deadlines. We visited Fromsoft, talked with Mr. Miyazaki and got a deep look behind the scenes of the game's creation. With the content we've been able to add as a result, a better understanding of the game is possible. The detailed attack data in the Arsenal & Attire chapter and the area breakdowns of the Progression Guide give you the power to plan new ways to play, long after you've seen the hidden ending.

This book isn't going to make Bloodborne easy. The maps might let you know where a Blood Rock is, and the text will tell you how to reach it, but you'll still have to somehow get past those Winter Lanterns without getting Frenzied to death before you can blink. The Bestiary will tell you to use Sedatives and the Training Manual says to keep your Insight low, and maybe if you can use the Lore Index you can figure out why having less Insight might make Frenzy weaker in the first place. There's a reason for everything in Bloodborne, and if you study its many parts close enough you might be able to figure them out. And that, we hope, is the real value of this guide: its ability to provide some insight.

Chapter Overview

About the Data

We've made every effort to update the data and content in this book so that almost everything you'll find on the pages that follow is accurate according to Bloodborne's final patch,1.09. Some values that have changed in patches since this book's first printing were sadly not possible to update, but this represents just a tiny fraction of the total data.

Lore Index

At the back of the book, in addition to the normal index, you'll find the Lore Index. Using this, you can find the lore text for every item as it appears throughout the guide, all sorted according to relevant topics you may want to read about.

Table of Contents

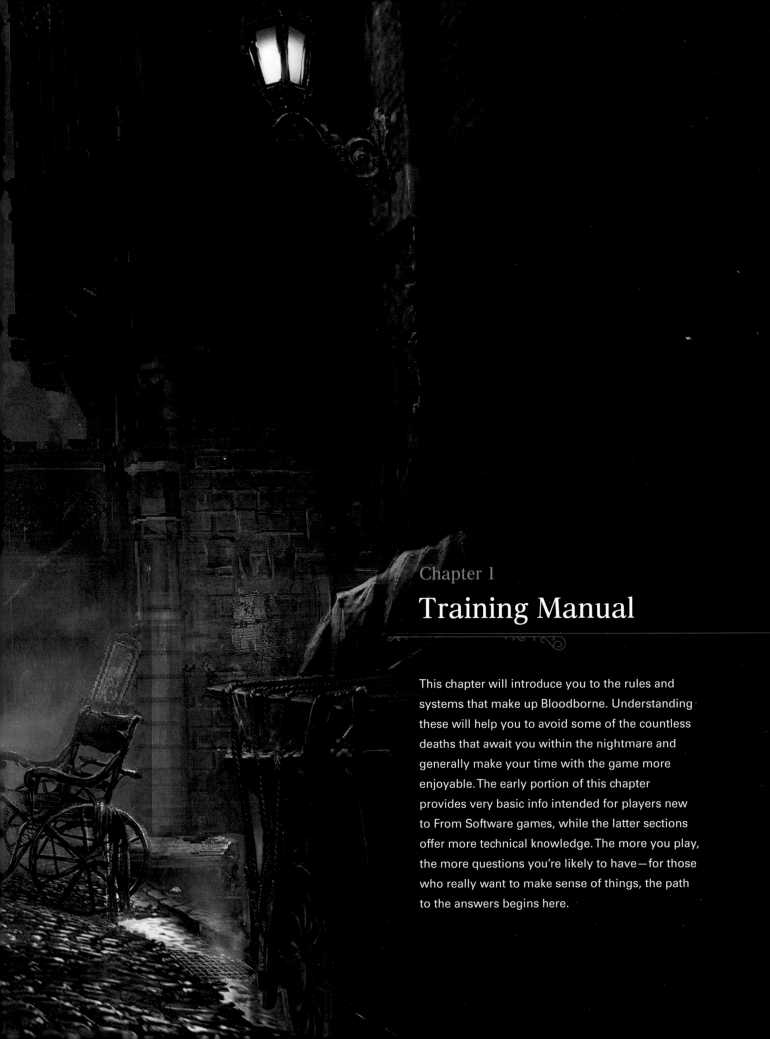

Chapter 1

Training Manual

This chapter will introduce you to the rules and systems that make up Bloodborne. Understanding these will help you to avoid some of the countless deaths that await you within the nightmare and generally make your time with the game more enjoyable. The early portion of this chapter provides very basic info intended for players new to From Software games, while the latter sections offer more technical knowledge. The more you play, the more questions you're likely to have—for those who really want to make sense of things, the path to the answers begins here.

Getting Started

This section will explain the finer points of starting a new character. It will also cover the HUD and basic in-game menus, as well as general system-related information that new players will need to get familiar with. If you are new and overwhelmed, this is the place to begin!

Saving & Loading

Bloodborne does not allow manual saves. Any time something happens, the game will auto-save. The game will also periodically auto-save even when nothing is going on. This means that if you fight through a difficult level and lose against the boss, you can't just load a save file at the boss. You'll need to play through the level again.

The game also cannot be paused, but you can quit via the menu at any time, and doing so will save your progress. When you load your game, your character will be in the same spot as it was when you quit. The exception to this rule is boss fights. If you quit in a boss fight, you'll be placed outside the boss's room and the boss will be fully healed. Of course, any healing items that you used before you quit will be gone. There is little to be gained by quitting mid-fight against a boss unless you want to fight the boss again from full health.

This is a screen you may see often, but don't get discouraged.

Quitting

You may be tempted to bypass the game's auto-save feature by turning off the console or exiting without using the in-game menus; that is a bad idea. Although rare, there is a chance that your save file will be corrupted. If that happens, your character and all the work you put into it will be gone, so always quit from the menu.

Character Creation

When creating a character, you're free to choose their name and gender, select an age and an origin and customize your their appearance. Name, gender, age and appearance are cosmetic only and offer no gameplay effects; your character's origin, however, does affect the game by determining your character's starting stats.

There are two primary considerations you should keep in mind when choosing your origin: the stat you want to focus on and the stat that you don't want to increase. All origins start with the same equipment, and eight out of the nine origins start at level 10. The Waste of Skin starts at level 4, but has exactly 6 fewer stat points than the others, so in the long run, they can all reach the same maximum level.

Origin	Lvl	Echoes	Vit	End	Str	Skl	Bld	Arc
Milquetoast	10	300	11	10	12	10	9	8
Lone Survivor	10	420	14	11	11	10	7	7
Troubled Childhood	10	360	9	14	9	13	6	9
Violent Past	10	180	12	11	15	9	6	7
Professional	10	240	9	12	9	15	7	8
Military Veteran	10	320	10	10	14	13	7	6
Noble Scion	10	540	7	8	9	13	14	9
Cruel Fate	10	500	10	12	10	9	5	14
Waste of Skin	4	10	10	9	10	9	7	9

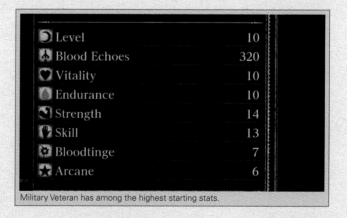

Level	10
Blood Echoes	320
Vitality	10
Endurance	10
Strength	14
Skill	13
Bloodtinge	7
Arcane	6

Military Veteran has among the highest starting stats.

Milquetoast

This is a good choice if you intend to increase all of your stats evenly. If you intend to keep one stat low, however, this might not be an ideal choice.

Lone Survivor

Survivors start with the highest base vitality, which means they have the highest starting hit points. With the importance of the Regain system, high HP is a true blessing.

Troubled Childhood

This origin gives you the highest endurance; if you are worried about stamina early in the game it can be a good choice.

Violent Past

If you have a history of violence, you'll find that your character has very high starting strength. The blunt force of the Hunter Axe goes well with your violent strength.

Professional

Professionals are focused in skill. The Threaded Cane will serve you better than the Hunter Axe with this origin.

Military Veteran

Veterans have good strength and skill, but they begin with the lowest arcane stat. This origin can be great if you don't want to use elemental weapons or magic items.

Noble Scion

Scions begin with high skill and the highest bloodtinge of any origin by far. This is great if you want to fight from range with guns, but, with the lowest starting vitality, you'll need the firepower!

Cruel Fate

Those branded with a cruel fate begin with the lowest bloodtinge but the highest arcane power. If you want to eschew firearms in favor of elemental weapons and magic items, this could be the origin for you.

Waste of Skin

Despite being the lowest level origin, the Waste of Skin is fairly well-rounded. It isn't the single lowest in any stat. If you plan to specialize in some stats and ignore others, this origin isn't a great choice. It is an option if you want a character that raises all stats evenly (or simply want to beat the game at the lowest level possible).

1

Menus & HUD

Here we'll look at the HUD and some of the key menus that you'll use often. Some of these elements are very useful and not fully explained within the game.

Messages

Many of the topics covered in this section are also given very brief explanations in the game, by way of the messages you'll find on he floor in early areas. When you see a glowing patch on the ground, a closer inspection will reveal that it's a note, hand delivered by the messengers. Examining it will bring up a tip on a basic gameplay element.

HUD

The HUD provides critical information that is necessary in order to effectively get through the game, including your health and stamina gauges. It is possible to turn the HUD off, but it's really not advised to do so. The screen here shows all of the HUD elements you can see during normal play, and a basic description is provided for each element.

❶ Health Gauge The size of your health gauge depends on your vitality stat.

❷ Stamina Gauge The size of your stamina gauge increases with your Endurance stat.

❸ Quick Item The currently selected Quick Item is shown here. Press ⊚ to use it or ♦ to select other Quick Items.

❹ Blood Vials The number here shows how many Blood Vials you are carrying. When you are at the maximum possible, the number will be blue.

❺ Quicksilver Bullets The number beside the bullet icon shows how many Quicksilver Bullets you currently have. If you're at the maximum the number will be blue, and if it drops to 0 you won't be able to shoot until you acquire more bullets.

❻ Blood Bullets This number only appears if you've pressed ♦ to generate Blood Bullets at the cost of health. The maximum number of Blood bullets is five.

❼ Weapon Mode This small symbol simply shows which mode your trick weapon is in; when the circle is filled the weapon is in its transformed mode.

❽ Blood Echoes This number is the amount of Blood Echoes you are currently carrying.

❾ Insight This number tells you how much Insight you currently have.

Weapon Info Menu

Most of the menus are easy to understand, but none are more important or quite as hard to fully grasp as the weapon menu. In the Inventory menu, pressing on one of the listed weapons (or when looking at a weapon in the shop), will bring up the detailed weapon info menu, which we'll take a close look at here.

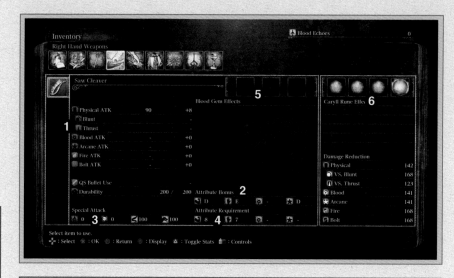

1 **Damage Types** These are the different types of damage a weapon can inflict. Enemies have separate defense values against each of these types, so it's important to know which type your weapon uses. For much more on this, see the Damage Calculation section later in this chapter, and consult the tables for your weapon in the Arsenal & Attire chapter.

2 **Attribute Bonuses** Attribute Bonuses are also known as "Scaling." They show how well a weapon scales with of your damage-increasing stats: Strength, Skill, Arcane and Bloodtinge. The scaling is graded on an alphabetic scale: E, D, C, B, A and S. A weapon with C for Strength won't gain much attack power as you raise your Strength stat, but if it also has S for Skill it will gain much more if you raise your Skill stat instead.

3 **Special Attacks** The numbers shown here detail your weapon's ability to deal out status ailments and racial damage bonuses. The first two will remain at 0 unless your weapon is Chikage, with it's built-in Rapid Poison, or has a Blood Gem equipped that allows it to inflict Slow Poison or Rapid Poison. The next two values show if the weapon can deal more or less than the default 100% damage against either Beast or Kin enemies.

4 **Attribute Requirements** These values show the minimum amount of a given stat, either Strength, Skill, Bloodtinge, Arcane, or a mix of these, that is required in order to wield the weapon.

5 **Blood Gem Slots** These three boxes at the top are where you'll see any Blood Gems you've fortified the weapon with. The Blood Gem Effects are listed below these, and there can be up to a maximum of three effects per Gem.

6 **Caryll Rune Slots** The four slots in the top right are for equipping Caryll Runes. There are three normal slots and one Oath Rune slot. The space below the slots details the effects of your equipped Runes. You'll need the Rune Workshop Tool in order to equip Runes.

Quick Items

When you press the Options button to bring up the main menu, the six slots you'll see on the bottom row are your Quick Items. The item displayed on your HUD (once you've set one) is the currently selected Quick Item, and you can press to use it instantly. If you haven't set any Quick Items yet, you should immediately do so. Simply select one of those bottom slots and choose an item from your list to put there. Then select the other slots (or press R2 and L2 to scroll between them while in your item list) to quickly set up the items you use most often for instant use. Once they are set up, you can use to scroll through them to find the one you need. It's a good idea to only set up items that you need in the current area or battle, and leave slots empty when you don't really need to fill them. This ensures that you won't have to scroll trough all six to get to the one you want in a hurry. Reorganize them as often as needed, but keep a couple of your most used items in the list as a constant point of reference. For example, if you always have Molotov Cocktails in the first slot and Antidotes in the fourth, you can use these to always know which way to scroll to the item you need.

You'll come to rely on Quick Items against bosses, especially those weak to fire. Remember to put the Molotovs and Oil Urns beside each other!

The bottom row of the main menu shows your equipped Quick Items.

Personal Effects

Pressing the right side of the touchpad brings up your Personal Effects menu. This gives you another six slots to access items from, much like the Quick Items. They are not quite as quick to use, though, because you must press the touchpad and then ⊗ to use them. This means they are best used for non-urgent items, such as the Beckoning Bell and Notebook, or for items you'll use often but don't want to take up a Quick Item slot with, such as the Monocular or Hand Lantern.

Leveling Up & Stats

You'll need to acquire 1 point of Insight in order to level up. Upon entering the Hunter's Dream with 1 point of Insight, you'll be greeted by an animate doll. The Doll will allow you to spend Blood Echoes gathered from defeated foes to level up your character's stats.

The equipment and items that you can use are determined by your stats. Your stats also determine how many hits you can take before dying, how many times you can attack before needing to rest, and how much damage you'll deal with various weapons.

Blood Echoes

Blood Echoes represent both currency and experience in the world of Bloodborne. They are primarily gained through defeating foes, but you can also get them from special Blood Echo items. Tougher foes typically award more Blood Echoes when killed. You'll spend these to level up or to buy items from the Messenger Shop.

If you die while carrying Blood Echoes, you'll lose them all, though you do have a chance to get them back. Return to the spot where you died and you'll find them glowing on the ground; interact with them to retrieve them all. If you die a second time before gathering them, they're lost forever. Be careful!

Where's My Blood?

Sometimes when you die, you'll make your way back to pick up your Blood Echoes, only to find nothing on the floor. Instead you might be confronted with the beast that killed you, now with the addition of glowing white eyes. This creature didn't just claim your life, it claimed your Blood Echoes, too. In order to retrieve your lost Echoes, you'll need to get revenge on the beast and kill it. Sometimes, it may not even be the exact enemy that killed you that has your Blood Echoes. If an enemy is positioned within 15 meters of the spot where you died they can also collect the Echoes. Not all enemies can collect Blood Echoes – the ones that can are listed here.

This particular Scourge Beast is very likely to take your Blood Echoes...

...and you're just as likely to reclaim them once you have a weapon.

Blood Echo-collecting Enemies

Scourge Beast	p266
Loran Cleric	p304
Bell Ringer	p287
Brainsucker*	p273
Beast Patient	p236
Labyrinth Rat	p233
Nightmare Apostle	p247
Rotted Corpse	p233
Hunting Dog	p238
Keeper's Hunting Dog	p305
Carrion Crow	p231
Gravekeeper Scorpion	p252
Lost Child of Antiquity	p244
Rabid Dog	p230
Large Snake Ball	p279
Snake Ball	p241
Maneater Boar	p270
Maneater Boar (Eyeballs)*	p270
Ashen Blood Beast Patient	p237
Large Nightmare Apostle	p289
Children of Rom	p344
Executioner	p269
Watcher's Gravediggers	p254
Kidnapper	p276
Skeletal Puppet	p249
Mad One	p274
Pilgrim	p252
Eye Collector	p277
Garden of Eyes	p285
Shadow of Yharnam	p338
Bloodlicker	p280
Keeper of the Old Lords*	p378
Snake Parasite	p240
Loran Silverbeast*	p281
Mergo's Attendants	p248
Mergo's Chief Attendant	p290
Cain's Servants	p242
Giant Lost Child	p282
Small Celestial Emissary	p241
Celestial Child	p247
Fluorescent Flower	p286
Winter Lantern	p284
Large Huntsmen	p231
Hemwick Grave Women	p238
Wheelchair Huntsmen	p229
Huntsman	p225
Huntsman's Minions	p267
Church Servants	p234
Church Giants	p271
Scholar	p245
Labyrinth Ritekeeper	p253
Labyrinth Watchers	p249
Labyrinth Warriors	p302
Labyrinth Madmen	p299
Watcher Chieftain*	p294
Merciless Watchers*	p296
Evil Labyrinth Spirit	p298
Undead Giant*	p301
Beast-possessed Soul*	p275

*Dungeon boss versions excluded

Leveling Up

Speak to the Doll and select "Channel Blood Echoes" to level up. You'll need to pay Blood Echoes to do so, and each additional level will cost more than the last.

When leveling up, you can choose which of your stats to increase. Your stats define what your character can or can't do; each stat gives you different benefits and allows you to use different equipment more effectively. If you want to use a massive hammer, you'll need strength. If you want to attack with a katana, you'll need skill.

You can preview your level gains before confirming them; watch the Attributes pane closely to observe the effects your changes will have. Remember that blue numbers represent increases. You can push the Help button at any time if you forget what a stat does.

Choosing which stat to level up can be confusing. Here's a handy flowchart! I want to...

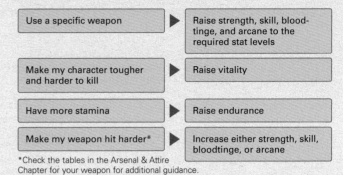

I want to...		Result
Use a specific weapon	▶	Raise strength, skill, bloodtinge, and arcane to the required stat levels
Make my character tougher and harder to kill	▶	Raise vitality
Have more stamina	▶	Raise endurance
Make my weapon hit harder*	▶	Increase either strength, skill, bloodtinge, or arcane

*Check the tables in the Arsenal & Attire Chapter for your weapon for additional guidance.

Blood Echoes Required Per Level

Lvl	Echoes	Lvl	Echoes	Lvl	Echoes	Lvl	Echoes	Lvl	Echoes	Lvl	Echoes	Lvl	Echoes	Lvl	Echoes	Lvl	Echoes	Lvl	Echoes
5	741	59	20777	113	80542	167	198044	221	392178	275	681841	329	1085927	383	1623333	437	2312954	491	3173686
6	758	60	21472	114	82135	168	200884	222	396616	276	688226	330	1094609	384	1634662	438	2327280	492	3191359
7	775	61	22181	115	83748	169	203751	223	401086	277	694650	331	1103337	385	1646044	439	2341665	493	3209097
8	793	62	22904	116	85381	170	206644	224	405590	278	701114	332	1112111	386	1657477	440	2356109	494	3226901
9	811	63	23640	117	87034	171	209564	225	410127	279	707617	333	1120931	387	1668964	441	2370612	495	3244770
10	829	64	24390	118	88707	172	212511	226	414697	280	714160	334	1129797	388	1680503	442	2385174	496	3262705
11	847	65	25154	119	90401	173	215484	227	419300	281	720743	335	1138710	389	1692095	443	2399795	497	3280706
12	1039	66	25932	120	92115	174	218485	228	423937	282	727366	336	1147668	390	1703740	444	2414476	498	3298773
13	1238	67	26724	121	93850	175	221513	229	428607	283	734029	337	1156674	391	1715438	445	2429216	499	3316905
14	1445	68	27530	122	95606	176	224568	230	433311	284	740732	338	1165726	392	1727189	446	2444016	500	3335104
15	1660	69	28351	123	97382	177	227650	231	438049	285	747476	339	1174825	393	1738993	447	2458876	501	3353369
16	1883	70	29186	124	99180	178	230760	232	442821	286	754259	340	1183971	394	1750851	448	2473796	502	3371700
17	2114	71	30036	125	100999	179	233897	233	447627	287	761084	341	1193164	395	1762762	449	2488775	503	3390098
18	2353	72	30901	126	102839	180	237062	234	452467	288	767949	342	1202404	396	1774727	450	2503815	504	3408562
19	2601	73	31780	127	104700	181	240255	235	457341	289	774855	343	1211691	397	1786746	451	2518915	505	3427093
20	2857	74	32675	128	106583	182	243476	236	462250	290	781802	344	1221026	398	1798818	452	2534075	506	3445691
21	3122	75	33585	129	108487	183	246725	237	467194	291	788790	345	1230408	399	1810945	453	2549296	507	3464356
22	3396	76	34510	130	110413	184	250002	238	472172	292	795819	346	1239838	400	1823126	454	2564577	508	3483088
23	3678	77	35450	131	112361	185	253307	239	477185	293	802889	347	1249316	401	1835361	455	2579919	509	3501887
24	3970	78	36406	132	114331	186	256641	240	482233	294	810001	348	1258841	402	1847650	456	2595322	510	3520754
25	4271	79	37377	133	116323	187	260004	241	487316	295	817154	349	1268415	403	1859994	457	2610786	511	3539688
26	4581	80	38364	134	118337	188	263395	242	492434	296	824349	350	1278037	404	1872392	458	2626311	512	3558689
27	4900	81	39367	135	120373	189	266815	243	497587	297	831586	351	1287707	405	1884845	459	2641897	513	3577758
28	5229	82	40386	136	122432	190	270264	244	502776	298	838864	352	1297425	406	1897353	460	2657545	514	3596895
29	5567	83	41421	137	124514	191	273742	245	508000	299	846185	353	1307192	407	1909916	461	2673254	515	3616100
30	5915	84	42472	138	126618	192	277249	246	513260	300	853548	354	1317007	408	1922534	462	2689024	516	3635373
31	6273	85	43539	139	128745	193	280785	247	518556	301	860953	355	1326871	409	1935207	463	2704856	517	3654714
32	6641	86	44623	140	130895	194	284351	248	523887	302	868400	356	1336784	410	1947936	464	2720750	518	3674123
33	7019	87	45724	141	133068	195	287946	249	529255	303	875890	357	1346746	411	1960720	465	2736706	519	3693601
34	7407	88	46841	142	135264	196	291571	250	534659	304	883422	358	1356757	412	1973559	466	2752724	520	3713147
35	7805	89	47975	143	137483	197	295226	251	540099	305	890996	359	1366817	413	1986454	467	2768804	521	3732762
36	8214	90	49126	144	139726	198	298910	252	545575	306	898615	360	1376927	414	1999405	468	2784946	522	3752446
37	8634	91	50294	145	141992	199	302625	253	551088	307	906276	361	1387085	415	2012412	469	2801151	523	3772199
38	9064	92	51479	146	144282	200	306370	254	556637	308	913980	362	1397294	416	2025475	470	2817418	524	3792020
39	9505	93	52681	147	146596	201	310145	255	562223	309	921727	363	1407552	417	2038594	471	2833748	525	3811911
40	9957	94	53901	148	148933	202	313950	256	567846	310	929517	364	1417860	418	2051769	472	2850141	526	3831871
41	10420	95	55138	149	151295	203	317786	257	572506	311	937351	365	1428218	419	2065001	473	2866597	527	3851900
42	10894	96	56393	150	153681	204	321652	258	579203	312	945229	366	1438626	420	2078289	474	2883115	528	3871999
43	11379	97	57666	151	156091	205	325549	259	584937	313	953150	367	1449084	421	2091634	475	2899697	529	3892167
44	11876	98	58956	152	158525	206	329477	260	590709	314	961115	368	1459592	422	2105036	476	2916342	530	3912405
45	12384	99	60265	153	160984	207	333436	261	596517	315	969124	369	1470151	423	2118495	477	2933050	531	3932713
46	12904	100	61592	154	163467	208	337426	262	602364	316	977177	370	1480760	424	2132010	478	2949822	532	3953091
47	13436	101	62937	155	165975	209	341447	263	608248	317	985274	371	1491420	425	2145583	479	2966657	533	3973539
48	13979	102	64300	156	168508	210	345499	264	614170	318	993415	372	1502131	426	2159213	480	2983556	534	3994057
49	14535	103	65682	157	171066	211	349583	265	620130	319	1001601	373	1512892	427	2172900	481	3000519	535	4014646
50	15103	104	67082	158	173649	212	353699	266	626128	320	1009831	374	1523705	428	2186645	482	3017546	536	4035305
51	15683	105	68501	159	176257	213	357846	267	632164	321	1018106	375	1534569	429	2200447	483	3034637	537	4056034
52	16275	106	69939	160	178890	214	362025	268	638238	322	1026426	376	1545484	430	2214307	484	3051792	538	4076834
53	16880	107	71396	161	181549	215	366236	269	644351	323	1034790	377	1556450	431	2228225	485	3069012	539	4097705
54	17497	108	72872	162	184234	216	370479	270	650502	324	1043200	378	1567468	432	2242201	486	3086296	540	4118647
55	18127	109	74367	163	186944	217	374754	271	656692	325	1051655	379	1578537	433	2256235	487	3103644	541	4139660
56	18770	110	75881	164	189680	218	379061	272	662921	326	1060155	380	1589658	434	2270327	488	3121057	542	4160744
57	19426	111	77415	165	192442	219	383401	273	669188	327	1068700	381	1600831	435	2284478	489	3138535	543	4181899
58	20095	112	78969	166	195230	220	387773	274	675495	328	1077291	382	1612056	436	2298687	490	3156078		

Vitality

Vitality determines the maximum amount of hit points (HP) you have. When your HP reaches 0, you die, so having a large maximum pool of HP is valuable by itself, but Bloodborne has specific systems that make having high HP even more important than you may initially assume.

Blood Vials, your main source of healing, restore a percentage of your maximum HP; the higher your vitality is, the more HP your healing items restore! Additionally, Bloodborne has a system called "Regain" that puts emphasis on being aggressive even after you've been hit by the enemy. This synergizes extremely well with high HP, as you can stay close and keep fighting without fear of a quick death.

HP Increase per Level of Vitality					
10	573	40	1325	70	1675
11	594	41	1346	71	1683
12	616	42	1366	72	1692
13	638	43	1386	73	1700
14	659	44	1405	74	1709
15	682	45	1424	75	1717
16	698	46	1442	76	1725
17	719	47	1458	77	1734
18	742	48	1474	78	1742
19	767	49	1489	79	1750
20	793	50	1500	80	1758
21	821	51	1508	81	1767
22	849	52	1517	82	1775
23	878	53	1526	83	1783
24	908	54	1535	84	1791
25	938	55	1544	85	1799
26	970	56	1553	86	1807
27	1001	57	1562	87	1814
28	1034	58	1571	88	1822
29	1066	59	1580	89	1830
30	1100	60	1588	90	1837
31	1123	61	1597	91	1845
32	1147	62	1606	92	1852
33	1170	63	1615	93	1860
34	1193	64	1623	94	1867
35	1216	65	1632	95	1874
36	1239	66	1641	96	1881
37	1261	67	1649	97	1888
38	1283	68	1658	98	1894
39	1304	69	1666	99	1900

Talk to the Doll to level up your character.

Stamina Increase per Level of Endurance					
10	91	21	112	31	136
11	93	22	115	32	139
12	95	23	117	33	141
13	97	24	119	34	144
14	98	25	121	35	146
15	100	26	124	36	149
16	102	27	126	37	152
17	104	28	129	38	154
18	106	29	131	39	157
19	108	30	133	40	160
20	110				

Slow Poison Resistance Increase per Level of Endurance					
10	30	40	107	70	128
11	36	41	–	71	129
12	42	42	108	72	130
13	48	43	109	73	131
14	54	44	110	74	–
15	60	45		75	132
16	62	46	111	76	133
17	65	47	112	77	134
18	68	48	113	78	–
19	70	49	–	79	135
20	73	50	114	80	136
21	76	51	115	81	–
22	78	52	–	82	137
23	81	53	116	83	138
24	84	54	117	84	139
25	86	55	118	85	–
26	89	56	–	86	140
27	92	57	119	87	141
28	94	58	120	88	142
29	97	59	121	89	–
30	100	60	–	90	143
31	–	61	122	91	144
32	101	62	123	92	–
33	102	63	124	93	145
34	–	64	–	94	146
35	103	65	125	95	147
36	104	66	126	96	–
37	105	67	–	97	148
38	–	68	127	98	149
39	106	69	–	99	150

Endurance

Your endurance determines your maximum stamina. You need stamina to attack and to defend. Bloodborne rewards players who attack frequently, so this is a very important stat. Endurance also increases your resistance to both Slow and Rapid Poison.

Rapid Poison Resistance Increase per Level of Endurance					
10	40	40	107	70	128
11	44	41	–	71	129
12	48	42	108	72	130
13	52	43	109	73	131
14	56	44	110	74	–
15	60	45		75	132
16	62	46	111	76	133
17	65	47	112	77	134
18	68	48	113	78	–
19	70	49	–	79	135
20	73	50	114	80	136
21	76	51	115	81	–
22	78	52	–	82	137
23	81	53	116	83	138
24	84	54	117	84	139
25	86	55	118	85	–
26	89	56	–	86	140
27	92	57	119	87	141
28	94	58	120	88	142
29	97	59	121	89	–
30	100	60	–	90	143
31	–	61	122	91	144
32	101	62	123	92	–
33	102	63	124	93	145
34	–	64	–	94	146
35	103	65	125	95	147
36	104	66	126	96	–
37	105	67	–	97	148
38	–	68	127	98	149
39	106	69	–	99	150

Strength

All right-hand weapons and most left-hand weapons require some level of strength to use. Many weapons also have their damage increased by raising your character's strength. Look through the Attack Power Increases tables in the Arsenal & Attire Chapter to see how much your character's strength will benefit your favorite weapon. Focus on strength if you want to engage in physical combat with heavy weapons.

Skill

Just as with strength, all right-hand weapons and most left-hand weapons require some level of skill to use. Many weapons also have their damage increased by your character's skill. Again, you can check the Attack Power Increases tables in the Arsenal & Attire Chapter to see how much your character's skill will benefit your favorite weapon. Raise this stat if you want to increase the physical damage of light weapons.

Bloodtinge

Bloodtinge is a requirement for and affects the attack power of many firearms, such as the Hunter Pistol, but it also affects the power of certain special weapons (primarily the Chikage). Once again, the Arsenal & Attire Chapter has tables that will show you which weapons pair well with bloodtinge. If you want to have powerful gun attacks, increase your bloodtinge.

Arcane

Similar to other stats, arcane is a requirement to use some weapons, and also increases the power of certain weapons, though it has a couple of other interesting points. First of all, most weapons have arcane scaling but don't actually use it by default. Instead, many weapons will only benefit from their natural arcane scaling when fitted with an elemental gem. Secondly, arcane scaling doesn't affect the physical damage of weapons; instead it will improve a weapon's arcane, fire, and bolt damage. Raising arcane is therefore important for those who use elemental weapons.

Increasing your arcane stat also raises your Discovery. This increases the odds of defeated enemies dropping items. It's not strictly required, but it does help with finding supplies while running Chalice Dungeons. If you want higher Discovery without putting points into arcane, you can always just equip an Eye Rune.

Finally, the arcane stat governs the usage of Magic Items. It determines which ones you can use and how powerful they are. These items are a special perk for those who invest heavily in arcane.

Discovery Increase per Level of Arcane

Lvl	Disc	Lvl	Disc	Lvl	Disc
10	106	24	150	38	186
11	109	25	154	39	188
12	112	26	157	40	190
13	115	27	160	41	192
14	119	28	163	42	194
15	122	29	166	43	195
16	125	30	170	44	197
17	128	31	172	45	200
18	131	32	174	46	202
19	135	33	176	47	204
20	138	34	178	48	206
21	141	35	180	49	208
22	144	36	182	50	209
23	147	37	184		

Physical Defense

As you level up, your physical defense will also increase. This is tied to your level. It doesn't matter which stat you increase; your physical defense will also go up. No matter which stats you choose to focus on, your character will become stronger and more resistant to enemy physical attacks. In other words, leveling up makes the game easier.

If you are having trouble, level up! In addition to any other benefits, you'll become harder to kill as your physical defense rises.

Defense Increase per Level

Lvl	Def	Lvl	Def	Lvl	Def	Lvl	Def	Lvl	Def	Lvl	Def	Lvl	Def
10	10	87	199	164	—	241	—	318	—	395	—	472	—
11	13	88	201	165	—	242	—	319	—	396	—	473	—
12	16	89	202	166	—	243	—	320	—	397	283	474	—
13	19	90	203	167	—	244	266	321	—	398	—	475	—
14	22	91	204	168	—	245	—	322	—	399	—	476	—
15	25	92	205	169	—	246	—	323	—	400	—	477	—
16	28	93	206	170	—	247	—	324	—	401	—	478	292
17	31	94	207	171	—	248	—	325	275	402	—	479	—
18	34	95	208	172	258	249	—	326	—	403	—	480	—
19	37	96	209	173	—	250	—	327	—	404	—	481	—
20	40	97	211	174	—	251	—	328	—	405	—	482	—
21	43	98	212	175	—	252	—	329	—	406	284	483	—
22	47	99	213	176	—	253	267	330	—	407	—	484	—
23	50	100	214	177	—	254	—	331	—	408	—	485	—
24	53	101	215	178	—	255	—	332	—	409	—	486	—
25	56	102	216	179	—	256	—	333	—	410	—	487	293
26	59	103	217	180	—	257	—	334	276	411	—	488	—
27	62	104	218	181	259	258	—	335	—	412	—	489	—
28	65	105	219	182	—	259	—	336	—	413	—	490	—
29	68	106	220	183	—	260	—	337	—	414	—	491	—
30	71	107	221	184	—	261	—	338	—	415	285	492	—
31	74	108	222	185	—	262	268	339	—	416	—	493	—
32	77	109	223	186	—	263	—	340	—	417	—	494	—
33	80	110	224	187	—	264	—	341	—	418	—	495	—
34	83	111	225	188	—	265	—	342	—	419	—	496	294
35	86	112	226	189	—	266	—	343	277	420	—	497	—
36	88	113	228	190	260	267	—	344	—	421	—	498	—
37	91	114	229	191	—	268	—	345	—	422	—	499	—
38	94	115	230	192	—	269	—	346	—	423	—	500	—
39	97	116	231	193	—	270	—	347	—	424	286	501	—
40	100	117	232	194	—	271	269	348	—	425	—	502	—
41	103	118	—	195	—	272	—	349	—	426	—	503	—
42	106	119	233	196	—	273	—	350	—	427	—	504	—
43	109	120	234	197	—	274	—	351	—	428	—	505	295
44	112	121	235	198	—	275	—	352	278	429	—	506	—
45	115	122	236	199	261	276	—	353	—	430	—	507	—
46	117	123	237	200	—	277	—	354	—	431	—	508	—
47	120	124	238	201	—	278	—	355	—	432	—	509	—
48	123	125	239	202	—	279	—	356	—	433	287	510	—
49	126	126	240	203	—	280	270	357	—	434	—	511	—
50	129	127	241	204	—	281	—	358	—	435	—	512	—
51	132	128	242	205	—	282	—	359	—	436	—	513	—
52	134	129	243	206	—	283	—	360	—	437	—	514	296
53	137	130	244	207	—	284	—	361	279	438	—	515	—
54	140	131	—	208	262	285	—	362	—	439	—	516	—
55	143	132	245	209	—	286	—	363	—	440	—	517	—
56	145	133	246	210	—	287	—	364	—	441	—	518	—
57	148	134	247	211	—	288	—	365	—	442	288	519	—
58	151	135	248	212	—	289	271	366	—	443	—	520	—
59	153	136	249	213	—	290	—	367	—	444	—	521	—
60	156	137	—	214	—	291	—	368	—	445	—	522	—
61	158	138	250	215	—	292	—	369	—	446	—	523	297
62	161	139	251	216	—	293	—	370	280	447	—	524	—
63	164	140	252	217	263	294	—	371	—	448	—	525	—
64	166	141	—	218	—	295	—	372	—	449	—	526	—
65	168	142	253	219	—	296	—	373	—	450	—	527	—
66	171	143	254	220	—	297	—	374	—	451	289	528	—
67	173	144	—	221	—	298	272	375	—	452	—	529	—
68	175	145	255	222	—	299	—	376	—	453	—	530	—
69	178	146	—	223	—	300	—	377	—	454	—	531	—
70	180	147	—	224	—	301	—	378	—	455	—	532	298
71	181	148	—	225	—	302	—	379	281	456	—	533	—
72	182	149	—	226	264	303	—	380	—	457	—	534	—
73	183	150	—	227	—	304	—	381	—	458	—	535	—
74	184	151	—	228	—	305	—	382	—	459	—	536	—
75	185	152	—	229	—	306	—	383	—	460	290	537	—
76	187	153	—	230	—	307	273	384	—	461	—	538	—
77	188	154	256	231	—	308	—	385	—	462	—	539	—
78	189	155	—	232	—	309	—	386	—	463	—	540	—
79	190	156	—	233	—	310	—	387	—	464	—	541	299
80	191	157	—	234	—	311	—	388	282	465	—	542	—
81	192	158	—	235	265	312	—	389	—	466	—	543	—
82	194	159	—	236	—	313	—	390	—	467	—		
83	195	160	—	237	—	314	—	391	—	468	—		
84	196	161	—	238	—	315	—	392	—	469	291		
85	197	162	—	239	—	316	274	393	—	470	—		
86	198	163	257	240	—	317	—	394	—	471	—		

Stamina

Stamina is an important resource. Attacking, rolling, dashing, back-stepping, and quickstepping all consume stamina; if you don't have enough, you won't be able to perform those actions. Being unable to roll or quickstep is a huge problem, as those are your primary means of defense.

Your stamina regenerates naturally over time, but it won't regenerate while you are running, attacking, rolling, etc. Shooting firearms doesn't consume stamina, but it does pause stamina regeneration. Using items does not interfere with your stamina regeneration. Always watch your stamina closely. If it gets low, try to either back away from the enemy or get behind it. Look for a safe spot where you can wait while your stamina refills. Quickstepping, rolling, and backstepping all cost 10 points of stamina.

Negative Stamina

No matter how much stamina your attacks costs, you can perform it as long as you have at least one point of stamina. The problem, though, is that your stamina will go into negative numbers, and you won't be able to take any action that consumes stamina until it recovers. This unfortunately includes rolling and quickstepping. You'll be absolutely helpless until you recover, and must wait until your stamina comes back.

There are many ways you can avoid this. One is by increasing your stamina gauge, either by improving your endurance or equipping Anti-Clockwise Metamorphosis Runes. Another is to raise your stamina regeneration by slotting the Hunter Oath Rune, equipping Radiant gems, or using Arianna's Blood. Or, you could simply be careful not to attack when your stamina is low! If you do find yourself in a negative stamina situation, remember you can still defend yourself by walking under or away from enemy attacks. It isn't ideal, but you might be surprised what can be dodged without even rolling.

Insight

Insight is another form of resource for your character. It appears next to the eye icon on the upper-right of the game screen. It can be used as currency in the Insight Shop or to participate in online multiplayer. See the Multiplayer section later in this chapter for more info on the importance of Insight for online play.

Insight also has other effects. High levels of Insight reduce your Beasthood and your Frenzy resistance; some enemies even become stronger if your Insight is high, which means that having a large stock of Insight can be a double-edged sword.

Your character may experience visual and auditory hallucinations at high levels of Insight. Or perhaps they are not hallucinations at all... either way, this is tied to the story, so we won't spoil it here. For the full list of potential Insight effects, check out p669 in the Hunter's Appendices chapter.

Beasthood

Your Beasthood stat determines the maximum strength of your Beast Transformation using Beast Blood Pellets or the Beast Claw's transformed mode. You won't literally transform into a beast, but raising the Beast Gauge will give you a serious increase in attack power, at the cost of a similarly meaningful decrease in defense. The higher your Beasthood is, the higher your maximum potential damage will be when using Beast Transformation.

Beasthood can't be gained like normal stats. Instead, it is conferred by attire. Having high Insight also reduces your Beasthood, so make sure to spend all of your Insight if you want to maximize Beasthood. For more on Beasthood, see the entry for Beast Blood Pellets in the Arsenal & Attire chapter.

Slash like a man possessed to get the most out of the Beast Transform!

Items and Equipment

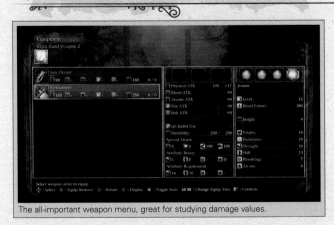
The all-important weapon menu, great for studying damage values.

This section will explain the basics of items and equipment in Bloodborne. Some of these topics are covered in greater detail in the Arsenal & Attire Chapter, beginning on p568.

Right-hand Weapons

You can equip two primary weapons at once. Only one will be available at any given time, but pressing ❍ well allow you to swap between them. Try to select two weapons that match your character's stats and complement each other; for example, you may choose a quick close-range weapon and a slow weapon that has more reach.

Left-hand Weapons

As with primary weapons, you can equip two left-hand weapons at once, and you can swap between them by pressing ⬅. Usually, you'll use a gun in your left hand, but sometimes you may want a torch or shield. Left-hand weapons are also referred to as "off-hand weapons," "sidearms," and, in the case of guns, "firearms."

Generally speaking, guns are a reliable form of ranged attack, most of which scale with your bloodtinge stat. That said, different guns are effective at different ranges and tasks, and some even scale with arcane rather than bloodtinge.

Quicksilver Bullets

These bullets are made by the hunter that uses them, specifically to take down beasts of the scourge. Even so, they are rarely enough to slay a beast, so you'll go through them in large quantities on your hunts. By default you'll carry a maximum of 20 bullets, but this number can be augmented with Caryll Runes later in the game, increasing the total to a maximum of 25. Most sidearms consume a single bullet per shot, but there are some exceptions, such as the Repeating Pistol requiring two bullets per shot, and the Cannon, which uses up 12 bullets to deliver a single, powerful blast. Arcane items also consume Quicksilver Bullets for their various effects, and again the rate of consumption varies from one bullet to seven.

You'll often find these bullets after defeating beasts, so you can usually maintain a good supply of them, as long as you don't use them too carelessly. If you do run out, there's always Blood Bullets, which you can read about in the Health & Damage section of this chapter.

Quicksilver Bullets are a common pickup, so don't hesitate to use them.

You can check exactly how many Quicksilver Bullets a gun or arcane item will use by looking for QS Bullet Use in the menus.

Attire

Attire refers to your four clothing slots: head, chest, gloves, and legs. Each piece of attire contributes to your overall defense and changes your character's appearance. While different pieces of attire do have different effects, the changes are typically not drastic enough to override aesthetic considerations. In other words, make sure you look good! Full attire details can of course be found in the Arsenal & Attire chapter.

Consumable Items

Consumable Items can be bought or found throughout the course of the game and can generally only be used once each, though there are some exceptions. They can either be used via the menu or by pressing Ⓞ while the item you want to use is selected in your quick inventory. Consumables are very powerful in Bloodborne, and can make your life a lot easier. There are five main categories: Attack Items, Support Items, Healing Items, Blood Echo Items, and Insight Items. You can find the details for each beginning on p566 of the Arsenal & Attire Chapter.

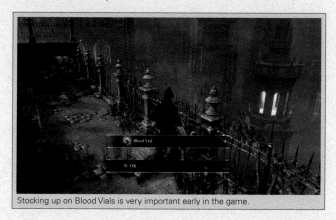
Stocking up on Blood Vials is very important early in the game.

Arcane Items

Arcane Items require a minimum level of the arcane stat to be used. Unlike weapons, these items can be equipped in your quick inventory and used via the Ⓞ button. Additionally, they don't disappear from your inventory after being used like normal items do; instead, they consume Quicksilver Bullets. These items provide a number of extra combat options and are a perk of using an arcane build that relies on elemental weapons. Additionally, having a high arcane stat increases the effects of many Arcane Items. See p580 for details.

Upgrading Weapons

Once you have access to the Hunter's Dream, you can approach the Workbench and interact to upgrade your weapons. Select "Fortify" from the menu to begin upgrading – this will cost you Blood Echoes and Blood Stones and is the single most important aspect of character progression, so choose wisely when spending Blood Stones.

There are four levels of Blood Stone: Blood Stone Shards, Twin Blood Stone Shards, Blood Stone Chunks, and Blood Rocks. Blood Stone Shards and Twin Blood Stone Shards will eventually be unlocked for purchase in the shop. Blood Stone Chunks can be found, looted from rare enemies, and (very rarely) dropped by foes. Only two Blood Rocks can be found in the main game; all other Blood Rocks must be plundered from Root Dungeons.

Required Stones for Upgrade

Upgrade Level	Required Stones
+1	3 Blood Stone Shards
+2	5 Blood Stone Shards
+3	8 Blood Stone Shards
+4	3 Twin Blood Stone Shards
+5	5 Twin Blood Stone Shards
+6	8 Twin Blood Stone Shards
+7	3 Blood Stone Chunks
+8	5 Blood Stone Chunks
+9	8 Blood Stone Chunks
+10	1 Blood Rock

Your weapon has a durability factor that decreases whenever you hit enemies or objects with it. When its durability reaches zero, a weapon will break and become ineffective. Before this happens (or to reverse it once it has), go to the Workshop desk and select "Repair Weapons." It costs Blood Echoes to do so, but it's necessary. Don't forget to repair periodically when doing long chains of Chalice Dungeons!

Storage

Once you have access to the Workshop in the Hunter's Dream, you can store and remove items freely by interacting with the large storage chest. This will enable you to keep items in reserve beyond what you can normally carry. Additionally, your stock of Blood Vials and Quicksilver Bullets (up to 600) will automatically be replenished from storage whenever you return to the Hunter's Dream (as long as you have them stored in the first place).

If your storage is almost full of an item, sell some off to gain Blood Echoes.

1

Gems & Runes

In Bloodborne, your weapon can be customized through the use of Blood Gems (gems) and your character can be customized using Caryll Runes (runes). Both of these topics are important enough to warrant having special, dedicated sections of this guide. To learn about Blood Gems, see p606 of the Arsenal & Attire Chapter. For Caryll Runes, go to p597.

New Game+

After completing Bloodborne, the game will automatically begin again. You'll keep your stats and most of your items, and your enemies will become stronger. You'll receive more Blood Echoes for defeating foes, and most of the treasures placed in the areas will once again be available. For the exact details of New Game+ changes, see p161 of the Hunting Grounds chapter.

Combat Explained

No matter how excellent your strategy is, it doesn't mean anything if you can't execute it. Read through the following section for tips on the basic controls and finer points of Bloodborne's combat.

Lock-On

Press R3 to focus on a nearby enemy. If there are multiple enemies present, you can then switch between them by moving the right stick. If there are no enemies nearby, this will orient the camera to face in the same direction as your character. If you press R3 while already locked-on, you'll break your lock-on.

Locking on to enemies can help you keep the camera on them and aim your attacks, but there are plenty of occasions when not locking on is much better. For example, fighting near ledges with lock-on can be risky, as your camera and your movement orientation are influenced by the enemy. Fighting small or agile foes is another example; the default aiming of your weapon's attacks while locked on may be insufficient. Consider breaking lock-on and aiming the attacks manually by moving the camera.

The first Huntsman. Use him to get familiar with lock-on.

Locking-on works from a good distance away.

In Bloodborne, even large foes tend to be agile, and the camera tracks their bodies (which are often above your character's head). If you are getting frustrated while fighting a boss because the camera is interfering with your movement or you can't see what you want to see, try unlocking and controlling the camera yourself. It's more challenging at first, but it will give you a greater degree of control and ultimately can be less frustrating.

If an enemy blocks your attack...

Lock-on lets you target multiple points on some enemies, including weak points.

...use a transformation attack to break their guard.

Camera

When you are not locked on, you can control the camera freely using the right stick. You can and should use this to examine the environment very closely. The camera helps to determine your movement controls, as well. If the camera touches a wall, it will be automatically adjusted by default; if you don't like that behavior, there is an option called "Camera Auto-Adjust" in the Controls section of the Game Options. Turn it off if you are having visibility or control issues caused by the camera in small spaces. You can also adjust the Camera sensitivity or flip the axis controls if you like.

Quick Camera Turn

As previously mentioned, pressing **R3** will immediately reset the camera to face the same direction as your character. Push **⊕** and then quickly press **R3** for a fast turn. Use this feature when you hear a suspicious noise behind your character!

Attacking

Pressing **R1** will allow you to perform a basic attack. These attacks tend to be quicker and consume less stamina than other attacks, but they also deal less damage in a single hit. They can be chained together easily, though, and are thus very important. **R2** attacks are slower, cost more stamina, and generally don't combo as well as **R1** attacks, but they usually deal more damage and have a stronger impact on the enemy. Weapons that are held in both hands also have **L2** attacks. These tend to have special properties; read about each weapon's attacks in the Arsenal & Attire Chapter for the full details.

Weapon Transformation

All of the weapons in Bloodborne are trick weapons with two modes: normal mode and transformed mode. Pressing **L1** will allow you to swap from one mode to the other. Most weapons are very different in normal mode and transformed mode, so read up on the pros and cons of each in the Arsenal & Attire Chapter's weapon section.

Transformation Attacks

Pressing the **L1** button while performing another action will prompt your character to execute a special transformation attack. This is a good way to change modes in the middle of combat, and the transformation attacks of many weapons combo very well. They also instantly break the guard of blocking foes, so use this against shield-wielding opponents.

Altered Attack Sequences & Alternate Animations

Be advised that the first **R1** attack following a transformation attack might not be the first **R1** in the chain. In order for your attacks to flow smoothly, you may see an alternate version of another attack, and some attacks may repeat in order for the chain to correct itself. The damage values for attacks with alternate animations don't change.

For example, if you perform normal mode **R1** > **L1** > **R1** with the Saw Spear, you'll see an alternate animation for the transformed **R1** (2). Additionally, for normal **R1** > **L1** > **R1** > **R1**, the alternate animation of transformed **R1** (2) will be followed by the regular version of transformed **R1** (2). From there, the chain will continue as normal.

Practice these different combos against early enemies.

Sidestepping attacks can cause a similar issue. In the first place, sidestepping to the left and attacking with an R1 (sidestep) will give a different animation than sidestepping to the right and performing an R1 (sidestep). If you follow up those attacks with a normal R1, they will begin the chain at different points. It's critical that you practice with your weapon of choice to master these details.

Quickstepping to the right direction can be critical against strong enemies.

Visceral Attacks

When an opponent has been staggered they are open for a lethal visceral attack – simply press R1 when directly in front or behind them. This attack is the same regardless of which weapon you're using, and has its own separate damage calculation, so its power doesn't depend on the weapon you use. Visceral attacks deal a lot of damage and are often the fastest possible way to end a fight. They provide a window of invincibility while executing them, and knock nearby enemies away. The enemy on the receiving end of the visceral attack will also be knocked away. You can even use this to knock a strong enemy off a cliff (or another high place) for an instant kill! Visceral attacks are able to benefit from the special effects of a number of Caryll Runes (see p598 for more on this).

Interrupts & Visceral Attacks

If you time your shots correctly, you can use gunshots to stop enemy attacks; this is called an interrupt. To do this, press L2 during the enemy's attack while holding a gun in your left hand. You also need to have enough ammo to shoot, of course. The timing can be difficult, and it varies for every attack. This is a high-risk, high-reward technique.

This isn't possible against every foe, but it can be used against most enemies, including some bosses. If you are successful, the enemy will be staggered and left open. Approach the opponent from the front and press R1 while it is staggered to execute a powerful visceral attack.

Visceral attacks aren't the only option while the enemy is staggered, though. You can also perform normal attacks – the first one that hits will get a very large damage bonus. Some weapons are fast enough to perform a fully charged R2 attack for massive damage. The

Cannon can also work wonders in this situation. Test out different attacks and see what works best for you.

Guns that can Interrupt	
Hunter Pistol	p559
Hunter Blunderbuss	p559
Repeating Pistol	p560
Ludwig's Rifle	p560
Evelyn	p561

Trick Weapons that can Interrupt	
Rifle Spear	p511
Reiterpallasch	p505

Charged Attack Staggers & Rear Visceral Attacks

By maneuvering to the opponent's back and landing a fully-charged R2 attack, you can cause most enemies to stagger. While in this state, you can either hit them for a large damage bonus or perform a rear visceral attack. Whether or not the rear visceral attack or another type of attack is more powerful depends on your stats, weapon upgrade level, gems, and runes. Experiment to see what is best for you whenever you make a major change to your character.

As with normal visceral attacks, your character is invincible while performing the attack, and nearby enemies will be knocked away. Even if another attack would deal more damage, sometimes it's worth using a rear visceral attack for these effects.

Shooting the enemy during certain attacks is one way to stager them...

...landing a charged R2 from behind is the other.

Health & Damage

The way you fight in Bloodborne is based not just on your ability to deal damage, but also on how well you can take it. The game provides some tools for managing your health that have serious implications on the combat, so we'll go through those here.

Blood Vials

Blood Vials are your primary source of healing in Bloodborne. They are always assigned to the △ button; there's no need to equip them in your quick inventory. You can hold a maximum of 20 by default, though this can be increased by equipping certain Runes. Blood Vials will heal you for 40% of your maximum HP. They are very quick to use, too, and you can move a little while doing so.

Be careful not to use too many, though. Bloodborne's Regain system is intended to help you heal without the use of Blood Vials, and it's easy to run out of Blood Vials if you don't make use of Regain at all. You can always buy more, but it's a waste of Blood Echoes that could be used for leveling up.

The Blood Vials in your inventory are replenished when you warp, but they are taken from your stock. These are not free refills. If you run out of Blood Vials in your stock, your inventory won't be replenished until you collect or buy more.

Regain

For a short period after taking damage, you'll have a chance to recover the health you lost. A small white marker will appear on your health bar to illustrate the amount of HP you can recover. After a short period, roughly two and a half seconds, the amount of HP that you can recover will begin to decrease until it is gone. Striking an enemy before this happens will allow you to Regain your lost health. The amount of HP recovered per hit varies by weapon and can be increased with gem effects.

The best way to Regain health is to roll or quickstep behind the enemy so that they have trouble hitting you; attack from that position. Always beware of quick spinning attacks and area-of-effect attacks. While it is true that you need to hurry if you want to utilize the Regain system, sometimes you need to simply fall back and use a Blood Vial. You have to find a balance, and the best method of healing will be determined by your enemy's power and aggressiveness. Against enemies that don't flinch when struck and attack quickly, Regain may be too risky; in those cases, use vials.

Regain is a key system in Bloodborne. Don't mistake its simplicity for a lack of importance. After being struck by an enemy attack, look for a chance to retaliate quickly to recover health.

Blood Bullets

By pressing ⬆, you can create Blood Bullets. At the cost of 30% of your maximum health, you'll make 5 bullets that function just like normal Quicksilver Bullets. You can only hold 5, and you should generally make sure that you have them with you. This will help you build a stockpile of Quicksilver Bullets.

Blood Bullets are especially critical for users of magic items and weapons that use a lot of bullets, like the Cannon, Flamesprayer,

Blood Vial refills are not free. Your inventory is replenished from your stock, and you'll need to buy more if you run out.

This is what your health gauge looks like when hitting the enemy would cause you to Regain lost health.

Creating Blood Bullets is best done when there's no enemies around.

Rosmarinus, and the Repeating Pistol. By using Blood Bullets to offset the cost, you can fire more shots or use more casts.

Don't worry about accidentally killing yourself while attempting to make Blood Bullets; your character can't die in this way. You won't be able to make bullets, though, if your health is at 30% or less. You also can't make bullets if you already have 5 Blood Bullets. The HP cost of this technique can also be used tactically to activate the Poorman gem effect.

If your character has a passive health regeneration effect from a Pulsing gem, you can essentially make Blood Bullets for free, though it takes time for your life to recover. The Regain system can also be used to regenerate health exchanged for bullets; if you are confident that you can defeat an enemy without being hit, you can make Blood Bullets just before engaging.

Status Ailments

Status Ailments are often more deadly than normal attacks. It is always better to avoid such affliction, as curing ailments in the middle of a battle can be tricky. Still, you will inevitably need to deal with status ailments at some point. When you are exposed to a status ailment, its associated bar will begin to fill up; when it is completely full, the status will be inflicted. You can cure it before the bar fills to prevent the ailment. Refer to the chart below for effects and possible cures.

Icon	Ailment	Effect	Cure
	Slow Poison	Gradual HP Loss (at a rate of 12pt + 0.1% * 40/1sec)*	Antidote
	Rapid Poison	Instant HP Loss (250pt + 3%)**	Antidote
	Frenzy	Instant HP Loss (70%)	Sedative

* Blood-starved Beast inflicts Slow Poison at a rate of 6pt + 0.2% * 40/0.2sec

** Blood Gems (including those used by NPCs) inflict Rapid Poison at a rate of 100pt + 10%

Note that Rapid Poisoning and Frenzy must be cured before the HP Loss occurs, as the damage is instantaneous. This means that fighting foes that inflict either of these requires you to be very careful. Sometimes, if you haven't used an Antidote or Sedative before engaging them, it might already be too late. If an enemy kills you very quickly and you're unsure why, these status ailments are possibly the cause; check their entry in the Bestiary chapter to see what they are capable of and how to avoid it.

Movement

Moving around during combat gives you full control over attack ranges and tactical positioning. It's also the key to evading enemy attacks and creating chances to land attacks of your own, so we'll take a look at some of the less obvious movement-related details here.

Rolling & Quickstepping

Pressing ◎ while holding a direction on the left stick will cause you to roll or quickstep. If you are locked on to the enemy, you will quickstep, and you'll roll if you are not locked on. There's no major difference between rolling and quickstepping.

During the middle of your roll or quickstep, you'll be invincible. The period of time in which you can't be hurt is known as your "invincibility frames," or "iframes." You may instinctively want to dodge away from enemy attacks, but in many cases it's actually better to dodge through them thanks to this invincibility. Doing so minimizes the time that you spend in contact with the enemy's attack and moves you into a better position.

Rolling or quickstepping costs 10 points of stamina. With shields being extremely unreliable in Bloodborne, this is your primary defensive technique. Aggressive play is good, but always try to save a bit of stamina to escape after your attacks.

Backsteps

If you just press ◎ without pressing a direction on the left stick, your character will perform a short backstep. This backstep has no invincibility frames at all. On the other hand, if you hold back on the left stick while pressing ◎, you'll perform a longer backstep, and it will have the invincibility frames of a normal roll. Either way, your backstep will cost 10 points of stamina.

Dodging through an attack both prevents you taking damage and positions you to counter attack!

Quickstepping is safest against gunshots, but strafing also works.

Backstep to make the enemy's attack miss...

...and then retaliate quickly.

So why would you ever use the short backstep? The main reason to do so is that you can perform special R1 and R2 attacks from the short backstep, and sometimes these moves are very useful. Attacking from the long backstep is just like attacking from a frontstep. Look at your chosen weapon's attack multipliers carefully and decide if using the short backstep is worthwhile. Both short and long backsteps have the same stamina cost; it's usually better to use the long one and have the invincibility frames.

Dashing & Jumping

Hold ◎ while moving to dash instead of walking. This will drain your stamina, but dashing is much faster than walking. This is a critical movement technique in Bloodborne. The enemies are all fast and aggressive, so staying mobile is vital for survival. You can perform special Dashing Attacks by pressing R1 or R2 while dashing; check the Arsenal data for your weapon to see what sort of attacks can be performed.

You can also jump by pressing ◎ while dashing. It's tricky at first, but you need to hold ◎ to dash and then quickly let go and press it again to jump. The command can be awkward, but jumping can let you take some very interesting shortcuts in some areas. Be warned that this will fail if you are very low on stamina. Also note that you can run in circles to build up speed for a jump.

Concealed Dash

When fighting against other players, attacks that are fast and cover a lot of ground are very useful. Dashing attacks, in particular, are great against human opponents. They're quick and hard to react to; unfortunately, the enemy can see them coming easily if you just dash forward. Luckily, there is a way to start a dash without it being obvious.

Lock onto the enemy, hold down ◎, and strafe to the side. Just before you want to attack, begin moving forward and then quickly press the attack button. If done with proper timing, the enemy won't even see your character begin dashing before the attack starts!

Jump Attack

Pressing ⬆ and R2 at the same time will prompt you to leap forth and deliver a jump attack. The main benefit of this technique is its long range; be careful, though, as you'll be wide open if you miss. Judge the distance carefully and use good timing to surprise your enemy.

Falling

Falling short distances will not harm you, but if you fall too far you'll take damage. Falls from great heights will outright kill you.

When your character lands after falling a long way, there will be a moment where you can't move; you can avoid this by rolling or backstepping just as you land. Alternatively, you can perform a special plunging attack by pressing R1 while falling. Finally, the Beast Rune has a hidden effect that lessens fall damage; you can use this to your advantage if you want to literally get the drop on the enemy.

Jumping attacks bring you forward, closing the gap...

...and landing with a powerful strike.

Enemy Behavior

This section covers some things about the way enemies behave and react that are critical to success in combat. Bloodborne is a game that encourages aggressive play, yet punishes those who aren't careful enough in battle. To succeed, you'll need to pay attention to how enemies react to your attacks, and try to keep each battle manageable.

Impact

When you hit an enemy, it will be stunned momentarily. A very brief stun is called a "flinch," while a longer stun is a "stumble." Whether the enemy flinches or stumbles depends on the impact of your attack. While the enemy is flinching or stumbling, you have time to begin your next attack; this is the basis of combo attacks in Bloodborne. Higher levels of impact will stun the enemy for longer and allow you more time to perform another attack (or escape if need be). Some attacks have massive impact and can knock an enemy down. Check the weapons sections, beginning on p476; each weapon has attack tables that assess the impact of each strike.

Excerpt from Burial Blade Attack Table

Attack	Dmg ×	Type	Stamina	Impact
R1	1.00	Physical / Arcane	23	Light
R1 (backstep)	1.05	Thrust / Arcane	12(+10)	Light

Flinching strong enemies requires powerful attacks.

Super Armor

Not all enemies can be stunned by a single attack. Many foes have a hidden statistic called "super armor" that prevents them from flinching or stumbling. Each of your attacks reduces the enemy's super armor; when it reaches zero ("breaks"), the enemy will flinch or stumble. The degree to which the enemy is stunned depends on the impact of the attack that breaks its armor. A light impact attack will stun the enemy as if it was a normal impact attack, a normal impact attack will act as a heavy impact attack, and so on. Always try to use the highest impact attack possible just as the enemy's super armor breaks.

Different foes have different amounts of super armor, and each of your attacks deal different amounts of super armor damage. Learning how many attacks each enemy can withstand from a specific weapon is a matter of practice. Particularly make a note of how many R1 attacks you need to use to break a foe's armor; once you remember that, you can use an R2 attack or a transformation attack for the final hit.

Once an enemy's super armor is broken, it is instantly refilled. Only one hit benefits from the upgraded impact before the process begins again. Some weapons are able to break the armor of enemies that have low amounts of super armor in a single strike; in that case, every hit will stun the enemy.

As you attack an enemy, its super armor will decrease, but it will regenerate if you wait too long between attacks. Furthermore, enemy super armor does not regenerate gradually; it is instantaneous. If you wait four seconds between attacks, the enemy will recover its super armor. Some enemies are very aggressive, so attacking constantly can be difficult. There are some tricks that you can use, however.

The most important trick is to roll or quickstep into the enemy. Whenever you touch the enemy with a roll or a quickstep, it counts as an attack and resets the countdown to armor recovery! You can use your roll or quickstep's invincibility to dodge the enemy's attacks while preventing the opponent from recovering super armor. If you stay close and aggressive, you can dominate otherwise tough foes with this technique, particularly in co-op. If you need to get away from the enemy for a moment but don't want to allow armor recovery, gunshots and throwing knives can reset the timer as well.

You can stun enemies by hitting them multiple times consecutively. Use a high impact attack to create the biggest stun.

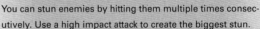

If you wait more than four seconds between attacks, the enemy will be harder to stun, but rolling or quickstepping into the enemy will reset the timer.

Red Eyes

Some enemies you'll encounter will have glowing red eyes, and this not only makes them appear more threatening, it actually strengthens them. Red-eyed enemies have greater attack power than their normal counterparts, and those you'll come across in Old Yharnam also have the ability to inflict Slow Poison when their attacks connect.

Luring

Sometimes, enemies will be waiting near traps or hazards that are very dangerous. You can lure the enemy out with Pebbles or Throwing Knives, or by running close enough to get their attention. After you have the enemy's attention, retreat back to a safer location to do battle. Always try to have a safe zone prepared. Pull the enemies to that spot with ranged attacks and deal with the traps separately.

Baiting

You can bait enemies to attack you by intentionally stepping into their attack ranges. Let the enemy get close enough to attack and then roll away. This is very important for fighting both normal enemies and bosses. For bosses, you can even bait specific moves; each attack tends to be used most often at a certain range. Stand at that distance, and you can fool the boss into performing only the moves that you want!

Damage Calculation

The following section explains how damage calculations are handled by the game. Some of the information is very technical; if you just want the basics for now, skim through and read the note boxes. You can always come back later if you want to learn more about the combat system.

Damage Types

The damage type of your attack determines which enemy defense value is used to reduce its damage and which gems can increase it. There are five main types: physical, blood, arcane, fire, and bolt. For example, if you attack with only fire, just the enemy's fire defense will reduce it. All other defenses are ignored.

Physical is a bit special in that it has two sub-types: blunt and thrust. Each physical attack is either normal physical, blunt, or thrust. The enemy will use the appropriate defense type depending on your attack. In other words, the enemy really has seven defense types: physical, blunt, thrust, blood, arcane, fire, and bolt. Gems that increase physical attack, however, also increase blunt and thrust damage. On the other hand, a gem that increases thrust won't raise normal physical or blunt damage.

- "Physical ATK UP" raises the power of physical, blunt, and thrust attacks.

- "Thrust ATK UP" raises the power of thrust attacks only.

- "Blunt ATK UP" raises the power of blunt attacks only.

The next important point to understand is that damage type is determined by your individual attack, not the weapon overall. Ludwig's Holy Blade does normal physical damage, but it also has separate blunt and thrust attacks. A "physical attack up" gem would raise the damage of all of the attacks, but a "thrust attack up" gem would only benefit the thrusts.

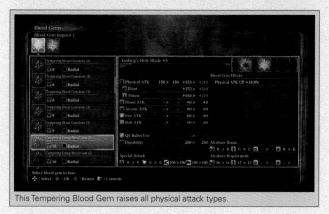

This Tempering Blood Gem raises all physical attack types.

Finally, know that attacks can have more than one type. For example, an attack can be both physical and arcane. In this case, the physical portion of the attack will benefit from physical gems and be reduced by the enemy's physical defense, while the arcane portion will be increased by arcane gems and reduced by arcane defense.

The tables in the weapons section of the Arsenal & Attire chapter will show you what type of damage each of your weapon's attacks deal. Remember that blunt and thrust are sub-types of physical damage. If you convert your weapon's physical damage into an element like fire, it no longer matters if an attack is thrust or blunt; the damage will be fire elemental.

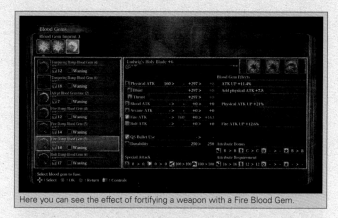

Here you can see the effect of fortifying a weapon with a Fire Blood Gem.

Some enemies are very weak against certain damage types. Try thrust attacks on Brainsuckers or bolt attacks against Celestial Emissaries.

In this table, you can see the damage types for two attacks from the Burial Blade's normal mode. Notice that they both have a mix of physical damage and arcane, but the R1 (backstep) attack will benefit from "Thrust ATK UP" gems and will be reduced by the enemy's thrust defense instead of normal physical defense. The arcane part of the attack is calculated separately; it benefits from "Arcane ATK UP" and will be reduced by only the enemy's arcane defense.

Excerpt from Burial Blade Attack Table

Attack	Dmg ×	Type	Stamina	Impact
R1	1.00	Physical / Arcane	23	Light
R1 (backstep)	1.05	Thrust / Arcane	12(+10)	Light

Attack Power

So how do you know how strong your weapon is? Open your Inventory and scroll to the Right Hand Weapons section. Select your weapon and press ⓘ to pull up the details pane. On the left side of the details pane, you'll see the attack values for your weapon. From top to bottom, you can see: physical attack, blunt attack, thrust attack, blood attack, arcane attack, fire attack, and bolt attack. The number on the left of each entry is the "base attack" of your weapon. The number on the right is the amount that the damage is increased by your stats; this is called "attack from scaling."

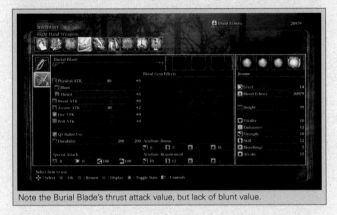

Note the Burial Blade's thrust attack value, but lack of blunt value.

As an example, let's look at the Burial Blade. Our character has 10 strength, 12 skill, and 15 arcane. Our base physical attack is 80, and we get +5 physical attack from scaling. That means our Burial Blade has 85 total physical attack power. We also have a base arcane attack of 30 and +2 arcane attack from scaling for a total of 32 arcane attack. So our attacks will use a physical attack value of 85 and an arcane value of 32. But what if our attack is a thrust?

If we use a thrust type attack, we'll use the Burial Blade's "thrust attack from scaling" instead of its "physical attack from scaling." It will be added to the normal base physical attack. In this case, its 80 base physical attack and +5 thrust attack from scaling, so the total attack power will be 85. It's the same as before in this case, but if we had a gem that increased only thrust damage, it could be higher! In that case, the thrust attack from scaling would increase. If our attack type is "Thrust / Arcane," it will use 85 thrust attack power and 32 arcane attack power.

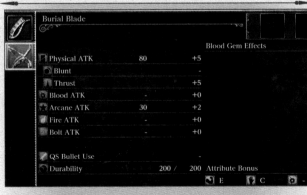

"Physical ATK UP" benefits physical, thrust, and blunt damage types but "Thrust ATK UP" and "Blunt ATK UP" only benefit their own sub-type.

Attack Damage Multipliers

Ok, so you know how strong your weapon's attack power is. Great! But that doesn't tell the whole story. Each individual attack is different, right? In fact, each and every attack that you can do has a hidden "attack damage multiplier." They aren't visible in the game, but they are available in the weapon tables starting on p481.

Excerpt from Burial Blade Attack Table

Attack	Dmg ×	Type	Stamina	Impact
R1	1.00	Physical / Arcane	23	Light
R1 (backstep)	1.05	Thrust / Arcane	12(+10)	Light

The damage multipliers (marked as Dmg × in the tables) are applied to your total attack power for each type. If you want more details and don't mind getting technical, read on.

Higher "Dmg ×" means the attack deals more damage!

From our previous example with the Burial Blade, we had 85 total physical attack power and 32 arcane attack power. Each of these is multiplied by the "Dmg ×" for the R1 attack (1.00), so the attack will deal 85 points of physical damage and 32 points of arcane damage. The physical damage will be reduced by the enemy's physical defense, and the arcane damage will be reduced by the enemy's arcane defense. The results are added together, and that's your actual damage! In the case of the R1 attack, the multipliers are 1.00, so the numbers don't change. Let's look at the R1 (backstep) now.

For the R1 (backstep), the multiplier is 1.05. The total thrust attack is 85. When we multiply it by "Dmg ×," we get 89. If we multiply the total arcane attack (32) times "Dmg ×" (1.05), we get 34. This attack deals slightly more damage than the normal R1 attack. The effect is more noticeable at higher levels.

> **Basic Formulas**
>
> **Base Attack + Attack from Scaling = Total Attack**
>
> **Total Attack × "Dmg ×" = Total Damage**
>
> **Total Damage − Enemy Defense = Actual Damage**
>
> Remember that this is calculated separately for each damage type and then added together.

Attacks Versus Open Foes

If your enemy is "open," it means they have missed an attack, rolled, performed a backstep, or otherwise left themselves open for an attack. In this situation, you can perform a counter hit for extra damage. The amount of bonus damage is determined by how open the enemy is. For example, after it misses with a normal swing, you may hit a foe for an extra 20% damage. If the enemy misses a really big, slow attack, you might deal an extra 40% damage. It doesn't stop there, either; it's pretty common to hit a cutlass-wielding Huntsman for a roughly 68% bonus.

Timing is very critical in performing these counter hits. If you are too early or too late, you'll deal less damage. You want to hit the enemy just after the attack ends but before it begins to recover. There is some margin for error; 40% bonus hits can become 20% bonus hits if your timing is only off by a little bit. If you miss the timing too much, though, you'll just hit for normal damage.

Spacing is key if you want to use counter hits. You need to stand in a position that baits an enemy into using a big attack but still lets you step out of range. Then, as the enemy attempts to recover, you can attack for a counter hit. Another method is to roll or frontstep behind the enemy; you'll often pass through their attack with your invincibility frames and recover just in time to counter. A more advanced technique is to backstep to dodge the enemy attack and then counter with a backstep attack. If your normal backstep doesn't move far enough to dodge the attack or its attack doesn't reach the enemy, check p19 for information on the two different ways to backstep.

> If an enemy misses an attack it will be "open." You can hit it for a big damage bonus.

The Finestrike gem effect can increase the amount of damage you deal against open foes. This will further increase the damage bonus of counter hits. When fighting normally, you may want to rely on other effects, but if you use certain long-range weapons, such as the Rifle Spear (p511) or Hunter Axe (p487), you may find this to be very useful indeed. The Rifle Spear in particular is extremely well-suited for attacking open foes.

Lead Elixirs can be used to perform counter hits more easily. Light enemy attacks will rebound off of you while you are under the effects of a Lead Elixir, and you receive a bonus while the enemy is in the rebound state. Attacks that don't rebound won't stagger you unless they are very heavy, which means you can perform a counter normally. When combined with the Regain system and good defense, you can use this to deal a large amount of damage to the enemy while completely negating their attacks via Regain.

Enemy Weak Points

Many enemies have specific weak points that can be struck for bonus damage. For example, striking the Cleric Beast's head will deal additional damage and can even temporarily stagger it. Hitting enemy weak points combines with other damage multipliers, so study each enemy and strike their vulnerable points. This system existed in previous From Software titles, but it is greatly expanded in Bloodborne. It rewards you for understanding your enemy and knowing your weapon's moveset perfectly.

Serrated Weapons & Righteous Weapons

Some enemies are weak against "serrated" weapons, and some are weak against "righteous" weapons. The bonus multipliers that they give stack with your attack damage multiplier, open foe bonus damage, gem effects, etc., leading to some highly damaging hits.

The Saw Spear is a well balanced serrated weapon.

Ludwig's Holy Blade is the most righteous of weapons.

Serrated weapons include the Saw Cleaver's normal mode, both modes of the Saw Spear, and the transformed mode of the Threaded Cane. Attacks from those deal an additional 20% damage to specific enemies.

Enemies Weak to Serrated Weapons

Scourge Beast	p266
Cleric Beast	p326
Father Gascoigne (Beast)	p328
Blood-starved Beast	p330
Vicar Amelia	p336
Abhorrent Beast	p386
Beast-possessed Soul	p275
Darkbeast Paarl	p334
Loran Silverbeast	p281
Watchdog of the Old Lords	p376
Bloodletting Beast	p390

Righteous weapons include the normal mode of the Kirkhammer (50% bonus), both modes of Ludwig's Holy Blade (50% bonus), both modes of Logarius' Wheel (30% bonus), and the normal mode of the Threaded Cane (20% bonus).

Enemies Weak to Righteous Weapons

Lost Child of Antiquity	p244
Forsaken Castle Spirit (Knife)	p245
Forsaken Castle Spirit (Head)	p245
Bloodlicker	p280
Evil Labyrinth Spirit	p298

Beasts & Kin

There are two types of "racial bonus" in Bloodborne – one versus beasts, and one versus kin. You can view your weapon's damage bonus (or penalty) by looking at your weapon info screen. This is tied directly to the Blood Gem system; check the Arsenal & Attire chapter for information on Beasthunter and Kinhunter gems.

🐾	Beast Damage	Percent of normal damage against beasts
🐍	Kin Damage	Percent of normal damage against kin

Multiplayer

As in previous From Software games, online multiplayer is woven deeply into the experience of Bloodborne. You can play the game entirely offline, but you'll be missing out on a whole lot if you do.

Notes

Once you've picked up the Notebook you can begin leaving notes on the ground, just like the ones the messengers have left around the Hunter's Dream for you. Other players will be able to see and read these notes as they play their game, so you can give them tips and warnings or point out things of interest. The notes are based on templates that allow you to combine words and simple phrases into a message.

Summoning Help

If you ring the Beckoning Bell, you will enter summoning mode. This costs one point of Insight, so it cannot be performed if you have none. You will be surrounded by a visual aura near your feet, and matchmaking will begin. In some early areas, an NPC character may answer your call if there's no one else around. The Beckoning Bell is unavailable for use in areas where the boss has been defeated. By using the Silencing Blank, you can return summoned allies to their worlds – this will not work for nemeses and infiltrators, however. Be warned that when you attempt to summon a co-op partner at level 30 or above, a Bell Ringer will appear as well, and begin to summon infiltrators to kill you. In some areas, regardless of these conditions, Bell Ringers will already be present. These areas are the Nightmare Frontier, Nightmare of Mensis and root dungeons with the Sinister Bell rite selected. Equipping the 'Impurity' rune will allow you to call upon the aid of various NPC allies, even if you're playing offline. You might need to meet other prerequisites such as completing specific quests before they'll become available to summon, but their help can be invaluable when you're plumbing the depths of a Chalice Dungeon or struggling against a difficult boss. For a full list of potential allies, check the NPC section starting on p632.

Offering Help

By ringing the Small Resonant Bell, you can attempt to join another player as a guest. You can do this even in areas where you've already killed the boss, but the player you're helping must not have killed that boss yet, since your goal will be to help the host defeat the area boss (unless you are summoned as a nemesis).
If the area boss is defeated while you are summoned as an ally, you will be rewarded with 1 Insight point and a portion of the boss' Blood Echoes before returning to your world. You can return at any point by using the Silencing Blank, though you will not receive any rewards; dying in the host's world or the host dying will yield the same results. While playing as a co-op guest, killing a nemesis or infiltrator will reward you with 30% of the total Blood Echoes that they would need in order to level up.

Boss Health

Having a summoned ally doesn't alter the health or difficulty of the enemies you'll fight, but it does affect the bosses. To ensure they are still a challenge, boss health is increased to 1.5x when a second co-op player enters your world, and to 2.0x when a third enters.

Infiltrating Another Player

By ringing the Small Sinister Bell, you can be summoned as an infiltrator by a Bell Ringer to the world of another player. Your goal as an infiltrator is to kill the host. Once the host has died, you will receive 1 point of Insight and 10% of the Blood Echoes required for the host to level up. If you are killed, or the host reaches the area boss, you will be sent back to your world unrewarded. The Silencing Blank can be used to return to your own world, which will also result in no rewards. Bell Ringers will appear to a host of level 30 and above with at least one summoned ally. A Bell Ringer can summon only one infiltrator at a time and will cease summoning until the current infiltrator has returned to their world.

Factional Conflict

Your Oath Memory Slot marks your factional alignment. There are four possible Oath types: 'Corruption' for Vileblood, 'Radiance' for Executioner, 'Hunter' for Hunter of Hunters, and 'None'. Executioner and Vileblood are naturally opposed to each other, and Hunter of Hunters has a set chance to oppose players with no affiliation. By using the Sinister Resonant Bell, you have a 5% chance of becoming a Bloodlust Hunter, which is in opposition to Hunter of Hunters. If you attempt to join a co-op session as a guest and the host is a member of an opposing faction, you will instead be summed with the task of killing the host as a nemesis. For example, if you bear the Radiance Rune and the server's matchmaking pairs you with a player bearing Corruption, you will be summoned as a nemesis, even if you intended to join co-op play! Similar to using the Sinister Resonant Bell, the rewards for killing the host are 10% of the Blood Echoes they require to level up and 1 point of Insight.

PvP

Once there's a Bell Ringer in your world, other players will be summoned to fight against you. Usually you need to have a co-op player with you for the Bell Ringer to appear somewhere in the area, but in Nightmare Frontier and Nightmare of Mensis they will always appear when you're online, so entering these areas makes PvP very likely. If you don't want to fight other players then you need to track down the Bell Ringer and kill her. She cannot appear in healing Church Workshop or Iosefka's Clinic, so these are safe areas. When a player engages you, remember that shooting them as they attempt to heal or use an item will interrupt them, allowing for a visceral attack. Don't let your opponents heal with impunity, or the battle can last a long time!

Chapter 2
Hunting Grounds

To the hunter, the nature of the hunting ground
is no less vital than the nature of the prey.
Knowledge of both provides a clear advantage.
The areas that you'll stalk in Bloodborne are rich
in complexity and filled with unseen paths, clever
shortcuts and obscure dead ends, all waiting to
be explored. This chapter will guarantee that you
see them all and learn their secrets, be they real
or part of a nightmare...

How to Use This Chapter

Welcome to the Hunting Grounds. This is no standard walkthrough, nor even a typical area guide; it's actually a hybrid chapter that shows you everything there is to know about each area while also providing a critical route to follow. On these pages we'll take you through the elements that make the chapter work.

Overview Pages

All areas begin with an overview page (or pages) on which you'll find the full area map alongside a breakdown of everything the area contains: enemies, NPCs, items and landmarks. We'll use an example overview page here to explain each element used.

❶ Area Details

We've come up with some small signifiers to give you an idea of an area's difficulty level and place within the game's overall flow. The first of these rates the area's difficulty. The second shows the character level and primary weapon level we recommend when entering the area. Finally, there's the time of day; key events in the game advance the time of day, and some areas can be tackled at different times. The time shown here is the one we recommend entering the area during.

❷ Enemies

This chart lists all of the enemies you'll encounter in the area. Each one has a page reference you can follow to find their full strategy page. For easy reference, we also show each enemy's HP and the amount of Blood Echoes they drop when defeated. Enemies are categorized into four distinct types: Regular, Hunter, Strong and Boss.

❸ Insight

There are actions you can take in each area that will cause you to gain Insight. We list each of these, along with the exact amount of Insight you'll gain. For details on what Insight is and what you can do with it, check out p669.

❹ NPCs

Some (but not all) areas are home to NPCs that ask for your help or just want to talk to you (or be rid of you). These are listed in small charts like this one, with a page reference in case you want to find out the full details surrounding a particular NPC.

❺ Items

Every area has items that you can find and pick up. We show their locations as numbered icons on the overview map, and these correspond to the numbers in the Item Legend list. You'll most often find items in chests or in glowing white balls on the floor, so look for those when searching with help from the map. Most items have black icons on the map, but some very important ones are colored gold to make them stand out. These gold icons are also placed next to the individual Focal Point headers so that you can quickly find and read about the area where you pick up the item.

❻ Bell Ringers

When you ring the Beckoning Bell, the help you call for will bring with it a Bell Ringer, who will summon opposing hunters. You'll need to find and kill her to avoid being invaded, so her location in each area is important. We've added the Bell Ringer icon to the overview maps to make this as easy as possible.

❼ Map Links

In the sample page you'll see that we use curving red lines to link places where one floor leads to another (usually via ladders or stairways) to make them visually as clear as possible.

❽ Landmarks

The area's most distinct or important parts are highlighted as landmarks on the overview map. We've split the map up so that only one of these appears on each of the walkthrough pages, so the page reference here lets you easily skip straight to that part of the area.

Walkthrough Pages

❾ Boss/World Change

Boss encounters are key points in the area at which you'll need to defeat a major foe. We'll always reference the relevant page in the Bestiary when you approach a boss, but we might gave some key tips in the text here to avoid having to flick back and forth too often.

❿ Route Lines

The route lines on the map are very important. They show two distinct things: the critical path through the area, colored red, and optional exploration paths, colored blue. Following the red route line will get you through the area in the most direct route, without missing anything of key importance. When the route diverges to blue exploration areas you'll have a choice to make, and reading the text linked to the corresponding blue point will help you to make the right one.

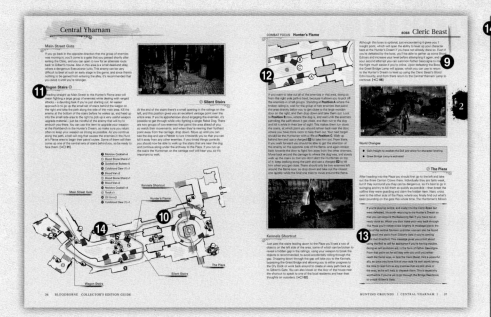

⑭ Maps

Each page has its own map, which is a section cut from the area's overall map. For these maps we sometimes include areas from different floors layered on top of each other in order to make the area's geography clear. In these cases, if an item is on a lower floor it will be slightly faded. If you pay attention to the route lines and icons, such as Levers, Lamps and Ambush Enemies, you should be able to make your way through an area with minimal surprises or missed opportunities, allowing you to read the text only when needed.

- 🔵 Lamp
- 🎚 Lever
- 👻 NPC
- 🔴 Regular Enemy
- 🦇 Hunter Enemy
- 🐾 Special Enemy Appearance
- 🌙 Wandering Nightmare
- ⚔ Strong Enemy
- 🐀 Boss
- 🏹 Sniper Enemy
- 🐍 Enemy Ambush
- 🚪 Locked Door
- 🔒 Locked Door (one side)
- 🔔 Bell Ringer
- ✉ Note

⑪ Focal Points

Each point along the route line is given a name, and corresponds to the text you'll find elsewhere on the page with the same name. The text is also color-coded according to the route lines, so if you only want to follow the critical path then you only need to read the red points.

⑫ Combat Focus

At times when there are a lot of enemies, or a very specific way to tackle a battle, we'll show the key positions on the cropped map. Usually we do this when focusing on a particularly challenging combat situation, so that we can show exact enemy locations, or useful defensive positions.

⑬ Event Box

Sometimes you'll find an item or meet a character that lets you do something very important in another area, though you may not realize it at the time. These boxes appear rarely, but when they do you'll know you've found or triggered something worth paying attention to.

Progression Guide

Starting on p200, near the end of this chapter, you'll find the Progression Guide, which provides an at-a-glance overview of each area's key items and events. A lot of useful data about each area has been included, such as the total amount of Blood Echoes you'll get there, the rank of the Blood Gems that drop and the amount and location of all Fortification Materials. Consult this for planning purposes or as a spoiler-free quick reference guide.

Accessing the Hunter's Nightmare

To access the Hunter's Nightmare and related areas you'll first need to make your way through Central Yharnam to the Cathedral Ward. Either purchase the Hunter Chief Emblem to open the gate, or advance through Old Yharnam and the Healing Church Workshop to reach the Grand Cathedral. Defeat Vicar Amelia in the Grand Cathedral and inspect the nearby skull to advance time to Night. Now, upon returning to the Hunter's Dream you'll find the Eye of a Blood-drunk Hunter at the foot of the Side Stairway. Take it, return to the Oedon Chapel in the Cathedral Ward and leave the building through the left exit to the Well area. Head over to where the Hunter's attire set was located and allow the Amygdala perched on the chapel to grab you. After a short cut-scene, you'll be transported to the Hunter's Nightmare. From this point onward, the gravestone near the rear entrance of the building in the Hunter's Dream will serve as your warp point to and from those areas.

Stand here and the Amygdala will grab you...

This is the location of the Hunter's Nightmare gravestone.

Hunter's Dream (Afternoon)

You awaken, drowsily, to the sight of an old graveyard chapel building, set among an idyllic garden. The drowsiness and the fog combine to make this feel like a dream. And if where you came from was reality, then this dream is a big improvement. There's much to learn here.

NPC

Name	Page
Doll	p635
Gehrman, the First Hunter	p634
Bath Messenger	p664
Insight Trade	p666
Stump Messenger	–

The Gravestones

A row of gravestones run along the stairway that leads to the Workshop's main entrance doors. Each of these stones is used for Chalice Rituals, with the exception of the lowest one, which is used for online matchmaking. More details on Chalice Dungeons can be found on p394. Messengers spill forth from a fountain in the alcove opposite the gravestones; they act as a shop, selling you goods in exchange for Blood Echoes. For details of what they'll sell you and when, see p664. [→☐ 01/02]

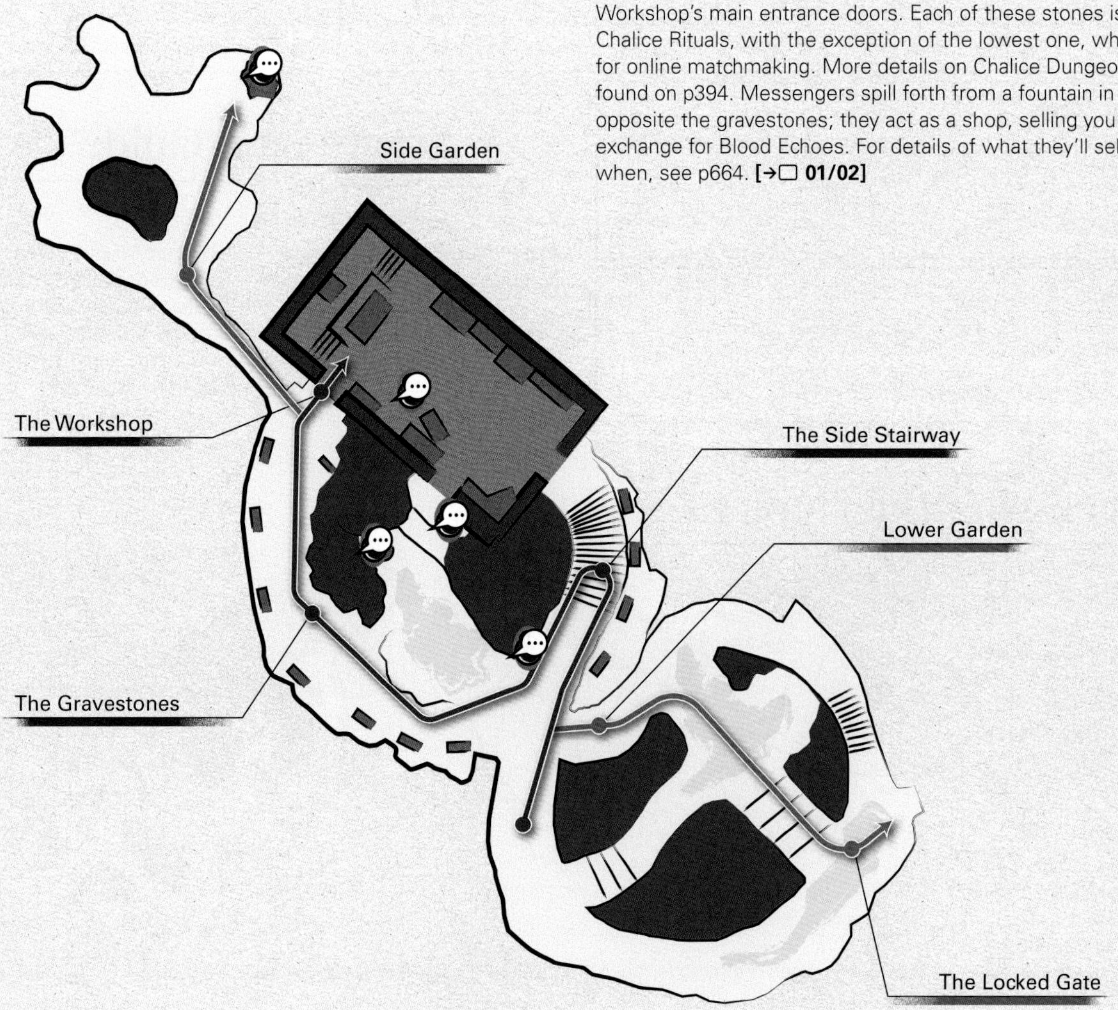

Side Garden

The Workshop

The Side Stairway

Lower Garden

The Gravestones

The Locked Gate

Wandering around the Lower Garden you'll come across a lot more Notes on the ground. Viewing them is worthwhile, even if you're familiar with games like Bloodborne, because they include many useful tips about things you could easily overlook. [→☐ 04]

The Side Stairway

More gravestones line the outer side of this stairway. These ones are used to awaken in various places in the real world. Initially you'll only be able to awake in Iosefka's Clinic, but the list of places will increase as you discover new areas and light more lamps. The Lamps in the early areas will generally be on the first Yharnam Headstone, but as you explore more you'll open up options on the other ones higher up the stairs. The first time you visit the Hunter's Dream there are Messengers on the stairway, offering you a choice of starting weapons, so make sure you don't miss them. At the bottom of this stair is a lifeless doll. If you return to the Hunter's Dream after acquiring some Insight the doll will awaken. You can talk to her or choose to level up your character by spending some Blood Echoes. Everything you need to know about the Doll can be found on p635.

The Workshop

The Workshop's interior is dusty and covered in old books. Gehrman, an old hunter in a wheelchair, sometimes appears here with advice for you. To the right of the fireplace is your storage box, and to its left is the workbench, which you'll come back often to use for weapon upgrading and equipping Blood Gems. There's also a small altar near the main entrance that will allow you to select and equip Caryll Runes once you've acquired a certain item. Opposite the fireplace there an open door, leading to a small ledge. Here you'll find another fountain, where Messengers are offering items to trade, but only when you have some Insight to spare. [→☐ 03]

The Locked Gate

At the furthest corner of the garden is a locked gate, and until very late in the game the area beyond it will remain inaccessible. We cover every accessible part of an area under each area's section, but to avoid spoilers, there are a few important exceptions made for places that you'll need to return to much later. This is one of those exceptions; at the point when you can open this gate, the related page in the Area Guide (which happens to be p160, for those who don't mind spoilers) will detail what lies behind it. [→☐ 05]

Side Garden

The Side garden is found to the left of the Workshop's main entrance doors. It is home nothing of interest, other than a small tree stump. Examining the stump reveals that Messengers may reside there, but you won't actually find them there until later visits. Once they appear you can use items you find in other areas to change the Messengers' appearance. [→☐ 06]

Central Yharnam

You awaken in a clinic full of rusty medical equipment. Madmen roam the streets, and the howls of beasts echo through the city. Behind shuttered doors, Yharnamites warn you of your plight; as an outsider wandering the streets on the night of the Hunt, you are alone. You also hear rumors of a Healing Church where you may find information on the Paleblood you seek, but first you must brave the beasts of Yharnam and the mindless hunters that stalk the alleyways. As the afternoon fades into evening, the nightly hunt begins...

Difficulty	Area **B** | Cleric Beast **B** | Father Gascoigne **A**
Recommended	Player Level **25-35** | Weapon Upgrade **+3**
Timezones	○ ◑ ☾ ●
Insight	Encounter the Cleric Beast ×1, Defeat the Cleric Beast ×3, Encounter Father Gascoigne ×1, Witness Father Gascoigne's transformation ×1, Defeat Father Gascoigne ×2

Enemies

Regular	HP	Echoes	Page
Huntsman (Torch & Axe)	150	48	p225
Huntsman (Torch & Shield)	70	48	p226
Huntsman (Sickle)	70	48	p226
Huntsman (Cleaver)	70	48	p226
Huntsman (Cutlass)	150	48	p227
Huntsman (Pitchfork)	150	48	p227
Huntsman (Rifle)	90	48	p227
Wheelchair Huntsman (Pistol)	80	58	p229
Rabid Dog	80	53	p230
Carrion Crow	70	29	p231
Large Huntsman (Torch & Saw)	225	73	p232
Large Huntsman (Spear)*	282	73	p232
Labyrinth Rat	98	62	p233
Rotted Corpse	239	56	p233

*Strong version protects Hunter's Garb: 358 HP, 257 Echoes.

Strong	HP	Echoes	Page
Scourge Beast	520	336	p266
Huntsman's Minion (Brick)	279	158	p267
Huntsman's Minion (Statue)	279	158	p268
Executioner	343	340	p269
Maneater Boar	423	431	p270

Boss	HP	Echoes	Page
Cleric Beast	3015	4000	p326
Father Gascoigne	2031	1800	p328

NPC

Name	Page	Name	Page
Iosefka	p645	Older Sister	p642
Iosefka (Imposter)	p646	Lonely Old Woman	p638
Gilbert	p635	Eileen the Crow	p636
Young Girl	p642		

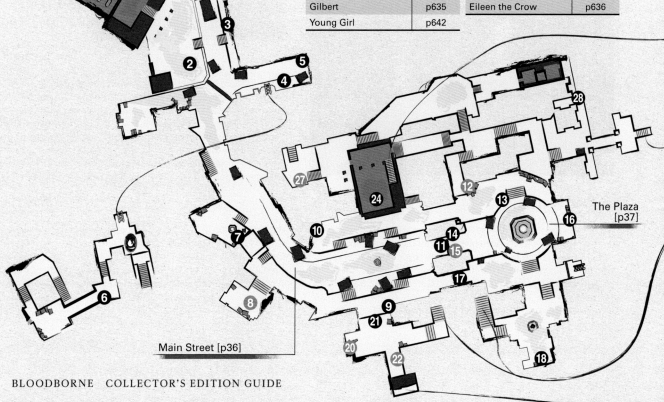

Start

The Clinic [p34]

The Plaza [p37]

Main Street [p36]

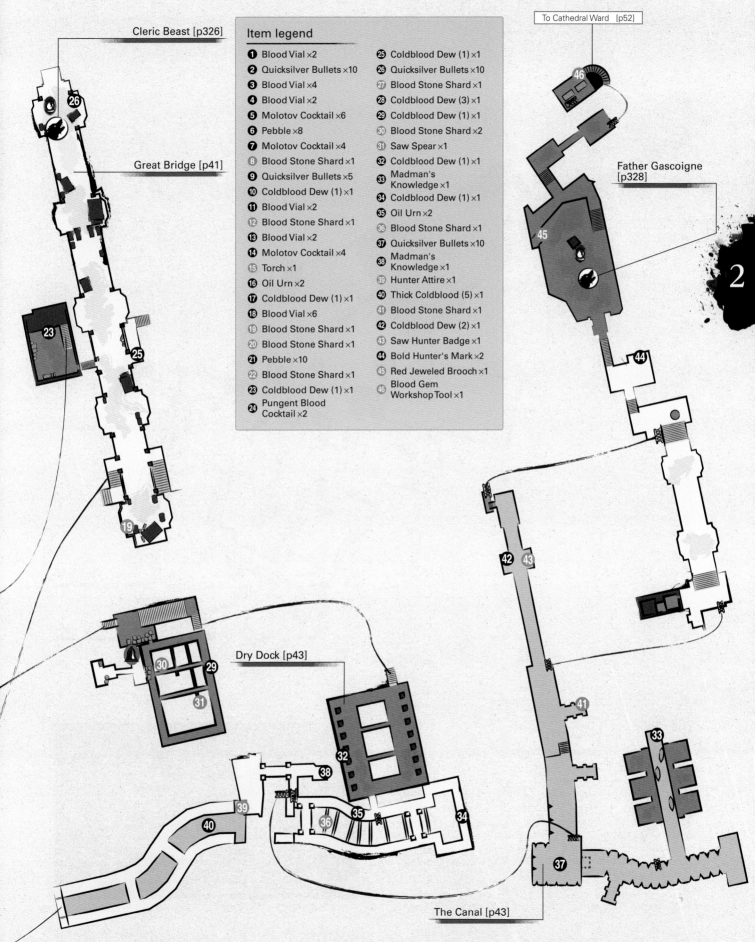

Cleric Beast [p326]

Great Bridge [p41]

To Cathedral Ward [p52]

Father Gascoigne [p328]

Dry Dock [p43]

The Canal [p43]

Item legend

1. Blood Vial ×2
2. Quicksilver Bullets ×10
3. Blood Vial ×4
4. Blood Vial ×2
5. Molotov Cocktail ×6
6. Pebble ×8
7. Molotov Cocktail ×4
8. Blood Stone Shard ×1
9. Quicksilver Bullets ×5
10. Coldblood Dew (1) ×1
11. Blood Vial ×2
12. Blood Stone Shard ×1
13. Blood Vial ×2
14. Molotov Cocktail ×4
15. Torch ×1
16. Oil Urn ×2
17. Coldblood Dew (1) ×1
18. Blood Vial ×6
19. Blood Stone Shard ×1
20. Blood Stone Shard ×1
21. Pebble ×10
22. Blood Stone Shard ×1
23. Coldblood Dew (1) ×1
24. Pungent Blood Cocktail ×2
25. Coldblood Dew (1) ×1
26. Quicksilver Bullets ×10
27. Blood Stone Shard ×1
28. Coldblood Dew (3) ×1
29. Coldblood Dew (1) ×1
30. Blood Stone Shard ×2
31. Saw Spear ×1
32. Coldblood Dew (1) ×1
33. Madman's Knowledge ×1
34. Coldblood Dew (1) ×1
35. Oil Urn ×2
36. Blood Stone Shard ×1
37. Quicksilver Bullets ×10
38. Madman's Knowledge ×1
39. Hunter Attire ×1
40. Thick Coldblood (5) ×1
41. Blood Stone Shard ×1
42. Coldblood Dew (2) ×1
43. Saw Hunter Badge ×1
44. Bold Hunter's Mark ×2
45. Red Jeweled Brooch ×1
46. Blood Gem Workshop Tool ×1

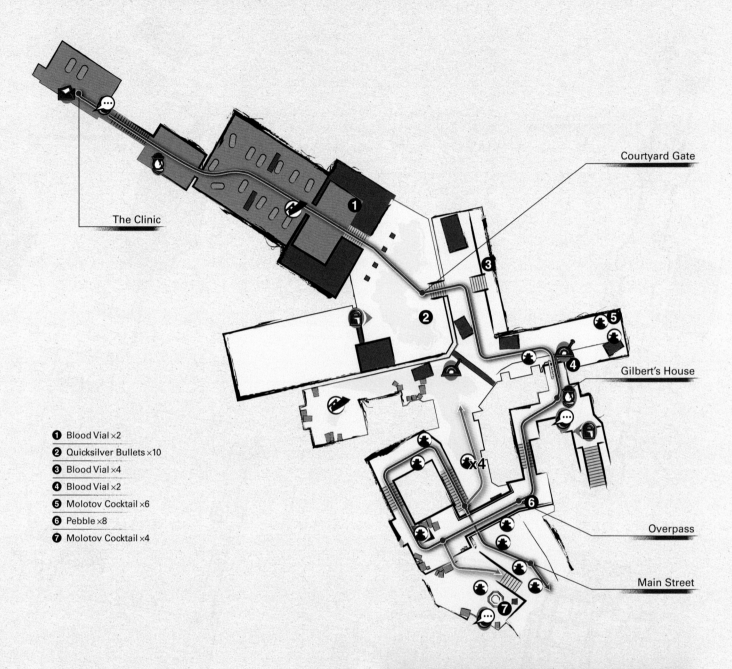

Courtyard Gate

The Clinic

Gilbert's House

Overpass

Main Street

❶ Blood Vial ×2
❷ Quicksilver Bullets ×10
❸ Blood Vial ×4
❹ Blood Vial ×2
❺ Molotov Cocktail ×6
❻ Pebble ×8
❼ Molotov Cocktail ×4

The Clinic

With the blood still wet on your contract you'll awaken in a small room in Iosefka's Clinic with a small note on a chair in front of you providing the only hint of what to do. There are two doors in the room: one of them cannot be opened from this side, so go through the other one and head down the stairs. You'll soon come across a Scourge Beast feasting on a corpse. Defeating it barehanded is difficult; your safest option is just to run past it. If it kills you, you'll be transported to the Hunter's Dream, where you can acquire your first weapons and then return to the Clinic to exact your revenge upon the beast. [→☐ 01]

01

Courtyard Gate

The courtyard outside the clinic has two gates. One is locked and can't be opened until later, so proceed through the other one (after picking up the item near it). Be careful as you move up the path to the right, because there's an enemy patrolling on the other side of the carriage ahead. Just past him there's a switch to lower a ladder, but if you don't have a weapon you'll need to lure him away from it before you try to climb up. While you're doing that it's well worth picking up the Firebombs at the end of the path; they'll be very useful in the upcoming sections. [→▢ 02]

Gilbert's House

Upon reaching the top of the ladder you'll find yourself outside Gilbert's house, by the Central Yharnam Lamp. If you have not yet been to the Hunter's Dream to collect your weapons, use the Lamp here to do that now, because proceeding without them would be extremely difficult. Gilbert knows the area well and often has hints about places that you may want to investigate, so it's worth checking back with him often. After you've been to the Hunter's Dream you can also return to the Clinic and speak with Iosefka to get a potent healing item. For more information on Iosefka, refer to p645, and turn to p635 to find out more about Gilbert. [→▢ 03]

Overpass

As you approach the Overpass you'll be able to pick up a number of Pebbles that you can use to quietly get the attention of an enemy, or separate one from a group. A Huntsman will attempt to ambush you when you reach the other side of the Overpass, so don't run ahead too quickly. Once you've dealt with him you can either head down the stairway, or drop through a gap in the railings for a small shortcut. [→▢ 04]

When you get to the top of the stairs overlooking Main Street, you'll notice a large group of Huntsmen slowly making their way up the street. While you can wait until they're much further up the street before proceeding, it's best to deal with them sooner rather than later, so that you don't accidentally run into them further along the street. Wait until they're just past the bottom of the stairs, and then use a Pebble to attract one of the rear enemies and separate it from the group; once it's down, do the same thing again for one or two more until you feel comfortable finishing off any that remain. [→▢ 05/06]

Central Yharnam

Main Street Gate

If you go back in the opposite direction that the group of enemies was moving in, you'll come to a gate that you passed shortly after exiting the Clinic, and you can open it now for an alternate route back to Gilbert's house. Also in this area is a small dead-end alley, where a dangerous Executioner lurks. This enemy can be very difficult to beat at such an early stage in the game, and since there's nothing to be gained from entering the alley, it's recommended that you avoid it until you're stronger.

Wagon Stairs ⑧

Heading straight up Main Street to the Hunter's Flame area will mean fighting a large group of enemies while dealing with ranged attacks – a daunting task if you're just starting out. An easier approach is to go up the small set of stairs behind the wagon on the right and take the path along the side of the main area. Kill the enemy at the bottom of the stairs before he wakes up, and head up into the small side area to the right to pick up a very useful weapon upgrade material – just be mindful of the enemy that will try to ambush you there. You can use this item to upgrade your weapon at the Workbench in the Hunter's Dream, so make sure you return often to keep your weapon as strong as possible. As you continue along the path, a bell will ring that causes the enemies in the Hunter's Flame area to begin their patrol routes. Some of them will then come up one of the central sets of stairs behind you, so be ready to face them. **[→□ 01]**

⑫ Silent Stairs

At the end of the stairs there's a small opening in the railings on the left, and this position gives you an excellent vantage point over the entire area. If you're apprehensive about engaging the enemies, it's possible to get through while only fighting a single Rabid Dog. There are two groups of two enemies that patrol the area ahead of you, so watch their movements, and when they're nearing their furthest point away from the carriage, drop down. Move up until you can see the dog and use a Pebble to lure it towards you so that you can kill it away from any other enemies. If you timed things correctly you should now be able to walk up the stairs that are near the dog and continue along under the archway to the Plaza. If you run up the stairs the Huntsman on the carriage roof will hear you, so it's important to walk.

⑦ Molotov Cocktail ×4
⑧ Blood Stone Shard ×1
⑨ Quicksilver Bullets ×5
⑩ Coldblood Dew (1) ×1
⑪ Blood Vial ×2
⑫ Blood Stone Shard ×1
⑬ Blood Vial ×2
⑭ Molotov Cocktail ×4
⑮ Torch ×1
⑯ Oil Urn ×2
⑰ Coldblood Dew (1) ×1

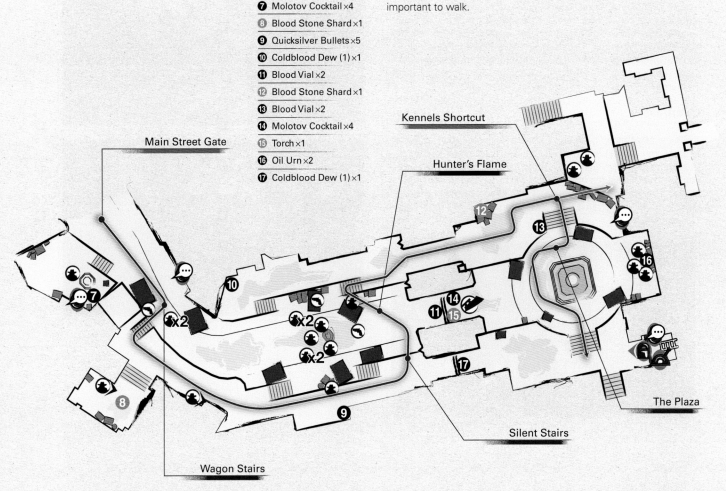

Main Street Gate

Kennels Shortcut

Hunter's Flame

The Plaza

Silent Stairs

Wagon Stairs

COMBAT FOCUS Hunter's Flame

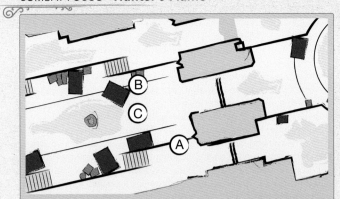

If you want to take out all of the enemies in this area, doing so from the right side path is best, because it allows you to pick off the enemies in small groups. Standing at **Position A** where the broken railing is, wait for the group of two enemies that patrol the area directly below you to get close to the large wooden door on the right, and then drop down and take them out. Look to **Position B** now, where the dog is, and wait until the enemies patrolling the path above it get close, and then run to the dog and kill it while in their line of sight. This makes them run down the stairs, at which point you should retreat back near the door, where you have more room to take them out. Your next target should be the Huntsman with a rifle at **Position C**. Walk up behind him and use a charged R2 to take him out. From there, if you walk forward you should be able to get the attention of the enemy on the opposite side of the flame, and again retreat back towards the door to fight him away from the other enemies. Move back around the carriage to where the dog was, and slowly walk up the stairs so that you don't alert the Huntsman on top of it; keep walking along the path and use a charged R2 to kill him when you get close. There should only be two enemies left around the flame now, so drop down and take out the closest one quickly while the final one tries to move around the flame.

Kennels Shortcut

Just past the stairs leading down to the Plaza you'll see a row of objects on the left side of the area, some of which can be broken to reveal a hidden gap in the railings; using your weapon to break the objects is recommended, to avoid accidentally rolling through the gap. Dropping down through the gap will take you to the Kennels, bypassing the Great Bridge and allowing you to either progress to the Dry Dock or work back around to create an easy path back up to Gilbert's Gate. You can also knock on the door of the house near the shortcut to speak to one of the local residents and hear their thoughts on outsiders. [→☐ 02]

⑮ The Plaza

After heading into the Plaza you should first go to the left and take out the three Carrion Crows there. Individually they are fairly weak, but if they surround you they can be dangerous, so it's best to go in swinging and try to kill them as quickly as possible – then break the coffins they were guarding and claim the hidden item. Next, cross over to the other side of the Plaza, where you finally find out what's been pounding on the gate this whole time. The Huntsman's Minion hits hard, but since it has its back to you, you can run up behind it and get close enough to hit it with a charged R2 attack as it is turning around. If you then follow up with a transform attack combo to keep it off balance, you can nearly kill it before you need to back off and let your stamina recover. Once it's dead, make sure you pick up the Torch, and then continue up the stairs towards the Well. [→☐ 03]

If you're playing online, and made it to the Cleric Beast but were defeated, it's worth returning to the Hunter's Dream so that you can acquire the Beckoning Bell if you have not already done so. When you then make your way back through The Plaza you'll notice a new brightly lit message just to the side of the central fountain (a similar one can also be found just down the stairs from Gilbert's Gate if you're coming from that direction). This message gives you a hint about using the Bell to call for assistance if you're having trouble. Doing so will summon aid, in the form of Father Gascoigne. From that point on he will stay with you until you either reach the Canal area, or face the Cleric Beast. He's a powerful ally, so once you have him at your side it's well worth taking the time to lead him to any enemies that are still alive in the area, as he will help to dispatch them. This is especially worthwhile if you've yet to go through the Bridge Residence to unlock Gilbert's Gate.

Central Yharnam

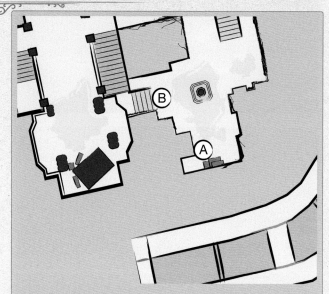

The Well can be difficult, especially if you run straight up the stairs, but if you're patient and tactical it can be done relatively safely. At first glance it appears that you only have to deal with one Rabid Dog patrolling the area between the top of the stairs and the Well, and another stationary one at **Position A**. When you reach the top of the stairs, however, a large group of enemies including a sniper and another Rabid Dog will come down the stairs at **Position B**. Try to deal with the two dogs that are already in the area first. Start by running up the stairs to the patrolling one and killing it as quickly as possible, and then throw a Pebble at the stationary one at the back if it hasn't spotted you already. Run back down the stairs so that it follows you, allowing you to kill it out of the patrolling group's line of sight.

Next, run back up the stairs so that the sniper and one or two of the patrolling enemies spot you, and then retreat again. Once the Huntsman with the rifle spots you he will rarely change position, so you can use the railings and the wall to the side of the stairs as cover from his shots, to avoid worrying about him while fighting the others. Repeat this tactic for any other patrolling enemies, and then move up and take out the rifleman. Finally, if you did not kill the Huntsman's Minion that was pounding on the door at the Plaza, it will approach from behind when you enter the Well area, so make sure you're prepared for it.

When you reach the top of the bridge, you can cross straight over it to find this small overlook area, where you'll be able to replenish your Pebble supply and pick up another Blood Stone Shard. You can drop off the ledge to get back down to the Hunter's Flame area if you wish, and if you've killed all the enemies then this can be a good time to head back and upgrade your weapon. On the opposite side of the area there's an alley leading to another ledge that you can drop off; you'll land on a series of wooden platforms. These will lead you down to the Aqueducts, where you'll be able to find some useful items, and if you wish to return there's a series of ladders that you can use to climb back up. **[→⬚ 01]**

01

Upon dropping down to the walkways above the Aqueduct, you'll be able to see a number of Large Huntsmen patrolling around the area. Try to watch their routes and pick them off one at a time to keep the fights manageable. If you're confident in your shooting skills, interrupting their attacks so that you can stagger them for a visceral attack is by far the quickest way to dispatch them. Near the opposite end of the Aqueducts there's a beam with an item on it about half-way down the wall, and if you line yourself up carefully you can drop onto the beam to retrieve it. Once you're on the beam, drop down again and kill the Labyrinth Rats below you quickly, because another Large Huntsman is around the corner nearby and you'll want to face him one-on-one. When the area is clear, go around the corner and pick up the Attire set the Large Huntsman was guarding, and then either backtrack along the Aqueducts and use the ladders to reach the Main Street Overlook, or drop down to the Canals and use the ladders there to get back to the Great Bridge via the Plaza. **[→⬚ 02]**

02

Canal Residence

Climbing this ladder will take you up to another small area above the canals, and if you head around to the right you can fight your way through a group of Carrion Crows to reach an item. After crossing the bridge there's a door on the right that you can knock on to speak with one of the local residents. In the opposite corner there's yet another ladder that will take you up towards the Plaza, but standing below it is a Huntsman's Minion; thankfully he has his back to you, so you can sneak up and use a charged attack to stagger him from behind. Next to the gate at the top of the ladder you'll notice a glow coming from the window, and if you approach it you can talk to the Young Girl inside the house. If you want, you can offer to help look for missing mother, and to help aid your search she'll give you the Tiny Music Box, which is useful in an upcoming boss battle. To find out more about the Young Girl's story, refer to p642. [→▢ 03]

Twin Wolves

As you make your way along the Great Bridge you'll encounter two Scourge Beasts. These can be very dangerous enemies, especially when you have to face two of them at once. Running straight up and fighting them head on can be problematic because of how aggressive they are, so if you want to fight them on the bridge, it's a good idea to weaken them from a distance with Molotovs, or Throwing Knives if you have any. Alternatively, you can run past them and head into the Bridge Residence, where you'll be able to fight them in relative safety using long ranged attacks, since they cannot pass through the doorway. [→▢ 04]

2

- ⑱ Blood Vial ×6
- ⑲ Blood Stone Shard ×1
- ⑳ Blood Stone Shard ×1
- ㉑ Pebble ×10
- ㉒ Blood Stone Shard ×1
- ㊳ Madman's Knowledge ×1
- ㊴ Hunter Hat ×1
  Hunter Garb ×1
  Hunter Gloves ×1
  Hunter Trousers ×1
- ㊵ Thick Coldblood (5) ×1

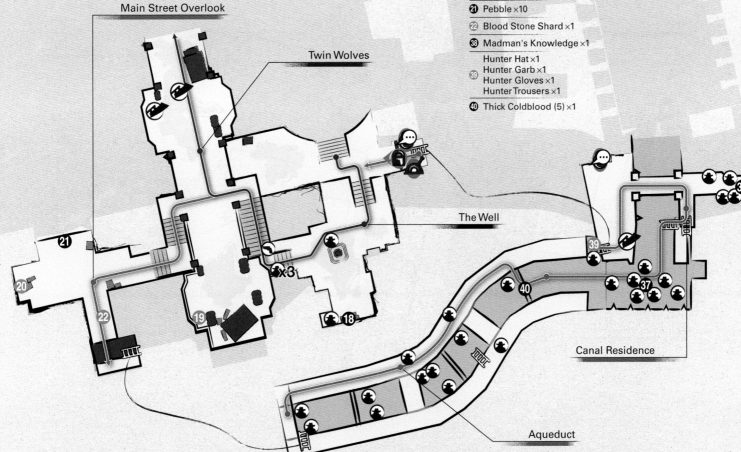

Main Street Overlook

Twin Wolves

The Well

Canal Residence

Aqueduct

Central Yharnam

Crumbled Stairs

Opposite the Bridge Residence you'll find a set of crumbled stairs near some breakable objects. You can drop down from here, making for another shortcut to the kennels area. This will allow you to skip going through the residence and dealing with the Cleric Beast if you wish, but is not recommended for your first time through the area. [→ ☐ 01]

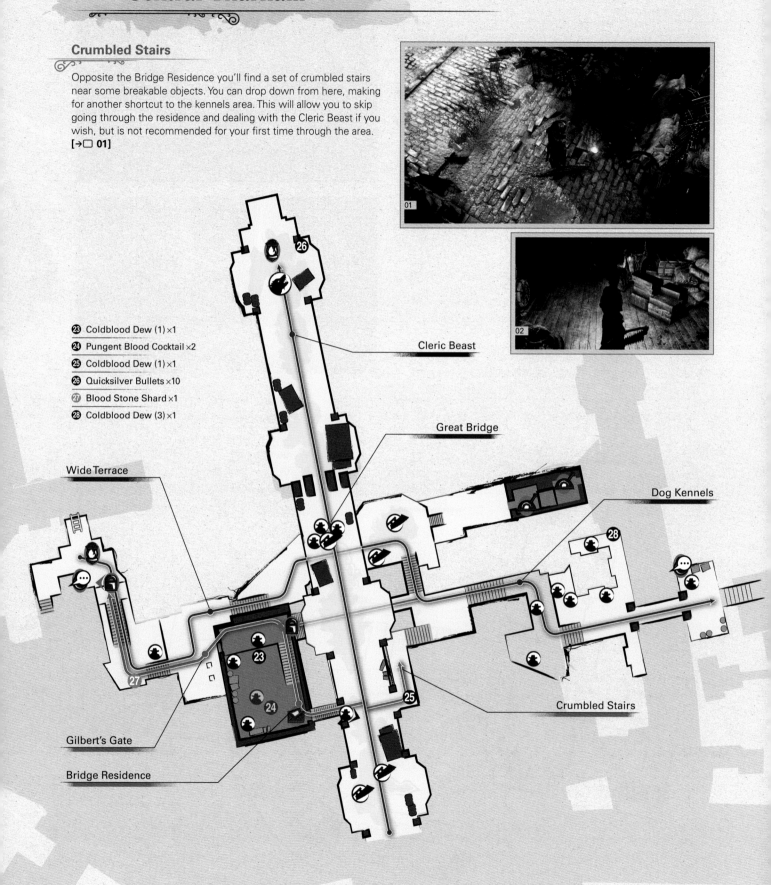

㉓ Coldblood Dew (1) ×1
㉔ Pungent Blood Cocktail ×2
㉕ Coldblood Dew (1) ×1
㉖ Quicksilver Bullets ×10
㉗ Blood Stone Shard ×1
㉘ Coldblood Dew (3) ×1

Cleric Beast

Great Bridge

Wide Terrace

Dog Kennels

Crumbled Stairs

Gilbert's Gate

Bridge Residence

Bridge Residence

Going through the residence will allow you to reach and unlock Gilbert's Gate and create an extremely useful shortcut back to the Great Bridge and later sections of the area; opening this shortcut is strongly recommended before you attempt to fight the Cleric Beast, so that you can quickly return if you're defeated. The residence itself is extremely dark, so it's worth equipping the Torch you acquired in the Plaza. There are two enemies hidden behind objects on the top floor – take them out first before proceeding downstairs. You'll be attacked by an enemy at the bottom of the stairs, so make sure you're ready for him, and then turn and start making your way towards the glowing item at the back of the room. When you get close you'll see a lifeless body in a wheelchair, but this enemy will spring to life when you walk past it for the item, so start attacking it as soon as you're in range. [→☐ 02]

Gilbert's Gate ㉗

After exiting the residence you'll need to run up some stairs (taking out an enemy and picking up the Blood Stone Shard along the way) to reach the switch at the top, so that you can finally unlock this gate. Once unlocked, you'll have a quick route from the Central Yharnam Lamp to both the Great Bridge and later sections of the area, making it the most important shortcut in the area. [→☐ 03]

Great Bridge

The final obstacle blocking your path to the end of the bridge is a group of enemies consisting of a Huntsman's Minion and three Carrion Crows. Conserving resources for the upcoming Boss fight is important, so it's best to try and separate the enemies to make the fight easier. To accomplish this, throw a Pebble at the Minion to lure it back towards you and fight it away from the other enemies; if you still have Throwing Knives left they can also be very useful for killing it as it tries to close in. Once it's down, move up and take out the remaining enemies before pushing onwards. [→☐ 04]

Although this boss is optional, just encountering it gives you 1 Insight point, which will open the ability to level up your character back at the Hunter's Dream if you have not already done so. Even if you're defeated by the boss, you'll be able to gather up some Blood Echoes and increase your level before attempting it again, and on your second attempt you can summon Father Gascoigne to make the fight much easier if you're online. Upon defeating the Boss, the Great Bridge Lamp will appear, which you can use to return to the Hunter's Dream to level up using the Cleric Beast's Blood Echo bounty, and from there return to the Central Yharnam Lamp to continue. [→☐ 05]

World Changes

- Gain Insight to awaken the Doll and allow for character leveling
- Great Bridge Lamp is activated

Wide Terrace

When you reach the steps at the top of the Wide Terrace you'll see two Huntsman's Minions patrolling the area below. Since fighting them both at the same time is very dangerous, you should try to separate them. One of them sometimes gets closer to the stairs than the other one, so if you stand roughly halfway between the stairs and the corner of the nearby building it should see you and come running. Lure this first one back to the stairs and kill it there, before moving up and finishing off the other one. At the far end of the Wide Terrace is an elevator that isn't usable yet, so follow the path up the stairs on the right. If you turn right again at the top of the stairs and go under the bridge, you'll be able to unlock another door on the bottom floor of the Bridge Residence, which will allow you to skip the Wide Terrace altogether on subsequent trips through the area.

Dog Kennels

There are a large number of caged Rabid Dogs in this area, and it's important to kill them as you come to them, because if left alone they will burst out of their cages when you reach the Canal Bridge and attack you from behind. Kill the two dogs on the upper part of the area first, and then go down the stairs and kill the two just to the left, before taking out the last two on the way to the bridge. Just before the bridge you'll be able to take a path to the left, where you'll see an item sitting on the ground near the end. Before picking it up, continue around the corner and take out another Rabid Dog that's hiding there.

Central Yharnam

Canal Bridge

As you cross the Canal Bridge you'll see another Rabid Dog barking angrily at a door, so run up and take it out while it's distracted. With the area now clear you can knock on the door the dog was interested in and speak with the Lonely Old Woman in the house. It turns out she's looking for a safe place to spend the night while the hunt is on, but since you know of no such place at this time, you can't help her yet. It's important to remember this location, however, so that you know to return once you do find a sanctuary. Check p638 to find out more about this character. [→ □ 01]

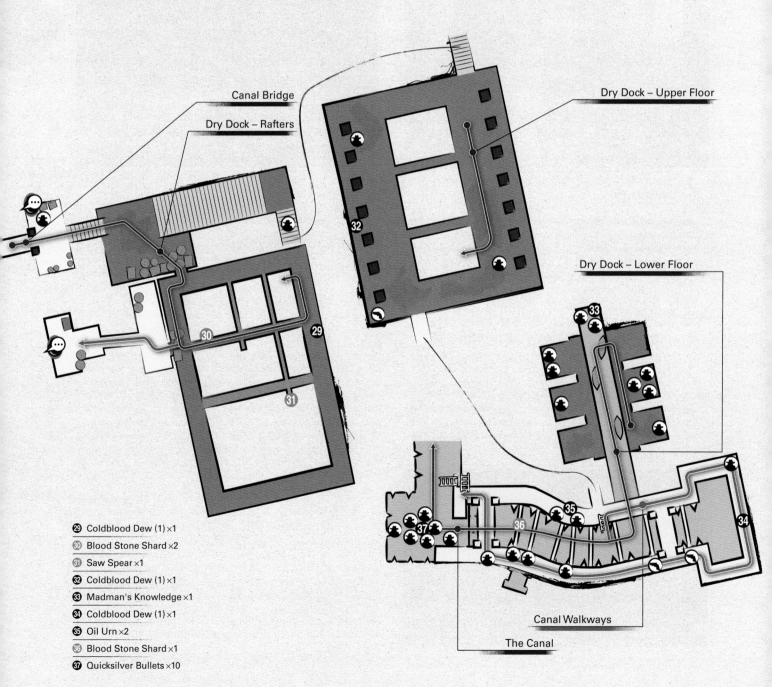

- ㉙ Coldblood Dew (1) ×1
- ㉚ Blood Stone Shard ×2
- ㉛ Saw Spear ×1
- ㉜ Coldblood Dew (1) ×1
- ㉝ Madman's Knowledge ×1
- ㉞ Coldblood Dew (1) ×1
- ㉟ Oil Urn ×2
- ㊱ Blood Stone Shard ×1
- ㊲ Quicksilver Bullets ×10

Dry Dock – Rafters ㉚ ㉛

Upon entering this building you'll notice a large set of stairs directly ahead, and while that is the obvious way to proceed, there is another, more lucrative way. Before progressing, however, it's worth approaching the top of the stairs and taking out the Large Huntsman that starts walking up them. Once he's down, break through the barrels and crates at top of the stairs to reveal an opening that you can drop through to reach the rafters. As you look out across the rafters you'll notice some more barrels on the right-hand side about halfway along. These are blocking another doorway that you can go through to reach a balcony, where you'll find the Eileen the Crow. If you go through all of her dialogue she will give you some items and a Gesture before telling you to continue with your hunt, but if you want to learn just what else Eileen is up to, refer to p636.

Back in the main room you'll notice two bodies hanging from the ceiling with items on them, but since they're too far out of reach, you need to break the chains holding them, so that they drop down to the floor below. Wide-arcing, long-range attacks are generally your safest option for breaking the chains, but you can also shoot them if you have the bullets to spare. When you're ready to proceed, go to one of the walkways around the outskirts of the rafters and drop down to the upper floor from there, taking care that you don't accidentally drop down to the lowest floor. [→☐ 02/03]

Dry Dock – Upper Floor

If you killed the Large Huntsman on the stairs when you first entered, you should only have to contend with two more of them on this floor: one stationary one with his back to you on the same side as the stairs, and another patrolling on the opposite side. If the one near the stairs has not detected you yet, you can walk up slowly and use a charged attack from behind; make sure you finish him off quickly, however, because a Huntsman armed with a rifle will come running out onto the walkway near the exit and start firing at you shortly after that. Once the Large Huntsman is down, run up to the Huntsman, using the pillars and coffins for cover, and kill him before going after the final Large Huntsman. The items on the bodies that you chopped down from the rafters are on either side of the central canal on the lower floor, meaning that you need to pick a side to drop down to get the first item you want. If you stand with the stairs to your back, it's recommended that you drop down onto the left side of the canal below, so that you can get the Saw Spear first.

Dry Dock – Lower Floor

There are a lot of Labyrinth Rats in the alcoves here, so kill them as you come to them, before picking up the Saw Spear. Once you have it, look to the back of the canal, where you'll find another alcove with some rats in it; drop down and take them out so that you can get the item they were guarding. To get the remaining item that you chopped down earlier you'll need to exit the Dry Dock and climb the ladder outside, so that you can get back to the Upper Floor, and then drop down again on the other side. There are more rats in the alcoves on that side too, so deal with them first before going for the item. [→☐ 04]

㊱ Canal Walkways

The ladder here leads up to the Canal Walkways, which you can use to re-enter the Dry Dock to get the remaining item on one of the bodies you chopped down from the Rafters. Before you start exploring the area, however, you'll need to deal with two-rifle carrying Huntsmen and a patrolling Large Huntsman. The Huntsmen with the rifles are the biggest initial threat, so try to use the statues on the sides of the nearby bridge to block their shots as you move in to take them out. Once they've been dealt with you can focus your attention on the Large Huntsman without having to worry about incoming gunfire.

If you follow the walkways along you'll be able to get some more items, as well as take out a large number of Carrion Crows that would otherwise drop down onto you if you were to run along the Canal below. Near the end of the walkway you can cross another bridge, where you'll find two more crows pecking away at a wooden coffin. Kill the crows and destroy the coffin to reveal the item that was hiding behind it. The final item in this area is dangling precariously on a beam below, so you need to line yourself up carefully and drop down onto it to retrieve it. If you miss the beam, simply climb the ladder and work your way back around to try again.

The Canal

At the end of the small canal is a wooden platform sticking out over an adjoining canal, from which you can access a ladder that leads up to the Canal Residence. If you look down below the platform you'll see an item surround by a large number of Rotted Corpses, and while they're dormant now, some of them will come to life when you get close to them, and the remaining ones will do so after you pick up the item. Try to finish off all of the ones that come to life when you drop down before picking up the item, so that you don't have to contend with them all at the same time. Once they've all been defeated, continue up the canal while taking out the enemies as you come to them.

Central Yharnam

Canal Exit ④

After descending the stairs in the canal, make sure you go into the small alcove on the right and get the Blood Stone Shard to help further upgrade your weapons. Just past that alcove you'll have to defeat some more Rotted Corpses, and there are also two Carrion Crows sitting on a beam; use Pebbles or your gun to knock them down so that you can fight them. At the end of the canal, just to the right of the Boar Tunnel, you'll find a ladder that you can use to access the Ambush Bridge above. Head up the ladder and activate the elevator to create a shortcut back here, and then decide whether to tackle the Boar Tunnel or the Ambush Bridge first. [→☐ 01-03]

Boar Tunnel ④

When you approach the entrance to this tunnel you'll see a large Maneater Boar at the other end guarding a pair of items. If you stay at the entrance to the tunnel the beast will eventually charge straight at you, and you can avoid this by stepping to one side as it draws near, after which you'll be able to turn around and attack it from behind. Or, with a full bar of Endurance, if you sprint straight towards it as soon as you enter the tunnel you can get behind it before it has time to charge. Once the beast is dead and you have the items, head back down the tunnel and up the ladder. Alternatively, if you crossed the Ambush Bridge first, you can climb down the ladder at the end of the bridge and sneak up behind the boar for an easy kill.

Ambush Bridge

Before you start crossing the bridge, make sure you've gone into the small building on the left and activated the elevator inside, as that will give you a straight path between here and the Central Yharnam Lamp – especially handy since there's a boss coming up. When you start crossing the bridge you'll notice a group of enemies on the other side, along with a mysterious ball just behind them; continue across the bridge until the enemies catch sight of you, and then backtrack quickly into one of the side alcoves along the bridge. A Huntsman with a torch will soon set the bale of hay ablaze and then a Huntsman's Minion will kick it along the bridge, killing any enemies in its path; make sure you're off to the side so that you don't get caught up in the destruction. Finish off any remaining enemies before crossing the bridge. After going up the first set of stairs leading on from the bridge you'll come to a small area with two enemies standing around an item; try to sneak up on them so that you can use a charged R2 and Visceral Attack follow-up on one of them to get an early advantage in the fight.

⑤ BOSS Father Gascoigne

The only thing standing between you and the next area now is Father Gascoigne, and if you've fully explored Central Yharnam you should have been able to upgrade your weapon to +2, which will aid you greatly in the battle. If you spoke to the Young Girl and got the Tiny Music Box after offering to find her mother, you can use it periodically in the fight to briefly disorientate Gascoigne, allowing you to get some easy hits in. Once he's been defeated, a new Lamp will appear near the fountain – make sure to light it, but don't use it just yet. Follow the path around to the upper part of the area and drop down onto a small rooftop to find the Red Jeweled Brooch that the Young Girl said her mother was wearing. The Brooch can be used to obtain a useful Blood Gem, or you can return it to the Young Girl; to help inform your choice, please refer to p642. [→☐ 04]

World Changes

- ● Tomb of Oedon Lamp is activated
- ● Gain access to the Cathedral Ward
- ● The Insight Trade shop opens up in the Hunter's Dream

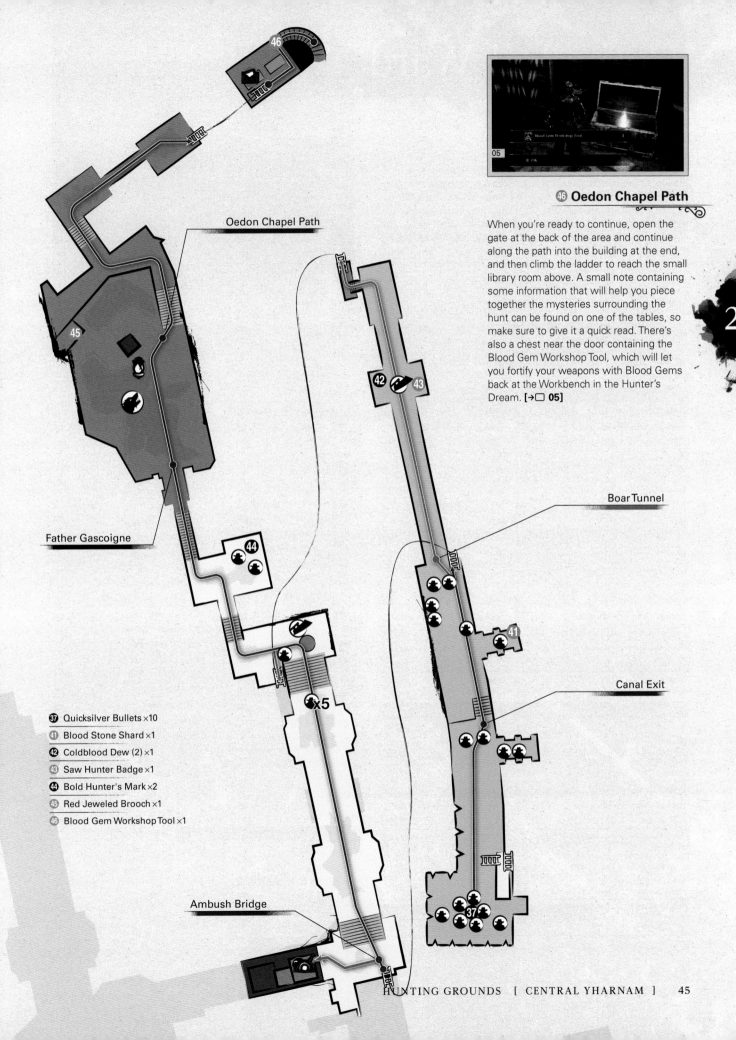

Oedon Chapel Path

Father Gascoigne

37 Quicksilver Bullets ×10
41 Blood Stone Shard ×1
42 Coldblood Dew (2) ×1
43 Saw Hunter Badge ×1
44 Bold Hunter's Mark ×2
45 Red Jeweled Brooch ×1
46 Blood Gem Workshop Tool ×1

Ambush Bridge

Boar Tunnel

Canal Exit

46 Oedon Chapel Path

When you're ready to continue, open the gate at the back of the area and continue along the path into the building at the end, and then climb the ladder to reach the small library room above. A small note containing some information that will help you piece together the mysteries surrounding the hunt can be found on one of the tables, so make sure to give it a quick read. There's also a chest near the door containing the Blood Gem Workshop Tool, which will let you fortify your weapons with Blood Gems back at the Workbench in the Hunter's Dream. [→☐ **05**]

2

Cathedral Ward

You push open the doors of Oedon Chapel. Within, a shadowy, robed creature asks you to search the city for survivors and bring them to the chapel for refuge. Stepping into the streets of the Cathedral Ward, you are beset by the servants of the Church as well as mad huntsmen. The scent of fading incense drifts through the streets; the residents are using the smell as a ward against the scourge of beasts, but the fragrance grows weaker by the hour. Though you can see your goal, Grand Cathedral, the main gates are barred – you'll need to find another way.

Difficulty	Area **B** | Vicar Amelia **B**
Recommended	Player Level **20-30** | Weapon Upgrade **+3**
Timezones	○ ◓ ☾ ●
Insight	Encounter Vicar Amelia ×1, Defeat Vicar Amelia ×3

To Hemwick Charnel Lane [p72]

Enemies

Regular	HP	Echoes	Page
Huntsman (Torch & Axe)	194	193	p225
Huntsman (Sickle)	125	171	p226
Huntsman (Cutlass)	194	193	p227
Huntsman (Pitchfork)	123	171	p227
Huntsman (Rifle)	158	214	p227
Huntsman (Rifle & Cutlass)	161	214	p228
Rabid Dog	141	184	p230
Carrion Crow*	123	110	p231
Church Servant (Cane)**	282	239	p234
Church Servant (Cane & Lantern)	282	258	p235
Church Servant (Cane & Flamesprayer)	233	257	p235
Church Servant (Cane & Pistol)	279	433	p235
Church Servant (Scythe)	343	464	p236
Church Servant (Crucifix)	429	742	p236
Large Huntsman (Torch & Saw)	287	257	p232
Large Huntsman (Plow)	358	257	p232
Wandering Nightmare	47	18	p671

*Cathedral Ward (Night): 125 HP/128 Blood Echoes
**In Cathedral Ward (Blood Moon): 343 HP/402 Blood Echoes

Strong	HP	Echoes	Page
Huntsman's Minion (Brick)	441	552	p267
Huntsman's Minion (Statue)	441	552	p268
Church Giant (Axe)	705	718	p271
Church Giant (Wrecking Ball)	705	718	p272
Brainsucker	150	449	p273
Executioner	404	1505	p269
Kidnapper	910	1368	p276

Hunter	HP	Echoes	Page
Yahar'gul Hunter (Tonitrus & Wooden Shield)	1030	3420	p313
Yahar'gul Hunter (Rifle Spear & Ludwig's Rifle)	886	3420	p313

Boss	HP	Echoes	Page
Vicar Amelia	5367	15000	p336

Item legend

① Madman's Knowledge ×1
② Top Hat ×1, Hunter Garb ×1, Hunter Gloves 1, Hunter Trousers ×1
③ Blood Vial ×6
④ Coldblood Dew (2) ×1
⑤ Molotov Cocktail ×4
⑥ Madman's Knowledge ×1
⑦ Madman's Knowledge ×1
⑧ Blood Stone Shard ×2
⑨ Monocular ×1
⑩ Blood Stone Shard ×3
⑪ Blood Stone Shard ×5
⑫ Tempering Blood Gemstone (1) ×1
⑬ Thick Coldblood (5) ×1
⑭ Thick Coldblood (4) ×1
⑮ Madman's Knowledge ×1
⑯ Madman's Knowledge ×1
⑰ Madman's Knowledge ×1
⑱ Madman's Knowledge ×1
⑲ Madman's Knowledge ×1
⑳ Twin Blood Stone Shards ×2
㉑ Shining Coins ×12
㉒ Tempering Blood Gemstone (2) ×1
㉓ Antidote ×1
㉔ Poison Knife ×12
㉕ Black Church Hat ×1, Black Church Garb ×1, Surgical Long Gloves ×1, Black Church Trousers/Dress ×1
㉖ Poison Knife ×18
㉗ Blood Vial ×2
㉘ Thick Coldblood (4) ×1
㉙ Quicksilver Bullets ×10
㉚ Thick Coldblood (5) ×1
㉛ Thick Coldblood (5) ×1
㉜ Thick Coldblood (6) ×1
㉝ Wooden Shield ×1
㉞ Numbing Mist ×6
㉟ Black Messenger Hat ×1
㊱ Thick Coldblood (5) ×1
㊲ Blood Vial ×7
㊳ Bloodshot Eyeball ×1
㊴ Bold Hunter's Mark ×3
㊵ Frenzied Coldblood (7) ×1
㊶ Twin Blood Stone Shards ×1
㊷ Lead Elixer ×3

NPC

Name	Page
Chapel Samaritan	p637
Alfred, Hunter of Vilebloods	p644
Arianna, Woman of the Night	p639
Bigoted Old Man	p640

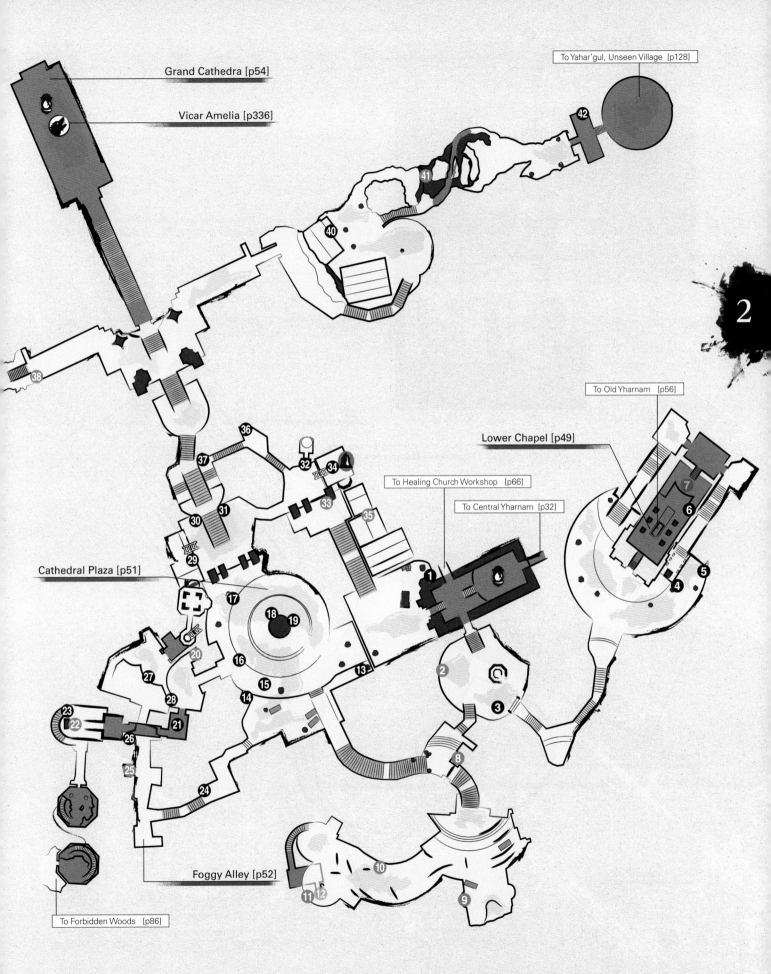

Grand Cathedra [p54]

Vicar Amelia [p336]

To Yahar'gul, Unseen Village [p128]

42

41

40

38

To Old Yharnam [p56]

Lower Chapel [p49]

To Healing Church Workshop [p66]

To Central Yharnam [p32]

36

37

32 34

33

31

35

30

29

Cathedral Plaza [p51]

7

6

5

4

1

17

18 19

16

20

27

2

15

28

3

13

14

23

22

21

26

8

25

24

Foggy Alley [p52]

10

11 12

9

To Forbidden Woods [p86]

2

Cathedral Ward

This Chapel acts as a sanctuary for those seeking safety during the night of the hunt. After speaking with the Chapel Samaritan you'll be able to inform anyone looking for a safe place about this location. If you return to Iosefka's Clinic in Central Yharnam and speak with her now, she'll also offer her services as a sanctuary, giving you two possible choices. To find out more about the sanctuary and how it works, go to p637. Be sure to activate the Cathedral Ward Lamp in the middle of the chapel, as you'll return to this area often. [→ ☐ 01/02]

World Changes

- With 15 Insight, Church Servants will become more powerful
- With 40 Insight, the creature attached to Oedon Chapel is visible

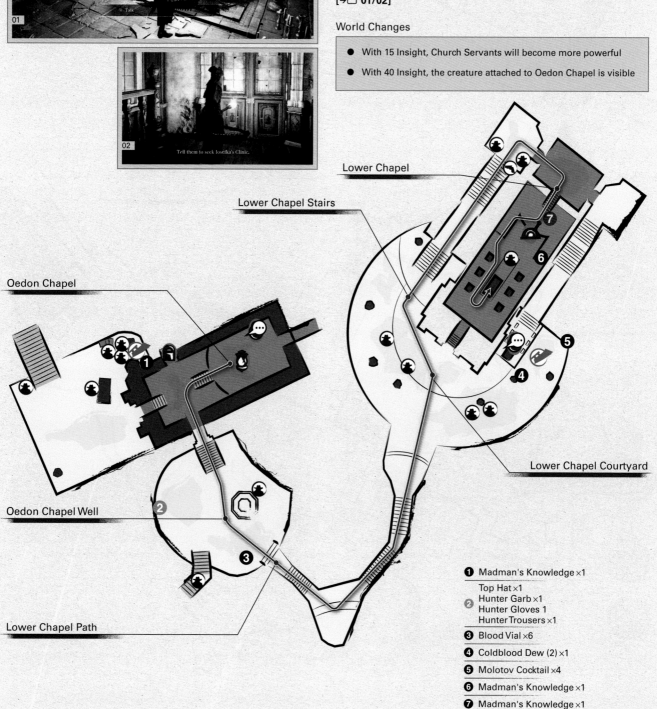

Lower Chapel

Lower Chapel Stairs

Oedon Chapel

Lower Chapel Courtyard

Oedon Chapel Well

Lower Chapel Path

❶ Madman's Knowledge ×1

❷ Top Hat ×1
Hunter Garb ×1
Hunter Gloves 1
Hunter Trousers ×1

❸ Blood Vial ×6

❹ Coldblood Dew (2) ×1

❺ Molotov Cocktail ×4

❻ Madman's Knowledge ×1

❼ Madman's Knowledge ×1

Oedon Chapel Well ❷

Upon stepping outside the chapel you'll encounter your first Church Servant approaching from a stairway on the other side of the well. Church Servants can inflict a lot of damage, so it can be safer to quickstep around their attacks, rather than try to interrupt them, at least until you're more familiar with the timing. The main threat here, though, is far more sinister and only reveals itself under certain conditions. There's an attire set that you can pick up from behind one of the large trees, but going near it will cause a mysterious portal to pass through the area. If you get too close to this portal you will be grabbed and instantly killed by an invisible being that is attached to the outside of the Oedon Chapel. You can still run and get the attire set – just make sure that you run back out of the area very quickly! [→☐ 03]

An important choice regarding how you want to proceed also needs to be made, and it will have a significant impact on the order in which you encounter other areas. The Plaza Gate near the middle of the Cathedral Ward is locked, and the only ways to open it are by operating the switch on the other side, or buying the Hunter Chief Emblem from the Bath Messengers for 10,000 Blood Echoes. To reach the other side of the gate without parting with your Blood Echoes, you'll have to go to Old Yharnam (p56) and defeat the boss there – that will cause the side door in the Oedon Chapel to open, allowing you to enter the Healing Church Workshop (p66). At the end of that area you can drop down to the other side of the Oedon Chapel Gate, giving you access to the rest of the Cathedral Ward.

If you buy the Emblem, you can interact with the gate to open it. This gives you the option to explore all of Cathedral Ward, and even head straight to Hemwick Charnel Lane. Old Yharnam is less challenging, though, and worth heading there first for the treasures it holds (chief among them a Holy Chalice), so that's the route we recommend.

Lower Chapel Path

This path leading down from the well will take you to the Lower Chapel, where you'll find the entrance to Old Yharnam. A single Church Servant patrols between the well and a small side area just after first set of stairs along the path. If you wait for him to come to a stop there you'll easily be able to sneak up behind him and use a charged R2 from behind. [→☐ 04]

Lower Chapel Courtyard

There are quite a few enemies patrolling the Lower Chapel Courtyard, so it's important not to go running straight ahead. Look at the chapel and wait for the patrolling group to move to the right-hand side of it;now you can circle around to the left and take out the enemy standing by the fire, and the one patrolling near him, before the others can see you. Then you simply need to get the attention of the Rabid Dog and lure it away from the other enemy before engaging it.

The Kidnapping Event

The small clearing just to the right-hand side of the Chapel is where an event happens after you've defeated the boss in Old Yharnam. A new enemy called a Kidnapper will appear in the clearing, and at two other locations in Cathedral Ward. We've marked their locations on the maps with a blue Strong Enemy icon. If one of these Kidnappers kills you, you'll be taken to Yahar'gul, Unseen Village. It can be a difficult area, so it's recommended that you do not trigger the event until you have cleared Hemwick Charnel Lane and have upgraded your weapon further.

Lower Chapel Stairs

At the top of these stairs you'll see a lone Huntsman looking down at you with a rifle. He's not as alone as he appears to be, so don't go running straight up. After going up a few of the stairs a Rabid Dog will come running down – wait for it to come all the way down and fight it out of the sniper's line of sight. A second Rabid Dog will do the same once you're further up the stairs, so make sure you trigger them one at a time. After opening the door, the path around the back of the Lower Church leads to a small shrine, where Alfred prays. Alfred is a fellow hunter of sorts, and if you agree to cooperate with him, he'll be more than willing to share all of the useful information he has on the church. He will also give you three Fire Papers and a new Gesture. If you want to learn more about Alfred and his quest, please turn to p644.

Lower Chapel

Upon entering the Lower Chapel from the rear you'll see a lever. Pulling this lever moves the large sarcophagus in the middle of the building, revealing a hidden stairway that leads down to Old Yharnam. There are ledges to either side of the lever that you can use to drop back down to the floor, and one of these has an item on it, so be sure to grab it first. There's only a single enemy in this part of the church, so try to find him quickly when you drop down to avoid being ambushed later.

Cathedral Ward

COMBAT FOCUS **Stairway Gate** ⑧ ⑨

Upon reaching this gate you'll encounter your first Church Giant at **Position A**, so approach with caution. These huge, lumbering enemies make up for their lack of speed with incredibly damag-

ing, long-reaching attacks. It's best to stay close and keep behind them, only attempting one or two attacks before moving. Once you've defeated it, you can close the nearby gate if you wish, so that you don't have to face it on subsequent trips through the area, but it's worth venturing down the stairs here first. Just past the bottom of the stairs you'll find a Huntsman's Minion standing with his back to you at **Position B** and a number of Carrion Crows surrounding him. Another Minion will approach from the path to the right, but if you stand near the stairs he won't see you, and will eventually come to a stop at **Position C** near the other one.

If you approach from the left of both Minions you can get close enough to use a charged R2 in the back of one of them before the crows can attack you, and then finish it off with a Visceral Attack or another charged R2. As soon as that's done, roll away from the enemy group, so that you don't have to contend with them all at once. Since the Minion is faster, it should catch you up before the Crows. If you're comfortable with the timing of its

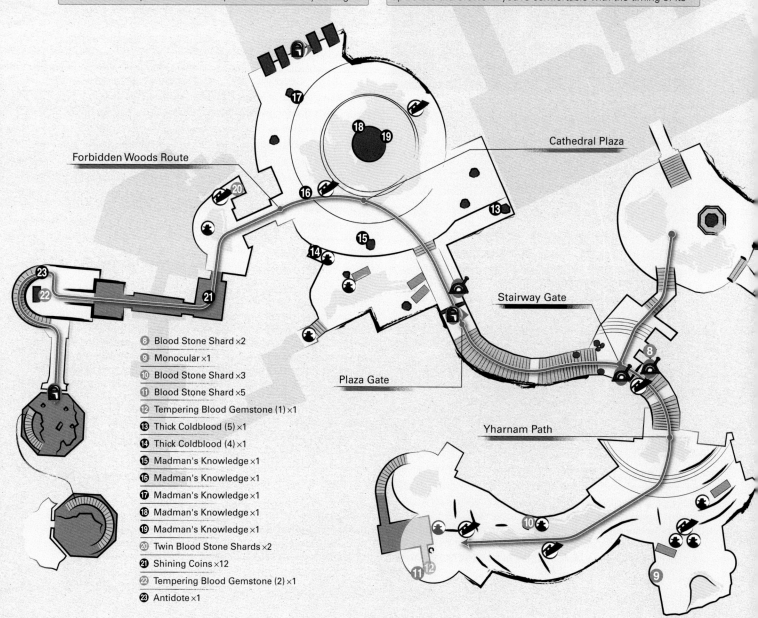

Forbidden Woods Route

Cathedral Plaza

Stairway Gate

Yharnam Path

Plaza Gate

⑧ Blood Stone Shard ×2
⑨ Monocular ×1
⑩ Blood Stone Shard ×3
⑪ Blood Stone Shard ×5
⑫ Tempering Blood Gemstone (1) ×1
⑬ Thick Coldblood (5) ×1
⑭ Thick Coldblood (4) ×1
⑮ Madman's Knowledge ×1
⑯ Madman's Knowledge ×1
⑰ Madman's Knowledge ×1
⑱ Madman's Knowledge ×1
⑲ Madman's Knowledge ×1
⑳ Twin Blood Stone Shards ×2
㉑ Shining Coins ×12
㉒ Tempering Blood Gemstone (2) ×1
㉓ Antidote ×1

attacks then it's worth trying to interrupt them, so that you can stagger it and finish it off quickly. Otherwise, you should use the fences in the area to impede its movement and bait it into attacking, so that you can retaliate while it recovers. After taking out the Crows, make sure you check around the back of the cart here, because you can find the very useful Monocular; using it switches the camera position to an over-the-shoulder view with a targeting reticule, which will allow you manually aim any ranged weapon with great precision.

Yharnam Path ⑩ ⑪ ⑫

Continuing along the path here can be quite lucrative, because between item pickups and killing a Wandering Nightmare you'll be able to acquire a number of upgrade materials for your weapons. The Wandering Nightmare is found near another Church Giant, but it's kneeling down at first, so if you're quick you can run past it and kill the Wandering Nightmare before it gets up. Going down the stairs at the end of this path will take you to a small room with a chest in it, where you'll be able to acquire another Blood Gem. [→□ 01-03]

Plaza Gate

Unless you purchase the Hunter Chief Emblem from the Bath Messengers in Hunter's Dream for 10,000 Blood Echoes, you will not be able to open this gate when you approach from the front. To reach the switch on the other side you'll have to clear the Healing Church Workshop and return here after accessing the other half of the Cathedral Ward. Be careful when you walk past the carts on the way to the Foggy Alley, because a Church Servant with a Flamesprayer will walk out from behind the last one; try to attack before he can start using the Flamesprayer, because once he does it can be difficult to close in. [→□ 04]

Cathedral Plaza

Two Church Giants patrol around the middle of this large plaza. Upon entering, the first thing you should do is take them both out. Their routes usually keep them far apart, so try to get close to one without the other seeing you, so that you don't have to contend with both at once. If you're entering here via the path from the Plaza Gate, you won't be able to run straight through to the Grand Cathedral Stairs, because the gate at the back of the plaza can only be opened from the other side.

⑳ ㉒ Forbidden Woods Route

This small alley leading off from the side of the Cathedral Plaza leads down into the Forbidden Woods, but you will not be able to get through the door at the end until you defeat Vicar Amelia in the Grand Cathedral and examine the altar. Beware of the Brainsucker that's waiting around the corner to the right near the start of the path, because it has a very deadly grab attack – either interrupt it with firearms or use thrust attacks to kill it quickly. About halfway along the path is a sarcophagus, and if you've previously spoken to Alfred he will move here once it becomes night; talk to him again to get some more information. [→□ 05]

Cathedral Ward

Foggy Alley ㉕

This narrow alley is home to a large number of local residents; anywhere you see a red lantern hanging next to a door or window, take the time to knock. You might gain a little more insight into the church and the hunts. Two of the residents here can be sent to sanctuaries if you fulfill certain conditions. Before Arianna will bring up the subject of looking for a safe place to go to, you will first need to beat one of the three bosses that are available to you at this time. This means that you will need to clear either Old Yharnam, Hemwick Charnel Lane, or defeat Vicar Amelia at the end of the Cathedral Ward. To read more about Arianna, refer to page p639. The Bigoted Old Man will not talk to you about sanctuaries until you have already sent Arianna to one, and since he doesn't trust you, when you inform him of a place he will always go to the opposite one. If you want to find out more about his quest, turn to p640.

Oedon Chapel Gate

Side Alley

Grand Cathedral – Lower Stairs

Rooftop View

Foggy Alley

Ladder Ambush

㉔ Poison Knife ×12

㉕ Black Church Hat ×1
Black Church Garb ×1
Surgical Long Gloves ×1
Black Church Trousers/Dress ×1

㉖ Poison Knife ×18

㉗ Blood Vial ×2

㉘ Thick Coldblood (4) ×1

㉙ Quicksilver Bullets ×10

㉚ Thick Coldblood (5) ×1

㉛ Thick Coldblood (5) ×1

㉜ Thick Coldblood (6) ×1

㉝ Wooden Shield ×1

㉞ Numbing Mist ×6

㉟ Black Messenger Hat ×1

㊱ Thick Coldblood (5) ×1

㊲ Blood Vial ×7

As soon as you enter the alley, a Large Huntsman with a plow and a rifle-bearing Huntsman will start walking towards you. To avoid having to fight the Large Huntsman in the alley while under fire from the other one, wait for it to get close and lure it back around towards the entrance. Fighting it near the entrance will also reduce the risks of waking up some of the other Huntsmen that are lying dormant on the floor along the alley. [→☐ **01/02**]

Ladder Ambush

There's a Huntsman patrolling on a ledge just ahead when you reach the top of the stairs at the end of the alley. If that enemy spots you it signals a small group of nearby enemies to come running down the stairs on the left towards you. If that happens, quickly run to those stairs and try to fight the enemies there, since they form a natural bottleneck. Following the fence along to the right from the top of those stairs will reveal an item behind an upright coffin at the end of a small path. [→☐ **03**]

Rooftop View

Climbing the long ladder the top of the tower here provides an excellent view over the entire Cathedral Ward. It's worth taking the time to have a look around to get a feel for how the different parts of the area connect. The way forward is through a small gap in the railings on the opposite side of the tower to the ladder, but running straight off the ledge would lead to quite a long fall, and a needless loss of health. If you approach the gap carefully and look down over the edge you'll see a small platform sticking out halfway down the tower – step off slowly you'll be able to drop onto it, and then drop down again to land on the rooftops below safely. Alternatively there's also a ladder that you can access just to the side of the railing if you want to avoid any risk. If, however, you're thinking of approaching this area from the Lower Stairs first, it's highly recommended that you do not go down the ladder. All of the enemies involved in the ambush will be standing directly in front of you, and with little room to move, that can be a very dangerous situation. It's a much better option to go through the Plaza and come back around from the other side.

Grand Cathedral – Lower Stairs

Regardless of which direction you approach these stairs from, the first thing you'll see is a group of Church Servants walking up the Grand Cathedral stairs; confronting them while they're still grouped up is very dangerous, so it's best to wait for them to move before advancing. Near the base of the stairs you'll find a handy switch that you can pull to open the gate on this side of Cathedral Plaza, allowing you to run through and open the Plaza Gate if you've not already done so. Going up and fighting that group of enemies from this position is also quite dangerous, because one of the Church Servants

is armed with a gun and he takes up position on a ledge overlooking the area. It's much better to go around through the Side Alley, so that you can attack those enemies from behind. [→☐ **04/05**]

㉝ ㉟ Oedon Chapel Gate

If you reach this area by going through the Healing Church Workshop, pulling the switch to open the gate here creates an extremely useful shortcut. It provides a direct path from the Cathedral Ward Lamp in the Oedon Chapel to the mid-point of the Grand Cathedral Stairs, so it's well worth opening. With that done, climb up the nearby ladder to reach the top of another tower, where you'll find some useful Numbing Mists. From there, drop down through the gap in the railings to land on another series of rooftops, with another item. Once you reach the end of the rooftops you can drop down onto the stairs. This is a good time to return to Hunter's Dream via the Cathedral Ward Lamp before heading up the stairs towards the Grand Cathedral.

Side Alley

Going up the stairs from the Oedon Chapel Gate will let you make use of a small alleyway that bypasses the bottom section of the Grand Cathedral stairs. The Church Servants that were walking up from the bottom of the Grand Cathedral Stairs will usually be coming down the stairs towards the end of this alley by the time you get here; fighting them here lets you deal with them away from the other enemies on the main stairs, so it's a much easier fight. [→☐ **06**]

Cathedral Ward

Grand Cathedral – Central Stairs

A Church Giant can usually be found patrolling up and down the central part of the stairs. Try to watch its movements and make sure you take out the two Church Servants on the ledges when it's not nearby. Similarly, further up the stairs, there is a more powerful version of the usual Church Servants, so try to keep the fight with the Church Giant as low as possible on the stairs to avoid dealing with both at once. The two crucifix-bearing Church Servants are far enough apart that you can take them on one at a time as long as you do not let the fight go too far up the stairs. [→ ☐ 01]

㊴ Grand Cathedral – Upper Stairs

Upon reaching the upper part of the stairs you'll have a number of possible directions to head in, and while the Grand Cathedral is temptingly close, going straight up to fight Vicar Amelia, the Cathedral Ward boss, is not the best choice. Heading around to the left of the Grand Cathedral will take you along a path that leads to Hemwick Charnel Lane, which is an excellent place to acquire some Twin Blood Stone Shards to further upgrade your weapon. You can pick up a number of these upgrade materials quite near the start of the area, so it can be well worth taking a quick trip there to grab some before heading into other areas.

Completing both Old Yharnam and Hemwick before facing Vicar Amelia will not only make the fight with her much easier, but if you go into Hemwick when you have less than 15 Insight you will not have to deal with the Mad Ones that would otherwise appear. Taking the path to the right leads to a dead end by The Cliffs, but it's a dead end with some useful items to pick up along the way. Be warned, however, that the enemies along that path are stronger than other enemies in the Cathedral Ward, so either avoid engaging them until you're stronger or be very careful when you do so. [→ ☐ 02]

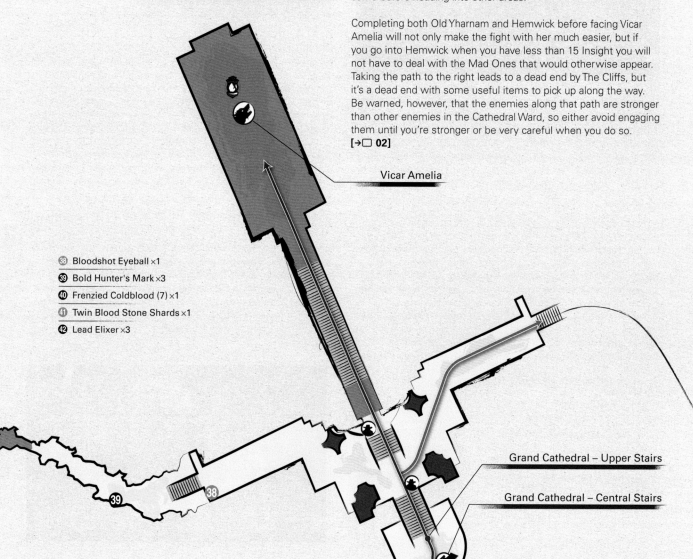

Vicar Amelia

㊳ Bloodshot Eyeball ×1
㊴ Bold Hunter's Mark ×3
㊵ Frenzied Coldblood (7) ×1
㊶ Twin Blood Stone Shards ×1
㊷ Lead Elixer ×3

Grand Cathedral – Upper Stairs

Grand Cathedral – Central Stairs

BOSS Vicar Amelia

Defeating Vicar Amelia progresses time from the evening to night, and that brings with it some changes. Many of the NPC questlines will progress, so make sure you check back with those you've previously spoken with . A new Lamp will appear in the Grand Cathedral upon Amelia's death, and if you interact with the altar at the rear of the cathedral you'll be able to view a cut-scene. A password is revealed, and you'll need it to get through the door that was blocking your access to the Forbidden Woods. [→☐ 03/04]

World Changes

- Changes time of day from evening to night
- Gain access to the Grand Cathedral Lamp
- Learn the password for the door leading to the Forbidden Woods

Shortly after you start going down this path you'll have a choice of routes, but going down the stairs to the right is a much riskier option. If you run straight ahead and drop off the cliff, however, you'll be able to land on one of the rooftops and get an item, and from there you can drop down and sneak up behind one of the Hunters and use a charged R2 from behind. If you manage to kill that first Hunter quickly and quietly, you'll also be able to sneak up on the second one nearby.

41 The Cliffs

The obvious path here is to head down the stairs on the right. This is is the fastest option if you just want to reach the bottom (and it will let you take out the Wandering Nightmare along the way) but doing so puts you in a very bad position. There are various ledges in the cliff on the way down, and Huntsmen with rifles have taken up positions on most of them, so if you run down through the cave they'll all begin firing when you exit. Two Executioners patrol near the base of the cliffs, and trying to fight them while dodging the incoming bullets can be very difficult.

A better approach is to take the route to the left of the stairs, as that will allow you to drop down onto the ledges one at a time and take out the riflemen from behind. It should be noted, however, that if you come down this route after completing Old Yharnam, a Kidnapper will also be waiting for you at the top of the cliffs, so take it out first before dropping down. Two more Wandering Nightmares are outside the room near the end of the path, and they tend to run in different directions when you approach. So you'll need to kill them quickly or return here again to get the one you missed. If you approach the door in the room at the end, another of the mysterious portals will start to move across the doorway; unless you have the Tonsil Stone in your possession, getting caught in the portal will instantly kill you. If you have the Tonsil Stone, however, you will be transported to the Lecture Building, which leads to the Nightmare Frontier. You can acquire the Tonsil Stone after entering the Forbidden Woods – for more on that, check out p649.

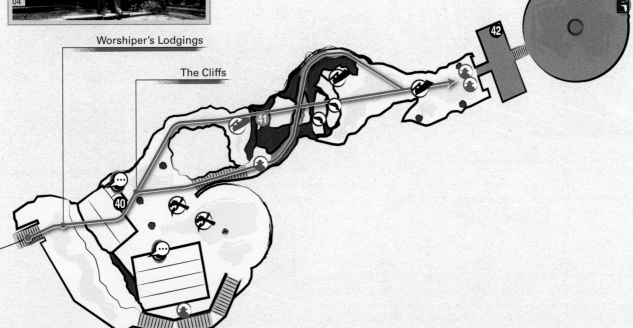

Worshiper's Lodgings

The Cliffs

Old Yharnam

A notice posted on the door warns that hunters should turn back; it's clearly directed at you. Discarding the warning, you step into the ruins of Old Yharnam. The entire town is a smoldering mess; charred corpses, strewn about in disgusting piles, still burn and fill the air with the stench of cooked flesh. You hear the cries of beasts echoing off of the dead city walls, and from afar a voice warns you to turn back, lest you become the hunted.

Difficulty	Area **B** | Blood-starved Beast **B**
Recommended	Player Level **25-35** | Weapon Upgrade **+3**
Timezones	○ ● ☾ ☾ ●
Insight	Encounter the Blood-starved Beast ×1, Defeat the Blood-starved Beast ×2

Enemies

Regular	HP	Echoes	Page
Beast Patient (Male)	190	141	p236
Beast Patient (Female)	225	155	p237
Ashen Blood Beast Patient	364	254	p237
Wandering Nightmare	46	11	p671
Carrion Crow	121	64	p231

Strong	HP	Echoes	Page
Scourge Beast	364	987	p266

Hunter	HP	Echoes	Page
Djura's Ally	997	795	p314

Boss	HP	Echoes	Page
Blood-starved Beast	3470	6600	p330

NPC

Name	Page
Retired Hunter Djura	p648

Item legend

1. Tempering Blood Gemstone (1) ×1
2. Antidote ×4
3. Pungent Blood Cocktail ×3
4. Blood Stone Shard ×1
5. Hunter's Torch ×1
6. Coldblood Dew (2) ×1
7. Blood Vial ×6
8. Coldblood Dew (2) ×1
9. Blood Stone Shard ×2
10. Blood Stone Shard ×1
11. Antidote ×3
12. Antidote ×3
13. Blood Stone Shard ×2
14. Fire Paper ×2
15. Bloodtinge Gemstone (1) ×1
16. Antidote ×1
17. Coldblood Dew (3) ×1
18. Blood Vial ×6
19. Tempering Blood Gemstone (1) ×1
20. Rifle Spear ×1
21. Charred Hunter Garb ×1 / Charred Hunter Gloves ×1 / Charred Hunter Trousers ×1
22. Coldblood Dew (2) ×1
23. Madman's Knowledge ×1
24. Molotov Cocktail ×4
25. Bloody Messenger Head Bandage ×1
26. Coldblood Dew (2) ×1
27. Antidote ×3

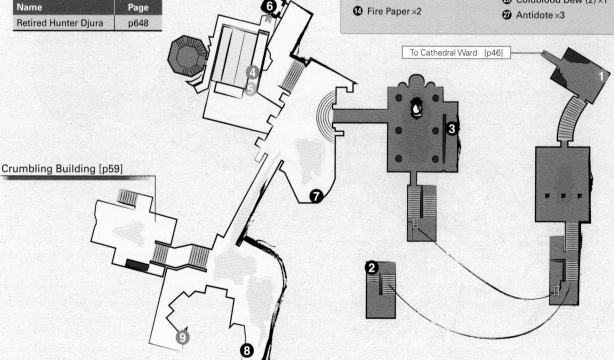

To Cathedral Ward [p46]

Crumbling Building [p59]

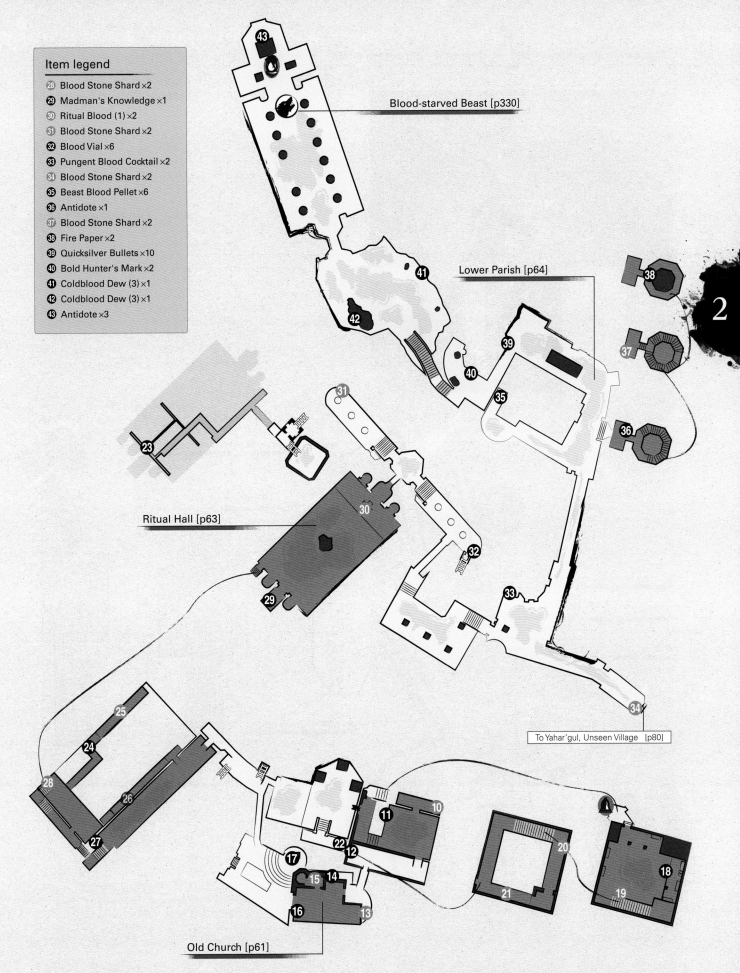

Item legend

- 28 Blood Stone Shard ×2
- 29 Madman's Knowledge ×1
- 30 Ritual Blood (1) ×2
- 31 Blood Stone Shard ×2
- 32 Blood Vial ×6
- 33 Pungent Blood Cocktail ×2
- 34 Blood Stone Shard ×2
- 35 Beast Blood Pellet ×6
- 36 Antidote ×1
- 37 Blood Stone Shard ×2
- 38 Fire Paper ×2
- 39 Quicksilver Bullets ×10
- 40 Bold Hunter's Mark ×2
- 41 Coldblood Dew (3) ×1
- 42 Coldblood Dew (3) ×1
- 43 Antidote ×3

Blood-starved Beast [p330]

Lower Parish [p64]

2

Ritual Hall [p63]

To Yahar'gul, Unseen Village [p80]

Old Church [p61]

Old Yharnam

❶ Lower Church Basement

After going down the first set of stairs you'll enter the extremely dark basement beneath the Lower Church, and a Scourge Beast will come running from the shadows, so have your weapon at the ready. The pillars in the room can be very useful, as you can use them to impede the beast's movement while you can move to an advantageous position. [→☐ 01]

Old Yharnam Lamp

When you reach the ladder after going the stairs from the dark room, you'll see an item on the other side of the staircase. To get the item you'll need to go down the ladder, and then go back up the stairs to reach the broken section of floor there. At the bottom of the stairway is a room that's home to the Old Yharnam Lamp. There's a small hallway to the side of this room, and if you go there and break the items along the wall, you'll find a hidden item. After kindling the flame on the Lamp, approach the nearby large double doors and read the warning notice; interact with the doors a second time to open them and enter Old Yharnam. [→☐ 02/03]

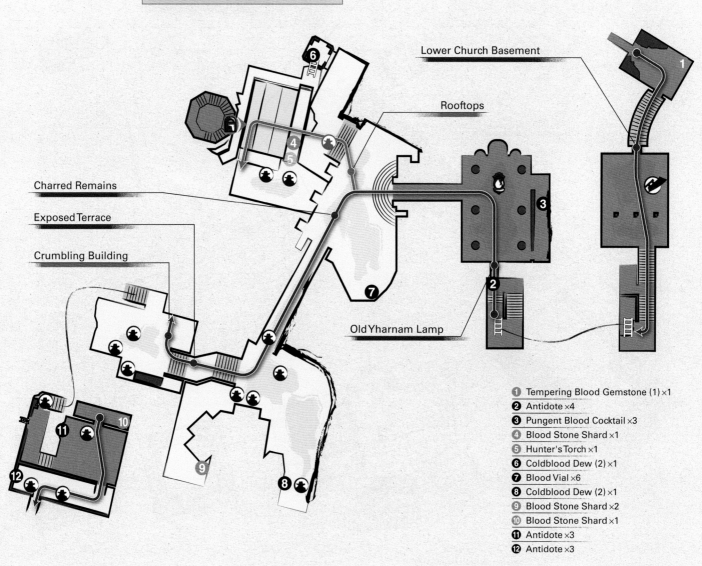

Lower Church Basement

Rooftops

Charred Remains

Exposed Terrace

Crumbling Building

Old Yharnam Lamp

❶ Tempering Blood Gemstone (1) ×1
❷ Antidote ×4
❸ Pungent Blood Cocktail ×3
❹ Blood Stone Shard ×1
❺ Hunter's Torch ×1
❻ Coldblood Dew (2) ×1
❼ Blood Vial ×6
❽ Coldblood Dew (2) ×1
❾ Blood Stone Shard ×2
❿ Blood Stone Shard ×1
⓫ Antidote ×3
⓬ Antidote ×3

Rooftops ④ ⑤

While the main route through the area takes you over the bridge to the left after you pass through the doors, it's worth exploring the area down the stairs to the right first. As you approach the stairs you'll see a Wandering Nightmare just ahead of you, so quickly chase after it and try to kill it before it drops off the ledge; you can still catch it if it does drop down, but it's much easier to keep track of up here. Once it's dead, drop over the ledge onto the wooden platform and get the item there, and then drop down the series of rooftops to reach the ground below. If you head around to the back of this area you'll be able to find another item hidden underneath the archways. Returning to near where you first dropped into this area, drop down through the gap onto a narrow ledge below, and then once more to reach solid ground. In this area you'll find a one-way gate that will act as a shortcut later on; for now, continue along the path and go up the ladder at the end. Upon reaching the top, drop down from the tower to reach the area you started in. [→☐ 04/05]

Charred Remains ⑨

As you start to cross the bridge Djura will start warning you to turn back and leave the area, and at the same time a Beast Patient will start approaching from the other side of the bridge. These enemies are one of the more common ones you'll encounter in Old Yharnam, so learning how to deal with them effectively will help you greatly in the long run. They are gravely afraid of fire, so if you have your Torch

out they will spend most of the time shielding their eyes rather than attacking, which gives you the perfect opportunity to strike. Once you reach the other side of the bridge, the smoke given off by the charred remains of corpses will obscure much of your view over the area, so be on alert for any Beast Patients running through the smoke to attack you. The two paths leading around the sides of the building at the back of this area both lead to items, but guarding the one to the left is a female Beast Patient with a hooded cloak covering its head. Because of the hood this enemy doesn't fear the light of the flame in the same way as the others, so you need to be a bit more proactive when fighting them. [→☐ 06]

Exposed Terrace

There are a quite a few enemies in this area, but it's important that you do not venture forward past the large statue in the middle, because if you do, Djura will start firing at you with a gatling gun from his position high up atop a tower in the distance. From that point on you'll always need to be aware of your surroundings and make sure that as often as possible you have a wall or other solid object between you and Djura. If his gunfire hits you then you'll need to roll quickly to try to get back behind cover, because he won't stop shooting until he loses sight of you. The enemies are a mix of both types of Beast Patient, so lure the hooded ones towards you and take them out while the non-hooded ones cower from the flame of your Torch. To continue on safely, look for a small gap in the railings on the right-hand side of the area and drop down through it to avoid having to contend with incoming gunfire. There are other routes you can take down to the floors below if you wish, but they bring with them a much higher degree of risk. [→☐ 07]

Crumbling Building

The most direct method to get off the rooftop is to drop down from the front of this building, so that you land in the courtyard below. Not only will you take significant damage from the fall by doing this, but there's not much cover in the courtyard, so avoiding the gunfire can be difficult. Alternatively, you can go down the stairs on the side of the building to reach a broken doorway, through which you can cross a small hallway to reach the floor below. There's a Beast Patient standing in front of the door, however, and you'll need to get past it while under fire from Djura – you may want to stand in the doorway and fight it, so that you have some cover.

Fireplace Room ⑩

If you dropped down through the gap in the railings you'll land on a small ledge outside this room – quietly walk through the doorway into the room and you'll be able to sneak up on a female Ashen Blood Beast Patient, a larger and more dangerous version of the smaller ones. The beast will not have its back turned for long, so as soon as you're in range, use a charged R2 to stagger it and follow up with a visceral attack. The area down the stairs leading out of this room is lined with explosive pots and Djura has a direct line of sight over it, so you'll need to be extremely careful. There are also a couple of Beast Patients to contend with, and it's best to clear them out first by running into the room to get their attention, and then quickly retreating back up the stairs to fight them behind cover. [→ ▢ 01]

⑩ Blood Stone Shard ×1
⑪ Antidote ×3
⑫ Antidote ×3
⑬ Blood Stone Shard ×2
⑭ Fire Paper ×2
⑮ Bloodtinge Gemstone (1) ×1
⑯ Antidote ×1
⑰ Coldblood Dew (3) ×1
⑱ Blood Vial ×6
⑲ Tempering Blood Gemstone (1) ×1
⑳ Rifle Spear ×1
　　Charred Hunter Garb ×1
㉑ Charred Hunter Gloves ×1
　　Charred Hunter Trousers ×1
㉒ Coldblood Dew (2) ×1

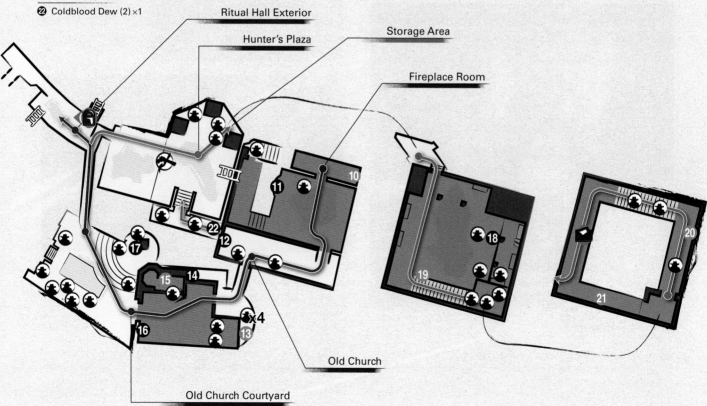

Ritual Hall Exterior

Hunter's Plaza

Storage Area

Fireplace Room

Old Church

Old Church Courtyard

Old Church ⑬ ⑮

The short wooden bridge leading to this area is extremely exposed, so make sure you run across it as quickly as possible to avoid being knocked off by Djura's gunfire; heading to the small area to the side of the building and killing the Carrion Crows there is the quickest way to get out of his line of fire. There's a small gap just to the right of the church door that leads to a narrow path with an item at the end, but to get it you need to be very careful. Djura has a direct line of sight on the path, so you need to run to the end very quickly and hide behind the wall there until he stops shooting, before making your way back out. Entering the church itself is not without danger, because once you reach the middle, an Ashen Blood Beast Patient will break through the door on the right. After defeating the creature, make sure you enter the small room it emerged from to find another hidden item. [→☐ 02-04]

Old Church Courtyard

There are a large number of enemies in this courtyard area, and most of them are obscured by the smoke rising up from the piles of charred corpses. To make matters worse, Djura will start firing on you as soon as you exit the door, and while the trees in the middle of the courtyard can provide some cover, trying to fight all of the enemies out there can quickly lead to being overwhelmed. The safest way to take on the enemies is to quickly run out to awaken some of them, and then retreat to the safety of the building and fight them there. Once you've cleared out a number of them, run straight across the courtyard and fight the remaining enemies near the wall at the back, since Djura can't reach you there.

Hunter's Plaza

As soon as you cross the bridge that leads to this area, Djura's Ally will emerge from the smoke that engulfs much of the plaza and start attacking you. This particular Hunter likes to keep his distance and use his firearm while backing away, so unlike other Hunters you may come across, he won't actually follow you very far if you decide you don't want to fight him. Since he rarely goes much past the stairs at the bottom of the plaza it can be difficult to fight him while Djura is still manning his gun. Your best option is to try to circle around the Hunter once he reaches the bottom of the stairs and cut off his retreat, keeping him in the small area that Djura cannot reach.

⑲ ⑳ ㉑ Storage Area

Behind one of the statues at the rear of the plaza you'll find a small gap in the railings that you can roll through to reach a narrow ledge. From there you can drop down through a series of ledges to reach a small balcony at the bottom. The doorway there will take you into a hidden storage area, where, after fending off a number of Beast Patients, you'll be able to pick up some very useful items including another Blood Gem from the chest near the base of the stairs. Halfway up the stairs you'll also be able to acquire the highly effective Rifle Spear, and at the top of the stairs you can get a new attire set. When you're ready to leave the area simply drop down through the doorway at the top of the stairs to land in a small area near the plaza – don't stay out in the open here, though, because Djura will open fire on you straight away. [→☐ 05]

Ritual Hall Exterior

There's a locked gate in this area that can only be opened from the other side later, which leaves you with two possible route options. Heading straight up the stairs into the Ritual Hall is the most direct route into the building, and it's worth exploring at least some of the area there to get the items before returning here and going up the nearby ladder. The route up the ladder will take you to the rafters of the building, where you'll be able to create an advantageous environment for the battle on the main floor, so it's the recommended option. [→☐ 06/07]

Old Yharnam

Djura's Tower

Once you reach the midpoint of the tower you'll have the option to climb another ladder to reach the top, where Djura is perched, or continue on to the Rafter's Access. There are a couple of ways that you can resolve things with Djura, so you'll have to make a choice as to how you wish to proceed. The first and most direct approach is to continue up the tower and kill him. Doing that will mean that you can freely explore the area below, and he'll drop the Powder Keg Badge for you. Alternatively, you can leave him alone and return here later after your first visit to Yahar'gul, Unseen Village for a much more diplomatic conclusion. For more details check p648. [→☐ 01]

If you face away from the ladder leading up to the very top of the tower, you'll see a small gap in the wooden railings that you can drop through to reach another wooden platform below. That platform will lead you through a hole in the wall and onto a bridge, where a female Beast Patient awaits. Try to lure the beast towards you and fight it on the platform, rather than the bridge, to avoid being accidentally knocked down during the fight. Once it's been defeated, cross the bridge and enter the Ritual Hall. [→☐ 02]

22 Coldblood Dew (2) ×1

23 Madman's Knowledge ×1

24 Molotov Cocktail ×4

25 Bloody Messenger Head Bandage ×1

26 Coldblood Dew (2) ×1

27 Antidote ×3

28 Blood Stone Shard ×2

29 Madman's Knowledge ×1

30 Ritual Blood (1) ×2

31 Blood Stone Shard ×2

32 Blood Vial ×6

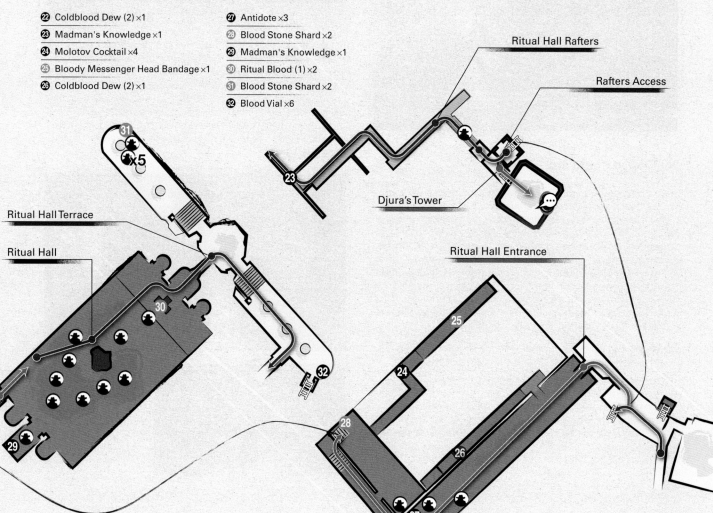

Ritual Hall Rafters ㉕

Follow the wooden walkway from the other side of the bridge until the second turn, and then pay close attention to a pair of wooden planks sticking out from the corner. Attached to these planks is a rope with an explosive pot hanging from the end of it – if you chop the planks, the pot will drop down and ignite a large bonfire on the floor below. The fire created by the explosion will kill a large number of the enemies surrounding the bonfire, and cause even the female Beast Patients to recoil from the heat, making things much easier. Just past the area where you drop the pot you'll come to a gap in the railings, leading out onto a beam that you can use to access another beam with an item on it.

Return to the midpoint of the first beam and look down below to the left to see another walkway, and then drop down onto that to reach an item. From that item you should be able to see another walkway along the wall a short distance away, with another item at the end of it. To reach it you'll need to perform a running jump to cross the gap. You need to be quite precise with the angle and timing of the jump, because if it's too short you'll land on the walkway below the one you want to reach, and if the angle is too sharp you may fall to the ground. If you do miss the walkway, you can always make your way back outside and climb up to try again. Once you have the item, simply drop down to the walkway below, and from there you can either drop off the end near the exit side to avoid most of the enemies, or drop off near the entrance to take them on. [→☐ 03]

03

Ritual Hall Entrance ㉘

While entering the Ritual Hall through the main entrance does not provide quite as many benefits as heading up to the rafters, there are a few items to be obtained, so it's worth taking a trip inside. There are quite a few female Beast Patients to either side of the first corridor you enter, so you need to be careful as you make your way along it – if you haven't been up to the rafters, the enemy on the bridge across the corridor will drop down when you get close. A short way along the corridor you'll see an opening on the right, and if you go through it you can drop down a series of walkways, leading to an item. From there, you can only drop down to the ground floor. If you continue along the first corridor you'll find another item near the banister at the top of the stairs, and halfway down the stairs you can exit out onto a large platform with yet another item on it, before continuing on to the main hall. [→☐ 04]

04

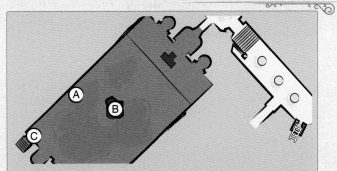

There are a large number of enemies to contend with in this area, but how you approach the situation will depend on the route you used to get here. If you're dropping down from the rafters you'll usually land close to **Position A**, not far from the large fire at **Position B**, created by dropping the explosive pot. Not only will that fire give you a significant advantage in the battle (because it causes most of the enemies to recoil from the heat), but you can also lure or knock them into the fire for quick victories. Try to work your way around the fire, clearing out enemies on one side before moving, so that you keep the encounters manageable.

If you came in through the main entrance then the battle will start near **Position C** when you first enter the hall. Once one of the enemies spots you a large number of them will come running, so try to force them through bottlenecks to control their movement, and never back yourself into a corner. The doorway and stairway you used to reach the hall make an ideal place for the battle, as you'll always be able to back up to create more space, and can even use the side door near the entrance to drop down onto the walkways. This lets you separate the enemies and approach them from behind. Regardless of which approach you take, once they've all been defeated, make sure you claim the items on the altar at the back of the room, because they're used in creating Chalice Dungeons and you'll be acquiring your first Chalice soon.

㉛ **Ritual Hall Terrace**

Upon exiting the Ritual Hall you have the option of heading left or right. Going left will take you to a small dead end area with a number of Carrion Crows and an item, while going right takes you along the main path. Near the end of this path you'll come to a small bridge on the right, but before going across it you should take the time to investigate the doorway a short distance past it. This doorway leads to a ladder that you can climb to reach the other side of the one-way gate you passed earlier, near the Ritual Hall Exterior. By unlocking this gate you'll create a shortcut that allows you to bypass the Ritual Hall on subsequent trips through the area.

Old Yharnam

Smoke-filled Room

Although this room may appear empty, the smoke and the pillars are in fact hiding a number of Beast Patients, lying on the ground just waiting to ambush you. Before dealing with them, however, your first focus should be on trying to kill the Wandering Nightmare that's hidden behind the pillar at the far end of the room. The easiest way to do this is to run behind the nearest pillar, and then follow the path down so that you approach the Wandering Nightmare from behind – kill it quickly before the Beast Patients get up. If you have your Torch out while dealing with the Wandering Nightmare, the Beast Patients will rarely close in to attack you, but you should still be aware of where they are just in case one gets brave. [→□ 01/02]

Lower Parish Bridge ㉞

Exiting the smoke-filled room will take you to the streets of Old Yharnam, where your primary enemies are Scourge Beasts. Following the road around to the right will lead you to a large wooden door that can only be opened from the other side; to reach that area you'll need to travel through Yahar'gul, Unseen Village (p80). There is an item near the door, however, so a quick trip down there is worthwhile before you follow the road around to left and continue onward.

Lower Parish Alley

A lone Scourge Beast can usually be found patrolling along this alley, and while you may fancy your chances against a single one, it has some backup nearby just waiting to ambush you. Clinging to the side of the building near the end of the alley is another Scourge Beast, and it will drop down to join the fight if you battle the first one in the area below. Try to lure the first one away and fight it near the start of the alley to avoid this happening. When you head into the alley you can either use a ranged attack to knock the hanging Scourge Beast down, or, if you go around the side of the building and pick up the item there, it will drop down naturally.

㊲ Lower Parish Tower

Just past the Alley you'll see a large house with an ornate door on the right-hand side of the street. When you get close to that door a Scourge Beast will come bursting through it, so make sure you're ready. If you go through the newly-opened door after defeating the beast you'll be able to climb up the spiral staircase inside, and halfway up there's a small room on the left with an item. Continuing up the stairs will take you to the other side of the one-way gate that you encountered near the Rooftops at the start of the area; opening this will create an extremely valuable shortcut back to the Lamp for you. Before leaving the area, however, make sure you continue to the top of the stairs, where you'll find another item. [→□ 03]

Lower Parish

As you round the corner here you'll be presented with two paths, both leading in the same direction. The path on the left is obscured by smoke, and a female Ashen Blood Beast Patient is hiding behind it, with a Scourge Beast waiting on the other side of the alley. Going through the smoke and fighting the Beast Patient first is the best approach, because if you were to go along the other path, you'd still have to fight the Scourge Beast, and the Beast Patient would then come running out of the alley to join in.

BOSS Blood-starved Beast

When you reach this area you should ignore the items near the top of the stairs, because a Wandering Nightmare is sitting nearby and will start running away when you get close; kill it first, and then come back up for the other items. Before heading in to face the Blood-starved Beast, you may want to enlist the aid of a friendly face that you encountered earlier. Just to the right of the path leading down to the Boss room you can find another brightly lit message if you're playing online and agreed to cooperate with Alfred back in the Cathedral Ward. If you have the Insight required, you can ring the Beckoning Bell to summon him. Alfred can help considerably with the fight, so if you're able, it's well worth bringing him in. [→□ 04]

World Changes

- Obtaining the Pthumeru Chalice allows for Chalice Dungeon creation
- Gain access to the Church of the Good Chalice Lamp

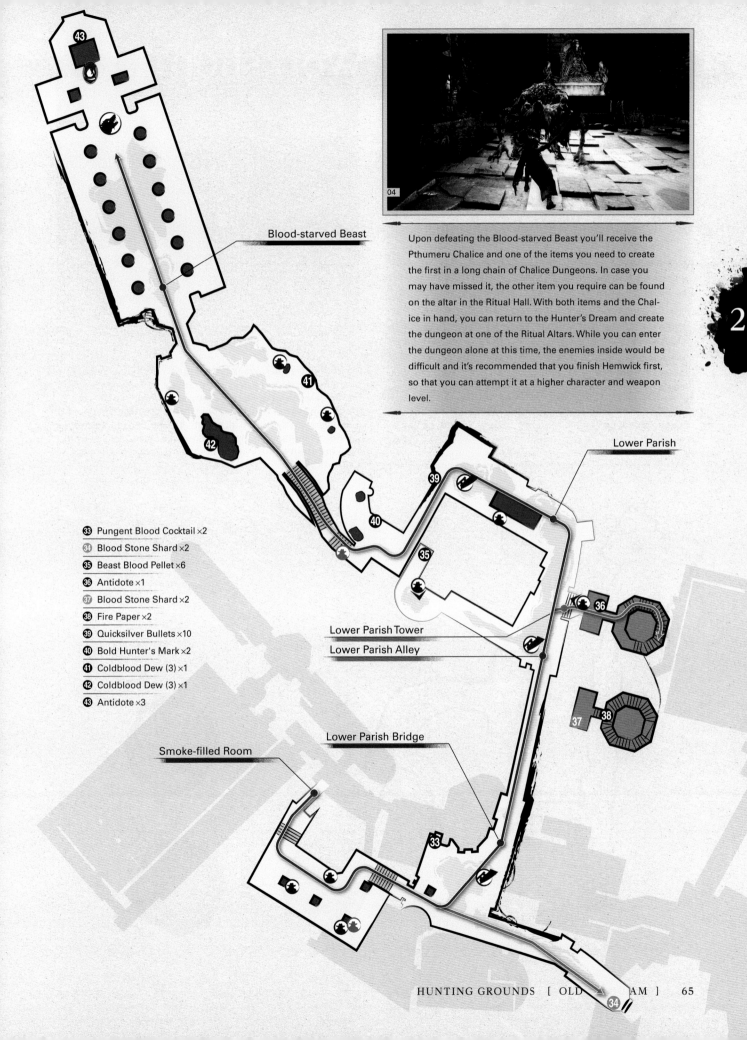

Blood-starved Beast

Upon defeating the Blood-starved Beast you'll receive the Pthumeru Chalice and one of the items you need to create the first in a long chain of Chalice Dungeons. In case you may have missed it, the other item you require can be found on the altar in the Ritual Hall. With both items and the Chalice in hand, you can return to the Hunter's Dream and create the dungeon at one of the Ritual Altars. While you can enter the dungeon alone at this time, the enemies inside would be difficult and it's recommended that you finish Hemwick first, so that you can attempt it at a higher character and weapon level.

2

Lower Parish

33 Pungent Blood Cocktail ×2
34 Blood Stone Shard ×2
35 Beast Blood Pellet ×6
36 Antidote ×1
37 Blood Stone Shard ×2
38 Fire Paper ×2
39 Quicksilver Bullets ×10
40 Bold Hunter's Mark ×2
41 Coldblood Dew (3) ×1
42 Coldblood Dew (3) ×1
43 Antidote ×3

Lower Parish Tower

Lower Parish Alley

Lower Parish Bridge

Smoke-filled Room

Healing Church Workshop

Enemies

Regular	HP	Echoes	Page
Huntsman (Rifle)	164	142	p227
Huntsman (Torch & Axe)	218	128	p225
Huntsman (Torch & Shield)	127	114	p226
Huntsman (Sickle)	215	128	p226
Huntsman (Cutlass)	271	142	p227
Huntsman (Pitchfork)	191	128	p227
Rabid Dog	145	142	p230
Carrion Crow	127	85	p231
Wheelchair Huntsman (Gatling Gun)	145	99	p229
Wheelchair Huntsman (Rifle)	145	99	p230
Wheelchair Huntsman (Flamesprayer)	145	99	p230
Wandering Nightmare	49	14	p671

Strong	HP	Echoes	Page
Huntsman's Minion (Brick)	455	469	p267
Beast-possessed Soul	656	795	p275
Kidnapper	910	1368	p276
Brainsucker	236	511	p273

The door of Oedon Chapel, once locked, now stands open. You remember, as if from a dream, the advice of Gehrman— seek out the Church's workshop, for they have much to offer you. The area is overrun with mad huntsmen, and the dilapidated buildings crumble to ruin all around. The footing is treacherous, but there is something familiar about this place. You can even smell the scent of the incense drifting up from the Cathedral Ward below...

Difficulty	Area **B**
Recommended	Player Level **25-35** | Weapon Upgrade **+3**
Timezones	○ ◑ ☾ ●
Insight	Enter the Abandoned Old Workshop ×2

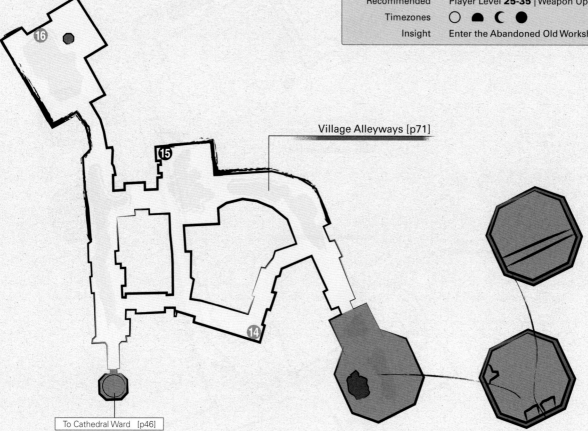

Village Alleyways [p71]

To Cathedral Ward [p46]

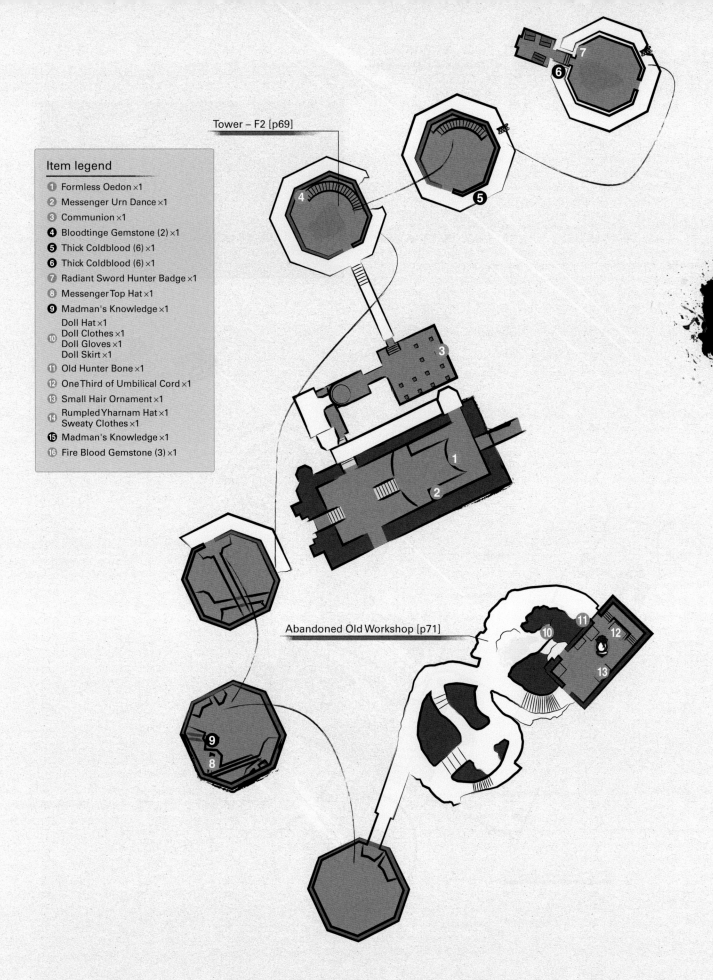

Item legend

1. Formless Oedon ×1
2. Messenger Urn Dance ×1
3. Communion ×1
4. Bloodtinge Gemstone (2) ×1
5. Thick Coldblood (6) ×1
6. Thick Coldblood (6) ×1
7. Radiant Sword Hunter Badge ×1
8. Messenger Top Hat ×1
9. Madman's Knowledge ×1
10. Doll Hat ×1
    Doll Clothes ×1
    Doll Gloves ×1
    Doll Skirt ×1
11. Old Hunter Bone ×1
12. One Third of Umbilical Cord ×1
13. Small Hair Ornament ×1
14. Rumpled Yharnam Hat ×1
    Sweaty Clothes ×1
15. Madman's Knowledge ×1
16. Fire Blood Gemstone (3) ×1

Tower – F2 [p69]

Abandoned Old Workshop [p71]

Healing Church Workshop

Oedon Chapel Elevator ❶ ❷

The door in the middle of the Oedon Chapel does not open until you have defeated the Blood-starved Beast in Old Yharnam. You'll eventually be able to reach the Upper Cathedral Ward from this path, but for now you can only explore this area. Coming here as soon as you can is advisable, however, because there are a number of useful items to be found. After stepping onto the elevator near the start of this section, if you turn around you'll be able to see an opening in the wall about halfway up the tower; time it correctly and you can step or roll off the elevator and onto a ledge. If you then follow the path outside and along the rooftops to the left, you'll reach a balcony above the main floor of the Oedon Chapel. The chest here contains a Formless Oedon Caryll Rune that increases the amount of Quicksilver Bullets you can hold by four, and a Messenger Skin can be found nearby. Once you have both items, simply drop back down to the main floor of the Oedon Chapel, and after going back through the door again, ride the elevator all the way to the top this time. [→⬜ 01-03]

01

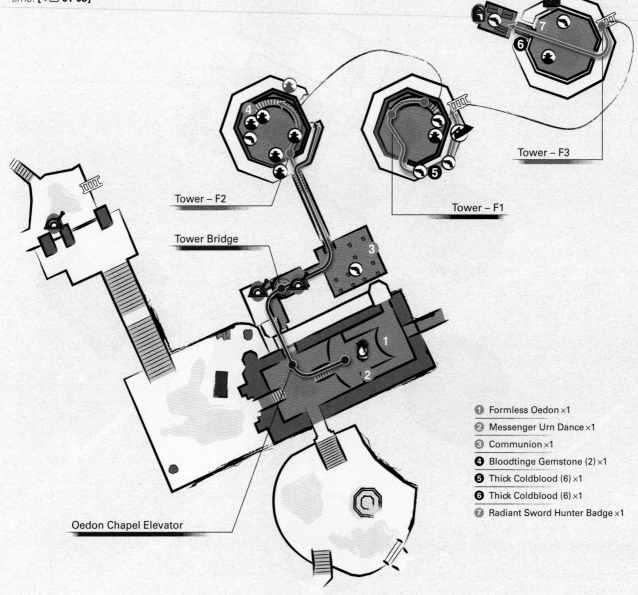

Tower – F3

Tower – F2

Tower – F1

Tower Bridge

Oedon Chapel Elevator

❶ Formless Oedon ×1
❷ Messenger Urn Dance ×1
❸ Communion ×1
❹ Bloodtinge Gemstone (2) ×1
❺ Thick Coldblood (6) ×1
❻ Thick Coldblood (6) ×1
❼ Radiant Sword Hunter Badge ×1

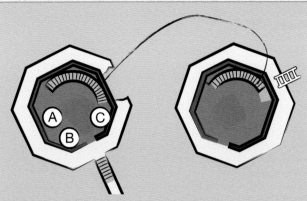

There are quite a few enemies in this room, so you should approach the door cautiously rather than running straight in. The major threat is the group of enemies at the back of the room, but there's also a Huntsman with a rifle at **Position A**, another enemy hidden just to the left on the other side of the doorway at **Position B**, and a final one with a shield at **Position C**. If you align yourself correctly near the doorway you can use a Pebble or gunshot to lure the enemy at **Position C** out of the room to dispatch him easily, and then if you quickly run into the room and back out, the enemy at **Position B** will follow you, so you can kill him outside too.

There are a couple of ways you can handle the remaining enemies, depending on your personal preference. One option is to run straight ahead to the group at the back and try to kill them quickly between the shots fired by the enemy at **Position A**. If you pace your initial run well, you can cause his first shot to miss and give yourself a small window to attack the enemies before he shoots again. Keep your view trained on him so you can evade accordingly. Alternatively, you can run in and take out the enemy at **Position A** first, which will alert the nearby group and cause them to close in on you; make sure you kill that first enemy quickly, so that you're done by the time the other two are within range.

Tower Bridge ③

When you reach the end of the elevator ride, make sure you sprint into the room at the top – there's a Wheelchair Huntsman armed with a gatling gun to the right of the doorway, and he'll attempt to gun you down as soon as you enter. If you run in quickly you can get past his firing angle and easily attack him from the side before he can turn. The bridge outside can also be tricky, because as soon as you start to cross it a Huntsman will come running towards you, while two others start firing down at you from the floor above. As before, the easiest way to handle this situation is to sprint across the bridge, past the enemy approaching you, and fight it on the walkway on the other side, below the riflemen. On this walkway there are two possible routes you can take: the path to the right leads down to the lower part of the area, whereas entering the room and heading upwards takes you up into the tower, towards the locked door that leads to the Upper Cathedral Ward. Opening that door requires a key that is unobtainable until much later in the game, but going up a bit before taking the path to the right is worthwhile, due to the items you can acquire.

Tower – F2

Quickly run over to the left side of this room after climbing the stairs, because there's a Wheelchair Huntsman with a chain-gun near the wall, and another Huntsman next to him. Try to get close to the Wheelchair Huntsman quickly – get to the side of him and take him out before he starts shooting.

Once both enemies have been killed, walk to the doorway, but don't exit out onto the ledge straight away. Just to the left of the doorway are the gun-wielding enemies that were firing down at you when you first crossed the bridge into this area, and you need to deal with them carefully, especially since there's also a Huntsman's Minion patrolling along the ledge. Before heading out to deal with the two ranged enemies, try to peek around the corner and get the attention of the Minion, so that you can lure it back inside and fight it there. Use the corner of the wall again to bait the riflemen into firing, and then quickly run and try to kill them before they finish reloading. Once the area's clear, continue around the ledge and climb the ladder.

If you follow the ledge around to the right once you reach this floor you'll be able to find a small note on the ground. Heading back around to the left will let you enter the room on this floor, where two Wheelchair Huntsmen with Flamesprayers are waiting for you. One of them is much closer than the other, so if you run in there and get to the side of him quickly, you can easily take him out before the other one gets near. With the room now clear, secure the items and then head back down to continue your exploration.

Healing Church Workshop

Tower – B1 (8)

The lower part of the tower is primarily made up of a number of small wooden ledges that you can drop onto to reach the bottom safely. Along the way there are a number of items you can get, as well gaining access to the Abandoned Old Workshop. It's impossible to do everything in one trip down, so it's recommended that you go to the workshop first. From there you can use the Lamp to warp back to the Hunter's Dream and return to the start of the area, so that you can proceed further down. To reach the entrance to the workshop you'll need to make two long drops, so make sure you have full health before you try, and enough Blood Vials to heal. For the first drop, walk out onto the bridge until you come to the first set of small horizontal planks, and from there turn around, so that you're aiming towards the ropes on the wall beneath the starting ledge. If you run off from that angle you should land on a small platform halfway down the tower. After healing, you can drop down again from there to reach the platform with the door leading to the workshop. [→□ 01/02]

- (8) Messenger Top Hat ×1
- (9) Madman's Knowledge ×1
- (10) Doll Hat ×1
  Doll Clothes ×1
  Doll Gloves ×1
  Doll Skirt ×1
- (11) Old Hunter Bone ×1
- (12) One Third of Umbilical Cord ×1
- (13) Small Hair Ornament ×1
- (14) Rumpled Yharnam Hat ×1
  Sweaty Clothes ×1
- (15) Madman's Knowledge ×1
- (16) Fire Blood Gemstone (3) ×1

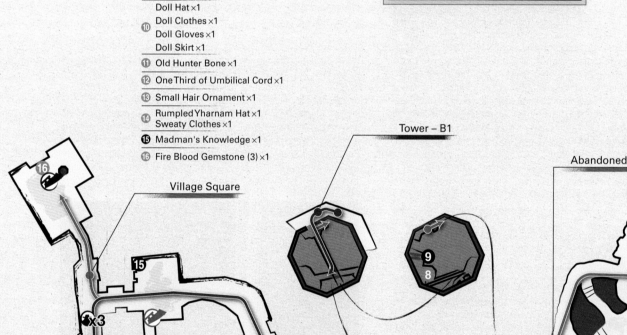

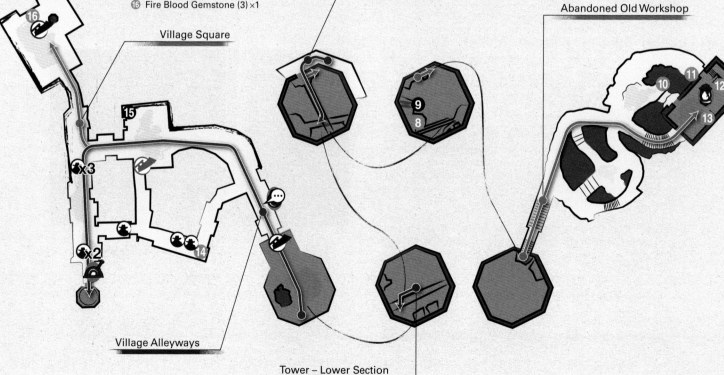

Village Square

Tower – B1

Abandoned Old Workshop

Village Alleyways

Tower – Lower Section

Abandoned Old Workshop ⑩ ⑪ ⑫ ⑬

This area is the real-world counterpart to the Hunter's Dream that hunters so frequently visit, so the layout should be immediately familiar. There are a number of items you can get in the grounds outside the workshop – of particular note is the Old Hunter's Bone, which allows you to drastically increase your roll and quickstep speed for a short period of time. Inside you'll find the inactive remains of the Doll, and the Abandoned Old Workshop Lamp. The item on the altar in the workshop is One Third of Umbilical Cord, which is one of the items required to get a different ending to the game. On one of the cabinets near the Lamp you'll also find a Small Hair Pin, which you can give to the Doll in Hunter's Dream to receive an item that you can turn into a useful Blood Gem. [→☐ 03/04]

Tower – Lower Section

To get all of the items on the way down the tower you'll need to start from the first ledge, rather than one near the entrance to the Abandoned Old Workshop. Make your way across the first bridge, and as you get near the end of it, drop down to the left to land on another bridge below, and then drop down again to the left to land on a platform below that. From there you can walk out along a narrow beam, near the end of which you can drop down to the right to land on another beam with an item on it, and then drop again to land on a large platform. If you look down over the edge near the middle of the higher section of this platform, you should see another item on a beam below, so drop down to get it. Next, drop down yet again to the bridge spanning the middle of the tower. When you're on the bridge you should see a large pile of crates to one end below; you can drop down onto the crates to reduce your fall damage, but doing that will also awaken the Beast-possessed Soul that's crouched near the doorway. If you land without alerting the beast you can easily sneak up behind it and use a charged R2 from behind. [→☐ 05/06]

⑭ Village Alleyways

After going through the door at the base of the tower and back on to the streets you'll soon come to a fork in the path, and while both routes eventually lead back to the same place, if you follow the path to left you'll be able to approach the patrolling enemy group from behind and get the drop on them. There's also a Kidnapper in this area, and the first time you're killed by this enemy you'll automatically be transported to Yahar'gul, Unseen Village. While going to that area is recommended, doing so via this Kidnapper is not; it's much better to finish going through this area so that you can unlock the Oedon Chapel Gate in the Cathedral Ward, and then let one of the other Kidnappers in that area kill you.

⑯ Village Square

At the end of the alley here you'll find a Brainsucker feasting on a corpse with its back to you. Try to sneak up behind it and used a charged R2 from behind for an easy victory. Make sure to pick up the Blood Gem from the body of the corpse the Brainsucker was feeding on, and then head all the way to the other end of the alley and ride the elevator up. It comes to a stop by a small ledge with an item on it; drop down from here to land near the Oedon Chapel Gate in Cathedral Ward. [→☐ 07]

Hemwick Charnel Lane

Smoke hangs heavy in the air, like a stiff body on the gallows. Passing through a small wooded area, mad huntsmen and their beasts prowl at every turn. You try to consider the true nature of your Hunt, but your mind stumbles and falters as your feet find a shallow grave. And another. An entire village of them. Within this bizarre cemetery, seemingly mad villagers dance about in some peculiar ecstasy; until they spot you, that is. You've entered Hemwick; keep your eyes peeled, if you'll keep them at all.

Difficulty	Area **B** | Witch of Hemwick **B**
Recommended	Player Level **30-40** | Weapon Upgrade **+3**
Timezones	○ ● ☾ ●
Insight	Encounter the Witch of Hemwick ×1, Defeat the Witch of Hemwick ×2

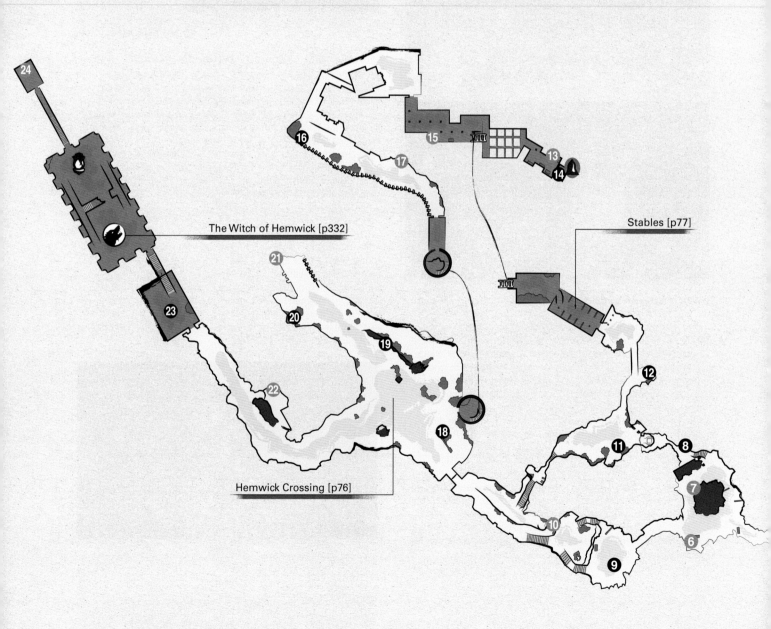

The Witch of Hemwick [p332]

Stables [p77]

Hemwick Crossing [p76]

Enemies

Regular	HP	Echoes	Page
Huntsman (Rifle)	152	266	p225
Huntsman (Rifle & Cutlass)	152	266	p228
Hunting Dog	195	365	p238
Hemwick Grave Woman (Sickle)	174	299	p239
Hemwick Grave Woman (Pole Iron)	228	299	p239
Hemwick Grave Woman (Hammer)	195	332	p239
Hemwick Grave Woman (Cleaver & Torch)	195	332	p240
Hemwick Grave Woman (Cleaver & Molotov)	228	332	p240
Wheelchair Huntsman (Pistol)	202	58	p229
Carrion Crow	152	199	p231
Wandering Nightmare	58	33	p671

Strong	HP	Echoes	Page
Mad One*	666	1426	p274
Huntsman's Minion (Brick)	544	797	p267
Executioner	348	2324	p269

*Boss support: 544 HP, 0 Echoes.

Boss	HP	Echoes	Page
The Witch of Hemwick	2611	11800	p332

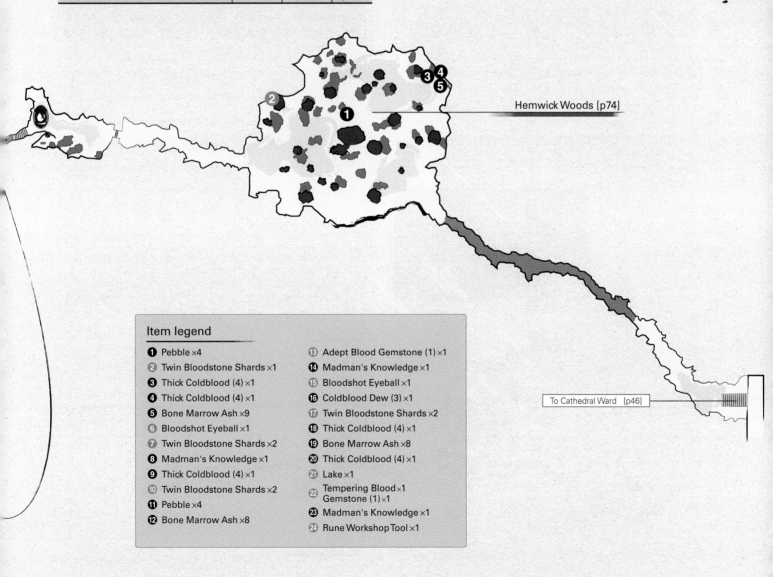

Hemwick Woods [p74]

To Cathedral Ward [p46]

Item legend

1 Pebble ×4
2 Twin Bloodstone Shards ×1
3 Thick Coldblood (4) ×1
4 Thick Coldblood (4) ×1
5 Bone Marrow Ash ×9
6 Bloodshot Eyeball ×1
7 Twin Bloodstone Shards ×2
8 Madman's Knowledge ×1
9 Thick Coldblood (4) ×1
10 Twin Bloodstone Shards ×2
11 Pebble ×4
12 Bone Marrow Ash ×8
13 Adept Blood Gemstone (1) ×1
14 Madman's Knowledge ×1
15 Bloodshot Eyeball ×1
16 Coldblood Dew (3) ×1
17 Twin Bloodstone Shards ×2
18 Thick Coldblood (4) ×1
19 Bone Marrow Ash ×8
20 Thick Coldblood (4) ×1
21 Lake ×1
22 Tempering Blood Gemstone (1) ×1
23 Madman's Knowledge ×1
24 Rune Workshop Tool ×1

Hemwick Charnel Lane

Hemwick Woods

Rifle-carrying Huntsmen and their Hunting Dogs guard the woods outside Hemwick. Trees often obscure their positions, so you'll need to be extremely cautious when moving through the area. The largest concentration of enemies is on the right-hand side of the woods, so it's best to stick to the left as much as possible if you just want to get through the area. A Hunting Dog patrols near the entrance to the woods, so wait for it to spot you and lure it back. Doing that should ensure that you don't wander into one of the Huntsmen's lines of sight.

If you walk along the left side of the area you can easily sneak around behind the first Huntsman and kill him before the nearby dog spots you. After killing the beast, quickly run and use the large tree further along for cover, while you close in to deal with the enemies on the other side of it. From there, run straight down the path and try to get close to the patrolling group before they spot you, so you can take them out quickly. Once they're down, go through the gate at the end of the path and activate the Hemwick Charnel Lane Lamp. [→ ☐ 01]

Even greater threats can be awakened in Hemwick if you venture into this area with 15 or more Insight, because only then will the fearsome Mad Ones crawl forth from their blood portals in the ground. Their locations have all been noted on the maps with a blue Strong Enemy icon, so you'll always know where one will appear even before you hear them screech. These enemies are very fast and aggressive, so whenever possible you should try to attack them while they are still appearing, and always fight them away from other enemies.

01

❷ COMBAT FOCUS **Big-game Hunter**

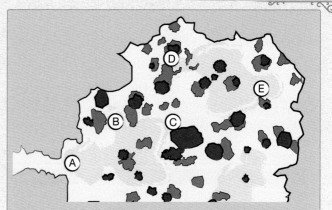

Before you try to clear out the entire woods, it's worth following the main route along the left to take out all of those enemies, so that you do not come under fire from them while dealing with the other enemies. Activating the Lamp first is also a good idea, so that you don't have far to travel if the worst happens. By starting from **Position A** at the top of the path you can work around the area counter-clockwise, which will let you approach some of the more dangerous groups of enemies from behind.

Your first target should be the Huntsman standing near a tree at **Position B** – use the gravestones for cover and close in quickly to take him out. A Hunting Dog that patrols the middle of the woods will often spot you around this time, as will another Huntsman at **Position C**, so try to use the nearby trees for cover while you deal with the beast. The Huntsman at **Position C** is standing near some explosive pots, and while you can shoot them and have the explosion kill him, doing so will alert all of the other enemies in the area, making the rest of the fight more difficult. Leave that enemy alone for now and continue around the edge of the area and quietly approach the two enemies standing near **Position D**. If done correctly you should be able to kill the first enemy from behind, and then quickly move up and kill the other one nearby before it can attack.

With those two enemies down you can approach the one at **Position C** without having to worry about coming under fire, so he should be your next target. The final group of four enemies is located at **Position E**, and if you're approaching from **Position C**

The Morgue

Double Stairs

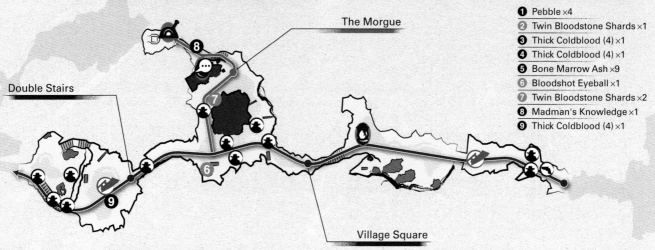

❶ Pebble ×4
❷ Twin Bloodstone Shards ×1
❸ Thick Coldblood (4) ×1
❹ Thick Coldblood (4) ×1
❺ Bone Marrow Ash ×9
❻ Bloodshot Eyeball ×1
❼ Twin Bloodstone Shards ×2
❽ Madman's Knowledge ×1
❾ Thick Coldblood (4) ×1

Village Square

The Morgue

If you head around to the right of the large statue in the square you'll find a set of wooden stairs leading up behind the morgue building, where corpses are awaiting burial. If you look closely at the back of the building you'll see that one of the boarded up windows has light shining from it, and if you approach it you'll be able to speak to the occupant. The path leading away from the back of the building will take you to the bottom of a shortcut elevator, but you'll need to activate it from above before you can use it.

Double Stairs

Running straight into this area can be extremely dangerous and you'll soon find yourself surrounded by enemies, so patience is the key to making it through safely. As you start heading up the first set

Hemwick Woods

Big-game Hunter

you can sneak up behind them. The two on the left as you look at the group are fairly close to each other, so you should try to get as close to them as possible and kill both of them quickly with some wide-arcing horizontal attacks before moving on to the final two enemies. Once the area has been cleared, you can freely roam around and gather all of the items.

Village Square ⑧ ⑦

A few Hemwick Grave Women are in the village square, but if you're patient and tactful it's possible to take them on in small manageable groups. When you first enter the square you'll see one kneeling down near a grave, while another dances around near the statue in the middle of the area; getting close to the kneeling enemy will cause the one behind to come running towards, you so take that one out first, and then quickly kill the one that was kneeling before it can attack. As you get close to the statue in the middle, another Grave Woman on the other side should spot you and come running, and a second one that's hiding behind the statue won't be far behind her. If you move backwards while they approach and fight them near the front of the square you can take them out one at a time without alerting the other enemies. Once they're both down, sneak up behind the enemy standing near the guillotine and finish her off.

of stairs, a Grave Woman will come running down – wait for her to come to you before you start attacking her. Come to a stop once you reach the top of the stairs, because a Hunting Dog will soon start coming down the furthest of the two sets of stairs in front of you, and shortly after that another Grave Woman will follow. The major threat here is a Grave Woman standing on the ledge ahead between the two staircases, because once you're in range, she'll start to throw Molotovs. If you hold your position at the top of the stairs, the patrolling Hunting Dog and Grave Woman will soon spot you and come running towards you, which allows you to take them on one at a time as they get close, without worrying about the Molotovs. Once they're both dead, run up either of the stairs and take out the Grave Woman quickly, before finishing off the remaining enemy and continuing up the next set of stairs. [→☐ 02]

Hemwick Charnel Lane

Village Gate ⑩

Before going too far up the path towards the gate, stop at the top of the first set of stairs and follow a small ledge around to the right to find a hidden item. A Huntsman's Minion patrols up and down the hill – fight it near the bottom, because a Grave Woman is standing on a ledge further up the hill and she'll start throwing Molotovs down at you when you get close. After killing the Minion, run up the hill as quickly as you can to avoid the Molotovs, and then double back along the ledge on the right and take out the Grave Woman. The gate at the top of the hill cannot be opened from this side, so you can ignore it for now. In this area you'll see another set of stairs leading down, but instead of taking them, walk along the narrow ledge to the side. At the end of the ledge you'll come to the top of a small alcove, where another Grave Woman is waiting for you to pass by below; from this position you can drop down with a plunging attack for an easy victory. [→ ☐ 01/02]

Cliffside Clearing

A large number of Carrion Crows are hiding in the tall grass in this area, so keep your eyes trained on the ground while you explore and gather items; try to spot them early, so you can use jumping attacks to take them out easily. The top of the elevator that leads

01

02

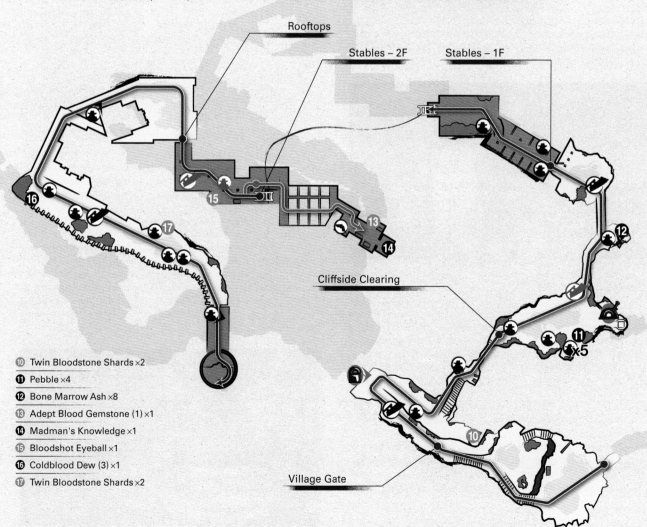

Rooftops

Stables – 2F Stables – 1F

Cliffside Clearing

Village Gate

⑩ Twin Bloodstone Shards ×2
⑪ Pebble ×4
⑫ Bone Marrow Ash ×8
⑬ Adept Blood Gemstone (1) ×1
⑭ Madman's Knowledge ×1
⑮ Bloodshot Eyeball ×1
⑯ Coldblood Dew (3) ×1
⑰ Twin Bloodstone Shards ×2

to the Village Square can also be accessed from here, giving you a nice shortcut between these two areas. If you only ventured into this area to gather enough materials to upgrade your weapon before going to another area, then this is also the ideal time to head back to the Lamp. Be very careful as you continue along the cliff side – as you round the corner near the bridge, a Grave Woman will ambush you from the side and try to knock you off the cliff. To counter this you should either be ready to evade the instant you see her, or angle yourself so that if she hit you, it won't push you off. On the other side of the nearby bridge you'll see a Huntsman's Minion patrolling in front of the Stables. Try to lure it back across the bridge towards you crossed and fight it there, because another Grave Woman will exit the Stables once you get close and fighting both can be quite dangerous. [→◻ 03/04]

Stables – 1F

There are a few enemies that will try to ambush you in the Stables, so you should proceed cautiously and always check your surroundings. A Grave Woman is laying in wait in the second stall on the right as you enter, so attack her quickly to kill her before she stands up. Near the end of the stalls a Hunting Dog will come running from the middle of the Stables, so try to use one of the stalls to block its movement and attack it safely from the other side of the wall. Once the area is clear, head to the back of the Stables and climb the ladder to the next floor. [→◻ 05]

⑬ ⑮ Stables – 2F

The first thing to do upon reaching this floor is run straight ahead and kill the Wandering Nightmare before it can disappear. If you then turn around you can double back around the ladder and go down the stairs behind the wall to reach a set of beams crossing the floor below. Once you reach the other side, be careful as you enter the room, because a Wheelchair Huntsman is waiting around the corner to the right; quickly run and get to his side before he can shoot you, and then finish him off before he reloads. Once he's down you can gather up all the items and head back across the beams and exit the Stables onto the Rooftops. [→◻ 06]

⑰ Rooftops

For the first part of the Rooftops you need to be extremely mindful of your positioning, because falling over the edge will send you plummeting to your death. Enemies will also try their best to push you off, so always try to stick to the wall on the left, so that even if you do get hit you will not get knocked back over the edge. After rounding the first couple of corners on the Rooftops you'll reach the top of a wall, where you'll see patrolling Grave Women with a Huntsman's Minion accompanying them. Watch their movements and try to lure the Grave Women towards you with Pebbles without the Minion detecting you, or lure the Minion first if he's closer and fight him away from the Grave Women. The order in which you kill them doesn't matter as much as making sure that you engage them separately to keep the fight manageable. Falling off the side of the wall is not quite as dangerous as falling off the rooftops, because there is solid ground not too far down, but you will land amongst a large group of Hunting Dogs, so it's best to keep your distance from the edge as you fight your way down the wall. [→◻ 07]

Hemwick Charnel Lane

Hemwick Crossing

At the end of the wall you'll come to a building that joins on to a tower, and you need to be careful as you approach the doorway, because a Grave Woman will jump out and ambush you when you get near. If you stay to the right of the doorway, her ambush attempt will usually miss and you can attack her as she recovers. There are two Executioners patrolling the area just outside the tower, and it's very important to avoid fighting both of them at once. The patrol route of one of them brings it very close to tower exit, so you should try to fight it in that area to ensure you're far enough away from the other one that it doesn't see you. The doorway of the tower is just small enough that the Executioners will rarely be able to fit through it, so you can use it to hold them in place and use hit-and-run attacks in relative safety. Once they've both been defeated, make sure you pull the switch to open the Village Gate, so that you can return to the Lamp if needed and have a quick route back again. [→ ☐ 01/02]

Cainhurst Carriage Event

The large obelisk in the middle of the Hemwick Crossing may not do anything on your first trip to Hemwick, but it is the trigger point for an event that can occur later. In the distance, you can see an island castle, behind the nearby tower; it's a destination most hunters never reach. After obtaining the Cainhurst Summons from the back of Iosefka's Clinic, however, if you return to this obelisk, a carriage will arrive, and if you board it you'll be taken directly to the castle.

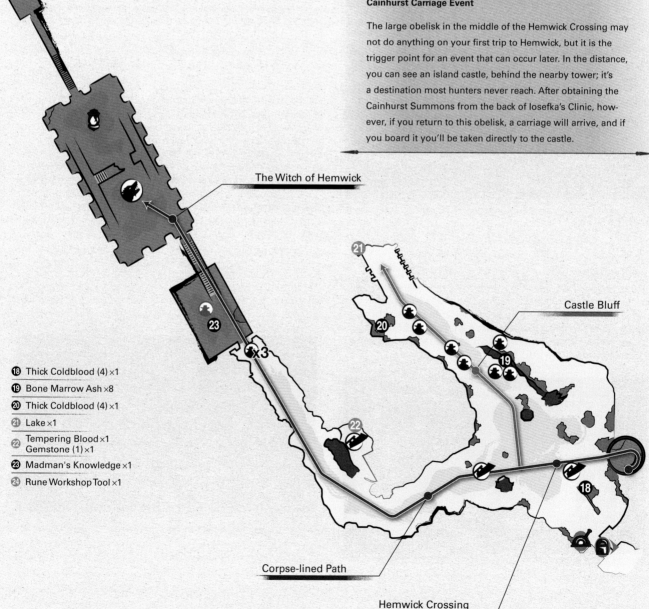

The Witch of Hemwick

Castle Bluff

⑱ Thick Coldblood (4) ×1
⑲ Bone Marrow Ash ×8
⑳ Thick Coldblood (4) ×1
㉑ Lake ×1
㉒ Tempering Blood ×1
    Gemstone (1) ×1
㉓ Madman's Knowledge ×1
㉔ Rune Workshop Tool ×1

Corpse-lined Path

Hemwick Crossing

Castle Bluff ㉑

The items on the bluff make for a tempting lure to draw you in, but to reach them you'll have to contend with a large pack of Hunting Dogs, and one wrong step can see you easily surrounded by them. If you move up just past the obelisk you should be able to draw a small group of the beasts towards you, and you can use the obelisk and nearby gravestones as cover while you separate and attack them. Further up the path you'll see a lone Hunting Dog, and again, let it come to you before you fight it, rather than advancing. Near the end of the path you'll see a final Hunting Dog standing next to a Grave Woman who likes to throw Molotovs; once the dog spots you, let it run towards you so that you can fight it outside the Grave Woman's throwing range, before finally moving up and killing her. With the area now clear you can go about picking up all of the items, but be especially careful when going for the one at the end of the broken section of road, because it's dangerously close to the edge and the footing is very uneven.

Corpse-lined Path ㉒

There are a few items to pick up along this path, and while the first half of it is clear, once you get halfway up there are some enemies you'll have to contend with. A group of Grave Women patrol the upper part of the main path, and at the end of a small side path an Executioner stands in wait. If you don't engage the patrolling group and wait for them to start walking back up the hill, you can sneak along the side path and take advantage of the fact that the Executioner is standing with his back to you by hitting it with a charged R2 attack. You'll need to kill the Executioner quickly, because the noise of the battle will usually attract the patrolling group, and you don't want to face both at the same time. Similarly, if you were to go after the group first, the Executioner would come out of the side path behind you so you'd want to fight them as far up the path as possible to give yourself the most time. [→☐ 03]

㉔ BOSS The Witch of Hemwick

Before heading into the boss room, if you break the three barrels just in front of the stairs leading down, the noise will cause a Wandering Nightmare to drop from the ceiling nearby, and you can kill it for some extra Bloodstone Shards. The Mad Ones that you face during the fight with the Witch have very poor visibility, so as long as you slowly walk around the area, they will not detect you unless you get close to them. When you defeat the boss, the new Witch's Abode Lamp will appear. Being able to return to this area will make the trip to the obelisk for summoning the carriage to Cainhurst Castle much quicker. [→☐ 04-06]

World Changes

- Gain access to the room containing the Rune Workshop Tool
- Witch's Abode Lamp is activated

If you follow the narrow hallway along from the back of the boss room and enter the small room at the end you can find the Rune Workshop Tool on the body of one of the Witch's victims. With this in hand you can now return to the Hunter's Dream and make use of it at the Memory Altar inside the workshop to memorize the inscriptions of powerful Caryll Runes. These runes have many different effects and you can memorize up to three normal ones at any time, with a fourth position reserved for rare Oath Runes.

Yahar'gul, Unseen Village (Evening)

Did you perish? No. As the coarse weave of the burlap sack chafes your skin, your mind slowly regains clarity. You slide onto the disgusting floor as an iron gate screeches to a close. You have been claimed by a fate far worse than death. You are trapped within a horrific city of madmen – kidnapped, but to what dark purpose? As you seek an escape from this Unseen Village, you hear terrified whispers ringing in your ears. Do they belong to another victim, or are these frightened murmurs your own?

Difficulty	Area **B** | Darkbeast Paarl **S**
Recommended	Player Level **35-45** | Weapon Upgrade **+4**
Timezones	
Insight	Arriving in the prison ×1, Encounter Darkbeast Paarl ×1, Defeat Darkbeast Paarl ×3

To reach this area you're going to have to go against your natural instincts and actually let a specific enemy kill you. After defeating the boss in Old Yharnam, Kidnapper enemies will be released in various areas, and the first time one of them kills you, a cut-scene will trigger during which you'll be transported to this area. The Kidnappers can be found in the following areas:

- Just outside the Oedon Chapel in the Cathedral Ward.

- To the side of the Lower Chapel in the Cathedral Ward.

- At the top of The Cliffs in the Cathedral Ward.

- In the Village Alleyways of the Healing Church Workshop.

- At the end of the Village Outskirts in the Forbidden Woods.

It's important to remember, however, that you will still lose your Blood Echoes when the Kidnapper kills you, so make sure you spend them first before triggering the event.

Enemies

Regular	HP	Echoes	Page
Huntsman (Bare Fists)	177	319	p228
Rabid Dog	202	593	p230
Wandering Nightmare	68	46	p671

Strong	HP	Echoes	Page
Kidnapper	910	1368	p276
Eye Collector	278	365	p277
Maneater Boar	758	3192	p270

Boss	HP	Echoes	Page
Darkbeast Paarl	4552	21000	p334

NPC

Name	Page
Adella, Nun of the Healing Church	p641

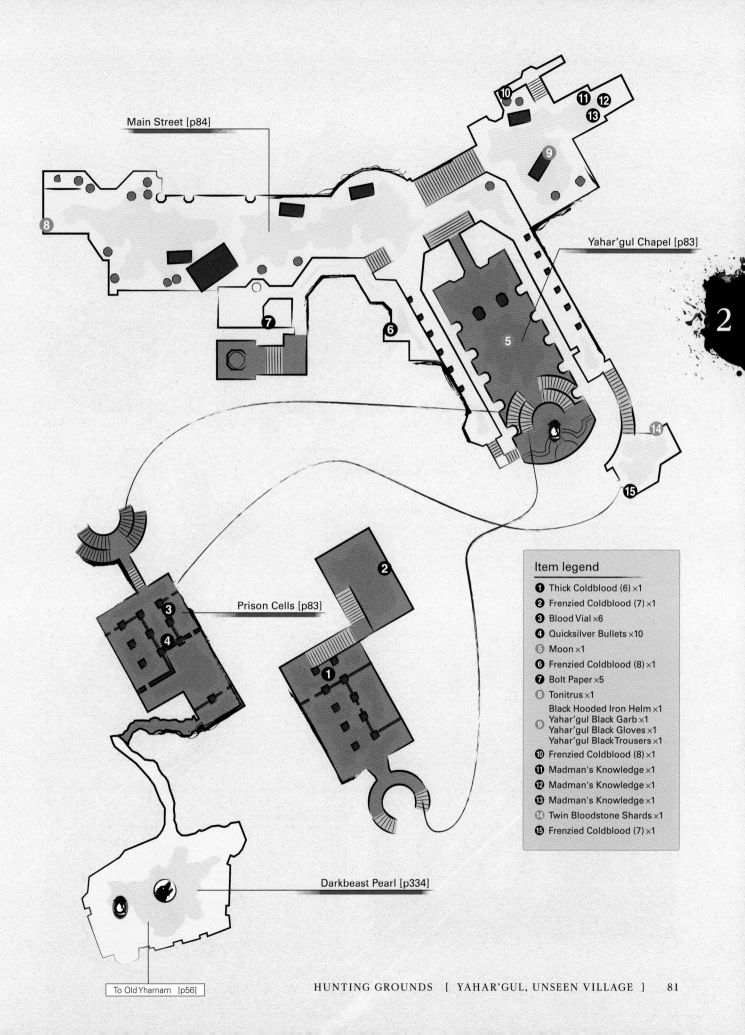

Main Street [p84]

Yahar'gul Chapel [p83]

Prison Cells [p83]

Darkbeast Pearl [p334]

To Old Yharnam [p56]

Item legend

1. Thick Coldblood (6) ×1
2. Frenzied Coldblood (7) ×1
3. Blood Vial ×6
4. Quicksilver Bullets ×10
5. Moon ×1
6. Frenzied Coldblood (8) ×1
7. Bolt Paper ×5
8. Tonitrus ×1
9. Black Hooded Iron Helm ×1
   Yahar'gul Black Garb ×1
   Yahar'gul Black Gloves ×1
   Yahar'gul Black Trousers ×1
10. Frenzied Coldblood (8) ×1
11. Madman's Knowledge ×1
12. Madman's Knowledge ×1
13. Madman's Knowledge ×1
14. Twin Bloodstone Shards ×1
15. Frenzied Coldblood (7) ×1

Yahar'gul, Unseen Village

Prisoner Holding Area

After being defeated by the Kidnapper and taken to Yahar'gul you'll awaken in the Prison Cell they use to hold their captives, but as luck would have it they've left the cell door unlocked. Exit through the door and head around to the left, where you'll find a staircase leading up. Halfway up the staircase you'll see an open doorway, and while that path will take you almost straight to the boss of the area, it's worth taking the time to continue up the stairs and activate the Hypogean Gaol Lamp at the top.

This version of Yahar'gul, Unseen Village is only available up until you defeat the boss in Byrgenwerth, changing the time to Blood Moon. At that point all of the Kidnappers get killed, and many other changes occur in the area, so if you want to check this place out, don't leave it too late!

Storeroom

If you head around to the right when you exit your cell, you'll come to a small storage area with an item and a number of Huntsmen sitting dormant on the floor. If you try to pick the item up, or walk too close to them, they'll begin to get up, so try and kill them quickly before they can fight back. Continue down the stairs and you'll come to another storeroom, where an Adella can be seen cowering in the corner. Trying to talk to the Nun will usually result in her asking to be left alone, but if you equip any church related garb (such as the Black or White Church Garb), she'll assume you're a member of the church and be much more responsive; you'll even get the option to send her to one of the sanctuaries you've opened up. To find out more about Adella, please turn to p641. [→ ☐ 01]

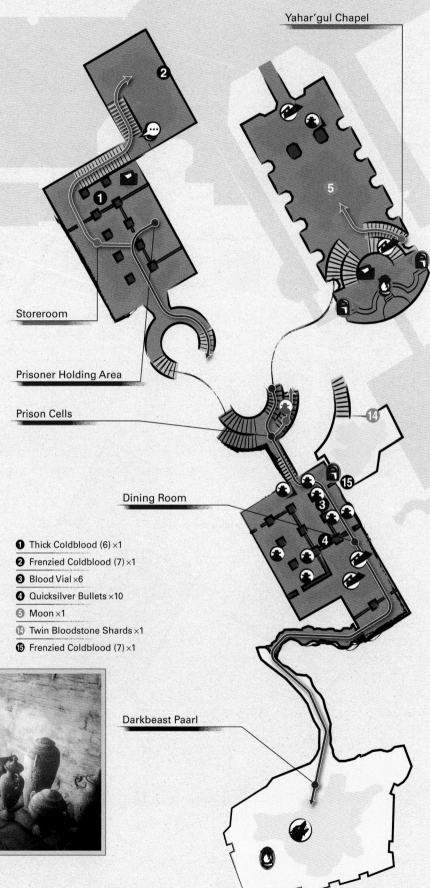

Yahar'gul Chapel

Storeroom

Prisoner Holding Area

Prison Cells

Dining Room

Darkbeast Paarl

❶ Thick Coldblood (6) ×1
❷ Frenzied Coldblood (7) ×1
❸ Blood Vial ×6
❹ Quicksilver Bullets ×10
❺ Moon ×1
⓮ Twin Bloodstone Shards ×1
⓯ Frenzied Coldblood (7) ×1

01   Please, leave me be...

Prison Cells

As you start going down these stairs you'll see an Eye Collector running across the doorway at the bottom, letting you know that you'll be in for a fight once you get down there. The direction she was running in, however, is meant to distract you from the real threat, which is a second Eye Collector hiding around the corner to the right on the other side of the doorway. If you were to just walk through the doorway, she would immediately grab you with a damaging attack. To avoid this, you should sprint down the stairs and roll through the doorway before taking her on. The other Eye Collector will usually start patrolling through the cells to the left, where there are also a number of Huntsmen sitting on the floor, so try to take her out without awakening them. Before advancing to the Dining Room, make sure you kill all of the dormant Huntsmen to ensure that they do not attack you from behind later. [→☐ 02/03]

Dining Room

In the middle of the Dining Room there are two Kidnappers standing around a table, and taking them both on at the same time can be quite challenging. There are two ways into the Dining Room; one through the small cell by the base of the stairs, and the other through the large cell on the other side of the room. If you approach the doorway in the small cell slowly you can get the Kidnapper on the far side of the table to spot you, so that you can lure it back into the cells and fight it away from the other one. The remaining Kidnapper stands with his back to you, and once he's on his own you can sneak up behind him and use a charged R2. After they've both been defeated, go through the hole in the wall at the back of the room and follow the tunnel along to drop back down into Old Yharnam, where Darkbeast Paarl awaits you. Once you drop down from the end of the tunnel, however, you will be unable to return, so make sure you are well equipped for the upcoming battle. [→☐ 04/05]

BOSS Darkbeast Paarl

After following the narrow path you will come face-to-face with Darkbeast Paarl, a fearsome creature that guards the route back into Old Yharnam. Upon defeating it, you'll acquire the Spark Hunter Badge to increase your shop inventory, and the Graveyard of the Darkbeast Lamp will become available. Before you leave, however, you should make sure to open the large wooden door nearby, so that you can use this Lamp as a shortcut to the back of Old Yharnam if needed. If you came straight to this point after you entered Yahar'gul, it's worth returning to the Hypogean Gaol Lamp so that you can explore the area. Entering Old Yharnam from this direction will let you climb up Djura's tower without him seeing you, so you'll be able to reach a peaceful resolution with him. To read more about Djura, please refer to p648. [→☐ 06]

World Changes

- Acquire the Spark Hunter Badge
- Gain access to the Graveyard of the Darkbeast Lamp

❺ Yahar'gul Chapel

There are two Kidnappers that you have to contend with in this room, and if you came here straight from the Prisoner Holding Area, they will both usually be positioned in the middle of the room on either side of an item. To make the fight much easier it's recommended that you use the Hypogean Gaol Lamp at the top of the room to leave and then return, as that will reset the Kidnappers to their starting positions. One of them will be walking down the stairs just in front of the Lamp, and the other will be approaching the middle from the doorway at the opposite end of the room. If you attack the one on the stairs nearby quickly you can fight it without any interference from the other one in the middle of the room. After taking them both out and grabbing the item in the middle of the room, start heading towards the door at the opposite end; make sure you go around the right-hand side of the large pillars rather than through the middle, because an Eye Collector is waiting to ambush you from behind the one on the right.

Yahar'gul, Unseen Village

Yahar'gul Chapel Stairs

After stepping onto the stairs outside Yahar'gul Chapel, you're faced with a number of possible routes to take, but don't start exploring just yet – a Maneater Boar will start walking up the stairs directly in front of you as soon as you enter the area, and if you wait near the door it will pass you by and you can sneak up behind it for an early advantage in the fight. Although you can see a number of bridges and buildings above and around you at this time, most of them are not accessible until you return here later on.

Side Alley

If you head around to the left from the Yahar'gul Chapel Stairs you'll be able to use this alley to reach one of the one-way doors that are near the Hypogean Gaol Lamp. By opening the door you'll be able to avoid having to go through the Yahar'gul Chapel to reach the Main Street outside, which will come in very handy later in the game. Along the alley you'll also find a Wandering Nightmare – be sure and kill it to gain some additional weapon upgrade materials. **[→☐ 01]**

01

⑧ COMBAT FOCUS Main Street–West

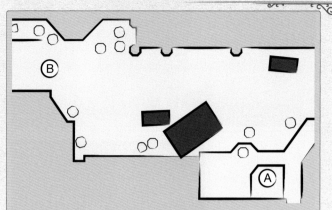

This large, open street has a number of enemies along it, but thankfully there are also a lot of things in the environment that you can use to your advantage when taking them on. The first threat you need to deal with is a Maneater Boar in a small alcove at **Position A**. If you were to run straight up the street, the Boar would come charging out at you and be very difficult to avoid. If, however, you stick to the left side of the street and approach slowly, you can get it to charge into a gap between the wall and a statue that is too narrow for it to fit through. While it's struggling to get free you can run in and attack it quickly, and if you see it start to attack, simply drop back to avoid it easily.

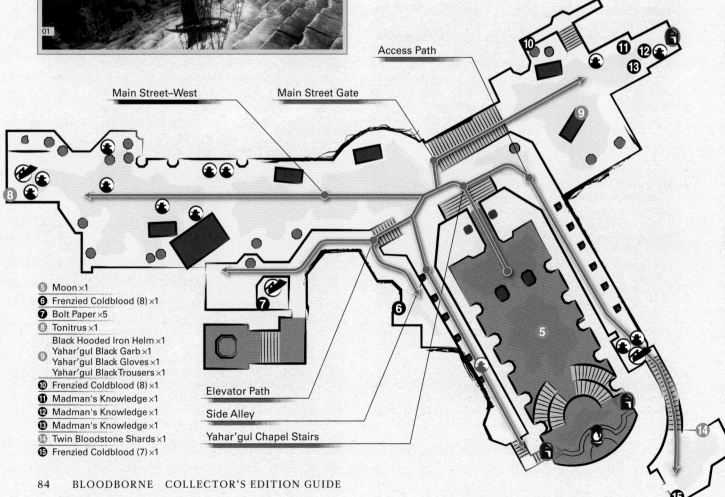

Access Path

Main Street–West

Main Street Gate

Elevator Path

Side Alley

Yahar'gul Chapel Stairs

⑤ Moon ×1
⑥ Frenzied Coldblood (8) ×1
⑦ Bolt Paper ×5
⑧ Tonitrus ×1
⑨ Black Hooded Iron Helm ×1
Yahar'gul Black Garb ×1
Yahar'gul Black Gloves ×1
Yahar'gul Black Trousers ×1
⑩ Frenzied Coldblood (8) ×1
⑪ Madman's Knowledge ×1
⑫ Madman's Knowledge ×1
⑬ Madman's Knowledge ×1
⑭ Twin Bloodstone Shards ×1
⑮ Frenzied Coldblood (7) ×1

Move up the street sticking to the left-hand side and you'll start to see pairs of Rabid Dogs patrolling the area just past a large wagon; try to attract them individually using Pebbles and fight them behind the wagon, away from the others. If you get spotted by a few of them, circle around the wagon so that you always keep it between you and the majority of the enemies, and try to attack them at the corners of the wagon using weapons with long reach. At the end of the street at **Position B** are two more Rabid Dogs and a Kidnapper. Try to take advantage of the dogs' speed and lure them back away from the Kidnapper, so that you can fight them separately. The two large statues on the right-hand side of the street can provide an excellent place to fight the dogs from; you can use the statues to block the attacks of the dogs as they run towards you, and then quickly attack them before they recover.

Elevator Path

By going up the small set of stairs near the Yahar'gul Chapel Stairs you can reach a small raised path that runs alongside the Main Street for a short distance. If you follow the path along to the left from the top of the stairs, you'll be able to find an item hidden in a small niche in the wall. Taking the path back around the other side of the building will lead you into a small room, at the end of which is the bottom of an elevator shaft. Unfortunately, you cannot activate the elevator yet, and will have to wait until you return here later. The stairs just outside the elevator room will take you up to a small paved area, where there's a break in the railings overlooking the Main Street. If you perform a running jump through the gap you can land on the roof of the large wagon, allowing you to use ranged attacks on the dogs below, if you have any. [→☐ 02/03]

9 Main Street Gate

Heading down the large set of stairs in front of Yahar'gul Chapel will take you to the area just in front of the large Main Street Gate, where you'll be able to acquire a large number of items. Just in front of the gate are a couple of Rabid Dogs, so make sure you deal with them first before moving around to pick up the items. The gate has clearly not been opened for some time, and remains firmly shut, so you cannot pass through it at this point in the game.

14 Access Path

Following the path around to the right from the Yahar'gul Chapel Stairs will allow you to reach a narrow access path lined with pillars, at the end of which are a Kidnapper and two Rabid Dogs that are slowly making their way towards you. As you get close to the enemies the dogs will be the first to see you. Once they do, wait for them to run towards you and use the pillars in the area to help block their attacks while you fight them. If you're quick, you should easily be able to kill them before the Kidnapper gets close, at which time you can again use the pillar as cover while he attacks, and then circle around and attack him from behind. The stairway at the end of the path leads to a small courtyard with a couple of items to pick up. The door in this area can also be opened from this side to give you another entrance point to the Prison Cells and back into the Yahar'gul Chapel. [→☐ 04]

2

Forbidden Woods

"Fear the old blood." You speak the password, an adage passed down from Vicar to Vicar across generations. The door creaks open, and the man who sits beyond is unmoving in death. Who asked for the password, if not he? Putting your fears aside, you take up the Hunt once more. This shrouded forest, long forbidden by the Church, holds a key to your journey. You step cautiously down the path into the foliage below as the sounds of beasts and men echo through the night.

Difficulty	Area **B** | Shadow of Yharnam **A**
Recommended	Player Level **40-50** | Weapon Upgrade **+5**
Timezones	○ ◑ ☾ ●
Insight	Defeat the Shadows of Yharnam ×2

Enemies

Regular	HP	Echoes	Page
Huntsman (Torch & Axe)	306	695	p225
Huntsman (Torch & Shield)	179	556	p226
Huntsman (Sickle)	301	556	p226
Huntsman (Cleaver)	301	556	p226
Huntsman (Cutlass)	381	695	p227
Huntsman (Pitchfork)	301	556	p227
Huntsman (Rifle)	230	695	p227
Huntsman (Rifle & Cutlass)	230	695	p228
Huntsman (Oil Urn)	301	556	p228
Huntsman (Molotov)	179	556	p228
Large Huntsman (Torch & Saw)	409	834	p232
Large Huntsman (Plow)	511	834	p232
Rabid Dog	204	521	p230
Carrion Crow	179	284	p231
Rotted Corpse	434	427	p233
Parasite Larva	230	142	p242
Wandering Nightmare	69	47	p671

Strong	HP	Echoes	Page
Executioner	409	4379	p269
Kidnapper	920	1706	p276
Church Giant (Bare Fists)	1023	2711	p272

NPC

Name	Page
Patches the Spider	p649

Item legend

1. Thick Coldblood (6) ×1
2. Twin Bloodstone Shards ×1
3. Pebble ×2
4. Madman's Knowledge ×1
5. Adept Blood Gemstone (2) ×1
6. Antidote ×4
7. Antidote ×3
8. Twin Bloodstone Shards ×1
9. Thick Coldblood (6) ×1
10. Blood Vial ×2
11. Twin Bloodstone Shards ×1
12. Quicksilver Bullets ×10
13. Beast Blood Pellet ×3
14. Thick Coldblood (6) ×1
15. Blood Vial ×5
16. Pungent Blood Cocktail ×4
17. Pungent Blood Cocktail ×3
18. Antidote ×4
19. Beast Blood Pellet ×6
20. Quicksilver Bullets ×6
21. Blue Elixir ×4
22. White Church Hat ×1
    White Church Garb ×1
    Surgical Long Gloves ×1
    White Church Trousers/Dress ×1
23. Antidote ×2
24. Frenzied Coldblood (7) ×1
25. Arcane Blood Gemstone (2) ×1
26. Nourishing Blood Gemstone (2) ×1
27. Dirty Blood Gemstone (3) ×1
28. Frenzied Coldblood (7) ×1
29. Blood Vial ×6
30. Beast Roar ×1
31. Molotov Cocktail ×11
32. Twin Bloodstone Shards ×1
33. Twin Bloodstone Shards ×1
34. Twin Bloodstone Shards ×2
35. Blood Vial ×6
36. Beast Blood Pellet ×4
37. Twin Bloodstone Shards ×1
38. Poison Knife ×8
39. Poison Knife ×3
40. Canon ×1

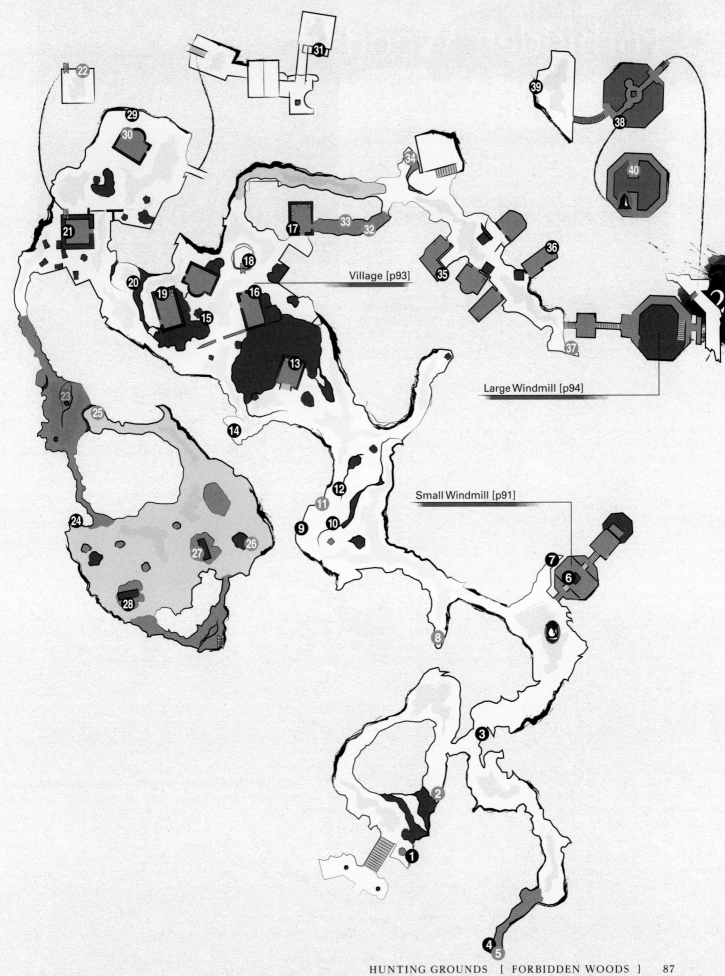

Village [p93]

Large Windmill [p94]

Small Windmill [p91]

Forbidden Woods

Enemies

Regular	HP	Echoes	Page
Snake Parasite	1023	1138	p240
Snake Ball	281	237	p241
Rotted Corpse	434	427	p233
Small Celestial Emissary	143	765	p241

Strong	HP	Echoes	Page
Small Celestial Emissary (Tendrils)	143	765	p278
Executioner	409	4379	p269
Large Snake Ball	716	1460	p279
Maneater Boar	767	2323	p270

Boss	HP	Echoes	Page
Shadow of Yharnam (Sword)	3645	18600	p338
Shadow of Yharnam (Sword & Candle)	2302	18600	p338
Shadow of Yharnam (Mace & Fireball)	2046	18600	p338

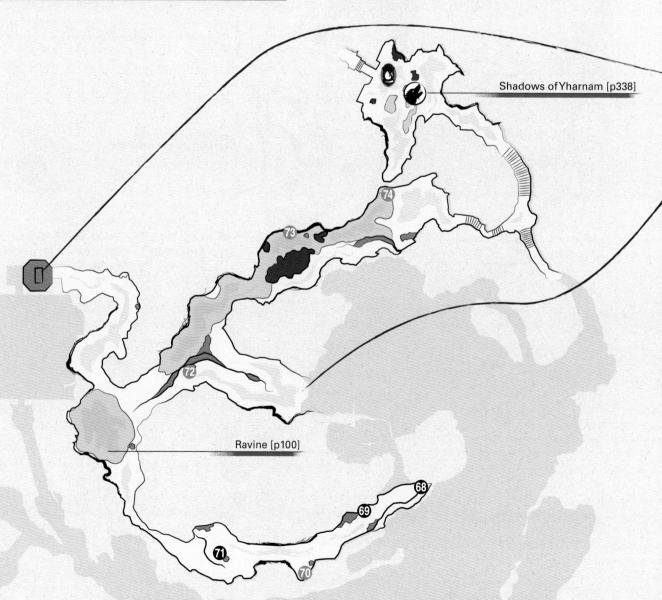

Shadows of Yharnam [p338]

Ravine [p100]

Item legend

41 Madman's Knowledge ×1		**59** Deep Sea ×1	
42 Twin Bloodstone Shards ×1		**60** Twin Bloodstone Shards ×1	
43 Frenzied Coldblood (7) ×1		**61** Twin Bloodstone Shards ×3	
44 Twin Bloodstone Shards ×2		**62** Frenzied Coldblood (8) ×1	
45 Shining Coins ×6		**63** Clockwise Metamorphosis ×1	
46 Twin Bloodstone Shards ×1		**64** Frenzied Coldblood (7) ×1	
47 Twin Bloodstone Shards ×1		**65** Graveguard Mask ×1	
48 Madman's Knowledge ×1			Graveguard Robe ×1
49 Madman's Knowledge ×1		**66** Graveguard Manchettes ×1	
50 Twin Bloodstone Shards ×2			Graveguard Kilt ×1
51 Twin Bloodstone Shards ×1		**67** Frenzied Coldblood (7) ×1	
52 Twin Bloodstone Shards ×2		**68** Madman's Knowledge ×1	
53 Twin Bloodstone Shards ×2		**69** Madman's Knowledge ×1	
54 Twin Bloodstone Shards ×1		**70** Anti-Clockwise Metamorphosis ×1	
55 Thick Coldblood (6) ×1		**71** Madman's Knowledge ×1	
56 Clear Deep Sea ×1		**72** Twin Bloodstone Shards ×1	
57 Bloodstone Chunk ×1		**73** Dissipating Lake ×1	
58 Shining Coins ×5		**74** Sharp Blood Gemstone (3) ×1	

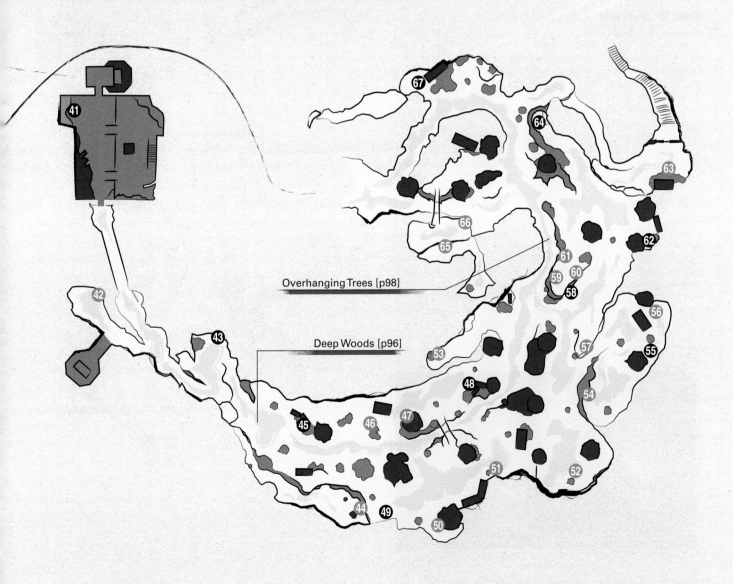

Overhanging Trees [p98]

Deep Woods [p96]

Forbidden Woods

1 Thick Coldblood (6) ×1
2 Twin Bloodstone Shards ×1
3 Pebble ×2
4 Madman's Knowledge ×1
5 Adept Blood Gemstone (2) ×1
6 Antidote ×4
7 Antidote ×3
8 Twin Bloodstone Shards ×1
9 Thick Coldblood (6) ×1
10 Blood Vial ×2
11 Twin Bloodstone Shards ×1
12 Quicksilver Bullets ×10
13 Beast Blood Pellet ×3
14 Thick Coldblood (6) ×1

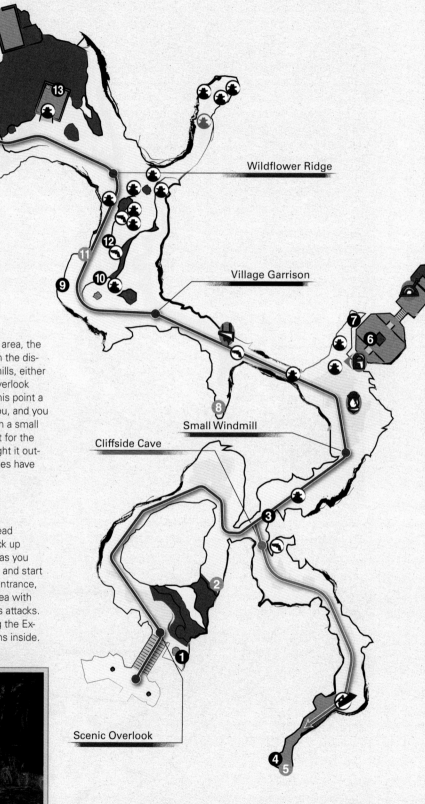

Scenic Overlook 2

Upon reaching the bottom of the stairs at the start of this area, the tops of two large, decrepit windmills are visible: one off in the distance and one close by. To reach the closest of the windmills, either follow the path along the top of the cliff, or drop off the overlook and use the ledges to reach the first fork in the path. At this point a Large Huntsman will start walking up the path towards you, and you should (just about) be able to see a Huntsman standing on a small cliff ahead. The Huntsman likes to throw oil flasks, so wait for the Large Huntsman to come up the path towards you and fight it outside of the Huntsman's throwing range. Once both enemies have been defeated, continue down towards the windmill.

Cliffside Cave 5

From the fork in the path, if you head up to the right (instead of down to the windmill) you can follow a narrow path back up the cliffs. There's a small cave at the end of the path, and as you approach it an Executioner will emerge from the entrance and start walking towards you; instead of fighting it near the cave entrance, wait for it walk further down the path and fight it in the area with the small fire, where there's much more room to evade its attacks. The rest of the area is clear of enemies, so after defeating the Executioner you can freely enter the cave and claim the items inside.
[→☐ 01]

01

02

Small Windmill ⑧

The Lamp near the Small Windmill can be quite difficult to see when you're running through the area, but since it's the only one in the woods it's extremely important that you activate it. The door leading into the windmill cannot be opened from this side, and you need to be careful as you get close to it, because there are Carrion Crows hiding in the grass. There's also a Huntsman patrolling the bridge nearby; try to get its attention either with a Pebble or by standing close to the bridge, so that it comes towards you. On the other side of the bridge is another Huntsman with a rifle, so by fighting the patrolling one on the side of the bridge near the Lamp you'll be out of the other's line of fire.

Shortly after crossing the bridge there are skeletal remains just in front of some suspiciously piled up wooded planks. Beneath those planks there's a pressure plate that will cause a spiked section of tree trunk to come swinging down between two nearby trees. To avoid triggering the trap, simply walk around to the side of the planks, otherwise, step on them, and then quickly run to the side so the swinging tree trunk misses you. [→☐ 02]

COMBAT FOCUS Village Garrison ⑪

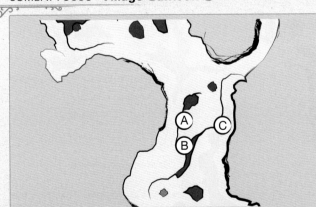

There are a large number of enemies huddled around campfires in this area, and the mix of fast-moving Rabid Dogs, along with ranged and melee Huntsmen can make it quite a difficult battle. The two Huntsmen at **Positions A** and **B** throw oil urns, and if you were to run in and start fighting the other enemies and dogs first, it's highly likely that one of them would hit you. Given the number of fires and torch-wielding enemies in the area, that can be very dangerous, so it's best to take them out as soon as possible. Upon reaching this area, follow the cliff along to the right and take out the Large Huntsman that's patrolling there, before heading to the top of the small alcove at **Position C**. You'll have a clear line of sight down to the enemy at **Position A** and the two

dogs near him, and how you continue will depend on what you have in your arsenal.

If you have a good ranged option, such as a Pistol or Throwing Knives, you should use them from the top of the cliff to take out the two dogs below, because the Huntsman is unable to throw the oil urns up to your position. You can then drop down to take him (and the one at **Position B**) out easily with no dogs to worry about. Without a ranged option you can drop down, and if you have a weapon with a wide arcing horizontal attack, such as the transformed Hunter Axe, you can get close enough to take all the enemies out in one or two quick hits. Alternatively, position yourself between the two dogs and try to kill them both with a charged R2 attack before quickly engaging the Huntsman nearby. Once that group is down, run back along the path and kill the second oil urn-wielder at **Position B**, before the other enemies can get too close. The remaining enemies can be separated quite easily, because the Axe users move a lot faster than those with the Shields. Try to lure them up the path and away from the fires, where you'll have more room to maneuver.

Wildflower Ridge

After getting past the Garrison there's a picturesque hill covered with flowers leading upwards on the left. The path going straight past the hill leads to a wooden platform, and stepping out onto it causes it to break, dropping you into the village. There's another path leading directly away from the hill, and along it are some items and a Wandering Nightmare to kill for some more weapon upgrade materials. Continue up the hill towards the ridge and a Large Huntsman will come walking out of a dilapidated shack just ahead; try to run in quickly and attack it before it spots you. Once it's defeated you can search the shack for items, and then continue on down the path towards the Woodland Village. Be careful as you get near the gate, however, because just in front of it there's another hidden pressure plate that releases a spiked log. [→☐ 03]

03

Forbidden Woods

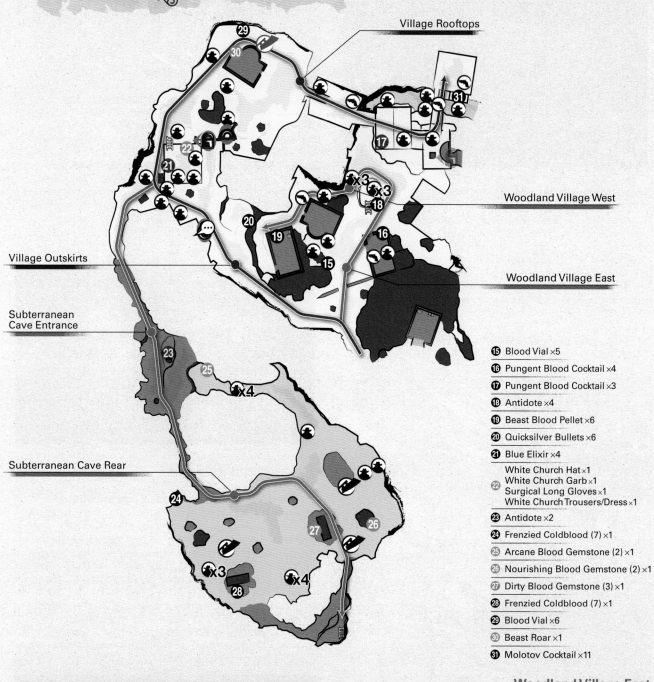

Village Rooftops

Woodland Village West

Village Outskirts

Woodland Village East

Subterranean
Cave Entrance

Subterranean Cave Rear

15 Blood Vial ×5

16 Pungent Blood Cocktail ×4

17 Pungent Blood Cocktail ×3

18 Antidote ×4

19 Beast Blood Pellet ×6

20 Quicksilver Bullets ×6

21 Blue Elixir ×4

22 White Church Hat ×1
White Church Garb ×1
Surgical Long Gloves ×1
White Church Trousers/Dress ×1

23 Antidote ×2

24 Frenzied Coldblood (7) ×1

25 Arcane Blood Gemstone (2) ×1

26 Nourishing Blood Gemstone (2) ×1

27 Dirty Blood Gemstone (3) ×1

28 Frenzied Coldblood (7) ×1

29 Blood Vial ×6

30 Beast Roar ×1

31 Molotov Cocktail ×11

Woodland Village East

When exploring the village, it's best to work your way around the buildings to ensure that nothing is missed. The first building on the right as you enter is a good place to start. Be careful as you enter the building, however, because two Huntsmen are waiting in ambush – take them out before going for the items. From the back of this building you should be able to see a large number of wooden planks in the middle of the village; they are in fact covering a large pit, in which there are a few Carrion Crows and an item. The building to the right of the large pit has an item in it, but since the gate in there is locked form this side, you may want to leave it until you get there from the other side. The path at the rear of the village leads to an oil-filled stream that runs below the Village Rooftops, and while you can make your way through it, it's much safer and more lucrative to follow the route along the Village Outskirts. [→☐ 01]

01

Woodland Village West

The buildings on the west side of the village can only be entered from behind, so it's best to start on the east side and approach this area from the rear. Before you can get into the buildings, however, you'll have to deal with a small group of Huntsmen, and a Large Huntsman. The Large Huntsman will often spot you first, so wait for it to come towards you and fight it away from the other enemies. If you follow the path leading behind the buildings, another Huntsman will walk out from behind the first building as you get close, so make sure you're ready for him. If you're making your way back to the entrance to reach the Village Outskirts path, be sure to watch out for the Huntsmen in front of the last building if you haven't already killed them.

Village Outskirts ㉒ ㉚

This path around the outskirts of the village allows you to skip entering the village altogether, and also lets you reach the rooftops at the end, so that you can easily take on the walkway enemies there. If you talk to the NPC in the shack on your way up he will have been taken over by Patches the Spider, and if you haven't already got it elsewhere, this is the ideal time to talk to him and get the Tonsil Stone. For more details on the mysterious Patches, refer to p649.

Just past that shack you'll come to a number of kennels with Rabid Dogs inside them, and it's best to kill them while they're caged to stop them becoming a problem later. The gate at the top of the hill in this area will close as soon as you get close to it, and if you haven't killed the Rabid Dogs by then, they will break free of their cages and attack you. Following the path between the kennels will take you to a branching path that leads down to the Subterranean Cave. Continuing along the main path until you reach the back of the nearby building, you'll notice a ladder leading to its roof, where a very useful Attire set awaits. More Rabid Dogs are patrolling in front of the building just beyond the one with the Attire set, so make sure you deal with them before going around back where a Kidnapper awaits (if you've been to Old Yharnam). When the area is clear, enter the house to get the Beast Roar, one of the fragments of the Great Ones. [→▢ 02]

Subterranean Cave Entrance

The tunnel to the cave is long and winding, with a number of pitfalls, so be careful of your footing. Once you reach the bottom of the first slope, make sure to run back beneath the overhang to get the item hidden there. You need to be extremely careful once you reach the bank of the lake, because not only are its waters poisonous, but there are also Bare Fist variants of the Church Giants patrolling, and numerous Parasite Larva. Fighting the enemies while in the poisonous water is dangerous, so always try to lure them to an area of solid ground. The first of the Church Giants is quite close to the entrance of the cave and there is more than enough solid ground to

fight him there. After killing him you can either explore the rest of the cave, or run straight across to the tunnel on the other side and use the ladders to reach the alternate entrance to Iosefka's Clinic. The small island near the tunnel is also an excellent place to fight the Church Giant that patrols near it – just make sure to take out the Parasite Larvae in the area first.

㉕ ㉖ ㉗ Subterranean Cave Rear

To reach the back of the cave it's best to hug the shore of the lake heading to the left from the entrance. Doing this you can make it most of the way without having to step into the poisonous waters. The island where another Church Giant is kneeling should be clearly visible, but it's a lot more dangerous than it appears, because of the group of Parasite Larvae swimming around near it. Fighting all of the enemies on that small island can be very problematic. Luckily, the Parasite Larvae have slow movement speed, so take advantage of this to lure the Church Giant to the small patch of land beyond the island and fight it there. If you notice the Parasite Larvae getting close, simply run back to the island again. Near that island you should also see a small inlet that leads to a narrow tunnel, at the end of which there's a Blood Gem. There's precious little dry land in the tunnel, however, and it's teaming with Parasite Larvae, so it's highly likely that you'll get poisoned when trying to reach the end; make sure you have plenty of healing items or some Antidotes at hand before attempting to get the Gem. [→▢ 03/04]

Village Rooftops

There are a number of enemies along these rooftops, many of which throw Molotovs, so taking them out from up here is much easier than having to contend with them down below in the Oil Swamp. Before running straight down the ramp onto the rooftops, look down to the left from the top of it and you'll find a Huntsman that was waiting to ambush you – drop down and kill him first. As you make your way along the rooftops, try to use the trees to block the Molotovs that are being thrown at you. When you reach the bridge where the first of the Molotov throwers is located, look down to the right-hand side to see a small ramp that leads underneath the bridge; this is an excellent hiding spot from other Hunters. After crossing the bridge you can drop down off the rooftop onto a small ledge above the Oil Swamp, where you'll find a large number of Molotovs, useful for getting rid of some of the Rotted Corpses in the swamp below.

Forbidden Woods

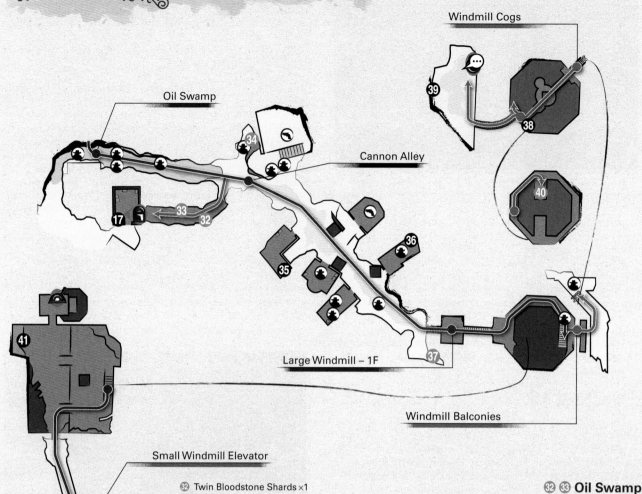

Windmill Cogs

Oil Swamp

Cannon Alley

Large Windmill – 1F

Windmill Balconies

Small Windmill Elevator

32 Twin Bloodstone Shards ×1
33 Twin Bloodstone Shards ×1
34 Twin Bloodstone Shards ×2
35 Blood Vial ×6
36 Beast Blood Pellet ×4
37 Twin Bloodstone Shards ×1
38 Poison Knife ×8
39 Poison Knife ×3
40 Canon ×1
41 Madman's Knowledge ×1
42 Twin Bloodstone Shards ×1

01

32 33 Oil Swamp

Separating the two halves of the village is this small, oily swamp area. As soon as you step into it you will become coated in oil, and any fire damage you receive will be doubled. This can be especially dangerous if you enter along the main path through the first half of the village, because a number of enemies will start throwing Molotovs down at you, which can be very difficult to avoid, especially since the swamp is filled with slow-moving Rotted Corpses. So it's recommended that you reach this area via the Rooftops. The oil can also work in your favor, however, as you'll be able to take out the Rotted Corpses very quickly using fire based attacks. At the end of the swamp, there's a narrow path doubling back on the right-hand side that leads to the other side of the one-way gate in the village. Opening it will allow you to bypass the swamp altogether on subsequent trips into the area. [→ 01]

Large Windmill – 1F

Upon entering the Large Windmill you'll see a Snake Parasite walking down a set of stairs on the opposite side of the room. Follow the walkway around to the left to reach those same stairs. Let the Snake Parasite keep walking, and it will eventually come to a stop near a fireplace with its back to you, so you can sneak up behind it and use a charged R2 for an easy victory. Near that fireplace there's a doorway that leads to the top of an elevator shaft, but the elevator needs to be activated from the bottom. Heading through the door opposite the one leading to the elevator will allow you to reach the dense forest that lies just beyond the windmill.

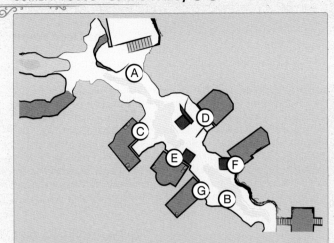

02

Blimey, don't scare me like that!

03 ⟋ Cannon

Before heading into the second half of the village, it's important to kill the small group of enemies around the building at **Position A**, especially the Huntsman with a rifle up on the roof, because you don't want him firing from behind as you try to advance through the village. As soon as you enter this part of the village, a Huntsman on top of the hill at **Position B** will start firing cannonballs at you; never stand out in the open where he has a direct line of sight on you. There is some makeshift cover you can use along the main path up the middle of the village, but most of that can be destroyed by the cannon fire. If you do hide behind it, never get too close to it.

The safest way to get through the area is by making use of the buildings on either side of the path and quickly dashing between them as you make your way towards the cannon. Not all of the buildings are empty, however, so you need to be careful when entering one. Clearing them as you proceed will ensure that you never get attacked from behind, and that each fight is manageable. The first building to head to is the one at **Position C** on the right, since it is closest, and also empty. Wait there for the cannon to fire, and then dash across to the house on the other side at **Position D**. There's a rifleman in this house – take him out quickly because another Huntsman will usually come running from the house on the other side shortly after you enter.

Once both enemies have been defeated, run across to the now empty house at **Position E**, and then move up again to **Position F** and kill the Large Huntsman in that house. Now that you're this close to the cannon it cannot hit you, so you can safely run across to the house at **Position G** and kill the two Huntsmen inside, before finally taking out the enemy behind the cannon. With him out of the way you can operate the cannon yourself if you wish, and it can be used as a nasty surprise against other Hunters.

Windmill Balconies

Just before the first set of stairs inside the windmill there's an opening in the wall on the left that you can use to drop down onto a balcony below. It's wise to stay clear of the edge of this balcony – falling off will lead to certain death. Be especially careful when fighting the Large Huntsman near the ladder; try to always stick near the wall to avoid being knocked off. From the top of the ladder, crossing the makeshift bridges and cogs leads to an opening on the other side, which leads out onto a rooftop overlooking the Cannon Alley. As well as some items you can also talk to the Afflicted Beggar on the roof (who you'll find feeding on some corpses in the corner), and for doing so you'll get a Gesture and have the option to send him to a sanctuary; depending on where you choose to send him it can have dire consequences for other NPCs, so make sure you check p643 first so that you're fully informed before making a choice. [→☐ 02]

④⓪ Windmill Cogs

The windmill is home to one last treasure if you know where to look. Just below the upper set of cogs and bridges you should be able to make out another walkway, and if you drop down and head around the side of one of the large cogs you'll find the Cannon near a corpse. The Cannon is the most powerful single hit firearm there is, and if you have the strength to wield it, it can be a fearsome weapon. Dropping down from here will take you back to the walkway you were initially on when you entered the building. [→☐ 03]

④② Small Windmill Elevator

Another Snake Parasite patrols the bridge just outside the windmill. The snakes have already burst from his head, so be careful; try to use attacks that flinch to stop the snakes from starting their attacks, or ranged attacks to weaken it before getting close. After crossing the bridge there's a trail leading back along the cliff to the right-hand side of the path, and up to a cave with an elevator inside. The elevator acts as a shortcut back up to the Small Windmill near the Lamp, so you can now get the items in the room there and open the one-way gate. Before proceeding any further into the woods it's highly recommended that you use the Lamp to return to the Hunter's Dream and use all of the weapon upgrade materials you've acquired in the first half of the area to strengthen your weapon, while also increasing your character's level.

Forbidden Woods

The Deep Wood

It's very easy to get disorientated and lose your sense of direction in the Deep Wood. Surroundings look similar and there's a dark fog clouding your view. The most important thing to remember is that the small lanterns hanging from the trees are there to illuminate the main path. If you ever get lost, all you need do is look for the lanterns along the path and use them to help regain your bearings. The major exploration areas are off to either side of the main path, so as long as you keep the outside edge of the area in your sights, you can easily find the path again, just by heading away from it. If you stick to the path then you'll have to contend with very few enemies until you reach the Snake Den, but you'll also miss out on a large number of items. [→ ☐ 01]

㊹ Executioner's Cliff

If you keep going straight ahead after the second lantern along the path, you can drop down onto a narrow ledge running along the side of the cliff. There's a small gap near the start of the ledge, but it can easily be crossed using either a roll or a jump. At the end of the ledge there's an item on a corpse. Don't go running straight for it, however, because there's an Executioner hiding behind a tree nearby. Approach from the left side of the tree and you can sneak up on him, so a weapon with long range has a chance for a charged strike on his back before he turns around. Try to lure the Executioner away from the edge and fight it in the middle of the area to avoid either of you falling off, and then claim the item once he's defeated. Rather than dropping down from the end of this area into the middle of the woods, it's better to return to the gap in the ledge you jumped over and drop down there in order to keep your bearings. [→ ☐ 02]

㊸ Frenzied Coldblood (7) ×1

㊹ Twin Bloodstone Shards ×2

㊺ Shining Coins ×6

㊻ Twin Bloodstone Shards ×1

㊼ Twin Bloodstone Shards ×1

㊽ Madman's Knowledge ×1

㊾ Madman's Knowledge ×1

㊿ Twin Bloodstone Shards ×2

51 Twin Bloodstone Shards ×1

52 Twin Bloodstone Shards ×2

53 Twin Bloodstone Shards ×2

54 Twin Bloodstone Shards ×1

55 Thick Coldblood (6) ×1

56 Clear Deep Sea ×1

57 Bloodstone Chunk ×1

58 Shining Coins ×5

59 Deep Sea ×1

60 Twin Bloodstone Shards ×1

61 Twin Bloodstone Shards ×3

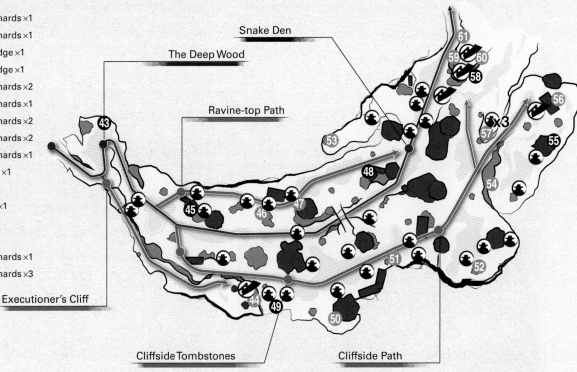

Snake Den

The Deep Wood

Ravine-top Path

Executioner's Cliff

Cliffside Tombstones

Cliffside Path

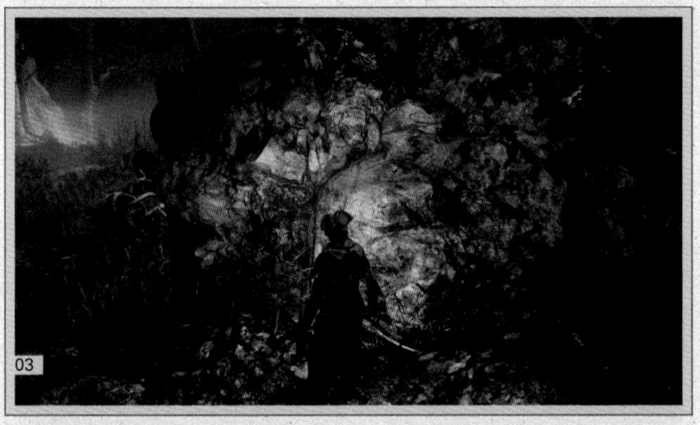

03

Ravine-top Path ㊻ ㊼

This path that runs along the top of the ravine is home to a number of very useful items. Following it to its end naturally leads you back onto the main path, near the middle of the woods. It's also a relatively narrow area, so it's quite easy to find your way back onto the main path at any point. The brush along this side of the woods is quite thick, so it can be difficult to spot the numerous Snake Balls hiding within it if you're moving quickly; it's better to progress slowly so that you can hear them hiss when you get close, giving you time to locate them and land a pre-emptive strike. **[→☐ 03]**

Cliffside Tombstones ㊿ ㊿

This side of the woods stretches much further away from the path than the other side, so you may want to use some Shining Coins to mark areas that you've already explored, or use the large tombstones as landmarks. There are a lot more enemies to contend with on this side of the woods, and an equally high number of items to collect. Try to keep the cliffside to your right, as that will help keep your bearings. With that in mind, head around the back of the first large tombstone and continue along the path from there. Clear out the Snake Balls in front of the next large tombstone before trying to pick up the item in front of it, and then continue along the cliff to reach another item behind a large tree. From here you should be able to see a Snake Parasite standing near a small fire – try to sneak up behind him to take him out easily. Just beyond that fire there's a large tree, to the left of which is a small path leading up a fallen tree trunk that you can use to cross over to the Ravine Path if you wish.

Cliffside Path (51) (52) (54) (56)

Continuing straight on from the fire will lead to another large tombstone that you can make your way around, and from there you should see another Snake Parasite, and an item by a tree to the right. It's very difficult to sneak up on this enemy, so it's best to run up and attack it quickly with flinching attacks to stop the snakes from attacking, or with ranged attacks. As you continue along the cliffside path you'll start to notice it split, with one path going down and away from the cliff, and another going up a hill alongside it. The path leading down will take you to the Snake Den, but approaching it from this side can be quite dangerous, because you run the risk of being spotted by the group of Snake Parasites in the alcove nearby. It's much safer to backtrack slightly and approach that area from further back. If you continue up the hill you'll find a Large Snake Ball waiting for you at the top; this enemy is far more dangerous than its smaller brethren. You should try to close in quickly so you don't have to contend with its ranged attacks, and then use the trees for cover, circling around behind it before attacking. Once it's been defeated, make sure to gather up all of the items in the area, including the one hiding behind the nearby tombstone. **[→☐ 04]**

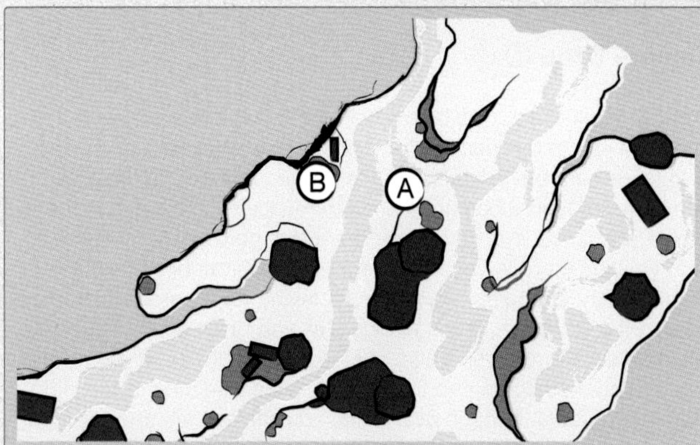

The heat from the fire burning in the center of the woods has attracted a large number of enemies, so this location should be approached with caution. The major threat in the area is the Large Snake Ball that starts moving into the area from **Position A**, but dealing with it while it's still surrounded by the large number of Snake Balls can be very difficult, so it's best to take them out first. Approaching the area along either the main path or the ravine top path provides plenty of trees for cover, but once you get down into the area, the best cover is from the plants at **Position B**. Many of the Snake Balls can be reached from this cover position and you can use hit-and-run style attacks against them between the Large Snake Ball's ranged attacks.

The Large Snake Ball will eventually move around the plants, so the simplest way to deal with it is to run around behind it and try to land a charged R2 before it turns around, and then try to stay behind it while attacking. If it has moved to a position that would make getting behind it awkward, or if you want to play it safe, you may want to retreat back up the main path and use ranged attacks to weaken it, while using the trees for cover.

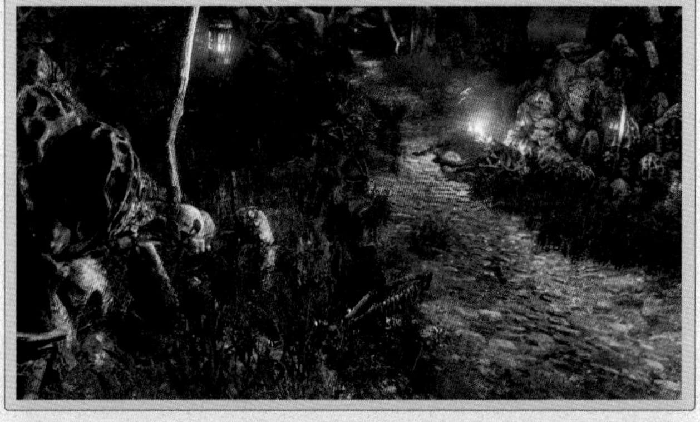

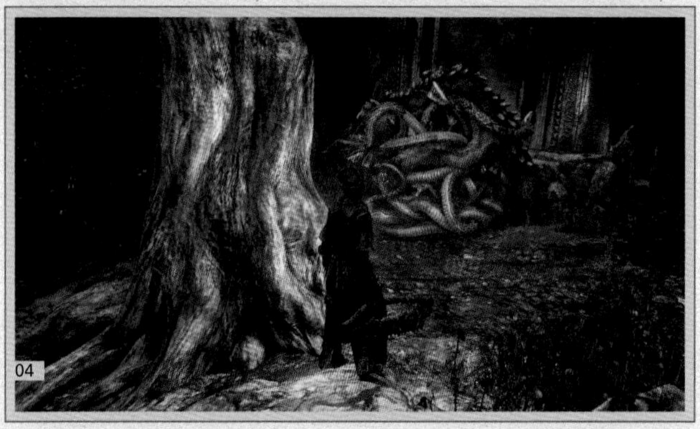

04

2

Forbidden Woods

Ravine Drop 53 65

After the Snake Den has been cleared out you can safely explore this area just to the side of it, starting with a small section of cliff that leads back along the top of the ravine, where you'll be able to find more Twin Bloodstone Shards. You'll also find a gap in the fence, and if you look down over the edge there are some ledges that you can drop down onto in order to reach the bottom of the ravine safely. Dropping down into the ravine from here will allow you to skip the latter part of the woods area and reach another shortcut elevator sooner, but you'll also miss out on a number of items. Near where you drop down into the ravine there's a section of the cliff that sticks out far enough over it that you can actually jump across to the other side, reaching a small area where you can acquire the Graveguard Mask. Once you jump across, however, you won't be able to jump back, so you'll have to either drop down into the ravine, or drop down where you picked up the Graveguard Mask and proceed from there. [→□ 01/02]

Overhanging Trees

The path leading on from the Snake Den winds beneath a series of overhanging trees, so it's very easy to follow and will eventually take you to a large crossroads, where a Snake Parasite patrols. From the crossroads, the path heading to the right will take you to the Twin Snakes area, and both the straight ahead path and the one to the left will eventually lead you to the same place, just outside the ravine area. The lamps on the trees signify that the path straight ahead is the main one. It's a dangerous route if you've not cleared

out the area, because as you round the corner a Large Snake Ball will start spraying poison at you from a small alcove on the right. Just past that area, there's also the option of going off the path to the cliff edge, from where you can drop down and skip a large section of the ravine.

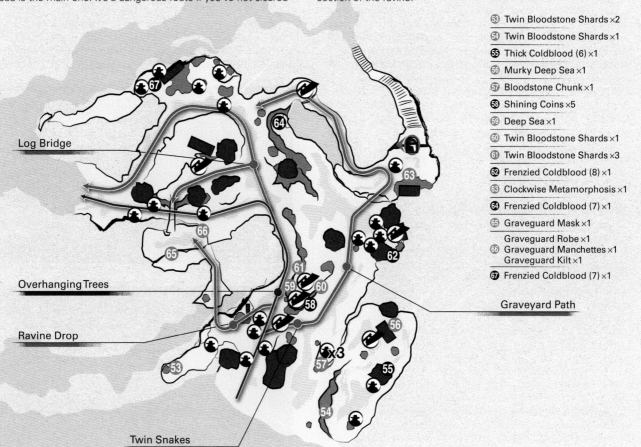

53 Twin Bloodstone Shards ×2
54 Twin Bloodstone Shards ×1
55 Thick Coldblood (6) ×1
56 Murky Deep Sea ×1
57 Bloodstone Chunk ×1
58 Shining Coins ×5
59 Deep Sea ×1
60 Twin Bloodstone Shards ×1
61 Twin Bloodstone Shards ×3
62 Frenzied Coldblood (8) ×1
63 Clockwise Metamorphosis ×1
64 Frenzied Coldblood (7) ×1
65 Graveguard Mask ×1
66 Graveguard Robe ×1
   Graveguard Manchettes ×1
   Graveguard Kilt ×1
67 Frenzied Coldblood (7) ×1

Log Bridge

Overhanging Trees

Ravine Drop

Twin Snakes

Graveyard Path

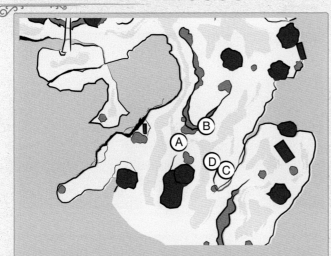

04

05

Before you reach the overhanging trees you'll see a small path at **Position A**. It leads to an item at **Position B** above a large alcove, where two Large Snake Balls can be found. Before heading straight for the item, however, it's best to deal with the group of Snake Parasite s that are in another alcove at **Position C**, otherwise they would attack you from behind. There's a tree in front of the second alcove at **Position D**; head around it slowly to lure one of the enemies out and fight it away from the others, and then round it a bit more to do the same with a second one. The final enemy there will usually have its back to you, so once the first two are out of the way, sneak up behind it for an easy victory.

Once the entire group has been defeated, return to **Position A** overlooking the Large Snake Balls and use any ranged attacks at your disposal to weaken them from this safe vantage point. Molotovs are especially effective, because their area of effect is large enough to hit both of them. After you've weakened them, drop off and use a plunging attack to hit them both, and finish them off quickly before they can attack. Clearing out all of these enemies will allow you to pick up a large number of Twin Bloodstone Shards, a Bloodstone Chunk and a Caryll Rune, so the rewards are more than worth it.

㊌ Graveyard Path

Following the path towards the cliff edge from the Twin Snakes alcoves, you'll see a large tree, beyond which is another group of enemies. The major threat, as usual, is the Large Snake Ball, but the tree provides more than enough cover from its ranged attacks, allowing you to safely wait behind it while all of the Snake Balls make their way towards you. When all of the enemies have been dispatched, grab the item that was hiding behind the tree you used for cover, and then go around behind the next large tree. From there, a series of ledges lead down into the graveyard area below, where a Snake Parasite is patrolling. The Clockwise Metamorphosis Rune is your reward for killing him. The gate leading out of this area can only be opened from the other side, so head up the narrow path near where you first dropped down. It leads to an overhang, overlooking another Large Snake Ball – a plunging attack from this height will deal a lot of damage, allowing you to finish it off with a combo. **[→☐ 03-05]**

㊏ Log Bridge

Just to the side of the main path at the large crossroads there's a ramp leading up to an area where a Maneater Boar patrols. If you're careful you can often use the rocky outcroppings in this area for cover and sneak up behind the beast and land a charged **R2**. Continuing further up the hill leads to a log bridge that you can cross in order to reach the remaining pieces of Graveguard Attire, and from there you can drop back down to the main path again. **[→☐ 06]**

03

06

Forbidden Woods

Ravine Access ⓻

The two paths leading down into the ravine provide a choice of routes, depending on where you want to go. Before you make your choice, be aware that one of the Maneater Boars from the ravine can patrol along this area. If you encounter it when you first get here, try to run towards the split in the path, so that if it charges, it does so into the wall, allowing you to easily circle around behind it. The upper path on the left provides a safer route to the back end of the ravine, avoiding the patrolling Maneater Boar most of the time, while the lower path on the right leads through the ravine towards the end of the area. [→☐ **01/02**]

ravine are two Small Celestial Emissaries with Tendrils, and they are much more dangerous than the regular ones. These enemies are capable of using multiple ranged magic attacks in quick succession, so by far the best way of dealing with them is to close in quickly and hit them with a thrust attack before they can open fire. A couple of regular ones will also emerge once you reach that point, so you'll need to take out the enemies as quickly as possible to avoid being surrounded. Once the area is clear, you can pick up the Anti-Clock-wise Metamorphosis Rune that increases your maximum Stamina, making the trip extremely worthwhile. [→☐ **04**]

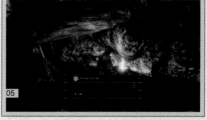

Lakeside Path

Upon reaching the lake there's the faint glow of a lantern coming from within the grass along the north shore. This serves as an excellent landmark to help orientate yourself, regardless of which route you took to reach the lake, or which direction you're heading in. Be careful as you continue up the hill from the lantern, because there's a Snake Parasite waiting to ambush you from behind a tree on the left about half way up. At the top of the hill there's an elevator that goes back up to the main floor of the Large Windmill, creating a useful shortcut back to the elevator in the Small Windmill. Since you're nearing the end of the area at this point, it's worth making the trip back to the Hunter's Dream and leveling up some more before you face the boss. [→☐ **03**]

⓻⓸ Boar Creek

Ravine Floor ⓾

Heading to the south from the lake will lead to a narrow tunnel and then to a section of the ravine where the Small Celestial Emissaries reside. After going up the small hill on the other side of the tunnel, be wary of picking up the item that's lying in plain sight, because there's an Emissary waiting in ambush behind the nearby tree – kill it before going for the item. In the middle of this section of the

A pair of Maneater Boars patrol this section of the ravine, so listen out for the sound of them stomping through the water in the distance to make sure you don't get caught by surprise. Once you hear one, it's best to track it down so that you can close in quickly to fight it, rather than have it spot you first and charge. There are some overhanging trees just above the water line on the left side of the creek as you walk along it, and you can actually go under their roots and clear out some Rotted Corpses to get a Caryll Rune. Near those trees you'll have the choice of either following the creek, or taking a path to the side of it; the path is generally the better option, as it will allow you to maneuver around the Maneater Boar in the area. [→☐ 05]

Narrow Pass

Heading up the hill at this fork will allow you to open the one-way gate that leads to the Graveyard Path, so if you have yet to get the Caryll Rune from that area, now is the perfect time to do so. With the gate open you also have another shortcut back to the boss area if you prefer to run straight through the woods rather than go through the ravine. The room at the bottom of the path is where you'll face the boss, so make sure you're fully prepared before entering.

06

The Shadows of Yharnam make for a tricky threesome, but you can make things a bit easier by using the tombstone in the center of the area to both split the group up and shield yourself from incoming magic attacks. For the full strategy see p338. Upon defeating the bosses you'll automatically receive the Blood Rapture Caryll Rune that restores your HP when using visceral attacks, and gain access to the Forbidden Grave Lamp. While the path to Byrgenwerth is directly ahead, it's recommended that you only go so far as to light the Lamp at the start of that area, and then go to Nightmare Frontier or Forsaken Cainhurst Castle to further level up your character and gain some more useful items first. [→☐ 06]

World Changes

- Gain access to the Forbidden Grave Lamp
- Open the way to Byrgenwerth

2

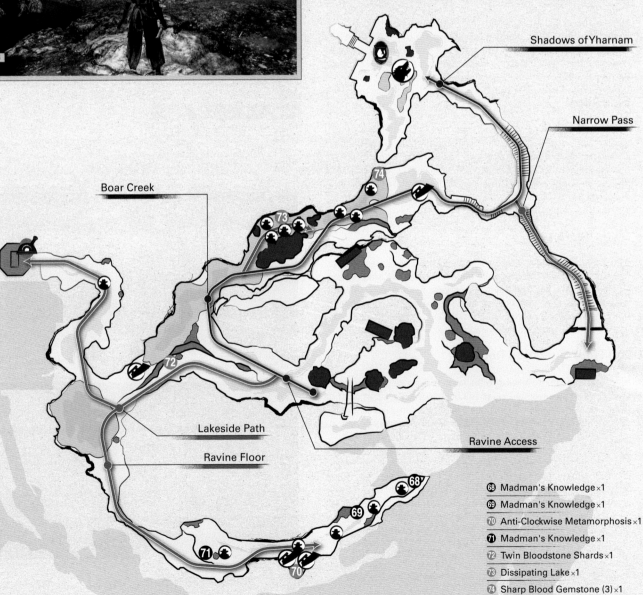

Shadows of Yharnam

Narrow Pass

74

Boar Creek

73

72

Lakeside Path

Ravine Floor

Ravine Access

68

69

71

70

68 Madman's Knowledge ×1

69 Madman's Knowledge ×1

70 Anti-Clockwise Metamorphosis ×1

71 Madman's Knowledge ×1

72 Twin Bloodstone Shards ×1

73 Dissipating Lake ×1

74 Sharp Blood Gemstone (3) ×1

Iosefka's Clinic

You know this place; you remember it from not long ago. Perhaps it is where you awoke? Or where your dream began? You see a different side of it now, though, and the shadows cast by the moonlight quicken your pulse. As you enter, a familiar voice calls out not in greeting, but in warning. The whispered talk of rescue and true salvation somehow invokes fear. Should you wish to continue as you are now, turn back. But if you seek the truth, no matter how dark, onward you must go.

Difficulty	Area **B**
Recommended	Player Level **40-50** | Weapon Upgrade **+5**
Timezones	○ ◑ ☾ ●
Insight	Entering via the Backdoor ×1

Graveyard Gate

Upon reaching this area, the first and most important thing to do is pull the switch to open the gate that leads back out to Central Yharnam. Doing so means that if you die, you'll have a quick route back here via either the 1st Floor Sickroom Lamp or the Central Yharnam Lamp. [→□ 01]

Side Alley

If you go through the already open gate near the top of the ladder, you'll be able to access this small alley that runs alongside the main clinic building. It may seem like the area is empty, but don't run through carelessly. Near the end of the alley you'll see a well with an item on it, but the Brainsucker just to the left of it will ambush you if you fail to pay him the required attention. Use a powerful thrust attack to take him out quickly. [→□ 02]

Clinic Rooftops

At the top of the ladder, there are some rooftops to cross in order to enter the clinic. While there are quite a number of Carrion Crows in this area, you can avoid them all by simply running along the left-hand side if you're in a rush. Given the ease with which they can be killed, however, and the high amount of Blood Echoes they reward you with, killing them can be quite lucrative.

2nd Floor Operating Room ❸

Following the corridor around to the right as soon as you enter the clinic building will eventually lead you back to the room that you first awoke in, after signing your contract. There are a few key differences since the last time you were here, however. For every person you have sent to Iosefka's Clinic Sanctuary so far, there will be an additional Small Celestial Emissary in the clinic, so you may well encounter one on the way to the room, as well as inside it. For more information about whom you can send to the Clinic and how, check p646. Unless you provoke them, these Emissaries will not attack, so you can simply leave them to carry on about their business if you wish. Inside the room you'll also find a new item sitting on the operating table you awoke upon. It's the Cainhurst Summons, a very important item that allows you to reach Forsaken Cainhurst Castle (via Hemwick Crossing in Hemwick Charnel Lane). [→□ 03]

Enemies

Regular	HP	Echoes	Page
Small Celestial Emissary	143	658	p241
Carrion Crow	179	284	p231

Strong	HP	Echoes	Page
Brainsucker	484	995	p273

NPC

Name	Page
Imposter Iosefka	p646

01

02

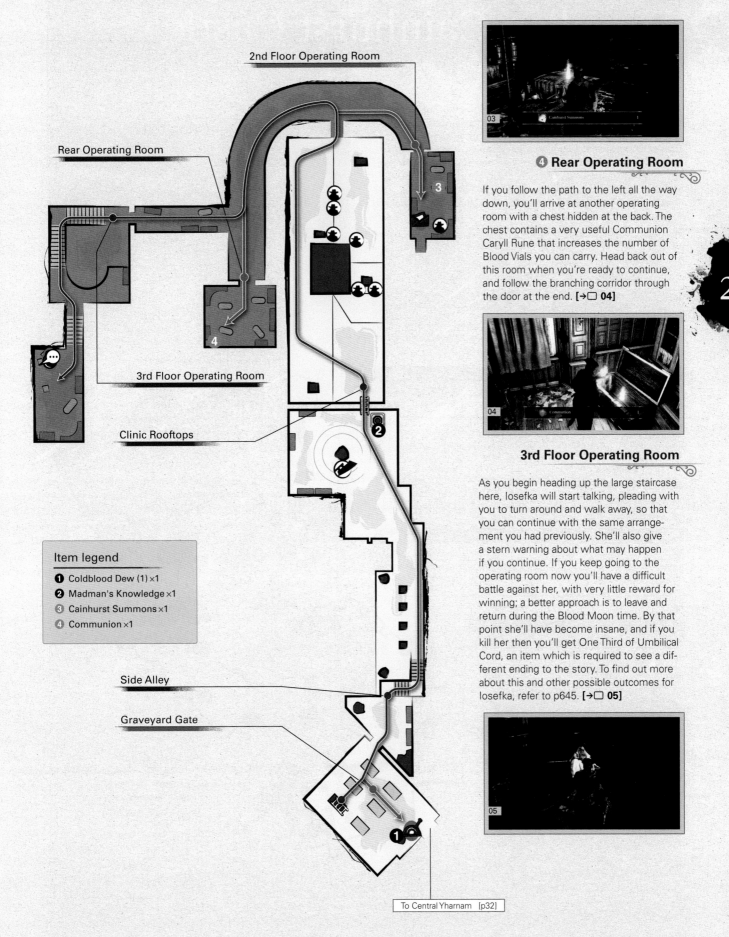

2nd Floor Operating Room

Rear Operating Room

3rd Floor Operating Room

Clinic Rooftops

Item legend

❶ Coldblood Dew (1) ×1
❷ Madman's Knowledge ×1
❸ Cainhurst Summons ×1
❹ Communion ×1

Side Alley

Graveyard Gate

To Central Yharnam [p32]

❹ Rear Operating Room

If you follow the path to the left all the way down, you'll arrive at another operating room with a chest hidden at the back. The chest contains a very useful Communion Caryll Rune that increases the number of Blood Vials you can carry. Head back out of this room when you're ready to continue, and follow the branching corridor through the door at the end. **[→☐ 04]**

3rd Floor Operating Room

As you begin heading up the large staircase here, Iosefka will start talking, pleading with you to turn around and walk away, so that you can continue with the same arrangement you had previously. She'll also give a stern warning about what may happen if you continue. If you keep going to the operating room now you'll have a difficult battle against her, with very little reward for winning; a better approach is to leave and return during the Blood Moon time. By that point she'll have become insane, and if you kill her then you'll get One Third of Umbilical Cord, an item which is required to see a different ending to the story. To find out more about this and other possible outcomes for Iosefka, refer to p645. **[→☐ 05]**

Forsaken Cainhurst Castle

You find an ancient letter, addressed to none other than yourself. Following its directions, you board a mysterious coach near the large gate of Hemwick. As the coach proceeds, a massive, ancient castle draws near. You approach, and a chill runs up your spine. From the corner of your eye you see movement, but, when you turn to look directly, the night is still. You would be fortunate if it was a mere ghost, for you have a growing sensation that this castle is home to apparitions far worse. Apparitions that smell strongly of blood.

Difficulty	Area **B** | Martyr Logarius **S**
Recommended	Player Level **45-55** | Weapon Upgrade **+6**
Timezones	◐ ◑ ☾ ●
Insight	Arrive in the area ×2, Encounter Martyr Logarius ×1, Defeat Martyr Logarius ×3, Enter the Queen's Chamber ×2,

Enemies

Regular	HP	Echoes	Page
Parasite Larva	510	210	p242
Cain's Servant (Cane)	595	560	p243
Cain's Servant (Cane & Candelabra)	595	560	p243
Cain's Servant (Rapier)	993	910	p243
Lost Child of Antiquity*	908	910	p244
Forsaken Castle Spirit (Knife)	737	490	p245
Forsaken Castle Spirit (Head)	397	490	p245
Wandering Nightmare	153	70	p671

*Stronger version on rooftop: 922 HP, 832 Echoes.

Strong	HP	Echoes	Page
Bloodlicker	1362	2310	p280

Boss	HP	Echoes	Page
Martyr Logarius	9081	25600	p342

NPC

Name	Page
Annalise, Queen of the Vilebloods	p647

Entrance Hall [p107]

Item legend

1. Numbing Mist ×2
2. Frenzied Coldblood (9) ×1
3. Tempering Blood Gemstone (3) ×1
4. Numbing Mist ×4
5. Frenzied Coldblood (9) ×1
6. Frenzied Coldblood (8) ×1
7. Numbing Mist ×4
8. Madman's Knowledge ×1
9. Madman's Knowledge ×1

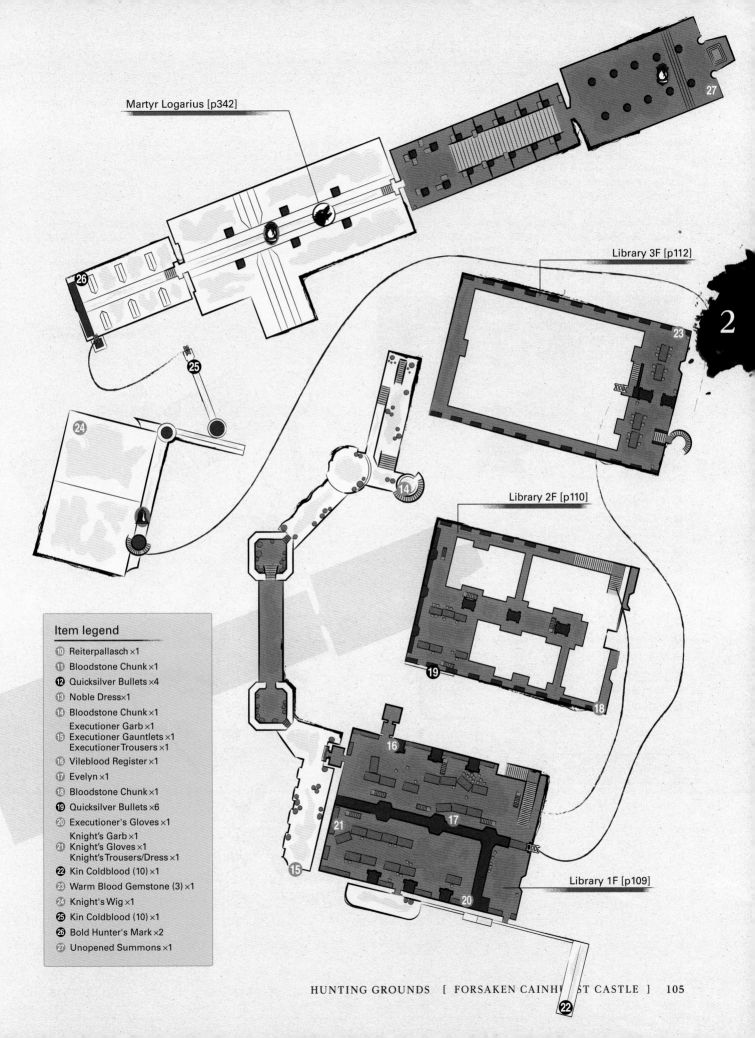

Martyr Logarius [p342]

Library 3F [p112]

2

Library 2F [p110]

Library 1F [p109]

Item legend

- ⑩ Reiterpallasch ×1
- ⑪ Bloodstone Chunk ×1
- ⑫ Quicksilver Bullets ×4
- ⑬ Noble Dress×1
- ⑭ Bloodstone Chunk ×1
- ⑮ Executioner Garb ×1
  Executioner Gauntlets ×1
  Executioner Trousers ×1
- ⑯ Vileblood Register ×1
- ⑰ Evelyn ×1
- ⑱ Bloodstone Chunk ×1
- ⑲ Quicksilver Bullets ×6
- ⑳ Executioner's Gloves ×1
- ㉑ Knight's Garb ×1
  Knight's Gloves ×1
  Knight's Trousers/Dress ×1
- ㉒ Kin Coldblood (10) ×1
- ㉓ Warm Blood Gemstone (3) ×1
- ㉔ Knight's Wig ×1
- ㉕ Kin Coldblood (10) ×1
- ㉖ Bold Hunter's Mark ×2
- ㉗ Unopened Summons ×1

Forsaken Cainhurst Castle

Castle Grounds

The grounds surrounding the castle are home to dangerous Bloodlickers, so the most important thing to do upon entering the area is to activate the Lamp before wandering too far in. From the Lamp you should also be able to see a torch burning on the side of wall near an archway in the distance; there is an elevator there that you can only activate later, but it's still worth exploring the area to get the item on the other side of the building. While crossing the grounds, try to get any Bloodlickers that you come across stuck amongst the groups of statues – this will limit their movement and make them easier to fight. Just like the gate leading into this area, the door to the castle's Entrance Hall will open automatically once you get close to it. [→☐ 01]

❸ Worm Gully

At the rear of the Castle Grounds you'll find a large gully, at the bottom of which there's a very useful Blood Gem; reaching it, however is not as easy as it appears. As you make your way down the gully you'll come across a couple of Parasite Larvae, and while the rest of the path to the gem seems to be clear, as you approach, large numbers of Parasite Larvae will emerge from the walls. If you want to kill all of the enemies, you should progress very slowly so that only a few emerge at a time, and you can retreat to fight them without causing more to appear. Alternatively, it's possible to sprint there and get out again without taking much damage if you're quick. There are also a couple of Bloodlickers patrolling the opposite side of the gully. They can be difficult to spot among the grey rocks, so be careful when walking around that area. [→☐ 02]

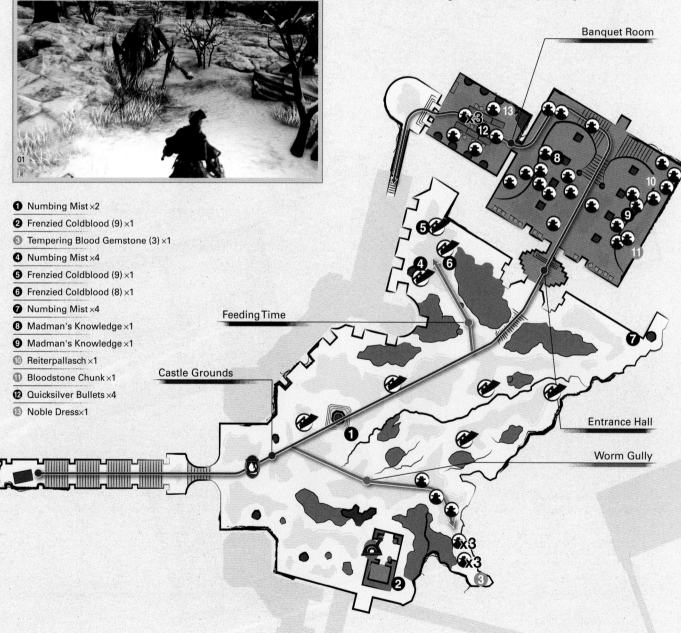

01

❶ Numbing Mist ×2
❷ Frenzied Coldblood (9) ×1
❸ Tempering Blood Gemstone (3) ×1
❹ Numbing Mist ×4
❺ Frenzied Coldblood (9) ×1
❻ Frenzied Coldblood (8) ×1
❼ Numbing Mist ×4
❽ Madman's Knowledge ×1
❾ Madman's Knowledge ×1
❿ Reiterpallasch ×1
⓫ Bloodstone Chunk ×1
⓬ Quicksilver Bullets ×4
⓭ Noble Dress ×1

Banquet Room

Feeding Time

Castle Grounds

Entrance Hall

Worm Gully

COMBAT FOCUS Feeding Time

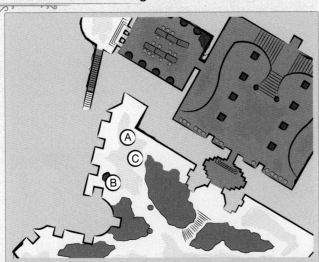

Fighting multiple Bloodlickers at the same time can be extremely dangerous, but if you employ a bit of stealth you can take advantage of the fact that this group are distracted by the corpses they're feeding on. The fully engorged Bloodlicker at **Position A** is unable to attack, so your primary focus should be dealing with the other two at **Positions B** and **C**. If you hug the rampart wall and walk slowly you can get close enough to the Bloodlicker at **Position B** to use a charged R2 on it (and a visceral attack follow-up), without attracting the attention of the one at **Position C**. If that wasn't enough to kill it, move back away from the remaining enemies before carrying on the fight, so that you don't disturb them. Because you can get close to the fully engorged enemy without any risk, if you walk along the castle wall towards it, you can cut across in front of it and get behind the Bloodlicker at **Position C**. With both of them out of the way you can kill the engorged one at your leisure, and then pick up all of the items from the corpses they were feeding on.

⑩ ⑪ Entrance Hall

Upon stepping inside the Entrance Hall you'll immediately hear the crying of multiple Forsaken Castle Spirits, but they will remain hidden and not pose a threat until you pick up one of the items in the area. Similarly, the Cain's Servants are focused on scrubbing the floors and will not engage you unless you attack them first. Clearing the room of all enemies can net you a large amount of Blood Echoes, so it's worth taking the time to do it. To make things easier you may want to kill off the Servants before picking up any items, so that you don't have to worry about them once the Castle Spirits materialize. Once you can see the Castle Spirits, they will initially be in a non-corporeal state and you won't be able to lock-on to them – only once they detect you will they become fully tangible. After clearing out the area, make sure to open the chest in the corner to the right of the large staircase to acquire the Reiterpallasch. **[→☐ 03/04]**

⑬ Banquet Room

Like the Entrance Hall, the Banquet room appears initially empty, but you'll be able to hear the crying of Castle Spirits, so you know they're in the area. An item sits out in plain sight between the two tables, and approaching it up will cause a large number of them to materialize around you, so it's best to run straight back towards the doorway to avoid being surrounded. Because of their slow movement speed they will be unable to keep up with you, and after making some space you can move through the room taking out the enemies as you approach them. **[→☐ 05]**

Forsaken Cainhurst Castle

You need to pay close attention to your surroundings while walking along the Castle Ramparts, because Lost Children of Antiquity try their best to blend into the environment and can be difficult to spot. These enemies have a good chance of dropping Twin Bloodstone Shards and a small chance to drop Bloodstone Chunks, so it's well worth killing all of them you come across. Upon reaching the top of the stairs when you first enter the Ramparts, if you look carefully you'll see a Lost Child posed among a group of statues on the left side of the path. As you approach, it will immediately spring to life and use a grab attack. To avoid this ambush, walk along the upper path on the right of this area until you're behind the enemy, and when you approach it the ambush will miss and you can attack it freely.

There is a tower to the left of the first of the ramparts. Climbing it yields an item, and an opportunity to use a charged R2 to the back of a Lost Child that's perched on the wall; killing it now will stop it from flying down and ambushing you later. Be careful as you approach the door at the end of the rampart, because there's another Lost Child waiting in ambush – use the statues on the left to easily block its grab attack. [→▢ **01/02**]

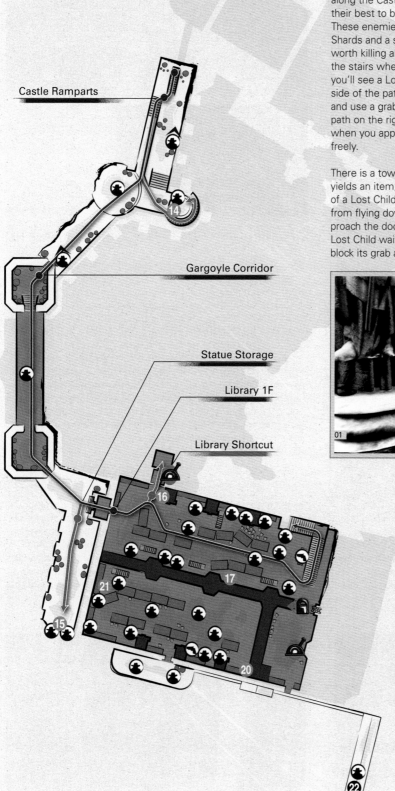

Castle Ramparts

Gargoyle Corridor

Statue Storage

Library 1F

Library Shortcut

⑭ Bloodstone Chunk ×1

⑮ Executioner Garb ×1
Executioner Gauntlets ×1
Executioner Trousers ×1

⑯ Vileblood Register ×1

⑰ Evelyn ×1

⑳ Executioner's Glove ×1

㉑ Knight's Garb ×1
Knight's Gloves ×1
Knight's Trousers/Dress ×1

㉒ Kin Coldblood (10) ×1

Gargoyle Corridor

There are no Lost Children of Antiquity along this section, so you will not have to worry about any ambushes. The only threat you need to contend with is a Servant with a rapier that patrols along the corridor. This enemy attacks extremely quickly if given the chance and is very agile, so the simplest way to deal with it is to use a firearm to knock it down. Doing that gives you the chance to close in safely and start attacking it the instant it stands up. [→□ 03]

Statue Storage ⓯

Two Lost Children sit atop a wall at the end of this area, guarding the Executioner Attire. While you can run up, grab it and leave, it's worth killing them for the chance of some more Bloodstones. Both of the enemies will jump down once you get close to them, so to make the fight easier, retreat back amongst the statues so that they are unable to attack you at the same time. The small group of statues in the middle of the area is perfect for this, as most weapons have enough range to hit the enemies on the other side of them. [→□ 04/05]

⓰ ⓱ Library 1F

Although there is a large number of Castle Spirits s in this room, because they move relatively slowly, it's quite easy to progress through the room and dispatch them systematically as you approach them. If a group of them starts moving towards you, however, it can help to use the tables to impede their progress and funnel them into more manageable numbers. A Servant at the back of the room will start firing at you with its blowgun if you go towards the back of the room, so try to clear out all of the enemies in the first half before progressing further. [→□ 06]

While you're in the back half of the room, make use of the protruding bookshelves to shield yourself from the incoming darts. The darts themselves deal very little damage, but if you do get hit, a mark will appear above you character, allowing Castle Spirits to detect you from a short distance away, even if they have no direct line of sight. To reach the chest on the right-hand side of the room you'll need to climb the small set of stairs in front of the tables that are blocking your access, and then run off the top, so that you land on those tables. Because there's little cover while going for the chest, it's best to leave it until you have killed the enemies in the room.

Library Shortcut

Just outside the doorway here you'll find a chest containing the Vile-blood Manifest, and beyond it is an elevator that will take you back up to the Castle Grounds, creating a shortcut back to the Lamp. Given the easy access you now have back to this room, it's worthwhile taking a trip back to the Hunter's Dream to use any Blood Echoes and Bloodstones you have acquired up to this point. [→□ 07]

Forsaken Cainhurst Castle

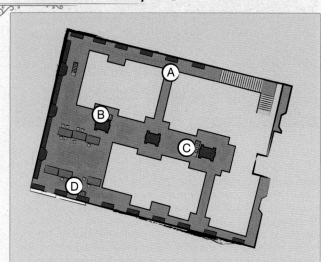

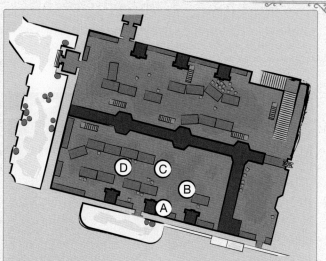

The darts from the candelabra-carrying Servants on this floor are different from the others in that instead of placing a mark on you, the darts simply inflict a lot of damage and flinch you. Fighting the other enemies while trying to avoid incoming darts can be difficult, so it's best to work your way around the room without being spotted by those particular Servants. Most of the other Servants here are also busy with their cleaning duties, so as long as you're walking slowly and don't go into their direct line of sight, you can move about relatively freely.

Start by walking across the bridge at **Position A**. Turn right and walk up behind the candelabra-carrying Servant at **Position B** and use a charged R2 on it, with a follow up attack if required. Done correctly you shouldn't detected by the other nearby Servant, or the one on the other side of the room. That nearby Servant should be left alone for now, because if you start fighting it the candelabra one will start firing at you. Back track past the bridge you crossed, and now take out the Servant that's cleaning at **Position C**.

If you look across the bridge ahead of you, you'll see a stationary Servant cleaning a window, and another one patrolling the balcony; wait for the patrolling one to start moving away, and then walk up behind the one that's cleaning and kill it quickly. You should have enough time to kill it and then hide behind the bookcase, so that the patrolling one doesn't see you when it comes back down, which will allow you to sneak up behind it as it starts to move away again. Walk up the balcony to the remaining candelabra Servant at **Position D** and kill it now. As soon as you do that, the other two Servants that are nearby will start coming towards you, so use your firearm to knock one of them down while you kill the other, and then finish off the one you knocked down. Only one enemy remains at this point, a Servant cleaning the floor on the opposite side of the room. Cross back over the bridge at **Position A** again and attack it from behind for an easy win.

The Executioner's Gloves, along with most parts of the Knight's Attire can be found in this room, but you'll have to fight your way through a number of enemies to reach them. In addition to the usual Castle Spirits, this room contains a slightly different type that will emit a high-pitched scream from its severed head. This will paralyze you if you're within its radius, leaving you totally open to attack from other enemies. The mark placed on you if you're hit by a dart from the Servant in this room becomes a serious threat, since it will cause the Castle Spirits to react much sooner than they otherwise would have.

The Servant is located at **Position A** – make killing it your first priority. There are quite a few Castle Spirits near the Servant, so try to hug the bookcase as you move around to the right in order to remain hidden, and start attacking as soon as it comes into view. If you do get hit with a dart, keep attacking until the Servant is dead, and then retreat out of the room and wait for the effect to wear off. The headless Castle Spirits should now be your focus. After killing the enemies near the Servant, head to the middle of the room and take out the row of Castle Spirits at **Positions B, C and D**. With those enemies down, the remaining Spirits can easily be picked off, leaving you free to loot the room.

Library Balcony

While you can drop straight down from the ledges to the balcony below, doing so would cause you to take unnecessary damage and miss out on an item, so it's better to navigate them properly. Follow the highest ledge to the end just past the window, and then drop down in the gap between it and the gargoyle to land on another ledge below, with an item on it. After picking up the item, turn around and walk back underneath the ledge you started on and drop down again. From this position, you can either keep going straight ahead and drop onto the wall near the Statue Storage area, or turn around and follow it along until you can drop onto the balcony. As soon as you touch the balcony, a Lost Child will come flying down to the middle of the area, and if you're quick, you can attack it while it's still trying to land. Killing that enemy quickly is advised, because a second one will fly down after a short time. [→☐ 01]

- Executioner Garb ×1
- ⑮ Executioner Gauntlets ×1
- Executioner Trousers ×1
- ⑯ Vileblood Register ×1
- ⑰ Evelyn ×1
- ⑱ Bloodstone Chunk ×1
- ⑲ Quicksilver Bullets ×6
- ⑳ Executioner's Gloves ×1
- ㉑ Knight's Garb ×1
  Knight's Gloves ×1
  Knight's Trousers/Dress ×1
- ㉒ Kin Coldblood (10) ×1

Castle Ledges

At the end of the balcony there's a small gap in the railings that you can walk through to drop onto a ledge. From there, you can climb a small rooftop to reach another ledge. About halfway along the second ledge you'll come to an open window that you can drop through, but before doing that it's worth continuing on to the next rooftop at the end. There's an item sitting the base of the tower on this rooftop, and if you look above it you'll spot a Lost Child perched higher up on the tower; if you have any ranged attack options, use them to knock the enemy off its perch, otherwise it will swoop down to ambush you when you pick up the item. [→☐ 02]

Secret Bookcase

There are no enemies in this section of the library, so once you enter you can pull the switch in the middle straight away to move a section of the bookcase nearby, restoring the ladder leading up to the third floor. With that section of the bookcase moved, you can easily return to the main part of the library, and therefore make use of the shortcut back to the Lamp if you wish. The upcoming boss fight can be difficult, so it's highly recommended that you make all possible preparations before continuing.

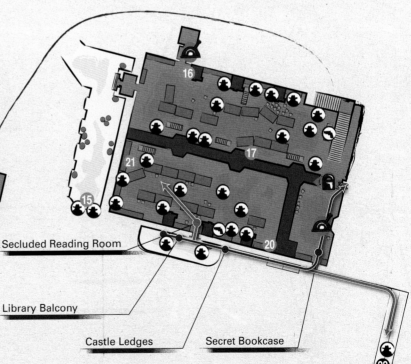

Library 2F

Secluded Reading Room

Library Balcony

Castle Ledges

Secret Bookcase

Forsaken Cainhurst Castle

Library 3F ㉓

Upon first reaching this floor you'll see a chest almost directly ahead of you, which contains a prized Warm Blood Gemstone that can be placed in any weapon slot to increase its Bloodtinge scaling. The only other thing on this floor is a Wandering Nightmare in the middle of the balcony on the opposite side, so it's worth going around and killing it for the Twin Bloodstone Shards that it drops, before looping back around and going up the stairs to the rooftop. [→ ▢ 01/02]

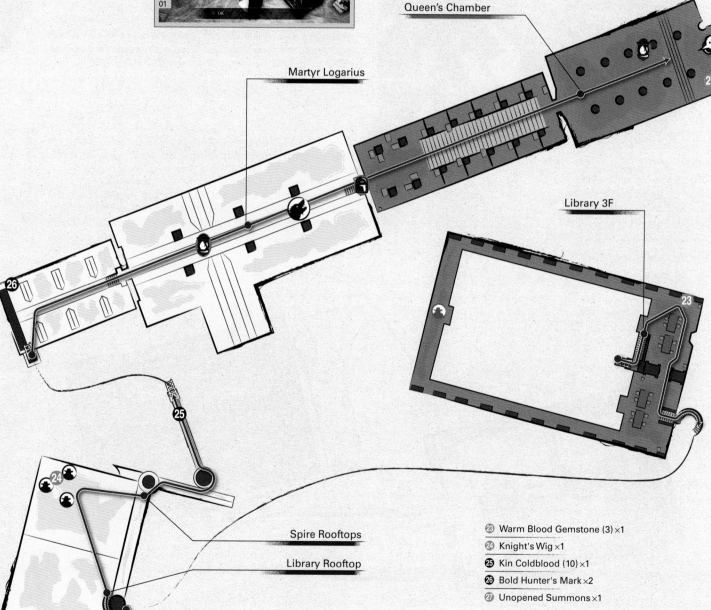

Queen's Chamber

Martyr Logarius

Library 3F

Spire Rooftops

Library Rooftop

㉓ Warm Blood Gemstone (3) ×1
㉔ Knight's Wig ×1
㉕ Kin Coldblood (10) ×1
㉖ Bold Hunter's Mark ×2
㉗ Unopened Summons ×1

Library Rooftop ㉔

When you first see the Lost Child patrolling the area around the item on this rooftop you'll notice that it has glowing red eyes, which indicates that it's a lot stronger than the normal versions. To add to the threat, if you get close to the item two more Lost Children will come swooping down from a tower in the distance; fighting all three at the same time is extremely dangerous. Luring the first enemy away from the item using a Pebble or other ranged attack from the ridge in the middle of the roof will allow you to fight it without having to worry about the other two flying in. When you get close to the item and trigger the enemies to fly in, try to attack one of them while it's still in the air to knock it down and gain an early advantage. [→☐ 03/04]

03

04

Spire Rooftops

One of the corners of the Library Rooftop has a spire protruding from it, and looking over the edge reveals that you can drop down onto another section of the rooftops. Follow the curvature of the spire rooftop around, until you're directly above a narrow section of rooftop below it, and then drop down again. Half way along this narrow section you'll come to another spire, and if you drop down onto that and follow it around you'll be able to drop down a final time onto a bridge. The ladder at the end of the bridge will take you up to another large rooftop. The lack of enemies just adds to the building tension; passing beneath the archway at the end of the upward sloping path will begin the battle with Martyr Logarius. [→☐ 05]

05

BOSS Martyr Logarius

The battle with Martyr Logarius can be very tough due to the sheer number of projectiles he can launch at you, so always try to use one of the spires on the rooftop to block them. When you finally defeat him not only will you gain access to the Logarius' Seat Lamp, but a new item will appear on the ground near the entrance. This item is the Crown of Illusions, and it is said to have the power to reveal an illusion. Equip it and walk towards the wall behind Logarius' throne – the path to the Queen's Chamber is revealed. [→☐ 06/07]

06

07

㉗ Queen's Chamber

Climbing the long set of stairs beyond the newly-revealed door will lead you to the chambers of the Vileblood Queen, Annalise, and she can be found sitting on her throne at the back of the room. Just before you reach her you'll find the Vileblood Queen's Chamber Lamp that you can light to travel straight back to this room. Off to one side in the corner is an Unopened Summons sitting on a table. If you pick it up you'll be able to give it to Alfred if you wish to help him complete his mission. When you approach the Queen there will be the option to kneel, and if you do so you can elect to join her, becoming one of the Vilebloods. Joining her and swearing the oath will also get you the Corruption Caryll Rune, Respect Gesture and the Cainhurst Badge to increase your shop inventory, so even if you do not intend to stay with the Vilebloods, it's worth joining up to get the items. For more information on Annalise check (p647), and for Alfred, see (p644).

World Changes

- Acquire the Crown of Illusions
- Acquire the Unopened Summons
- Gain access to the Logarius' Seat Lamp
- Gain access to the Vileblood Queen's Chamber Lamp

2

Lecture Building 1F

You were given a strange stone, and told to seek the ancient, shrouded church. There was a promise of strength, granted by the godhead. At the appointed location, you find a vat of some bizarre substance. Surely, it is used for some ritual. As you examine the room, you feel pressure building around you. The air feels heavy... except it isn't the air. This pressure is demonic in nature! Your consciousness is squeezed out; when you awaken, you find yourself in... a school? Or a nightmare? No, this is certainly both.

Difficulty	Area **B**
Recommended	Player Level **35-45** | Weapon Upgrade **+6**
Timezones	◯ ◖ ☾ ●
Insight	Arriving in the area ×2

Enemies

Regular	HP	Echoes	Page
Scholar (Bare Hands)	153	702	p246
Scholar (Flask)	153	702	p246

NPC

Name	Page
Patches the Spider	p649

Item legend

1. Lecture Theater Key ×1
2. Student Uniform Student Trousers ×1
3. Augur of Ebrietas ×1
4. Madman's Knowledge ×1
5. Madman's Knowledge ×1
6. Red Jelly ×2

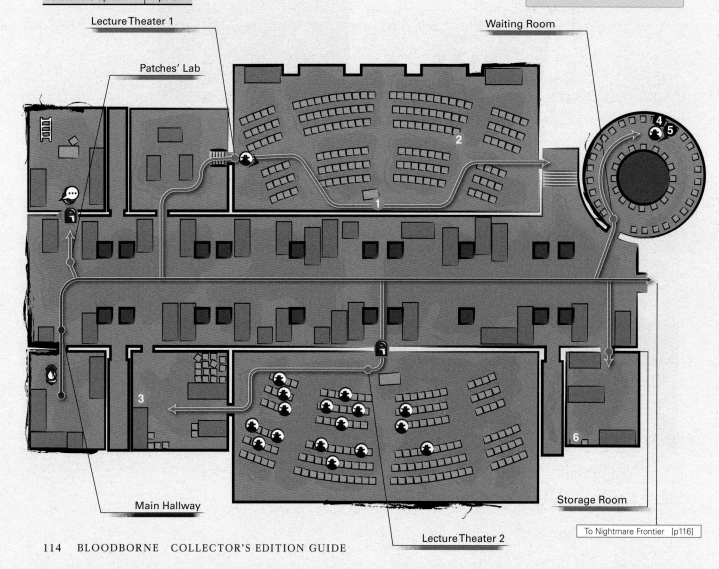

Lecture Theater 1

Patches' Lab

Waiting Room

Main Hallway

Lecture Theater 2

Storage Room

To Nightmare Frontier [p116]

Main Hallway

The Lecture Building Lamp is right in front of you when arrive in this area, so light it straight away before proceeding through the nearby door. There are no enemies in the Main Hallway, so if you're in a rush and simply want to get through the area without exploring, you can run straight along it and open the door at the other end to be transported to Nightmare Frontier. [→□ 01]

Patches' Lab

Directly across from the room that you start in there is a locked one-way door with a broken window, through which you can see the face of a very mysterious creature. If you approach the door you'll be able to talk to it, and while most of what it says may initially appear to be riddles filled with obscurities, there are some hidden truths and potential clues to be found in its words. [→□ 02]

Lecture Theater 1 ❶ ❷

If you enter the door slightly further along the hallway from Patches' Lab you'll find yourself in another lab, from which you can enter one of the large Lecture Theaters. Quickly move to the side of the door-way once you pass through it, because a Student will drop from the ceiling in an attempt to ambush you; while it recovers from the fall, move around behind it and kill it before it can retaliate. The body of a former student can be found slumped in a chair near the middle of the room, and on it you can find the Lecture Theater Key that will let you open the door to the other Lecture Theater on this floor. Another body is located near the end of the middle row of seats, and on this one you'll find the Student Attire.

❸ Lecture Theater 2

A very large group of Students will begin to close in on you as soon as you enter this room, so you'll need to quickly decide how you want to handle them. If you want to use items with large areas of effect to try and take out multiple enemies at once, such as Molotovs, then you're better off staying in the room and trying to group up as many as possible before using one. If you want to use conventional weapons, however, then it's best to retreat back through the doorway and fight them from there. This way it'll be easier to control their numbers, and you can use the pillars just outside the door for some extra cover. There are no items inside the room itself, so once all of the enemies have been killed, exit through the other door and open the chest in the room beyond it to receive the Augur of Ebrietas. [→□ 03]

Waiting Room

After entering this room, follow the path around counter clockwise until you see two items on the floor. Instead of running ahead towards them, look up to the ceiling, where you'll see a Student waiting to drop down and ambush you. Now that you've discovered its hiding place you can use range attacks from a safe distance to knock it down and then close in to finish it off quickly, before grabbing the items.

❻ Storage Room

The final room to explore on this floor has no enemies in it and only a single chest, the content of which is some Red Jelly. This is an item required in some Chalice Dungeon crafting rituals, and will come in useful when you want to progress through even deeper dungeons to find better Blood Gems. [→□ 04]

Nightmare Frontier

A dark, swirling force tugs at your mind as you pass through the doorway, and you awaken to find yourself in a twisted, disgusting landscape rife with hellish monsters. The stench of thick poison and raw flesh wafts through the air, and your pulse quickens. Echoing off of the nightmarish crags and valleys, you hear a faint, maniacal chuckling. This place appears as if it was patched together from the night terrors of the wicked; what manner of creature could possible find pleasure here?

Difficulty	Area **A**	Amygdala **B**
Recommended	Player Level **50-60**	Weapon Upgrade **+6**
Timezones	◯ ◐ ☾ ◑
Insight	Arrive in the area ×2, Encounter Amygdala ×3, Defeat Amygdala ×3

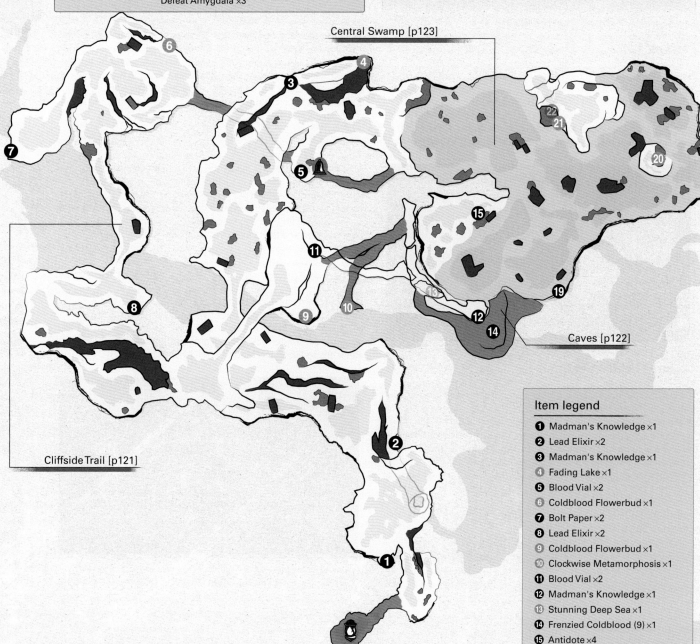

Central Swamp [p123]

Caves [p122]

Cliffside Trail [p121]

Item legend

❶ Madman's Knowledge ×1
❷ Lead Elixir ×2
❸ Madman's Knowledge ×1
❹ Fading Lake ×1
❺ Blood Vial ×2
❻ Coldblood Flowerbud ×1
❼ Bolt Paper ×2
❽ Lead Elixir ×2
❾ Coldblood Flowerbud ×1
❿ Clockwise Metamorphosis ×1
⓫ Blood Vial ×2
⓬ Madman's Knowledge ×1
⓭ Stunning Deep Sea ×1
⓮ Frenzied Coldblood (9) ×1
⓯ Antidote ×4

Enemies

Regular	HP	Echoes	Page
Wandering Nightmare	69/78	54/56	p671
Large Wandering Nightmare*	97	648	p672
Crawler	281	486	p246

*Stronger version in second half of area: 110 HP, 676 Echoes.

Strong	HP	Echoes	Page
Loran Silverbeast*	153	702	p281
Giant Lost Child	639	1458	p282
Large Crawler**	434	1134	p283
Winter Lantern	523	2759	p284

*Parasite Attack: 115 HP, 702 Echoes, Crawling: 153 HP, 702 Echoes, Patrol: 174 HP, 732 Echoes.

**Stronger version in second half of area: 494 HP, 1182 Echoes.

Hunter	HP	Echoes	Page
Hunter of Despair (Hunter's Axe & Hunter's Pistol)	829	4050	p315
Hunter of Despair (Threaded Cane & Flamesprayer)	829	4050	p315

Boss	HP	Echoes	Page
Amygdala	6404	21000	p340

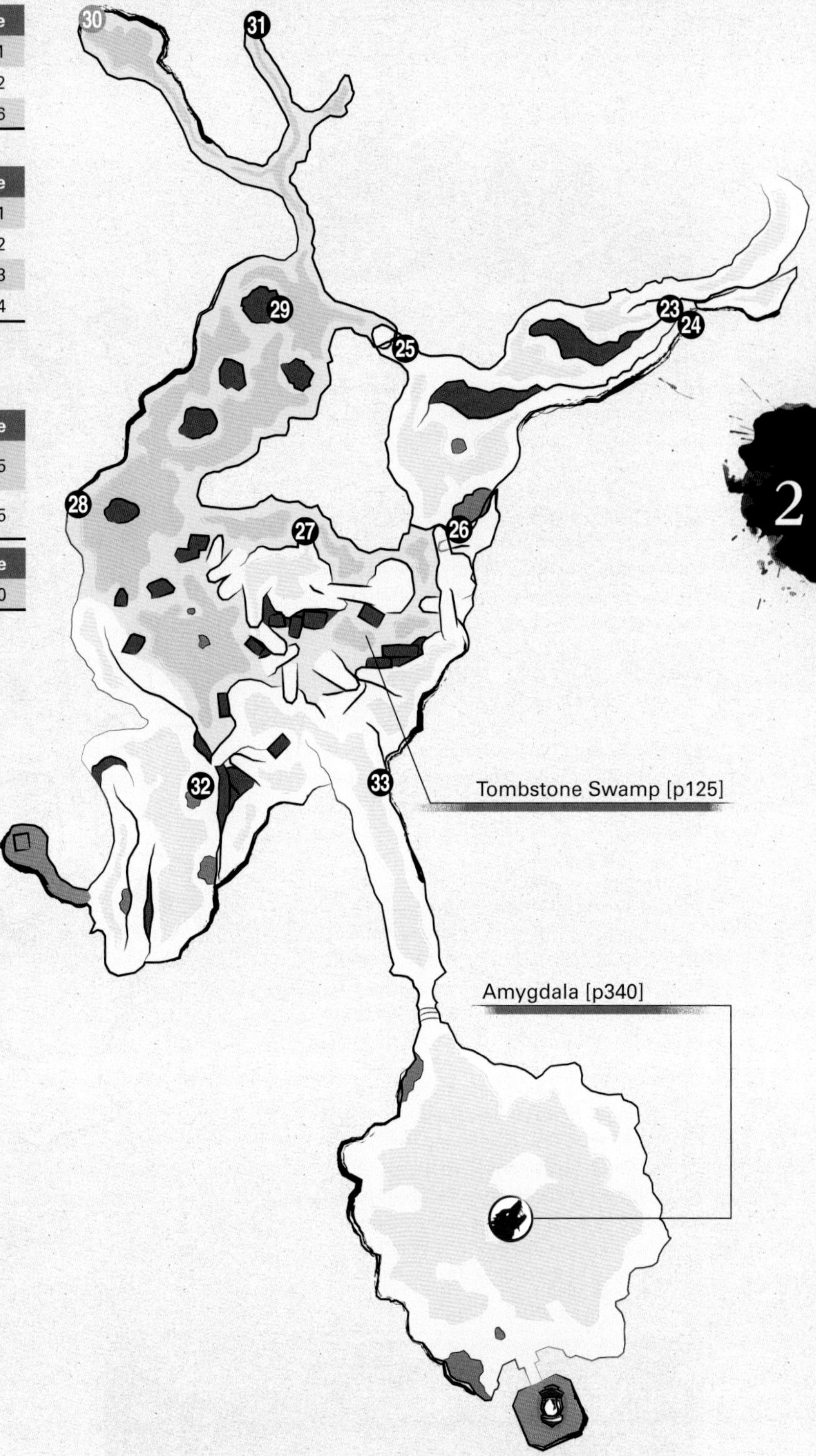

Item legend

- **16** Lead Elixir ×2
- **17** Antidote ×3
- **18** Messenger's Gift ×1
- **19** Madman's Knowledge ×1
- **20** Coldblood Flowerbud ×2
- **21** Clear Deep Sea ×1
- **22** Frenzied Coldblood (8) ×1
- **23** Frenzied Coldblood (8) ×1
- **24** Lead Elixir ×3
- **25** Madman's Knowledge ×1
- **26** Bold Hunter's Mark ×3
- **27** Frenzied Coldblood (9) ×1
- **28** Madman's Knowledge ×1
- **29** Frenzied Coldblood (9) ×1
- **30** Great Deep Sea ×1
- **31** Kin Coldblood (10) ×1
- **32** Blood Vial ×3
- **33** Madman's Knowledge ×1

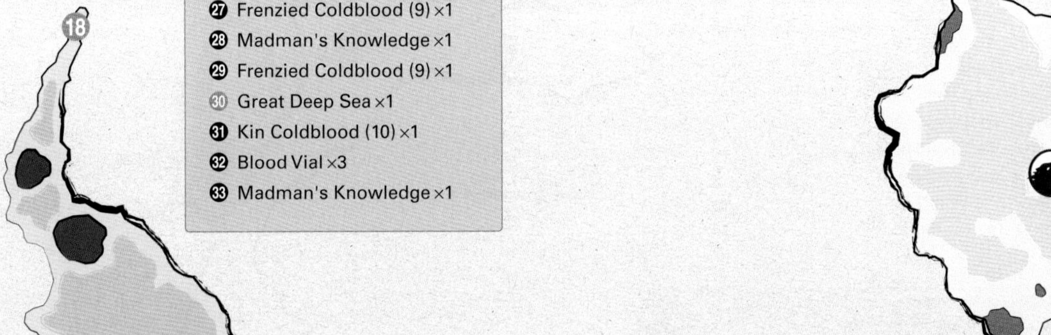

Tombstone Swamp [p125]

Amygdala [p340]

2

Nightmare Frontier

Rocky Path

Nightmare Frontier features a number of highly poisonous swamps, so before proceeding it's recommended that you equip Attire that raises your Slow Poison resistance, and have a full complement of Antidotes. There's a Lamp right where you start, so use it to return to Hunter's Dream for supplies if needed. Most of the enemies here blend in very well with the environment, so you'll need to keep your eyes focused for the slightest bit of movement and listen out for the sounds of nearby enemies. Just outside the cave you start in you'll find a Wandering Nightmare near the edge of the cliff; this area has an extremely large number of these enemies so you can acquire a lot of Bloodstone Shards if you kill them all.

Further along the path you'll encounter a Loran Silverbeast. These aggressive enemies can be very difficult to deal with once they start attacking. The best way to deal with them is to use fire based attacks. Near the path leading to the Cliffside Cave, you can follow another path that leads down to a ledge. This ledge overlooks the swamp below, where a Silverbeast and a Large Wandering Nightmare can be seen. Like its smaller cousins, the Wandering Nightmare will try to run away once it spots you, so try to use a Pebble to lure the Silverbeast away to a safe distance before fighting it. This way you can focus on the Wandering Nightmare when you go down to the ledge. [→☐ 01/02]

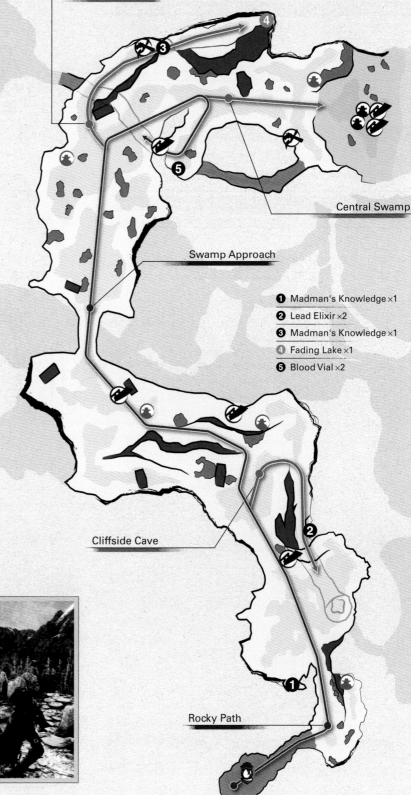

Hunter's Ledge

Central Swamp

Swamp Approach

❶ Madman's Knowledge ×1
❷ Lead Elixir ×2
❸ Madman's Knowledge ×1
❹ Fading Lake ×1
❺ Blood Vial ×2

Cliffside Cave

Rocky Path

Cliffside Cave

Along the side of the cliff face you'll notice a path running down into a cave, where a faint green light is emanating. The light is coming from a switch that's used to call an elevator, but before it can be used you'll need to activate it from down below. Just outside the cave entrance there's a corpse with an item on it sitting on a ledge. To reach it, simply drop down onto the ledge from the path that runs above the cave. [→ 03-05]

Swamp Approach

Shortly after crossing the bridge you'll see a messenger holding a bright blue lantern. These act as beacons pointing out paths that you can follow. Be very cautious as you make your way down this path, because there are a couple of Hunters in the vicinity, and you need to avoid having to fight them both at the same time. Shortly after you pass the lantern, the glow of the first Hunter's torch should come into view atop a ledge in the distance; try to stick to the left side of the path as you approach, so that you give the Silverbeast in the tunnel on the right a wide berth. The second Hunter is further down the path on the Central Swamp Shore, so lure the first one further back up the path before fighting it. While you can continue on and cross the Central Swamp straight away if you wish, doing so will skip a large part of the area, so it's recommended that you head through the tunnel with the Silverbeast after exploring the shoreline. [→ 06]

Central Swamp

A second Hunter awaits you on the shore of the swamp, and since there are also other enemies down there, as soon as you see him start running towards you, retreat back up the path. Similarly, there is a Silverbeast on the edge of the swamp very close to a Wandering Nightmare, and unless you lure the Silverbeast away before the Wandering Nightmare detects you, it's unlikely that you'll be able to kill it. A very large group of Crawlers will start closing in from within the swamp once you reach the shore. If you have some Molotov Cocktails you can use them to weaken the entire group as they slowly approach. When fighting them with normal weapons, it's best to let them reach solid ground first, so that you don't have to fight them in the poisonous waters of the swamp. The glow from another blue lantern messenger can be seen to one side of the shore, signaling the entrance to a small tunnel. This tunnel leads back around to an area just in front of the other tunnel with the Silverbeast.

❹ Hunter's Ledge

There is a gap in the ledge where the first Hunter enemy you encountered initially stood, and you can cross it either by either jumping or rolling over it. Following the ledge along on the other side will take you to a corpse with a Fading Lake Caryll Rune on it that can reduce the Fire damage you take. [→ 07/08]

Nightmare Frontier

Boulder Valley

Like most Wandering Nightmares, the one you encounter at the end of the tunnel here will run away as you approach, but this one is also trying to lure you out into an ambush. Just outside the tunnel on a ledge to the left, there's a Giant Lost Child waiting to throw a huge boulder at you. When chasing after the Wandering Nightmare, make sure you stick close to the rocky outcropping just outside the tunnel, so that you can use it for cover.

Unless you have been increasing your Vitality significantly, it's highly likely that a direct hit from one of the boulders will kill you, and since there are a large number of Giants in this area you'll need to be very careful. Killing them all along this route will make exploring the swamps below much easier when you get down there.

To reach the first Giant you'll need to continue along the path and follow it around to the left, but since there's also another Wandering Nightmare nearby, you may want to kill that first before turning your attention to the Giant. Alternatively, you can use ranged attacks on the Giant, and after a few hits it will come running down towards you, letting you kill it away from the Wandering Nightmare. It's also possible to use the huge tombstones as cover, as the boulders can't pass over the top of them unless you're very far away from them. [→ 🖳 01/02]

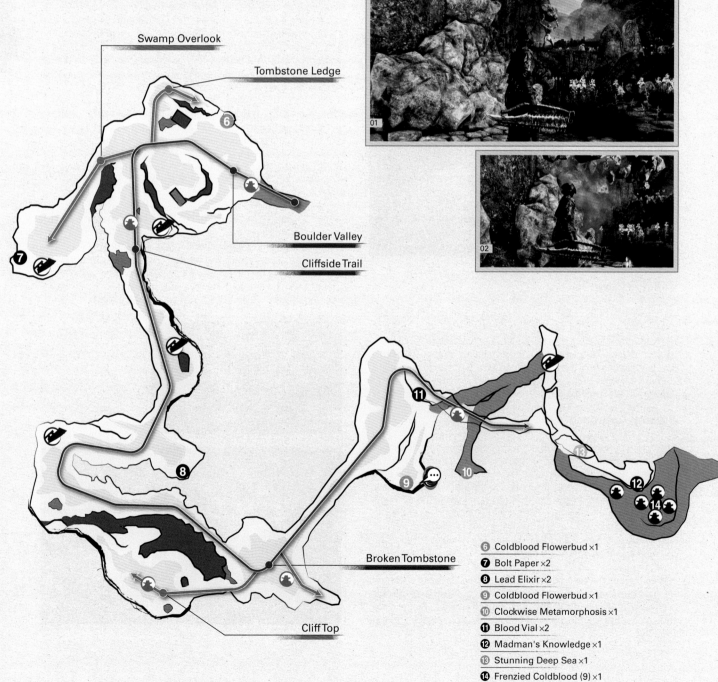

Swamp Overlook

Tombstone Ledge

Boulder Valley

Cliffside Trail

Broken Tombstone

Cliff Top

6 Coldblood Flowerbud ×1
7 Bolt Paper ×2
8 Lead Elixir ×2
9 Coldblood Flowerbud ×1
10 Clockwise Metamorphosis ×1
11 Blood Vial ×2
12 Madman's Knowledge ×1
13 Stunning Deep Sea ×1
14 Frenzied Coldblood (9) ×1

Tombstone Ledge ⑥

There is a path hidden behind the pair of large tombstones here. Following it will take you along a ledge to reach the item on a corpse that you could see after first exiting the tunnel. There's a gap halfway along, but simply running across is enough to get you over it. The item is one that's involved in the crafting of some Chalice Dungeons, so if you're interested in creating those, it's worth taking the trip to pick it up. [→☐ 03]

Swamp Overlook

While fighting the Giant in this area you will be under constant bombardment from another one along the Cliffside Trail, so it's best to employ hit-and-run attacks on it while using the large tombstones for cover when you see an incoming boulder. Fighting from that side of the area also greatly reduces the risk of getting knocking into the swamp below if you do get hit. [→☐ 04]

Cliffside Trail

The entire time you're walking along this trail, a Giant at the end of it will be throwing boulders down at you. Try to keep your camera on it as much as possible to ensure that you have plenty of time to avoid incoming boulders. There's a Silverbeast near the start of the trail standing next to a large tombstone, and trying to fight it out in the open while dealing with the incoming boulders can be very dangerous. Running straight past the Silverbeast and taking cover behind the large tombstone while fighting it is one option, or you can lure it back down the trail out of the Giant's throwing range. From this trail you can see down into the swamp below, and if you have any attack items, such as Throwing Knives or Molotovs, you can use them on some of the Crawlers to weaken them before you reach them. [→☐ 05]

Broken Tombstone

There's a Wandering Nightmare in the middle of this location, so when you approach from the Cliffside Trail, try to run past it quickly to prevent it running over the edge. A large tombstone can also be seen jutting out from the edge; if you walk along to the end of it, the base will crumble and it will collapse, creating a shortcut back to the start of the area. It's important to remember, however, that if you use the Lamp to resupply at Hunter's Dream, all of the Giants that you killed will reappear. So if you want to explore the swamps, it's recommended that you head back down the Cliffside Trail and kill them again first. [→☐ 06]

Cliff Top

The small path leading back away from the Broken Tombstone will take you to the highest point of the cliff side, where a lone Wandering Nightmare resides. Try to get around to the side of the enemy as quickly as you can, and aim to steer it away from the edge overlooking the trail. Otherwise it will run off the edge, forcing you to drop back down to follow it. [→☐ 07]

2

Nightmare Frontier

Lower Caves ❾ ❿

If you look up to the right while crossing the bridge here you'll see a small ledge on the cliff face overlooking the swamp. Patches the Spider is hanging there on the cliff, just above where a number of Shining Coins have been laid out to lead you down towards an item. If you follow the coins down, a cut-scene will trigger, and Patches will knock you down into the Swampy Gorge below. If you want to get the item at the end of the ledge you'll need to make your way back around to get it. Just beyond the bridge are a complex series of caves and tunnels that you can use to reach different parts of the swamps, and with the correct route you can get all of the items within them in one pass.

Start by going to the end of the tunnel straight ahead from the bridge and sneak up behind the Giant standing at the end; try to kill this enemy without causing it fall off, so that you don't have to contend with it after heading down to the swamp. Once it has been killed, take the branching path you passed on the way to the enemy and get the Clockwise Metamorphosis Caryll Rune from the corpse at the end. Exit the cave the way you came in, and then take the path to the side of the cave entrance that leads up and over it to reach the item there. [→☐ 01/02]

Upper Caves ⓭

Another Wandering Nightmare can be found near the start of this path, so try to kill it quickly before it falls over the ledge and into the swamp below. If you follow the ledge around you can drop down off the end onto another ledge below. This leads to an item on a corpse, overlooking a cave filled with Crawlers. Molotov Cocktails can hit the large group of enemies from this position, so if you have a couple to spare they provide an easy means of killing them all. After dropping down, make sure to take the path leading back up out of the cave to get the Stunning Deep Sea Caryll Rune sitting just outside. Finally, head back down through the cave and drop down to the ground below along the bottom edge of the swamp.

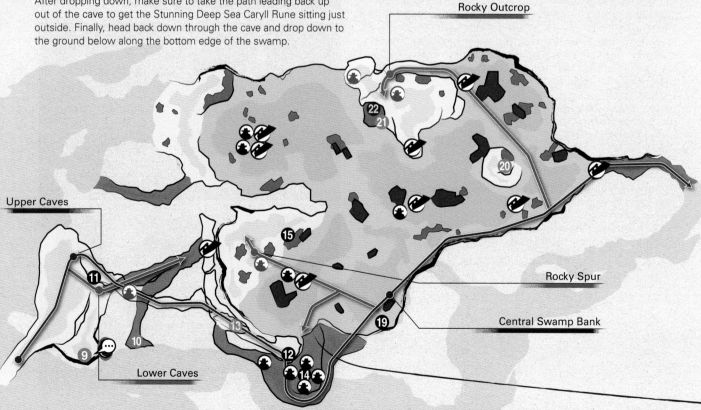

Rocky Spur

The Antidotes that can be found on this spur of land are worth collecting, because they'll be extremely useful as you explore and make your way through the swamps. There's a large group of Crawlers in the swamp close to the spur, but it's worth ignoring them initially, because a Wandering Nightmare is sitting near the edge of the spur, and you'll want to kill it before it disappears. With that out of the way you can wait for the group of Crawlers to get close to the land, so that you don't get poisoned while fighting them in the swamp.

Swampy Gorge ⑱

This swamp is where you'll end up if you triggered the event with Patches earlier, and there's precious little dry land to be found here. If you're low on Antidotes and Healing Items, it's recommended head back out to the Central Swamp, rather than continuing to explore. There are many riches to be found here, however, so as long as you have plenty of supplies it's well worth exploring. When you do find land, make sure to let the Slow Poison build-up subside. Because the swamp greatly reduces your movement speed, consider using ranged attacks on any Wandering Nightmare that you come across to ensure they don't escape; using Molotov Cocktails on the group of them near the rear of the gorge is also very effective.

At the back of the gorge you'll encounter a Winter Lantern. This enemy's primary attack is line-of-sight based, so try to use the walls to block its view so in order to close in safely. Staying within its gaze for more than a few seconds can cause a lethal amount of Frenzy buildup. Your prize for reaching the end of the gorge is the Messenger's Gift, which lets you take on the appearance of a Messenger.

⑳ **Central Swamp Bank**

The narrow stretch of land that runs along the base of the cliff on this side of the swamp gives you just enough room to avoid the boulders thrown by the Giant on the Rocky Outcrop in the middle. There are some large tombstones scattered along the way that will provide some additional cover from the Giant on the outcrop, but the other one near the cave entrance at the end will still have a direct line of sight. A group of Crawlers also block your way towards the end, but it's much better to run straight past them and kill the Giant first. Killing that enemy will also make exploring the rest of the swamp much easier, so it's recommended that you kill it before venturing out into the poisonous waters. [→☐ 03/04]

㉑ **Rocky Outcrop**

Two Crawlers will attempt to block your access to the small path leading to the top of this Rocky Outcrop. Try to run around them as quickly as possible to get out of the swamp, and then fight them on dry land. Once you're on the outcrop, the Giant will usually ignore you until you get close to it, so use the time to take out the two Wandering Nightmares first. If you're careful when fighting the Wandering Nightmares, the Giant shouldn't become aware of your presence. This will allow you to sneak up behind it for an advantage in the fight. After killing all of the enemies, walk over to where a corpse with an item is hanging over the edge, and then drop down to find a hidden cave below with another item in it.

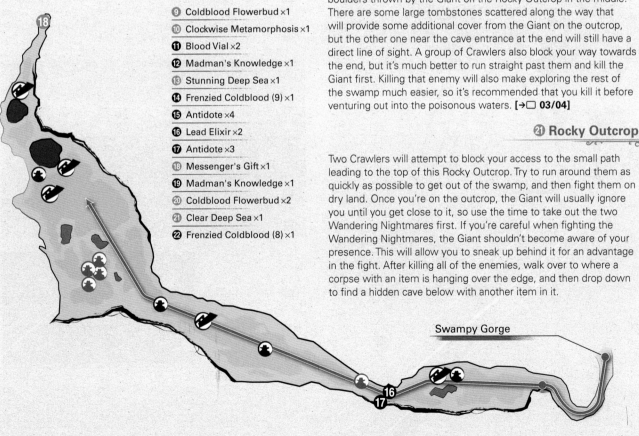

⑨ Coldblood Flowerbud ×1
⑩ Clockwise Metamorphosis ×1
⑪ Blood Vial ×2
⑫ Madman's Knowledge ×1
⑬ Stunning Deep Sea ×1
⑭ Frenzied Coldblood (9) ×1
⑮ Antidote ×4
⑯ Lead Elixir ×2
⑰ Antidote ×3
⑱ Messenger's Gift ×1
⑲ Madman's Knowledge ×1
⑳ Coldblood Flowerbud ×2
㉑ Clear Deep Sea ×1
㉒ Frenzied Coldblood (8) ×1

Swampy Gorge

Nightmare Frontier

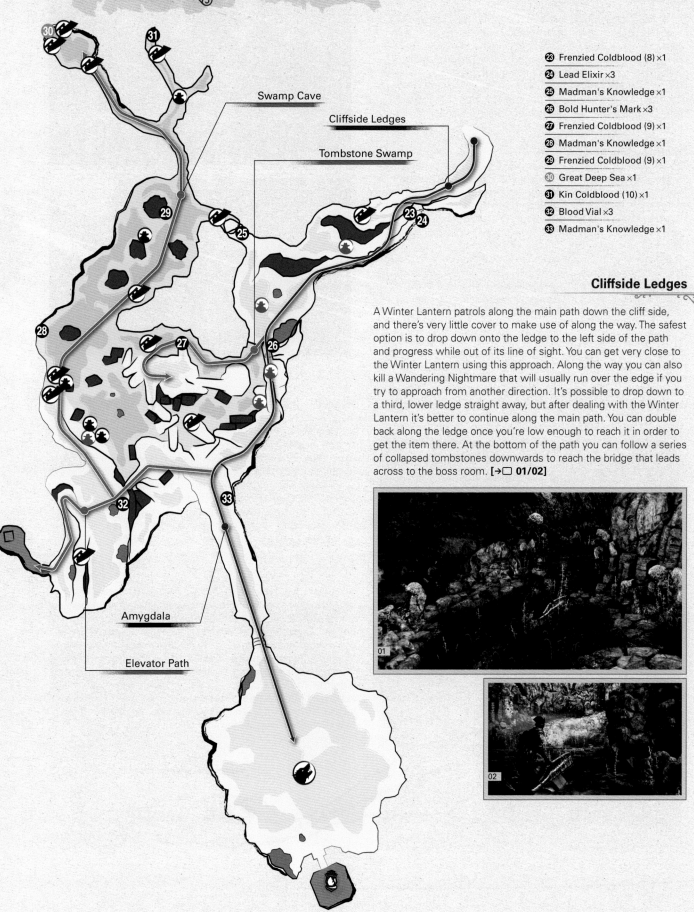

Swamp Cave

Cliffside Ledges

Tombstone Swamp

㉓ Frenzied Coldblood (8) ×1
㉔ Lead Elixir ×3
㉕ Madman's Knowledge ×1
㉖ Bold Hunter's Mark ×3
㉗ Frenzied Coldblood (9) ×1
㉘ Madman's Knowledge ×1
㉙ Frenzied Coldblood (9) ×1
㉚ Great Deep Sea ×1
㉛ Kin Coldblood (10) ×1
㉜ Blood Vial ×3
㉝ Madman's Knowledge ×1

Cliffside Ledges

A Winter Lantern patrols along the main path down the cliff side, and there's very little cover to make use of along the way. The safest option is to drop down onto the ledge to the left side of the path and progress while out of its line of sight. You can get very close to the Winter Lantern using this approach. Along the way you can also kill a Wandering Nightmare that will usually run over the edge if you try to approach from another direction. It's possible to drop down to a third, lower ledge straight away, but after dealing with the Winter Lantern it's better to continue along the main path. You can double back along the ledge once you're low enough to reach it in order to get the item there. At the bottom of the path you can follow a series of collapsed tombstones downwards to reach the bridge that leads across to the boss room. [→ ◻ 01/02]

01

02

Amygdala

Elevator Path

Numerous large tombstones jut out of the swamp in this area, creating makeshift bridges and sections of land that you can use to get out of the swamp. Because of the amount of overhangs and hard-to-reach areas, you need to listen carefully for the sounds of the many Wandering Nightmare enemies; they will normally detect you long before you can see them here. The small island in the middle can only be accessed from the side closest to the cave entrance, so try to stick to the mainland as much as possible before cutting across the swamp to reach it. There's sufficient land on the island to give you a good place to fight the nearby Crawlers, and you should try to clear them out before going for the item that's sitting on the tip of the one of the tombstones. [→☐ 03]

At the top of this path just in front of the elevator you can clearly see a Silverbeast patrolling around. If you time your approach for when it's facing away from you, it's possible to get quite close before it detects you. There are a couple of different paths you can take up to the elevator, so if the Silverbeast does spot you early, you can often run around it using one of the paths to get the drop on it from above. Because this area can be such a drain on your healing items, activating the elevator is extremely important. It lets you return the Lamp to resupply before exploring the nearby swamp or fighting the boss. [→☐ 05]

Swamp Cave ③⓪

There's little ground to stand on in this cave, and you'll have to battle past a large number of enemies to get the items. Before venturing inside, it's highly recommended that you activate the nearby elevator, so that you can quickly return here if the worst happens. As you enter the cave you'll start to hear the song of a Winter Lantern, but before closing in to kill it you should use the pillars in the area to block its line of sight and try to clear out some of the Crawlers.

The cave narrows considerably just past the Winter Lantern and splits shortly after that, giving you two possible routes to take. Going straight ahead will lead you to an opening, where three Crawlers are guarding a Great Deep Sea Caryll Rune. After killing the first Crawler it's worth trying to get past the other two to reach the dry land at the back of this area, so that you can fight them there. If you follow the tunnel along to the right from the first fork, you'll soon come to a second one, at which point you should take the left route, since it's the only one that leads to an item. [→☐ 04]

BOSS Amygdala

The arms of the giant false God, Amygdala can actually be quite difficult to hit with normal weapons, so you may want to consider using ranged weapons to attack its head directly for some easy damage. After defeating Amygdala you can enter the small room at the back of the area and light the Amygdala's Chamber Lamp to leave the area. [→☐ 06]

World Changes

- ● Acquire the Lower Loran Chalice
- ● Gain access to the Amygdala's Chamber Lamp

Upon defeating Amygdala you will also receive the Ailing Loran Chalice, which will allow you to create the Ailing Loran Dungeon. The Coldblood Flowerbud you can find in this area is one of the necessary ritual materials for this dungeon, but you'll need Ritual Blood (4) x9 as well, so heading into other dungeons first is necessary.

Byrgenwerth

The night is now well underway; you survived the treacherous journey through the Forbidden Woods and overcame every guardian that was set before you. Byrgenwerth, an ancient place of learning, lies before you. Within lie secrets untold; the answers you seek may lie with them, but there's something unnerving about this place. The skittish tapping of spider legs can be heard in the night, reflected from some concealed location, and the moon looms larger still.

Difficulty	Area **B** | Rom, the Vacuous Spider **S**
Recommended	Player Level **55-65** | Weapon Upgrade **+7**
Timezones	○ ◐ ☾ ◑
Insight	Speak with Provost Willem x2, Encounter Rom, the Vacuous Spider x2, Defeat Rom, the Vacuous Spider x2

College Path

Be careful as you walk down the path towards Byrgenwerth, because about halfway along a Garden of Eyes is waiting in ambush behind a large tree on the right. If you walk along that side of the path and use the tree for cover, you can mask your approach until you're close, and then quickly round the tree to attack it. The grab attack of the Garden of Eyes inflicts a large amount of Frenzy build-up, so if you have any Sedatives it's worth equipping them to your Quick Items for ease of use. Once you reach the Lamp, instead of following the path around to the right, keep going straight and drop down the levels. Doing so will usually allow you to get behind another Garden of Eyes that's patrolling around down the bottom.

Item legend

1. Madman's Knowledge ×1
2. Arcane Lake ×1
3. Madman's Knowledge ×1
4. Great One's Wisdom ×1
5. Sedative ×5
6. Pearl Slug ×1
7. Student Uniform ×1
   Student Trousers ×1
8. Lunarium Key ×1
9. Empty Phantasm Shell ×1

Enemies

Strong	HP	Echoes	Page
Garden of Eyes	910	945	p285
Fluorescent Flower	758	1418	p286
Brainsucker	605	1527	p273

Hunter	HP	Echoes	Page
Yurie, the Last Scholar (Threaded Cane & Rosmarinus)	2281	5453	p316

Boss	HP	Echoes	Page
Rom, the Vacuous Spider	5058	22600	p344

NPC

Name	Page
Provost Willem	p640

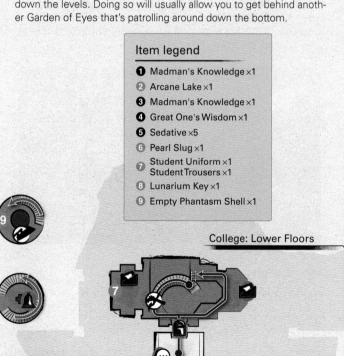

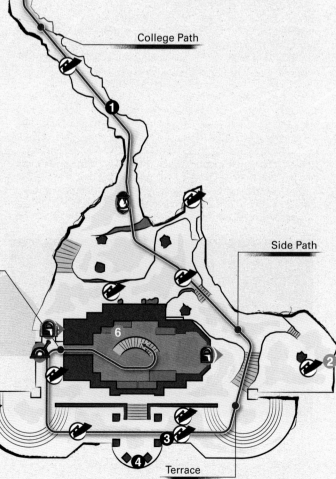

College Path

Side Path

College: Lower Floors

College: Upper Floors

Lunarium

Terrace

Rom, the Vacuous Spider

Side Path ②

As you approach the stairway leading around the side of the building, a Garden of Eyes will come running down the stairs towards you. Lure it backwards, rather than running forward to fight it, otherwise you'll get the attention of another one waiting around the corner to the left. After going up those stairs, the main path leads down to the Terrace on the right, but straight ahead there's a raised area with a large tree in the middle, behind which a Brainsucker is waiting. If you head to the right as soon as you reach the top of the stairs and walk behind the tree, you can get behind the Brainsucker for an easy charged R2 opportunity. [→☐ 01]

Terrace

While the Terrace may seem quite safe when you first approach, running straight ahead will take you into a very nasty ambush. When you get close to the base of the Lunarium, two Gardens of Eyes will jump down from the top and land on the front edge of the terrace, near the lake. At the far end of the Terrace a Fluorescent Flower, difficult to see through the fog, is standing guard. Avoiding the Fluorescent Flower's fireballs while fighting the Gardens of Eyes is very difficult, so to make things easier, stay on the upper part of the Terrace and advance until you see the Gardens of Eyes drop down. One of them should spot you and come running around the wall towards you. Wait for it to come to you before fighting it, and then go around the wall and take out the second one. The Fluorescent Flower is best dealt with by attacking the glowing "flower" part with ranged attacks while using the pillars for cover. After reaching the other side of the building, make sure to pull the switch and open the gate, so that you have a quick path back in if you need it.

College: Lower Floors ⑥ ⑦

Once you're inside the college building you can find a chest containing a Holy Chalice ritual material tucked in behind one of the storage units on the left. You can also open the door on the other side of the room to create another access point. As soon as you begin heading up the stairs, an enemy Hunter will start making her way down; if you quickly retreat back down the stairs and hide underneath them you can often get the drop on her when she reaches the bottom. Upon reaching the top of the stairs, make sure you get the Student Attire from the chest at the back of the seating area on the left, and there's also a note to read on one of the sofas. The door leading out to the Lunarium is locked, so you'll need to continue exploring the building to find the key; be sure to inspect the bookcase on your way around to the ladder, because there is another note tucked amongst the books that you can read. [→☐ 02]

College: Upper Floors ⑧ ⑨

After climbing the ladder and reaching this floor, the key that's required to open the Lunarium can be found sitting on a work bench directly ahead of you. Before going back down and unlocking the door, however, it's worth continuing up the stairs to the top floor and killing the Garden of Eyes there, so that you can get the Empty Phantasm Shell.

Lunarium

Provost Willem, the old master of Byrgenwerth College, can be found sitting in his favorite rocking chair out on the Lunarium, gazing up to the moon. Talking to him will only cause him to utter the faintest of groans, while using his cane to point to towards the lake. There is little else to be gained from Provost Willem, so you can kill him if you wish. Doing so will reward you with the Eye Caryll

Rune, which significantly increases your Discovery rate. Following Provost Willem's directions, however, is advised; if you walk to the end of the Lunarium and look down into the lake you'll notice some mysterious ripples emanating from an area of the lake below. To find out just what secrets are hidden below the surface, take the plunge and jump right in.

BOSS Rom, the Vacuous Spider

Rom is not hostile when you first enter the area, so you can run right up to him without risk, and only once you hit him will the fight begin. The Children of Rom that he summons during the fight can all drop Blood Vials and Quicksilver Bullets, so if you find yourself running low, kill some of them to replenish your supplies. Upon killing Rom, a mysterious apparition will appear in the middle of the lake, and when you approach it a cut-scene will trigger. After the scene you'll find yourself back in the Cathedral Ward, standing in front of a newly-opened door. Going through that door takes you back into Yahar'gul, Unseen Village, where things are quite different than before. Time will also have moved forward at this point, and night will have turned to Blood Moon; make sure to check back with any NPCs whose quests you've been following, as many of them will have advanced at this point. If you drop down into the lake again from Byrgenwerth, a new Lamp will appear so that you can leave the area again.

World Changes

- Changes time of day from night to Blood Moon
- The door in Cathedral Ward that leads to Yahar'gul, Unseen Village (Blood Moon) will open.
- Hypogean Gaol Lamp is destroyed

Yahar'gul, Unseen Village (Blood Moon)

Enemies

Regular	HP	Echoes	Page
Huntsman (Torch & Axe)	518	485	p225
Huntsman (Torch & Shield)	403	347	p226
Huntsman (Sickle)	403	347	p226
Huntsman (Cleaver)	403	347	p226
Huntsman (Cutlass)	518	485	p227
Huntsman (Pitchfork)	518	485	p227
Huntsman (Rifle)	461	347	p227
Huntsman (Molotov)	403	347	p228
Wheelchair Huntsman (Pistol)	374	485	p229
Wheelchair Huntsman (Rifle)	374	485	p230
Wheelchair Huntsman (Gatling Gun)	374	554	p229
Rabid Dog	461	762	p230
Hemwick Grave Woman (Sickle)	403	624	p239
Hemwick Grave Woman (Pole Iron)	518	624	p239
Hemwick Grave Woman (Hammer)	461	693	p239
Hemwick Grave Woman (Cleaver & Torch)	461	693	p240
Hemwick Grave Woman (Cleaver & Molotov)	518	693	p240
Wandering Nightmare	155	69	p671

You learned true horror on your last visit to Yahar'gul. This time, the Unseen Village is a sight beyond horror. Massive, hulking, twisted creatures drag themselves along the streets. Giant demons cling to buildings as if they were mere flies on the wall. In the midst of it all, cultists swirl about in apparent ecstasy. Bells ring out, beckoning. Beckoning to the beasts. Beckoning to the moon itself. Beckoning to you.

Difficulty	Area **S** | The One Reborn **A**
Recommended	Player Level **60-70** | Weapon Upgrade **+8**
Timezones	○ ◐ ☾ ●
Insight	Encounter The One Reborn ×1, Defeat The One Reborn ×3

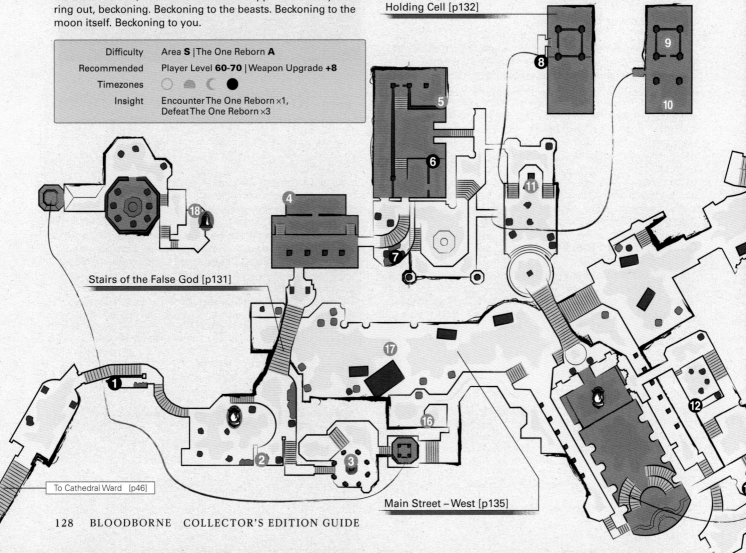

Strong	HP	Echoes	Page
Scourge Beast (Skeletal)	1844	3881	p266
Huntsman's Minion (Brick)	1441	2079	p267
Huntsman's Minion (Statue)	1441	2079	p267
Bell Ringer	518	901	p287
Cramped Casket	864	1455	p288

Strong	HP	Echoes	Page
Yahar'gul Hunter (Threaded Cane & Flamesprayer)	1891	5198	p316
Yahar'gul Hunter (Beast Claw & Hunter Pistol)	1891	5198	p317
Yahar'gul Hunter (Rifle Spear & Cannon)	1891	5198	p317

Boss	HP	Echoes	Page
The One Reborn	10375	33000	p346

Item legend

1. Frenzied Coldblood (8) ×1
2. Bloodstone Chunk ×1
3. Iron Yahar'gul Helm ×1
4. Bolt Damp Blood Gem (4) ×1
5. Heir ×1
6. Frenzied Coldblood (8) ×1
7. Bolt Paper ×3
8. Frenzied Coldblood (8) ×1
9. Upper Cathedral Key ×1
10. Tiny Tonitrus ×1
11. Bloodstone Chunk ×1
12. Frenzied Coldblood (8) ×1
13. Blood Vial ×8
14. Bloodstone Chunk ×2
15. Bloodstone Chunk ×2
16. Bloodstone Chunk ×2
17. Bloodstone Chunk ×2
18. Bloodstone Chunk ×1
19. Frenzied Coldblood (8) ×1
20. Blood Vial ×6
21. Tempering Damp Blood Gem (5) ×1
22. Arcane Lake ×1
23. Madman's Knowledge ×1
24. Madman's Knowledge ×1

2

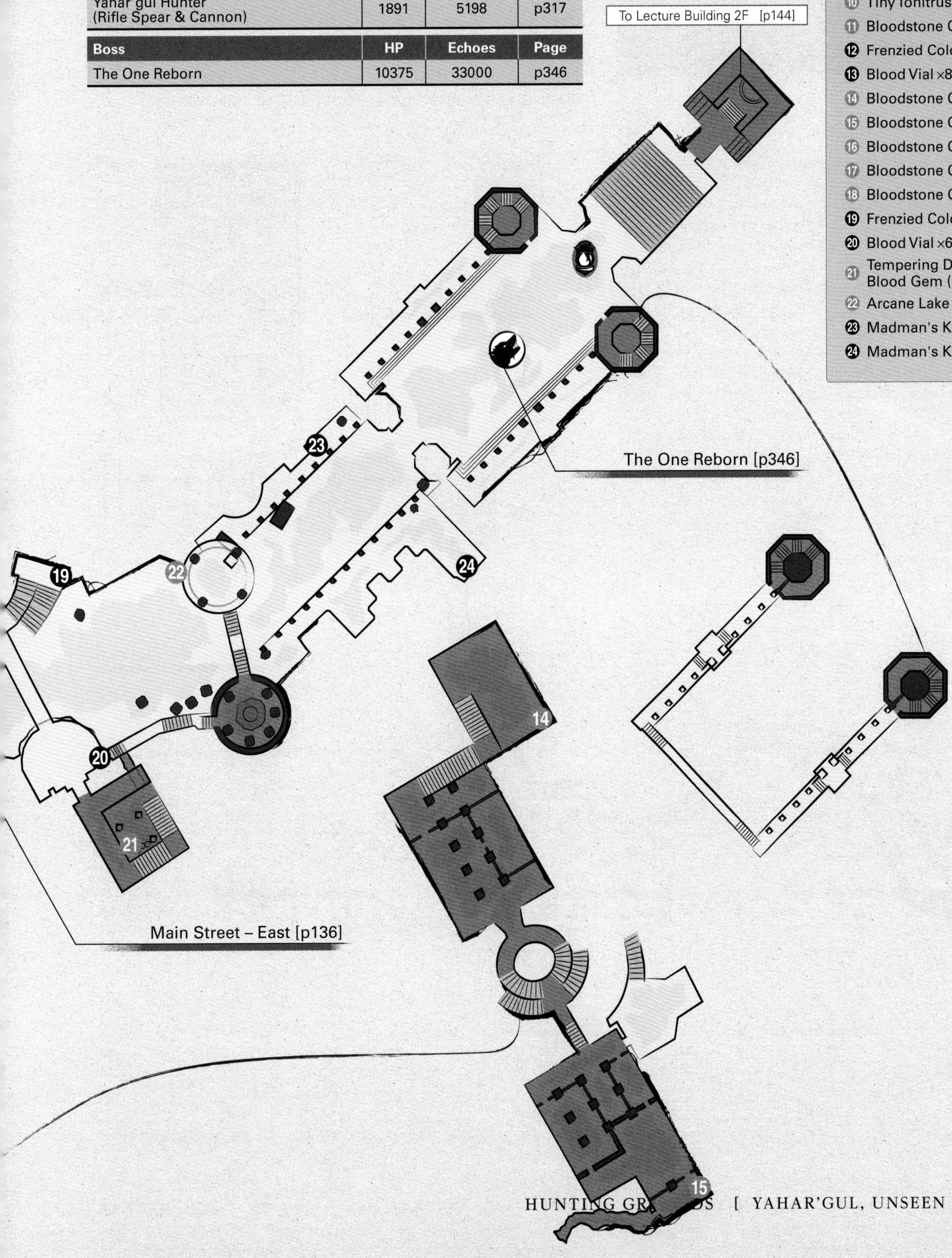

To Lecture Building 2F [p144]

The One Reborn [p346]

Main Street – East [p136]

Yahar'gul, Unseen Village

01

Entry Stairs ❷

The door in Cathedral Ward that leads to this area will open after you defeat Rom, the Vacuous Spider in Byrgenwerth. Sprint straight ahead through the door without stopping in order to avoid being grabbed by the False God. Reaching the bottom of the stairs, you'll hear a bell chime and a couple of Huntsmen will spawn from the ground ahead of you. While you've faced these enemies before, they are not to be underestimated here. Their blood aura is being placed there by a nearby Bell Ringer, and it grants them a huge defensive boost. To make matters worse, any enemy killed will always be brought back after a short period of time, until the Bell Ringer is dead. Killing her will also cause the blood aura to be removed from any enemies still alive, and not only will they be severely weakened after that, but it causes them to writhe in pain briefly, giving you a small window to attack. These reappearing enemies will only grant Blood Echoes the first time you kill them, although they can keep dropping items.

After making it past the first two enemies you'll come to a stairway, and as soon as you start walking down it another Huntsman will come around the corner at the bottom and run towards you; make sure you kill him before doubling back along the stairs to get the item there. At the bottom of the stairs you'll find the Yahar'gul, Unseen Village Lamp. It's important that you light it, because the Hypogean Gaol Lamp has been destroyed, making this Lamp your only way back here for now. [→ 🗖 01]

❸ Elevator Plaza

The stairway here leads down to an elevator, and along the way a Bloodstone Chunk can be found in a corner behind a statue. There are a lot of Bloodstone Chunks to be found in this area, and if you gather them all you can significantly increase the overall strength of your arsenal. At the bottom of the stairs you'll see another item on a corpse near a statue, and while it may be tempting to run straight ahead and get it, a Wheelchair Huntsman with a rifle has his sights on it from around the corner to the left. Hide behind one of the pillars until after he fires a shot, and then quickly close in and kill him while he reloads. The other Huntsman that's standing just outside the elevator room may spot you, so deal with him before finally picking up the item. You cannot make use of the elevator at this time, so continue along the main route once you've looted the area.

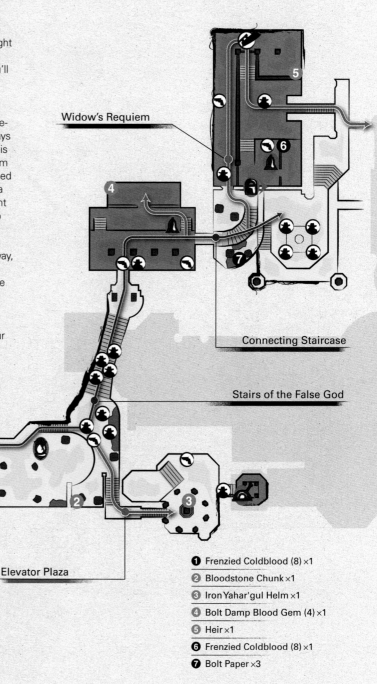

Widow's Requiem

Connecting Staircase

Stairs of the False God

Entry Stairs

Elevator Plaza

❶ Frenzied Coldblood (8) ×1
❷ Bloodstone Chunk ×1
❸ Iron Yahar'gul Helm ×1
❹ Bolt Damp Blood Gem (4) ×1
❺ Heir ×1
❻ Frenzied Coldblood (8) ×1
❼ Bolt Paper ×3

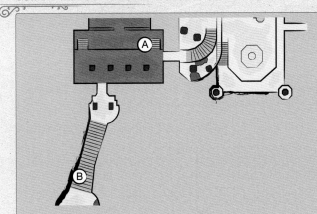

About halfway down this small curved staircase there's a gap in the railings on the right that you can drop through. By doing this you'll be able to skip the large room at the end of the stairs entirely. If you choose to go through the room you can bypass the Sacrifice Square initially, but if you want the Upper Cathedral Ward Key you'll have to fight the enemies there when you come back around. The ledge you land on after dropping through the gap also has some useful Bolt Papers on it, so grab them before dropping down again to Sacrifice Square.

❺ COMBAT FOCUS **Widow's Requiem**

As if the intimidating visage of the False God hanging from the side of the building wasn't enough, there's also the extremely large number of Huntsmen lining the stairs, all of whom are being strengthened by a Bell Ringer in the room at the bottom, at **Position A**. The False God is not content to sit idly by here – when you near the middle of the staircase he'll move his hand across the stairs in an attempt to grab you. This attack does not affect the Huntsmen, however, and they can pass safely through it. Because these enemies are under the control of a Bell Ringer, speed is very important here – you don't want to have enemies begin reappearing in the middle of the fight. The easiest way to handle the start is to consider the enemies on the stairs as two groups: those before the False God's grab area, and those after it. The major threat in the first group is the Huntsman with a rifle at **Position B**, but before you can deal with him you'll first need to clear out some of the other enemies. Approaching the top of the stairs, the first of the other Huntsmen will spot you; retreat and lure him backwards, so that you can fight him out of the rifleman's line of sight. Once he's been defeated, go a bit further down the stairs to get the attention of the next enemy and do the same thing. Killing those two enemies will put enough space between the rifleman and the next two enemies for you to run down and kill him before they can close in.

It's best to run straight past the group of enemies at the bottom at this time, and make the Bell Ringer your next target.. If you were to start fighting them, there's a strong chance that the first group will start to reappear and you'll get caught in the middle, with your movement limited due to the False God's attack. When you enter the room at the bottom of the stairs, head around to the left rather than the right, because there's another Huntsman waiting just inside the door on the right. While you're fighting the Bell Ringer, keep in mind that a couple of the Huntsmen will sometimes follow you into the room. As soon as the Bell Ringer is dead, quickly return to the second group of enemies and try to kill some of them while they writhe in pain from her death, before killing the rest in their now weakened state.

The door that leads into this room cannot be opened from the outside – you can only enter via the large hole in the wall to side of it. Shortly after entering the room, the Bell Ringer at **Position A** will ring her bell and a number of enemies will burst from the ground. The most immediate threat is a Huntsman that will appear behind you at **Position B**. Try to kill him quickly, because a Huntsman's Minion will also appear at the opposite end of the corridor and start closing in on you straight away. Once those enemies have been killed, go through the gate at **Position C**, which will cause the Bell Ringer to ring her bell once more, summoning a second group of enemies.

A new Huntsman with a rifle will appear at **Position D** in the corridor, but he can't fire through the bars, so as long as you don't go back in there he's not a threat. Similarly, the Huntsman in the middle of the room should be ignored until you've dealt with the Bell Ringer and her new Wheelchair Huntsman guardian. The Bell Ringer should be your first target, because contending with her attacks while fighting the Wheelchair Huntsman can be difficult. It does mean that you'll need to be mindful of his shots; try to keep him in view at all times so that you know when he's finished reloading and can dodge accordingly. Once the Bell Ringer has been killed it should be no problem to finish off the dazed Wheelchair Huntsman and severely weakened Huntsman.

Yahar'gul, Unseen Village

Sacrifice Square

Four Hemwick Grave Women are gathered around the middle of this square, and if you're dropping down from the Connecting Staircase you should be able to kill the one closest to you before the others can react. Luring the remaining enemies around the railings and down the stairs can also help split them up and stop them from surrounding you, making the rest of the fight easier. The stairs themselves will take you down to the Holding Cell, but approaching along this path will not allow you to get the Upper Cathedral Ward key from within the cell.

Holding Cell ⑨ ⑩

From the top of the stairs leading away from the Widow's Requiem room, if you follow the railing along to the right, you'll find a gap that you can drop through in order to reach a ledge below. On that ledge you can find an item near the end, so grab that before going through the nearby door. There's a Huntsman's Minion with its back to you on the right as soon as you go through the door, and while it may be tempting to attack it, it's better to leave it alone and walk around to the left. In the middle of this area you'll find a Bell Ringer, and killing her will not only make fighting the two nearby Minions much easier, but also make the Rooftop Attack much easier to handle. Near the door you entered the upper part of the Holding Cell through, you'll find a gap in the low wall that you can drop through to land in the

cell below, where the key to the Upper Cathedral Ward is sitting on a corpse. The remaining Minion here will start coming after you as soon as you leave the cell. Try to fight him near the exit to the room so that you're out of the line of sight of the Wheelchair Huntsman with the gatling gun. Once all of the enemies have been killed you can safely claim the Tiny Tonitrus from the chest.

⑪ COMBAT FOCUS Rooftop Attack

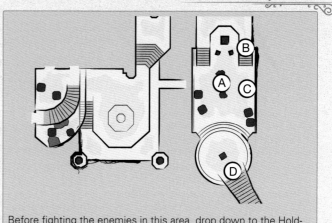

Before fighting the enemies in this area, drop down to the Holding Cell and kill the Bell Ringer there to significantly weaken them

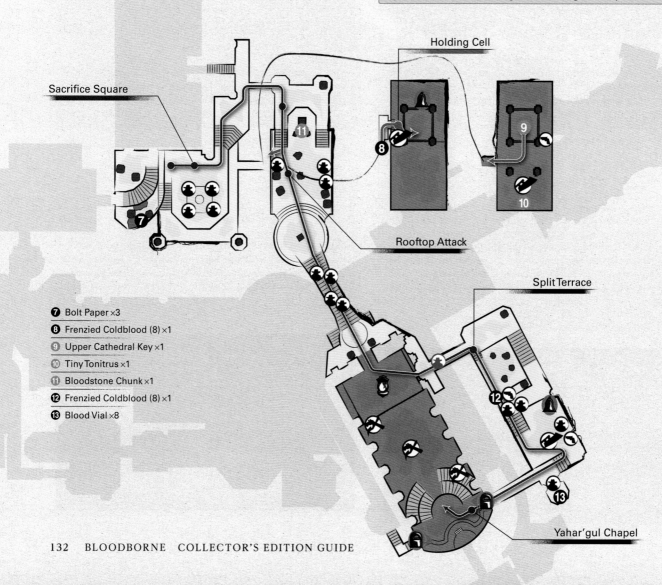

Sacrifice Square

Holding Cell

Rooftop Attack

Split Terrace

Yahar'gul Chapel

❼ Bolt Paper ×3

❽ Frenzied Coldblood (8) ×1

❾ Upper Cathedral Key ×1

❿ Tiny Tonitrus ×1

⑪ Bloodstone Chunk ×1

⑫ Frenzied Coldblood (8) ×1

⑬ Blood Vial ×8

all. Once you go past the trees at **Position A**, the False God on the side of the building ahead will start firing down into the area using a continuous beam that traces across the ground. While the initial beam does not deal damage, after a short time the ground it struck will explode; watch for the glowing sections of the floor and stay clear of them to avoid taking damage. Try to do as much fighting as possible without going past those trees so that you don't have to contend with the False Gods attacks, and that will mean luring the enemies back towards you.

Begin by going down the stairs at **Position B**, which will cause one of the Grave Women at **Position C** to come running towards you. After you deal with her, use a Pebble or ranged attack on the one facing away from you to lure it back towards you. A second group of Grave Women will have made their way up the stairs at the back of the area and come to a stop near **Position D**, and among them is a Molotov-thrower; not only will you need to lure the other enemies away from the False God, but also from her. The other three move fairly quickly, so all you have to do is quickly run far enough past **Position A** to get their attention, and then retreat back to the stairs and fight them there. When all that remains is the final Molotov-thrower, try to time your approach between False God's attacks and kill her quickly before running down the stairs to the safety of the Yahar'gul Chapel Lamp.

COMBAT FOCUS **Split Terrace**

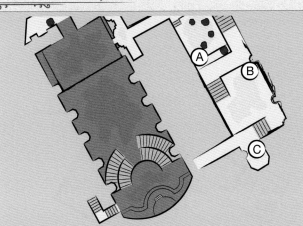

There's another Bell Ringer strengthening the enemies in this area, but it's worth taking out some of the other enemies along the way to her. Instead of going down the main stairs here, head up to the small garden area and drop through the gap in the railings at **Position A**. You'll land on a ledge with a Huntsman carrying a rifle, so take him out as quickly as possible. As long as you're fairly quick here, taking him out first ensures that he won't be able to shoot you in the back later. Just below the ledge you're on are two Rabid Dogs – if you have any strong ranged options, you can kill both of them from the safety of the ledge, otherwise drop down and use a plunging attack to weaken one before finishing them off.

At the far end of the second half of the terrace you'll see a couple of Huntsmen and a Huntsman's Minion. Before going after them, drop down to the left of the stairs leading down and kill the Bell Ringer at **Position B**. As soon as she is dead, quickly run up and kill the two Huntsmen while they're stunned, so that you can deal with the Minion on its own. The final enemy to take care of is just past the end of the terrace, hiding behind a pillar at **Position C**. Be sure to take him out before going for the item there, to avoid being attacked from behind.

COMBAT FOCUS **Yahar'gul Chapel**

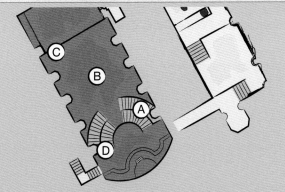

This area might be familiar to you, but you no longer have the safety of the Hypogean Gaol Lamp, and the enemies here are quite different than before, so you'll need to be careful. Three Hunter enemies have taken up positions in the room: one with a Threaded Cane & Flamesprayer on the stairs at **Position A**, another with Beast Claws & Hunter's Pistol in the middle of the room at **Position B**, and finally, one armed with a Rifle Spear & Cannon at **Position C**. The Clawmark Caryll Rune (dropped by the Hunter with the Beastclaw) makes for a tempting prize, but acquiring it leads to a difficult battle with these Hunters. You can bypass the room altogether if you opened the one-way door leading outside during your first visit to this area, but then you won't get the Rune.

As soon as you hit one of the enemies they'll all come running towards you to join the fight, so the initial attack needs to inflict as much damage as possible to weaken one of them before the others get close. The best candidate for this is the enemy at **Position A**. He's far away from the other two, and if you go down the two sets of stairs near **Position D** and walk slowly, you can get behind him and use a charged R2 and visceral attack for maximum damage. Try to inflict some more damage quickly once he gets up – if he's still alive when you see the other two, it's best to break off your attack so that they don't overwhelm you.

The network of stairs in this area are actually very useful for fighting the group of enemies, because you will usually have a place to retreat to, and the different walls and levels are ideal for separating the group. This is especially important with the Hunter that's armed with the Cannon, because fighting either of the other two while under the threat of Cannon fire is very difficult. Whenever you manage to separate them into a one-on-one situation, try to interrupt their attacks and aim for visceral attack follow-ups. If there's more than one around, it's safest to go for single hits or short combos before moving again.

Yahar'gul, Unseen Village

Storeroom & Prison Cells ⑭ ⑮

Going down the central staircase in Yahar'gul Chapel will let you reach these areas, and even if you explored them during the first time you can come to this area, there are some items down here that make a second visit worthwhile. This time, when you go down the stairs to the Prison Cells, a Scourge Beast will be waiting for you, and if you go to the back of the Dining Room you'll find some Bloodstone Chunks on the body of a Kidnapper. Similarly, when you go towards the Storeroom you'll have to fight another new Scourge Beast. Down at the bottom of the Storeroom you'll find another Kidnapper corpse with more Bloodstone Chunks on it, so be sure you grab them before moving on. [→☐ 01]

⑯ Elevator Path

Huntsmen now occupy most of the Elevator Path, all strengthened by a Bell Ringer on the paved area overlooking Main Street. Before exploring the rest of this area, it's worth following the path to the right, running straight past the Huntsman and killing the Bell Ringer at the end, so that the other enemies are much easier to kill. If you've been picking up all of the Bloodstone Chunks along the way, it's also worth taking the elevator to get back to the Lamp at the start of the area for a quick stop at the Hunter's Dream to upgrade your weapons. While you're going up in the elevator you may also notice that the stained glass window that you pass is broken, and you can roll through it to reach a previously inaccessible area. [→☐ 02]

⑭ Bloodstone Chunk ×2
⑮ Bloodstone Chunk ×2
⑯ Bloodstone Chunk ×2
⑰ Bloodstone Chunk ×2
⑱ Bloodstone Chunk ×1

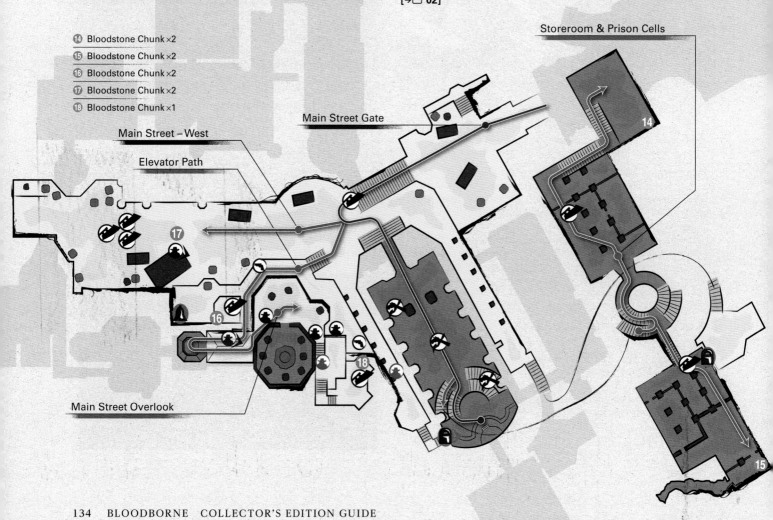

Storeroom & Prison Cells

Main Street Gate

Main Street – West

Elevator Path

Main Street Overlook

Main Street has now been overrun by Cramped Caskets, and while these enemies may move slowly, once they start attacking they are extremely aggressive. If you can hit them with attacks that flinch then you can often keep them from attacking; if they've already started, it's best to wait until they slam down on the ground, as that allows you to move in and begin attacking while they recover. To make travelling down this section of Main Street easier, you may want to clear out the Elevator Path area first, because you'll be under constant fire from the Huntsmen with rifles there.

A Cramped Casket now resides in the small alcove at **Position A** that used to be occupied by a Maneater Boar; as before, use the statue near the wall on the left to block its movement, and then quickly move around and attack it. Once it's defeated, be sure to head into the alcove and pick up the Bloodstone Chunks at the back. About halfway up the street you'll come across a suspiciously rocking wagon at **Position B**, in front of which are some more tempting Bloodstone Chunks.

Do not try to pick these up, however, because when you get close, a Cramped Casket will launch itself out of the wagon at you; quickly roll out of the way to avoid its ambush attempt. Try not to move past the wagon while fighting that Cramped Casket, because a group of three more are gathered just beyond it. Walking just past the wagon will cause one of them to head towards you, which will allow you to draw it away from the others when you're ready to fight. You can lure one of the remaining two away with a Pebble, or walk up slowly behind one and use a charged R2 for an early advantage.

⑱ Main Street Overlook

Approach the end of the rooftop here carefully, because two Rabid Dogs will come running at you; try to use one of the walls nearby as cover and attack them as they appear, one at a time. The room you can enter just past the rooftop contains a small bath, and if you inspect it you'll be transported to another bath, located near the Main Street Overpass. By travelling to that area via the bath you can kill all of the enemies on the bridge and overpass straight away without having to travel down the street. Down the stairs, just past the room with the bath, you'll come across a Wandering Nightmare. Be sure you have a weapon at the ready to kill it before it escapes. There's a Scourge Beast facing away from you near a wall at the bottom of the stairs, and if you approach it quietly you can easily land a charged R2 and Visceral Attack. [→☐ 03/04]

Main Street Gate

Unlike the first time you came to this area, there are no enemies here. So if you didn't previously pick up all the items, you can do so now without fear. The large Gate at the end is also open now, giving you direct access to the rest of the Main Street. [→☐ 05]

Yahar'gul, Unseen Village

Main Street – East ㉒

As soon as you reach the top of the stairs leading up to the bridge, a Scourge Beast will start to walk across it from the other side, so if you want to kill the Huntsman in the middle first, you'll need to be quick. Alternatively, you can wait at the top of the stairs, using the wall to block the Huntsman's shots, and then fight the Scourge Beast once it crosses the bridge. [→☐ **01**]

A new type of Cramped Casket is found in this area, and unlike the normal version, this one will exclusively attack you with bone spears from a distance. There are two of these enemies in total: one at **Position A**, and one at **Position B**. Staying behind cover so they can't hit you is the key to getting through this area safely. Clearing out the Bell Ringer at the end of the Main Street Overpass along with the Huntsman with a rifle on the bridge will also help, but you can still make it through without doing that if you're careful. Start by approaching the back of the wagon at **Position C**, as that will give you cover from both of the long range Cramped Caskets. Wait there until you see a normal Cramped Casket coming down the stairs on the left. Walk around the left side of the wagon so that it sees you, and then lure it back towards you so that you can fight it from behind cover.

With that first Cramped Casket down, advance to the side of the next wagon at **Position D**. From there, you should be able to lure another normal Cramped Casket back towards the side of the wagon, where you can fight it while behind cover. Now all that's left is to focus on the two long-range Cramped Caskets, so quickly run across the street towards the one at **Position A**, and try to fight it near the wall of the building, so that the statues block incoming fire from the other one. When only the final one is left, stand behind the statues and wait for it to fire, and then quickly close in kill it before it can fire again.

㉑ Main Street Access

There is a Huntsman with a rifle on the stairs leading down in this room, but the railings and pillars in the area provide plenty of cover as you approach. Once you reach the top of the stairs, simply wait for him to fire, and then close in and kill him before he can reload. If you walk slowly down the stairs, you can get behind the Scourge Beast there and kill it using a charged R2 and visceral attack combo. Going through the door here will let you get back out onto Main Street, and if you haven't already killed them, you can go out and safely get rid of the nearby ranged Cramped Caskets if you hug the wall. [→☐ **02**]

㉒ Main Street Overpass

The small bath here is where you'll appear if you use the one at the Main Street Overlook. You can also use this one to be transported back there, so you can quickly access the elevator and return to the Lamp when you need to. Continuing through the door will take you out on to the overpass. As soon as the Bell Ringer at the other end spots you, she'll summon a Huntsman that you'll have to contend with before you can kill her. The ladder near the Bell Ringer will take you down to the midsection of the tower, from where you can drop down to the roof of a wagon, and again to reach the floor. [→☐ **03**]

03

04

End of the Road

Provided you have killed the long range Cramped Caskets, you won't have to worry about any more enemies in this area, so you can explore freely. At the end of the raised areas to either side of the street you'll be able to find some Madman's Knowledge. Once you have them it's time to head through the large archway at the bottom and face off against the boss.

BOSS ## The One Reborn

The red-robed Bell Ringers that are on the upper level of the boss room will constantly throw homing fireballs at you if you try to attack the boss straight away. So the first thing you should do is use the stairs at the back to get up there and kill them all. For the full strategy, check out p346. Once The One Reborn has been defeated, you'll automatically receive three Yellow Backbone Holy Chalice ritual materials, and the new Advent Plaza Lamp will appear.

If you go up the stairs just past the Lamp you'll come to a small room, at the back of which there's a mysterious mummy sitting in a chair. Inspecting the mummy will cause you to be transported to Lecture Building 2F. Since you should have the Upper Cathedral Ward key now, it's recommended that you use the Lamp to return to the Cathedral Ward Lamp. From there you can go through the Healing Church Workshop to reach the door at the top, and finally enter the Upper Cathedral Ward. [→ 04]

World Changes

- Inspecting the mummy opens the path to Lecture Building 2F
- Gain access to the Advent Plaza Lamp

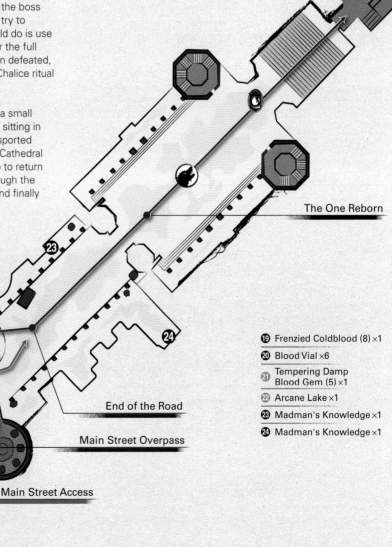

The One Reborn

Main Street – East

Main Street Bridge

End of the Road

Main Street Overpass

Main Street Access

⑲ Frenzied Coldblood (8) ×1
⑳ Blood Vial ×6
㉑ Tempering Damp Blood Gem (5) ×1
㉒ Arcane Lake ×1
㉓ Madman's Knowledge ×1
㉔ Madman's Knowledge ×1

Upper Cathedral Ward

The Upper Stratum of the Church is a place shrouded in secrecy. The highest class of clergy, the Choir, make their home here. The Choir, an organization of scholars and dreamers, seem to know something. It's as if they've been treated to a glimpse of the truth, and peered into the heavens themselves. After all, here we stand, feet planted in the earth, but might the cosmos be very near us... only just above our heads?

Difficulty	Area **B** | Celestial Emissary **B** | Ebrietas, Daughter of the Cosmos **A**
Recommended	Player Level **60-70** | Weapon Upgrade **+8**
Timezones	○ ◐ ☾ ●
Insight	Defeat the Celestial Emissary ×2, Encounter Ebrietas, Daughter of the Cosmos ×3, Defeat Ebrietas, Daughter of the Cosmos ×3

Enemies

Regular	HP	Echoes	Page
Celestial Child	345	131	p247
Carrion Crow	483	436	p231
Church Servant (Cane)	1105	873	p234
Church Servant (Cane & Lantern)	1105	982	p235
Church Servant (Scythe)	1105	1091	p236
Small Celestial Emissary	387	436	p241
Wandering Nightmare	49	14	p671

Strong	HP	Echoes	Page
Brainsucker	725	3273	p273
Scourge Beast	1451	1637	p266

Boss	HP	Echoes	Page
Celestial Emissary	2764	22400	p348
Ebrietas, Daughter of the Cosmos	12493	28800	p350

Reaching Upper Cathedral Ward

Getting to Upper Cathedral Ward requires the Upper Cathedral Key, which can be found in Yahar'gul, Unseen Village (Blood Moon). Upon reaching the rooftop that connects via a large stairway to Yahar'gul Chapel, you can drop off a gap in the railing to the right side, to land by the Holding Cell below. You must drop into the cell from above to retrieve the key. Once you have the key, head all the way to the top of the Healing Church Workshop, where you can use it to unlock the door to Upper Cathedral Ward.

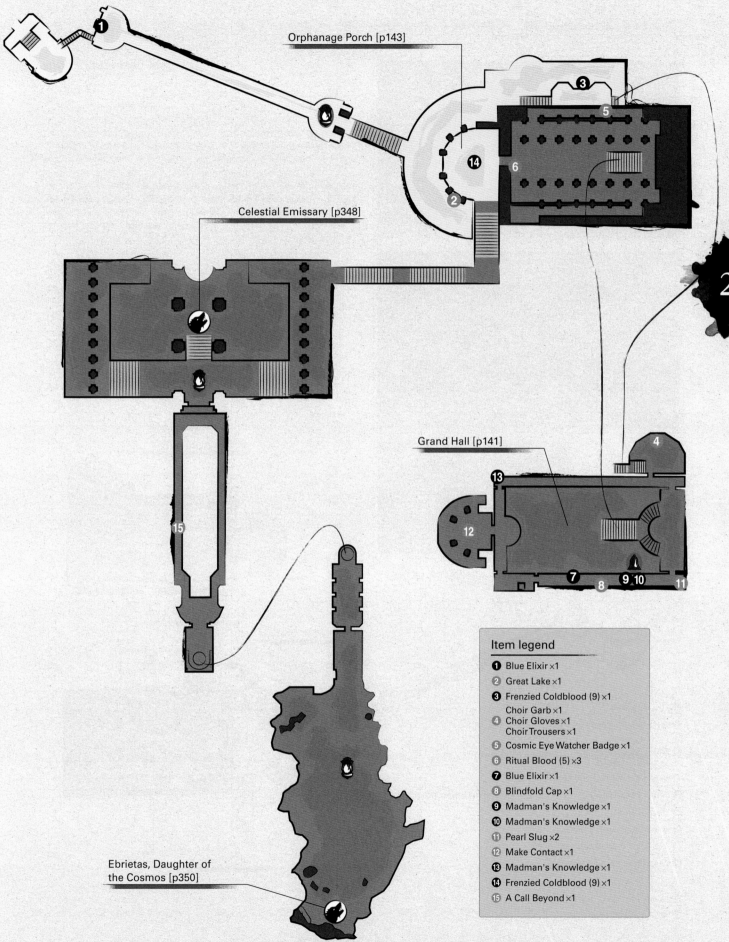

Orphanage Porch [p143]

Celestial Emissary [p348]

Grand Hall [p141]

Ebrietas, Daughter of
the Cosmos [p350]

Item legend

1 Blue Elixir ×1
2 Great Lake ×1
3 Frenzied Coldblood (9) ×1
4 Choir Garb ×1
  Choir Gloves ×1
  Choir Trousers ×1
5 Cosmic Eye Watcher Badge ×1
6 Ritual Blood (5) ×3
7 Blue Elixir ×1
8 Blindfold Cap ×1
9 Madman's Knowledge ×1
10 Madman's Knowledge ×1
11 Pearl Slug ×2
12 Make Contact ×1
13 Madman's Knowledge ×1
14 Frenzied Coldblood (9) ×1
15 A Call Beyond ×1

Upper Cathedral Ward

Upper Cathedral Bridge

There's a Celestial Child here, leaning up against the wall directly ahead of you upon first entering the area. While these enemies move and attack very slowly, they inflict an extreme amount of Frenzy build-up when they hit you. Always have some Sedatives in your Quick Items while in this area, and be especially careful when fighting large groups of these enemies. While you're crossing the bridge, a pair of Church Servants will start walking across; try to take out the one with the lantern first, so that you don't have to deal with his ranged attacks while fighting the other one. After battling your way past a few more Celestial Children and making it to the other side of the bridge you'll be able to activate the Upper Cathedral Ward Lamp. [→☐ 01/02]

❷ Statue Balcony

This small balcony area has a very large number of Celestial Children on it. Try to take them out with either jumping attacks from range, or by attacking a group of them with wide-arcing horizontal attacks to reduce the risk of getting hit. Clearing them all out will allow you to pick up the Great Lake Caryll Rune from a corpse near a statue, a very useful reward that increases all of your defenses by 4%. [→☐ 03]

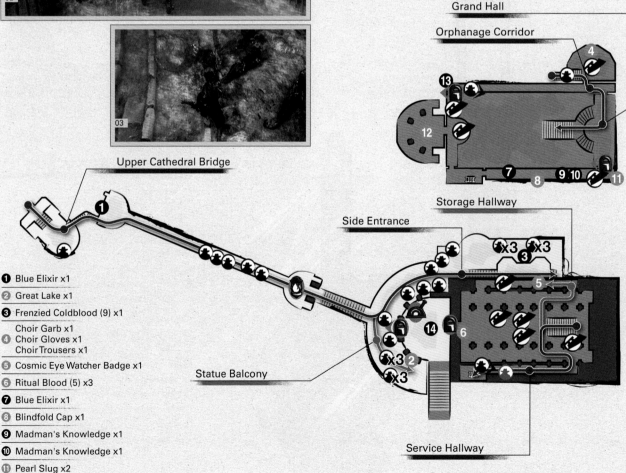

❶ Blue Elixir x1

❷ Great Lake x1

❸ Frenzied Coldblood (9) x1

❹ Choir Garb x1
   Choir Gloves x1
   Choir Trousers x1

❺ Cosmic Eye Watcher Badge x1

❻ Ritual Blood (5) x3

❼ Blue Elixir x1

❽ Blindfold Cap x1

❾ Madman's Knowledge x1

❿ Madman's Knowledge x1

⓫ Pearl Slug x2

⓬ Make Contact x1

⓭ Madman's Knowledge x1

Side Entrance ④

Numerous Celestial Children will emerge from amongst the statues around this side of the building, so progress slowly and try to kill all of them as they appear, to avoid ending up being surrounded. To the left of the stairs in this area you can fight your way through a group of Carrion Crows to reach another item. A Church Servant is standing guard at the top of the stairs – try to run up and fight him on the flat ground at the top rather than on the stairs. Once at the top of the stairs, if you enter the room quietly, you can sneak around and get behind the Brainsucker that's feeding on a body and land a charged R2 in his back for a visceral attack chance. [→☐ 04/05]

Orphanage Corridor

Paths leading to either side are available to you after entering this corridor. While heading to the right will let you get an item now, the door there can only be opened from the other side, and you'll be coming back through there later. For now it's best to head left and go through the door there instead, to enter the Orphanage's Grand Hall.

Grand Hall ⑥

The large chandelier hanging from the ceiling of the Grand Hall dominates the room, but if you look closely at it you'll also notice that a group of Scourge Beasts have made it their home. When you reach the halfway point as you walk down the stairs, the enemies will spot you and the chandelier will come crashing to the floor.

As soon as they hit the ground, the Scourge Beasts will start running towards you – your safest option by far is to retreat up the stairs and go back through the doorway. The Scourge Beasts are too big to fit through the doorway, which is good, because fight all of them out in the open would be extremely dangerous.

From the safety of your position behind the doorway you can bait the Scourge Beasts into attacking, and then easily hit them during the recovery using a weapon with good reach. If there are a couple of them near the door, try using Molotovs to hit them all for a large amount of damage. Once all three have been killed, descend the stairs once again, but keep an eye out for a forth Scourge Beast that patrols around down there; try to lure it to the other side of the banister so that it can't close in on you, and attack it from beyond its reach. The large door at the far end of the hall is currently locked, and the key can be found on the floor above. [→☐ 06/07]

⑤ Storage Hallway

There's a Brainsucker that patrols up and down this hallway. Try to time your approach when you see it walking away, because avoiding its magic attacks in the narrow area can be very difficult. Clearing the area, however, is well worth it, because you can pick up the Cosmic Eye Hunter Badge to further increase your shop inventory.

Service Hallway

Near the end of the hallway here you'll see a Wandering Nightmare, and while it will be tempting to just run straight ahead after it, you need to be very careful. On the other side of the door at the far end of the hallway there's a Brainsucker waiting to ambush you as you run through it. If you want to kill the Wandering Nightmare you need to try and do so without it going past that point. By approaching from the right-hand side of the doorway you can turn your camera around to spot the Brainsucker, causing it to attempt its ambush early and completely miss. If the Wandering Nightmare is still alive at this point, you can run past the Brainsucker to try and kill it, but be mindful of the Brainsucker's magic attacks. [→☐ 08]

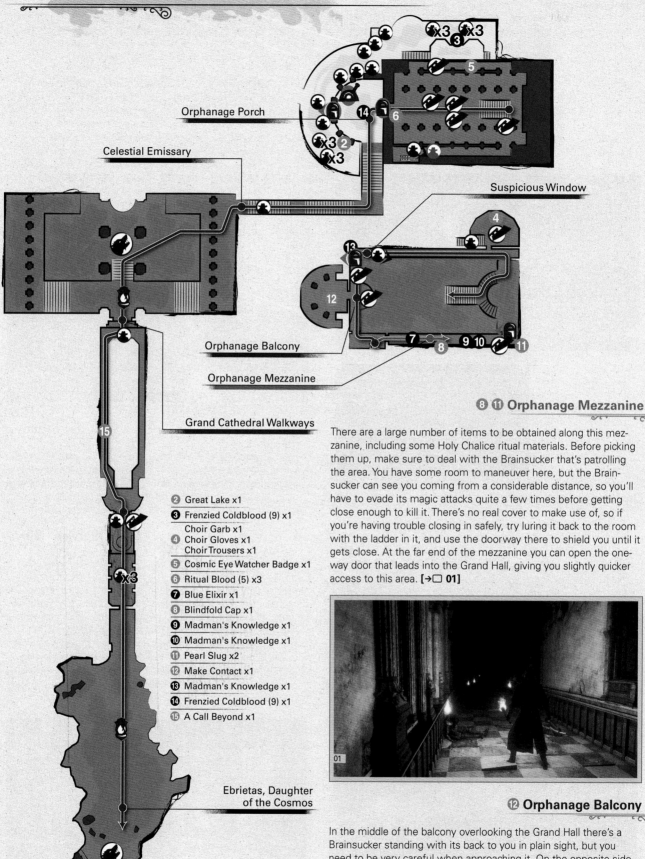

Orphanage Porch

Celestial Emissary

Suspicious Window

Orphanage Balcony

Orphanage Mezzanine

Grand Cathedral Walkways

② Great Lake x1

③ Frenzied Coldblood (9) x1

④ Choir Garb x1
Choir Gloves x1
Choir Trousers x1

⑤ Cosmic Eye Watcher Badge x1

⑥ Ritual Blood (5) x3

⑦ Blue Elixir x1

⑧ Blindfold Cap x1

⑨ Madman's Knowledge x1

⑩ Madman's Knowledge x1

⑪ Pearl Slug x2

⑫ Make Contact x1

⑬ Madman's Knowledge x1

⑭ Frenzied Coldblood (9) x1

⑮ A Call Beyond x1

Ebrietas, Daughter
of the Cosmos

⑧ ⑪ Orphanage Mezzanine

There are a large number of items to be obtained along this mezzanine, including some Holy Chalice ritual materials. Before picking them up, make sure to deal with the Brainsucker that's patrolling the area. You have some room to maneuver here, but the Brainsucker can see you coming from a considerable distance, so you'll have to evade its magic attacks quite a few times before getting close enough to kill it. There's no real cover to make use of, so if you're having trouble closing in safely, try luring it back to the room with the ladder in it, and use the doorway there to shield you until it gets close. At the far end of the mezzanine you can open the one-way door that leads into the Grand Hall, giving you slightly quicker access to this area. [→☐ 01]

⑫ Orphanage Balcony

In the middle of the balcony overlooking the Grand Hall there's a Brainsucker standing with its back to you in plain sight, but you need to be very careful when approaching it. On the opposite side of the balcony near the one-way door is a second Brainsucker, and it will immediately start using its magic attacks when it sees you. If you're careful and don't walk past the middle of the balcony, you can sneak up behind the first Brainsucker without getting hit, because all of the other Brainsucker's attacks will hit either the rail or the top of the stairs near it. When the first one has been killed, wait near the rail, and then try to time your approach between its attacks and kill it. Doing so gets you the Orphanage Key, required to unlock the door below. Before continuing, however, make sure you go through the large door in the middle of the balcony and retrieve the Make Contact Gesture from the poor soul out there. [→ 02]

Suspicious Window

After opening the one-way door you'll notice an item on the ground to the left, and while you can pick it up safely, as soon as you start walking back along the corridor, a blue-eyed Scourge Beast will burst through the window. As soon as this happens, quickly run back through the door so that it can't follow you, and attack it from there to remain safe. Once it has been defeated, continue along corridor into the Grand Hall, and then use the Orphanage Key to unlock the door at the front.

Orphanage Porch

The first thing to do once you're out on the porch is to pull the switch and open the front gate, creating a quick path back to the Lamp. There are a couple of boss battles coming up, so if you have a large amount of Blood Echoes it's worth going back to the Hunter's Dream now and leveling up some before facing them. Continue up the stairs when you're ready, and as you start to cross the bridge at the top, a lone Small Celestial Emissary will come running across to attack you; its appearance is an omen of what's to come.

BOSS Celestial Emissary

Only one of the Small Celestial Emissaries at the start of this fight is the Celestial Emissary that you're trying to kill, and while they all look the same, there is a defining characteristic that you can look for. The Celestial Emissary generally does not close in to attack you, so always look for one that's hanging back while the others advance. Upon its defeat you'll automatically receive the Communion Caryll Rune, which increases the amount of Blood Vials you can carry by four. The Lumenflower Gardens Lamp will also appear in the area, and if you're running low on healing items, it's worth using it to go back to the Hunter's Dream and resupply, because there is still more to do here. Just behind the Lamp there's a large window, and if you get close to it you'll see an area on the other side that you can reach by either breaking the window with your weapon, or rolling through it. Once you're on the other side, however, you won't be able to leave until you either kill the next boss, or it kills you, so be sure you're prepared.

World Changes

- Gain access to the Lumenflower Gardens Lamp

The walkways on the other side of the window are actually high above the Grand Cathedral, where you faced Vicar Amelia, and from the place you start you have a nice view down to the altar at which she was praying. A Celestial Child is also nearby when you first drop down, so don't get too distracted by the view and make sure you kill it quickly before you get hit. The item that's hanging over the banister along the right-hand walkway is A Call Beyond, which is extremely powerful if you have the stats to use it. Two Small Celestial Emissaries are waiting in ambush on the other side of the large archway at the end of the walkways, and one of them is the very deadly Tendril version, so you need to be careful. If you approach the arch along the left-hand side of it, you can spot the normal Celestial Emissary and cause it to come running out to attack you, letting you kill it out of the field of view of the other one. Once it's dead, round the corner and quickly kill the Tendril one before it can launch any of its magic attacks.

BOSS Ebrietas, Daughter of the Cosmos

You can find Ebrietas dormant at the far end of the Altar of Despair, and she will remain so until you hit her to begin the fight. While her head may be her weak point, it can be dangerous to stand in front of her. You may want to try standing between her tails, where it's somewhat safer, and attack her from there. Once she's been defeated the Altar of Despair Lamp will appear in the middle of the area. [→ 03]

World Changes

- Gain access to the Altar of Despair Lamp
- Acquire the Great Isz Chalice
- The Altar of the Despair becomes accessible

The Great Isz Chalice can be used to access parts of the Labyrinth previously unreachable, but to break the seal you will need a large number of materials. A total of nine Ritual Blood (5), three Pearl Slugs and 25 Arcane Haze will first need to be acquired before you can attempt to claim some of the treasures found in Isz. Behind where Ebrietas was laying dormant you can also find the remains of a False God that are still emanating a great deal of power; if Vileblood Queen Annalise happens to die, you can retrieve her Queenly Flesh and bring it to this altar to resurrect her. For more information, please refer to p647.

Lecture Building 2F

Once again, you've returned for more education. The leaders of Yahar'gul, the School of Mensis, seem attuned to this institution, adrift as it is in the nightmare. The presence of massive Church Giants betrays a connection between Mensis and the Healing Church, but you don't have time to think on that. Let the fear pull you onward; all that lies between madness and yourself, is sheer terror.

Difficulty	Area **B**
Recommended	Player Level **60-70** | Weapon Upgrade **+8**
Timezones	◯ ☁ ☾ ●
Insight	Set eyes upon Patches the Spider ×2

Enemies

Regular	HP	Echoes	Page
Scholar (Bare Hands)	458	1361	p246
Scholar (Flask)	458	1361	p246

Strong	HP	Echoes	Page
Church Giant (Flame Fist)	3129	4082	p272

NPC

Name	Page
Patches the Spider	p649

Item legend

❶ Sedatives ×6
❷ Bloodstone Chunk ×1
❸ Communion ×1

To Nightmare of Mensis [p146]

Patches' Lab Revisited

Lecture Theater 1 Balcony

2F Waiting Room

Lecture Theater 2 Balcony

Main Hallway

Main Hallway ❷

The 2nd floor Lecture Building Lamp is in the same room that you start in – be sure to light it before venturing past the door. As with the 1st floor, if you simply want to get through the area, you can run straight along the Main Hallway and open the door at the opposite end. Doing so will transport you to the Nightmare of Mensis, but this time you'll need to fight your way past some Scholars along the way. There are also Scholars on the opposite side of the floor, and they'll do their best to hit you with projectile attacks as you enter their range, so try to use the pillars for cover if you stop to fight. [→☐ 01]

01

2F Waiting Room

You can freely enter this room and pick up the item at the back, but you need to be careful when making your exit, because a Scholar hanging above the door will drop down and ambush you. Keep your camera aimed up slightly as you approach the door and you should be able to spot the Scholar on the ceiling; either advance slowly so that it misses you when it drops, or use a ranged attack to knock it down first. [→☐ 02/03]

02

03

Lecture Theater 2 Balcony

If you look up and to the right after going through the door and out onto the balcony, you'll notice another Scholar hanging from the ceiling, waiting to ambush you. This one lets you run beneath it safely, however, and will only drop down once you're about halfway along the balcony. Because they move so slowly (and because it drops down so far behind you), you can just keep running and leave it alone if you wish, or double back and finish it off. Just past another Scholar at the end of the balcony you'll find a note on the ground that you can read, and there's another one in the nearby room.

❸ Lecture Theater 1 Balcony

As long as you hug the wall, you can make it through the door and onto the balcony without the Church Giant outside spotting you. Even if it does spot you, it can't follow you through the door, so you're safe once you're on the other side. There are no enemies along this stretch of the balcony, so you can just run along it and go through the door at the other end, where you'll find a chest containing a Communion Caryll Rune that increases the amount of Blood Vials you can carry. You can't get back to the Main Hallway from here, so you'll need to backtrack along the balcony and exit that way. [→☐ 04]

04

05

Patches' Lab Revisited

The Church Giant in this area is standing very close to a hatch with a ladder. That ladder leads down to Patches' Lab on the 1st floor, and to reach it you can either run past the enemy and drop straight down, or kill it first so that you can use the ladder safely. Once you're in the lab you can talk to Patches to receive the Beg for Life Gesture, and if you talk again you'll have the option to decide whether or not you think ill of him. Selecting 'no' will lead to him becoming friendly, and you'll receive an Anti-Clockwise Metamorphosis Caryll Rune that boosts your maximum Stamina. To find out more about Patches, please refer to p649. [→☐ 05]

Nightmare of Mensis

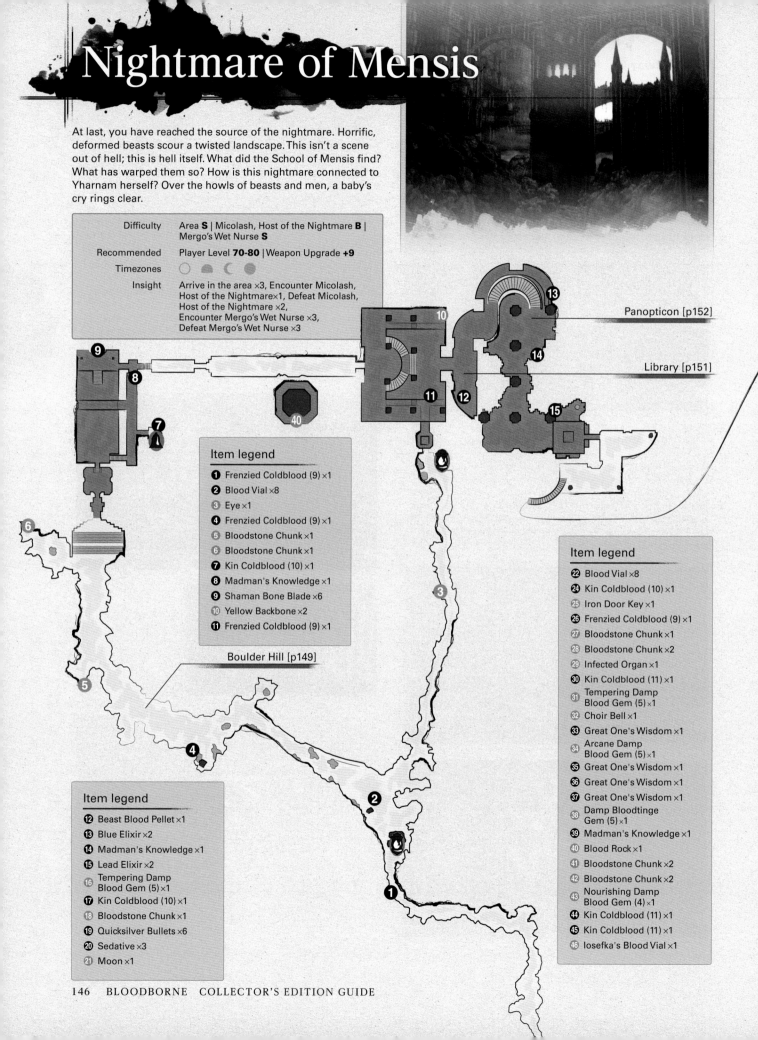

At last, you have reached the source of the nightmare. Horrific, deformed beasts scour a twisted landscape. This isn't a scene out of hell; this is hell itself. What did the School of Mensis find? What has warped them so? How is this nightmare connected to Yharnam herself? Over the howls of beasts and men, a baby's cry rings clear.

Difficulty	Area **S** | Micolash, Host of the Nightmare **B** | Mergo's Wet Nurse **S**
Recommended	Player Level **70-80** | Weapon Upgrade **+9**
Timezones	○ ◐ ☾ ●
Insight	Arrive in the area ×3, Encounter Micolash, Host of the Nightmare ×1, Defeat Micolash, Host of the Nightmare ×2, Encounter Mergo's Wet Nurse ×3, Defeat Mergo's Wet Nurse ×3

Panopticon [p152]

Library [p151]

Item legend

1 Frenzied Coldblood (9) ×1
2 Blood Vial ×8
3 Eye ×1
4 Frenzied Coldblood (9) ×1
5 Bloodstone Chunk ×1
6 Bloodstone Chunk ×1
7 Kin Coldblood (10) ×1
8 Madman's Knowledge ×1
9 Shaman Bone Blade ×6
10 Yellow Backbone ×2
11 Frenzied Coldblood (9) ×1

Boulder Hill [p149]

Item legend

12 Beast Blood Pellet ×1
13 Blue Elixir ×2
14 Madman's Knowledge ×1
15 Lead Elixir ×2
16 Tempering Damp Blood Gem (5) ×1
17 Kin Coldblood (10) ×1
18 Bloodstone Chunk ×1
19 Quicksilver Bullets ×6
20 Sedative ×3
21 Moon ×1

Item legend

22 Blood Vial ×8
24 Kin Coldblood (10) ×1
25 Iron Door Key ×1
26 Frenzied Coldblood (9) ×1
27 Bloodstone Chunk ×1
28 Bloodstone Chunk ×2
29 Infected Organ ×1
30 Kin Coldblood (11) ×1
31 Tempering Damp Blood Gem (5) ×1
32 Choir Bell ×1
33 Great One's Wisdom ×1
34 Arcane Damp Blood Gem (5) ×1
35 Great One's Wisdom ×1
36 Great One's Wisdom ×1
37 Great One's Wisdom ×1
38 Damp Bloodtinge Gem (5) ×1
39 Madman's Knowledge ×1
40 Blood Rock ×1
41 Bloodstone Chunk ×2
42 Bloodstone Chunk ×2
43 Nourishing Damp Blood Gem (4) ×1
44 Kin Coldblood (11) ×1
45 Kin Coldblood (11) ×1
46 Iosefka's Blood Vial ×1

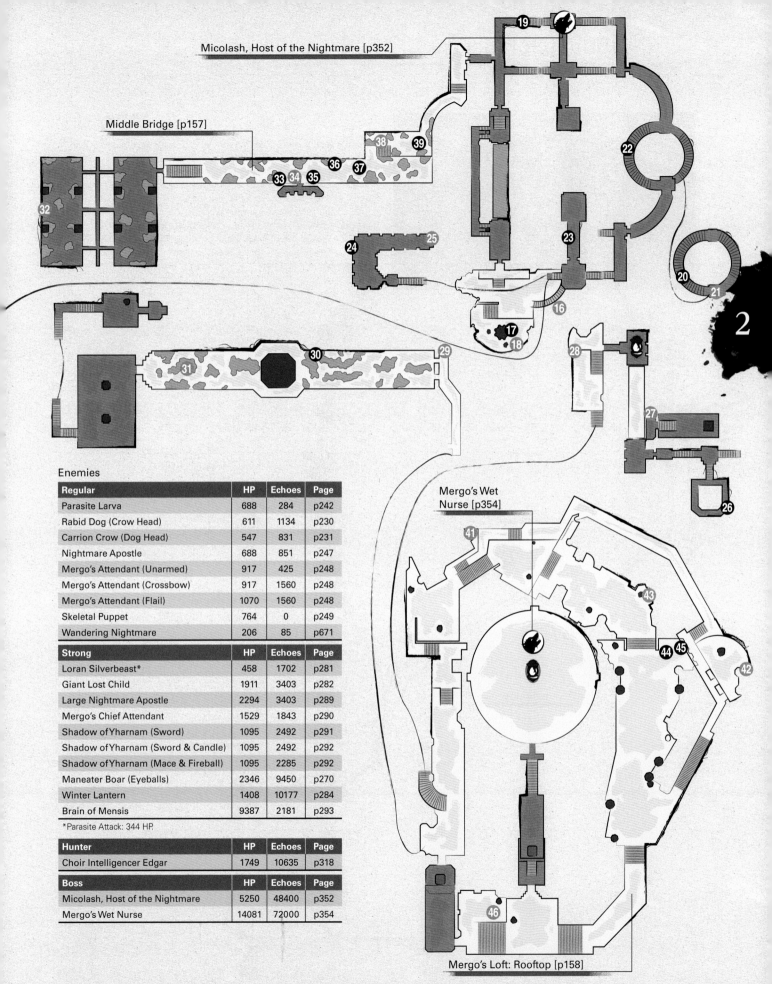

Micolash, Host of the Nightmare [p352]

Middle Bridge [p157]

Mergo's Wet
Nurse [p354]

Enemies

Regular	HP	Echoes	Page
Parasite Larva	688	284	p242
Rabid Dog (Crow Head)	611	1134	p230
Carrion Crow (Dog Head)	547	831	p231
Nightmare Apostle	688	851	p247
Mergo's Attendant (Unarmed)	917	425	p248
Mergo's Attendant (Crossbow)	917	1560	p248
Mergo's Attendant (Flail)	1070	1560	p248
Skeletal Puppet	764	0	p249
Wandering Nightmare	206	85	p671

Strong	HP	Echoes	Page
Loran Silverbeast*	458	1702	p281
Giant Lost Child	1911	3403	p282
Large Nightmare Apostle	2294	3403	p289
Mergo's Chief Attendant	1529	1843	p290
Shadow of Yharnam (Sword)	1095	2492	p291
Shadow of Yharnam (Sword & Candle)	1095	2492	p292
Shadow of Yharnam (Mace & Fireball)	1095	2285	p292
Maneater Boar (Eyeballs)	2346	9450	p270
Winter Lantern	1408	10177	p284
Brain of Mensis	9387	2181	p293

*Parasite Attack: 344 HP.

Hunter	HP	Echoes	Page
Choir Intelligencer Edgar	1749	10635	p318

Boss	HP	Echoes	Page
Micolash, Host of the Nightmare	5250	48400	p352
Mergo's Wet Nurse	14081	72000	p354

Mergo's Loft: Rooftop [p158]

Nightmare of Mensis

01

Nightmare Trail

There are no threats in the area when you start, so head through the tunnel at your leisure. When you get outside, off in the distance you should be able to see a Loran Silverbeast standing with its back to you. As long as you approach quietly you can sneak up behind it and use a charged R2. Don't let the Loran Silverbeast go too far up the trial, because there's a Wandering Nightmare that's better left undisturbed until you're ready to fight it. When you round the corner near the end of the trail you'll be under the gaze of the Brain of Mensis, so quickly run ahead and take cover near the Nightmare of Mensis Lamp. [→☐ 01]

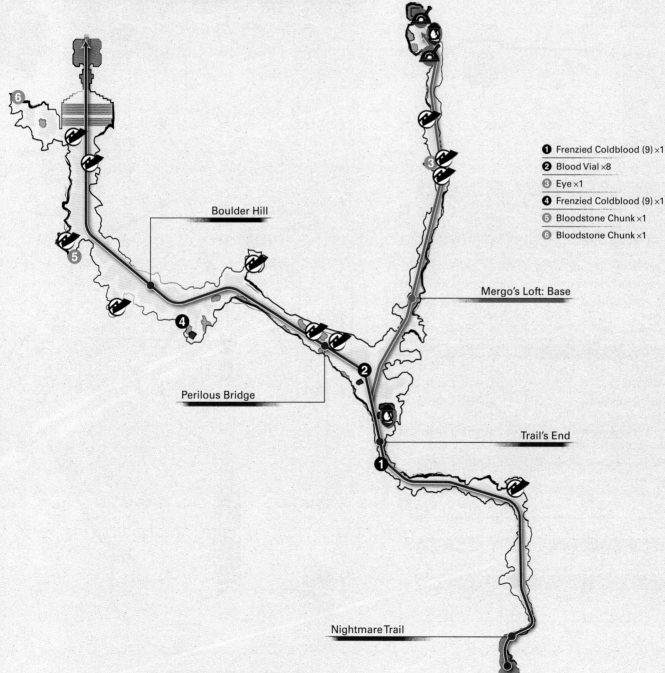

Boulder Hill

Mergo's Loft: Base

Perilous Bridge

Trail's End

Nightmare Trail

1 Frenzied Coldblood (9) ×1
2 Blood Vial ×8
3 Eye ×1
4 Frenzied Coldblood (9) ×1
5 Bloodstone Chunk ×1
6 Bloodstone Chunk ×1

Watching over this entire area from its position on the Middle Bridge is the Brain of Mensis; any time you're in its field of view your health will slowly drop, and Frenzy will build up. Thankfully there's a lot of cover available in the area, and as long as you're standing directly behind something it will not be able to see you. There's a small window between when the Brain first spots you and when your health begins to drop, so if you listen for the sound it makes when it detects you, you can often get behind cover before taking damage. Enemies can also be damaged by the Brain's gaze, however, so it can be beneficial to try and lure them into its field of view – so that they are already weakened when you start to fight them. [→☐ **02/03**]

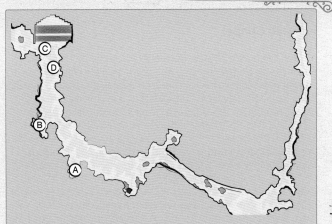

The hill leading up to the chapel has a number of Giant Lost Children along it. While here you'll need to stay aware of your surroundings and try to keep your camera aimed up the hill as much as possible, so that you can spot any incoming boulders. The first enemy at **Position A** will not actually throw boulders as you approach from this direction, so you can quickly close in and fight it on the small ledge it's standing on. Once you reach the enemy at **Position B**, however, a third one near the top of the hill at **Position C** will start throwing boulders down at you.

02

Instead of fighting the one at **Position B** straight away, it's better to run up the hill and deal with the one at **Position C**, because boulders thrown by the one down at **Position B** cannot reach you there. Another Giant is crouched down at **Position D**, and you'll have to run past it to reach the one at **Position C**, waking it up in the process. If you kill the Giant at **Position C** quickly, however, you can have it out of the way before the crouched one is ready to fight. Once the enemies at the top of the hill have been killed you can run back down the hill and finish off the remaining one without having to worry about incoming boulders.

03

Mergo's Loft: Base ❸

There's not a lot of cover available along this path, so you should try to sprint across the open areas to avoid being exposed to the Brain of Mensis for very long, and then wait for the Frenzy build-up to subside whenever you reach some cover. There's a group of Giant Lost Child enemies about halfway along the path, and the safest way to deal with them is to run straight past them to the Mergo's Loft: Base Lamp. This should entice them to move out from behind their cover to follow you, exposing themselves to the Brain's gaze in the process. The area around the Lamp is outside Brain's field of view, so you won't have to worry about it while fighting the enemies there. The switches in the area control elevators, but they need to be activated from the other end, so you cannot make use of them yet.

Perilous Bridge

While there's quite a lot of cover available on this bridge, fighting any of the Silverbeasts nearby on it is extremely dangerous – not only because of the likelihood that a fight will take you out from behind cover, but also because of the bottomless drop on either side. It's much safer to lure the first enemy away from the start of the bridge and kill it before crossing, and then once you get close to the other side, quickly run across and fight the other enemy there. [→☐ **04**]

04

Nightmare of Mensis

Infested Chapel

A Large Nightmare Apostle, along with some smaller Nightmare Apostles, can be seen hanging from the roof of the chapel when you get near the entrance, and as you'd expect, they will not remain there for long. If you were to run straight to the middle of the chapel, all of them would descend at once, which can make the fight quite difficult. To make things easier, use ranged attacks to lure them down one at a time. After the first couple, you'll have to use the Chapel Hallway to reach the rest without being detected, but doing so will allow you to fight the Large Nightmare Apostle on its own. If you do trigger them to fall, the fight is best handled near the entrance doorway, as the Large Nightmare Apostle cannot fit through it. The smaller ones will still come through the door, so make sure you back away far enough that you're out of range of the large one's attacks before fighting them. [→☐ 01/02]

Chapel Hallway

In the middle of this hallway another Nightmare Apostle can be found hanging from the ceiling, but you can run straight past it without it dropping down and get the item at the end if you wish. The small bridge leading out to the side of the hallway has a couple more of them hanging above it, and if you walk out onto the bridge, the two above it and the one in the hallway will drop down to attack you from either side. If that happens, drop down off the bridge to create more space to fight them. [→☐ 03/04]

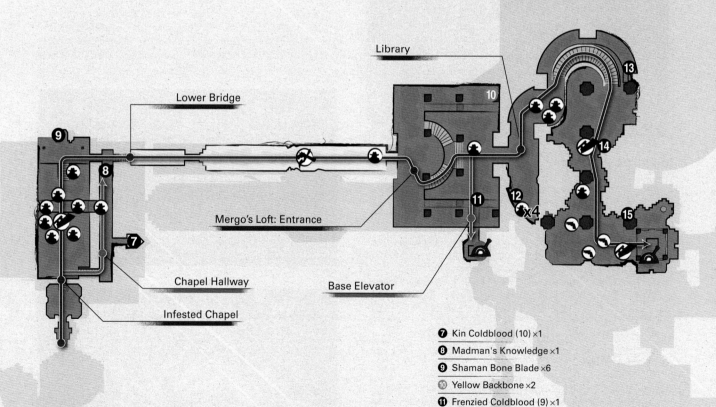

7 Kin Coldblood (10) ×1

8 Madman's Knowledge ×1

9 Shaman Bone Blade ×6

10 Yellow Backbone ×2

11 Frenzied Coldblood (9) ×1

12 Beast Blood Pellet ×1

13 Blue Elixir ×2

14 Madman's Knowledge ×1

15 Lead Elixir ×2

Base Elevator

The elevator that you can access here will take you down to a small room near the Mergo's Loft: Base Lamp, giving you quick access to a Lamp without having to fight any enemies or worry about the Brain of Mensis. Because of the ease with which you can now re-enter Mergo's Loft, it's worth returning to the Hunter's Dream to spend any Blood Echoes you've acquired thus far in the area. [→☐ 07]

Lower Bridge

The Hunter that you face on this bridge can be quite difficult to fight, due to the fact he'll often use Rosmarinus while walking backwards. The wide area of effect on that weapon makes getting past the spray on the narrow bridge problematic. To counter that, try to stay as close to him as possible and use the sides of the gate in the middle of the bridge to restrict his movement.

Mergo's Loft: Entrance ⑩

Unarmed Mergo's Attendants patrol this area, but they will not become hostile unless you actually attack them. So they can be left alone unless you want the extra Blood Echoes. The chest on the balcony contains some useful Chalice Dungeon materials, so be sure to grab those before going down the stairs towards the Panopticon. [→☐ 05/06]

Library

Upon entering the Library you'll notice a lot more unarmed Mergo's Attendants walking around, and as before, they will remain non-combative until you hit them. Heading around to the right will lead you to a small dead end, where an item can be found hidden behind a screen. When you reach the top of the stairs to the left, look for a small balcony entrance behind the mirror nearby, that you can follow along to reach another item. [→☐ 08/09]

Nightmare of Mensis

COMBAT FOCUS Panopticon

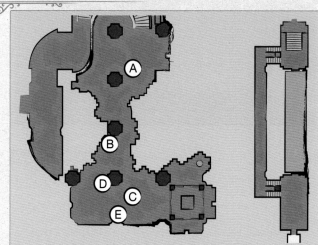

The Panopticon is home to all types of Mergo's Attendants, and the constant threat of falling off the edges of the broken floor during an encounter makes the positioning with which you fight them very important. The most immediate threat is the Mergo's Chief Attendant that patrols between the cages near **Position A**; try to fight it as close to the stairs as you can, so that you keep the fight away from other enemies and give yourself the most room to maneuver. Interrupting their slow attacks and using a visceral attack while they're staggered is the fastest way to kill them, but for an easier option you can try quickstepping through their attacks and hitting them while they recover.

An unarmed Attendant can be found hiding behind a pillar at **Position B**, but unlike the other ones this one will attack you straight away, so be ready for it as you pass the pillar. Towards the back of the room at **Positions C, D** and **E** are three more Attendants, this time all armed with crossbows. You can approach them by going around the right-hand side of the pillar in the middle, but from that direction they all have good lines of sight over each other. Before you can go around the left side of that pillar safely, however, you'll have to contend with another Mergo's Chief Attendant standing near the elevator at the back. When you get close to that pillar, the Chief Attendant will spot you and start walking towards you, so wait for him to come past it and fight him there. When you go around the pillar you can use the first broken cage full of books for cover while you fight the enemy at **Position C**, before running down and killing the one at **Position D** near the screen to the side of the pillar. Use the other broken cage in the area to cover your approach while you close in and finish off the enemy at **Position E**.

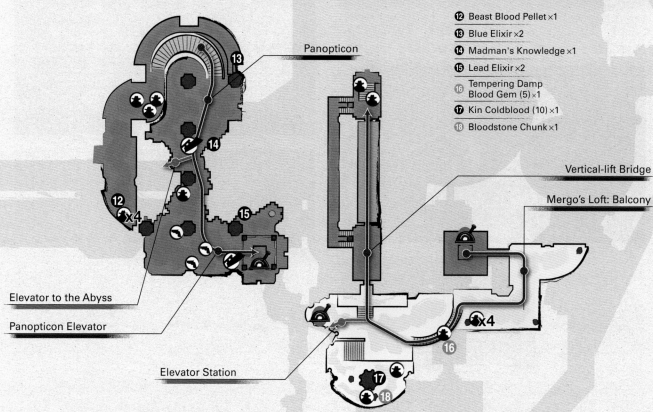

Panopticon

- 12 Beast Blood Pellet ×1
- 13 Blue Elixir ×2
- 14 Madman's Knowledge ×1
- 15 Lead Elixir ×2
- 16 Tempering Damp Blood Gem (5) ×1
- 17 Kin Coldblood (10) ×1
- 18 Bloodstone Chunk ×1

Vertical-lift Bridge

Mergo's Loft: Balcony

Elevator to the Abyss

Panopticon Elevator

Elevator Station

Elevator to the Abyss

While it won't be here during your first time through the Panopticon, a series of events later in the area can cause a new cage elevator to become available at this point. Use it, and you'll descend into the abyss below to face off against an ancient evil. [→□ 01/02]

Panopticon Elevator

Before stepping onto the elevator here, go through the gap in the rail on the left and follow the path around to reach an item hanging over the edge, behind the pillar. It's worth noting that even if you used a lot of items getting through the Panopticon room, you're better off continuing, rather than going back to the Base Elevator, because you'll be able to open up another path to a Lamp shortly. [→□ 03]

Mergo's Loft: Balcony ⑯

The cage hanging directly in front of you when you enter this area contains a Dog-headed Carrion Crow that will come crawling out as you approach; these enemies attack in the same way as their traditional-looking counterparts, so don't let their appearance intimidate you. After following the path around to the right you'll find another group of Carrion Crows, feeding on the seemingly dead corpse of a Rabid Dog. When two of the crows have been killed, the dog will spring to life, so try to attack it while it's still lying down. At the top of the nearby stairs, you can double back around to the right and roll off the edge into the hanging cage to get the item that you could see in there while going up the stairs.

⑱ Elevator Station

On your way to the Elevator Station you'll come to a set of stairs leading down to the left, where a pair of Crow-headed Rabid Dogs are guarding some items. If you go down there, try to use the trees in the area to the block the dogs' attack attempts, and then kill them while they recover. Only one elevator at the station is currently active, but you can use it to descend to the path just in front of the Mergo's Loft: Base Lamp. This allows you to get straight back here without having to fight any enemies. There's a boss fight coming up shortly, so making use of the Lamp is highly recommended. [→□ 04]

Vertical-lift Bridge

While the reasons for having a bridge and a hallway cross the same room and lead to the same area may not be apparent at first, the metal bridge will get moved shortly, so you'll have to use the hallway during subsequent trips here. When you reach the other side, two Skeletal Puppets will spring to life on the steps, so have your weapon at the ready. Walking a short distance along the corridor beyond those enemies will trigger the start of the boss battle, so make sure you're well prepared before continuing. [→□ 05/06]

Nightmare of Mensis

COMBAT FOCUS **Micolash, Host of the Nightmare Pt.1**

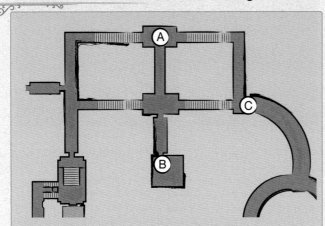

This boss encounter differs from the others in the game in that it takes place over a large portion of the area, and it is primarily a game of cat & mouse. Micolash starts at **Position A**, and your primary objective should be to get him into the dead end room at **Position B**. When you approach him, he will nearly always run away in the direction of the room, so he doesn't take much persuading. Any time you hit him before getting him into that room, however, he'll disappear in a cloud of smoke, and you'll need to track him down again; killing him in this manner does take slightly longer, but it lets you avoid dealing with his attacks. For more information on the attacks Micolash can use, check p352.

To impede your progress in tracking him down, numerous Skeletal Puppets will spring to life around the room, and while you can kill these enemies, doing so is only temporary and they will spring back up again after a short period of time. Unless one of them is blocking your way, it's best to just avoid and run around them. There are two Skeletal Puppets in the first room that you trap Micolash in, but they will not become active until you get around half way into the room, which means you can lure Micolash back slightly and fight him near the entrance to avoid dealing with them. Once you get his health down to around 50%, Micolash will vanish and the nightmare fog at **Position C** will dissipate, allowing you to continue to the next part of the area.

- ⑲ Quicksilver Bullets ×6
- ⑳ Sedative ×3
- ㉑ Moon ×1
- ㉒ Blood Vial ×8
- ㉔ Kin Coldblood (10) ×1
- ㉕ Iron Door Key ×1
- ㉖ Frenzied Coldblood (9) ×1
- ㉗ Bloodstone Chunk ×1

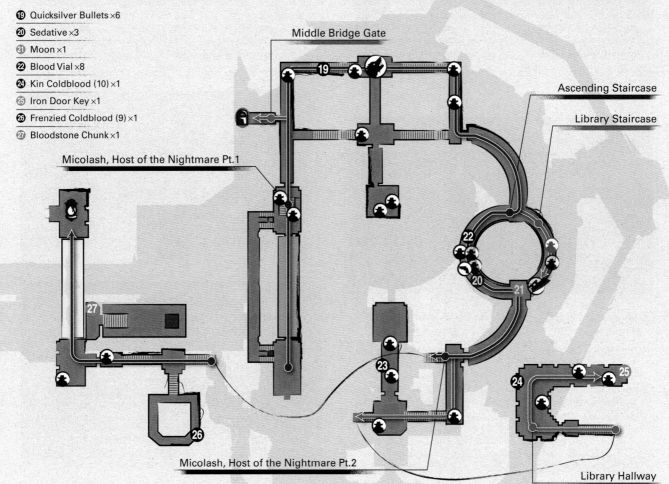

Micolash, Host of the Nightmare Pt.1

Middle Bridge Gate

Ascending Staircase

Library Staircase

Micolash, Host of the Nightmare Pt.2

Library Hallway

Middle Bridge Gate

You can get the key to this gate in the area where you fight Micolash for a second time. Once you have it, you can return here to access the Middle Bridge if you wish. At this time the Brain of Mensis is still in position on the bridge and it's extremely difficult to gather the items out there while that's the case. You'll have another chance to access the bridge later, after dealing with the Brain, so it's much safer to leave the items until then.

Library Staircase ㉑

You'll reach this large staircase on the way to the second part of the fight with Micolash, and you can either head down straight away and explore, or carry on and finish the boss fight first. The first enemy you'll run into while going down the stairs is a Wandering Nightmare, and you should try to kill it before it can run too far down. About halfway down the stairs a pair of crossbow-wielding Mergo's Attendants stand guard, so try to use the natural curvature of the wall for cover and time your approach between their shots. Another crossbow-wielding Attendant is at the bottom of the stairs, this time accompanied by a Chief Attendant, so you need to be a bit more careful. Hug the inside wall as normal, and then move out to get the attention of the Chief Attendant and lure it back up the stairs away from the other enemy before fighting it. Once all of the enemies have been defeated, you can safely pick up the very useful Moon Caryll Rune, that lets you receive more Blood Echoes for killing enemies. [→☐ 01]

Ascending Staircase

Heading up the spiral staircase will take you closer to the second encounter with Micolash, but before you get to him there are some other enemies blocking your way. The first one you'll come to is a flail-using Mergo's Attendant, and just behind that is another crossbow-user; try to lure the enemy with the flail down the stairs and fight it out of the other one's line of sight. When you reach the top of the stairs, go through the archway to continue the fight with Micolash.

Library Hallway ㉕

You can access this area during the fight with Micolash, or leave exploring it until after you've defeated him. The most important item here is the Iron Door Key, that lets you open the gate to the Middle Bridge in the first part of the Micolash fight. There's also a Kin Coldblood tucked away in front of one of the bookcases that you can use for some extra Blood Echoes.

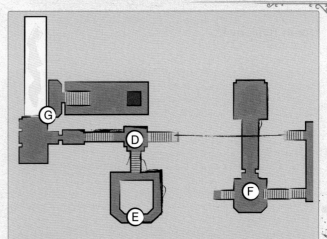

The basic goal is to once again trap Micolash in a room with no escape so that you can fight him, but this time he takes a bit of a scenic route to get there. Micolash always starts at **Position D** halfway up the stairs, and if you run straight towards him, he'll go running to **Position E**, and then drop down to **Position F**. If you follow the same route he took you'll drop down behind him and he'll go running straight ahead into the dead-end room. Don't follow him in, though, because this time a gate is shut, locking him in, and if you're too close you'll be locked in with him. While you can fight him like that, you can get a significant advantage by approaching from a different location. Make your way back up to the room at the top of the stairs, where Micolash entered the mirror, and go to **Position G**, where you'll find a broken section of rail that you can drop through to land on a small balcony.

Grab the item here, and then go through the nearby doorway and into the room beyond, where you'll find a hole in the floor. If you look down you should see Micolash standing below you. Although you may be tempted to drop straight down with a plunging attack, he will often move out of the way and avoid it. It's better to use ranged attacks from up here, where you're totally safe; Bone Marrow Ash-strengthened Pistol shots or Poison Throwing Knives are especially effective. If you run out of ranged options you can drop down and finish him off via conventional means. Upon defeating Micolash a cut-scene will trigger, during which the Vertical-lift Bridge will rise to its upper position. You can now access it from the room at the top of the area. After crossing the bridge you'll also be able to light the Mergo's Loft: Middle Lamp, so now is the perfect time to resupply.

Nightmare of Mensis

Upper Balcony ㉘

At the top of the first flight of stairs here you can double back around to the right to reach a small balcony, where two Dog-headed Carrion Crows are guarding an item. The item in question is two Bloodstone Chunks, so it's worth taking a quick trip in there to kill them and retrieve it, before continuing up the stairs. [→□ 01]

Upper Elevator Dock

To the right at the top of the stairway is another area with multiple elevators. The elevator in the room is not usable yet, but the cage elevator can be operated, and will take you back down to the Elevator Platform. From there, you can take the other elevator down to easily reach the Mergo's Loft: Base Lamp if you need to. When you step onto the elevator you may notice that the cage door is broken and doesn't shut; that should be your first clue that there is something hidden nearby. Keep looking at the building during the elevator's descent and you'll notice an open window at about the halfway point. Since the cage door is broken you can roll out of the elevator and through the window to reach the Upper Bridge. [→□ 02]

01

02

- ㉘ Bloodstone Chunk ×2
- ㉙ Infected Organ ×1
- ㉚ Kin Coldblood (11) ×1
- ㉛ Tempering Damp Blood Gem (5) ×1
- ㉜ Choir Bell ×1
- ㉝ Great One's Wisdom ×1
- ㉞ Arcane Damn Blood Gem (5) ×1
- ㉟ Great One's Wisdom ×1
- ㊱ Great One's Wisdom ×1
- ㊲ Great One's Wisdom ×1
- ㊳ Damp Bloodtinge Gem (5) ×1
- ㊴ Madman's Knowledge ×1
- ㊵ Blood Rock ×1

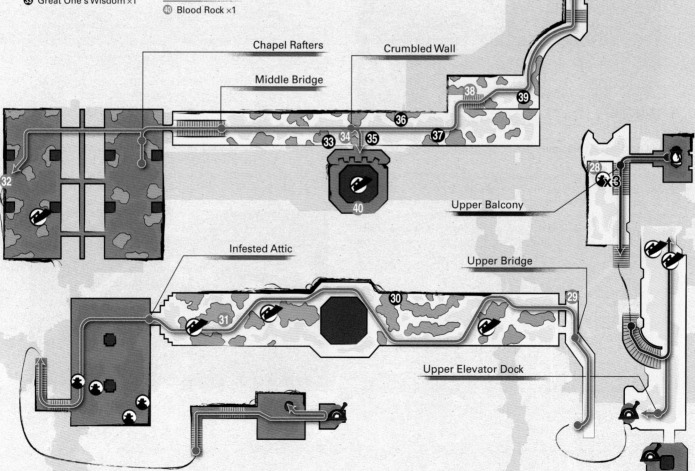

Chapel Rafters

Crumbled Wall

Middle Bridge

Upper Balcony

Infested Attic

Upper Bridge

Upper Elevator Dock

Upper Bridge ㉙ ㉛

Before heading out onto the bridge, be sure to open the nearby chest to get the Inflicted Organ ritual material. You should already be able to hear the song of the Winter Lantern from the bridge. Try to watch its movements through the archways and only go out onto the bridge when it's safe to do so. Use the cover on the bridge to work your way along it, and take out the Winter Lantern once you're close enough. You can skip killing these enemies and still make it across safely by using the cover, but since they have a high chance of dropping very powerful Blood Gems, it's worth trying to kill them. There are two more Winter Lanterns on the second half of the bridge, and it's much easier to kill each one as you come to it rather than sneak past them. Just to be safe, however, you may want to put some Sedatives in your Quick Items if you have them. A very powerful Droplet-shaped Blood Gem that increases your Physical Attack by 18% can also be found here, so make sure you pick it up before moving on. [→☐ 03]

Infested Attic

This attic area is infested with a number of Human-headed Nightmare Apostles. Try to progress slowly and only fight them one at a time. If you get surrounded, retreat back through the doorway. The corridor at the back leads to another room with a hole in the floor, and there's a switch on a small ledge just outside. Pulling the switch will release the chains holding the Brain of Mensis in place, sending it crashing down to the abyss below. This will allow you to traverse the start of the area without having to worry about its gaze. After pulling the switch, return to the hole and drop through it. [→☐ 04]

㉜ Chapel Rafters

A Winter Lantern is patrolling on the other side of this room, so as soon as you land, quickly run behind one of the nearby pillars, so that you're out of its line of sight. Try to position your camera so that you can see where the Winter Lantern is, and when it's all the way to one side of the room, quickly move down and cross the beams at the opposite end. Be careful while crossing, because a fall from this height would mean certain death. Once you're on the other side, hide behind one of the pillars again and wait for the Winter Lantern to get close to you before attacking it. When the area is all clear, grab the Choir Bell from the chest, and then cross back over to the other side of the room to reach the Middle Bridge.

㉞ ㉟ Middle Bridge

With the Brain of Mensis dropped from its housing you're free to explore the Middle Bridge at your leisure, since there are no other enemies in the area. There are a large number of items to pick up from the corpses of the Brain's victims, including some more useful Droplet Blood Gems. If you go down the stairway near the end of the bridge, there's a path you can follow to reach the other side of the iron gate, leading back into the area where you faced Micolash.

㊵ Crumbled Wall

Near the centre of the Middle Bridge there is a crumbled section of wall that you can walk through. This lets you reach the top of a room just to the side of the bridge, with a large hole in the middle. Look down over the edge first, and drop down very carefully. At the back of this room you'll find a precious Blood Rock, an item of extreme rarity. With it, you'll finally be able to upgrade one of your weapons to +10 when you return to the Hunter's Dream. The only way out of this room is through a small hole in the wall that leads out onto a ledge, from which you can drop down onto the Lower Bridge.

While you're in this area it's the perfect time to head back into the Panopticon and use the now active Elevator to the Abyss to reach what remains of the Brain of Mensis. It cannot fight back and does not inflict Frenzy, so there is no risk in heading down there for the large amount of Blood Echoes and a rare Chalice Dungeon material that it drops. Before killing it, however, if you've been to the Upper Cathedral Ward and got the "Make Contact" Gesture, strike the pose in front of the Brain and hold it for a while to be rewarded with a high level Moon Caryll Rune. Once it's been killed, return to the Panopticon and use the Base Elevator to get back outside, from where you can use the cage elevators to get back up to the Upper Elevator Dock. [→☐ 05/06]

Nightmare of Mensis

ing Nightmare for some more Bloodstones, and skip fighting the Maneater Boars along Boar Alley. Be careful when you reach the stairs at the end of the path, however, because there are two Shadows of Yharnam in a small balcony area at the top.

Instead of going straight onto that balcony, walk slowly along the path until you see one of the enemies standing in an archway with its back to you – begin the fight with a charged R2 for an early advantage. Similar caution should be employed when you reach the top of the stairs just past the balcony, because there's a group of four Shadows of Yharnam patrolling in that area. Watch their patrol route and stick close to the wall at the top of the stairs; you can usually lure one or two of the enemies towards you at a time, so that you don't have to fight the entire group at once. You can also wait for them to have their backs to you and throw Pebbles to lure them for a slightly safer approach. [→☐ 04]

⁴³ Boar Alley

At the top of the main stairs you'll see a Maneater Boar standing a short distance ahead, with its back to you. Approach it quietly and use a charged R2 from behind, following up with a visceral attack for an easy victory. Two more Maneater Boars patrol up and down the alley. Stay behind cover and wait for them to begin walking away, so that you can run up behind them and attack them before they can turn around. If you do get spotted early and one of them charges, make use of the trees and railings in the area to block the attack, and then kill it during the recovery period.

You'll also run into the patrolling Shadows of Yharnam along this route. As you get near the alley it's worth hugging the building on the left and using it to hide your presence, so that you can use Pebbles to lure them out one at a time. It is possible to get the Maneater Boars to charge straight into them, but the timing required to set it up is quite difficult, so it will usually be easier to kill them all yourself.

⁴⁶ Mergo's Loft: Rooftop

Standing outside the entrance to the boss area, you'll find the distraught Pthumerian Bride crying in anguish over the loss of her child. You cannot talk or interact with her, but if you return to where she is standing after defeating Mergo's Wet Nurse, she will graciously thank you and disappear. If you continue along the path past the bride, you'll arrive at an elevator that will take you back down to the Upper Elevator Dock. From there, you have quick access back down to the Mergo's Loft: Base Lamp. The upcoming boss fight is very difficult, so it's highly recommended that you make the trip and resupply before confronting it.

Rooftop Path

Two Shadows of Yharnam can be seen walking away in the distance when you head down this path – try to catch up with them and engage them as quickly as possible. A third one that uses ranged attacks is standing atop a wall just beyond the first two, and fighting them before you get in range of his attacks is much easier. If you have any Shaman Bone Blades, it can be worth using one here to make the two enemies fight each other. Otherwise, once you've engaged them you should bring the fight away from the third one to avoid getting too close to him. [→☐ 01-03]

Rooftop Stairs ⁴¹

When you reach the base of this large stairway there are three possible routes that you can take: the main stairs going up, a smaller set of stairs going down to the left, and a ledge to the far left. The narrow ledge will take you around the side of the building to a hidden item, and the stairway going down leads to a small dead end area, which is where you'll land if you want to exit the Moonlit Path at this end.

Moonlit Path ⁴²

Following the rail around to the left after reaching the top of the Rooftop Stairs will lead you to a broken section that you can drop through in order to reach this path. If you took this path accidentally, you can take the small set of stairs nearby and drop down into another path, leading back around to the base of the Rooftop Stairs. By continuing along the path, you'll be able to kill a Wander-

BOSS Mergo's Wet Nurse

It can be extremely difficult to get close to this boss due to the large radius of its multi-hit attacks, so you may want to consider using Bone Marrow Ash-strengthened Pistol shots to weaken it from range. Upon defeating the boss you'll automatically receive One Third of Umbilical Cord, which is one of the items required to see the true ending, and the Wet Nurse's Lunarium Lamp will appear in the middle of the room. [→☐ 05]

World Changes

- Gain access to the Wet Nurse's Lunarium Lamp
- Acquire One Third of Umbilical Cord

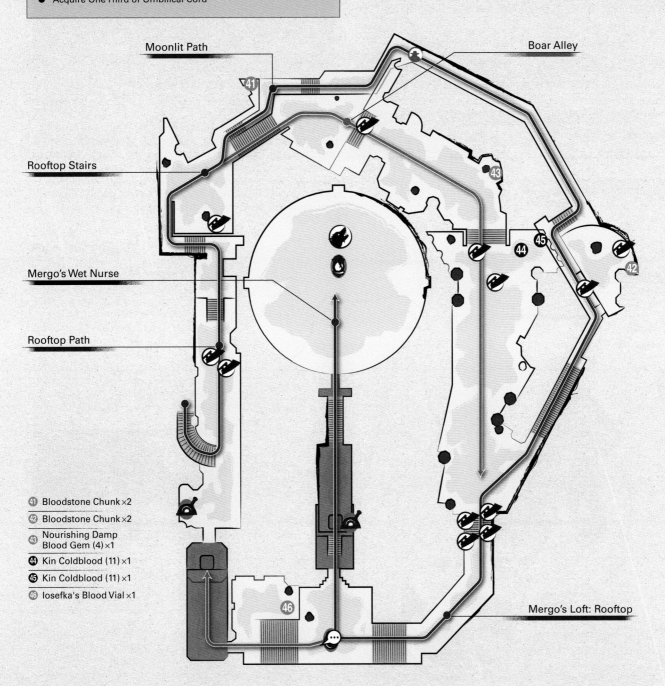

Moonlit Path

Boar Alley

Rooftop Stairs

Mergo's Wet Nurse

Rooftop Path

Mergo's Loft: Rooftop

㊶ Bloodstone Chunk ×2
㊷ Bloodstone Chunk ×2
㊸ Nourishing Damp Blood Gem (4) ×1
㊹ Kin Coldblood (11) ×1
㊺ Kin Coldblood (11) ×1
㊻ Iosefka's Blood Vial ×1

2

Hunter's Dream (Late Blood Moon)

The workshop, home to the hunters and their tools, is an inferno. The Doll greets you calmly and informs you that Gehrman awaits by the great tree. As you draw near, you see his face. The lines of worry seem somehow deeper in the moonlight. You can barely hear his ancient voice over the rustling of flowers in the wind, but he speaks to you of mercy. He speaks to you of the end. The first hunter is here. You are here. The moon is present.

Difficulty	Area – | Gehrman, the First Hunter **S** | Moon Presence **S**
Recommended	Player Level **70-80** | Weapon Upgrade **+9**
Timezones	○ ◐ ☾ ●
Insight	Encounter Gehrman, the First Hunter ×1, Defeat Gehrman, the First Hunter ×3, Encounter the Moon Presence ×5, Defeat the Moon Presence ×5

Enemies

Boss	HP	Echoes	Page
Gehrman, the First Hunter	14293	128000	p356
Moon Presence	8909	230000	p358

NPC

Name	Page
Doll	p635
Gehrman, the First Hunter	p634
Bath Messenger	p664
Insight Trade	p666
Stump Messenger	–

Workshop

Return to the Hunter's Dream after defeating Mergo's Wet Nurse and you'll find that things have taken a turn for the worse, as the end of the night rapidly approaches. Although the Workshop is now ablaze, you can still enter and make use of the facilities within, and all of the tombstones outside also remain fully functional. Carry out any last minute upgrades now, and attend to any unfinished business before heeding the doll's advice and making your way to The Great Tree.

The Great Tree

The gate that was once locked in the Lower Garden is now open. Head through it to reach Gehrman, who sits below The Great Tree. If you want to see the true ending to the game, make sure that you've used three One Third of Umbilical Cord items before speaking with Gehrman. No matter which outcome you choose, you'll automatically begin New Game+ upon completion, so make sure you do everything you want to do before continuing. [→□ 01]

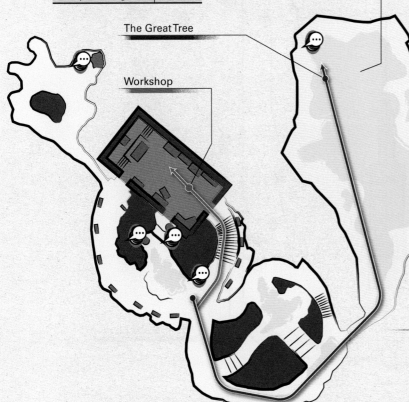

Gehrman, the First Hunter

The Great Tree

Workshop

01

BOSS Gehrman, the First Hunter

After talking to Gehrman for a while he'll present you with a question, and your answer will determine how the nightmare ends.

Yharnam Sunrise Ending

- If you choose "Submit your life" during the conversation with Gehrman, the game will come to an end without any further battles.

Honoring Wishes Ending

- Refuse Geherman when he poses the question and you will have to face him in battle.

Childhood's Beginning Ending

- Use three One Third of Umbilical Cord item before talking to Gehrman, and then select "Refuse" when prompted. You will then face Gehrman as usual, immediately followed by the Moon Presence.

Gehrman is an extremely agile enemy that attacks aggressively while constantly moving around, making it very difficult to stay locked on to him. Be careful with your attacks because he can interrupt your attacks with his gunshots' be patient and wait for him to make the first move, and you can interrupt him instead. Once he's been defeated, you'll automatically receive the Old Hunter Badge and, if you have not used three One Third of Umbilical Cord items, the game will come to an end. If you did use them, however, there will be one final challenge to overcome…

BOSS Moon Presence

Assuming you've met the requirements, the battle with the Moon Presence will begin as soon as you defeat Gehrman, so you'll have very little time to compose yourself. If you need a bit more time (or just want to resupply), you can exit the game and load your save file, and you'll reappear outside of the boss room with full access to the shops and other areas. This also happens if you die in the battle, so don't worry too much. Once you're fully stocked up, make your way back towards The Great Tree to begin fighting the Moon Presence. The head or limbs should be your primary targets during this intense battle; damaging them sufficiently will cause the creature to stumble or stagger, allowing you to get more hits in.

> **Congratulations on making it through the night, but a new day is dawning, and a new nightmare will surely follow…**

One Third of Umbilical Cord Locations

Area	Location	Page	Info
Healing Church Workshop	Abandoned Old Workshop	p71	After entering the Workshop you'll find the item sitting on the altar.
Cathedral Ward	Oedon Chapel	p48	Fulfill certain conditions within Arianna's quest (p639).
Iosefka's Clinic	3rd Floor Operating Room	p103	Enter the room during the Blood Moon when Imposter Iosefka is still alive and kill her.
Nightmare of Mensis	Mergo's Loft: Rooftop	p158	Defeat Mergo's Wet Nurse.

New Game+

Upon starting New Game+ all of the Key Items you acquired on your previous playthrough will be stripped away. You do, however, get to keep all of your other items, including all dungeon materials and Chalices. All of your stats and weapons will also carry over.

The biggest change in New Game+ is to the enemy's stats; they all hit much harder and have more health. The increase to their stats is dependent on the area, with earlier parts of the game getting a much bigger increase than later ones, so you'll need to be on your toes right from the start. The values in the table below show you how much enemy stats are multiplied by in each area on your first NG+ playthrough. The values are not absolute, though; many enemies have unique multipliers as required to keep the balance intact. This means they should only be taken as a rough guideline for how the New Game+ system works.

The only enemies that are not affected by these changes are the ones found in dungeons; they will remain the same regardless of how many playthroughs you've done. If you chose the Yharnam Sunrise ending, you'll also notice a new Tombstone in the Hunter's Dream that the Doll will sometimes pray at; maybe she has fond memories of someone she once knew?

Enemy stat changes by area

Area											
Central Yharnam (1st Half)	7.9	15.5	1.4	2.5	2.5	2.5	2.5	1.5	1.5	1.5	1.5
Central Yharnam (2nd Half)	6.4	19.1	1.3	2.3	2.3	2.3	2.3	1.4	1.4	1.4	1.4
Old Yharnam	5.3	9.5	1.3	2.1	2.1	2.1	2.1	1.4	1.4	1.4	1.4
Cathedral Ward (Evening)	5.2	5.2	1.4	1.9	1.9	1.9	1.9	1.4	1.4	1.4	1.4
Cathedral Ward (Night)	5.2	5.5	1.3	1.8	1.8	1.8	1.8	1.4	1.4	1.4	1.4
Cathedral Ward (Blood Moon)	4.5	6.9	1.3	1.7	1.7	1.7	1.7	1.3	1.3	1.3	1.3
Hemwick Charnel Lane	4.5	6.6	1.3	1.6	1.6	1.6	1.6	1.4	1.4	1.4	1.4
Forbidden Woods	4.0	5.3	1.3	1.4	1.4	1.4	1.4	1.2	1.2	1.2	1.2
Yahar'gul (Evening)	4.0	6.0	1.3	1.4	1.4	1.4	1.4	1.3	1.3	1.3	1.3
Lecture Building 1F and Nightmare Frontier (1st half)	4.0	5.1	1.3	1.4	1.4	1.4	1.4	1.2	1.2	1.2	1.2
Nightmare Frontier (2nd half)	3.5	6.9	1.4	1.4	1.4	1.4	1.4	1.2	1.2	1.2	1.2
Byrgenwerth	2.5	5.1	1.2	1.3	1.3	1.3	1.3	1.2	1.2	1.2	1.2
Forsaken Cainhurst Castle	1.9	4.6	1.2	1.3	1.3	1.3	1.3	1.2	1.2	1.2	1.2
Yahar'gul (Blood Moon)	1.9	4.2	1.2	1.2	1.2	1.2	1.2	1.1	1.1	1.1	1.1
Upper Cathedral Ward	1.6	4.1	1.2	1.2	1.2	1.2	1.2	1.1	1.1	1.1	1.1
Lecture Building 2F and Nightmare of Mensis (1st half)	1.5	3.9	1.2	1.1	1.1	1.1	1.1	1.1	1.1	1.1	1.1
Nightmare of Mensis (2nd half)	1.5	3.2	1.1	1.1	1.1	1.1	1.1	1.0	1.0	1.0	1.0

Beyond New Game+

The increase in difficulty does not stop after your first playthrough – you can keep making things more and more difficult all the way up to your 7th playthrough. The Game Cycle chart shows the multipliers for further rounds of NG+. These are applied to the values in the above table, and not to the game base values. This means that while these multipliers are always static, the resulting stat increases may seem inconsistent, because they are being applied to the guideline values which can be slightly different on a per-enemy basis.

Game Cycle		
3	1.07	1.10
4	1.10	1.25
5	1.125	1.50
6	1.15	2.00
7	1.20	2.50

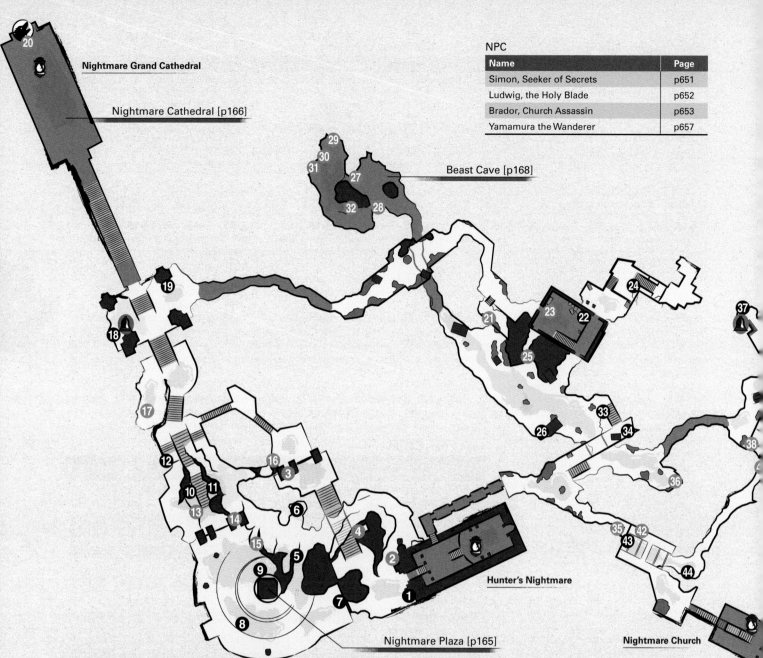

Nightmare Grand Cathedral

Nightmare Cathedral [p166]

Beast Cave [p168]

Hunter's Nightmare

Nightmare Plaza [p165]

Nightmare Church

NPC

Name	Page
Simon, Seeker of Secrets	p651
Ludwig, the Holy Blade	p652
Brador, Church Assassin	p653
Yamamura the Wanderer	p657

Enemies

Regular	HP	Echoes	Page
Old Hunter (Beast Cutter & Blunderbuss)	1727/3331	842/1126	p255
Old Hunter (Beasthunter Saif)	1520/3109	771/994	p256
Old Hunter (Beasthunter Saif & Piercing Rifle)	829	811	p256
Old Hunter (Boom Hammer & Torch)	1865/3559	913/1237	p257
Beast Patient (Male)	552	203	p236
Ashen Blood Beast Patient	1451	507	p237
Church Servant (Cane)	2064	871	p234
Huntsman (Torch & Axe)	760	355	p225
Huntsman (Sickle)	483	338	p226
Huntsman (Cleaver)	483	270	p226
Huntsman (Cutlass)	760	338	p227
Huntsman (Delayed Molotov)	483	331	p228
Old Hunter's Hound	483	372	p230
Labyrinth Rat	535	1198	p233
Carrion Crow	483	220	p231
Wandering Nightmare (Small)	186	27	p671

Strong	HP	Echoes	Page
Nightmare Executioner (Axe)	3455	2366	p306
Nightmare Executioner (Church Cannon)	3455	2366	p307
Bloodlicker	1658	517	p308
Blood-starved Beast	5183	2366	p330
Eye Collector	760	304	p277

Hunter	HP	Echoes	Page
Djura's Disciple	3196	7326	p321
Bestial Hunter	4134	6105	p321
Church Doctor (Ludwig's Holy Blade & Repeating Pistol)	3332	8820	p322
Church Doctor (Threaded Cane)	2194	11025	p323
Yahar'gul Hunter (Church Pick & Repeating Pistol)	2739	9923	p323

Boss	HP	Echoes	Page
Ludwig the Accursed	16658	34500	p360
Laurence, the First Vicar	21243	29500	p363

Hunter's Nightmare (OH)

Difficulty	Area **B** | Ludwig the Accursed **A** | Laurence, the First Vicar **A**
Recommended	Player Level **80** | Weapon Upgrade **+9**
Timezones	○ ◐ ☾ ●
Insight	Reach the Hunter's Nightmare for the first time ×2
	Reach the Underground Corpse Pile and encounter Ludwig the Accursed ×1
	Defeat Ludwig the Accursed ×3
	Encounter Laurence, the First Vicar in the Nightmare Grand Cathedral ×1
	Defeat Laurence, the First Vicar ×3

In Yharnam, there are whispered rumors of hunters who go drunk with blood – they are whisked away into a horrible nightmare, where they engage in an eternal hunt. According to gossip, though, this is a special fate reserved only for hunters who are overcome by the scourge of the beast. It may be common hearsay, but you feel reassured that this fate could never befall you; whatever monstrosity it is that delivers hunters to this awful fate should have no business with a sane hunter like yourself. But perhaps you shouldn't have carried the eye of a blood-drunk hunter in your pocket...

2

For more information on how to access this area, please refer back to p171

Item legend

1. Frenzied Coldblood (8)
2. Twin Blood Stone Shards ×1
3. Old Hunter Cap
4. Old Hunter Gloves
5. Blood Vial ×3
6. Frenzied Coldblood (9)
7. Blood Vial ×6
8. Madman's Knowledge ×1
9. Madman's Knowledge ×1
10. Quicksilver Bullets ×4
11. Molotov Cocktail ×4
12. Blood Vial ×3
13. Beast Cutter
14. Twin Blood Stone Shards ×3
15. Twin Blood Stone Shards ×3
16. Old Hunter Trousers
17. Old Hunter Garb
18. Molotov Cocktail ×3
19. Blood Vial ×6
20. Eye Pendant
21. Twin Blood Stone Shards ×1
22. Delayed Molotov ×5
23. Boom Hammer
24. Beast Blood Pellet ×3
25. Old Hunter Top Hat
26. Frenzied Coldblood (8)
27. Blood Stone Chunk ×1
28. Twin Blood Stone Shards ×1
29. Amygdalan Arm
30. Twin Blood Stone Shards ×2
31. Twin Blood Stone Shards ×2
32. Blood Stone Chunk ×1
33. Blood Vial ×3
34. Quicksilver Bullets ×6
35. Constable's Gloves
36. Constable's Trousers
37. Frenzied Coldblood (9)
38. Constable's Garb
39. Beasthunter Saif
40. Butcher Mask, Garb, Gloves, Trousers
41. Madman's Knowledge ×1
42. Twin Blood Stone Shards ×2
43. Blood Vial ×2
44. Oil Urn ×3
45. Whirligig Saw
46. Blood Vial ×6
47. Pebble ×1
48. Blood Vial ×3
49. Frenzied Coldblood (9)
50. Frenzied Coldblood (9)
51. Fist of Gratia
52. Blood Stone Chunk ×1
53. Great One's Wisdom
54. Laurence's Skull
55. Church Cannon

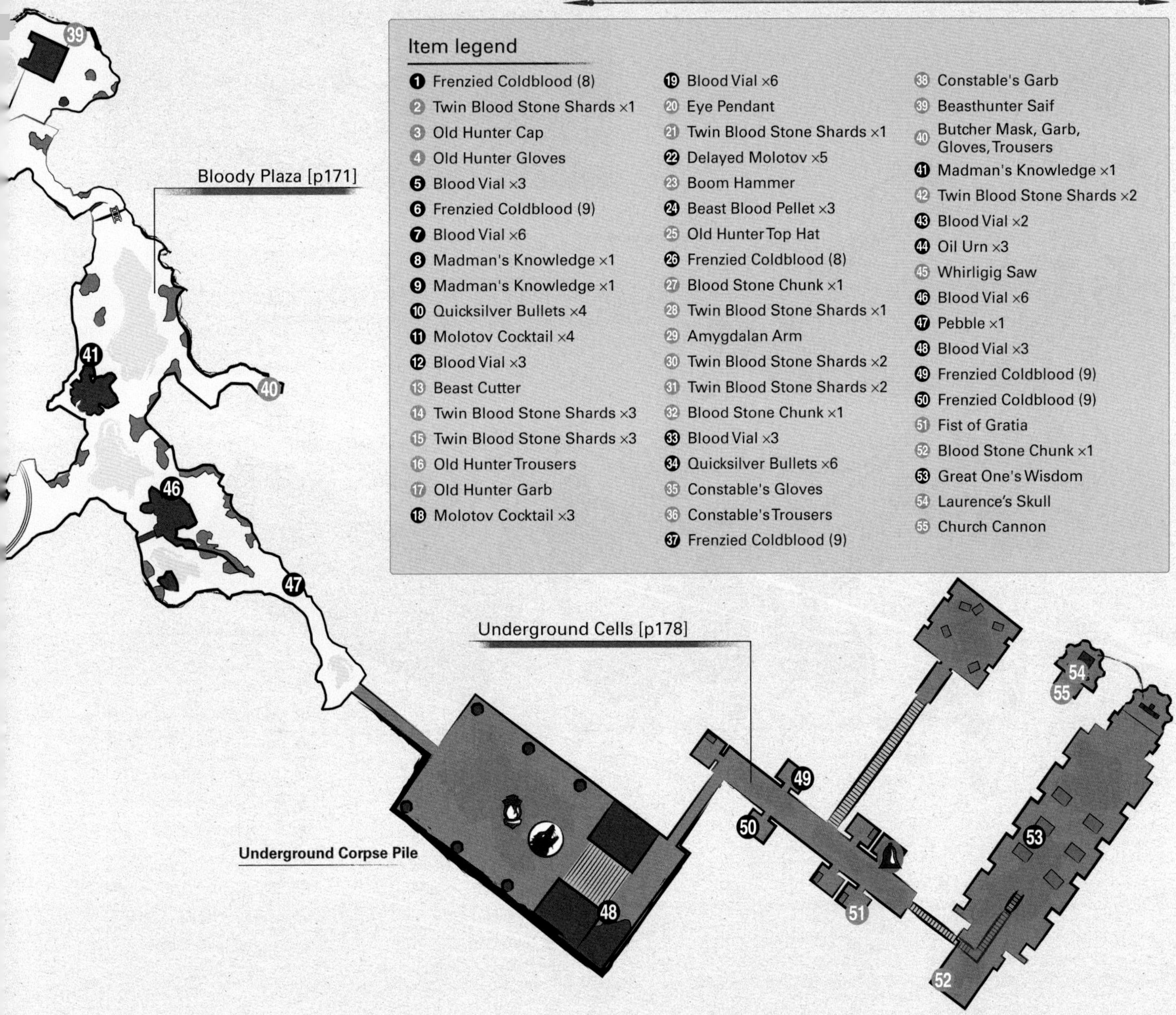

Bloody Plaza [p171]

Underground Cells [p178]

Underground Corpse Pile

Hunter's Nightmare

Nightmare Chapel ❶ ❷

After being squeezed out of existence by Amygdala you'll find yourself in an eerily familiar area. Before moving ahead too far to investigate, make sure you light the Hunter's Nightmare lamp in the room. Stepping outside of the chapel reveals the world to be a twisted nightmare version of the Cathedral Ward, but do not expect past knowledge to be enough to get by on.

If you approach the bottom of the chapel stairs, an Old Hunter will start to make his way slowly down towards you, and while you can skip this enemy if you want, it's worth taking the time to fight him. You'll encounter Old Hunters frequently during this area, so learning how to fight them is extremely important. Since you can fight this one on its own and near a lamp, there is no better time to practice. The stairway here leads up to a large gate that you cannot open from this side, so when you're ready to continue, head up the narrow path to the side of the stairs. [→☐ 01]

❹ Rooftop Path

As you start to round the corner about halfway along this path, you'll see a pair of Beast Patients further ahead of you; if you hang back without alerting them, another Old Hunter will appear over the crest of the hill and kill them for you, netting you some easy Blood Echoes. The Old Hunters will often tend to kill any other beasts in the area if they spot them first, and you can use this to your advantage if you pay attention.

Due to the distances here, it's best to wait until the Beast Patients have been killed before moving up to take on the Old Hunter. Near that halfway point of the path there's a partially exposed rooftop that

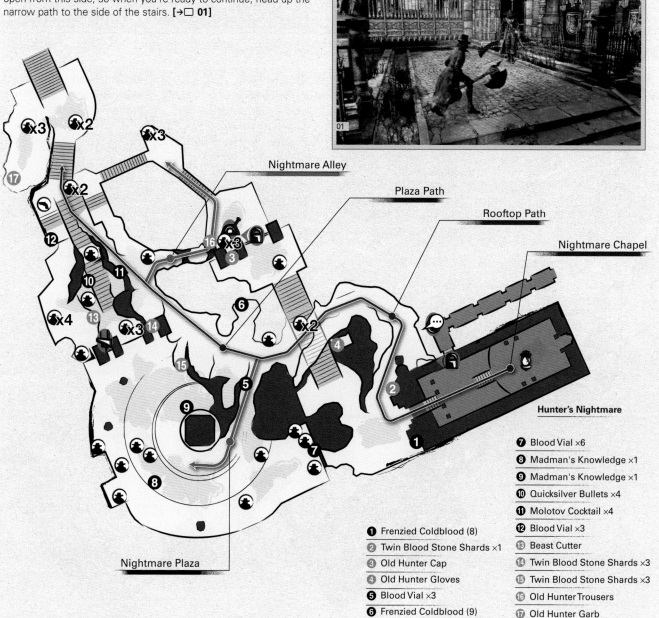

01

Hunter's Nightmare

❼ Blood Vial ×6
❽ Madman's Knowledge ×1
❾ Madman's Knowledge ×1
❿ Quicksilver Bullets ×4
⓫ Molotov Cocktail ×4
⓬ Blood Vial ×3
⓭ Beast Cutter
⓮ Twin Blood Stone Shards ×3
⓯ Twin Blood Stone Shards ×3
⓰ Old Hunter Trousers
⓱ Old Hunter Garb

❶ Frenzied Coldblood (8)
❷ Twin Blood Stone Shards ×1
❸ Old Hunter Cap
❹ Old Hunter Gloves
❺ Blood Vial ×3
❻ Frenzied Coldblood (9)

Nightmare Alley
Plaza Path
Rooftop Path
Nightmare Chapel
Nightmare Plaza

As you make your way down into the plaza, a number of Beast Patients will begin to congregate near an archway at **Position A**, so hold your ground and wait for them to finish grouping up. In addition to that main group, there's also a group of three Beast Patients around the corner to the left at **Position B**, and another group far to the right at **Position C**. While it may seem like a large amount of enemies, the Beast Patients in this area are a lot more timid than usual and spend most of their time recoiling in fear. You're not the only one hunting them either; there are Old Hunters hidden at **Positions D and E** and you can use the natural hatred both enemies have for each other to take advantage of the situation.

Start making your way towards the largest group of enemies at **Position A** and try to dodge past the first couple that you come to, so that you can get close to the wall just to right of the gate in this area. As soon as you reach that point, the nearby Old Hunter should come out from behind the wall and begin attacking the Beast Patients. Since the Beast Patients are a lot easier to kill than the Old Hunter, wait for him to engage a couple of them, and then try to move around to his back and either use a charged R2 or a couple of quick R1 attacks while he's distracted. If you don't manage to kill him in your first attempt, simply back off a bit until he switches focus back to Beast Patients and try again.

A short while after you start the fight, the Old Hunter at **Position E** will emerge. He'll engage the Beast Patients near him at **Position C**, but since there are not many enemies over there to keep him occupied he'll soon start making his away over to you. This means that taking out the first Old Hunter quickly is important, to avoid fighting them both in the same area. If you run out of Beast Patients near **Position A** before killing both of the Old Hunters, lure them back down to **Position B** so that the ones there can take their attention.

you can drop down onto for some Attire. It's also possible to lure the Old Hunter onto the rooftop, and once there he sometimes gets stuck, which allows you to drop down to the stairs below and use ranged attacks to kill him.

❻ ⑭ ⑮ **Plaza Path**

This narrow path that follows alongside the plaza provides you with an alternate route to the Nightmare Cathedral Stairs, just in case you want to avoid the fight in the plaza. Just as you reach the narrow gap between the large arch and a tower, you'll see a section of rooftop leading down to the plaza, and if you follow it you'll be able to find an item hidden on a ledge. Be careful, however, as you will not be able to go back the way you came, and if you haven't already cleared out the plaza you'll have to fight or run past a large number of enemies to get back to where you were.

Just as you pass through that narrow gap, a pair of Old Hunter's Hounds will come running towards you. Wait for them to reach you before attacking them, because there is another Old Hunter just up ahead on the right. Behind that Old Hunter is a path that you can take to open a shortcut. This path splits near the end, and it's better to go up the slope on the right, as the platform will block the shots of the Old Hunter that will start attacking you. [→☐ 02]

❸ ⑯ **Nightmare Alley**

Be careful when dropping down to this area because there's an item on a ledge that you can drop onto, and it's very easy to overshoot it if you're running too fast or rolling. When you land you'll also have to face a small group of Carrion Crows, so begin attacking straight away before they get a chance to react. Pulling the nearby lever will open the large gate next to it, creating a shortcut between the Nightmare Chapel and the narrow stairs leading up to the middle of the Nightmare Cathedral Stairs. At the mid-point of those narrow stairs there's a group of Beast Patients huddled in the corner with their backs to you – either spare them or finish them off. [→☐ 03]

Hunter's Nightmare

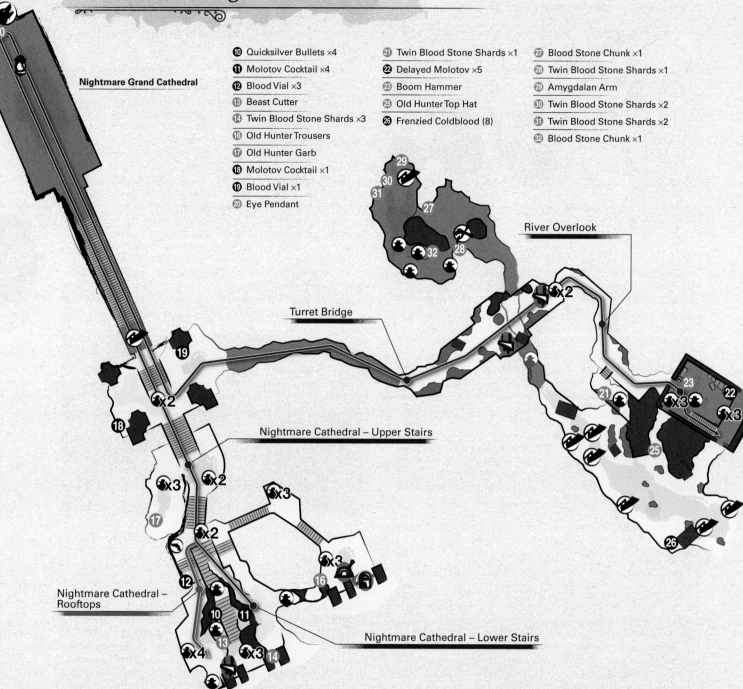

Nightmare Grand Cathedral

10 Quicksilver Bullets ×4
11 Molotov Cocktail ×4
12 Blood Vial ×3
13 Beast Cutter
14 Twin Blood Stone Shards ×3
16 Old Hunter Trousers
17 Old Hunter Garb
18 Molotov Cocktail ×1
19 Blood Vial ×1
20 Eye Pendant

21 Twin Blood Stone Shards ×1
22 Delayed Molotov ×5
23 Boom Hammer
25 Old Hunter Top Hat
26 Frenzied Coldblood (8)

27 Blood Stone Chunk ×1
28 Twin Blood Stone Shards ×1
29 Amygdalan Arm
30 Twin Blood Stone Shards ×2
31 Twin Blood Stone Shards ×2
32 Blood Stone Chunk ×1

River Overlook

Turret Bridge

Nightmare Cathedral – Upper Stairs

Nightmare Cathedral – Rooftops

Nightmare Cathedral – Lower Stairs

Nightmare Cathedral – Lower Stairs 10 11

As soon as you reach this point you'll come under fire from a Old Hunter with a Piercing Rifle so you'll need to use the environment for cover. If you're coming from the Plaza Path you can use the platform as cover, but if you're approaching from Nightmare Alley you'll need to use the statues at the top of the stairs. This enemy usually fires twice in quick succession before pausing briefly and firing again, so stay behind cover until you see him fire twice, and then run over and attack him quickly. If you did not previously clear out the Plaza, you'll also have a couple of Beast Patients and another Old Hunter at the bottom of the stairs, but if you want to take them out, it's far better to follow the path along the Nightmare Cathedral – Rooftops rather than to go straight down the stairs.

12 13 Nightmare Cathedral – Rooftops

To reach this area you'll need to drop down from the ledge at the top of the Lower Stairs, after which you can follow a narrow pathway to reach the rooftops. Along the rooftops are a number of completely docile Beast Patients that will not attack you regardless of how close you get. If you attack one of them, however, they will all become hostile. To make matters worse, attacking them gets the attention of a nearby Old Hunter and he will drop down from the tower at the end of the rooftops and start attacking whatever is closest. As before, try to get him to focus on the Beast Patients first, and then run up and attack him. Make sure to grab the Beast Cutter weapon that's sitting at the end of the path before dropping back down.

If you previously avoided the Plaza, you'll also have to fight your way past another Old Hunter at the base of the Lower Stairs after you drop off the rooftops. This Old Hunter will also become alerted if you attack the group of Beast Patients above, but if that happens, you can hide at the back of the rooftops out of sight until he forgets about you. Then you can drop down and land a hit on him for an early advantage in the fight. Also in this area is a pressure plate that, when stepped on, activates a nearby turret that fires directly back towards the pressure plate. You can use this to attack the Old Hunter after you start fighting him, but you need to be careful not to get shot yourself.

Nightmare Cathedral – Upper Stairs ⑰ ⑱ ⑲ ⑳

As soon as you start making your way up these stairs you'll see a group of Beast Patients coming towards you from just ahead, but do not run up to attack them. Shortly after you see the Beast Patients, two Huntsmen near the top of the stairs will unleash a giant flaming ball of hay towards you – as soon as you see it coming you should run back down the stairs and onto one of the side platforms to avoid it. Thankfully, it should also take care of the Beast Patients for you. That's not the only trick those Huntsmen have up their sleeve, however, because once they start rolling the hay ball down towards you, they'll turn around and try to open the Nightmare Cathedral doors.

Unfortunately for them, a rather angry Nightmare Executioner is standing on the other side. This enemy is very deadly and you should be extremely careful when engaging him; if at any point you see him raise his axe vertically, you should close in as quickly as possible and attempt to land a charged R2 to his back before he can complete the attack. Not only does this attack cause a large blast around him, but afterwards he'll power himself up and become even more dangerous. After you've defeated him, enter the Cathedral and retrieve the Eye Pendant before coming back out and continuing along the path. [→☐ 01/02]

While there is no lamp in the Nightmare Cathedral at this time, if you return here later after obtaining a specific key item, you can trigger an event that will cause the lamp to appear. For more information on this, please refer to p180.

As soon as you exit the tunnel and look out over this bridge you'll come under fire from a number of turrets. Try to stay on the left-hand side of the path, as it has the most cover available. The turrets are being controlled by a Huntsman on a pressure plate just behind them, which means you have to cross the bridge to reach him. There is plenty of cover scattered along the bridge, and there are short breaks in the turrets' firing patterns – use these to move safely from cover to cover. Be careful as you approach the body of an Amygdala near the middle of the bridge, because there's another pressure plate just before it; stepping onto that plate will cause a turret on the opposite side of the bridge to fire on your position.

The best way to continue from the middle of the bridge is to keep hugging the left-hand side as much as possible, since that will keep you out of the turrets' line of fire. Once you get close enough to the turrets you can either destroy them, or wait for the Huntsman to step off the pressure plate and come after you. Behind that first line of turrets you'll also find a second Huntsman standing on another pressure plate that controls a turret shooting in the opposite direction to the others; simply attack him to knock him off the pressure plate to stop the turret from firing. [→☐ 03]

㉑ River Overlook

When you reach the bottom of the hill, a group of Huntsmen and a Old Hunter will be approaching. These particular Huntsmen primarily attack by throwing Delayed Molotovs. Avoiding the constant blasts while fighting the Old Hunter is very difficult, but thankfully the Huntsmen will not pursue you very far, so you can lure the Old Hunter back up the hill and fight him away from the other enemies, If the turrets are all still intact, you can even lure him up to the bridge and use them to kill him. [→☐ 04]

Hunter's Nightmare

Nightmare Residence

Nightmare Gate

Beast Cave

Bridge over the River of Blood

River of Blood – Downstream

Chapel Tunnel

Hunter's Nightmare

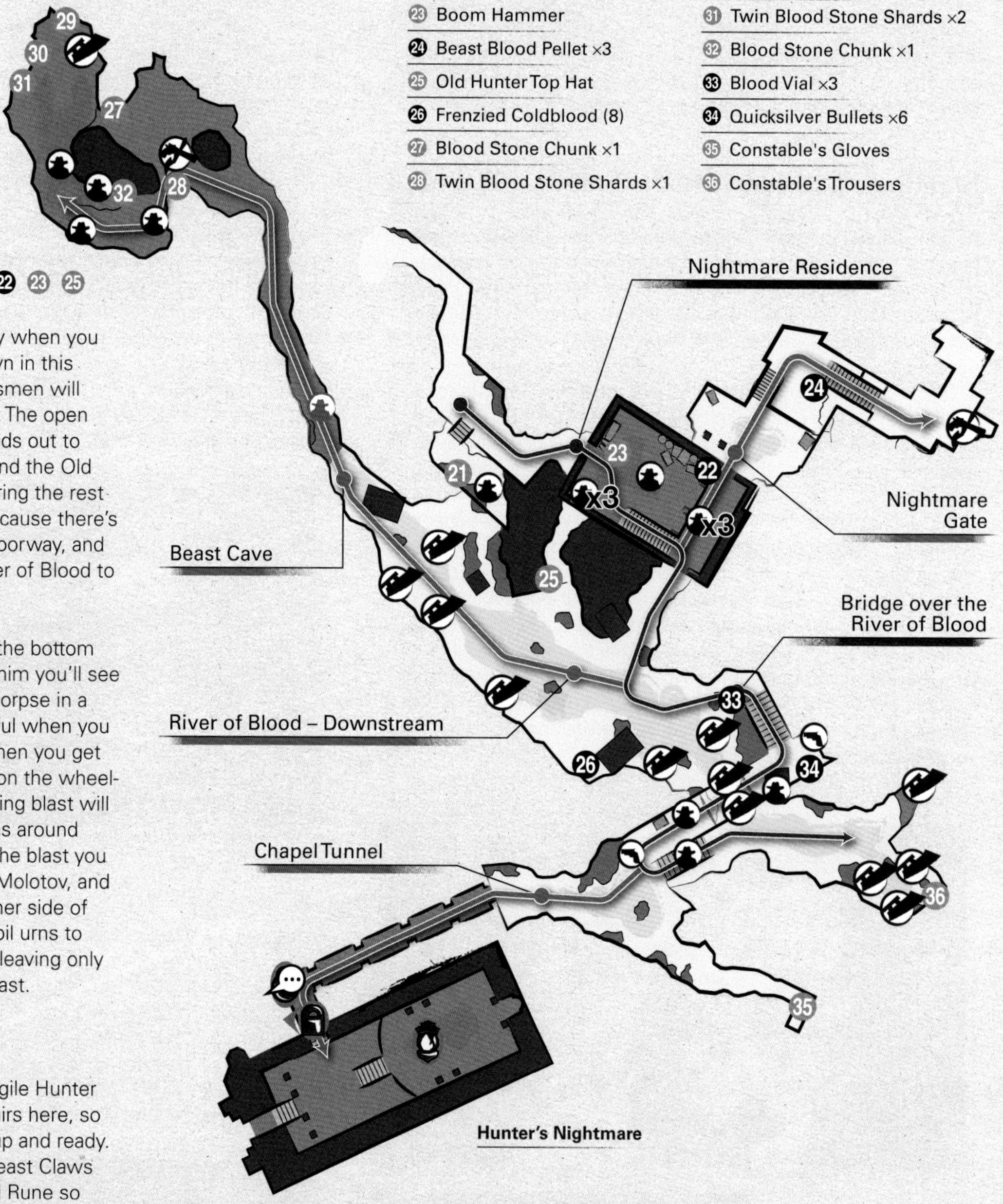

Nightmare Residence ㉒ ㉓ ㉕

Have your weapon at the ready when you get near the stairs leading down in this house, because a pair of Huntsmen will come running up to attack you. The open doorway on the upper floor leads out to a small ledge where you can find the Old Hunter Top Hat. It's worth clearing the rest of the house first, however, because there's no way back up through that doorway, and you'd have to go along the River of Blood to get back into the house.

There's another Huntsman on the bottom floor waiting for you, and past him you'll see an item on the floor next to a corpse in a wheelchair. Be extremely careful when you approach the item, because when you get close to it, a Delayed Molotov on the wheelchair will activate and the ensuing blast will cause a large number of oil urns around the room to explode. To avoid the blast you can either trigger the Delayed Molotov, and then quickly run back to the other side of the room, or shoot one of the oil urns to detonate them all beforehand, leaving only the easily avoidable Molotov blast.

Nightmare Gate ㉔

An extremely aggressive and agile Hunter awaits you at the top of the stairs here, so make sure you're fully healed up and ready. The enemy is equipped with Beast Claws and the Beast's Embrace Caryll Rune so you'll need to contend with that weapon's alternate moveset, which includes a lot of quick attacks, and long range jumping attacks. Upon defeating him you'll automatically get the Firing Hammer Badge, adding some new items to the shop inventory.

River of Blood – Downstream ㉖

There are a number of Bloodlickers along this section of the river, but if you take a cautious approach, you can pick them off one at a time and avoid getting ganged up on. Closest to you is one stationary Bloodlicker, and another one that patrols up and

down a short section of the river; the patrolling one will not move very far from the end of its patrol route even if it detects you, so use a pebble and lure the stationary one back and take it out first, and then kill the patrolling one. Just past those enemies you'll see two more Bloodlickers with their backs to you; use a pebble to lure one of them away from the other before killing it, which will let you sneak up on the undisturbed one and use a charged R2 to start the fight. Once all of the Bloodlickers have been taken care of, continue up the river past the large carriage and try to kill the Wandering Nightmare there before it can get too close to the cave entrance.

㉗ ㉘ ㉙ ㉚ ㉛ ㉜ Beast Cave

Be careful as you get near the end of the tunnel leading into this cave, because just inside it Djura's Disciple is waiting with a deadly Gatling Gun in hand. It can be quite hard to approach this enemy while he's constantly firing at you, so it's best not to take a direct approach. Instead, run towards the circular rock formation beside him. By moving around this rock you can easily block his shots and time your attacks for when he gets close. You'll also be able to easily move away to let your stamina restore. After killing him you'll get to take his Gatling Gun with you.

Further into the cave you'll see two more openings, both of which lead to the same place where a Blood-starved Beast is laying in wait. If you go to the opening directly opposite the entrance you can spot the beast and lure it towards you with a ranged attack. Since the ledge there stops it from reaching you, you can keep using ranged attacks to whittle its health down. If you decide to take the beast on at close range, it's worth remembering that it's susceptible to the effects of Pungent Blood Cocktails, so you can use them to create openings to attack. Killing the beast is extremely worthwhile, because doing so will allow you to claim the Amygdalan Arm weapon that it was guarding. [→☐ 01]

01

COMBAT FOCUS Bridge over the River of Blood ㉝ ㉞

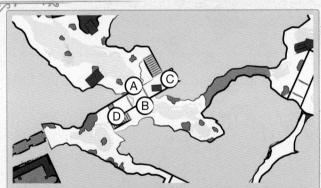

As you approach the bridge that crosses the river, a Huntsman will spot you and signal your arrival to a Old Hunter nearby, who will then run to **Position A** on the bridge. This Old Hunter is armed with a rifle, and trying to fight the group of Bloodlickers just below him will put you right in his crosshairs. Similarly, there's another Old Hunter on the other side of the bridge at **Position B** covering that section of the river. Trying to fight the Bloodlickers in the tight confines under the bridge, without straying into the line of fire from one of the Old Hunters above is very dangerous, so it's best to take out the Hunters first. With that in mind, hug the left side of the river and sprint up the stairs on that side to avoid the Hunter's shots, and then stop behind the overturned carriage at **Position C**.

You're totally safe at this position because the Hunters won't move and the Bloodlickers won't follow you this far if they detected you, so you can take a moment to survey the area. Once you're behind the carriage you'll also be out of the Old Hunter's line of sight, and if you stay there they'll forget about you after a

short while. There are other enemies on the bridge that you need to be aware of before moving out to attack anyone: the first is another Huntsman just on the other side of the carriage, and then a third one on the stairs at the opposite side of the bridge at **Position D**. Your first goal should be to take out the two Huntsmen on the bridge, and you can do this by taking advantage of the fact that the Old Hunters won't move. If you target and try to shoot the Huntsman just on the other side of the carriage, the sound will cause him to come running around to where you are so you can kill him behind cover.

The Huntsman that issued the signal is just beyond the Old Hunter at **Position A**, and since firearms or Pebbles don't have the range to reach him, you'll need to use a Throwing Knife or similar thrown weapon. Once you hit him, he'll come running down towards you again so that you can fight him behind the carriage. You should only have the two Old Hunters left on the bridge now, and how you deal with them will depend on what you have left in your arsenal. If you still have plenty of ranged options you can stick near the carriage and use them to pick off one of the Hunters while ducking back behind cover when they turn to shoot. Alternatively, you'll need to rush up to one of them and try to take him out as quickly as possible while keeping an eye on the other one and dodging whenever he shoots.

Since you'll get spotted by the Old Hunter at **Position B** regardless, it's generally best to go for him first; when you run behind the other one he'll usually try to use a melee attack on you, and rolling to avoid that should put you within range of the one at **Position B** with a bit of time before you have to worry about dodging again. Try to kill that enemy quickly, and then retreat back to take on the other Old Hunter, because the Huntsman at **Position D** will usually start coming up the stairs once the fighting starts and begin throwing Delayed Molotovs.

Once all of the enemies on the bridge have been killed, all that's left to deal with are the Bloodlickers under the bridge. To do that, start by going down the stairs at **Position D**. These Bloodlickers do not venture far out from beneath the bridge, so you can sneak up behind them and use a charged ⓡ2 attack, then retreat up the stairs to safety, wait for them to reset and repeat until they're dead.

㉟ **Chapel Tunnel**

When the Path splits on this side of the bridge splits, take the one going left, because it leads to a dead-end where you can get another piece of the Constable's Attire set. After collecting that, take the path to the right, enter the tunnel and speak to Simon when you reach him. For more information on Simon and the question he poses you, please refer to p651. A short distance past Simon you'll come to a large door that you can open, which leads back into the Nightmare Chapel and the lamp within it. [→☐ 02]

02

River of Blood – Upstream ㊱

There's a large group of Bloodlickers near the cliff at the back of this area, but if you just want to proceed you can ignore them and head straight into the nearby tunnel. If you want the piece of Constable's Attire they're guarding, however, you'll need to kill them all. The easiest way to do this is to lure them out one at a time using Pebbles, and fight them away from the main group. Should you happen to get the attention of more than one, they will only follow you to the base of the stairs near the bridge behind you, so you can always run back up to safety. [→ ⬚ 01]

Corpse Canal ㊲

A Old Hunter's Hound will come running down to attack you just as you reach the collapsed tower in this area, so have your weapon at the ready. After defeating it and rounding the corner near the tower, another Hound will come running around a corner ahead. Instead of coming after you it will stand its ground and bark, so you'll have to move up and take it out. The path the Hound was guarding leads to an item you can grab before moving on. When you round the top of the tower a Old Hunter will start walking towards you from the

01

㉝ Blood Vial ×3
㉞ Quicksilver Bullets ×6
㉟ Constable's Gloves
㊱ Constable's Trousers
㊲ Frenzied Coldblood (9)
㊳ Constable's Garb
㊴ Beasthunter Saif
㊵ Butcher Mask, Garb, Gloves, Trousers
㊶ Madman's Knowledge ×1
㊷ Twin Blood Stone Shards ×2
㊸ Blood Vial ×2
㊹ Oil Urn ×3
㊺ Whirligig Saw
㊻ Blood Vial ×6
㊼ Pebble ×1

River of Blood – Upstream

Corpse Canal

Balance Beams

Bloody Plaza

Corpse Ravine

Nightmare Church

Nightmare Church

far end of the canal, and although he walks quite slowly, it's best to wait for him to come to you; there are a large number of Carrion Crows along that section of the canal and it's much easier to fight him away from them. Once you've battled past all of the Crows, climb the ladder to get out of the canal and head along the path directly ahead. [→☐ 02]

Balance Beams ㊳ ㊴

From the top of the ladder, if you follow the railing to the left you'll come to a gap through which you can drop down onto a wooden beam below. Crossing that beam will lead you to the top of the section of wall, where you'll find the constable's Garb. After picking that up, drop down and make your way back up the ladder again. Head left from the top of the ladder again, and this time look for a gap just to the right of the pulley system that you can drop through, but make sure you're well prepared before you do. The Beasthunter Saif weapon is in this area, but before you can pick it up safely, you'll need to defeat a tough Old Hunter that's also using it. [→☐ 03]

Bloody Plaza ㊵ ㊶ ㊻

When you drop down into the plaza, a Nightmare Executioner with a Church Cannon will start walking towards you from the opposite end while firing grenades at you, so it's best not to stand around in the open. At the same time, a second Nightmare Executioner with an Axe will start making his way into the plaza from a path on the left. It's important to avoid having to fight both of these enemies at the same time. The best way to accomplish this is to quickly sprint up along the right-hand side of the plaza until you come to a large circular statue that you can use for cover. Move around to the back of the statue, and after waiting for the Nightmare Executioner to fire, run up and attack him before he can fire again.

If you keep the fight far enough away from the second Nightmare Executioner, he won't become aware of what's going on, and will then take up a stationary position near the middle of the area with his back to you. After killing the first one, you can then quietly approach the second one and use a charged R2 to stagger him for a Visceral Attack follow-up.

It's worth heading down the path the second Nightmare Executioner came from, because you'll be able to get the Butcher Attire set. If you've been to the Forbidden Woods, met with Valtr, joined the League, and have the Impurity Caryll Rune equipped you'll also find the summon point for Younger Madaras Twin at the end of this path. If you choose to summon this NPC, you won't be able to summon Henriett from her summon point near the Nightmare Church, but you will be able to summon Valtr at the Mouth of the River. [→☐ 04]

Nightmare Church

Before heading down the stairs inside the Church, make sure you light the lamp to the side of the sarcophagus to give yourself a restart point in this area. A Wandering Nightmare can be found at the bottom of the stairs, and you'll need to be quick to catch up to it and kill it before it can disappear. Just to the left from the base of the stairs you can also find the summon point for Henriett (providing you haven't already summoned Younger Madaras Twin). Choosing to summon Henriett will lock you out of summoning both Younger Madaras Twin and Valtr if you're a member of the League, which will mean you'll only have one partner to help you instead of two. [→☐ 05]

㊷ ㊸ ㊹ ㊺ Corpse Ravine

If you follow the path along in this area you'll come to a wooden bridge that leads to a ledge with an item on it. Be very careful as you start to cross the bridge, because a tough Old Hunter will drop down and attack you from behind. Try to fight this enemy on one of the ledges rather than the bridge to reduce the risk of getting knocked down to the area below, where there are numerous Carrion Crows. Dropping down afterwards, however, is worthwhile, because after fighting through the crows and following the ravine along, you'll be able to acquire the Whirligig Saw. Once you have the weapon you'll need to drop down from the stone tablet into the Corpse Canal area again and make your way back to where you started this detour.

Mouth of the River ⁴⁷

Hiding behind the wall at the top of the hill here is an Eye Collector with its back to you, so take advantage of the opportunity that presents itself and use a charged R2 from behind. From there, if you drop down to where all of the bodies are piled up in front of a gate you'll see that one of them is futilely banging away on the gate, and if you kill this enemy it will drop a number of Blood Vials. If you're a member of the League and haven't summoned Henriett in this area, you'll also find the summon point for Valtr hidden behind a rock, and you'll be able to bring him and Younger Madaras Twin with you into the upcoming boss fight if he's still alive. When you've made all of your preparations, go through the nearby tunnel to reach the room where you will face Ludwig the Accursed. [→☐ 01/02]

BOSS Ludwig the Accursed ⁴⁸

Ludwig can be an extremely difficult fight, so it's highly recommended that you bring at least one of the NPC summons in this area into the fight with you. This is especially true if you've joined the League and can bring both Younger Madaras Twin and Valtr with you, as they will be able to hold the boss's attention most of the time allowing you to attack freely. Upon defeating Ludwig you'll automatically receive a Guidance Caryll Rune, and the Underground Corpse Pile lamp will appear in the room.

If you inspect the room after killing Ludwig, you'll find his severed head lying on the ground close to where you killed him, and if you approach it, you'll be able to strike up a conversation with it.

Ludwig's head is key to obtaining the highly coveted Holy Moonlight Sword, and there are a few ways you can go about it. The most direct method is to simply kill the head either before or after talking to it, at which time it will drop the weapon for you. Alternatively, if you equip a chest piece of church attire before talking to it, he will ask you a question; answer yes to the question to receive the sword. [→☐ 03/04]

⁴⁹ ⁵⁰ ⁵¹ Underground Cells

When you get near the top of the stairs you'll hear a mysterious voice coming from up ahead. Once you get to top, if you turn to the left you'll see that the voice was coming from a person in a prison cell. The occupant of the cell is called Yamamura the Wanderer, but until you find the key to his cell there is nothing you can do for him. If you want to find out how to acquire the key now, please refer to p185. At the far end of this corridor there is a Church Messenger along with a Wheelchair Huntsman, and it's best to kill them before exploring the cells.

The easiest way to deal with them is to take advantage of the fact that the Church Messenger moves faster than the Wheelchair Huntsman. Run along the corridor and go through the large open gate on the left, then descend the stairs a little. Once there, wait for the Church Messenger to walk just past the gate, and then run up and kill the Wheelchair Huntsman, who should be trailing behind him, and then kill the Church Messenger. With the area now clear you can explore freely, so start by going all the way down the stairs from the open gate and approaching the door to start a conversation

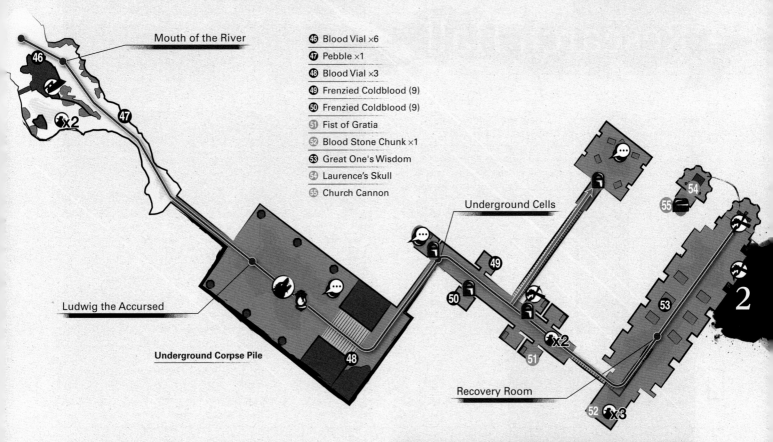

Mouth of the River

- 46 Blood Vial ×6
- 47 Pebble ×1
- 48 Blood Vial ×3
- 49 Frenzied Coldblood (9)
- 50 Frenzied Coldblood (9)
- 51 Fist of Gratia
- 52 Blood Stone Chunk ×1
- 53 Great One's Wisdom
- 54 Laurence's Skull
- 55 Church Cannon

Underground Cells

Ludwig the Accursed

Underground Corpse Pile

Recovery Room

with the occupant of the cell, a man named Brador. For information on this character and the role he plays, please refer to p653. Before leaving the Underground Cells, make sure to pick up the Fist of Gratia from one of the open cells; it's the only melee weapon that you can equip in your left hand. [→▢ 05/06]

Recovery Room 52 53 54 55

Before venturing too far into this room, double back around from the top of the stairs and kill the group of Labyrinth Rats in the dark alcove. On the opposite side of the room is the surgery altar that you need to reach, but it is being guarded by two Church Doctors and you'll need to defeat them first. The one in the Black Church Garb will almost exclusively use Ludwig's Holy Blade and is extremely aggressive, constantly rushing towards you and attempting to stay within melee range. The one in the White Church Garb, however, is primarily ranged focused and will use the Blacksky Eye to launch projectiles at you unless you get very close.

The White Garb Doctor also moves a lot slower than the one in Black Garb, so the best approach is to always try and keep them as far apart as possible. Since the one in Black Garb will always run to you, it's best to focus on taking that one out first, while using the beds in the room to block incoming projectiles from the one in White Garb. Once both of them have been killed, approach the altar at the back and insert the Eye Pendant to trigger a cutscene and move to the Research Hall. [→▢ 07]

There is a hidden area you can access now if you wish by first taking the elevator back down. Once it stops, step onto it again to make it rise, and then quickly jump off; the hidden altar will come into view, and if you pull the lever to lower the elevator and step onto it you'll reach another hidden room containing some highly coveted items.

05

06

07

Research Hall (OH)

Beyond the river of blood in the Hunter's Nightmare lies a clock-tower. As you enter, you see deformed creatures dressed as medical patients scurrying about and moaning to themselves. Sinister-looking medical equipment and odd fluids are stored on shelves. As you gaze up the stairs leading above, you feel a tingling sensation within your mind; it's almost like the sound of water. Drip, drip.

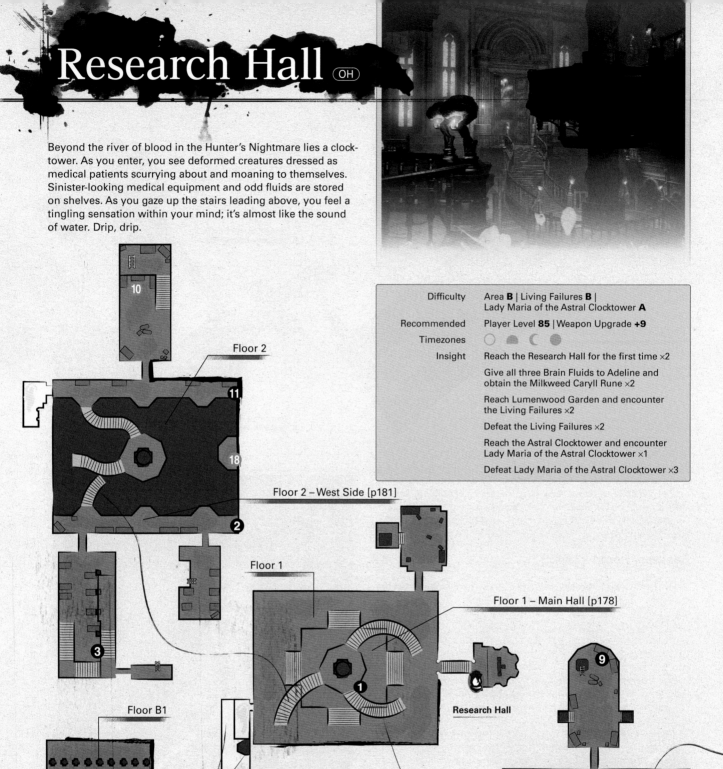

Floor 2

Floor 2 – West Side [p181]

Floor 1

Floor 1 – Main Hall [p178]

Research Hall

Floor B1

Floor 3

Difficulty	Area **B** | Living Failures **B** | Lady Maria of the Astral Clocktower **A**
Recommended	Player Level **85** | Weapon Upgrade **+9**
Timezones	○ ◐ ☾ ◑
Insight	Reach the Research Hall for the first time ×2
	Give all three Brain Fluids to Adeline and obtain the Milkweed Caryll Rune ×2
	Reach Lumenwood Garden and encounter the Living Failures ×2
	Defeat the Living Failures ×2
	Reach the Astral Clocktower and encounter Lady Maria of the Astral Clocktower ×1
	Defeat Lady Maria of the Astral Clocktower ×3

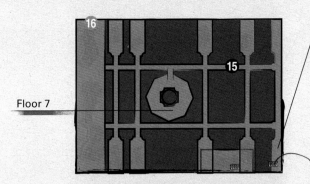

Floor 7

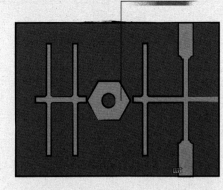

Research Hall Rafters [p184]

Floor 8

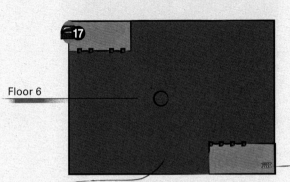

Floor 6

Floor 5 [p183]

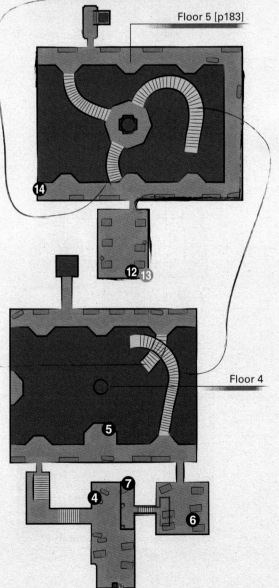

Floor 4

Enemies

Regular	HP	Echoes	Page
Labyrinth Rat	535	1198	p233
Carrion Crow	535	653	p231
Wheelchair Huntsman (Pistol)	841	980	p229
Wheelchair Huntsman (Rosmarinus)	841	762	p230
Wheelchair Huntsman (Gatling Gun)	841	762	p229
Clocktower Patient (Fists)	688	1089	p258
Clocktower Patient (Acid Bottles)	458	1198	p258
Clocktower Patient (Infected Hand)	382	1307	p259
Clocktower Patient (Crawling)	688	1198	p259
Clocktower Patient (Leaping)	1299	1525	p259
Clocktower Patient (Headless)	688	653	p260
Clocktower Patient (Head)	688	1307	p260

Strong	HP	Echoes	Page
Clocktower Patient (Transfusion Stand)	3058	3594	p309
Clocktower Patient (Magic)	688	1307	p309

Boss	HP	Echoes	Page
Living Failures	20646	22000	p366
Lady Maria of the Astral Clocktower	14081	39000	p368

NPC

Name	Page
Adeline, Research Hall Patient	p654

Item legend

- ❶ Blue Elixir ×2
- ❷ Blood Vial ×2
- ❸ Sedatives ×3
- ❹ Blood Vial ×5
- ❺ Antidote ×2
- ❻ Quicksilver Bullets ×3
- ❼ Dirty Damp Blood Gem (5)
- ❽ Madman's Knowledge ×1
- ❾ Beast Blood Pellet ×6
- ❿ Decorative Old Hunter Garb & Decorative Old Hunter Trousers
- ⓫ Frenzied Coldblood (9)
- ⓬ Blue Elixir ×1
- ⓭ Enlarged Head
- ⓮ Blue Elixir ×4
- ⓯ Great One's Wisdom
- ⓰ Blood Stone Chunk ×1
- ⓱ Finestrike Damp Blood Gem (5)
- ⓲ Loch Shield
- ⓳ Quicksilver Bullets ×4
- ⓴ Underground Cell Key
- ㉑ Lethal Damp Blood Gem (5)
- ㉒ Kin Coldblood (10)
- ㉓ Kin Coldblood (10)
- ㉔ Blacksky Eye
- ㉕ Pulsing Damp Blood Gem (5)

2

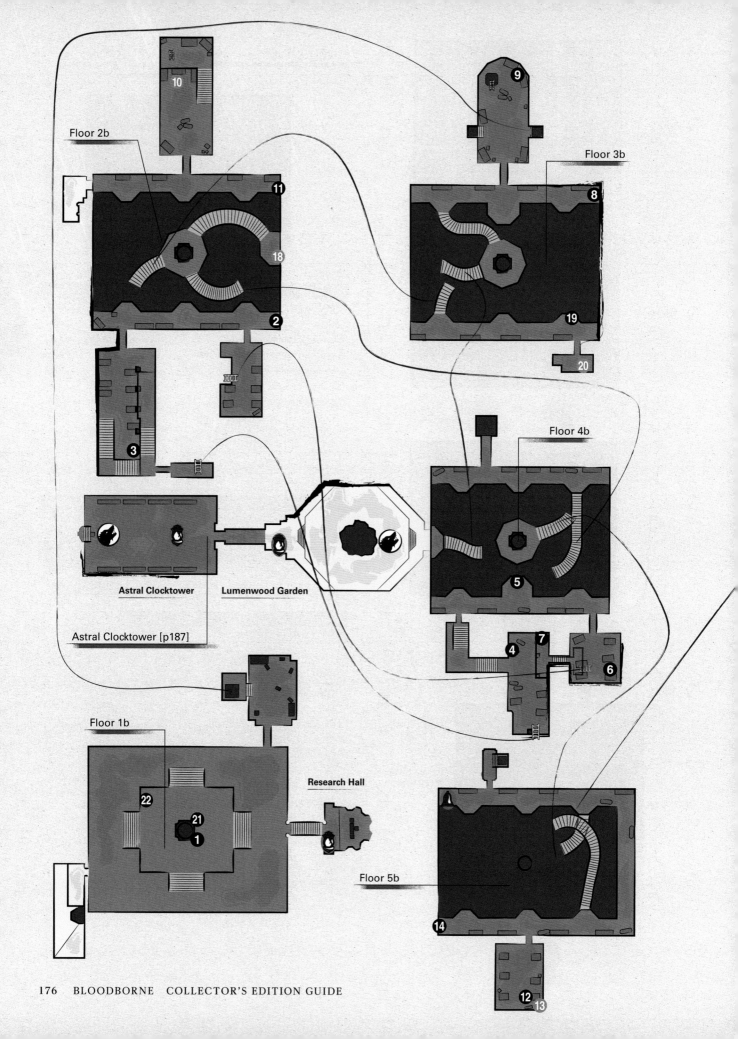

Floor 2b

10

11

18

2

3

Astral Clocktower

Astral Clocktower [p187]

Lumenwood Garden

Floor 1b

22

21

1

Research Hall

9

Floor 3b

8

19

20

Floor 4b

5

4

7

6

Floor 5b

14

12

13

Research Hall (OH)

Difficulty	Area **B** | Living Failures **B** | Lady Maria of the Astral Clocktower **A**
Recommended	Player Level **85** | Weapon Upgrade **+9**
Timezones	○ ◑ ◐ ◗
Insight	Reach the Research Hall for the first time ×2
	Give all three Brain Fluids to Adeline and obtain the Milkweed Caryll Rune ×2
	Reach Lumenwood Garden and encounter the Living Failures ×2
	Defeat the Living Failures ×2
	Reach the Astral Clocktower and encounter Lady Maria of the Astral Clocktower ×1
	Defeat Lady Maria of the Astral Clocktower ×3

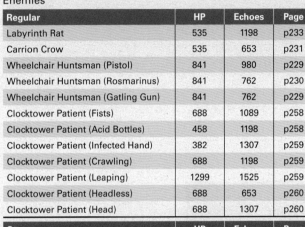

This second set of overview maps shows the position of the stairs after they have been raised by operating the device in the rafters.

Floor 6b

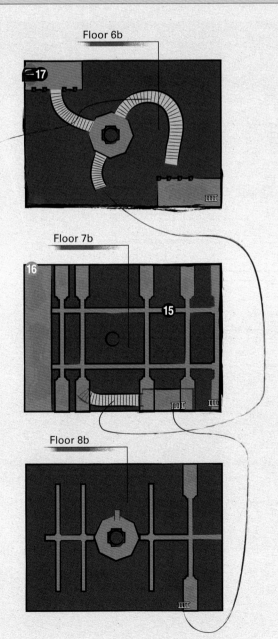

Floor 7b

Floor 8b

Enemies

Regular	HP	Echoes	Page
Labyrinth Rat	535	1198	p233
Carrion Crow	535	653	p231
Wheelchair Huntsman (Pistol)	841	980	p229
Wheelchair Huntsman (Rosmarinus)	841	762	p230
Wheelchair Huntsman (Gatling Gun)	841	762	p229
Clocktower Patient (Fists)	688	1089	p258
Clocktower Patient (Acid Bottles)	458	1198	p258
Clocktower Patient (Infected Hand)	382	1307	p259
Clocktower Patient (Crawling)	688	1198	p259
Clocktower Patient (Leaping)	1299	1525	p259
Clocktower Patient (Headless)	688	653	p260
Clocktower Patient (Head)	688	1307	p260

Strong	HP	Echoes	Page
Clocktower Patient (Transfusion Stand)	3058	3594	p309
Clocktower Patient (Magic)	688	1307	p309

Boss	HP	Echoes	Page
Living Failures	20646	22000	p366
Lady Maria of the Astral Clocktower	14081	39000	p368

NPC

Name	Page
Adeline, Research Hall Patient	p654

Item legend

- ❶ Blue Elixir ×2
- ❷ Blood Vial ×2
- ❸ Sedatives ×3
- ❹ Blood Vial ×5
- ❺ Antidote ×2
- ❻ Quicksilver Bullets ×3
- ❼ Dirty Damp Blood Gem (5)
- ❽ Madman's Knowledge ×1
- ❾ Beast Blood Pellet ×6
- ❿ Decorative Old Hunter Garb & Decorative Old Hunter Trousers
- ⓫ Frenzied Coldblood (9)
- ⓬ Blue Elixir ×1
- ⓭ Enlarged Head
- ⓮ Blue Elixir ×4
- ⓯ Great One's Wisdom
- ⓰ Blood Stone Chunk ×1
- ⓱ Finestrike Damp Blood Gem (5)
- ⓲ Loch Shield
- ⓳ Quicksilver Bullets ×4
- ⓴ Underground Cell Key
- ㉑ Lethal Damp Blood Gem (5)
- ㉒ Kin Coldblood (10)
- ㉓ Kin Coldblood (10)
- ㉔ Blacksky Eye
- ㉕ Pulsing Damp Blood Gem (5)

Research Hall

Research Hall Entrance

As soon as the altar elevator comes to a stop you'll find the Research Hall lamp directly in front of you, so before doing anything else, make sure to light it. If you wish to head back down to the Recovery Room, simply step back onto the altar and it will descend. [→ ☐ 01]

01

There are no real enemies on this floor so there's no need to be on guard and you can freely explore the area. There are, however, two Wandering Nightmares that you should deal with first to make sure they don't escape. The first of these is near a pillar just to the left of the entrance. The second one is on the stairs at the back of the pool of liquid, and it's best if you approach it from the side so that it runs into the low wall nearby. The pool of liquid is extremely toxic, so try to avoid stepping into it whenever possible, and make sure to sprint to the middle and back when attempting to pick up the item there.

Also near the pool you'll find a non-hostile Clocktower Patient that you can speak with, and although it asks you to help find its eyes, there is nothing you can do to help it other than put an end to its suffering. There are also two doors on this floor, but at the moment you're unable to open either of them; the Laboratory Floor 1 door

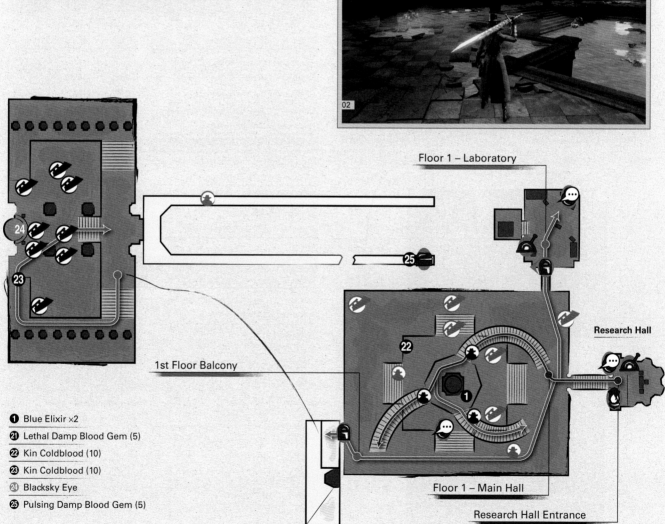

02

Floor 1 – Laboratory

1st Floor Balcony

Research Hall

22

Floor 1 – Main Hall

Research Hall Entrance

❶ Blue Elixir ×2

㉑ Lethal Damp Blood Gem (5)

㉒ Kin Coldblood (10)

㉓ Kin Coldblood (10)

㉔ Blacksky Eye

㉕ Pulsing Damp Blood Gem (5)

can only be opened from the other side, and the 1st Floor Balcony door requires a key. Your only way forward at this time is to head up the large wooden staircase, but be careful as you approach the landing, because you'll encounter some hostile Clocktower Patients. There are two at first, but another two will approach from the stairs to the right. Once they've been killed, you can either take the stairs on the right to reach Floor 2 – West Side, or the stairs on the left if you want to go to Floor 3 – East Side. [→☐ 02]

Floor 1 – Laboratory

To be able to enter this room you'll need to go up to Floor 3 – East Side, and then use the elevator in the Laboratory there to descend down to this Laboratory. There are no items to pick up in the room, but you will be able to talk to Adeline, whom you'll find strapped to a chair in the corner. She is desperate for you to bring her some Brain Fluid, and unlike the Patient you encountered in the Main Hall, you can actually fulfill her request. There are a total of three Brain Fluids you can give to her, and doing so will net you some very good rewards, including the key to the 1st Floor Balcony, and the Milkweed Caryll Rune. For full details on the Adeline's quest refer to p654. [→☐ 03]

03

COMBAT FOCUS   1st Floor Balcony ㉓ ㉔

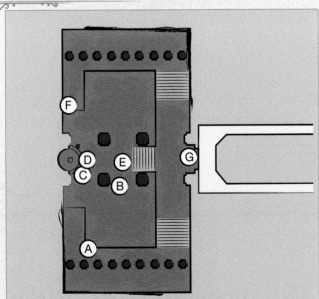

After going through the door you'll find yourself on a small balcony with a gap in the railing that you can drop through to land on a rooftop. You can then drop down again to the floor below. Once you land, follow the path around to the left to reach an item on a corpse hanging over the end. Below in the garden area you'll see a large number of Clocktower Patients – these ones are signifi-

cantly more dangerous than the normal ones, because they all have access to extremely damaging long range magical attacks. As soon as you drop down into the garden area they will all stop working and stand guard, and if one of them spots you, any within range will start attacking you.

The best way to deal with these enemies is to take advantage of the fact that they won't move unless you get close to them, and if they lose sight of you for a while they'll go back to standing guard. With that in mind, go to **Position A**, and then drop down and use a plunging attack on the Patient below, following up with some normal strikes if it's still alive. Once it's dead, quietly walk over to the one at **Position B** just to the right of the large pillar, and then use a charged R2 to stagger it and then finish it off. If done correctly, you should not alert any of the other nearby enemies.

Move back away from the pillar again before going down and hugging the back wall until you're behind the Patient at **Position C**, and then once again use a charged R2 and follow-up to kill it quickly. That will alert the enemy at **Position D** nearby, so quickstep back behind the large pillar and stay out of sight until it stops attacking you. Repeat the process for reaching the enemy at **Position C** to get behind the one at **Position D** and finish it off in the same manner. The final enemy in this part of the room (at **Position E**) will usually detect you during this process. If it does, quickly get behind the pillar again until it stops attacking, and then go around the other side of the pillar to get behind it and kill it.

Go up the nearby steps to get out of the garden area, and then run around the path to **Position F**, where you'll be overlooking another Patient below. As before, use a plunging attack to weaken it and then finish it off quickly. The remaining two enemies in the area are too close to each other to sneak up on, so the best thing to do is run up and attack them to try and kill them before they can retaliate. Once all of the enemies have been killed you can safely claim the Blacksky Eye item from the corpse in the middle of the room. After collecting your prize, cross to the other side of the room and break the window at **Position G** to gain access to the Recovery Room Balcony.

Research Hall

Recovery Room Balcony ㉕

There's a Wandering Nightmare along the left side of this Balcony, so it's worth going that way first to kill it before it escapes. Go around to the other side of the Balcony and you'll come to a hole in the floor that you can jump across to reach a chest containing a Blood Gem. Once you have the contents of the chest, drop down through the hole to land on a small ledge below, and from there drop down onto one of the beds in the Recovery Room. By accessing the Recovery Room in this manner, the usual altar elevator should be in its raised position (if it's not, step onto the altar to trigger the elevator, and then step off quickly before it gets too high), which will reveal a hidden altar.

Stepping onto this second altar does not trigger the elevator, so approach it and pick up Laurence's Skull. After picking up that item, pull the lever to operate the elevator, and then quickly run onto the hidden alter to be lowered down to a secret area with a chest containing the Church Cannon. Step onto the hidden altar to return to the Recovery Room, and then pull the lever there to lower the elevator again so you can access the normal altar and return to the Research Hall.

Now that you have Laurence's Skull, you can access one of the toughest challenges the new areas have to offer. Take the skull back to the Nightmare Grand Cathedral in the Hunter's Nightmare (p167), where you first picked up the Eye Pendant. When you approach the smoldering body at the back of the room you'll trigger a cutscene. As soon as that cutscene is over you'll have to face Laurence, the First Vicar. For full details of that fight refer to p363. Upon killing him you'll automatically get the Beast's Embrace Rune, and a new Nightmare Grand Cathedral lamp will appear in the room.

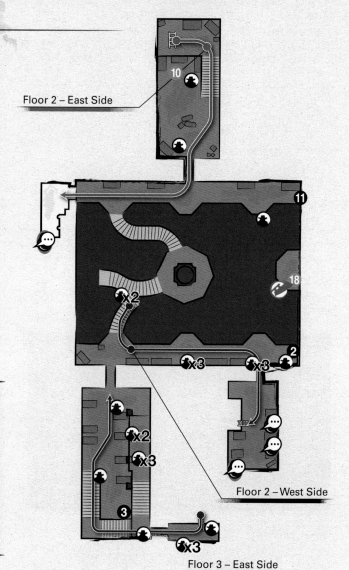

Floor 2 – East Side

Floor 2 – West Side

Floor 3 – East Side

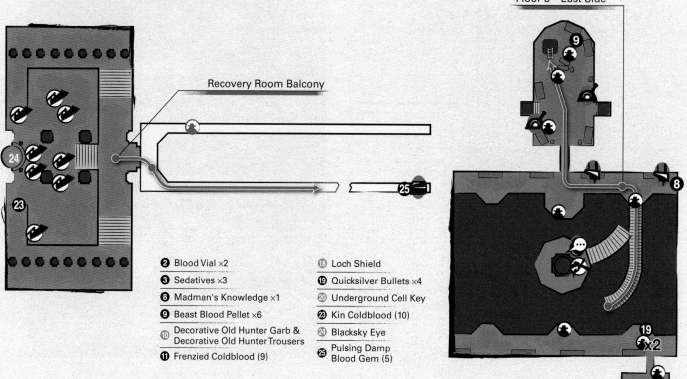

Recovery Room Balcony

❷ Blood Vial ×2

❸ Sedatives ×3

❽ Madman's Knowledge ×1

❾ Beast Blood Pellet ×6

❿ Decorative Old Hunter Garb & Decorative Old Hunter Trousers

⓫ Frenzied Coldblood (9)

⓰ Loch Shield

⓳ Quicksilver Bullets ×4

⓴ Underground Cell Key

㉓ Kin Coldblood (10)

㉔ Blacksky Eye

㉕ Pulsing Damp Blood Gem (5)

Be careful as you approach the shelving units on this floor, because there are pressure plates just in front of some of them that when stepped on, cause the jars of chemicals on the shelves to explode. If you get hit by the liquid you'll take a large amount of damage, so step on the pressure plate and then wait for the jars to explode before moving on. Halfway along the balcony there's a Church Messenger standing on a ledge, and while you can run up and attack him to knock him off, that won't kill him; it's best to wait and let him move away from the ledge so that you can kill him without knocking him off and have him turn up unexpectedly later.

There is only one room you can enter on this floor, but it's quite an important one because it acts as the shortcut hub for the entire area. Guarding the room are three Wheelchair Huntsmen, however, and you'll need to deal with them first. Thankfully they're all fairly spread out in the room and two of them have their backs to you so killing them is fairly straightforward. Once the room is clear, you'll have a few paths you can take. At the back of the room is an open trapdoor with a ladder you can use to reach Floor 2 – East Side (you can also drop down from the ledge outside this room to reach the same location), and while you can't use the elevator on the left, the one on the right will take you down to the Laboratory on Floor 1. Once you're in that room not only will you be able to speak with Adeline, but you can also open the door to create a shortcut back from the lamp. [→☐ 01]

01

It's recommended that you access this floor via the trapdoor in the Laboratory on Floor 3 rather than dropping onto the staircase outside, because it will put you in a better position for fighting the enemies in the Laboratory. From the bottom of the ladder, if you walk towards the nearby ledge you'll see an enemy directly below you, so drop off and use a plunging attack on it. These particular Clocktower Patients are extremely agile and tend to leap around a lot, so try to finish this first one off before it can start moving around.

When tackling other enemies of this type, remember that it's possible to knock them over by shooting them with any firearm; this makes fighting them much easier. After clearing the room, make sure to pick up the Decorative Hunter Attire and then exit out onto the balcony. If you go left along the balcony you'll come to an enemy guarding an item, and going to the right will lead you out to another non-hostile Clocktower Patient that you can talk to, or kill. The large wooden stairs on this floor don't lead anywhere at this time, but if you head up them, two Labyrinth Rats will drop down that you can kill for some extra Blood Echoes.

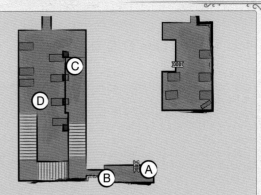

There are two doors you can enter on this floor, both of which contain ladders that lead up to the Patient Room on Floor 4. The entrance to the Laboratory is directly in front of you when you first reach this floor and it contains a large number of Clocktower Patients. The main thing that makes this room problematic are the enemies on the mezzanine throwing acid bottles down at you. While you can go underneath the mezzanine to avoid them, doing so limits your movement options for dealing with the other enemies. A better approach is to head left along the balcony towards the Patient Room, but stop and turn around when you get close to it, because a group of Clocktower Patients will come running out of the Laboratory towards you. After dealing with those enemies, enter the Patient Room, where you'll find more non-hostile patients that you talk to and kill if you like.

Climb up the ladder in this room to reach the Patient Room on Floor 4, and after dealing with the Clocktower Patient there, approach the ladder that leads back down to Laboratory on Floor 2. If you look down just to the left of the ladder you'll see a Clocktower Patient below you at **Position A**; step off the ledge and use a plunging attack on it. The other Patients nearby at **Position B** have their backs to you when you approach from this side, so you can start the fight with a fully charged ☐R2☐ for an early advantage.

After killing those enemies, go through the doorway and turn to the right to the see the area where the acid bottle-throwing Patients are standing. Start going down the stairs towards them, but be ready to move back once you get to the bottom of them, because the Patient at **Position C** will come running towards you. Fighting that enemy near the top of the stairs should mean the acid-throwers don't hear you, so you can then sneak up behind the first one and use a charged ☐R2☐ in its back to stagger it for a Visceral Attack follow-up. Doing that will usually alert the other enemies to your presence, so be ready to evade towards the other acid-thrower and take it out quickly, before another Patient approaches from **Position D**. All that's left now is to drop down and take out the last couple of Patients in the area below.

2

Research Hall

Floor 4 – West Side ❹ ❺ ❻ ❼

To reach this floor you will need to climb up one of the ladders on Floor 2, and while they both lead to the same room, the ladder in the Patient Room will put you in a much better starting position against the first enemy you'll encounter. This enemy is a tougher version of the Clocktower Patients, and it patrols back and forth along a small section of the room. If you took the ladder from Floor 2 Patient Room, a narrow tunnel will hide you from the enemy's sight, allowing you to watch its movements and time your approach so you can hit it from behind.

After killing that enemy, follow the stairs up and start running along the balcony until you come to a ledge with an item on it; you can drop down from the ledge onto the landing below to reach Floor 4 – East Side if you wish. Further along the balcony you'll come to a set of stairs going up, and at that time two Clocktower Patients will come out of the nearby Patient Room and attack you. After defeating them, approach the doorway leading into the Patient Room, but do so very slowly because just inside to the left there's another Clocktower Patient waiting to ambush you. If you inch into the room slowly you can attack and kill it before the ambush triggers, and then deal with the other enemy in the room normally.

The small set of stairs in that room leads out onto a ledge overlooking the other Patient Room on this floor. To proceed from this floor you need to go up the large stairs from the balcony. When you do so it's best to sprint, because you'll come under fire from a Wheelchair Huntsman with a Gatling Gun on Floor 5. When you reach the landing halfway up those stairs, you'll have the option of either going down the stairs on the right to reach the Floor 5, or taking the stairs directly ahead to reach a ladder that goes up to the Rafters. [→ ☐ 01]

01

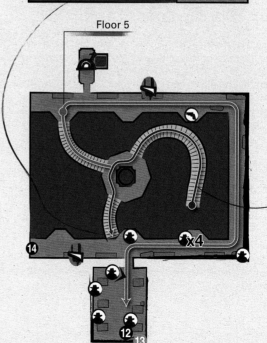

Floor 5

❹ Blood Vial ×5

❺ Antidote ×2

❻ Quicksilver Bullets ×3

❼ Dirty Damp Blood Gem (5)

❽ Madman's Knowledge ×1

❾ Beast Blood Pellet ×6

⓬ Blue Elixir ×1

⓭ Enlarged Head

⓮ Blue Elixir ×4

⓱ Finestrike Damp Blood Gem (5)

⓳ Quicksilver Bullets ×4

⓴ Underground Cell Key

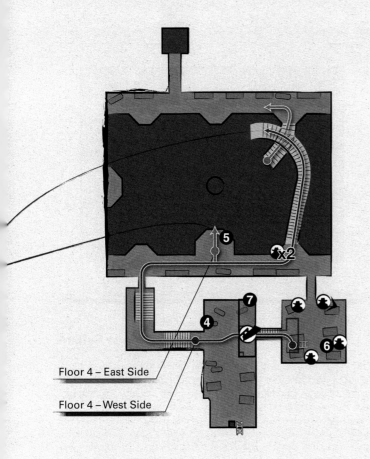

between Floor 3 and Floor 5. If that elevator is down on Floor 3, you can drop down the shaft from this floor and land on top of it. From there you can drop through the hatch in the roof to reach Floor 3. Alternatively, to leave this floor you will have to return to the landing you dropped onto at the start, and then jump across to the balcony on Floor 3 – East Side. [→☐ 02]

Floor 4 – East Side

Floor 4 – West Side

Floor 4 – East Side

If you're attempting to reach this area by dropping onto the landing from Floor 4 – West Side, the first thing you'll have to face is an enemy Hunter blocking your path to the stairs. It's possible to drop down without being detected, which will allow you to sneak around to the side of him and use a charged R2; it's difficult to get much closer before attacking because the nearby Clocktower Patient Head will start talking and alert him to your presence. By attacking aggressively from the start you can knock the Hunter off the landing for an easy win. The Clocktower Patient Head in this area is non-hostile and you can talk to it if you wish. Its main secret, however, is that attacking it will cause it to drop one of the Brain Fluids that Adeline so covets.

There are no other items or enemies on this floor, and the open doorway only leads to an elevator shaft for the elevator that runs

12 13 14 Floor 5

Unlike the other Floors in the Research Hall, the balcony on this one wraps around so you can access both sides. The Laboratory door directly in front of the stairs you use to reach this floor leads to an elevator that you can use to go back down to the Laboratory on Floor 3 where the other elevator is, in case you need to return to the lamp. Be careful as you move along the balcony on this floor, because there are pressure plates again that will trigger the acid bottles on nearby shelving units to explode. Just past the first of those pressure plates you'll be able to finally take out the Gatling Gun-wielding Wheelchair Huntsman that was shooting at you earlier.

If you continue along to the other side of the balcony you'll encounter a headless variation of the Clocktower Patients; these enemies will wander around harmlessly unless you attack them, at which point they'll retaliate. Finally on this side you'll come to a Patient room that you can enter, and inside are a number slowly pulsating Clocktower Patient Heads, and a couple of items at the back of the room.

The Heads are not initially hostile, but once you pick up the Enlarged Head Attire at the back of the room they will all start attacking. Instead of picking the item up first, it's best to attack the Heads as you come to them, as that puts you in a much better position for starting the fight. All of their attacks inflict Frenzy build-up, so if you get hit even once or twice, it's best to back off and let your Frenzy levels go back down. Before trying to exit the room, however, look above the door and you'll see another sneaky Head attached to the wall, and if you go back through the doorway it will drop down and grab you. To avoid this ambush, use any kind of ranged weapon to knock it down from its hiding spot first, and then kill it normally. [→☐ 03/04]

Research Hall

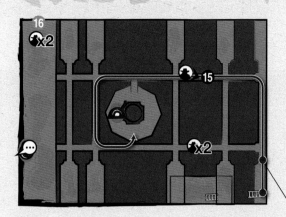

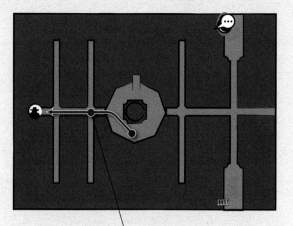

Research Hall Rafters   Research Hall Upper Rafters

8 Madman's Knowledge ×1

9 Beast Blood Pellet ×6

15 Great One's Wisdom

16 Blood Stone Chunk ×1

17 Finestrike Damp Blood Gem (5)

19 Quicksilver Bullets ×4

20 Underground Cell Key

Research Hall Rafters **15** **16**

The Rafters span the entire Research Hall and you can freely walk along any of the beams. Two Labyrinth Rats also patrol along the beams, so be very careful if you attempt to fight them on the narrow sections. Similar caution should also be employed when going for the item that's on a corpse hanging off one of the beams, because when you get close to it, a Carrion Crow will drop down and attack you. From the starting point of the Rafters, if you take the first left, and then left again, you can drop down onto a small platform with a ladder on it that leads to the Upper section of the Rafters.

Cross the Rafters to the other side of the hall and you'll find a pair of Carrion Crows in the corner guarding another item, along with a non-hostile Clocktower Patient that you can speak with. The main reason for coming up here, however, is the large mechanism in the centre that you can operate, because doing so will raise the entire staircase structure and allow you access to new parts of the area. Once the stairs have been moved, however, they cannot be moved back, so you'll need to take slightly different routes to move between the floors. [→ □ **01**]

Research Hall Upper Rafters

You can reach the Upper Rafters via the Ladder from the floor below, or if you activate the mechanism to raise the stairs you'll automatically end up here. On one side of these rafters you'll find another non-hostile Head that you can talk to, and then if you attack it you'll get a second Brain Fluid for Adeline. Going the other way you'll find a Carrion Crow sitting on the end of a beam, and when you approach it, it will fly down to the ledge below as if showing you the path to take. Follow the Crow and drop down from the end of the beam, and if you kill it you'll get a handy Guidance Caryll Rune. [→ □ **02**]

If you've collected both of the Brain Fluids so far, you will now be able to go down and give them both to Adeline in the Laboratory on Floor 1 and get the Balcony Key in return, allowing you to enter the 1st Floor Balcony.

17 Back through the Hall

Now that you've moved the stairs, you can access the door that leads to the boss room. To reach that door, cross back over the rafters and drop down to the platform with the ladder going to the Upper Rafters, where you'll be able to use some stairs to go down. When you reach the landing, if you go down the stairs on the left you can reach a small platform where you'll find some Carrion Crows guarding a chest containing a Blood Gem. Going down the stairs to the right on that landing will take you down to Floor 5. Once there, run around the balcony to the Laboratory and use the elevator to go down to Floor 3. Exit the Floor 3 Laboratory and follow the balcony along to the right until you come to a set of stairs, and then follow them up and open the large door to face off against the Living Failures. [→▢ 03]

Floor 3 – West Side ⑱ ⑲ ⑳

To access this part of the Research Hall, make your way to the Laboratory on Floor 3 – East Side. Just outside the room there's a ledge you can drop from to reach a landing on the stairs below. If you go up the stairs to the left from this landing you'll be able to reach Floor 4 – East Side if you haven't already been there, and if you take the stairs going down from there you'll reach a small platform. On this platform you'll find a Crawling Clocktower Patient that you'll need to kill before picking up the Loch Shield from the nearby corpse. This shield is extremely handy, as it greatly reduces all non-physical damage. From that platform you can also drop down to Floor 1 if you wish, but be careful because raising the stairs released a large number of Crawling Clocktower Patients down there. You'll also find a couple of new items in the toxic pool, so it's worth battling past the new enemies to get them.

The set of stairs going up to the right from that landing bring you to the West Side of Floor 3. Follow the balcony along on this floor, killing the Clocktower Patients as you come to them until you reach the Patient Room. Just to right in side of this door, a Clocktower Patient with an infected hand is waiting to ambush you with a grab as you enter. To counter this ambush attempt, step through the doorway and then quickly evade backwards so the grab misses you. After killing the enemy you'll be able to claim the item on a corpse here, which is the Underground Cell Key. [→▢ 04]

> Now that you have the Underground Cell Key, it's recommended that you go back to the Underground Cells and get all of the items inside the cells it unlocks. One of the cells does, however, contain a very dangerous Hunter, who will reward you with the Church Pick weapon upon his defeat.

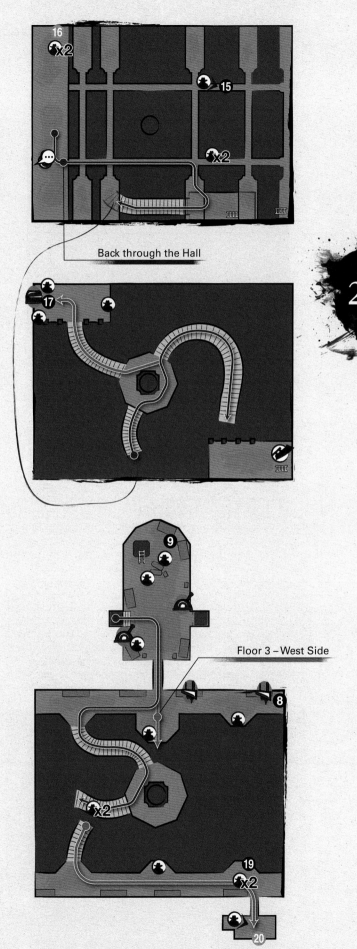

Back through the Hall

Floor 3 – West Side

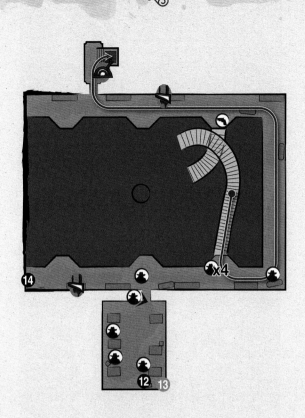

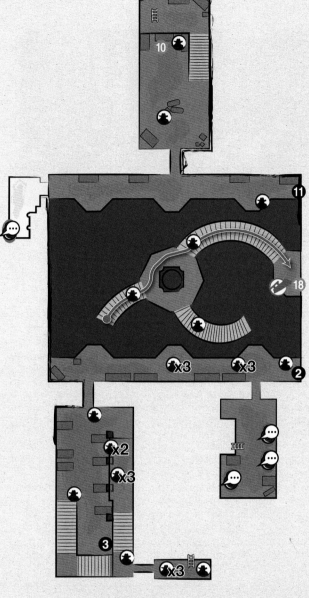

BOSS Living Failures

At the start of this battle you'll only have to face one or two of these enemies, but as the fight progresses, more and more will gradually appear in the area. While each one only has a relatively small amount of health and can be killed off, you need to defeat enough of them to deplete their overall shared HP pool. Because they have quite high physical resistance, your best means of killing them is to use elemental attacks, or try to interrupt them and use Visceral Attacks, since they will still deal significant damage. Once you've killed enough of them to finish the fight you'll automatically get the Astral Clocktower Key, and the Lumenwood Garden lamp will appear at the back of the area near the locked door. [→☐ 01/02]

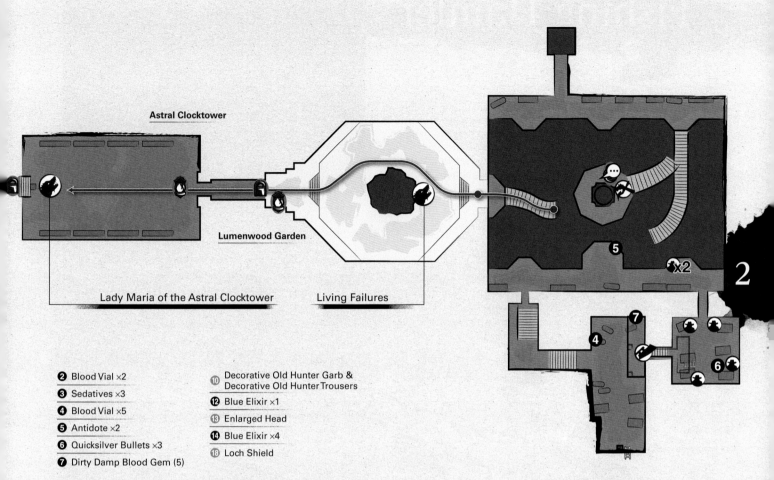

Astral Clocktower

Lumenwood Garden

Lady Maria of the Astral Clocktower

Living Failures

x2

2

2 Blood Vial ×2
3 Sedatives ×3
4 Blood Vial ×5
5 Antidote ×2
6 Quicksilver Bullets ×3
7 Dirty Damp Blood Gem (5)

10 Decorative Old Hunter Garb &
Decorative Old Hunter Trousers
12 Blue Elixir ×1
13 Enlarged Head
14 Blue Elixir ×4
18 Loch Shield

03

04

BOSS Lady Maria of the Astral Clocktower

Upon entering the Astral Clocktower you'll notice a mysterious figure sat in a chair on the opposite side of the room; approach the chair and inspect the corpse to trigger a cutscene. As soon as that cutscene is over the fight with Lady Maria will begin, so make sure you're ready beforehand. Maria can quickly cover a lot of ground with her attacks, but you can use this to your advantage in the early phase of the fight because quickstepping forward and to the side slightly will evade a great deal of her attacks.

Once you've defeated her you'll find the Celestial Dial on the ground near the entrance, and the new Astral Clocktower lamp will appear nearby. With the Celestial Dial in hand, approach the large clock face and hold it up when prompted to trigger the clock mechanism to turn. Once the clock has stopped moving there will be a new opening that you can walk through to reach the Fishing Hamlet. [→☐ 03/04]

Fishing Hamlet OH

The smell of rotten fish assails your nose. Baleful chants echo through the fog, and the sea breeze relentlessly washes you in the pungent stench of decay. Yet there's something else hanging thick in the air. Wrath... despair... and a sense of... longing? Ahead, you see a small fishing village and wonder what cursed horrors await you in the depths of this fetid nightmare.

Difficulty	Area **A** | Orphan of Kos **S**
Recommended	Player Level **90** | Weapon Upgrade **+9**
Timezones	○ ◑ ☾ ●
Insight	Reach the Fishing Hamlet for the first time ×4
	Encounter the Orphan of Kos ×5
	Defeat the Orphan of Kos ×5
	Slay the Orphan of Kos' remaining shadow after the battle to end the nightmare ×3

Fishman Street [p191]

Dilapidated Building [p192]

Fishing Hamlet

Lighthouse Hut

Lighthouse Hut [p194]

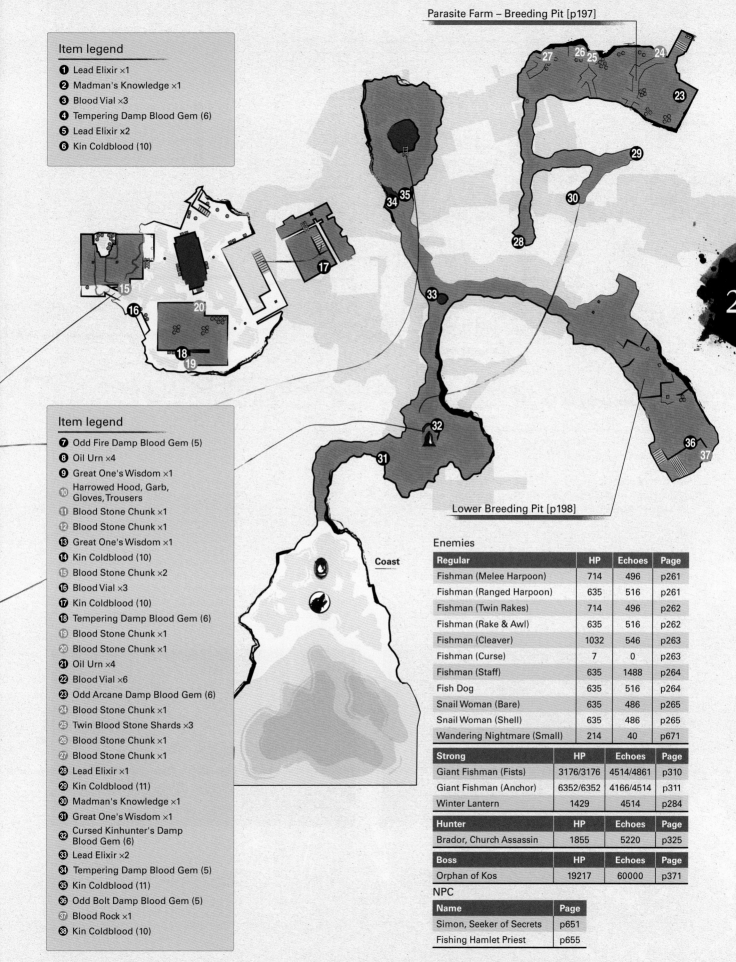

Item legend

1. Lead Elixir ×1
2. Madman's Knowledge ×1
3. Blood Vial ×3
4. Tempering Damp Blood Gem (6)
5. Lead Elixir ×2
6. Kin Coldblood (10)

Item legend

7. Odd Fire Damp Blood Gem (5)
8. Oil Urn ×4
9. Great One's Wisdom ×1
10. Harrowed Hood, Garb, Gloves, Trousers
11. Blood Stone Chunk ×1
12. Blood Stone Chunk ×1
13. Great One's Wisdom ×1
14. Kin Coldblood (10)
15. Blood Stone Chunk ×2
16. Blood Vial ×3
17. Kin Coldblood (10)
18. Tempering Damp Blood Gem (6)
19. Blood Stone Chunk ×1
20. Blood Stone Chunk ×1
21. Oil Urn ×4
22. Blood Vial ×6
23. Odd Arcane Damp Blood Gem (6)
24. Blood Stone Chunk ×1
25. Twin Blood Stone Shards ×3
26. Blood Stone Chunk ×1
27. Blood Stone Chunk ×1
28. Lead Elixir ×1
29. Kin Coldblood (11)
30. Madman's Knowledge ×1
31. Great One's Wisdom ×1
32. Cursed Kinhunter's Damp Blood Gem (6)
33. Lead Elixir ×2
34. Tempering Damp Blood Gem (5)
35. Kin Coldblood (11)
36. Odd Bolt Damp Blood Gem (5)
37. Blood Rock ×1
38. Kin Coldblood (10)

Parasite Farm – Breeding Pit [p197]

Lower Breeding Pit [p198]

Coast

Enemies

Regular	HP	Echoes	Page
Fishman (Melee Harpoon)	714	496	p261
Fishman (Ranged Harpoon)	635	516	p261
Fishman (Twin Rakes)	714	496	p262
Fishman (Rake & Awl)	635	516	p262
Fishman (Cleaver)	1032	546	p263
Fishman (Curse)	7	0	p263
Fishman (Staff)	635	1488	p264
Fish Dog	635	516	p264
Snail Woman (Bare)	635	486	p265
Snail Woman (Shell)	635	486	p265
Wandering Nightmare (Small)	214	40	p671

Strong	HP	Echoes	Page
Giant Fishman (Fists)	3176/3176	4514/4861	p310
Giant Fishman (Anchor)	6352/6352	4166/4514	p311
Winter Lantern	1429	4514	p284

Hunter	HP	Echoes	Page
Brador, Church Assassin	1855	5220	p325

Boss	HP	Echoes	Page
Orphan of Kos	19217	60000	p371

NPC

Name	Page
Simon, Seeker of Secrets	p651
Fishing Hamlet Priest	p655

Fishing Hamlet

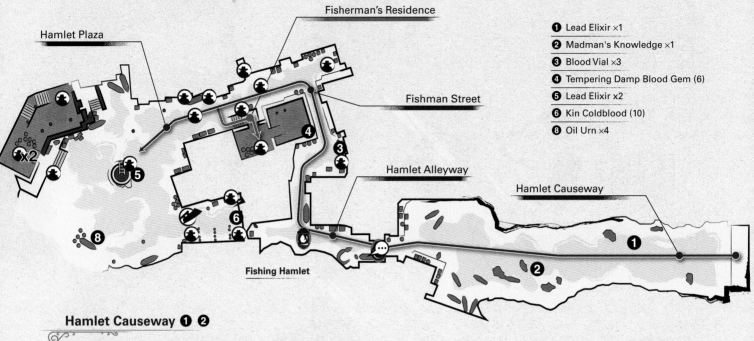

Fisherman's Residence

Hamlet Plaza

Fishman Street

Hamlet Alleyway

Hamlet Causeway

Fishing Hamlet

1 Lead Elixir ×1
2 Madman's Knowledge ×1
3 Blood Vial ×3
4 Tempering Damp Blood Gem (6)
5 Lead Elixir ×2
6 Kin Coldblood (10)
8 Oil Urn ×4

Hamlet Causeway **1** **2**

After dropping down from the Astral Clocktower you'll land on a narrow dirt path that's flanked on either side by water. Be very careful when exploring this area because the land does not extended very far out from the path and it drops off suddenly. Along the path you'll find a couple of items, and since they're near the edge of the land, make sure to aim your camera down to give you a better view through the water.

As you get close to the village, the mysterious figure of the Fishing Hamlet Priest will start walking towards you while rambling incoherently. After you've listened to his initial dialogue, you can talk to him for more information. You cannot, however, kill this character; even if you deplete all of his health he will simply stand up and continue walking through the area. Follow the path along between the buildings to enter the Fishing Hamlet proper, and just after that you'll come to the Fishing Hamlet lamp. [→▢ **01**]

3 Hamlet Alleyway

When you near the end of the first building along this alley you'll see a large creature walk past an open window up ahead, and while you will have to face it later, you don't have to worry about it right now. After rounding the corner there's an item near a building on the other side of the small courtyard, and just in front of it you can see the fin of a submerged creature swimming back and forth. The creature is a Fishman, and if you wait too long or approach the item it will leap out of the water and attack you, so it's best to run up and kill it first before it can retaliate. [→▢ **02**]

If you talk to the Fishing Hamlet Priest while you have the Milkweed Caryll Rune equipped, he will react to your Lumenwood appearance and speak to you differently. At the end of that dialogue he will give you the Accursed Brew.

Fishman Street

Upon turning the corner here, a Fishman will step out of a small alcove just ahead on the right. Hold your ground instead of running over and attacking it because a group of four more Fishmen will also start running towards you from further ahead. The group will reach you in a staggered fashion rather than all at once, so if you retreat back and use the corner to hinder their movements you can take them out one at a time as they reach you. [→☐ 03/04]

Fisherman's Residence ❹

There's a Fishman standing with his back to you just outside the entrance to this house. If you walk up the stairs quietly, you can sneak up behind it and use a charged ®R2® to stagger it for an easy victory. This is the building that you saw the creature in earlier, but since you just killed it, you can safely enter and get the item in the corner. There's another item up on a broken staircase, but you can only reach it by entering via the upper floor later. [→☐ 05/06]

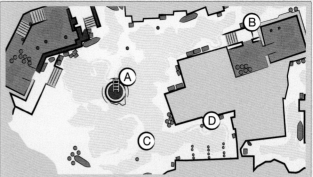

2

Be careful as you approach this open clearing – if you run in recklessly it's very easy to attract the attention of a large number of enemies and become overwhelmed quickly. The most immediate threat is a Fishman (Curse) sat near the well at **Position A**. This enemy will fire large volleys of homing skulls at you that have considerable range and tracking capabilities, which makes fighting other enemies in the area problematic. Just in front of that enemy are two more Fishmen, and they will come running towards you as soon as the other one starts firing skulls at you. The easiest way to take them out is to retreat back to **Position B** outside of the skull's range before fighting the other Fishmen.

Once those first two enemies have been killed, run back towards the well and kill the Fishman there. He has very little health so it will only take a single hit. Be sure not to go past the well, however, otherwise you'll get the attention of a bomb-throwing Fishman in the large building nearby, as well as the other Fishmen along the water bank. If you look to **Position C** you should see another Fishman that has already spotted you, but instead of attacking you it just patrols back and forth as if daring you approach. If you do start approaching, a Giant Fishman will come walking out from behind the building nearby and start attacking you. This enemy is extremely dangerous and can inflict a massive amount of damage, so you need to be very cautious.

Along the side of that building you'll notice some oil urns with a small flame flickering in them; if you time it correctly you can move forward until you hear the Giant Fishman, and use a firearm or explosive to detonate them and damage it. By far the safest option for dealing with the Giant Fishman here is to retreat back down to the Fisherman's Residence. The giant enemy cannot pass through the doorway of the residence, so you can safely wait for one of its attacks to miss, and then hit it while it recovers. Once it's dead, go back to where you first encountered it and head round the corner to reach an area with an item and another Fishman. Be careful as you approach that item because a second Fishman will appear from under the building at **Position D** – so make sure you kill the first one quickly.

Fishing Hamlet

Plaza Well

If you look closely at the well in the middle of the plaza you'll notice that there is a ladder that you can use to reach a cave below the plaza. Within that cave an Anchor-wielding Giant Fishman patrols around a central column. Once its health reaches around 40%, a second Giant Fishman will drop down from the ceiling. Fighting both of those enemies at this point is extremely difficult, and you can have a much easier time be approaching this area through a tunnel you'll access later. If you choose to fight them now, the central column can help you a lot, since you can use it to restrict both the movement and attack angles of the Giant Fishmen by constantly moving around it. Poison Knives can also be very effective here, because the Poison can take off large amounts of health while you're waiting for a safe time to attack. The second Giant Fishman will drop the Rakuyo weapon when it's killed, so whichever approach you take, it's worth taking the time to kill them. [→ 01]

01

COMBAT FOCUS Dilapidated Building ❼

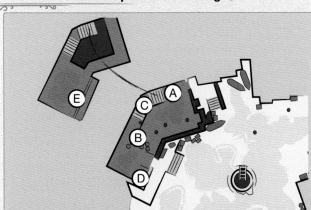

There are a lot of enemies in and around this large building, so as is often the case, a cautious approach is best. Start by approaching the building while hugging the right-hand side of the plaza – that will allow you to get close while remaining undetected – and then enter slowly through the doorway when you reach it. There's a Fishman just inside at **Position A** with its back to you, and if you're quiet you can sneak up behind it and use a charged R2 to stager it for a quick finish.

There are three more Fishmen to contend with on this floor, but if you engage them in the correct order you'll only have to face them one at a time. The first one has its back to you in the middle near some oil-filled urns at **Position B**, the second is under the stairs nearby at **Position C**, and the final one is in the far corner

of the room at **Position D**. If you shoot or throw a Molotov at the oil urns, the ensuing explosion will kill the enemy at **Position B** without alerting the others. You can then use a ranged attack on the enemy under the stairs at **Position C** to lure it towards you and fight it out of the other enemy's line of sight. When only the enemy at **Position D** remains, run over and kill it before quietly going up the stairs.

At the top of the stairs another Fishman will spot you; retreat back down the stairs so that it follows you and fight it on the floor below to avoid alerting a second Fishman on the upper floor a **Position E**. Go back up the stairs after dispatching that first foe, sneak up behind the one at **Position E** and use a charged R2 to stagger it and a visceral attack follow-up. Once all the enemies in the house have been defeated, run along the narrow ledge near the stairs to get the item at the end, and then go back down the stairs and out the front door to start cleaning up the last few Fishmen.

Just after you exit the house, a nearby Fishman will come running towards you, so move back inside and fight it there to avoid alerting the other enemies. The remaining two are standing near the water's edge just off to the side of the house. If you're quiet you can sneak up behind the first one and use a charged R2 to stagger it for a quick kill, leaving only one to finish off afterwards. Try not to stand around in the open too much while fighting it, however, because there's another Fishman further up the hill that will start throwing harpoons down at you, so keep the fight behind the nearby wall.

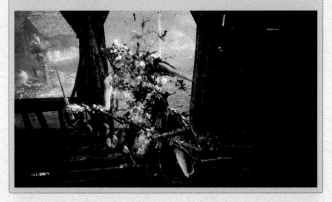

❾ ❿ ⓫ Cliffside Trail

If you look along the base of the cliff you'll notice a series of oil urns highlighting a narrow path that you can follow to reach the rooftops. After picking up the item at the start of the first rooftop you come to, continue around the left-hand side to find a ladder that you can kick down to create a shortcut back to the lamp. Next to the ladder there's a hole in the wall that you can walk through to enter a building, and once inside you'll find a walkway leading to an adjacent building. Be very careful when you enter this second building, because there's a sneaky Fishman clinging to the roof just waiting to drop down and ambush you with a grab attack.

The easiest way to avoid being grabbed is to slowly move into the room while hugging the wall on the right to cause it to drop down, and then quickly move backwards to avoid the grab. Another Fishman can be seen hacking up the remains of a poor villager at the opposite end of this building, and while it's distracted you can sneak up behind it and use a charged R2. Once the area is clear, make sure to pick up the item from the corpse the Fishman was chopping, because it's a full Attire set. Then go down the broken staircase to claim the item you could see when you entered the lower floor of this building earlier.

Lighthouse Path

If you peek out from behind the tree at the base of the hill you can safely bait the Fishman further up into throwing a harpoon into the tree. Once it does, you can quickly run up and attack it during the recovery. Try to kill it as quickly as possible, because once you reach that point a Fish Dog will come running down from behind the large tree nearby. This enemy is largely similar to other dog type enemies, the main difference being that it has an area of effect attack that, while doing no damage, will cause your character to stumble back-wards. The best way to deal with it is to use a firearm to shoot it and knock it over to stop it from attacking, and then kill it as it gets up.

Around this time a large group of enemies will start making their way towards you from further up the hill, so as soon as you've killed that Fish Dog, run up and take cover behind the large tree. The group of enemies consists of another Fish Dog, two melee Fishmen, and two more that will hang back and throw harpoons. The Fish Dog will usually reach you first, so stick behind the tree while fighting it to shield yourself from the harpoons and hamper the approach of the two melee Fishmen, and then pick them off one

at a time as they round the tree. Be careful when you run up to take on the two harpoon throwing Fishmen, because there's yet another one further up the hill that will start throwing harpoons down at you while you attack them. Using hit-and run style tactics from behind the cover of the nearby wall is the safest way to kill them.

⑫ ⑬ Lighthouse Approach

Start making your way up towards the next harpoon Fishman, but don't attack it. When you get near it a Fishman (Curse) will start firing projectiles down at you. On top of that, another Giant Fishman will come running down from a path on the right, and you don't want to have to contend with all three at once. The Giant Fishman should be your first priority since it is by far the biggest threat, and there are a couple of ways you can go about dealing with it.

If you're comfortable fighting these enemies out in the open, then retreat back down to the large tree and fight it there, so that you can use the tree for cover if needed. For a safer approach, carry on sprinting up the hill past all of the enemies and enter the Light-house Hut. The Giant Fishman will be unable to enter, so you can pick it off with ranged attacks, or wait for it to attack and then use melee strikes while it recovers. After it's dead, run back and kill the Fishman (Curse) before taking out the other Fishman to secure the area. When it's safe to do so, look for a narrow path between the buildings nearby that you can follow to find an item.

2

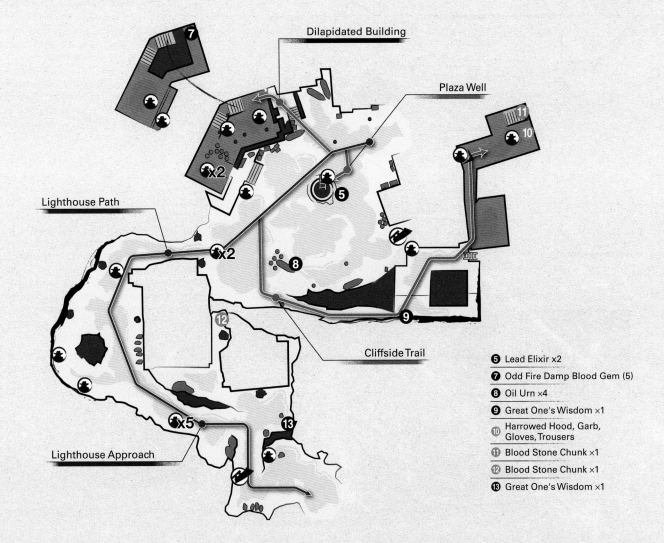

Dilapidated Building

Plaza Well

7

11

10

Lighthouse Path

x2

x2

5

8

9

12

Cliffside Trail

x5

13

Lighthouse Approach

⑤ Lead Elixir x2

⑦ Odd Fire Damp Blood Gem (5)

⑧ Oil Urn ×4

⑨ Great One's Wisdom ×1

⑩ Harrowed Hood, Garb, Gloves, Trousers

⑪ Blood Stone Chunk ×1

⑫ Blood Stone Chunk ×1

⑬ Great One's Wisdom ×1

Fishing Hamlet

Lighthouse Hut ⑭

The Lighthouse Hut lamp is directly in front of you upon entering the building, so before doing anything else, make sure you light it. Just to the side of the doorway you entered through you'll find an injured and collapsed Simon if you've been following his quest; talk to him a couple of times and you'll get Simon's Bowblade and the Underground Cell Inner Chamber Key as a parting gift. The gate in the room does not open from this side. The opening in the side wall of the house leads to a path you can follow down to another gate that you cannot open from this side. There is, however, and item in that area that you can pick up now if you wish.

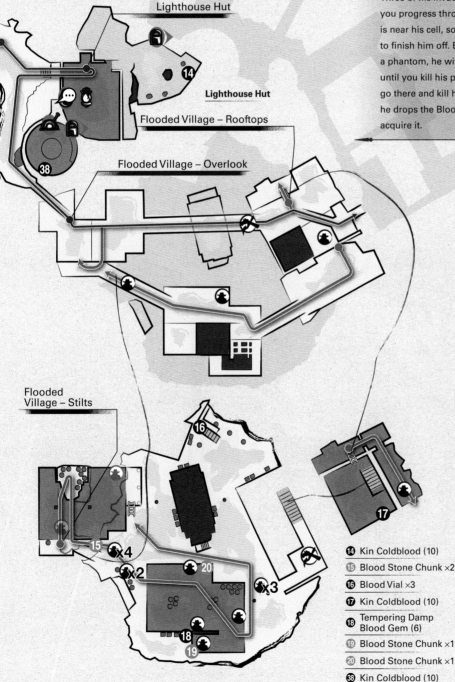

Lighthouse Hut

⑭

Lighthouse Hut

Flooded Village – Rooftops

Flooded Village – Overlook

㊳

Flooded Village – Stilts

⑯

⑮ x4

x2

⑳

x3

⑱

⑲

The Underground Cell Inner Chamber Key opens the final cell in the Underground Cells area – a cell that houses Brador. After reaching the Lighthouse Hut, Brador will start invading your world in fixed locations until you go to his cell and kill him. But that does not mean you should rush there and finish him off straight away. There are four places in total that Brador will invade, and for each of those locations you kill him in you will get a piece of his Attire set, so if you want the full set, you'll have to kill him at each location.

Three of his invading locations you'll encounter naturally as you progress through the rest of this area, and the forth one is near his cell, so you can leave it for last when you go there to finish him off. Even after you kill him when he invades as a phantom, he will still keep appearing in those locations until you kill his physical body in the cell. Another reason to go there and kill him once you have the full Attire set is that he drops the Bloodletter weapon, and that is the only way to acquire it.

Flooded Village – Overlook

When you reach the top of the hill, follow the path around to a pair of wooden planks, and then walk along them to reach the large rooftop below. If Brador is still alive, you'll start hearing a bell ring as soon as you reach this rooftop to indicate that you're near one of his invading points, but he won't appear just yet so you can still survey the area.

You can drop off either side of the rooftop to reach a platform below that gives access to the large house, but whether you intend to clear the area or simply run through it, a better option is to cross the wooden bridge leading off from the rooftop. Once you start walking on the bridge, however, Brador will invade on the other side and start coming towards you, so retreat back and fight him on the large rooftop where you have more room. After crossing the bridge you'll come to another rooftop, and if you just want to push through the area, you can go straight up the next set of planks and enter the Parasite Farm. [→☐ 01]

01

⑭ Kin Coldblood (10)
⑮ Blood Stone Chunk ×2
⑯ Blood Vial ×3
⑰ Kin Coldblood (10)
⑱ Tempering Damp Blood Gem (6)
⑲ Blood Stone Chunk ×1
⑳ Blood Stone Chunk ×1
㊳ Kin Coldblood (10)

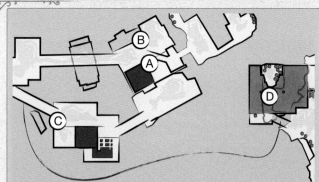

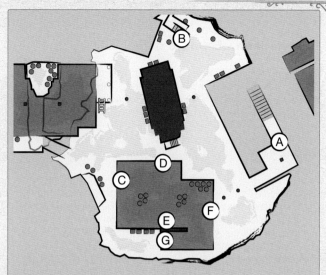

There are a large number of Fishmen in this part of the village, and it's very easy to be overrun by them, especially if you happen to drop off to the Stilts area below. The safest approach is to sweep and clear the rooftops and building interiors one at a time, while also using your elevated position to pick off some of the enemies below in safety. To begin with, start by slowly walking through the gap at **Position A** to reach a Fishman (Staff). If this enemy spots you it can fire barrages of lightning strikes that appear directly above you, so take advantage of the situation and deliver a charged R2 to its back before finishing it off.

Backtrack slightly now and descend the ladder at **Position B** to reach a wooden platform. From there, walk slowly through the nearby doorway and sneak up behind the Fishman at the opposite end of the building, so that you can use a charged R2 to stagger it for an easy kill. Exit through the next doorway and follow the platform around until you reach another wooden bridge. From here you should be able to see a Fishman (Staff) standing towards the end of the next rooftop, and another Fishman patrolling along behind him. Wait for the patrolling Fishman to be at his closest point to you, and then cross the bridge so he spots you. Try to fight him on the section of rooftop just after the bridge. Be careful when fighting in this area, however, because there is a large hole on the other side of the apex, and if you drop through it you'll be surrounded by the group of enemies in the room below. After killing that enemy, sneak up behind the Fishman (Staff) and kill it.

If you now go to **Position C** (just to the left of the next wooden bridge) and look down, you should be able to see a very large enemy group standing near some oil urns. By either shooting, or using a Molotov to make the urns explode, it's possible to kill nearly all of them, and then you can finish off the rest using any ranged options you have. Another group of enemies consisting of two Fish Dogs and a Fishman patrol the area below the other side of the bridge, so if you still have plenty of ranged attacks left you can pick them off from this position.

Cross the nearby wooden bridge now and approach the open doorway on the other side; as soon as you enter the building, a Wandering Nightmare will start running towards a hole in the floor – try to kill it before it reaches its goal. If it does drop down, it's important that you don't follow it, because the area is surrounded by a large number of oil urns, and a nearby Fishman will throw a bomb to detonate them as soon as you land. The best way to deal with the situation is to blow them up yourself before dropping down by either shooting them or using a Molotov, and if you're quick, this will also kill the Wandering Nightmare if it did drop down. After clearing the trap, drop down yourself and immediately roll towards **Position D** and kill the Fishman there. Follow the path around underneath the building to reach an item near the ledge, and then drop down into the water below.

One of the main reasons to kill as many enemies from the rooftops as possible is because down here among the Stilts (at **Position A**) you'll be invaded by Brador if he's still alive. He will only invade after you have gone up the stairs near that position and entered the building, so it's important that you stay far away from there if you have other enemies chasing you.

If you haven't already taken out any of the enemies, you'll be faced with a large numbers of enemies now, and while your first instinct may be to run through the nearby open doorway, there are more enemies in there, so you can end up making things worse. A better option is to run past the ladder (which will take you back up to the rooftops in case you need to get out) and around the back of the building to the left, until you come to the small set of stairs at **Position B**. You can use these stairs as a bottleneck to funnel the enemies towards you, and at any time you get pushed back, you can drop down and loop back behind them.

Once you're done with them (or if you killed them earlier) slowly go through the doorway at **Position C**. Inside this building are four more Fishmen; if you make your way through it slowly and quietly, it possible to take them on one at a time. Start by sneaking around behind the one at **Position D** before killing it, and then take out the one near the opposite wall at **Position E**. From there you can walk around behind the next one at **Position F**, before killing the final one at **Position G**. Once the building has been cleared, exit through the nearby door and follow the building wall around to find an item hidden outside. The only thing left now is to enter the building at **Position A** to get the item there, and then be ready to fight Brador once again when you leave.

Parasite Farm – Entrance ㉑ ㉒

Be very careful when moving around in this area; one wrong step and you can easily fall to your death. Most of the Fishmen in this area are busy tending to the parasites, but while they'll often have their backs to you, they will always detect you when you get close. You'll still have an advantage against them, however, since they'll have to get up and turn around, during which time you can start attacking them.

To start with, hug the wall on the right as you enter, and then drop down onto the narrow ledge along the wall and follow it along to the first Fishman you can kill. Once that enemy is dead, go up the nearby ramp and do the same to the one at the top of it. Just past that second Fishman you'll see a Fishman (Staff) patrolling up and down another ramp; wait for it to start moving up the ramp and then sneak up behind it and attack it with a charged R2 if you get close enough, otherwise just attack it normally before it can start firing lightning bolts. Follow the path around to the right when you reach the top of that ramp, and then immediately turn left under the overhang and take out the Fishman there before getting the nearby item. [→ □ 01/02]

01

02

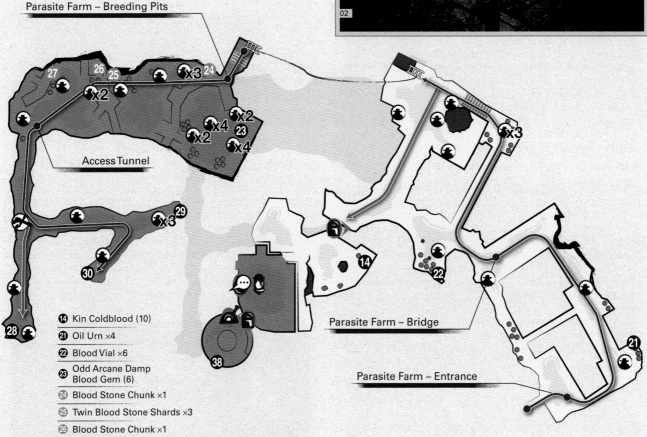

Parasite Farm – Breeding Pits

Access Tunnel

Parasite Farm – Bridge

Parasite Farm – Entrance

⑭ Kin Coldblood (10)

㉑ Oil Urn ×4

㉒ Blood Vial ×6

㉓ Odd Arcane Damp Blood Gem (6)

㉔ Blood Stone Chunk ×1

㉕ Twin Blood Stone Shards ×3

㉖ Blood Stone Chunk ×1

㉗ Blood Stone Chunk ×1

㉘ Lead Elixir ×1

㉙ Kin Coldblood (11)

㉚ Madman's Knowledge ×1

㊳ Kin Coldblood (10)

Parasite Farm – Bridge

From this location you'll be able to spot a group of Fishmen on the other side of a narrow beam, and another group on a large platform that includes two Staff-wielding Fishmen. If you were to go for the platform first, you'd have to deal with both mages at once, so it's best to go down the narrow beam. As soon as you step onto it, the three Fishmen on the other side will start running towards you, so move back on to solid ground and take them out one at a time as they reach you.

When it's safe, cross the narrow beam, and then go up the stairs and quickly take out the Fishman (Staff) at the top. Shortly after you start attacking it another Fishman will come after you from the left, so keep the camera trained that way to see it coming. The second Fishman (Staff) will usually detect you during the fighting, but the large column nearby will easily shield you from its attacks until you're ready to go around and face it. The only enemy left after that should be a lone Fishman on the other side of the platform with its back to you. This one you can sneak right up behind to stagger it with a charged R2. The way forward is down a ladder at the back of this platform, but before you go down there, it's worth crossing back over the bridge and opening the gate there to create a shortcut back to the Lighthouse Hut lamp. [→☐ 03/04]

Parasite Farm – Breeding Pits ㉓ ㉔ ㉕ ㉖ ㉗

At the bottom of the ladder you'll come to an area with a number of large pits filled with parasites that are divided by wooden walkways between them. Some of the large shells in these pits actually contain enemies called Snail Women, so it's best to attack any shells you come across just to avoid being attacked from behind later. Their attacks don't have a lot of range and are quite slow, but they often wake in groups so you'll have to contend with a few at a time. The best way to deal with them is to use a weapon that has long reach, and try to hit the exposed torso rather than the shell from outside of their attack range.

The first pit you come to can be skipped by simply following the walkway along and dropping down into the second pit when you come to it. If you do go into the first pit then there are some planks at the end that you can walk up to reach the second pit. When you

reach the tunnel leading out of this area, look just to the right of it and you'll see a small mound of parasites piled up over a wooden plank. You can walk over them to reach a small side area containing a Bloodstone Chunk. [→☐ 05/06]

㉘ ㉙ ㉚ Access Tunnel

A short distance into the tunnel the path will split, with one branch going straight ahead and another off to the left. When you reach that point, two shell-less Snail Women will come swimming down from directly ahead to attack you. If Brador is still alive, you should also start hearing the sound of a bell in this area to indicate you're near one of his invading locations. The path going straight is a dead-end so it's worth going that way first to get the item. Be ready as you approach it, because Brador will appear directly behind you. Since he appears quite close to you here, try to attack him will he is still materializing to get an early lead.

When heading down the other section of the tunnel, another shell-less Snail Woman will attack you almost straight away. Be ready to evade when you see her, and then at the far end of the tunnel there are two more of them, along with a Fishman (Curse). The best course of action there is to run past the two Snail Women and kill the Fishman first so you don't have to worry about evading its projectiles, and then finish off the Snail Women. Once everything is dead, go into the small alcove along this branch of the tunnel, and carefully drop down into the cave below. [→☐ 07]

Fishing Hamlet

Elevator Cave ③① ③② ③⑧

There's a large circular pit directly ahead when you land in this cave, so make sure you don't accidentally run into it, because even though it won't kill you outright, you will take a lot of damage. To get the item at the bottom of the pit safely, use the ladder that's on one side of it. Not too far from the pit there's a lever that you can pull, and doing so will lower an elevator platform over the pit. If you step onto the elevator it will take you up to a small room containing an item and a gate you can open that leads back into the Lighthouse Hut. As well as the elevator there are also two tunnels leading out from this cave – one takes you deeper into the caves for some exploration, and the other leads to a boss fight.

Culvert Intersection ③③

The item that you can see near the pillar at the far end of this tunnel may appear tempting, but do not be lured in by the bait because two Winter Lanterns are patrolling the area just to the left of it. Before fighting these creatures, make sure your insight it as low as possible, have attire that has high frenzy resistance, and have sedatives at the ready. You can circle around the pillar to try to stay out of their gaze to reduce the frenzy build-up. If you just want to run along to the Lower Breeding Pit, you can sprint through the intersection and keep running to escape their gaze. [→☐ 01]

01

Tunnel to the Well ③④ ③⑤

To explore this section of the tunnel you will have to deal with both of the Winter Lanterns, but the reward for beating them is making another hard fight easier. From the ledge at the end of the tunnel you'll be looking down into the cave below the Plaza Well with the two Giant Fishmen. It's possible to fight them from here and make that encounter much safer. Although you'll see one of them clinging to the ceiling, you cannot actually hit it at this time. Use a ranged attack such as a throwing knife to hit the one at the back of the cave so that it comes closer.

If you have Poison Throwing Knives they can also be very effective here for taking off large amounts of health. When they're close to the ledge, you can just move back out of the range of their attacks, and use a jumping attack to hit them during their recovery. If you drop down from the ledge you won't be able to get directly back up, so you'll need to climb the ladder out of the well and make your way back around to the Fishing Hamlet lamp so that you can warp to the Lighthouse Hut again.

③⑥ ③⑦ COMBAT FOCUS Lower Breeding Pit

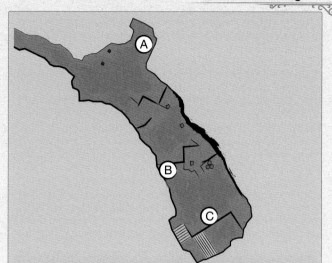

There are a large number of shell-less Snail Women near the entrance to this area, but if you approach it slowly you can lure them towards you either one at a time or in small manageable groups. If you need to create more space when fighting them, just retreat back down the tunnel. A Fishman (Staff) is also patrolling around the back of the first pit. As long as you don't rush in and pick off the Snail Women slowly, he'll usually have moved to a stationary position further in. Head to **Position A** as soon as you enter the first pit, because there are a few more Snail Women in an alcove there and it's best to kill them before going any further in.

The only things you should have to kill in the second section of the pit are a couple of Snail Women in their shells, near the wooden planks leading to the next section. Before killing them, however, go to **Position B** and you'll see a Fishman (Staff) standing on the other side of the wooden fence. You can attack and kill him through the fence before he can retaliate for an easy victory. Another Snail Woman will drop down near it so you can kill her safely from here too.

In the third section of the pit the patrolling Fishman (Staff) from earlier can be found at **Position C**, and two more shell-less Snail Women on the platform just behind it. If you're quick, you can run up and kill the Fishman before either of the Snail Women reaches you. This will allow you to then take both of them out normally afterwards. Now that the room is clear of threats, you can go up the stairs to the top of the platform and claim a highly coveted Blood Rock.

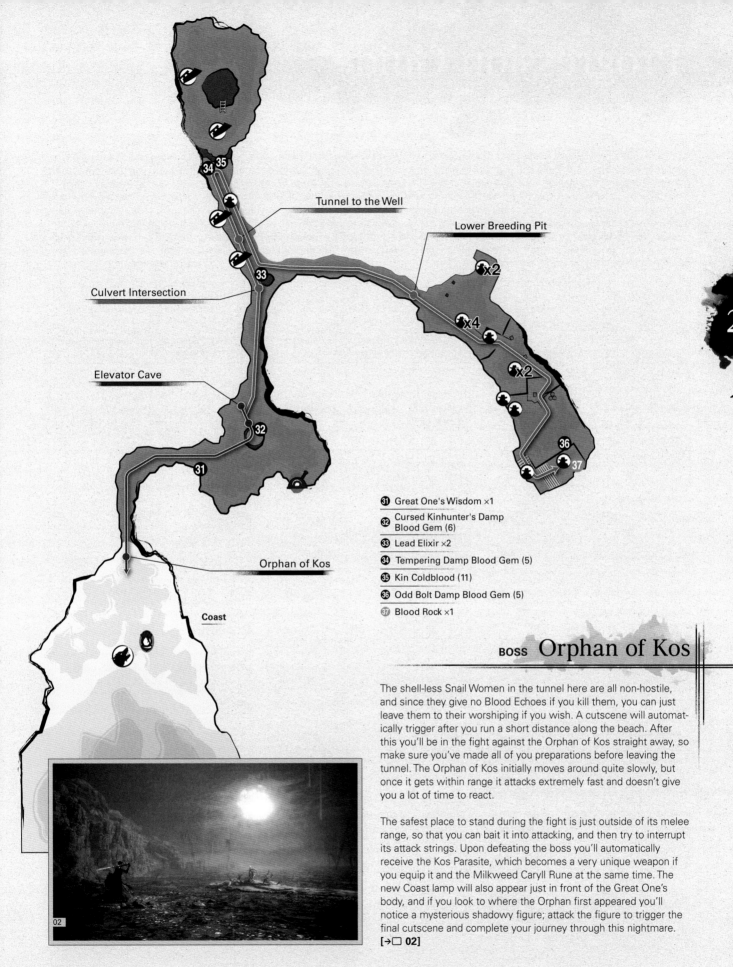

Tunnel to the Well

Lower Breeding Pit

Culvert Intersection

Elevator Cave

Coast

Orphan of Kos

31 Great One's Wisdom ×1

32 Cursed Kinhunter's Damp Blood Gem (6)

33 Lead Elixir ×2

34 Tempering Damp Blood Gem (5)

35 Kin Coldblood (11)

36 Odd Bolt Damp Blood Gem (5)

37 Blood Rock ×1

BOSS Orphan of Kos

The shell-less Snail Women in the tunnel here are all non-hostile, and since they give no Blood Echoes if you kill them, you can just leave them to their worshiping if you wish. A cutscene will automatically trigger after you run a short distance along the beach. After this you'll be in the fight against the Orphan of Kos straight away, so make sure you've made all of you preparations before leaving the tunnel. The Orphan of Kos initially moves around quite slowly, but once it gets within range it attacks extremely fast and doesn't give you a lot of time to react.

The safest place to stand during the fight is just outside of its melee range, so that you can bait it into attacking, and then try to interrupt its attack strings. Upon defeating the boss you'll automatically receive the Kos Parasite, which becomes a very unique weapon if you equip it and the Milkweed Caryll Rune at the same time. The new Coast lamp will also appear just in front of the Great One's body, and if you look to where the Orphan first appeared you'll notice a mysterious shadowy figure; attack the figure to trigger the final cutscene and complete your journey through this nightmare.

[→☐ 02]

Progression Guide

Welcome to the progression guide. Here we present a high-level overview of the game breaking down the most important items and events in each area. Along with our recommended route through the game, this section compiles useful information that can provide some insight into how difficult or lucrative an area might be. The recommended path matches the full walkthrough (starting on p30), so it's easy to move between both sections depending on the level of guidance you desire. For those who want even less detail, the chart below shows only the most crucial steps required to get through the game with everything needed to achieve the Childhood's Beginning ending. The other endings do not require specific materials, and you can you find out how to achieve them on p161.

Color Coding

The same color coding as in the main walkthrough is used here for the events in each area. Red steps are required to progress the game, while blue signifies optional steps that are still very useful and will lead to a smoother playthrough.

Hunter's Dream | p30
Acquire a trick weapon and firearm, return to Central Yharnam.

Central Yharnam | p41 & p44
Kill Cleric Beast and Father Gascoigne, collect the Blood Gem Workshop Tool, proceed to Cathedral Ward.

Cathedral Ward | p49
Open the entrance to Old Yharnam,

Old Yharnam | p64
Kill Blood-starved Beast.

Healing Church Workshop | p71
Enter the Abandoned Old Workshop to get the One Third of Umbilical Cord. Proceed up the elevator at the end of the Village Alleyways to return to Cathedral Ward, and onward to Hemwick Charnel Lane.

Hemwick Charnel Lane | p79
Kill the Witch of Hemwick and collect the Rune Workshop Tool, return to Cathedral Ward.

Cathedral Ward (cont.) | p55
Kill Vicar Amelia and examine the altar in the Grand Cathedral. Die from a Kidnapper to be transported to Yahar'gul, Unseen Village.

Yahar'gul, Unseen Village (Evening) | p83
Kill Darkbeast Paarl and return to the Hunter's Dream.

Hunter's Dream (cont.) | p29
Pick up the Eye of a Blood-drunk Hunter and return to Cathedral Ward..

Cathedral Ward (cont.) | p49
Proceed to the Oedon Chapel Well and allow yourself to be grabbed by the Amygdala, transporting you to the Hunter's Nightmare. After, return to Cathedral Ward and proceed to the Forbidden Woods.

Forbidden Woods | p101
Kill Shadows of Yharnam, proceed to Brygenwerth.

Byrgenwerth | p127
Kill Rom, the Vacuous Spider and be transported to Yahar'gul, Unseen Village.

Yahar'gul, Unseen Village (Blood Moon) | p137
Acquire the Upper Cathedral Key, kill The One Reborn and enter the Lecture Building 2F.

Lecture Building 2F | p144
Proceed to Lecture Building 1F.

Lecture Building 1F | p114
Proceed to the Nightmare Frontier.

Nightmare Frontier | p125
Kill Amygdala and return to Lecture Building 2F and proceed to Nightmare of Mensis.

Nightmare of Mensis | p154 & p159
Kill Micolash, Host of the Nightmare and Mergo's Wet Nurse and claim the One Third of Umbilical Cord. Return to the Forbidden Woods and enter Iosefka's Clinic.

Iosefka's Clinic | p102
Kill Iosefka (Imposter) to receive the One Third of Umbilical Cord, then pick up the Cainhurst Summons. Return to Hemwick Charnel Lane and be escorted to Forsaken Castle Cainhurst.

Forsaken Cainhurst Castle | p113
Kill Martyr Logarius and return to the Healing Church Workshop. Ascend the Workshop Tower and enter the Upper Cathedral Ward.

Upper Cathedral Ward | p143
Kill Celestial Emissary and Ebrietas, Daughter of the Cosmos. Return to Hunter's Nightmare.

Hunter's Nightmare | p166
Grab the Eye Pendant from the Nightmare Grand Cathedral, then kill Ludwig the Accursed. Collect Laurence's Skull and kill Laurence, the First Vicar. Proceed to the Research Hall.

Research Hall | p186
Kill Living Failures and Lady Maria of the Astral Clocktower, proceed to Fishing Hamlet.

Fishing Hamlet | p199
Kill Orphan of Kos and attack the mysterious shadowy figure that remains, return to the Hunter's Dream.

Hunter's Dream | p160
Consume One Third of Umbilical Cord x3 and kill Gehrman, the First Hunter and Moon Presence.

Central Yharnam

Difficulty	Area **B**	Cleric Beast **B**	Father Gascoigne **A**
Blood Gem Rank	**1**
Timezones	○ ◐ ☾ ●
Blood Echoes	From Enemies **14640**	From Items **5450**
Insight	Encounter the Cleric Beast ×1, Defeat the Cleric Beast ×3, Encounter Father Gascoigne ×1, Witness Father Gascoigne's transformation ×1, Defeat Father Gascoigne ×2

Upgrade Materials

	✦	✦	✦
From Pickups	10	–	–
From Wandering Nightmare	–	–	–

Chalice Dungeon Materials

Material Name	Acquired By
–	–

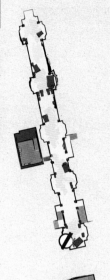

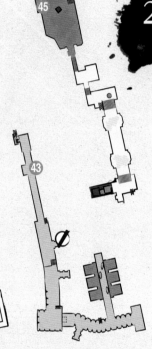

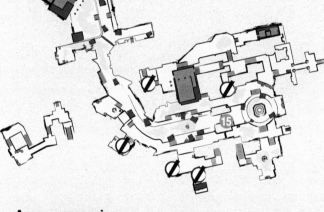

Area progression

Pick up the Torch in the Plaza. p37

Kill the Cleric Beast to acquire the Sword Hunter Badge and gain Insight to allow character leveling in the Hunter's Dream. p41

Enter the Dry Docks to acquire the Saw Spear. p43

Get the Saw Hunter Badge from the Boar Tunnel. p44

Kill Father Gascoigne to acquire the Oedon Tomb Key so you can reach the Cathedral Ward. p328

Open the chest at the end of the Chapel Path to get the Blood Gem Workshop Tool. p45

Item legend

✦	–	Bloodstone Shard	p585
15	p37	Torch	p563
31	p43	Saw Spear	p484
39	p38	Hunter Hat Hunter Garb Hunter Gloves Hunter Trousers	p622
43	p44	Saw Hunter Badge	p595
45	p45	Red Jeweled Brooch	p586
45	p45	Blood Gem Workshop Tool	p606

Cathedral Ward

Difficulty	Area **A**	Vicar Amelia **B**	
Blood Gem Rank	**2-3**	
Timezones	○ ◐ ☾ ●	
Blood Echoes	From Enemies **41855**	From Items **10900**	
Insight	Encounter Vicar Amelia ×1, Defeat Vicar Amelia ×3	

Upgrade Materials

	∅	∅	∅
From Pickups	10	3	–
From Wandering Nightmare	6	4	–

Chalice Dungeon Materials

Material Name	Acquired By
Bloodshot Eyeball	Loot Corpse

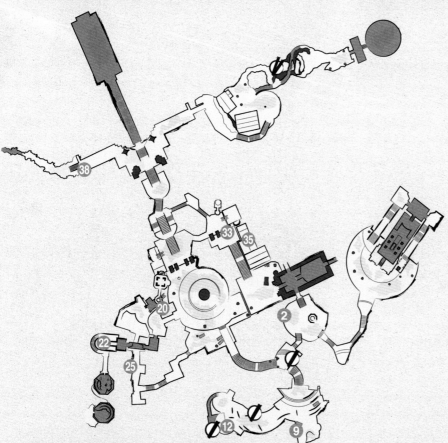

Item legend

∅	–	Bloodstone Shard	p585
∅	–	Twin Bloodstone Shards	p585
2	p48	Top Hat Hunter Garb Hunter Gloves Hunter Trousers	p622
9	p51	Monocular	p576
12	p51	Tempering Blood Gemstone (2)	–
25	p52	Black Church Hat Black Church Garb Surgical Long Gloves Black Church Trousers/ Dress	p617
33	p53	Wooden Shield	p563
35	p53	Black Messenger Hat	p590
38	p54	Bloodshot Eyeball	p404

Area progression

Buy the Hunter Chief Emblem from the Bath Messenger in the Hunter's Dream to skip Old Yharnam, Healing Church Workshop and Yahar'gul Victim City (Evening). p48

◀ OR ▶

Go to and complete Old Yharnam (opens the door in the Oedon Chapel that leads to the Healing Church Workshop). p56

▼

Go to and complete Healing Church Workshop (requires completion of Old Yharnam). p66

Go to and complete Hemwick Charnel Lane (requires completion of Healing Church Workshop or purchasing of the Hunter Chief Emblem). p72

▼

Kill Vicar Amelia and examine the altar in the Grand Cathedral to get the Forbidden Woods password (requires completion of Healing Church Workshop or purchasing of the Hunter Chief Emblem). p336

▼

After obtaining the Tonsil Stone (enter the Forbidden Woods and speak with any residential NPC before reaching Byrgenwerth), go to the room at the end of The Cliffs and get caught in the False God's attack to access Lecture Building 1F. p55

Old Yharnam

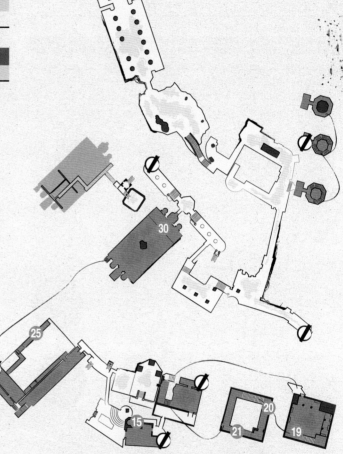

Difficulty	Area **B**	Blood-starved Beast **B**	
Blood Gem Rank	**1-2**	
Timezones	○ ◑ ☾ ◐	
Blood Echoes	From Enemies **23841**	From Items **5000**	
Insight	Encounter the Blood-starved Beast ×1, Defeat the Blood-starved Beast ×2	

Upgrade Materials

	⊘	⊘	⊘
From Pickups	12	–	–
From Wandering Nightmare	9	–	–

Chalice Dungeon Materials

Material Name	Acquired By
Ritual Blood (1)	Collect at the altar in the Ritual Hall

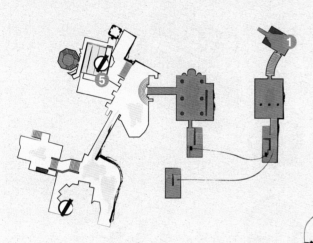

Area progression

Get the Hunter's Torch from the Rooftops	p59

▼

Get the Rifle Spear from the Storage Area	p61

▼

Defeat Djura at the top of his tower to get the Powder Keg Badge, or leave him alive for a peaceful resolution after completing Yahar'gul, Unseen Village (Evening).	p62

▼

Defeat the Blood-starved Beast to open up the Healing Church Workshop, acquire the Pthumeru Chalice and cause Kidnappers to appear in various areas. Allow a Kidnapper to kill you in order to access Yahar'gul, Unseen Village (Evening).	p330

Item legend

⊘	–	Bloodstone Shard	p585
①	p58	Tempering Blood Gemstone (1)	–
⑤	p59	Hunter's Torch	p563
⑮	p61	Bloodtinge Gemstone (1)	–
⑲	p51	Tempering Blood Gemstone (1)	–
⑳	p61	Rifle Spear	p511
㉑	p21	Charred Hunter Garb Charred Hunter Gloves Charred Hunter Trousers	p618
㉕	p63	Bloody Messenger Head Bandage	p590
㉚	p63	Ritual Blood (1)	p403

Healing Church Workshop

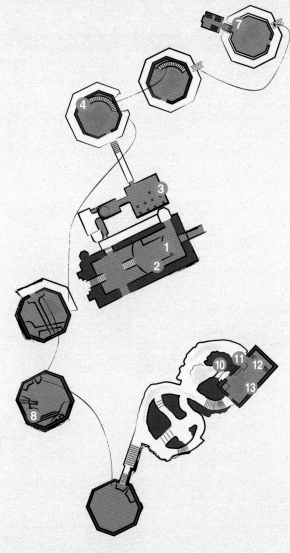

Difficulty	Area **B**			
Blood Gem Rank	**3-4**			
Timezones	○ ◗ ☾ ●			
Blood Echoes	From Enemies **6077** | From Items **5400**			
Insight	Enter the Abandoned Old Workshop ×2			

Upgrade Materials

	⊘	⊘	⊘
From Pickups	–	–	–
From Wandering Nightmare	–	2	–

Chalice Dungeon Materials

Material Name	Acquired By
–	–

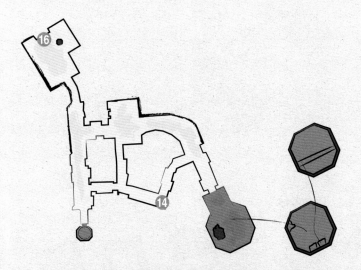

Item legend

❶	p68	Formless Oedon	p602
❷	p68	Messenger Urn Dance	p590
❸	p69	Communion	p602
❹	p69	Bloodtinge Gemstone (2)	–
❼	p69	Radiant Sword Hunter Badge	p596
❽	p71	Messenger Top Hat	p589
❿	p71	Doll Hat Doll Clothes Doll Gloves Doll Skirt	p622
⑪	p71	Old Hunter Bone	p580
⑫	p71	One Third of Umbilical Cord	p594
⑬	p71	Small Hair Ornament	p588
⑭	p71	Rumpled Yharnam Hat Sweaty Clothes	p624
⑯	p71	Fire Blood Gemstone (3)	–

Area progression

Go up the Oedon Chapel Elevator and access the hidden path to reach the Formless Oedon Caryll Rune.	p68
Go to Tower F3 to get the Radiant Sword Hunter Badge.	p69
Enter the Abandoned Old Workshop to get the Old Hunter Bone, One Third of Umbilical Cord and the Small Hair Ornament.	p71

Hemwick Charnel Lane

Difficulty	Area **B** | Witch of Hemwick **B**
Blood Gem Rank	**4-5**
Timezones	○ ● ☾ ◓
Blood Echoes	From Enemies **46645** | From Items **7000**
Insight	Encounter the Witch of Hemwick ×1, Defeat the Witch of Hemwick ×2

Upgrade Materials

	∅	∅	∅
From Pickups	–	7	–
From Wandering Nightmare	–	2	–

Chalice Dungeon Materials

Material Name	Acquired By
Bloodshot Eyeball	Guillotine, Corpse
Bloodshot Eyeball	Barn, Corpse
Bloodshot Eyeball	Defeat Witch of Hemwick

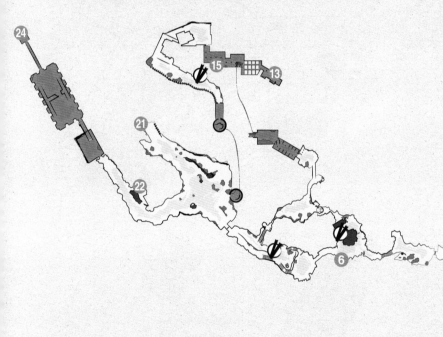

Area progression

Kill the Witch of Hemwick to reach the room containing the Rune Workshop Tool.	p332

▼

Return to Hemwick Crossing after obtaining the Cainhurst Summons from Iosefka's Clinic, and then approach the large obelisk in the middle to summon the carriage that will take you to Forsaken Cainhurst Castle.	p78

Item legend

∅	–	Twin Bloodstone Shards	p585
6	p75	Bloodshot Eyeball	p404
13	p77	Adept Blood Gemstone (3)	–
15	p77	Bloodshot Eyeball	p404
21	p79	Lake	p600
22	p79	Tempering Blood Gemstone (1)	–
24	p79	Rune Workshop Tool	p605

Yahar'gul, Unseen Village (Evening)

Difficulty	Area **B** | Darkbeast Paarl **S**	
Blood Gem Rank	**5-6**	
Timezones	○ ● ☾ ◐	
Blood Echoes	From Enemies **45832** | From Items **11800**	
Insight	Arriving in the prison ×1, Encounter Darkbeast Paarl ×1, Defeat Darkbeast Paarl ×3	

Upgrade Materials

	⊘	⊘	⊘
From Pickups	–	1	–
From Wandering Nightmare	–	6	–

Chalice Dungeon Materials

Material Name	Acquired By
–	–

Item legend

⊘	–	Twin Bloodstone Shards	p585
5	p83	Moon	p597
8	p84	Tonitrus	p517
9	p85	Black Hooded Iron Helm Yahar'gul Black Garb Yahar'gul Black Gloves Yahar'gul Black Trousers	p626

Area progression

Obtain the Moon Caryll Rune from the Yahar'gul Chapel.	p83

▼

Get Tonitrus from Main Street - West.	p84

▼

Kill Darkbeast Paarl to acquire the Spark Hunter Badge and open up the back way into Old Yharnam so that you can speak with Djura and peacefully get the Powder Keg Badge.	p334

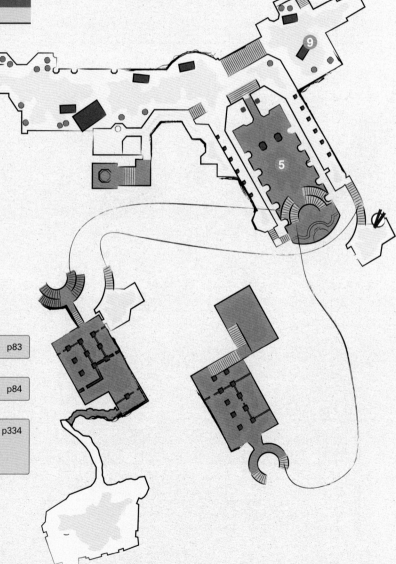

Forbidden Woods

Difficulty	Area **A** | Shadows of Yharnam **A**
Blood Gem Rank	**7-8**
Timezones	○ ◐ ☾ ●
Blood Echoes	From Enemies **125318** |
	From Items **20200**
Insight	Defeat the Shadows of Yharnam ×2

Upgrade Materials

	⊘	⊘	⊘
From Pickups	–	26	1
From Wandering Nightmare	–	3	–

Chalice Dungeon Materials

Material Name	Acquired By
–	–

Item legend

⊘	–	Twin Bloodst. Shards	p585	40	p95	Cannon	p561
⊘	–	Bloodstone Chunk	p585	56	p97	Clear Deep Sea	p601
5	p90	Adept Blood Gemstone (2)	–	59	p97	Deep Sea	p601
22	p93	White Church Hat White Church Garb Surgical Long Gloves White Church Trousers/Dress	p625	63	p99	Clockwise Metamorphosis	p598
				65	p99	Graveyard Mask	p621
25	p93	Arcane Blood Gemstone (2)	–	66	p98	Graveyard Robe Graveyard Manchettes Graveyard Kilt	p621
26	p93	Nourishing Blood Gemstone (2)	–	70	p100	Anti-Clockwise Metamorphosis	p598
27	p93	Dirty Blood Gemstone	–	73	p100	Dissipating Lake	p600
30	p93	Beast Roar	p582	74	p101	Sharp Blood Gemstone (3)	–

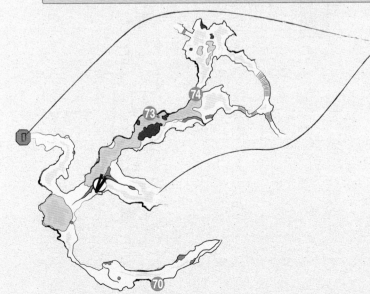

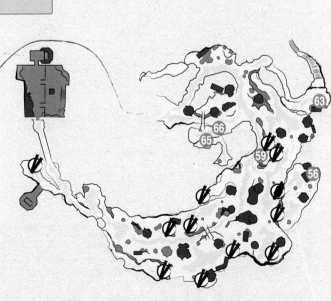

Area progression

Talk to any residential NPC between seeing the area name come up and entering Byrgenwerth to get the Tonsil Stone.	p589

▼

Pick up the Beast Roar from the Village Outskirts.	p93

▼

Go through the Subterranean Cave to reach the back of Iosefka's Clinic, where you can find the Cainhurst Summons.	p93

▼

Get the Cannon from the Windmill Cogs.	p95

▼

Go to the Graveyard Path to get the Clockwise Metamorphosis Caryll Rune.	p99

▼

Get the Anti-Clockwise Metamorphosis Caryll Rune from the Ravine Floor.	p100

▼

Kill the Shadows of Yharnam to open the path to Byrgenwerth.	p338

Iosefka's Clinic

Difficulty	Area **B**
Blood Gem Rank	**1**
Timezones	○ ● ☾ ●
Blood Echoes	From Enemies **3357** | From Items **350**
Insight	Entering via the backdoor ×1

Upgrade Materials

	⬦	⬦	⬦
From Pickups	–	–	–
From Wandering Nightmare	–	–	–

Chalice Dungeon Materials

Material Name	Acquired By
–	–

Item legend

③	p102	Cainhurst Summons	p588
④	p103	Communion	p602

Area progression

Get the Cainhurst Summons from the 2nd Floor Operating Room.	p102

▼

Get the Communion Caryll Rune from the Rear Operating Room.	p103

▼

Return here during the Blood Moon and kill Iosefka (Imposter) to get One Third of Umbilical Cord.	p103

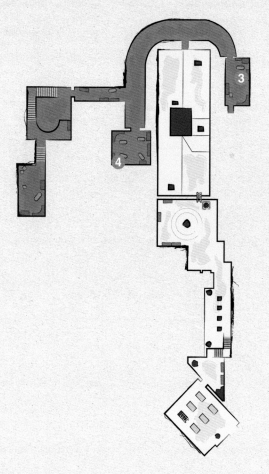

Forsaken Cainhurst Castle

Difficulty	Area **B** | Martyr Logarius **S**
Blood Gem Rank	**9-10**
Timezones	◯ ◔ ☾ ◑
Blood Echoes	From Enemies **87892** | From Items **24000**
Insight	Arrive in the area ×2, Encounter Martyr Logarius ×1, Defeat Martyr Logarius ×3, Enter the Queen's Chamber ×2

Upgrade Materials

	🔩	🔩	🔩
From Pickups	–	–	3
From Wandering Nightmare	–	–	2

Chalice Dungeon Materials

Material Name	Acquired By
–	–

Item legend

🔩	–	Bloodstone Chunk	p585
③	p106	Tempering Blood Gemstone (3)	–
⑩	p107	Reiterpallasch	p505
⑬	p107	Alluring Dress	p616
⑮	p109	Executioner Garb Executioner Gauntlets Executioner Trousers	p619
⑯	p109	Vileblood Register	p577
⑰	p109	Evelyn	p561
⑳	p110	Executioner's Gloves	p582
㉑	p111	Knight's Garb Knight's Gloves Knight's Trousers/Dress	p623
㉓	p112	Warm Blood Gemstone (3)	–
㉔	p113	Knight's Wig	p623
㉗	p113	Unopened Summons	p588

Area progression

Go to the obelisk in the Hemwick Crossing part of Hemwick Charnel Lane after getting the Cainhurst Summons from Iosefka's Clinic to reach the area.	p78

▼

Acquire the Reiterpallasch from the Entrance Hall.	p107

▼

Get the Vileblood Register from the Library 1F.	p109

▼

Get Evelyn from the Library 1F.	p109

▼

Go to the Secluded Reading Room to get the Executioner's Gloves.	p110

▼

Defeat Martyr Logarius and equip the Crown of Illusions to reveal the Queen's Chambers.	p342

▼

Get the Unopened Summons from the Queen's Chambers.	p113

▼

Talk to the Queen and join the Vilebloods to get the Cainhurst Badge.	p113

Lecture Building 1F

Difficulty	Area **B**
Blood Gem Rank	**6-7**
Timezones	○ ◐ ☾ ◑
Blood Echoes	From Enemies **12636** | From Items —
Insight	Arriving in the area ×2

Upgrade Materials

	∅	∅	∅
From Pickups	–	–	–
From Wandering Nightmare	–	–	–

Chalice Dungeon Materials

Material Name	Acquired By
–	–

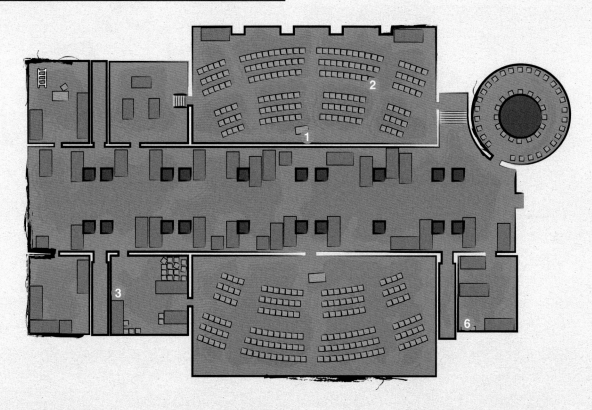

Area progression

After obtaining the Tonsil Stone, go the room at the end of the Cliffs in the Cathedral Ward and get caught in the False God's attack to be transported to this area.   p55

▼

Go through Lecture Theater 2 to get Augur of Ebrietas.   p115

▼

Open the door at the end of the Main Hallway to reach the Nightmare Frontier.   p115

Item legend

❶ p115	Lecture Theatre Key	p587
❷ p115	Student Uniform Student Trousers	p624
❸ p115	Augur of Ebrietas	p581
❻ p115	Red Jelly	p404

Nightmare Frontier

Difficulty	Area **A** | Amygdala **B**
Blood Gem Rank	**6-7**
Timezones	○ ◐ ☾ ●
Blood Echoes	From Enemies **87650** | From Items **29000**
Insight	Arrive in the area ×2, Encounter Amygdala ×3, Defeat Amygdala ×3

Upgrade Materials

	⊘	⊘	⊘
From Pickups	–	–	–
From Wandering Nightmare	34	9	4

Chalice Dungeon Materials

Material Name	Acquired By
Coldblood Flowerbud	Corpse
Coldblood Flowerbud	Corpse
Coldblood Flowerbud	Corpse

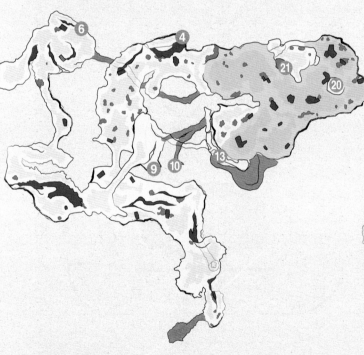

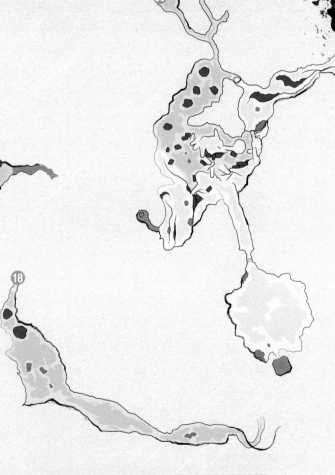

Area progression

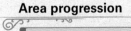

Go to the Lower Caves to get the Clockwise Metamorphosis Caryll Rune.	p122

▼

Venture to the end of the Swampy Gorge to get Messenger's Gift	p123

▼

Defeat Amygdala to acquire the Lower Loran Chalice.	p340

Item legend

④	p119	Fading Lake	p600
⑥	p120	Coldblood Flowerbud	p403
⑨	p122	Coldblood Flowerbud	p403
⑩	p122	Clockwise Metamorphosis	p598
⑬	p122	Stunning Deep Sea	p601
⑱	p123	Messenger's Gift	p582
⑳	p123	Coldblood Flowerbud	p600
㉑	p123	Clear Deep Sea	p601
㉚	p125	Great Deep Sea	p602

Byrgenwerth

Difficulty	Area **B** | Rom, the Vacuous Spider **S**
Blood Gem Rank	**8-9**
Timezones	◯ ◖ ☾ ◑
Blood Echoes	From Enemies **38558** | From Items **20000**
Insight	Speak with Master Willem ×2, Encounter Rom, the Vacuous Spider ×2, Defeat Rom, the Vacuous Spider ×2

Upgrade Materials

	⊘	⊘	⊘
From Pickups	–	–	–
From Wandering Nightmare	–	–	–

Chalice Dungeon Materials

Material Name	Acquired By
Pearl Slug	Inside University Building, Chest

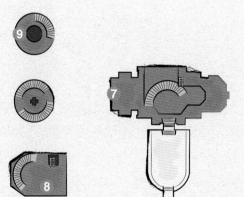

Area progression

Obtain the Lunarium Key and the Empty Phantasm Shell from the College: Upper Floors. — p127

▼

Kill Master Willem to get the Eye Caryll Rune. — p127

▼

Jump into the lake, defeat Rom, the Vacuous Spider, and then approach the ghost of Yharnam to be transported back to Cathedral Ward with the doors to Yahar'gul, Unseen Village (Blood Moon) open in front of you. — p344

Item legend

②	p127	Arcane Lake	p599
⑥	p127	Pearl Slug	p404
⑦	p127	Student Uniform Student Trousers	p616
⑧	p127	Lunarium Key	p587
⑨	p127	Empty Phantasm Shell	p580

Yahar'gul, Unseen Village (Blood Moon)

Difficulty	Area **S** | The One Reborn **A**
Blood Gem Rank	**12-13**
Timezones	◯ ◖ ◑ ●
Blood Echoes	From Enemies **124552**
	From Items **15000**
Insight	Encounter The One Reborn ×1, Defeat The One Reborn ×3

Upgrade Materials

	⊘	⊘	⊘
From Pickups	–	–	11
From Wandering Nightmare	–	–	4

Chalice Dungeon Materials

Material Name	Acquired By
Yellow Backbone	Defeat boss, The One Reborn

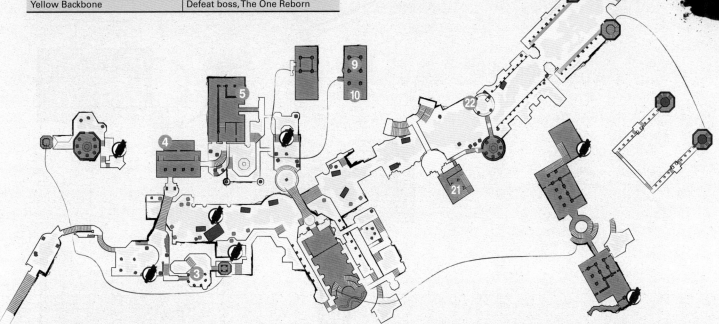

Area progression

Go to the Holding Cell to acquire the Upper Cathedral Key and Tiny Tonitrus. — p132

▼

Kill The One Reborn and inspect the mummy in the next room to be taken to Lecture Building 2F. — p346

Item legend

⊘	–	Bloodstone Chunk	p585
③	p130	Iron Yahar'gul Helm	p626
④	p131	Bolt Damp Blood Gem (4)	–
⑤	p131	Heir	p599
⑨	p132	Upper Cathedral Key	p587
⑩	p132	Tiny Tonitrus	p580
㉑	p136	Tempering Damp Blood Gem (5)	–
㉒	p137	Arcane Lake	p599

Upper Cathedral Ward

Difficulty	Area **B** | Celestial Emissary **B** | Ebrietas, Daughter of the Cosmos **A**
Blood Gem Rank	**10-11**
Timezones	○ ◒ ☾ ●
Blood Echoes	From Enemies **89084** | From Items **10000**
Insight	Defeat the Celestial Emissary ×1, Encounter Ebrietas, Daughter of the Cosmos ×2, Defeat Ebrietas, Daughter of the Cosmos ×3

Upgrade Materials

	⊘	⊘	⊘
From Pickups	–	–	–
From Wandering Nightmare	–	–	2

Chalice Dungeon Materials

Material Name	Acquired By
Ritual Blood (5)	Orphanage, Corpse
Pearl Slug	Orphanage, Corpse

Item legend

② p140	Great Lake	p600
④ p141	Choir Garb Choir Gloves Choir Trousers	p619
⑤ p141	Cosmic Eye Watcher Badge	p596
⑥ p141	Ritual Blood (5)	p403
⑧ p141	Blindfold Cap	p619
⑪ p141	Pearl Slug	p404
⑫ p142	Make Contact	p676
⑮ p143	A Call Beyond	p581

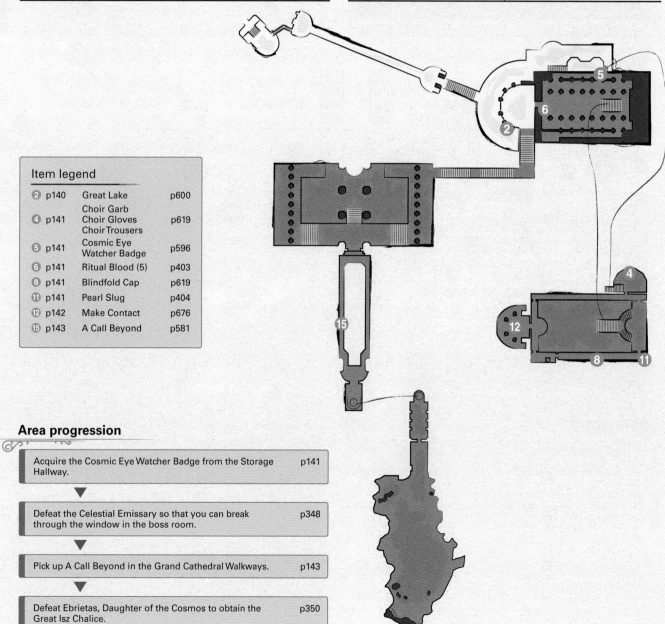

Area progression

Acquire the Cosmic Eye Watcher Badge from the Storage Hallway.   p141

▼

Defeat the Celestial Emissary so that you can break through the window in the boss room.   p348

▼

Pick up A Call Beyond in the Grand Cathedral Walkways.   p143

▼

Defeat Ebrietas, Daughter of the Cosmos to obtain the Great Isz Chalice.   p350

Lecture Building 2F

Difficulty	Area **B**
Blood Gem Rank	**13-14**
Timezones	○ ◑ ☾ ●
Blood Echoes	From Enemies **21124** | From Items –
Insight	Set eyes upon Patches the Spider ×2

Upgrade Materials

	⌀	⌀	⌀
From Pickups	–	–	1
From Wandering Nightmare	–	–	–

Chalice Dungeon Materials

Material Name	Acquired By
–	–

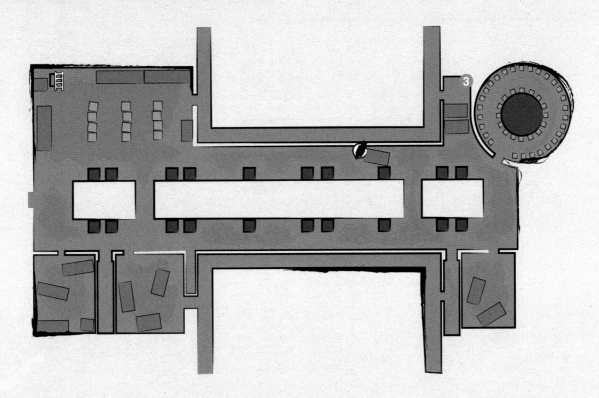

Area progression

Go along the Lecture Theater 1 Balcony to get the Communion Caryll Rune.	p145

▼

If you did not obtain the Tonsil Stone and access Nightmare Frontier previously, you can go there now by going down the ladder in Patches' Lab to reach 1F, and follow the Main Hallway along on that floor to reach the door that takes you there.	p116

▼

Go through the door at the end of the Main Hallway to reach Nightmare of Mensis.	p146

Item legend

⌀	–	Bloodstone Chunk	p585
❸	p145	Communion	p602

Nightmare of Mensis

Difficulty	Area **S** | Micolash, Host of the Nightmare **B** | Mergo's Wet Nurse **S**
Blood Gem Rank	**13-14**
Timezones	○ ◐ ☾ ◑
Blood Echoes	From Enemies **331796**
	From Items **66000**
Insight	Arrive in the area ×3, Encounter Micolash, Host of the Nightmare ×1, Defeat Micolash, Host of the Nightmare ×2, Encounter Mergo's Wet Nurse ×3, Defeat Mergo's Wet Nurse ×3

Chalice Dungeon Materials

Material Name	Acquired By
Yellow Backbone	Loot chest
Infected Organ	Loot chest
Living String	Defeat 'Brain of Mensis'

Upgrade Materials

	🔩	🔩	⏱
From Pickups	–	–	7
From Wandering Nightmare	–	–	9

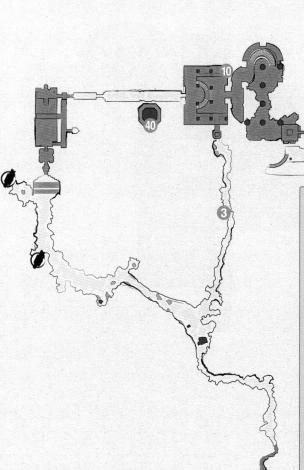

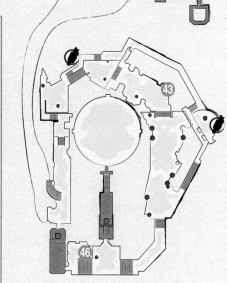

Item legend

🩸	–	Bloodstone Chunk	p585
3	p149	Eye	p597
10	p151	Yellow Backbone	p405
16	p153	Tempering Damp Blood Gem (5)	–
21	p155	Moon	p597
25	p155	Iron Door Key	p587
29	p157	Infected Organ	p404
31	p157	Tempering Damp Blood Gem (5)	–
32	p157	Choir Bell	p581
34	p157	Arcane Damp Blood Gem (5)	–
38	p157	Damp Bloodtinge Gem (5)	–
40	p157	Blood Rock	p585
43	p158	Nourishing Damp Blood Gem (4)	–
46	p158	Iosefka's Blood Vial	p566

Area progression

Pick up the Eye Caryll Rune from Mergo's Loft: Base.	p149

▼

Get the Moon Caryll Rune from the Library Staircase.	p155

Go to the Chapel Rafters and get the Choir Bell.	p157

▼

Drop down through the Crumbled Wall on the Middle Bridge to reach the room containing the Blood Rock.	p157

▼

Defeat Mergo's Wet Nurse to obtain One Third of Umbilical Cord.	p354

Hunter's Nightmare OH

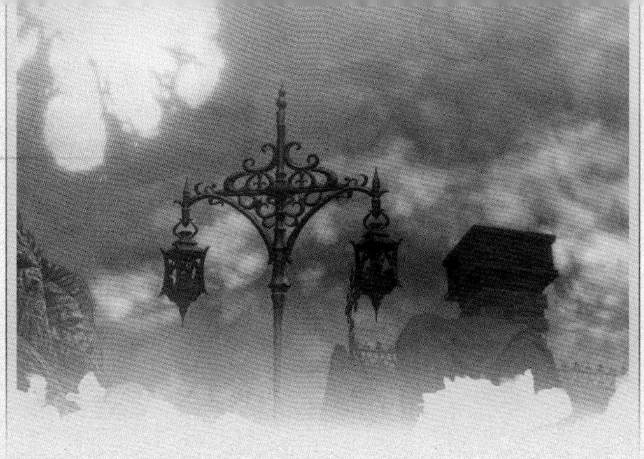

Difficulty	Area **B** | Ludwig the Accursed **A** | Laurence, the First Vicar **A**
Blood Gem Rank	**15**
Timezones	
Blood Echoes	From Enemies **148215**
	From Items **26000**
Insight	Reach the Hunter's Nightmare for the first time ×2, Reach the Underground Corpse Pile and encounter Ludwig the Accursed ×1, Defeat Ludwig the Accursed ×3, Encounter Laurence, the First Vicar in the Nightmare Grand Cathedral ×1, Defeat Laurence, the First Vicar ×3

Upgrade Materials

From Pickups	–	15	3
From Wandering Nightmare	–	–	2

Chalice Dungeon Materials

Material Name	Acquired By
–	–

2

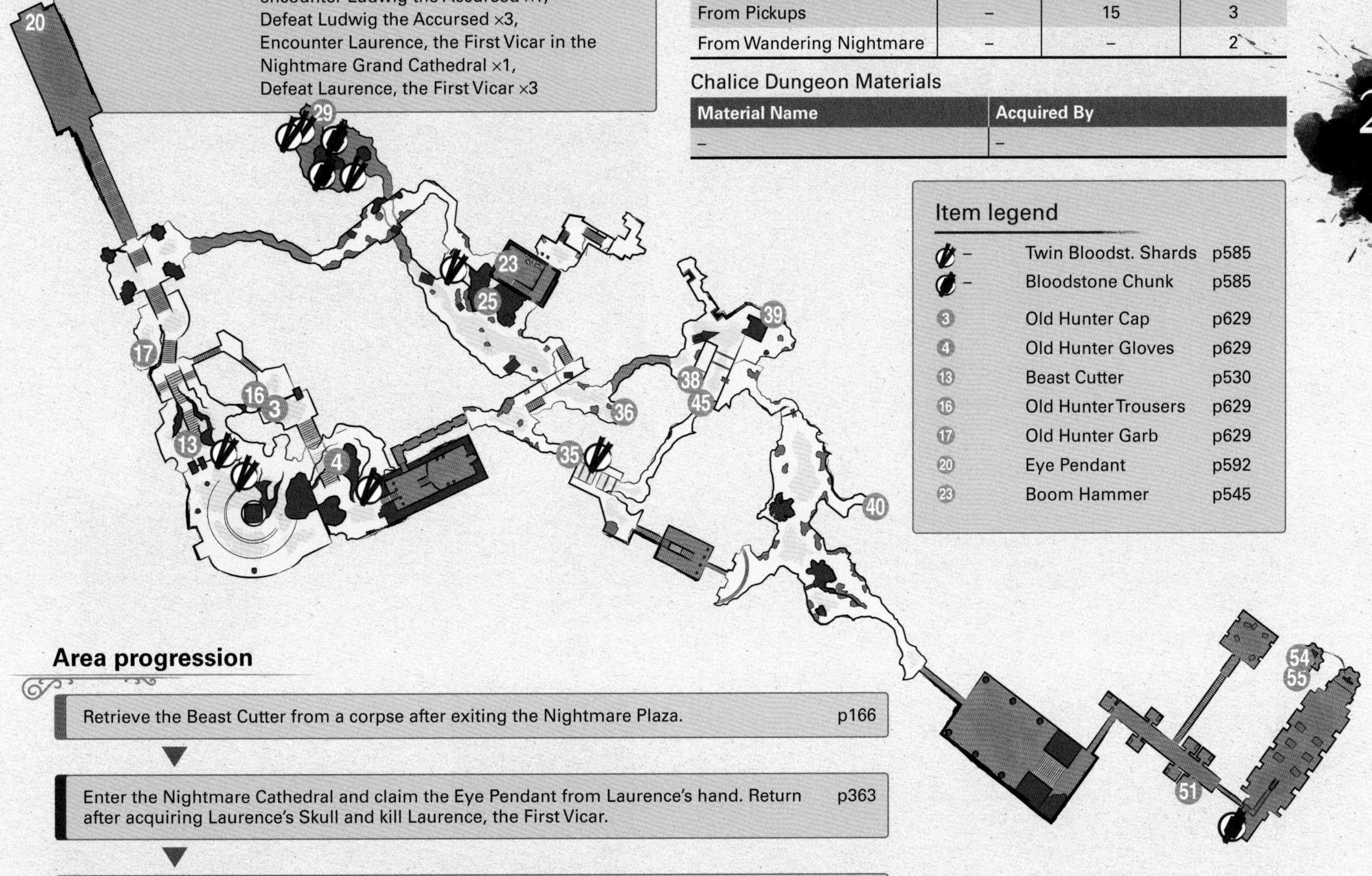

Item legend

–	Twin Bloodst. Shards	p585
–	Bloodstone Chunk	p585
③	Old Hunter Cap	p629
④	Old Hunter Gloves	p629
⑬	Beast Cutter	p530
⑯	Old Hunter Trousers	p629
⑰	Old Hunter Garb	p629
⑳	Eye Pendant	p592
㉓	Boom Hammer	p545

Area progression

Retrieve the Beast Cutter from a corpse after exiting the Nightmare Plaza. p166

▼

Enter the Nightmare Cathedral and claim the Eye Pendant from Laurence's hand. Return after acquiring Laurence's Skull and kill Laurence, the First Vicar. p363

▼

Procure the Boom Hammer from a trapped corpse on the lowest floor of the Nightmare Residence. Travel onward to the Nightmare Gate and defeat the Bestial Hunter to claim the Firing Hammer Badge. p168

▼

Dispatch Djura's Disciple inside the Beast Cave, rewarding the Gatling Gun. The Amygdalan Arm can also be found on a corpse in the cave depths behind the Blood-starved Beast. p168

▼

Drop off a ledge after the Balance Beams to find the Beasthunter Saif on a nearby corpse. p171

▼

Retrieve the Whirligig Saw from a body at the end of the Corpse Ravine. p171

▼

Kill Ludwig the Accursed in the Underground Corpse Pile. Speak to Ludwig, the Holy Blade (Head) while wearing Black Church Garb, White Church Garb, Choir Garb, Executioner Garb, Tomb Prospector Garb and respond "No". Upon returning to the Underground Corpse Pile, Simon, Seeker of Secrets will bestow the Holy Moonlight Sword. p360

Item legend

㉕	Old Hunter Top Hat	p628
㉙	Amygdalan Arm	p553
㉟	Constable's Gloves	p627
㊱	Constable's Trousers	p627
㊳	Constable's Garb	p627
㊴	Beasthunter Saif	p527
㊵	Butcher Mask, Garb, Gloves, Trousers	p627
㊺	Whirligig Saw	p547
(51)	Fist of Gratia	p565
(54)	Laurence's Skull	p592
(55)	Church Cannon	p565

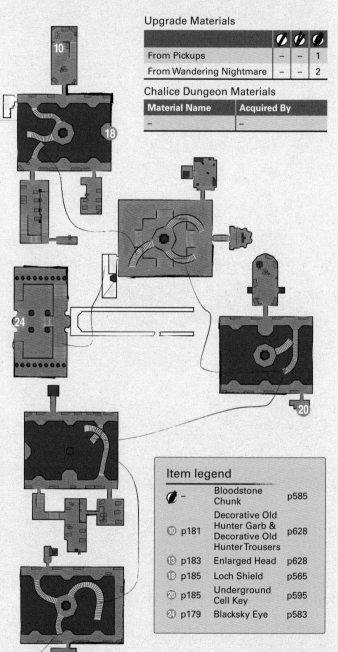

Claim the Fist of Gratia from a corpse in the Underground Cells. After acquiring the Underground Cell Key from the Research Hall, return and defeat the Yahar'gul Hunter for the Church Pick. After obtaining the Underground Cell Inner Chamber Key, return and murder Brador, Church Assassin, which rewards the Bloodletter. — p172

Raise the hidden altar in the Recovery Room to obtain Laurence's Skull, then take the altar platform back downward to find the Church Cannon. — p173

Return to the main floor and ride the elevator upward to the Research Hall. — p173

Research Hall (OH)

Difficulty	Area **B**	Living Failures **B**	Lady Maria of the Astral Clocktower **A**
Blood Gem Rank	**16**
Timezones	○ ◑ ◐ ◑
Blood Echoes	From Enemies **176694**
	From Items **21000**
Insight	Reach the Research Hall for the first time ×2, Give all three Brain Fluids to Adeline and obtain the Milkweed Caryll Rune ×2, Reach Lumenwood Garden and encounter the Living Failures ×2, Defeat the Living Failures ×2, Reach the Astral Clocktower and encounter Lady Maria of the Astral Clocktower ×1, Defeat Lady Maria of the Astral Clocktower ×3

Area progression

Raise the central staircase using the mechanism in the Research Hall Upper Rafters. — p184

Eliminate a Carrion Crow in the Research Hall Upper Rafters, picking up a Guidance Caryll Rune. — p184

Retrieve the Loch Shield from Floor 1 - Main Hall after raising the central stairs. — p185

Access floor 3b after raising the central stairs and procure the Underground Cell Key. — p185

Give Brain Fluid x3 to Adeline, Research Hall Patient to receive the Balcony Key and the Milkweed Caryll Rune. Access the 1st Floor Balcony and claim the Blacksky Eye. — p179

Kill Living Failures in the Lumenwood Garden. — p366

Kill Lady Maria of the Astral Clocktower, rewarding the Celestial Dial. Use the Celestial Dial to Interact with the clock face, opening the path to the Fishing Hamlet. — p368

Upgrade Materials

	⊘	⊘	⊘
From Pickups	–	–	1
From Wandering Nightmare	–	–	2

Chalice Dungeon Materials

Material Name	Acquired By
–	–

Item legend

⊘	–	Bloodstone Chunk	p585
10	p181	Decorative Old Hunter Garb & Decorative Old Hunter Trousers	p628
13	p183	Enlarged Head	p628
18	p185	Loch Shield	p565
20	p185	Underground Cell Key	p595
24	p179	Blacksky Eye	p583

Fishing Hamlet OH

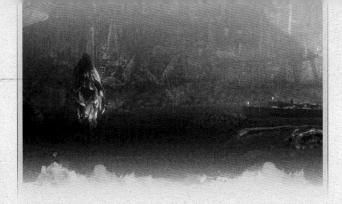

Difficulty	Area **A** | Orphan of Kos **S**	
Blood Gem Rank	**17**	
Timezones	○ ◐ ☾ ●	
Blood Echoes	From Enemies **158236**	
	From Items **52000**	
Insight	Reach the Fishing Hamlet for the first time ×4, Encounter the Orphan of Kos ×5, Defeat the Orphan of Kos ×5, Slay the Orphan of Kos' remaining shadow after the battle to end the nightmare ×3	

Upgrade Materials

	⬦	⬦	⬦
From Pickups	–	3	9
From Wandering Nightmare	–	–	3

Chalice Dungeon Materials

Material Name	Acquired By
–	–

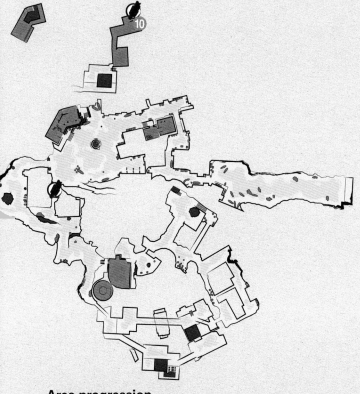

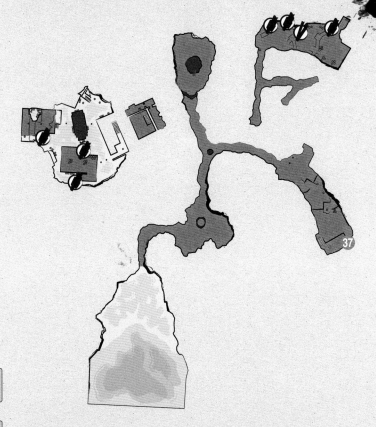

Area progression

Speak to the Fishing Hamlet Priest with the Milkweed Caryll Rune equipped; they will offer the Accursed Brew.	p190

▼

Enter the Plaza Well and dispatch the pair of Giant Fishmen to obtain the Rakuyo.	p192

▼

Confront Simon, Seeker of Secrets in the Lighthouse Hut to obtain Simon's Bowblade and the Underground Cell Inner Chamber Key.	p194

▼

Claim the Blood Rock from the Lower Breeding Pit.	p198

▼

Kill Orphan of Kos, rewarding the Kos Parasite. Attack the mysterious shadowy figure to complete the journey through the nightmare.	p371

▼

Return to the Hunter's Dream, use all three One Third of Umbilical Cord, and kill Gehrman, the First Hunter and the Moon Presence.	p356

Item legend

⬦	–	Twin Blood Stone Shards	p585
⬦	–	Bloodstone Chunk	p585
10	p192	Harrowed Hood, Garb, Gloves, Trousers	p628
37	p198	Blood Rock	p585

Chapter 3
The Bestiary

The scourge that enveloped Yharnam has left some truly beastly specimens in its wake, and anything that isn't a beast is well on its way to becoming one. If you're going to hunt these creatures, you'll need to know all you can about them. Even the biggest and most dangerous beasts have their weaknesses, and can be easy prey for a hunter who knows them well enough. Reading the following pages will allow you to get to know them in intimate detail.

How to Use This Chapter

This is a huge chapter full of data and strategies. For the most part it should be very clear and easy to use, but there are few things that require a decent explanation, so we'll go over those here.

Categories & Groups

We've presented the enemies in four categories: Regular, Strong, Hunter and Boss, so that each type gets the required space and detail. We've chosen to designate enemies as Strong based on how much of a threat they can be. So a Brainsucker, for example, is small and can be killed in a couple of hits once you're familiar with it, but it's still a very serious threat due to its incapacitating magic and Insight-stealing grab. Some enemies are very similar to each other, such as the many variants of the Huntsmen, and in these cases we've grouped them up to avoid repetition. Each variant still has its own data and strategy, though.

Item Drops

For the most part, items dropped by enemies are decided simply by a random per cent chance from that enemy's own list of potential items. In this case we list all of the items and the exact chance of each one being selected. When an enemy appears in a dungeon, it sometimes has one or more of its drops determined by the dungeon's Depth, in order to give better rewards for more challenging dungeons. Such items are selected from a pool of similar items, and these pools are shown here. The upshot of this is that an enemy might drop a Tomb Mold (1) in the Depth 1 Pthumerian Root Labyrinth, but would drop a Tomb Mold (5) instead in a Depth 5 Isz Gravestone dungeon.

Enemy Data

This is the good stuff. The data you'll find here tells you, in raw numbers, exactly what each enemy is weak against. It also reveals what items they can drop, and the exact chances of them dropping each one, as well as how much HP they have and how many Blood Echoes they give when defeated. As you can see in the example here, this data is provided separately for every area the enemy appears in.

Item Legend

Icon	Label
	Physical DEF
	Blunt DEF
	Thrust DEF
	Blood DEF
	Arcane DEF
	Fire DEF
	Bolt DEF
	Slow Poison RES
	Rapid Poison RES
	Beast
	Kin

Item Drop Pools

Pool Name	Depth 1	Depth 2	Depth 3	Depth 4	Depth 5
Blood Stone Shard Pool A	Blood Stone Shard	Blood Stone Shard	Blood Stone Shard	Twin Blood Stone Shards	Twin Blood Stone Shards
Blood Stone Shard Pool B	Blood Stone Shard	Blood Stone Shard	Twin Blood Stone Shards	Twin Blood Stone Shards	Twin Blood Stone Shards
Blood Stone Shard Pool C	Blood Stone Shard	Blood Stone Shard	Twin Blood Stone Shards	Twin Blood Stone Shards	Blood Stone Chunk
Ritual Blood A	Ritual Blood (1)	Ritual Blood (2)	Ritual Blood (3)	Ritual Blood (4)	Ritual Blood (5)
Ritual Blood B	Ritual Blood (2)	Ritual Blood (3)	Ritual Blood (4)	Ritual Blood (5)	Ritual Blood (5)
Coldblood Flowerbud Pool A	Blood Vial	Blood Vial	Coldblood Flowerbud	Coldblood Flowerbud	Blooming Coldblood Flower
Coldblood Flowerbud Pool B	Blood Vial	Blood Vial	Coldblood Flowerbud	Coldblood Flower Bulb	Blooming Coldblood Flower
Tomb Mold Pool	Tomb Mold (1)	Tomb Mold (2)	Tomb Mold (3)	Tomb Mold (4)	Tomb Mold (5)
Sage's Wrist Pool	Blood Vial	Sage's Wrist	Sage's Wrist	Sage's Hair	Sage's Hair
Inflicted Organ Pool	Blood Vial	Blood Vial	Inflicted Organ	Inflicted Organ	Yellow Backbone

Enemies list per pool

Blood Stone Shard Pool A	Large Snake Ball [50%], Hunting Dog [30%], Snake Ball [4%]
Blood Stone Shard Pool B	Kidnapper ×1 [45%] x2 [25%], Keeper's Hunting Dog [33%], Large Snake Ball [18%], Undead Giant (Twin Curved Blades) & (Club & Hook) ×2 [15%], Hunting Dog [4%]
Blood Stone Shard Pool C	Keeper's Hunting Dog [15%], Undead Giant (Twin Curved Blades) & (Club & Hook) ×2 [5%], Large Snake Ball [1.5%]
Ritual Blood A	Labyrinth Ritekeeper [4%]

Ritual Blood B	Kidnapper [25%], Merciless Watcher [20%], Shadow of Yharnam [15%]
Coldblood Flowerbud Pool A	Loran Cleric [8%]
Coldblood Flowerbud Pool B	Loran Cleric [8%]
Tomb Mold Pool	Watcher's Gravedigger (Pickaxe) ×1 [8%] ×2 [0.7%], Labyrinth Rat ×1 [4%] ×2 [0.4%]
Sage's Wrist Pool	Labyrinth Madman [15%]
Inflicted Organ Pool	Labyrinth Warrior [15%]
Blooming Coldblood Flower	Loran Cleric [8%]
Bloodshot Eyeball	Eye Collector [4%]
Pearl Slug	Garden of Eyes [4%]

Dungeon Data

For enemies that also (or exclusively) appear in dungeons, we've included their base dungeon stats only, because their exact stats at any given point are calculated from these base values. Each enemy has different Levels they can be, from Level 1 to Level 4. These levels correspond roughly (but not exclusively) with the Layer you'll encounter them on. We've provided all of the possible multipliers here, and the basic formula is:

$$\text{Total Value} = \text{Base} \times A \times B \times C$$

The Base value represents a stat that a Level 1 enemy has, so the stats we provide show, for example, how many Blood Echoes that enemy would give in a Depth 1 Pthumeru dungeon with no other multipliers in effect. An example of a Base value is the 67 Blood Echoes a basic Level 1 Labyrinth Watcher in the Preset Pthumeru Labyrinth would give. To continue the example, and apply the multipliers to that base value, if you encounter a Level 3 version of that same enemy in a Depth 5 Cursed Pthumeru Ihyll Root dungeon it would give you 5468 Blood Echoes when killed. That's just for Blood Echoes, though; there are different multipliers for HP and Physical defense, all of which you'll find here. Not all stats use all multiplier types; dungeon enemy physical defense values are determined by the dungeon depth only, and the elemental values are completely unaffected by multipliers.

Basic Information Example

Basic Information																
Chalice Dungeon Base Level	123	67	Item Drops	Blood Vial ×1 [8%]		68	68	68	68	46	58	60	120	180	–	–

Blood Echo Multipliers

Multiplier A – Depth

Depth	Multiplier
1	1.0
2	2.32
3	7.53
4	31.71
5	45.17*

*61.83 for Pthumeru Ihyll

Multiplier B – Level

Layer	Multiplier
1	1.0
2	1.05
3	1.1
4	1.2

Multiplier C – Additional Rite

Additional Rite	Multiplier
Cursed Offering	1.2

HP Multipliers

Multiplier A – Depth

Depth	Multiplier
1	1.0
2	1.45
3	3.83
4	6.46
5	6.91*

*7.63 for Pthumeru Ihyll

Multiplier B – Level

Layer	Multiplier
1	1.0
2	1.05
3	1.075
4	1.15

Physical Defense Multiplier

Multiplier A – Depth

Depth	Multiplier
1	1.0
2	1.04
3	1.29
4	1.40
5	1.43*

*1.45 for Pthumeru Ihyll

Bosses

Covering bosses requires some extra detail, so we've added sections for how to prepare for the battle and how to take advantage of the environment you fight them in, as well as an overview of their behavior. The absolute most important strategies are distilled into a single Key Strategies box, so you can read this first if you just want some quick help.

Enemy Index

This index lists all the enemies covered in the chapter, and allows you to find the one you want without flipping through and risking spoilers in the art-work images.

Regular Enemies

Huntsman

A basic enemy encountered throughout Yharnam and the surrounding areas. Huntsmen patrolling the streets of Central Yharnam will travel set routes which you can use to either avoid or ambush them; they also sometimes guard fixed positions. These foes are weak on their own, but almost never appear alone – the greatest danger they present is their ability to swarm you in large numbers if you're not careful. Their close-range torch attacks are especially deadly, because they leave almost no time to react and can hit you several times in a row; on the other hand, their weapon attacks have longer reach, but are much slower and more predictable.

There are a wide variety of Huntsmen, but they all share some basic traits and can be killed with a few hits from your weapon. The trick to eliminating risk is to separate them and fight them one at a time, using pebbles if necessary. Some, such as the Torch & Shield variant, are more defensive and require a slightly different approach, but most, when fought alone are best tackled by cutting them down before they can attack. The ones that use longer combos, such as the Sickle and Cleaver variants, tend to give you easy chances for landing charged R2 attacks from behind while they recover from their attack string. The Cutlass and Pitchfork variants are the most dangerous, and should be considered the highest threat among a group of them, due to their ability to strike from the back of the group and still reach you.

Huntsman (Torch & Axe)

Avoid standing close to them, because they can use an extremely fast poke with their torch that can easily hit you out of your attacks – instead, stay just outside their melee range and wait for them to act. If they attack with the torch, wait for them to finish swinging and strike during their recovery; if they close in with the axe, quickstep toward them and through the attack, then hit them from behind. They turn around too quickly to use a charged R2 after evading through an attack, so a quick R1 combo will work out better. Be careful when pursuing these enemies, because they can use a multi-hit torch attack while walking backwards, and it's easy to get caught in it if you're overly aggressive.

Basic Information	■	⚔	Item Drops										
Central Yharnam	150	48	Blood Vial ×1 [21%], Quicksilver Bullets ×2 [10%], Molotov Cocktail ×1 [5%]	70	70	70	70	67	65	75	120	180	— —
Cathedral Ward	194	193	Blood Vial ×1 [21%], Quicksilver Bullets ×2 [10%], Molotov Cocktail ×1 [5%]	77	77	77	77	67	65	75	120	180	
Healing Church Workshop | Executioner	218	128	Blood Vial ×1 [21%], Quicksilver Bullets ×2 [10%], Molotov Cocktail ×1 [5%], Pungent Blood Cocktail ×1 [0.5%]	77	77	77	77	72	65	65	120	180	
Healing Church Workshop	271	142	Blood Vial ×1 [21%], Quicksilver Bullets ×2 [10%], Molotov Cocktail ×1 [5%]	77	77	77	77	67	65	75	120	180	
Forbidden Woods	306	695	Blood Vial ×1 [21%], Quicksilver Bullets ×2 [10%], Molotov Cocktail ×1 [5%], Pungent Blood Cocktail ×1 [0.5%]	86	86	86	86	67	65	75	120	180	
Yahar'gul (Blood Moon)	518	485	Blood Vial ×1 [10.5%], Quicksilver Bullets ×2 [5%], Molotov Cocktail ×1 [2.5%]	95	95	95	95	67	65	75	120	180	
Hunter's Nightmare	760	355	Blood Vial ×1 [21%], Quicksilver Bullets ×2 [10%], Molotov Cocktail ×1 [5%]	96	96	96	96	92	89	103	120	180	

Huntsman (Torch & Shield)

Transformation attacks are the easiest way to knock aside their shields and set them up for a quick R1 combo, especially if you use one after quickstepping towards them to close the distance. Ranged attacks and thrown weapons are largely ineffective against their shields, so you should always close in and fight them in melee range. You can also break their guard just by attacking them several times, but this consumes large amounts of stamina for no good reason and can prevent you from being able to finish them once you've gotten past their shields.

Basic Information

Location	■	⬥	Item Drops											
Central Yharnam	70	48	Blood Vial ×1 [21%], Quicksilver Bullets ×2 [10%], Molotov Cocktail ×1 [5%]	68	68	68	68	67	65	75	120	180	—	—
Healing Church Workshop	127	114	Blood Vial ×1 [21%], Quicksilver Bullets ×2 [10%], Molotov Cocktail ×1 [5%]	75	75	75	75	67	65	75	120	180		
Forbidden Woods	179	556	Blood Vial ×1 [21%], Quicksilver Bullets ×2 [10%], Molotov Cocktail ×1 [5%], Pungent Blood Cocktail ×1 [0.5%]	83	83	83	83	67	65	75	120	180		
Yahar'gul (Blood Moon)	403	347	Blood Vial ×1 [10.5%], Quicksilver Bullets ×2 [5%], Molotov Cocktail ×1 [2.5%]	95	95	95	95	67	65	75	120	180		

Huntsman (Sickle)

Maintain a distance of at least two meters from them to ensure that you have time to respond to their attacks – you can either move in and hit them with an R1 chain during their recovery or position yourself behind them during their combo and hit them with a charged attack from behind. Avoid standing at extremely close range, because their attacks are very fast and you won't have enough time to react to them at that range. Because their attacks lack range, it can be quite effective to bait them into attacking and then move back outside their range again, so that you have a clean opening when they finish their combo.

Basic Information

Location	■	⬥	Item Drops											
Central Yharnam	70	48	Blood Vial ×1 [8%]	70	70	70	70	67	65	75	120	180	—	—
Cathedral Ward	125	171	Blood Vial ×1 [8%]	77	77	77	77	67	65	75	120	180		
Healing Church Workshop	215	128	Blood Vial ×1 [8%]	77	77	77	77	67	65	75	120	180		
Forbidden Woods	301	556	Blood Vial ×1 [8%]	88	88	88	88	67	65	75	120	180		
Yahar'gul (Blood Moon)	403	347	Blood Vial ×1 [4%]	95	95	95	95	67	65	75	120	180		
Hunter's Nightmare	483	338	Blood Vial ×1 [8%]	96	96	96	96	92	89	103	120	180		

Huntsman (Cleaver)

Treat them the same as those with sickles – stand no closer than two meters away and bait their attacks, then strafe or quickstep out of the way and hit them while they recover. You can also strafe counterclockwise or quickstep forward through their attacks to position yourself behind them for a charged strike, which will allow you to perform a visceral attack. In general, R1 or transform attack combos work best to dispatch them individually; if facing a group, switch to an attack with a large horizontal arc to ensure that you hit all of them.

Basic Information

Location	■	⬥	Item Drops											
Central Yharnam	70	48	Blood Vial ×1 [8%]	70	70	70	70	67	65	75	120	180	—	—
Healing Church Workshop	215	114	Blood Vial ×1 [8%]	77	77	77	77	67	65	75	120	180		
Forbidden Woods	301	556	Blood Vial ×1 [8%]	88	88	88	88	67	65	75	120	180		
Yahar'gul (Blood Moon)	403	347	Blood Vial ×1 [4%]	95	95	95	95	67	65	75	120	180		
Hunter's Nightmare	483	270	Blood Vial ×1 [8%]	96	96	96	96	92	89	103	120	180		

Huntsman (Cutlass)

Their thrust attack has a long windup and is easy to identify; simply strafe to either side or quickstep forward to position yourself behind them for a charged R2. Interrupting this attack is also relatively easy because of the heavily telegraphed animation, so if there are no other enemies around, it can be a very effective means of taking them out. To avoid their horizontal slashes, quickstep forward through the swing or backward and out of its reach. After baiting any of their attacks, simply perform a quick R1 chain to finish the job.

Basic Information

	■	⚔	Item Drops	🗍	🌑	🔺	✴	★	✎	🎵	💀	🔻	🐾	🐍
Central Yharnam	150	48	Blood Vial ×2 [32%]	72	72	72	72	67	65	75	120	180	—	—
Cathedral Ward	194	193	Blood Vial ×2 [32%]	79	79	79	79	67	65	75	120	180		
Healing Church Workshop	271	142	Blood Vial ×2 [32%]	79	79	79	79	67	65	75	120	180		
Forbidden Woods	381	695	Blood Vial ×2 [32%], Pungent Blood Cocktail ×1 [0.5%]	88	88	88	88	67	65	75	120	180		
Yahar'gul (Blood Moon)	518	485	Blood Vial ×2 [16%]	95	95	95	95	67	65	75	120	180		
Hunter's Nightmare	760	338	Blood Vial ×2 [32%]	99	99	99	99	92	89	103	120	180		

Huntsman (Pitchfork)

You can knock these Huntsmen out of their running thrust with a shot from a firearm, and since they like to use this attack as they close in on you, it's best to have your gun at the ready. With careful timing you can also use a jumping or thrusting attack of your own to hit them just as they come into range. Their attacks in general have a lot more reach than other Huntsmen, so you'll need to stay further back than usual, and their attacks have a wider arc, so they're more difficult to evade. At close range they'll also use a very hard to evade shove attack that will often hit you even if you're at their side. Standing out of reach of their pitchforks and waiting for them to begin an attack, so that you can quickstep towards and through it to strike them from behind, is the most effective means of fighting them. Their overhead slam is easy to interrupt, however, so if you see it in time you can stagger them and finish them off quickly with a visceral attack.

Basic Information

	■	⚔	Item Drops	🗍	🌑	🔺	✴	★	✎	🎵	💀	🔻	🐾	🐍
Central Yharnam	150	48	Blood Vial ×1 [8%]	70	70	70	70	67	65	75	120	180	—	—
Cathedral Ward	123	171	Blood Vial ×1 [8%]	77	77	77	77	67	65	75	120	180		
Healing Church Workshop	191	128	Blood Vial ×1 [8%]	77	77	77	77	72	65	65	120	180		
Forbidden Woods	301	556	Blood Vial ×1 [8%]	86	86	86	86	67	65	75	120	180		
Yahar'gul (Blood Moon)	518	485	Blood Vial ×1 [4%]	95	95	95	95	67	65	75	120	180		

Huntsman (Rifle)

If you encounter riflemen among a group of other enemies, it's best to eliminate them first – otherwise they will continually bombard you while you fight. Unfortunately, this is often easier said than done, as the snipers are usually located in spots that can't be reached without running through a group of foes. To evade their gunfire, quickstep or roll sideways relative to their position; if you have a Blue Elixir, you can use it before entering their line of sight to prevent them from seeing you while you fight, or to sneak past the other enemies and deal with the riflemen. The best time to attack them is during their long reload cycle (which takes a full two seconds) when they can't defend themselves – use that time to close in and get to their side before they can fire again. You can also use thrown weapons such as Molotovs or Throwing Knives to pick off the sharpshooters without getting close to their allies, or lure other enemies out of the snipers' field of vision and get rid of them in a safe spot before advancing.

Basic Information

	■	⚔	Item Drops	🗍	🌑	🔺	✴	★	✎	🎵	💀	🔻	🐾	🐍
Central Yharnam	90	48	Quicksilver Bullets ×3 [100%]	65	65	65	65	67	65	75	120	180	—	—
Cathedral Ward	158	214	Quicksilver Bullets ×3 [100%]	72	72	72	72	67	65	75	120	180		
Healing Church Workshop	164	142	Quicksilver Bullets ×3 [100%]	72	72	72	72	67	65	75	120	180		
Hemwick Charnel Lane	152	266	Quicksilver Bullets ×4 [15%], Quicksilver Bullets ×3 [80%], Bone Marrow Ash ×2 [5%]	73	73	73	73	67	65	75	120	180		
Forbidden Woods	230	695	Quicksilver Bullets ×3 [99.5%], Pungent Blood Cocktail ×1 [0.5%]	80	80	80	80	67	65	75	120	180		
Yahar'gul (Blood Moon)	461	347	Quicksilver Bullets ×3 [25%]	95	95	95	95	67	65	75	120	180		

3

Huntsman (Rifle & Cutlass)

Treat them like the riflemen when at long range, and like the swordsmen when up close – approach using cover to block their bullets and quickstep behind them to attack from their blind spot. They are still vulnerable while reloading and switching weapons, giving you plenty of time to mow them down with an R1 chain before they can react. Quickstepping attacks are a great way to deal damage and immobilize them as you approach and allow you to immediately follow through with an R1 combo.

Basic Information			Item Drops											
Cathedral Ward	161	214	Quicksilver Bullets ×3 [100%]	72	72	72	72	67	65	75	120	180	—	—
Hemwick Charnel Lane	152	266	Quicksilver Bullets ×4 [15%], Quicksilver Bullets ×3 [80%], Bone Marrow Ash ×2 [5%]	79	79	79	79	67	65	75	120	180		
Forbidden Woods	230	695	Quicksilver Bullets ×3 [99.5%], Pungent Blood Cocktail ×1 [0.5%]	80	80	80	80	67	65	75	120	180		

Huntsman (Bare Fists)

Interrupting their attacks is possible, but doing so is not really an effective use of bullets; it's much more economical to simply run up and hit them while they're getting up, so that they don't even get the chance to start attacking. If they do get up, remember that their attacks have extremely short range, so using weapons with long reach will let you attack them safely. This is also true if you come across a group of them; you can back up out of their range and use wide-arcing attacks from weapons such as the transformed Hunter's Axe or Ludwig's Holy Blade to take out the whole group without fear.

Basic Information			Item Drops											
Yahar'gul (Evening)	177	319	Blood Vial ×1 [4%]	90	90	90	90	67	65	75	120	180	—	—

Huntsman (Oil Urn)

These Huntsmen are capable of throwing their Oil Urns a considerable distance, so the first thing that may alert you to one being in the area is getting hit, especially in the darker areas of the woods. If you do get coated in oil, make sure to stay away from any other enemies nearby that have fire-based attacks until it wears off. Once you've located the Huntsman throwing them, lure other enemies back out of its throwing range and fight them in a safer spot. Oil Urn Huntsmen represent no real threat without their allies, so once you've eliminated any others that are capable of inflicting fire damage (such as those carrying torches or Molotovs) you can pick them off at your leisure with melee attacks.

Basic Information			Item Drops											
Forbidden Woods	301	556	Blood Vial ×1 [21%], Oil Urn ×1 [5%]	86	86	86	86	67	65	75	120	180	—	—

Huntsman (Molotov)

The splash damage from their Molotovs can make it difficult to approach them with other enemies around, so try to stay out of their reach until after you've defeated any melee-oriented foes in the area. If you can reach them with Molotovs or Throwing Knives, try to defeat them from a distance in order to avoid having to fight your way through a group of other enemies or make a side trip to reach them. They have weak melee attacks, but may continue hurling Molotovs at close range; evade their throws with carefully-timed rolls or quicksteps as you approach, then strike them down with R1 combos during their recovery.

Basic Information			Item Drops											
Forbidden Woods	179	556	Blood Vial ×1 [21%], Molotov Cocktail ×1 [10%]	86	86	86	86	67	65	75	120	180	—	—
Yahar'gul (Blood Moon)	403	347	Blood Vial ×1 [10.5%], Molotov Cocktail ×1 [5%]	95	95	95	95	67	65	75	120	180		
Hunter's Nightmare	483	331	Blood Vial ×1 [21%], Molotov Cocktail ×1 [10%]	96	96	96	96	92	89	103	120	180		

Wheelchair Huntsmen

Wheelchair-bound residents of Yharnam equipped with various firearms, these enemies are barely mobile and unable to do anything but shoot – they effectively act as stationary gun turrets. What they lack in mobility, however, they more than make up for in firepower. Due to the ranged nature of most of their attacks, they are most threatening when they see you coming from a distance and you're forced to close in while under fire. Once you do get close, however, their lack of melee attack and very slow turning ability means that they're all but defenseless. Those using pistols and rifles have an extremely long reload time between each shot (around 5 seconds), so once you see them fire you'll know you have a small window of opportunity to close in and get to the side of them, where it's safe.

Wheelchair Huntsmen with gatling guns can pack a deadly punch and are able to fire sustained bursts at an incredible rate. Each round that hits you will cause you to flinch, making it difficult to escape once they've got you in their sights, so rather than running straight at them, it's best to approach at an angle so that their shots miss. Unlike the other Wheelchair Huntsmen, the ones armed with either a Flamesprayer or Rosmarinus have no means of hitting you at long range, but they are a serious threat at mid range. When you get close, they'll spray jets of fire in sweeping frontal arcs, which are wide enough to reach you if you're standing beside them, so make sure you get right round to their back once you get close.

3

Wheelchair Huntsman (Pistol)

Watch for them to level their pistols and take aim, then roll or quickstep out of the way or simply strafe sideways. After they've fired, run in and get behind them while they're reloading – at this point they're completely helpless and you can attack them without fear of being hit. They cannot be interrupted or staggered, but have very low health and will fall quickly to a chain of R1 attacks.

Basic Information			Item Drops											
Central Yharnam	80	58	Quicksilver Bullets ×4 [100%]	64	64	64	64	55	65	40	120	180	—	—
Hemwick Charnel Lane	202	58	Quicksilver Bullets ×4 [100%]	77	77	77	77	55	65	40	120	180		
Yahar'gul (Blood Moon)	374	485	None	86	86	86	86	55	65	40	120	180		
Research Hall	841	980	Quicksilver Bullets ×4 [76%], Antidote ×2 [12%], Sedatives ×1 [4%], Beast Blood Pellet ×1 [4%]	91	91	91	91	78	92	57	120	180		

Wheelchair Huntsman (Gatling Gun)

These enemies are most dangerous at long range, where they have enough room and time to start shooting at you. Observe them carefully before you move in and try to bait them into firing, then hide until they stop to reload; try to use any available cover to block their fire as you approach. Once you get past their long-range barrage, they're completely helpless; a couple of R1 attacks will finish them. Alternately, if they have you pinned down and unable to advance, a Molotov or a couple of Throwing Knives will finish them off from a distance; their health is low enough that even normal pistol shots are effective for this purpose.

Basic Information			Item Drops											
Healing Church Workshop	145	99	Quicksilver Bullets ×4 [100%]	70	70	70	70	55	65	40	120	180	—	—
Yahar'gul (Blood Moon)	374	554	None	86	86	86	86	55	65	40	120	180		
Research Hal	841	762	Quicksilver Bullets ×6 [76%], Antidote ×2 [12%], Sedatives ×1 [4%], Beast Blood Pellet ×1 [4%]	91	91	91	91	78	92	57	120	180		

Wheelchair Huntsman (Rifle)

Approach these snipers the same way as the ones with gatling guns – use their long reload cycle and any available cover to move in safely, and then hit them with quick R1 attacks from up close, or thrown weapons at a distance. As with all Wheelchair Huntsman enemies, the best place to stand is behind them, but you won't be there very long – one or two basic R1 attacks are enough to deplete their low health.

Basic Information	■	⚓	Item Drops	◻	◐	▲	✸	★	❂	⌐	☠	▽	⚔	∿
Healing Church Workshop	145	99	None	70	70	70	70	55	65	40	120	180	—	—
Yahar'gul (Blood Moon)	374	485	None	86	86	86	86	55	65	40	120	180		

Wheelchair Huntsman (Flamesprayer/Rosmarinus)

The easiest way to deal with these enemies is to run up to them as quickly as possible and try to get around behind them before they can start using their flamesprayers. Once you're there you can easily finish them off with a quick combo before they can turn around. If you can't get close to them, or they've already started firing, it can be worth using your own ranged attacks to hit them from outside the range of their flamesprayers – just make sure to keep moving backwards so that you stay out of range.

Basic Information	■	⚓	Item Drops	◻	◐	▲	✸	★	❂	⌐	☠	▽	⚔	∿
Healing Church Workshop | **Flamesprayer**	145	99	Quicksilver Bullets ×4 [100%]	70	70	70	70	55	65	40	120	180	—	—
Research Hall | **Rosmarinus**	841	762	Quicksilver Bullets ×4 [67%], Antidote ×2 [15%], Sedatives ×1 [6%], Beast Blood Pellet ×1 [6%]	91	91	91	91	78	92	57	120	180		

Rabid Dog/Old Hunter's Hound

Fast, agile attack dogs usually found in the company of Huntsman enemies, but also sometimes locked in cages and unable to attack. Beware that if you wait too long before attacking caged Rabid Dogs, they may eventually break out of their kennels and attack. They move quickly and are highly evasive, dashing in to perform lunging bites and immediately leaping backward to avoid your counter-attack. They can be extremely dangerous in groups due to their swift movement, but their low health and weakness to fire make them easy prey if you can manage to land an attack; they also suffer additional damage from serrated weapons, such as the Saw Cleaver and the Saw Spear. A later version of this foe sports the head of a Carrion Crow, and there's a stronger version known as an Old Hunter's Hound that appears alongside Old Hunter enemies, but they behave in the exact same manner.

If possible, try to eliminate them with thrown items or ranged attacks before they detect you – Molotovs and Throwing Knives are very effective due to their low health, but are very likely to miss during battle due to these foes' agility and quick evasive responses. If they see you at a distance, time a thrust attack to hit them as they leap at you; shooting them with a pistol or scattergun will knock them to the ground, cancelling their attack and giving you an opportunity to hit them as they get back up. Try not to let them get near you as they turn quickly, making it difficult to avoid their bite attacks at close range.

Basic Information	■	⚓	Item Drops	◻	◐	▲	✸	★	❂	⌐	☠	▽	⚔	∿
Central Yharnam*	80	53	None	60	60	60	60	62	55	65	120	180	✕	—
Cathedral Ward**	141	184	None	66	66	66	66	62	55	65	120	180		
Healing Church Workshop	145	142	None	66	66	66	66	62	55	65	120	180		
Yahar'gul (Evening)	202	593	None	72	72	72	72	62	55	65	120	180		
Forbidden Woods	204	521	None	74	74	74	74	62	55	65	120	180		
Yahar'gul (Blood Moon)	461	762	None	81	81	81	81	62	55	65	120	180		
Nightmare of Mensis | **Crow Head**	611	1134	None	86	86	86	86	62	55	65	120	180		
Chalice Dungeon Base Level	141	84	None	68	68	68	68	67	55	65	120	180		
Hunter's Nightmare | **COld Hunter's Hound**	483	372	None	82	82	82	82	85	75	89	120	180		

*When in cage, 38 Blood Echoes and no drops.   **Dog near main gate has 172 HP/834 Blood Echoes. Preset Chalice Dungeons: Central Pthumerian Labyrinth, Hintertomb, Lower Pthumerian Labyrinth, Pthumeru Ihyll

Carrion Crow

Large, jet-black birds that lie on the ground, blend into shadows and can be very hard to spot in dark areas or among the rubble littering Yharnam's streets. They flock together in tightly-clustered groups and are almost never encountered alone; trying to fight too many at once can quickly lead to death, so take care not to walk into a nest of them. If you approach them head on, they'll usually fly into the air to perform a combo with their claws and beaks; this attack inflicts several hits in quick succession and causes you to flinch, which can prove lethal if several Carrion Crows use it on you at once. They'll also sometimes attack you up close with short-ranged pecks, but these are easily avoided by staying behind them and out of their reach. A later variation of this enemy has the head of a Rabid Dog, but attacks in exactly the same way as the normal version.

Jump attacks from outside the range of their flying combo will allow you to strike them before they can react; you can also bait their flying attack and quickstep sideways, positioning yourself to strike once they've landed. Their peck has very short range but is quick and difficult to avoid; the best strategy is to stay to their sides and take advantage of their slow movements to hit them with far-reaching attacks or thrown weapons before they can counterattack. Molotovs and Throwing Knives are effective at a distance; sweeping horizontal swings from weapons such as the transformed Hunter's Axe can be used to mow down groups of them from behind if you can sneak up undetected.

Basic Information	◼	⬩	Item Drops	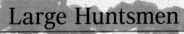										
Central Yharnam	70	29	Pebble ×1 [6%], Pebble ×2 [3%], Antidote ×1 [1%]	56	56	56	56	35	50	40	120	180	×	—
Cathedral Ward*	123	110	Pebble ×1 [6%], Pebble ×2 [3%], Antidote ×1 [1%]	62	62	62	62	35	50	40	120	180		
Old Yharnam	121	64	Pebble ×1 [6%], Antidote ×1 [3%], Antidote ×2 [1%]	60	60	60	60	35	50	40	120	180		
Healing Church Workshop	127	85	Pebble ×1 [6%], Pebble ×2 [3%], Antidote ×1 [1%]	62	62	62	62	35	50	40	120	180		
Hemwick Charnel Lane	152	199	Pebble ×1 [6%], Pebble ×2 [3%], Antidote ×1 [1%]	63	63	63	63	35	50	40	120	180		
Forbidden Woods	179	284	Pebble ×1 [6%], Pebble ×2 [3%], Beast Blood Pellet ×1 [0.5%]	69	69	69	69	35	50	40	120	180		
Iosefka's Clinic	179	284	Pebble ×1 [6%], Pebble ×2 [3%], Beast Blood Pellet ×1 [0.5%]	69	69	69	69	35	50	40	120	180		
Upper Cathedral Ward	483	436	Pebble ×1 [6%], Pebble ×2 [3%], Antidote ×1 [1%]	77	77	77	77	35	50	40	120	180		
Nightmare of Mensis | Dog Head	547	831	Pebble ×1 [6%], Pebble ×2 [3%], Antidote ×1 [1%]	83	83	83	83	35	50	40	120	180		
Hunter's Nightmare	483	220	Pebble ×1 [6%], Pebble ×2 [3%], Beast Blood Pellet ×1 [1%]	77	77	77	77	48	68	55	120	180		
Research Hall	535	653	Guidance ×1 [100%]	79	79	79	79	49	71	57	120	180		

*Cathedral Ward (Night): 125 HP/128 Blood Echoes

Large Huntsmen

These slow-moving enemies suffer from advanced stages of the Scourge, and while that makes them stronger than normal Huntsmen, they are not quite transformed enough to suffer the attack bonuses against beasts, and do not take additional damage from fire. They are, however, quite vulnerable to interrupts due to their slow and predictable attacks, so it's worth having a firearm at the ready when you approach one. The most common version you'll come across is armed with a torch and a crosscut saw, and at close range they'll often perform combos where they swing both of their weapons in horizontal arcs. Quickstepping through one of these attacks gives you an opportunity to land a charged R2. They also have a hard knockdown attack that slams you to the ground when it connects – if it hits you, immediately roll to the side, because they'll often follow up with a downward stab using their torch.

The less common Spear version also has a similar knockdown attack and downward stab follow-up, and you can evade that one in the same way. While this version shares the same generally slow attacks as the others, its spear has considerably more range, so you'll need to take that into account when approaching one. The plow-carrying version use their weapon in much the same way as the saw ones, with an even greater emphasis on slow, overhead attacks that slam you down to the ground if they connect. Because these overhead attacks are so slow, however, it gives you plenty of time to interrupt them, or quickstep behind them for an R1 chain or charged R2 strike. Their range is slightly longer than the size of their makeshift weapons might suggest, so be careful not to get too close to them during their combos.

Large Huntsman (Torch & Saw)

Avoid standing in front of them at close range to reduce the risk of getting caught in their combo, and try to keep at least two meters away if you plan on baiting their attacks and interrupting them. Take advantage of their slow recovery to nail them with a chain of R1 attacks, but be sure to save enough stamina to quick-step away if you can't finish them off. Transform attack combos can also be effective, because they flinch the enemy enough to keep them from attacking.

Basic Information			Item Drops											
Central Yharnam	225	73	Blood Vial ×2 [79%], Bloodstone Shard ×1 [16%], Oil Urn ×1 [5%]	91	91	91	91	50	78	85	120	180	×	—
Cathedral Ward	287	257	Blood Vial ×2 [79%], Bloodstone Shard ×1 [16%], Oil Urn ×1 [5%]	96	96	96	96	50	78	85	120	180		
Forbidden Woods	409	834	Blood Vial ×2 [79%], Twin Bloodstone Shards ×1 [16%], Oil Urn ×1 [5%]	107	107	107	107	50	78	85	120	180		

Large Huntsman (Spear)

These Large Huntsmen are often found guarding a fixed area and rarely patrol, so if you pay attention to the environment, you can usually sneak around and use a charged R2 from behind. When you're at mid range against this enemy it will tend to use single slow, strong hits rather than the quick combo it uses up close, so if you're attempting to bait it into attacking, it's much easier to do so at that range. If you see it draw the spear to the side it will use a wide horizontal attack, so quickstep forward to avoid it. If it pulls the spear down, it will use an upwards strike that will send you flying up into the air; quickstep to the side to get round it.

Because of the slow speed of both of those attacks they are prime interrupt bait, so attempting to stagger them is a very viable strategy. Once you get close they'll tend to use a quick combo comprising of horizontal swings, so it's best to quickstep forward through the attacks, and then use a quick R1 combo from behind while they recover.

Basic Information			Item Drops											
Central Yharnam	282	73	Blood Vial ×2 [79%], Bloodstone Shard ×1 [16%], Oil Urn ×1 [5%]	91	91	91	91	50	78	85	120	180	×	—
Central Yharnam | **Strong**	358	257	Blood Vial ×2 [79%], Bloodstone Shard ×1 [16%], Oil Urn ×1 [5%]	96	96	96	96	50	78	85	120	180		

Strong version protects Hunter's Garb.

Large Huntsman (Plow)

While the size of the plow may appear small, the attacks have a much bigger horizontal radius than you may think, so make sure to always quickstep forward through them, rather than to the side. Most of the attacks this enemy uses come in the form of slow, powerful overhead strikes, and while they are extremely damaging if they connect, they're also relatively easy to interrupt, so it's worth taking the risk if you want a quick victory. They do, however, have a much quicker combo that they'll sometimes use when you're at close range – if they use it, quickstep or strafe away and wait at a safe distance until they stop swinging.

Basic Information			Item Drops											
Cathedral Ward	358	257	Blood Vial ×2 [79%], Bloodstone Shard ×1 [16%], Oil Urn ×1 [5%]	96	96	96	96	50	78	85	120	180	×	—
Forbidden Woods	511	834	Blood Vial ×2 [79%], Twin Bloodstone Shards ×1 [16%], Oil Urn ×1 [5%]	107	107	107	107	50	78	85	120	180		

Labyrinth Rat

Giant rats inhabiting the central sewers of Yharnam in large colonies. While not too dangerous on their own, they are never encountered alone and can become a serious problem in groups if you don't have a few Molotovs handy. Labyrinth Rats use basic claw swipes, forward lunges and a bite combo; their attacks have enough windup for you to quickstep out of the way and counterattack, but it's still a good idea not to let them get too close. They're not quite as agile as Rabid Dogs, but they move quickly and will keep up the pressure by constantly running toward you if you try to back off. They will also sometimes leap sideways immediately after striking in an attempt to avoid your counterattack. Although Labyrinth Rats cannot be staggered or interrupted, you can knock them out of their attacks by shooting them.

In many spots where groups of Labyrinth Rats are visible below you, you can hit several at once with a single Molotov from a safe vantage point – just be careful not to stand too close to the edge, or you risk falling into the lower area and being swarmed. If you have no choice but to face them on even ground, try to avoid being seen by several at once – fighting a group leaves very few safe openings for you to attack, though thrust attacks from weapons like the Saw Spear in transformed mode will stop them in their tracks at a safe distance. If you do end up fighting several at once, back away from them and wait for a chance to use a sweeping horizontal attack to hit all of them at the same time – if you can keep up the combo long enough to kill one or two of them, you can buy yourself enough breathing room to mop up any that remain.

Basic Information	▪	♣	Item Drops											
Central Yharnam	98	62	Throwing Knife ×2 [5%], Throwing Knife ×1 [15%]	63	63	63	63	80	40	30	200	270	X	—
Chalice Dungeon Base Level	123	53	Ritual material E ×2 [0.4%], Ritual material E ×1 [4%]	62	62	62	62	80	40	30	200	180		
Research Hall	535	1198	Poison Knife ×2 [5%], Poison Knife ×1 [15%]	85	85	85	85	114	57	42	200	270		

Preset Chalice Dungeons: Pthumerian Labyrinth, Central Pthumerian Labyrinth, Hintertomb, Lower Hintertomb, Lower Pthumerian Labyrinth, Cursed Pthumerian Defilement, Ailing Loran, Lower Loran, Isz Gravestone, Pthumeru Ihyll

Rotted Corpse

Rotting remains of drowned scourge victims that aren't quite dead, these slow-moving enemies have little ability to attack and aren't much of a threat, even in large numbers. That said, don't take them lightly – rushing blindly into a group can still lead to the situation getting out of hand. Rotted Corpses can only attack the area directly in front of them; they'll use a slow, short-range vomit projectile, a quick overhead slam and a shove combo, but not much else. They can be hard to spot, because they are always partly submerged in stagnant water and are motionless until you approach; pay careful attention to your surroundings in these situations to avoid ambushes.

Stay behind them or to their sides; from these positions you can beat them to death with R1 chains at little risk to yourself. Sweeping horizontal swings such as the Hunter Axe's L2 and charged R2 attacks in transformed mode are very effective for eliminating large groups; if you have no choice but to fight them head-on, use jump attacks from outside their reach to prevent them from hitting you as you approach.

Basic Information	▪	♣	Item Drops											
Central Yharnam	239	56	Blood Vial ×1 [20%], Bold Hunter's Mark ×1 [2%]	84	84	84	84	65	75	70	120	210	—	—
Forbidden Woods	434	427	Blood Vial ×1 [24%], Sedatives ×1 [1%]	98	98	98	98	65	75	70	120	210		
Chalice Dungeon Base Level	158	83	Blood Vial ×1 [20%], Bold Hunter's Mark ×1 [2%]	88	88	88	88	65	75	70	120	210		

Preset Chalice Dungeons: Hintertomb, Lower Hintertomb, Isz Gravestone

3

Church Servants

Church Servants can be found throughout the Cathedral Ward, where they aim to defend the church from all those that seek to harm it. Found on their own or in pairs, these enemies can usually be seen moving methodically and with purpose along short patrol routes, often with an end destination that you can follow them to. Church Servants can be interrupted and staggered, and are particularly weak against charged blows from transformed weapons. Transformation attacks aren't very effective at flinching them, though, so you're better off just using normal combos. The most common weapon employed by these enemies is the Cane, which uses a very simple and limited set of attacks (either an overhead spike or a horizontal swing) to great effect. Sometimes they will use a short combo, but the hits are slow enough that you can always escape even if one connects.

Occasionally you'll come across Servants that carry an additional weapon along with their Canes to augment their offensive capabilities, so make sure and pay attention to their off-hand when you approach them so that you don't run into any surprises. Some will be armed with Repeating Pistols, which they use to take potshots at you from a distance, and others use Flamesprayers to blanket the area in front of them with fire. Not all Servants use Canes, however, and some instead use a completely different and much more deadly fighting style with their scythes. These weapons have very long reach and can easily clip you as you're quickstepping past an attack if your timing if even slightly off, and Servants with this weapon a lot more aggressive than their Cane-wielding counterparts.

Then comes the black sheep of the Church servants – literally. These black-robed clergymen wield an unusual crucifix weapon in the shape of the Hunter's Mark, which they use to perform surprisingly fast overhead slams and forward thrusts. They are also capable of an extremely swift grab attack, which looks almost exactly like their normal thrust attack and gives almost no warning. Their most interesting ability, however, is the fact that they can switch between two fighting stances: the first has their weapon held vertically at the ready, the second in a much more aggressive posture with the crucifix held horizontally and pointing toward you. When they are in the second stance it can be extremely difficult to predict their attacks, especially their grab; furthermore, all of their attacks cause frenzy and can be lethal if you get hit too many times.

> If you enter the Cathedral Ward with 15 or more Insight, many of the Church Servants will undergo some changes that make them considerably more dangerous. The lanterns carried by the Cane & Lantern Servants will become covered with eyeballs and they'll now be able to use two magic attacks not otherwise accessible to them. The first is a large spherical blast that strikes in all directions, and the other shoots out small orbs that home in on you. The homing orb attack can be dangerous if there are other enemies nearby, as it will pass through them on its way to you, but environmental obstacles will block it. For the Scythe users, their weapon becomes coated in a magical aura that adds elemental damage to their attacks, and for the Crucifix wielders, a dark aura coats the weapon that dramatically increases the strength of their attacks, and the amount of frenzy buildup they cause.

Church Servant (Cane)

All of their cane attacks have clearly telegraphed animations that only strike a small area in front of them, and both of these things combined make them very easy to interrupt, even if you're not yet familiar with the enemy. The small strike area of their attacks also makes them very easy to evade, so if you want to conserve bullets, quickstepping through the attacks to get to their back can be just as effective. Because they lack any kind of ranged attacks, if you're using a long ranged weapon or firearms you can attack them from outside of their range as they slowly walk towards you.

Basic Information			Item Drops											
Cathedral Ward*	282	239	Blood Vial ×2 [19%], Blue Elixir ×1 [1%]	99	99	99	99	80	71	65	150	180	—	—
Upper Cathedral Ward	1105	873	Blood Vial ×2 [20%], Blue Elixir ×1 [1%]	124	124	124	124	80	71	65	150	180		
Hunter's Nightmare/ Research Hall	2064	871	Blood Vial ×2 [21%], Blue Elixir ×1 [1%]	128	128	128	128	114	101	92	150	180		

*Cathedral Ward (Blood Moon): 343 HP/402 Blood Echoes

Church Servant (Cane & Lantern)

In general, you should treat this type of Church Servant the same as you would those armed only with canes: try to interrupt their melee attacks if possible or quickstep through them and attack from behind. Pay close attention to their lanterns – if they're draped with eyes, you'll need to be ready to quickstep backward if they use their spherical magic blast, or sideways if they cast the homing orbs. The homing orbs can be problematic if this enemy spots you early and starts firing them at you before you can close in, however, because they can fire them off quite quickly and it can be difficult to evade through multiple projectiles safely. If this happens, try to either use cover as you approach, or hide behind it until they lose track of you and stop casting, giving you the window you need to close in.

Both of these attacks give enough warning for you to safely get out of the way; the homing projectiles move very slowly and you can usually avoid them simply by strafing away.

Basic Information

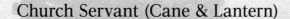

	■	⚕	Item Drops	🔲	🌑	🔺	⚙	⭐	🍃	♫	💀	🔻	🗡	✂
Cathedral Ward*	282	258	Blood Vial ×2 [21%], Quicksilver Bullets ×3 [21%], Blue Elixir ×1 [1%]	99	99	99	99	80	71	65	150	180	—	—
Upper Cathedral Ward	1105	982	Blood Vial ×2 [21%], Quicksilver Bullets ×3 [21%], Blue Elixir ×1 [1%]	124	124	124	124	80	71	65	150	180		

*Cathedral Ward (Blood Moon): 343 HP/433 Blood Echoes

Church Servant (Cane & Flamesprayer)

These Servants will generally use their Flamesprayer when you're at mid range, and will use either a straight ahead blast of fire, or a horizontal sweep. If you try and strafe around them during this attack they'll keep moving and try to realign themselves while continuously firing, which can lead to problems if you don't pay close attention to the area you're fighting in. You can quickstep through the flames, however, and try to either get behind the enemy, or the weapon so that the flames don't hit you. They turn quite slowly while they're trying to realign themselves, so if you do get around the flame, you can usually strike them from the sides or behind before they can catch up to you.

Basic Information

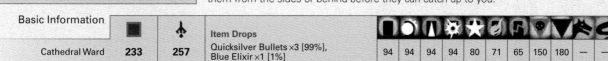

	■	⚕	Item Drops	🔲	🌑	🔺	⚙	⭐	🍃	♫	💀	🔻	🗡	✂
Cathedral Ward	233	257	Quicksilver Bullets ×3 [99%], Blue Elixir ×1 [1%]	94	94	94	94	80	71	65	150	180	—	—

Church Servant (Cane & Pistol)

The primary threat this enemy poses is if they seem you coming and can start firing at you, so if you spot them early enough, try to use the environment to your advantage and get around behind them undetected. If they do spot you, try to use cover to mask your approach, or take cover until they've fired both shots, and then quickly move up while they're reloading. Once you do get up close, place a bigger emphasis on evading attacks rather than interrupting so that you don't take a bullet when they decided to mix in some gunfire with their Cane attacks. Like other Servants, once you get around to their side or back there's little they can do, and you should be able to finish them off with a quick R1 combo.

Basic Information

	■	⚕	Item Drops	🔲	🌑	🔺	⚙	⭐	🍃	♫	💀	🔻	🗡	✂
Cathedral Ward	279	433	Quicksilver Bullets ×3 [99%], Blue Elixir ×1 [1%]	96	96	96	96	80	71	65	150	180	—	—

3

Church Servant (Scythe)

Trying to quickstep through their swings is risky and unreliable; it's best to stay out of their range and bait their attacks from a safe distance, and then rush in and hit them while they recover. Their horizontal slashes can still hit you if you're behind them as they turn to face you, so leave yourself plenty of room to evade and wait until they finish swinging to move in and attack. If you're confident, you can interrupt them from outside the range of their scythes at much less risk to yourself.

Basic Information

	■	⚑	Item Drops										
Cathedral Ward	343	464	Blood Vial ×3 [42%], Blue Elixir ×1 [1%]	101	101	101	101	80	71	65	150	180	—	—
Upper Cathedral Ward	1105	1091	Blood Vial ×3 [42%], Blue Elixir ×1 [1%]	124	124	124	124	80	71	65	150	180		

Church Servant (Crucifix)

Wait for them to attack, and then quickstep forward to position yourself behind them and let loose with a chain of R1 swings or stagger them with a charged R2. Most of their attacks won't hit you in this position, though they will sometimes perform a 360-degree horizontal swing, which can strike you here if you are standing extremely close; be prepared to strafe or quickstep backward to avoid it. Alternately, stand out of range of their thrusts and wait for them to attack so that you can interrupt them. When they lower their crucifixes and switch to the aggressive battle stance, avoid standing in front of them at all costs – this is when they'll use their grab attack, which has a near-instant startup and leaves almost no time for you to escape. Also beware that any hit they land will build up your frenzy meter, so if you get hit too many times in quick succession, back off and let it decrease.

Basic Information

	■	⚑	Item Drops										
Cathedral Ward	429	742	Blood Vial ×2 [21%], Quicksilver Bullets ×3 [21%], Blue Elixir ×1 [1%]	101	101	101	101	80	71	65	150	180	—	—

Beast Patient (Male)

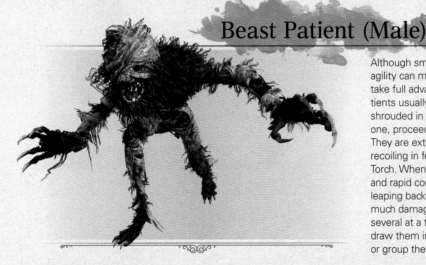

Although small and relatively weak on their own, their speed and agility can make them very dangerous in large numbers and they'll take full advantage of that fact with clever ambush tactics. Beast Patients usually appear in groups and are often hidden behind obstacles, shrouded in steam or smoke, or otherwise out of sight; if you see one, proceed with caution, as there are probably more hiding nearby. They are extremely fearful of fire and will often shield their eyes while recoiling in fear at that sight of any flame, including the one from your Torch. When they do attack they employ simple claw swipes, lunges and rapid combos, and will frequently try to dodge your attacks by leaping backwards or to the side; their individual hits don't deal too much damage, but can add up quickly, especially if you're fighting several at a time. The scent from Pungent Blood Cocktails will also draw them in, so you can throw one to stop them from pursuing you or group them together to hit all of them at once with a Molotov.

Beast Patients fall quickly due to their low health; a single Molotov will kill them and is a great way of dealing with tightly-clustered groups. They can be interrupted, but it's more effective just to hit them a few times with R1 attacks due to their low health and defense; simply stand back and wait for them to act, then move in and mow them down during their recovery. Trying to stay behind these enemies is difficult due to their agility, but you can evade most of their attacks by quickstepping forward through them or sideways and out of the way When fighting more than one at a time, try to have your Torch out in one hand because the flame will tend to keep them at bay for while, allowing you to work your way through the group one at a time if you're quick. Even attacking them with the Hunter's Torch can be very effective during the early stages of the game, but when you encounter them later in dungeons you're much better off using fire elemental weapons to dispatch them quickly.

Basic Information

	■	⚑	Item Drops										
Old Yharnam	190	141	Random gem based on area ×1 [4%], Blood Vial ×1 [8%]	86	86	86	86	66	50	60	120	270	×	—
Chalice Dungeon Base Level	158	81	Random gem based on area ×1 [2%], Blood Vial ×1 [8%]	90	90	90	90	66	50	60	120	180		
Hunter's Nightmare	552	203	Random gem based on area ×1 [4%], Blood Vial ×1 [8%]	110	110	110	110	90	68	82	120	270		
Hunter's Nightmare	Weak	138	203	Random gem based on area ×1 [4%], Blood Vial ×1 [8%]	110	110	110	110	90	68	82	120	270		

Preset Chalice Dungeons: Ailing Loran, Lower Loran

Female Beast Patients

These Beast Patients share the same basic attacks as the other types, and those with glowing red eyes will also inflict poison build-up if they hit you. The hooded cloak they wear shields their eyes so they do not recoil in fear at the sight of small flames like the male versions, but they do still share the same weakness to fire attacks. They usually appear in groups both with other females and males, and having your Torch out while fighting mixed groups can be very beneficial, because it will allow you to focus on the females while the males recoil from the flame. You can further use this to your advantage by luring females over to recoiling males so that they group up and you take multiple enemies out at once with well placed Molotovs. At close range they will often use a swift shoulder charge, which can be difficult to avoid; if you're just outside their reach, they may try to close the distance with a combo attack, which carries them forward as they perform it. In addition, they will often perform a close-range grab attack that causes enormous poison build-up and is almost guaranteed to fill your meter instantly.

3

Beast Patient (Female)

Handle them the same way as the males – stand back and wait for them to strike, then dash in and perform a quick-step attack or an R1 chain to finish them quickly and easily. Molotovs are helpful for dealing with tightly-clustered groups, especially in the enclosed spaces and narrow pathways of Old Yharnam. Most thrust attacks from long weapons, such as Rifle Spear or the transformed Saw Spear, can hit them from a safe distance and help minimize the risk of being poisoned if they manage to hit you, though carrying a few Antidotes is always a good plan just in case. If you're being chased by several Beast Patients and need to create some breathing room, you can distract them with a Pungent Blood Cocktail; you can also toss one into any of the fires scattered throughout Old Yharnam and they will throw themselves into the flames after it.

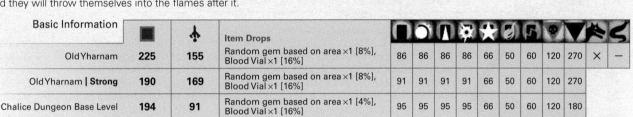

Basic Information	■	🔱	Item Drops	🜂	🌑	🔺	✴	★	🌙	🎵	☠	🔻	⚔	🗡
Old Yharnam	225	155	Random gem based on area ×1 [8%], Blood Vial ×1 [16%]	86	86	86	86	66	50	60	120	270	X	—
Old Yharnam | **Strong**	190	169	Random gem based on area ×1 [8%], Blood Vial ×1 [16%]	91	91	91	91	66	50	60	120	270		
Chalice Dungeon Base Level	194	91	Random gem based on area ×1 [4%], Blood Vial ×1 [16%]	95	95	95	95	66	50	60	120	180		

Strong versions appear before facing Blood-starved Beast.
Preset Chalice Dungeons: Ailing Loran, Lower Loran

Ashen Blood Beast Patient

Fight them as you would the smaller females, but watch out for their grab attack at close range – they will slowly raise both hands above their heads, spread their arms and lunge forward, giving you plenty of time to strafe or quickstep out of the way. Interrupting or staggering these slow-moving enemies is the easiest way to defeat them, but quickstepping forward through any of their attacks and hitting them with an R1 combo while they recover is effective too. Beware of the poison build-up from their attacks, though, because it can increase very quickly; if you do get hit it's better to be cautious and use an Antidote rather than run the risk of getting poisoned.

Basic Information	■	🔱	Item Drops	🜂	🌑	🔺	✴	★	🌙	🎵	☠	🔻	⚔	🗡
Old Yharnam	364	254	Random gem based on area ×1 [8%], Blood Vial ×2 [30%], Antidote ×2 [10%]	97	97	97	97	74	60	70	120	180	X	—
Chalice Dungeon Base Level	229	128	Random gem based on area ×1 [8%], Blood Vial ×2 [30%]	99	99	99	99	74	50	70	120	180		
Hunter's Nightmar	1451	507	Random gem based on area ×1 [8%], Blood Vial ×2 [30%], Antidote ×2 [10%]	123	123	123	123	101	82	96	120	180		

Preset Chalice Dungeons: Ailing Loran, Lower Loran

THE BESTIARY [REGULAR ENEMIES] 237

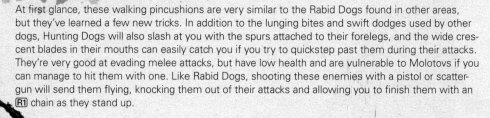

Hunting Dog

At first glance, these walking pincushions are very similar to the Rabid Dogs found in other areas, but they've learned a few new tricks. In addition to the lunging bites and swift dodges used by other dogs, Hunting Dogs will also slash at you with the spurs attached to their forelegs, and the wide crescent blades in their mouths can easily catch you if you try to quickstep past them during their attacks. They're very good at evading melee attacks, but have low health and are vulnerable to Molotovs if you can manage to hit them with one. Like Rabid Dogs, shooting these enemies with a pistol or scattergun will send them flying, knocking them out of their attacks and allowing you to finish them with an R1 chain as they stand up.

The safest and easiest way to deal with these agile creatures is to knock them down with a pistol shot or a scattergun blast, then quickstep toward them and attack with a couple of quick R1 swings before they finish recovering. Blunderbusses in particular are useful for dealing with groups of Hunting Dogs due to their ability to knock down several of these enemies at once. They will usually dodge Molotovs or Throwing Knives, but gunshots tend to be too quick for them to evade. When they lunge at you, quickstep sideways and counterattack with an R1 combo, though beware that they will sometimes leap away from you immediately after attacking. You can use Pungent Blood Cocktails either defensively to distract them while you escape, or offensively to group them together and hit several at once with Molotovs.

Basic Information			Item Drops														
Hemwick Charnel Lane	195	365	Twin Bloodstone Shards ×1 [4%], Bloodstone Shard ×1 [30%]		68	68	68	68	70	62	50	120	180	×	—
Chalice Dungeon Base Level	158	100	Bloodstone B ×1 [4%], Bloodstone A ×1 [30%]		66	66	66	66	70	62	50	120	180		

Preset Chalice Dungeons: Pthumeru Ihyll

Hemwick Grave Women

These graveyard-dwelling madwomen have very low health, but are usually found in groups, using their numbers to make up for their individual weakness; luring them out one at a time using Pebbles will help to greatly reduce the threat they pose. When not patrolling in groups, they'll often hide and attempt to ambush you either with direct attacks or using shoves to try and knock you off cliffs, so be careful anytime you round a corner in areas where Grave Women are located. They can be interrupted and staggered, and due to their frailty, rolling into them will send them reeling off balance and generally give you enough time to follow through with a quick R1 chain before they regain their footing. Rolling into them will also knock them out of their attacks, which can be useful if you're facing down a group of them; remember that you must perform a roll, and not a quickstep, so it's best to fight them without locking on.

The sickle-and-cleaver carrying Grave Women attack in a similar manner, using quick slashes and combos to try and overwhelm you, but the short reach of their attacks means you can often hit them from outside of their range. The sickle-users will occasionally use a slower overhead swing with a long windup that causes them to lose their balance afterward, giving you an opportunity to counterattack. The red-hot pole irons carried by some Grave Women inflict fire damage and can easily cause you to flinch, making it difficult to escape further attacks. The weight of their weapons prevents them from being able to use long combos so you generally only have to worry about evading single hits, but the range they can use their attacks from does make closing in on them more difficult than other Grave Women.

Wooden Mallets also become a fearsome weapon in the hands of some Grave Women, and they'll use them to perform powerful horizontal swings and overhead smashes. Mallet wielders have the slowest attack speed due to the weight of their weapon, making them extremely vulnerable to interrupts if you can spare the bullets. The final type of Grave Woman does not use a melee weapon as her primary form of offense, and instead prefers to stand back in out-of-reach spots from which they'll bombard you with Molotovs. They're especially dangerous when other enemies are nearby, since they have impeccable aim, can hit you at great distances and the splash damage of their Molotovs is hard to avoid. Once you you're close to them, however, they'll begin using the same cleaver attacks as the torch-bearers.

Hemwick Grave Woman (Sickle)

Make good use of their weak hips and fight them locked off, using your roll to keep them from attacking while you finish them. Rolling attacks are the best way to hit them before they can recover; if they do manage to get back on their feet before you kill them, simply roll into them again and repeat. It's also possible to quickstep forward through their attacks and position yourself behind them, where they can't hit you; at this point you can stagger them with a charged R2 attack or finish them off with an R1 chain.

Basic Information	■	⚔	Item Drops	⬜	◯	△	✦	★	⬗	♫	☠	▽	⚔	⌇
Hemwick Charnel Lane	174	299	Random gem based on area ×1 [2.5%], Blood Vial ×1 [8%]	77	77	77	77	70	68	72	120	240	—	—
Yahar'gul (Blood Moon)	403	624	Random gem based on area ×1 [1%], Blood Vial ×1 [4%]	92	92	92	92	70	68	72	120	240		

Hemwick Grave Woman (Pole Iron)

Molotovs and Throwing Knives allow you to attack from outside the reach of these foes' weapons, and as such they are more practical here than against other types of Grave Women. If you plan to use melee attacks, don't approach too quickly – they will sometimes try to hit you with their shove attack as you attempt to quickstep past them. Instead, stand a safe distance away to bait them into taking a swing at you, and then roll toward them during their recovery and knock them off balance. Interrupts do not work well on them, due to the precise timing required by most of their attacks, but a couple of R1 swings will get the job done just as quickly. One of the most common attacks they use when approaching is a running stab so be cautious even when you're outside of their normal attack range; if you make them miss with this attack it has a very long recovery time, giving you ample opportunity to close in and finish them off.

Basic Information	■	⚔	Item Drops	⬜	◯	△	✦	★	⬗	♫	☠	▽	⚔	⌇
Hemwick Charnel Lane	228	299	Random gem based on area ×1 [2.5%], Blood Vial ×1 [8%]	77	77	77	77	70	68	72	120	240	—	—
Yahar'gul (Blood Moon)	518	624	Random gem based on area ×1 [1%], Blood Vial ×1 [4%]	92	92	92	92	70	68	72	120	240		

Hemwick Grave Woman (Mallet)

Stay just outside their reach and bait them into attacking, and then either interrupt them or quickstep forward through their swings and hit them from behind with a quick R1 combo. If you do get close to them they'll often try to use a quick shove to try and knock you out of your attacks, so it's best to keep near the edge of their mallet range. Two or three hits are usually enough to finish them due to their low health and their melee attacks are easy to evade. As with the other Grave Women, don't lock on – instead, exploit their weakness by rolling into them and following up with a rolling R1 attack to defeat them before they can respond.

Basic Information	■	⚔	Item Drops	⬜	◯	△	✦	★	⬗	♫	☠	▽	⚔	⌇
Hemwick Charnel Lane	195	332	Random gem based on area ×1 [2.5%], Blood Vial ×2 [16%]	77	77	77	77	70	68	72	120	240	—	—
Yahar'gul (Blood Moon)	461	693	Random gem based on area ×1 [1%], Blood Vial ×2 [8%]	92	92	92	92	70	68	72	120	240		

Hemwick Grave Woman (Cleaver & Torch)

They can be interrupted and staggered, but the interrupt timing on many of their attacks is very precise and it's easier to simply hit them with a couple of R1 swings. Stunning them with a roll and immediately following through with a rolling R1 attack is the safest and most effective way to deal with them, although Throwing Knives are useful for defeating them before they can bring the fight to you. Due to their quick attacks, trying to quickstep past them is risky; instead, stand just out of their reach and wait for them to swing, and then move in while they recover and finish them with an R1 combo.

Basic Information	■	⚔	Item Drops											
Hemwick Charnel Lane	195	332	Random gem based on area ×1 [5%], Blood Vial ×1 [16%], Quicksilver Bullets ×2 [5%]	77	77	77	77	70	68	72	120	240	—	—
Yahar'gul (Blood Moon)	461	693	Random gem based on area ×1 [2.5%], Blood Vial ×1 [8%], Quicksilver Bullets ×2 [2.5%]	92	92	92	92	70	68	72	120	240		

Hemwick Grave Woman (Cleaver & Molotovs)

You can sometimes kill them with pistol shots, Throwing Knives or Molotovs of your own without having to directly approach them, which can also prevent you from having to fight other enemies while they're bombarding you from above. If all else fails, lure any other enemies out of their range and fight in a safe spot before coming back to deal with the Molotov-throwers afterward. Rolling R1 attacks are still the most effective way to deal with them at close range due to their frail hips, but you'll need to carefully roll or quickstep out of the way of their projectiles as you approach. Try to kill them quickly once you get in range and if they draw their cleavers, roll into them immediately to knock them off balance.

Basic Information	■	⚔	Item Drops											
Hemwick Charnel Lane	228	332	Random gem based on area ×1 [2.5%], Blood Vial ×1 [8%], Molotov Cocktail ×2 [10%]	77	77	77	77	70	68	72	120	240	—	—
Yahar'gul (Blood Moon)	518	693	Random gem based on area ×1 [1%], Blood Vial ×1 [4%], Molotov Cocktail ×2 [5%]	92	92	92	92	70	68	72	120	240		

Snake Parasite

360-degree radius, spit a frontal cloud of poison, and perform rapid forward combo attacks which have strong directional tracking. The host and snakes together will sometimes perform a grab attack, which is certain to inflict slow poison on the spot; they can use a stationary version of this move at close range and a running version from up to three meters away. The host can also summon Snake Balls using a high-pitched whistle, potentially complicating the encounter. Snake Parasites have high physical defense, but take respectable damage from elemental attacks such as Molotovs.

Avoid standing close to these opponents for more than a couple of seconds at a time – they can attack you from any direction and their snakes' rapid strikes will quickly poison you. Instead, take advantage of their slow speed and bait their attacks from just outside their reach, then quickstep forward and hit them from behind with R1 combos, or use far-reaching charged R2 swings from weapons such as the Rifle Spear or Hunter's Axe. It is possible to interrupt them, but doing so is impractical due to their unpredictability and the precise timing required. If fighting more than one at a time, Molotovs or other ranged weapons are the safest solution; these enemies have strong super armor and trying to hit several at once with sweeping horizontal attacks will almost always cause you to trade blows. If you have no choice but to clear several of them out of an area in order to proceed, lure them one at a time with Pebbles and fight them away from the other enemies.

At first glance these enemies resemble the axe-wielding Hunts-men, but a colony of parasitic snakes will burst from their heads as soon as they detect you. Snake Parasites use their axes in a similar fashion to Huntsmen that carry the same weapon, but their snakes' attacks are much less predictable and will build up your slow poison meter if they hit you. The snakes can strike around the host in a

Basic Information	■	⚔	Item Drops											
Forbidden Woods	1023	1138	Random gem based on area ×1 [25%], Blood Vial ×3 [20%], Blood Vial ×2 [55%]	132	102	102	120	120	75	66	999	180	—	—

Exposed version has 588 HP.

Snake Ball

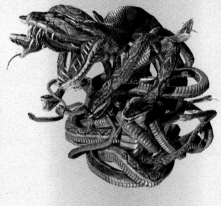

Clumps of intertwined snakes found throughout the Forbidden Woods, and in some Chalice Dungeons. Extremely slow-moving enemies with relatively low health, Snake Balls present little danger when alone, but are usually positioned to ambush you in groups from behind trees, boulders and other objects. Their attacks are rapid, hit multiple times and cause slow poison buildup, making them a real threat if they manage to surround you. They have very short reach, however, and their limited ability to pursue you makes it easy to get away if you need to retreat. Beware that they often appear alongside more agile enemies, such as Huntsmen and Snake Parasites, so examine the surrounding area carefully before you approach them.

Jump attacks or far-reaching R2s from transformed weapons such as the Hunter Axe or Rifle Spear will hit them from outside their attack range, allowing you to defeat them at no risk to yourself with proper timing. Though they have no real weakness to elemental attacks, their blunt defense is particularly low, so weapons such as Tonitrus or the Kirkhammer can kill them in one or two hits. Even when dealing with a group of these enemies, it's still possible to pick them off one at a time due to their incredibly slow movement speed – just pay attention to your surroundings and make sure there aren't any other enemies behind you. If there are faster enemies such as Snake Parasites or Large Huntsmen nearby, lure those away and deal with them first, then mop up any remaining Snake Balls.

Basic Information

Location	HP	Echoes	Item Drops											
Forbidden Woods	281	237	Random Murky gem based on area ×1 [4%], Bloodstone Shard ×1 [8%]	95	76	76	76	40	80	85	999	180	—	—
Chalice Dungeon Base Level	194	29	Random Murky gem based on area ×1 [2%], Bloodstone A ×1 [4%]	83	66	66	66	40	80	85	999	180		

Has poison version. Preset Chalice Dungeons: Hintertomb

Small Celestial Emissary

Small alien creatures with squid-like heads and mottled blue skin. They attack only with very basic slaps, shoves and flailing combos, but hit surprisingly hard for enemies their size and have extremely high defense. They are incredibly weak against thrust attacks, however, and Molotovs or Throwing Knives are a good way to damage them if you have no other means of dealing thrust damage. Many of their attacks are slow and give you plenty of time to interrupt them; they can also be staggered, but doing so is difficult because they recover quickly from their attacks and will usually turn to face you before you can strike them from behind with a charged R2 swing.

Use thrust attacks to kill them quickly. A strong thrust attack from a weapon such as the Rifle Spear or Saw Spear, even non-upgraded, can kill them in a single hit. Throwing Knives are also useful if you need to kill them without getting close; two or three will usually be enough to do the job. Other types of damage will eventually wear them down, but doing so takes quite a bit longer. Interrupts are very effective and will allow you to finish them with a single visceral attack, regardless of your weapon's damage type. Staggering them from behind is much more difficult and should be avoided unless an obvious opportunity arises.

Basic Information

Location	HP	Echoes	Item Drops											
Healing Church Workshop	387	436	None	297	330	0	165	160	60	50	120	180	—	×
Forbidden Woods	143	765	Random gem based on area ×1 [30%], Blue Elixir ×1 [1%]	265	294	0	147	160	60	50	120	180		
Iosefka's Clinic	143	658	Different drops (all 100%): Iosefka's Blood Vial ×1, Pungent Blood Cocktail ×3, Beast ×1, Formless Oedon ×1, Sedatives ×1, Arianna's Shoes ×1, or Oedon Writhe ×1	265	294	0	147	160	60	50	120	180		
Upper Cathedral Ward	387	436	None	297	330	0	165	160	60	50	120	180		
Chalice Dungeon Base Level	116	77	Random gem based on area ×1 [4%], Quicksilver Bullets ×2 [30%], Blue Elixir ×1 [1%]	246	273	0	136	160	60	50	120	180		

Boss support gives no Blood Echoes. Preset Chalice Dungeons: Isz Gravestone

Parasite Larva

Large parasitic worms first encountered in the Forbidden Woods; a pair of them will also emerge from the corpses of defeated Loran Silverbeasts in the Nightmare of Mensis. Extremely straight-forward enemies, Parasitic Larvae will slither toward you and perform lunging bites from just outside the range of your melee attacks. Despite their simplicity, they are very difficult to hit due to their small size and horizontal attacks will often pass over them entirely. When encountered away from a host, they usually appear in large groups; in these situations they are extremely dangerous due to their fast attacks and high evasion. Molotovs and Throwing Knives are marginally effective for dealing with Parasitic Larvae, but will often miss if they are actively engaged in attacking you.

Use jump attacks as they're approaching you to hit them before they can strike, or time a charged R2 attack from a weapon with long reach, such as the Rifle Spear, to activate as soon as they enter your range. Do not engage more than one at a time if possible; lure them individually with Pebbles or Throwing Knives to avoid being surrounded. Try to use vertical attacks and overhead swings, such as the Hunter Axe's basic R2; these are much more likely to connect than horizontal slashes.

Basic Information	■	✈	Item Drops										
Forbidden Woods	230	142	None	101	101	101	72	440	290	440	10	90	—	—
Forsaken Cainhurst Castle	510	210	None	109	109	109	78	440	290	440	10	90		
Nightmare of Mensis	688	284	None	118	118	118	84	440	290	440	10	90		
Chalice Dungeon Base Level	158	33	Coldblood Dew (1) ×1 [10%], Coldblood Dew (2) ×1 [7%], Coldblood Dew (3) ×1 [3%]	91	91	91	65	440	290	440	10	90		

Cain's Servants

These small hunchbacked creatures can be found tending to their duties within the walls of Cainhurst Castle, and you'll first encounter them scrubbing the floors in the castle's Entrance Hall. These cane-carrying servants are extremely focused on their duties and won't attack without provocation, so you can leave them to carry on their work if you wish. If you do attack one, they'll retaliate with simple swings of their canes, but since they move very slowly and can't strike behind them, it's easy to get around them and finish them off with a quick R1 chain.

Once you reach the castle's library you'll encounter servants that carry candelabras along with their canes; these servants are always hostile and will pelt you with bullets of ice from extreme range using their canes as blowguns. Their blowgun attacks have two different properties, depending upon where you encounter them: the servants on the lower floor of the library will shoot you with bullets that inflict almost no damage, but mark you with a red glyph, which causes the surrounding Forsaken Castle Spirits to become much more aggressive. Servants on the upper balconies fire bullets that have no additional effects, but inflict substantial damage if they hit you.

The most dangerous Cainhurst servants, however, wield rapiers and use a completely different set of attacks than the other types. They strike rapidly with quick thrusts, slashes and multi-hit combos, and will sometimes intentionally delay a slash to trick you into letting your guard down. They move quickly, are highly evasive and turn swiftly to face you, making their attacks extremely difficult to avoid. All Servants do share a similar weakness, however, and it is often the key to taking them out safely. Shooting them with any pistol or blunderbuss will knock them over for a short period of time, during which you can close in and put yourself in an advantageous position to hit them as they get up. If you're fighting multiple enemies at once and a Servant is among them, it can be worth shooting them every now and then just to keep them out of the fight, leaving you free to engage the other enemies.

Cain's Servant (Cane)

Since you'll normally encounter this enemy while they're busy cleaning, you can nearly always start your attack on them with a charged R2 from behind for a quick victory. If you're fighting them normally, baiting their slow attacks, and then quickstepping past them so that you can hit them from behind is generally the easiest method to deal with this type of Servant. Since there will usually be other enemies in the area along with these Servants try to keep the fight away from them so that you don't accidentally disturb their cleaning duties.

Basic Information			Item Drops											
Forsaken Cainhurst Castle	595	560	Blood Vial ×1 [22%]	90	90	90	90	50	68	45	120	180	—	—

Cain's Servant (Cane & Candelabra)

These enemies are only a threat at a distance – once you get close, they're sitting ducks. It's best to eliminate the blowgun snipers first to prevent them from harassing you as you fight other enemies, especially if those enemies are knife-wielding Forsaken Castle Spirits. If you have Blue Elixirs you can use them to mask your presences while you fight other enemies out in the open so that you don't have to worry about incoming darts. On the upper levels, use the bookshelves for cover as you approach the servants with blowguns – they can provide safe spots to fight servants wielding rapiers if one spots you before you reach your target.

Basic Information			Item Drops											
Forsaken Cainhurst Castle	595	560	Quicksilver Bullets ×2 [22%]	90	90	90	90	50	68	45	120	180	—	—

Cain's Servant (Rapier)

Knock them down by shooting them, and then attack as they're standing up. If you don't have enough stamina to finish them or are using a weapon that's too slow to keep them trapped in the combo, back off and shoot them again. Do not attempt to quickstep past them or through their attacks, as their thrusts have strong directional tracking and carry a high risk of hitting you in the process. Jump attacks can be effective for hitting them from outside their attack range but must be carefully timed in order to avoid being hit first. Faster weapons in their basic modes, such as the Threaded Cane, Saw Spear and Ludwig's Holy Blade, make it easier to trap these servants in a combo and prevent them from being able to counterattack.

Basic Information			Item Drops											
Forsaken Cainhurst Castle	993	910	Blood Vial ×2 [95%], Numbing Mist ×1 [5%]	95	95	95	95	50	68	45	120	180	—	—

Lost Child of Antiquity

Bat-like creatures with human heads encountered on the ramparts and roof of Cainhurst Castle. They are often perched in the distance or positioned behind obstacles, where they can't be easily seen, and will move in to attack when you pass certain points. While very slow, they also hit quite hard and can knock you down with a slow overhead slam; they can perform a combo with up to five hits, which will send you flying if the final blow connects, and will sometimes use a running grab attack which carries them forward as they execute it. They'll try to strike you with supersonic projectiles at mid range, and will also sweep a sonic blast in a forward arc when you're close to them. While these enemies can be interrupted and staggered, shooting them during any of their attacks (but outside of the interrupt timing window) will knock them onto their backs, where they'll flail about helplessly on the ground for several seconds before getting back up; this offers a prime opportunity to hit them with your strongest attacks at no risk to yourself.

Regardless of whether you prefer to interrupt them or simply knock them down, the most effective strategy against these foes is to shoot them during any of their attacks and make the most of the ensuing opportunity. They are very slow, giving you plenty of time to simply strafe or quickstep behind them and stagger them with a charged R2 swing. If you aren't interested in the Bloodstone Shards they can drop, you can score an easy kill by luring them with their backs to a ledge and shooting them when they attack, causing them to fall to their deaths.

Basic Information Special Weakness: Righteous			Item Drops											
Forsaken Cainhurst Castle	908	910	Twin Bloodstone Shards ×1 [28%], Bloodstone Chunk ×1 [1.5%]	199	199	199	199	90	76	80	120	180	—	—
Forsaken Cainhurst Castle | Strong	922	832	Twin Bloodstone Shards ×1 [28%], Bloodstone Chunk ×1 [1.5%]	203	203	203	203	90	76	80	120	180		
Chalice Dungeon Base Level	282	125	Random Nourishing gem based on area ×1 [8%], Twin Bloodstone Shards ×1 [18%], Bloodstone Chunk ×1 [1.5%]	165	165	165	165	90	76	80	120	180		

Strong version on rooftop. Preset Chalice Dungeons: Pthumeru Ihyll

Forsaken Castle Spirits

Ghostly apparitions wandering the interior areas of Cainhurst Castle, these enemies are initially invisible when you enter the first indoor areas, but will reveal themselves and become hostile when you pass certain points or attempt to pick up items. Forsaken Castle Spirits move extremely slowly and won't make much effort to pursue you, so you can leave them alone if you're so inclined. In combat, they normally use a limited set of forward stabs and slashes with their knives, and will sometimes perform quick combos; if you have been marked by a Cain's Servant with a blowgun, however, they will become very aggressive and begin actively hunting you down.

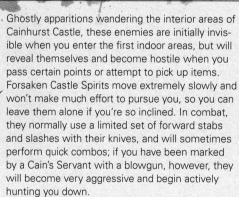

Forsaken Castle Spirits variants carrying their own heads are incapable of damaging you directly and can only use a single move: a paralyzing scream which will set you up for grab attacks by the ones carrying knives. They pose no threat without other enemies to support them, but are extremely dangerous in the presence of knife-wielding spirits; if you have to fight your way through the rooms they inhabit, this variant should be your priority target. Both versions cannot be damaged with normal physical attacks while in their non-corporeal state, but elemental attacks work just fine, so if you equip an elemental weapon you can often get some damage in before they react. Their elemental weakness also means that you can use Molotovs from a distance to weaken them before you close in, which is especially effective if there are a few of them in close proximity and you can hit them all.

Forsaken Castle Spirit (Knife)

Forsaken Castle Spirits represent little threat on their own, because their knife attacks have short range and don't inflict much damage. It's possible to interrupt and stagger them, and while interrupts are effective against their predictable attacks, staying behind them long enough to hit them with a charged ⓡ2 before they turn can be difficult, because they recover relatively quickly. Because of their high physical defense, visceral attacks are a good method of dispatching them if you lack any elemental weapons.

If you're using a weapon with a charged thrust attack, such as Ludwig's Holy Blade or the Saw Spear, you can time the thrust so that they walk into it at the edge of the weapon's range, thanks to their slow movement speed. If you've been marked by a Cain's Servant, however, they become faster and a lot more aggressive, so it's best to wait until the mark wears off before engaging them.

Basic Information				Item Drops												
Special Weakness: Righteous	⬛	✦														
Forsaken Cainhurst Castle	737	490		None	159	159	159	159	160	120	40	300	300	—	—

Forsaken Castle Spirit (Head)

If there are any other enemies nearby, try to lure them away and create some room to maneuver, so that you won't immediately be swarmed and stabbed to death if you're paralyzed by the scream attack. If you're unable to separate these spirits from the group, stand back and hit them with Molotovs from outside the range of their scream instead. The range of the scream is clearly visible thanks to the on-screen effect; once you've seen them use it and know the general radius, you can wait just outside it, so you won't have far to run in once them screaming stops. Without other types of enemies nearby, these spirits are helpless and inflict no damage, so even if you do get paralyzed you have nothing to fear.

Basic Information				Item Drops												
Special Weakness: Righteous	⬛	✦														
Forsaken Cainhurst Castle	397	490		None	146	146	146	146	160	120	40	300	300	—	—

Scholars

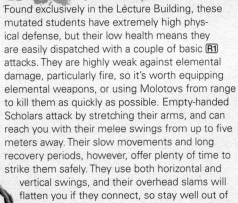

Found exclusively in the Lecture Building, these mutated students have extremely high physical defense, but their low health means they are easily dispatched with a couple of basic ⓡ1 attacks. They are highly weak against elemental damage, particularly fire, so it's worth equipping elemental weapons, or using Molotovs from range to kill them as quickly as possible. Empty-handed Scholars attack by stretching their arms, and can reach you with their melee swings from up to five meters away. Their slow movements and long recovery periods, however, offer plenty of time to strike them safely. They use both horizontal and vertical swings, and their overhead slams will flatten you if they connect, so stay well out of their range and move in to hit them once they miss.

When fighting them in groups, make sure to pay attention to ones at the back of the pack, because they can often still reach you due to the range of their melee strikes. Because so many of them will be able to attack you when they're grouped up, it's dangerous to fight them at close range unless you're taking them out in one hit. If you're not able to kill them in a single hit, fall back and use Molotovs to take them out from safety. In spite of their gooey consistency, they are vulnerable to both interrupts and staggers, but their attacks can be somewhat unpredictable and difficult to anticipate, so it's better to conserve your bullets for more difficult foes.

Scholars carrying flasks will use them to throw acid at you from long range and perform wide-ranging area attacks up close. When they rear up and hold their flasks to their mouths, they'll release a circular pool of acid on the ground around them; this move leaves more than enough time for you to quickstep behind them for a charged ⓡ2 strike. They will also splash acid in a 180-degree frontal arc with their flasks. After throwing two to four acid projectiles at you, they'll stop to refill their flasks by vomiting into them, offering an opportunity to hit them before they can attack again.

Scholar (Bare Hands)

Bait their attacks from at least five meters away, and then quickstep toward them while they recover and hit them with an R1 chain or a charged R2 swing, which will often be enough to finish them off. Alternately, you can jab them with a torch or blast them with the Flamesprayer for easy kills. Avoid rushing carelessly into the midst of large groups of these enemies, particularly in the large lecture theater; while they are little threat on their own, their long reach makes it very difficult to get away when several of them are hitting you at once. Because they turn quite slowly and their attacks take a while to recover, you can run around the entire group and hit the ones at the back before they can react, and then repeat this process as necessary to keep them from being able to mount an offensive.

Basic Information	■	♠	Item Drops											
Lecture Building 1F	153	702	Quicksilver Bullets ×3 [18%], Sedatives ×1 [2%]	263	356	113	188	160	50	60	120	180	—	—
Lecture Building 2F	458	1361	Quicksilver Bullets ×3 [18%], Sedatives ×1 [2%]	299	406	128	214	160	50	60	120	180		

Scholar on ceiling has no drops.

Scholar (Flask)

Use any available cover to block their acid projectiles while you close in on them, and then strike with R1 combos once you're close enough. Their area attacks and projectiles linger for a while, and can damage you for the entire duration of their animation, so avoid walking into dissipating clouds of acid. This is especially important when there are a group of Scholars, because the damage accumulation can quickly ramp up if you get caught in a large pool. You can bait their circular acid-vomiting attack by staying relatively close to them, and you'll have more than enough time to move around behind them for an easy stagger.

Basic Information	■	♠	Item Drops											
Lecture Building 1F	153	702	Quicksilver Bullets ×3 [18%], Sedatives ×1 [2%]	263	356	113	188	160	50	60	120	180	—	—
Lecture Building 2F	458	1361	Quicksilver Bullets ×3 [18%], Sedatives ×1 [2%]	299	406	128	214	160	50	60	120	180		

Crawler

Octopus-like enemies found in the poison pools of the Nightmare Frontier. Extremely slow-moving and vulnerable to thrust attacks, they attack with flailing swings of their tentacles, which they will sometimes chain into a combo. Although not especially dangerous on their own, the thick poison in which they are found severely impedes your movement speed, making it extremely difficult to avoid their attacks. They usually appear in groups alongside the larger variant, and to make matters worse, the Giant Lost Children surrounding some of the swamps will constantly bombard these areas with boulders, creating a nearly unapproachable melee combat situation. Fortunately, Molotovs are effective for damaging the tightly-clustered groups, and Throwing Knives are equally effective against individuals; these ranged options will allow you to engage Crawlers from a distance without having to venture into the poison.

Rather than waste all of your Throwing Knife supplies on a sustained assault, use them instead to lure these enemies out of the poison and onto dry land, where you can face them without the enormous disadvantages involved in trying to fight them on their home turf. Use thrust attacks when possible, and don't bother trying to stagger or interrupt them, as they're immune. Focus instead on staying behind them to avoid their attacks while you wear them down. As a much more elaborate, but immensely satisfying, alternative to fighting these enemies directly, you can hit the Giant Abandoned Children near the poison pools with Shaman Bone Blades, causing them to throw boulders at the Crawlers and potentially wiping out entire groups at once.

Basic Information	■	♠	Item Drops											
Nightmare Frontier	281	486	Thick Coldblood (6) ×1 [2%], Thick Coldblood (5) ×1 [8%], Thick Coldblood (4) ×1 [10%]	98	113	15	75	100	100	60	999	90	—	—

Nightmare Frontier (2nd half): 320 HP/507 Blood Echoes.

Celestial Child

Tiny larvae found in the Upper Cathedral Ward. Extremely weak and barely able to mount much of an offense, they move slowly, attack with pitiable bites and head swings, and will occasionally vomit a small amount of acid at extremely close range. While their low health, weakness to thrust attacks and general helplessness might lead you to believe they're no threat, beware: their attacks inflict an enormous amount of frenzy buildup and can easily kill you if you fail to take them seriously. That said, they're no threat at all as long as you don't let them hit you, so weapons or attacks with long enough reach to hit them from outside of their very short range will allow you to pick them off with near-impunity.

Jump attacks initiated out of their reach will crush them before they can hit you, regardless of the weapon you're using; normal R1 and R2 swings from transformed weapons with long range, such as the Hunter Axe or the Threaded Cane, are equally effective. Celestial Children turn slowly and can't hit you while you're behind them, so maintain this position by strafing or quickstepping as necessary and eliminate them with an R1 combo or a solid thrust attack.

Basic Information

			Item Drops		◧	◑	◨	✿	★	◗	♫	◉	▽	⚔	⚘
Upper Cathedral Ward	345	131	Madman's Knowledge ×1 [0.1%]		330	330	0	55	140	5	1	120	999	—	×
Chalice Dungeon Base Level	88	21	Madman's Knowledge ×1 [0.1%]		264	264	0	44	140	5	1	120	999		

Preset Chalice Dungeons: Isz Gravestone

Nightmare Apostle

Spider-like creatures encountered mainly on the ground floor of the chapel in the Nightmare of Mensis and in Chalice Dungeons; there's also a variant with a human head, but both share identical attacks and behavior. They attack by stabbing and slashing with their long legs, and will also occasionally sit up on their abdomens to perform a rapid multi-hit combo. They lunge forward during most of their attacks, effectively giving them much longer range than their small stature might suggest, but are completely unable to hit you while you're behind them. The Nightmare Apostles on the ground floor initially hang from a large web and can either be knocked down with ranged attacks or drawn down by getting close to them; by striking them one at a time with Throwing Knives you can avoid having to fight too many at once, although you will still eventually need to get close enough that any apostles remaining in the web will drop down to attack.

When first entering the chapel, use Throwing Knives or Poison Throwing Knives to knock them down from the web one at a time and eliminate them individually before knocking down more. When the large one inevitably gets involved, retreat into the small antechamber at the entrance, or even all the way outside, where it can't reach you, and fight the small ones there. Quickstep forward through their attacks to position yourself behind them, and do your best to stay there while you let loose with a R1 combos. Much like with Rabid Dogs, shooting them will knock them over, giving you a chance to attack. They are immune to visceral attacks and have no particular weakness to any element or damage type, so all weapons are equally effective.

Basic Information

			Item Drops		◧	◑	◨	✿	★	◗	♫	◉	▽	⚔	⚘
Nightmare of Mensis	688	851	Quicksilver Bullets ×2 [30%]		83	83	83	83	66	50	55	200	180	—	—
Chalice Dungeon Base Level	158	57	Quicksilver Bullets ×2 [30%]		64	64	64	64	66	50	55	200	180		
Chalice Dungeon Base Level **| Human Head**	158	57	Quicksilver Bullets ×4 [30%], Sedatives ×1 [5%]		64	64	64	64	66	50	55	200	180		

Summoned version gives 19 Blood Echoes and no drops. Preset Chalice Dungeons: Lower Hintertomb, Lower Pthumerian Labyrinth, Ailing Loran, Lower Loran, Isz Gravestone, Pthumeru IhyllPreset Chalice Dungeons: Lower Hintertomb, Lower Pthumerian Labyrinth, Ailing Loran, Lower Loran, Isz Gravestone, Pthumeru Ihyll

Mergo's Attendants

Short enemies clad in chainmail, found in the Library and Panopticon areas within the Mergo's Loft section in the Nightmare of Mensis. The unarmed versions are not aggressive for the most part, and will usually just wander around the area while completely ignoring you, although one will occasionally take a swing at you if you stay close to it for too long. They will become hostile if you go out of your way to hit them first, but lacking weapons of any kind, they use only basic shoulder charges and punches that are easily dealt with.

Attendants armed with crossbows like to hide behind pillars, mirrors and other obstacles in the prison area, just below where their unarmed comrades appear. Their crossbow bolts inflict rapid poison build-up, making them very dangerous at long range; they are also positioned so that you cannot easily attack one without stepping into the others' line of sight. Encountered only during the battle with Micolash, you will find flail-wielding attendants on the spiral staircase connecting the lower and upper sections of the boss area. They use only very simple short-range melee attacks with their flails and aren't much of a threat by themselves, but you'll still need to be careful if you encounter a group of them at once.

Mergo's Attendant (Unarmed)

Due to their lack of aggression, you can attack them from any direction with little fear of reprisal; still, it's safest to stay behind them so they can't hit you right away when your attacks turn them hostile. Elemental weapons and Molotovs are effective, as are interrupts and staggers, but like other weak enemies, it's more efficient simply to use R1 attack chains or charged R2s. In the uncommon event that they attack you without provocation, simply quickstep forward through their attacks and finish them with an R1 combo from behind.

Basic Information	■	♠	Item Drops	◻	◐	◭	✦	★	⬗	♫	☠	▽	⚑	⚞
Nightmare of Mensis	917	425	Random Dirty gem based on area ×1 [1.5%]	214	214	86	143	85	75	45	120	180	—	—

Mergo's Attendant (Crossbow)

Make good use of the surrounding environment for cover and try to lure them out of each others' range before engaging them. If they refuse to cooperate, peek out from behind an obstacle just long enough to hit them with a thrown weapon or a gunshot; even if they don't pursue you, you'll eventually wear them down. You can evade their shots with sideways quicksteps, but if you have to approach them out in the open, it's best to just move diagonally so that the arrows naturally miss by the time they reach you. Once the coast is clear enough for you to fight any remaining crossbowmen out in the open, you're free to cut them down with melee attacks at your leisure because they have little ability to defend themselves up close.

Basic Information	■	♠	Item Drops	◻	◐	◭	✦	★	⬗	♫	☠	▽	⚑	⚞
Nightmare of Mensis	917	1560	Random Dirty gem based on area ×1 [8%]	214	214	86	143	85	75	45	120	180	—	—

Mergo's Attendant (Flail)

The stairway you encounter these enemies on doesn't give you much room to maneuver, so you may need to bait their swings from afar and close the distance with a jump attack during their recovery. If you have room to quick-step through their attacks and position yourself behind them, do so and follow up with an R1 chain; you may be able to hit both at once in this manner, but be prepared to quickstep away if one of them recovers quickly enough to hit you. In general, however, they can be treated in much the same way as the unarmed version, just with slightly more range on their attacks.

Basic Information	■	♠	Item Drops	◻	◐	◭	✦	★	⬗	♫	☠	▽	⚑	⚞
Nightmare of Mensis	1070	1560	Random Dirty gem based on area ×1 [8%]	214	214	86	143	85	75	45	120	180	—	—

Skeletal Puppet

Slow but unpredictable enemies that appear almost exclusively during the boss fight with Micolash. They don't move around too much, but their attacks are swift and can cause you to stumble or knock you down. Skeletal Puppets have very high defense, inflict large amounts of damage and can hit you several times in quick succession, making them formidable enemies in their own right; additionally, the ones that appear as minions of Micolash will not die until the fight ends, and will get back up if defeated before then. With resourceful use of Shaman Bone Blades, however, these foes can be turned against Micolash while he is trapped in one of the balcony rooms, serving as distractions and potentially inflicting tremendous amounts of damage upon him while he is unable to flee.

Ignore the ones in Micolash's boss area unless you plan to turn them against him with a Shaman Bone Blade, though avoid standing near them for any longer than necessary to minimize unnecessary damage to yourself. If you encounter them elsewhere, quickstep forward through their attacks and hit them from behind with an R1 combo or stagger them with a charged R2. It is possible to interrupt their melee attacks, but the precise timing required and their erratic movements make this a tricky proposition; moreover, Molotovs and Throwing Knives are only marginally effective against them.

Basic Information																
Nightmare of Mensis	764	0	Item Drops: None	88	88	88	88	68	68	82	120	210	—	—	

Labyrinth Watchers

Labyrinth Watchers are simple enemies that you'll only encounter inside Chalice Dungeons, and since they are one of the more common foes you'll encounter there, learning how to deal with them effectively is very important. Many of the different Watchers have ranged attacks to compliment their melee weapons, so even though they're weak, you'll still need to approach them cautiously if they're aware of your presence. Cleaver carrying Watchers are capable of throwing Molotov Cocktails a considerable distance, while those carrying daggers tend to favor poison knives or urns that inflict a tremendous amount of slow poison build-up. If you see one holding a lantern you can take comfort in the fact that they don't have a ranged attack, but they can use their lantern to alert nearby enemies and make them come running to its aid, so taking them out quickly and quietly is of upmost importance.

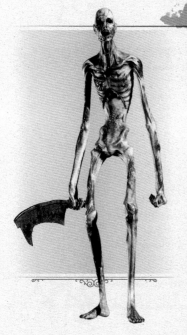

Outside of their weapons, the main difference you need to look out for is their attire. Watchers that have nothing on can be rolled into to knock them off balance giving you a small window to attack, those wearing clothes, however, will remain unaffected if you roll into them. Most types of Labyrinth Watcher can also be encountered through floor traps, that when stepped on summon a small group of them around you. Similarly, you'll often find that Bell Ringers summon these enemies, and during that time they are a lot more aggressive and will actively seek you out even if you are quite far away from the Bell Ringer; locate and kill the Bell Ringer to cause all of the Labyrinth Watchers under her control to die immediately.

Basic Information																
Chalice Dungeon Base Level	123	67	Item Drops: Blood Vial ×1 [8%]	68	68	68	68	46	58	60	120	180	—	—	

Summoned version gives 19 Blood Echoes and no drops. Preset Chalice Dungeons: Pthumerian Labyrinth, Central Pthumerian Labyrinth, Hintertomb, Lower Hintertomb, Lower Pthumerian Labyrinth, Cursed Pthumerian Defilement, Ailing Loran, Lower Loran, Isz Gravestone, Pthumeru Ihyll

3

Labyrinth Watcher (Cleaver)

Labyrinth Watchers wielding cleavers will continuously throw Molotov Cocktails at you from a distance, and will sometimes throw two in quick succession, requiring you to dodge twice. The second throw can be identified when they draw their arms back after executing the first, so keep an eye out for that animation and dodge accordingly. Once you get close to them they'll switch to melee attacks consisting largely of slow swings that have little range; simply quickstep through one of their attacks to get behind them and finish them off with an R1 chain before they recover. Weapons with long reach can also hit them from outside their melee range, but you'll still need to be close enough to them to get them to stop using Molotovs.

Basic Information			Item Drops											
Chalice Dungeon Base Level	**123**	**67**	Blood Vial ×1 [8%]	68	68	68	68	46	58	60	120	180	—	—

Some can throw knives and then drop Poison Knife [8%]. Strong version gives 114 Blood Echoes. Non-throwing Fire, Poison and Strong versions drop random gem [4%]. White clothes version has 77 Physical Defense.

Labyrinth Watcher (Dagger)

Dagger-wielding Labyrinth Watchers are quite common, so stocking up on antidotes before entering a dungeon will save you a lot of trouble and help conserve healing items. In battle, focus on taking these foes out first, since they will continually bombard you with poison projectiles while you're occupied with other enemies. If nearby enemies are preventing you from being able to safely eliminate a dagger-wielding Labyrinth Watcher, lure them back to an area you've already cleared and deal with them before engaging the Watcher. Once you get close to them you can treat them in much the same way as the Cleaver-carrying Watchers.

Basic Information			Item Drops											
Chalice Dungeon Base Level	**123**	**67**	Blood Vial ×1 [8%]	68	68	68	68	46	58	60	120	180	—	—

Some can throw knifes. Strong version gives 114 Blood Echoes. Poison and Strong versions drop random gem [4%]. Twin Dagger and Black clothes version have 194 HP. Twin Dagger gives 114 Blood Echoes. Black clothes fire version has 211 HP and drops Fire Paper [6%], White clothes fire version has 229 HP and drops Quicksilver Bullets ×2 [8%]. Dressed version have 80 Physical Defenses.

Labyrinth Watcher (Cleaver & Lantern)

Depending on your loadout, their ability to draw other enemies towards them can actually be a very useful thing. With a weapon that has wide-arcing horizontal attacks, or ones with large areas of effect such as the Flamesprayer, let this Watcher call to the others and then take them all out in one fell swoop once they converge on you. If the room you're in is large, fall back to a room you've already cleared and funnel the group through the connecting passage to prevent them all from attacking you at once. Dealing with them on their own is still a safer option, however, and if that's the route you want to take it's best to try and sneak up on them and kill them before they can ring their lantern. They lack the long range threat of the normal cleaver wielding Watchers so you can approach without fear, and once you get close, they'll use the same easy to deal with cleaver attacks.

Basic Information			Item Drops											
Chalice Dungeon Base Level	**194**	**67**	Blood Vial ×1 [8%], Quicksilver Bullets ×2 [8%]	77	77	77	77	46	58	60	120	180	—	—

Strong version gives 114 Blood Echoes. Poison and Strong versions drop random gem [4%].

Labyrinth Watcher (Halberd)

Despite wielding halberds, these Labyrinth Watchers' attacks don't reach especially far, though their horizontal swings make it more difficult to circle behind them. All of their melee swings are slow and easy to interrupt (offering plenty of opportunities for visceral attacks), but since they have such low health, it's generally better to conserve your bullets for other enemies and quick-step through their attacks and use a quick R1 combo to finish them off. Since they have extremely low super armor, transform attacks can be used to keep them flinched and eliminate their ability to fight back.

Basic Information	■	↟	Item Drops	▢	◐	△	✦	★	⟋	♫	☠	▽	⚔	⟋
Chalice Dungeon Base Level	194	67	Random gem based on area ×1 [4%], Blood Vial ×2 [14%]	80	80	80	80	46	58	60	120	180	—	—

Regular versions don't drop random gem. White clothes version has 229 HP. Strong version gives 114 Blood Echoes. Fire versions drop Fire Paper [4%].

Labyrinth Watcher (Twin Axes)

Labyrinth Watchers armed with dual axes have roughly the same reach as those carrying cleavers; their attacks have considerable forward momentum, but very weak tracking, making it possible to stand behind them with little risk to yourself. In battle they use very basic horizontal and vertical chops, as well as a dual overhead swing with long windup and recovery periods, and while their attacks aren't quite as slow as the halberd-wielders, they're still predictable enough to make interrupting them easy.

Basic Information	■	↟	Item Drops	▢	◐	△	✦	★	⟋	♫	☠	▽	⚔	⟋
Chalice Dungeon Base Level	194	67	Blood Vial ×2 [8%]	80	80	80	80	46	58	60	120	180	—	—

Strong version gives 114 Blood Echoes. White clothes version has 229 HP. Non-throwing Fire, Poison and Strong versions drop random gem [4%]. Fire versions drops Fire Paper [4%]. Fire, Poison and Strong versions drop random gem [4%]. Naked version has 68 Physical Defenses.

Labyrinth Watcher (Bare Hands)

These enemies will not attack you even when threatened and can be safely ignored or killed for their blood echoes. If you're using a Caryll Rune that gives you a bonus for visceral attacks, you can use these enemies as a way to stock up on bullets or Blood Vials by using a charged attack from behind to stagger them and then performing an easy visceral attack.

Basic Information	■	↟	Item Drops	▢	◐	△	✦	★	⟋	♫	☠	▽	⚔	⟋
Chalice Dungeon Base Level	105	67	Blood Vial ×1 [8%]	68	68	68	68	46	58	60	120	180	—	—

Pilgrim

These enemies are easily identified by their telltale ghostly glow and are typically found wandering the labyrinths alone. They are not initially hostile but will fight back when provoked, unleashing a short-range magical explosion before immediately reverting to their non-hostile state; their explosion attack has a long windup and leaves plenty of time for you to quickstep backward out of range. They have no super armor whatsoever and are highly vulnerable to R1 combo attacks, which will prevent them from ever using their magic blast.

Like the bare-fisted Labyrinth Watchers, this enemy can be ignored or easily killed and poses no real threat. You can deal enough damage with a combo to kill it before it even has the chance to retaliate. You can also use it to gain Quicksilver Bullets or Blood Echoes if you've equipped a Caryll Rune that rewards you for visceral attacks; just move to its back for a charged R2 to stagger it and then land the visceral attack.

Basic Information														
			Item Drops											
Chalice Dungeon Base Level	285	214	Blood Vial ×10 [40%], Quicksilver Bullets ×12 [60%]	77	77	77	77	120	120	120	999	180	—	—

Preset Chalice Dungeons: Pthumerian Labyrinth

Gravekeeper Scorpion

Gravekeeper Scorpions can be dangerous opponents due to their high defense, immunity to visceral attacks and ability to inflict rapid poison. These small arachnids have low health, but move quickly and are very aggressive; they will constantly run toward you in an attempt to keep you at close range, attacking with their claws and stingers as soon as you're within reach. Although they cannot strike directly behind them, they will immediately perform a defensive sidestep to face you if you attempt to take up this position. Their melee attacks have very short reach, however, and longer weapons such as the Rifle Spear and the transformed Hunter Axe can hit them from beyond their range. Purely physical damage sources are useless, due to their high defense, but they'll take heavy damage from elemental attacks, particularly lightning; they also lack super armor and by augmenting a fast weapon such as the Kirkhammer or Ludwig's Holy Blade with Bolt Paper, you can stun them to death with a single R1 combo. Gravekeeper Scorpions will explode in a burst of poison mist when killed; the mist will build up your rapid poison meter if it touches you, so be sure to carry a few Antidotes for emergencies.

Stand about three meters away from them while strafing to either side; this will cause all of their attacks to miss, allowing you to counterattack during their recovery. If you plan on using physical attacks, power up your weapon with Bolt Paper first or switch to a weapon that inflicts elemental damage, such as Tonitrus or the Burial Blade. If you have Rosmarinus or the Flamesprayer, blast them with it while backing away as they chase you; alternately, you can lock off and aim a Molotov at the ground in front of you to strike them as they approach.

Basic Information														
			Item Drops											
Chalice Dungeon Base Level	79	59	Random Dirty gem based on area ×1 [4%]	1848	792	1848	1320	40	80	70	999	180	—	—

Preset Chalice Dungeons: Central Pthumerian Labyrinth, Lower Pthumerian Labyrinth, Isz Gravestone, Pthumeru Ihyll

Gel

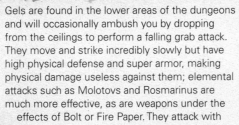

Gels are found in the lower areas of the dungeons and will occasionally ambush you by dropping from the ceilings to perform a falling grab attack. They move and strike incredibly slowly but have high physical defense and super armor, making physical damage useless against them; elemental attacks such as Molotovs and Rosmarinus are much more effective, as are weapons under the effects of Bolt or Fire Paper. They attack with simple body swings telegraphed long in advance, though they'll sometimes vary the timing to trick you into dropping your guard and attacking too soon. Gels are weak against lightning and can be struck down quickly by an electrified Tonitrus or physical weapons augmented with a Blood Gem or Bolt Paper.

Destroy Gels from outside their attack range with Rosmarinus or Flamesprayer blasts, or power up your weapons with Bolt Paper and cut them down with R1 combos. If you have no Bolt Paper, hit them with the Hunter's Torch or Tonitrus; avoid standing near them for too long, though, or you risk being flattened by their slam attacks. Gels will rear up slowly before all of their attacks, signaling that they're about to strike – at this point, quickstep backward to avoid being hit. They are immune to visceral attacks, so don't bother trying to interrupt or stagger them; save your Quicksilver Bullets for the Flamesprayer or Rosmarinus.

Basic Information			Item Drops										
Chalice Dungeon Base Level	105	124	Oil Urn ×2 [5%], Shining Coins ×3 [10%], Pebble ×3 [10%]	1848	1848	1320	1320	50	70	50	999	999	—	—

Preset Chalice Dungeons: Pthumerian Labyrinth, Central Pthumerian Labyrinth, Hintertomb, Lower Pthumerian Labyrinth, Ailing Loran, Lower Loran, Isz Gravestone

Labyrinth Ritekeeper

Ritekeepers use only magic and are incapable of melee attacks of any kind; their spells cannot be interrupted, but you can stagger them with charged R2 swings. They have low health and no super armor at all, so they can be easily stunned with R1 combos before they have a chance to respond. They'll launch slow-moving fireballs at you from a distance and use a spherical area attack at close range. Their fireballs have extremely long range and can travel backward, to strike behind the Ritekeeper, but have very poor tracking and can be avoided by quickstepping sideways. The area attack is centered on the skull in their left hand and has a radius of three meters; you can escape it by quickstepping backward.

Quickstep past them and strike from behind with R1 combos, or stagger them and follow through with visceral attacks. Ritekeepers are initially hunched over when you first encounter them, but will stand up when you get too close; they move and turn slowly in their squatting stance, but are somewhat faster when standing upright. Striking their exposed legs will cause them to sit back down again and can help prevent them from evading your attacks, but be careful of their area attack as you move in to strike. Dodge their fireballs by quickstepping forward past them and their area attack by quickstepping backwards; when you move in to attack, avoid approaching head-on and instead try to dash in from the side.

Basic Information			Item Drops										
Chalice Dungeon Base Level	158	78	Random gun type gem ×1 [2%], Ritual material A ×1 [4%]	77	77	77	77	74	64	78	120	180	—	—

Strong version has 211 HP/87 Blood Echoes and drops random gun type gem at 20%.
Preset Chalice Dungeons: Central Pthumerian Labyrinth, Cursed Pthumerian Defilement, Pthumeru Ihyll

Watcher's Gravediggers

Gravediggers carrying pickaxes are generally found alone, either using their tools for their intended purposes or standing guard. Those that are busy working will keep doing so unless you get very close to them; if there are other enemies in the area, lure them away and finish them off first before getting close. Their overhead attacks may be slow, but they have strong tracking and will hit you if you try to strafe around them; quickstep forward through the swings and position yourself behind them for a quick combo before they can turn around.

Hook-wielding Gravediggers attack slightly faster than the pickax variant, but their swings have less range. They'll often perform melee combos of up to four slashes, as well as a unique three-hit chain ending with a grab – the latter consists of a diagonal overhead swing, a horizontal slash and a forward snare, so if you see that series of attacks, be ready to evade the grab. Hook-wielding Gravediggers don't actually attack with their lanterns and are incapable of striking behind them. You'll also run into Gravediggers that like to use firearms at a distance, so any time you approach one you should always check to see if it's carrying a gun first so that you can adjust your approach accordingly.

Watcher's Gravedigger (Pickaxe)

Due to the slow and heavily telegraphed nature of their attacks you'll have plenty of opportunities to interrupt and stagger the pickaxe variant, and that's by far the easiest way to take them out in normal combat. Since you'll often find them working away at walls, you'll also be able to sneak up them and hit them from behind with a charged R2 for an easy victory. Once you're behind them they have no way to attack you directly, but their overhead swings do have a slight backwards arc that can clip you if you're too close, so be ready to evade backwards just in case. Because they have no super armor, however, once you begin your offense they should not be able to retaliate unless you run out of stamina.

Basic Information			Item Drops										
Chalice Dungeon Base Level	246	96	Blood Vial ×2 [29%], Ritual material E ×2 [0.7%], Ritual material E ×1 [8%]	80	112	80	80	50	65	70	120	180	—

Preset Chalice Dungeons: Hintertomb, Lower Hintertomb, Cursed Pthumerian Defilement, Isz Gravestone

Watcher's Gravedigger (Hook & Lantern)

As with the pickaxe variant, if you move around to its back it will spend all its efforts attempting to face you, and since these sickle-users don't have the large overhead strikes, once you are behind them you're generally pretty safe. While their hooks do have decent attack range, weapons such as the Rifle Spear and Ludwig's Holy Blade can easily hit them from outside their range, and if you don't kill them with your first hit, you can easily retreat back and do it again before they close in. If you decide to try and quickstep through their attacks, be mindful of the grab they'll often attempt at the end of their short combos because it redirects itself quite well and you'll need to keep strafing to stay at their back. Their lanterns are purely decorative, so when fighting them you can ignore them and focus all of your attention on the hook.

Basic Information			Item Drops										
Chalice Dungeon Base Level	246	96	Blood Vial ×3 [10%], Blood Vial ×2 [30%]	80	112	80	80	50	65	70	120	180	—

Preset Chalice Dungeons: Hintertomb, Lower Hintertomb, Cursed Pthumerian Defilement, Pthumeru Ihyll

Watcher's Gravedigger (Rifle, Hook & Lantern)

These Gravediggers have excellent vision and can spot you approaching from far away, but they are also naturally inquisitive and you can use both of these things to your advantage. If they spot you, hide behind cover and they'll start moving towards you to investigate, and if you keep repeating this process you can pull them away from other enemies from a much greater distance than your normal ranged attacks would otherwise allow. They also have relatively short memories, so if you stay behind cover for a while they will forget about you and start returning to their original position, at which time you can run up and attack them from behind before they can turn around. Once you do get close they'll switch out their gun for a hook and should be treated the same way as the normal hook variants.

Basic Information			Item Drops										
Chalice Dungeon Base Level	229	85	Quicksilver Bullets ×3 [100%]	77	108	77	77	50	65	70	120	180	—

Preset Chalice Dungeons: Hintertomb, Lower Hintertomb, Cursed Pthumerian Defilement, Pthumeru Ihyll

Old Hunters  OH

These fallen hunters are one of the standard enemy types in the early areas of the Hunter's Nightmare. They use a variety of weapons including the Beast Cutter, Boom Hammer, Beasthunter Saif and Piercing Rifle, with each type utilizing a different fighting style from the others. These lost souls are perpetually engaged in an endless hunt and, together with their hounds and the basic Huntsmen, represent one of two opposing team types in the nightmare; the other team consists of the Beast Patients and Nightmare Executioners, and you will periodically encounter both sides already engaged in battle with each other when you enter areas in which they are present in close proximity. You can use this to your advantage and attack one side while they are distracted with the other, or in certain cases lead a group of Old Hunters toward a Nightmare Executioner and let them attack one another (such as at the entrance to the Nightmare Grand Cathedral)... after all, the enemy⁰ of an enemy is a friend.

Old Hunter (Beast Cutter & Hunter Blunderbuss) OH

Old Hunters wielding Beast Cutters are the first of this enemy type to be encountered in the Hunter's Nightmare. These powerful opponents will alternate between the weapon's normal and transformed modes, using quick slashes at close range and slower whip attacks at a distance, though they will primarily stick to the transformed state. Their whip swings have wide arcs and considerable delays that can be difficult to anticipate, and they will intersperse their melee attacks with shotgun blasts which can cause flinching if they connect. They will also frequently quickstep backward to dodge attacks and establish enough distance to use their whips effectively. While their high health and attack power make them especially dangerous to players accessing the Hunter's Nightmare early in the game, they represent a real threat even to full-fledged hunters and should always be approached with caution. Be especially careful of the one with red eyes as this version is considerably stronger.

Strategy

The simplest way to deal with these opponents is to stand just outside their melee range, wait for them to initiate one of their slow whip attacks, interrupt it and quickstep forward to perform a visceral attack. It is important to take the delay of their whip swings into consideration when using this strategy, as well as to be prepared for a blunderbuss shot; the incoming blast can be identified by the sound of the gun cocking just before firing and should be dodged by quickstepping forward through it. Charged attacks from heavy weapons such as the transformed Kirkhammer will flatten these hunters, but they will usually back away before the attack finishes charging and are difficult to stagger from behind as a result. The safest opportunities to strike them with melee attacks occur while standing behind them after quickstepping forward through their whip swings; their recovery period leaves enough time for two to three hits before they attack again, depending upon the weapon used. In certain locations they can be ambushed with near-impunity while their attention is focused on the resident Beast Patients.

Basic Information	■	⚔	Item Drops	🏠	⬤	▲	✿	★	🌀	🎵	☠	▽	🐾	〜
Hunter's Nightmare	1727	842	Random gem based on area ×1 [16%], Blood Vial ×3 [20%]	148	148	148	148	96	96	96	200	180	—	—
Hunter's Nightmare | Red Eyes	3331	1126	Vermin ×1 [100%]	148	148	148	148	96	96	96	200	180		

3

Old Hunter (Beasthunter Saif) OH

The fastest and most agile of the Old Hunters. These foes alternate between both forms of the Beasthunter Saif, using wide swings in sword mode and rapid combo attacks in cleaver mode, though they tend to favor the cleaver. Although they do not carry firearms, their cleaver attacks have considerable forward momentum and allow them to strike quickly from outside their obvious melee range. They are quite a bit more aggressive than the variant armed with Piercing Rifles, and will frequently use evasive quicksteps and offensive lunges. They can foil attempts to quickstep past them with a backstepping horizontal transformation attack and will occasionally use a slow, heavy overhead slash to bait players into attacking preemptively. A saif-wielding Old Hunter with red eyes can be encountered on a ledge just before the Bloody Plaza this enemy has more health and higher attack power than the standard version, but otherwise behaves the same way.

Strategy

Attempting to bait interrupts from outside their melee range is somewhat riskier than with other Old Hunters due to the speed and long reach of this variant's lunging cleaver attacks, but is still an effective strategy in open areas with plenty of room to maneuver. The best opportunities to strike them with melee attacks are after quickstepping forward past them, though beware that their recovery speed is slightly faster than the Old Hunters armed with heavier weapons and it may be necessary to quickstep away early to avoid a counterattack. Charged attacks from heavier weapons such as the transformed Kirkhammer will instantly flatten these enemies but they will often quickstep away before the attack has time to activate, making it difficult to stagger them from behind. These Old Hunters can be picked off from relative safety while they are distracted by the Beast Patients found in certain areas of the nightmare.

Basic Information			Item Drops										
Hunter's Nightmare	1520	771	Random gem based on area ×1 [16%], Blood Vial ×3 [20%]	148	148	148	148	96	96	96	200	180	—	—
Hunter's Nightmare | Red Eyes	3109	994	Vermin ×1 [100%]	148	148	148	148	96	96	96	200	180		

Old Hunter (Beasthunter Saif & Piercing Rifle) OH

A much less aggressive variant of the Old Hunters armed with the Beasthunter Saif. This version acts as a sniper and will not move from its initial position until forced to defend itself, at which point it will switch to slow and infrequent individual attacks with the saif's sword mode. These enemies will occasionally perform a short combo consisting of a couple of sword slashes ending with a gunshot, but are otherwise quite passive. They have relatively low health and will rarely attempt to evade attacks or reposition themselves, making them easy targets at close range.

Strategy

Close the distance to these enemies using the environment for cover or quicksteps to avoid their rifle shots, then simply mow them down with R1 combos. Attempting to interrupt their attacks or stagger them is generally a waste of time and bullets; standard melee combos and charged R2 swings are much more efficient thanks to their low health and lack of any truly dangerous close-range attacks. They will also fall relatively quickly to attacks by the Beast Patients found in certain areas of the nightmare, and can alternatively be ambushed while their attention is diverted toward the opposing team.

Basic Information			Item Drops										
Hunter's Nightmare	829	811	None	148	148	148	148	96	96	96	200	180	—	—

Old Hunter (Boom Hammer & Torch) `OH`

The toughest of the Old Hunters. These formidable opponents have enormous amounts of health and attack with slow, powerful swings and quicker torch jabs. Many of their attacks inflict an extremely heavy knockdown effect that sends players flying, and they will frequently power up their next single strike even further by igniting their Boom Hammers' furnaces. Their overhead attacks have long delays and fairly strong tracking, and they will occasionally perform jumping overhead slams which carry them forward a short distance. While most of their combo attacks are slow and consist of no more than three hits, they can also alternate hammer strikes with faster torch jabs. Their delayed horizontal and vertical swings are relatively easy to interrupt, however, and their jump attacks and overhead slams have long recovery periods that leave them open to counterattack. They aren't especially good at dodging and are considerably more vulnerable to charged `R2` strikes than most of the other Old Hunters, but will still occasionally attempt to avoid attacks by repositioning themselves. A subtype of this enemy with red eyes can be found on the rooftops near the plaza; it has higher attack power but is otherwise identical to the others.

Strategy

Stay just outside the reach of their jump attacks and bait them into using one of their slow swings, then interrupt them. Alternately, quickstep forward past them through one of their swings and perform an `R1` combo or knock them down with a charged attack from a heavy weapon like the Kirkhammer while they recover. A single hit from the Fists of Gratia will cause them to stumble and knock them out of their attacks, and a single hit from the Beast Roar will send them flying as long as it connects mid-swing (otherwise, two hits are required during their idle stance in order to knock them down). As they are part of the opposing team type to the Beast Patients and Nightmare Executioners, it is possible to take advantage of their distraction with other targets and ambush them while their backs are turned.

Basic Information															
	■	⚴	Item Drops												
Hunter's Nightmare	**1865**	**913**	Random gem based on area ×1 [16%], Blood Vial ×4 [20%]	148	148	148	148	96	96	96	200	180	–	–
Hunter's Nightmare | Red Eyes	**3559**	**1237**	Vermin ×1 [100%]	148	148	148	148	96	96	96	200	180		

Clocktower Patients `OH`

These unfortunate victims of the Healing Church's shady experiments comprise the largest and most diverse enemy group in the expansion areas. Each variant uses a different set of attacks from the others and many of them incorporate gimmicks unique to their own subtype; most are susceptible to interrupts and staggers, but the Crawling version is immune. Additionally, although very few opportunities for exploiting this mechanic exist, the Clocktower Patients are handled as an opposing team type to the Wheelchair Huntsmen found in certain locations throughout the Research Hall; notably, a Wheelchair Huntsman armed with a Gatling gun is positioned on an inaccessible ledge overlooking a staircase and will mow down a group of patients attempting to climb the stairs as you approach. Fortunately, with the exception of the patients armed with transfusion stands detailed in the Strong Enemies section of this chapter, members of this enemy group generally have low health and will fall to a few `R1` attacks; the main danger they pose is their tendency to attack in large groups with swift combos, so keep an ear out for their telltale screams and proceed with caution if you suspect an ambush.

Clocktower Patient (Fists) OH

The most common enemy type in the Research Hall. These patients attack with swift headbutts and flailing arm combos which can inflict large amounts of damage if multiple hits connect. They fall relatively quickly to melee attacks but can be extremely dangerous in groups, and are indeed frequently encountered tightly clustered in dark rooms or narrow pathways which offer little space to maneuver. Many of their basic attacks carry them forward a short distance and can thwart attempts to dodge backward. They detect by sound and will be immediately alerted if they hear the noises of objects shifting in the environment from player movements or attacks, such as glass shattering or lab equipment being knocked over.

Strategy

When fighting only one, quickstep forward past them as they attack and cut them down with a quick R1 combo from behind. If faced with a group, lure them one at a time with gunshots or thrown weapons from a safe distance and deal with them individually. Interrupting their attacks is possible but impractical due to the large numbers in which they are usually encountered and their relatively low health. Frontal charged attacks from weapons with long reach such as the Rifle Spear are especially effective for eliminating them at a safe distance, and the super armor granted during charged attacks in general can be helpful for dealing with groups in an emergency. One hit from the Beast Roar will send them flying and can be used in some locations to knock them off of open stairways or balconies to their deaths.

Basic Information				Item Drops										
Research Hall	688	1089		Blood Vial ×1 [8%]	99	99	99	99	108	89	89	120	180	—	—

Clocktower Patient (Acid Bottles) OH

These Clocktower Patients primarily attack from a distance with bottles of corrosive acid in much the same way as Huntsmen that throw Molotov Cocktails. They move very little even when forced into melee combat, but are considerably less passive than their bare handed counterparts and will immediately begin using arm swipes when approached. These attacks are slow and easily avoided, however, making this enemy type much less dangerous at close range. While some have a bit more health than others, they are weak enemies overall and are easy prey to a few R1 swings or ranged attacks.

Strategy

Quickstep forward past their projectiles and strike them with an R1 combo. Their recovery from the throwing animation leaves enough time that a strong weapon can finish them before they have an opportunity to counterattack, diminishing the need to quickstep past them and attack from behind. As with most of the other Clocktower Patients, interrupting their attacks is largely a waste of bullets as a few hits with a melee weapon will finish the job just as quickly. They can be eliminated at range using Molotov Cocktails, Throwing Knives or gunshots, especially those from firearms augmented with Bone Marrow Ash.

Basic Information				Item Drops										
Research Hall	458	1198		Blood Vial ×1 [8%]	99	99	99	99	108	89	89	120	180	—	—

Clocktower Patient (Infected Hand) **OH**

One of the least common Clocktower Patient types, almost exclusively found hiding around corners in darkened rooms lying in wait to spring an ambush. Such situations typically involve the patient performing a grab attack from the side which will inflict slow poison if it connects; afterward they will perform slow whip-like swings with the sagging flesh of their infected arms and will continue attempting to use the grab. The danger they pose is almost solely dependent upon the element of surprise, without which they are extremely weak enemies with low health and will die in one or two hits from most weapons.

Strategy

Knowing where they are ahead of time is the key to avoiding their ambushes. For their exact locations, please refer to the Hunting Grounds chapter. While their grab is quite easy to interrupt, doing so is a waste of bullets; simply quickstep forward past the grab or their whip attacks and strike them a couple of times during their recovery. A couple of Throwing Knives or a few shots from most firearms at higher upgrade levels will do them in from a distance, but are once again a less efficient alternative to melee attacks.

Basic Information			Item Drops										
Research Hall	382	1307	Random Murky Blood Gem ×1 [8%], Quicksilver Bullets ×8 [92%]	99	99	99	99	108	89	89	120	180	—	—

Clocktower Patient (Crawling) **OH**

These slow-moving Clocktower Patients are generally very weak and vulnerable, though they can be troublesome in groups and are capable of attacking from a short distance with their tentacles. They will crawl aimlessly about until they detect a player, at which point they will inchworm closer and attack with short-range headbutts. Their melee attacks do have some forward momentum, however, and can inflict considerable damage despite being relatively easy to avoid.

Strategy

Their tentacle attacks are preceded by a very obvious scream during which they will rear up off the ground, providing ample time to quickstep backward and out of range. Firearms or thrown weapons can be used to pick them off at a distance if desired, but are inefficient owing to the enemy's slow movement and general vulnerability. Jump attacks with larger weapons such as the Kirkhammer, Whirligig Saw or Ludwig's Holy Blade can be used to strike them from outside their reach before they have an opportunity to initiate an attack, and quickstepping forward past them or to their sides provides plenty of time to cut them down before they can respond. Avoid standing behind them at pointblank range for too long, however – they can perform a relatively quick sideways headbutt which will reach this blind spot.

Basic Information			Item Drops										
Research Hall	688	1198	Quicksilver Bullets ×2 [4%], Quicksilver Bullets ×1 [4%]	99	99	99	99	116	89	89	120	180	—	—

Clocktower Patient (Leaping) **OH**

One of the least common variants of the Clocktower Patient, found only in a couple of locations throughout the Research Hall. These enemies crawl rapidly on all fours in an almost spiderlike motion and strike with far greater speed than most of the other types, using rapid leaping attacks, flailing lunges, headbutts and short-range arm swipes. They have considerably more health than the other patients and can inflict heavy damage, but can be knocked over by gunshots in the same way as the dog-type enemies found in other areas. They are also susceptible to visceral attacks, though the timing required to interrupt them is extremely precise and their movements so unpredictable that attempting to do so is a difficult proposition.

Shoot them to knock them down, then close in and strike with R1 combos as they recover. If the first combo doesn't finish them, shoot them again before they can attack and perform another. Interrupts against this enemy type are more likely to occur by accident than by design, but by all means capitalize on such opportunities should one arise. All of these enemies' attacks can be avoided simply by quickstepping forward past them, at which point a timely gunshot during their recovery will render them helpless long enough to close in and finish them off.

Basic Information														
Research Hall	**1299**	**1525**	Item Drops Random gem based on area ×1 [12%], Blood Vial ×2 [88%]	142	142	142	142	108	89	89	200	270	—	—

Clocktower Patient (Headless) OH

Clocktower Patients with their heads missing entirely. They have no means of detecting players other than by direct contact and will roam aimlessly about until struck, at which point they will take a swing in the general direction of the attack and immediately return to wandering around. These enemies are effectively harmless and can be completely ignored without fear of reprisal, though they might be better served by a merciful coup de grâce.

Strategy

As these enemies will completely ignore player characters unless attacked first, they can be slaughtered with impunity using any desired means. Their feeble counterattacks can be interrupted and they can be staggered from behind with charged attacks, but a simple R1 combo is more than enough to put them out of their misery.

Basic Information														
Research Hall	**688**	**653**	Item Drops Blood Vial ×1 [8%]	99	99	99	99	108	89	89	120	180	—	—

Clocktower Patient (Head) OH

These large, shapeless blobs are actually a type of Clocktower Patient in the final stages of deformity and are found only in the Research Hall patient room containing the Bloated Head. One will drop from the ceiling just inside the door and perform a grab attack; the others will not turn hostile until after the Bloated Head has been picked up and will thereafter attack with omnidirectional tentacle swings and by spraying streams of blood. Their attacks cause Frenzy buildup, which can be extremely dangerous if several hits connect in rapid succession; however, they are almost immobile and suffer from long recovery periods between attacks.

Strategy

Thrown weapons such as Molotov Cocktails are effective for eliminating them from a safe distance, as are jump attacks timed to land during the recovery period after these enemies withdraw their tentacles. Thrust attacks from long weapons such as the Rifle Spear and the Holy Moonlight Sword are effective as well, and normal R1 combos can be used as long as they are timed during the enemy's recovery. Beware, however, that several of these opponents appear in very close proximity to one another and the timing of their attacks may overlap, making it dangerous to strike them up close until their numbers have been thinned out. Tools such as the Tiny Tonitrus and the Executioner's Gloves are also effective for eliminating these patients from a safe distance, though we advise resisting the temptation to use A Call Beyond while standing in their midst.

Basic Information														
Research Hall	**688**	**1307**	Item Drops Madman's Knowledge ×1 [2%], Frenzied Coldblood (8) ×1 [2%], Blue Elixir ×1 [2%]	320	406	85	213	125	92	85	120	180	—	—

Fishmen OH

Fishmen are the most common enemy type encountered in the Fishing Hamlet. While they use a variety of different makeshift weapons, most behave in more or less the same way – their movements and attacks are slow, but they are protected by super armor during their evasive steps and sometimes make deliberate efforts to attack in groups. Each subtype is equipped to support the others in battle and in certain cases they will work together to spring elaborate ambushes; these typically consist of a firebomb-throwing Fishman who will detonate a cluster of explosive-packed fishing buoys as you approach, followed immediately thereafter with a charge by a group of Fishmen, Fish Dogs and Giant Fishmen with melee weapons. While they can be quite dangerous in groups, these enemies are individually quite weak and pose relatively little threat as long as you take care to pick them off one by one. When entering a new area, survey the space ahead of you carefully to determine potential hiding places and traps; if you spot even a single Fishman closing in on you, retreat to a section you've already cleared and lure the target toward you by itself rather than advancing into the open where you'll likely be set upon by several more.

Fishman (Melee Harpoon) OH

One of several basic enemy types encountered in the Fishing Hamlet. This variant wields a harpoon and will initially close in with a running thrust attack, then switch to slow jabs and slashes. They will also frequently perform a long windup followed by a short-range attack in which they drive their harpoons into the ground in front of them, leaving themselves vulnerable. Although protected by super armor during their evasive steps, these enemies are vulnerable to stunlocks from faster weapons such as the Kirkhammer's longsword or the Tonitrus during their idle stance and attack animations. They move and strike very slowly, providing many opportunities for interrupts.

Strategy

Quickstep forward past them when they strike and hit them with an R1 combo while they recover. Alternately, stay just outside their reach and wait for them to take a swing, then interrupt them and follow up with a visceral attack. Their downward stab provides a particularly good opportunity for interrupts and is so slow that it even leaves enough time to quickstep behind them and stagger them with a charged attack. R1 combos are most effective due to this foe's susceptibility to stunlocks, and arcane weapons such as the Holy Moonlight Sword will deal particularly heavy damage to them.

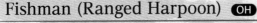

Basic Information														
	■	⚓	Item Drops		⬒	◑	⬟	✦	★	◈	♫	☠	▽	⟡	⤸
Fishing Hamlet	714	496	Blood Vial ×2 [32%]		120	120	120	120	105	115	240	200	180	—	—

Fishman (Ranged Harpoon) OH

This variant of the harpoon-wielding fishmen can be distinguished by the quiver of harpoons on its back. It will throw these in a straight line at long range and switch to excruciatingly slow melee attacks up close, usually only one swing at a time. The windup on its throw is very obvious even from a distance and leaves plenty of time to evade or take cover behind an object. These enemies share the same weaknesses as the melee-oriented harpooners: susceptibility to stunlocks, poor tracking, low arcane defense and an unusually passive temperament.

Approach them using quicksteps to evade their ranged attacks and mow them down with combos before they have an opportunity to respond. Interrupting their melee attacks is pointless as a simple R1 chain will do the job just as efficiently; a single charged attack from a heavier weapon like the transformed Hunter Axe or Kirkhammer will usually finish them as well. Attempting to trade ranged attacks with them is not recommended due to both the unnecessary expenditure of resources on a relatively weak enemy and the risk of being hit by a harpoon.

Basic Information														
Fishing Hamlet	635	516	Item Drops Oil Urn ×2 [28%]	120	120	120	120	105	115	240	200	180	—	—

Fishman (Twin Rakes) OH

A speed-oriented variant of the basic enemies in the Fishing Hamlet. These Fishmen move much more quickly and attack more aggressively than the harpooners, making far better use of their dodges and pressing their advantage with rapid combos of up to five consecutive hits. They also use a few individual lunge attacks and slashes which carry them forward some distance, enabling them to punish attempts to quickstep away from them. They will keep their distance while strafing sideways and suddenly dart in to perform a quick strike, but these feints have no directional tracking after the attacks begin and are easily foiled by a timely forward quickstep.

Strategy

Their five-hit combo offers a series of prime opportunities to interrupt them, though this should not be attempted at extremely close range as the attacks carry them forward a short distance. Quickstepping forward past them will cause nearly all of their attacks to miss and position them for a counterattack from behind during their recovery; ordinary R1 chains are best-suited to this purpose due to the enemy's relatively low health and susceptibility to stunlocks, though a single charged attack from a strong weapon at this point will usually finish them as well. Take advantage of their weakness to arcane damage if possible; otherwise simply cut them down with melee combos as they recover from their attacks.

Basic Information														
Fishing Hamlet	714	496	Item Drops Blood Vial ×2 [32%]	120	120	120	120	105	115	240	200	180	—	—

Fishman (Rake & Awl) OH

Although these enemies are capable of relatively swift combo attacks at close range, their primary weapons are small bombs similar in effect to Molotov Cocktails which they will lob in arcing trajectories from a distance. This variant appears in only a few places throughout the hamlet, generally perched in spots which afford them greater throwing range and are not immediately accessible with melee attacks. In such situations they will typically target not the player but a cluster of explosive urns in the player's vicinity, dealing far more damage with the ensuing blast than their individual bombs inflict. They aren't terribly dangerous up close, though their three-hit combo strikes deceptively quickly compared to their otherwise lethargic movements. As with other members of their species, they are susceptible to arcane damage and stunlock from melee combos.

Strategy

Quickstep forward through their projectiles and close the distance, then eliminate them with R1 combos. Don't bother interrupting their attacks unless a particularly convenient opportunity presents itself; they fall quickly enough to ordinary R1 chains and can usually be ambushed from behind before being alerted. Pay particular attention to the environment and be wary of the presence of explosive urns, which usually indicate a fiery ambush by one of these devious Fishmen. The urns can either be detonated preemptively by striking them with Molotov Cocktails from a safe distance or simply left alone until the bombardier has been dealt with; however, attempts to destroy them with melee attacks will usually result in the Fishmen detonating them first and are therefore strongly discouraged.

Basic Information														
Fishing Hamlet	635	516	Item Drops Oil Urn ×2 [28%]	120	120	120	120	105	115	240	200	180	—	—

Fishman (Cleaver) OH

This uncommon variant of the Fishing Hamlet's basic enemy type uses heavy cleaver attacks and a fairly swift running grab. They can perform combos of up to four hits but will usually use slower individual swings or their grab outside of extremely close range. Though predictable and easy to interrupt, their attacks hit hard and have a significant knockback effect. Like other enemies of this family, they are weak against arcane damage and stunlocks in addition to suffering from low mobility.

Strategy

Interrupts are more worthwhile against these enemies than most of the other Fishmen due to their higher HP, so stay just outside their melee range and bait one of their individual swings or combos. Do not attempt to interrupt their grab; although possible, doing so is extremely risky as their erratic movements during this attack will frequently cause bullets to miss and can result in the grab connecting even if the shot is correctly timed. Quickstepping past them through one of their melee attacks and stunlocking them with an R1 chain is still a viable strategy as well, though they tend to be encountered in enclosed spaces where room to maneuver is limited.

Basic Information														
Fishing Hamlet	1032	546	Random gem based on area ×1 [8%], Blood Vial ×1 [8%]	120	120	120	120	105	115	240	200	180	—	—

Fishman Mage (Curse) OH

By far the weakest enemy in the Fishing Hamlet but also one of the most dangerous, these fishmen sit cross-legged on the ground and continuously launch large volleys of homing skulls which inflict arcane damage and have extremely strong tracking. A single attack of any kind will kill them and in fact they should be top-priority targets owing to the tremendous threat they pose at range, but they are usually surrounded by other enemies which must be dealt with before they can be reached with melee attacks.

Strategy

Before taking any offensive action against these foes, survey their vicinity for other enemies and determine the locations of any other potential threats. Find an object or terrain feature that can be used as cover and be prepared to retreat behind it to avoid an incoming cloud of skulls. Use the Monocular to aim a thrown weapon such as a Molotov Cocktail or Throwing Knife at the Fishman from behind cover before its next attack; it will generally be necessary to point the crosshairs well above the target itself in order to compensate for the projectile's arc, but in this way it is possible to eliminate these dangerous foes with relatively little risk. If most or all of the surrounding enemies have been eliminated, dash straight toward the target between volleys and strike with a single R1 attack or a gunshot as soon as it is within range. There is a small zone in this enemy's immediate vicinity where the skulls cannot reach, affording a narrow margin of safety from which to eliminate it.

Basic Information														
Fishing Hamlet	7	0	None	97	97	97	97	142	124	435	200	180	—	—

Fishman Mage (Staff) OH

Immediately recognizable by their long staves, these Fishmen use only two attacks: a targeted lightning bolt that strikes the player's current location from a distance and a larger AoE thunder burst centered at their feet, which they will cast at close range. They move quite slowly and are all but defenseless in melee combat, but should nonetheless be treated as priority targets due to their ability to deal heavy damage from far away. Although it is possible to stagger them from behind, a single charged attack from most weapons will usually just kill them outright.

Strategy

A roll or quickstep in any direction will avoid their targeted thunderbolts, while a backward quickstep is generally enough to escape their AoE. Close the distance and cut them down as quickly as possible if there is a direct path to their location; if not, use the Monocular to manually target them with thrown weapons such as Molotov Cocktails. They are susceptible to poison, making Poison Knives equally effective for this purpose; either way, make every effort to eliminate these dangerous enemies from afar if they are not immediately accessible on foot. As their close-range area-of-effect attack is slow and easy to avoid, they can be dispatched with relative impunity using melee weapons.

Basic Information	■	⚔	Item Drops	⬚	◐	◭	✲	★	✿	♫	☠	▽	⤢	⤡
Fishing Hamlet	635	1488	Random Bolt Gem ×1 [20%], Quicksilver Bullets ×5 [80%]	97	97	97	97	142	124	435	200	180	—	—

Fish Dog OH

All but unrecognizable as anything canine at first glance, these bizarre creatures betray their true nature as soon as they begin their attack. They behave in exactly the same way as the more familiar dog-type enemies in other areas, with the exception of one attack unique to the Fishing Hamlet variant: an AoE scream which inflicts no damage but causes stumbling. Gunshots will still knock them down and leave them completely helpless, at which point one or two normal attacks will usually finish them.

Strategy

Handle them in the same way as any other dog-type foes: knock them down with a gunshot and follow up with either a jump attack, a few more gunshots or a forward quickstep and a couple of R1 swings. Their scream attack presents little if any danger unless other enemies are present, but even then its effect is so short-lived that it will rarely prove decisive. Still, these enemies should be lured away from groups and eliminated individually as their speed and evasive abilities make them somewhat more dangerous than their masters.

Basic Information	■	⚔	Item Drops	⬚	◐	◭	✲	★	✿	♫	☠	▽	⤢	⤡
Fishing Hamlet	635	516	None	90	90	90	90	93	60	172	120	180	—	—

Snail Women OH

These odd enemies are found only in and around the subterranean aquaculture farms beyond the lighthouse in the Fishing Hamlet; the subtype living in large spiral shells are immobile and can be picked off with almost complete impunity, but those without shells are considerably more mobile and can become troublesome in groups. Both variants have very low HP and defense, but you'll usually have to deal with them in large numbers due to the tight quarters in which you'll encounter them. In certain spots they can be found hanging from rafters and will drop down to attack as you pass by, so keep your eyes not only on the path ahead of you, but the space above you as well.

Snail Woman (Bare) OH

Though their unnatural movements and hideous screams may seem intimidating at first, these slug-like creatures are actually only capable of performing a single mid-range jump attack and have no means of striking close proximities at all. They will constantly attempt to position themselves at the distance required for this attack to connect, but can only back away helplessly if prevented from doing so. They move relatively quickly and can become problematic in numbers or if given enough room to use their jump attack, but fall very quickly to a paltry few R1 swings and are easy pickings when encountered alone.

Strategy

Use quicksteps to close in and attack them at pointblank range with R1 combos – they will be completely unable to retaliate and can be eliminated in this manner with utter impunity. A few shots from an upgraded firearm such as the Repeating Pistol or Piercing Rifle will do them in from a safe distance, as will a few Throwing Knives; Molotov Cocktails can be helpful for dealing with groups. Their jump attack can be avoided by quickstepping either sideways or forward past them as they execute it, at which point they can be swiftly eliminated with melee attacks.

Basic Information														
			Item Drops											
Fishing Hamlet	635	486	Random Fool Blood Gem ×1 [8%], Quicksilver Bullets ×2 [8%]	90	90	54	90	240	105	1498	200	180	—	—

Snail Woman (Shell) OH

Some of the giant snail shells scattered throughout the underground farms in the Fishing Hamlet are inhabited by the slug-like creatures found in the same area. This variant is nearly immobile owing to the weight of their shells; they will attack with flaccid horizontal arm swipes at close range and will also occasionally rear up off the ground to perform a grab. The damage they incur will be drastically reduced if an attack strikes their shells; the full amount will only be dealt by direct hits to the white slug body.

Strategy

Thrust attacks are the easiest way to target these enemies' weak point, but most weapons have at least one move which can be used for this purpose and if all else fails, jump attacks will suffice in a pinch. Stay just outside the target's melee range until after it finishes swinging, then move in and strike from the front. Both the arm swipes and the grab attack can be avoided with a sideways or backward quickstep, at which point a chain of well-placed R1 swings will settle matters once and for all.

Basic Information														
			Item Drops											
Fishing Hamlet	635	486	Random Poorman Blood Gem ×1 [8%], Quicksilver Bullets ×2 [8%], Oil Urn ×1 [4%]	90	90	54	90	240	105	1498	200	180	—	—

Strong Enemies

Scourge Beast

Scourge Beasts are fast, aggressive and tough; they attack quickly and often strike several times in a row. They have a weakness to fire, so Molotovs and Fire Paper are very effective, as are serrated weapons such as the Saw Cleaver and the Saw Spear. They also flinch and stumble easily, so transformation attacks can be useful with fast weapons. If you have enough stamina to kill a Scourge Beast in one chain, keep swinging; if not, save enough to quickstep a safe distance away and recover. Visceral attacks are the fastest way to damage them, but their unpredictable attacks make it difficult to interrupt or stagger them. The variants found in Yahar'gul and the Upper Cathedral Ward differ in appearance and elemental weaknesses, but behave in exactly the same way as those encountered in Central Yharnam.

Strategy

In some areas you can lure Scourge Beasts to narrow doorways and other borders that stop them from following you, then use ranged weapons or far-reaching melee attacks to kill them with little risk to yourself – this is especially useful in early areas, or if you're being chased while low on health. Quickstepping forward through their attacks to get behind them works well – they turn slowly, so this is your chance to use an R1 chain or land a charged attack from behind to stagger them. The Flamesprayer is highly effective against Scourge Beasts, especially if you're forced to fight more than one at a time; when powered up with Bone Marrow Ash, it will tear them to shreds in seconds. Another useful strategy is to throw a Pungent Blood Cocktail and hit them from behind with a charged attack while they are chasing it; this item can also be used to buy yourself time to escape if you aren't able to fight your way out of the encounter.

Basic Information
Special Weakness: Serration

	■	⚔	Item Drops	🝓	🌑	△	✦	★	🗲	🝞	👁	▽	⚔	🝜
Central Yharnam	520	336	Blood Vial ×3 [92%], Blood Stone Shard ×1 [8%]	108	108	108	108	75	48	65	200	270	×	—
Old Yharnam	364	987	Blood Stone Shard ×2 [8%], Blood Stone Shard ×1 [87%], Beast Blood Pellet ×1 [5%]	108	108	108	108	75	48	65	200	270		
Yahar'gul (Blood Moon) | Skeletal	1844	3881	Blood Stone Chunk ×1 [4%], Twin Bloodstone Shards ×2 [15%], Twin Bloodstone Shards ×1 [76%], Beast Blood Pellet ×1 [5%]	135	135	135	135	75	48	65	200	270		
Upper Cathedral Ward	1451	1637	Blood Stone Chunk ×1 [4%], Twin Bloodstone Shards ×2 [10%], Twin Bloodstone Shards ×1 [15%], Blood Stone Shard ×2 [28%]	206	206	28	138	75	48	65	200	270		
Chalice Dungeon Base Level	370	157	Random gem based on area ×1 [25%], Blood Vial ×4 [15%], Blood Vial ×3 [60%]	106	106	106	106	75	50	65	200	180		

Scourge Beast in Iosefka's Clinic has 146 of 364 HP.
Preset Chalice Dungeons: Ailing Loran, Lower Loran, Isz Gravestone

Key Attacks

Name	Interrupt	Notes
Gnawing Grab	Yes	Quickstep in any direction; dodge forward through it to get behind them.
Lunge	Yes	Quickstep left or right.

The Scourge Beasts can be a real threat...

...Throwing Knives can help...

...or take advantage of their weakness to Fire.

Huntsman's Minions

These brutes hit hard and move surprisingly quickly for such large opponents. The brick-carrying Minion is the more common of the two types that you'll encounter and you'll need to pay attention to spot the rare statue type as you approach them, so that you can adjust your tactics accordingly. Both types will walk up to you slowly when they spot you, and once they're a few meters away they'll tend to close the remaining distance with their Shoulder Charge. This attack can be difficult to avoid, because of their size and the range they use it from, so when you see them drop their shoulder and start the attack, it's often better to go for an interrupt rather than evade. At close range, the Brick Minion will often perform a furious Brick Combo attack consisting of multiple swift blows with the bricks they carry. While this attack can provide another interrupt opportunity, it's safer to quickstep behind them – but remember to keep moving around them because they will turn slightly after each hit of the combo.

If you stay behind them for too long after they recover from a previous attack, they'll perform a quick 360-degree Turnaround Spin, which will strike you if you're extremely close; it's best to either go for a charged R2 straight away once you get behind them, or use a couple of quick R1s, and then move away before they use the spin attack. The statue-wielding Minion is very similar to the version armed with bricks, and shares almost all of the same moves, with the exception of the Brick Combo. However, they also use several new techniques, and are somewhat less predictable as a result. Both versions of their slow overhead slam leave plenty of time to move around and stagger them from behind, but they also have an increased ability to hit you while you're behind them using their Statue Spin. Their attacks in general are much slower than the brick Minion's, and have much longer recovery, so you'll have plenty of time to strike once you evade an attack. Beware, though, that they will deliberately vary the number and timing of hits in their combos to trick you into letting your guard down or attacking too early.

Shoot the Huntsman's Minion to interrupt him as he charge towards you.

The statue variant has the same change attack. Shoot him, too!

Huntsman's Minion (Brick)

Interrupting their Shoulder Charge, Brick Combo or Downward Slam is by far the most effective way of dealing with these hulking enemies. Look for the starting animation of the Shoulder Charge as they approach and interrupt it for a quick victory. The Downward Slam and Brick Combos both have about the same range, so if you stand back out of that range, you can reduce the odds of them using those attacks and often bait them into using the Shoulder Charge. Alternately, strafing or quickstepping behind them when they use their Downward Slam will give you enough time to stagger them with a charged strike – just be sure that it will connect before they're able to use the Turnaround Swing. Short R1 chains can be very effective during their attack recovery, but leave yourself enough stamina to quickstep away if you can't finish them off.

Basic Information

	■	✦	Item Drops											
Central Yharnam	279	158	Blood Vial ×4 [5%], Blood Vial ×2 [85%], Shining Coins ×3 [5%], Shining Coins ×2 [5%]	123	82	103	103	90	95	100	250	180	—	—
Cathedral Ward	441	552	Blood Vial ×4 [5%], Blood Vial ×2 [85%], Shining Coins ×3 [5%], Shining Coins ×2 [5%]	132	88	110	110	90	95	100	250	180		
Healing Church Workshop	455	469	Blood Vial ×4 [5%], Blood Vial ×2 [85%], Shining Coins ×3 [5%], Shining Coins ×2 [5%]	132	88	110	110	90	95	100	250	180		
Hemwick Charnel Lane	544	797	Blood Vial ×4 [5%], Blood Vial ×2 [85%], Shining Coins ×3 [5%], Shining Coins ×2 [5%]	135	90	113	113	90	95	100	250	180		
Yahar'gul (Blood Moon)	1441	2079	Blood Vial ×4 [2.5%], Blood Vial ×2 [17.5%], Shining Coins ×3 [2.5%], Shining Coins ×2 [2.5%]	162	108	135	135	90	95	100	250	180		

Key Attacks

Name	Interrupt	Notes
Shoulder Charge	Yes	Medium-range running attack with a Downward Slam follow-up. Best chance to perform an interrupt; otherwise quickstep forward or sideways.
Brick Combo	Yes	Multiple hits with individual tracking; quickstep forward or sideways.
Downward Slam	Yes	Close range, long windup; quickstep forward past them.
Turnaround Swing	Yes	Short-range 360-degree spin attack; strafe or quickstep backward.

Huntsman's Minion (Statue)

Stand well outside their melee range to bait the Shoulder Charge, and then interrupt them when they use it – if you stay out of the reach of their other attacks, they'll perform it almost exclusively. Once you're close to them, most of their moves are slow enough react to and evade with a backward quickstep, but you'll need to watch out for their Fast Statue Combo and Left Hook. The Left Hook has much shorter range than their other attacks, however, so as long as you maintain some distance they'll rarely use it and will stick to their more telegraphed attacks. The best chances to stagger them are during their slow downward slam attacks, which give you enough time to quickstep behind them and finish charging an R2 attack before they turn.

Basic Information

	■	✦	Item Drops											
Central Yharnam	279	158	Blood Vial ×4 [5%], Blood Vial ×2 [85%], Shining Coins ×3 [5%], Shining Coins ×2 [5%]	123	82	103	103	90	95	100	250	180	—	—
Cathedral Ward	441	552	Blood Vial ×4 [5%], Blood Vial ×2 [85%], Shining Coins ×3 [5%], Shining Coins ×2 [5%]	132	88	110	110	90	95	100	250	180		
Yahar'gul (Blood Moon)	1441	2079	Blood Vial ×4 [2.5%], Blood Vial ×2 [17.5%], Shining Coins ×3 [2.5%], Shining Coins ×2 [2.5%]	162	108	135	135	90	95	100	250	180		

Key Attacks

Name	Interrupt	Notes
Shoulder Charge	Yes	Interrupt it or quickstep forward or sideways.
Left Hook	Yes	Extremely fast punch with the empty left hand. Instant startup; avoid standing close to them.
Slow Statue Combo	Yes	Up to three slow, diagonal swings; can delay the third hit. Quickstep backward or forward past them.
Fast Statue Combo	Yes	Three rapid overhead slams; quickstep forward or backward.
Downward Slam	Yes	Quickstep forward.
Turnaround Swing	Yes	Strafe or quickstep backward.
Statue Spin	Yes	Up to three 360-degree spins; makes them dizzy and has a long recovery. Strafe or quickstep backward until they stop spinning.
Windup Statue Slam	Yes	Frontal overhead slam with long windup; quickstep forward through it.

Executioner

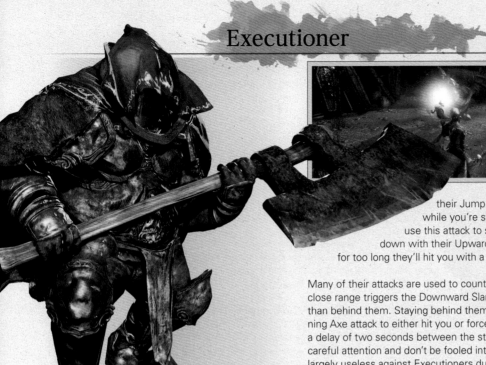

These powerful enemies have enormous range and a protective battle stance that drastically reduces the damage they take from the front when they aren't performing an action. Executioners can dish out huge amounts of damage very quickly and knock you down with most of their attacks. If you hang back and try to shoot them, they'll immediately use their Jump Attack to close the distance and hit you while you're stuck in the animation; they'll also sometimes use this attack to strike you on the ground after knocking you down with their Upward Chop. If you stand directly in front of them for too long they'll hit you with a fast Headbutt, or attempt a lethal grab attack.

Many of their attacks are used to counter your actions. Strafing around them at close range triggers the Downward Slam, which will hit you if you're anywhere other than behind them. Staying behind them for too long results in them using the Spinning Axe attack to either hit you or force you to back away. Their Running Slash has a delay of two seconds between the start of its animation and the attack itself; pay careful attention and don't be fooled into dodging too early. Ranged weapons are largely useless against Executioners due to their ability to block damage from the front; however, interrupts and to a lesser extent staggers are very effective. Don't stand in front of them while they get back up after being knocked down, though – they'll often use their Headbutt the moment they're back on their feet.

Strategy

They can be defeated using interrupts – with correct timing, this will place you at relatively low risk and is the quickest way to end the fight. The best times to interrupt them are during any hit of their combo attack and when they use Spinning Axe, Downward Slam or especially Running Slash attacks. You can use forward quicksteps to get behind them during their slower attacks, but watch out for their Spinning Axe attack, as trying to quickstep through this move is usually not possible. If you are able to sneak behind them just as they finish a Spinning Axe, Jump Attack or Downward Slam, you'll have just enough time to hit them with a charged blow. Executioners are weak against bolt and blunt damage. Since Tonitrus deals both of these, it's the ideal Executioner-slayer – capable of killing them in a single combo. Weapons such as the Kirkhammer in its transformed state or the Hunter Axe's standard R2 are also effective. They are susceptible to poison and can be defeated at range with Poison Knives and some patience, but bear in mind that if they block your knives, they'll also take reduced poison buildup.

Basic Information	■	✦	Item Drops										
Central Yharnam	343	340	Random gem based on area ×1 [20%], Blood Vial ×4 [24%], Blood Vial ×3 [52%], Pungent Blood Cocktail ×1 [4%]	149	92	149	115	115	160	70	300	999	—	—
Cathedral Ward	404	1505	Random gem based on area ×1 [20%], Blood Vial ×4 [24%], Blood Vial ×3 [52%], Pungent Blood Cocktail ×1 [4%]	234	144	234	180	115	160	70	300	999		
Hemwick Charnel Lane	348	2324	Random gem based on area ×1 [20%], Blood Vial ×4 [24%], Blood Vial ×3 [52%], Pungent Blood Cocktail ×1 [4%]	219	135	219	169	115	160	70	300	999		
Forbidden Woods	409	4379	Random gem based on area ×1 [20%], Blood Vial ×4 [24%], Blood Vial ×3 [52%], Pungent Blood Cocktail ×1 [4%]	239	147	239	184	115	160	70	300	999		

Key Attacks

Name	Interrupt	Notes
Jump Attack	Yes	Quickstep sideways. Will hit you on the ground, but can roll away in time to avoid it.
Spinning Axe	Yes	720-degree horizontal spin attack; quickstep backward.
Upward Chop	Yes	Fast close-range uppercut, sometimes followed by a jump attack; quickstep sideways or backward.
Headbutt	Yes	Near-instant, frontal, extremely close range. Avoid standing in front of them at close range
Combo	Yes	Up to three hits; interrupt them or quickstep forward.
Grab	Yes	Two versions – stationary and running. Quickstep backward.
Running Slash	Yes	Runs forward several steps and performs a delayed counterclockwise chop; interrupt it or quickstep left.
Downward Slam	Yes	Frontal horizontal area attack that hits to either side of them; strafe or quickstep backward.

Maneater Boar

If these gigantic pigs spot you from far away, they'll charge in to perform a tackle with their massive bodies. At close range they attack with a straightforward set of head swings, body presses and clouds of poisonous mist. In spite of their size, Maneater Boars are very predictable opponents and their attack patterns create many openings to interrupt and stagger them. Their attacks tend to strike wide areas and can also damage other enemies, so use this to your advantage if the situation allows. Maneater Boars will chase Pungent Blood Cocktails, allowing you to set them up for a stagger or trick them into hitting their allies; they are also affected by Shaman Bone Blades, which will cause them to actively hunt down and attack any other enemies nearby. The Maneater Boars encountered in the Nightmare of Mensis sport additional eyes, but attack in exactly the same way as the others.

Strategy

Due to their limited attacks and inability to strike behind them, Maneater Boars are easily defeated simply by strafing or quickstepping behind them and repeatedly using charged swings. They recover so slowly that it is possible to hit them with a second charged strike as they stand up from the first, though they will sometimes leap backward to reposition themselves and prevent a second stagger. Maneater Boars use two versions of their Body Press: a quick, short-range variation and a longer one in which they rear up on their hind legs, take several steps forward and crash down on the area in front of them; both of these are telegraphed early enough to make interrupting them relatively easy. In certain areas they can also be tricked into performing their Charging Tackle into pitfalls or groups of other enemies. It's safe to use R1 chains or transformation attacks while standing behind them or at their sides; just be sure to avoid standing directly in front of them. Molotovs are highly effective, as is the Flamesprayer; when you have access to Bone Marrow Ash, a single bullet's worth of augmented Flamesprayer fire will tear these foes to shreds.

Basic Information

Location	■	🗡	Item Drops											
Central Yharnam	423	431	Blood Vial ×4 [20%], Blood Vial ×2 [80%]	105	79	105	105	68	65	80	250	180	×	—
Yahar'gul (Evening)	758	3192	Blood Vial ×4 [20%], Blood Vial ×2 [80%]	120	90	120	120	68	65	80	250	180		
Forbidden Woods	767	2323	Blood Vial ×4 [20%], Blood Vial ×2 [80%]	123	92	123	123	68	65	80	250	180		
Nightmare of Mensis | Eyeballs	2346	9450	Blood Vial ×4 [20%], Blood Vial ×2 [80%]	148	111	148	148	68	65	80	250	180		
Chalice Dungeon Base Level	529	379	Random Radiant gem based on area ×1 [16%], Blood Vial ×4 [10%], Blood Vial ×2 [74%]	105	78	105	105	68	65	80	250	180		
Chalice Dungeon Base Level | Boss	2646	1240	Lethal Bloodstone Gem (2) [100%]	105	78	105	105	68	45	80	250	180		

Preset Chalice Dungeons: Hintertomb (Boss)

Key Attacks

Name	Interrupt	Notes
Charging Tackle	No	Long-range linear charge attack; quickstep or roll twice sideways.
Body Press	Yes	Forward body slam with varying forward momentum and delay; quickstep sideways or stay beside/behind them.
Thrashing Combo	Yes	Strikes both in front of them and behind; quickstep backward. Used only the Chalice Dungeon boss version.
Poison Belch	No	Strafe backward or sideways and stay out of the cloud.

Maneater Boars will chase Pungent Blood Cocktails...

...even if it leads them into a pitfall.

Church Giants

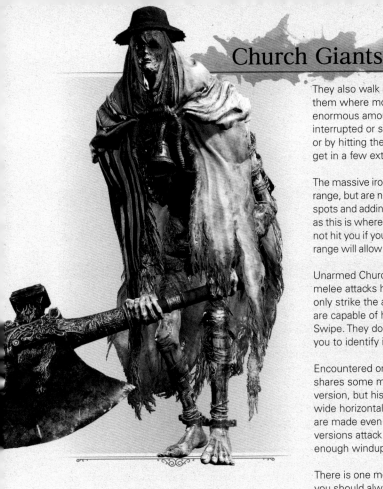

They also walk and turn extremely slowly, allowing you to position yourself behind them where most of their attacks can't reach you. They have very high defense, enormous amounts of health, high fire and bolt resistance, and they cannot be interrupted or staggered normally; breaking their super armor with a charged attack or by hitting their heads will bring them to their knees momentarily and allow you to get in a few extra hits.

The massive iron wrecking balls wielded by some Church Giants have extremely long range, but are nearly incapable of striking close to their bodies, creating enormous blind spots and adding to their already glaring weaknesses. Avoid standing in front of them, as this is where the majority of their attacks are targeted, although most of these will not hit you if you stand extremely close. Positioning yourself behind them at pointblank range will allow you to evade everything they have, even their 360-degree spins.

Unarmed Church Giants are a bit faster than those with weapons and their basic melee attacks have less windup, but they also have shorter reach and will usually only strike the area directly in front of them. Unlike the other Church Giants, these are capable of hitting you while you're directly behind them using their Turnaround Swipe. They don't use this attack often, though, and it has just enough windup for you to identify it and back out of the way before it hits you.

Encountered only once in Lecture Building 2F, this Church Giant with Flame Fists shares some moves (like the Running Haymaker) with the normal bare fisted version, but his regular melee attacks are slightly different. They mainly consist of wide horizontal hook punches, slow combo attacks and vertical slams, all of which are made even more dangerous by the fact that their fists are on fire. Both unarmed versions attack a fair bit faster than those wielding weapons, but they still have just enough windup to see them coming and quickstep through them.

There is one move that can be used by all Church Giants, and while they rarely use it, you should always be on the lookout for it. If you're standing reasonably close in front of them they'll sometimes raise their leg up and use a powerful stamp, so powerful that it actually breaks their leg. When that happens you'll be able to see the bone sticking out of thier knee, and if you attack it you'll do considerably more damage than normal and have the ability to stagger them. Standing in front of them does put you at greater risk from their other attacks, however, so you'll need to be careful.

These massive towering giants can inflict tremendous damage and will send you flying any time one of their attacks connect, but their long windup and recovery periods leave them vulnerable, and make them much less frightening than they first appear.

Church Giant (Axe)

When approaching one of these enemies, bait an attack from as far away as possible, and then quickstep through it to get behind them. Stay in this position by strafing or quickstepping while attacking with R1 combos or charged R2s; Church Giants are immune to visceral attacks, but fully-charged swings and transformation attacks will tear through their super armor and help keep them from being able to act. Watch out for their Fast Frontal Sweep; it will not reach you directly behind them, but may clip you if they use it while turning to face you. To lower the risk of being struck by this attack, circle them clockwise; the swing starts above their right shoulder and ends at the ground to their left, so it's less likely to hit you if you're directly beneath the axe when they initiate it.

Basic Information

	■	🗡	Item Drops											
Cathedral Ward	705	718	Blood Vial ×3 [54%], Bloodstone Shard ×1 [43%], Blue Elixir ×1 [3%]	134	134	134	134	163	290	290	300	180	—	—

Middle part: 718 HP/835 Blood Echoes; last part: 859 HP/1205 Blood Echoes.

Key Attacks

Name	Interrupt	Notes
Axe Thrust	No	Forward stab with extremely long reach; quickstep to either side.
Ground Stab	No	Downward stab that hits directly at their feet; quickstep backward.
Running Overhead Chop	No	Dashing downward chop with poor tracking. Travels forward four meters. Quickstep toward them.
Fast Overhead Chop	No	Close-range frontal chop; quickstep backward to either side.
Slow Overhead Chop	No	Extremely long windup; quickstep forward or to either side.
Fast Frontal Sweep	No	Frontal 180-degree radius; quickstep backward.
Slow Frontal Sweep	No	Frontal 210-degree radius with longer range than the fast version; quickstep backward twice.

Church Giant (Wrecking Ball)

As with the other Church Giants, focus on staying directly behind them while you let loose with your strongest melee attacks. As long as you stand as close to them as possible, their 360-degree spins will pass over your head; take advantage of this blind spot while continually readjusting your position with strafes and quicksteps to deal the most damage with the least risk of being hit. Their overhead smashes strike in a straight line and are easily avoided by quickstepping to either side, though beware that they will alternate between using their vertical slams and frontal 180-degree sweeps; also note that if their first attack is a horizontal swing, they may use a second, slower frontal sweep with a wider arc and longer reach immediately afterward.

Basic Information

			Item Drops											
Cathedral Ward	705	718	Blood Vial ×3 [54%], Bloodstone Shard ×1 [43%], Blue Elixir ×1 [3%]	134	134	134	134	163	290	290	300	180	—	—

Key Attacks

Name	Interrupt	Notes
Frontal Sweep	No	Frontal 180-degree radius, sometimes followed by a second sweep; quickstep backward.
Running Overhead Slam	No	Running downward slam with four meters' forward momentum; quickstep toward them.
Frontal Combo	No	Up to four frontal overhead slams with long reach; quickstep backward.
Spinning Combo	No	One frontal strike followed by up to two 360-degree spins. Extremely slow; quickstep or strafe backward.

Church Giant (Bare Fists)

Clear out all the Parasite Larvae near these enemies first by luring them into the side caverns where the giants can't reach. When you've cleared a safe spot in which to fight the giants, preferably on the sand along the walls or the islands jutting out of the poison, lure them towards you one at a time with gunshots or thrown weapons, and then take them down with R1 combos. Keep an eye out for their Turnaround Swipe, and be prepared to strafe or quickstep away from them if they use it. If you've already picked up the Cannon from the windmill before exploring this area, you can use it to simultaneously blast the giants and wipe out any Parasite Larvae caught in the explosion.

Basic Information

			Item Drops											
Forbidden Woods	1023	2711	Twin Bloodstone Shards ×1 [25%], Bloodstone Shard ×1 [72%], Blue Elixir ×1 [3%]	149	149	149	149	163	290	290	300	180	—	—

Key Attacks

Name	Interrupt	Notes
Running Stomp	No	Carries them forward four meters. Slow with long windup; quickstep forward past them.
Turnaround Swipe	No	360-degree swipe attack used to hit behind them; quickstep backward.

Church Giant (Flame Fists)

This Church giant is the only one of his kind that can be staggered without having to wait for it break its leg, and there are a couple of ways you can go about it. The first method is to attack his head when he lowers it during or after one of his attacks. Be sure to clear out any Scholars in the area, and then bait him into using an attack that causes him to lower his head so that you can strike it and stagger him; overhead or jumping attacks will generally give you the best chance of hitting his head. You can also stagger him from behind with a charged R2 strike, but you must still initiate the visceral attack from the front. R1 combos and transformation attacks are marginally effective, but far from ideal. Apart from the minor differences between their movesets, this giant fights almost identically to those in the Forbidden Woods and can be handled in the same way if you're having trouble landing a visceral attack.

Basic Information

			Item Drops											
Lecture Building 2F	3129	4082	Bloodstone Chunk ×1 [4%], Twin Bloodstone Shards ×1 [93%], Blue Elixir ×1 [3%]	180	180	180	180	163	290	290	300	180	—	—

Key Attacks

Name	Interrupt	Notes
Running Haymaker	No	Four-meter sprint followed by a slow downward punch; quickstep forward past them.
Turnaround Swipe	No	360-degree arm chop with several minor variations; quickstep backward.
Windup Punch	No	Raises right arm and slams fist into the ground. Very slow; strafe or quickstep backward.

Brainsucker

Brainsuckers give the impression of being weak and helpless, but they are wolves in sheep's clothing. They have extremely high physical defense but very low health, and are highly weak against thrust attacks as well as fire and bolt damage; in early areas a single Molotov or single strong thrust attack will kill them. Throwing Knives work well against Brainsuckers and offer a way of attacking from a safe distance. Despite these weaknesses, they have a number of extremely dangerous attacks which make them serious threats if not dealt with immediately: they can inflict severe damage or paralyze you with long-range blasts, steal your Insight with their grab attacks and send you flying with their Head Swing. In most areas you'll find them scavenging corpses with their backs to you, allowing you to approach slowly from behind and kill them before they detect you. In Upper Cathedral Ward they patrol narrow hallways, so sneaking up on them will be much tougher. Apart from their grabs and projectiles, Brainsuckers use simple combos and arm swipes in melee combat; those encountered in the Cathedral Ward will not use any of their magic attacks, but are still dangerous if you give them time to grab you.

Strategy

Whenever possible, sneak up behind them and use a charged thrust attack to finish them before they have a chance to attack you. If you aren't able to defeat them in one shot, back off and wait for them to use their slow grab or a normal combo, then hit them with a thrust attack or a Molotov during their recovery. They aren't good at dodging, so you can stand at a safe distance and hit them with a few Throwing Knives, but beware that they'll start using their energy projectiles at longer range and you'll need to time your throws carefully in order to avoid being hit. Don't attempt to knock them out of their grab attacks with gunshots or melee swings; killing the Brainsucker before it can finish them is the only way to stop these moves. Due to the danger they present, Brainsuckers are top-priority targets and should be defeated first when other enemies are around. If they haven't yet spotted you, lure any other targets in the opposite direction and fight them a safe distance away. Defeating a Brainsucker will not restore any Insight stolen from you during the fight, so try to avoid being hit by their grab attacks.

Basic Information

	■	✈	Item Drops										
Cathedral Ward	150	449	Quicksilver Bullets ×4 [25%], Quicksilver Bullets ×3 [70%], Shaman Bone Blade ×1 [5%]	344	344	83	138	164	50	60	200	270	—	—
Healing Church Workshop	236	511	Quicksilver Bullets ×4 [8%], Quicksilver Bullets ×3 [20%], Shaman Bone Blade ×1 [2%]	413	413	99	165	180	50	60	200	270
Iosefka's Clinic	484	995	Quicksilver Bullets ×4 [25%], Quicksilver Bullets ×3 [70%], Shaman Bone Blade ×1 [5%]	422	422	101	169	164	50	60	200	270
Byrgenwerth	605	1527		506	506	122	203	180	50	60	200	270
Upper Cathedral Ward	725	3273	Quicksilver Bullets ×4 [8%], Quicksilver Bullets ×3 [20%], Shaman Bone Blade ×1 [2%]	516	516	124	206	180	50	60	200	270
Chalice Dungeon Base Level	148	214	Random gem based on area ×1 [18%], Quicksilver Bullets ×4 [25%], Quicksilver Bullets ×3 [52%], Shaman Bone Blade ×1 [5%]	336	336	81	134	164	50	60	200	180
Chalice Dungeon Base Level | Root Dungeon	185	228	Random gem based on area ×1 [25%], Quicksilver Bullets ×4 [25%], Quicksilver Bullets ×3 [45%], Shaman Bone Blade ×1 [5%]	413	413	99	165	180	50	60	200	180
Chalice Dungeon Base Level | Boss	617	1069	Tempering Blood Gemstone (3) [100%], Arcane Damp Blood Gem (6) [100%]	413	413	99	165	180	50	60	200	180

Preset Chalice Dungeons: Isz Gravestone, Lower Hintertomb (Boss), Isz Gravestone (Boss)

Key Attacks

Name	Interrupt	Notes
Stationary Grab*	Yes	Slow short-range grab. Strafe or quickstep backward.
Quick Grab*	Yes	Short-range grab with slight forward momentum.
Running Grab*	Yes	Mid-range running grab attack. Quickstep forward past them or to either side.
Dark Blast	No	Used by dungeon boss version. Fires long-range arcane damage blast; strafe or quickstep sideways.
Paralyzing Blast	No	Long-range paralyzing blast followed by a running grab if it connects; strafe or quickstep sideways.
Paralyzing Wave	No	Short-range circular paralysis blast in a one-meter radius; strafe or quickstep backward.
Head Swing	Yes	Used when head is expanded. 360-degree whip with I knockdown effect; quickstep backward.

*Expands their heads and drains two points of Insight

Mad One

First encountered alongside The Witch of Hemwick, these scythe-wielding demons will appear elsewhere along the Charnel Lane after nightfall if you have at least 15 Insight, announcing their arrival with a flash of red light and a scream. These agile opponents attack with vertical and horizontal slashes and swift combos, but are incapable of reaching directly behind them. They have fairly high physical defense and aren't weak to elemental damage, but can be interrupted and staggered; their slow Overhead Slash is the best opportunity to do this and set them up for a visceral attack. While their individual swings aren't too difficult to avoid, their Scythe Combo can hit up to seven times and they will adjust to track you after each swing; in spite of the danger, this technique gives you seven opportunities to stagger them if you can get out of the way in time. The Mad Ones that appear with The Witch of Hemwyck have much shorter detection range and move more slowly than those found outside; if they're killed, the witch will summon them in increasingly large numbers based on the amount of damage she's taken.

Strategy

Quickstep behind them and use R1 chains or charged attacks while they turn to face you; alternately, stand in front of them at a safe distance and bait their Overhead Slash, then interrupt it and perform a visceral attack. The Overhead Slash gives you enough time to quickstep forward and use a charge attack to stagger them, or to simply let loose with a chain of R1 swings; just be sure to save enough stamina to quickstep away if they manage to catch you in a combo. In general, it's best to stay behind them and strike from their blind spot. Try to avoid fighting any other enemies if you're already being attacked by a Mad One; their scythes inflict heavy damage and their swift combos can easily immobilize you, especially if you're being hit by other foes at the same time. When you see the telltale red glow which signals that a Mad One is about to appear, retreat to the safety of an area you've already cleared and eliminate it before advancing.

Basic Information

			Item Drops										
Hemwick Charnel Lane	666	1426	Random gem based on area ×1 [25%]	123	123	123	123	75	75	75	200	180	—	—
Hemwick Charnel Lane | Boss support	544	0	None	113	113	113	113	75	75	75	200	180		
Chalice Dungeon Base Level	58	19	None	112	112	112	112	75	75	75	200	180		

Key Attacks

Name	Interrupt	Notes
Scythe Combo	Yes	Up to seven hits with individual tracking; quickstep forward through it or sideways if you're caught in it.
Overhead Slash	Yes	Slow overhead slash; interrupt it or quickstep forward.
Diagonal Slash	Yes	Frontal 180-degree arc; quickstep backward.
Jump Attack	Yes	Swift, forward overhead jumping slash with little forward momentum; quickstep sideways.

Shooting Mad Ones to interrupt them is risky...

...but it's the quickest way to kill them.

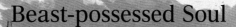

Beast-possessed Soul

A unique enemy found only at the bottom of the Healing Church Workshop and in certain Chalice Dungeons, the Beast-possessed Soul attacks with swift, far-reaching claw combos and with fire magic, despite its weakness to fire. The one encountered in the Workshop basement will be asleep with its back to you, and will only wake up if you run too close to it or land on any of the breakable rubble as you drop down from the rafters. You can interrupt its physical attacks, but not its fire techniques, and it can be staggered, allowing you to hit it from behind with a charged R2 strike while it's asleep and begin the battle with a visceral attack or another charged R2. The Beast-possessed Soul is weak against serrated weapons, so using Fire Paper on a Saw Cleaver or Saw Spear will inflict heavy damage. Throwing Knives are also reasonably effective if you need a ranged option. You'll face this beast in an enclosed room with no other enemies present, so you won't have to worry about being ambushed during the battle; however, pay close attention to your surroundings to avoid being backed into a corner.

Strategy

When first entering the Healing Church Workshop basement, be careful not to land on any breakable objects as you drop down – this will wake the Beast-possessed Soul and cost you an opportunity to attack it from behind. Walk slowly toward it and hit it from behind with a charged R2 swing; if you follow up with a visceral attack, you can quickstep toward it after that for an extra hit or two. This foe will chase Pungent Blood Cocktails, which you can use to set it up for further visceral attacks; it is incapable of striking directly behind it, so try to stay in this position as much as possible and attack with R1 combos or charged R2s if you have no blood cocktails on hand. Alternately, you can stand facing it at a safe distance and bait it into taking a swing at you, then interrupt it; however, you must be prepared to shoot it out of its fireball attacks and evade its grab. Molotovs are very useful for damaging it from a distance, though be careful not to throw one while the beast is charging a fireball unless you have enough time to evade it afterward. Poison Knives are effective, especially against the boss version of this enemy, and the pillars in the boss room can be used for cover between throws.

Basic Information

Basic Information Special Weakness: Serration	■	♠	Item Drops	🔲	🌙	🔺	✴	★	🗡	🔪	💀	🔻	🐺	🐍
Healing Church Workshop	656	795	Beast [100%]	110	110	110	110	70	50	70	120	300	✕	—
Chalice Dungeon Base Level	635	276	Random gem based on area x1 [25%], Blood Vial x4 [25%] or x3 [45%], Beast Blood Pellet x1 [5%]	106	106	106	106	70	50	70	120	180		
Chalice Dungeon Base Level | Boss	2205	1226	Radiant Blood Gemstone (3) [100%], Fire Damp Blood Gem (5) [100%]	106	106	106	106	70	50	70	120	180		

Preset Chalice Dungeons: Central Pthumerian Labyrinth, Ailing Loran (both Boss versions)

Key Attacks

Name	Interrupt	Notes
Single Fireball	No	Short delay and some tracking; quickstep sideways or shoot him out of it.
Double Fireball	No	Short delay and some tracking; quickstep sideways twice in opposite directions or shoot him out of it.
Burning Leap	Yes	Leaps forward two meters and creates a circular wave of fire with a very short radius; quickstep sideways.
Flame Whip	No	Frontal mid-range 90-degree arc; quickstep sideways.
Claw Combo	Yes	Up to six slashes with heavy stun, ending with slow headbutt; quickstep sideways and stay behind him.
Gnawing Grab	Yes	Slow windup but long reach; boosts his attack power if it connects. Strafe or quickstep away.

Sneak up on the Beast-possessed Soul and charge an R2.

To start the fight with a visceral attack follow up.

Kidnapper

You'll need to let a Kidnapper defeat you in order to infiltrate the Unseen Village of Yahar'gul (see p80 for more information on this event). Kidnappers have high defense, but are very weak to poison; Poison Knives are a good idea. They can be interrupted and staggered, and give you plenty of opportunities to do so, making visceral attacks or charged attacks the best ways to defeat them.

Kidnappers aren't very aggressive when you first encounter them; they'll walk slowly toward you and occasionally throw a punch. However, after losing 20% of their health they'll reinforce their attack damage with Madness Boost, become more vicious and begin using new moves. While under the effects of the attack boost, they'll move faster and perform punches, kicks and short combos. They'll respond to any damage you deal by leaping backward as a feint, then rushing back in to counter with a scissor kick. They'll also begin using a close-range grab and two attacks with their sacks: a frontal overhead slam and a 360-degree spin that will send you flying. Finally, they'll gain access to a spherical energy wave and a vortex spell that drags you toward them, both of which inflict no damage, but will cause you to stumble.

Strategy

As mentioned above, visceral attacks are the most effective strategy against these opponents. Once they've used Madness Boost, their melee attacks or sack swings are your best chances to interrupt them. Another reliable strategy is to bait them into backstepping by shooting them, then quickstep toward them as they counter with the scissor kick and stagger them with a charged attack while they recover. Kidnappers take only moderate damage from Molotovs and Throwing Knives, but have extremely low resistance to Poison Knives – a mere two or three will usually poison them. You can also sometimes use environmental hazards or other enemies to do the job for you – the Kidnapper near the Lower Chapel can be shoved into the nearby bonfire and burned to death, while those in Yahar'gul can be lured into the path of a charging Maneater Boar.

Basic Information

Location	■	✦	Item Drops	🗍	◐	◭	✳	★	🪶	🜂	💀	▽	⚔	⚒
Cathedral Ward	910	1368	Twin Bloodstone Shards ×1 [30%], Bloodstone Shard ×2 [65%], Bolt Paper ×1 [5%]	144	144	144	144	76	78	80	70	120	—	—
Healing Church Workshop	910	1368	Twin Bloodstone Shards ×1 [30%], Bloodstone Shard ×2 [65%], Bolt Paper ×1 [5%]	144	144	144	144	76	78	80	70	120		
Yahar'gul (Evening)	910	1368	Twin Bloodstone Shards ×1 [30%], Bloodstone Shard ×2 [65%], Bolt Paper ×1 [5%]	144	144	144	144	76	78	80	70	120		
Forbidden Woods	920	1706	Twin Bloodstone Shards ×1 [30%], Bloodstone Shard ×2 [65%], Bolt Paper ×1 [5%]	147	147	147	147	76	78	80	70	120		
Chalice Dungeon Base Level	388	234	Ritual material B ×1 [25%], Bloodstone B ×2 [25%], Bloodstone B ×1 [45%], Bolt Paper ×1 [5%]	129	129	129	129	76	78	80	70	120		

Appears after Old Yharnam. Preset Chalice Dungeons: Pthumerian Labyrinth, Central Pthumerian Labyrinth, Lower Pthumerian Labyrinth

Key Attacks

Name	Interrupt	Notes
Madness Boost	No	Used when below 80% health, covers them in a red aura and increases their attack power.
Stun Blast	No	Area attack with wide radius. Inflicts no damage, but causes stumble; quickstep backward repeatedly.
Vacuum Vortex	No	Inflicts no damage, but causes you to stumble and drags you toward them; quickstep backward.
Jump Attack	Yes	Quick jump attack that carries them forward two meters; quickstep toward them or sideways.
Sack Smash	Yes	Slow overhead slam using their sacks. Will flatten you if it lands; interrupt or strafe backward.
Sack Swing	Yes	360-degree sack swing with slow windup and knockdown effect; interrupt it or quickstep backward.
Chokehold Grab	Yes	Short-range grab attack with slow startup; quickstep backward.

Eye Collector

Eye Collectors are a non-boss[*] variant of the Witch of Hemwick; they move considerably faster and attack much more aggressively, but are incapable of using magic and will use their grabs or basic melee attacks most of the time instead. They are straightforward enemies with average defense; Throwing Knives and Molotovs are effective, but ordinary physical attacks make more sense, given these foes' inability to strike behind them. Eye Collectors can be interrupted and staggered relatively easily due to their predictable behavior and small repertoire of moves; they also turn slowly, enabling you to stay behind them and avoid their attacks with relative ease.

Strategy

Standing in front of them is lethal, especially at close range; they will often use the fast version of their grab attack before you can react, and will go out of their way to position themselves as close to you as possible before performing it. Quickstep behind them and maintain that position using further quicksteps or strafes, while launching your attack with R1 combos or charged R2 swings; beware that while three Throwing Knives are generally enough to kill them, the arc of Molotovs will often cause them to miss if you throw one at an Eye Collector that's moving toward you. Generally, you're better off saving your consumable items altogether – these enemies have low enough health that a visceral attack or a solid R1 combo will get the job done more efficiently.

3

Basic Information

	■	✦	Item Drops	🔲	◑	▽	✱	★	🍃	🌀	💀	▽	🐺	⚡
Yahar'gul (Evening)	278	365	Pebble ×6 [35%], Pebble ×3 [61%], Bloodshot Eyeball ×1 [4%]	84	84	84	84	140	65	140	200	180	—	—
Chalice Dungeon Base Level	194	78	Pebble ×6 [35%], Pebble ×3 [61%], Bloodshot Eyeball ×1 [4%]	72	72	72	72	160	70	160	200	180		
Chalice Dungeon Base Level | Strong	264	94	Pebble ×6 [25%], Pebble ×3 [51%], Bloodshot Eyeball ×1 [4%], Random gem based on area ×1 [20%]	72	72	72	72	70	73	90	200	180		
Hunter's Nightmare	760	304	Pebble ×6 [35%], Pebble ×3 [61%], Bloodshot Eyeball ×1 [4%]	96	96	96	96	220	96	220	200	180		

Preset Chalice Dungeons: Hintertomb (Regular), Lower Hintertomb (Regular)

Key Attacks

Name	Interrupt	Notes
Eye Gouge	Yes	Slow stationary grab attack; strafe or quickstep backward.
Running Eye Gouge	Yes	Mid-range running grab attack; quickstep forward past it.

Don't get too close...

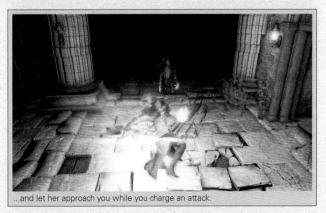

...and let her approach you while you charge an attack.

Small Celestial Emissary (Tendrils)

Identical to the other Small Celestial Emissaries in most respects, the key difference lies in the two lethal attacks used only by this variant. While both share the same high physical defense, low health and severe weakness to bolt, fire and thrust attacks, the energy projectiles used by this type have very long range and inflict enormous arcane damage, making them far more dangerous than their bare-headed cousins. Fortunately, you'll only encounter Small Celestial Emissaries with tendrils in zones with plenty of obstacles to use as cover from their projectiles; they are highly vulnerable in close combat, so you can lure them toward you by getting their attention and then duck back into one of these safe spots to fight them up close. Throwing Knives are highly effective against these enemies; Molotovs will kill them in one hit. They can also be interrupted and staggered, but getting close enough to do so can be very difficult.

Strategy

Try to sneak up on them without being seen, then throw a Molotov or a couple of Throwing Knives to eliminate them before they have a chance to use their dangerous projectiles. Failing that, wait for them to finish using one of their energy attacks and advance as quickly as possible while they recover; if you're able to bring them within melee range before they attack again, hit them with thrust attacks to inflict the highest possible damage and eliminate them before they can react. Don't go out of your way to try to interrupt or stagger them, as this may take valuable time and exposes you to danger. If you want to be sure to kill them in a single hit, use Bolt Paper on a weapon with a strong thrust attack, such as the Saw Spear.

Basic Information

			Item Drops										
Forbidden Woods	143	765	Random gem based on area ×1 [30%], Blue Elixir ×1 [1%]	265	294	0	147	160	60	50	120	180	—	✕

Key Attacks

Name	Interrupt	Notes
Cosmic Blast	No	Fast long-range projectile with moderate tracking; quickstep sideways or use cover to block it.
Triple Laser	No	Fires three linear lasers in quick succession. Tracks in all directions and can hit you behind them; quickstep sideways or use obstacles to block it.
Flailing Combo	Yes	Rapid multi-hit combo with slight forward momentum and flinch effect; quickstep sideways or backward.

The beam attacks are lethal...

...but when you get close a single thrust attack will do the job.

Large Snake Ball

These clusters of giant snakes encountered in the Forbidden Woods behave much like the smaller version, but are capable of spitting venom at you from far away and will occasionally summon four normal Snake Ball enemies to aid them in battle. Their high health and defense can make them difficult to kill, but Throwing Knives (or the Augur of Ebrietas, if you have a high enough Arcane stat) deal decent damage and are useful for defeating them from outside the reach of their powerful melee at-

tacks. In close combat, Large Snake Balls have an extremely limited moveset consisting only of forward bites; while these attacks are easy to dodge simply by strafing around the target, they also inflict heavy damage and slow poison.

They turn very slowly and cannot attack behind them, but they're immune to visceral attacks and cannot be interrupted or staggered. While a single Large Snake Ball isn't extremely dangerous on its own, several of them often appear very close to each other and they are almost always found near groups of the smaller Snake Balls; pay close attention to your surroundings when fighting and be careful not to walk into an ambush.

3

Strategy

Stay behind them by strafing or quickstepping and hit them with R1 combos or Flamesprayer blasts augmented with Bone Marrow Ash. An alternate, safer tactic is to charge the transformed R2 with the Rifle Spear from just outside their melee range and then dodge backwards after it hits. Beware of any other nearby enemies when fighting, though; if necessary, use ranged attacks or thrown weapons to lure away faster opponents, such as Snake Parasites. Throwing Knives are effective at range, though you'll need to dodge blasts of venom if you get too far away. Due to their incredibly slow movement and minimal ability to chase you, it's possible simply to ignore these enemies as long as you can put an obstacle or terrain difference between yourself and their projectiles as soon as you're out of their reach; still it's a good idea to carry a large supply of Antidotes when passing through their territory.

Basic Information	■	⚔	Item Drops	🗋	◑	◇	✿	★	🍃	🎵	☠	▽	🐺	⤵
Forbidden Woods	716	1460	Random Murky gem based on area ×1 [30%], Twin Bloodstone Shards ×1 [8%], Bloodstone Shard ×2 [62%]	147	59	118	118	45	85	90	999	180	—	—
Chalice Dungeon Base Level	493	265	Random Murky gem based on area ×1 [30%], Bloodstone C ×1 [1.5%], Bloodstone B ×2 [18%], Bloodstone A ×2 [50%]	132	53	106	106	40	80	85	999	180		

Key Attacks

Name	Interrupt	Notes
Venom Spit	Yes	Launches venom in a straight line at extremely long range; roll sideways or use obstacles to block it.

Dash around behind the Snake Ball...

...and aim to stay there while you hack it to death.

Bloodlicker

Large, insect-like enemies encountered in Cainhurst's Castle Grounds and Chalice Dungeons. They move and attack very quickly and inflict heavy damage, making them dangerous opponents. A large number of them appear scattered throughout the area and their pale skin blends in with their surroundings, making them difficult to spot and increasing the likelihood of ambush by several at once. Some Bloodlickers patrol, while others sit in fixed locations; those on patrol can spot you from a considerable distance.

They're highly defensive and will constantly back away from you in order to keep you in front of them. They use fast horizontal arm swipes, far-reaching jump attacks and a multi-hit tongue combo, and can strike directly behind them with a backward kick, making it dangerous to stand in this position for too long. If you attempt to use an item while in range, they will immediately punish you with their jump attack; however, they have little ability to hit you if you stand at least 90 degrees to their left, and you can reliably avoid their attacks by staying in this position using strafes and quicksteps. Bloodlickers are weak against thrust attacks and fire damage, so using weapons boosted with Fire Paper is a good idea, especially one with a thrust attack that can track them. They cannot be interrupted or staggered, making it impossible to use visceral attacks, but ordinary melee swings and transformation attacks work well.

Strategy

Keep a close eye on your surroundings while crossing the Castle Grounds to ensure that none of the Bloodlickers in the area are able to sneak up on you. Avoid fighting several at once, as doing so will leave you virtually no opportunities to attack. Instead, lure them one at a time with thrown weapons or simply allow one to see you and retreat to a safe spot to fight. Stand directly to their left when at close range and strike with quick single R1 attacks, while strafing or quickstepping counterclockwise to maintain your position; avoid using combos in this situation. Bloodlickers will hiss immediately before using their frontal attacks, so be prepared to quickstep behind them as soon as you hear this cue. Molotovs are viable if you haven't yet been spotted, but will usually miss if you have. Try to use the fountain and the statues dotting the area to obstruct the Bloodlickers' movement and get them stuck, preventing them from hitting you with their jump attacks while you use Blood Vials.

Try to stay at their side when attacking Bloodlickers.

Basic Information
Special Weakness: Righteous

			Item Drops										
Forsaken Cainhurst Castle	1362	2310	Random gun type gem ×1 [16%]	70	117	70	117	88	77	85	150	90	—	—
Chalice Dungeon Base Level	405	211	Random gun type gem ×1 [16%]	56	94	56	94	88	77	85	150	90		

Three "stomach" sizes; bigger means slightly better Physical, Blunt, Thrust & Blood defense values. Preset Chalice Dungeons: Pthumerian Labyrinth, Central Pthumerian Labyrinth, Hintertomb, Lower Hintertomb, Lower Pthumerian Labyrinth, Cursed Pthumerian Defilement, Ailing Loran, Lower Loran, Isz Gravestone, Pthumeru Ihyll

Key Attacks

Name	Interrupt	Notes
Jumping Slam	No	Swift forward jump attack with variable range; quickstep sideways or forward.
Tongue Combo	No	Multiple rapid hits with very little forward momentum; quickstep forward or backward.

Loran Silverbeast

Loran Silverbeasts move quickly and can cover vast distances with their lunge attacks. They have high physical defense, but extremely low health and are weak against fire. They also take extra damage from serrated weapons, such as the Saw Spear. These strange foes use basic combo attacks with their claws and torches when bipedal, and much faster forward lunges and claw swipes while on all fours; they can also mix their parasite attacks into their melee combos and will try to force you to abandon your attack chains using their Electric Burst. Their claws extend to well over a meter in length when they swipe at you, giving their swings much longer reach than the length of their arms; be sure to take this into account when dodging their attacks. Silverbeasts begin in their torch stance nearly every time you encounter them, and will switch to the unarmed stance when their health drops below 50%. In either stance, they can't attack directly behind themselves, making this the safest place to stand. Only the Silverbeasts in the Nightmare of Mensis will use their parasite attacks and Bile Spray. They will chase Pungent Blood Cocktails and are susceptible, though highly resistant, to poison. Beware that the Silberbeasts in the Nightmare of Mensis will spew out two Parasite Larvae upon death, unless the finishing blow was dealt by a fire attack.

Strategy

Fire attacks are the fastest way to eliminate Loran Silverbeasts, especially in the Nightmare of Mensis to prevent Parasite Larvae from bursting out of their corpses upon defeat. Use Fire Paper if your weapon allows it, or consider the Flamesprayer or the Hunter's Torch for the task. These foes can be interrupted and staggered, but doing so is difficult and largely impractical without Pungent Blood Cocktails; very few of their attacks are slow enough to reliably interrupt and the best opportunities to stagger them require you to get past their flame breath or forward leaps. Try to stay a short distance behind them in melee combat, especially when they switch to their unarmed stance; the hitbox of their unarmed lunge attack covers their entire body and lasts for the duration of the lunge, placing you at high risk of being hit if you stand too close, either beside or in front of them.

3

Basic Information
Special Weakness: Serration

			Item Drops											
Nightmare Frontier	153	702	Random gem based on area ×1 [25%]	700	700	700	500	86	86	500	500	90	×	—
Nightmare Frontier | Parasite Attack	115	702	Random gem based on area ×1 [25%]	665	665	665	475	86	86	500	500	90		
Nightmare Frontier | Crawling	153	702	Random gem based on area ×1 [25%]	613	613	613	438	86	86	500	500	90		
Nightmare Frontier | Patrol	174	732	Random gem based on area ×1 [25%]	714	714	714	510	86	86	500	500	90		
Nightmare of Mensis	458	1702	Random gem based on area ×1 [16%]	798	798	798	570	86	86	500	500	90		
Nightmare of Mensis | Parasite Attack	344	1702	Random gem based on area ×1 [16%]	758	758	758	542	86	86	500	500	90		
Chalice Dungeon Base Level	105	122	Random gem based on area ×1 [25%], Blood Vial ×3 [30%], Blood Vial ×2 [41%], Bastard of Loran ×1 [4%]	539	539	539	385	86	86	500	500	90		
Chalice Dungeon Base Level | Boss	423	1568	Tempering Damp Blood Gem (6) [100%]	493	493	493	352	86	86	500	500	90		

Preset Chalice Dungeons: Ailing Loran, Lower Loran, Lower Loran (Boss)

Key Attacks

Name	Interrupt	Notes
Torch Stance		
Fire Breath	No	Sweeps fire breath from left to right in a frontal 180-degree arc; quickstep backward or toward their right side.
Forward Fire Breath	No	Breathes a three-meter column of fire straight at you with slightly delayed tracking; quickstep sideways.
Jump Attack	Yes	Heavy jumping attack that carries them forward and will knock down if it hits; quickstep forward or sideways.
Gnawing Grab	Yes	Frontal grab attack with stationary and moving versions. Quickstep sideways or forward.
Electric Burst	No	Charges electricity for one second and releases sparks in an area of effect; quickstep backward.
Parasite Whip	Yes	Multiple versions with varying range; strikes in a forward line up to three meters away. Quickstep sideways.
Bile Spray	No	Small frontal area of effect; quickstep sideways or forward past them.
Unarmed Stance		
Forward Lunge	Yes	Extremely quick lunge attack followed by up to two bites; travels forward up to four meters. Quickstep sideways.
Electric Burst	No	Same as in Torch Stance; quickstep backward.
Parasite Whip	Yes	Mid-range whip attack reaching up to three meters away; quickstep sideways or backwards.

Giant Lost Child

These boulder-lobbing giants are positioned in hard-to-reach perches in the Nightmare Frontier and guarding the castle approach in the Nightmare of Mensis. They will constantly bombard you with giant rocks while you are within their line of sight. A direct hit from one of these massive projectiles is almost certain to spell instant death, and the shrapnel can damage you even after the initial impact. Although their melee attacks inflict heavy damage and will usually knock you down, they are extremely slow in combat and are quite vulnerable at close range. They use very basic punches, kicks and a ground-pounding combo, all of which can be avoided with forward or sideways quicksteps and nearly all of which leave plenty of time to stagger them with a charged R2 swing from behind. Their predictable swings are very easy to interrupt and even ordinary R1 combos will inflict heavy damage due to their low defense.

Strategy

When crossing areas watched by Giant Lost Children, use Blue Elixirs before entering their field of vision and try to run past them before the effect wears off; if you have no elixirs, ignore any other nearby enemies and keep moving to avoid the flying boulders. When you enter their melee range, immediately dash or quickstep behind them and stay there for the rest of the battle; they will be unable to hit you in this position, allowing you to cut them down with near-impunity. Visceral attacks are among the best way to defeat these foes, as their slow swings provide ample opportunities to interrupt or stagger them. Alternately, simple R1 combos or transformation attacks will get the job done just as effectively. You can also use a Blue Elixir to sneak up on a Giant Lost Child and strike it with a Shaman Bone Blade, causing it to throw rocks at any other enemies in its massive range for virtually guaranteed kills. Beware that if you approach undetected and throw the giant off a cliff with a visceral attack, you should check to make sure that you've actually killed it – these foes are usually perched on low cliffs overlooking solid ground and will often survive the fall if your visceral attack doesn't finish them. Apart from Blue Elixirs and Shaman Bone Blades, don't waste your consumable items on these enemies; they are easily defeated with melee weapons and aren't very dangerous in close combat as long as you stay behind them.

Basic Information

			Item Drops											
Nightmare Frontier	639	1458	Bloodstone Shard ×3 [8%], Bloodstone Shard ×1 [28%], Lead Elixir ×1 [2%]	225	225	225	150	50	50	50	70	120	—	—
Nightmare of Mensis	1911	3403	Twin Bloodstone Shards ×3 [8%], Twin Bloodstone Shards ×1 [28%], Lead Elixir ×1 [2%]	257	257	257	171	50	50	50	70	120		

Key Attacks

Name	Interrupt	Notes
Boulder Throw	No	Throws an enormous boulder at extreme range. Direct hit inflicts lethal damage; debris has a lingering hitbox. Targets your location at the time the boulder is thrown; keep moving or roll in any direction.
Leaping Punch	Yes	Jump attack that travels forward four meters; quickstep forward or sideways.
Running Kick	Yes	Slow mid-range goal kick; quickstep forward or sideways.
Ground Pound	Yes	Short-range combo attack with slow startup; quickstep in any direction.

Sneaking up on these giants is often possible...

...allowing you to land an easy visceral attack.

Large Crawler

Larger and tougher than the ordinary Crawlers, these bizarre creatures are found only in the poison swamps of the Nightmare Frontier alongside their smaller kin. They hit harder and have more health, but behave in very much the same way as the smaller version, except that they can occasionally send a cloud of poison your way. Large Crawlers have high physical defense and cannot be interrupted or staggered, but are weak against bolt damage and thrust attacks. Large Crawlers cannot attack behind them, although it can be difficult to determine which part of them is "behind;" when in doubt, remember that they'll always face you head-on, so you can simply allow them to pursue you for a few moments and quickstep around to the far side of their bodies. In this position you'll be safe from all of their attacks and can freely use your strongest thrusts or charged R2 swings, but beware of any other Crawlers in the vicinity and keep an eye out for boulders thrown by Giant Lost Children.

Strategy

Use ranged attacks to get their attention, and wait for them to pursue you onto dry land, where you can fight without the disadvantages of standing ankle-deep in poisonous sludge. In close combat, do your best to stay behind them – their Tentacle Combo inflicts heavy damage and can be very dangerous if you become trapped in it. Use thrust attacks against them if possible; the Rifle Spear's charged R2 attack is an ideal choice, due to its combination of range and damage. Large Crawlers move extremely slowly and are easily outrun if you want to ignore them; their individual tentacle attacks can be avoid by quickstepping forward or sideways and as long as you keep moving, their Poison Gas will never touch you.

Basic Information

	■	⚔	Item Drops		🗋	⬤	▲	✦	★	🗲	🎵	☠	▽	⚔	⤸
Nightmare Frontier	434	1134	Thick Coldblood (6) ×1 [4%], Thick Coldblood (5) ×1 [16%], Thick Coldblood (4) ×1 [20%]		146	169	23	113	130	130	80	999	90	—	—
Nightmare Frontier | **Strong**	494	1182	Thick Coldblood (6) ×1 [4%], Thick Coldblood (5) ×1 [16%], Thick Coldblood (4) ×1 [20%]		149	172	23	115	130	130	80	999	90		

Stronger version in second half of Nightmare Frontier.

Key Attacks

Name	Interrupt	Notes
Poison Gas	No	Large, slow-moving cloud of poison gas that travels slowly forward. Lasts five seconds; strafe or quickstep away in any direction.
Tentacle Combo	No	Frontal multi-hit combo with moderate forward momentum and tracking; quickstep sideways or forward.

Get behind the crawler to avoid the Poison Gas...

...and use a charged attack while it recovers.

Winter Lantern

Grotesque creatures with few attacks but a lethal gimmick, Winter Lanterns will constantly damage you and build up your frenzy meter with their gaze. This ability will affect you from absurd distances and cannot be avoided by any means other than putting an obstacle between yourself and your target, making it almost impossible to approach these enemies without taking damage; due to the danger of frenzy buildup, a full inventory of Sedatives is highly recommended when facing them. At close range they will exclusively use a running grab with a very wide hitbox; this attack carries them forward up to two meters and has decent tracking, requiring you to dodge as late as possible in order to avoid being hit at the end of a quickstep. Winter Lanterns have below-average defense and completely predictable attack patterns, making them incredibly easy to interrupt and stagger.

Strategy

Try to minimize the damage and frenzy buildup from their gaze by approaching them behind cover to the fullest possible extent, then hitting them with gunfire or thrown weapons and ducking back to safety as they navigate to you. Their Chewing Grab is the only melee attack they have, so once you have a sense of its timing you can reliably interrupt it and finish them with a visceral attack; you may also quickstep behind them when they perform it and let loose with R1 combos or stagger them with charged R2 swings, but take care not to dodge too early – there is a full second of delay between the initiation of their grab and its first active frames. While it is possible to temporarily stop their gaze attack by stabbing them with a Shaman Bone Blade, doing so is largely a waste – it will not cause their gaze to damage other enemies, and you could just as easily defeat them with an R1 combo in the time it takes to use the blade.

Basic Information

	■	✦	Item Drops	⬜	⬤	◭	✷	★	↻	♫	☠	▽	⤳	⤧
Nightmare Frontier	523	2759	Random Blood Gem based on Pthumeru Dungeon ×1 [33%], Quicksilver Bullets ×3 [62%], Pebble ×10 [5%]	89	89	89	89	70	70	70	70	450	—	—
Nightmare of Mensis	1408	10177	Random Blood Gem based on Pthumeru Dungeon ×1 [33%], Quicksilver Bullets ×3 [62%], Pebble ×10 [5%]	103	103	103	103	70	70	70	70	450		
Fishing Hamlet	1429	4514	Random gem based on dungeon ×1 [33%], Quicksilver Bullets ×3 [62%], Pebble ×10 [5%]	105	105	105	105	105	105	105	70	450		

Key Attacks

Name	Interrupt	Notes
Chewing Grab	Yes	Mid-range running grab with a wide hitbox that extends one meter to either side; quickstep forward past them as late as possible or backward twice as soon as they initiate it.
Malevolent Gaze	No	Inflicts constant damage and frenzy buildup while in their line of sight. Can only be avoided by breaking line of sight, but hitting them with a Shaman Bone Blade will temporarily negate it.

Avoid the Chewing Grab at all costs...

...and hit as hard as you can, becuase even with Sedatives, Frenzy is lethal.

Garden of Eyes

end of a short combo when you're stunned and less able to evade it; beware that the active frames of this attack begin late in its animation at the top of the leap, so you'll need to dodge about half a second after they initiate it. Carrying a large supply of Sedatives is a good idea when exploring Byrgenwerth; if you have none, you can obtain five from a corpse behind the closed gate to the patio.

Strategy

Simple but very dangerous enemies encountered at Byrgenwerth, these once-human test subjects were used by Provost Willem as living vessels for the cultivation of eyes. They attack with a limited set of very basic punches and slams, but inflict heavy damage and are capable of using a grab that inflicts a large amount of frenzy buildup. They are weak to most types of damage, especially elemental. These enemies are very aggressive and will constantly run you down, keeping you at close range and giving you as little room as possible to evade their grab. They can be interrupted and staggered, but the timing required to do so is quite precise. While they can perform the grab on its own, they will more frequently use it at the

Strafe or quickstep backward to avoid their combos and when they use their Flying Grab, quickstep sideways. Try to stay behind them, as none of their attacks will hit you there, although the tracking on their aerial grab is strong enough that you may still need to quickstep sideways if they use it. If you feel confident in your ability to interrupt their melee swings, do so and finish them with visceral attacks; otherwise stay behind them and use R1 combos or back off and chip away at them with ranged weapons. The Flamesprayer can be fired while walking, allowing you to strafe around them while dishing out heavy fire damage; you can also use it to counterattack after baiting them into swinging at you and strafing backward out of their reach.

Basic Information

	■	🏹	Item Drops	⬛	🌑	🔺	⚙	★	〰	◉	▽	⚡	〜
Byrgenwerth	910	945	Quicksilver Bullets ×4 [10%], Quicksilver Bullets ×3 [15%], Sedatives ×1 [5%]	104	104	104	104	42	72	68	999	999	—	—
Chalice Dungeon Base Level	285	110	Random gem based on area ×1 [20%], Quicksilver Bullets ×4 [25%], Quicksilver Bullets ×3 [51%], Pearl Slug ×1 [4%]	92	92	92	92	42	72	68	999	999		

Key Attacks

Name	Interrupt	Notes
Flying Grab	No	Aerial grab attack with strong tracking and slight forward momentum, often at the end of a melee combo; quickstep sideways or backward.
Two-Handed Slam	Yes	Heavy melee attack that will cause you to stumble; strafe or quickstep backward.

Trying to interrupt the Garden of Eyes is dangerous, but worthwhile.

The Flamesprayer can make short work of them.

Fluorescent Flower

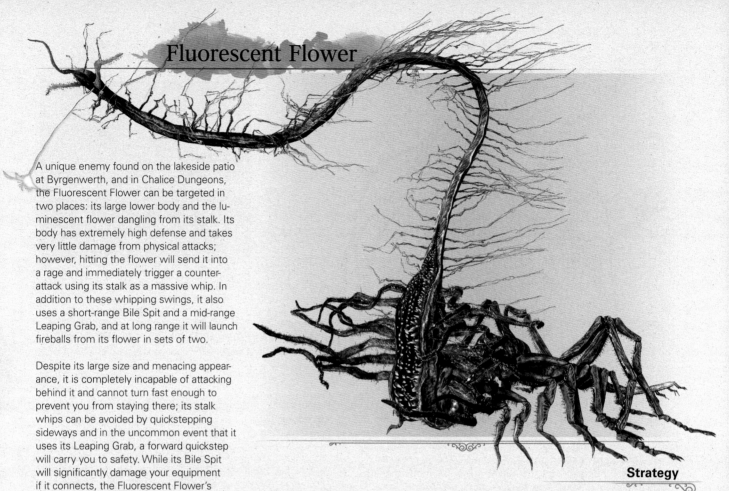

A unique enemy found on the lakeside patio at Byrgenwerth, and in Chalice Dungeons, the Fluorescent Flower can be targeted in two places: its large lower body and the luminescent flower dangling from its stalk. Its body has extremely high defense and takes very little damage from physical attacks; however, hitting the flower will send it into a rage and immediately trigger a counter-attack using its stalk as a massive whip. In addition to these whipping swings, it also uses a short-range Bile Spit and a mid-range Leaping Grab, and at long range it will launch fireballs from its flower in sets of two.

Despite its large size and menacing appearance, it is completely incapable of attacking behind it and cannot turn fast enough to prevent you from staying there; its stalk whips can be avoided by quickstepping sideways and in the uncommon event that it uses its Leaping Grab, a forward quickstep will carry you to safety. While its Bile Spit will significantly damage your equipment if it connects, the Fluorescent Flower's only truly dangerous move is its long-range Double Fireball; you'll need to approach it using the nearby pillars for cover or conceal your presence with a Blue Elixir in order to avoid being hit. Contrary to its venomous appearance, it is highly vulnerable to status ailments and can be poisoned by striking its flower with a single Poison Knife.

Strategy

You can use vertical attacks with overhead arcs such as the transformed L2 combo of Ludwig's Holy Blade to strike the flower directly, but doing so requires that you position yourself in harm's way; it's much safer to simply target the flower from farther away and kill the creature in a few shots from your pistol. If you have even one Poison Knife, you can throw it at the dangling flower to poison the entire enemy and simply take cover inside the university building until it dies. For a faster (though still slightly risky) kill, you can lure one or two of the nearby Garden of Eyes enemies toward the Fluorescent Flower and stab it with a Shaman Bone Blade, causing them to attack each other and often resulting in the flower's defeat.

Basic Information														
	■	⚶	Item Drops											
Byrgenwerth	758	1418	None		585	585	585	390	290	290	290	10	90	—	×
Chalice Dungeon Base Level	264	185	Arcane Haze ×3 [8%], Arcane Haze ×2 [30%], Arcane Haze ×1 [62%]		495	495	495	330	290	290	290	10	90		

Projectiles version: 342 Blood Echoes, drops random gem based on area ×1 [8%].
Preset Chalice Dungeons: Pthumerian Labyrinth, Lower Pthumerian Labyrinth, Pthumeru Ihyll

Key Attacks

Name	Interrupt	Notes
Double Fireball	No	Launches two long-range fireballs in quick succession. Fireballs do not track but travel quickly; roll or quickstep sideways.
Leaping Grab	No	Leaps forward four meters and performs a frontal grab; quickstep sideways.
Bile Spit	No	Close-range frontal projectile that creates a lingering pool of acid on the ground with a small spherical area of effect; strafe backwards.

Getting close is the hard part...

...you just need a single strong hit to the flower...

...and it'll be dead in no time.

Bell Ringer

Although weak and largely defenseless on their own, Bell Ringers will continuously summon other enemies until you locate and defeat them. Enemies summoned by Bell Ringers can be identified by their red auras and will receive defense bonuses until the Bell Ringer is killed. You'll hear the bell's telltale ring even if the Bell Ringer is located far away (which they usually are). Although tracking down each and every Bell Ringer might seem like a frustrating game of hide-and-seek, killing them is worth the trouble if you're trying to explore an area. Upon the Bell Ringer's death, all of the enemies under her control will grab their heads and stumble for several seconds; at this point they will lose their defense boosts and will no longer reappear when defeated. In dungeons, the Bell Ringer's death will instantly kill the enemies she has summoned. When you do manage to hunt down a Bell Ringer and force her into battle, she'll offer little resistance with weak swings and slow combos using her dagger. You're likely to cut her down before you ever see her Dark Mist attack, but if she uses it as you approach, simply back off until the darkness fades and then move in for the kill. Bell Ringers have low defense and health and are vulnerable to interrupts and staggers, making them equally susceptible to nearly any form of attack.

Strategy

Finding each Bell Ringer's hiding spot is the hard part – with that accomplished, there's not much they can do to stop you from painting the cobblestones with their innards. While it's a good idea to stay behind them in order to avoid their dagger slashes and combo attacks, they have very low super armor and a frontal R1 chain will prevent them from ever hitting you as long as your opening attack lands first. Thrown weapons or consumable items are a waste; melee weapons will get the job done faster and much more efficiently.

Basic Information

	⬛	⬥	Item Drops										
Yahar'gul (Blood Moon)	518	901	Quicksilver Bullets ×3 [30%], Quicksilver Bullets ×2 [70%]	89	89	89	89	45	68	72	250	300	—	—
Yahar'gul (Blood Moon) | Boss support (red robe)	345	901	Quicksilver Bullets ×3 [3%], Quicksilver Bullets ×2 [7%]	89	89	89	89	45	68	72	250	300		
Chalice Dungeon Base Level	211	114	Quicksilver Bullets ×3 [30%], Quicksilver Bullets ×2 [70%]	73	73	73	73	45	68	72	250	300		
Hunter's Nightmare	1036	710	None	90	90	90	90	52	93	99	250	300		
Research Hall	1147	2287	None	94	94	94	94	54	96	102	250	300		
Fishing Hamlet	1191	1042	None	99	99	99	99	57	102	108	250	300		

Preset Chalice Dungeons: Pthumerian Labyrinth, Central Pthumerian Labyrinth, Hintertomb, Lower Pthumerian Labyrinth, Lower Pthumerian Labyrinth, Ailing Loran, Lower Loran

Key Attacks

Name	Interrupt	Notes
Sinister Summon	No	Continually spawns regular enemies. Summoned enemies will receive a massive defense boost until the summoner is killed.
Dark Mist	No	Circular area attack with a six-meter radius; quickstep backward or strafe out of the effect area.

Bell Ringers are always the highest priority target...

...so get in there quickly and take her down.

Cramped Casket

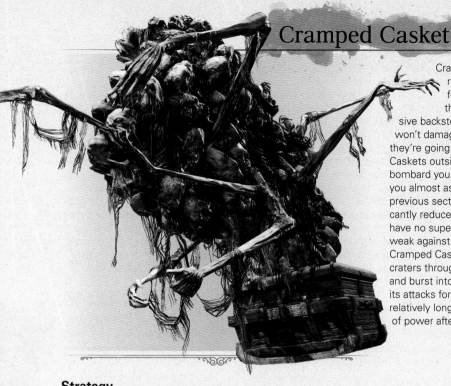

Cramped Caskets attack quickly and have enormous range; they use rapid punch combos, arm slams and forward body presses. They respond to attacks from their sides or rear with either a Heavy Sweep or a defensive backstep, repositioning them to face you. Since the backstep won't damage you, you should always play it safe and assume they're going to use the sweep instead. Some of the Cramped Caskets outside the boss area in Yahar'gul (2nd visit) will constantly bombard you with Rotting Spears, even at close range. They'll spot you almost as soon as you pass through the gateway from the previous section of town, though you can use a Blue Elixir to significantly reduce their detection range. Fortunately, Cramped Caskets have no super armor and are vulnerable to stunlocks; they're also weak against bolt damage, and three Molotovs will kill them. If a Cramped Casket touches one of the burning corpses situated in craters throughout the streets of Yahar'gul it will take heavy damage and burst into flames, drastically reducing its speed and weakening its attacks for sixty seconds; while this provides an advantage for a relatively long period of time, beware that each corpse will run out of power after being touched several times.

Strategy

Stay beside or behind them and use single R1 attacks with a transformed weapon; you'll need to constantly watch for a Heavy Sweep, but with close attention to the enemy and a little patience you'll wear them down fairly quickly. If you have a heavier weapon with a far-reaching charge attack such as Ludwig's Holy Blade or the Hunter Axe, you can back off and begin charging an R2 strike as the Cramped Casket approaches; if you time the charge so that it activates just as the enemy enters your range, it will inflict heavy damage and stun the target long enough for you to quickstep away and recover your stamina to repeat the process. The Flamesprayer

is particularly useful against these foes due to your ability to walk backward while firing it; by using it in this manner while a Cramped Casket moves toward you, you'll inflict continuous damage while it's committed to an attack that can no longer reach you. Aim to lure them toward the nearest burning corpse, then finish them while they're weakened. If you allow a Cramped Casket to stay in the corpse's effect area, it will continue taking damage but will deplete the corpse's energy. As there are fewer of these corpses than there are Cramped Caskets, it's better to do this only once per enemy, so that you can use a single corpse to weaken multiple opponents.

Basic Information

			Item Drops											
Yahar'gul (Blood Moon)	864	1455	Random Hunter gem ×1 [8%], Random Kinhunter gem ×1 [8%]	211	162	97	162	67	67	67	200	180	—	—
Chalice Dungeon Base Level	264	197	Random Hunter or Kinhunter gem ×1 [8%]	180	139	83	139	67	67	67	200	180		

Key Attacks

Name	Interrupt	Notes
Assimilating Grab	No	Extremely swift close-range grab attack. Too fast to avoid on reaction; stay out of its reach if possible.
Heavy Sweep	No	Fast, 180-degree body sweep with clockwise and counterclockwise versions; quickstep backward or sideways.
Rotting Spear	No	Used only by Cramped Caskets outside the boss area. Launches a spear of bone as a linear ranged attack. Quickstep sideways or use obstacles to block it.

If the Cramped Casket touches the burning corpse it will take damage...

...making finishing it off much easier.

Large Nightmare Apostle

Giant spider-like enemy hanging from a web just inside the Mensis keep. It will remain in its web until you get too close or hit it with a ranged attack, allowing you to knock down some of the smaller Nightmare Apostles with Throwing Knives and thin their numbers before engaging it. It's too large to fit through either the keep entrance or the smaller doorway to the right, so you can trap it at either of these choke points and bombard it with ranged attacks from the other side. In close combat the Large Nightmare Apostle swings or jabs its long legs forward; while it can hit behind it with its Reverse Dark Sphere, it cannot strike directly to its sides. It has average physical defense, but is slightly weak against blunt attacks and cannot be interrupted or staggered; despite its spidery appearance it is susceptible to poison and is also affected by Shaman Bone Blades, six of which can be found on a corpse leaning against the far wall directly behind it. A Cannon shot, boosted with Bone Marrow Ash, can make dealing with this enemy much easier, and can decimate the smaller apostles if any of them wander into the area of effect.

Strategy

First, eliminate as many of the smaller ones as possible, by knocking them down one by one with Throwing Knives (the Monocular can help with this) and luring them into the entrance antechamber to fight. When only the large apostle remains, climb the steps to the right of the entrance and eliminate the small apostles in the hall, then proceed through the doorway onto the bridge behind the large apostle. You can attack it a few times while it's still hanging in the web, so make the most of the opportunity and hit it with a Bone Marrow Ash Cannon shot. While it is possible to continue raining attacks down on the large apostle from the bridge, beware that it can still hit you there with its overhead leg stabs and the bridge itself will often obstruct your ranged weapons. If you plan to abuse the large apostle's size by getting it stuck in a doorway through which it can't fit, use the keep entrance –many of the apostle's attacks will pass over your head there. From the relative safety of the antechamber, you can strike with ranged attacks; however, be sure you actually have enough ammunition to kill the apostle before taking up this position, since getting back into the keep with a giant spider occupying the entrance is a tricky proposition.

Alternately, you can immediately head for the bridge while eliminating only the small apostles directly blocking your path, then drop down behind the large apostle and stab it with a Shaman Bone Blade as it descends from the web. This will turn all of the smaller apostles against it, almost certainly resulting in its death; it will usually take out a few of the smaller ones in the process, making this a highly effective strategy provided you make a swift exit immediately after stabbing the large apostle.

Basic Information

Basic Information	■	⚔	Item Drops	🌑	🌓	⌁	✸	★	🔥	♫	☠	▽	⚒	↯
Nightmare of Mensis	2294	3403	Quicksilver Bullets ×8 [27%]	150	90	150	150	165	75	160	250	180	—	—
Chalice Dungeon Base Level	529	282	Quicksilver Bullets ×8 [27%]	121	73	121	121	165	75	160	250	180		

Key Attacks

Name	Interrupt	Notes
Dark Sphere	No	Spherical area attack with a three-meter radius; quickstep backward.
Reverse Dark Sphere	No	Fires three orbs of darkness directly backward; quickstep sideways.
Leg Combo	No	Alternating leg swings ending with a long-range forward stab; quickstep forward past it when it rears up.

If you must fight up close, stay to its side.

You can always run to safety, because it can't fit through this opening.

Mergo's Chief Attendant

Simple but tough, chief attendants fight using slow combos and single blows with their giant axes and chain flails. All of their attacks inflict rapid poison build-up, but most are heavily telegraphed and very easy to interrupt; their slower axe attacks, such as the Guillotine Slam, also leave plenty of time to stagger them from behind with a charged R2 swing. They have a lot of health, and high physical defense. Combining blunt or thrust attacks with bolt damage is a good idea, making Tonitrus an ideal choice. Chief attendants cannot strike behind them, making this the safest place to stand given their slow movement and attacks. Beware that they always appear in the vicinity of smaller attendants equipped with various weapons, and watch your surroundings carefully to avoid being ambushed; if you've already cleared a safe spot to which you can fall back, try to lure them there rather than fighting them out in the open.

Strategy

Visceral attacks are the most effective means of defeating chief attendants, especially when they use their slow axe attacks. Stand just outside the range of their chain whips and wait for them to swing, then interrupt them; alternately, quickstep behind them when they use a slow move like the Guillotine Slam and use R1 combos or stagger them with charged R2 strikes. The attacks that inflict rapid poison build-up are slow and can be avoided by quickstepping forward or to the side. When fighting the Chief Attendants in the prison area beneath the lift bridge, be careful not to quickstep into one of the pits in the area, and beware of the smaller attendants armed with crossbows, as their bolts will also build up your rapid poison meter.

Basic Information

			Item Drops											
Nightmare of Mensis	1529	1843	Random Dirty Blood Gem ×1 [30%]	252	101	101	168	85	77	50	200	300	—	—

Key Attacks

Name	Interrupt	Notes
Guillotine Slam	Yes	Frontal downward chop with the axe held lengthwise; strafe backward or quickstep forward.
Chain Whip	Yes	Mid-range whip attack with the chain flail in their left hand; can be repeated or alternated with axe attacks. Quickstep sideways or backward.

THe Guillotine Slam is lethal, but easily evaded.

Trying to interrupt from a short distance away is by far the best strategy.

Shadows of Yharnam

These non-boss versions of the Shadows of Yharnam are encountered in the Rooftop area of Mergo's Loft in the Nightmare of Mensis. They have considerably less health and defense compared to boss versions, and they'll only use from Phase 1 of the boss fight so you don't have to worry about them transforming and using any of their snake attacks. Both of the versions that carry swords are limited to basic swings, but the one carrying the candle can still perform a basic fire breath attack so you'll need to keep an eye out for it. The attacks from the mace-carrying Shadow are extremely slow (and in some cases deliberately delayed), and that makes them predictable and easy to interrupt. Because both of their basic fireball attacks have respectable range and can knock you down if they connect, however, they do still pose the biggest threat and should be targeted first if possible. Since you'll often encounter these enemies in groups, if you have a Shaman Bone Blade you should try to hit the mace carrying Shadow with it and let him take out the other enemies for you. All of the Shadows are also quite agile so ranged attacks are generally ineffective once they've been alerted to your presence, but since they lack super armor, fighting them up close is much more effective anyway.

Shadow of Yharnam (Sword)

Either lure them one at a time using Pebbles or Throwing Knives and slice them to death with R1 combos, or lure several at once and mow them down with a powered-up Cannon shot or Flamesprayer burst. Their sword attacks can be interrupted relatively easily and their combos leave enough time for you to stagger them from behind if you respond quickly enough; try to stay behind them where they'll have difficulty hitting you while you launch your attack. You can also lure them toward one of the Maneater Boars that appear near their patrol routes and bait it into attacking them, or stab them with a Shaman Bone Blade and stand back as they slaughter one another.

Basic Information	■	✦	Item Drops					★						
Nightmare of Mensis	1095	2492	Blood Vial ×3 [20%], Blood Vial ×2 [20%]	108	108	108	108	60	90	68	200	180	—	—
Chalice Dungeon Base Level	246	143	Blood Vial ×3 [15%], Blood Vial ×2 [15%], Ritual material B ×1 [15%]	79	79	79	79	60	90	68	200	180		

Key Attacks

Name	Interrupt	Notes
Upward Slash	Yes	Quick upward slash that will launch you if it connects; interrupt it or quickstep sideways.
Sword Combo	Yes	Rapid combo of up to five slashes; quickstep backward.

Shadow of Yharnam (Sword & Candle)

Handle it in the same way as the variant armed only with a sword by interrupting its sword attacks, or staggering it from behind after evading an attack. Its fire breath has a long windup and hitting it with a gunshot or thrown weapon during the animation will cancel the attack; you can use this technique as an opportunity to dart in and strike with melee attacks, but beware that the shadow will turn to face you while blowing flames in your direction. If you manage to get behind it while it's still blowing flames, however, you'll have plenty of time to get some hits in.

Basic Information

			Item Drops										
Nightmare of Mensis	1095	2492	Blood Vial ×3 [20%], Quicksilver Bullets ×3 [20%]	108	108	108	108	60	100	68	200	180	—	—
Chalice Dungeon Base Level	246	131	Blood Vial ×3 [15%], Quicksilver Bullets ×3 [15%], Ritual material B ×1 [15%]	79	79	79	79	60	100	68	200	180		

Key Attacks

Name	Interrupt	Notes
Upward Slash	Yes	Quick upward slash that will launch you if it connects; interrupt it or quickstep sideways.
Sword Combo	Yes	Rapid combo of up to five slashes; quickstep backward.
Fire Breath	No	Short-range frontal fire breath with directional tracking; quickstep backward.

Once they start using their Fire Breath, begin strafing around them...

...and land a charged attack from behind, for a visceral attack follow-up.

Shadow of Yharnam (Mace & Fireball)

Be careful of its fireball attacks if there are other shadows nearby; trying to fight the sword-wielders while being bombarded with fireballs can quickly get out of hand and result in death. This variant in particular is a good candidate for Shaman Bone Blades, as using one on it without being detected can cause it to incinerate its allies before they figure out that it's turned against them; you can also lure it toward the nearby Maneater Boars and let them handle the heavy lifting for you. If you want to be safe, it's best to use a Pebble to lure it away from any other enemies, and they stay close to it and try to interrupt one of its mace swings.

Basic Information

			Item Drops										
Nightmare of Mensis	1095	2285	Blood Vial ×3 [20%], Quicksilver Bullets ×3 [20%]	108	108	108	108	160	90	160	200	180	—	—
Chalice Dungeon Base Level	246	160	Blood Vial ×3 [15%], Quicksilver Bullets ×3 [15%], Ritual material B ×1 [15%]	79	79	79	79	160	90	160	200	180		

Key Attacks

Name	Interrupt	Notes
Triple Homing Fireball	No	Launches three long-range homing fireballs; quickstep sideways or forward through them.
Triple Raining Fireball	No	Throws three fireballs in an overhead arc. Fireballs converge on your location as they descend; quickstep backward or sideways.

Brain of Mensis

The Brain of Mensis hangs in the tower in the middle of the bridge between the keep and Mergo's Loft. It will continuously assault you with its gaze while you are outside the castle. You can approach it on an upper section of the bridge and strike it with ranged attacks, but it is completely invincible at this point and cannot be defeated by normal means.

Strategy

3

To destroy the brain, you'll need to jump out of one of the shortcut elevators to access a hidden path and pull the lever at the other end; this will release the chains from which it's suspended and drop it out of the tower, freeing the area from its damaging gaze. After the boss fight with Micolash, a cage elevator will descend to the prison area on the ground floor directly below the lift bridge; by riding this elevator, you can reach the now-helpless brain and destroy it. It will no longer be able to use its gaze attack after falling from the tower and has no other means of fighting back, so you can simply walk up and beat it to death with no opposition.

Basic Information				Item Drops		▢	◉	◗	✦	★	⬮	⌐	☠	▽	⌁	⟋
Nightmare of Mensis	**9387**	✈ **2181**		Living String [100%]		236	142	142	236	290	290	290	999	999	—	—

Key Attacks

Name	Interrupt	Notes
Evil Eye	No	Line-of-sight gaze attack that constantly damages you and rapidly builds up your frenzy meter; break line of sight or pull the lever to drop the brain out of its tower.

Pulling this lever will finally rid you of the Brain of Mensis.

Make Contact, then use your most powerful attack to finish the Brain off.

Watcher Chieftains

As slow as are they powerful, these brutes use purely melee attacks. They use a variety of combos, almost all with a slow build-up, making them easy to interrupt. If you stand a short distance away from them, they'll often use their Running Overhead Slam, which is one of their faster moves. It can be avoided by quickstepping to the side just as they begin running. While their club attacks are slow, swings from their lanterns are not, and they can hit you almost instantly during their Club & Lamp Combo so be careful if you're standing within the lantern's range. They'll tend finish the combo regardless of the distance you stand from them, so you may need to use a couple of quicksteps to evade the whole thing.

Chieftains with heated clubs share all of the same attacks as the other variant, but have a few extra moves in their repertoire. Although they may look threatening, they'll inflict far less damage compared to other Watchers, even with the added fire effect on their club. From the edge of their reach they will most commonly use their Double Jab, and after each jab they will momentarily hold their club outward to bait you into walking into its scorching base. This is your best chance to interrupt them for a visceral attack since this attack can be interrupted the entire time the club is held out.

Their overhead combo is almost identical to the other variant's three-hit overhead combo, but instead ends with a single jab, which is also briefly held out outwards. When standing close to or against them, they'll use their Lantern Smack; although this will inflict minimal damage, it may open you to being hit by a follow-up attack, so it's best to avoid standing too close to them. Like the other club-wielding variant, when behind them they will occasionally use a Backside Swing, which you can quickstep backwards to avoid, once you see them raise their to ready the attack.

The Watcher Chieftain left a bit too much exposed.

This is the ideal range for baiting an attack.

Watcher Chieftain (Club & Lantern)

Use a fire weapon, or apply some Fire Paper and aim to stay just outside their reach, so that they'll use one of their combos. Once they do, you can either try to interrupt one of the attacks, or wait for it to miss and begin an attack of your own as they recover. Against most of their attacks, such as the Two-hand Overhead Smash, you can also quickstep towards them to pass through the attack, leaving the Watcher open long enough for a quickly-charged attack from behind. This also takes the range of their attacks out of the equation; the Two-hand Overhead Smash has deceptively long range, and can easily hit you even after a backdash. As long as you are sure the attack they use isn't a combo-starter it's safe to quickstep through their attacks to position yourself at their back, and then land one or two quick attacks before moving away again to avoid their Backside Swing. Their slow movement speed also makes them quite susceptible to ranged attacks and you can use them to whittle down their health as they slowly close in on you.

Basic Information

			Item Drops											
Chalice Dungeon Base Level	555	316	Random gem based on area ×1 [25%], Blood Vial ×3 [30%], Quicksilver Bullets ×4 [25%], Ritual material B ×1 [20%]	131	71	119	119	49	69	162	200	180	—	—
Chalice Dungeon Base Level | Boss	793	1126	None	131	71	119	119	48	69	162	200	180	—	—

Preset Chalice Dungeons: Pthumerian Labyrinth, Pthumerian Labyrinth (Boss), Central Pthumerian Labyrinth, Lower Pthumerian Labyrinth, Lower Pthumerian Labyrinth (Boss), Pthumeru Ihyll

Key Attacks

Name	Interrupt	Notes
Two-hand Overhead Smash	Yes	Interrupt the long windup, or quickstep past this and use charged attacks from behind.
Overhead Swing Combo	Yes	Three delayed one-handed overhead swings; quickstep through it.
Club Combo		Two downward swings followed an upward third; quickstep through it.
Club & Lamp Combo	Yes	Up to five hits; quickstep backwards and interrupt this while backing up.
Running Overhead Slam	Yes	Used when standing at mid range ahead; quickstep to either side as early as possible, or interrupt it.
Backside Swing	Yes	Used at close range from either side or behind; quickstep back once the Chieftain draws its arm back.

Watcher Chieftain (Heated Club & Lantern)

The most effective way to deal with these enemies is to stay about three meters away and wait for them to attack; they will almost exclusively use their Double Jab from this range, despite you being out of its reach. This opens them to be repeatedly interrupted, allowing you to use visceral attacks or charged R2 attacks to end the encounter quickly. When tackling them head on, treat them as you would the other variant of Watcher Chieftains; apply a Fire Paper to your weapon before approaching them, quickstep through their attacks, then position yourself behind them to attack.

Basic Information

			Item Drops											
Chalice Dungeon Base Level	555	316	Random gem based on area ×1 [25%], Blood Vial ×3 [30%], Quicksilver Bullets ×4 [25%], Ritual material B ×1 [20%]	131	71	119	119	49	69	162	200	180	—	—

Preset Chalice Dungeons: Pthumerian Labyrinth, Lower Pthumerian Labyrinth, Cursed Pthumerian Defilement

Key Attacks

Name	Interrupt	Notes
Double Jab	Yes	Two outward jabs, both briefly held in place to bait you walking into it; quickstep though this to position yourself behind them or interrupt it.
Lantern Smack	Yes	Fast, close-range attack; avoid standing close for too long and quickstep backward.
Walking Two-hand Thrust	Yes	Groans before walking forward and thrusting with both hands held briefly out to bait you walking into it; repeatedly quickstep back to avoid its tracking.
Overhead Swing & Jab Combo	Yes	Two delayed one-handed overheads followed by a jab; quickstep through it.
Running Overhead Slam	Yes	Used when standing at mid range ahead; quickstep to either side early as possible, or interrupt it.
Backside Swing	Yes	Used at close range from either side or behind; quickstep back once they draw their arm back.

Shoot as they approach to weaken them.

Molotovs and other long range options are reliable for wearing them down.

Merciless Watchers

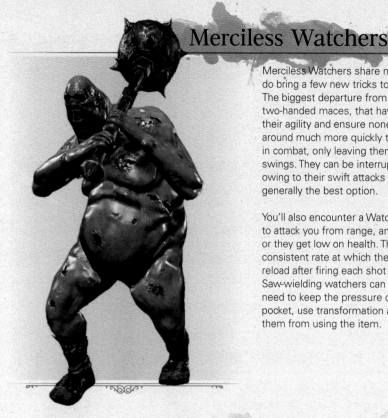

Merciless Watchers share much in common with Watcher Chieftains, but they do bring a few new tricks to the table that you're going to need to watch out for. The biggest departure from the Chieftains are the Watchers equipped with large two-handed maces, that have also decided to ditch their heavy grab to increase their agility and ensure none of their movements are restricted. These variants move around much more quickly than the others, and will roll continuously when engaged in combat, only leaving themselves vulnerable during the recovery periods after their swings. They can be interrupted and staggered, but doing so is extremely difficult owing to their swift attacks and constant rolling, so sticking to quick R1 strikes is generally the best option.

You'll also encounter a Watcher that comes armed with a scattergun that it will use to attack you from range, and will only switch to their clubs once you get close, or they get low on health. Their gunshots are predictable, due to the slow and consistent rate at which they're fired, and they are completely vulnerable as they reload after firing each shot so this is your best chance to close in and attack them. Saw-wielding watchers can use recovery items to fully restore their health, so you'll need to keep the pressure on them. Once you see them reach for their left side pocket, use transformation attacks to quickly break their super armor and prevent them from using the item.

Merciless Watcher (Mace)

To inflict optimal damage in an extremely short period of time, hit them with short bursts of Flamesprayer or Rosmarinus fire as they roll or while they recover after attacking. Striking them with repeated melee swings is difficult due to their continuous rolling, but you'll have brief opportunities to use R1 combos after most of their attacks. When you're within reach of their melee attacks, they'll often perform a Rolling Overhead Swing or Front Flip Slam immediately after recovering from a roll. The Front Flip Slam has a longer recovery period and leaves them open to charged attacks from behind. At short range, they will use a slow Overhead Swing with strong tracking and up to two delayed follow-up strikes; the animation on this attack is heavily telegraphed so look to interrupt it. From slightly further out they tend to favor the Running Underhand Swing, which they can delay for up to a second to trick you into dodging too early, so it's much safer to try and interrupt it.

Basic Information

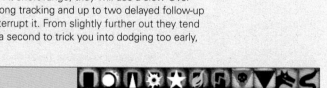

	■	⚶	Item Drops											
Chalice Dungeon Base Level	555	316	Random gem based on area ×1 [25%], Blood Vial ×3 [30%], Quicksilver Bullets ×4 [25%], Ritual material B ×1 [20%]	131	71	119	119	49	69	162	200	180	—	—

Preset Chalice Dungeons: Pthumerian Labyrinth, Cursed Pthumerian Defilement, Pthumeru Ihyll

Key Attacks

Name	Interrupt	Notes
Back Slam	Yes	Quick startup but long recovery; quickstep away from their rolls and get behind for a charged attack.
Front Flip Slam	Yes	Usually used after close-range rolls; very fast with a long recovery. Quickstep away and circle behind for a charged attack during the recovery.
Overhead Swing	Yes	Easiest to interrupt; slow windup with good tracking followed by two more delayed overhead swings. Quickstep away and interrupt the follow-ups.
Running Overhead Swing	Yes	Delayed startup; quickstep behind it and attack during its recovery.
Rolling Overhead Swing	Yes	Quick vertical swing sometimes used after rolling; quickstep to either side and attack during its recovery.
Slow Sweeping Combo	Yes	Frontal 180-degree arc with short reach; quickstep backward to avoid.
Rapid Sweeping Combo	Yes	Quickstep backward to escape or forward to position yourself behind them; attack from behind while they continue the combo.
Running Underhand Swing	Yes	Drags club on ground and performs upward swing with strong tracking; quickstep left to avoid it.

Merciless Watcher (Scattergun, Club & Lantern)

Since you'll have to contend with incoming fire while you approach this enemy, make sure to make use of any available cover in the area, and then close in while they're reloading. Once you're inside their gun range they will start attacking you with their lantern, but since this attack does a negligible amount of damage, you can just keep attacking them and easily recover the health. If you're attacks are doing decent damage you can often kill them before they can pull their club out, and if you're having trouble doing that, you may want to use some Fire Paper to increase your damage when going up against these enemies. Look to bait them into using their Two-hand Overhead Club Smash after they pull their club out by standing at the edge of their reach; once you see the attack coming, quickstep through it and attack them from behind.

Basic Information	◼	♠	Item Drops										
Chalice Dungeon Base Level	555	316	Random gem based on area ×1 [25%], Blood Vial ×3 [30%], Quicksilver Bullets ×4 [25%], Ritual material B ×1 [20%]	131	71	119	119	49	69	162	200	180	—	—
Chalice Dungeon Base Level | Boss	1058	1126	None	131	71	119	119	48	69	162	200	180		

Preset Chalice Dungeons: Pthumerian Labyrinth, Pthumerian Labyrinth (Boss), Central Pthumerian Labyrinth, Lower Pthumerian Labyrinth, Lower Pthumerian Labyrinth (Boss), Pthumeru Ihyll

Key Attacks

Name	Interrupt	Notes
Scatter Shot	Yes	Quickstep through the shot and attack while they are reloading.
Lantern Smack	Yes	Same attack used by the heated club Watcher Chieftain; avoid standing against them too long while they are using their scattergun.
Two-hand Overhead Club Smash	Yes	Same attack used by the club & lantern Watcher; best chance to interrupt this enemy.
Overhead Swing Combo	Yes	Up to three hits, same one used by the club & lantern Watcher Chieftain; quickstep past this to their back and attack.
Club & Lamp Combo	Yes	Same five hit combo used by the club & lantern Watcher; quickstep backwards and interrupt this while backing up.
Backside Swing	Yes	Same close-range attack used by the club & lantern Watcher; from either side or behind; quickstep back as they draw their arm back.
Running Overhead Slam	Yes	Same attack used by the club & lantern Watcher; interrupt this or quickstep to either side.

Merciless Watcher (Saw)

These enemies are aggressive and powerful, but their low mobility and complete lack of long-ranged attacks make them incredibly vulnerable to throwing items from a distance. From close range, they will use their Sawing Combo, Overhead Cleave & Sawing Combo, and Two-Hand Swings; all of their attacks should be avoided by quickstepping forward through them, or back away from them rather than to the sides because of their tracking. If you choose to backstep away from an attack, you'll often be able to interrupt the subsequent hits of their combo, and if you went forward through it, you'll have amble time to hit them in their back before they recover.

Basic Information	◼	♠	Item Drops										
Chalice Dungeon Base Level | Boss	1058	1126	None	131	71	119	119	48	69	162	200	180	—	—
Chalice Dungeon Base Level	1058	1126	None	131	71	119	119	48	69	162	200	180		

Preset Chalice Dungeons: Pthumerian Labyrinth (Boss), Lower Pthumerian Labyrinth, Lower Pthumerian Labyrinth (Boss), Cursed Pthumerian Defilement, Pthumeru Ihyll

Key Attacks

Name	Interrupt	Notes
Sawing Combo	Yes	Seven hit Frontal repeated sawing attack; quickstep through it.
Overhead Cleave & Sawing Combo	Yes	Up to six hit combo, cleaves overhead and saws repeatedly, then repeats this in the reverse order; quickstep back and interrupt the subsequent hits.
Side Swings	Yes	Used when standing to either of their sides; quickstep left so the second swing goes over your head, or quickstep back to interrupt it.
Two-hand Swings	Yes	Quickstep back and out of range, the second attack will usually be canceled once you are out of reach.
Health Restoration Item	No	Quickly pulls an item from their pocket when low on health and eats it, completely restoring their health.
Running Overhead Slam	Yes	Same attack used by the club & lantern Watcher; interrupt this or quickstep to either side.

Evil Labyrinth Spirit

Evil Labyrinth Spirits make their presence known through their laughter, which can be heard from a distance. Once they've spotted you, they will aggressively chase you while flailing their knife, screaming. Their attacks are simple and lacking in range, though they inflict Frenzy build-up, which is enough to make them a real threat. Their long combos also carry them forward a good distance. They will attack with a variety of stabs and slashes, all of which are easily avoided by retreating away from them. Their Running Stab is the lone exception, and will need to be avoided by quickstepping to either side, or forwards in order to behind them. Occasionally they will disappear into a puff of smoke and appear behind you for a surprise attack, though as long as you avoid standing still, their surprise attacks after reappearing will almost never reach you.

Strategy

Far-reaching attacks will make short work of this enemy – the Rifle Spear and Ludwig's Holy Blade are especially effective against Evil Labyrinth Spirits; their thrust attacks can be used to hit them from outside of their reach, and Ludwig's Holy Blade also has a special attack bonus against kin. If there is a ladder in the room they reside in, lead them up it and drop back down, so that you can attack them while they are still climbing. You can also quickstep through their attacks to get behind them and perform a charged attack, though a simple R1 combo will often serve to kill them.

Basic Information																	
Special Weakness: Righteous																	
Chalice Dungeon Base Level	**185**	**112**	Item Drops Random gem based on area ×1 [8%]					380	380	380	380	75	75	75	999	999	–	–

Preset Chalice Dungeons: Central Pthumerian Labyrinth, Hintertomb, Cursed Pthumerian Defilement, Pthumeru Ihyll

Key Attacks

Name	Interrupt	Notes
Shoulder Charge	Yes	Best chance to perform an interrupt; otherwise quickstep forward or sideways.
Brick Combo	Yes	Multiple hits with individual tracking; quickstep forward or sideways.
Downward Slam	Yes	Close-range, long windup; quickstep forward past them.
Turnaround Swing	Yes	Short-range 360-degree spin attack; strafe or quickstep backward.

Lure them into climbng ladders to attack them freely.

Quickstepping through their attacks gives you a chance for an R1 combo.

Labyrinth Madmen

Labyrinth Madmen are extremely fast and aggressive enemies that come sprinting towards you while flailing attacks as soon as they spot you. They have excellent vision and can spot you from a considerable distance away, so it's important to listen out for the shrill scream they make as they run because they can cover that distance very quickly. Twin sickle-wielding madmen can inflict a tremendous amount of damage and their rapid attacks give you only brief openings in which to hit them. This threat is compounded by the fact that they are not easily flinched, even with heavy weapons, so you'll only ever get the chance to hit them once or twice before having to back off.

Single sickle Madmen are slightly less aggressive than those with two, and they tend not to run around as much once they're close to you. The key differences, however, are their lower amount of super armor, which means they're much easier to deal with once you start attacking them, and the fact that they'll occasionally decide to walk around slowly without attacking, allowing you to regain stamina or heal. Unlike other enemies, it's also recommended that you do not to try and stay behind them while attacking because many of their attacks reach far behind them. In a macabre display, the final type of Madman carries a rotting corpse in both hands which is used as a surprisingly effective weapon. Each attack from these enemies emits a small cloud of toxic fumes that cause large amounts of rapid poison buildup, making them incredibly dangerous.

Labyrinth Madman (Twin Sickles)

The short range on their attacks is this enemy's main weakness, and it's something you'll need to take full advantage of when fighting them. Using a weapon with long reach will help a lot, allowing you to keep even further back from them and reduce the odds of getting hit. Most of their attacks can be evaded by simply walking backwards away from them, which will then let you attack them once or twice during their recovery. The main exception to this is the Jumping Overhead Slash that they use while running; if you see this attack coming, either quickstep to the side and get a couple of hits in, or try to interrupt it for a damaging visceral attack.

Basic Information														
	■ 370	⚔ 246	Item Drops		128	128	128	128	76	52	34	120	180	✕	—
Chalice Dungeon Base Level	370	246	Random gem based on area ×1 [25%], Quicksilver Bullets ×5 [15%], Quicksilver Bullets ×4 [45%], Ritual material F ×1 [15%]												

Preset Chalice Dungeons: Hintertomb, Lower Hintertomb, Ailing Loran

Key Attacks

Name	Interrupt	Notes
Running Diagonal Overhead Slash	Yes	Often used while running. Quickstep backward to dodge this.
Jumping Overhead Slash	Yes	Quick and high damage attack commonly used while running. Quickstep to either side to avoid its forward momentum.
Diagonal Overhead Slash	Yes	High damage but has long buildup and recovery; quickstep backward.

The Rifle Spear can stop them in their tracks.

Quickstep around the Jumping Overhead Slash and retaliate with a fast attack.

Labyrinth Madman (Sickle)

Unlike the madmen wielding two sickles, you can cause this enemy to flinch relatively easily by using quick üs, and this can be an especially effective tactic if you're using weapons with long reach such as the Rifle Spear. One of their more commonly used attacks Overhead Swinging Combo, which ends with a heavily delayed third hit to bait you walking into it; if you evade the first two hits, it's worth trying to interrupt the last one since it has such a lengthy animation. From close range they may use up to two kicks; although these will do little damage, they are fast and hard to evade, so if you get hit with one it's important to be slightly defensive in case they're using it to setup another attack. When using shorter weapons, quickstep past and through their attacks and hit their backs a few times before quickstepping backward to get away from them before they can turn around and attack again.

Basic Information			Item Drops										
	■	✈		128	128	128	128	76	52	34	120	180	✕	—
Chalice Dungeon Base Level	370	246	Random gem based on area ×1 [25%], Quicksilver Bullets ×5 [15%], Quicksilver Bullets ×4 [45%], Ritual material F ×1 [15%]										

Preset Chalice Dungeons: Hintertomb, Lower Hintertomb, Ailing Loran, Lower Loran

Key Attacks

Name	Interrupt	Notes
Running Overhead Slash	Yes	Quickstep forward past this to avoid its sideways tracking.
Double Sweep	Yes	Slower and hard hitting two hit combo. Quickstep backward.
Overhead Swinging Combo	Yes	Short range three hit combo with a heavily delayed third hit. Quickstep back and away from this.

Labyrinth Madman (Corpse)

Take advantage of their elemental weaknesses and apply a Fire or Bolt Paper to your weapon from a safe distance before moving in. Poisoning is easiest way to deal with them since it will only take two Poison Knives to inflict the status, and they will be almost stationary during their attacks. For fighting them with melee weapons, quickstep backward out of their attacks and hit them once or twice during their recoveries the same as you would the other madmen. If they use their Overhead Slam Combo you can quickstep through the first swing and position yourself behind for a charged attack, but avoid quickstepping through their other attacks because their heavy overhead tracking and wide sweeps will generally catch you.

Basic Information			Item Drops										
	■	✈		128	128	128	128	76	52	34	120	180	✕	—
Chalice Dungeon Base Level	370	246	Random gem based on area ×1 [25%], Quicksilver Bullets ×5 [15%], Quicksilver Bullets ×4 [45%], Ritual material F ×1 [15%]										

Preset Chalice Dungeons: Lower Hintertomb, Ailing Loran, Lower Loran

Key Attacks

Name	Interrupt	Notes
Overhead Slam Combo	Yes	Slams the corpse ahead letting out poison fumes, then hits again as it is swung back for another overhead slam; quickstep through and past them during the first swing..
Running Overhead Swing	Yes	Quickstep forward past this while they are running.
Toxic Swing	Yes	Low reaching swing which emits a large cloud of poison fumes. Quickstep backward

Undead Giant (Hatchet & Cannon)

These hulking monstrosities have a large hatchet fused to their left arm, and a dangerous cannon chained to their right arm. Occasionally they are found with a large pink growth which can be attacked for massive amounts of damage until it bursts. From long range, they'll aim and fire cannon balls at you continuously. Upon impact, these will cause an explosion covering a large area, which you'll need to quickstep sideways repeatedly to properly evade. They may still use their cannon at close range, though only when you're standing in front of them or slightly ahead of their cannon. They can also use a powerful kick with good tracking when you get up close. Taking these enemies on in close combat from the front is dangerous; from a little further away their frontal melee attacks are made up of telegraphed horizontal and vertical swings from their hatchet arm, and are all easily evaded with a quickstep backward. The safest place to stand is behind them, since they will attack less frequently and only using their Turnaround Swing. All of their attacks cannot be interrupted, nor can they be staggered with a single charged attack from behind; however, they can be staggered by attacking their legs, which will open them to visceral attacks to their head. This can only be done once, and then you'll need to wait until after they have used their limb recovery, indicated by a swirling red particle effect, in order to do it again. Once they've lost 50% of their health, they will begin to use their Roaring Slam to create a large area-of-effect shockwave – because of how heavily telegraphed this attack is, you'll have plenty of time to quickstep away from it. They are weakest to fire damage, making the Flamespayer and weapons augmented with Fire Paper very useful for taking them out quickly.

Strategy

Carry a few antidotes with you, since these enemies are usually found in poison swamps; bait them into the swamps to poison them while using antidotes to avoid taking damage. Apply a Fire Paper to your weapon before approaching them and try to enter the range of their melee attacks as soon as possible to reduce the chance of them using their cannon shots. Immediately position yourself at their back, where you'll only need to deal with their Turnaround Swing – easily avoided by quickstepping back. Between their attacks and during their recoveries, attack their legs as often as possible to stagger them for visceral attacks. A decently upgraded Flamesprayer is effective by itself, though with Bone Marrow Ash applied it will inflict more damage.

Basic Information	■	✈	Item Drops												
Chalice Dungeon Base Level	952	446	None		132	132	92	132	160	120	70	300	180	—	—
Chalice Dungeon Base Level | Boss	3175	1425	Hintertomb Root Chalice [100%]		132	158	92	132	160	120	70	300	180		

Preset Chalice Dungeons: Hintertomb, Hintertomb (Boss), Lower Hintertomb

Key Attacks

Name	Interrupt	Notes
Cannon Shot	No	Long range attack with heavy damage, cannon ball explodes upon impact; repeatedly quickstep to either side until you are out of the range of the cannon ball and its explosion.
Roaring Slam	Yes	Heavily telegraphed by their roaring, slams both arms down, creating a high damage area-of-effect shockwave; quickstep backwards.
Kick	Yes	Try not to stand too close to their front and they won't use it.
Turnaround Swing	Yes	Telegraphed swing reaching to behind them; quickstep back to avoid this.

Attack the tumor.

Cannon attacks have a huge radius.

Evading the Turnaround Swing is very important.

Labyrinth Warriors

Labyrinth Warriors are among the strongest opponents you'll encounter in the dungeons, and should be approached with due caution. Those armed with a greatsword in both hands can inflict large amounts of damage with accurate swings, and to make things worse, they'll often have additional elemental effects on their weapons. As they approach you they'll often use their Running Sweep, which has an immense amount of tracking and forward momentum so you'll need to quickstep through it at the last second to evade it successfully. These enemies lack any long range attacks and will generally only walk toward you, so if needed you can run away to create some space with which to heal, buff or use ranged attacks. Although slightly weaker than those with greatswords, warriors carrying crossbows & swords have the advantage of ranged attacks. Once you they have spotted you they will open fire with their crossbows, firing one shot roughly every 6 seconds so you'll need to approach them either from behind cover, or while strafing diagonally to make the shots miss. Labyrinth Warriors wielding morning stars are aggressive and dangerous enemies; both the chain and the spiked head can strike you for multiple hits. From close range, they will use a string of overhead swings or their faster Flailing Combo. Their Flailing Combo consists of five swings and will appear to have ended before the last hit to bait you into walking into it. This attack will continue regardless of the distance you stand from them, creating many openings to interrupt it. Some warriors even employ shields to increase their defensive capabilities, and they will occasionally hold their shields up defensively and walk around while focused on you. From a distance they often use their Running Shield Smash or Running Overhead Cleave, both of which have strong tracking and will be followed by a Turnaround swing if you quickstep to past them to their back. Since both of these attacks have very telegraphed animations, it's better to try and interrupt them rather than evade.

Labyrinth Warrior (Greatsword)

Try to take advantage of their elemental weaknesses by applying an Empty Phantasm Shell or Fire Paper to your weapon before approaching them, because you'll want to end things as quickly as possible. The Hunter's Blunderbuss will flinch them out of all of their attacks, so if you are having a hard time avoiding their Running Sweep you can shoot them out of it with this weapon and possibly interrupt it for a visceral attack. From within their range they will often use their Overhead Cleave, which has heavy initial tracking like all of their overhead attacks, but thanks to a long buildup you'll have plenty of time to interrupt it. Because their tracking makes it difficult to evade their attacks, it's generally best to position yourself just out of their reach so that you can back away from their attacks and punish them during the recovery. Keep a close lookout for their Overhead & Sweeping combo and evade it at all costs – if you are hit by the first swing, the second is a guaranteed follow-up.

Basic Information			Item Drops												
Chalice Dungeon Base Level	335	309	Random gem based on area ×1 [25%], Blood Vial ×4 [15%], Blood Vial ×3 [45%], Ritual material G ×1 [15%]	175	175	117	117	52	91	122	10	180	—	—

Preset Chalice Dungeons: Lower Pthumerian Labyrinth, Cursed Pthumerian Defilement, Pthumeru Ihyll

Key Attacks

Name	Interrupt	Notes
Running Sweep	Yes	Greatsword is dragged creating sparks as they run and use a high damage sweep; interrupt this when the sparks appear or quickstep back at the last second.
Overhead Cleave	Yes	High damage, but very long windup; back up and interrupt this or circle to back for a charged attack after their swing has missed.
Overhead & Sweeping Combo	Yes	Swings greatsword overhead, hits again bringing it back, then uses a sweep; quickstep back twice and interrupt this.
Side Stab	Yes	Stabs while you are standing to their sides; strafe to the right against them so that it misses.

Labyrinth Warrior (Crossbow & Sword)

The six seconds between each of their crossbow shots are just enough time to peek out from behind cover and use ranged attacks against them of you want to fight them from outside of their melee range. Once you're within six meters of them they'll switch to their swords and use melee attacks which, while having short range and little forward momentum, do have considerable tracking and are very difficult to evade. From the front they will use simple one handed attacks and combos or a more powerful Two-hand Combo, all of which are easily interrupted and avoided by standing out of range and quickstepping forward or backward. If you're behind them, however, they will attempt to catch you with a Turnaround Swing that you can evade by quickstepping to either side, so make sure you only attack them once or twice before preparing to evade.

Basic Information			Item Drops											
Chalice Dungeon Base Level	335	309	Random gem based on area ×1 [25%], Blood Vial ×4 [15%], Blood Vial ×3 [45%], Ritual material G ×1 [15%]	175	175	117	117	52	91	122	10	180	—	—

Preset Chalice Dungeons: Lower Pthumerian Labyrinth, Pthumeru Ihyll

Key Attacks

Name	Interrupt	Notes
Crossbow Shot	Yes	Shots fired will inflict around as much damage as their one handed sword swings; quickstep to the side or through their shots.
Two-hand Combo	Yes	Two-hands the sword for higher damage, up to three hits; keep just out of their reach while moving back up to avoid their forward momentum
Side Stab	Yes	Used when standing at either of their sides; quickstep to the right and attack.
Turnaround Swing	Yes	Stabs while you are standing to their sides; strafe right against them so it misses and attack.

Labyrinth Warrior (Morning Star)

These warriors have more range than the other types, which means you'll need to stand further away if you're attempting bait them into attacking so that you can move back and strike them in the recovery once they miss. The transformed R2s of weapons such as the Threaded Cane and Hunter Axe are especially useful against these enemies because they can flinch them very easily, so once you start attacking, keep going until your stamina has been exhausted. When at long range, they will run slowly after you and use either their Spinning Swing or Running Overhead Swing; both of these attacks can be evaded with a well timed quickstep to the side, but you may want to take advantage of the telegraphed animation and go for an interrupt instead to end the fight quickly.

Basic Information			Item Drops											
Chalice Dungeon Base Level	335	309	Random gem based on area ×1 [25%], Blood Vial ×4 [15%], Blood Vial ×3 [45%], Ritual material G ×1 [15%]	175	175	117	117	52	91	122	10	180	—	—

Preset Chalice Dungeons: Cursed Pthumerian Defilement

Key Attacks

Name	Interrupt	Notes
Spinning Swing	Yes	Long range swing reaching almost 360 degrees and far ahead of them; move back a good distance and use throwing items against them.
Flailing Combo	Yes	Fast combo with up to five swings which can each hit multiple times and continues regardless of your distance; quickstep back and interrupt this or use throwing items.
Running Overhead Swing	Yes	Reaches far ahead of them; quickstep to either side as soon as they swing and attack them during their recovery.

Labyrinth Warrior (Sword & Shield)

These enemies share many of the same sword attacks used by the crossbow-wielding variant, though they have a larger set of moves and can be found sometimes with elemental effects applied to their weapon. Although they can be staggered with a charged attack from behind, the fact that they are quite quick to turn and will often use their Turnaround Swing make it quite difficult to actually do so. The best means of staggering them is to stand outside their range to try and bait them into using their running attacks so that you can interrupt them. When they bring their shields up, use transform attacks to break their guard and hit them while they are stunned.

Basic Information			Item Drops											
Chalice Dungeon Base Level	335	309	Random gem based on area ×1 [25%], Blood Vial ×4 [15%], Blood Vial ×3 [45%], Ritual material G ×1 [15%]	175	175	117	117	52	91	122	10	180	—	—

Preset Chalice Dungeons: Pthumeru Ihyll

Key Attacks

Name	Interrupt	Notes
Swinging Combo	Yes	Quick flurry of attacks with up to four hits; quickstep back and interrupt this or quickstep forward past them and use a charged attack from behind.
Turnaround Swing	Yes	Same attack used by the crossbow and sword variant; quickstep back to avoid this.
Running Shield Smash	Yes	Runs towards you from a long distance; quickstep back or to either side just before they swing to avoid its heavy initial tracking.
Running Overhead Cleave	Yes	Acts and is avoided similarly to their Running Shield Smash but hits much harder.

Loran Cleric

Loran Clerics are usually found hidden away in the corners of a room, from where they will continuously cast fireballs at you. Their fireballs aren't too powerful, but they travel very far – thankfully, they don't track well and are easily avoided by strafing. At mid to long range they will cast one or two quick fireballs, and occasionally a Large Fireball, which will deal a much larger amount of damage if it hits you. When approached at close range they'll begin to perform basic, interruptible swings using their staff. Their melee attacks are slow, deal relatively low damage can be and easily avoided, though they do have a heavy knockback effect. From behind, they are completely defenseless and will only attempt to turn to face you, making for an easy kill. Their most dangerous attack is their Flame Ring, which is incredibly difficult to avoid and will cover almost the entire area and deal obscene amounts of damage.

Strategy

Equip a serrated weapon, such as the Saw Cleaver or Saw Spear, which inflict extra damage due to their bonuses against beasts. Prioritize getting behind Loran Clerics as quickly as possible and use R2 strikes to flinch them out of their attacks. If they begin to charge for their Flame Ring, quickly line yourself up with their backs and use a charged R2 to stagger them for a Visceral Attack; their Flame Ring is most commonly used after being visceral attacked from behind, so with good timing you can repeatedly stagger them while they attempt to use it. You can also stand at close range to bait their slow melee attacks for interrupts; avoid quickstepping to the side when dodging, since they can turn around quickly before each swing.

Basic Information			Item Drops											
	■	✦	Random gem based on area ×1 [8%], Ritual material C ×1 [8%], Ritual material D ×1 [8%], Blooming Coldblood Flower ×1 [8%]			75	75	75	75	288	74	292	120	300	—	—
Chalice Dungeon Base Level	**176**	**98**												

Preset Chalice Dungeons: Ailing Loran

Key Attacks

Name	Interrupt	Notes
Large Fireball	No	Holds staff with both hands to cast a large fireball. Quickstep to either side.
Flame Ring	No	Massive circular wave of fire. Flinch them out of this attack using [R2] attacks.

The Large Fireball is important to avoid.

They are completely defensless once you're behind them.

Keeper's Hunting Dog

Keeper's Hunting Dogs are usually found in pairs alongside a Keeper of the Old Lords. Though they may appear quite menacing, their only truly dangerous attack is their arcing Flame Breath, which is used less often than their other attacks. They will use it when you stand in front of them and will move their heads to spread it across a wide area – this leaves openings for you to quickstep past it to the opposite direction their head is facing. They will move just as erratically as Rabid Dogs and attack with quick successions of bites, often using the Pouncing Bite when at a distance. Despite their size, they can be knocked over by your gunfire, much like Rabid Dogs, and because they appear in pairs, the Hunter's Blunderbuss' wide scattering shots are especially useful for handling these enemies.

Strategy

Lead Keeper's Hunting Dogs away from their master, if he's present, and try to pick them off separately. Since they are found in pairs, the far-reaching sweeps of the transformed Hunter Axe is great for hitting them when they are together. You can use the Hunter Blunderbuss to knock them over and quickstep forward to attack them as they are getting up; this is by far the most effective way of dealing with these enemies, as you can knock them out of any of their attacks, including their Flame Breath. They are also prone to the effects of Pungent Blood Cocktails, so if you have any you can use them to distract both dogs while you get some easy hits in. Once they're distracted, it can also be worthwhile using a Shaman Bone Blade on one of them to make it attack the other one, along with anything else in the area.

Basic Information				Item Drops											
Chalice Dungeon Base Level	**285**	**105**		Bloodstone C ×1 [1.5%], Bloodstone B ×1 [33%]		73	73	73	73	68	188	68	120	180	×	—

Preset Chalice Dungeons: Lower Pthumerian Labyrinth, Cursed Pthumerian Defilement, Lower Loran, Isz Gravestone

Key Attacks

Name	Interrupt	Notes
Flame Breath	Yes	Breathes fire in a wide arc ahead of it from side to side; quickstep through whichever side is open and attack their sides, or fall back to knock them over with gunfire.
Pouncing Bite	Yes	Fast and hard-to-avoid pouncing attack; quickstep to either side as soon as possible.

Shooting them with a Blunderbuss is great for keeping them down.

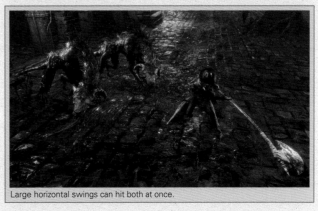
Large horizontal swings can hit both at once.

Nightmare Executioners 🅞🅗

Enormous, powerful enemies found in the Hunter's Nightmare. While they have some similarities with the Executioners encountered in and around Yharnam, they have a large arsenal of new tricks up their tattered sleeves and should be handled quite differently. Nightmare Executioners armed with axes have incredibly long reach and their attacks tend to carry them forward considerable distances, making it dangerous to take them on from the front; they are also good at punishing attempts to quickstep past them with wide horizontal swings. While only one of these enemies in a single location carries the Church Cannon, he is positioned at a bottleneck at the end of a large, open area with no obstructions for you to use as cover from his explosive cannonballs; he'll fire both long- and short-range shots and will also use his cannon as a melee weapon. Both of these subtypes have tremendous amounts of health and wearing them down can be difficult, but both are susceptible to normal interrupts and staggers.

Nightmare Executioner (Axe) 🅞🅗

Axe-wielding Nightmare Executioners alternate between horizontal and vertical melee swings of varying speeds and can perform combos of up to five consecutive hits, many of which have wide arcs and reach directly behind them; they will also perform an extremely swift forward shove attack with their axes at pointblank range and can repeat this move almost immediately, making it extremely dangerous to stand near to them for any length of time. At close to mid range they'll use a jumping vertical chop which comes out very quickly and covers a great deal of ground; often they will deliberately time this attack to punish the use of consumable items such as Blood Vials. At mid range they favor a running attack consisting of several steps forward followed by a counterclockwise horizontal chop; this move has a wide arc and very long reach, and the extended delay before the swing can give misleading indications of when to dodge it. They will use both of these attacks to close the distance between themselves and their targets, making it difficult to escape their surprisingly rapid advance. They will sometimes perform a short-range grab attack, rearing their heads back shortly before jabbing the ground in front of them with their tentacles. The startup animation for this attack is easily identified and leaves enough time to back out of range before it activates, providing a prime opportunity for an interrupt. Their most dangerous technique, however, is the Cosmic Explosion – a massive spherical area attack centered on their axe, which inflicts arcane damage and adds smaller bursts of arcane energy to all of their subsequent attacks. Nightmare Executioners are aggressive towards other enemies of the Nightmare, and will engage them in combat if their paths happen to cross.

The Cosmic Explosion strikes an extremely large spherical area centered on the axe...

...but also has a long recovery period and leaves time for you to move behind them and perform a chain of visceral attacks.

Strategy

The safest way to fight these enemies is from a distance. Stay outside the range of their melee combos and bait their jumping cleave or running slash, then either interrupt these attacks or quickstep past them and swing one or two times during their recovery. They recover fairly quickly and will counterattack straight away, so be prepared to back off immediately after striking; additionally, pay close attention to their attacks and try to quickstep through each swing in the opposite direction if you're unable to move out of range in time. When their health drops below 67% they will use Cosmic Explosion; this attack has a lingering hitbox, so dodging through it with invincibility frames is not possible. They will take halved damage while charging the buff and it cannot be interrupted, but they can be knocked out of it with a Cannon shot, two hits from the Fists of Gratia, a single use of the Beast Roar or any other attack that breaks their super armor. If knocked out of the buff, they will not attempt to use it again. Immediately after the initial explosion, there is enough time to quickstep behind them and stagger them with a charged 🆁🅶 swing. Their recovery period after the ensuing visceral attack leaves enough time for them to be staggered again; in this manner it is possible to trap then in a chain of visceral attacks and prevent them from taking further actions.

Nightmare Executioners are susceptible to slow poison, though poisoning them is an inefficient strategy for players with more advanced equipment and is generally only useful to those tackling the Hunter's Nightmare very early in the game. They can also be lured into the vicinity of the Old Hunters and Old Hunters' Hounds prowling the surrounding areas, which will result in the two sides attacking one another and can be useful for weakening these powerful opponents before engaging them directly.

Basic Information														
Hunter's Nightmare	3455	2366	Item Drops Blood Vial ×6 [24%]		268	165	268	206	220	137	82	300	999	—	—

Key Attacks

Name	Interrupt	Notes
Jump Attack	Yes	Quickstep sideways or forward past it.
Axe Shove	Yes	Quickstep backward or avoid standing in front of them at pointblank range.
Running Slash	Yes	Interrupt it or quickstep clockwise through it late in the animation.
Tentacle Grab	Yes	Strafe backward out of range during the windup and interrupt it just as they strike.
Cosmic Explosion	No	Used only once when their HP drops below 67%. Break their super armor to knock them out of it or immediately quickstep away several times when they begin using it.

Nightmare Executioner (Church Cannon) OH

These Nightmare Executioners are much less aggressive than their axe-wielding counterparts, but their ability to strike distant targets with heavy munitions still poses a considerable threat. At long range they will level their Church Cannons directly at their mark and launch explosive cannonballs that create large fire-elemental explosions wherever they land; at short to mid range they will fire at the ground in front of them to create a forward area attack. The splash damage generated by each detonation is cumulative with a direct hit from the projectile in much the same way as the player-obtainable version of this weapon, meaning that being caught on the edge of a blast is far less lethal than taking a explosive cannonballs straight to the face. These enemies use the same tentacle grab attack as the axe type, but do not use the axe variant's Cosmic Explosion and therefore cannot augment their attacks with the same dangerous effects. The cannoneers will, however, use their artillery as makeshift melee weapons at close range, performing slow individual swings and combos of up to three hits. Their super armor can be easily broken using the Fists of Gratia, the Beast Roar or Cannon shots, but doing so is much less vital than with the axe type due to this version's more passive fighting style and simpler attack patterns.

Strategy

Quickstep forward through their cannon shots and bring them into melee range, then either bait and interrupt their attacks or quickstep forward through the swings and strike from behind. Set them up by moving in close to trigger their three-hit combo and immediately quickstepping backward out of reach when they initiate it – the first attack will miss and leave them open to being interrupted when they begin the second or third. Another good opportunity to interrupt these opponents is when they perform their grab attack, and they are slow enough that a well-calculated charged strike can stagger them from behind. When they level their cannons straight at you, quickstep forward through the shot and move in close; when they aim downward at the ground, quickstep backward twice if positioned at mid range or forward twice past them to avoid the blast. Note that they will use their ground blast in an attempt to drive you out of their blind spots; the tracking on these close shots is quite strong and precise timing is required to dodge the explosion by quickstepping past them. Additionally, beware of splash damage in these situations – the residual flames reach slightly behind the Executioner and can clip you even if you successfully avoid the initial explosion. Slow poison offers weaker players a marginally safer strategic alternative, but is still far from efficient for those capable of dealing reasonable damage with ordinary physical attacks.

Quickstep forward through their long-range shots...

...and interrupt their slow, predictable melee attacks.

Basic Information														
Hunter's Nightmare	3455	2366	Item Drops Quicksilver Bullets ×10 [24%]		268	165	268	206	220	137	82	300	999	—	—

Key Attacks

Name	Interrupt	Notes
Ranged Cannonball	No	Quickstep forward through it at least twice as soon as possible after they level their launchers.
Close Cannonball	No	Quickstep backward at mid range or forward past them at close range and avoid standing too close until the blast dissipates.
Tentacle Grab	Yes	Strafe backward out of range during the windup and interrupt it just as they strike.
Bludgeon Combo	Yes	Strafe or quickstep backward depending on their distance from you and interrupt the second or third swing.

Bloodlicker OH

These fully-engorged Bloodlickers are encountered in large numbers along the river of blood in the Hunter's Nightmare. Though they use the same tongue whips and arm combos as those found in Cainhurst and the Chalice Dungeons, this variant does not share the same leap attacks; instead, they focus on projectiles and group ambushes. At long range they will spit streams of blood which have strong tracking and cause slow poison buildup, and will begin using a delayed body slam when engaged up close. All members of a given group will attack together if one is provoked, and all will simultaneously disengage and return to their starting positions if you retreat far enough for even one to lose interest. With the dense distribution of other enemy types throughout many of the same enclosed areas as these, it is almost impossible to avoid fighting several foes at a time.

Strategy

Cannon shots augmented with Bone Marrow Ash are an effective and economical way of dealing heavy damage to entire groups of these enemies with a single blow. Hunter tools such as A Call Beyond and the Tiny Tonitrus are effective for this purpose as well, as are Molotov Cocktails and charged attacks with wide arcs such as that of the transformed Hunter Axe. When fighting more than one at a time, try to use the uneven terrain to obstruct their blood spit attack and separate them as much as possible. When they lose interest and disengage, they can be struck with jump attacks or projectiles on the way back to their starting locations before they can turn around to resume the offensive. In general, quickstep forward through their attacks and perform R1 combos while positioned at their sides; avoid standing behind them as they will respond with a swift backward kick. Charged attacks from heavy weapons such as the transformed Kirkhammer will knock them down or send them flying, though keep in mind that they cannot be interrupted or staggered.

Basic Information														
Special Weakness: Righteous			Item Drops		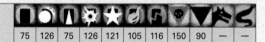									
Hunter's Nightmare	1658	517	Random gun type gem ×1 [16%]		75	126	75	126	121	105	116	150	90	—	—

Key Attacks

Name	Interrupt	Notes
Blood Spit	No	Quickstep sideways each time they launch a stream of blood or use the environment for cover.
Body Slam	No	Quickstep forward past them. Be careful to account for the short delay.
Rear Kick	No	Quickstep sideways or avoid standing directly behind them.
Tongue Combo	No	Quickstep forward past them.
Arm Combo	No	Quickstep forward past them once to twice and continue strafing to stay behind them.

Use a shield to help prevent being poisoned as you approach.

Strike from the side to avoid their swift front and rear counterattacks.

Clocktower Patients OH

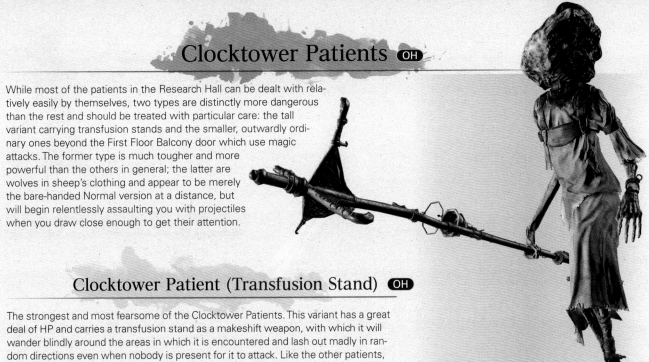

While most of the patients in the Research Hall can be dealt with relatively easily by themselves, two types are distinctly more dangerous
than the rest and should be treated with particular care: the tall
variant carrying transfusion stands and the smaller, outwardly ordinary ones beyond the First Floor Balcony door which use magic
attacks. The former type is much tougher and more
powerful than the others in general; the latter are
wolves in sheep's clothing and appear to be merely
the bare-handed Normal version at a distance, but
will begin relentlessly assaulting you with projectiles
when you draw close enough to get their attention.

Clocktower Patient (Transfusion Stand) OH

The strongest and most fearsome of the Clocktower Patients. This variant has a great
deal of HP and carries a transfusion stand as a makeshift weapon, with which it will
wander blindly around the areas in which it is encountered and lash out madly in random directions even when nobody is present for it to attack. Like the other patients,
these detect by sound, and knocking over or destroying objects in the environment
such as bottles or medical equipment will immediately alert them to your presence.
They use only basic horizontal, vertical and thrust attacks with their transfusion
stands, but can chain their swings in long and extremely rapid combos whose potent
stunlock effect will trap you if too many hits connect. Their indiscriminate flailing is
easy to interrupt but they have exceptionally long reach, strong tracking and considerable forward momentum during their combos, making it dangerous to approach
these enemies from the front; to make matters worse, they are protected by super
armor during almost all of their combos and their attacks inflict either heavy hitstun or
outright knockdown. They are extremely susceptible to poison and can still be knocked
down with charged swings from heavy weapons
like the transformed Kirkhammer; however, beware
that their recovery after such attacks is very quick
and they will be invulnerable to further knockdown
until their super armor resets, so the Kirkhammer's
followup charge strike will fail to send them flying
and will leave you vulnerable to attack.

Strategy

Quickstep forward past them to avoid their swings, then hit them from behind with up to three melee attacks
while they recover. Be prepared to quickstep away immediately afterward or even break off your attack
early – these enemies can strike behind them with some of their horizontal sweeps and the tracking
on their combos causes them to turn very quickly, so evasive action may become necessary with
little warning. Alternately, stand just outside the reach of their attacks and continue backing up
until they commit to a combo, then interrupt it. While many of their individual swings have short
cooldown periods, the recovery times of their complete combos are generally long enough that they
can be staggered from behind with careful positioning and a timely charged R2 attack. Slow poison is extremely effective against these enemies, but once they are aware of your presence they will chase you down
relentlessly and you'll have to wait out the poison in a spot they can't reach, such as a ladder or other high perch.
With a bit more work, they can also be lured toward ledges and either knocked off with charged attacks or baited into
jumping off by themselves; the transformed charge attack of the Hunter Axe is ideal for this purpose. The sustained
L2 attack of the transformed Whirligig Saw will tear straight through their super armor, and a direct hit from the
weapon's jump attack in this form will break it instantly.

Basic Information	■	⚜	Item Drops											
Research Hall	3058	3594	Random gun type gem ×1 [20%], Blood Vial ×4 [80%]	99	99	99	99	108	89	89	120	180	—	—

Key Attacks

Name	Interrupt	Notes
Combo Attacks	Yes	Quickstep forward through them or stay at the outer edge of mid range and continuing backing away while waiting for an opportunity to interrupt them.

Clocktower Patient (Magic) OH

These wolves in sheep's clothing are found only in the area past
the locked First Floor Balcony door in the Research Hall. Although
outwardly identical to the ordinary bare-handed Clocktower Patients,
this version uses the same arcane-based magic attacks as the Small
Celestial Emissaries with head tendrils encountered in the Forbidden Woods and the Isz Chalice Dungeons. Because you'll have no
choice but to face a large group of them at one time with relatively
limited room to maneuver, these enemies present great danger and
should be treated with care.

The Loch Shield will absorb most of the damage from their arcane attacks, but beware that blocking too many at once will deplete your stamina and break your guard. If this occurs, you'll be left vulnerable to further attacks for a few moments and will more than likely be struck with the full brunt of the next projectile. Use the pillars and other elements of the nearby terrain to separate these foes from one another as much as possible; ranged attacks such as Throwing Knives, Molotov Cocktails and arrows from Simon's Bowblade are effective as well, but you'll have very few opportunities for interrupts or staggers due to this enemy type's focus on ranged attacks. If you must rely solely on melee weapons, focus on one patient at a time with R1 combos and keep an eye on your surroundings – you'll need to be prepared to retreat behind a pillar or other cover at a moment's notice.

Basic Information															
Research Hall	688	1307	Item Drops		99	99	99	99	108	89	89	120	180	—	—
			Blood Vial ×1 [8%]												

Key Attacks

Name	Interrupt	Notes
Cosmic Blast	No	Single long–range projectile with moderate tracking; quickstep sideways or use cover to block it.
Triple Laser	No	Fires multiple linear lasers in quick succession. Tracks in all directions and can hit you behind them; quickstep sideways or use obstacles to block it.

Giant Fishmen OH

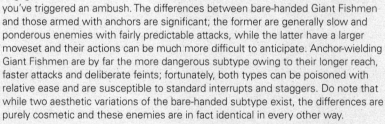

These monstrous brutes serve as the token "tank" enemies in the Fishing Hamlet. While encountered in only a few locations, they tend to be positioned in spots where they are either not immediately visible or cannot be engaged in combat at all until you've triggered an ambush. The differences between bare-handed Giant Fishmen and those armed with anchors are significant; the former are generally slow and ponderous enemies with fairly predictable attacks, while the latter have a larger moveset and their actions can be much more difficult to anticipate. Anchor-wielding Giant Fishmen are by far the more dangerous subtype owing to their longer reach, faster attacks and deliberate feints; fortunately, both types can be poisoned with relative ease and are susceptible to standard interrupts and staggers. Do note that while two aesthetic variations of the bare-handed subtype exist, the differences are purely cosmetic and these enemies are in fact identical in every other way.

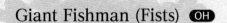

Giant Fishman (Fists) OH

These powerful enemies have large reserves of health and very high defense against physical attacks, but are quite weak to arcane damage; their considerable super armor can be broken with two hits from the Fists of Gratia, but the Beast Roar and most charged attacks are largely ineffective for this purpose. At close range they will attack with quick shoves, slower individual arm slams and combos consisting of up to three hits. They will usually end their combos with either a two-handed overhead slam or a grab attack, though they may abandon the sequence entirely if you back too far away. They will also use two separate variations of the grab on its own: a fast version that strikes directly in front of them at close range and a slow version preceded by several lumbering steps forward. Their other attacks include a slow left-handed uppercut, the two-handed slam by itself and a long-range sliding tackle. The tackle and the faster grab are their most dangerous attacks; the former because it hits multiple times and covers ground quickly, and the latter because it leaves very little time to respond. Despite their great size and strength, these opponents can be set up for visceral attacks by interrupting or staggering them in the usual ways.

Strategy

Before engaging a Giant Fishman, eliminate any weaker enemies in the vicinity if possible. Leaving enough room to maneuver is crucial; backing yourself into a corner while fighting these dangerous opponents will more than likely result in death, as will interference from other Fishmen. Use any available sources of arcane damage such as the Holy Moonlight Sword or A Call Beyond to end the battle quickly and pay careful attention to the enemy's movements for the telegraphs of particular attacks. Provided no other enemies are present, the most effective tactic is to stand just outside the target's melee range and bait any of its slow swings, then strafe backward out of range and interrupt the attack. All variations of the grab can be interrupted, as can the sliding tackle as long as the bullet connects early in the animation – specifically, before the enemy's body hits the ground. The tackle can be avoided by quickstepping either sideways or forward through it; resist the temptation to quickstep backward

as doing so will allow the attack to connect. Due to these enemies' slow turning speed and generally poor tracking, it is possible to avoid every last one of their melee attacks by standing behind them at pointblank range; strafing sideways is usually enough to hold this position, though an occasional sideways quickstep may also be necessary. Breaking their super armor with the Fists of Gratia will immobilize them long enough to stagger them with a charged strike, and their recovery from knockdown is slow enough that they can be staggered again as they stand up and struck with consecutive visceral attacks. All of their moves except the close-range grab can be reliably avoided by quickstepping forward through the attack, which will also position you to perform an R1 combo from the safety of their blind spot; the grab in question can be thwarted with a single backward quickstep.

Basic Information

Basic Information	■	⚔	Item Drops										
Fishing Hamlet	3176	4514	Random gem based on area ×1 [25%], Blood Vial ×5 [20%], Blood Vial ×4 [55%]	195	90	150	150	114	118	270	200	180	–	–
Fishing Hamlet | Strong	3176	4861	Rakuyo ×1 [100%]	195	90	150	150	114	118	270	200	180		

Key Attacks

Name	Interrupt	Notes
Gnawing Grab (Standing)	Yes	Close range. Strafe or quickstep backward and try to capitalize on the chance to interrupt it.
Gnawing Grab (Running)	Yes	Quickstep forward past it at close range or backward at least twice from mid range; can also interrupt it.
Sliding Tackle	Yes	Quickstep left or right, or interrupt it by shooting him at the beginning of the animation before he hits the ground.
Uppercut	Yes	Strafe clockwise around him at pointblank range; otherwise quickstep left or interrupt it.
Overhead Slam	Yes	Quickstep backward out of range or interrupt it near the end of the animation. Beware of the long delay before the slam.

Circle behind them as they use one of their slower moves...

...then stagger them with a charged R2 and trap them in a chain of visceral attacks.

Giant Fishman (Anchor) OH

These monstrous fishmen are the most dangerous enemies in the expansion areas, bar none. They have rock-solid defense, more health than some bosses and a repertoire of incredibly devious attacks which put their unarmed counterparts to shame. The anchor-wielding variant's combat behavior differs drastically from the unarmed type owing to the addition of a makeshift weapon; these enemies do not use grab attacks, but their swings have incredibly long reach and powerful stunlock capabilities. They utilize a combination of rapid strikes and delayed feints, and will incorporate both into combos of up to five hits; additionally, many of their individual swings have considerable forward momentum or reach directly behind them. At close range they will perform a quick three-hit melee combo followed by an overhead slam if you are still within reach afterward; they will also use a separate series of up to five slow horizontal swings which alternate between counterclockwise and clockwise, and will punish attempts to hide behind them with a swift backward uppercut. Another of their close to mid-range combos consists of up to three vertical slams at different intervals; they will generally only execute the followup swings if the first hit connects and will occasionally use a horizontal sweep instead of a third vertical blow. At mid to long range they will sometimes run forward for about three seconds and perform a counterclockwise swing with an extremely wide arc; they also use a far more dangerous version of the unarmed variant's sliding tackle at all ranges. For all their ferocity, however, they are still susceptible to visceral attacks via ordinary interrupts and staggers, and can be poisoned with a paltry four Poison Knives. They share their species' weakness to arcane damage, making weapons like the Holy Moonlight Sword and tools such as the Executioner's Gloves and A Call Beyond particularly useful for dealing with them.

Strategy

As these enemies can reach every position in their immediate vicinity with at least one of their attacks, standing close to them for any length of time is not recommended. The safest strategy is to keep them at mid to long range and wait for an opportunity to interrupt one of their more predictable moves, then follow up with a visceral attack. Opportunities to strike them with melee weapons can be exploited during the recovery periods after their combos and heavy individual swings, but remain ever watchful for their swift counterattacks and be prepared to quickstep through an incoming strike at a moment's notice. Their jump attack, downward slams, running horizontal sweep, uppercut and slower combos offer the best chances to interrupt them; the recovery of their heavier attacks will also occasionally leave enough time to stagger them from behind. Their sliding tackle is only superficially similar to the version used by their unarmed counterparts; it can still be interrupted but the bullet must connect after they hit the ground rather than before. Extremely precise timing is required to interrupt this attack without trading hits; however, even if you do trade on a successful interrupt, there will still usually be enough time to recover and initiate the visceral attack. To avoid the tackle, quickstep twice sideways as the enemy hits the ground and begins sliding, or once sideways and then once

backward; an additional backward quickstep may be necessary after the initial slide in order to escape the subsequent flailing. Their jump attack can be avoided by quickstepping to either side or forward past them as they jump, or simply interrupted midair; beware that they will immediately perform this move in an attempt to punish the use of Blood Vials or other consumable items if you do so while within its reach. Their five-hit horizontal combo can be avoided by quickstepping backward out of range or sideways in the opposite direction of each swing, but it is NOT safe to stand behind these enemies or remain at close range during this combo as all of the swings strike in a nearly 360-degree radius and will reach directly behind them; either dodge the first swing and immediately back out of range of the rest or simply interrupt one of the following strikes and perform a visceral attack. At mid range it is possible to avoid their downward slam combo with one to two backward quicksteps; in closer proximity it is necessary to quickstep forward counterclockwise past the enemy's left side and continue strafing toward its back. The windup on their forward uppercut is very obvious and provides plenty of warning; if you must dodge rather than interrupt it, quickstep forward counterclockwise past the enemy's left side just before it swings or move in to pointblank range and strafe counterclockwise around its body and the swing will miss. Do NOT attempt to quickstep clockwise through the swing as its enormous hitbox has a high probability of beating out your invincibility frames. To avoid the faster three-hit melee combo, quickstep forward clockwise toward the enemy's right side underneath the first swing and continue strafing clockwise at pointblank range, staying behind it for the remainder of the combo. If it follows up with the slam, continue to strafe clockwise at pointblank range or quickstep past it in a clockwise direction just before it brings its arms down.

Basic Information																
Fishing Hamlet	6352	4166	Random gun type gem ×1 [25%], Blood Vial ×5 [20%], Blood Vial ×4 [55%]			195	90	150	150	114	118	270	200	180	–	–
Fishing Hamlet | Strong	6352	4514	None			195	90	150	150	114	118	270	200	180		

Key Attacks

Name	Interrupt	Notes
Dashing Swing	Yes	Extremely long delay; interrupt it or dodge late in the animation by quickstepping through the attack in the opposite direction of the swing.
Rising Anchor	Yes	Interrupt it or quickstep forward counterclockwise past the enemy's left side just before the swing.
Downward Slam	Yes	At mid range, quickstep backward once to twice; if any closer, quickstep forward counterclockwise past the enemy's left side and continue strafing toward its back. Easily interrupted.
Leaping Smash	Yes	Quickstep forward past the attack or interrupt it.
Backward Uppercut	Yes	Strafe or quickstep counterclockwise if standing on the enemy's left side or clockwise through the attack from any other close-range location. Positioning and timing are unfavorable for interrupts.
Sliding Tackle	Yes	Quickstep twice sideways as the enemy hits the ground and begins sliding, or once sideways followed by once backward.

Quickstep twice sideways as soon as they launch into their slide attack.

Skirt well outside their melee range while you wait for a chance to interrupt a slow attack.

Hunter Enemies

Yahar'gul Hunter (Rifle Spear & Ludwig's Rifle)

This Yahar'gul hunter and his Tonitrus-wielding partner guard the path to the village from the Cathedral Ward and will attack together if you charge in carelessly, but it's possible to fight them separately if you lure his partner away first. This hunter wields a Rifle Spear and can shoot at you with it in its transformed state; he also wields Ludwig's Rifle, a scattergun with considerably longer range than the Hunter Blunderbuss, and will take full advantage of its longer reach to harass you from a distance while his partner pummels you at close range.

Eliminate the other hunter before attacking this one – his scatter shots are much less dangerous without an ally to support him. Interrupt him and perform visceral attacks when possible; otherwise quickstep forward through his scatter shots and hit him with quickstepping attacks or R1 combos. He'll usually evade slower thrown weapons like Molotovs, but Poison Knives or gems that add poison effects to your weapons are effective for wearing him down.

Equipment

Right Hand 1	Rifle Spear +5	Head	Black Hooded Iron Helm
Right Hand 2	Bare Hands	Body	Yahar'gul Black Garb
Left Hand 1	Ludwig's Rifle +5	Hands	Yahar'gul Black Gloves
Left Hand 2	Bare Hands	Feet	Yahar'gul Black Trousers

Basic Information

			Item Drops												
Cathedral Ward	886	3420	Quicksilver Bullets ×10 [100%]	252	228	203	194	151	141	151	173	155	—	—

Yahar'gul Hunter (Tonitrus & Wooden Shield)

This Yahar'gul hunter guards the village approach and is positioned farther ahead of his rifle-toting comrade, allowing you to lure him away without the other hunter noticing. He wields a Tonitrus and a Wooden Shield, and will block both melee attacks and ranged weapons such as firearms or Throwing Knives. He has no ranged weapons of his own, though, so he's incapable of interrupting you and can only attack with his Tonitrus. It's very easy to break his guard with transformed R1 attacks from two-handed weapons like the Kirkhammer or the Hunter Axe, and his slow swings are equally easy to interrupt.

Walk just close enough to get his attention without alerting the other hunter and lure him back up the steps. Interrupt his attacks or quickstep forward through them and hit him with R1 combos; alternately, you can simply break his guard when he tries to block and hit him with heavy attacks while he's stunned. Firearms and thrown weapons like Molotovs or Poison Knives are not enough to knock aside his shield, so it's better to deal with him using melee attacks and rely on your equipped gems to inflict any desired status effects.

Equipment

Right Hand 1	Tonitrus +5	Head	Black Hooded Iron Helm
Right Hand 2	Bare Hands	Body	Yahar'gul Black Garb
Left Hand 1	Wooden Shield	Hands	Yahar'gul Black Gloves
Left Hand 2	Bare Hands	Feet	Yahar'gul Black Trousers

Basic Information

			Item Drops												
Cathedral Ward	1030	3420	Bolt Paper ×4 [100%]	252	228	203	194	151	141	151	173	155	—	—

Bloody Crow of Cainhurst

An extremely agile opponent encountered in the Grand Cathedral after fulfilling certain requirements. For detailed information on how to access this battle, check out the NPC section in the Hunter's Appendices chapter. The Bloody Crow of Cainhurst wields the Chikage, a lethal weapon that inflicts rapid poison build-up in its transformed state and can deal tremendous amounts of damage in a very short time. He'll continually use an Old Hunter Bone to maintain the Quickening status throughout the fight, making him extremely difficult to hit; he'll also use Blood Vials when his health is low and will throw Numbing Mist at you to prevent you from doing the same. The Corrupted Hunter is very proficient at interrupts, and will make a deliberate effort to set you up for visceral attacks, making him one of the most dangerous hunters you'll face in single combat.

Well-timed interrupts are your best chance of victory, but beware that the Bloody Crow of Cainhurst is extremely good at evading gunshots when under the effects of the Old Hunter Bone. Hitting him with a Numbing Mist will prevent him from using Blood Vials; other thrown weapons are generally not worth using as he will evade them. The fastest way to defeat him is to power up the Cannon with Bone Marrow Ash, interrupt one of his attacks with a gunshot from the Reiterpallasch and blast him with a cannon shot during the stagger state, but you'll still need to land an interrupt first. combos and other ordinary melee attacks aren't very effective due to his tremendous evasive abilities, but he will frequently walk straight into charged attacks if you initiate them from mid range and time the charge correctly.

Equipment

Right Hand 1	Chikage +10	Head	Cainhurst Helmet
Right Hand 2	Bare Hands	Body	Crowfeather Garb
Left Hand 1	Repeating Pistol +10	Hands	Cainhurst Gauntlets
Left Hand 2	Bare Hands	Feet	Cainhurst Leggings

Basic Information

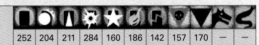

			Item Drops											
Cathedral Ward	3510	6238	Blood Rapture ×1 [100%]	252	204	211	284	160	186	142	157	170	—	—

Djura's Ally

Djura's Ally patrols the area at the foot of Djura's Tower in Old Yharnam. He can be hard to see among the columns of smoke rising from the corpses, but will usually spot you first and make his way to you. There are a number of Beast Patients in the area and you'll need to keep an eye on them while facing him; he'll also make a point of refusing to leave the cover of Djura's gatling gun, forcing you to deal with intermittent barrages from above while you fight. Djura's Ally will occasionally use a Blood Vial when his health is low and will take potshots at you with his pistol from outside the range of his melee attacks; Poison Knives are helpful for damaging him without exposing yourself to Djura's cover fire, but he'll often dodge thrown weapons or bullets.

Lure him toward the ladder leading up to Djura's perch and fight him on the makeshift wooden staircase – Djura can't target you in this spot and Djura's Ally will stray just close enough for you to use hit-and-run tactics when he moves in. Interrupts are most effective, especially since he'll have to approach you through a narrow pathway; however, beware that he'll often use jump attacks that have long reach if his weapon is transformed. You can also wait for him to approach and quickstep toward him to perform an combo when he attacks, or strafe backward out of his reach and perform a jumping attack of your own while he's recovering from a miss.

Equipment

Right Hand 1	Saw Spear +3	Head	Black Hood
Right Hand 2	Bare Hands	Body	Charred Hunter Garb
Left Hand 1	Hunter Pistol +3	Hands	Charred Hunter Gloves
Left Hand 2	Bare Hands	Feet	Charred Hunter Trousers

Basic Information

			Item Drops											
Old Yharnam	997	795	Bone Marrow Ash ×6 [100%]	229	212	168	220	132	286	159	131	146	—	—

Hunters of Despair

The Hunters of Despair wait at the edge of the poison pond leading to the final section of the Nightmare Frontier and will attack together when you approach. While it's extremely difficult to get their attention individually, the terrain provides plenty of cover and obstacles which can be used to separate them and make the battle a bit easier. The axe-wielding hunter uses the standard axe moveset and favors jump attacks, but will also make frequent use of its sweeping swings and forward stabs. She tends to prefer close combat but will occasionally shoot at you from long range. The cane-wielding hunter will periodically switch modes with his weapon and make use of its wide, sweeping arcs to prevent you from quickstepping past him; this can be particularly dangerous due to the many obstacles and terrain differences in the area where you'll encounter him. He'll occasionally throw a Poison Knife at you if you back out of range of his blunderbuss, and will pepper you with scattergun blasts from a distance while his partner closes in with her axe.

Try to eliminate any Loran Silverbeasts in the area before engaging the hunters. Interrupts work well against the axe-wielding hunter's slow attacks, but you'll have to lure her out of range of the cane-wielding hunter's blunderbuss in order to safely follow through with a visceral attack. R1 combos are effective after quickstepping forward through both hunters' swings; you can also lead them into the swamp until they become poisoned, then simply hang back until it finishes them or wears off. Stabbing the nearest group of Crawlers with a Shaman Bone Blade will cause the hunters to rush into the poison and begin fighting them, serving the dual purpose of weakening them directly and exposing them to the toxic muck.

Equipment (Hunter Axe & Torch)

Right Hand 1	Hunter Axe +5	Head	Yharnam Hunter Cap
Right Hand 2	Bare Hands	Body	Yharnam Hunter Garb
Left Hand 1	Hunter's Torch +5	Hands	Yharnam Hunter Gloves
Left Hand 2	Hunter Pistol +5	Feet	Yharnam Hunter Trousers

Equipment (Threaded Cane & Flamesprayer)

Right Hand 1	Threaded Cane +5	Head	Black Church Hat
Right Hand 2	Bare Hands	Body	Black Church Garb
Left Hand 1	Hunter Blunderbuss +5	Hands	Surgical Long Gloves
Left Hand 2	Bare Hands	Feet	Black Church Trousers

Basic Information

			Item Drops											
Nightmare Frontier (Hunter Axe)	829	4050	Lead Elixir ×1 [100%]	228	211	228	203	211	244	228	184	166	—	—
Nightmare Frontier (Threaded Cane)	829	4050	Lead Elixir ×1 [100%]	203	203	237	268	252	236	244	214	209	—	—

Old Hunter Henryk

Henryk is the first opponent you'll help Eileen defeat over the course of her quest, and she'll fight alongside you during the battle either from the start or after a brief period of time depending upon when you initiate the encounter. Henryk uses a Saw Cleaver and Hunter Pistol, and will sometimes toss a Throwing Knife at you from a distance. He is wildly aggressive and extremely trigger-happy, and will blindly rush you down with quick R1 combos and transformation attacks. If you get far enough away from Henryk during the fight he'll occasionally use the Roar gesture, giving you an opportunity to dash in for a few free hits. If he scores an interrupt on you, he'll often follow up with a charged R2 strike rather than a visceral attack.

Take advantage of Henryk's single-minded aggression and lead him straight into an R1 combo from a weapon with wide horizontal swings such as the Hunter Axe or the Saw Spear; alternately, back away from and wait for him to take a swing at you, then interrupt him and perform a visceral attack. When Eileen joins the fight, you can use her as a distraction and hit Henryk from behind with a charged R2 strike and follow up with either a visceral attack or another charged blow. The tombstones in the area can be used to obstruct his gunshots but may also impede your ability to evade; if the terrain becomes a problem, lure Henryk up the stairs and fight him in the open area in front of the gate.

Equipment

Right Hand 1	Saw Cleaver +6	Head	Henryk's Hunter Cap
Right Hand 2	Bare Fists	Body	Henryk's Hunter Garb
Left Hand 1	Hunter Pistol +6	Hands	Henryk's Hunter Gloves
Left Hand 2	Bare Fists	Feet	Henryk's Hunter Trousers

Basic Information

			Item Drops											
Central Yharnam	1716	5198	Heir ×1 [100%]	228	228	211	194	177	228	316	119	169	—	—

Yurie, the Last Scholar

You'll be attacked by this member of the Healing Church Choir as you explore the second floor of Byrgenwerth. She uses the Threaded Cane, a very swift weapon whose transformed attacks strike wide frontal arcs and will almost always hit you if you try to quickstep through them. Most of the time she'll switch between both stances and occasionally fire a quick burst from her Rosmarinus, but she can also cast Augur of Ebrietas and A Call Beyond. Fighting her in the ground floor's interior area will ensure a battle free of interruptions, but the outdoor patio is populated by strong enemies that can defeat her very quickly with resourceful use of Shaman Bone Blades.

Interrupt her and perform visceral attacks; do not attempt to quickstep through her swings, especially when she switches her weapon to its whip mode. You'll need to stay three to four meters away or be prepared to quickstep sideways in order to avoid Augur of Ebrietas; if she casts A Call Beyond, quick-step twice sideways or once forward through the blasts. R1 combos are effective, but you'll need to wait until she stops swinging before quickstepping in to attack; you can also back off and time a charge attack so that she runs into it just as you swing. If you have any Shaman Bone Blades, you can run outside, stab a Garden of Eyes and lure it toward her when she runs out after you; if these enemies hit her with their grab attack, it will inflict frenzy and tear off an enormous portion of her health.

Equipment

Right Hand 1	Threaded Cane +7	Head	Blindfold Cap
Right Hand 2	Bare Hands	Body	Choir Garb
Left Hand 1	Rosmarinus +7	Hands	Choir Gloves
Left Hand 2	Bare Hands	Feet	Choir Trousers

Basic Information

			Item Drops											
Byrgenwerth	2281	5453	Blue Elixir ×3 [100%]	186	194	194	203	323	252	260	181	163	—	—

Yahar'gul Hunter (Threaded Cane & Flamesprayer)

One of three Yahar'gul hunters guarding the ground floor of the chapel during your return trip to the village. The trio is a group encounter, and as soon as one of them detects you, the other two will immediately rush to your location and attack together. This one attacks with both of the Threaded Cane's forms but prefers its whip mode; he'll usually lash at you from just out of reach, but will occasionally strafe you with his Flame-sprayer. He also carries a Tiny Tonitrus, which he'll use for mid-range surprise attacks on rare occasions, so be prepared to get out of the way if he uses it.

A Flamesprayer of your own can come in very handy during this encounter, especially since this par-ticular hunter's whip attacks can be very difficult to interrupt. Trying to fight all three hunters head-on is suicide, so try to use the narrow staircases and banisters to separate them; funneling them into a staircase is a particularly effective strategy if you're using the Flamesprayer or the Cannon as doing so will severely limit their ability to avoid the area of effect. Hit-and-run tactics are the safest bet; strike only once at a time before backing off and be sure to leave yourself enough stamina to escape.

Equipment

Right Hand 1	Threaded Cane +9	Head	Black Hooded Iron Helm
Right Hand 2	Bare Hands	Body	Yahar'gul Black Garb
Left Hand 1	Flamesprayer +9	Hands	Yahar'gul Black Gloves
Left Hand 2	Bare Hands	Feet	Yahar'gul Black Trousers

Basic Information

			Item Drops											
Yahar'gul (Blood Moon)	1891	5198	Madman's Knowledge ×1 [100%]	252	228	203	194	151	141	151	178	160	—	—

Yahar'gul Hunter (Beast Claw & Hunter Pistol)

One of the trio of Yahar'gul hunters guarding the chapel during your second trip through the village. This scantly-clad madman is the only one of the three that will be immediately visible when you enter the room and will be standing in full view, but don't be fooled into approaching him – as soon as you do, you'll be attacked from behind by the third hunter. Though this hunter's attacks lack range, he's capable of unleashing long, rapid combos which are nearly impossible to escape; and with the other two attacking you at the same time, the situation becomes even more dangerous.

Shooting him at any point during his combos has a high chance to stagger him, but be sure the others are far enough away that you'll actually have time to perform a visceral attack afterward. Weapons with longer range, such as the transformed Hunter Axe and Saw Spear, can hit him from outside his reach, and his lack of armor leaves him highly susceptible to poison; however, he will often evade thrown weapons such as Poison Knives and Molotovs. As with the others, use hit-and-run tactics and do your best to separate him from them before attempting to interrupt his attacks; when you do strike, use only one or two attacks at a time and be sure to save enough stamina to quickstep away afterward.

Equipment

Right Hand 1	Beast Claw +9	Head	Iron Yahar'gul Helm
Right Hand 2	Bare Hands	Body	Nothing
Left Hand 1	Hunter Pistol +9	Hands	Nothing
Left Hand 2	Bare Hands	Feet	Nothing

Basic Information

Yahar'gul (Blood Moon)	1891	5198	Item Drops Clawmark ×1 [100%]		60	40	9	19	19	29	9	75	77	–	–

Yahar'gul Hunter (Rifle Spear & Cannon)

By far the most dangerous of the three chapel guards, owing to his long reach and massive firepower, this Yahar'gul hunter hides immediately to the right of the building's street-level entrance and will wait for you to run past him before moving in to attack. In combat he'll mainly use the basic attacks of his Rifle Spear and won't transform it very often; he'll rarely fire his Cannon, but you must be prepared for him to do so at any time, as a direct hit will usually mean instant death. His quick attacks can be difficult to interrupt and to make matters worse, the long reach of his spear makes it equally difficult to get close to him. He'll usually evade thrown weapons and often melee attacks as well, and his spear's reach makes it difficult to hit him with frontal charge attacks before he can knock you out of them. He isn't good at dealing with jump attacks from well outside his range, though, and such surprise attacks will usually hit him before he can react.

Separate him from the others and try your best to interrupt his attacks; if that doesn't work, back far enough away from him to initiate a jump attack and time it so that you hit him just as he enters its range. As with the others, hit-and-run damage is the slow but sure way to wear him down; using the environment to prevent him from getting a clean shot at you with his Cannon is crucial, and the curved stairwells provide the best means of doing so. You'll have a hard time getting behind him to use R1 combos; instead, back off and wait for him to miss an attack, then quickstep forward and counterattack before he can act again. If he does take a shot at you with his Cannon, quickstep toward him if you're close or backward if farther away to avoid being hit by the splash damage.

Equipment

Right Hand 1	Rifle Spear +9	Head	Black Hooded Iron Helm
Right Hand 2	Bare Hands	Body	Yahar'gul Black Garb
Left Hand 1	Cannon +5	Hands	Yahar'gul Black Gloves
Left Hand 2	Bare Hands	Feet	Yahar'gul Black Trousers

Basic Information

Yahar'gul (Blood Moon)	1891	5198	Item Drops Quicksilver Bullets ×20 [100%]		252	228	203	194	151	141	151	178	160	–	–

Choir Intelligencer Edgar

Choir Intelligencer Edgar guards the lower bridge to Mergo's Loft in the Nightmare of Mensis. He attacks very aggressively and tends to prefer using the heavy transformed swings of Ludwig's Holy Blade, though he'll also occasionally fire a short burst with his Rosmarinus or cast Augur of Ebrietas. He's extremely aggressive and will respond quickly to your attacks, but his tendency to use only slow swings makes him very vulnerable to interrupts; it also often causes him to run face-first into charge attacks with long reach such as those of the transformed Hunter Axe. He's vulnerable to poison but will often dodge projectiles such as Poison Knives, so it's more effective to set your weapon with poison gems if you plan to wear him down in this manner.

As usual, interrupts are the best strategy – you can catch him during one of his heavy two-handed swings or his R2 thrust attacks. Be cautious about quickstepping forward through his swings as their wide horizontal arcs will often clip you; instead, stand outside the reach of his melee attacks and wait for him to miss, then quickstep toward him and strike before he has a chance to recover. If you're using a weapon with long reach and strong forward thrusts such as Ludwig's Holy Blade or the Saw Spear, take advantage of his habit of walking into charged attacks and bait him into doing just that.

Equipment

Right Hand 1	Ludwig's Holy Blade +9	Head	Nothing
Right Hand 2	Bare Hands	Body	Student Uniform
Left Hand 1	Rosmarinus +9	Hands	Nothing
Left Hand 2	Bare Hands	Feet	Student Trousers

Basic Information

			Item Drops											
Nightmare of Mensis	1749	10635	Sedatives ×3 [100%]	116	106	106	144	200	106	116	136	119	—	—

Izzy's Admirer

Izzy's Admirer stands behind a large pile of dead Maneater Boars amid a giant nest of Labyrinth Rats. You'll enter through a tunnel on the opposite side of the room out of sight of both the prospector and the rats, and will need to clear the giant rodents out in order to safely engage the hunter. The pile of dead pigs offers some cover as the Admirer will prioritize chasing you around it rather than over it, but the broken cages lying in the muck won't slow him down and should not be counted on for any amount of protection. He'll transform his weapon as soon as he sees you and will use it exclusively in its transformed mode until defeated; beware that the more hits he lands on you in rapid succession, the more powerful a damage bonus he'll receive.

Lure the rats toward you one at a time with Throwing Knives and fight them in the tunnel through which you entered. Using a Blue Elixir before approaching them will help ensure that you're not seen by the others, but isn't necessary as long as you maintain enough distance from the pack. With the rats out of the way, you can safely engage the Admirer – the safest tactic is to lead him in circles around the pile of dead Maneater Boars and begin charging a transformed R2 attack as soon as you have an opening, then release it just as he enters your range to inflict damage and stun him long enough for you to back off and repeat the process. If you have any Shaman Bone Blades, you can lure him back into the entry tunnel and use them on the Gel at the intersection; its resistance to physical attacks will keep it alive long enough for it to deal enormous damage to the Admirer or even defeat him outright.

Equipment

Right Hand 1	Beast Claw	Head	Tomb Prospector Hood
Right Hand 2	Bare Fists	Body	Charred Hunter Garb
Left Hand 1	Bare Fists	Hands	Charred Hunter Gloves
Left Hand 2	Bare Fists	Feet	Charred Hunter Trousers

Basic Information

			Item Drops											
Chalice Dungeon Base Level	454	479	Random gem based on area ×1 [20%]	270	242	213	236	168	300	177	139	154	—	—

Preset Chalice Dungeons: Ailing Loran

Nameless Tomb Prospector (Ludwig's Holy Blade & Rosmarinus)

This hunter waits in the corner of a long rectangular chamber littered with gravestones. A few Gravekeeper Scorpions wander the area, but all of them can be lured away and eliminated before getting the hunter's attention. In combat he'll switch between both of his weapon's modes and occasionally cast Augur of Ebrietas; on rare occasion he'll also spray bursts of sacred mist with his Rosmarinus, but usually he'll just stick to physical attacks. He's very good at dodging ranged attacks and will often evade thrown weapons like Molotovs and Poison Knives, but quick R1 combos are very effective against him.

Interrupt his slow transformed attacks or quickstep through them and hit him from behind with R1 combos. Keep an eye out for Augur of Ebrietas and be prepared to quickstep sideways if he casts it; you can also quickstep forward past him if you're close enough and attack before he recovers from the casting animation. If you have any Shaman Bone Blades, you can use one on the nearby Gravekeeper Scorpions to create a temporary distraction.

Equipment

Right Hand 1	Ludwig's Holy Blade +3	**Head**	Tomb Prospector Hood
Right Hand 2	Bare Fists	**Body**	Tomb Prospector Garb
Left Hand 1	Hunter's Torch +3	**Hands**	Tomb Prospector Gloves
Left Hand 2	Rosmarinus +3	**Feet**	Tomb Prospector Trousers

Basic Information

Chalice Dungeon Base Level	454	422	Item Drops											
			Random gem based on area ×1 [20%]	223	232	268	228	276	244	244	193	189	—	—

Preset Chalice Dungeons: Isz Gravestone

Nameless Tomb Prospector (Kirkhammer & Repeating Pistol)

You'll encounter this hunter twice during your time in the Pthumeru Ihyll dungeon, but for the most part you'll be able to use the same tactics against him both times. He will use both forms of the Kirkhammer, but does tend to favor the heavier transformed mode and will immediately swap their torches out for Repeating Pistol. From a distance he'll try to pepper you with gunshots, then as you get close he'll run away and drop Rope Molotovs behind him to get you as pursue. Both times you face him there are pools of oil nearby, so if you have fire weapons you can greatly increase your damage by fighting him in one, just make sure not to over-pursue and get hit by one of his Rope Molotovs.

Interrupts are most effective against the slow transformed swings of the prospectors' Kirkhammer, and you can quickstep in to initiate an R1 combo if they try to throw Molotovs at you from mid range. Quickstepping past them and attacking from behind will create opportunities for R1 combos with faster weapons, but slower ones will give them enough time to recover between swings and hit you with Rope Molotovs. The prospector is highly evasive and will almost always dodge thrown weapons like Poison Knives unless he's in the recovery of an attack. If you're having trouble interrupting his attacks, it's worth using a Shaman Bone Blade on one of the nearby enemies to have them do some of the work for you. This is especially true for the second encounter because there are some extremely powerful Labyrinth Warriors nearby that you can make use of.

Equipment

Right Hand 1	Kirkhammer +3	**Head**	Tomb Prospector Hood
Right Hand 2	Bare Fists	**Body**	Tomb Prospector Garb
Left Hand 1	Hunter's Torch +3	**Hands**	Tomb Prospector Gloves
Left Hand 2	Repeating Pistol +3	**Feet**	Tomb Prospector Trousers

Basic Information

Chalice Dungeon Base Level	454	422	Item Drops											
			Random gem based on area ×1 [20%]	223	232	268	228	276	244	244	193	189	—	—

Preset Chalice Dungeons: Pthumeru Ihyll

Younger Madaras Twin (OH)

The younger Madaras twin is one of the strongest non-boss enemies in the early game and poses a particularly serious threat to players traversing the Forbidden Woods for the first time. He primarily uses the normal mode of his Hunter Axe and will immediately augment it with Fire Paper when engaged in combat; he'll also occasionally throw in a shotgun blast, especially if you are out of reach of his melee attacks. He will frequently perform a forward roll followed by a physical attack, leaving himself open to interrupts, but moves too quickly for most charged attacks to reliably stagger him.

Strategy

Be mindful of the other enemies in the area before you engage him, particularly the Carrion Crows near the elevator room entrance. If you enter the area from the Hunter's Dream via the lamp, you'll appear behind him and can begin the fight by ambushing him with a charged strike. Watch for him to roll toward you and shoot him as soon as he follows up with a swing, then hit him with a visceral attack. If you've already obtained the Beast Roar from a later section of the woods, you can use it to knock him down and attack him while he recovers; however, beware that sending him flying off one of the nearby ledges to his death will make it difficult to retrieve the item he drops. You can limit his ability to evade your attacks by backing him up against the elevator hut or one of the nearby tombstones, but be careful not to become trapped yourself.

Equipment

Right Hand 1	Hunter Axe +7	Head	Butcher Mask
Right Hand 2	Bare Fists	Body	Butcher Garb
Left Hand 1	Hunter Blunderbuss +4	Hands	Butcher Gloves
Left Hand 2	Bare Fists	Feet	Butcher Trousers

Basic Information

Location			Item Drops										
Forbidden Woods	2574	4158	Madaras Whistle [100%]	244	159	244	168	211	177	252	200	211	—	—

Djura's Disciple OH

The long, narrow cave in which you'll encounter Djura's Disciple forces you into the sights of his Gatling Gun, granting him a significant tactical advantage. He will only pursue you as far as the cave entrance and will retreat back inside if you try to lure him too far, but he loses this advantage if engaged farther into the cavern where the path widens. Bear in mind that while you'll need a light source in order to be able to see properly in this area, the darkness has no effect on this enemy's ability to track you. When forced into close combat he will draw his Saw Spear and will use transformation attacks to switch between its forms; he'll continue using his Gatling Gun even at close range and will also occasionally throw Poison Knives. While the section of the cave in which Djura's Disciple waits is free of enemies, the adjoining chambers are not; straying too far in will attract the attention several Beast Patients and a Blood-starved Beast.

Strategy

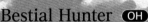

The Wooden Shield can be used to block the hail of bullets from the disciple's Gatling Gun, but watch your stamina – if your guard is broken you'll be left open to a barrage of crippling hits. You can also use the large pile of rocks in the center of the chamber as cover from the gunfire, and the Hand Lantern is extremely helpful for illuminating your surroundings if you prefer not to dedicate your gun slot to a torch during the fight. Like other NPC Hunters, Djura's Disciple will periodically roll toward you and perform a physical attack, but without a light source it can be difficult to exploit the opportunity for an interrupt. Visceral attacks in general are less effective in the cave for this reason, but it is possible to lure the disciple far enough outside that neither the light nor the tight spaces will be problematic. You can take advantage of his relatively short leash by luring him to the cave entrance, allowing him to lose interest and attacking him from behind as he walks back in.

Equipment

Right Hand 1	Saw Spear +5	Head	Black Hood
Right Hand 2	Bare Fists	Body	Charred Hunter Garb
Left Hand 1	Gatling Gun +5	Hands	Charred Hunter Gloves
Left Hand 2	Bare Fists	Feet	Charred Hunter Trousers

Basic Information

			Item Drops											
Hunter's Nightmare	3196	7326	Gatling Gun [100%]	229	212	168	220	132	286	159	171	186	—	—

Bestial Hunter OH

This enemy can be found at the dead end in the Hunter's Nightmare where Gilbert's house would be located in Central Yharnam. He uses the Beast Claw paired with the Beast's Embrace rune, granting him access to the weapon's alternate moveset; combined with his enormous reserves of health, this makes him an especially dangerous opponent no matter when you choose to face him. While the Bestial Hunter does not use firearms, he is a nimble enemy with powerful

melee attacks whose fighting style places a heavy emphasis on evasion; he rolls and quicksteps frequently in battle, and will almost always dodge thrown weapons such as Molotov Cocktails. He will exclusively use the Beast Claws' transformed mode in combat and will occasionally perform the roar attack; he will also periodically attempt to hit you from a distance with the leaping dive, but this move will usually miss at close range. Despite his appearance, the Bestial Hunter is not affected by the damage bonuses from serrated weapons or Beasthunter gems.

Strategy

Stand just outside the reach of his claw swipes and interrupt him when he performs a slow attack. Trapping him in a corner with melee combos is effective as well, but his heavy use of evasive quicksteps can turn the tables if you press your advantage too far. The Wooden Shield will deflect his light attacks and can be used to set him up for retaliatory R1 combos; charged attacks are effective as well, though staggering from behind is difficult due to his high mobility. The Whirligig Saw's transformed L2 attack is especially effective for stunlocking him and a hit from the Beast Roar will send him flying. Fast weapons such as the Blades of Mercy are useful for trapping him in combos and preventing his escape; slower attacks will often miss if not timed carefully, but can be initiated after quickstepping forward through his swings to increase the chances of striking him during his recovery.

Equipment

Right Hand 1	Beast Claw +7	Head	Nothing
Right Hand 2	Bare Fists	Body	Nothing
Left Hand 1	Bare fists	Hands	Nothing
Left Hand 2	Bare Fists	Feet	Old Hunter Trousers

Basic Information

			Item Drops											
Hunter's Nightmare	4134	6105	Firing Hammer Badge [100%]	264	254	264	60	50	70	40	156	147	—	—

Church Doctor (Ludwig's Holy Blade & Repeating Pistol) OH

One of two Healing Church doctors encountered in the Recovery Room. This one focuses primarily on melee attacks and will switch between both modes of her Holy Blade; she will also take potshots at you with her Repeating Pistol and will occasionally toss a Poison Knife your way. She has a great deal of health and can deal damage very quickly if measures are not taken to separate her from the other doctor; she will follow you as far as the cell block if you attempt to retreat, but will give up partway to the Underground Corpse Pile and begin walking back to her starting position if drawn too far from it. Beware that she initially hides behind a pilaster on the right side of the room past the beds and will rush in to ambush you as you approach the other doctor kneeling before the altar.

Strategy

Separate the two doctors using the beds as obstacles and eliminate the other one first as she has lower HP and her ranged attacks make her considerably more dangerous. Afterward, lure this enemy out to the open area in front of the altar so that you have more room to maneuver and either bait and interrupt her attacks from just out of reach or quickstep forward past them and strike with R1 combos. Pay close attention to her at range as she will attempt to shoot you if she can't reach you with her sword; you can also use the Wooden Shield to block the shots and force her into using melee attacks instead.

Equipment

Right Hand 1	Ludwig's Holy Blade +7	Head	Black Church Hat
Right Hand 2	Bare Fists	Body	Black Church Garb
Left Hand 1	Repeating Pistol +7	Hands	Surgical Long Gloves
Left Hand 2	Bare Fists	Feet	Black Church Trousers

Basic Information

			Item Drops											
Research Hall	3332	8820	Madman's Knowledge ×1 [100%]	203	203	237	268	252	236	244	216	211	—	—

Church Doctor (Threaded Cane) `OH`

One of two Healing Church doctors encountered in the Recovery Room, this one kneeling in plain sight before the altar at the far end of the hall. She carries only a Threaded Cane and no firearms, but is equipped with the Blacksky Eye and will use it to bombard you with a constant barrage of ranged attacks from far away. Due to her relatively low health and the considerable danger posed by her projectiles, this doctor will fall relatively quickly to a sustained assault and should be considered the priority target. She will rarely strike with her cane and instead primarily uses the Blacksky Eye; she will also make relatively little effort to avoid close-ranged attacks and will spend most of her time strafing around you while launching projectiles.

Strategy

Eliminate this doctor first using the beds in the middle of the room to separate her from her associate. Backing her into a corner or against a wall can help prevent her from escaping, at which point a couple of combos from a sufficiently fortified weapon are usually enough to cut her down; her ranged attacks are much less dangerous when you use the beds for cover as this forces her into melee combat for which she is poorly equipped. Bear in mind that because this enemy does not use physical attacks very frequently, you'll have fewer opportunities to interrupt her and perform visceral attacks.

Equipment

Right Hand 1	Threaded Cane +7	Head	White Church Hat
Right Hand 2	Bare Fists	Body	White Church Garb
Left Hand 1	Bare Fists	Hands	Surgical Long Gloves
Left Hand 2	Bare Fists	Feet	Nothing

Basic Information

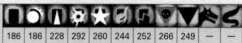

			Item Drops										
Research Hall	2194	11025	Quicksilver Bullets ×10 [100%]	186	186	228	292	260	244	252	266	249	—	—

Yahar'gul Hunter (Church Pick & Repeating Pistol) `OH`

This hunter can be found in a locked cell below the Recovery Room. He will attack on sight when you unlock and enter the cell, and his Church Pick can be very dangerous in the enclosed space due to its long reach and sweeping attacks. He will switch between both forms of his weapon using transformation attacks and will throw an occasional Molotov Cocktail your way; he can also be particularly aggressive with gunshots if backed into a corner. He does sometimes use charged attacks, though he'll usually stick with ordinary light and heavy swings. His initial position in the cell is close enough to the hallway that he can be struck with attacks which extend through the wall, and he will immediately move toward the much thinner cell door if hit in this manner, making it even easier to reach him. You will automatically receive the Church Pick even if he dies from an attack through the door or walls, allowing you to obtain the weapon before actually finding the key to the cell.

Strategy

Hit him through the wall using jump attacks with larger weapons such as the transformed Kirkhammer or Ludwig's Holy Blade, or charged attacks with longer weapons such as the Rifle Spear. Area attacks such as the Beast Roar or the transformed `L2` attack of the Beast Claw with the Beast's Embrace rune equipped will knock him down, after which he'll move toward the door in an attempt to reach you and inadvertently position him to be struck much more easily with little risk of retaliation. Should you choose to face him head-on, avoid fighting in his cell; instead, lure him out into the hallway where you have more room to maneuver. His attacks with both of the Church Pick's forms are fairly swift and can be tricky to interrupt, but the standard strategy of staying just out of his reach and baiting him to set himself up by taking a swing is still reasonably effective. The narrow hallway impedes his ability to evade melee combos, so quickstepping forward past him during his attacks and striking from behind with an R1 chain is an equally viable tactic.

Equipment

Right Hand 1	Church Pick +8	Head	Black Hooded Iron Helm
Right Hand 2	Bare Fists	Body	Yahar'gul Black Garb
Left Hand 1	Repeating Pistol +8	Hands	Yahar'gul Black Gloves
Left Hand 2	Bare Fists	Feet	Yahar'gul Black Trousers

Basic Information			Item Drops											
Research Hall	2739	9923	Church Pick [100%]	252	228	203	194	151	141	151	205	187	—	—

Church Doctor (Threaded Cane & Repeating Pistol) OH

You'll encounter this Healing Church doctor on a platform in the Research Hall next to one of the NPC patients that drop Brain Fluid. Although he initially stands with his back to you, he will automatically detect your presence when you approach and will begin attacking with both forms of his Threaded Cane, occasional gunshots and the odd Poison Knife. He is quite aggressive and fighting him on the narrow staircase is particularly risky owing to the danger of falling, but this can also work to your advantage should he accidentally quickstep off the edge and fall to his death. Beware the long reach of his swings when he transforms the cane – the lack of room to maneuver makes it extremely difficult to avoid his horizontal whip attacks.

Strategy

Ideally, knock him off the staircase and let almighty gravity do the rest. This is most easily accomplished with a single hit from the Beast Roar or a charged R2 attack from the transformed Hunter Axe, but R1 combos from faster weapons like the Blades of Mercy will usually stunlock him long enough to push him backward and off the edge. Interrupting his attacks is easier when he is using his weapon in cane mode; alternately, charged attacks from heavy weapons such as the Kirkhammer have enough super armor that they'll usually take precedence over his comparatively lighter attacks and flatten him if timed correctly. Should the first hit of the Kirkhammer's transformed R2 chain land, the follow-up will send him flying backward and virtually guarantees a kill if it connects when he has his back to a ledge. If you are equipped with A Call Beyond, you can target him with it before he detects your presence and position yourself at such an angle that the blasts will knock him off the platform without ever having to engage him directly.

Equipment

Right Hand 1	Threaded Cane +7	Head	Black Church Hat
Right Hand 2	Bare Fists	Body	Black Church Garb
Left Hand 1	Repeating Pistol +7	Hands	Surgical Long Gloves
Left Hand 2	Bare Fists	Feet	Black Church Trousers

Basic Information			Item Drops											
Research Hall	2899	7718	Sedatives ×5 [100%]	203	203	237	268	252	236	244	246	241	—	—

Brador, Church Assassin Ⓞ🅗

Brador will begin invading in set locations after you reach the Fishing Hamlet. For information on the exact spots in which he invades, please refer to the Hunting Grounds chapter. Although he has lower health than all of the other hunter enemies in the expansion areas, he can be an extremely deadly opponent owing to his unique weapon and devious fighting style. Upon invading he will immediately transform his weapon and will use it almost exclusively in this mode until he is defeated; he will also continuously drink Lead Elixirs, granting him potent super armor and a deflection effect which causes lighter melee attacks to bounce off of him. The transformed Bloodletter has long reach and brutally high attack speed, and knocking Brador out of his swift combos is next to impossible while he is under the effects of a Lead Elixir. His wanton use of this double-edged sword comes with a trade-off, however: the elixir's effects also impair his movement speed, leaving him far more vulnerable to ranged attacks and AoEs. He will vary his swings between light and heavy, horizontal and vertical, and can still quickstep even with the movement penalty, but leaves himself completely vulnerable while consuming Lead Elixirs.

Strategy

Wait for him to consume a Lead Elixir, then stand just outside his reach and bait one of his attacks to set him up for an interrupt. Alternately, if you have the Gatling Gun, allow him to use an elixir and then mow him down with a sustained volley while backing away from him; his impaired movement will leave him helpless and unable to escape the stream of bullets. Hunter tools such as the Tiny Tonitrus, Executioner's Gloves and Blacksky Eye can be used for this purpose as well, but A Call Beyond is less effective in certain enclosed locations such as the cell block as most of the projectiles will collide with walls before they have a chance to reach their mark. You may also wait for the effects of Brador's current elixir to wear off, then allow him to use another and immediately quickstep forward to perform an R1 combo while he is locked in the animation. He is susceptible to poison, which is considerably more effective against him than other hunters thanks to his lower health and self-inflicted inability to dodge Poison Knives. He will also have great difficulty dodging Bone Ashed Cannon or Church Cannon blasts after using an elixir, so make good use of this tactic if you have the necessary equipment and eliminate him before he has a chance to attack.

Equipment

Right Hand 1	Bloodletter +9		Head	Brador's Testimony
Right Hand 2	Bare Fists		Body	Beast Hide Garb
Left Hand 1	Ludwig's Rifle +9		Hands	Bloodied Armbands
Left Hand 2	Bare Fists		Feet	Bloodied Trousers

Basic Information

Location			Item Drops										
Hunter's Nightmare/ Fishing Hamlet	1855	5220	Brador Attire, one piece for killing each projected appearance; Bloodletter, upon killing his physical body	221	245	177	202	159	123	159	184	178	—	—

Bosses

Cleric Beast

Preparation

Firstly, stock up on Blood Vials, Quicksilver Bullets and Molotov Cocktails before facing the Cleric Beast. If you've obtained the Saw Hunter Badge from the Boar Tunnel, you can also buy a full load of Throwing Knives. Oil Urns will amplify the damage from Molotovs and are particularly effective in this fight due to the Cleric Beast's weakness to fire; a few can be found throughout Central Yharnam and collecting them is well worth it. You can purchase a weapon that inflicts bonus damage against beast-type enemies from the shop after obtaining the Saw Hunter Badge, or pick up a Saw Spear in the Drydock, and if you're still wearing your starting equipment, you can replace it with the Yharnam Hunter set from the shop or the slightly better Hunter set found in the Aqueduct. Search Central Yharnam for Bloodstone Shards before the battle to upgrade your weapons, and don't hesitate to spend those spare blood echoes on gaining a couple of levels. Note that you won't be able to level up until you've returned to the Hunter's Dream with Insight. You can earn one by encountering Cleric Beast or Father Gascoigne, or by gathering Madman's Knowledge, two of which are located in Central Yharnam.

Overview

You'll face the Cleric Beast at the far end of the Great Bridge spanning Central Yharnam. It attacks with straightforward claw swipes, slams, lunges and leaps, and becomes more aggressive when its health drops to 70%. While this boss moves slowly, its lunging attacks cover long distances and its horizontal swings have considerable range; additionally, many of its attacks have heavy forward momentum and will hit you if you try to evade by backing away. The Cleric Beast uses no magic or projectiles of any kind; its only means of hitting you at a distance are its jump attacks and forward lunges.

Basic Information Special Weakness: Serration			Item Drops											
Central Yharnam	3015	4000	Sword Hunter Badge [100%]	103	123	103	103	165	50	165	999	999	✕	—

Key Attacks

Phase 1	Interrupt	Notes
One-Two Slam	No	Slams left arm on the ground in front of it, jumps forward and slams right arm. Roll forward through it.
One-Armed Grab	No	Executed with the left arm. Slow windup; roll behind it or quickstep backward.
Overhead Slam Combo	No	Quicker version of the Overhead Smash with up to three hits; quickstep forward past it.
Lunging Swipe	No	Lunges forward and swipes a wide frontal arc with its left arm; quickstep forward or to the right.
Recovery	No	Surrounds itself in a red aura and heals its injured limbs or head. Repairs body damage, not HP.

Phase 2	Interrupt	Notes
Two-Armed Grab	No	Slower windup; strafe or quickstep backward.
Double Slam Combo	No	Slow three-hit combo ending with a downward slam; quickstep in any direction.
Slow Overhead Smash	No	Delayed ground slam with a delayed follow-up if you're close; quickstep forward or backward.
Jump Attack	No	Leaps high into the air and performs a falling slam; dash or roll forward as it passes over you.

Environment

The boss area is a long, narrow bridge littered with rubble and abandoned horse-drawn carriages. The smaller carriages will be destroyed if the Cleric Beast hits them with any of its attacks, giving you a little more room to maneuver; if you run out of ammunition, a corpse at the far end holds 10 Quicksilver Bullets. It's very easy to get backed into a corner and end up fighting in close quarters, which puts you at a severe disadvantage, so try to fight using the full length of the bridge to keep a safe distance between yourself and the boss when you're not attacking.

Strategies

Key Strategies

The Cleric Beast's head and all four of its limbs can be injured separately, stunning it and giving you a few seconds to pile on additional attacks; its wounded limbs will also take 50% more damage. Hitting its head with gunshots, thrown weapons or melee attacks will stagger it, allowing you to inflict heavy damage with visceral attacks; it will eventually heal any damaged parts of its body, restoring their defense to normal but also allowing you to injure them again. The Cleric Beast is highly weak against fire and will take heavy damage from Molotovs, especially if you hit it with an Oil Urn first; its head also takes double damage, so you can douse it in oil and then hit it in the face with a Molotov to cut off a huge chunk of its health. Weapons with damage bonuses against beasts such as the Saw Cleaver and the Saw Spear are very effective on this boss.

Phase 1

The Cleric Beast has two targetable points on its body: one mid-abdomen, the other on its head. The best way to begin the battle is to target its head with gunshots, Throwing Knives or Molotovs to stagger it, then follow through with a visceral attack. The safest place to stand is directly behind the boss, though be warned that it will occasionally rotate its upper body to strike beside and behind it with its arms. By standing back just far enough to avoid these swings, you can attack the boss as it recovers from its actions or attempts to turn toward you. Most of the Cleric Beast's heavy attacks have forward momentum and will almost always connect if you attempt to evade by backing up; instead, quickstep forward or sideways in the opposite direction of the swing. Due to the boss' hunched posture, rolling or quickstepping through its legs is impossible most of the time; the best approach is to fight it without locking on and evade its close-range attacks by rolling behind it, where it will have trouble hitting you. Standing directly in front of it places you in range of its fastest attacks and should be avoided if at all possible, although doing so will often trigger its slow grab attacks and provide you with opportunities to hit its head with your melee weapons. If you need to heal, back off and put as much distance as possible between yourself and the boss – if you are far enough away to be out of reach of its jump attack, there's nothing it can do to prevent you from using a few Blood Vials.

Phase 2

When its health has been reduced to 70% the Cleric Beast will roar, announcing the start of Phase 2. From this point onward it will begin attacking more aggressively with longer combos and lunges, and striking its head becomes much harder. You can still hit it with Oil Urns and Molotovs during its recovery periods, dealing large amounts of damage from outside its melee range; if you have any Throwing Knives, you can use them to deal damage from a safe distance. The Cleric Beast will begin using stronger variations of its grab and combo attacks during this Phase, but you can avoid them in the same manner as their Phase 1 versions. Due to the boss' more frequent attacks and erratic movement during Phase 2, locking onto it in close combat can decrease your ability to keep track of it and evade its attacks; if you experience this problem, continue fighting while locked off.

Father Gascoigne

Preparation

Leveling up before facing Gascoigne is a very good idea; to do so, you'll need to get at least one point of Insight before returning to the Hunter's Dream. The Doll will then be available to use. If you are having trouble, increase your Vitality. Every level up will raise your defense, but raising your Vitality also increases your HP for extra survivability. You should also fully explore Central Yharnam in order to find eight Bloodstone Shards; you can use these at the workbench in the Hunter's Dream to upgrade your weapon to +2, greatly increasing your damage. If you don't have any Molotovs for Phase 3, consider buying some from the shop. Finally, make certain that you've started the Little Girl's quest and received the Tiny Music Box from her. This can be used to stun Gascoigne during the fight. Before the fight, equip your Tiny Music Box and Molotovs in your Quick Items, as well as Throwing Knives if you choose to use them. It's recommended to remove other items so that they don't get in the way during the battle. If you have done all of this and are still having trouble, you can stockpile Blood Echoes safely between the Central Yharnam Lamp and the Dog Kennels; every additional point of Vitality will help. You can also go online and use a Beckoning Bell to summon another player for help at the cost of one point of Insight.

Overview

You'll face Father Gascoigne after crossing Central Yharnam's Lower Bridge. During Phase 1, he will attack you with his Hunter Axe and a blunderbuss. He uses the normal Hunter Axe moveset with a couple of additions, such as the Rising Shear. He will also shoot at you when you are at medium range; be warned that he will sometimes shoot you if you dodge backwards away from his melee.

After losing 20% of his health, he can transform his weapon to begin Phase 2. Sometimes the timing of this transformation varies; he likes to have some space before he extends his axe. His attacks are a bit slower in this Phase, but he has a lot more range. His spin slash hits twice, so be careful when dodging forward. He will start using jumping attacks to close the distance, but be warned that, unlike a player using the Hunter Axe, he can still shoot you. After losing 70% of his health, he will change into a beast, and Phase 3 begins. He will become very fast and aggressive, but he gains weaknesses to both fire and saw attacks.

Basic Information

Special Weakness: Serration (Beast only)

		■	✦	Item Drops											
Central Yharnam	2031	1800		None	95	95	95	95	80	65	120	999	999	—	—
Central Yharnam | Beast	2031	1800		Oedon Tomb Key [100%]	126	126	126	126	160	50	120	999	999	X	—

Key Attacks

Human Form	Interrupt	Notes
Scattergun Burst	No	Quickstep forward through it.
Horizontal Chop	Yes	Quickstep in the opposite direction of the swing.
Spark Uppercut	Yes	Interrupt it or quickstep sideways.
Jump Attack	Yes	Interrupt it or quickstep forward or sideways.
Charged Spin	Yes	Used after transforming his axe; identical to the player version of the charged R2. Quickstep backward.

Beast Form	Interrupt	Notes
Aerial Dive	No	Leaps high into the air, hovers momentarily and dives at your current location; roll toward him.
Downward Slam	Yes	Raises arms slowly and slams the ground; strafe backward and interrupt it or quickstep forward past him.
Claw Combo	Yes	Fast hits with heavy forward momentum. Quickstep forward or sideways and strafe behind him.
Howl	No	Not an offensive move; mainly an opportunity for you to get in a few free hits or oil him.

Environment

The graves and trees can get in the way of your attacks and movement, but Gascoigne can get stuck on them as well. There are also stairs that lead up to an upper terrace, a clear, open space with plenty of room for you to move; and there's a broken rail that will allow you to jump down to heal when needed.

Where you choose to fight Gascoigne should be based on which aspect of the fight causes you the most trouble. If you are getting stuck on obstacles, fighting upstairs may be better for you. If his gunshots are more annoying to deal with, having the trees and graves to block them may be more valuable. Be warned that in Phase 3, Gascoigne can destroy the small graves with his attacks; the large, central monument can still be used to slow him down, however.

Strategies

Key Strategies

During his first Phase, quickstepping and using charged attacks is a good idea until you're familiar with Gascoigne's attacks. Use interrupts when up close once you begin to recognize his slower attacks. When he transforms his weapon you can switch to using your Throwing Knives to move him into Phase 3 of the fight. While he's transforming, use a Molotov, then use the environment and the Music Box to slow him down while you finish him with more Molotovs.

Phase 1

During Phase 1, focus on quickstepping through Gascoigne's attacks and counterattacking with an R1 > L1 combo. You should dodge toward Gascoigne so that you pass through his attack and get behind him. The R1 will cause him to flinch, and the L1 will cause him to stumble. After the L1, be ready to roll toward him again; after a slight pause, he will either attack you again or quickstep and shoot his gun. Roll through his attack or his bullets and attack him again, but don't bother trying to continue the combo after the first L1; sometimes you can, but he will often quickstep back and shoot you out of it.

If he hits you once or twice, back off and heal. If you stay in the lower area, try to position a tree or large tombstone between you and Gascoigne; if on the upper level, drop down on the small roof to heal, then drop down to the ground and head back upstairs. When attacking, stay close so that he doesn't shoot often. When healing, make sure you have cover to block bullets. The one attack to watch out for is his Rising Shear; it's slightly slower than his normal attack, so you need to dodge forward a little bit later.

An alternate strategy for this Phase is to shoot him during his attacks for an interrupt. When he staggers after the interrupt, you can use a Visceral Attack to deal a lot of damage quickly. If you are confident in your timing, this is an easy way to win.

Phase 2

Phase 2 is largely the same as Phase 1. You can fight him in the same way, but there are a couple of new attacks to watch out for.

His Jumping Attack is used from long range and hits hard, so either stay close or be ready to dodge it. His Spin Attack hits twice in the area around him, so you need to dodge either backward out of its range, or forward, through the attack.

Once again, gunshot interrupts are a viable alternate strategy; just remember that the timing will be slightly later since he is holding the two-handed version of the axe. You can also back off a bit and use Throwing Knives if you like, since shoots less often during this Phase. The downside to this tactic is that it puts you in the range from which he likes to use his Jumping Attack. If you keep space behind you to dodge backwards, this can be ok; consider fighting upstairs if you want to use this method.

Phase 3

Phase 3 will begin with his transformation. Use your Tiny Music Box just as the transformation ends – he will stumble before finally roaring and shaking himself free from the stun. While he is stunned quickly use your Molotovs, making sure you're locked on and not too far away. Two Molotovs will greatly weaken him; if you manage to land three, he will be nearly dead.

To finish Gascoigne off, there are three main strategies: running away and using items, dodging through his attacks and striking him from behind, and using gunshot interrupts. If you choose to run away and use Molotovs and Throwing Knives, try to use the large central monument to slow him down, and only throw an item while he's recovering from a missed attack.

Option two is to stay close; as in Phase 2, if he lands his Downward Slam, be prepared to dodge past him instead of away. This will position you well, and also prevent him punishing your escape with a Jump Attack. Additionally, try baiting Gascoigne to do his Claw Combo and immediately circling around to your right to reach his back. You are safe behind him once he initiates the combo, which provides you plenty of time to heal or get damage in. If you have a quick weapon, you can easily land a charged R2 attack with this strategy followed by a Visceral Attack for major damage.

The final strategy is by far the most risky; Gascoigne can be interrupted using gunshots in this Phase, but he is so fast and aggressive that one miss can end your life. This method is stylish, but not for the faint of heart. If you do get hit, remember the monument or the drop to the roof as ways to buy time and heal.

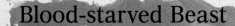

Blood-starved Beast

Overview

The Blood-starved Beast resides in the abandoned Church of the Good Chalice in Old Yharnam. During Phase 1 it moves very slowly and isn't very aggressive. It will spend most of its time strafing sideways or walking toward you and will occasionally perform basic claw swipes or a lunging slash. Phase 2 begins when its health drops below 70%, at which point it will roar and cover itself in a permanent aura that adds extremely potent slow poison build-up to all of its melee attacks. It fights more aggressively during this Phase and will begin sprinting toward you to use its claw attacks; it will also start using a fast lunging grab attack that can reach you from far away. In addition to its Phase 1 attack chains, it will perform a more rapid five-hit combo. When you reduce its health to 30% it will initiate Phase 3 with its Poison Blast attack, which causes it to continuously emit toxic mist that builds up slow poison if you stand too close. It will become even more aggressive and unpredictable during this Phase, relentlessly chasing you down and attacking with long combos; its grab attack is much more common and it will use its Poison Blast at regular intervals when its toxic proximity effect wears off.

Preparation

Weapons that inflict bonus damage against beasts, such as the Saw Spear and the Saw Cleaver, are useful for this battle, so upgrading one beforehand is a good idea. If you haven't already obtained the Flamesprayer from Gilbert in Central Yharnam, be sure to do so; it's also well worth making a side trip to Hemwick Woods to pick up some Bone Marrow Ash. Pungent Blood Cocktails are an extremely effective tool in this fight. Be sure you have your weapon upgraded to +3 by this point – there are numerous Blood Stone Shards available in Old Yharnam and the Cathedral Ward. Also, be sure your weapon is slotted with Blood Gems for maximum damage, such as the Red Jeweled Brooch found in the Tomb of Oedon. If you've already met Alfred in the Cathedral Ward and exhausted his dialogue, you'll be able to summon him outside the church to assist you during the battle if you're playing online.

Basic Information

Special Weakness: Serration

	■	♠	Item Drops	⌐	○	△	⚙	★	♫	⬡	▽	⚡	∿
Old Yharnam	3470	6600	Pthumeru Chalice [100%]	108	108	108	108	160	55	160	999	180	×	—
Chalice Dungeon Base Level	635	333	Random gun type gem x1 [100%]	114	114	114	114	160	70	160	999	180		
Chalice Dungeon Base Level | Boss	2910	1397	Lower Hintertomb Chalice [100%], Ailing Loran Root Chalice [100%]	114	114	114	114	160	55	160	999	180		
Hunter's Nightmare	5183	2366	Random gun type gem x1 [100%]	137	137	137	137	220	75	220	999	180		

Preset Chalice Dungeons: Hintertomb (Boss), Ailing Loran (Boss)

Key Attacks

Phase 1	Interrupt	Notes
Lunging Slash	Yes	Delayed long-range lunge; quickstep forward or to the left.
Slow Combo	Yes	Up to three hits with long reach, but slow startup; quickstep forward past its right side or strafe clockwise at close range.
Fast Combo	Yes	Up to three hits with quick startup and long reach; quickstep forward past it.

Phase 2	Interrupt	Notes
Poison Grab	Yes	Lunging mid– to long-range grab; extremely quick and inflicts slow poison. Quickstep forward or sideways.
Rage Combo	Yes	Up to five rapid hits with extremely quick startup; quickstep forward.

Phase 3	Interrupt	Notes
Poison Blast	No	Large spherical area attack. Inflicts damage and generates an aura that builds up slow poison; avoid staying near it.
Jump Combo	Yes	Mid-range jump followed by two quick slashes; quickstep forward past it.

Environment

The church battlefield consists of a long rectangular nave with aisles on both sides and a semi-circular ambulatory at the far end. The nave is large and open, providing plenty of room to fight on even ground; the ambulatory surrounds an altar, which can be used for cover, but the narrow aisles restrict your evasive ability and the pillars supporting them don't provide safe cover. In general, keep the fight to the length of the nave, so that you have plenty of room to dodge; use the altar to obstruct the boss if you need time to heal, but try to stay out of the aisles. If you run out of Antidotes, you can obtain three more from a corpse behind the altar.

Strategies

Key Strategies

The Blood-Starved Beast can be trivialized with the right consumable setup. He is susceptible to Pungent Blood Cocktails and can easily be lured into a corner. Use Fire Paper on your weapon and toss a Pungent Blood Cocktail into a corner of the room. You'll have several seconds to freely attack the beast before you need to toss another cocktail.

Otherwise, staying very close to the boss and circling to your left can avoid all of the Blood-Starved Beast's attacks. Attacking it from behind while it's recovering from its own attack is ideal – it has no back attacks to punish you.

Phase 1

The Blood-starved Beast is most vulnerable during the first Phase, due to its slow movement and minimal aggression. You can avoid all of its attacks by circling clockwise around it at a very close distance, or quickstepping to be safe. Beware that both its Slow & Fast Combos can clip you if you close in to attack before the combo finishes. If you're using a fast weapon, you can employ charged R2 attacks from behind followed by a Visceral Attack. If you're confident in your timing, you can interrupt all of the Blood-Starved Beast's attacks – just be aware that doing so later in the fight can be extremely risky. Remember to stay close, and take advantage of his scream that signals Phase 2; a few R1 hits or a charged R2 to the back can add some significant damage.

Phase 2

Watch out for the boss' grab during this Phase and try to avoid being hit – even a glancing blow from its claws will inflict an enormous amount of slow poison build-up. Watch for it to stop walking and stare forward for a moment; that signals an oncoming grab attack. You can still avoid all of its attacks by rotating or quickstepping past it in a clockwise direction – do your best to stay behind it, as it cannot reach you in this position. Continue using Pungent Blood Cocktails to lure it into a vulnerable area, or punish its attacks from behind. Be aware of the scream that signals Phase 3 and punish it appropriately with a charged R2 from behind and a Visceral Attack or several R1 attacks.

Phase 3

Your priority during this Phase is to finish the boss as quickly as possible, though you'll also need to pay careful attention to its attacks in order to avoid being poisoned or grabbed. Make every effort to stay behind the boss and don't get greedy with your melee attacks; attempting to interrupt it during this Phase is extremely risky, due to its unpredictability.

As in the previous Phases, you can avoid all of its attacks with very close clockwise rotation or quicksteps, but be aware of its poison aura if it has successfully used Poison Blast. When the Blood-starved Beast retreats and begins emitting jets of brown mist, it is readying its Poison Blast; while this move has heavy super armor, you can cancel it by repeatedly striking the boss' head with quick R1 attacks or landing a charged R2 from behind followed by a Visceral Attack. Pungent Blood Cocktails still attract Blood-Starved Beast in this Phase, so use them as necessary for some free damage.

The Witch of Hemwick

Be sure you've obtained the Radiant Sword Hunter Badge from the Healing Church Workshop to make Bone Marrow Ash available for purchase from the Bath Messengers in the Hunter's Dream. Stock up on Blood Vials, Quicksilver Bullets and Bone Marrow Ash; if you've already acquired the Powder Keg Hunter Badge from Djura in Old Yharnam, buy a full load of Oil Urns as well. Finally, if you've picked up any Numbing Mists and haven't used them yet, this is a good time to add them to your Quick Items; this measure is optional, but can provide a helpful advantage during the battle.

Overview

Although the witch herself is weak and straightforward for a boss enemy, she uses several diversionary tactics to complicate the fight. During the first Phase, the witch you'll face is actually a doppelganger; the real one will not join the battle until the clone's health falls below 50%. Both witches are invisible outside a narrow radius of two to three meters; moreover, the real witch's health bar will not be displayed at any point during Phase 1, even after she joins the battle and begins taking damage. Each witch will always begin the battle in a fixed position: the clone starts off in the corner to the left of the entrance, while the real witch will appear in the opposite corner to the right of the exit. Neither witch is especially aggressive during this Phase; most of the time they'll slowly wander the perimeter of the room and completely ignore you, but will occasionally perform a single melee attack or their Dark Wave if you get too close. They will teleport away from you after being hit, usually to the opposite end of the room or onto the walkways, and will continuously summon Mad Ones up to a total of four. These Mad Ones have extremely short detection range and move very slowly during Phase 1, but can become a serious problem if they corner you.

Phase 2 begins when you reduce either witch's health to 0. At this point you'll have 50 seconds to defeat the remaining witch before the first one stands back up with 20% health. Both witches will begin bombarding you with repeated Paralysis Blasts during this Phase and will immediately follow up with their Eye Gouge while you're stunned; they will also summon Mad Ones more frequently and will continue using their Dark Wave attack at mid range. The Mad Ones' movement speed and detection range will increase during this Phase, and they'll become more aggressive and persistent in hunting you down.

Basic Information			Item Drops												
Hemwick Charnel Lane	2611	11800	Bloodshot Eyeball ×4 [100%]		79	79	79	79	70	73	90	200	180	—	—

Key Attacks

Phase 1	Interrupt	Notes
Dark Wave	No	Spherical area attack with a two-meter radius; quickstep forward through it or backward to escape.
Summon	No	Summons up to four Mad Ones in quick succession; shoot or attack the witch to cancel the summoning.

Phase 2	Interrupt	Notes
Paralysis Blast	No	Long-range projectile that paralyzes, followed by an Eye Gouge if it connects. Roll or quickstep sideways.
Eye Gouge	Yes	Running grab attack used after a Paralysis Blast. Unavoidable if paralyzed; otherwise quickstep sideways.

Environment

The partially-collapsed bridge connecting the outer walkways effectively divides the room into two square halves, though you can move freely between them through the broken section in the middle. Running on the walkways generates loud noise that will immediately alert any summoned Mad Ones to your exact location no matter how far away they are; you can prevent this by tilting the left stick gently to walk, but it can also be used to lure the Mad Ones onto the walkways and away from the witches if you need more room to fight.

Strategies

Key Strategies

Reduce both witches' health to critical levels during Phase 1 and keep careful track of their positions to finish them in quick succession and completely bypass the battle's second Phase. Their incredibly slow movements during the first Phase allow you to stagger them consecutively with charged strikes and trap them in a chain of visceral attacks until you run out of stamina; alternately, you can power up your Cannon or Flamesprayer with Bone Marrow Ash, strike one of the witches from behind with an oil urn, stagger her with a charge attack before she teleports and blast her during the stagger state for heavy damage. Hitting the witches with Numbing Mist surrounds them in a white cloud, which can be used to track them from far away. If you're having problems with the Mad Ones, you can enter the fight with 0 Insight and they will not appear. Note that the first time you enter the fight, you'll be granted 1 Insight and will have to spend it for this to work.

Phase 1

Walk far enough into the boss room to initiate the fight, then turn left and engage the doppelganger witch. You may use any desired means to fight her, but chaining visceral attacks is the quickest and most effective way to deal damage. Keep an eye on the Mad Ones and run up the walkway to divert them if you need more room to fight; if you drop down from the longer half of the broken bridge

spanning the arena, every Mad One in the room will move slowly to that spot and then lose track of you provided you don't enter their detection range before they get there. The witches' melee attacks and Dark Wave can damage the Mad Ones, but don't count on them to use either one – most of the time they won't attack at all. If they do use their Dark Wave, either quickstep toward them just before they cast to negate the damage with your invincibility frames or quickstep backward as soon as possible to avoid the attack entirely. Reduce the clone's health to around 20% and memorize her current location, then head for the far end of the room and track down the real witch; if you haven't already attacked her, she'll still be wandering around near the exit. If you have any Numbing Mists, hit her with one before attacking so that you can track her location; otherwise deal as much damage as possible using any of the Key Strategies before she can teleport away. Focus on defeating the real witch first and when she falls, immediately return to the doppelganger's position and finish her off before she has a chance to initiate Phase 2.

Phase 2

If you're unable to defeat both witches before this Phase begins, you'll have to deal with their Paralysis Blasts and constant attacks from more aggressive Mad Ones. Using the walkways to draw the Mad Ones away from the witches becomes much more important at this point, but the barrage of paralyzing magic will make it dangerous to stay in one place for too long. You can use the terrain and even the Mad Ones themselves to block these projectiles; you can also use the projectiles to get a fix on the witches' locations. Apart from the increased pressure and less frequent opportunities to safely attack the witches, the overall strategy during this Phase remains the same: reduce their health to critical levels and strike them down at close intervals to bring the fight to an end.

Darkbeast Paarl

Preparation

Purchase a full load of Molotovs and if you have any Oil Urns, save them for this battle. Be absolutely sure you've obtained the Radiant Sword Hunter Badge from the Healing Church Workshop so that you can stock up on Bone Marrow Ash and Fire Paper; if you haven't already acquired the Flamesprayer from Gilbert in Central Yhar-nam, do so or buy one from the shop in the Hunter's Dream. The Saw Spear is an excellent choice for this fight as the boss is weak against both thrust attacks and anti-beast weapons; Henryk's attire is useful due to its comparatively high lightning defense. By using the Monocular to aim, you can hit him with Molotovs and Throwing Knives from outside the boss area after encountering him for the first time and triggering him to wake up; by alternating between Oil Urns and Molotovs in this manner, you can reduce his health by more than half before even passing through the Nightmare Fog.

Overview

Darkbeast Paarl is an extremely agile and aggressive boss whose attacks can be incredibly difficult to avoid. He will constantly circle you outside the reach of your melee attacks and will immediately back up if you advance toward him, preventing you from being able to hit him or use the blind spot underneath him to avoid his melee swings. He will continuously reposition himself to keep you at mid range while leaping in to strike with wide horizontal sweeps and overhead slams, and will perform combos of up to four hits with massive range and highly-varied timing. Dealing heavy damage to Paarl's head in a short period of time will stagger him and allow you to perform a frontal visceral attack; repeatedly striking his limbs will knock him down and dispel his lightning aura, at which point he'll

Basic Information				Item Drops											
Special Weakness: Serration	■	✈				120	144	120	120	75	85	300	999	999	✕	—
Yahar'gul (Evening)	4552	21000		Spark Hunter Badge [100%]		120	144	120	120	75	85	300	999	999	✕	—
Loran Darkbeast Base Level	2822	1724		Lower Ailing Loran Root Chalice [100%]		112	135	112	112	75	85	300	999	999		

Preset Chalice Dungeons: Lower Loran (Loran Darkbeast)

Key Attacks

Phase 1	Interrupt	Notes
Lunging Sweep	No	Long-range horizontal slash with an extremely wide arc; quickstep forward through it.
Leaping Burst Slash	No	Long-range downward slash that creates a forward blast of lightning after 0.5 second delay; quickstep backward or forward.
Soaring Pounce	No	Long-range jumping slam. Combined hitboxes cover an enormous area; quickstep directly or diagonally backward.
Charge Punch	No	Charges for two seconds and performs a downward punch.; the attack creates a frontal sphere of electricity after 0.5 second delay. Quickstep backward.
Burst Combo	No	Up to four hits: a frontal sweep, two overheads that create spherical blasts of lightning and a horizontal slash. Quickstep backward.
Lunging Bite	No	Mid-range counterclockwise bite attack; strikes a frontal 90-degree arc on his right side. Quickstep backward.
Thunder Slam	No	Frontal vertical slam that creates a large sphere of lightning 0.5 seconds after the initial impact and trails sparks clockwise in a 90-degree arc; quickstep backward.
Static Discharge	No	Massive spherical area attack centered on his head; quickstep backward 2-3 times, or quickstep once the instant he raises his head to evade using invincibility frames.

Phase 2	Interrupt	Notes
Forward Static Discharge	No	Used to end combos. Slams both arms down and generates an enormous forward spherical area attack; quickstep backward or sideways as late as possible to pass through it.

take 50% more damage until he restores it. Almost all of Paarl's physical attacks leave lingering trails of lightning that will damage you on contact; some of them also generate large spherical blasts of electricity either in front of him or to his sides. He uses the same set of attacks during both Phases of the battle, but during the second Phase his swings will generate forward waves of sparks and the radius of the lightning blasts they generate will double.

Environment

The perimeter is dotted with a few irregular features such as trees and buttresses, but is otherwise completely open and provides no cover at all. Backing Darkbeast Paarl into one of the acute corners can help prevent him from evading your attacks, but be careful not to be cornered yourself, as his wide swings can make it almost impossible to escape.

Strategies

Key Strategies

Quickstep forward through Paarl's attacks, and try to focus on one specific part of his body. When he uses his Static Discharge, roll through it and attack while he recovers. Repeatedly attacking Paarl's limbs will stun him and dispel his lightning, allowing you to deal more damage. He'll regenerate the lightning if you let him get away, so focus on staying close by dodging through his attacks. If you alternate attacking different legs, you can stun lock him on the ground with enough damage and skip Phase 2 completely.

Phase 1

During this Phase you can handle Darkbeast Paarl in one of two ways: either stay underneath him to avoid his dangerous frontal attacks and quickstep through his Static Discharge, or continually back away from him by strafing and quickstepping out of his reach. If you're relying on melee weapons, stay underneath him. In order to reach this position you'll have to quickstep forward around his head, bearing slightly to your left; if you dash directly towards him you'll be blocked by his head and left front leg, leaving you vulnerable to his attacks. Make every possible effort to stay directly beneath him and avoid standing to his sides; he'll frequently try to drive you away with close-range swipes and slashes that will knock you down or cause you to stumble, setting you up for further combos or follow-ups. Power up your weapons with Fire Paper and aim for his legs to knock him down, but watch for him to curl up and begin charging electricity – these are signs that he's about to unleash his Static Discharge attack, and you'll need to pay close attention to his posture and audio to time your quickstep correctly. Watch for him to raise his head and listen for his scream – time your quickstep as close as possible to the first frame of either of these cues, and don't attack after he curls up or you risk being hit by the blast. The safest opportunities to recover your health are after quickstepping away from his combos and while underneath him, but be sure you'll recover from the animation before he does.

Phase 2

Darkbeast Paarl will initiate this Phase by backing away from you and intensifying his lightning aura when his health drops to 66%. From this point onward it is no longer safe to stand in front of him due to his extremely unpredictable attacks, massive frontal lightning blasts and constant bombardment of sparks; your only choice is to stay beneath him. Beware that in this Phase he will sometimes end his combo attacks with his nearly inescapable Forward Static Discharge; the only way to reliably avoid this attack is to stay under him, which will prevent him from using it altogether. Destroying his lightning aura during this Phase will temporarily disable all of his lightning projectiles and area attacks until he restores it; take full advantage of this opportunity to deal as much damage as you can while he's weakened. The only safe times to heal are when you're directly beneath him and during the start-up of his Static Discharge.

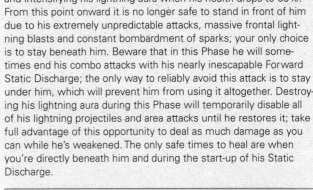

Vicar Amelia

Preparation

Weapons with damage bonuses against beasts, such as the Saw Cleaver and the Saw Spear, are very helpful for this battle, so consider upgrading one if you haven't already done so. You should also have the Radiant Sword Hunter Badge at this point, which will allow you to purchase Fire Paper in the Hunter's Dream; you may either buy a few from the shop or find some on a corpse in the Cathedral Ward. Another corpse in the same area holds three Numbing Mists, which are helpful for this battle. The Flamesprayer is extremely effective against Vicar Amelia, as are Molotovs and Oil Urns; and as always, stock up on Blood Vials and Quicksilver Bullets before heading out.

Overview

Vicar Amelia moves relatively slowly, but can cover long distances with her jumping attacks. In close combat she uses sweeping horizontal swings with long reach as well as a forward shockwave and a few basic combos. She is highly weak against both fire and weapons that deal extra damage to beasts, making the Saw Cleaver or the Saw Spear ideal weapons for this battle when used with Fire Paper. The Flamesprayer is highly effective as well, especially when used with Oil Urns and Bone Marrow Ash. You can injure her head and all four of her limbs by hitting them repeatedly; doing so will cause her to stumble, and the injured limb will take an additional 50% damage. Trying to get behind her is tricky and requires proper timing due to the delay on most of her melee attacks; staying there is effectively impossible, because she will immediately backstep away and reposition herself facing you. During the first Phase of the battle she will move and attack slowly, usually only using one or two swings at a time but occasionally chaining up to three. During the second Phase, she will begin recovering her health every time it drops below 50% and will attack much more aggressively, running or leaping toward you and adding several more hits to her combos.

Basic Information

Special Weakness: Serration			Item Drops			113	135	113	113	160	55	160	999	999	✕	—
Cathedral Ward	5367	15000	Gold Pendant [100%]													

Key Attacks

Phase 1	Interrupt	Notes
Axe-Handle Smash	No	Mid-range forward shockwave that grows as it travels; quickstep sideways as soon as her fists hit the ground.
Jumping Slam	No	Mid-range jump attack that travels forward four meters; quickstep sideways.
Cross Sweep	No	Spreads both arms and performs a frontal 180-degree pincer slash. Looks like a grab, but isn't. Quickstep sideways or forward past her.
Gnashing Grab	No	Right-handed close-range grab attack with a one-second windup; quickstep backward.
Uppercut Sweep	No	Delayed short-range launcher that strikes a frontal 120-degree arc; quickstep into the attack or away from it as soon as you see sparks from her claws.

Phase 2	Interrupt	Notes
Recovery	No	Clasps claws together in prayer and recovers health; attack her to cancel it or hit her with Numbing Mist to disable it.
Super Axe-Handle Slam	No	Roars, then performs an Axe-Handle Slam that creates a long-range shockwave. Quickstep to either side.
Bite	No	Short-range bite with near-instant startup. Too fast to evade reliably; avoid standing directly in front of her at close range.
Jumping Double Slam	No	Stronger version of the Jumping Slam performed with both fists; quickstep sideways.
Tantrum Combo	No	Slowly raises both arms above her head and performs a rapid multi-hit combo; quickstep sideways or backward.

Environment

The boss area is an empty rectangular chapel with no unusual features, forcing you to fight Vicar Amelia head-on with no cover and nowhere to hide. The layout of this arena gives you quite a bit of room to maneuver, which is essential to avoiding Amelia's jump attacks and wide, sweeping swings – just keep the fight to the center of the room as much as possible and try to avoid being backed into a corner.

Strategies

Key Strategies

Repeatedly attacking Vicar Amelia's hind legs will stagger her, allowing you to perform a visceral attack from the front; you may also choose to hit her with a Flamesprayer blast during this time, which will inflict enormous amounts of damage if you use a pinch of Bone Marrow Ash and strike Amelia with an Oil Urn before staggering her. Quick R1 combos with the Saw Cleaver or Saw Spear in their one-handed modes are extremely effective if you augment your weapons with Fire Paper, providing a substantial boost to your melee damage.

Phase 1

During this Phase you should focus on injuring Amelia's hind legs to stagger her, whether using melee attacks, Molotovs or the Flamesprayer. You can avoid her melee attacks by quickstepping either toward her or sideways in the opposite direction of the swing, but beware that most of her attacks have delays of up to a full second and require you to dodge late in order to avoid being hit. Her Uppercut Sweep is particularly dangerous in this regard and you must pay close attention to its timing – either quickstep backward twice as soon as she begins using it, or once sideways in the opposite direction when she swings. Beware that if you stand beside her at very close range, you'll need to keep an eye out for her sideways swipes; if she tries to hit you with one, quickstep backward.

Phase 2

When Vicar Amelia's health falls to 50%, she will begin using her Recovery technique to restore it, and will fight more aggressively. You can temporarily disable her ability to heal herself by striking her with a Numbing Mist, but your most important objective during this Phase is to avoid her much faster combo attacks while dealing as much damage as you can. You may need more than one quickstep to evade her Phase 2 attacks, so keep a close eye on your stamina; continue to focus on injuring her limbs to buy yourself enough time for a few attacks and beware that she will now change up her mid-range shockwave attack with a long-range version that can hit you from across the room. This attack can still be avoided by quickstepping sideways and offers a chance to hit her a few times if you're close to her when you dodge it. Try to keep her at mid range if you can, and avoid standing close enough that you'll need more than one quickstep to get away. Continue to wear her down with your melee attacks and Fire Paper, and if you have no Numbing Mist when she begins healing herself, dash in and hit her with R1 combos or transformation attacks to cancel her recovery.

Shadow of Yharnam

If you've cleared your way far enough into the Chalice Dungeons that Shaman Bone Blades are available from the Insight Shop, bring three; if you plan to use the Cannon, be sure to bring some Bone Marrow Ash. Bolt Paper and weapons that inflict additional arcane damage, such as the Burial Blade, are very effective against two of the shadows, but the third is resistant to lightning and arcane, so you'll need a backup weapon with a purely physical damage type. The Chikage is also a good choice, as all three shadows are equally weak against its physical and blood damage; scatterguns are useful for their ability to hit multiple targets, so consider bringing a Hunter Blunderbuss or Ludwig's Rifle as well.

Overview

The two swordsmen are weak against lightning and arcane damage, but the mace-wielding shadow is resistant to both elements; all three have low physical and blood defense, so melee weapons with either of these damage types such as the Chikage are most effective against them. The shadows with scimitars both use the same fighting style, though the one carrying a candle can also breathe fire and isn't as aggressive with its sword attacks; in addition to basic horizontal and vertical slashes, they'll sometimes perform longer combos and heavy swings that can knock you down or launch you into the air. The mace-wielder usually attacks with homing fireballs, though it'll occasionally take a swing at you with its mace if you're close; it's the least aggressive of the three and has the lowest maximum health, but the damage from its fireballs can become a serious problem. During Phase 1, the bosses are limited to their basic attacks; the swordsmen will chase you around the boss area while the mace-wielder bombards you with fireballs from afar. When Phase 2 starts, all three shadows will begin using their stronger attacks and the one carrying a candle will cover its blade with fire. The swordsmen will use their knockdown attacks much more persistently, and will begin performing long-range stabs and launchers. Any shadows remaining at the start of Phase 3 will periodically summon a trio of giant snakes, which will strike you individually at mid to long range.

Environment

The boss area's uneven border creates a large number of nooks and corners which can become deathtraps if you're backed into them, but the tombstones are essential for separating your enemies and blocking the fireballs thrown by the mace-wielding shadow. The nooks can also work against the bosses, though, and can be used to trap them if their constant backsteps are proving troublesome.

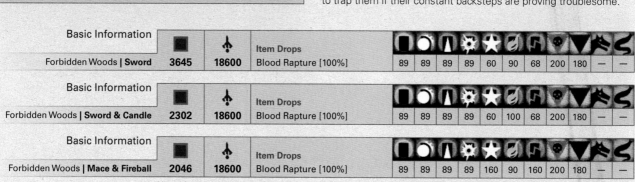

Basic Information															
Forbidden Woods | Sword	3645	18600	**Item Drops** Blood Rapture [100%]	89	89	89	89	60	90	68	200	180	—	—
Basic Information															
Forbidden Woods | Sword & Candle	2302	18600	**Item Drops** Blood Rapture [100%]	89	89	89	89	60	100	68	200	180	—	—
Basic Information															
Forbidden Woods | Mace & Fireball	2046	18600	**Item Drops** Blood Rapture [100%]	89	89	89	89	160	90	160	200	180	—	—

Note: You can only get one Blood Rapture Rune, and it will drop from whichever enemy you kill last.

Key Attacks

Phase 1	Interrupt	Notes
Sword, Sword & Candle		
Upward Slash	Yes	Swift close-range launcher used in combos and on its own; quickstep forward or backward.
Running Slash	Yes	Mid-range running knockdown attack; quickstep forward or sideways.
Sword Combo	Yes	Up to five rapid hits and a delayed sixth swing; quickstep backward.
Sword & Candle		
Fire Breath	No	Mid-range fire breath with continuous tracking; quickstep backward or sideways.
Mace & Fireball		
Triple Homing Fireball	No	Launches three long-range homing fireballs; quickstep sideways or forward through them.

Phase 2	Interrupt	Notes
Sword, Sword & Candle		
Whip Thrust	Yes	Long-range forward thrust with slightly delayed startup; quickstep sideways.
Whip Uppercut	Yes	Identical to the sword-only version. Long-range launcher with slightly delayed startup; quickstep in any direction.
Mace & Fireball		
Triple Raining Fireball	No	Throws three arcing mid-range fireballs that converge on your location and create large spherical explosions; quickstep backward or forward.

Phase 3	Interrupt	Notes
Sword, Sword & Candle, Mace & Fireball		
Snake Summon	No	Summons three giant snakes that perform long-range strikes or mid-range sweeping bites depending on their distance from you. Snakes appear in random locations; keep moving and roll in any direction when they attack.

Strategies

Key Strategies

Above all, focus on one shadow at a time to avoid triggering the next Phase with all three still alive. Interrupts are the best way to deal with the swordsmen; staggers are equally effective on the two shadows that use fire attacks. Shaman Bone Blades will turn the bosses against each other and can drastically turn the tide of the battle if used at the right time. All three shadows have no super armor and any melee attack will cause them to flinch; charge attacks from heavier weapons such as the transformed Hunter Axe and Burial Blade will knock them down, and are helpful for keeping them at a safe distance during Phases 1 and 2. If you have a Shadow in a one-on-one situation, you can exploit their defensiveness by alternating an R1 attack followed by a few steps forward while locked on. Most of the time, they will dash away after being hit, so by walking the distance they just dashed and using R1 again, you can lock them in an infinite cycle.

Phase 1

Hit-and-run tactics are the safest strategy while being pursued by all three shadows; the giant tombstone is especially helpful for separating them, though beware that the mace-wielder's fireballs can sometimes curve around it. Interrupt the Sword Shadow and finish it with visceral attacks, or stab it with a Shaman Bone Blade before it gets up and lure it toward the others. Don't get greedy with melee combos during this Phase; instead, use single R1 swings or quick-stepping attacks, so that you can keep moving out of your enemies' reach. We recommend defeating one of the swordsmen first to reduce the pressure during later Phases, but the mace-wielder is the easiest target during Phase 1 and getting rid of it early will prevent you from having to constantly watch for its fireballs.

Phase 2

When one shadow's health drops below 30% or all three reach 50%, snakes will burst from their bodies and they will begin using their Phase 2 attacks. Finish the weakest shadow as quickly as possible and continue using hit-and-run tactics on the remaining two; as before, focus on a single shadow and use the tombstones for cover, but beware that the sword-wielders' whip attacks can hit you through the giant tombstone. Interrupts, staggers and knockdown attacks are still the most effective melee strategy during this Phase and with one of the swordsmen gone, you'll have safer and more frequent opportunities to interrupt the other.

Phase 3

When all three shadows drop below 25% health or only one remains standing with a full life bar, the survivors will begin summoning giant snakes that will attack you from far away. If the snakes appear near you, stand as close to them as possible and roll sideways to avoid their attacks; otherwise watch them carefully and dash or roll away when they strike. Finish any weakened stragglers immediately and pressure the remaining shadow with melee attacks to minimize its opportunities for summoning the snakes; if you're having trouble hitting it, back it into a corner along the outer edge of the arena.

Amygdala

Preparation

Bring the Cannon and a single-shot firearm like the Hunter Pistol or Evelyn, and be sure to purchase a full load of Bone Marrow Ash and Quicksilver Bullets; the Repeating Pistol is optional for higher burst damage, but consumes ammunition twice as quickly. Throwing Knives and Molotovs are useful for backup ranged damage if you run out of bullets, and Oil Urns are handy if you plan on using Molotovs or the Flamesprayer; Fire and Bolt Paper are equally effective for increasing the power of your melee attacks.

Overview

Amygdala is an enormous opponent with incredibly long reach, but it also has several glaring weak points you can exploit to make the fight much easier. First, its head will take tremendous damage, even from normally weak sources such as pistols; second, focused attacks on its head will eventually stagger it and allow you to perform a frontal visceral attack; and third, there is a blind spot directly beneath its left thigh in which none of its attacks can hit you except a slow and easily-avoided stomp. During Phase 1 it will use far-reaching overhead smashes and wide vertical sweeps with its long arms, and will attack the area in front it with exploding lasers. In Phase 2 its slam and punch attacks will create explosions of energy and it will begin using a stronger version of its acid attack with a much wider area of effect; it will also fight somewhat more aggressively than the previous Phase. At the beginning of Phase 3, Amygdala will rip off two of its own arms and begin wielding them as clubs, drastically increasing the range of its physical attacks, and will be more persistent about repositioning itself using its leap.

Basic Information

Basic Information	⬛	✈	Item Drops	🗃	◔	△	✦	★	🍃	🎵	☠	▽	🐾	〰
Nightmare Frontier	6404	21000	Ailing Loran Chalice [100%]	128	153	128	128	70	70	70	999	999	—	—
Chalice Dungeon Base Level	3175	1739	Great Pthumeru Ihyll Chalice [100%]	130	156	130	130	70	70	70	999	999		

Preset Chalice Dungeons: Cursed Pthumerian Defilement

Key Attacks

Phase 1	Interrupt	Notes
Pinpoint Lasers	No	Fires multiple small bursts of light in a frontal cone-shaped area; each creates a delayed explosion one second after landing. Quickstep or run sideways.
Straight Laser	No	Sweeps a long-range laser forward, then backward in a straight line; a series of explosions follow the laser's path after a one-second delay. Quickstep or run sideways.
Oscillating Laser	No	Sweeps a laser forward in a zigzag pattern, followed by a series of explosions along the same path one second later; quickstep sideways or backward.
Giant Leap	No	Leaps into the air and lands facing you. Only used to reposition itself and won't deliberately try to land on you; stand still and it will miss.
Stomp	No	Used with one or both feet when you're directly beneath its legs; lock off and walk away from whichever leg is being used for the attack.
Acid Pool	No	Excretes a pool of acid onto the ground below its head; quickstep away in any direction.

Phase 2	Interrupt	Notes
Large Acid Pool	No	Excretes a large amount of acid from its head and shakes it to either side; quickstep backward.
Energy Punch	No	Charges energy on its hands and slams the ground in front of it; quickstep backward and/or sideways, or stay under its legs and it won't use this attack.

Phase 3	Interrupt	Notes
Arm Club	No	Tears off two of its arms and uses them as clubs. Extremely long range; quickstep backward several times or stay under its legs where it can't hit you.

Environment

The boss area is an irregularly-shaped enclosure littered with debris and large poles. While Amygdala can and eventually will destroy the poles, beware of the uneven ground along the inside edge of the arena; the elevation difference in some places is enough to prevent you from being able to walk over it and can leave you with deceptively little room to back away from the boss' attacks. Keep the fight to the center and don't let yourself become trapped in a corner or against the outer wall, and watch out for debris and other obstacles when backing up.

Strategies

Key Strategies

Power up your firearms with Bone Marrow Ash and aim for Amygdala's head – a Cannon shot boosted in this manner will instantly stagger it and allow you to follow through with a visceral attack for even more damage, and when you no longer have enough ammunition to fire the Cannon, you can switch to your pistol and use the rest of your Bone Marrow Ash to make each shot hit much harder. You can also hit Amygdala in the head with melee attacks during its recovery, and the transformed overhead slashes of Ludwig's Holy Blade will reach during the boss' idle stance.

Phase 1

Stand at long range and bait one of Amygdala's overhead slam attacks or wait for it to approach you, then shoot its head with the Cannon or other firearm powered up with Bone Marrow Ash and follow through with a visceral attack when it staggers. Staggering it in this manner will injure its head and you'll be unable to stagger it again for a short time, but it will eventually heal the injury with a quick red flash, at which point you can repeat the process. If solely using melee weapons, avoid standing directly beneath Amygdala's head or the core of its body and don't rush directly toward its legs while it's idle – it can strike all of these spots with downward punches and swipes, and will deliberately target the most direct path to its feet in an effort to catch you as you move in. Instead, stand directly beneath its left thigh and do not lock on; you can walk slowly to maintain this position while avoiding all of Amygdala's attacks and step out quickly during its recovery periods to attack its head and

hands, or simply attack its body without moving from its blind spot. Its legs and tail take almost no damage but you can hit its pelvis and lower body with overhead swings for average damage, allowing you to chip away at it in relative safety.

Phase 2

When its health drops to 70% Amygdala will roar, announcing the beginning of Phase 2. Although it will begin using more powerful versions of its overhead slams that generate explosions at the points of impact, the strategy during this part of the fight remains the same: either stand at long range and bait its attacks for an opportunity to blast its head, or stand under its left thigh and strike its head and body with melee attacks. Its arms remain viable targets as well, but don't get greedy – its ventral punch attacks will create multiple large explosions from this Phase onward, making it far more dangerous to stand directly beneath it. By hitting Amygdala's head with a Bone Marrow Ash Cannonball when it has about 40% health remaining and following through with a visceral attack, you can finish it off before or immediately after it initiates Phase 3.

Phase 3

When Amygdala's health falls below 30% it will rip off two of its arms and begin using them as clubs. Standing in front of it is far more dangerous during this Phase due to the vastly increased range of its melee attacks and it will reposition itself much more frequently using its leap, but even now the strategy remains the same. Although it's harder to target Amygdala's head with gunfire from beneath its legs, you can charge your gun with Bone Marrow Ash in the safety of its blind spot and rush out to shoot while it recovers from an attack; you can still target its remaining arms, but beware that it will continue using its exploding punches if you stand under it for too long.

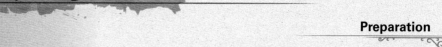

Martyr Logarius

Preparation

It's much easier to interrupt Logarius with single-shot firearms like the Hunter Pistol and Evelyn, so bring one along and don't forget to stock up on Quicksilver Bullets. Stock up on Bone Marrow Ash and Blood Vials, and be sure you have a weapon with fast one-handed charge attacks such as Ludwig's Holy Blade or one of the saws. Fire Paper is optional but not necessary; it will add a few extra points of damage to your attacks, but not enough to make it a priority purchase. If you've obtained the Reiterpallasch from the lower sections of the castle, consider equipping it in your second weapon slot – you can use it as a right-handed gun for strategies involving the Cannon or the Flamesprayer.

Overview

Logarius is an extremely fast and agile opponent, but many of his attacks are highly predictable and provide excellent opportunities to interrupt him. During Phase 1 he'll bombard you from long range with large clouds of dark spirits and use quicker versions of these spells up close; his melee attacks at this stage consist of slow scythe combos and faster sword slashes. He'll respond to frontal attacks and punish you for standing too close by using either a nearly instant frontal skull blast or a delayed explosion. He'll immediately use these techniques or a quick sword slash after standing up from a visceral attack. At the start of Phase 2 he'll perform his Spirit Wave, surrounding himself with an aura that deflects bullets and grants him an enormous amount of super armor. Then he'll assault you with swift melee combos and flying slashes while periodically summoning a cloud of swords that will rain down on you from above. Logarius is strong against all elemental attacks, but is least resistant to fire; his physical defense is much lower, however, so melee weapons augmented with Fire Paper will inflict the most damage.

Basic Information

			Item Drops										
Forsaken Cainhurst Castle	9081	25600	Crown of Illusions [100%]	133	133	133	133	290	160	180	999	999	—	—

Key Attacks

Phase 1	Interrupt	Notes
Homing Skulls	No	Launches a wave of small homing skulls; quickstep sideways or forward through them, or block them with the terrain.
Skull Blast	No	Close-range forward spherical area attack. Near-instant; quickstep backward or avoid standing too close to him.
Delayed Skull Blast	No	Creates a small stationary skull and immediately quicksteps backward, then detonates the skull after one second. Quickstep away in any direction.
Skull Sphere	No	Charges a large sphere of skulls above him and sends it slowly toward you. No tracking whatsoever; quickstep forward under or around it.
Exploding Skull Sphere	No	Same as Skull Sphere, but used at longer range and explodes in a larger spherical blast on contact; run around it or use the terrain for cover.

Phase 2	Interrupt	Notes
Spirit Wave	No	Massive spherical area attack with a five-meter radius. Cannot be interrupted; quickstep backward at least three times.
Aerial Dive	Yes	Three versions. Hovers in the air and dives at you after one to two seconds' delay; interrupt it or roll toward him when he flies toward you.
Phantom Swords	No	Drives a sword into the ground, releasing a spherical attack and a cloud of swords that constantly rain down on you. Quickstep backward twice from the initial blast; shoot or attack the sword in the ground to disperse the others.

Environment

You'll face Logarius on the rooftop of Cainhurst Castle. The roof has multiple slopes and obstacles that you can use for cover during the battle; however, beware that there are no railings or other barriers preventing you from falling off the edge. The spires can be used to block Logarius' projectile attacks and create enough room for you to use Blood Vials if necessary, but pay attention to your position to avoid being backed up against them; the gabled slopes can cause his melee attacks to pass over your head if he's far enough above you and can also provide limited cover from his ranged attacks.

Strategies

Key Strategies

Interrupt Logarius' attacks during both Phases, especially the second Phase when his super armor prevents you from knocking him out of his animations. If you have the Reiterpallasch, you can use its transformed gunshots to interrupt Logarius with a powered-up Cannon in your left hand and deal severe damage during his stagger state, rather than perform a visceral attack. When he covers himself in his spirit aura, make every possible effort to break his super armor – doing so will dispel the aura and stagger him, allowing you to use the aforementioned technique or a visceral attack.

Phase 1

Bait Logarius' Skull Blasts from long range and quickstep forward past them to hit him with melee attacks, or stand no closer than mid range and wait for a chance to interrupt his scythe combos. Don't stand close to him during combat or as he's standing up after a visceral attack, or you risk being hit by his extremely quick counterattacks; instead, back off and watch his movements while you wait for a chance to hit him. By dealing heavy damage to Logarius in a short enough period of time, you can delay or even bypass the trigger for his Spirit Wave when he switches to his Phase 2

attacks, preventing him from using his super armor aura. While his Skull Blasts and slower melee attacks leave enough time for you to quickstep behind him and stagger him with a charged attack, he will always backstep away from you as soon as he recovers, making it impossible to stay in that position for very long.

Phase 2

At around 70% health, Logarius will drive his scythe into the ground and begin channeling energy, signaling the start of Phase 2. While channeling, he will not flinch, but he can be hit with a charged R2 attack from behind for a Visceral Attack. In this phase, Logarius will begin using extremely swift combos with both his scythe and sword; at any time after this point, he may also perform his Spirit Wave if you don't keep constant pressure on him. His flying attacks provide the best opportunities to deal damage during Phase 2; when he dives in from a high angle you can roll toward him and strike from behind with a charged attack when he lands, and when he approaches low to the ground you can interrupt him with gunfire. When Logarius drives his sword into the ground, back away and strafe sideways until it becomes targetable, then shoot it from a distance or quickstep forward and hit it with a melee attack. If you need space to use Blood Vials, put one of the spires between yourself and Logarius but stand well back – his area attacks and some of his normal swings can still reach you on the other side if you're too close. Do not attempt to mount a frontal attack on Logarius at close range during this Phase, and be extremely careful if you have to quickstep toward him; his instant melee attacks can easily stun you long enough for him to trap you in a longer combo.

Rom, the Vacuous Spider

Preparation

Stock up on Bolt Paper, Quicksilver Bullets and Blood Vials. Shaman Bone Blades can be helpful during the second and third Phases if you have access to them; Molotovs and Throwing Knives are only marginally useful. If you've obtained and upgraded the Tonitrus from Yahar'gul, bring it along as it's extremely effective; also consider bringing a weapon with sweeping horizontal swings such as the Hunter Axe or Ludwig's Holy Blade for dealing with the small spiders.

Overview

Rom will not be hostile the first time you enter the boss area, so you can take your time getting prepared. During the first Phase he won't attack you at all and you'll only have to deal with the small spiders; during the second, he'll summon another group of spiders and begin using his magic attacks. When you're close to Rom, he'll use a large spherical magic blast to drive you away; at mid range he'll perform a much wider area attack that causes boulders of ice to rise from the lake beneath you; and if you're outside the range of those spells he'll rain ice boulders down on you from above. Rom will summon a final group of spiders at the beginning of Phase 3 and will begin using a flailing thrash attack if you stand close to him for too long, but will otherwise continue to use his spells in the same manner as during Phase 2. For their part, the spiders are only a threat when they're close to you; if you draw Rom far enough away from them, they'll forget about you and begin aimlessly wandering the area.

Basic Information

	■	✦	Item Drops	🚪	◐	🔔	⚙	★	🗡	🎵	🔲	▽	🐾	〰
Byrgenwerth	5058	22600	Kin Coldblood (12) [100%]	130	130	130	130	80	72	45	999	999	—	—
Chalice Dungeon Base Level	1764	1325	Lower Pthumeru Root Chalice [100%]	112	112	112	112	80	72	45	999	999		

Preset Chalice Dungeons: Lower Pthumerian Labyrinth

Basic Information

	■	✦	Item Drops	🚪	◐	🔔	⚙	★	🗡	🎵	🔲	▽	🐾	〰
Byrgenwerth | Children of Rom	252	0	Madman's Knowledge ×1 [1%]	91	91	91	91	72	62	48	120	300	—	—
Chalice Dungeon Base Level | Children of Rom	88	17	Madman's Knowledge ×1 [1%]	70	70	70	70	72	60	48	120	300		

No Blood Echoes during boss battle. Preset Chalice Dungeons: Lower Pthumerian Labyrinth

Key Attacks

Phase 1	Interrupt	Notes
Rom, the Vacuous Spider		
None		
Children of Rom		
Headbutt Dive	No	Mid-range forward jump attack; quickstep forward or sideways.
Web Shot	No	Mid-range forward web attack; quickstep sideways.
Rear Web Blast	No	Mid-range backward web shot; quickstep sideways.

Phase 2	Interrupt	Notes
Rom, the Vacuous Spider		
Magic Blast	No	Spherical area attack with a four-meter radius; quickstep away from Rom twice to avoid it.
Rising Meteors	No	Massive ring-shaped area attack; strikes between two and eight meters from his body but won't reach at point blank range. Quickstep forward or backward.
Meteor Barrage	No	Rains meteors on your current position regardless of range; stand still as soon as he uses it and they won't hit you.

Phase 3	Interrupt	Notes
Rom, the Vacuous Spider		
Thrash Combo	No	Thrashes from side to side at close range. Quickstep backward and wait for him to stop thrashing.

Environment

The Moonside Lake is a completely flat and open battleground with no obstacles or terrain features of any kind. Although it has no visible boundaries, the area is effectively an enormous circle and you cannot travel beyond the outer edges; even so, its size leaves more than enough room for you to separate Rom from the smaller spiders and fight him a safe distance away.

Strategies

Key Strategies

Rom and his children are very weak against lightning, so use the Tonitrus or power up other weapons with Bolt Paper to inflict the most possible damage. Both Rom and the small spiders take drastically reduced damage from attacks to their heads, so you'll have to quickstep beside or behind them in order to reach their weak points. Weapons with wide horizontal attacks are well-suited to dealing with the small spiders and can eliminate several at once, especially when augmented with Bolt Paper. While fighting Rom, focus on attacking only one of his sides – these spots can be injured with repeated attacks, after which point they'll take additional damage when hit.

Phase 1

Rom will not attack at all during this Phase, so ignore him and focus instead on his children – the first group will not disappear when he summons more, so take your time and eliminate them before things heat up. Quickstep toward them and strike their bodies with melee attacks, but avoid hitting their heads as you'll inflict very little damage by doing so. Beware of their jumping headbutt and web attacks as both deal heavy damage, and don't fight more than one at a time if possible to avoid being surrounded. When all the small spiders are gone, power up your weapon with Bolt Paper and hit Rom's sides with your strongest attacks until he teleports away from you.

Phase 2

When Rom's health drops below 75% he'll teleport to the opposite side of the lake and summon another group of spiders; at this point he'll also begin attacking you directly with his spells. You can either defeat the spiders or ignore them and lure Rom away, but it's better to get rid of them now since they will not disappear even when he summons the final group. When you're within three to four meters of him, he'll raise his head and tail while a swirling vortex of energy surrounds him, then release a spherical blast of energy after a short delay. While this attack lingers too long for you to pass through it using your invincibility frames, it does leave enough time for you to quickstep backward twice and out of its range. At a distance of two to eight meters, Rom will roll over onto his back and summon a ring of ice boulders out of the lake beneath you after a short delay. The boulders strike an enormous ring-shaped area centered on Rom, but will miss you if you're standing against his sides; you can also escape

them by quickstepping backward two to four times. If you're out of reach of both of these spells, Rom will rear up and summon barrages of ice boulders that will rain down on you from the sky no matter how far you are from him; these projectiles track your current location in real time, but will always target a small circle around and will never strike your exact position. To avoid being hit, stop moving as soon as he begins casting and watch the boulders carefully before dodging; alternately, you can prevent Rom from using this attack by staying close enough for him to reach you with the other two.

Phase 3

When you reduce his health to 50% Rom will teleport again and summon a final group of spiders. He will continue to use his spells in the same manner as during Phase 2, but will also begin using a flailing combo attack at extremely close range. This attack is easily avoided by quickstepping backward, but has a very fast start-up and is likely to clip you if you're attacking while pressed directly against his side; he'll also wait until you're in the middle of a combo before initiating it to prevent you from being able to evade in time. Continue attacking Rom's sides and eliminate any spiders that get close enough to attack you; otherwise, focus on defeating him and ignore his children.

The One Reborn

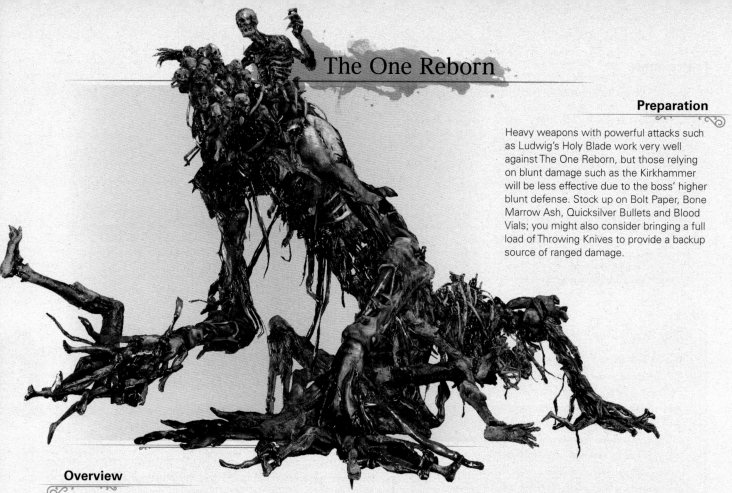

Heavy weapons with powerful attacks such as Ludwig's Holy Blade work very well against The One Reborn, but those relying on blunt damage such as the Kirkhammer will be less effective due to the boss' higher blunt defense. Stock up on Bolt Paper, Bone Marrow Ash, Quicksilver Bullets and Blood Vials; you might also consider bringing a full load of Throwing Knives to provide a backup source of ranged damage.

Overview

The One Reborn is supported by six Bell Ringers that will constantly supply it with dark energy; they'll also begin bombarding you with homing fireballs if you damage the boss while they're still alive. The One Reborn will initially launch clumps of severed limbs at you and rain gore down on your current position, and will use a massive area attack to hit you both on the ground and in the upper galleries. Its arm attacks will generate spheres of darkness at the points of impact, inflicting additional damage and making them harder to avoid; if you try to circle behind it and attack its rear half, it will fill the area around it with acid and force you to retreat. When facing

this boss on the ground level it will use overhead arm slams and horizontal swipes with massive range, and will kick at you with the legs surrounding its core if you stand against its body for too long. If you fight in the galleries, it will stretch its body up to reach you with forward punches and horizontal swings, and will continue pelting you with projectiles. The large corpse atop its front half, the lower central core of its body and all four of its large arms can be injured once each to knock it down for several seconds, allowing you to let loose with your strongest attacks at no risk to yourself; the large corpse receives heavily-increased damage and is your priority target once you've knocked the boss down.

Basic Information

			Item Drops											
Yahar'gul (Blood Moon)	10375	33000	Yellow Backbone x3 [100%]	135	162	135	135	290	70	40	999	999	—	—

Key Attacks

Phase 1	Interrupt	Notes
Corpse Blast	No	Slightly delayed long-range linear projectile with splash damage on impact; quickstep sideways or block it with the terrain.
Raining Gore	No	Long charge period followed by several seconds of corpses raining down on you. Follows your current location; keep moving until the corpses stop falling.
Evil Explosion	No	Massive spherical area attack with a five-meter radius centered on the uppermost corpse; can hit both levels of the area. Quickstep away three times.
Acid Pool	No	Regurgitates an enormous amount of acid from the rear half of its body. Spreads outward to cover a huge area; get to higher ground.
Acid Spray	No	Spits acid from the rear half of its body. Targets a sweeping mid-range 180-degree arc; quickstep backward or move to its other end.

Environment

The Bell Ringers are all positioned in the galleries, so you'll need to ignore the boss when the battle begins and head straight for the stairways to eliminate them; a corpse at one end of the bridge connecting the balconies holds ten Quicksilver Bullets in case you run out of ammunition. The ground level of the plaza is lined by slightly raised arcades that restrict your evasive options and are not normally safe places to stand, but the difference in elevation allows you to retreat to these areas to avoid the boss' pools of acid. When all of the Bell Ringers are dead, you may choose to fight the boss either on the ground or in the galleries; your decision will determine how it attacks and the methods you can use to damage it.

Strategies

Key Strategies

Before you do anything else, head straight for the balconies and eliminate the Bell Ringers. From that point on, it's entirely up to you whether to fight on the ground or in the galleries; the galleries are better suited to strategies involving the Cannon or sidearms, as they allow you to target weak points from above, though taking up that position also severely limits the attacks the boss can use and makes melee combat much simpler. Fighting on the ground gives you direct access to all four of the boss' large limbs and allows you to focus on knocking it down, at which point you can target the large corpse atop its body with heavy attacks for extreme damage, but also places you at greater risk of being hit by its arms and legs.

Phase 1

After eliminating the Bell Ringers, remain in the gallery to fight or wait for the boss to approach and perform a plunging attack when it's within reach. If you fight in the galleries, it will use three attacks: a straight punch, an alternating double swipe and a headbutt. If it winds up with its left arm, it's about to use the straight punch – quickstep to either side and counterattack while it withdraws its arm. If it draws back its right arm, it'll perform a counterclockwise horizontal swing followed by a clockwise swing in the opposite direction after a short delay; you can avoid these by quickstepping through them into the attack or by backing up against the wall, but

beware that in the lower sections of the balconies backing up won't always leave you enough room. If the boss leans back slowly, it'll perform a forward headbutt after a brief delay; you can avoid this by backing up against the wall, and it offers an excellent opportunity to counterattack. You can also peek through the broken sections of the railing and shoot the large targetable corpse from above; when it takes enough damage the boss will collapse, at which point you can perform a plunging attack for tremendous damage.

On the ground, you'll have to stand at mid to long range and bait its arm attacks, then strike its arms as it recovers from the swing. When one of its arms sustains enough damage the boss will fall over, allowing you to reach the large corpse atop its body; this is your best chance to deal damage without the risk of taking any, so hit it with your strongest attacks before it gets up again. Do your best to stay away from the boss' lower central core; the smaller legs lining this part of its body will constantly kick at you and leave very few safe opportunities to strike with melee weapons. If you circle behind the boss and attack its lower end, it will lift that half of its body and begin attacking you with its two rear arms; if you plan on attacking these limbs you'll have to stand back and wait for a chance to move in safely. Causing it to reverse its stance also brings the large corpse atop its front half low enough for you to reach it with melee attacks, though it will quickly switch back when you do so. When one of its arms sustains enough damage the boss will fall over, allowing you to reach the large corpse atop its body; this is your best chance to deal damage without the risk of taking any, so hit it with your strongest attacks before it gets up again. Alternatively, if you focus on damaging one of its large legs, you can stagger it again while it is already down. Moving from leg to leg like this can stun the boss up to four times in a row, after which you can focus on the large corpse on top to finish it off.

Celestial Emissary

Preparation

The Celestial Emissary is extremely weak against thrust attacks and bolt, so the Saw Spear and the Rifle Spear are good choices for this battle; it also affected by attack bonuses against kin, making Ludwig's Holy Blade an ideal weapon for the job. Pick up plenty of Bolt Paper and Blood Vials, and consider bringing a full load of Bone Marrow Ash to take advantage of the Emissary's low blood defense. Throwing Knives will deal respectable damage from a distance once you've run out of bullets; Molotovs are optional but can be helpful for this purpose.

Overview

When you first enter the boss area, the only enemies present will be a group of Small Celestial Emissaries, one of which is the true boss. When you've figured out which one this is and dealt it enough damage to trigger Phase 2, it will transform into a giant version of the smaller emissaries and attack you with basic punches, kicks and stomps. After reducing the boss' health further and initiating Phase 3, it will sprout tendrils from its head and begin targeting you with energy projectiles when you're out of reach of its melee attacks. The other small emissaries will continue to follow you throughout all three Phases and will attack if they get close enough to do so, but their movement speed is slow and they can be led away from the boss long enough for you to attack it several times before they return; they will also reappear in the center of the arena if you kill them, so it's better to just lead them away and focus on the boss.

Environment

You'll face the Celestial Emissary in a rectangular courtyard with raised pathways along the perimeter surrounding a garden in the center. The colonnades on each side and the large pillars in the garden offer plenty of cover from the boss' ranged attacks when it begins using them; the smaller emissaries can be led all the way to the ends of the raised pathways overlooking the fountain and will walk slowly back down the steps rather than jump off the edge to pursue you.

Basic Information

	■	⚓	Item Drops											
Upper Cathedral Ward	2764	22400	Communion [100%]	235	261	26	131	170	60	55	300	180	—	✕
Chalice Dungeon Base Level	1499	1482	Arcane Damp Blood Gem (6) [100%]	188	209	21	105	170	60	55	300	180		

Preset Chalice Dungeons: Isz Gravestone

Key Attacks

Phase 1	Interrupt	Notes
None		

Phase 2	Interrupt	Notes
Slap Combo	No	Frontal flailing combo with moderate forward momentum; quickstep sideways or forward past it.
Stomp	No	Close-range downward stomp with small area of effect; strafe or quickstep backward.

Phase 3	Interrupt	Notes
Multi-Laser	No	Multiple small blasts in quick succession with minor tracking. If close, quickstep sideways; if farther away, strafe or roll sideways or block it using the terrain.
Aura Blast	No	Long-range projectile with moderate tracking; strafe or roll in any direction.

Strategies

Key Strategies

Deal as much damage as possible before triggering Phase 2, and when the boss' health is just above 60%, strike it with a powerful charged thrust attack from a weapon boosted with Bolt Paper; alternately, power up the Cannon or Flamesprayer with Bone Marrow Ash and immolate the entire group of emissaries at once. If you aren't able to finish off the boss before its minions get involved, lead them to the end of one of the walkways and drop into the garden; they'll take the long way back around rather than fall off after you, giving you plenty of time to attack the boss before they return.

Phase 1

To figure out which of the small emissaries is the real boss, you can lock on to each emissary until you find the one that does not display a health bar. The boss emissary will also follow you but won't attack. Once you've determined which of them is the true boss, reduce its health to about 70% with melee attacks and lead the other emissaries away from it if possible. At this point, power up your melee weapons with Bolt Paper and lay into the boss emissary. Get in as much damage as you can as the boss transforms; it won't hurt you when he does, but it will knock you down. It's worth getting the damage in and, with enough, you can even kill the boss before it leaves Phase 1.

Phase 2

When the boss' health drops below 60% it will assume its true form and begin Phase 2. It will only use a few extremely basic melee attacks at this point and will not follow you very far onto the raised walkway, so you can lure the smaller emissaries away at your leisure and return your attention to the boss. You can avoid its melee attacks by quickstepping forward or sideways, but standing behind it is a better strategy as none of its attacks can reach you there as long as you keep one to two meters' distance from its feet; its stomp attacks will hit you if you're pressed against it at pointblank range, but you can avoid them simply by strafing backward. Avoid

standing in front of the boss at all costs – its melee attacks have forward momentum and long reach, making them difficult to dodge.

Phase 3

When the boss' health falls below 30% it will grow tendrils and begin using its energy projectiles. You'll have to avoid these attacks while you lure the smaller emissaries away, but the pillars and columns in the area give you plenty of cover and will keep you safe as long as you watch the boss carefully while moving. The Multi-Laser is its most dangerous move – each small blast inflicts heavy individual damage and has minor tracking capability, so you're better off hiding behind obstacles than trying to dodge them. The giant emissary will still usually prioritize its melee attacks when you're in range, so staying behind it is still the best way to damage it without having to deal with its projectiles; continue hitting it with thrusts from its blind spot and it will quickly fall.

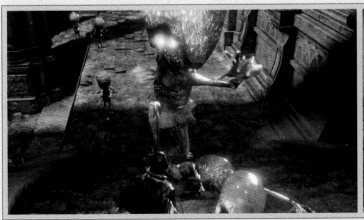

Ebrietas, Daughter of the Cosmos

Preparation

Ebrietas is weak against bolt and thrust attacks, so bring as much Bolt Paper as you can carry and a weapon capable of inflicting thrust damage – Ludwig's Holy Blade is ideal due to both its heavy R2 thrusts and its damage bonus against kin of the cosmos. Use a strong single-shot firearm such as the Hunter Pistol and stock up on Bone Marrow Ash, Quicksilver Bullets and Blood Vials; it's also a good idea to purchase 20 Throwing Knives so that you can continue to attack at range after running out of ammunition. Most importantly, buy as many Sedatives as you can hold – you'll need them to nullify Ebrietas' frenzy attacks. Both the Flamesprayer and the Cannon are capable of tearing down as much as 35% of her health in seconds, and can provide an important edge if you're struggling with this difficult battle; Oil Urns will make the Flamesprayer even more effective, so bring a few if you plan to use it.

Overview

You'll need to attack Ebrietas in order to initiate the battle, and any hits you land on her before her life bar appears will not inflict any damage. During the first Phase she'll crawl slowly toward you and attack from far away using her long tentacles; when you get close enough she'll try to crush you with her Head Smash. At mid to long range she'll periodically use her Forward Charge, a dangerous attack that can be extremely difficult to avoid; she'll also use a frontal grab attack which is much more easily evaded

Basic Information			Item Drops											
Upper Cathedral Ward	12493	28800	Great Isz Chalice [100%]	252	336	101	168	170	60	55	999	999	—	×
Chalice Dungeon Base Level	2857	1568	Isz Root Chalice [100%]	205	273	82	136	170	60	55	999	999		

Preset Chalice Dungeons: Isz Gravestone

Key Attacks

Phase 1	Interrupt	Notes
Head Smash	No	Mid-range downward hammer attack with her head; quickstep backward one to two times depending on your distance from her.
Forward Charge	No	Long-range linear charge attack; quickstep backward two to three times or sideways at least three times.
Tentacle Slam	No	Forward tentacle slam with long reach; quickstep once to either side.
Crushing Grab	No	Close-range frontal grab attack; quickstep backward.
Forward Blood Spit	No	Inflicts frenzy. Two consecutive mid-range projectiles with linear trajectories and large spherical hitboxes; quickstep sideways.
Sweeping Blood Spit	No	Inflicts frenzy. Frontal 150-degree arc of large spherical projectiles; quickstep backward.

Phase 2	Interrupt	Notes
Cosmic Radiation	No	Surrounds herself in a spherical aura that constantly damages you while in it. Cannot be evaded; avoid standing near her for too long or counteract it using regain.
Star Shower	No	Charges cosmic energy and releases three clusters of projectiles with strong tracking; quickstep sideways three to four times or dash sideways until all three bursts land.
Two-Stage Charge	No	Long-range flying ram attack followed by a head smash upon landing; quickstep backward. Or, quickstep once to avoid the charge and sideways to dodge the follow-up slam.

and will not usually reach you in the first place. Beware of Ebrietas' Blood Spit – a single hit from one of these attacks is almost guaranteed to max out your frenzy meter, so you'll need to keep your Sedatives close at hand in case of emergencies. At the beginning of Phase 2, she'll surround herself in an aura that will constantly damage you as long as you're within its field of effect, and will begin using an even more dangerous charge attack as well as her Star Shower spell. She'll also become far more aggressive at this point, and will begin using faster melee combos with longer reach and more hits.

Environment

This area is longer than it is wide and although there are no obstacles in the center, the edges are littered with rubble that creates tight corners and niches where you can become trapped if you're not careful. Keeping the battle to the full length of the cavern is essential for avoiding Ebrietas' ram attacks and giving you enough room to retreat if you need to use Blood Vials; pay close attention to your surroundings and do not under any circumstances allow yourself to be backed into a wall. After defeating Ebrietas you'll be able to access the altar at the far end of the chamber, allowing you to offer the Flesh of a Queen and advance the associated quest.

Strategies

Key Strategies

Target Ebrietas' head with your strongest attacks and do your best to stagger her. She'll expose her head after her ram attacks and Head Smash, so your goal during both Phases should be to bait these attacks from as far away as possible and quickstep in to strike before she lifts her head. The vertical L2 attacks and especially the charged R2 thrusts of the transformed Holy Blade are ideal for this purpose, and the weapon can be further augmented with Bolt Paper for a small increase in damage. The Cannon and the Flamesprayer are very helpful for this purpose – when powered up with Bone Marrow Ash, direct hits from either of these weapons can inflict high damage and instantly stagger Ebrietas, allowing you to perform either a visceral attack or another powered-up blast while she's vulnerable.

any of the tactics described in the Key Strategies box. Focus on baiting either the Head Smash or Forward Charge so that Ebrietas lowers her head, then move in to strike; stay as far away as possible to avoid her tentacle attacks and if you aren't able to back away them in time, quickstep through them in the opposite direction of the swing. If she uses her Blood Spit ability, evade it according to the move table and be sure your Sedatives are equipped for easy access. If you're using the Cannon or Flamesprayer strategies outlined in the Key Strategies box, the best time to unload on Ebrietas is when just over 50% of her health remains; doing so at this point in the battle will minimize the time you'll have to spend dealing with her extremely dangerous Phase 2 attacks.

Phase 2

When Ebrietas' health drops below 50%, she'll lower her head and channel her Cosmic Radiation, which gives you a few seconds to inflict serious damage to her head. She'll also begin using her Phase 2 moveset, as well as far deadlier slams and swings with her tentacles. At this point it is no longer safe to stand anywhere near her; you'll need to use the full length of the arena and keep her as far away as possible while you bait her ram attacks or Head Smash, and continue to attack her head when she exposes it. The most dangerous combo in this Phase is her Star Shower followed by her Two-Stage Charge. To deal with this, always make sure you have room to run away. When she uses her Star Shower spell, immediately unlock and sprint away for a few seconds, then run perpendicular to her until all three clusters of her Star Shower have fired. This avoids Star Shower, and also positions you safely to avoid a follow up Two-Stage Charge. Most of her attacks can be avoided in this Phase by simply quickstepping away, though you'll also need to be aware of your position so that you don't back yourself into a corner. If you need to get past Ebrietas and into the open, evade her next attack and dash or quickstep past her as she recovers; beware that if you don't leave yourself enough space for this purpose in the first place, you're likely to get hit anyway.

Phase 1

Ebrietas' most dangerous attack during this Phase is her Forward Charge – to reliably escape it, you'll need to leave yourself plenty of room to back up and must begin quickstepping backward as soon as you see her shake her head. Ebrietas' head has extremely low defense, with the red interior portion between the two outer halves being its weakest point – if you manage to strike this area with any type of attack, she'll suffer tremendous damage and cringe away for a couple of seconds, giving you time to perform one to two follow-up strikes. If you deal heavy damage to her head in a short enough period of time she'll stagger, at which point you may use

Micolash, Host of the Nightmare

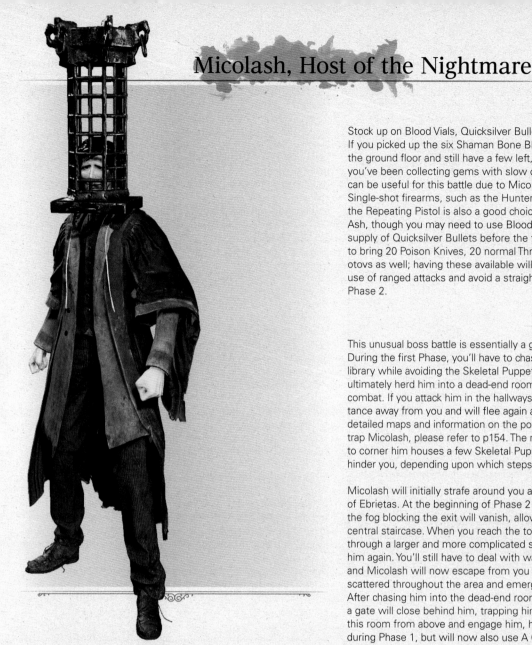

Preparation

Stock up on Blood Vials, Quicksilver Bullets and Bone Marrow Ash. If you picked up the six Shaman Bone Blades from the corpse on the ground floor and still have a few left, bring them with you; if you've been collecting gems with slow or rapid poison effects, they can be useful for this battle due to Micolash's low poison resistance. Single-shot firearms, such as the Hunter Pistol or Evelyn, are ideal; the Repeating Pistol is also a good choice if used with Bone Marrow Ash, though you may need to use Blood Bullets if it depletes your supply of Quicksilver Bullets before the fight ends. It's a good idea to bring 20 Poison Knives, 20 normal Throwing Knives and 10 Molotovs as well; having these available will allow you to extend your use of ranged attacks and avoid a straight fight with Micolash during Phase 2.

Overview

This unusual boss battle is essentially a game of cat and mouse. During the first Phase, you'll have to chase Micolash around the library while avoiding the Skeletal Puppets wandering the area and ultimately herd him into a dead-end room, where he'll be forced into combat. If you attack him in the hallways, he'll teleport a short distance away from you and will flee again as soon as you approach. For detailed maps and information on the positions you'll need to use to trap Micolash, please refer to p154. The room in which you'll need to corner him houses a few Skeletal Puppets that can either help or hinder you, depending upon which steps you took to prepare.

Micolash will initially strafe around you and periodically cast Augur of Ebrietas. At the beginning of Phase 2 he'll teleport away and the fog blocking the exit will vanish, allowing you access to the central staircase. When you reach the top, you'll have to pursue him through a larger and more complicated series of rooms and corner him again. You'll still have to deal with wandering Skeletal Puppets, and Micolash will now escape from you by jumping into the mirrors scattered throughout the area and emerging in a different location. After chasing him into the dead-end room in the center of this area, a gate will close behind him, trapping him inside; when you enter this room from above and engage him, he'll fight the same way as during Phase 1, but will now also use A Call Beyond.

Basic Information

			Item Drops		169	134	125	179	232	124	125	144	132	—	—
Nightmare of Mensis	5250	48400	Mensis Cage [100%]												

Key Attacks

Phase 1	Interrupt	Notes
Augur of Ebrietas	No	Same as the player version. Mid-range forward tentacle attack; quickstep sideways or backward.

Phase 2	Interrupt	Notes
A Call Beyond	No	Same as the player version. Rains small blasts of energy on a spherical area with frontal homing capability; quickstep sideways or forward.

Environment

The battle with Micolash takes place throughout an enormous section of the loft's upper floors. This area consists of several square rooms connected by a series of narrow hallways and is filled with thick fog, making it difficult to keep track of the boss if he gets too far away. While neither Micolash nor the Skeletal Puppets found throughout the halls are aggressive enough that you'll need to take cover at any point, the labyrinthine corridors can make it difficult to get your bearings and provide Micolash with considerable cover from you. For a more detailed explanation of how to use this environment to your advantage, please refer to p155.

Strategies

Key Strategies

Normal R1 combos are the best way to deal damage; poison is also effective and will continue to damage him even after he teleports away. You can turn the Skeletal Puppets in the trap rooms against him by stabbing them with Shaman Bone Blades, providing distractions and temporary allies; during Phase 2 you can power up your firearms with Bone Marrow Ash and snipe him from above the dead-end room once he's trapped inside.

Phase 1

Micolash has low health and no super armor, so ordinary R1 combos are the best way to deal with him. You'll have to watch out for his Augur of Ebrietas spell, as it will knock you down if it hits you, but is easily avoided with a sideways quickstep and offers you an opportunity to attack him while he recovers. The Skeletal Puppets in the trap room pose more of a threat than Micolash, so try to stay away from them and keep track of their locations to avoid being attacked while dealing with him. Quickstepping attacks will often clip Micolash before he can move out of the way, and heavy blows with knockdown effects, such as the transformed R2 charge attacks of the Burial Blade and the Hunter Axe, work quite well. It's best to save your Shaman Bone Blades for Phase 2 unless you plan to snipe Micolash from above without engaging him directly.

Phase 2

Trap Micolash in the dead-end room and loop around to the upper floor overlooking his location. At this point you can either use Bone Marrow Ash on your pistol or Cannon and rain death on him from above, or drop into the room with a plunging attack and fight directly. Poison Knives are especially effective from this perch, due to Micolash's low poison resistance, and will deal continuous damage while you hit him with other ranged attacks such as pistol shots, Molotovs or Throwing Knives. If you choose to face Micolash directly, he will fight in the same way as during the first Phase; however, beware that he will also begin casting A Call Beyond, which can be hard to avoid in the enclosed space.

Mergo's Wet Nurse

Preparation

The Chikage is an excellent weapon for this fight, especially when set with gems that add rapid poison build-up to its attacks; the Repeating Pistol is also highly effective when used with Bone Marrow Ash and allows you to deal considerable damage from out of reach of most of the boss' attacks. Purchase a full load of Quicksilver Bullets and Blood Vials, and consider bringing 20 Poison Knives to take advantage of the boss' low poison resistance.

Overview

Mergo's Wet Nurse is a slow-moving enemy with predictable attacks, but hits like a freight train and has an astronomical amount of health. Apart from using its Blender Combo a bit more frequently and generally being slightly more aggressive in the second Phase, Mergo's Wet Nurse will attack in very much the same way throughout the battle. During Phase 1 its Nightmare Veil attack will create just as many problems for itself as it will for you – it won't be able to keep track of you in the darkness and will instead blindly attack the area in front of it, giving you a chance to hit it several times before the veil

Basic Information

| Nightmare of Mensis | 14081 | 72000 | Item Drops: One Third of Umbilical Cord [100%] | 148 | 177 | 148 | 148 | 75 | 75 | 75 | 250 | 180 | — | — |

Key Attacks

Phase 1	Interrupt	Notes
Uppercut Slash	No	Heavily-delayed upward diagonal launcher; strikes its left side and directly in front of it. Quickstep backward during the delay or clockwise if close.
Downward Slash	No	Heavily-delayed frontal overhead slash with all arms at once; quickstep backward once or sideways up to twice.
Flying Slash	No	Long-range gliding horizontal scissor slash; quickstep forward as late as possible.
Cross Combo	No	Slow combo composed of three delayed slashes using all of its arms; quickstep clockwise toward it through the first attack.
Blender Combo	No	Constant barrage of extremely rapid frontal slashes with slight forward momentum; quickstep through it behind the boss and punish.
Teleport Ambush	No	Folds its wings and vanishes; appears elsewhere in the arena a few seconds later, ambushing you with a Flying Slash if you're close enough. Back up against a wall so you can see the entire room and respond according to its distance from you.
Nightmare Veil	No	Blankets the area in darkness, drastically reducing visibility. Cannot be cancelled or dispelled early; keep moving and wait until it wears off.
Nightmare Blades	No	Only used while Nightmare Veil is in effect. Long-range stab attacks with stretched arms; roll or quickstep sideways, or run out of its reach.

Phase 2	Interrupt	Notes
Deathly Duo	No	Used only while Nightmare Veil is in effect. Summons a clone that attacks from beside you at regular intervals; dash counterclockwise along the edge of the arena and don't stop moving until the effect ends.

lifts. This technique becomes far more dangerous during Phase 2, at which point the boss will create a doppelganger of itself and both will actively hunt you down in the darkness. Most of its moves are heavily telegraphed and have lengthy recovery times, allowing you to quickstep in afterward and hit it before it can react.

Environment

The battlefield has no obstacles and offers no cover at all, but its circular shape means you'll never become trapped in a corner and gives you plenty of room to maneuver. When the boss blankets the area in darkness during Phase 2 of the battle, the loft's circular shape actually works to your advantage – you can lead the boss around the perimeter while at the same time running out of range of the clone's constant attacks from the side.

Strategies

Key Strategies

Mergo's Wet Nurse is unusually weak against poison, especially rapid poison, so make use of any gems you've collected to imbue your weapon with the effect before initiating the battle. Stay very close to the boss and circle or quickstep to its back when possible. None of its attacks hit behind it, which gives you ample opportunity to deal damage from its back. Being behind the boss when its Blender Combo starts gives you the largest opening to deal damage, but be sure to be directly behind it or you can be clipped by its flailing blades. During Nightmare Veil, keep moving and play defensively.

Phase 1

Don't let the boss' slow movements tempt you to rush in and attack carelessly – its combo attacks have unusual delays that can be difficult to anticipate until you've seen them a few times and become accustomed to their timing. Focus on dodging through its attacks and working your way directly behind the boss. You can get attacks in from its side, but you'll need to get behind it quickly if it starts using its Blender Combo. If you get clipped, remain calm and use Regain to recover small hits taken.

Phase 2

The second Phase begins when the boss' health falls below 70%, though its basic attack patterns won't change drastically until it uses Nightmare Veil. Continue to fight in the same manner as you did during Phase 1 until it initiates the Phase 2 version of this technique, then immediately disengage and dash counterclockwise around the perimeter of the room. As long as you keep moving and don't get stuck on the columns or staircases, the real boss will never catch up to you and the doppelganger's attacks won't be able to track you fast enough to keep up with your position. Manage your stamina carefully during this time and continue sprinting until the Nightmare Veil wears off, then resume the strategies outlined in Phase 1.

Gehrman, the First Hunter

Preparation

Buy as many Blood Vials, Molotovs, Throwing Knives and Quicksilver Bullets as you can carry, and don't forget to stock up on Bone Marrow Ash. Gehrman is immune to poison, but has no other strengths or weaknesses, so you're free to use the weapon combination of your choice; however, the Reiterpallasch's ability to perform right-handed interrupts is extremely useful when combined with the Cannon or the Flamesprayer. Fit your weapons with gems that increase their attack power, and equip the Clawmark and Oedon Writhe runes to make your visceral attacks inflict more damage and restore Quicksilver Bullets.

Overview

Gehrman is one of the fastest and most agile opponents you've faced up to this point, and can cover tremendous distances in an instant with his quicksteps. He can be interrupted and staggered, but is also capable of doing the same to you, and his near-bottomless reserves of health can cause the fight to drag on. During the first Phase he'll use his Burial Blade in scythe mode and will attack with wide, sweeping slashes. When Phase 2 begins, Gehrman will revert his weapon to sword mode and will begin using his scattergun in addition to much longer combos with his blade. If he interrupts you with a scattergun blast at close or mid range, he'll dash in and attempt to follow through with a visceral attack for massive damage; the only way to prevent this is to time your attacks carefully and avoid giving him easy opportunities to interrupt you. At the beginning of Phase 3 he'll use a more powerful version of the Quickening spell which grants him a large amount of super armor, and will begin switching between his weapon's normal and transformed modes; his attacks during this Phase are more aggressive and include an aerial projectile with a large splash damage radius, an enormous spherical area attack and a gunshot that will instantly stagger you if it hits.

Basic Information

				Item Drops										
Hunter's Dream (Late Blood Moon)	14293	128000		Old Hunter Badge [100%]	150	150	150	150	65	70	65	999	999	—	—

Key Attacks

Phase 1	Interrupt	Notes
Scythe Combos	Yes	Delayed charge attacks and faster quicksteps; many variations. Quickstep backward one to three times.
Jumping Cleave	Yes	Slightly delayed two-hit aerial combo; quickstep sideways.

Phase 2	Interrupt	Notes
Sword Combos	Yes	Quick one-handed slashes with heavy forward momentum; many variations. Quickstep to the left one to two times.
Scattergun Blast	Yes	Used on its own or at the end of combos; can stagger you. Quickstep sideways twice.
Visceral Attack	No	Used if one of his Scattergun Blasts staggers you at close range; time your attacks carefully and try to limit his opportunities to stagger you.

Phase 3	Interrupt	Notes
Advanced Quickening	No	Surrounds himself in a blue aura that grants the effects of the Quickening spell and strong super armor; cannot knock him out of this move.
Moonlight Wave	No	Faces the moon with arms spread and charges for five seconds, then performs a massive spherical area attack; quickstep backward two to three times.
Stagger Shot	Yes	Sometimes used immediately after transforming his weapon. Single fiery shot that instantly staggers you if it connects; quickstep sideways.
Two-Stage Cleave	Yes	Long sidestep followed by a quickstepping slash in the opposite direction. Quickstep backward just before he performs the slash.
Air Blade	No	Hovers in the air and throws a blade of wind with strong tracking and a large spherical zone of splash damage; quickstep backward two to three times.
Transformation Attack	Yes	Two-hit scythe combo ending with a transformation attack that switches his weapon to sword mode; often followed by a sword slash or a Stagger Shot. Quickstep backward before each hit.

Environment

You'll face Gehrman in the meadow beyond the locked gate in the Hunter's Dream. This battleground has an irregularly-shaped border and a few crucifixes dotting the center, but no other notable obstacles; its most important feature is its moderate slope, which can cause some of Gehrman's attacks to pass over you if you're far enough below him. The open field provides plenty of space for you to fight, but also places Gehrman at a significant advantage due to his far higher mobility; its borders are fairly straight in most places, but be careful not to be backed into a corner near the gate or at the foot of the tree.

Strategies

Key Strategies

Interrupts are by far the most effective way to fight Gehrman, especially if you're equipped with the Clawmark and Oedon Writhe runes to boost their effects. Visceral attacks can be used in this manner to deal damage and restore your invaluable Quicksilver Bullets, but aren't always the best use of a stagger – if you use a transformed Reiterpallasch to interrupt Gehrman and immediately blast him with a Bone Marrow Ash Cannon shot while he's down, you'll inflict far more damage. If you aren't able to interrupt Gehrman, focus on baiting his combos and slow melee attacks, then strike him afterward as he recovers. If you need to heal, back as far away from him as you can before doing so – several quicksteps are usually necessary to reach the minimum safe distance.

effort to evade during this Phase, so you can wear him down from a distance with thrown weapons like Oil Urns and Molotovs, but pay careful attention to your distance from him to avoid committing to the throwing animation while he's close enough to hit you with one of his dashing attacks.

Phase 2

When Gehrman's health drops below 75% he'll revert his Burial Blade to sword mode and initiate Phase 2. His sword combos have heavy forward momentum but very poor tracking, so the best way to avoid them is by quickstepping sideways, particularly to the left; their long recovery periods will give you plenty of time to attack him afterward. During this Phase Gehrman will occasionally perform an ordinary forward roll followed by either a melee attack or a Scattergun Blast; this provides a good opportunity to interrupt him as he's coming out of the roll, since the timing is the roughly same for both attacks. Though he'll fight much more aggressively during this Phase, you should continue to interrupt him whenever possible and punish his combo attacks as he recovers.

Phase 3

When his health falls to 50% Gehrman will begin Phase 3 with his Advanced Quickening spell, which makes him invisible during his quicksteps and grants him a large amount of super armor; your R1 combos will no longer cause him to flinch while this ability is in effect, so you'll have to be much more careful about when and how you attack. You can hit Gehrman a few times while he's charging his Moonlight Wave attack if you're close to him when he uses it, but be sure to leave yourself enough time to get out of the way. Apart from his new Phase 3 attacks, he'll essentially switch between his Phase 1 and 2 fighting styles, so you should approach him according to which weapon mode he's using. Interrupts are much trickier at this point but are still the fastest way to defeat him; otherwise continue to punish his combos with one or two attacks at a time.

Phase 1

Avoid all of Gehrman's attacks except the Jumping Cleave by quickstepping backward one to two times; if he uses this move, quickstep sideways instead. All of his attacks during this Phase have pinpoint directional tracking and are almost guaranteed to hit you if you try to quickstep forward or sideways; the only option is to quickstep away from the first hits in his combos and either time a gunshot so that it interrupts him during one of the subsequent strikes, or wait for him to finish swinging and attack while he recovers. Most of his combos and individual swings leave enough time for you to hit him with a quickstepping attack afterward, but don't get greedy – it's extremely important to avoid dashing toward Gehrman too early and running straight into a delayed swing. He won't make much

Moon Presence

Preparation

As this fight will take place immediately after defeating Gehrman, with no rest period in between, you might want to quit to the title screen and reload your save file to exit the boss area and access the shops. Purchase as many Blood Vials and Quicksilver Bullets as you can carry, and bring plenty of Bone Marrow Ash; it's also worthwhile to create some Blood Bullets as well since the boss fight takes place in the same area and you can purchase more Blood Vials to replace those used restoring your health afterward. The Moon Presence has equal defensive values with no strengths or weaknesses, and cannot be interrupted, so feel free to bring your favorite weapon combination. The Cannon can be extremely helpful for this fight due to its ability to instantly stagger the boss. Set your weapons with as many attack bonus gems as you can fit, and consider equipping the Clawmark and Oedon Writhe runes to improve the effectiveness of your visceral attacks.

Overview

The Moon Presence is an extremely aggressive opponent from the start, and will alternate between putting intense pressure on you at close range and leaping backward to evade your attacks and reposition itself for another strike. Dealing enough damage to its head will knock it into a stagger state and enable you to follow through with a visceral attack; repeated blows to its arms will injure them and cause it to stumble for a few seconds, setting it up for further combos. Any injured part of its body will take drastically increased damage, including its head; it will eventually repair this damage with its Regeneration move, but this will also allow you to stagger it again with focused attacks on its face. During the first Phase it will use only physical attacks with its tentacles and arms; its combos and individual swings are very swift and can be exceedingly difficult to avoid, but it has a few slower moves that leave openings for you

Basic Information													
Hunter's Dream (Late Blood Moon)	8909	230000	Item Drops None	137	137	137	137	75	75	75	999	999	—	—

Key Attacks

Phase 1	Interrupt	Notes
Overhead Whip	No	Forward overhead whip attack; quickstep backward one to two times.
Spinning Whip	No	Two-hit 360-degree spin attack used when you're behind it; repositions it facing you at a distance. Quickstep backward when it crouches.
Jumping Slam	No	Long-range jump attack; quickstep sideways one to two times.
Charging Combo	No	Forward dash combo with heavy momentum; quickstep sideways or diagonally backward.
Seeking Combo	No	Same as Charging Combo but with strong tracking; will hold its head before performing this version. Quickstep backward until it stops attacking.
Regeneration	No	Holds its head and emits white particles of energy. Repairs head and limb damage, but doesn't actually restore HP.

Phase 2	Interrupt	Notes
Doom Gaze	No	Holds its head and releases a flash of light that instantly reduces your HP to 1 regardless of range. Cannot be dodged or blocked; run toward it immediately and attack its head with R1 combos to regain your health.
Numbing Shower	No	Frontal spherical area attack with a five-meter radius; rains blood that temporarily blocks your ability to use Blood Vials if any of it touches you. Quickstep backward two to three times.
Numbing Cloudburst	No	Summons small clouds from the ground which explode in showers of blood; temporarily blocks your ability to use Blood Vials if it connects. Dash through the clouds to dissipate them or out of range to avoid the blood.
Desperation Combo	No	Forward running attack with flailing arms; quickstep sideways or diagonally backward.

to counterattack. The Moon Presence becomes far more dangerous during Phase 2, at which point it will begin using a gaze attack that instantly reduces your health to 1, regardless of how far away you are from it; it will also try to disable your healing with wide-ranging area attacks and will continue to pummel you with melee combos.

Environment

You'll face the Moon Presence in the same meadow as Gehrman, so avoid being backed into a corner and make full use of the open space so that you have room to maneuver freely. In this case, however, you may also choose to back the boss into one of the corners at the base of the tree or in front of the gate if its constant backsteps are making it difficult to hit; while you'll suffer certain disadvantages in this position, so will the boss, and its large size will restrict its movement in the corners while leaving you just enough room to evade.

Strategies

Phase 2

When you reduce the Moon Presence's health to 70% it will become even more aggressive and begin using its Phase 2 moveset, including the potentially lethal Doom Gaze attack. At this point, keep it at mid to long range, but don't get too far away – the Doom Gaze actually offers the best opportunity to attack its head, and you'll regain most of your lost health in the process. Alternately, you can use its incredibly long recovery after this attack as a chance to blast its head with the Cannon and perform a visceral attack; this will still recover a substantial amount of your health and can potentially inflict far more damage. You can either bait this attack exclusively by staying at long range, or move in a little closer and look for other opportunities; regardless, continue to dodge its melee attacks with sideways quicksteps and attack during its recovery periods.

Key Strategies

Aim for its head at every possible opportunity and if you're having trouble hitting it with the Cannon, wait until it uses its Overhead Whip and blast it in the face during its recovery. Take advantage of the damage bonus against its injured head or limbs and attack these parts of its body until it repairs them, and above all, don't get greedy with your melee attacks – be absolutely sure to leave yourself enough stamina to get out of the way after a combo. In general, the best place to stand is directly behind the Moon Presence; you'll have to watch out for its Spinning Whip, but will be safe from its much more dangerous combo attacks. When it uses its Doom Gaze, dash in and hit it as many times as you can before it recovers – doing so will not only inflict damage, but restore most of your health via regain.

Phase 1

Sideways quicksteps are the best way to avoid the Moon Presence's Phase 1 attacks; you'll also need to quickstep forward in a clockwise or counter-clockwise direction in order to get around it and strike from out of reach of its arms. Aim for its head when it provides you with openings to do so – the best chance during this Phase is after avoiding its Overhead Whip. When it uses this move, wait until the first of its tentacles touches the ground in front of it, then quickstep forward and unleash a strong attack; this is also the best time to shoot it in the head with the Cannon if using the associated strategy as it will be unable to dodge the shot. Do your best to stay beside or behind it and target its arms when you can't reach its head; it will try to hit you with its Spinning Whip in these positions, but gives just enough warning that you can quickstep backward and out of the way. Be careful not to use up all your stamina on combo attacks – it's only safe to hit the boss with one or two heavy swings at a time before it counterattacks or leaps away from you.

Ludwig, the Accursed/Ludwig, the Holy Blade OH

Preparation

Arcane Lake runes and equipment with high arcane defense are extremely helpful for damage mitigation. If you prefer a more offense-oriented approach, stack Oedon Writhe or Clawmark runes so that you can carry more ammunition or inflict greater damage with visceral attacks. Ludwig takes the most damage from fire attacks in both of his forms, although the damage increase from Fire Paper on its own will be relatively insignificant. Take advantage of Ludwig's weakness to serrated damage and bring a Saw Cleaver, Beast Cutter or the Whirligig Saw; the damage bonuses from Beasthunter gems will affect him in his first form but not his second, so Tempering or Nourishing gems that provide unconditional bonuses are preferable for this battle. If you meet the stat requirements for the Cannon, bring it along with some Bone Marrow Ash to help stagger Ludwig and set him up for visceral attacks. Depending upon what eligibility requirements you meet, you can summon a variety of NPCs in the area outside the boss room to help you: Valtr, Henriett or the younger Madaras twin. While Henriett can only be summoned on her own, it's possible to bring both Valtr and younger Madaras twin into the fight with you.

Overview

This boss fight consists of two completely different opponents in succession, with the transition between them occurring halfway through the battle. In his "Accursed" form Ludwig will use basic combos with his claws, leaping body slam attacks, a forward tackle, a series of advancing bites and two variations of a frontal water blast, and will use a rear kick and a flailing stomp attack to drive you away if you stand next to him for too long. In his "Holy Blade" form he will draw the Holy Moonlight Sword, a weapon familiar to many fans of From Software titles, and perform its signature ranged magic wave attacks as well as several melee combos and AoEs. He will no longer use the water geysers nor his equine kicks or jump attacks in this form, and instead relies solely on his sword for the remainder of the battle.

Environment

The boss room consists of a large, roughly square lower area with a set of steps leading up to a narrow dais at the far end. Keeping the fight to the large area and away from the corners is crucial; you'll need plenty of room to avoid Ludwig's attacks in both of his forms and becoming trapped in a corner can quickly prove fatal. Likewise, avoid backing Ludwig into one of the corners and make every effort to lure him back to the center of the room if this occurs; be especially cautious of the elevation difference on the steps and the dais as it can foul the hit detection of visceral attacks if you are too far above or below Ludwig when he staggers.

Basic Information Special Weakness: Serration			Item Drops											
Hunter's Nightmare | **Accursed**	16658	34500	Guidance [100%]	140	140	140	140	126	98	126	999	999	✕	—
Hunter's Nightmare | **Holy Blade**				140	140	140	140	252	119	168	999	999	—	—

During Phase 1, quickstep forward through Ludwig's claw swipes to avoid them and attack him as he ends the combo.

During Phase 1, look for openings to attack Ludwig's head in order to stagger him.

Key Attacks

Phase 1	Interrupt	Notes
Claw Swipes		Quickstep forward through them or sideways in the opposite direction of each swing. Can also quickstep backward several times to avoid them at mid range.
Rear Kick		Strikes directly behind him with a swift kick. Quickstep sideways or simply avoid standing in this position.
Headbutt		Extremely quick forward launcher used at close to pointblank range. Quickstep sideways one to two times.
Stomp		Strikes in a 360-degree radius around his body at extremely close range. Quickstep away from him one to two times.
Retreating Slash		Rapid frontal 180-degree slash while backstepping. Used if you pressure him too much from the front; to avoid it, quickstep backward once or forward through it.
Leaping Slam		Rapid short-range jumping slam, usually used after other attacks as a followup. Quickstep backward or sideways one to two times.
High Jump	No	Slower jump attack with very long reach, preceded by a scream. Quickstep forward past it at close range or backward several times at mid to long range.
Bite Combo		Multiple hits with heavy forward momentum and minor tracking. Quickstep sideways two to three times as he approaches.
Charging Tackle		Used after his health drops below 80%. Preceded by exhaling a puff of yellow gas. Quickstep twice to either side when he begins charging.
Drop Ambush		Used after his health drops below 80%. The blood dripping from the ceiling marks his location; run directly away from his position in a straight line.
Forward Geyser		Used after his health drops below 80%. Rapid long-range blast of water in a straight line. Quickstep sideways once to twice.
Sweeping Geyser		Used after his health drops below 80%. Sweeps a geyser of water in a counterclockwise arc. Run or quickstep counterclockwise, or move to his side.

Phase 2	Interrupt	Notes
Fast Combo		Preceded by a roar. Raises his sword to his left shoulder and performs two quick frontal slashes, a slower overhead cut and an upward swing. Quickstep right twice consecutively through the horizontal swings, right again through the overhead and continue strafing counterclockwise during the uppercut.
Heavy Combo		Frontal arcing counterclockwise slash followed by either a single diagonal swing from the opposite direction or three overhead chops and an upward cleave. Quickstep backward two to three times to avoid the entire combo or quickstep forward through the first hit, sideways through each of the three overheads and forward or sideways through the final upward slash.
Run-in Combo		Dashes toward you from long distance and performs a horizontal slash followed by either a slower diagonal slash or a series of vertical overhead cuts. Quickstep forward past each swing toward his rear.
Forward Cross		Two extremely rapid diagonal slashes which strike directly ahead of him; generally used to punish pointblank strafing. Quickstep once sideways.
Uppercut Rush	No	Running uppercut slash sometimes followed up with a diagonal cut. Strikes a large forward and backward vertical arc on his right side and has long reach. Quickstep forward past it toward his left side, or quickstep once sideways.
Moonlight Wave		Slow horizontal charge slash followed by a horizontal wave of moonlight. Quickstep forward through the wave, or twice sideways at longer range when time permits.
Double Moonlight Wave		Two diagonal slashes in opposite directions which create two waves of moonlight at opposite angles. Quickstep sideways to avoid the first and immediately quickstep sideways again to avoid the second.
Moonlight Stab		Performs a forward thrust covered in arcane energy. Quickstep once in any direction to avoid it; it will miss completely if you are standing at pointblank range.
Moonlight Ring		Charges for about three seconds, then stabs his sword into the ground. Creates a small circular burst of energy centered on the sword; quickstep backward one to two times to escape.
Moonlight Onslaught		Slowly raises his sword above his head, then creates a massive spherical explosion centered on the sword followed after about two seconds by a massive forward blast of energy which lasts another three seconds. Quickstep in any direction immediately before the explosion to dodge through, then quickstep forward past him and stand to either side or behind him to avoid the sustained energy blast.

Key Strategies

Ludwig's left and right sides can be injured individually and will take additional damage from all attacks thereafter; he will also be temporarily stunned when one side is injured, allowing for a few more swings before he recovers. Unlike many other bosses Ludwig will not regenerate damaged limbs, so take full advantage of this and focus on one side for optimal damage or injure them sequentially to keep him immobilized. Repeated blows to the head during Phase 1 will stagger him, at which point you can perform a visceral attack on his face. If you have a Cannon, it can be used with Bone Marrow Ash to attack Ludwig's head and stagger him very quickly. During Phase 2 Ludwig will stagger after sustaining enough damage, at which point a visceral attack can be initiated from the front of his torso. His sides can no longer be injured at this point, but breaking his super armor will still cause him to stumble. The transformed L2 attack of the Whirligig Saw is supremely effective for quickly injuring Ludwig's legs, especially when augmented with Fire Paper; during Phase 2 it is one of the fastest and easiest ways to stagger him.

Phase 1 (Ludwig the Accursed)

Ludwig will usually begin the battle by closing the distance with a High Jump, so be prepared to dodge as soon as he approaches; with careful positioning you can quickstep to the side when he lands and strike his head with melee attacks as he recovers. Targeting his head is extremely difficult during his normal combos, but his jump attacks and other moves with long recovery periods offer safe opportunities to do so and you should make use of every such

To successfully perform a visceral attack during Phase 2, you must initiate it from this position.

chance you reasonably can in order to earn a visceral attack. Ordinary gunshots to the head will also stagger him, especially when augmented with Bone Marrow Ash; the Repeating Pistol and Evelyn are especially effective for this purpose depending upon your stat allocation. In general, quickstep forward through his claw swipes and

The localized Moonlight Ring attack offers a perfect opportunity to use Blood Vials.

strike his legs a couple of times; just be prepared to get out of the way immediately to avoid his counterattacks. Focus on one side at a time to injure them as quickly as possible; this will stun Ludwig and buy you more time to pile on additional attacks. You can also sneak in a hit or two by dodging his Bite Combo if you are close enough to him when the attack ends, and his High Jump leaves him open long enough to execute a charged attack on his head. Beware that standing directly behind him at close range will trigger his Rear Kick, and he'll use his Headbutt to punish attempts to close in on him from straight ahead. When Ludwig's HP drops below 80% he will begin using his Charging Tackle, Drop Ambush and both Geyser attacks, offering a new set of opportunities to strike him either as he recovers from the Drop Ambush or after quickstepping counter-clockwise to his left side while he is performing the Sweeping Geyser.

Phase 2 (Ludwig, the Holy Blade)

Ludwig will remain idle for a couple of seconds after the cutscene, so take advantage of this opportunity to use Blood Vials or create Blood Bullets if necessary. From this point forward he will abandon his entire Phase 1 moveset and use only sword swings, arcane-based projectiles and area attacks. He will use three distinct melee combos with limited variations: a Fast Combo at close range, a Heavy Combo at close and mid range, and a Run-in Combo at long range. Generally speaking, these offer limited opportunities to quickstep past him through the swings and counterattack; his slower individual moves such as the Moonlight Wave, Moonlight Stab, Moonlight Ring and especially the Moonlight Onslaught offer much more reliable openings when correctly evaded and require considerably less focus on evasion of consecutive hits. Quickstepping forward through the Moonlight Wave and the Moonlight Stab at close range will buy time for one or two swings; the Moonlight Ring has a long and obvious wind-up which provides a large window for either attacks or Blood Vial use; and by quickstepping toward Ludwig at close range the instant before he releases the initial explosion of the Moonlight Onslaught, you can completely avoid the damage using your invincibility frames and buy yourself an extended period of time to strike with R1 combos before he performs the second half of the attack. If you successfully dodge the initial explosion in this manner and come out of your quickstep close to Ludwig's body, all you'll need to do to avoid the forward follow-up blast is strafe around him in either direction at pointblank range; this allows you to exploit a second and even longer period of vulnerability to strike with further R1 combos while he is committed to the attack.

Laurence, the First Vicar OH

weapon such as the Beast Cutter or Saw Cleaver will be effective, but the Whirligig Saw's multi-hit jump attack and sustained L2 chain in transformed mode make it an especially good choice. Laurence is subject to the damage bonuses from Beasthunter gems, so attaching three of these to one of the aforementioned weapons will maximize your damage potential against him; however, elemental weapon buffs such as Bolt Paper are largely ineffective. Single-shot firearms like the Hunter Pistol and Evelyn are very useful for injuring Laurence's head and staggering him, especially when powered up with Bone Marrow Ash; the Cannon and Church Cannon are much less efficient for this purpose due to the high risk of a missed shot. If you have met Valtr in the Forbidden Woods and are equipped with the Impurity rune, you can summon him just inside the cathedral door to assist you.

Preparation

Fading Lake runes and equipment with high fire defense such as the Charred Hunter set will help cut down the damage from Laurence's attacks. Alternately, Clawmark runes will allow you to end the fight faster with powerful visceral attacks; you may also opt to stack Communion or Oedon Writhe runes in order to carry more ammunition or Blood Vials. Bring a few Lead Elixirs for the second phase of the fight as these can be incredibly useful for preventing the lava from stunlocking you; if you've already obtained the Loch Shield, consider bringing it along as well to block the AoEs. Any serrated

Quickstep or dash to Laurence's side and strike while he uses his Lava Launcher attack.

Overview

The first phase of this battle will play out much like the fight with the original Cleric Beast, though Laurence is by no means a mere clone and in fact has a number of unique tricks in his arsenal. First and foremost, the majority of his attacks either leave lingering trails of flame or create explosions on impact. Laurence becomes a completely different enemy during the second phase, at which point his lower body will melt away and leave only his torso and head; in this form his severed abdomen continuously leaves a trail of damaging lava as he moves and he will begin using an entirely different set of attacks from Phase 1. His moveset is far more limited during the second phase but also much less familiar and predictable, consisting of crawling slam combos, delayed arm swipes and attacks that cover large areas in lingering pools of lava.

Environment

You'll face Laurence in a rectangular hall identical to Yharnam's Grand Cathedral, where you originally faced Vicar Amelia. Keeping the fight to the room's long axis and taking care not to back yourself into the corners is crucial; you'll need to be especially wary of the pilasters jutting out of the walls at intervals as you can become caught on these while skirting the edges of the hall. If Laurence backs into a corner or against a wall, lure him back toward the center of the room so that you have enough space to dodge his attacks.

Basic Information Special Weakness: Serration	■	✦	Item Drops														
Hunter's Nightmare	21243	29500	Beast's Embrace [100%]	148	178	148	148	200	744	200	999	999	×	—

Key Attacks

Phase 1	Interrupt	Notes
One–Armed Grab		Executed with the left arm. Slow windup; roll or quickstep behind him or quickstep backward.
Two–Armed Grab		Frontal grab with a slow windup; strafe or quickstep backward out of range.
Fire Slam		Single frontal open-palmed ground slam that generates a small explosion. Resembles the first hit of the Overhead Claw, but has no followup. Quickstep backward at mid range or forward past him at close range.
Double Slam		Two advancing ground punches in rapid succession. Both punches create small explosions. Quickstep backward twice at mid range or forward twice past the attacks at close range.
Heavy Double Slam		Slower version of the Double Slam that generates larger explosions. Quickstep twice forward clockwise past the first hit from anywhere inside mid range; if on the outer edge of mid range or farther, quickstep backward three times.
Retreating Slam		Quick frontal ground slam that generates a small explosion, followed immediately by a backstep that repositions him facing you. Quickstep backward once or forward through the attack.
Lunging Swipe		Lunges forward and swipes a wide frontal arc with his left arm, leaving a trail of lingering flames; quickstep forward or counterclockwise through the swing.
Slam Combo		Two slow ground punches followed by a downward slam that generates a small explosion of flames; quickstep backward one to two times at mid range or forward past him if extremely close.
Left Combo A	No	Four-hit combo with his left arm starting with a ground punch followed by two horizontal swipes and a frontal shove. The shove inflicts heavy knockdown. Quickstep forward or sideways through each swing in the opposite direction.
Left Combo B		Five-hit combo with his left arm starting with a ground punch followed by four horizontal slashes. The final three slashes are performed leaning forward and have increased range. Quickstep backward three to five times at mid range or forward past him at close range.
Right Combo		Opens with a right-handed horizontal slash and alternates between left and right for three more horizontal swings. The fourth swing will be either a close-range swipe or a mid-range forward dive depending on your distance from him. Quickstep forward past him through each attack at close range or backward three to four times at mid range.
Variable Combo		Can chain an unlimited number of horizontal slashes, ground punches and forward shoves in random order. Quickstep forward through each attack at close range or backward out of reach at mid range.
Advancing Lunge		Extremely quick two-hit forward lunge with almost no warning. Both hits generate explosions. Mainly used at short range, but has very long reach. Quickstep forward past his right side one to two times.
Flying Press		Jumps high into the air and performs a rapid falling body slam. Can change direction midair and has strong tracking; quickstep or roll toward him and he will pass over you.
Overhead Claw		Mid–range overhead slam with his left arm that creates a small explosion of flames, sometimes followed by an upward swing which generates a much larger explosion. Preceded by a scream and has a long windup; he also digs his claws into the ground on the first hit, in contrast to the open-palmed Fire Slam. Quickstep forward past him from close range or backward from mid range.
Recovery		Surrounds himself in a red aura and heals injured limbs. Doesn't actually restore HP; simply repairs body damage.

Phase 2	Interrupt	Notes
Lava Launcher		Long-range forward conical stream of lava that remains on the ground for several seconds and inflicts residual damage. Quickstep or strafe sideways as needed, or quickstep forward toward his right side.
Rear Lava Gush	No	Close-range frontal AoE slam while gushing a large pool of lava behind him out of his severed abdomen. Quickstep away from him two to three times at close range and beware that he will follow up with a horizontal swipe if you stand in front of him for too long.
Crawling Combo		Drags himself forward using up to seven overhead claw slams often ending with a left-handed horizontal slash. Quickstep left twice and continue strafing or quickstepping clockwise as he circles you.
Delayed Slam		Single overhead slam with his left arm after a long windup, sometimes followed by a horizontal swipe. Has strong tracking and must be dodged very late, just before he brings his arm down – quickstep sideways or forward past it.

Target Laurence's head from a distance with gunfire to stagger him...

...then quickstep in close and hit him with a visceral attack.

Strategies

Key Strategies

Target Laurence's head with pistols or the Piercing Rifle to stagger him, then follow through with a visceral attack. Staggering him works in exactly the same manner as with the original Cleric Beast; he will eventually repair the damage to his head, allowing you to injure it and stagger him again. You can also injure Laurence's limbs, but unlike most other bosses this will only stun him temporarily and does not actually increase the damage he receives. The Whirligig Saw's transformed L2 attack will quite literally tear Laurence to shreds, especially if you've also set it with Beasthunter gems; fast weapons with serrated bonuses such as the Saw Cleaver and the Saw Spear are also ideal for dishing out heavy damage as quickly as possible. If you're having trouble with the lava stunlocking you to death during Phase 2, try using a Lead Elixir – it'll give you enough super armor to walk through the flames without flinching, though you'll need to keep a close eye on your HP. The Loch Shield will absorb the impact and most of the damage from his AoEs, though it is not effective for blocking the actual physical swings themselves.

The Rear Lava Gush offers an excellent opportunity to deal damage, but watch out for the followup swing!

Phase 1

In general, quickstepping forward through Laurence's combos and baiting his grab attacks provide some of the safer opportunities to attack him from behind with R1 chains or to heal yourself if necessary; strafing backward out of range of his two-hit forward lunges and performing a jump attack after he misses the second swing is another good chance to deal damage. A third such opportunity comes while he is recovering injured limbs since he is helpless during this animation; additionally, injuring a limb will cause him to stumble and buy a little extra time for another attack or two. If you aim to injure his arms or legs, it is often easier to lock off and circle him manually while using dodge rolls to avoid his backward swipe attacks - the two targetable points on his body are very high and will often foul attempts to strike low enough to injure his legs. When fighting locked-on, be sure to target the lower point (on his abdomen) as attempting to dodge his attacks while locked onto his head makes it harder to

avoid taking damage. It is possible, though extremely difficult, to avoid the explosions created by his slam attacks using the quickstep's invincibility frames to dodge through them; however, beware that the large explosion on the second hit of his Overhead Claw (when he pulls his claw out of the ground) is large enough that it extends a short distance behind him and can still clip you coming out of a quickstep with poor positioning. You can also attack him one or two times after dodging his Fire Slam, but be sure not to get caught at pointblank range when the AoE occurs. If you are behind him at fairly close range, it is possible to avoid his Slam Combo simply by strafing sideways and strike during his recovery period after the final hit. Alternately, to avoid this combo from the front, quickstep backward away from him. When the AoE from the third hit dissipates, he will be left recovering for a few seconds during which it is possible to quickstep forward and attack him.

Phase 2

When Laurence's HP falls below 40% the bottom half of his body will disintegrate leaving only his torso, arms and head. In this state his mobility is drastically reduced and he loses access to his entire Phase 1 moveset. His severed torso constantly spews lava that lingers on the ground for a short period of time, causing fire damage and flinching if you touch it. The best time to attack Laurence or restore your HP during this phase is during his Lava Launcher; he will telegraph this attack with very obvious shudders and screams, providing enough warning for you to quickstep toward his right side and strike several times while he is spitting lava. This move has moderate lateral tracking and leaves large pools of lava on the ground which cause fire damage and heavy stunlock; the stream of lava itself inflicts damage and hits multiple times, and a direct hit with this attack will usually stunlock you to death. The Whirligig Saw's transformed L2 is ideal for piling on damage from Ludwig's right side during this move as it can be used while strafing clockwise to avoid the boss' frontal attack area. Another good chance to attack comes during the Rear Lava Gush, though you'll need to dodge the frontal AoE before positioning yourself to strike his head and will also need to avoid the horizontal follow-up swing at the end.

Living Failures

Preparation

The Failures are affected by the damage bonus from Kinhunter gems, so set your weapons with these if you have any on hand. Lightning damage from the Tonitrus is effective against the Failures, as are thrusting weapons such as the Rifle Spear; the longsword component of the Kirkhammer and both forms of Ludwig's Holy Blade also have thrust attacks and are perfectly serviceable alternatives. The Chikage is an especially good choice for this fight as its blood damage will cut through the Failures' high defense, and Bolt Paper provides a marginal damage boost as well. The Piercing Rifle augmented with Bone Marrow Ash can drill a powered-up shot through an entire group of Failures at once; Bone Ashed shots from the Cannon are slightly less economical but proportionally more devastating when several Failures are clustered together, and the Tiny Tonitrus offers yet another viable alternative if your stat spread allows for its use. Armor and runes that reduce arcane damage are helpful for softening the constant blows from energy projectiles; the Failures are vulnerable to both interrupts and staggers, so you may alternately opt to stack a few Clawmark runes instead. Yamamura the Wanderer can be summoned just outside the boss area if you meet the conditions for him to appear; he wields the Chikage and a Piercing Rifle, making him a particularly valuable ally against the horde of foes you'll face.

Overview

This boss fight follows the "Battle Royale" format: four Living Failures will be present in the arena at any given time, with new ones immediately spawning in to replace the fallen. The individual enemies will have either 1223, 1957 or 2447 HP; the fight ends when you have slain enough Failures to inflict a combined total of 20,646 damage. The Failures have very few attacks – two smaller projectiles, a collective meteor attack similar to the one used by Rom at the Moonside Lake, and a generic set of basic physical attacks similar to those of the giant Celestial Emissary boss in the Upper Cathedral Ward. The main problems you'll face in this fight are being outnumbered and having to constantly watch for incoming projectiles, but the giant lumenflowers in the center of the arena provide enough cover for you to divide and conquer with a bit of patience.

Basic Information			Item Drops										
Research Hall	20646	22000	Astral Clocktower Key [100%]	239	273	102	171	256	92	71	250	180	—	×

Key Attacks

Phase 1	Interrupt	Notes
Headbutt	Yes	Rapid short-range headbutt usually used to counter melee attacks. Interrupt it or quickstep once sideways or backward.
Frontal Slam	Yes	Short-range overhead slam similar to but slightly slower than the headbutt. Interrupt it or quickstep away in any direction.
Astral Orb	No	Charges and launches a large orb of energy in a slow arc. Strafe or quickstep in any direction to avoid it.
Cosmic Missiles	No	Charges and fires a barrage of multiple homing blasts of energy. Strafe, run or quickstep to one side until all the projectiles have missed or use the giant flower in the center of the arena for cover. Can also knock them out of it.
Meteor Swarm	No	Used by all Failures simultaneously when the boss health bar drops below 60%. Calls down a shower of giant meteors. The meteors always approach from the right side of the arena (facing the exit); take cover behind the giant flower until the meteors disappear.

Environment

The boss room consists of an octagonal garden surrounded by balconies along six of its opposing sides. Several giant lumenflowers occupy a slightly elevated mound in the center, providing crucial cover from the Failures' endless bombardment of projectiles. In order to persevere, you'll need to make good use of this obstacle to separate your enemies and avoid their attacks; it is also prudent to stay off of the balconies lining the edges of the arena as they offer few tactical advantages and in fact place you in a desperately vulnerable position with no protection from the terrain.

Use the giant lumenflowers to separate the Failures, then pick them off with visceral attacks.

Strategies

Key Strategies

Use the giant flowers to separate the Failures, then pick them off one at a time by interrupting their melee swings and following up with visceral attacks. Thrust attacks provide a viable alternative if you prefer a more direct approach; charged attacks can be effective as well depending on the weapon, but charged thrusts in particular will deal the most damage. Avoid engaging more than one enemy at a time; try to focus on the same one until it falls and back off to reposition yourself if you find your opponents gathered too close for you to safely approach.

Phase 1

Your goal during this battle will be to separate the Failures as much as possible and pick them off one by one before the others can interfere. Exploiting their vulnerability to interrupts and staggers is an important part of this strategy; the safest way to defeat them is simply to skirt them just outside melee range and bait them into taking a swing at you, then interrupt it and quickstep in to perform a visceral attack. You'll need to stay on your toes and watch for their projectile attacks – not just from whichever Failure you happen to be targeting at any given time, but also from any others that may be behind you or outside your line of sight. Never attempt to approach a group of these enemies head-on; trying to dash in for a visceral attack in these situations will almost always cause you to be struck and

sent flying. If the Failures are positioned close together, strike them from a distance with area attacks such as the Tiny Tonitrus or a Bone Ashed Cannon shot. The Beast Roar is very helpful for clearing a bit of breathing room – a single hit from it will instantly cause the Failures to flinch, and will also knock them out of their Cosmic Missiles attack if it connects early in the animation. In addition, the Beast Roar can be used to deflect the Astral Orb projectile with proper timing; it will also deflect the smaller Cosmic Missiles, but does not last long enough to protect you from an entire barrage and cannot deflect the large meteors. The Loch Shield will turn aside the Astral Orb attack and will block the Cosmic Missiles until you run out of stamina, but too many hits from the smaller projectiles will break your guard as will a single meteor. Apart from visceral attacks, the best opportunities to strike these foes with melee combos are while they charge their Astral Orb or Cosmic Missiles; striking them during these times has the added bonus of potentially breaking their super armor and stunning them out of the attack. It is possible to safely hit them a few times after quickstepping forward through their arm swings, but greater care is required due to the increased risk of retaliation. When the Failures begin using their Meteor Swarm attack, they will all enter a summoning animation that leaves them completely helpless for several seconds; this is a perfect chance to stagger them from behind with charged attacks or simply let loose with melee combos, but be sure you are in the cover of the giant lumenflowers before you do so. Try to keep the battle to the left half of the arena relative to your position when you first enter the boss room – any Failures that are also in the cover of the lumenflowers when the meteors fall can be cut down with impunity until the attack ends. Do note, however, that attacking a Failure while it is summoning the meteors will knock it out of the animation and allow it to resume its normal attacks, so be sure to focus on one enemy at a time during the meteor barrage in order to avoid prematurely freeing them.

View of the meteors' trajectory from the boss room entrance. They will always approach from this direction.

To avoid the Meteor Swarm, stand on the opposite side of the giant lumenflowers as they approach.

Lady Maria of the Astral Clocktower `OH`

Preparation

Lead Elixirs can be helpful to avoid constantly being knocked out of your attacks as the elixir's effect grants temporary super armor, but some of Maria's heavier swings will still cause you to flinch and stumble so it's generally better to avoid them altogether. High-defense builds with physical damage reduction runes will be able to make the best use of this strategy; otherwise stack two or three Clawmark, Communion or Oedon Writhe runes to boost your offensive capabilities or Blood Vial capacity. Maria is equally susceptible to both lightning and arcane attacks, but is somewhat more resistant to fire; Bolt Paper and the Empty Phantasm Shell will provide respectable increases to the damage of your melee attacks and hunter tools such as the Executioner's Gloves, Tiny Tonitrus, Blacksky Eye and A Call Beyond offer effective ranged options. The Beast Roar is extremely useful for its ability to knock Maria down in a single hit; by alternating it with physical swings at the correct intervals, it is possible to lock Maria in an almost inescapable rhythm of attacks.

Overview

Maria wields the Rakuyo, a double-sided blade that breaks into a sword and a dagger, and carries an Evelyn pistol. Her fighting style is superficially similar to the hunter NPCs encountered in numerous other locations throughout the game and includes rolls, quicksteps, gunshots and transformation attacks; she is also susceptible to both interrupts by firearms and staggers from charged `R2` strikes. Make no mistake, though – she is anything but a generic hunter and in fact uses a multitude of completely unique moves and gimmicks, especially during the second and third phases of the battle. Maria has a permanent Quickening effect identical to that granted by the Hunter Bone and is a highly mobile, evasive and aggressive opponent. She is susceptible to stunlocks during her idle animations but has super armor on most of her combo attacks and individual swings, and from Phase 2 onward she will extend her blades to ridiculous lengths by manipulating her own blood. During Phase 3 her attacks will leave trails of damaging fire and she will begin attempting to stagger you, following up with a visceral attack if she succeeds.

Environment

The boss room is a rectangular chamber with a narrow set of steps leading up to a small mausoleum at the far end. Like most other arenas of this shape, the main danger is becoming trapped in the corners or against the pilasters lining the walls; you must also be careful not to let Maria back you up to the steps as there is no avenue of escape from atop the mausoleum other than directly past her. In general, keep the fight to the center of the room as much as possible and lure Maria away from the walls or corners if necessary; however, bear in mind that if using specific strategies such as trapping her in an infinite combo with the Beast Roar, backing her into a corner or against a wall can actually work to your advantage and help prevent her from escaping.

Basic Information			Item Drops												
Research Hall	14081	39000	Celestial Dial [100%]	147	147	147	147	103	177	103	999	999	—	—

Key Attacks

Phase 1	Interrupt	Notes
Iai Blow	Yes	Extremely fast long-range strike with a delayed startup and strong lateral tracking. Quickstep forward past it just before she strikes or interrupt it by timing your shot so that the bullet connects as she begins the dash.
Launcher Combo	Yes	Quick two-hit combo that will launch you into the air, sometimes used as part of longer combos. Interrupt her or quickstep forward past the swings.
Double Overhead Slash	Yes	Heavy slash with a slightly delayed startup and super armor, used on its own and in combos. Interrupt it or quickstep forward past it and continue strafing sideways in the same direction to avoid subsequent swings.
Double Lateral Slash	Yes	Heavy horizontal slash with both blades. Quickstep forward through it or sideways in the opposite direction of the swing, or interrupt it.
Cross Slash	Yes	Lunging scissor-type cross slash. Quickstep forward past it or interrupt her.
Transformation Attacks	Yes	Used periodically to switch between weapon modes. Interrupt her or quickstep forward past both versions of the attack.

Phase 2	Interrupt	Notes
Dive Bomb	No	Leaps high in the air, pauses and performs a forward dive at a fixed angle. Tracks laterally and creates an explosion when she lands; quickstep forward underneath her at shorter range and backward at mid range.
Blood Burst	Yes	Raises the blade above her head and performs a small frontal short- to mid-range area attack with a slightly delayed startup marked by blue particle effects. Interrupt it or quickstep forward past her just before she strikes.
Blood Stinger	Yes	Lowers the blade to her side and performs a mid- to long-range diagonal slash attack with a delayed startup marked by blue particle effects, sometimes followed by a second identical slash. Quickstep sideways one to two times just before she strikes.
Blood Lance	Yes	Levels the blade at her shoulder and performs a heavily-delayed long-range thrust attack in a straight line; the windup is marked by blue particle effects and she'll sometimes immediately follow up with a wide horizontal slash with the same reach. Quickstep sideways just before the first attack and either sideways through the second at a distance or forward past it at close range.

Phase 3	Interrupt	Notes
Flying Cross	Yes	Resembles the Cross Slash but with a delayed startup and fairly obvious telegraph. This move will instantly stagger you and if it connects, Maria will immediately attempt a visceral attack. Can be interrupted from a safe distance; otherwise quickstep forward past it.

Strategies

Key Strategies

During Phase 1 you may either quickstep forward past Maria's attacks and strike from behind with melee combos during her recovery or simply bait and interrupt her swings. Gunshots and projectiles are largely useless at long range as she will usually dodge them, but skirting just out of reach of her attacks and tempting her to take a swing will force her to commit to an attack animation and provide you with an opportunity to interrupt her. During Phases 2 and 3 it is no longer safe merely to quickstep forward through her attacks as the extended reach of her blades and the trails of fire left by her attacks will often strike behind her or in a 360-degree radius; you'll still need to use the evasive components of this tactic to avoid her forward combos, but the most reliable ways to damage her remain baiting opportunities for interrupts or knocking her down with the Beast Roar.

Phase 1

During this phase Maria will walk slowly toward you and begin launching attacks when she reaches mid range. Exploit this behavior to anticipate when she will strike and either interrupt her or quickstep forward through her swings and counterattack from behind. Some of Maria's delayed attacks such as her double slashes and Iai Blow

leave enough time to interrupt them on reaction; it is also possible to set her up for an interrupt by baiting her to begin a combo, dodging the first hit and shooting her when she begins the second. Attacking Maria in the middle of one of her combos is strongly discouraged as there is a risk of hitting her while her super armor is in effect and becoming trapped in the rest of the combo when she absorbs the hit. Never attempt to dodge by backing up if you are anywhere inside mid range as almost all of Maria's attacks carry her forward by at least the length of a quickstep. Dodging diagonally forward past her will avoid nearly all her attacks during this phase, though the timing will be slightly delayed for her heavier swings. Maria is susceptible to stunlocks during her idle and walking animations, and can be trapped in combos with heavy weapons such as the transformed Kirkhammer and Ludwig's Holy Blade if the first hit causes her to flinch. She is especially vulnerable to being stunlocked after finishing a combo but will sometimes backstep away and escape after one or two hits; at this point she will usually initiate an immediate and fairly predictable melee counterattack, opening herself up to an interrupt. Beware that Maria also has super armor during her recovery from being knocked down and if she is flattened with the first hit of a Kirkhammer charge combo, the followup swing will NOT send her flying if it connects and will instead leave you open to a counterattack. Faster weapons such as the Kirkhammer's longsword and the transformed Blades of Mercy ARE effective for stunlocking Maria as she recovers from being knocked down; this can be used to set her up for extremely long combos such as a visceral attack followed by an R1 chain as she regains her footing. She'll usually be focused on attempting to counterattack at this point, so she will often not bother trying to quickstep out of the combo. Be sure you conserve enough stamina to quickstep forward past her after the last hit of the R1 chain, though, as fully depleting your reserves will give her an opening to counterattack. Reduce Maria's health to just above 60%, then interrupt her and perform a visceral attack (and ideally an R1 combo as she stands up) to minimize the amount of time you'll have to spend fighting her far more dangerous Phase 2 attacks.

This is the start-up pose for the Blood Lance. Watch out for the swift follow-up if you're close!

Phase 2

When Maria's HP drops below 60% she will use a spherical area attack in which she impales herself with her blades, causing a small explosion centered on herself. She has infinite super armor and cannot be staggered during this attack; at this point the length of her weapons will increase drastically and she will begin using her Phase 2 moves in addition to those from Phase 1. Bear in mind that while the animations for her Phase 1 attacks are still the same, these swings can now reach you from much greater distances due to the increased length of her blades. The safest opportunities to use Blood Vials are largely limited to the recovery periods of her slower moves and while standing behind her after quickstepping forward through one of her combos; do not under any circumstances attempt to heal yourself while standing in front of her unless she is very far away from you and even then, keep a close eye on her to be sure she isn't about to hit you with a Blood Lance. Interrupts are riskier during this phase due to the increased range of Maria's attacks, but are still the best way to finish her quickly. Baiting her melee combos at mid range (leaving enough room to quickstep backward away from the first attack and calculate the timing of a gunshot to interrupt a subsequent swing) is the most reliable means of dealing damage. She can still

The Blood Burst starts as shown here. It's very quick, but you can still interrupt it with careful timing.

be stunlocked with melee combos, but will counterattack more aggressively if she escapes. Reduce her health to just above 30% and interrupt one of her swings, then hit her with a visceral attack and an R1 combo as she stands up in order to help end Phase 3 as quickly as possible.

This pose signals the Blood Stinger. Watch for the follow-up slash after you dodge the initial attack.

Phase 3

When Maria's HP drops below 30%, she will run away from you and float into the air for a few seconds, then generate a large AoE explosion around herself and power up her swords. She can be attacked during this move but it has infinite super armor and she is immune to staggering for its duration. The AoE lingers just long enough that the quickstep's invincibility frames cannot be used to dash through it; if you decide to attack Maria during this time, quickstep backward twice when the sound of swirling blood begins to fade. Maria will continue using all of her previous attacks during this phase, but their range will increase even further and they will now leave lingering trails of flame which will damage you on contact. The radii of her area attacks such as the Blood Burst increase substantially at this point and she will begin using a slower version of her Cross Slash to stagger you, following up immediately with a visceral attack if it connects. Attempting to bait interrupts from the front is now extremely risky; quickstepping forward past her swings and counterattacking from behind is still fairly reliable, but it is almost impossible to avoid taking damage from the trails of fire. Lead Elixirs will prevent flinching due to residual fire damage, but direct hits with Maria's blades will still cause heavy hitstun. Make every effort to end the battle quickly when this phase begins – taking too much time greatly increases the risk of being clipped and killed by a stray slash from across the arena.

This is the start-up pose for the Flying Cross. This move is easy to interrupt, but will stagger you if it connects.

Orphan of Kos

Preparation

Equipment and runes that reduce physical or arcane damage can be helpful for a defense-oriented approach, but you may find that Communion or Clawmark runes provide more substantial benefits during this fight. Despite being the offspring of Kos, the boss is NOT part of the Kin family and thus is not affected by Kinhunter attack bonuses, so use either Tempering, Nourishing or Adept gems instead depending upon which weapon you choose. The Orphan of Kos has no particular strengths or weaknesses to specific damage types, but fast weapons with decent reach such as the Kirkhammer's longsword and the Saw Cleaver will fare better than those with slower attacks. A notable exception is the Whirligig Saw, which can deal damage very quickly during the limited safe openings with its transformed L2 attack. The Cannon and Church Cannon can instantly knock the boss out of certain attacks which would otherwise require complex evasive action or multiple hits from the Fists of Gratia, and will deal heavy damage if augmented with Bone Marrow Ash. For Bloodtinge builds, the Evelyn or Repeating Pistol are also good candidates for Bone Marrow Ash; alternately, the arrows from Simon's Bowblade can inflict tremendous amounts of damage with high Bloodtinge if the weapon is set with three high-level Damp gems. Arcane builds will need tools with faster activation times such as the Executioner's Gloves, Tiny Tonitrus or Blacksky Eye and will find comparatively few safe opportunities to use A Call Beyond.

Overview

The Orphan of Kos is one of the most aggressive bosses in the game, particularly during the second phase of the battle. He is susceptible to interrupts and staggers during both phases, but landing them can be extremely difficult during Phase 2 due to his speed and highly unpredictable movements. He can swing his blade around him on an elastic tendon to strike at multiple ranges from a single position, and many of his combos create small zones of splash damage that can hit you on the ground while you're helpless. He is protected by super armor during all of his attacks, but is vulnerable to being stunlocked during his walking and idle animations; however, he will rarely stand still long enough for a full R1 combo to connect. His relentless attack patterns during Phase 2 give a whole new meaning to the term "Heat Up;" his movements become extremely erratic and difficult to predict at this point, and he will begin using several rapid, wide-ranging area attacks that can be exceedingly tricky to avoid.

Environment

You'll face the Orphan of Kos in a small coastal inlet consisting of a gently-sloped beach leading down to a wider stretch of shallow water. The corpse of the Great One, Kos, lies in the center of the beach and a collection of boulders and dead shrubs line the rock walls leading down to the water's edge. In terms of environmental collision, the water is actually the best place to fight as it provides a wide, flat and completely unobstructed battlefield free of obstacles of any kind; however, do note that there is a hard boundary some distance out to sea where the water deepens and it is possible to back yourself up against this invisible wall if you don't pay attention to your position. Keeping the battle in the shallow water as far away from Kos' corpse as possible is crucial during Phase 2 – the boss will periodically use a massive area attack that originates from the corpse and spreads quickly outward, so the farther you are from the beach, the more time you'll have to avoid it.

Many of this boss' attacks have deceptively long reach and will hit you if you attempt to quickstep backward.

3

The long start-up of Bolts of Sorrow provides a good chance to attack the boss...

...but don't get greedy – keep a close eye on the corpse of Kos!

Basic Information

			Item Drops												
Fishing Hamlet	19217	60000	Kos Parasite [100%]	183	183	183	183	274	205	228	999	999	—	—

Key Attacks

Phase 1	Interrupt	Notes
720 Swing	Yes	Swings his sword in a short-range 360-degree ring followed immediately by a mid-range 360-degree ring. Interrupt it at the very beginning of the animation or quickstep backward from the first swing and forward past the second, or quickstep backward three times to out-range both swings.
Uppercut Swing	Yes	Delayed mid-range forward uppercut used on its own and at the end of combos; strikes directly behind him when the blade returns to his hand. Interrupt it or quickstep forward past his left side.
Leaping Dive	Yes	Leaps into the air and performs a forward dive at a fixed angle after a very short delay. Almost impossible to interrupt due to unfavorable targeting; quickstep forward past it at close range or backward one to two times at mid range.
Airborne Strike	Yes	Leaps into the air and strikes the ground in front of him with a close to mid-range sword slam while hovering. Nearly impossible to interrupt; quickstep forward past it at close range or backward twice from mid range.
Guillotine Slam	Yes	Slow two-handed downward chop performed at close range, sometimes to open a combo. Reaches slightly farther than it looks like it should; interrupt it from no less than two quicksteps' distance away or quickstep forward past it if any closer. Be prepared for follow-up swings.
Visceral Grenade	Yes	Rips a chunk of flesh from his abdomen and throws it at you from all ranges. Tracking is unavoidable; the only way to escape is to block it with the terrain or quickstep sideways the instant before it explodes. Shooting him before he throws the projectile will destroy it, cancelling the attack.
Visceral Groundburst	Yes	Rips a chunk of flesh from his abdomen and drives it into the ground at his feet, creating a large frontal explosion. Extremely difficult to avoid at close range but quickstepping twice forward past him has the best chance of success; otherwise quickstep backward twice to escape. Shooting him before he strikes the ground will destroy the chunk of flesh and cancel the attack.

Phase 2	Interrupt	Notes
Double Uppercut	Yes	Two-hit frontal launcher followed by at least one downward slam if it connects. Interrupt it or quickstep forward past him at close range; otherwise quickstep back one to two times.
Feint Rush	Yes	Extremely quick two-hit long-range dash attack in a straight line. Very difficult to avoid if not anticipated; interrupt it or quickstep sideways one to two times to avoid it.
Ferocious Dive	Yes	Heavier version of his jump attacks from Phase 1, but with stronger tracking. He can repeat it up to three times consecutively at different intervals; quickstep forward underneath him at close range or backward twice per jump attack at mid range until you are out of reach.
Visceral Assault	No	Throws multiple chunks of flesh at the ground in a line creating a wall of large explosions in front of him, sometimes used to end combos or immediately after a Visceral Groundburst. After the first wave he will often leap 90 degrees to your side and perform the attack again. Virtually impossible to dodge at close range; quickstep backward twice to avoid each wave or break his super armor with a Cannon shot to knock him out of it.
Visceral Bombardment	No	Flies into the air and rains Visceral Grenades on a large circular target area beneath him. Each projectile creates an initial explosion and a forward wave of smaller explosions that moves outward along the ground. Quickstep backward up to three times from mid range or stand directly beneath him if already at close range when he initiates the attack.
Bolts of Sorrow	No	Screams for about three seconds. Roughly 1.5 seconds into the scream a massive bolt of lightning will strike the corpse of Kos in the middle of the beach and release large waves of lightning outward from that spot in six directions. Three waves will always head directly toward you and the center of these will always target your position when the attack activates; lock off and watch Kos' corpse when he begins screaming, then run or quickstep sideways to slip through the gap between the waves of lightning. A Cannon shot during the first second of the scream will break his super armor and cancel the attack, but he cannot be staggered out of it from behind.

Strategies

Key Strategies

During Phase 1 the boss will walk slowly toward you at a distance and begin attacking when he reaches mid range. Standing close to him for any length of time is not safe as he uses extremely rapid melee combos with heavy hitstun which can strike around him at all angles; the only safe opportunities to attack him at close range are after dodging one of his combos or individual swings, and you'll only have time to swing once to twice before he recovers and launches a counterattack. The strafe-and-bait strategy works relatively well during Phase 1 if you intend to fish for interrupts, but carries far greater risk during Phase 2 due to the ceaseless onslaught of rapid knockdown attacks. Ranged chip damage is a viable strategy during Phase 2 if you can hit hard enough to make it worthwhile; Simon's Bowblade with Blood Bullets, three Oedon Writhe runes and three high-level Damp gems is ideal for this purpose and will afford you far more safe opportunities to attack the boss than close-range weapons.

Phase 1

Quickstep forward past his combo attacks, hit him once or twice and strafe or quickstep out of range before he can turn to face you. The safest strategy (although still risky) is to stay no closer than mid range and bait him into using one of his slower attacks such as the Uppercut Swing or Guillotine Slam, then interrupt him. If he uses a faster attack and you aren't confident in your ability to time an interrupt correctly, quickstep backward one to two times and try again. Apart from the special attacks listed in the table above, the Orphan of Kos uses a generic set of rapid close-range melee combos consisting of horizontal and vertical swings with widely-varied timing. Many of these are delayed long enough that quickstepping immediately after being struck will cause you to get hit again by the next attack; however, he will frequently mix up his combos to prevent you from reliably anticipating them. The only safe opportunities to heal are during the recovery of one of his slower attacks and when far away from him at long range; the forward momentum of his melee attacks will usually enable him to hit you if you attempt to use Blood Vials up close. It's worth trying to shoot him out of his Visceral Grenade and Visceral

Groundburst if you identify them quickly enough; the Visceral Grenade in particular can be extremely difficult to dodge correctly due to the precise timing required, especially if you're caught along the walls or in the narrow area near the entrance of the boss room. Reduce the Orphan's health to just above 50%, then interrupt him and perform a visceral attack to help reduce the amount of time you'll have to spend dealing with his dangerous Phase 2 attacks.

Phase 2

When the Orphan's health drops below 50% he will generate a small explosion centered on his own body and sprout wings, signaling the beginning of Phase 2. He attacks far more aggressively during this phase and will constantly chase you down at a fast dash; moreover, his melee combos and special moves become much less predictable and tend to strike wider areas at longer ranges. He will now often dodge to your side before initiating physical attacks and uses many swings that reach directly behind him, so you'll have to either chip him out from a distance with ranged attacks or take what limited opportunities you safely can to strike him from behind during the short recovery periods after his combos. In general, make every effort to keep him no closer than mid range and to stay behind him if he does manage to close the gap. Baiting his more predictable attacks from a distance and interrupting them is still the safest strategy, but requires a great deal of attention to his movements in order to avoid miscalculating a dodge. The best opportunities to heal are when he is far away and during the longer recovery periods of his moves; also beware that he will sometimes attempt to trick you by following up with another attack when he appears to have ended a combo. Beware that he can now also repeat certain attacks in immediate succession – as many as three consecutive times in the case of his Ferocious Dive. Be absolutely sure to keep the fight to the water during this phase; if you're anywhere near the corpse of Kos when the Orphan uses Bolts of Sorrow, you may be unable to get out of the way in time. This move also offers one of the best opportunities to attack the boss without fear of reprisal, ideally by knocking him out of it with a Bone Ashed Cannon shot before he can summon the lightning.

Overhead view of Bolts of Sorrow. Note that the center lightning blast will always target your location at the time of the attack.

3

Undead Giant (Twin Curved Blades)

Preparation

Rather than face the Undead Giant immediately after unlocking the gate leading to it, return to the Hunter's Dream to stock up on Blood Vials, Fire Paper, Quicksilver Bullets and Bone Marrow Ash. Bringing a decently upgraded Cannon or Flamesprayer into this fight can make it safer, but the quickest way to win is up close using a weapon with strong Bolt damage.

Overview

An Undead Giant is the first boss you will encounter in the Preset Chalice Dungeons. The two blades fused into both of its arms are used as its primary means of offense; its swings cover a wide range to its sides, while both its thrusts and overhead slices feature heavy tracking and long reach. From the front, its combos are long and slow, stringing up to a maximum of five hits. During its combos it can damage you as it walks if you come into contact with its legs; this will deal a miniscule amount of damage, but it can very briefly cause you to flinch and open you to the Undead Giant's attacks. Standing close to its legs from the front is a bad idea, as it may use its dangerous Kick, which is somewhat faster than its other attacks. Once you're behind the Undead Giant, it will attack much less often, using single swings from its sides and its Spinning Slice. When standing at a distance ahead of it, the Undead Giant will use its dangerous Leaping Blade Slam; while it's airborne its legs can re-peatedly hit you. After its health drops to 50% it will begin using its Roaring Slam and Walking Thrust, which are both highly dangerous, though it will not change its behavior otherwise.

Basic Information

	◼	⚔	Item Drops	🔲	⚪	🔺	⚙	⭐	🔥	🎵	☠	🔻	⚡	✂
Chalice Dungeon Base Level	952	446	Random Adept gem based on area ×1 [12,5%], Random gem based on area ×1 [12,5%], Bloodstone C ×1 [5%], Bloodstone B ×2 [15%]	132	132	92	132	160	120	70	300	180	—	—
Chalice Dungeon Base Level | Boss	3175	1425	Adept Blood Gemstone (2) [100%]	132	158	92	132	160	120	70	300	180		

Preset Chalice Dungeon: Pthumerian Labyrinth (Boss)

Key Attacks

Phase 1	Interrupt	Notes
Leaping Blade Slam	No	Leaps forward into the air and lands with both blades. Avoid by quickstepping to either side.
Kick	No	Used by either leg; avoid standing close to their legs for too long and quickstep back or to the side to avoid.
Recovery	No	Surrounds its injured parts with a red aura which restores their defense.
Spinning Slice	No	Slices while spinning almost 360 degrees when standing behind it. Quickstep back once.

Phase 2	Interrupt	Notes
Roaring Slam	No	Roars and slams with both blades, sending out an area-of-effect shockwave; quickstep back as it roars.
Walking Thrust	No	High damage right handed-thrust with heavy tracking and knockback. Quickstep back twice to evade.

Environment

The boss area is a circular chamber, strewn with bones and armor. Although this chamber offers plenty of room to maneuver and distance yourself to heal, you will need lots of space to quickstep back from its attacks and combos. If you aren't paying close attention you may end up backing yourself into a wall.

Strategies

Key Strategies

Get behind the Undead Giant as soon as you can, and aim to stay there. It can only hit you with its Spinning Slice in this spot, so quickstep backwards once you see it begin to attack. Use Tonitrus or a weapon augmented with a Bolt Blood Gem to quickly shred off enormous portions of its health. Otherwise, apply a Bolt Paper to increase your weapon's damage and focus on hitting the large growth on the outer side of the its left knee; this will burst, depleting 25% of the Undead Giant's total health. By hitting its head and each of its limbs, you can injure these parts separately, which will cause them to take 50% more damage; after some time the specifically injured limbs will have their defenses restored by the Recovery move, though this will allow you to injure them again. You can also stagger it by hitting its left and right legs, opening it up for a visceral attack.

Phase 1

Be prepared to roll or quickstep out of the way at a moment's notice once you have entered the room; the Undead Giant will spawn in the center, giving it just enough space to use its Leaping Blade Slam. Position yourself behind it as soon as possible; from behind you will only need to avoid a few attacks, instead of its long combos from the front. Its single right and left arm swipes used from behind are easily avoided by sticking directly to the center of its back, though you will need to watch carefully for when it draws its right arm to the left to use its Spinning Slice. You'll need to quickstep back to properly evade it. Utilize the Key Strategies detailed above; once you have decreased the defense of a part of its body by injuring it, you can attack it with the powered up Cannon or Flamesprayer for an absurd amount of damage. When you need to heal, quickstep repeatedly out of its reach during its combos and heal while it continues, to prevent it from using its Leaping Blade Slam.

Phase 2

When the Undead Giant's health has been reduced by 50%, it will use its Roaring Slam and begin to bleed profusely, signaling its second phase. Its Roaring Slam will create a high-damage (but short range) area shockwave; quickstep backward when it roars and wait for the shockwave to pass, then move in and hit it a few times. The Undead Giant will gain one other dangerous attack: its Walking Thrust. This attack targets a frontal area at mid range and will track you until its third step, at which point it will thrust; dodge this by quickstepping to either side slightly after the second step forward. Aside from the two moves gained during this phase, little else changes, so continue to handle it similarly to the first phase by sticking to its back, where it won't even use its Walking Thrust.

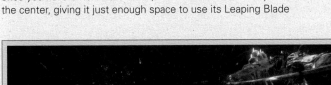

Watchdog of the Old Lords

Preparation

Stock up on Blood Vials and bring an upgraded weapon with a damage bonus against beasts, such as the Saw Cleaver or Saw Spear. Be sure to fortify your weapons with blood gems that increase your physical damage or provide attack bonuses against beasts; don't bother with Fire or Bolt Paper, as they will do little to increase your damage against this boss. Small firearms are practically useless against this boss, as it cannot be staggered, but if you have a Cannon, stock up on Bone Marrow Ash and Quicksilver Bullets to put your ammunition to good use.

Overview

The Watchdog of the Old Lords is a large flaming beast; as its appearance would indicate, it incorporates fire into the majority of its attacks and has high defense against this element. Its defenses to both elemental and arcane attacks are strong, which means that, Molotovs, Fire Paper and Bolt Paper will do very little against it; using a decently upgraded weapon fused with physical attack-increasing Blood Gems is imperative for putting out good damage. It is slightly weak to thrust attacks, so the Saw Spear is a very good choice. It will almost constantly attempt to move into close range to use its side-to-side bites and Flame Bark Combo. During its third phase it will chase you even more aggressively and begin to use a massive area-of-effect explosion. When standing in front of it, it may use a rearing paw slam or stomping combo, during which its head will be left wide open to your attacks. Its Flame Wave swipe can be used from close to mid range and will become a Double Flame Wave Swipe during its second phase. It is possible to get behind it, though this is more often than not a waste of time, as it will very quickly turn around to face you. Occasionally from any range it will use its Lava Vomit, which leaves it extremely vulnerable during its long build-up.

Basic Information Special Weakness: Serration	■	♦	Item Drops	▮	●	▲	✹	★	🔥	ϟ	☠	▼	🐺	∿
Chalice Dungeon Base Level	**970**	**519**	Random Fire gem based on area ×1 [100%]	110	110	110	110	160	9939	160	999	999	×	–
Chalice Dungeon Base Level **| Boss**	**3528**	**1696**	Central Pthumeru Chalice [100%], Cursed Sharp Damp Blood Gem (5) [100%]	110	132	110	110	160	9939	160	999	999		

Preset Chalice Dungeons: Pthumerian Labyrinth (Boss), Cursed Pthumerian Defilement (Boss)

Key Attacks

Phase 1	Interrupt	Notes
Flame Wave Swipe	No	Left swipe sending a wave of fire outward. Quickstep to either side or through the wave.
Flame Bark Combo	No	Barks quick bursts of fire ahead multiple times; quickstep repeatedly backward to avoid this.
Lava Vomit	No	Vomits lingering pools of lava ahead. Back away during its long build-up to avoid walking into the lava pools.
Flaming Charge	No	Lights up and charges; quickstep to either side and out of the way.
Pounce Attack	No	Pounces with heavy tracking. Dash or quickstep forward past it while it's airborne.
Stomping Combo	No	Stomps multiple times with its front and hind legs when standing against them. Quickstep backward to avoid.

Phase 2	Interrupt	Notes
Double Flame Wave Swipe	No	Same as the Flame Wave Swipe, but followed by a delayed second hit from the right paw. Quickstep left twice during the first swipe to move out of the second's range.

Phase 3	Interrupt	Notes
Explosion	No	Absorbs heated particles before using a massive explosion. Gain as much distance possible by repeatedly quickstepping backward.

Environment

The Watchdog of the Old Lords is fought in a massive circular arena which gives plenty of space to maneuver toward it and back away from its attacks. The boss area is completely empty, save for the statues lining its walls, and provides no obstructions to be used as cover. Consequently, you will need to fight the Watchdog of the Old Lords head – on and out in the open.

Strategies

Key Strategies

By hitting its head and each of its four legs separately, these parts can be injured once per fight and will receive 50% more damage as a result. Injuring its head or any of its limbs will also cause it to stumble, opening it to your attacks. You'll need to move out again quickly, though, as it will use a medium range explosion once it has stood up. The Cannon is extremely effective for injuring the boss' limbs; the best time to fire is as it recovers after its attacks. The only safe position from which to fight this boss is in front of it – you'll have to wait for an opening in its attacks and strike during its recovery.

Phase 1

During this phase the Watchdog of the Old Lords will trot at a pace slightly slower than your own running speed. If you need to heal, you can outrun it by dashing, though generally you should keep close to avoid triggering its dangerous Pounce Attack or Flaming Charge. Stay at mid range to bait its attacks while continuously backing up from them. Occasionally it will use its Flame Wave Swipe, which will send a wave of fire outwards; quickstep directly through this to counter attack and quickstep back to retain your distance ahead of it. During the brief recovery periods after its attacks, strike the head using the transformed mode of your weapon, before quickstepping back out; if you have successfully injured the head, lay in as many hits as possible before moving out from its counter attack as it stands back up. When its throat begins to swell in preparation for its Lava Vomit, run in and attack its legs, as this will serve as a prime opportunity to deal some damage and possibly cancel the attack by injuring it.

Phase 2

When The Watchdog of the Old Lords' health has dropped to 70% it will begin to use its Double Flame Wave Swipe. Quickstep left twice during the first swipe to move out of the reach of the second and attack the Watchdog's side during its swing. It will also begin to use a further-reaching forward bite which can be used by itself or inserted into its biting combos; give yourself a bit more space when backing up to avoid this. Aside from these two new attacks, the strategy during this phase will remain largely the same as the first: continue to bait its attacks from ahead while backing up and counterattack during its recoveries.

Phase 3

Once you have reduced its health to 40%, be ready to quickstep immediately and repeatedly away to avoid its massive Explosion, which will signal the beginning of its final phase. Its Explosion will be used occasionally throughout the remainder of the fight, so be ready to escape at a moment's notice. From here on out, it will attack more aggressively and move towards you at a faster pace, though you will only need to quickstep backward as you are backing up to keep your distance when it gets too close. Like the previous phase, the general strategy will remain largely the same.

Keeper of the Old Lords

Preparation

Purchase a full load of Poison Knives and consider using a weapon that inflicts additional arcane damage, such as the Burial Blade or the Blade of Mercy. The Rosmarinus can be helpful if you have access to it, especially when augmented with Bone Marrow Ash; bring a firearm that only consumes one bullet at a time, such as the Hunter Pistol or Hunter Blunderbuss, and remember to stock up on ammunition. If you've already obtained the Empty Phantasm Shell, bring it along and use it to augment purely physical weapons with additional arcane damage. If you've acquired any Blood Gems that add poison effects to your weapons, equipping them before heading out will help end the fight more quickly once you've run out of Poison Knives.

Overview

The Keeper of the Old Lords fights very much like a hunter NPC, but is capable of using several fire attacks not accessible to players. During Phase 1 it will walk slowly toward you at long range and begin using its mid-range fire attacks when you're close enough; it will also occasionally take a swing at you with its sword, but tends to prefer its Flash Fire at short range. The Keeper will often respond to attacks during this phase with a quick horizontal slash followed by a backstep, even if the damage was inflicted by a ranged weapon, and will make relatively little effort to avoid Molotovs and Throwing Knives. At the beginning of Phase 2 it will cover its sword in flames and begin using its Fire Slash, usually only one or two swings at a time from mid range, but up to five if it manages to trap you in a close-range combo. It'll also pursue you more aggressively and evade your ranged attacks more frequently during this phase, and the bursts of flame from its Fire Slashes will severely limit your opportunities to interrupt its attacks.

Basic Information

	■	⚔	Item Drops										
Chalice Dungeon Base Level | Boss	2540	1425	Central Pthumeru Root Chalice [100%], Cursed Sharp Damp Blood Gem (5) [100%]	99	99	99	99	30	70	75	120	210	—	—
Chalice Dungeon Base Level	529	356	Random Sharp gem based on area ×1 [30%], Blood Vial ×3 [30%], Blood Vial ×2 [40%]	99	99	99	99	30	70	75	120	210		

Preset Chalice Dungeons: Central Pthumerian Labyrinth (Boss), Lower Pthumerian Labyrinth (Strong), Cursed Pthumerian Defilement (Strong), Cursed Pthumerian Defilement (Boss), Lower Loran & Isz Gravestone (Strong)

Key Attacks

Phase 1	Interrupt	Notes
Flash Fire	No	Frontal short-range burst of fire with a small spherical area-of-effect; quickstep forward past it.
Flamethrower	No	Two consecutive mid-range bursts of flame in frontal cone-shaped arcs; quickstep backward at mid range or forward past them if close.
Heat Wave	No	Strikes a wide circular radius with flame; quickstep backward once or twice.

Phase 2	Interrupt	Notes
Fire Slash	Yes	Up to five sword swings that create narrow forward bursts of flame; quickstep forward past them if close or sideways if at mid-range.

Environment

The boss room forms a short-armed cross with four pillars surrounding the center in ordinal positions. The narrow corners along the perimeter are dangerous places for close-quarters combat, but also provide the advantage of preventing the boss from being able to evade thrown weapons such as Poison Knives; this is particularly important during Phase 2 if you're incorporating poison into your battle strategy. You can use the pillars for cover if you need to create some breathing room or use items, but it's best to keep your hand-to-hand combat to the center of the room if possible, in order to ensure that you have enough room to maneuver.

Strategies

Key Strategies

Interrupts are highly effective during the first phase, but become impractical during the second due to the high risk of trading hits in the process. To minimize the risk of taking damage unnecessarily, reduce the Keeper's health to just over 70% and hit it with four Poison Knives before it transitions to the second phase, then move in and attack a couple of times while it powers up its sword with fire. Immediately retreat and stay away from it until the poison wears off, then lure it into one of the narrow spaces behind the pillars and hit it with four more Poison Knives. If you have a Pistol or similarly timed firing weapon, you can repeatedly fire on Keeper from mid range and it will eventually try to backstep attack, which will result in it being parried. A quick dash in will grant you the Visceral Attack. Be sure to watch your bullet count, though!

Phase 1

Interrupt the Keeper's melee swings and use visceral attacks, or augment your weapon with arcane or fire damage and attack with transformed R1 combos. You can avoid all of its attacks by quickstepping forward past or through them, which will place you behind the Keeper and give you a brief opportunity to counterattack; if you're having trouble hitting it, try locking off and rolling behind it, as doing so gives you more control and positions you closer to it after your dodge. Avoid using non-transformed light attacks, as they won't stun the Keeper long enough for you to get out of the way before it recovers; heavy R1 or L2 swings from large weapons will inflict a strong enough stumble effect to prevent it from immediately counterattacking, but most transformation attacks are too slow to be of any use and will only leave you vulnerable for extended periods of time.

Phase 2

When the Keeper's health falls below 70% it will cover its sword in flames, increasing its attack power and causing all of its melee attacks to throw waves of fire. You can still interrupt its sword swings during this phase, but doing so requires you to position yourself beyond their range before shooting it, and leaves you with very little time to reach it before it recovers from staggering and stands up. If using melee weapons exclusively, you'll need to keep the fight to the center of the room and continue to quickstep or roll forward past the Keeper's attacks before striking with heavy R1 swings; it will retreat as soon as it recovers, so you'll need to be quick in order to hit it before it escapes. Backing the Keeper against a pillar or into a corner will make it harder for you to evade its attacks, but also helps prevent it from evading yours; you can also power up your Rosmarinus with Bone Marrow Ash and lure the boss through one of the narrow spaces behind the pillars, then quickstep forward through one of its attacks and blast it with sacred mist while it's unable to escape.

Undead Giant (Club & Hook)

Bring a strong weapon with heavy-hitting attacks like Ludwig's Holy Blade or the Kirkhammer, or take advantage of its weakness to thrust attacks with a Saw Spear or Rifle Spear. Alternatively, a Chikage set with rapid poison gems will be very effective in its transformed state. If you choose a weapon that can receive augmentations from items, bring some Bolt Paper; also consider bringing the Tiny Tonitrus if you have it. Poison Knives are optional but can be used with almost no risk; other thrown weapons will deal very little damage and aren't generally worth using. The Cannon is useful but not necessary; it will deal heavy damage when used with Bone Marrow Ash and since the boss cannot be interrupted, you won't have many other uses for your ammunition during this battle.

Overview

This Undead Giant variant uses only a few basic attacks consisting mainly of horizontal slashes with its hook and vertical slams with its club. It moves extremely slowly during both phases of the fight, and will hold its attacks until it's extremely close to you in order to prevent you from escaping. Beware that it can use the weighted chains hanging from its back as whips, and will do so if you stand behind or beside it for too long; it will also kick you if you stand in front of it at point blank range. It has several weak points including its head, its legs and a large lump of flesh on its right hip; all of these spots can be targeted for extra damage or additional effects. You can also quickstep forward through its legs in order to escape its frontal attacks. During Phase 1 it will use only slow melee attacks and combos, and will occasionally throw in a grab attack. During Phase 2 it will begin using a much more dangerous chain whip attack with longer reach and will increase the speed of its club combos; it'll also begin using a slam attack that strikes a small spherical area around its body with a damaging shockwave.

Environment

The arena is a large rectangular cavern with no obstacles or terrain differences. While the area is open and unobstructed, it's still very easy to be backed into a corner or against a wall due to your opponent's size and sweeping attacks, so pay constant attention to your position and try to use the full length of the room to maintain enough space to evade.

Basic Information				
	■	⚓	Item Drops	
Chalice Dungeon Base Level	3175	1425	Adept Blood Gemstone (3) [100%]	

Preset Chalice Dungeon: Lower Pthumerian Labyrinth

132	158	92	132	160	120	70	300	180	—	—

Key Attacks

Phase 1	Interrupt	Notes
Beatdown Combo	No	Up to five slow hits, usually vertical club smashes but sometimes ends with a horizontal hook slash; strafe or quickstep backward, or quickstep forward.
Fishhook Grab	No	Close-range grab attack; quickstep backward once or twice.
Spinning Flail	No	360-degree spin attack with very fast startup, used if you attack from behind; quickstep backward when it starts.
Front Kick	No	Single forward kick with fast startup, used with either foot; quickstep sideways or backward.

Phase 2	Interrupt	Notes
Shockwave Slam	No	Spherical area attack centered on itself. Slow and obvious windup; quickstep backward.
Chain Cyclone	No	Horizontal slash followed by 360-degree trailing attacks from the chains attached to its back. Slow windup but long reach; quickstep backward.
Pulverizer Combo	No	Up to five fast slams with its club, sometimes ending with a hook slash instead; can hit you repeatedly on the ground. Strafe or quickstep backward.

Strategies

Key Strategies

Aim for the boss' legs – injuring them will stagger it and allow you to perform a frontal visceral attack, or a Bone Marrow Ash Cannon shot if you're using the necessary equipment. Destroying the lump of flesh on its right hip will instantly deplete 25% of its health, but try to avoid doing so until just before its hit points drop below half; this will minimize the time you have to spend dealing with its deadlier Phase 2 attacks. Striking its head with vertical swings such as the transformed L2 attacks of Ludwig's Holy Blade will eventually cause it to stumble, setting it up for a longer combo; it will also walk straight into carefully-timed charge attacks such as those of the transformed Holy Blade and Hunter Axe. If you need to heal, simply quickstep backward three to four times before using your Blood Vials – the boss has no way of closing the distance quickly enough to stop you from doing so.

Phase 1

Wait for the Undead Giant to use one of its slow melee attacks or combos, then quickstep forward through the swing and strike its legs. When it staggers, circle in front of it to perform a visceral attack or simply hit it with a Bone Marrow Ash Cannon blast; when you've injured one of its legs, switch sides and begin focusing your attacks on the other to stagger it again. It will eventually repair the limb damage, identifiable by a swirling red particle effect around the area being healed, at which point you can re-injure the limb to stagger the giant yet again. Don't get greedy with R1 combos, though – attacking more than once before quickstepping away places you at risk of being hit with a Spinning Flail. Wait until the boss' health is just over 50%, then destroy the lump of flesh on its right hip to instantly cut that amount in half and begin Phase 2.

Phase 2

The second phase begins when the Undead Giant's health drops below 25%, and although it won't move any faster, it will fight more aggressively and make frequent use of its Chain Cyclone attack. Beware that it can perform both clockwise and counter-clockwise versions of this move, and will try to catch you off guard by alternating them. Regardless of which version it uses, the best way to avoid them is to quickstep backward once or twice. This is the best time to use your Poison Knives; eight to nine will inflict poison on the boss, allowing you to do so twice with a full load of 20, and if you back well away before using them the boss will be completely unable to evade. Continue focusing your melee attacks on its legs to stagger it, and if both legs are injured, fall back and let it repair them so you can injure them again; you can still evade all of its attacks by quickstepping forward through them, but if you're at mid range or farther, you're often better off just quickstepping away.

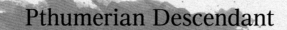

Pthumerian Descendant

Preparation

Bring a single-shot firearm such as the Hunter Pistol or Evelyn and a full load of Quicksilver Bullets. Avoid using the Repeating Pistol as you'll need as many opportunities as possible for interrupts; Bone Marrow Ash is only necessary if you plan to use the Cannon. If you've already obtained the Clawmark or Oedon Writhe runes, equip them beforehand and set your weapons with your best attack bonus gems. Weapons with heavy transformed modes such as the Kirkhammer and Ludwig's Holy Blade are well-suited to this fight, as are those with additional arcane damage, such as the Burial Blade. If you've already obtained the Empty Phantasm Shell, use it to augment purely physical weapons with additional arcane damage; otherwise stock up on Fire Paper.

Overview

The Pthumerian Descendant is an extremely aggressive opponent with swift attacks, and will constantly run you down in an attempt to keep you at close range. His melee swings and combos consist almost exclusively of rapid horizontal slashes; his only notable special abilities are a boomerang technique with his scythes and a long-range aerial dive. Although he will attempt to trick you into lowering your guard by varying the timing of his swings and quickstepping toward you without taking any immediate action, the Pthumerian Descendant uses only a very small set of melee attacks, which are predictable enough for you to interrupt them; he can also be staggered from behind, but doing so is nearly impossible due to his swift responses. During Phase 1 he will alternate between walking slowly toward you and lunging forward to perform his scythe combos, and

Basic Information

	■	⚔	Item Drops										
Chalice Dungeon Base Level	529	322	Random Nourishing gem based on area ×1 [100%]	110	110	110	110	51	56	154	250	180	—	—
Chalice Dungeon Base Level | Boss	2205	1625	Lower Pthumeru Chalice [100%], Tempering Damp Blood Gem (6) [100%]	110	110	110	110	52	60	154	250	180		

Preset Chalice Dungeons: Central Pthumerian Labyrinth (Boss), Pthumeru Ihyll (Boss)

Key Attacks

Phase 1	Interrupt	Notes
Boomerang Sickle	No	Forward ranged attack that can hit you once in each direction; quickstep sideways at close to mid range or backward twice at long range.

Phase 2	Interrupt	Notes
Double Boomerang Sickle	No	Throws two consecutive Boomerang Sickles; quickstep sideways once or twice at close to mid range or backward twice at long range.
Aerial Cleave	Yes	Jumps into the air, pauses briefly and performs a diving slash at your current position; quickstep forward under him or sideways.

will frequently throw his scythe at you if you're outside the range of his other attacks. At the beginning of Phase 2 he will separate his scythe into two and will begin using his Aerial Cleave technique; he'll also use heavier melee attacks and make a more focused effort to keep you at close range, but will otherwise fight in the same way as the first phase.

Environment

The arena is an enormous circular room lined with statues at intervals along the edges. The room is free of obstructions, but the niches between the statues can trap you if the boss manages to back you into one; you'll need to keep the fight to the open area in the center to ensure that you have enough room to escape his Boomerang Sickle and bait his other attacks. Staying at long range is especially important during Phase 2; at this point you'll need to use the full diameter of the room to maintain the distance necessary to bait the boss' Aerial Cleave without backing into one of the niches or getting caught on a statue.

Strategies

Key Strategies

Interrupts are the most effective way of defeating the Pthumerian Descendant, but you'll have to constantly strafe and quickstep backward while waiting for opportunities and immediately quickstep back in to perform a visceral attack before he stands up again. During Phase 2 the safest strategy is to keep him at long range and constantly back away from him to bait his Aerial Cleave, then quickstep forward or sideways when he dives and hit him with heavy attacks before he can escape; however, you'll still have to stay on constant watch for his Double Boomerang Sickle and must be prepared to quickstep out of the way if he uses it.

Phase 1

Keep the boss at mid to long range and bait him into rushing you with a sickle attack. When he swings, interrupt him and immediately quickstep forward to follow up with a visceral attack before he can recover; even if you're too late, you can still score a few hits before he stands up and take partial advantage of the damage bonus while

he's staggered. Do not attempt to quickstep through his combos and counterattack him; he has super armor during his attacks and you're almost guaranteed to trade blows rather than knocking him out of his swings. If he gets too close and initiates a combo before you can escape, quickstep forward through it and use additional quicksteps to establish some distance from him before he turns to face you again.

Phase 2

When his health drops below 50%, the Pthumerian Descendant will split his scythe into two and transition to his second phase. At this point he'll become even more persistent about rushing you down and attacking at close range, but as long as you constantly back away from him and keep a watchful eye out for his Double Boomerang Sickle, you can continue to bait and interrupt his melee combos. Alternately, keep him at long range either by constantly quickstepping away from him or locking off and running around the perimeter of the room while manually aiming your camera at him; this will prevent him from reaching you with any attacks other than his Double Boomerang Sickle and Aerial Cleave. Dodge the boomerang attack or simply continue running away from the boss to avoid it and wait for him to use the Aerial Cleave; when he does, roll under him and counterattack with one to two transformed R1 swings of a heavy weapon like Ludwig's Holy Blade before he can backstep out of your reach.

Forgotten Madman & Madman's Escort

Preparation

Stock up on Bone Marrow Ash, Pungent Blood Cocktails, Quicksilver Bullets and Blood Vials. Setting your weapons with Blood Gems that add poison effects can be helpful; otherwise just stack as many attack bonuses as you can fit and bring some Fire Paper to further boost your damage. The Reiterpallasch is extremely useful for its ability to perform right-handed interrupts and is most effective when paired with the Cannon or a Flamesprayer, and the Hunter Axe's transformed charge attack is very useful for keeping the madmen at a safe distance.

Overview

You'll start off facing only the Forgotten Madman; his escort won't join the battle until you've reduced his health by 25%. The madman frequently switches between both of his weapon's forms with transformation attacks, and will continually maintain an arcane augmentation on his sword throughout the battle using the Empty Phantasm Shell; he'll also occasionally cast Augur of Ebrietas and A Call Beyond. The escort does not use magic, but will often fire long, sustained blasts with his Flamesprayer while walking toward you, and tends to prefer the heavier transformed stance of his Kirkhammer. Both are susceptible to poison but have extremely quick responses and will frequently dodge thrown weapons such as Poison Knives, making Blood Gems a more reliable alternative for poisoning them. Both opponents are extremely aggressive and will constantly rush directly at you, giving you very little room to act without using the environment to separate them.

Basic Information Forgotten Madman														
Chalice Dungeon Base Level	1212	713	Item Drops	213	195	232	194	276	237	252	199	185	—	—
			Lower Hintertomb Root Chalice [100%]											

Preset Chalice Dungeon: Lower Hintertomb

Basic Information Madman's Escort														
Chalice Dungeon Base Level | Boss support	454	713	Item Drops	213	195	232	194	276	237	252	199	185	—	—
			Lower Hintertomb Root Chalice [100%]											

Preset Chalice Dungeon: Lower Hintertomb. Last one defeated drops Lower Hintertomb Root Chalice.

Equipment Madman's Escort

Right Hand 1	Kirkhammer +3
Right Hand 2	Bare Hands
Left Hand 1	Flamesprayer +3
Left Hand 2	Bare Hands

Head	Madman Hood
Body	Madman Garb
Hands	Madman Manchettes
Feet	Madman Leggings

Equipment Forgotten Madman

Right Hand 1	Ludwig's Holy Blade +3
Right Hand 2	Bare Hands
Left Hand 1	Ludwig's Rifle +4
Left Hand 2	Bare Hands

Head	Madman Hood
Body	Madman Garb
Hands	Madman Manchettes
Feet	Madman Leggings

Environment

The boss room forms a short-armed cross, with narrow corners and an open center flanked by four pillars in ordinal positions. Fighting in the tight corners restricts your evasive options and is extremely dangerous if both madmen are still alive, but fighting in the center of the room is equally difficult, because it exposes you to attack from both of them at the same time. The four pillars are essential for separating the bosses and buying yourself time to heal or prepare an ambush, and you'll need to make constant use of them to avoid being stunlocked to death.

Strategies

Key Strategies

Inflict as much damage as possible on the Forgotten Madman before Phase 2 begins and finish him as quickly as you can when his escort shows up. This is most easily accomplished by reducing his health to around 80%, powering up the Cannon with Bone Marrow Ash and interrupting him with a gunshot from the Reiterpallasch – by shooting him with the cannon while he's staggered rather than using a visceral attack, you'll inflict a far larger amount of damage. Use the pillars to separate your enemies and focus your attacks on the madman; when he falls, finish the escort with interrupts or gunshots boosted with your remaining Bone Marrow Ash.

Phase 1

Reduce the madman's health to about 80%, then power up your weapons with Bone Marrow Ash (and Fire or Bolt Paper if you haven't already used it) and interrupt him. Whether you use one of the Key Strategies or simply follow through with a visceral attack at this point is up to you; the goal is simply to deal as much damage to him as possible before his escort appears and complicates the battle. While the madman isn't extremely dangerous on his own, be careful to time your attacks so that he can't retreat or knock you out of them; if you try to hit him when he isn't in the middle of performing an action, he'll instantly quickstep away or counter with a faster swing.

Phase 2

When the Forgotten Madman's health drops below 75%, the Madman's Escort will appear at the rear of the room and join the fight. The madman is your priority target at this point and you should eliminate him before dealing with the escort; if you've followed the Key Strategies, the madman will begin this phase with only about

25% of his health remaining and will fall quickly to R1 combos. Power up your firearms with Bone Marrow Ash and bombard the madman with high-damage ranged attacks from a safe distance. If you're unable to use ranged attacks at all, use the pillars to separate your targets and wait for an opportunity to interrupt the madman, then finish him with a visceral attack – the invincibility frames during the animation will prevent the escort from damaging you until you recover. With the madman out of the way, finish the escort with visceral attacks or R1 combos; you can also time charged attacks so that he walks straight into them.

Abhorrent Beast

Preparation

An upgraded Flamesprayer will help a lot here, as will having some Bone Marrow Ash on hand; if it's already available at the shop in the Hunter's Dream, buy the maximum stock of 10 (even if you don't use them all for this battle, they'll be useful against other strong enemies later on). You might also consider buying as many Poison Knives as you can if they're in stock, though you can find six on the rooftop for free. Up to 20 normal Throwing Knives are a good idea if poison ones aren't on sale yet; Fire Paper is extremely helpful if you plan to use melee weapons, so bring a few if you have any left over from earlier areas. If you have an upgraded weapon that inflicts bonus damage against beasts, such as the Saw Cleaver or the Saw Spear, use it. Of course, if you fight the Abhorrent Beast at a point when you already have an upgraded Cannon, that'll help too.

Overview

The Abhorrent Beast moves and strikes quickly, has incredibly long reach and is extremely aggressive, leaving little opportunity to damage him or restore your health. Many of his moves cause knockdown or will launch you into the air; the rest will cause you to stumble and can make it nearly impossible to escape his combos.

He is highly weak against fire and incurs additional damage from serrated weapons, such as the Saw Spear; he also has extremely low status resistance and a single Poison Knife will poison him. He has effectively limitless super armor, to the extent that even a direct hit from the Cannon won't break his stride. He'll become increasingly aggressive as his health decreases, putting even more pressure on you to calculate your dodges carefully. You can injure his arms and head separately; once any of these parts have been injured, they will receive 50% more damage. By striking the head you can eventually stagger him, which will injure the head and open the beast up for a visceral attack.

Basic Information
Special Weakness: Serration

			Item Drops												
Forbidden Woods	2046	6811	Beast ×1 [100%]	123	123	123	123	70	70	295	70	999	×	—
Chalice Dungeon Base Level	1058	525	Random Bolt gem based on area ×1 [100%]	101	101	101	101	70	70	295	70	999		
Chalice Dungeon Base Level | Boss	2099	1753	Lower Loran Chalice [100%], Bolt Damp Blood Gem (6) [100%]	101	101	101	101	70	70	295	70	999		

Preset Chalice Dungeons: Ailing Loran (Boss), Lower Loran (Boss)

Key Attacks

Phase 1	Interrupt	Notes
Dash Punch	No	Fast long–range punch; if you use an item when he isn't performing another action, he'll punish you with this attack. Quickstep forward through it.
Punch Combo	No	Three swift punches with long reach and tracking; quickstep forward and stay behind him to avoid it.
Storm Hammer	No	Downward hammer attack which creates a lightning bolt; targets a spherical area directly in front of him. If extremely close quickstep forward past him to avoid it; from farther away, quickstep backward or sideways.
Backward Chop	No	Counterclockwise horizontal swipe with his arm used if you strike him from the sides or behind. Targets a backward 180–degree arc; dodge it by quickstepping away from him.

Phase 2	Interrupt	Notes
Tornado Blast	No	Throws a blast of wind forward. Quickstep forward past him if you're close, or backward if farther away.

Phase 3	Interrupt	Notes
Leaping Storm Hammer	No	Leaps forward and generates a large burst of lightning. Enormous area of effect; inescapable if he uses it while you're on the ground, but can be avoided by quickstepping toward him as soon as he initiates it.
Double Storm Hammer	No	Stationary double arm slam that generates a large spherical burst of electricity. Targets a frontal area reaching two meters forward. If extremely close, quickstep past him; if farther away, quickstep backward.
Flying Slash	No	Lunges forward and performs a horizontal slash, usually as part of a combo; quickstep forward.
Uppercut	No	Launcher usually mixed into a combo; extremely quick, but you can avoid it by quickstepping forward.

Environment

You'll first be able to face the Abhorrent Beast atop a roof in the Forbidden Woods. This encounter is not technically a boss fight, so there are no fog barriers preventing you from retreating back into the windmill or falling off the roof; you can use this to your advantage by standing in the hallway out of reach of the Beast's melee attacks to recover your health or bombard him with projectiles. The elevation difference where the two slopes meet can be used to block the Beast's projectiles if it's on the opposite side from you, and can occasionally cause its attacks to pass over your head if you're standing far enough below it. When fighting him in the Forbidden Woods. the Beast cannot leave the rooftop under any circumstances, so don't waste your time trying to make him fall into the river.

Strategies

Key Strategies – Forbidden Woods

Attack the Afflicted Beggar and trigger him to transform, and then immediately run back into the hallway through which you first accessed the rooftop. The most effective way to use this strategy is to run far enough into the windmill that the Beast leaves combat and returns to his starting position with his back to you; at this point you can walk up slowly behind him without being detected and hit him with a Bone Marrow Ash–boosted Flamesprayer blast, then run back into the windmill before he can counterattack. None of his melee attacks will reach you if you stand far enough inside, but you'll still be able to hit him with Molotovs, Throwing Knives and the Cannon. When he transitions to his second phase he'll begin throwing blasts of wind into the hallway, so you'll need to time your ranged attacks carefully to avoid being struck while you're vulnerable.

Key Strategies – Chalice Dungeon

Quickstep through his attacks as often as possible and strike his arms during the recovery; his punching combo is especially susceptible to this, allowing you to get a few hits in safely each time. Eventually, his arms will become injured and take 50% more damage, making this strategy very effective. Alternately, if you are having a hard time avoiding his attacks, you can use poison. A single Poison Knife will poison the Abhorrent Beast, making them incredibly useful – throw one while luring him in a circle around the room, and then throw another once the effect has worn off. Most of his attacks have low forward momentum and will not reach far ahead, making them easy to avoid by quickstepping and continually backing up. You can almost kill the Abhorrent Beast with 20 Poison Knives, and although it will take a while, this is the safest way of handling him.

Phase 1

During this phase you can avoid all of his physical attacks by quickstepping forward through them and using additional quicksteps to stay behind him. He'll deliberately delay some of his swings to trick you into dodging too early, though. Stay beside or behind him, as most of his attacks won't reach there, but be prepared to quickstep away after hitting him once to avoid his Backward Chop.

When he uses his Storm Hammer, don't quickstep forward through it unless you're at extremely close range – it's active long enough to outlast your invincibility frames. The best opportunities to attack are after quickstepping forward past his slower swings. These openings can be used to recover your health if necessary; you can also back away from him until he uses a slower attack, then quickstep backward and use a Blood Vial before his attack animation ends. Don't attempt to use consumable items during his idle animation unless you're very far away from him – he'll respond to any such attempts with a swift dashing punch that will negate the HP you regain from Blood Vials and completely cancel slower items like Molotovs.

Phase 2

At 80% health, he'll announce phase 2 with a roar that charges his body with electricity. From this phase onward he will increase the number of hits in his combos, use his Tornado Blast attack and begin knocking you down and hitting you on the ground with arm slams or Storm Hammers. Stay behind him as much as possible, using your attacks and items only after he's committed to attacks; you'll have enough time to hit him with a single attack before he uses his Backward Chop, so quickstep backward immediately after striking.

Phase 3

When the Beast's health drops to 50% he'll charge himself up with even more electricity and become even more aggressive. He'll also begin making a focused effort to knock you down and hit you while you're helpless on the ground. He'll also start incorporating his Tornado Blast technique and all three Storm Hammer variations into his melee combos. From this point onward, avoid being hit by the Tornado Blast at all costs – if it knocks you down, he'll immediately use a Flying Slash or a Leaping Storm Hammer to hit you on the ground. Both of these attacks offer additional opportunities to hit him or use items, though, so be prepared to quickstep forward when you identify them in order to take advantage of the openings.

Pthumerian Elder

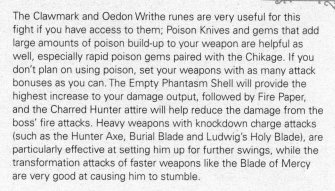

Preparation

The Clawmark and Oedon Writhe runes are very useful for this fight if you have access to them; Poison Knives and gems that add large amounts of poison build-up to your weapon are helpful as well, especially rapid poison gems paired with the Chikage. If you don't plan on using poison, set your weapons with as many attack bonuses as you can. The Empty Phantasm Shell will provide the highest increase to your damage output, followed by Fire Paper, and the Charred Hunter attire will help reduce the damage from the boss' fire attacks. Heavy weapons with knockdown charge attacks (such as the Hunter Axe, Burial Blade and Ludwig's Holy Blade), are particularly effective at setting him up for further swings, while the transformation attacks of faster weapons like the Blade of Mercy are very good at causing him to stumble.

Overview

The Pthumerian Elder will move very slowly during the first half of the battle, though he'll frequently cover great distances by teleporting several times in a row. His consecutive teleports will always be in the same direction as the first, a trick you can use to help keep track of his location if he escapes you. At close range he'll use a few basic melee attacks and combos consisting of wide horizontal swings, forward thrusts and frontal overhead chops; from a distance, he'll shoot at you with his Fire Crossbow. Most of his attacks have very long reach and some, particularly his Spear Combo, also have extremely quick start ups that can be difficult to anticipate. His slower attacks are relatively easy to interrupt, however, and leave you just enough time to do so from out of their range before quickstepping in for a visceral attack. The elder becomes far faster and more aggressive during Phase 2, at which point he'll bombard you with consecutive

Basic Information

			Item Drops											
Chalice Dungeon Base Level	564	322	Random Nourishing gem based on area ×1 [100%]		110	110	110	110	52	60	154	250	180	—	—
Chalice Dungeon Base Level | Boss	2381	1625	Short Ritual Root Chalice [100%]		110	110	110	110	52	60	154	250	180		

Preset Chalice Dungeon: Lower Hintertomb

Key Attacks

Phase 1	Interrupt	Notes
Fire Crossbow	No	High-speed, long-range projectile; quickstep sideways or forward through it.
Fire Cleave	Yes	360-degree counterclockwise horizontal slash with slow windup and dark-red flame; quickstep in any direction as late as possible.
Spear Combo	Yes	Up to three hits starting with a forward thrust. Long reach and extremely fast startup; quickstep forward if close or backward if at mid range or beyond.
Hook Combo	Yes	Diagonal hook slash followed by one of two identical overheads with slightly different timing; quickstep forward past each hit or backward out of reach.
Scythe Combo	Yes	Diagonal slash with slow windup followed by a horizontal slash and a vertical chop; interrupt it or quickstep backward.

Phase 2	Interrupt	Notes
Repeating Fire Crossbow	No	Up to four consecutive Fire Crossbow shots; quickstep forward or sideways before each shot.
Rising Skewer	No	Strikes your current location from below with a spear. Extremely quick and difficult to identify; roll or quickstep in any direction.
Diving Slice	No	Flies into the air, hovers for 1.5 seconds and performs a flying slash toward your current position. If close, quickstep forward; if far, quickstep right.
Flame Lance	Yes	Charging forward thrust attack with fast start up and extremely long reach; quickstep forward or sideways as late as possible.
Sunburst	Yes	Overhead attack with a spiked ball of fire, followed by a delayed explosion at the point of impact; quickstep forward past him or backward twice.
Fireball Rain	Yes	Spins staff above his head, raining fireballs in a large circular area, followed by a horizontal slash. Interrupt the slash or quickstep backward.

Fire Crossbow shots from long range and rapid combo attacks with heavy stun effects up close. In addition, some of his combo attacks will create waves of fire that travel forward, and he'll gain the ability to strike you anywhere on the battlefield with his Rising Skewer; he'll also begin chaining his Flame Lance, Sunburst and Rising Skewer techniques into his melee combos and will often perform a Sunburst followed immediately by a Flame Lance.

Environment

The battlefield is an enormous circular platform with a raised perimeter and no obstacles other than the railing along the outside edge. While this provides plenty of open ground on which to fight, be careful not to become trapped in the corners near the entrance and exit – these spots are dangerous not only because they restrict movement but because they lack railings, and although the elder cannot fall from them, you can. In general, try to keep the fight to the middle of the arena, as backing the boss against the edge leaves you less room to evade his attacks and launch your own.

Strategies

Key Strategies

Interrupts are most effective against the Pthumerian Elder, but require careful timing and positioning; the easiest attacks to interrupt are his Fire Cleave, Fireball Rain and the first hit of his Scythe Combo. Alternatively, bait him into finishing one of his combos by quickstepping forward through the first two hits, then quickstep behind him when he initiates the third and stagger him with a charged R2 attack. Be on the lookout for his quick forward thrusts, especially during Phase 2; you can interrupt these as well, but the timing required is extremely precise.

Phase 1

Keep no less than five meters of distance from the boss and wait for him to use a slow swing, such as his Fire Cleave or the first attack in his Scythe Combo, then interrupt him. You'll need to quickstep forward immediately in order to perform a visceral attack before he recovers, but even if you're too late, you'll still have time to take advantage of the damage bonus from his stagger state. If you prefer to use ordinary melee attacks, stand out of reach and wait for the elder to begin a combo, then strafe backward until he cancels it and quickstep forward to hit him a few times before he teleports (or, quickstep forward through the first two swings and stagger him with a charged attack from behind as he performs the third). Hit him with transformation attacks when he finishes his combos to make him stumble and knock him out of any follow-up swings; alternatively, use these openings knock him down with charged R2s as you'll have enough time to hit him with another as he stands up.

Phase 2

Keep him at long range and don't let him get anywhere near you. Dodge his Fire Crossbow shots and keep a careful eye out for him to perform a quick flourish with his flame scythe before slamming it into the ground, a signal that he's about to use his Rising Skewer. Bait his Diving Slice and quickstep forward though the attack, then immediately perform an R1 or L2 combo with a heavy weapon such as the transformed Hunter Axe or Ludwig's Holy Blade. If you time your attack correctly, your swings will cause him to stumble and prevent him from launching further attacks after he lands, forcing him to retreat; at this point, retreat to long range again and repeat the process.

Bloodletting Beast

Preparation

Use an upgraded weapon with a damage bonus against beasts, such as the Saw Spear or Saw Cleaver; these weapons are also useful for reaching the Bloodletting Beast's head when in their transformed modes. The Bloodletting Beast is weakest to fire damage, so bring as many Fire Paper, Oil Urns and Molotov Cocktails as you can to this fight. Likewise, the Flamesprayer is highly effective against it, so stock up on Quicksilver Bullets, and, as per usual, enough Blood Vials to last the fight.

Overview

The Bloodletting Beast is an extremely aggressive boss that will take great effort to keep you at close range, and will constantly chase you before initiating some of its attacks. During the first phase it will primarily attack with its arms at mid range, but will also occasionally end a combo with a forward bite; from farther away it will use its Right Arm Punch or Lunging Swipe. The headless, parasite-infested Bloodletting Beast will perform a unique mid- to long-range projectile attack in which it launches a swarm of parasites that each hit individually and inflict rapid poison build-up; this technique is not used by the other version. It's possible to roll or quickstep

directly through the beast's legs, but the only safe opportunity to do so is during the ground-punching combo; attempting this maneuver at any other time will usually trigger its close-range Double Arm Slam or Backstep Stomp.

Repeated blows to its head will injure it and cause it to stagger, allowing you to perform a frontal visceral attack; all four of its limbs can be injured as well, and will receive 50% more damage afterwards. It will eventually heal any injuries to its limbs or head, but in the process it will make them vulnerable to injury again, giving you

Basic Information
Special Weakness: Serration

	◼	⬩	Item Drops	🌀	🔔	🔪	⚙	★	🍃	🌊	💀	🔻	⚔	✂
Chalice Dungeon Base Level	635	472	Random Tempering gem based on area ×1 [100%]	106	106	106	106	68	68	120	999	999	×	—
Chalice Dungeon Base Level | Boss	2998	1710	Defiled Chalice [100%], Pthumeru Ihyll Root Chalice [100%]	106	127	106	106	68	58	120	999	999		

Preset Chalice Dungeons: Lower Pthumerian Labyrinth (Boss), Pthumeru Ihyll (Boss)

Key Attacks

Phase 1	Interrupt	Notes
Right Arm Punch	No	Long build-up but near instant and far reaching punch with heavy tracking. Back up during its windup and quickstep right half a second after its fist unfurls.
Left Arm Grab	No	Frontal grab attack used at close range; bites and slams you if it successfully connects. Quickstep backward early as possible.
Double Arm Slam	No	Low reach attack used when standing near its legs. Quickstep backward.
Turnaround Swipe	No	Swipes with one arm while turning to face you when you are behind it. Quickstep back.
Backstep Stomp	No	Stomps to jump back and distance you from its legs. Quickstep back as it raises its left leg.
Parasite Swarm	No	Used only by the Bloodletting Beast (Parasites). Leans forward and releases a swarm of parasites that fly toward your location from long range; each hit inflicts rapid poison build-up. Quickstep forward under them or sideways two to three times.

Phase 2	Interrupt	Notes
Right Arm Slash	No	Uses the same buildup as the Right Arm Punch. Back up far as possible and quickstep a split second after its first unfurls.
Flailing Combo	No	Flails its arms wildly to hit multiple times. Quickstep back twice to avoid this.

more opportunities to perform visceral attacks. During its second phase it will no longer restore its wounded extremities and will start using its Right Arm Slash and Flailing Combo; in addition, many of its previous attacks and combos will be extended, notably its Lunging Swipe. The parasite-infested Bloodletting Beast's missing head will be replaced by a gigantic parasite at the beginning of this phase; the parasite will perform basic forward bite attacks that inflict rapid poison build-up if they connect.

Environment

The boss area is an immense hemispherical chamber with eight large pillars lining its outer ring. These pillars can be destroyed by the Bloodletting Beast during its attacks and should not under any circumstance be used as cover. Although you will need to face the Bloodletting Beast out in the open, the massive size of the area affords plenty of room to maneuver which you will need to avoid The Bloodletting Beast's long reaching attacks.

Strategies

Key Strategies

An upgraded Flamesprayer coupled with Bone Marrow Ash will drastically reduce the Bloodletting Beast's health, and is the most effective way of handling it. This will also easily injure its body parts and stagger it, at which point you can follow through with a visceral attack. Throwing an Oil Urn at it will also boost the damage of the Flamesprayer, and you can also use them to boost the damage from your Molotovs or weapon after applying a Fire Paper. Be sure to disengage your target lock at close range, as locking on at this distance will result in extremely disadvantageous camera angles.

Phase 1

Before opening the door to its boss room, apply a Fire Paper to your weapon; once you have entered the room, the Bloodletting Beast will take a moment before beginning to attack. During this period you can throw a Molotov, Oil Urn or possibly both before it can approach you. It's too risky to attempt to stay behind it at this point, so keep a medium distance ahead of it while quickstepping and backing up from its moves. Due to its hunched posture you can hit its head with melee attacks to injure and stagger it, though you'll need to use a weapon with an extended reach to reliably hit it. Alternately, you can use throwing items and gunshots to reach it. Your best opportunities to attack it in this phase are during the brief recovery periods after its attacks and while it occasionally circles you; even then you'll only be able to hit it once or twice before needing to quickstep out to evade its next attack.

Phase 2

The Bloodletting Beast will roar, initiating the second phase of the fight. After this, it will no longer restore the defenses of its injured body parts, which in turn will remove the chance to stagger it; however, new openings to attack will appear during its extended combos. Quickstep through the first hit of each of its combos (past it or through the opening between its legs), then position yourself behind it, where you can strike while it is mid combo. Its Flailing Combo provides a long opening to do some damage as well; quickstep back to a safe distance and throw Oil Urns and Molotovs at it. In stark contrast to the first phase, standing ahead of it is now far more dangerous due to its longer combos and feints, and you'll need to circle behind it as often as possible.

Yharnam, Pthumerian Queen

Preparation

Stock up on Blood Vials, Quicksilver Bullets and Antidotes, and if you have Oedon Writhe or Clawmark runes, equip them before heading to the dungeon. Consider bringing a Reiterpallasch and a Cannon, but pick up plenty of Bone Marrow Ash regardless of what firearm you choose. Bring a weapon with a pure physical damage type and set it with your strongest attack bonus gems; the Rifle Spear is the best weapon for this battle, due to its long reach, and will allow you to strike from outside the reach of the boss' paralysis attack.

Overview

The Pthumerian Queen has strong elemental and arcane defenses as well as an enormous amount of health. She will start Phase 1 with her hands bound, and will use only blood magic attacks until the next phase begins. Her spells inflict rapid poison build-up and cannot be interrupted, although they will be cancelled if she is hit while casting. She can be staggered from behind, but her Paralysis Cry attack will almost always hit you before you have time to finish charging. Once her health has been reduced to 80% she will break her cuffs and draw a dagger, with which she'll perform physical attacks in addition to her blood magic; at this point her Blood Spears will be replaced by Triple Blood Spears and she will begin using her other Phase 2 moves. Her melee attacks are all interruptible and consist of basic slashes and stabs from close range; the Gliding Stab is performed at mid range and has a heavy knockback. She'll occasionally teleport and reappear with two clones, but you can tell them apart by their appearance: only the real queen is pregnant. The clones use the queen's knife attacks and Blood Spears, and present considerable danger when left alive; however, a single gunshot or melee attack will destroy them. After her health falls to 50% she will cover her dagger with blood, extending its reach and adding a rapid poison effect to her melee attacks; from this point on, she will begin using her Phase 3 moves and will always use her Rising Blood Spear attack six times in a row.

Basic Information

	■	✦	Item Drops										
					75	75	75	75	115	95	115	250	270	—	—
Chalice Dungeon Base Level	246	115	None		75	75	75	75	115	95	115	250	270	—	—
Chalice Dungeon Base Level | Boss	2822	1069	Yharnam Stone [100%]		75	90	75	75	115	95	115	250	270		

Preset Chalice Dungeon: Pthumeru Ihyll (Boss)

Key Attacks

Phase 1	Interrupt	Notes
Blood Spears	No	Shoots up to three consecutive blood spears; move to either side or run diagonally towards her.
Blood Burst	No	Large spherical explosion of blood used at mid to close range. Quickstep back once she raises both arms.
Blood Spray	No	Sprays a forward arc of rapid poison build-up inflicting blood from side to side. Quickstep backward.
Paralysis Cry	No	The baby in her womb will cry, emitting a short-range paralyzing wave. Quickstep back the moment the cry begins.

Phase 2	Interrupt	Notes
Telekinesis	No	Holds her womb, creating a large telekinetic area around herself; quickstep repeatedly backward out of it.
Triple Blood Spears	No	Launches three blood spears at once up to three times; replaces her Blood Spears move. Roll or quickstep to either side away from each shot.
Gliding Stab	Yes	Easy to interrupt, quickstep to either side while she is gliding; the initial tracking will catch an early dodge.
Rising Blood Spear	No	Stabs her palm, creating a blood spear beneath you; can be done up to three times. Lock off and run in any direction to avoid them.
Blood Spear Wave	No	Stabs her palm three times sending a wave of blood spears across the ground in a different direction each time. Quickstep out of the way according to the direction they come from.

Phase 3	Interrupt	Notes
Blood Geyser	No	Stabs the floor creating multiple rapid bursts of blood in a large area around her; blood rains down for a short period after. Quickstep backward twice.

Environment

The boss area is a massive dome, empty save for the large altar in the center. The altar can be used reliably as cover for healing or Antidotes use during the first phase, though during later phases it can obstruct your vision, making Queen Yharnam's Rising Blood Spears difficult to avoid.

Strategies

Key Strategies

During Phase 1, use the Rifle Spear's standard R2 attack from outside the reach of Queen Yharnam's Paralysis Cry to knock her out of her casting animations and prevent her from attacking while you wear her down. From Phase 2 onward, use the Reiterpallasch to interrupt her melee attacks and immediately follow up with a Bone Marrow Ash Cannon shot while she's staggered. When you run out of ammunition, continue interrupting her swings and use visceral attacks to regain your Quicksilver Bullets with the power of the Oedon Writhe rune, then repeat the procedure.

Phase 1

Stand just outside the reach of her Paralyzing Cry and strike her with single R2 attacks using the Rifle Spear. Use only one thrust at a time and do not charge the attack – your goal is to hit the queen first and prevent her from taking action while at the same time avoiding the dangerous paralysis attack. If you time your strikes correctly and strafe backward after each one to compensate for your forward momentum, you can keep her completely helpless throughout the entirety of Phase 1 and prevent her from ever having a chance to attack. If you don't have a Rifle Spear, wait for her to perform an action and quickstep toward her as she recovers afterward. Hit her with a quickstepping attack followed immediately by a transformation attack to make her stumble, then quickstep backward twice to escape the incoming counterattack. You'll need to be patient and repeat this procedure many times to wear her down and trigger Phase 2, so keep an eye on your stamina and don't get greedy with your attacks.

Phase 2

When the queen's health drops below 80%, she'll break free of her handcuffs and draw a dagger. From this point onward she will use a set of very basic physical attacks which can be easily interrupted, and will continue using her previous moves in addition to her new Phase 2 abilities. In spite of her wider arsenal of attacks, the Rifle Spear will still reach her from outside the range of her Paralyzing Cry and you should continue to use it in the same manner as during

Phase 1; by timing your thrusts carefully you will be able to continually knock her out of her attacks and prevent her from being able to act until the third phase begins. Without a Rifle Spear you'll need to continue using the alternative melee strategy from Phase 1, darting in to strike with transformation attacks and retreating immediately afterward. Another effective strategy from this phase onward is to power up the Cannon with Bone Marrow Ash, then interrupt the queen's physical attacks with a gunshot from the Reiterpallasch. When she staggers, blast her with the Cannon to take advantage of the damage bonus and inflict a tremendous amount of damage; if you run out of ammunition, create a few Blood Bullets and use the Oedon Writhe rune to restore your standard ammunition with ordinary visceral attacks.

Phase 3

When the queen's health drops below 50% she'll cover her dagger in blood, extending its range and effectively turning it into a sword. All of her physical attacks will inflict rapid poison build-up from this point onward, but even now, the Rifle Spear will still reach her from outside her melee range and can be used in the same way as during previous phases to keep her helpless while you chip away at her nearly bottomless reserves of health. If you choose not to use the Rifle Spear, you'll need to continue following the alternate melee strategy from both previous phases instead, using hit-and-run tactics to gradually wear her down or inflicting burst damage with visceral attacks and the cannon. Regardless of what strategy you use, be especially careful of the queen's Blood Geyser attack – it strikes an extremely wide area and rains poisonous blood for a brief period of time following the initial bursts of blood, so you'll have to get as far from her as possible if you're unable to stop her from using it.

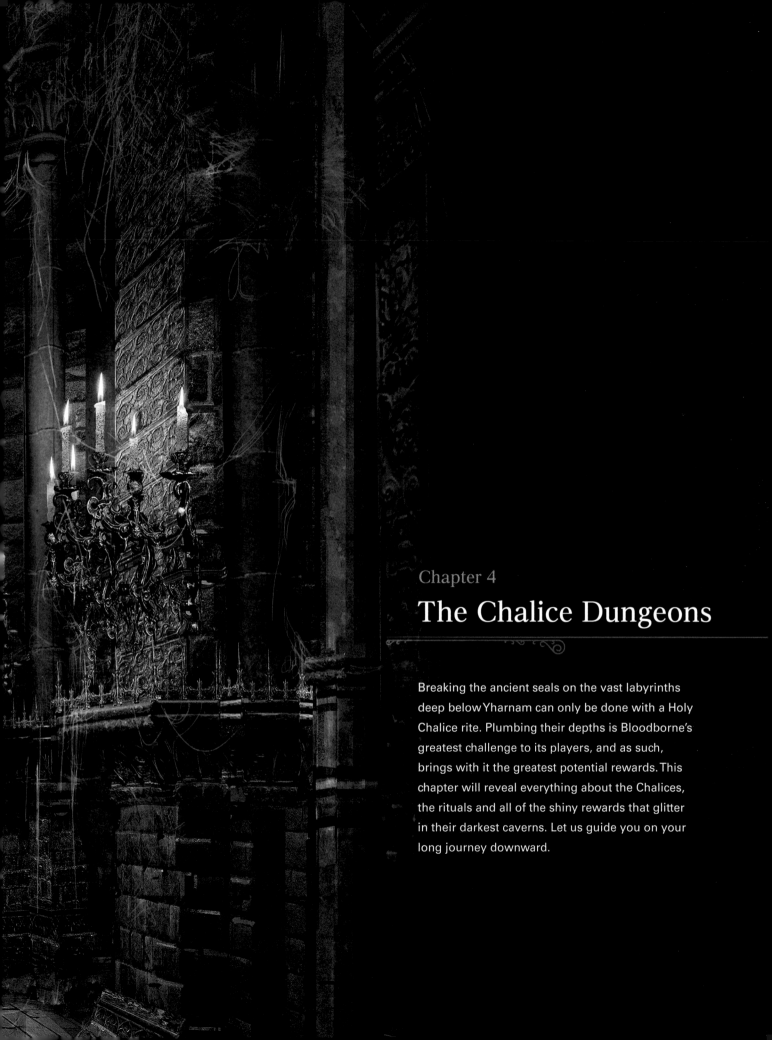

Chapter 4

The Chalice Dungeons

Breaking the ancient seals on the vast labyrinths
deep below Yharnam can only be done with a Holy
Chalice rite. Plumbing their depths is Bloodborne's
greatest challenge to its players, and as such,
brings with it the greatest potential rewards. This
chapter will reveal everything about the Chalices,
the rituals and all of the shiny rewards that glitter
in their darkest caverns. Let us guide you on your
long journey downward.

Chalice Dungeon Overview

The Chalice Dungeons are a large part of Bloodborne, but they are an entirely optional part. The role they play in the game's overall structure is another mystery for players to solve. Here we'll lay out the basics.

These gravestones are your Chalice Dungeon hub.

Preset Chalices

These labyrinthine dungeons must be unlocked through rituals, each of which carries a cost in materials and Blood Echoes – the deeper the dungeon, the more costly the ritual is to complete. Reaching their deepest depths is no small undertaking, and your path there begins when you acquire your first Chalice, by defeating the Blood-starved Beast in Old Yharnam. This Chalice lets you perform the ritual to create the Pthumerian Labyrinth.

In order to craft the first labyrinth you'll also need a 'Ritual Blood (1)', which you can find in Old Yharnam at an Altar on your way to the boss. You can also purchase them from the Messenger Bath shop in the Hunter's Dream after acquiring the Radiant Sword Hunter Badge and defeating the Blood-starved Beast.

Completing the Pthumerian Labyrinth rewards you with the Central Pthumeru Chalice, which you can use to make the next dungeon, which in turn will reward you with another Chalice. From this point onwards you can progress through the dungeons in tandem with the main quest. There are two more Chalices that can only be found in the main game, and many more to be found by clearing the dungeons you build. All three main game Chalices are listed here.

Pthumeru Chalice	Defeat the Blood-starved Beast
Lower Loran Chalice	Defeat Amygdala
Great Isz Chalice	Defeat Ebrietas, Daughter of the Cosmos

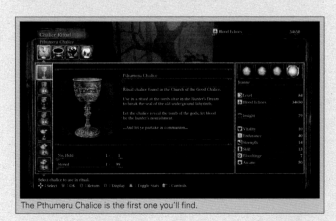
The Pthumeru Chalice is the first one you'll find.

Root Chalices

Many dungeons will reward you, upon defeating bosses, with either a Preset Chalice or a Root Chalice. Root Chalices always have the word 'Root' in their names and are used to create randomly generated versions of the dungeon the Chalice is named after. So the Central Pthumeru Root Chalice, for example, will create a randomly generated version of the Central Pthumerian Labyrinth.

Ritual Altars

To conduct your rituals, you can use any of the six 'Ritual Altars' lined along the path to the left of where you always enter the Hunter's Dream. These altars are where you'll be able to craft or dismantle Chalice Labyrinths and search for other player-created labyrinths online. Treat this area of the Hunter's Dream essentially as the Chalice Labyrinth hub. There are only six Ritual Altars, so you will eventually have to dismantle some of your crafted labyrinths by selecting the 'Remove Chalice' option when you wish to craft newer labyrinths, or improve root labyrinths by performing additional rites with newer materials when re-crafting them. Preset labyrinths will always remain the same when re-crafted, which is worth bearing in mind in case you wish to hunt for specific items and materials.

Makeshift Altar

Once you collect the Short Ritual Root Chalice from defeating the boss on layer 3 of the Lower Hintertomb dungeon, you'll be able to access online functions relating to dungeons from this altar. Selecting Dungeon Quick-search will let you join any accessible dungeon, and Co-op Quick-search will look for Beckoning Bell Chimes within dungeons and send you to those asking for aid. The final Adversarial Quick-search option will let you invade someone that's in a Root Dungeon with the Sinister Bell Additional Rite active.

Area Types

The underground labyrinth is extremely large, and changes its form the deeper it goes. Each part has its own unique appearance and tendencies, though, and these are divided into four distinct areas: Pthumeru, Hintertomb, Loran and Isz.

Pthumeru

- The standard area type, usually with a basic room structure.
- No particular elemental type dominates.
- Kidnappers appear often.
- Merciless Watchers guard floor levers

Hintertomb

- Hintertomb dungeons are dark and have a strong tendency towards poison.
- Bodies of water in Hintertomb dungeons are often poison swamps.
- Smoke coming out of burners is a poisonous fog.
- Some enemies have the Poison special effect, signified by a purple mist around their weapons.
- Watcher's Madmen guard floor levers.

Loran

- Every Loran dungeon is covered entirely in sand.
- Loran dungeons are sometimes near to gigantic crevices, separating rooms with perilous rope bridges.
- They are home to many beast-type enemies. Beast Patients are the most common enemy type.
- Blood Gems that appear in Loran dungeons have a high chance to be Fire or Bolt elemental.
- Loran Silverbeasts guard floor levers.

Isz

- Isz dungeons are closely connected to the Cosmos, giving them an other-worldly appearance.
- Kin-type enemies and bosses appear often.
- Celestial Children appear in great numbers.
- Blood Gems that appear in Isz dungeons have a tendency towards Damp.
- Brainsuckers guard floor levers.

Dungeon Structure

Each individual labyrinth has its own unique layout, but they all follow the same basic pattern. All dungeons start with a chamber of the seal, which is a small room with a lamp in it. That leads into a linking corridor, which in turn leads to the layer Lamp. Linking rooms can have doorways on the right or left that lead to optional paths, the goal of which is a treasure room with a coffin to loot. Once you've opened the coffin it's safe to head back to the linking room to progress.

Every labyrinth has at least one locked exit gate per layer. Once that door is unlocked you'll have a clear path to the boss, though there's usually a linking room behind the door that may contain another optional path. The layer Lamp is very often near the locked exit gate, as in the example here. This ensures that if the boss defeats you, it won't take you very long to get back and try again. With Lamps being as frequent as they are you'll never have to travel far to reach one, so taking frequent trips back to the Hunter's Dream to repair your weapon, upgrade your character and ensure you're fully stocked up on consumables is highly recommended.

Doors/Gates

While the doors and gates you come across in dungeons may initially just feel like they're there to halt your progress, they do convey useful information once you know what to look for. At the start of each layer you'll come across one or more bronze doorways, and a pair of statues holding flaming torches will surround one of them. Those torches are used to let you know that the path beyond that doorway is the one that will eventually lead you to the room containing a lever that must be pulled to open an exit gate.

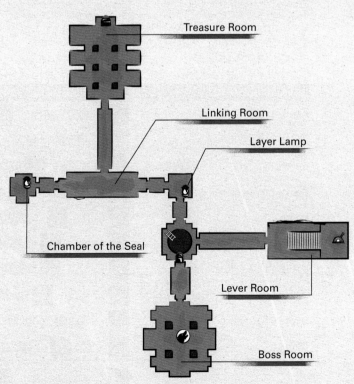

Treasure Room

Linking Room

Layer Lamp

Chamber of the Seal

Lever Room

Boss Room

4

The door without the flames will always lead you to optional parts of the layer, where you can get some extra loot. Finding the locked exit gate is rarely a problem because they are almost always placed in plain sight, as if taunting you, and they're easily identifiable due to the statues holding a blue flame on either side. Once you pull the lever associated with that gate, those flames will turn from blue to a normal yellow flame, letting you know it has been unlocked. Some floors have multiple exit gates to open, so you can't always assume that going through one is going to take you straight to the boss.

Gate Lever Rooms

These rooms will usually be some of the most heavily-defended ones in the dungeons, and you'll often have to battle your way past large groups of regular enemies, a single strong one, or sometimes a combination of both. A cautious approach is called for when entering one of these rooms, and with patience you'll often be able to lure the enemies out one at a time to make the fight easier, and sometimes you can take advantage of room layouts to let you get behind enemies without them noticing.

Treasure Rooms

Similar to the Gate Lever rooms, these rooms should be one of your primary targets in any dungeon. You'll often have to make your through a challenging gauntlet of traps and enemies to make it to these rooms, but once inside there's often only a single enemy guarding the chest(s). The contents of these chests are often large quantities of valuable materials for creating dungeons.

Secret Paths

Once you start recognizing each room type, you'll notice that the door placements in each one will either be open or blocked off depending on how the room is arranged in the layer/dungeon you're in. These blocked off doorways are the most common places to find hidden walls, so a good methodical way to discover them is to simply attack every blocked off doorway that you come across. Short, dead end corridors or long pathways leading to seemingly nothing can also signify that a hidden wall is nearby, so it's important to check those as well. A single hit with a weapon is all it takes to remove the illusionary wall.

Floor Messengers

Certain doorways and openings into rooms will have unlit lamps on the floor near them and when you enter those rooms, helpful messengers will light the lamp with a blue flame. Once the lamps are lit you can use them as markers to let you know which rooms you've been into in case you find yourself getting lost.

Bosses

Additionally, dungeon bosses can sometimes drop upgrade materials depending upon the Depth rating and the actual floor on which they're encountered. If you're willing to take a chance and can handle the encounters, they can be a potentially good source of materials if you're looking to upgrade a lot of weapons or just want to put some extra upgrades on a specific weapon before you'd normally encounter the materials to do so. Also note that the percentages shown in the table below are base values only and do not take into account any additional drop rate modifiers from "Eye" Runes or the "Milkweed" Oath Rune.

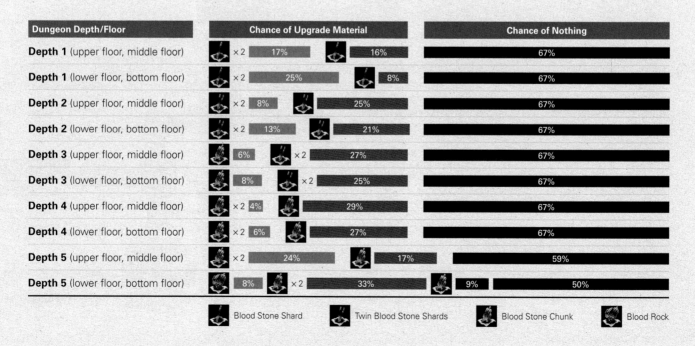

Dungeon Depth/Floor	Chance of Upgrade Material			Chance of Nothing
Depth 1 (upper floor, middle floor)	Blood Stone Shard ×2 17%	Twin Blood Stone Shards 16%		67%
Depth 1 (lower floor, bottom floor)	Blood Stone Shard ×2 25%	Twin Blood Stone Shards 8%		67%
Depth 2 (upper floor, middle floor)	Blood Stone Shard ×2 8%	Twin Blood Stone Shards 25%		67%
Depth 2 (lower floor, bottom floor)	Twin Blood Stone Shards ×2 13%	Blood Stone Chunk 21%		67%
Depth 3 (upper floor, middle floor)	Blood Stone Chunk 6%	Twin Blood Stone Shards ×2 27%		67%
Depth 3 (lower floor, bottom floor)	Blood Stone Chunk 8%	Twin Blood Stone Shards ×2 25%		67%
Depth 4 (upper floor, middle floor)	Blood Stone Chunk ×2 4%	Blood Stone Chunk 29%		67%
Depth 4 (lower floor, bottom floor)	Blood Stone Chunk ×2 6%	Blood Stone Chunk 27%		67%
Depth 5 (upper floor, middle floor)	Blood Stone Chunk ×2 24%	Blood Rock 17%		59%
Depth 5 (lower floor, bottom floor)	Blood Stone Chunk 8%	Blood Stone Chunk ×2 33%	Blood Rock 9%	50%

Blood Stone Shard   Twin Blood Stone Shards   Blood Stone Chunk   Blood Rock

Dungeon Gameplay

While most of the skills you acquire from the main game will carry over into the dungeons, there are a few differences. In this section we'll go over some basic tips about the different types of elements found in dungeons that will aid you in your exploration.

Dungeon Dwellers

You'll encounter some familiar enemies from the main game in dungeons, but for the most part you'll have to contend with new enemies and have to formulate new strategies to deal with them. Some of the layer bosses will sometimes return in later dungeons as regular enemies, so you'll need to adapt to fighting them with other enemies present. The opposite is also true; enemies that you have encountered normally (such as Brainsuckers) can show up as bosses with much higher stats, forcing you to again reevaluate how you approach them. It's also important to remember that most Strong enemies within dungeons drop Basic Materials that are used in dungeon creation, so killing them all is extremely important if you want to create multiple dungeons.

The Keeper of the Old Lords is a boss, with a suitably large amount of HP.

He also appears in later dungeons as a strong enemy.

Bell Ringers

One other thing worth noting is that Bell Ringers are among the greatest threats in Chalice Dungeons, because they continually summon more enemies you'll have to deal with. Locating them quickly is therefore very important, so get used to the places they tend to appear in. By far the most common places are on the ledge in the multi-level room with stairways on either side, and at the very top of the three-story circular room with the stone elevator platform in the middle.

Hand Lantern

If you haven't already done so, it's worth investing in the Hand Lantern from the Bath Messenger in the Hunter's Dream, because it can get very dark in some rooms (especially in Loran Dungeons) so every little helps. This is especially true if you primarily use a transformed 2-handed weapon and cannot carry a Torch normally. Equip the Hand Lantern in your Personal Effects to keep your Quick Item slots free for other things.

Stay Powerful

Your character and weapon levels matter even more in the dungeons than they do in the main game, so making sure your weapons are as upgraded as possible and taking frequent trips back to the Hunter's Dream to level up are very important. If this is your first playthrough it's recommended to stick with one main right and left hand weapon and focus on fortifying them. A second right hand weapon can still be very useful, especially if you're making weapons to take advantage of enemy elemental and type weaknesses; having dedicated fire and arcane/bolt weapons will help you considerably against some of the tougher opponents you'll encounter in dungeons.

Using the Environment

Most rooms in the dungeons are connected via doorways or narrow tunnels, and thanks to this, if you enter a room that contains a formidable number of enemies, you can always retreat back and funnel the enemies through it so that you can deal with them in more manageable numbers. Doing this is an almost essential tactic once you start getting into the high difficulty dungeons, so becoming comfortable with doing it early on will help you considerably in the long run. Always check the ceilings when entering rooms, because the dangling roots and murky corners are often home to Nightmare Apostles and Gels that are just waiting to drop down onto you.

Room Types

Although there are many different types of rooms used in the dungeons, if you pay attention as you go through them, you can start to get familiar enough with the types to almost know what's coming up just by looking into a room. The different types of dungeons will often try to camouflage the rooms by covering them in roots or similar environmental objects – try to disregard these while keeping track of the room types.

Depth Order

Finally, while you can bypass some of the earlier dungeons if you wish, it's recommended that you do them all in the order of depth so that you can used to the way things work as you build up to the more difficult ones. The depth two and three dungeons can be a very good source of Blood Echoes if you tackle them at the appropriate level, especially the Root versions with some Additional Rites. Once you get up to the depth four and five dungeons, however, it's recommended that you attempt them in co-op with other players, because while you may be able to handle the normal enemies on your own, the bosses can be extremely challenging even with a team.

Run off the side of the stairway to avoid the flaming boulder.

Pools of oil can be a serious hazard.

Traps & Hazards

Hoards of enemies are not the only things you'll have to contend with in dungeons – there are also numerous fiendish traps that are trying their best to kill you. Once you know where the traps are, and how they work, you can even use them to your advantage by luring enemies into them for easy kills.

Fire Arrows

Fire arrow traps are one of the most common you'll encounter, and they are capable of inflicting a tremendous amount of damage. These traps are activated by a stepping onto a pressure plate on the floor, causing between one and three statues somewhere else in the room to shoot a fire arrow. The arrows always fly directly at the pressure plate, but they can come from any direction depending on the placement of the statues. Locating the pressure plate on the floor is not always easy, so you'll need to carefully check the floor before entering a room to find them. The safest means of negating these traps, however, is to destroy the statues that fire the arrows, because then you can step on the pressure plate as often as you want without fear of arrows. The large clay statues that fire the arrows are fairly easy to locate in most rooms, as they will usually be along one of the outer walls, however, they are sometimes placed next to pillars, so be sure to check those too.

Ambush

Similar to the Fire Arrow traps, these ambush traps are also triggered by pressure plates, but most of the time they are hidden, so you won't be able to tell exactly where they are. That doesn't mean that there's nothing you can do to avoid them, however, because the pressure plates are often within raised motifs on the floors of some rooms, so as long as you stay out of those areas you can avoid triggering this trap. If you do trigger it, a group of between two and four Labyrinth Watchers will appear around you in a puff of smoke and immediately start attacking you. It's best to roll past them quickly to try and create some space, rather than trying to contend with attackers from all sides.

Boulder

Boulder traps are nearly always found in T-shaped corridors, and your first clue that one is in the area will be the noise made by the boulder. There will be a loud crash as the boulder drops down at once end of the corridor, followed by a rumbling as it makes its way along it. When you reach to the junction in the corridor, stop and watch to see which direction the boulder is rolling in; depending on which way you want to go, you'll either need to follow behind the boulder after it passes you, or quickly run in the opposite direction and try to get past the point at which the boulders are dropping down. Most of these corridors have small alcoves along them that you can duck into to avoid the boulder.

Flaming Boulder

You'll encounter Flaming Boulder traps exclusively in the spiral staircase rooms. Every time you start going up one of these stairways, listen out for the sound of the boulder rolling down towards you. If you hear one coming, simply run off the side of the stairs to safety and wait for the boulder to roll by.

Swinging Axes

Swinging Axes can often be found along narrow stone bridges in the sewer-types areas of dungeons. Each of the axes swings at a consistent pace, so the first thing you should do is watch them to get familiar with how long it takes them to swing past you each time.

Next, check the configuration of the axes; sometimes there will be a single one followed by a gap, and then two more after that that are close together, and other times it will be the opposite way round. To get past the axes, get as close as you can by turning the camera to the side so that you get a better view, and then as soon as the first one passes you, start running. Very rarely will you be able to make it past all of the axes in a single sprint, so make sure you've identified where the safe gap that you can stand in is. If you're near the end and it looks like you might get hit, it's worth trying to roll forward to safety, since a roll moves slightly quicker than running.

Crumbling Floors

If you step onto a weak section of floor, it will collapse and you'll be dropped into an area below, usually into a room filled with enemies. Spotting these sections of floor is extremely difficult and the only signs are slightly separated bricks on the floor; most pitfalls are in the middle of rooms or corridors, so if you're concerned, just stick to the walls and you can avoid them. Keeping track of which floor you're on in a layer will help too, because if you're on the bottom floor, you won't have to worry about them at all.

Guillotines

Guillotine traps are some of the more dangerous ones you'll encounter, due to their speed and lethal amounts of damage they inflict. Like many other traps they are triggered by a pressure plate on the floor, but the guillotine will also be extremely close to it, so if you're just running through and area and trigger one, you won't have

time to react. You'll nearly always find these traps in just inside doorways at the start of narrow corridors, usually obscured by smoke, so it's always best to approach these areas cautiously. To get past it you either need to jump over the pressure plate, or a much safer approach is to walk slowly onto it to trigger the trap, and then move past the guillotine while it resets.

Warp

These traps are quite rare and will only appear in some of the later dungeons on the landings of some staircases. The trap area consists of a faint ring of candles on the floor, and if you step into it, they will light up and you will be warped to a nearby room. The rooms that you end up in will always be ones that are filled with enemies, but as with the crumbling floors, depending on the route you took through the dungeon you may have already cleared out the enemies in the room the trap sends you to.

Bloodlickers

The Bloodlickers from Forsaken Cainhurst Castle also turn up in dungeons, and their appetite for blood is just as strong here. After killing any strong enemy, and then heading off to other parts of the layer, there's a chance that when you return to the room you killed it in a Bloodlicker will appear to feed on the corpse. There's no indication that this has happened, so you won't know until you come face-to-face with one after reentering a room. In some of the higher depth dungeons these enemies can be very deadly, so you'll need to consider carefully whether to take one on or simply run past it.

4

Chalice Rituals

Conducting a ritual to create a Chalice Dungeon is fairly straightforward; when you've got a Chalice and the required ritual materials, approach a Chalice altar and select the Chalice Ritual option. In the Chalice Ritual menu you'll see the list of all your collected chalices in the large window on the left of your screen. Along the top of this window are four tabs, one for each class of Chalice, which affects the area that labyrinth will be set in. The central window shows the details of the ritual, including the Depth of the created dungeon, which is essentially the difficulty level, with 1 being the lowest and 5 being the maximum.

The depth affects the required level for certain Basic and Rite Materials. For example, Depth 2 labyrinths will require Ritual Blood (2) and Tomb Mold (2), which can be acquired from the corresponding depth labyrinths or from certain chests and enemies from the previous Depth. The ocst in Blood Echoes is also shown, along with the required materials, both for the ritual and any possible Additional Rites. If you have all of the required materials and are certain you want to use them, select the Conduct Ritual option to create the dungeon.

Additional Rites

When using a Root Chalice to create randomly generated dungeons you'll usually have the possibility to conduct Additional Rites, at the cost of more materials. These rites add effects that can drastically change the conditions within each dungeon, usually making them much more challenging. They do carry some reward, however, usually in the form of increased item drops and Blood Echoes. There are four possible Additional Rites, and we'll explain each of them here.

Fetid Offering

Enemies are strengthened when this rite is used. They will have their stats boosted and appear with a smoky red visual effect to signify their upgrade. This makes the dungeon harder, but rewards you with more Blood Echoes. It also increases the amount of items that will drop from defeated enemies, making it very much worth the effort to kill those powered-up enemies.

Rotted Offering

This rite triggers one of, or a combination of, the following difficulty-increasing effects:
• The Eye Collector appears and summons Mad Ones.
• Tomb Prospector Hunters often appear as enemies.
• The Labyrinth Ritekeeper appears. It will patrol large rooms, gather other enemies around it and then strengthen them. Even when the Ritekeeper is killed, the enemies will retain their powered-up status.

It also increases the chance of getting very powerful Blood Gem effects, but this comes at the cost of strong negative effects. The chart here shows the chances of each effect. The chances are different in Hintertomb dungeons compared to other types, but in all cases the total chance adds up to 100%, so one of the effects is guaranteed to occur.

Rotted Offering Effects

	Non-Hintertomb	Hintertomb
Eye Collector	16%	24%
Tomb Prospectors	17%	13%
Labyrinth Ritekeeper	17%	13%
Eye Collector+Tomb Prospectors	17%	25%
Eye Collector+Labyrinth Ritekeeper	17%	25%
Tomb Prospectors+Labyrinth Ritekeeper	16%	0%

Cursed Offering

The Cursed Offering adds by far the most challenge, because in Cursed dungeons your HP is cut in half. Unless you have exceptionally high vitality this will make even the most basic enemies deadly, and forces a more careful approach. As with the other offerings, it does come with some real rewards, though; enemies defeated in Cursed dungeons give 20% more Blood Echoes and the items you'll find will be of higher rarity. Blood Gems you find will have a very high chance of having the 'Cursed' effect.

Sinister Bell

With this rite activated, the Bell Ringers appear frequently in the dungeon. As long as they are alive, competing players can enter the same layer, with the goal of killing you in order to earn Insight. If you're playing offline, this offering will cause the Bell Ringers to summon powerful NPC hunters instead of other players. Sinister Bell is only possible in dungeons created from the 'Sinister' Chalice type, so it can't be combined with other Additional Rites. It is the best way to play extended sessions of PvP and gain Insight, but it doesn't come with any rewards, such as higher drop rates.

Random Effects

The Additional Rites aren't the only things that affect the characteristics of Root Dungeons. There are three random effects that can be applied every time you perform a ritual, regardless of whether you use any Additional Rites. These effects, along with the chances

of each one occurring, are detailed here. These are all independent of each other, so it's possible to have all of them appear in a single dungeon if you're lucky (or unlucky).

Random Effects

Effect	Special Enemy/Shop	4th Layer	Poison
Total Chance	40%	20%	20%

Special Characters

This effect gives a chance for a special Beast-possessed Soul enemy to appear that will attempt to kill not just you, bother enemies as well. This can be used to your advantage, if you can lure this beast towards other deadly foes. It also gives the chance of a shop or a rare shop appearing, each with their own lineup of consumables for sale. The shops appear in the usual messenger baths, but the rare shop is run by Patches the Spider, and can occur only after you've encountered him in the main game. When he appears, he'll be dangling from the ceiling, offering a selection of useful items at vastly inflated prices. See the Shop section in the Hunter's Appendices chapter for the full list of items and prices.

Special Enemy/Shop Breakdown

Special Enemy/Shop	Chance
Shop	7%
Beast-possessed Soul	10%
Rare Shop	3%
Shop+ Beast-possessed Soul	14%
Rare Shop+Beast-possessed Soul	6%

4th Layer

This effect unlocks a dungeon's hidden 4th layer. The wall that blocks the path to the 4th layer will disappear after defeating the 3rd layer boss, so you should always pay attention before leaving a dungeon, just in case this happens. All enemies on the 4th layer, including the boss, give an extra 20% more Blood Echoes when defeated. 4th layer bosses also have a slightly higher chance of dropping the best possible Blood Gems.

Poison

When this effect is active, many of the enemies appear in the dungeon will appear with a purple poison mist around their weapons. This means that their attacks can inflict Slow Poison, so you'll need to be fully stocked with Antidotes. It has no effect on drops or rewards.

Hidden Effects

There are, along with Additional Rites and Random Effects, some other completely hidden characteristics a dungeon can take on when created. These are mostly related to the enemies you'll find in the dungeon and how large its structure is. Many won't have a noticeable effect on the dungeon, but there are a few that can really shake things up. The most notable are the Spider Dungeon effect, in which the basic enemies are replaced by Children of Rom, which of course means the boss will be Rom, the Vacuous Spider. Another is the Boss Rush effect, in which you'll have to battle a few bosses one after the other, in a room that's exclusive to the effect.

Ritual Materials

Ritual materials are the various, usually disgusting items you need to collect in order to perform Chalice rituals. They range from basic mold to festering organs, so Chalice rituals aren't a business for the faint of heart.

Basic Materials

Basic and Rite crafting materials can be found mainly in the Chalice Labyrinths from loot chests or enemy drops, with the rarer ones required to craft specific labyrinths also found in the main quest. Progressing though the game, acquiring Hunter Badges, defeating bosses and clearing labyrinths will also unlock certain Basic Materials in both Bath Messenger Blood Echoes and Insight shops in the Hunter's Dream. Ritual Blood and Tomb Mold basic materials have a numerical value in brackets next to them. These correspond to the depth/difficulty of a labyrinth, and can also be found on the same depth or one depth below. The highest level of both of these items (5), cannot be purchased from shops and can only be found inside dungeons.

Arcane Haze

Certain Chalice Labyrinths will require a Basic Material named 'Arcane Haze'. You can acquire these by hunting the Fluorescent Flower enemies found in some dungeons, or by extracting them from your unused crafting materials at the workbench. To do the latter, you'll need the Workshop Haze Extractor, found on the second layer of the Lower Pthumeru Labyrinth.

Ritual Blood

Material used in a Holy Chalice ritual. One of the basic ingredients used to satiate a Holy Chalice is this incoagulable blood. When all is melted in blood, all is reborn.

Purchasing info

Shop Type	Material	Cost	Unlock Req.
Bath Messenger	Ritual Blood (1)	2500	Obtain the Pthumeru Chalice (p405)
	Ritual Blood (2)	6000	Obtain the Defiled Chalice (p407)
	Ritual Blood (3)	12000	Obtain the Great Pthumeru Ihyll Chalice (p407)
	Ritual Blood (4)	24000	Defeat Yharnam, Pthumerian Queen (p392)

Tomb Mold

Material used in a Holy Chalice ritual. Mold that grows from rotten flesh and blood inside the old labyrinth. Matures to bear giant spores.

Purchasing info

Shop Type	Material	Cost	Unlock Req.
Bath Messenger	Tomb Mold (1)	2000	Obtain the Sinister Hintertomb Chalice (p409)
	Tomb Mold (2)	5000	Obtain the Defiled Chalice (p407)
	Tomb Mold (3)	10000	Obtain the Great Pthumeru Ihyll Chalice (p407)
	Tomb Mold (4)	20000	Defeat Yharnam, Pthumerian Queen (p392)

Coldblood Flowerbud

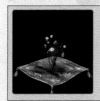

Material used in a Holy Chalice ritual. Pale vegetation that commonly grows on coldblood in a place long ago abandoned.

Purchasing info

Shop Type	Cost	Unlock Req.
Insight Trade	2	Obtain the Ailing Loran Chalice (p406)

Coldblood Flower Bulb

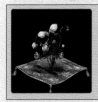

Material used in a Holy Chalice ritual. Pale vegetation that commonly grows on coldblood in a place long abandoned, said to mature slowly in close proximity to death, and eventually bloom.

Loran Clerics have a small chance to drop this

Blooming Coldblood Flower

Material used in a Holy Chalice ritual. Pale vegetation that commonly grows on coldblood in a place long abandoned, that has bloomed into a bright red stygian flower.

Arcane Haze

Material used in a Holy Chalice ritual. The tiny smatterings of haze that are found in certain ritual materials. Sometimes required for special rites. The additional rite Sinister Bell makes the bell-ringing woman appear, and when she rings a sinister bell, hunters from other worlds will be beckoned as adversaries.

Bloodshot Eyeball

Material used in a Holy Chalice ritual. An exquisite eyeball removed quickly after death, or perhaps even before. Used to unlock the seal of the old labyrinth hintertombs.

Purchasing info

Shop Type	Cost	Unlock Req.
Insight Trade	2	Defeat the Witch of Hemwick (p332)

Living String

Special material used in a Holy Chalice ritual. The Immense brain that Mensis retrieved from the nightmare was indeed lined with eyes on the inside, but they were of an evil sort, and the brain itself was terribly rotten. But even still, it was a legitimate Great One, and left a relic. A living relic, at that, which is a precious thing indeed.

Purchasing info

Shop Type	Cost	Unlock Req.
Insight Trade	10	Defeat the Brain of Mensis (p293)

Red Jelly

Material used in a Holy Chalice ritual. Stillborn infants born of a creature of unknown origin, of the type found in some corners of the old labyrinth.

Purchasing info

Shop Type	Cost	Unlock Req.
Insight Trade	5	Clear Pthumeru Ihyll Dungeon (p468)

Pearl Slug

Material used in a Holy Chalice ritual. Of all the strange lifeforms that reside in the nooks and crannies of the old labyrinth, the slugs are clear signs of the left-behind Great Ones.

Purchasing info

Shop Type	Cost	Unlock Req.
Insight Trade	3	Obtain the Great Isz Chalice (p407)

Rite Materials

Sage's Wrist

Special material used in a Holy Chalice ritual. A body part of a saint, sacrificed by the Healing Church in their search for Truth. The additional rite Fetid Offering invigorates the Watchers, making them more treacherous than normal, but also making them worthy prey for a special hunt.

Sage's Hair

Special material used in a Holy Chalice ritual. A body part of a saint, sacrificed by the Healing Church in their search for Truth. The additional rite Fetid Offering invigorates the Watchers, making them more treacherous than normal, but also making them worthy prey for a special hunt.

Inflicted Organ

Special material used in a Holy Chalice ritual. Special body parts collected by the Healing Church. What was this gruesome bait used to lure? The additional rite Rotted Offering beckons ungodly forces, normally terrifying things, but also worthy prey for a special hunt.

Yellow Backbone

Special material used in a Holy Chalice ritual. Special body parts collected by the Healing Church. What was this gruesome bait used to lure? The additional rite Rotted Offering beckons ungodly forces, normally terrifying things, but also worthy prey for a special hunt.

Bastard of Loran

Special material used in a Holy Chalice ritual. Remains of a Loran infant infected by the scourge. A harbinger of curses and symbol of defilement. The additional rite Curse defiles dungeons in which hunters' HP is greatly eroded, but what better place to seek cursed blood gems but in the midst of defilement?

Preset Dungeon List

There are ten Preset Chalice Labyrinths in Bloodborne. Each labyrinth is comprised of three layers, with the exception of the Lower Pthumeru Labyrinth, which has four layers. Clearing these labyrinths will reward you with loot, key items, weapons and more Chalices to unlock more challenging dungeons. Here is a complete list of Preset Chalice Labyrinths in the order we recommend to tackle them. We also list the page on which you'll find each dungeon's layer-by-layer guide.

Central Pthumeru Chalice

A chalice that breaks the labyrinth seal. But only a Root Chalice changes the shape of the old labyrinth when used in a ritual. The old labyrinth was carved out by the Pthumerians, superhuman beings that are said to have unlocked the wisdom of the eldritch Truth.

Acquired From	Pthumerian Labyrinth **L3 Boss:** Watchdog of the Old Lords
Dungeon Created	Central Pthumerian Labyrinth
Depth	2
Required Ritual Material	Ritual Blood (2) ×6 Blood Echoes × 1800
Layer Boss	**L1:** Beast-possessed Soul **L2:** Keeper of the Old Lords **L3:** Pthumerian Descendent
Key Rewards	**L1 Boss:** Radiant Blood Gemstone (3) **L2 Coffin:** Hintertomb Chalice **L2 Boss:** Central Pthumeru Root Chalice **L3 Boss:** Lower Pthumeru Chalice
Page	p418

Pthumeru Chalice

Ritual chalice found in the Church of the Good Chalice. Use in a ritual at the tomb altar in the Hunter's Dream to break the seal of the old underground labyrinth. Let the chalice reveal the tomb of the gods; let blood be the hunter's nourishment. ...And let ye partake in communion...

Acquired From	Old Yharnam Boss: Blood-starved Beast
Dungeon Created	Pthumerian Labyrinth
Depth	1
Required Ritual Material	Ritual Blood (1) ×2 Blood Echoes ×1000
Layer Boss	**L1:** Undead Giant (Twin Curved Blades) **L2:** Merciless Watcher ×2, Watcher Chieftain ×1 **L3:** Watchdog of the Old Lords
Key Rewards	**L1 Boss:** Adept Blood Gemstone (2) **L2 Boss:** Pthumeru Root Chalice **L3 Boss:** Central Pthumeru Chalice
Page	p412

Hintertomb Chalice

A chalice that breaks a labyrinth seal. Hintertombs are the peripheral catacombs of the old underground labyrinth. To this day, the Watchers continue to expand the hintertombs, unceremonious catacombs filled with graves and death.

Acquired From	Central Pthumerian Labyrinth **L2 Coffin:** Hintertomb Chalice
Dungeon Created	Hintertomb
Depth	2
Required Ritual Material	Ritual Blood (2) ×3 Bloodshot Eyeball ×3 Blood Echoes ×1800
Layer Boss	**L1:** Maneater Boar **L2:** Undead Giant (Hatchet & Cannon) **L3:** Blood-starved Beast
Key Rewards	**L1 Boss:** Lethal bloodstone gem (2) **L2 Boss:** Hintertomb Root Chalice **L3 Boss:** Lower Hintertomb Chalice
Page	p424

Lower Hintertomb Chalice

A chalice that breaks a labyrinth seal. Hintertombs are the peripheral catacombs of the old underground labyrinth. To this day, the Watchers continue to expand the hintertombs, unceremonious catacombs filled with graves and death.

Acquired From	Hintertomb **L3 Boss:** Blood-starved Beast
Dungeon Created	Lower Hintertomb
Depth	3
Required Ritual Material	Ritual Blood (3) ×6 Bloodshot Eyeball ×6 Blood Echoes ×3200
Layer Boss	**L1:** Brainsucker **L2:** Forgotten Madman & Madman's Escort **L3:** Pthumerian Elder
Key Rewards	**L1 Boss:** Tempering Blood Gemstone (3) **L2 Boss:** Lower Hintertomb Root Chalice **L3 Bath Messenger Shop:** Sinister Hintertomb Root Chalice **L3 Boss:** Short Ritual Root Chalice (to access online)
Page	p430

Lower Pthumeru Chalice

A chalice that breaks the labyrinth seal. But only a Root Chalice changes the shape of the old labyrinth when used in a ritual. The old labyrinth was carved out by the Pthumerians, superhuman beings that are said to have unlocked the wisdom of the eldritch Truth.

Acquired From	Central Pthumerian Labyrinth **L3 Boss:** Pthumerian Descendent
Dungeon Created	Lower Pthumerian Labyrinth
Depth	3
Required Ritual Material	Ritual Blood (3) ×9 Blood Echoes × 3200
Layer Boss	**L1:** Merciless Watcher ×2, Watcher Chieftain ×1 **L2:** Undead Giant (Club & Hook) **L3:** Rom The Vacuous Spider **L4:** Bloodletting Beast
Key Rewards	**L1 Boss:** Tempering blood gemstone (3) **L2 Coffin:** Workshop Haze Extractor **L2 Boss:** Adept Blood Gemstone (3) **L3 Boss:** Lower Pthumeru Root Chalice **L4 Bath Messenger Shop:** Sinister Lower Pthumeru Root Chalice **L4 Boss:** Defiled Chalice
Page	p436

Ailing Loran Chalice

A chalice that breaks a labyrinth seal. Loran is a tragic land that was devoured by the sands. The tragedy that struck this ailing land of Loran is said to have its roots in the scourge of the beast. Some have made the dreaded extrapolation that Yharnam may be next.

Acquired From	Nightmare Frontier Boss: Amygdala
Dungeon Created	Ailing Loran
Depth	4
Required Ritual Material	Ritual Blood (4) ×9 Coldblood Flowerbud ×4 Blood Echoes ×5500
Layer Boss	**L1:** Beast-possessed Soul **L2:** Blood-starved Beast **L3:** Abhorrent Beast
Key Rewards	**L1 Boss:** Fire Damp Blood Gem (5) **L2 Coffin:** Beast Claw (weapon) **L2 Boss:** Ailing Loran Root Chalice **L3 Boss:** Lower Loran Chalice
Page	p444

Defiled Chalice

A chalice that breaks a labyrinth seal. Only, this defiled chalice is cursed. Curses are caused by inciting the anger of the Great Ones, and used to hex others. Special materials are required to complete the ritual. To try one's hand at cursed, first seek the Bastard of Loran.

Acquired From	Lower Pthumerian Labyrinth **L4 Boss:** Bloodletting Beast
Dungeon Created	Cursed Pthumerian Defilement
Depth	4
Required Ritual Material	Ritual Blood (4) ×9 Bastard of Loran ×2 Arcane Haze ×22 Blood Echoes ×5500
Layer Boss	**L1:** Keeper of the Old Lords **L2:** Watchdog of the Old Lords **L3:** Amygdala
Key Rewards	**L1 Boss:** Cursed Sharp Damp Blood Gem (5) **L2 Boss:** Cursed and Defiled Root Chalice **L3 Boss:** Great Pthumeru Ihyll Chalice
Page	p450

Great Isz Chalice

A chalice that breaks a labyrinth seal. Great chalices unlock deeper reaches of the labyrinth. The Great Isz Chalice became the cornerstone of the Choir, the elite delegation of the Healing Church. It was also the first Great Chalice brought back to the surface since the time of Byrgenwerth, and allowed the Choir to have audience with Ebrietas.

Acquired From	Upper Cathedral Ward Boss: Ebrietas, Daughter of the Cosmos
Dungeon Created	Isz Gravestone
Depth	5
Required Ritual Material	Ritual Blood (5) ×9 Pearl Slug ×3 Arcane Haze ×25 Blood Echoes ×11500
Layer Boss	**L1:** Brain Sucker **L2:** Celestial Emissary **L3:** Ebrietas, Daughter of the Cosmos
Key Rewards	**L1 Boss:** Arcane Damp Blood Gem (6) **L2 Boss:** Arcane Damp Blood Gem (6) **L3 Bath Messenger Shop:** Sinister Isz Root Chalice **L3 Boss:** Isz Root Chalice
Page	p462

Lower Loran Chalice

A chalice that breaks a labyrinth seal. But only a Root Chalice changes the shape of the Chalice Dungeon when used in a ritual. There are trace remains of medical procedures in parts of ailing Loran. Whether these were attempts to control the scourge of the beast, or the cause of the outbreak, is unknown.

Acquired From	Ailing Loran **L3 Boss:** Abhorrent Beast
Dungeon Created	Lower Loran
Depth	5
Required Ritual Material	Ritual Blood (5) ×9 Blooming Coldblood Flower ×4 Blood Echoes ×11500
Layer Boss	**L1:** Loran Silver Beast **L2:** Abhorrent Beast **L3:** Loran Darkbeast
Key Rewards	**L1 Boss:** Tempering Damp Blood Gem (6) **L2 Boss:** Bolt Damp Blood Gem (6) **L3 Bath Messenger Shop:** Sinister Lower Loran Root Chalice **L3 Boss:** Lower Ailing Loran Root Chalice
Page	p456

Great Pthumeru Ihyll Chalice

A chalice that breaks a labyrinth seal. Great chalices unlock deeper reaches of the labyrinth. Pthumeru Ihyll was the title of both the Pthumerian monarch and its capital. This reveals that while early Pthumerians were mere humble guardians of the slumbering Great Ones, their descendants felt entitled to name themselves a leader.

Acquired From	Cursed Pthumerian Defilement **L3 Boss:** Amygdala
Dungeon Created	Pthumeru Ihyll
Depth	5
Required Ritual Material	Ritual Blood (5) ×9 Red Jelly ×4 Arcane Haze ×25 Living String ×1 Blood Echoes ×11500
Layer Boss	**L1:** Pthumerian Descendant **L2:** Bloodletting Beast (Parasite) **F3:** Yharnam, Pthumerian Queen
Key Rewards	**L1 Boss:** Tempering Damp Blood Gem (6) **L2 Boss:** Pthumeru Ihyll Root Chalice **L3 Bath Messenger Shop:** Sinister Pthumeru Ihyll Root Chalice **L3 Boss:** Yharnam Stone
Page	p468

Root Dungeon List

The Chalices in this list all create randomly generated Root Dungeons. You can acquire these Chalices by clearing layers in the Preset Dungeons. For each one, the required materials listed; they require more materials than the Preset Chalices, and some of them have the possibility of adding Additional Rites. Depth 5 Root dungeons contain some the game's most valuable rewards in their treasure rooms, including Lost and Uncanny weapons, Blood Rocks, high level Caryll Runes and the highest ranking Blood Gems, along with plenty of ritual materials.

Pthumeru Root Chalice

Root Chalice that breaks multiple labyrinth seals. Root Chalices, used in rituals to break old labyrinth seals, are said to change the labyrinth's form each time. The old labyrinth was carved out by the Pthumerians, superhuman beings that are said to have unlocked the wisdom of the eldritch Truth.

Acquired From	Pthumerian Labyrinth Layer 2 Boss
Dungeon Created	Pthumerian Labyrinth
Depth	1
Required Ritual Material	Ritual Blood (1) ×2 Tomb Mold (1) ×3 Blood Echoes ×1000
Additional Rite(s)	–

Central Pthumeru Root Chalice

Root Chalice that breaks multiple labyrinth seals. Root Chalices, used in rituals to break old labyrinth seals, are said to change the labyrinth's form each time. The old labyrinth was carved out by the Pthumerians, superhuman beings that are said to have unlocked the wisdom of the eldritch Truth.

Acquired From	Central Pthumerian Labyrinth Layer 2 Boss
Dungeon Created	Pthumerian Labyrinth
Depth	2
Required Ritual Material	Ritual Blood (2) ×8 Tomb Mold (2) ×6 Blood Echoes ×1800
Additional Rite(s)	Sage's Wrist ×2 = Fetid Offering

Hintertomb Root Chalice

Root Chalice that breaks multiple labyrinth seals. Root Chalices, used in rituals to break old labyrinth seals, are said to change the labyrinth's form each time. The hintertombs are unceremonious homes to graves and death, cesspools of noxious snakes and insects.

Acquired From	Hintertomb Layer 2 Boss
Dungeon Created	Hintertomb
Depth	2
Required Ritual Material	Ritial Blood (2) ×8 Tomb Mold (2) ×10 Bloodshot Eyeball ×3 Blood Echoes ×1800
Additional Rite(s)	Sage's Wrist ×2 = Fetid Offering

Lower Hintertomb Root Chalice

Root Chalice that breaks multiple labyrinth seals. Root Chalices, used in rituals to break old labyrinth seals, are said to change the labyrinth's form each time. The hintertombs are unceremonious homes to graves and death, cesspools of noxious snakes and insects.

Acquired From	Lower Hintertomb Layer 2 Boss
Dungeon Created	Lower Hintertomb
Depth	3
Required Ritual Material	Ritual Blood (3) ×12 Tomb Mold (3) ×3 Bloodshot Eyeball ×6 Blood Echoes ×3200
Additional Rite(s)	Sage's Wrist ×4 = Fetid Offering Inflicted Organ ×3 = Rotted Offering

Sinister Hintertomb Root Chalice

Root Chalice that breaks multiple labyrinth seals. When used in a ritual, this sinister chalice summons the Sinister Resonant Bell. The bell-ringing woman appears to be a mad Pthumerian. The Hintertombs are unceremonious homes to graves and death, cesspools of noxious snakes and insects. Note: Additional rite Sinister Bell is for online use only. The bell-ringing woman does not appear offline.

Acquired From	Lower Hintertomb Layer 3 Shop 10000 Blood Echoes
Dungeon Created	Lower Hintertomb
Depth	3
Required Ritual Material	Ritual Blood (3) ×12 Tomb Mold (3) ×3 Bloodshot Eyeball ×6 Blood Echoes ×3200
Additional Rite(s)	Arcane Haze ×19 = Sinister Bell

Sinister Lower Pthumeru Root Chalice

Root Chalice that breaks multiple labyrinth seals. When used in a ritual, this sinister chalice summons the Sinister Resonant Bell. The bell-ringing woman appears to be a mad Pthumerian. The old labyrinth was carved out by the Pthumerians, superhuman beings that are said to have unlocked the wisdom of the eldritch Truth. Note: Additional rite Sinister Bell is for online use only. The bell-ringing woman does not appear offline.

Acquired From	Lower Pthumerian Labyrinth Layer 4 Shop 9000 Blood Echoes
Dungeon Created	Lower Pthumerian Labyrinth
Depth	3
Required Ritual Material	Ritual Blood (3) ×12 Tomb Mold (3) ×8 Blood Echoes ×3200
Additional Rite(s)	Arcane Haze ×19 = Sinister Bell

4

Lower Pthumeru Root Chalice

Root Chalice that breaks multiple labyrinth seals. Root Chalices, used in rituals to break old labyrinth seals, are said to change the labyrinth's form each time. The old labyrinth was carved out by the Pthumerians, superhuman beings that are said to have unlocked the wisdom of the eldritch Truth.

Acquired From	Lower Pthumerian Labyrinth Layer 2 Boss
Dungeon Created	Lower Pthumerian Labyrinth
Depth	3
Required Ritual Material	Ritual Blood (3) ×12 Tomb Mold (3) ×8 Blood Echoes ×3200
Additional Rite(s)	Sage's Wrist ×4 = Fetid Offering Inflicted Organ ×3 = Rotted Offering

Ailing Loran Root Chalice

Root Chalice that breaks multiple labyrinth seals. Root Chalices, used in rituals to break old labyrinth seals, are said to change the labyrinth's form each time. There are trace remains of medical procedures in parts of ailing Loran. Whether these were attempts to control the scourge of the beast, or the cause of the outbreak, is unknown.

Acquired From	Ailing Loran Layer 2 Boss
Dungeon Created	Ailing Loran
Depth	4
Required Ritual Material	Ritual Blood (4) ×14 Coldblood Flower Bulb ×3 Tomb Mold (4) ×3 Blood Echoes ×5500
Additional Rite(s)	Sage's Hair ×3 = Fetid Offering Inflicted Organ ×5 = Rotted Offering

Cursed and Defiled Root Chalice

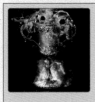

Root chalice that breaks multiple labyrinth seals. This cursed chalice makes a special ritual possible, but must not be used lightly, as the resulting transformation can be utterly drastic. The old labyrinth was carved out by the Pthumerians, superhuman beings that are said to have unlocked the wisdom of the eldritch Truth.

Acquired From	Pthumerian Defilement Layer 2 Boss
Dungeon Created	Pthumerian Defilement
Depth	4
Required Ritual Material	Ritual Blood (4) ×10 Tomb Mold (4) ×6 Blood Echoes ×5500
Additional Rite(s)	Sage's Hair ×3 = Fetid Offering Inflicted Organ ×5 = Rotted Offering Bastard of Loran ×3 = Curse

Lower Ailing Loran Root Chalice

Root Chalice that breaks multiple labyrinth seals. Root Chalices, used in rituals to break old labyrinth seals, are said to change the labyrinth's form each time. There are trace remains of medical procedures in parts of ailing Loran. Whether these were attempts to control the scourge of the beast, or the cause of the outbreak, is unknown.

Acquired From	Lower Loran Layer 3 Shop 18000 Blood Echoes
Dungeon Created	Lower Loran
Depth	5
Required Ritual Material	Ritual Blood (5) ×13 Blooming Coldblood Flower ×4 Tomb Mold (5) ×5 Red Jelly ×1 Blood Echoes ×11500
Additional Rite(s)	Sage's Hair ×6 = Fetid Offering Yellow Backbone ×6 = Rotted Offering Bastard of Loran ×3 = Curse

Sinister Lower Loran Root Chalice

Root Chalice that breaks multiple labyrinth seals. When used in a ritual, this sinister chalice summons the Sinister Resonant Bell. The bell-ringing woman appears to be a mad Pthumerian. There are trace remains of medical procedures in parts of ailing Loran. Whether these were attempts to control the scourge of the beast, or the cause of the outbreak, is unknown. Note: Additional rite Sinister Bell is for online use only. The bell-ringing woman does not appear offline.

Acquired From	Lower Loran Layer 3 Boss
Dungeon Created	Lower Loran
Depth	5
Required Ritual Material	Ritual Blood (5) ×13 Blooming Coldblood Flower ×4 Tomb Mold (5) ×5 Red Jelly ×1 Blood Echoes ×11500
Additional Rite(s)	Arcane Haze ×32 = Sinister Bell

Isz Root Chalice

Root Chalice that breaks multiple labyrinth seals. Root Chalices, used in rituals to break old labyrinth seals, are said to change the labyrinth's form each time. According to the Choir, the land of Isz lies in contact with the cosmos, which allowed the Great Ones to function on transcendental planes of thought.

Acquired From	Isz Gravestone Layer 3 Shop 20000 Blood Echoes
Dungeon Created	Isz Gravestone
Depth	5
Required Ritual Material	Ritual Blood (5) ×13 Tomb Mold (5) ×5 Pearl Slug ×3 Red Jelly ×1 Blood Echoes ×11500
Additional Rite(s)	Sage's Hair ×6 = Fetid Offering Yellow Backbone ×6 = Rotted Offering Bastard of Loran ×3 = Curse

Sinister Isz Root Chalice

Root Chalice that breaks multiple labyrinth seals. When used in a ritual, this sinister chalice summons the Sinister Resonant Bell. The bell-ringing woman appears to be a mad Pthumerian. According to the Choir, the land of Isz lies in contact with the cosmos, which allowed the Great Ones to function on transcendental planes of thought. Note: Additional rite Sinister Bell is for online use only. The bell-ringing woman does not appear offline.

Acquired From	Isz Gravestone Layer 3 Boss
Dungeon Created	Isz Gravestone
Depth	5
Required Ritual Material	Ritual Blood (5) ×13 Tomb Mold (5) ×5 Pearl Slug ×3 Red Jelly ×1 Blood Echoes ×11500
Additional Rite(s)	Arcane Haze ×32 = Sinister Bell

Pthumeru Ihyll Root Chalice

Root Chalice that breaks multiple labyrinth seals. Root Chalices, used in rituals to break old labyrinth seals, are said to change the labyrinth's form each time. The Pthumerian monarch was traditionally a woman who assumed a name with classical roots.

Acquired From	Pthumeru Ihyll Layer 2 Boss
Dungeon Created	Pthumeru Ihyll
Depth	5
Required Ritual Material	Ritual Blood (5) ×15 Tomb Mold (5) ×15 Red Jelly ×2 Blood Echoes ×11500
Additional Rite(s)	Sage's Hair ×6 = Fetid Offering Yellow Backbone ×6 = Rotted Offering Bastard of Loran ×3 = Curse

Sinister Pthumeru Ihyll Root Chalice

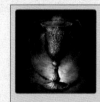

Root Chalice that breaks multiple labyrinth seals. When used in a ritual, this sinister chalice summons the Sinister Resonant Bell. The bell-ringing woman appears to be a mad Pthumerian. The Pthumerian monarch was traditionally a woman who assumed a name with classical roots. Note: Additional rite Sinister Bell is for online use only. The bell-ringing woman does not appear offline.

Acquired From	Pthumeru Ihyll Layer 3 Shop 16000 Blood Echoes
Dungeon Created	Pthumeru Ihyll
Depth	5
Required Ritual Material	Ritual Blood (5) ×15 Tomb Mold (5) ×15 Red Jelly ×2 Blood Echoes ×11500
Additional Rite(s)	Arcane Haze ×32 = Sinister Bell

Pthumerian Labyrinth

Defeating the Blood-starved Beast in Old Yharnam will allow you to craft the first Chalice Dungeon. In order to craft this dungeon you'll need two 'Ritual Blood (1)'s, which can be found in the Ritual Hall of Old Yharnam. You can also purchase them from the Messenger Bath shop in the Hunter's Dream after acquiring the Radiant Sword Hunter Badge and defeating the Blood-starved Beast. The first of the Pthumerian dungeons, this labyrinth will ease you into the job of tomb prospecting.

Recommended	Player Level **30+**	Weapon Upgrade **+3**

Layer 1

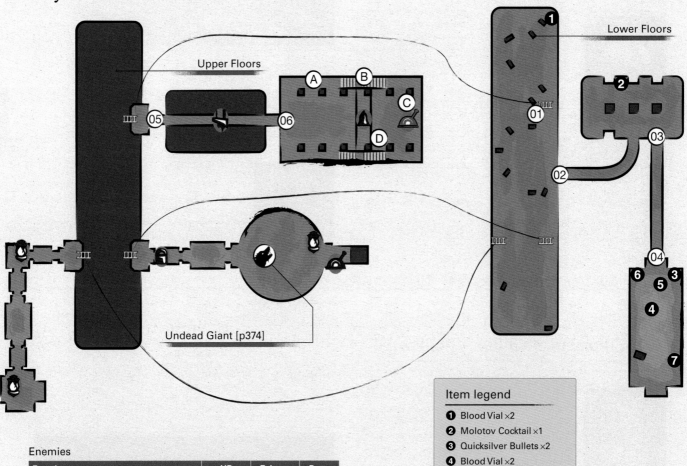

Undead Giant [p374]

Item legend

1. Blood Vial ×2
2. Molotov Cocktail ×1
3. Quicksilver Bullets ×2
4. Blood Vial ×2
5. Shining Coins ×3
6. Quicksilver Bullets ×2
7. Molotov Cocktail ×2

Enemies

Regular	HP	Echoes	Page
Labyrinth Rat	123	53	p233
Labyrinth Watcher (Cleaver)	123	67	p250
Labyrinth Watcher (Dagger)	123	67	p250
Labyrinth Watcher (Twin Axes)	194	67	p251

Strong	HP	Echoes	Page
Watcher Chieftain (Club & Lantern)	555	316	p294
Bell Ringer	211	114	p287
Kidnapper	388	234	p276

Boss	HP	Echoes	Page
Undead Giant (Twin Curved Blades)	3175	1425	p374

Ritual Info

Chalice	Pthumeru Chalice
Ritual Materials	Ritual Blood (1) ×2
Blood Echoes	1000
Floor Depth	1

Step 01

The pool of liquid at the base of the ladder here is in fact oil, so you'll need to approach with caution – especially since the Labyrinth Watcher at the top of the ladder will start throwing molotov cocktails at you when you get close. Instead of trying to climb the ladder with the enemy waiting at the top, run past the oil so that you're underneath the ledge. This will cause it walk off and drop down so that you to kill it easily.

Step 02

A Kidnapper is lurking just past the tunnel, so watch out for him when entering this area to explore the rooms beyond. [→☐ 01]

Step 03

This room is directly below the swinging axe trap, and it's where you will end up if you get knocked off while trying to cross the bridge. If you have not already killed the Bell Ringer in the lever room, the Labyrinth Watchers that she spawns will keep dropping off the bridge into this room; listen out for the sounds of one in the area while you explore so that they don't catch you unaware.

Step 04

Numerous Labyrinth Rats have taken up residence in this cave. There are a couple of rats near the entrance to the cave so take them out first before going deeper in towards the main group. It doesn't take a lot to kill the rats, so you can be quite aggressive when dealing with them. If they start surrounding you, however, make use of the nearby cart to try and split the group. [→☐ 02]

Step 05

You will need to cross a stone bridge hazarded by three swinging axes here to reach the floor lever room for this level. Negotiating this hazard can be tricky, thanks to the Labyrinth Watcher on the

other side throwing extremely potent poison daggers at you. Run past the first swinging axe to get in range, and then use your Hunter's Pistol, other ranged weapon such as Throwing Knives, to take out the Labyrinth Watcher. The next two axes are close together and you'll need to make it past both of them in one go; watch their movement, and time your dash for when they just start to move away from the middle of the bridge. [→☐ 03]

Step 06

The first thing to deal with in this room is the Bell Ringer, because killing her will stop her from spawning more Labyrinth Watchers. She's usually patrolling along the ledge in the middle of the room, so after taking out any Labyrinth Watchers that come after you initially, run up and kill her before she spawns more. A normal Labyrinth Watcher also patrols up and down the stairs near **Position A**; wait for it to come down the stairs and kill it there, so that you don't have to worry about it later.

Head up the stairs at **Position B** next, but make sure not to run once you get near the top; there are quite a few enemies up here, but if you walk you can get close to most of them without being detected, which will make the fight much easier. A Labyrinth Watcher has taken up position behind a cloud of incense at **Position C** near the top of the stairs, and it will start throwing poison knives at you as soon as it sees you. If you keep walking forward, the knives will get blocked by the nearby pillar. Once you reach the pillar, the Labyrinth Watcher will run around it, so deal with it up close.

Hug the wall at the back of the room and slowly follow it along behind the lever until you reach the Labyrinth Watcher on the other side, and then kill it. You should be able to walk up behind the Merciless Watcher now and use a charged R2 in its back, with Visceral Attack follow-up. If that doesn't finish it off, quickly move in and try to kill it before it turns around and attacks you. There is one more Labyrinth Watcher standing near the front of this upper section at **Position D**, and if you manage to kill the Merciless Watcher without causing much noise, you can often sneak up behind this enemy for an easy victory. [→☐ 04]

Pthumerian Labyrinth – Layer 2

Enemies

Regular	HP	Echoes	Page
Labyrinth Watcher (Dagger)	129	70	p250
Labyrinth Watcher (Cleaver)	129	70	p250
Labyrinth Watcher (Cleaver & Lantern)	204	70	p250
Labyrinth Watcher (Halberd)	204	70	p251

Strong	HP	Echoes	Page
Bell Ringer	222	120	p287
Kidnapper	407	246	p276
Merciless Watcher (Mace)	583	332	p296

Boss	HP	Echoes	Page
Merciless Watcher (Scattergun & Lantern), Merciless Watcher (Saw), Watcher Chieftain (Club & Lantern)	1111 1111 833	1182 1182 1182	p294

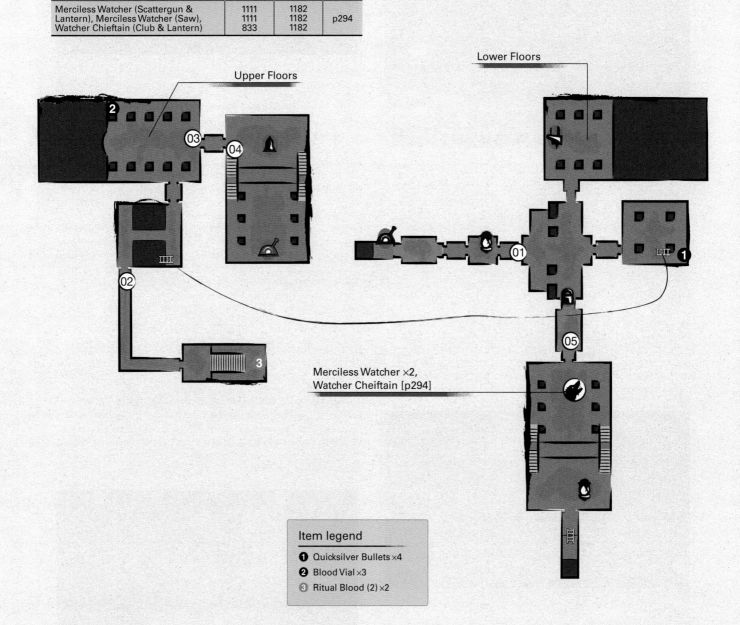

Upper Floors

Lower Floors

2

03

04

02

3

01

1

05

Merciless Watcher ×2,
Watcher Cheiftain [p294]

Item legend

❶ Quicksilver Bullets ×4

❷ Blood Vial ×3

❸ Ritual Blood (2) ×2

Step 01

Directly ahead from the entrance there's a pressure plate on the floor that when stepped on will cause a small group of Labyrinth Watchers to appear in front of you; it's worth triggering the trap straight away so that you can deal with the enemies while you're expecting them, rather than accidentally triggering it later. The wooden coffin leaning against the wall just past that pressure plate also has another Labyrinth Watcher hiding it, so run up and attack it after clearing out the other enemies. [→□ 01]

Step 02

Take out the Labyrinth Watchers scattered along this corridor, but be careful when you enter the room at the end, because as you cross over the motif in the middle of the floor, a group of Labyrinth Watchers will appear around you. Quickly retreat back through the doorway before they close in on you and fight them as they come through it. A Kidnapper stands in wait at the bottom of the stairs in this room, so you should head down there as quickly as possible so that you can fight him on the flat ground rather than on the stairs. Once he's dead, open the chest to claim the two Ritual Blood (2) materials. [→□ 02-06]

Step 03

There is no door anymore: Rush to the opening of this room in order to funnel in the Labyrinth Watchers summoned by the Bell Ringer so you can funnel them through and any other regular Labyrinth Watchers. Once you have cleared a path, head straight in and vanquish the Bell Ringer. Run to the middle of the room, where you can find the Bell Ringer patrolling – kill her to stop anymore Labyrinth Watchers spawning.

Step 04

At the bottom end of this room a Merciless Watcher is standing guard never the lever you need to pull. If you walk down the stairs closest to the room entrance and hug the wall, you can sneak around behind him and land a charged R2 in his back for an easy victory. If he does happen to spot you, run around the nearby cart and keep it between you and him while he attacks, and then hit him during his recovery periods.

Step 05

The Watcher Chieftain in this fight has less health and moves slower than the other two enemies. So it's worth trying to lure the other two away first, and then go back and focus on the chieftain to kill. Upon completing this fight you will automatically receive the Pthumeru Root Chalice, which will allow you to create randomly generated Pthumeru dungeons.

Enemies

Normal	HP	Echoes	Page
Labyrinth Watcher (Dagger)	132	74	p250
Labyrinth Watcher (Cleaver)	132	74	p250
Labyrinth Watcher (Cleaver & Lantern)	209	74	p250
Labyrinth Watcher (Twin Axes)	209	74	p251
Wandering Nightmare	51	15	p671
Pilgrim	306	235	p252

Strong	HP	Echoes	Page
Bell Ringer	227	125	p287
Fluorescent Flower	284	204	p286
Kidnapper	417	257	p276
Watcher Chieftain (Heated Club & Lantern)	597	348	p295
Merciless Watcher (Scattergun, Club & Lantern)	597	348	p297

Boss	HP	Echoes	Page
Watchdog of the Old Lords	3793	1866	p376

Upper Floors

Item legend

1. Ritual Blood (2) ×1
2. Ritual Blood (2) ×1
3. Tomb Mold (1) ×3
4. Blood Vial ×3
5. Blood Vial ×2
6. Coldblood Dew (3) ×1
7. Bold Hunter's Mark ×1
8. Molotov Cocktail ×2
9. Quicksilver Bullets ×4
10. Tomb Mold (1) ×3
11. Blood Vial ×3
12. Ritual Blood (2) ×4

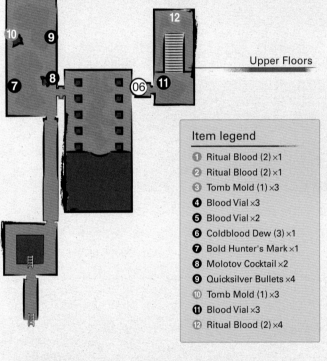

Lower Floors

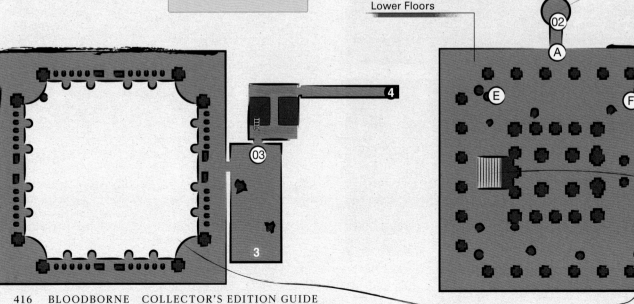

Step 01

Be careful as you open the door leading into the pit room, because there's a Labyrinth Watcher patrolling around the other side and it can be quite close when you open the door. The exit gate is directly in front of you, but since you need to unlock it first, approach the edge of the pit so that you can see the Labyrinth Watcher down there, and then drop down and kill it.

Step 02

There's a Bell Ringer patrolling the raised section in the middle of this large garden area and a large group of enemies that she spawned will be waiting for you near the end of the tunnel that leads into the garden at **Position A**. Try to fight them back from the end of the tunnel, because there's also a Labyrinth Watcher on the raised section in the middle that will operate the cannon at **Position B** once you're within range. Head around to the right from the end of the tunnel once the initial group of enemies has been dealt with, until you come to a large set of stairs. The Bell Ringer will have spawned more enemies by this time, so kill them as they come running down the stairs, and then quickly run up and kill her before she can spawn anymore.

If you head to **Position C** just to the side of the cannon you should have a clear line of sight to one of the Fluorescent Flowers. Use ranged attacks to target the flower part and kill it easily from here. It's a much better choice to kill it from range if you can, because there's also a Wandering Nightmare close to it, and it's quite likely that it would disappear before you could kill the Fluorescent Flower at close range. From **Position D** you can see a second Fluorescent Flower, but from here it's much harder to target its flower, so you can either try luring it forward first with a Throwing Knife or Molotov Cocktail, or, head down there and use the pillars for cover until you're within range, and then shoot the flower to kill it. A Blue Elixir will also let you get close if you have one.

There are a couple more Labyrinth Watchers standing under the raised section, but unless you go under there they won't see you. The major remaining threat is a Kidnapper that patrols the entire area, so you'll need to watch out for him as you go around collecting the items. The Fluorescent Flowers often drop Arcane Hazes, and you'll need a large number of them for crafting some of the later dungeons, so it's worth remembering that you can get to them here quite quickly. If you want, you can also skip nearly all of the combat in this area by pulling the switch at either **Position E** or **F** to lower a cage elevator near their respective positions. By getting into the cage elevator you can go straight up to the balcony that runs around the garden and avoid having to deal with the enemies.

Step 03

Regardless of which way you're approaching from, it's worth coming up to this room to get the three Tomb Mold (1) items from the chest at the back. You'll also find a Pilgrim wandering around the room, but since it's non-hostile you can simply leave it alone if you wish. The same cannot be said, however, of the three Labyrinth Watchers that can ambush you when you get near the doorway that leads out onto the balcony area. If you head out onto the balcony after they spawn you can force them to bunch up in the doorway, making them easier to kill.

Step 04

A Watcher Chieftain stands guard over the lever in this room, but if you walk around the right-hand side as you enter and follow the wall along, you can get quite close to him before he spots you. There's a pressure plat that triggers a flame arrow trap in this area as well, and the Chieftain is positioned such that you can step on the plate, and then move out of the way to hit him with the arrow. **[→☐ 01]**

Step 05

While you can just proceed straight to the boss after unlocking the gate, it's worth taking the path off to the right first, because there are quite a few items you can get, including a number of important dungeon crafting materials.

Step 06

The Merciless Watcher that stands guard over the coffin at the bottom of this room wields a pistol, so while it's approaching you, stand behind one of the statues at the top of the stairs to use it as cover. Once he's close, wait for him to reload before attacking him. The coffin contains four Ritual Blood (2), so if you picked up the other two on this level, you will have enough to create the Central Pthumerian Labyrinth with the Chalice you get from the boss at the end. **[→☐ 02]**

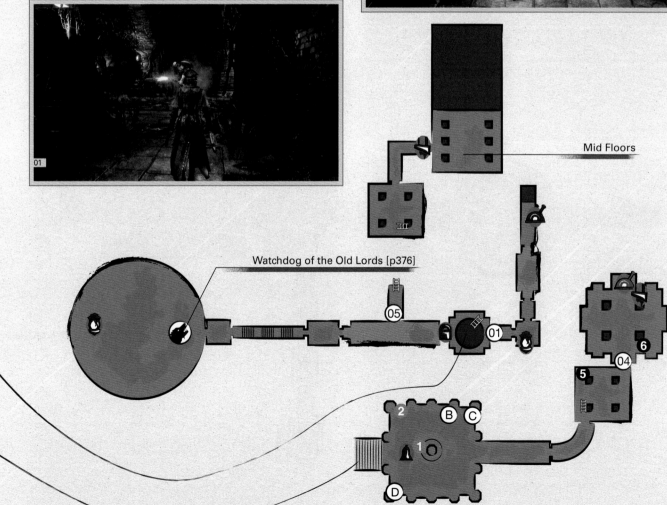

Mid Floors

Watchdog of the Old Lords [p376]

Central Pthumerian Labyrinth

You can tackle this labyrinth straight after completing the first Pthumerian Labyrinth, but it's recommended to level up your character to around 40 and your main weapon to +4 or +5 to make things easier. If you explored the Pthumerian Labyrinth thoroughly, you should have the six Ritual Blood (2) that are required to craft this Chalice Dungeon at the Ritual Altar. The Hintertomb Chalice can be found in a Coffin on the second level of this labyrinth.

Recommended	Player Level **40+**	Weapon Upgrade **+6**

Layer 1

Enemies

Regular	HP	Echoes	Page
Labyrinth Watcher (Dagger)	178	155	p250
Labyrinth Watcher (Twin Axes)	281	155	p251
Labyrinth Watcher (Cleaver)	178	155	p250
Rabid Dog	204	195	p230

Strong	HP	Echoes	Page
Bell Ringer	306	264	p287
Kidnapper	563	543	p276
Watcher Chieftain (Club & Lantern)	805	733	p294

Boss	HP	Echoes	Page
Beast-possessed Soul	3198	2844	p275

Ritual Info

Chalice	Central Pthumeru Chalice
Ritual Materials	Ritual Blood (2) ×6
Blood Echoes	1800
Floor Depth	2

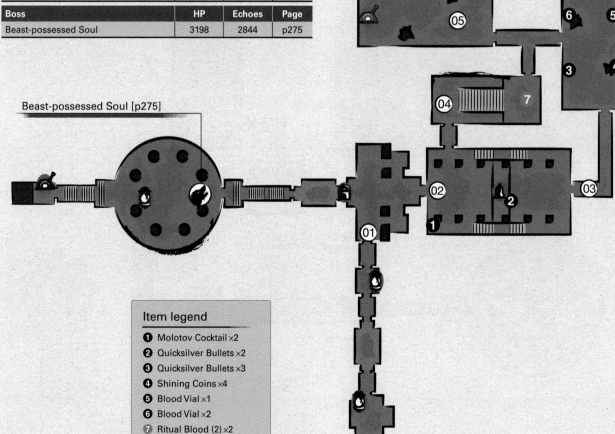

Beast-possessed Soul [p275]

Item legend

1. Molotov Cocktail ×2
2. Quicksilver Bullets ×2
3. Quicksilver Bullets ×3
4. Shining Coins ×4
5. Blood Vial ×1
6. Blood Vial ×2
7. Ritual Blood (2) ×2

Step 01

The coffin leaning against the wall just to the left of the entrance to this room has a Labyrinth Watcher hiding inside. Attack it as soon as you're in range to foil its ambush attempt. [→☐ 01]

Step 02

There's a Bell Ringer on the ledge in the middle of this room, but before running in there to kill her, wait near the entrance and let the enemies she spawned come towards you, so that you can kill them. There are more Labyrinth Watchers on the upper part of this room and they'll start throwing Molotov Cocktails down at you once you're in range. Taking out the initial group of enemies will mean you'll have as few obstacles as possible between you and the Bell Ringer when you go after her. [→☐ 02]

Step 03

Numerous Labyrinth Watchers lay dormant in this corridor. It's best to take them out one at a time as you come to them, in order to avoid being attacked form behind later on. [→☐ 03-05]

Step 04

The Labyrinth Watchers standing guard over the chest at the top of the stairs in this room all throw Molotov Cocktails, so instead of trying to enter from the bottom of the stairs while avoiding their attacks, it's better to approach from the top later.

Step 05

Before attempting to go after the Watcher Chieftain that's guarding the lever in this room, it's best to first take out the other enemies, so that you can fight it one-on-one. The first of the Labyrinth Watchers will generally be quite close to the entrance, so try to take it out first, and then move up and take out the two dogs while the second Labyrinth Watcher stands up near the wall on the left. Once everything else has been killed, move up and keep the tree in the area between you and the Watcher Chieftain, so that you can safely bait it into attacking and kill it while it's recovering. [→☐ 06/07]

Central Pthumerian Labyrinth – Layer 2

Enemies

Regular	HP	Echoes	Page
Gravekeeper Scorpion	120	144	p252
Gel	160	302	p253
Labyrinth Rat	187	129	p233
Labyrinth Watcher (Dagger)	187	163	p250
Labyrinth Watcher (Halberd)	295	163	p251
Labyrinth Watcher (Cleaver)	187	163	p250
Labyrinth Watcher (Twin Axes)	295	163	p251
Rabid Dog	215	205	p230
Labyrinth Ritekeeper	241	190	p253

Strong	HP	Echoes	Page
Kidnapper	591	570	p276
Watcher Chieftain (Club & Lantern)	845	770	p294
Merciless Watcher (Scattergun, Club & Lantern)	845	770	p297

Boss	HP	Echoes	Page
Keeper of the Old Lords	3867	3471	p378

Step 01

The Gravekeeper Scorpions in this room have attacks that inflict a large amount of Rapid Poison buildup, so you should always try to fight them one at a time, and don't hesitate to retreat if the buildup starts to get too high.

Step 02

There are a large number of oil urns covering half of the middle section of this room. On the floor above, A Labyrinth Watcher likes to throw Molotov Cocktails down at you once you're in its sights. The safest thing to do here is to either shoot some of the urns yourself to blow them up and get rid of the threat, or stick to the other side of the room, where there are no urns.

Step 03

Be extremely careful as you enter this tunnel, because there's a Gel on the ceiling hidden amongst the vines hanging down, and it will drop straight onto you with a grab attack if you try to walk beneath it. Train your camera up to the vines and try to locate the Gel before entering the tunnel – use a ranged attack to knock it down. Gels often inhabit places such as this, so any time you're about to enter one, always check the ceiling first. [→☐ 01]

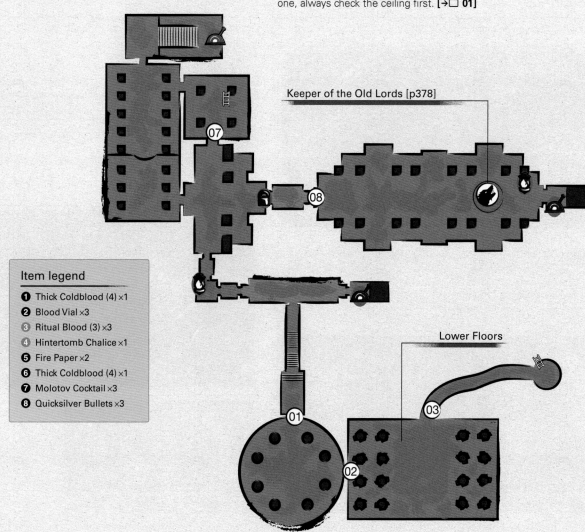

Keeper of the Old Lords [p378]

Lower Floors

Item legend

1. Thick Coldblood (4) ×1
2. Blood Vial ×3
3. Ritual Blood (3) ×3
4. Hintertomb Chalice ×1
5. Fire Paper ×2
6. Thick Coldblood (4) ×1
7. Molotov Cocktail ×3
8. Quicksilver Bullets ×3

Step 04

There are some very important Ritual Blood (3) items to be found in the chest in this room. Before you try to get them, it's worth going around the room and killing all of the dormant Labyrinth Watchers, so that they don't ambush you.

Step 05

The large central drawbridge in this room can be activated by operating the device at the top of the series of ladders just to the right when you enter. Lowering it will give you a path back to the upper part of the circular room near the start of the Level. [→□ 02]

Step 06

The Hintertomb Chalice can be found inside a coffin in this room, but to reach it you'll need to fight your way past a large amount of enemies. As soon as you open the door, Labyrinth Watchers, Labyrinth Rats and Rabid Dogs will start approaching, so stick near the doorway and try to fight them as they funnel through it. If you see a decently-sized group forming, you may want to use a Molotov Cocktail to severely weaken them. The Watcher Chieftain near the loot coffin will also move towards the door when you open it – try to kill as many of the other enemies as you can before he gets close. If there are quite a few enemies still around when you see him, drop back down to the area below to create some more space and take out the enemies as they try to follow you.

Step 07

There are two Labyrinth Ritekeepers near the top of the ladder in this room, along with a Kidnapper that patrols between them. Trying to fight the Kidnapper while evading the slow-moving projectiles from the Ritekeepers can be very difficult. It's best to kill the Ritekeeper closest to the top of the ladder straight away, and then wait for the Kidnapper to spot you and drop back down, so that he follows. Kill the Kidnapper as soon as he drops down, and then climb back up and finish off the other Ritekeeper.

Step 08

The Keeper of the Old Lords uses a lot of fire-based attacks, so it can be very beneficial to equip Attire with high fire defense before facing him. You can also make use of the pillars in the room to help shield you from his attacks. Upon defeating him you'll automatically receive the Central Pthumeru Root Chalice, which will allow you to create randomly generated Central Pthumerian Dungeons.

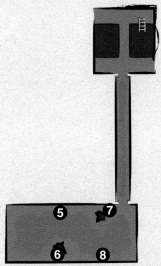

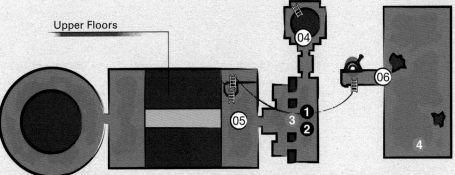

Upper Floors

Enemies

Regular	HP	Echoes	Page
Labyrinth Watcher (Cleaver & Lantern)	302	171	p250
Labyrinth Watcher (Cleaver)	192	171	p250
Labyrinth Watcher (Dagger)	192	171	p250
Labyrinth Watcher (Twin Axes)	302	171	p251
Labyrinth Watcher (Halberd)	302	171	p251
Evil Labyrinth Spirit	288	286	p298
Labyrinth Ritekeeper	246	199	p253

Strong	HP	Echoes	Page
Bell Ringer	329	291	p287
Watcher Chieftain (Club & Lantern)	865	806	p294
Merciless Watcher (Scattergun, Club & Lantern)	865	806	p297
Kidnapper	605	597	p286

Boss	HP	Echoes	Page
Pthumerian Descendant	3437	4147	p382

Pthumerian Descendant [p382]

Upper Floors

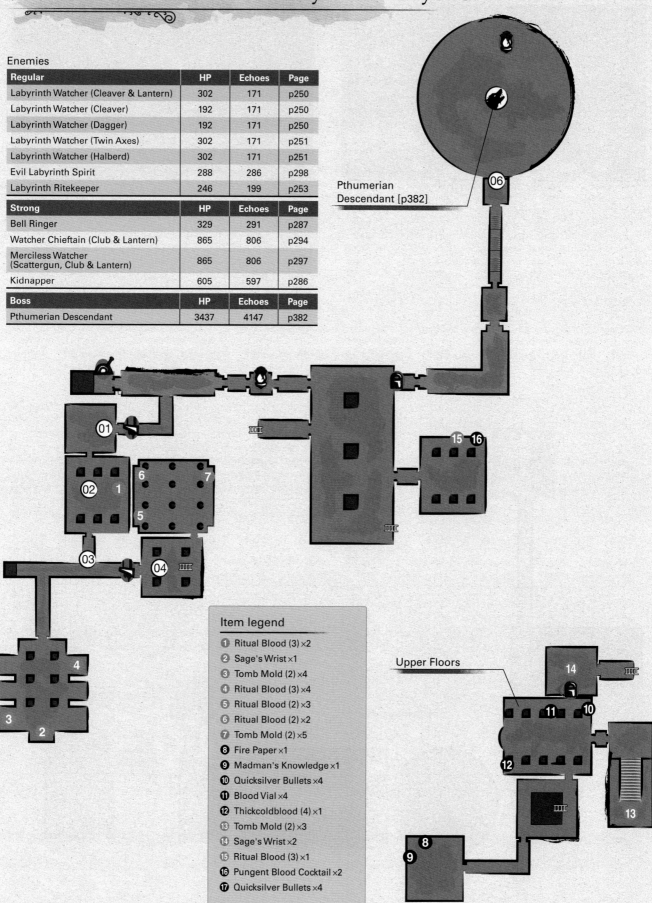

Item legend

1. Ritual Blood (3) ×2
2. Sage's Wrist ×1
3. Tomb Mold (2) ×4
4. Ritual Blood (3) ×4
5. Ritual Blood (2) ×3
6. Ritual Blood (2) ×2
7. Tomb Mold (2) ×5
8. Fire Paper ×1
9. Madman's Knowledge ×1
10. Quicksilver Bullets ×4
11. Blood Vial ×4
12. Thickcoldblood (4) ×1
13. Tomb Mold (2) ×3
14. Sage's Wrist ×2
15. Ritual Blood (3) ×1
16. Pungent Blood Cocktail ×2
17. Quicksilver Bullets ×4

Step 01

The Labyrinth Watcher with the lantern that patrols the middle of this room will shake its lantern and awaken all of the other enemies in the room if it spots you. Try and hide to the side of the doorway until it has its back to you, and then quickly run up and kill it. [→☐ 01]

Step 02

A Watcher Chieftain is standing guard near a chest in the middle of this room, but if you walk slowly around to the left as soon as you enter you can get behind him for an easy charged R2.

Step 03

Come to a stop when you reach the fork in this corridor, because giant boulders are being periodically dropped from a hole in the ceiling along the path to the left, after which they'll roll down the length of the corridor to a hole in the floor at the opposite end. It's advised that you follow the path around to the right first, because the room it leads to is a dead end. Wait for a boulder to roll past, and then follow it down to the room. When you come back from that room, wait for a boulder to drop in the hole, and then quickly run up to the entrance to the corridor and wait there until another boulder passes before continuing.

Step 04

Another lucrative room in terms of Holy Chalice rite materials can be found beyond the door on the bottom part of this room, so make sure you clear it out before going up the ladder.

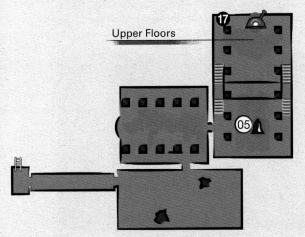

Step 05

The Labyrinth Watchers that have been spawned by the Bell Ringer in this room will often detect you before you can enter, so try to kill them as they funnel through the doorway. Once the initial group has been killed, quickly run straight ahead and kill the patrolling Bell Ringer. A Merciless Watcher with a gun is standing guard near the lever in this room, so after going down the stairs towards it, use the pillars for cover, and once it's close enough, kill it when it begins reloading. [→☐ 02]

Step 06

The Pthumerian Descendant is extremely aggressive and agile, and its attacks can be very difficult to interrupt. It's safest to use a series of quicksteps to try and evade its combos, and then get a couple of hits in during the recovery. For defeating it you will automatically receive the Lower Pthumeru Chalice, which will allow you explore even deeper parts of the Pthumeru Labyrinth. [→☐ 03/04]

4

Hintertomb

Before crafting the Hintertomb, you should go to Hemwick Charnel Lane to level up and collect Twin Bloodstone Shards for your main weapon. You can also find the Bloodshot Eyeballs there that are a requirement in this dungeon's Chalice Ritual. Defeating the Witch of Hemwick boss will unlock Bloodshot Eyeballs for purchase at the Insight shop in the Hunter's Dream. The major difference between Hintertomb and Pthumerian labyrinths is that many enemies encountered in the Hintertombs will attack with poison, made visible by a purple could around their attacking weapon.

| Recommended Player Level **40+** | Weapon Upgrade **+6** |

Layer 1

Enemies

Regular	HP	Echoes	Page
Labyrinth Watcher (Dagger)	178	155	p250
Labyrinth Watcher (Cleaver)	178	155	p250
Labyrinth Watcher (Halberd)	281	155	p251
Labyrinth Watcher (Twin Axes)	281	155	p251
Watcher's Gravedigger (Pickaxe)	357	223	p254
Watcher's Gravedigger (Rifle, Hook & Lantern)	332	197	p254
Rabid Dog	204	195	p230

Strong	HP	Echoes	Page
Eye Collector	281	181	p277
Bell Ringer	306	264	p287
Evil Labyrinth Spirit	268	260	p298
Labyrinth Madman (Twin Sickles)	537	571	p299

Boss	HP	Echoes	Page
Maneater Boar	3837	2877	p270

Ritual Info

Chalice	Hintertomb Chalice
Ritual Materials	Ritual Blood (2) ×3, Bloodshot Eyeball ×3
Blood Echoes	1800
Floor Depth	2

Step 02

An Eye Collector will either rush down to attack you if you did not draw the enemies through the tunnel at Step 01, or ambush you with a grab when you enter this room – try to stick close to the wall on the left as you enter and move slowly. This should cause her to miss, and you can kill her before she recovers. The only other enemies in the room are some Labyrinth Watchers, so take them out as you come to them on your way to the lever at the far end.

Step 03

A group of enemies that have been summoned by a Bell Ringer are gathered just beyond the door here, so before opening it, strike the door with your weapon to kill the enemies on the other side. Once you've opened the door, quickly run up to the staircase on the right and use it to reach the Bell Ringer on the ledge in the middle of the room. The other staircase in this room has been blocked off at the top by a cart, so continue up the one on the right and kill the Watcher's Gravedigger at the top. [→☐ 02]

Step 01

There are some oil urns standing near a cage in the middle of the open area here, and some Labyrinth Watchers on the floor above that will throw Molotov Cocktails down as you exit the tunnel. To avoid the risk of getting blown up as you pass by, shoot the oil urns with a gun from a safe distance. The loud noise this causes will usually make some of the other enemies from the floor above drop down to investigate, so make sure you're ready to take them on. [→☐ 01]

A Watcher's Gravedigger armed with a gun will start firing at you from the top of the stairs to the right as soon as you enter this room, so quickly run forward and use the statues at the bottom of the stairs for cover. Wait for it to reload, and then run up the stairs using the statue at the top for cover, and kill the Gravedigger while it's reloading. [→☐ 03]

Step 05

While you would normally be thankful for the cover that can come from pillars in a boss room, the Maneater Boar here can break through those pillars with its charge attack, so never assume you're safe behind them. Upon defeating the boss you'll receive a random Blood Gem. [→☐ 04]

Maneater Boar [p270]

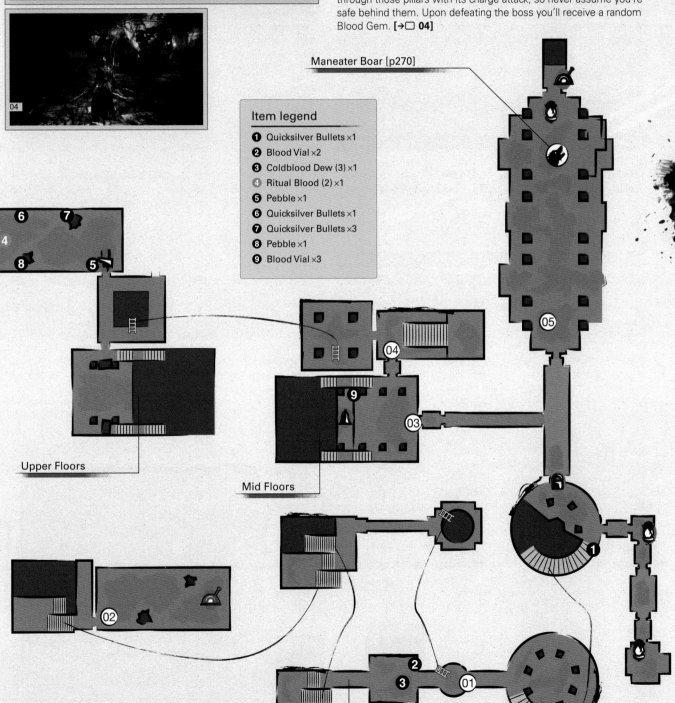

Item legend

❶ Quicksilver Bullets ×1
❷ Blood Vial ×2
❸ Coldblood Dew (3) ×1
❹ Ritual Blood (2) ×1
❺ Pebble ×1
❻ Quicksilver Bullets ×1
❼ Quicksilver Bullets ×3
❽ Pebble ×1
❾ Blood Vial ×3

Upper Floors

Mid Floors

Lower Floors

Hintertomb – Layer 2

Enemies

Regular	HP	Echoes	Page
Labyrinth Watcher (Dagger)	187	163	p250
Labyrinth Watcher (Cleaver)	187	163	p250
Labyrinth Watcher (Twin Axes)	295	163	p251
Labyrinth Watcher (Cleaver & Lantern)	295	163	p250
Labyrinth Watcher (Halberd)	295	163	p251
Watcher's Gravedigger (Hook & Lantern)	375	234	p254
Watcher's Gravedigger (Rifle, Hook & Lantern)	349	207	p254
Watcher's Gravedigger (Pickaxe)	375	234	p254
Rabid Dog	215	205	p230
Snake Ball	295	71	p241
Labyrinth Rat	187	129	p233
Wandering Nightmare	72	34	p671
Rotted Corpse	241	202	p233
Gel	160	302	p253

Strong	HP	Echoes	Page
Undead Giant (Hatchet & Cannon)	1450	1086	p301
Labyrinth Madman (Sickle)	563	599	p300
Labyrinth Madman (Twin Sickles)	563	599	p299
Evil Labyrinth Spirit	282	273	p298
Bloodlicker	617	514	p280
Bell Ringer	321	278	p287

Boss	HP	Echoes	Page
Undead Giant (Hatchet & Cannon)	4834	3471	p301

Step 01

There's a Bell Ringer in the room on the mid level ledge down to your right. Funnel any Labyrinth Watchers she may have summoned through the entrance to this room to kill them one by one before entering. Then, turn right and head down the stairs until you reach the ledge in the middle of the room, where you should find the Bell Ringer.

Step 02

Entering this room from the path at the top will put you in a much better position than from the door at the bottom of the stairs, because there's a Watcher's Gravedigger with a gun standing at the top of them. By using the top path you can kill the enemy near to the Gravedigger, and still be able to sneak up behind it and use a charged R2. Another Gravedigger, this time armed with a pickaxe, is at the bottom of the stairs. Once it spots you, wait for it to reach the top of the stairs and fight it there.

Step 03

The Labyrinth Madman guarding the coffin in this room is extremely fast and aggressive, so you should make sure to take out the Rabid Dog in the room first. Try using the trees to block the Madman's dashes, and attack him whenever you see an opening.

Step 04

If you quietly walk around to the right after entering this room you'll be able to sneak up behind the Watcher's Gravedigger standing in the middle and land a charged R2 on it. When you come back into this room after pulling the lever to open the gate later, a Bloodlicker may have taken up residence where the Gravedigger was previously standing to feed off his corpse.

Step 05

A toxic liquid that inflicts Slow Poison and slows your movement coats the floor of this corridor, so try to run through it as quickly as possible while avoiding the poison throwing knives coming from the Labyrinth Watcher near the opposite end. Getting hit by even one of those knives while in the poisonous liquid will be enough to poison you.

Step 06

The middle of the raised motif on the floor just inside this room is actually a pressure plate that, when stepped on, will cause a group of four Labyrinth Watchers to appear around you. Either avoid stepping on it or be ready for the enemies when they appear.

Step 07

The floor of this large cavern primarily consists of a poisonous swamp, but there are some patches of dry land scattered about, so try to run between them and stay out of the swamp as much as possible. A lone Undead Giant can be seen near the center of the room and the cannon it's armed with is extremely dangerous; if you intend to fight this enemy, it's recommended that you drop down off the walkway near the entrance and approach it from behind, so that you can get close without it detecting you.

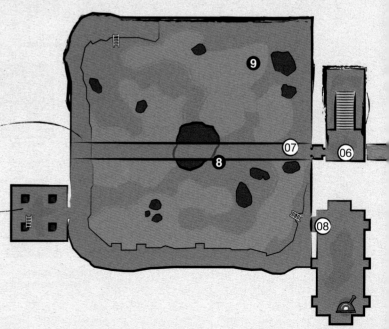

Step 08

A very large group of Labyrinth Rats swarm near the entrance to this room, and just on the other side of them is a Wandering Nightmare; try to lure some of the rats out of the room and kill them there, so that you have a clearer path to the Wandering Nightmare. Even once the rats are dead you'll need to be very quick in killing it, because shortly after you enter the room a Labyrinth Madman will start running towards you, and they can close the distance very quickly. If you need to create some space when you're ready to fight it, run around some of the broken cages in the room.

Step 09

The group of oil urns in the middle of the room here should give you a hint that if you were to go out there, a Labyrinth Watcher on the floor above would start to throw Molotov Cocktails down at you. There's also a very large group of enemies in the next part of the room and if you shoot the urns, the sound of the explosion will lure a lot of them towards you, which is actually beneficial. The Labyrinth Rats will be the first ones to reach you, so take those out as they round the corner, and then wait for the Watcher's Gravediggers and do the same. Now when you enter the room you'll be able to concentrate on the Gels and Rotted Corpses in the water.

Step 10

The Undead Giant here is a slightly stronger version of the one from the large cavern earlier, and as such your main goal should be to stay close enough so that it doesn't use its cannon. Once you defeat it you will get the Hintertomb Root Chalice, which lets you create randomly generated Hintertomb Dungeons.

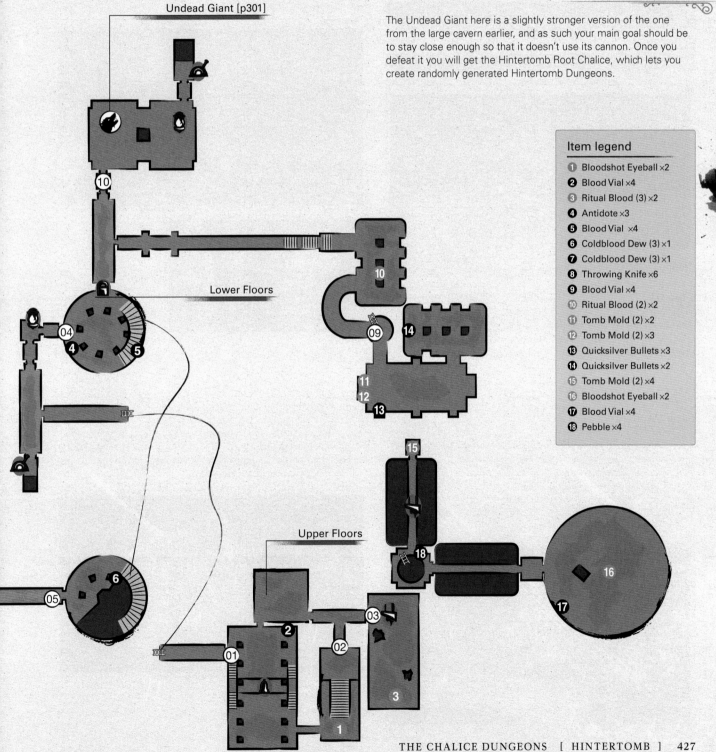

Undead Giant [p301]

Lower Floors

Upper Floors

4

Item legend

1. Bloodshot Eyeball ×2
2. Blood Vial ×4
3. Ritual Blood (3) ×2
4. Antidote ×3
5. Blood Vial ×4
6. Coldblood Dew (3) ×1
7. Coldblood Dew (3) ×1
8. Throwing Knife ×6
9. Blood Vial ×4
10. Ritual Blood (2) ×2
11. Tomb Mold (2) ×2
12. Tomb Mold (2) ×3
13. Quicksilver Bullets ×3
14. Quicksilver Bullets ×2
15. Tomb Mold (2) ×4
16. Bloodshot Eyeball ×2
17. Blood Vial ×4
18. Pebble ×4

Enemies

Regular	HP	Echoes	Page
Labyrinth Watcher (Twin Axes)	302	171	p251
Labyrinth Watcher (Cleaver)	192	171	p250
Watcher's Gravedigger (Pickaxe)	383	245	p254
Watcher's Gravedigger (Hook & Lantern)	383	245	p254
Watcher's Gravedigger (Rifle, Hook & Lantern)	357	217	p254
Wandering Nightmare	73	36	p671

Strong	HP	Echoes	Page
Labyrinth Madman (Twin Sickles)	577	628	p299
Bell Ringer	329	291	p287

Boss	HP	Echoes	Page
Blood-starved Beast	4536	3565	p330

01

Step 01

After killing the group of Labyrinth Watchers by taking them out one at a time through the narrow entryway to this room, run straight ahead to kill the patrolling Bell Ringer. There's also a second Bell Ringer at the top of the stairs in this room, so kill any Labyrinth Watchers that are in your way, and then run up and kill her to prevent more of them from spawning. [→ □ 01]

Step 02

If you sneak around to the left-hand side of this room after entering it you can get around to the back of the Labyrinth Madman and Watcher's Gravedigger that are standing guard by the coffin at the back of the room. Once you're close enough, use a charged R2 in the back of the Madman, since he's the greatest threat. If he survives, follow up with a Visceral Attack and then take out the Gravedigger. [→ □ 02]

02

Step 03

When you first enter this room a Watcher's Gravedigger will start firing at you from the top of the stairs, and while it may be tempting to run up there and attack it, a more cautious approach is called for. Out of sight at the top of the stairs is a Labyrinth Madman, and he'll start running down the stairs as soon as you step on to them. Wait for the Gravedigger to reload, and then step onto the stairs so that the Madman starts running at you – now lure him back out of the room and fight him there, so that you don't have to worry about the Gravedigger. [→ □ 03/04]

03

04

Step 04

As you approach the junction here you'll begin to hear the sounds of the giant boulders crashing down and rolling along the corridor. There is nothing in the room to the left at the junction, so wait for a boulder to roll past, and then follow along behind it to the right to reach the room at the end. There are four Watcher's Gravediggers armed with guns in that room, but if you make your way around the outside of it, you can use the pillars for cover while you systematically take out the enemies. [→ □ 05]

05

Step 05

In addition to the poison that the Blood-starved Beast exudes towards the latter part of the battle, you'll also have to contend with the fact that a large portion of the middle of the room is covered in a poisonous liquid. Try to keep the fight on the outer edges of the room where the ground is solid, to reduce the risk of getting poisoned. Upon defeating the boss you'll get the Lower Hintertomb Chalice that lets you explore new depths within the Hintertomb section of the labyrinth. [→ ☐ 06]

Blood-starved Beast [p330]

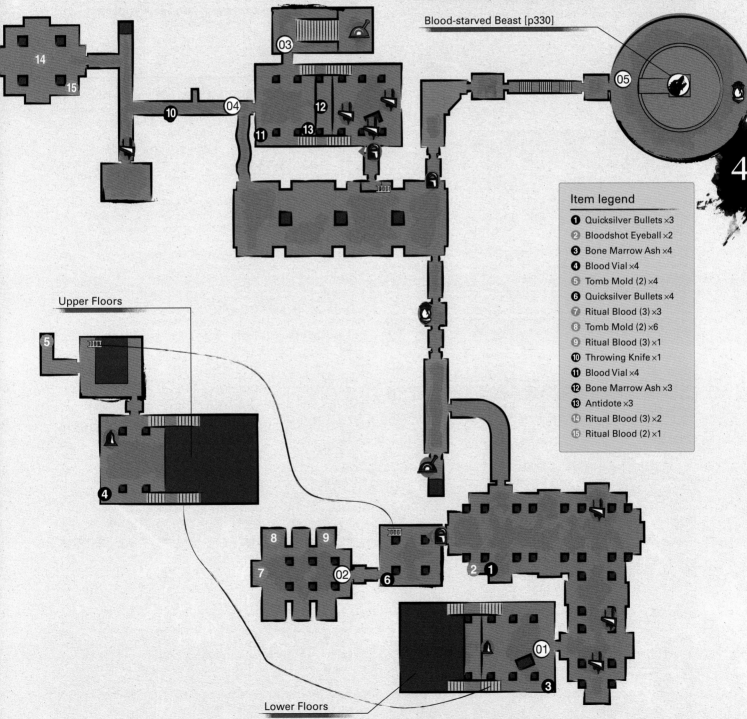

Upper Floors

Lower Floors

Item legend

1. Quicksilver Bullets ×3
2. Bloodshot Eyeball ×2
3. Bone Marrow Ash ×4
4. Blood Vial ×4
5. Tomb Mold (2) ×4
6. Quicksilver Bullets ×4
7. Ritual Blood (3) ×3
8. Tomb Mold (2) ×6
9. Ritual Blood (3) ×1
10. Throwing Knife ×1
11. Blood Vial ×4
12. Bone Marrow Ash ×3
13. Antidote ×3
14. Ritual Blood (3) ×2
15. Ritual Blood (2) ×1

4

Lower Hintertomb

It's recommended to tackle this labyrinth before the Lower Pthumerian Labyrinth, in order to collect the Short Ritual Root Chalice. With this, you can access the online matchmaking functions for the Chalice Dungeons from the Makeshift Altar in the Hunter's Dream. Working with an online co-op team for Depth 4 and 5 dungeons is strongly recommended. You should have more than enough of the required Ritual Blood (3) and Bloodshot Eyeballs for the Chalice Ritual from the previous dungeon. Depth 3 enemies are significantly stronger, so wait until you're at least at level 70 or higher, with your main weapon up to +8. Finally, as a Hintertomb dungeon, remember that many enemies will attack with poison, so carry a full stock of Antidotes.

Recommended	Player Level **70+**	Weapon Upgrade **+8**

Layer 1

Enemies

Regular	HP	Echoes	Page
Labyrinth Rat	472	399	p233
Wandering Nightmare	180	105	p671
Labyrinth Watcher (Cleaver)	472	505	p250
Labyrinth Watcher (Dagger)	472	505	p250
Labyrinth Watcher (Cleaver & Lantern)	744	505	p250
Labyrinth Watcher (Halberd)	744	505	p251
Labyrinth Watcher (Twin Axes)	744	505	p251
Watcher's Gravedigger (Hook & Lantern)	943	723	p254
Watcher's Gravedigger (Rifle, Hook & Lantern)	878	640	p254
Nightmare Apostle	606	429	p247

Strong	HP	Echoes	Page
Labyrinth Madman (Corpse)	1419	1852	p300
Labyrinth Madman (Sickle)	1419	1852	p300
Bloodlicker	1553	1589	p280

Boss	HP	Echoes	Page
Brainsucker	2366	8050	p273

Step 01

Guarding the coffin at the top of the stairs is a Watcher's Gravedigger (Rifle, Hook & Lantern) and a Labyrinth Madman (Corpse). As you approach the doorway to this room, the Gravedigger will see you and start to approach; peek out from the side of the doorway at **Position A** to lure him further down until he will descend no more, and then stay hidden so that he turns around and starts to go back up. Quickly sprint up the stairs after him and try to kill him as quickly as possible, before the Madman closes in. By taking the Gravedigger out first you will have the freedom to move around the room when trying to evade the Madman's attacks.

Step 02

The low visibility in this room hides a number of dangers. A Labyrinth Watcher patrols around the room, and if he spots you he will ring his lantern to attract nearby Labyrinth Watchers from the corridor above, if you've not already killed them. Two of those enemies can throw Molotovs, and since this room has a number of explosive

Ritual Info

Chalice	Lower Hintertomb Chalice
Ritual Materials	Ritual Blood (3) ×6, Bloodshot Eyeball ×6
Blood Echoes	3200
Floor Depth	3

oil jars, that can be very dangerous. Try to stay out of the patrolling Watcher's line of sight by using the cave wall for cover, and then when he has his back to you, close in and kill him before he can ring the lantern. Be careful when going for the item under the arch on the right as you enter, because there is Gel hanging above it.

Step 03

Watch the floors carefully in this area in front of the exit gate, as there are three floor switch traps that can summon Labyrinth Watchers. There are a few Labyrinth Watchers sleeping on the job that you can ambush here, too and it's wise to clear them all out before going for the items, so that they don't get the drop on you.

Step 04

At the top of the ladder in this room are two Gravediggers with guns waiting to ambush you, so instead of climbing straight up there, go to **Position B** just to the left of the first pillar in the room. From this position you should be able to see one of them standing near the top of the ladder; use a Pistol or other ranged attack to hit him, causing him to climb down the ladder, and during that time you can attack him freely. Once the first one is down, climb up the ladder and quickly take out the remaining one.

Step 05

After opening the door to the floor lever room, retreat back into the previous room, because two Labyrinth Watchers will come running at you straight away and if you fight them at the doorway you'll also come under fire from a Gravedigger in the middle of the room ahead. Run into the room and take out the Gravedigger once the first two enemies have been killed, and then hug the wall down the stairs from **Position C**, so you can sneak around behind the Labyrinth Madman that is guarding the lever and use a charged attack in his back.

Step 06

There's a Labyrinth Watcher patrolling near the entrance of this room, so try and lure him towards you once you've opened the door, so that you don't alert the Labyrinth Madman standing at the back of the room. After taking the watcher out, sneak along the right-hand side of the room to get behind the Madman and use a charged attack from behind. Make sure to search all of the chests in this room once the enemies have been killed, because they contain a number of Holy Chalice rite materials.

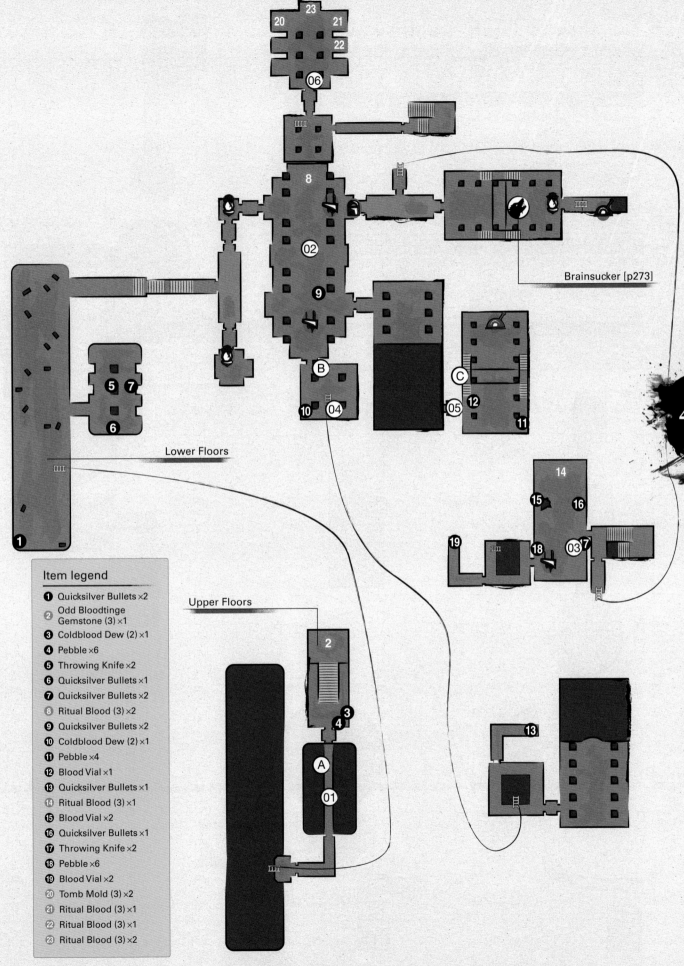

Brainsucker [p273]

Lower Floors

Upper Floors

Item legend

1. Quicksilver Bullets ×2
2. Odd Bloodtinge Gemstone (3) ×1
3. Coldblood Dew (2) ×1
4. Pebble ×6
5. Throwing Knife ×2
6. Quicksilver Bullets ×1
7. Quicksilver Bullets ×2
8. Ritual Blood (3) ×2
9. Quicksilver Bullets ×2
10. Coldblood Dew (2) ×1
11. Pebble ×4
12. Blood Vial ×1
13. Quicksilver Bullets ×1
14. Ritual Blood (3) ×1
15. Blood Vial ×2
16. Quicksilver Bullets ×1
17. Throwing Knife ×2
18. Pebble ×6
19. Blood Vial ×2
20. Tomb Mold (3) ×2
21. Ritual Blood (3) ×1
22. Ritual Blood (3) ×1
23. Ritual Blood (3) ×2

Lower Hintertomb – Layer 2

Enemies

Regular	HP	Echoes	Page
Labyrinth Watcher (Bare Hands)	423	530	p251
Labyrinth Watcher (Dagger)	495	530	p250
Labyrinth Watcher (Cleaver & Lantern)	781	530	p250
Labyrinth Watcher (Cleaver)	495	530	p250
Labyrinth Watcher (Twin Axes)	781	530	p251
Watcher's Gravedigger (Pickaxe)	990	759	p254
Watcher's Gravedigger (Hook & Lantern)	990	759	p254
Rotted Corpse	636	656	p233

Strong	HP	Echoes	Page
Undead Giant (Hatchet & Cannon)	3833	3526	p301
Eye Collector	781	617	p277
Labyrinth Madman (Twin Sickles)	1490	1945	p299
Bloodlicker	1631	1668	p280

Boss	HP	Echoes	Page
Forgotten Madman	4880	5637	p384
Madman's Escort	1828	5637	p384

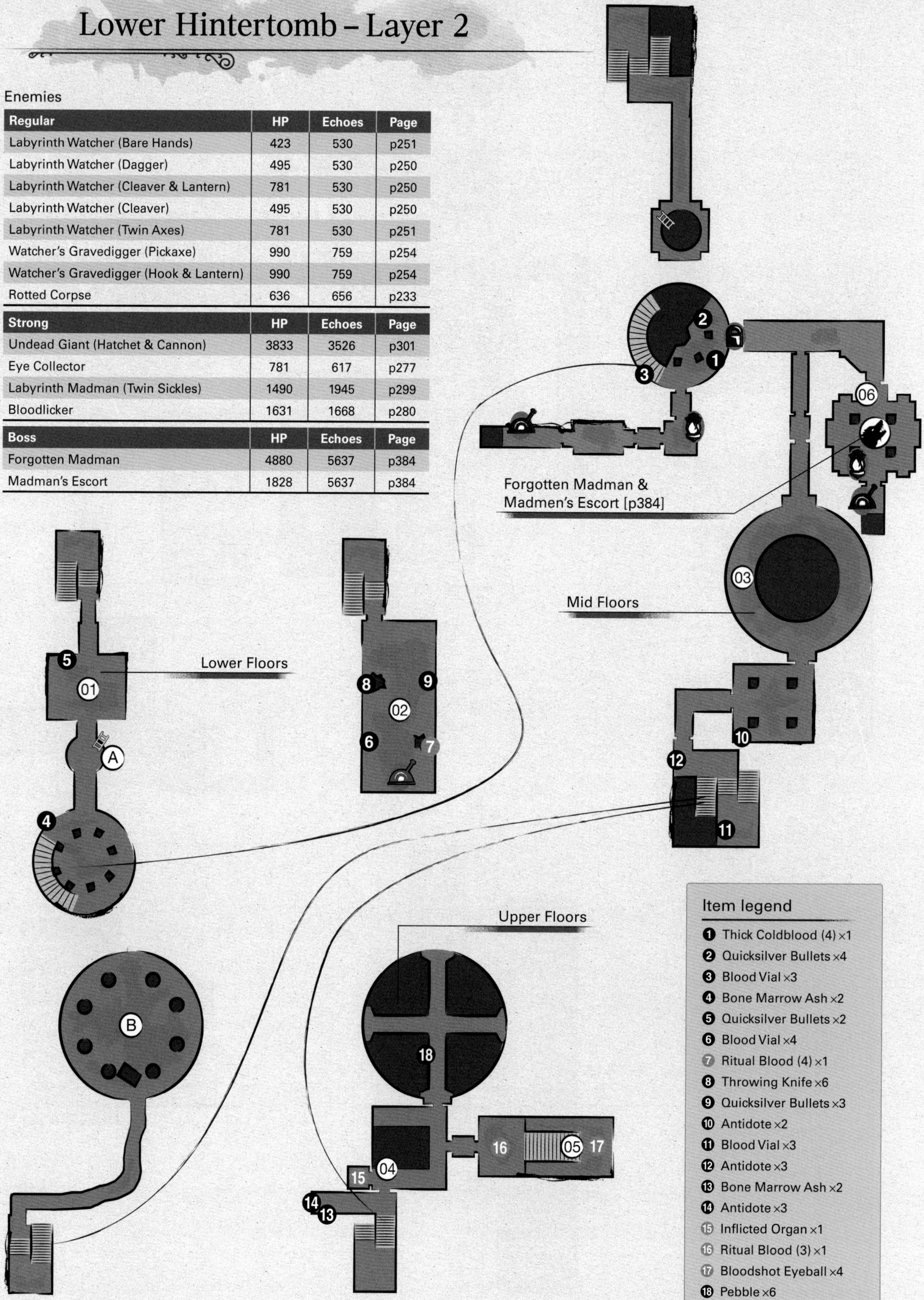

Forgotten Madman &
Madmen's Escort [p384]

Mid Floors

Lower Floors

Upper Floors

Item legend

1. Thick Coldblood (4) ×1
2. Quicksilver Bullets ×4
3. Blood Vial ×3
4. Bone Marrow Ash ×2
5. Quicksilver Bullets ×2
6. Blood Vial ×4
7. Ritual Blood (4) ×1
8. Throwing Knife ×6
9. Quicksilver Bullets ×3
10. Antidote ×2
11. Blood Vial ×3
12. Antidote ×3
13. Bone Marrow Ash ×2
14. Antidote ×3
15. Inflicted Organ ×1
16. Ritual Blood (3) ×1
17. Bloodshot Eyeball ×4
18. Pebble ×6

Step 01

There's a large group of Labyrinth Watchers in this room, so if you want to fight them, it's best to lure them back into the tunnel so that you can bunch them up reduce the risk of getting surrounded. Keeping the fight near the start of the room will also ensure that you don't alert the Eye Collector on the floor above, because if you do she'll come running down and join in. Once all of the Labyrinth Watchers have been killed, take out the Gravedigger that's standing on the right just as you enter the room. You can, if you wish, bypass this group of enemies entirely by climbing up the ladder at **Position A** and taking the hallway on the floor above where only the Eye Collector blocks your path. [→☐ 01]

Step 02

Unless you use a Blue Elixir there's no way to sneak around behind the Labyrinth Madman that's guarding the lever in this room, so the best method to deal with him is to use the trees to block his initial rush, and then circle around it and hit him when his attacks miss.

Step 03

If you wish, you can avoid fighting the Undead Giant (Cannon) at **Position B**, as Blood Echoes are all you gain from killing him and the paths leading out of both floors of this room eventually lead to the same place. As long as you walk through this area you can make it safely past him to the door on the other side, but any attempt at running will wake him from his slumber. If you decide to take him on, then you can either wear him down from this walkway using ranged options, or drop down and fight him face-to-face; even though he'll turn around when you hit the ground, it's still worth dropping down behind him to start the fight so that you have time to close in on him. Once the fight starts, lure him to one of the pillars and stand a safe distance behind it, so that his attacks miss and you can attack during their recovery. [→☐ 02]

Step 04

As soon as you enter this room you'll see a blue light emanating from behind a gate on the left that's being used to illuminate a tempting chest. Before opening the gate and going for the contents, however, look closely into the room to spot the Labyrinth Watcher hiding inside; if your weapon has good range, attack him through the gate so to kill him before opening it.

Step 05

A Labyrinth Madman stands guard over a coffin chest at the bottom of the stairs in this room, and he'll start rushing towards you as soon as you get near the top of those stairs. By standing to the side of the stairs, however, you can often get him to drop back down once he gets near the top, and if you're quick you can use a plunging attack before he runs away. If he reaches the top of the stairs, you can just roll across from the ledge you're on to the stairs and he'll usually drop down when he tries to follow you. [→☐ 03/04]

Step 06

The Forgotten Madman and his Madman's Escort reward you with the Lower Hintertomb Root Chalice and a single Ritual Blood (3) upon slaughtering them. You'll battle the Forgotten Madman first, and then the Madman's Escort will join in after a short period of time, so it's imperative that you do as much damage as possible to the Forgotten Madman before the Escort appears. Try to interrupt his attacks to stagger him, so that you can follow up with the attack of your choice. Once the Escort appears, bait him into using his Flamesprayer, and then lure the Forgotten Madman away so that you can fight him one-on-one. If you have a well-upgraded gun you can also use that to finish off the weakened enemy in relative safely, especially with some Bone Marrow Ash.

Item legend

1. Madman's Knowledge ×1
2. Bone Marrow Ash ×4
3. Blood Vial ×3
4. Quicksilver Bullets ×3
5. Bloodshot Eyeball ×2
6. Bone Marrow Ash ×4
7. Odd Bloodtinge Gemstone (3) ×1
8. Antidote ×4
9. Inflicted Organ ×2
10. Ritual Blood (4) ×1
11. Blood Vial ×4
12. Thick Coldblood (6) ×1
13. Quicksilver Bullets ×2
14. Blood Vial ×3
15. Thick Coldblood (5) ×1
16. Quicksilver Bullets ×4
17. Thick Coldblood (6) ×1
18. Antidote ×2
19. Ritual Blood (4) ×2
20. Quicksilver Bullets ×5

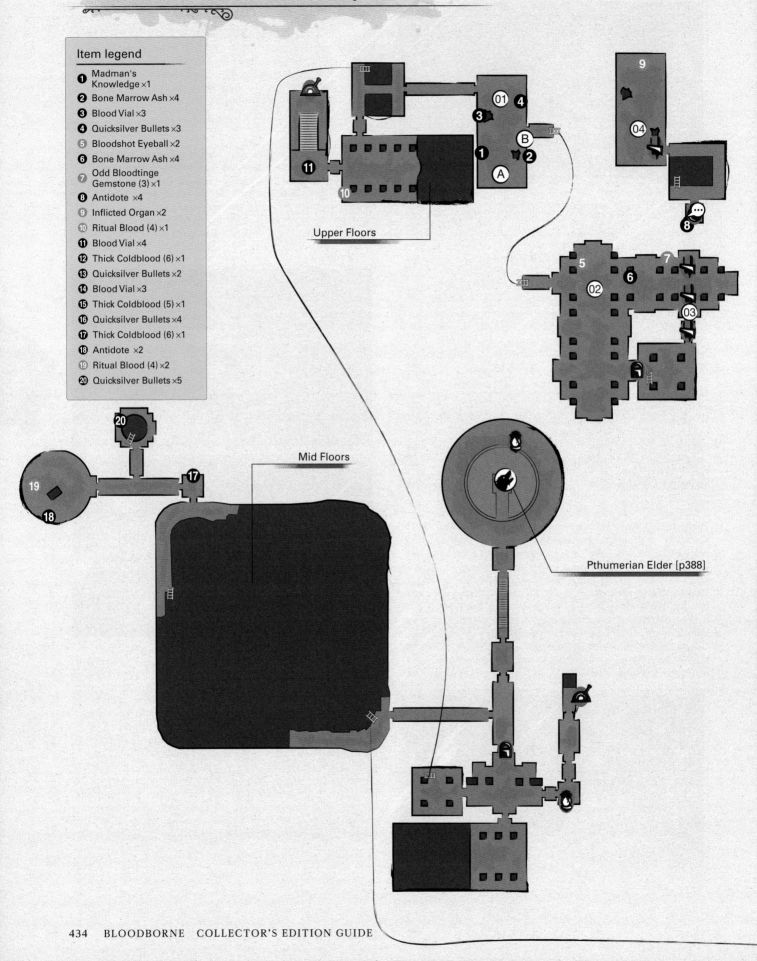

Upper Floors

Mid Floors

Pthumerian Elder [p388]

Enemies

Regular	HP	Echoes	Page
Labyrinth Watcher (Cleaver)	507	555	p250
Labyrinth Watcher (Dagger)	507	555	p250
Labyrinth Watcher (Twin Axes)	800	555	p251
Labyrinth Watcher (Halberd)	800	555	p251
Watcher's Gravedigger (Hook & Lantern)	1014	795	p254
Watcher's Gravedigger (Pickaxe)	1014	795	p254
Watcher's Gravedigger (Rifle, Hook & Lantern)	944	704	p254
Wandering Nightmare	194	116	p671
Nightmare Apostle	651	472	p247
Labyrinth Rat	507	439	p233

Strong	HP	Echoes	Page
Undead Giant (Hatchet & Cannon)	3924	3694	p301
Labyrinth Madman (Sickle)	1525	2038	p300
Labyrinth Madman (Twin Sickles)	1525	2038	p299
Bloodlicker	1669	1748	p280

Boss	HP	Echoes	Page
Pthumerian Elder	9815	13460	p388

Step 01

There's a Labyrinth Watcher manning a cannon at **Position A** on the other side of this room, so you'll need to be extremely careful. Take cover behind the tree just to the right as you enter the room, and as soon as you see a shot impact that tree, run up to the left-hand side of the next tree at **Position B**, which will put you out of the cannon's line of fire. From there you can simply flank around behind the cannon and kill the Labyrinth Watcher.

Step 02

A large group of Labyrinth Watchers stands in front of you when you enter this room, with a great many more scattered around the rest of the room, so rushing straight in could prove costly. Many of the enemies in this room are also armed with poisonous weapons, so getting hit brings with it even greater dangers than normal. Try to lure the enemies in the initial group towards you one at a time, either by using Pebbles or slowly walking forward until one spots you.

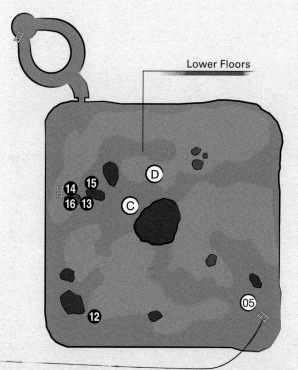

Lower Floors

Once they're down, work your way around the room taking out the enemies as you come to them; since most of the Gravediggers in the room are hard at work, you can usually sneak up behind them.

Step 03

The floor switch immediately in front of the doorway that activates the guillotine trap can be avoided with a well-timed running jump. Otherwise, simply wait for it the blade to fall then run past as it. In the room beyond the trap there's a Gravedigger standing on the floor above as soon as you enter; use a ranged attack on him so that he drops down and you can fight him before going up the ladder, where you'll find a second one waiting for you. [→☐ **01**]

01

Step 04

The treasure room is full of poisonous Nightmare Apostles, most of which are in the first half of the room as you enter. Towards the back half of the room, there's a Labyrinth Madman with two more Nightmare Apostles hanging from the ceiling above him. Aim to clear out all of the patrolling Apostles before engaging the Madman by luring them back towards the entrance one at a time. Be careful when doing this, however, as there is a pressure plate on the floor just in front of the door that will cause flaming arrows to fire towards the doorway. Once they've all been defeated, go far enough into the room to get the attention of the Madman and lure him back before fighting him, so that the two remaining Apostles hanging from the ceiling do not get drawn into the fray. Before entering this room, make sure to visit the Blood Echoes shop nearby to purchase the Sinister Hintertomb Root Chalice for 10000 Blood Echoes.

Step 05

There are a lot of enemies in the swamp area, but the primary threats are the two cannon-wielding Undead Giants at **Positions C** and **D**. Both of these enemies have an excellent field of view over the area, and unless you use a Blue Elixir, it will be impossible to reach the ladder on the other side of the room without at least one of them seeing you. Going for that ladder is worthwhile though, because the room you can reach from the top of it contains a number of useful items. If you follow the walkway around to the left when you enter, and then drop down and continue along the cave wall, you can get fairly close to the ladder before being spotted by one of the giants; once you see him start to move, try to bait him into firing his cannon. Then, after evading the shot, make a dash for the ladder and climb up it. Fighting both of the giants out in the open is extremely dangerous, so you should only attempt it if you're either very confident in your skills or have other players with you. Both of the giants are susceptible to poison, however, so once you're on the ledge at the back of the room, you can get keep luring them into the swamp to slowly whittle their health down. After killing one of them through this method, you may want to go down and fight the second one to speed the process up. If you manage to kill both of them, clear out the remaining enemies in the swamp so that you can gather all the loot.

Lower Pthumerian Labyrinth

If you have the Short Ritual Root Chalice you can form and join online co-op teams in order to raid Chalice Labyrinths. It's recommended to take on this and all following Chalice Labyrinths in co-op. At Depth three, enemies are as strong and as resilient as in the previous Lower Hintertomb Labyrinth, but the Lower Pthumerian Labyrinth is longer, and there are larger groups of enemies to contend with. It also has some important items to plunder, such as the Sinister Lower Pthumeru Root Chalice (from a secret Bath Messenger shop for 9000 Blood Echoes on level four), and the Workshop Haze Extractor (in a coffin on level two).

| Recommended | Player Level **80+** | Weapon Upgrade **+8** |

Layer 1

Enemies

Regular	HP	Echoes	Page
Nightmare Apostle	606	429	p247
Labyrinth Watcher (Cleaver)	472	505	p250
Labyrinth Watcher (Dagger)	472	505	p250
Labyrinth Watcher (Halberd)	744	505	p251

Strong	HP	Echoes	Page
Kidnapper	1488	1762	p286
Bell Ringer	809	858	p287
Labyrinth Warrior (Greatsword)	1285	2327	p302
Labyrinth Warrior (Crossbow & Sword)	1285	2327	p302
Bloodlicker	1553	1589	p280

Boss	HP	Echoes	Page
Merciless Watcher (Scattergun, Club & Lantern)	4057	8479	p297
Watcher Chieftain (Club & Lantern)	3041	8479	p294
Merciless Watcher (Saw)	4057	8479	p296

Ritual Info

Chalice	Lower Pthumeru Chalice
Ritual Materials	Ritual Blood (3) ×9
Blood Echoes	3200
Depth	3

Step 01

Attacking the wall at **Position A** in this room will reveal a hidden path that takes you up to a chest containing a Sage's Wrist. Once you have that, you can either backtrack the way you came, or drop down off the ledge to reach a room near the start of the level. [→◻ **01**]

Step 02

As you approach this room, Nightmare Apostles summoned by a Bell Ringer up ahead will start running toward you – try to take them on in the doorway so they can't surround you. There's also a pressure plate just in front of the door that triggers a number of flaming arrow traps, so taking the fight into the room can be dangerous. The room itself may appear clear, but if you look up you'll see a number of Nightmare Apostles hanging from the ceiling; rather than trying to fight them now, it's best to continue to the next room and kill the Bell Ringer there to stop her from summoning enemies first. Once she's been killed you can return here and either use ranged attacks to knock the Apostles down one at a time, or advance slowly through the room so that you don't have to fight the entire group at once. [→◻ **02**]

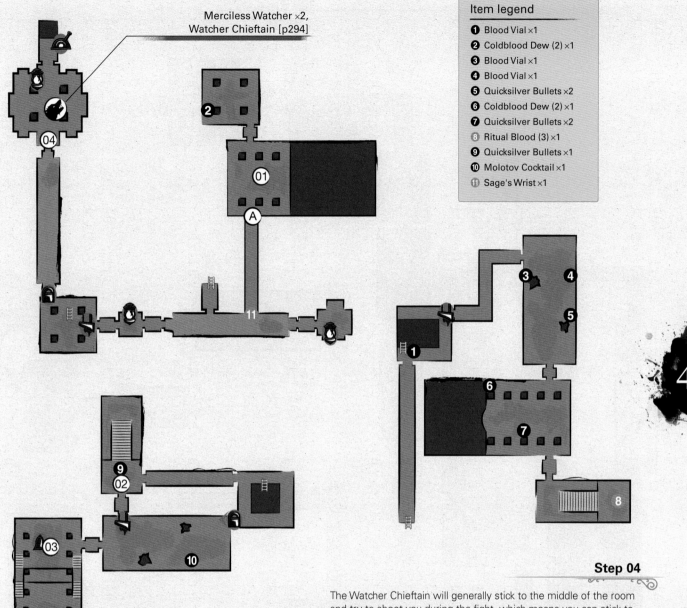

Merciless Watcher ×2,
Watcher Chieftain [p294]

Item legend

❶ Blood Vial ×1
❷ Coldblood Dew (2) ×1
❸ Blood Vial ×1
❹ Blood Vial ×1
❺ Quicksilver Bullets ×2
❻ Coldblood Dew (2) ×1
❼ Quicksilver Bullets ×2
❽ Ritual Blood (3) ×1
❾ Quicksilver Bullets ×1
❿ Molotov Cocktail ×1
⓫ Sage's Wrist ×1

4

Step 04

The Watcher Chieftain will generally stick to the middle of the room and try to shoot you during the fight, which means you can stick to the outskirts of the room and use the pillars for cover. If you keep moving around the room from pillar to pillar you should also be able to keep both Merciless Watchers approaching you from the same direction; wait for one to get close, and then after getting a couple of hits in, move on to the next pillar again before one can circle around you. [→☐ 03]

Step 03

The Bell Ringer you're after is straight ahead of you when you enter this room, so take her out as quickly as possible before she can summon too many enemies. Once she's down, check behind you just in case any of the Apostles from the previous room followed you in, because you'll want to deal with them before continuing. The Labyrinth Watcher standing guard over the lever at the bottom room has a commanding view of the area with his crossbow, but that can actually be used to your advantage. While you cannot normally sneak up behind him, if you go part of the way down one of the staircases so that he spots you, and then retreat, he'll move over to that side slightly. As long as you get him to move over enough, you can then walk down the other staircase and get around behind him for a charged R2.

03

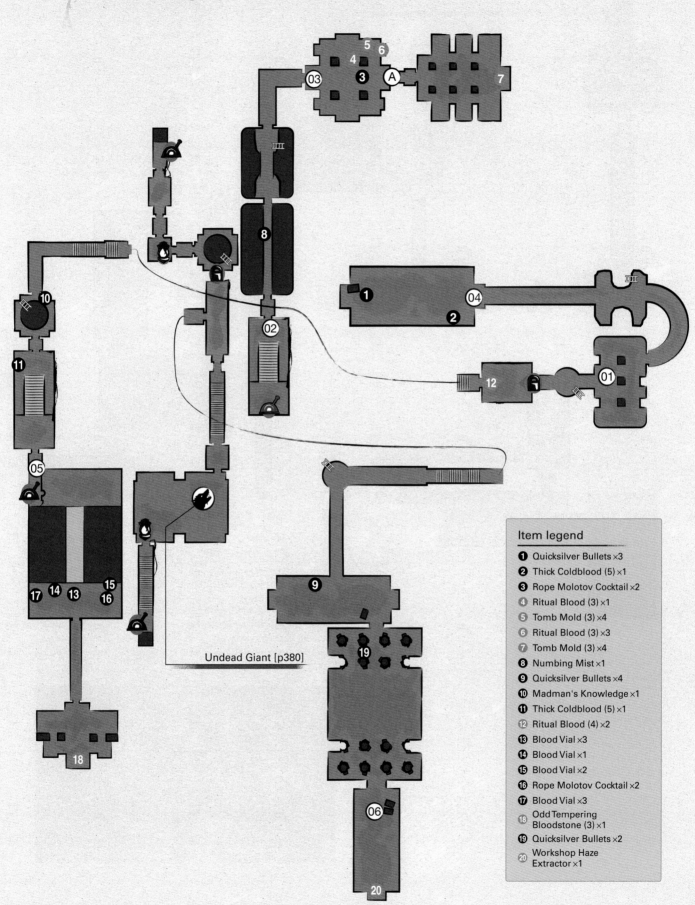

Undead Giant [p380]

Item legend

1. Quicksilver Bullets ×3
2. Thick Coldblood (5) ×1
3. Rope Molotov Cocktail ×2
4. Ritual Blood (3) ×1
5. Tomb Mold (3) ×4
6. Ritual Blood (3) ×3
7. Tomb Mold (3) ×4
8. Numbing Mist ×1
9. Quicksilver Bullets ×4
10. Madman's Knowledge ×1
11. Thick Coldblood (5) ×1
12. Ritual Blood (4) ×2
13. Blood Vial ×3
14. Blood Vial ×1
15. Blood Vial ×2
16. Rope Molotov Cocktail ×2
17. Blood Vial ×3
18. Odd Tempering Bloodstone (3) ×1
19. Quicksilver Bullets ×2
20. Workshop Haze Extractor ×1

Enemies

Regular	HP	Echoes	Page
Labyrinth Watcher (Cleaver & Lantern)	781	530	p250
Labyrinth Watcher (Cleaver)	495	530	p250
Labyrinth Watcher (Halberd)	781	530	p251
Labyrinth Watcher (Twin Axes)	781	530	p251
Labyrinth Watcher (Dagger)	495	530	p250
Labyrinth Rat	495	419	p233
Gel	423	980	p253
Rabid Dog	568	664	p230
Gravekeeper Scorpion	318	466	p252

Strong	HP	Echoes	Page
Watcher Chieftain (Heated Club & Lantern)	2235	2498	p294
Merciless Watcher (Saw)	4260	8903	p297
Bloodlicker	1631	1668	p280
Kidnapper	1562	1850	p276

Boss	HP	Echoes	Page
Undead Giant (Club & Hook)	12783	11267	p380

Step 01

A Labyrinth Watcher with a Lantern patrols this area, and if he spots you he'll ring the lantern, causing all of the Labyrinth Watchers on the bridge above to descend the ladder at the end of the tunnel on the opposite side of the room. This can actually work in your favor, because that ladder is just at the edge of their range, so they'll often get caught between trying to climb up and down it, and fighting them there is much easier than on the bridge. Be careful as you progress through the tunnel, however, because there's a Gel hanging from the ceiling near the end; use a ranged attack to knock it down as soon as it comes into view.

Step 02

There's a Merciless Watcher standing guard over the lever in this room at the top of the stairs, but fighting him there can be difficult, because there's not much room to move. It's better to lure him down to the bottom of the stairs, where you can use the statues to block his movement and easily make his attacks miss. [→☐ 01]

Step 03

While the large number of Holy Chalice rite materials that you can get in here would be reason enough to visit the room, there are even more secrets to uncover. If you strike the wall at **Position A** you'll reveal a hidden path that leads down to another room,

where you'll be able to acquire even more treasures. A number of Wandering Nightmares also occupy that room, but because of their positions it can be very difficult to kill them all before they disappear. To get any that you miss, simply leave the dungeon and make your way back here again.

Step 04

There's a very large group of Labyrinth Rats here, and there are a couple of ways you can go about dealing with them, depending on what you have at hand. Because the rats move about a lot, if you're patient, you can usually move forward just enough to get one or two of them to spot you at a time, and then drop back to fight them away from the group. If, however, you have some Pungent Blood Cocktails and Molotovs, you may want to try and lure a group of them back to the tunnel entrance, where there's a pool of oil, and then throw the Blood Cocktail into it so that the rats swarm in there. Once they're all bunched up, throw some Molotovs to kill them quickly. [→☐ 02/03]

Step 05

Pulling the lever here will lower the nearby drawbridge so that you can reach the other side of the room, where a large amount of items can be looted from corpses. Once you drop down, however, you won't be able to get back up, and will have to drop down again to the tunnels below to continue. If you decide to drop down, try to line yourself up above the Labyrinth Watcher manning the cannon below, so that you can kill it with a plunging attack.

Step 06

You need to approach the enemies in this room very cautiously if you haven't cleared out the upper part of the drawbridge room, because if you need to retreat, the Labyrinth Watchers up there will start firing their canons down at you. For the first group of Labyrinth Watchers, try to lure then to you one at a time to keep the fight manageable. Once they're down, lure the Warrior Chieftain away from the Watchers at the back and try to get him stuck on the cages in the room. The coffin here contains the Workshop Haze Extractor Key Item, which is used for extracting Arcane Hazes from ritual crafting items at the Workbench in the Hunter's Dream.

Lower Pthumerian Labyrinth – Layer 3

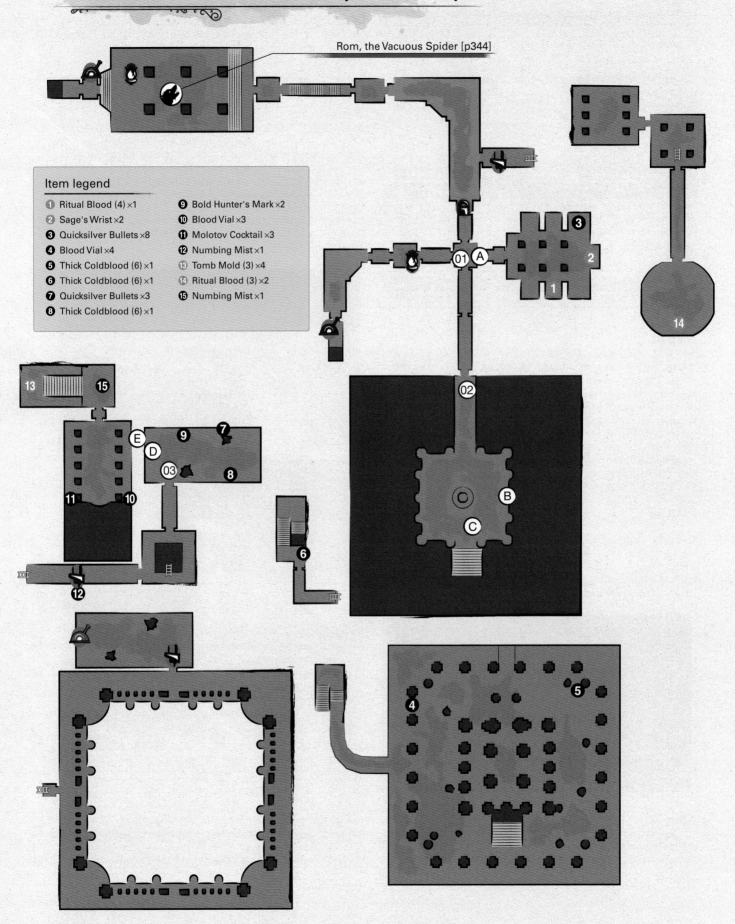

Rom, the Vacuous Spider [p344]

Item legend

1 Ritual Blood (4) ×1
2 Sage's Wrist ×2
3 Quicksilver Bullets ×8
4 Blood Vial ×4
5 Thick Coldblood (6) ×1
6 Thick Coldblood (6) ×1
7 Quicksilver Bullets ×3
8 Thick Coldblood (6) ×1
9 Bold Hunter's Mark ×2
10 Blood Vial ×3
11 Molotov Cocktail ×3
12 Numbing Mist ×1
13 Tomb Mold (3) ×4
14 Ritual Blood (3) ×2
15 Numbing Mist ×1

Enemies

Regular	HP	Echoes	Page
Children of Rom	363	141	p344
Labyrinth Watcher (Twin Axes)	800	555	p251
Labyrinth Watcher (Cleaver)	507	555	p250
Labyrinth Watcher (Halberd)	800	555	p251
Labyrinth Watcher (Dagger)	507	555	p250
Rabid Dog	581	696	p231
Nightmare Apostle	651	472	p247

Strong	HP	Echoes	Page
Labyrinth Warrior (Greatsword)	1381	2559	p302
Bloodlicker	1669	1748	p280
Bell Ringer	870	944	p287
Kidnapper	1599	1938	p276
Keeper's Hunting Dog	1175	870	p305
Keeper of the Old Lords	2181	2949	p378
Fluorescent Flower	1088	1532	p286
Merciless Watcher (Scattergun, Club & Lantern)	2288	2617	p297

Boss	HP	Echoes	Page
Rom, the Vacuous Spider	7271	10975	p344

Step 01

A hidden passageway can be revealed if you strike the wall at **Position A** in this room, and if you follow it along you'll be able to reach another room with some chests to plunder. There are no enemies in the treasure room, so you can explore at your leisure. [→☐ 01]

Step 02

There's a Bell Ringer near the fountain directly ahead when you enter this room, so quickly run forward and kill her before she can summon too many enemies. If done correctly you can kill her without alerting the Labyrinth Watcher at **Position B** and Kidnapper at **Position C**, so sneak up behind them one at a time and use charged R2 attacks. There are a large number of Fluorescent Flowers on the lower part of this room, and a Keeper of the Old Lords with two Keeper's Hunting Dogs are patrolling the area directly below the fountain. If you have ranged attack options, such as a Pistol or Throwing Knives, it's well worth using them on some of the Fluorescent Flowers from the corners of this upper area. You usually only be able to reach one of the two in the corners, but that will help you out in the long run.

Once you're ready to head down, going clockwise around the outside of the room from the bottom of the stairs is best; by doing that you'll be able to use the pillars for cover as you approach the remaining Fluorescent Flowers, and still keep an eye on the middle for the patrolling enemy group. Two more Fluorescent Flowers have taken up residence in the area below the fountain, but you should try to deal with the patrolling group first. When you encounter the group, take advantage of the fact that the dogs move faster and try to lure them away and around some of the pillars to separate them. Depending on where you first see them, and if they come out from beneath the fountain, it can be worth going back up the stairs and trying to use plunging attacks on them from above. Because of the sheer number of Fluorescent Flowers here, it can be worth repeatedly killing them for Arcane Hazes, so that you don't have to break down your other materials to get them. [→☐ 02]

Step 03

This room can be highly challenging, because you'll have to take on a Labyrinth Watcher, Keeper of the Old Lords, two Keeper's Hunting Dogs, three Nightmare Apostles and eventually a Kidnapper; playing with a co-op partner is definitely advised. You can bypass this area and head straight for the level boss if you wish, but you're reward for pushing through the challenge will be even more Holy Chalice rite materials. The Keeper of the Old Lords will usually stay in place at **Position D**, to the left of the doorway, unless he sees you. So it's best to lure some of the other enemies out of the room, without actually going in there. By sticking to the alley just in front of the door, you can usually get the Labyrinth Watcher to spot you, and he'll reliably be accompanied by the two Keeper's Hunting Dogs, since they're the fastest enemies.

If you have any Pungent Blood Cocktails, use them to keep the two dogs in place while you damage them and kill the Watcher. If you don't have any, you should retreat back to the ladder room, drop down, and try to separate them and attack them as they land. The Nightmare Apostles move quite slowly and it takes some time for them to reach you, but that doesn't mean that you shouldn't try to kill the first few enemies as quickly as possible; defeating them before the Apostles arrive will make things much easier, because you can soon get overwhelmed if you have to fight all of them at once. When you finally enter the room, try to lure the Keeper away from his starting position to avoid the risk of drawing the Kidnapper at **Position E** into the fight. [→☐ 03]

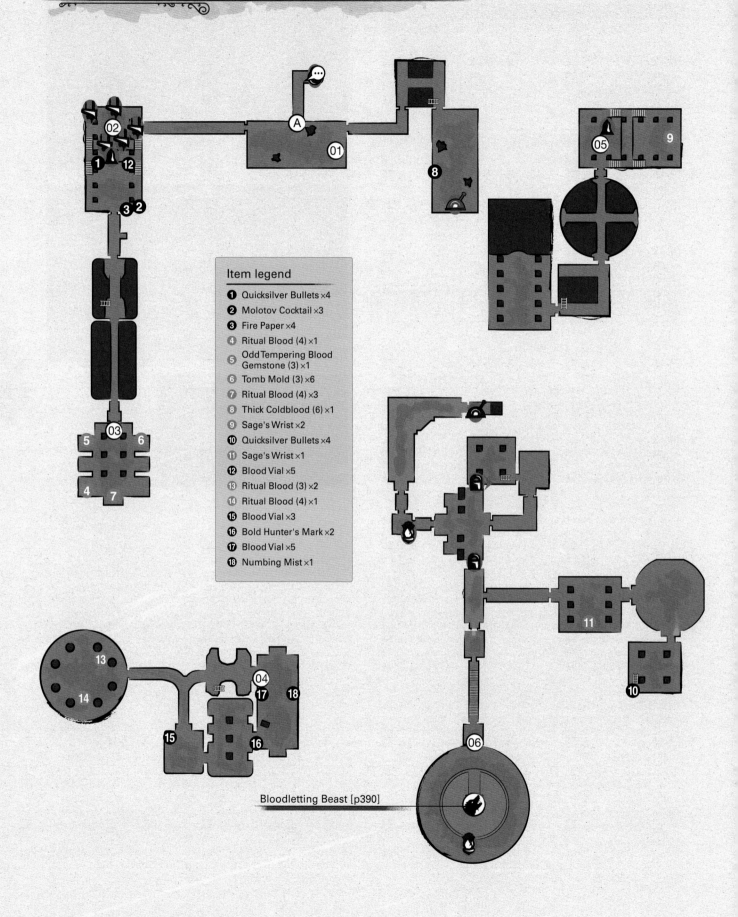

Item legend

1. Quicksilver Bullets ×4
2. Molotov Cocktail ×3
3. Fire Paper ×4
4. Ritual Blood (4) ×1
5. Odd Tempering Blood Gemstone (3) ×1
6. Tomb Mold (3) ×6
7. Ritual Blood (4) ×3
8. Thick Coldblood (6) ×1
9. Sage's Wrist ×2
10. Quicksilver Bullets ×4
11. Sage's Wrist ×1
12. Blood Vial ×5
13. Ritual Blood (3) ×2
14. Ritual Blood (4) ×1
15. Blood Vial ×3
16. Bold Hunter's Mark ×2
17. Blood Vial ×5
18. Numbing Mist ×1

Bloodletting Beast [p390]

Enemies

Regular	HP	Echoes	Page
Labyrinth Watcher (Cleaver)	542	605	p250
Labyrinth Watcher (Dagger)	542	605	p250
Labyrinth Watcher (Twin Axes)	855	605	p251
Wandering Nightmare	207	127	p671
Nightmare Apostle	697	515	p247
Gravekeeper Scorpion	348	533	p252
Gel	463	1120	p253
Labyrinth Rat	542	479	p233

Strong	HP	Echoes	Page
Keeper's Hunting Dog	1257	949	p305
Keeper of the Old Lords	2333	3217	p378
Watcher Chieftain (Club & Lantern)	2447	2855	p294
Watcher Chieftain (Heated Club & Lantern)	2447	2855	p295
Merciless Watcher (Saw)	4665	10175	p297
Bloodlicker	1786	1907	p280
Kidnapper	1711	2114	p276
Labyrinth Warrior (Greatsword)	1477	2792	p302
Bell Ringer	930	1030	p287

Boss	HP	Echoes	Page
Bloodletting Beast	13220	15452	p390

Step 01

There's a hidden passage in this room behind the wall at **Position A**, but before you can reach it you'll need to fight your way past a very large group of enemies. A Keeper of the Old Lords along with two Keeper's Hunting Dogs will usually be positioned near the back of the room, and hanging from the ceiling are a number of Nightmare Apostles. As always, trying to separate the enemies and fighting them in small groups is the key to victory. As long as the Keeper and the two Dogs are at the back of the room, you can advance slowly and knock the Apostles down one at a time without being detected.

If the Keeper and the dogs have started patrolling, however, you should try to use Pebbles to lure the dogs out one at a time. If you attract the attention of multiple enemies, fall back to the previous room with the ladder and try to get them to fall off, so that you can use plunging attacks. Once all of the enemies have been killed, hit the wall to reveal the hidden passage and head to the Blood Echoes shop at the end of this path selling the Sinister Lower Pthumeru Root Chalice for 9000 Blood Echoes. [→☐ 01]

Step 02

As you approach the doorway leading into this room, a large group of summoned Nightmare Apostles will round the corner and try to attack you – try to sprint past them quickly to get into the room and kill the Bell Ringer on the ledge to the left. If the apostles have already blocked your path, you should retreat back along the tunnel quickly to try and separate them somewhat before you turn and engage them.

Step 03

A Labyrinth Watcher will usually attack you as soon as you enter this room, so make sure you're ready for him. Up next is a Merciless Watcher that's standing near the back of the room – try to use the pillars to flank him during the fight. Once the enemies have been killed, loot all of the chests in the room for a number of useful items, including some Ritual Blood (4)s. [→☐ 02]

Step 04

The low visibility in this room can make seeing the enemies quite difficult, especially the numerous Gels that are clinging to the ceiling. A large group of Labyrinth Rats are gathered in the middle of the room – try to lure some of them to you using ranged attacks from the entrance of the room before you go in. The first Gel is hanging just inside the room, so once you're ready to enter, make sure it doesn't drop on you. If you climb the mound of dead pigs you can get a better view of the room; aim to take out the first few Gels so that you have some room in which to fight the Kidnapper that's near the middle.

Step 05

When you approach the opening to this room you will likely have to deal with a mob of summoned Nightmare Apostles from the Bell Ringer. Occupy the entrance to this room and funnel them through one at a time so as not to get swarmed. Once you have cleaved yourself a path, rush in and kill her quickly. Finish off the patrolling Labyrinth Watchers once she's down, and then walk down one of the sets of stairs and sneak past the Merciless Watcher, so that you can use a charged R2 from behind.

Step 06

The boss of this level is the Bloodletting Beast, and defeating him will reward you with the Defiled Chalice. He can knock down the support pillars circling this room if you attempt to use them as cover, so it's best to keep on the move and use the size of the room to your advantage by using ranged attacks.

Ailing Loran

In order to get the Chalice needed to craft the Ailing Loran Labyrinth, you have to defeat Amygdala at the end of the Nightmare Frontier. Doing so also unlocks the Coldblood Flowerbud ritual item in the Insight shop back at the Hunter's Dream, which you need at least four of in order to perform the ritual. As this is likely your first Depth four Chalice Labyrinth, it's strongly advised to try it with a cop-op partner. If you venture in solo, you're going to have to be very patient when moving from room to room, drawing out enemies one at a time and using interrupts and Visceral Attacks to maximize your damage output. There are a lot of Beast type enemies in this dungeon, so bringing Fire weapons is highly recommended.

| Recommended | Player Level **100+** | Weapon Upgrade **+9** |

Layer 1

Enemies

Regular	HP	Echoes	Page
Nightmare Apostle	1022	1807	p247
Beast Patient (Male)	1022	2569	p236
Beast Patient (Female)	1255	2886	p237
Ashen Blood Beast Patient	1481	4059	p237
Wandering Nightmare	304	444	p671
Labyrinth Watcher (Twin Axes)	1255	2125	p251
Gel	679	3932	p253

Strong	HP	Echoes	Page
Scourge Beast	2393	4978	p266
Bell Ringer	1365	3615	p287
Loran Silverbeast	679	3869	p281
Labyrinth Madman (Twin Sickles)	2393	7801	p299
Labyrinth Madman (Sickle)	2393	7801	p300
Bloodlicker	2620	6691	p280

Boss	HP	Echoes	Page
Beast-possessed Soul	14264	38876	p275

Ritual Info

Chalice	Lower Loran Chalice
Ritual Materials	Ritual Blood (4) ×9, Coldblood Flowerbud ×4
Blood Echoes	5500
Depth	4

Step 01

Creatures that are being spawned by a Bell Ringer within this room will start to attack you as you draw near it, so be ready to fight your way past them. When you make it to the room just before this one, you can lure the enemies up the stairs, and then drop down and sprint past them if you wish. Once you're in this room, turn left and go up the stairs straight away to reach the Bell Ringer walking around at the top.

Step 02

There are quite a few male and female Beast Patients in this room, along with a Wandering Nightmare and Nightmare Apostle at the far end. You should try to kill as many of the Beast Patients as possible without going too far into the room, so you can create a clear path to the Wandering Nightmare and fight it without having to worry about the other enemies.

Step 03

A group of female Beast Patients patrol around the central pillar in this large room – try to lure them towards you one at a time without going past the pillar yourself. Standing directly behind the pillar is a Ashen Blood Beast Patient, so you'll want to clear out as many of the smaller females as you can before moving up to take him on. If you walk up along the side of the pillar you can get close enough to him to use a charge R2 without getting detected, giving you a significant early advantage in the fight. [→⬜ 01/02]

Step 04

Try to stay clear of the section of floor at **Position A** in this room, because it will crumble beneath you if you step onto it. You'll drop down to a tunnel on the floor below, and have to make your way back up again. There are a couple of sleeping Beast Patients along the wall on the opposite of the room, so try to attack them before they get up and keep an eye on your surroundings to ensure that the fights never stray too close to breakable section of floor.

Step 05

A small group of Nightmare Apostles guard the chests in this room, but even though there aren't many of them, you should be careful, because these enemies can inflict large amounts damage very quickly. By going around to the left after entering the room you'll be able to see one of them up ahead, so use a Pebble or Throwing Knife to lure it towards you quietly. Once that first one is down you can work your way around the room taking out the others as you come to them. If a couple chase after you at once, remember that you can shoot them to knock them over and buy yourself some time. The chests in this room contain some high-level materials, so the reward for dispatching the Apostles is well worth it.

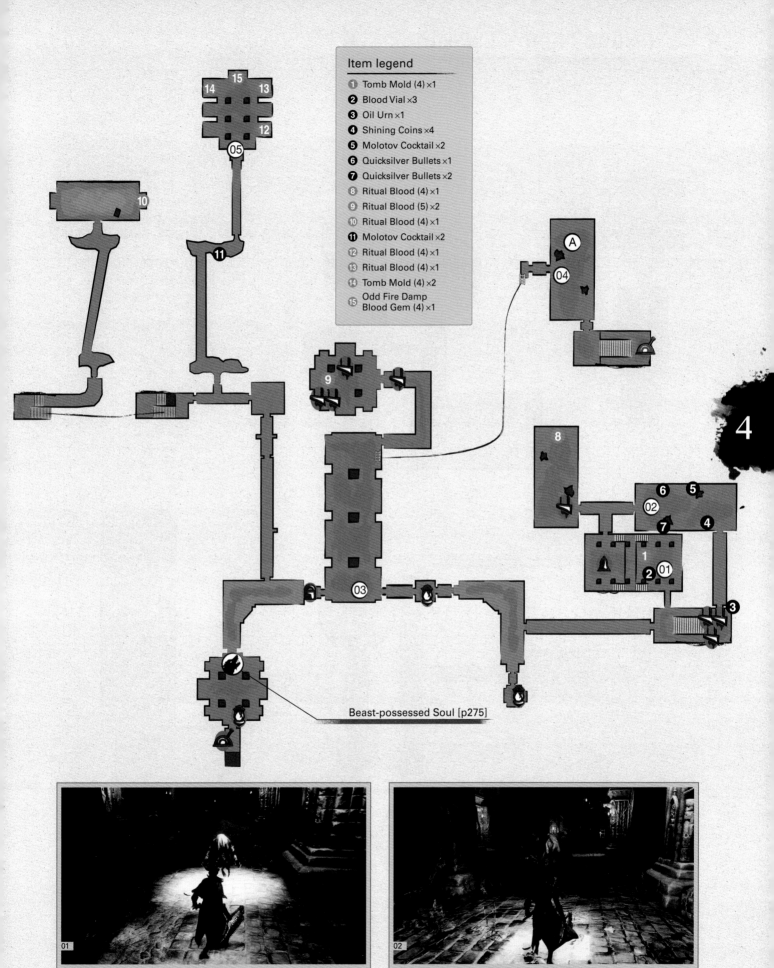

Item legend

1. Tomb Mold (4) ×1
2. Blood Vial ×3
3. Oil Urn ×1
4. Shining Coins ×4
5. Molotov Cocktail ×2
6. Quicksilver Bullets ×1
7. Quicksilver Bullets ×2
8. Ritual Blood (4) ×1
9. Ritual Blood (5) ×2
10. Ritual Blood (4) ×1
11. Molotov Cocktail ×2
12. Ritual Blood (4) ×1
13. Ritual Blood (4) ×1
14. Tomb Mold (4) ×2
15. Odd Fire Damp Blood Gem (4) ×1

Beast-possessed Soul [p275]

Ailing Loran – Layer 2

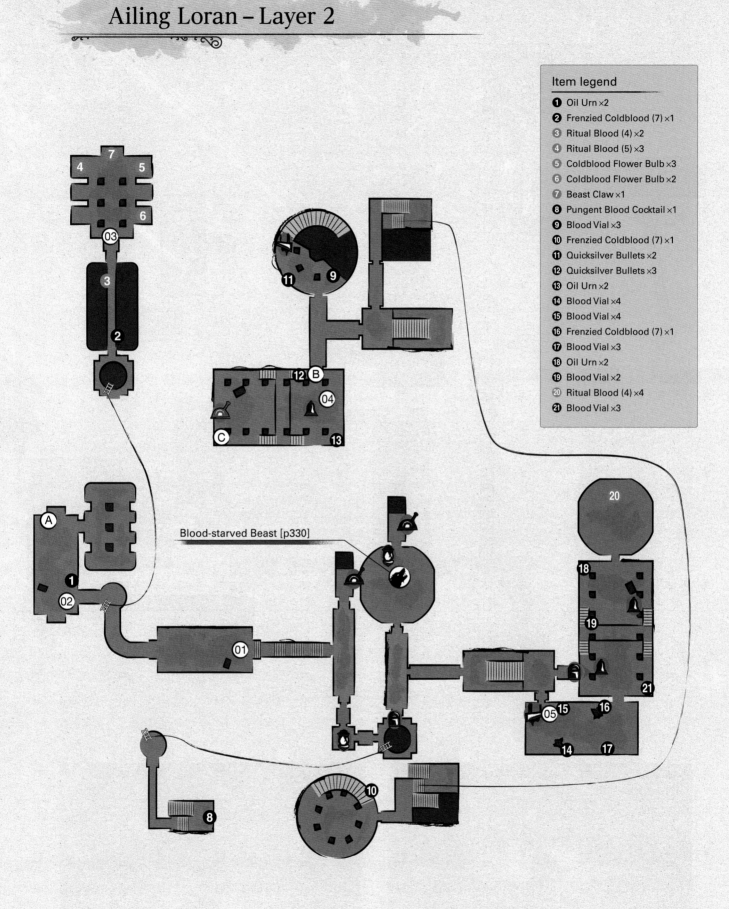

Blood-starved Beast [p330]

Item legend

1. Oil Urn ×2
2. Frenzied Coldblood (7) ×1
3. Ritual Blood (4) ×2
4. Ritual Blood (5) ×3
5. Coldblood Flower Bulb ×3
6. Coldblood Flower Bulb ×2
7. Beast Claw ×1
8. Pungent Blood Cocktail ×1
9. Blood Vial ×3
10. Frenzied Coldblood (7) ×1
11. Quicksilver Bullets ×2
12. Quicksilver Bullets ×3
13. Oil Urn ×2
14. Blood Vial ×4
15. Blood Vial ×4
16. Frenzied Coldblood (7) ×1
17. Blood Vial ×3
18. Oil Urn ×2
19. Blood Vial ×2
20. Ritual Blood (4) ×4
21. Blood Vial ×3

Enemies

Regular	HP	Echoes	Page
Labyrinth Rat	835	1765	p233
Gel	713	4129	p253
Labyrinth Watcher (Cleaver)	835	2231	p250
Labyrinth Watcher (Dagger)	835	2231	p250
Labyrinth Watcher (Twin Axes)	1318	2231	p251
Labyrinth Watcher (Halberd)	1318	2231	p251
Beast Patient (Male)	1073	2697	p236
Ashen Blood Beast Patient	1555	4262	p237
Nightmare Apostle	1073	1898	p247

Strong	HP	Echoes	Page
Scourge Beast	2513	5227	p266
Loran Silverbeast	713	4062	p281
Bloodlicker	2751	7025	p280
Bell Ringer	1433	3796	p287
Loran Cleric	1195	3263	p304

Hunter	HP	Echoes	Page
Izzy's Admirer	3084	15949	p318

Boss	HP	Echoes	Page
Blood-starved Beast	19765	46514	p330

Step 01

The Labyrinth Rats in this room tend to group up, so you may want to consider using Molotovs or even a well placed Cannon shot to take out a few of them in one shot. If they start to close in on you, retreat back through the tunnel and up the stairs, where you'll be able to funnel them through the narrow doorway.

Step 02

Another large group of Labyrinth Rats awaits you in this room, along with a Labyrinth Watcher near the entrance, but unlike the previous room, this one has an additional threat in the form of a Beast Claw-wielding Hunter at **Position A**. There's a large pile of pig carcasses blocking the Hunter's view, so if you keep the fight with the rats near the room's entrance, you can kill them all without him getting involved. The Hunter attacks very aggressively, so if you don't want to risk trying to interrupt him, consider using Bone Marrow Ash-buffed Pistol shots while backing away to take him out from range. [→☐ 01]

Step 03

This is a treasure room well worth taking a trip to, because not only does it contain a number of high-level dungeon creation materials, but you'll also be able to acquire the Beast Claw weapon that you need in order to get the Hunter's Essence Trophy. The coffin containing it is guarded by a Loran Silverbeast, so make sure you equip a fire weapon to make the fight much easier. [→☐ 02]

Step 04

There's a Bell Ringer summoning enemies in this room, use the entryway to funnel in any summoned Nightmare Apostles one at a time so as not to get overwhelmed. Find the Bell Ringer wandering around the open area just ahead, so run straight for her and kill her. Once she's be dealt with, go down the staircase at **Position B** and try to lure all of the Labyrinth Watchers towards you, so you can fight them near the stairs. A Loran Cleric is standing in the corner of the room at **Position C**, and fighting the other enemies near those stairs allows you to kill them without alerting him. When you engage him, be careful of where you take cover, because his projectiles can destroy the pillars in this room.

Step 05

A large number of summoned Nightmare Apostles will start coming after you as soon as you reach the room before this one, because there are not one, but two Bell Ringers summoning them. Fighting your way through the large group can be very dangerous – try to use the trees in that room to help you run around the Apostles, so that you can go straight for the Bell Ringers. One of them patrols around the upper part of the room, so take her out first, and then quickly drop down to the lower part to kill the other one. [→☐ 03]

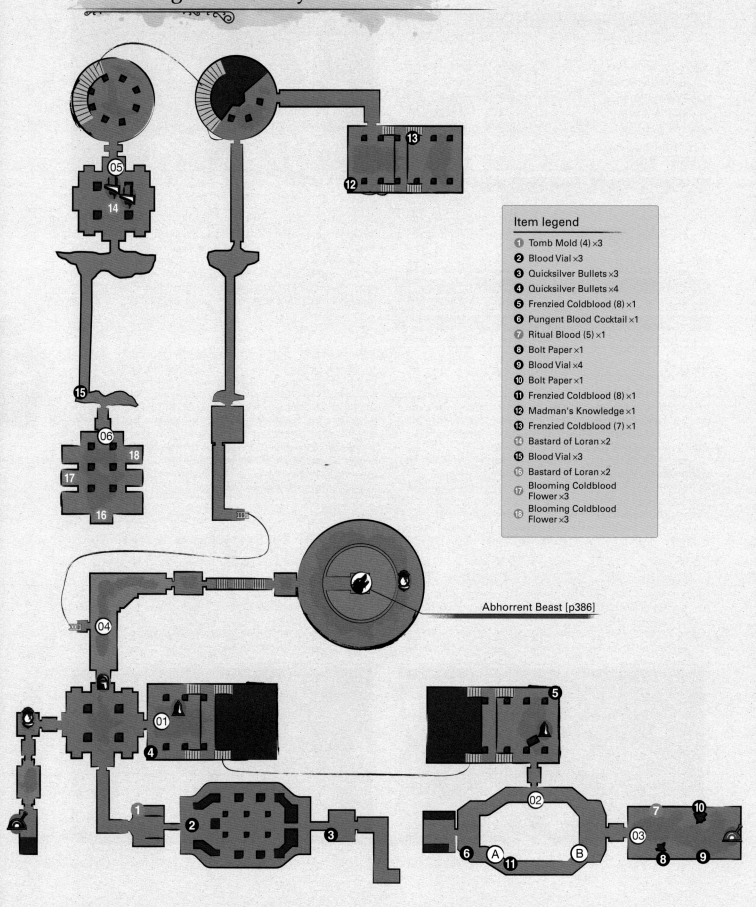

Abhorrent Beast [p386]

Item legend

1. Tomb Mold (4) ×3
2. Blood Vial ×3
3. Quicksilver Bullets ×3
4. Quicksilver Bullets ×4
5. Frenzied Coldblood (8) ×1
6. Pungent Blood Cocktail ×1
7. Ritual Blood (5) ×1
8. Bolt Paper ×1
9. Blood Vial ×4
10. Bolt Paper ×1
11. Frenzied Coldblood (8) ×1
12. Madman's Knowledge ×1
13. Frenzied Coldblood (7) ×1
14. Bastard of Loran ×2
15. Blood Vial ×3
16. Bastard of Loran ×2
17. Blooming Coldblood Flower ×3
18. Blooming Coldblood Flower ×3

Enemies

Regular	HP	Echoes	Page
Beast Patient (Male)	1099	2825	p236
Ashen Blood Beast Patient	1592	4465	p237
Labyrinth Watcher (Dagger)	855	2337	p250
Labyrinth Watcher (Cleaver)	855	2337	p250
Labyrinth Watcher (Halberd)	1349	2337	p251
Nightmare Apostle	1099	1988	p247
Wandering Nightmare	327	488	p671

Strong	HP	Echoes	Page
Scourge Beast	2573	5476	p266
Labyrinth Madman (Corpse)	2573	8581	p300
Labyrinth Madman (Twin Sickles)	2573	8581	p299
Bloodlicker	2816	7360	p280
Loran Silverbeast	730	4255	p281
Bell Ringer	1467	3976	p287
Loran Cleric	1224	3418	p304

Boss	HP	Echoes	Page
Abhorrent Beast	14596	61146	p386

Step 01

There are two Bell Ringers in this room, so you're going to have to contend with a lot of summoned Nightmare Apostles. The first Bell Ringer patrols the bottom part of the room – locate her first and take her out quickly. The second one can be found at the top of the stairs, so use whichever staircase is free of Apostles to reach her and take her out before the Apostles catch up to you. [→ 01]

Step 02

There are Loran Clerics hidden amongst the pillars on either side of the walkway in this room, at **Positions A** and **B**. They're far enough apart that you can take them on one at a time without the other being able to interfere, but you'll need to take care that you don't accidentally knock them down into the room below, where you may potentially run into them later.

Step 03

If you have any Blue Elixirs, it's recommended that you use one in this room, and then walk along one of the side walls, so that you can get behind the Labyrinth Madman that's guarding the lever. Once there, you can land a charged R2 from behind, with a Visceral Attack follow-up to finish him off easily.

Step 04

As soon as you open the door here, a Scourge Beast on the other side will leap forward and try to attack you; roll backwards immediately after opening the door to avoid the attack. The beast can't follow you through the doorway, so you can simply use long-range weapons or attacks to safely kill it. [→ 02]

Step 05

There's a Wandering Nightmare sat atop a treasure chest in this room, but if you want to kill it before it can disappear you'll need to take a bit of a risk. Standing around the chest are a number of male and female Beast Patients, and on the floor around it are pressure plates that trigger flaming arrow traps. If you want to kill the Wandering Nightmare, you'll have to run between them and try to kill it quickly before they close in. The only way to avoid having to do this is if you're carrying some Pungent Blood Cocktails, because then you'll be able to throw one to distract the Beast Patients long enough for you to kill the Wandering Nightmare. The chest in this room contains two Bastard of Loran items, which you'll need to make some of the upcoming dungeons. [→ 03/04]

Step 06

More Bastards of Loran (along with other materials) can be acquired in this room, so it's worth crossing over the bridge to come here. You only have to contend with a lone Loran Silverbeast before you can loot the room, so as long as you have a fire weapon or can use Fire Paper on your weapon of choice you should be able to dispatch him fairly quickly.

Cursed Pthumerian Defilement

After going through Ailing Loran you should have the two Bastards of Loran and nine Ritual Blood (4) needed for crafting this Dungeon. For the 22 Arcane Hazes, you may want to kill some Fluorescent Flowers on the third level of the first Pthumerian Labyrinth in the garden plaza. Alternately, you can use the Workshop Haze Extractor you collected from the Lower Pthumerian Labyrinth to extract the Arcane Hazes you need. In order to avoid sacrificing the rare, ritual crafting items you have amassed so far, use only the materials you can also purchase at either the Blood Echoes or Insight Bath Messenger shops in the Hunter's Dream.

The most challenging aspect of this 'cursed' Depth four Chalice Labyrinth is that your HP is lowered by 50%. Needless to say, having a character build with high Vitality will help a lot here. All Blood Gems collected from this and other cursed labyrinths are, naturally, cursed. This means adding them to your equipped weapon is going to have some kind of detrimental effect on your character or that particular weapon's performance, but the gem's benefits can also be higher than usual.

| Recommended | Player Level **100+** | Weapon Upgrade **+9** |

Layer 1

Item legend

1. Ritual Blood (4) ×2
2. Quicksilver Bullets ×2
3. Ritual Blood (4) ×1
4. Shining Coins ×3
5. Molotov Cocktail ×2
6. Quicksilver Bullets ×1
7. Quicksilver Bullets ×2
8. Blood Vial ×2
9. Molotov Cocktail ×1
10. Quicksilver Bullets ×2
11. Rope Molotov Cocktail ×2
12. Ritual Blood (4) ×2
13. Blood Vial ×2
14. Cursed Odd Tempering Damp Blood Gem (5) ×1

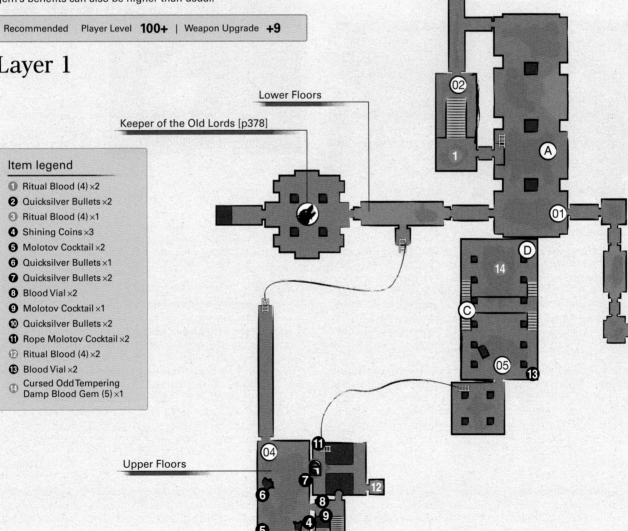

Lower Floors

Keeper of the Old Lords [p378]

Upper Floors

Enemies

Regular	HP	Echoes	Page
Labyrinth Watcher (Dagger)	796	2549	p250
Labyrinth Watcher (Cleaver)	796	2549	p250
Labyrinth Watcher (Halberd)	1255	2549	p251
Labyrinth Watcher (Twin Axes)	1255	2549	p251
Labyrinth Ritekeeper	1022	2968	p253
Watcher's Gravedigger (Hook & Lantern)	1591	3653	p254
Watcher's Gravedigger (Pickaxe)	1591	3653	p254
Watcher's Gravedigger (Rifle, Hook & Lantern)	1481	3234	p254

Strong	HP	Echoes	Page
Watcher Chieftain (Heated Club & Lantern)	3590	12024	p295
Bloodlicker	2620	8029	p280

Boss	HP	Echoes	Page
Keeper of the Old Lords	16431	54224	p378

Ritual Info

Chalice	Defiled Chalice
Ritual Materials	Ritual Blood (4) ×9, Bastard of Loran ×2, Arcane Haze ×22
Blood Echoes	5500
Depth	4

Step 01

Quickly run forward as soon as you enter this room, because the pool of liquid in front of the door is oil, and there's a Labyrinth Rite Keeper off to the right at **Position A** that's looking to fry you in it. As you start to run forward, a Labyrinth Watcher behind you on the left will start to give chase, but keep going until one of the large pillars in the room is blocking the Rite Keeper's fireballs, so that you can fight the Watcher without worrying about them. Once the watcher has been killed, keep using the pillar for cover as you close in on the Rite Keeper to kill it. **[→□ 01]**

Step 02

There's a Watcher's Gravedigger at the base of the stairs just to the right inside this doorway, and if you walk in quietly, you can usually sneak up behind him and use a charged R2. Once he's down, go up the stairs towards the chest, but do not walk straight across the raised motif; there's a hidden pressure plate that will cause four Labyrinth Watchers to appear around you.

Step 03

The lever in this room is guarded by a Merciless Watcher who, thanks to your low HP, can easily kill you in a single hit. It's recommended to use a Blue Elixir before entering the room and sneak around the outskirts so that you can get behind him and use a charged R2 and Visceral Attack to reduce the risk of getting hit. If you don't have a Blue Elixir you may want to use some ranged attacks to weaken him first, especially if you can use some Bone Marrow Ash-buffed Pistol shots. This fight will teach you to be precise and flawless and abate your hubris, and prepare you for trials to come. **[→□ 02/03]**

Step 04

A lone Watcher's Gravedigger patrols near the entrance to this room, and while it may be tempting to run in and fight him, doing so would be extremely dangerous. A Labyrinth Right Keeper is standing at **Position B** near the back of the room, and as soon as you enter she'll start launching fireballs at you. Lure the Gravedigger back towards the entrance, so that the tree in the room blocks the incoming fireballs and you can fight him without worrying about them. Once he's down, dash to the second tree and use it for cover, and when you see an opening, move around and take out the Rite Keeper.

Step 05

There are three Watcher's Gravediggers with guns in this room, so you'll need to always be aware of your surroundings. A number of Labyrinth Watchers also patrol around the bottom of the room – try to take them out as close to the back of the room as possible so that the Gravedigger standing in the middle of the upper part doesn't spot you. If you need to get closer, use the pillars for cover. Once all of the Watchers are dead, go up the stairs at **Position C**. There's another pillar just ahead from the top of the stairs, and a Gravedigger is standing just to the right of it; quickly move forward and stand behind the pillar so that you don't get shot. If you hold that position for a while, the Gravedigger will forget about you, and at that time you can walk around the pillar and land a charged R2. After you've killed him, walk along the back wall of the room to get behind the next Gravedigger at **Position D** and do the same to him, before moving up and finishing off the one in the middle.

4

Enemies

Regular	HP	Echoes	Page
Labyrinth Watcher (Dagger)	835	2677	p250
Labyrinth Watcher (Cleaver)	835	2677	p250
Labyrinth Watcher (Twin Axes)	1318	2677	p251
Labyrinth Watcher (Cleaver & Lantern)	1318	2677	p250
Labyrinth Watcher (Halberd)	1318	2677	p251
Watcher's Gravedigger (Rifle, Hook & Lantern)	1555	3396	p254
Watcher's Gravedigger (Hook & Lantern)	1671	3836	p254
Wandering Nightmare	319	559	p671

Strong	HP	Echoes	Page
Labyrinth Warrior (Morning Star)	2275	12346	p303
Merciless Watcher (Saw)	7186	44989	p297
Bloodlicker	2751	8430	p280
Labyrinth Madman (Sickle)	2513	9829	p300
Evil Labyrinth Spirit	1257	4475	p298

Boss	HP	Echoes	Page
Watchdog of the Old Lords	23963	67763	p376

Step 01

The pressure plate at **Position A** in this room will cause a small group of Labyrinth Watchers to appear around you when stepped on, so it's best to stick to the outskirts of the room at all times to ensure that you don't accidentally step on it. The enemies that get summoned by the trap are very aggressive and it can be difficult to evade all of their attacks, so it's better not to take a risk when you have such low health.

Step 02

There's a Labyrinth Warrior standing in the middle of this room that you'll need to kill before you can open the chests. If you walk slowly around to the left as soon as you enter you can get round behind him for a charged R2. Killing this enemy as quickly and quietly as possible is quite important, because there's a Labyrinth Madman on the floor just above this area, and if he hears you there's a strong chance that he'll drop down and join in.

Step 03

After killing a Labyrinth Watcher near the doorway in this room, you'll need to fight your way past a Labyrinth Madman in order to get the contents of the coffin at the bottom of the stairs. The speed and aggression that these enemies attack with make them extremely difficult to handle when you can't afford to take a single hit. To make the fight easier, you may want to consider using a Blue Elixir so that you can sneak around behind him and use a charged R2 for an early advantage. Alternatively, try to use some ranged attacks to weaken him from the top of the stairs as he approaches.

Step 04

It's recommended that you use the elevator in the middle of this room to reach the upper floor, because taking on the next room starting from there is much easier. Once you reach the upper walkway, make sure to go around and get the items from the chest before progressing.

Step 05

Opening the door to this room, you'll see a Watcher's Gravedigger with a gun standing in front of you, so walk up behind him slowly and use a charged R2. There are a lot of enemies on the different floors in this room, so you'll need to progress very carefully in order to take them out with as little risk as possible. Look down into the middle of the room and you should see another Gravedigger standing on the middle floor to the right, at **Position B**. A large group of Labyrinth Watchers will also start patrolling around the room between the bottom and middle floor.

Watch the patrolling group of enemies, and when they're on the opposite side of the room to the Gravedigger, drop down and walk back around behind the Gravedigger, so that you can land a charged R2 from behind. Check the position of the patrolling group again, and then use whichever staircase on this floor is furthest from them to reach the upper floor, where you'll need to take out a lone Labyrinth Watcher. How you deal with the patrolling group is down to personal preference. By staying far away and making use of the different floors you can use Pebbles to lure them one at a time, or you can get above them and use Molotovs to weaken the whole group before moving in. There's another Gravedigger that patrols around the bottom floor as well, so make sure you keep an eye out for him while you're dealing with the Watcher group. Once they've all been killed, go down to **Position C** and follow the path around behind the main stairs to find a Wandering Nightmare, and if you go through the broken bars nearby you'll be able to kill the two hard-at-work Gravediggers. [→☐ 01/02]

Step 06

At the top of the stairs guarding the lever is a nasty combination of a Labyrinth Madman and a Watcher's Gravedigger with a gun, so you need to lure one of the enemies away. To lure the Gravedigger down, simply stay near the doorway so that he can see you, and then move to the side so that he walks down to investigate, and keep repeating that. Once he's close enough you can use Throwing Knives to weaken him before closing in to kill him. Luring the Madman is somewhat easier, because you can just fire a shot in his general direction and he'll come running.

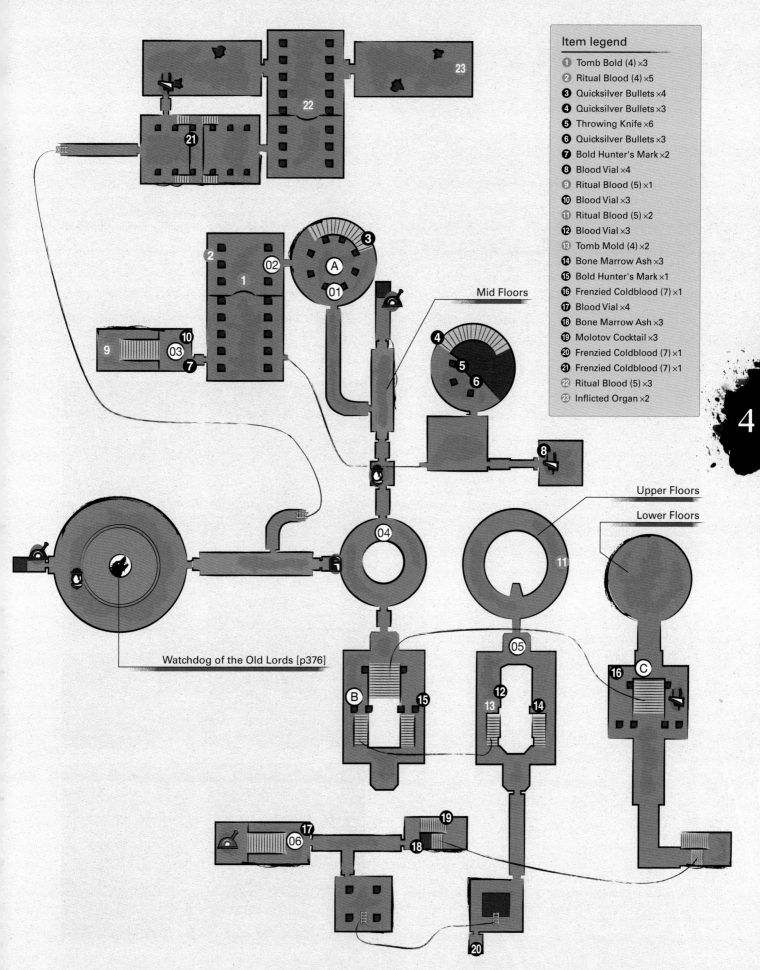

Item legend

1. Tomb Bold (4) ×3
2. Ritual Blood (4) ×5
3. Quicksilver Bullets ×4
4. Quicksilver Bullets ×3
5. Throwing Knife ×6
6. Quicksilver Bullets ×3
7. Bold Hunter's Mark ×2
8. Blood Vial ×4
9. Ritual Blood (5) ×1
10. Blood Vial ×3
11. Ritual Blood (5) ×2
12. Blood Vial ×3
13. Tomb Mold (4) ×2
14. Bone Marrow Ash ×3
15. Bold Hunter's Mark ×1
16. Frenzied Coldblood (7) ×1
17. Blood Vial ×4
18. Bone Marrow Ash ×3
19. Molotov Cocktail ×3
20. Frenzied Coldblood (7) ×1
21. Frenzied Coldblood (7) ×1
22. Ritual Blood (5) ×3
23. Inflicted Organ ×2

Mid Floors

Upper Floors

Lower Floors

Watchdog of the Old Lords [p376]

Enemies

Normal	HP	Echoes	Page
Labyrinth Watcher (Twin Axes)	1349	2804	p251
Labyrinth Watcher (Halberd)	1349	2804	p251
Labyrinth Watcher (Cleaver)	855	2804	p250
Labyrinth Watcher (Dagger)	855	2804	p250
Labyrinth Rat	855	2218	p233
Watcher's Gravedigger (Hook & Lantern)	1711	4018	p254
Watcher's Gravedigger (Pickaxe)	1711	4018	p254

Strong	HP	Echoes	Page
Keeper's Hunting Dog	1982	4395	p305
Keeper of the Old Lords	3679	14901	p376
Watcher Chieftain (Heated Club & Lantern)	3859	13227	p295
Merciless Watcher (Mace)	3859	13227	p296
Bloodlicker	2816	8832	p280
Labyrinth Warrior (Greatsword)	2330	12934	p302

Boss	HP	Echoes	Page
Amygdala	22079	72790	p340

Step 01

There is a Keeper of the Old Lords and two Keeper's Hunting Dogs patrolling around the middle of this room, so be very careful when you enter. If you stay near the doorway they won't see you, so you can plan your approach from there. The best course of action is to try to separate the two dogs from the Keeper, and you can do that by watching their patrol route, and either walking out far enough to get their attention, or by throwing a Pungent Blood Cocktail. The Blood Cocktail is the better choice if you have one, since it gives you a large window to attack them freely. You can also hit them with a Shaman Bone Blade at that time to have them fight each other, and potentially the Keeper too, if he's close enough.

If the Keeper hasn't already gotten involved in the fight, wait for him to get to the furthest point on his route, and then run and hide behind the pillar at **Position A**. Once there you'll be able to wait until he walks past the pillar so that you can run and attack him from behind quickly. If you get into trouble in the fight, remember that you can retreat back to the room with the Lamp and the enemies will not follow you there. [→☐ 01-03]

Step 02

A large group of Labyrinth Rats are swarming around the entrance to this room, so you may want to use some Molotovs or a Bone Marrow Ash-buffed Cannon shot to thin them out. The most important thing is that you keep near the entrance to the room, because there's a Merciless Watcher around the corner to the right and you don't want him to get involved while you're still fighting the rats.

Step 03

As you approach the doorway leading into this room, try to hug one of the walls so that you can hide to the side of the doorway when you reach it, because there's a large group of Labyrinth Watchers along with a Watcher Gravedigger patrolling near the entrance. By using the door for cover you can watch the movement of the group

undetected while you plan how to take them on. They're packed quite close together, so large area-of-effect attacks such as Molotovs and Cannon shots can be effective, or you can wait for them to move past the door, and then run up behind the group and use wide-arcing attacks. If they start to surround you, retreat back to the corridor and funnel them through the doorway. Another Watcher's Gravedigger patrols around a small area near the back of the room, where a number of Labyrinth Watchers also sit dormant. If you hide behind the pillars as you approach this area you can get close enough to the Gravedigger to attack him from behind as he passes you by.

Step 04

Only a single Merciless Watcher with a mace is guarding the chest in this room, but because these enemies are so agile you should still be careful. If you're familiar enough with their attacks then you can interrupt and stagger them for a quick win, but if you want to be safe you can use the trees in the room to bait them into attacking while you circle round and hit them during their recovery period.

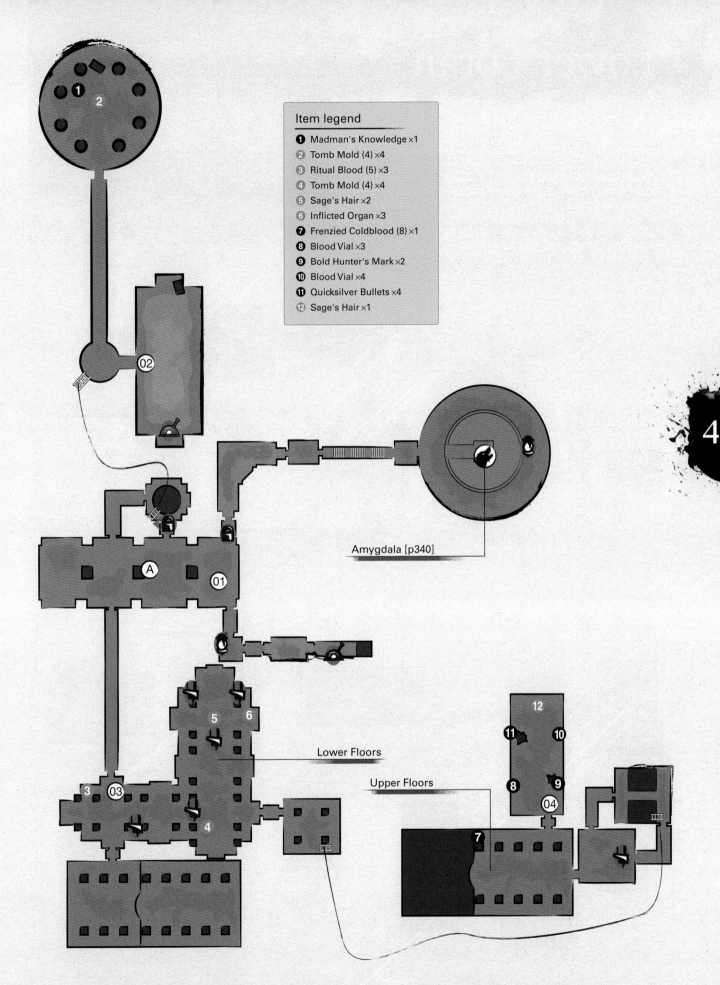

Item legend

1. Madman's Knowledge ×1
2. Tomb Mold (4) ×4
3. Ritual Blood (5) ×3
4. Tomb Mold (4) ×4
5. Sage's Hair ×2
6. Inflicted Organ ×3
7. Frenzied Coldblood (8) ×1
8. Blood Vial ×3
9. Bold Hunter's Mark ×2
10. Blood Vial ×4
11. Quicksilver Bullets ×4
12. Sage's Hair ×1

Amygdala [p340]

Lower Floors

Upper Floors

Lower Loran

This is likely to be your first Depth five Chalice Dungeon, because the ritual to create it has the lowest material requirements. Even with the use of fully upgraded weapons and well-times interrupts and visceral attacks, battles will be long and intense at this Depth. It is highly advised to tackle Depth five Chalice Labyrinths with a full online co-op team. When working together as a team, always look to draw enemies away from groups, to outnumber and team up on them.

Recommended | Player Level **140+** | Weapon Upgrade **+10**

Layer 1

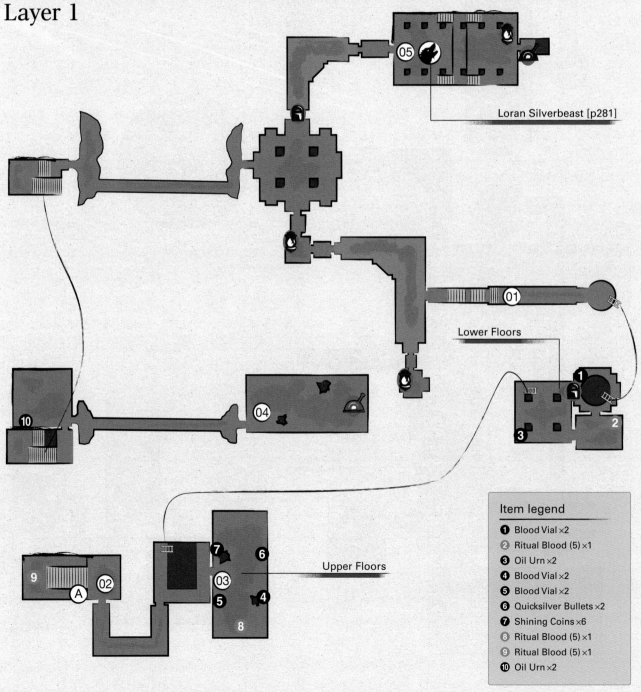

Loran Silverbeast [p281]

Lower Floors

Upper Floors

Item legend

1. Blood Vial ×2
2. Ritual Blood (5) ×1
3. Oil Urn ×2
4. Blood Vial ×2
5. Blood Vial ×2
6. Quicksilver Bullets ×2
7. Shining Coins ×6
8. Ritual Blood (5) ×1
9. Ritual Blood (5) ×1
10. Oil Urn ×2

Enemies

Regular	HP	Echoes	Page
Labyrinth Rat	851	2394	p233
Gel	726	5601	p253
Beast Patient (Male)	1093	3659	p236
Ashen Blood Beast Patient	1584	5782	p237
Labyrinth Watcher (Cleaver)	851	3026	p250
Labyrinth Watcher (Halberd)	1342	3026	p251
Labyrinth Watcher (Twin Axes)	1342	3026	p251
Nightmare Apostle	1093	2575	p247

Strong	HP	Echoes	Page
Scourge Beast	2560	7092	p266
Loran Silverbeast	726	5511	p281
Labyrinth Madman (Sickle)	2560	11112	p300
Bloodlicker	2802	9531	p280

Boss	HP	Echoes	Page
Loran Silverbeast	2927	70827	p281

Ritual Info

Chalice	Lower Loran Chalice (5)
Ritual Materials	Ritual Blood (5) ×9, Blooming Coldblood Flower ×4
Blood Echoes	11500
Depth	5

Step 01

The Scourge Beast in this tunnel will likely be your first real test in a Depth 5 Dungeon, so it's a good measure of how damaging and resilient your character is against enemies of this strength. If it's taking too long to kill the beast, it may be worthwhile going back to a Depth 4 Dungeon and leveling up some more. Remember to study up on what damage types the different enemies are weak against, to make sure you're always using the most effective means of killing them; since this is a Loran dungeon there are going to be a lot of Beast type enemies, so having a good fire weapon is highly recommended.

Step 02

The edge of the raised motif on the floor that's closest to the stairs in this room acts as a trigger point for a trap that will cause four Labyrinth Watchers to appear nearby. Not only will springing the trap unleash those enemies, but it will also awaken a Loran Silverbeast that's otherwise sitting down below at **Position A**. As long as you don't trigger that trap, you can either walk down the stairs to get behind the Silverbeast and use a charged R2, or you can drop down and using a plunging attack on it from above. [→□ 01/02]

Step 03

A Labyrinth Madman stands between you and the contents of the chest in this room, and he will start coming after you almost immediately after you enter the room so you won't have a lot of time to prepare for him. If you have a Blue Elixir, you can use it before entering the room, and then cross over to the opposite side of the room, walk around behind him, and use a charged R2 for an early advantage. Alternatively, you can lure him near the tree and use it to circle around so that you can hit him when his attacks miss. [→□ 03]

Step 04

The lever you need to pull is being guarded by a Loran Silverbeast, so unless you have a strong fire weapon it's going to be a difficult battle. If you have some Molotov Cocktails or the Flamesprayer you can lure it to one of the trees, and then circle around until an opportunity presents itself, or you can use a Blue Elixir before entering the room and sneak around behind him to start the fight with a charged R2. When you exit the room you can save yourself some time by dropping off the ledge to your right and landing on the platform below, instead of crossing both of the bridges again.

Step 05

Another, stronger Loran Silverbeast is the boss you'll need to defeat on this floor. He always approaches you from the flight of stairs to your left, giving you a momentary elevated advantage. You can also use the support pillars on this upper floor to your advantage to shield you from his flaming ranged attacks. Circle around the pillar at a safe distance until he fires up, and then flank around and attack him from behind while he recovers.

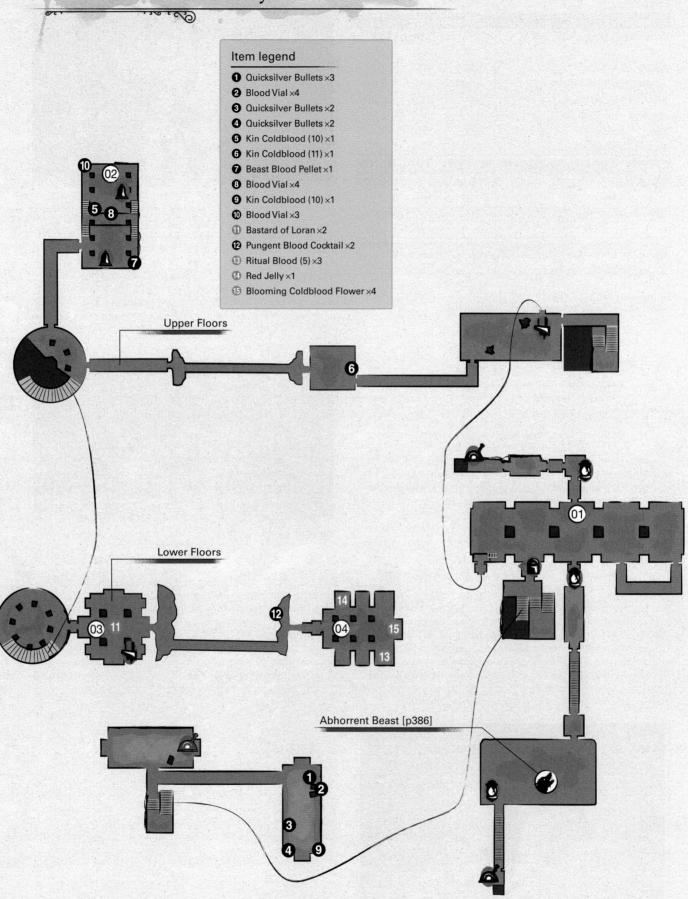

Item legend

1. Quicksilver Bullets ×3
2. Blood Vial ×4
3. Quicksilver Bullets ×2
4. Quicksilver Bullets ×2
5. Kin Coldblood (10) ×1
6. Kin Coldblood (11) ×1
7. Beast Blood Pellet ×1
8. Blood Vial ×4
9. Kin Coldblood (10) ×1
10. Blood Vial ×3
11. Bastard of Loran ×2
12. Pungent Blood Cocktail ×2
13. Ritual Blood (5) ×3
14. Red Jelly ×1
15. Blooming Coldblood Flower ×4

Upper Floors

Lower Floors

Abhorrent Beast [p386]

Enemies

Regular	HP	Echoes	Page
Beast Patient (Male)	1148	3842	p236
Beast Patient (Female)	1409	4316	p237
Ashen Blood Beast Patient	1664	6071	p237
Wandering Nightmare	341	664	p671
Large Wandering Nightmare	487	5075	p671
Nightmare Apostle	1148	2703	p247
Labyrinth Rat	894	2514	p233
Labyrinth Watcher (Cleaver)	894	3178	p250

Strong	HP	Echoes	Page
Scourge Beast	2688	7446	p266
Bell Ringer	1533	5407	p287
Labyrinth Madman (Corpse)	2688	11667	p300
Bloodlicker	2942	10007	p280
Loran Silverbeast	763	5786	p281

Boss	HP	Echoes	Page
Abhorrent Beast	15249	83142	p386

Step 01

Upon entering this room you'll see a large group of female Beast Patients patrolling around an area just ahead to the left, and there's also a male Ashen Blood Beast Patient standing behind the pillar at **Position A**. If you have a highly upgraded fire weapon, it's possible to kill the Beast Patients in a single hit even at this level, and if that's the case all you need to do is lure them towards you in manageable numbers. Try to kill them all without going past the pillar, as that will allow you to walk up behind the Ashen Blood Beast Patient and kill it with a charged R2 from behind. [→☐ 01/02]

This room can be very difficult if you do not come prepared, and since the rewards are only consumables and the Blood Echoes from defeating the enemies, only enter if you want a challenge, especially if you're on your own. On the upper part of the room there are two Scourge Beasts and a Bell Ringer, and there's a second Bell Ringer walking around down on the lower part of the room. As usual, both Bell Ringers will be summoning Nightmare Apostles. Pungent Blood Cocktails will be your best friend if you're here solo, because you can use them to keep the Scourge Beasts busy while you take on the Bell Ringers and put an end to their summoning.

If possible you should ignore the Nightmare Apostles and only attack them if you can't run around them, so that you can take full advantage of the time given to you by the Blood Cocktails. You'll still need to use at least two or three of them to give yourself enough time to kill both Bell Ringers. You can speed things up slightly if you also happen to have a Shaman Bone Blade, because you can use it on one of the Scourge Beasts while it's distracted by a Blood Cocktail and let it do some of the work for you. When taking the room on in co-op, divide the tasks between players, with two of them on Bell Ringer duty while another deals with the Beasts. [→☐ 03/04]

Step 03

A large group of enemies consisting of male and female Beast Patients are guarding the chest in the middle of this room, so make sure you either use Fire Paper on your weapon or have a fire weapon equipped before going in, to make things much easier. If you deal enough damage with your weapon of choice to kill these enemies in one hit, you should be able to work your way through the group relatively safely, but if you start to get surrounded, just fall back to the doorway and funnel the enemies through there.

Step 04

Only a single Loran Silverbeast guards the chests in this room, and since you can get a number of extremely valuable materials, it's well worth the trip across the bridge. Just before entering this room you can pick up a pair of Pungent Blood Cocktails – use one of them to distract the Silverbeast long enough for you to get behind it for an easy kill.

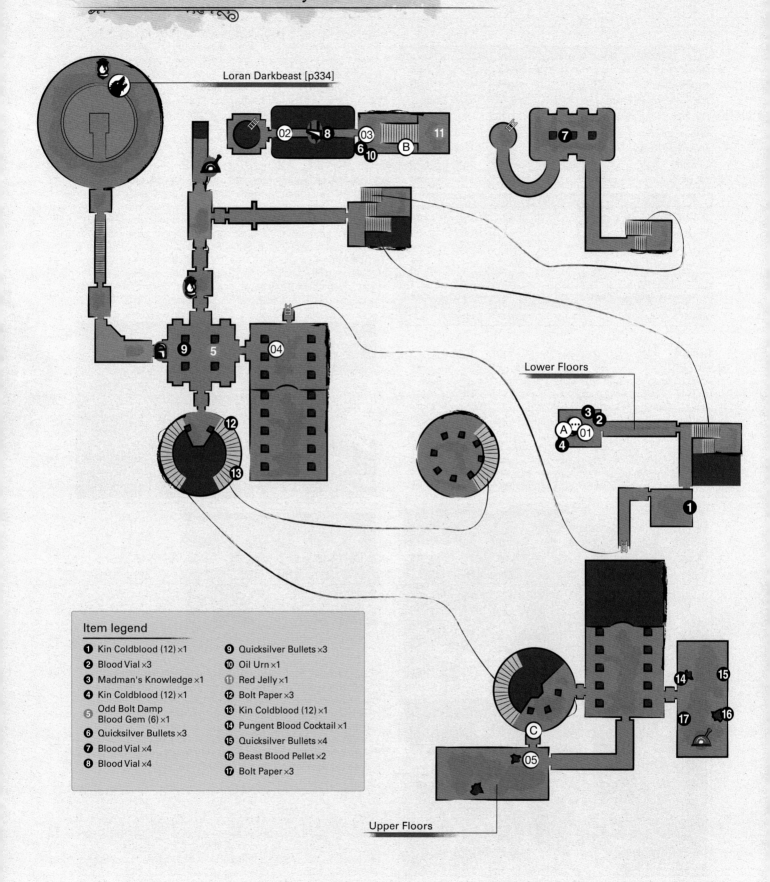

Loran Darkbeast [p334]

02 8 03
6
10 B 11
7

Lower Floors

3 2
A 01
4

9 5 04

12

13

1

Item legend

1. Kin Coldblood (12) ×1
2. Blood Vial ×3
3. Madman's Knowledge ×1
4. Kin Coldblood (12) ×1
5. Odd Bolt Damp Blood Gem (6) ×1
6. Quicksilver Bullets ×3
7. Blood Vial ×4
8. Blood Vial ×4
9. Quicksilver Bullets ×3
10. Oil Urn ×1
11. Red Jelly ×1
12. Bolt Paper ×3
13. Kin Coldblood (12) ×1
14. Pungent Blood Cocktail ×1
15. Quicksilver Bullets ×4
16. Beast Blood Pellet ×2
17. Bolt Paper ×3

14 15
17 16

C
05

Upper Floors

Enemies

Regular	HP	Echoes	Page
Beast Patient (Male)	1175	4025	p236
Ashen Blood Beast Patient	1703	6360	p237
Labyrinth Rat	915	2633	p233
Gel	781	6161	p253
Labyrinth Watcher (Cleaver)	915	3329	p250
Nightmare Apostle	1175	2832	p247
Wandering Nightmare	350	696	p671

Strong	HP	Echoes	Page
Loran Silverbeast	781	6062	p281
Scourge Beast	2752	7801	p266
Labyrinth Madman (Sickle)	2752	12223	p300
Bloodlicker	3012	10484	p280
Keeper's Hunting Dog	2120	5217	p305
Keeper of the Old Lords	3935	17689	p378

Boss	HP	Echoes	Page
Loran Darkbeast	20990	85660	p334

Step 01

A Bath Messenger shop can be found at **Position A** in this room, and along with the usual assortment of consumables, you'll also be able to buy the Sinister Lower Loran Root Chalice for 18000 Blood Echoes. This Chalice will let you create randomly generated dungeons that can also have the Sinister Bell Additional Rite activated if you're playing online, which means there will be Bell Ringers in the dungeon that summon other players. There are also some corpses you can loot in the room for some items, so grab them before you leave. [→▢ 01/02]

Step 02

When crossing the stone bridge here you'll have to negotiate four swinging axe hazards, and because they are all close together, you have to make it past them in one go. Position yourself close to the first swinging axe by adjusting the camera so that it's facing the side of your character to give you the best perspective. Wait for the first axe to be directly in front of you, and then begin your sprint. You can make it past all four axes safely using this method from both sides.

Step 03

There are two Loran Silverbeasts guarding the chest in this room: one at the top of the stairs, and one sitting with its back to you at **Position B**. If you walk slowly you can get close enough to the one at **Position B** to use a charged R2 and a Visceral Attack follow-up to kill it without alerting the other one. To make fighting the one at the top of the stairs easier, you may want to throw a Pungent Blood Cocktail up there once you're around halfway up to distract it and allow you to safely move in for the kill. [→▢ 03]

Step 04

If you enter this room quietly, you can walk around to the left to get behind the Labyrinth Madman standing in the middle and use a charged R2 from behind to begin the fight. Once he's down, if you approach the closed door in the room you'll notice that there's a Scourge Beast on the other side; you can attack it safely through the door.

Step 05

There are two ways you can enter this room, but the doorway at **Position C** gives you the best chance of trying to lure out some of the enemies to pick them off. Along with Beast Patients and a Nightmare Apostle, you'll also find a Keeper of the Old Lords and two Keeper's Hunting Dogs patrolling around the room. Try to peek into the room and lure out the Nightmare Apostle along with any Beast Patients that come into view using Pebbles or Throwing Knives, and then kill them outside away from the other enemies.

It's also worth trying to lure the two Hunting Dogs away from the Keeper by using a Pungent Blood Cocktail if you can. While they're distracted, try to locate the Keeper quickly and interrupt his attacks to stagger him, and then use a Shaman Bone Blade if you have one, or the follow-up of your choice if you don't. If you do connect with the Bone Blade, he should easily be able to take care of all the other enemies in the room for you. Alternatively, if the Pungent Blood Cocktail pulls the Hunting Dogs too far from the Keeper, you should use a Shaman Bone Blade on one of them instead, because it will still deal a lot of damage before its killed. Without using any Shaman Bone Blades you'll need to keep throwing Pungent Blood Cocktails to keep the dogs distracted while you kill them using fire-based attacks; Beast Blood Pellets will help speed this process up considerably.

Isz Gravestone

The Great Isz Chalice required for this dungeon is acquired by defeating Ebrietas, Daughter of the Cosmos. You can find her by reaching the Altar of Despair after clearing the Upper Cathedral Ward. Defeating her also unlocks the Pearl Slug basic ritual crafting item in the Insight Trade shop in the Hunter's Dream, three of which are needed in the crafting of this dungeon. You can also collect one Pearl Slug on the ground floor of the Byrgenwerth College Building, and another two in the Upper Cathedral Ward if you wish to save spending your Insight.

The celestial, other-worldly Isz dungeons seem ancient and overgrown, with all sorts of weird and wonderful foliage from floor to ceiling, making it hard to spot the many traps you'll encounter. As with all Depth five Chalice Dungeons, it's highly recommended to take this one on in an online co-op team in order to maximize your chances of success. The whole team should be focusing on interrupting and staggering enemies. It's also worth bringing a weapon that's strong against Kin type enemies, since you'll be running into them here.

> Recommended   Player Level **140+** | Weapon Upgrade **+10**

Layer 1

Step 01

There's a Wandering Nightmare around the corner to the left (at **Position A**) in this room, but if you want to kill it before it can disappear you'll need stay clear of the entrance to the room and lure all of the other enemies out of there first. The large group of Labyrinth Rats are the real concern, and after they spot you you may want to fall back to the circular room with the ladder, because you'll be able to use the cage there as cover. If you see them group up, consider using some Molotovs or other area of effect attacks. There's a Labyrinth Watcher near the entrance, but he moves much slower than the rats, so you shouldn't have to worry about him till they're dead.

Step 02

At the midpoint of this staircase is a new kind of trap that you'll need to be especially wary of. The trap area is marked by a circular ring of candles, and if you step into the circle you'll immediately be warped down to the room from Step 01. If you haven't already cleared out that room you'll be surrounded by enemies and in an extremely bad situation; your best option is to run back out of the room to create some distance. [→ 🔲 **01**]

Step 03

Along with the Brainsucker guarding the lever at the top of the stairs in this room, there are also some Celestial Children at the bottom of them. While the Celestial Children do move quite slowly, it's still best to take them all out before going up the stairs and fighting the Brainsucker, just in case one of them hits you in the back; the Frenzy buildup from their attacks is very strong, and getting Frenzied would almost certainly lead to death. When you take on the Brainsucker, remember to use thrusting attacks to take it down quickly.

Enemies

Regular	HP	Echoes	Page
Labyrinth Watcher (Halberd)	1342	3026	p251
Labyrinth Watcher (Cleaver)	851	3026	p250
Labyrinth Watcher (Dagger)	851	3026	p250
Labyrinth Watcher (Twin Axes)	1342	3026	p251
Labyrinth Rat	851	2394	p233
Wandering Nightmare	325	632	p671
Celestial Child	609	949	p247

Strong	HP	Echoes	Page
Keeper's Hunting Dog	1972	4743	p305
Keeper of the Old Lords	3660	16081	p378
Bloodlicker	2802	9531	p280
Brainsucker	1024	9666	p273

Boss	HP	Echoes	Page
Brainsucker	4269	48287	p273

Ritual Info

Chalice	Great Isz Chalice
Ritual Materials	Ritual Blood (5) x9, Pearl Slug x3, Arcane Haze x25
Blood Echoes	11500
Depth	5

01

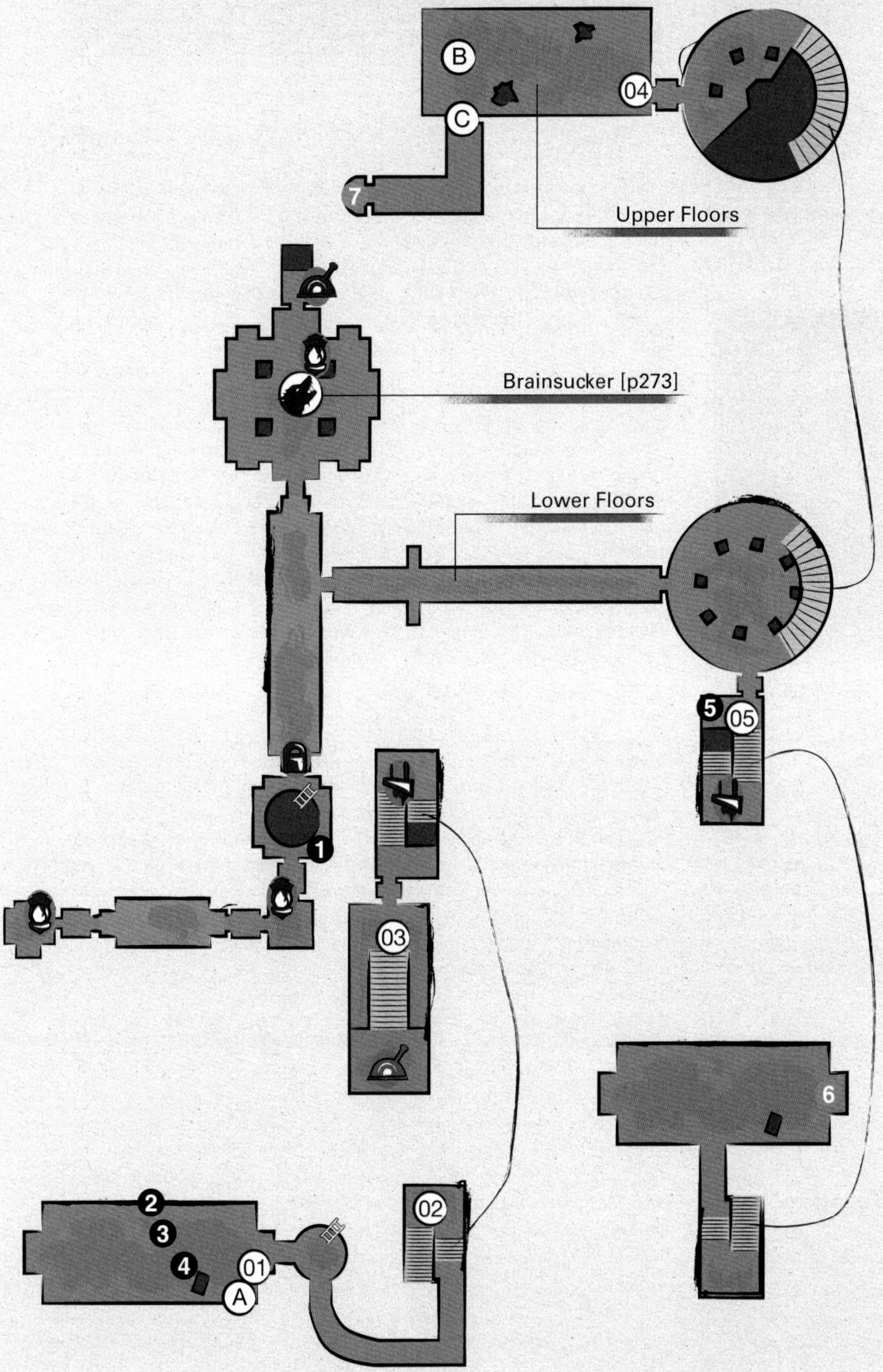

Be extremely cautious as you approach this room, because there are a lot of dangerous enemies inside. The Primary threats are a Keeper of the Old Lords along with his two Keeper's Hunting Dogs, as well as a number of Celestial Children and a Nightmare Apostle. To start with, slowly walk up to the door so that you can see inside and watch the patrol route of the Keeper and his two Dogs; wait for them to get far way, and then try to kill off some of the smaller enemies near the entrance.

When the patrolling group starts to come back towards you, use a Pungent Blood Cocktail to pull the Dogs away from the Keeper. Once they're distracted, you can use a Shaman Bone Blade to make them kill each other. If you don't have one of those, you should lure the dogs down to the bottom of the spiral staircase and fight them there, so that you can use the pillars for cover. The dogs have a large amount of health, so you may want to use more Blood Cocktails if you have them.

After killing them, head back into the room and try to finish off the remaining small enemies without the Keeper detecting you, so that they're not in the way when you fight him. Try to keep the fight with him towards the entrance half of the room; there's a Wandering Nightmare at **Position B** near the back that you don't want to disturb until you're ready. Also in this room at **Position C** is a wall that you can hit to reveal a hidden passage leading to a chest. [→ □ 02]

Step 05

The warp trap at the halfway point on the stairs here will take you straight into the room with the Keeper of the Old Lords and a number of other enemies, so if you haven't' already cleared that room out, make sure you avoid the trap at all costs.

B

C

7

04

Upper Floors

Brainsucker [p273]

Lower Floors

5   05

03

6

02

2

3

4   01

A

Item legend

1 Blood Vial ×2
2 Quicksilver Bullets ×2
3 Quicksilver Bullets ×2
4 Quicksilver Bullets ×1
5 Poison Knife ×2
6 Ritual Blood (5) ×2
7 Ritual Blood (5) ×1

Enemies

Regular	HP	Echoes	Page
Wandering Nightmare	341	664	p671
Labyrinth Rat	894	2514	p233
Labyrinth Watcher (Dagger)	894	3178	p250
Labyrinth Watcher (Cleaver)	894	3178	p250
Labyrinth Watcher (Bare Hands)	763	3178	p251
Nightmare Apostle	1148	2703	p247
Celestial Child	639	996	p247
Small Celestial Emissary	843	3652	p241
Gravekeeper Scorpion	574	2798	p252
Gel	763	5881	p253
Rotted Corpse	1148	3937	p233

Strong	HP	Echoes	Page
Brainsucker	1075	10150	p273
Bloodlicker	2942	10007	p280

Boss	HP	Echoes	Page
Celestial Emissary	10890	70289	p348

Step 03

You can find a couple of Pearl Slugs to help replenish your supplies after creating the dungeon in this room, and thankfully the enemies that are present in the room all move very slowly, so you can run past them if you wish. If you decide to take on the Gels, make sure you use fire based attacks, because anything else would take an extremely long time to kill them.

Step 04

The only enemy on the upper floor of this room is a small Celestial Emissary patrolling to the left of where you enter, so kill it before picking up all the items. If you go down the stairs at **Position A**, you'll find another small Celestial Emissary near the bottom; kill it and then collect all of the items on the middle floor. After going down the large stairs to the bottom floor, follow the passage around to the right to reach a Wandering Nightmare that's hiding near the back. Be careful when walking around on this floor, however, because there are a couple of pressure plates that will summon groups of Labyrinth Watchers if stepped on.

Step 01

A large number of Nightmare Apostles dangle from the ceiling in this room, but because of the lengths of cloth that are suspended between the roots, you won't be able to use ranged attacks to knock them down. You can, however, trigger them to drop in manageable numbers by walking slowly into the room. After the one closest to the entrance has been killed, walk along the right-hand wall and get the ones on that side to drop down one at a time. The two remaining ones on the other side of the room will drop down at the same time when you approach, so shoot one of them to knock it over while you kill the other one. [→☐ 01]

Step 02

Take out the small group of Celestial Children on the upper part of this room without getting too close to the stairs if possible, because there's a Brainsucker down there guarding the lever. The Brainsucker here does not use any magical attacks, so go down the stairs until it spots you, and then try to time a charged R2 to connect as it comes running in. [→☐ 02]

Step 05

While on first inspection it may appear that this room only has the two Brainsuckers guarding the coffin at the other end, there is in fact a small Celestial Emissary hidden behind the pillar on the left at **Position B**. If you walk around to the left of that pillar you can sneak up behind him and use a charged R2 for an easy victory. Of the two Brainsuckers, only the one on the left as you look into the room will use magic, so it poses by far the biggest threat. Your strategy for taking on both of them should revolve around staying safe from its paralyzing ranged attacks.

By continuing to walk along the side of the room you can use the next pillar ahead to block the magical attacks of the closest Brainsucker once it starts using them, and at the same time, the other Brainsucker will come running around to fight you in close range. The magic-using Brainsucker does not move very much, so as long as you keep the fight behind the pillar, you can remain safe from its magic. Once the first one has been killed, stay hidden behind the pillar for a while and the other one will lose track of you. When that happens you can sneak around the pillar and use a charged R2 in its back.

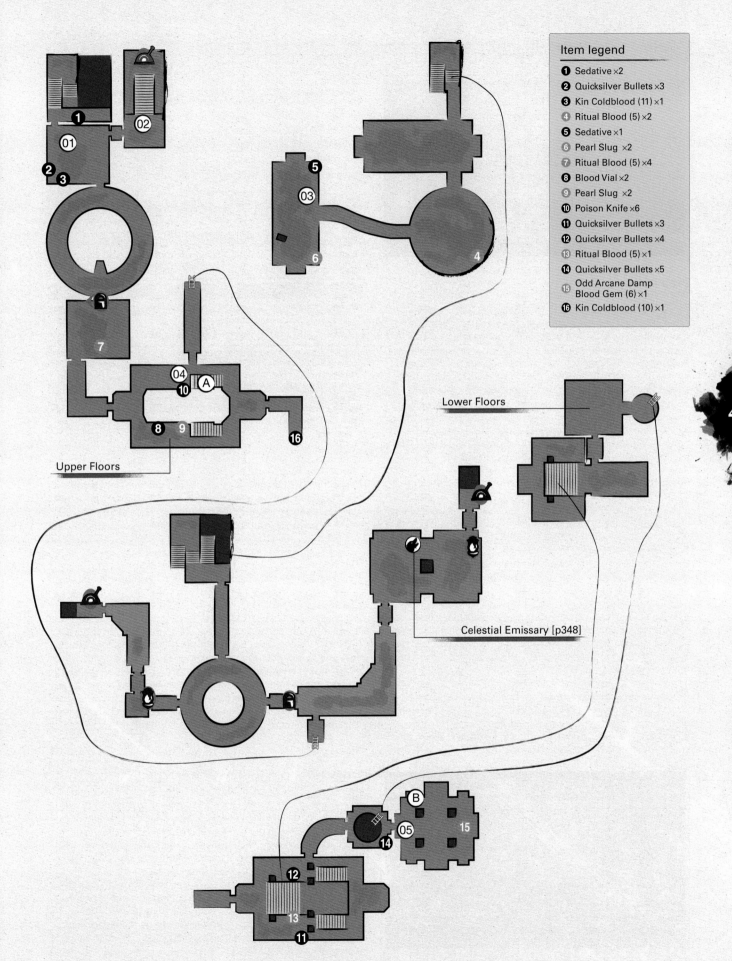

Celestial Emissary [p348]

Upper Floors

Lower Floors

Item legend

1. Sedative ×2
2. Quicksilver Bullets ×3
3. Kin Coldblood (11) ×1
4. Ritual Blood (5) ×2
5. Sedative ×1
6. Pearl Slug ×2
7. Ritual Blood (5) ×4
8. Blood Vial ×2
9. Pearl Slug ×2
10. Poison Knife ×6
11. Quicksilver Bullets ×3
12. Quicksilver Bullets ×4
13. Ritual Blood (5) ×1
14. Quicksilver Bullets ×5
15. Odd Arcane Damp Blood Gem (6) ×1
16. Kin Coldblood (10) ×1

4

01

Enemies

Regular	HP	Echoes	Page
Gravekeeper Scorpion	588	2932	p252
Wandering Nightmare	350	696	p671
Labyrinth Watcher (Halberd)	1443	3329	p251
Labyrinth Watcher (Cleaver)	915	3329	p250
Labyrinth Watcher (Dagger)	915	3329	p250
Labyrinth Watcher (Cleaver & Lantern)	1443	3329	p250
Small Celestial Emissary	863	3826	p241
Gel	781	6161	p253
Watcher's Gravedigger (Pickaxe)	1830	4770	p254
Labyrinth Rat	915	2633	p233
Celestial Child	655	1043	p247

Strong	HP	Echoes	Page
Scourge Beast	2752	7801	p266
Brainsucker	1101	10633	p273
Bloodlicker	3012	10484	p280

Hunter	HP	Echoes	Page
Nameless Tomb Prospector (Ludwig's Holy Blade & Rosmarinus)	3377	20968	p319

Boss	HP	Echoes	Page
Ebrietas, Daughter of the Cosmos	21250	77909	p350

Step 01

As soon as you enter this room you'll see a Gravekeeper Scorpion hiding behind a tombstone just ahead, so if you have any Arcane-based weapons, it's worth equipping them here. Try to keep the fight near the entrance, because a Hunter is standing at **Position A** not too far away, and you don't want to draw him into the fight prematurely. Once the Scorpion is down, move up and start fighting the Hunter, and if you need cover or just want to create some space, use the two carts in the corner nearby. Two more Scorpions can be found down to the left side of the room, and you should try to lure them back towards you, because there's a Wandering Nightmare further in and you should avoid disturbing it until you're ready so that it doesn't disappear. [→☐ 01]

Step 02

If you want to get the Blood Gem from the chest at the top of this room, you're going to have to fight your way through a very large number of enemies. In total you'll have to face four non-magic using Brainsuckers, two magic-using Small Celestial Emissaries and two Scourge Beasts. The first enemy you should deal with is a Brainsucker facing the wall on the right at **Position B**, but shortly after you enter the room, the Small Celestial Emissary at **Position C** will begin launching spells at you. If you start walking to the right upon entering the room, you should be able to get behind the pillar near the Brainsucker and use it for cover. Once there, wait for an opening to use a charged R2 from behind against the Brainsucker, and then finish it off with a Visceral Attack, so that you can use the invincibility to avoid any incoming magic.

Run to the opposite side of the room now, and while using the pillars there for cover, hit the Brainsucker on the stairs at **Position D** with a ranged attack to lure it to you, so that you can fight it from behind the pillar. The Celestial Emissary at **Position C** should be your next target. As you move further into the room, however, not

02

only will you have to use the pillars to block the attacks from that one, but the second one on the upper part of the room will also starting attacking. Wait for an opening, and then quickly run up the stairs to the ledge and fight the Celestial Emissary there while you're close to the wall, so that the one above cannot hit you. After killing it, walk along the ledge and take out the Brainsucker that's crouching with its back to you at the other end.

Depending on how much noise you make during those fights, one of the Scourges Beasts may jump down from the upper part, so make sure you keep watch just in case. Continue up the stairs near the Brainsucker you just killed, and when you near the top, throw a Pungent Blood Cocktail towards the coffin to distract the Scourge Beasts, and then quickly run up and take out the remaining Celestial Emissary. A final Brainsucker can also be found on the opposite side of this area at **Position E**, so keep the fight with the Scourge Beasts away from it by throwing Blood Cocktails near the stairs you came up. If you manage to kill them without disturbing the Brainsucker, you'll be able to walk over and use a charged R2 from behind since it's facing away from you. [→☐ 02]

Step 03

There's a large group of Small Celestial Emissaries patrolling around the middle of this room, but thankfully none of them use magic so you only have to be careful once you get close to them. Because they're bunched up so tightly, you may also want to use some Molotovs to weaken them as you approach. Try not to go too far into the room while fighting them, however, because two Scourge Beasts are lurking back there, obscured by the smoke. When you want to close in to take them on, throw a Pungent Blood Cocktail towards the smoke so that you can safely approach and attack them while they're distracted. There's a Wandering Nightmare along the back wall of the room, with another group of patrolling Celestial Emissaries nearby; run up and kill the Wandering Nightmare first, and then deal with this group of Celestial Emissaries in the same manner as the first.

Ebrietas, Daughter of the Cosmos [p350]

A lone Scourge Beast prowls the floor in this room, and if you hide behind the pillars you can often get close enough to attack it without being detected. Once the beast has been defeated, climb up the ladder and follow the path around to reach a Bath Messenger where, among other things, you'll be able to purchase the Sinister Isz Root Chalice for 20000 Blood Echoes.

Item legend

1. Blue Elixir ×2
2. Sedative ×3
3. Quicksilver Bullets ×4
4. Blue Elixir ×2
5. Odd Arcane Damp Blood Gem (5) ×1
6. Blood Vial ×5
7. Great One's Wisdom ×1
8. Kin Coldblood (12) ×1
9. Quicksilver Bullets ×3
10. Sage's Hair ×6
11. Red Jelly ×1
12. Red Jelly ×1
13. Tomb Mold (5) ×5
14. Kin Coldblood (12) ×1
15. Great One's Wisdom ×1
16. Quicksilver Bullets ×3
17. Yellow Backbone ×3

Lower Floors

Upper Floors

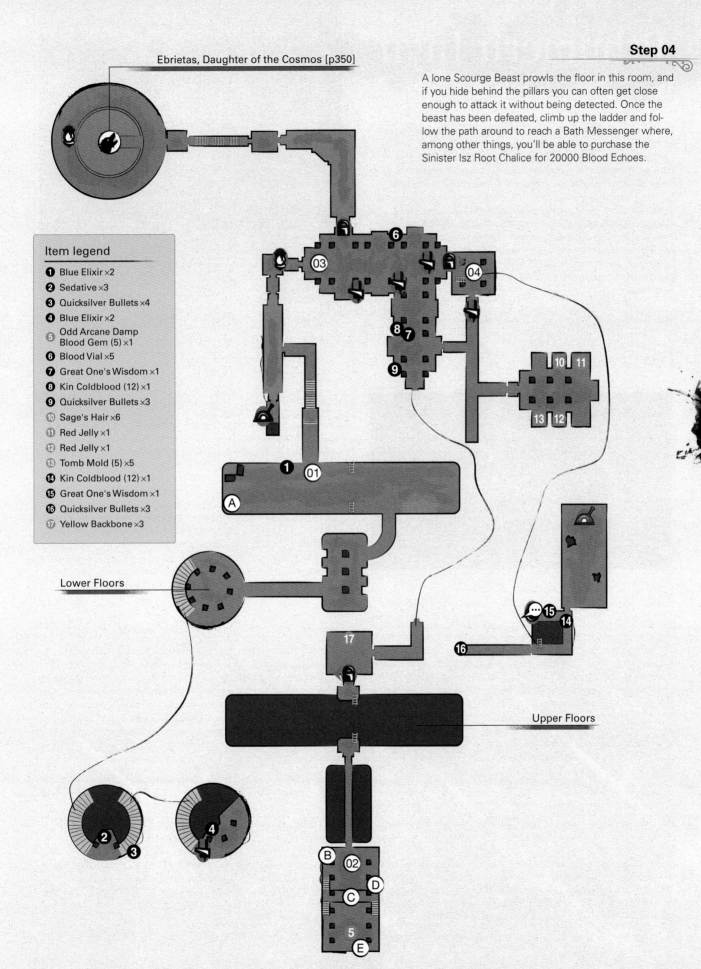

Pthumeru Ihyll

Two of the four Red Jellies you are going to need to help craft this dungeon can be found in a chest in the Lecture Building, and the other two can be found in the Lower Loran dungeon. You can get the required Arcane Hazes from the first Pthumerian Labyrinth from the Fluorescent Flowers on the third level garden plaza area, or use the Workshop Arcane Haze Extractor to extract them from any surplus basic ritual materials you can spare. The Living String is the hardest ritual item to get. You have to seek out and defeat the hidden Brain of Mensis in the Nightmare of Mensis area – for more information on how to do that, please refer to p156. As with all Depth five Chalice Dungeons, it is strongly advised to take this on in an online co-op team.

| Recommended | Player Level **140+** | Weapon Upgrade **+10** |

Layer 1

Step 01

Be careful as you enter this room, because a pressure plate just inside the door will trigger a flaming arrow trap when stepped on, and getting hit by even a single arrow will result in massive HP loss. A large group of Labyrinth Watchers are patrolling around the middle of the room not far from a Merciless Watcher, so try to lure them back towards the entrance side of the room to eliminate the risk of getting the Merciless Watcher involved. When it comes time to fight him, rush in and fight him at close range, since he has a gun and won't swap it for his club until his HP is low. When you're right next to him the shots from his gun will miss, and the swings from his lantern do negligible damage, so you can easily restore any HP you lose just by hitting him.

Step 02

A Merciless Watcher can just about be seen standing in the middle of this dark room as you enter, but don't go running straight ahead to fight him. If you hug the wall and walk around either side of the room you can get behind him to start the fight with a well placed charged R2 and follow-up of your choice to significantly weaken him. During this fight there's a strong chance that one of the Labyrinth Watchers on the floor above may drop down; keep listening for the sounds he makes to know if he's coming. [→□ 01]

Step 03

Above you on a walkway to the left, a Labyrinth Watcher will start throwing Poison Knives down at you as soon as you enter this room; if you hit him with a couple of ranged attacks of your own, you'll be able to knock him back far enough that his knives will hit the floor near his feet. Try to lure the two Hunting Dogs and Rabid Dog away from the Watcher Chieftain at the back of the room, and remember that you can shoot them to knock them over for a much easier fight. There's also a Labyrinth Watcher on either side of the room, so it's a good idea to take one of them out, and then stay on that side when fighting the other enemies, so that you don't have to worry about incoming Poison Knives. When it comes to fighting the Chieftain you can make use to the pillars to restrict his movement, or you can try to lure him near some of the explosive urns and shoot them to inflict massive damage.

Step 04

To reach the lever at the bottom of the stairs in this room you'll need to get through a club-wielding Merciless Watcher, and by far the best way to start the fight is to use a Blue Elixir. After using one if you drop down from the side of the stairs you can walk around behind him and start the fight with a charged R2 from behind. If that's not an option, you should attack him with ranged attacks from the top of the stairs while he slowly makes his way towards you, and then use a well timed jumping attack once he's in range to inflict heavy damage.

Step 05

A Tomb Prospector stands in wait beneath the bridge at the far end of this room, as if challenging you to approach. If you accept the challenge and want to fight him, there are plenty of things in the environment nearby that you can use to your advantage. A couple of wooden carts near the bridge provide excellent cover if you require some, and just past the bridge is a pool of oil, so if you have a fire weapon that's an excellent place to fight him. Be careful if you see him start to run away, however, because he'll often use Rope Molotovs if you give chase.

Enemies

Regular	HP	Echoes	Page
Labyrinth Watcher (Dagger)	940	4143	p250
Labyrinth Watcher (Twin Axes)	1482	4143	p251
Labyrinth Watcher (Cleaver)	940	4143	p250
Labyrinth Watcher (Halberd)	1482	4143	p251
Watcher's Gravedigger (Rifle, Hook & Lantern)	1749	5256	p254
Watcher's Gravedigger (Hook & Lantern)	1879	5936	p254
Labyrinth Rat	940	3277	p233
Nightmare Apostle	1207	3525	p247
Rabid Dog	1077	5194	p230
Hunting Dog	1207	6184	p238

Strong	HP	Echoes	Page
Merciless Watcher (Scattergun, Club & Lantern)	4239	19541	p297
Merciless Watcher (Saw)	8081	69629	p297
Watcher Chieftain (Club & Lantern)	4239	19541	p294
Bloodlicker	3094	13048	p280
Evil Labyrinth Spirit	1413	6926	p298

Hunter	HP	Echoes	Page
Nameless Tomb Prospector (Kirkhammer & Torch)	3468	26096	p319

Boss	HP	Echoes	Page
Pthumerian Descendant	16843	100486	p382

Ritual Info

Chalice	Great Pthumeru Ihyll Chalice
Ritual Materials	Ritual Blood (5), Red Jelly ×4, Arcane Haze ×25, Living String ×1
Blood Echoes	11500
Depth	5

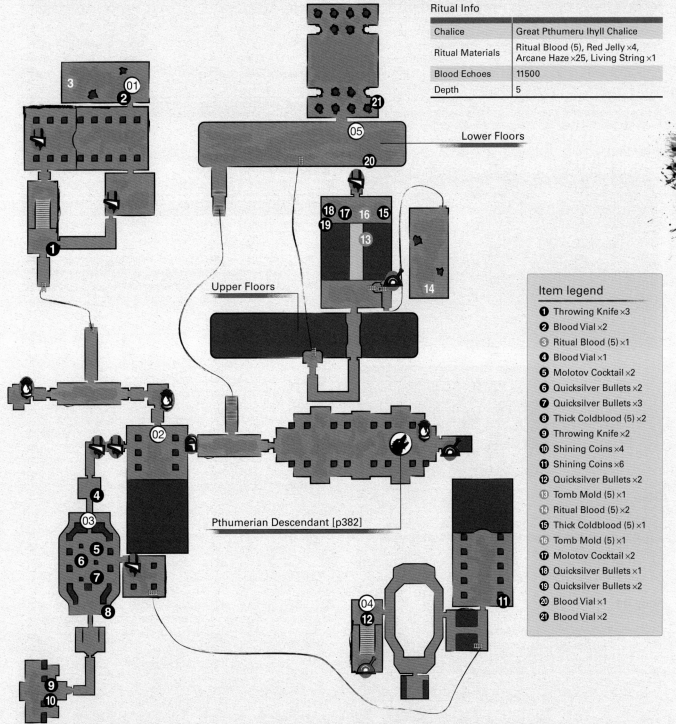

Lower Floors

Upper Floors

Pthumerian Descendant [p382]

Item legend

1. Throwing Knife ×3
2. Blood Vial ×2
3. Ritual Blood (5) ×1
4. Blood Vial ×1
5. Molotov Cocktail ×2
6. Quicksilver Bullets ×2
7. Quicksilver Bullets ×3
8. Thick Coldblood (5) ×2
9. Throwing Knife ×2
10. Shining Coins ×4
11. Shining Coins ×6
12. Quicksilver Bullets ×2
13. Tomb Mold (5) ×1
14. Ritual Blood (5) ×2
15. Thick Coldblood (5) ×1
16. Tomb Mold (5) ×1
17. Molotov Cocktail ×2
18. Quicksilver Bullets ×1
19. Quicksilver Bullets ×2
20. Blood Vial ×1
21. Blood Vial ×2

4

Step 01

All of the liquid on the floor of this massive cavern is oil, so it can be very useful if you lure enemies into it and attack them with fire weapons. The only enemies here are Labyrinth Watchers, and they will blindly come running towards you as soon as they detect you, so luring them into the oil is relatively easy.

Step 02

The four Ritual Blood (5) items contained within the chest at the back of this room make for tempting bait to lure you into this Nightmare Apostle nest. Numerous Apostles run about on the floor, but even more are hanging down from the ceiling, so you need to be very mindful of your position, and don't go recklessly running into the room. Try to fight all of the ones on the ground without progressing past the first tree, because that's the point at which some of the ones hanging from the ceiling will start to drop down. Once the first few are out of the way, systematically work your way through the room, shooting them down one at a time as you come to them. The Apostles often drop Quicksilver Bullets, so you should never run short of them, and it's even worth shooting them as they approach you so that they get knocked over and are easier to fight. [→ ☐ 01/02]

01

02

Step 03

You'll be entering this garden plaza area on the upper balcony, so use this opportunity to take out the Labyrinth Watchers and Watcher's Gravediggers that are scattered along it so that they don't become a problem later. Instead of dropping down to the main floor, go through the door on the opposite side into the elevator room.

Step 04

Taking the elevator down straight away in this room would put you in an extremely bad situation, because along with two Lost Children of Antiquity there are two Labyrinth Rite Keepers and you don't have a lot of room to evade their fireballs. A much safer option is to go around the upper part of the room until you see the Keepers down below, and then use ranged attacks to kill them from there.

Enemies

Regular	HP	Echoes	Page
Labyrinth Watcher (Twin Axes)	1556	4350	p251
Labyrinth Watcher (Cleaver)	986	4350	p250
Labyrinth Watcher (Dagger)	986	4350	p250
Labyrinth Watcher (Halberd)	1556	4350	p251
Labyrinth Rat	986	3441	p233
Watcher's Gravedigger (Pickaxe)	1973	6233	p254
Watcher's Gravedigger (Rifle, Hook & Lantern)	1837	5519	p254
Watcher's Gravedigger (Hook & Lantern)	1973	6233	p254
Wandering Nightmare	377	909	p671
Nightmare Apostle	1267	3701	p247
Rabid Dog	1131	5454	p230
Lost Child of Antiquity	2262	8116	p244
Labyrinth Ritekeeper	1267	5065	p253
Gravekeeper Scorpion	634	3831	p252
Strong	**HP**	**Echoes**	**Page**
Merciless Watcher (Saw)	8485	73111	p297
Merciless Watcher (Mace)	4451	20518	p296
Watcher Chieftain (Club & Lantern)	4451	20518	p294
Bloodlicker	3248	13700	p280
Labyrinth Warrior (Crossbow & Sword)	2687	20063	p302
Boss	**HP**	**Echoes**	**Page**
Bloodletting Beast (Parasite)	24045	111030	p390

The floor of the walkway you're on will shield you from their attacks, so you can just keep using your Throwing Knives or Molotovs until they're dead. The two Lost Children are pretending to be statues, so once you're on the lower floor, look for them amongst the pots and shoot them to awaken them one at a time.

Step 05

As you approach the central area of the garden plaza you'll see a Watcher Chieftain and a Wandering Nightmare patrolling around near the fountain. If you want to kill the Wandering Nightmare, you'll need to lure the Chieftain back towards you. Throwing Knives are best to accomplish that, since they don't produce any sound. Once the Chieftain is down, run up and take out the Wandering Nightmare while staying clear of the top of the stairs. A Labyrinth Warrior with a crossbow is standing with his back to you at the top of the stairs, so if you haven't disturbed him yet you can sneak up behind him and use a charged R2 into Visceral Attack combo to kill him.

Killing the Warrior makes enough noise to get the attention of the Gravedigger and two Rabid Dogs that are further down the stairs, so it's worth retreating back and using the fountain for cover straight away. If the dogs follow you, use the fountain to block the Gravedigger's shots while you kill them. The Gravedigger will eventually lose interest in you and turn around again if you stay hidden behind the fountain, so when you see him do that, walk up and use a charged R2 from behind for an easy victory. There are some more Labyrinth Watchers and Watcher's Gravediggers around the outskirts of the room, but they're spread out enough that they're easy to pick off one at a time.

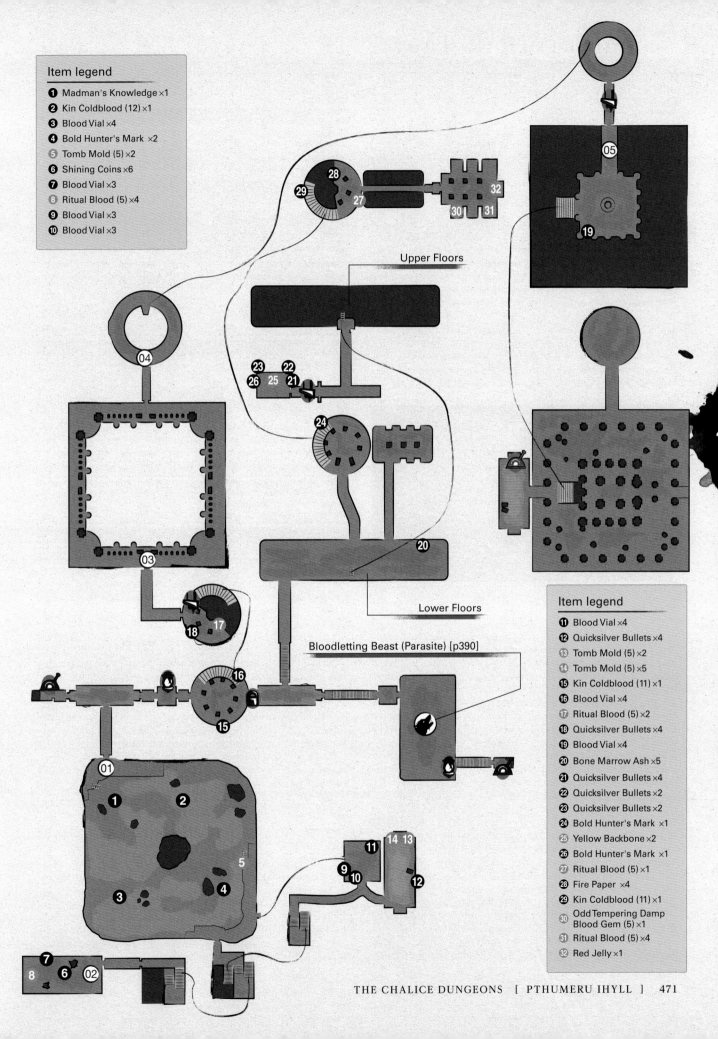

Item legend

1. Madman's Knowledge ×1
2. Kin Coldblood (12) ×1
3. Blood Vial ×4
4. Bold Hunter's Mark ×2
5. Tomb Mold (5) ×2
6. Shining Coins ×6
7. Blood Vial ×3
8. Ritual Blood (5) ×4
9. Blood Vial ×3
10. Blood Vial ×3

Upper Floors

Lower Floors

Bloodletting Beast (Parasite) [p390]

Item legend

11. Blood Vial ×4
12. Quicksilver Bullets ×4
13. Tomb Mold (5) ×2
14. Tomb Mold (5) ×5
15. Kin Coldblood (11) ×1
16. Blood Vial ×4
17. Ritual Blood (5) ×2
18. Quicksilver Bullets ×4
19. Blood Vial ×4
20. Bone Marrow Ash ×5
21. Quicksilver Bullets ×4
22. Quicksilver Bullets ×2
23. Quicksilver Bullets ×2
24. Bold Hunter's Mark ×1
25. Yellow Backbone ×2
26. Bold Hunter's Mark ×1
27. Ritual Blood (5) ×1
28. Fire Paper ×4
29. Kin Coldblood (11) ×1
30. Odd Tempering Damp Blood Gem (5) ×1
31. Ritual Blood (5) ×4
32. Red Jelly ×1

Step 01

Hidden in a dark corner of this room you'll find a Bath Messenger that sells some handy consumables, along with the Sinister Pthumeru Ihyll Root Chalice for 16000 Blood Echoes. Before making any purchases, however, you should take out the Watcher's Gravedigger that patrols along the opposite side of the room, so that he doesn't attack you while you're browsing in the shop.

Step 02

There's a Labyrinth Watcher just to the left as you enter this room, but ignore it for now and run straight ahead to where the Watcher's Gravedigger is and take him out first, since he poses a bigger threat. Once both enemies have been killed, use either of the staircases to get down to the lower part of the room and use Pebbles or Throwing Knives to lure the remaining Labyrinth Watchers away from the Merciless Watcher one at a time. You can fight them near the bottom of the sitars, and even run along the ledge without alerting the Merciless Watcher to your presence. After killing them all, sneak along one of the side walls so that you can get around behind the Merciless Watcher undetected and use a charged R2. [→◻ 01]

01

Step 03

It's best to enter this room through the tunnel that you can access from the bottom part of the room with the Bath Messenger, because it allows you to approach the enemies from an advantageous position. When you exit the tunnel you'll see a Watcher's Gravedigger with a gun standing near the stairs straight ahead; after he spots you, hide behind one of the support columns of the nearby archway so that he starts walking towards you, and then quickly run over and kill him. That should ensure none of the other enemies become aware of your presence, which will make dealing with them much easier. A Wandering Nightmare can usually be found somewhere around the central fountain, so try to locate it, and if it's not too near one of the other enemies, kill it quickly.

Next you'll need to kill the Gravedigger standing with his back to you at **Position A**, so sneak up behind him and use a charged R2 for an easy victory. Continue around the area clockwise, taking out the next Gravedigger at **Position B**, followed by the Watcher Chieftain at **Position C** (both of whom also have their backs to you). If you look over the edge of the area near **Position C** you should see two Rabid Dogs standing below, and it's worth using some ranged attacks to either kill them outright, or lure them up the stairs towards you. The remaining threats are the Fluorescent Flowers that are in each of the corners of the lower part of the room. While you're still on the upper section, it's worth using some ranged attacks on the ones you can reach, as it's much safer taking them out from up there. When

Enemies

Regular	HP	Echoes	Page
Watcher's Gravedigger (Hook & Lantern)	2020	6530	p254
Watcher's Gravedigger (Rifle, Hook & Lantern)	1880	5782	p254
Watcher's Gravedigger (Pickaxe)	2020	6530	p254
Labyrinth Watcher (Halberd)	1593	4557	p251
Labyrinth Watcher (Dagger)	1010	4557	p250
Labyrinth Watcher (Cleaver)	1010	4557	p250
Labyrinth Watcher (Twin Axes)	1593	4557	p251
Wandering Nightmare	386	952	p671
Rabid Dog	1158	5714	p230
Gravekeeper Scorpion	649	4013	p252
Labyrinth Rat	1010	3605	p233
Lost Child of Antiquity	2316	8503	p244

Strong	HP	Echoes	Page
Merciless Watcher (Mace)	4557	21495	p296
Merciless Watcher (Saw)	8687	76592	p297
Merciless Watcher (Scattergun, Club & Lantern)	4557	21495	p297
Bloodlicker	3326	14353	p280
Fluorescent Flower	2168	12584	p286
Labyrinth Warrior (Sword & Shield)	2751	21019	p303
Labyrinth Warrior (Greatsword)	2751	21019	p302

Hunter	HP	Echoes	Page
Nameless Tomb Prospector (Kirkhammer & Repeating Pistol)	3728	28705	p319

Boss	HP	Echoes	Page
Yharnam, Pthumerian Queen	23172	72715	p392

you finally have to go down to finish them off, work your way around the room taking them out as you come to them while using the pillars for cover. If you get close enough, it should only take a couple of hits to the flower to finish one off.

Step 04

Try to lure the Gravekeeper Scorpion near the entrance of this room back towards you, so that you can fight it away from the Tomb Prospector that's standing near the opposite wall. If he hasn't detected you, sneak around the right-hand side of the room so that you can get behind him and start with fight with a charged R2 from behind. There's a pool of oil in the tunnel you use to reach this room, so if you have a strong fire weapon you may want to lure him back into it. The other end of the room has two more Gravedigger Scorpions as well as two Labyrinth Warriors, so make sure you use Pebbles to lure them away one at a time to keep the fights manageable. The two Labyrinth Warriors both have Fire element weapons, so don't enter the pool of oil near them during the fight.

Step 05

Along with a gun toting Merciless Watcher, there's also two Lost Children of Antiquity guarding the lever in this room; one pretending to be a statue near the front of the upper part, and another clinging to the ceiling. Use ranged attacks from the stairs to knock them down one at a time so that you can fight them away from the Merciless Watcher. Once they've been defeated, sneak around the upper part of the room so that you can get behind the Merciless Watcher and use a charged R2 to start the fight.

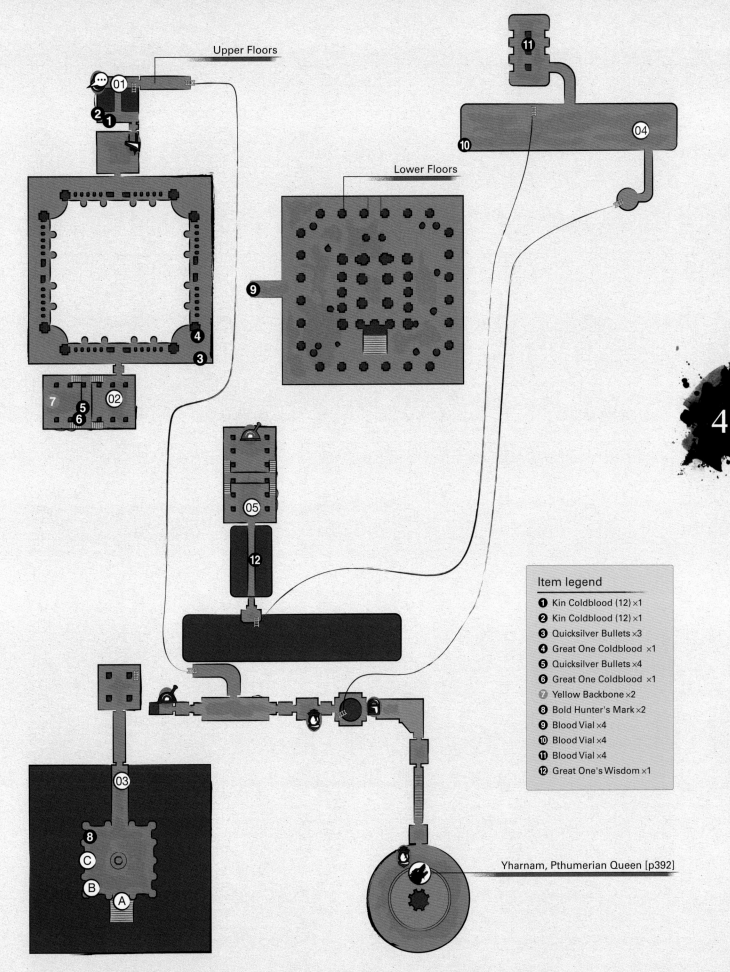

Upper Floors

01

02

Lower Floors

9

04

11

10

05

12

03

8
C
©
B
A

Yharnam, Pthumerian Queen [p392]

Item legend

1. Kin Coldblood (12) ×1
2. Kin Coldblood (12) ×1
3. Quicksilver Bullets ×3
4. Great One Coldblood ×1
5. Quicksilver Bullets ×4
6. Great One Coldblood ×1
7. Yellow Backbone ×2
8. Bold Hunter's Mark ×2
9. Blood Vial ×4
10. Blood Vial ×4
11. Blood Vial ×4
12. Great One's Wisdom ×1

4

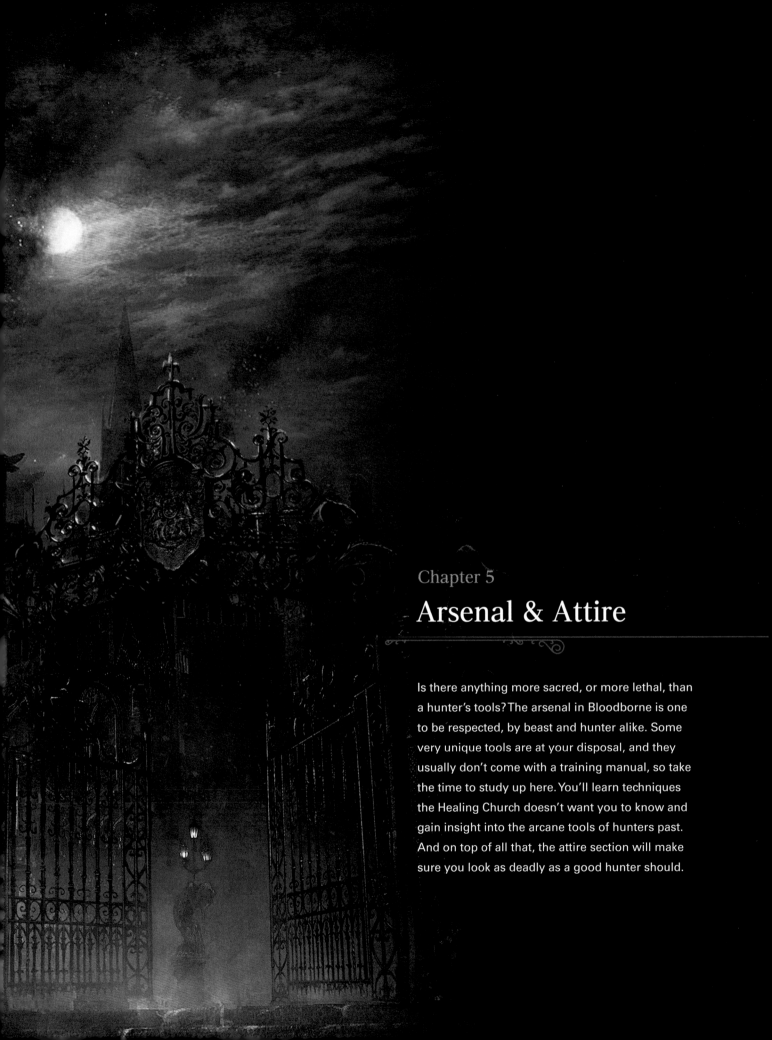

Chapter 5
Arsenal & Attire

Is there anything more sacred, or more lethal, than a hunter's tools? The arsenal in Bloodborne is one to be respected, by beast and hunter alike. Some very unique tools are at your disposal, and they usually don't come with a training manual, so take the time to study up here. You'll learn techniques the Healing Church doesn't want you to know and gain insight into the arcane tools of hunters past. And on top of all that, the attire section will make sure you look as deadly as a good hunter should.

How to Use this Chapter

On the following pages, you'll find a treasure trove of valuable weapon data. Every column is packed with useful data for comparing between weapons (and even different attacks of the same weapon). Pay particular attention to the attack tables for your favorite weapon; there are often small nuances in the numbers that you may otherwise miss!

Weapon Attack Data

The weapon attack data tables cover the key information about each attack. To ensure you know what each entry means, they are all explained in detail here.

Excerpt from Burial Blade Attack Table

Attack ❶	Dmg × ❷	Type ❸	Stamina ❹	Impact ❺
R1	1.00	Physical / Arcane	23	Light
R1 (backstep)	1.05	Thrust / Arcane	12(+10)	Light

❶ **ATTACK** This column is the name of the attack. Attacks are named for the input command required to execute them. Check out the notes column for additional info.

❷ **ATTACK DAMAGE MULTIPLIERS** Each attack has a different multiplier. Your attack's power is equal to the attack power of your weapon times this multiplier. Higher multipliers mean stronger attacks. Refer to the Training Manual if you want to learn more about damage calculation.

❸ **TYPE** Damage type determines which gems will boost your attack and which defense the enemy will use to reduce the damage. If multiple types are listed, the attack has two separate damage components that are calculated separately. The Training Manual has additional information on damage types.

❹ **STAMINA** Each attack costs a different amount of stamina. Numbers in parentheses indicate the cost of the additional action required to execute the attack. For example, a backstep attack requires a backstep, which costs 10 stamina.

❺ **IMPACT** When you hit an enemy, it will be stunned momentarily. Impact is an assessment of how heavy the stun will be. The scale is Light > Normal > Heavy > Massive. Attacks with Massive Impact often cause knockdowns. Refer to the Training Manual for additional information on Impact.

Damage from Upgrades

As you upgrade a weapon, the base attack values and scaling increase. For scaling, "E" is the worst, "A" is the second best, and "S" is the highest value. E < D < C < B < A < S.

Excerpt from Burial Blade Damage Upgrades Table

Weapon Level	Attack 🗡	Attack ★	Scaling 🦴	Scaling ✋	Scaling ★
4	112	42	E	C	D
5	120	45	E	B	C

Average Attack Increase (Stat)

These tables will show you the approximate damage increase you will gain per point of a stat with a +10 weapon. There are three main ranges: < 26, 26 to 50, and 51 to 99. The Damage per Point is how much each point of the stat will raise your attack power in that range. The Estimated Attack Gained is how much attack power will gain from that range in total.

For example, if you have 12 points of skill and you are using a +10 Burial Blade, you will gain about 3.69 attack power by going to 13 skill. If you went all the way from 12 to 25, you would gain about 23 attack power. The numbers are approximate due to in-game rounding. You can plan your character stats based on the damage ranges of your favorite weapon.

Burial Blade Average Physical Attack Increase (Skill) Table

Stat Range	Damage per Point	Estimated Attack Gained
13 to 25	3.69	48
26 to 50	1.68	42
50 to 99	0.37	18

Available Gem Slots

This table will show you which gem slots are available for each version of your weapon. Slots are gained at upgrade levels 1, 3, and 6.

Burial Blade Available Gem Slots

Weapon Type	Weapon Level		
	1	3	6
Normal	Radial	Waning	Radial
Uncanny	Radial	Triangular	Radial
Lost	Radial	Triangular	Waning

Acquisition

Here you'll find the list of locations where the different versions of your weapon can be found. Uncanny and Lost weapons have to be found in Root Dungeons before they become available for purchase at the Bath Messengers, but the Normal versions can be acquired through the main game.

Burial Blade Acquisition

Type	Obtained from	Reference	Badge Required for Purchase
Normal	Shop	p665	Old Hunter Badge
Uncanny	Lower Loran Root Chalice	N/A	N/A
Lost	Great Pthumeru Ihyll Root Chalice	N/A	N/A

Attack Diagrams

The attack diagrams on the following pages (and with an example here) are another way to show the attack speed information. In addition to giving you a visual reminder of what the attack looks like, they show the first and last hit frames (in red) visually to help you recognize them.

Normal Mode R1

To aid you in comparing weapons, the charts in this section show you visually which of them have the fastest attacks and which take the longest to recover. The scale at the top of each table represents the duration of the slowest attack in frames – use that to work out the relative speeds of each attack based on the lengths of the bars. Bloodborne runs at 30 frames per second, and the average attack takes 15 frames to become active, which equals half a second.

The bold unit lines denote every 5th frame while the regular lines denote each single frame. Each bar has three segments; the first is the time until the attack is active, the second red segment is the active frame (the short time in which the attack can hit), and the third is the recovery period. For charged attacks, the blue bar is the time until the flash. During this period you can be knocked out of the attack, but you can also release the attack early. The recovery period ends at the exact moment where you can cancel the animation into another one, such as Quickstep or another attack.

The recovery time of charged attacks is important when staggering an enemy from behind – the shorter the recovery of the attack that caused the stagger, the more time you'll have to take advantage of it. You can also follow up stagger or interrupt with a powerful strike that will deal extra bonus damage while a visceral attack is possible. The exact values change a little from enemy to enemy, but the table here shows an example from the point when your attack connects against a Huntsman.

Huntsman	Visceral Attack Possible Until	Enemy Recovers
Stagger	52	72
Interrupt	56	64

R1 Attacks

Normal R1 Attacks: If you look at the table, you'll notice the Saw Cleaver, Saw Spear, Blade of Mercy and Beast Claw have the fastest R1s. The Blade of Mercy is the fastest among them, but deals the least physical damage; this is made up for with its arcane attack, though that won't help against all foes. A key thing these weapons have in common is low range. You'll have to sacrifice speed for better reach, but you still have some good options. The Rifle Spear's R1s reach the furthest, but only strike directly ahead. For shorter, but broader swings with comparable speed, use the Burial Blade, Ludwig's Holy Blade or Kirkhammer.

Transformed R1 Attacks: A common advantage of transforming a weapon is increasing range; if you're willing to trade, the Blade of Mercy, Reiterpallash and both incarnations of the Beast Claw have the fastest R1 attacks of all. The Blade of Mercy's R1s will finish before many weapons even reach their first hitbox frame! The Hunter Axe R1s hit fairly quick, but take longer to recover; it's worth it though, as they're versatile with amazing reach. For the best reach possible, use either the Threaded Cane or Beast Cutter, The Threaded Cane focuses on Skill and the Beast Cutter focuses on Strength, so you have options to suit your build.

Normal R1 Attacks

Weapon (Stamina use)	Duration (based on 40 frames max)
Saw Cleaver (20)	
Saw Spear (20)	
Hunter Axe (25)	
Threaded Cane (17)	
Burial Blade (23)	
Blade of Mercy (15)	
Kirkhammer (16)	
Ludwig's Holy Blade (16)	
Reiterpallasch (18)	
Chikage (23)	
Rifle Spear (18)	
Stake Driver (19)	
Tonitrus (23)	
Logarius' Wheel (30)	
Beast Claw (15)	
Beasthunter Saif (30)	
Beast Cutter (25)	
Church Pick (20)	
Holy Moon. Sword (25)	
Simon's Bowblade (20)	
Rakuyo (23)	
Boom Hammer (25)	
Whirligig Saw (18)	
Bloodletter (23)	
Amygdalan Arm (25)	
Kos Parasite (24)	
Beast Claw (Rune) (15)	

Transformed R1 Attacks

Weapon (Stamina use)	Duration (based on 51 frames max)
Saw Cleaver (24)	
Saw Spear (25)	
Hunter Axe (27)	
Threaded Cane (17)	
Burial Blade (28)	
Blade of Mercy (11)	
Kirkhammer (30)	
Ludwig's Holy Blade (36)	
Reiterpallasch (16)	
Chikage (25)	
Rifle Spear (20)	
Stake Driver (15)	
Tonitrus (23)	
Logarius' Wheel (32)	
Beast Claw (14)	
Beasthunter Saif (25)	
Beast Cutter (30)	
Church Pick (25)	
Holy Moon. Sword (35)	
Simon's Bowblade (30)	
Rakuyo (23)	
Boom Hammer (50)	
Whirligig Saw (30)	
Bloodletter (25)	
Amygdalan Arm (25)	
Kos Parasite (28)	
Beast Claw (Rune) (18)	

5

R2 Attacks

Normal R2 Attacks: Again, if you don't mind its short range, the Blade of Mercy has the fastest R2 of any weapon. The Threaded Cane's R2 comes in a close second, and it deals solid damage. If you're looking for something with better reach, try the Holy Moonlight Sword; for a weapon of this size, the speed and damage of its R2 are tremendously good. Ludwig's Holy Blade, the Kirkhammer and Boom Hammer all pretty good, and if you look at the table you'll notice their speeds are exactly the same. The Kirkhammer and Ludwig's are both weaker, but their thrust damage may work out better, since not as many enemies are weak to the Boom Hammer's blunt damage.

Transformed R2 Attacks: The transformed R2 chain of the Rakuyo is faster than Blade of Mercy's, but deals considerably less damage. That being said, you'll deal more damage in less time using the Blade of Mercy. You'll still find good use with the Rakuyo's chain though, since it will allow you to deal thrust damage consistently and quickly. Another weapon with a thrusting R2 is the Saw Spear, which is quick with better range. If you need a strong attack for handling crowds, the Saw Cleaver's R2 is the fastest for this. The R2 of the church pick is similarly good for this purpose, but slightly slower; on the other hand, it deals serration and righteous damage, so it may be the better choice yet.

Normal R2 Attacks

Weapon (Stamina use)	Duration (based on 60 frames max)
Saw Cleaver (35)	
Saw Spear (35)	
Hunter Axe (45)	
Threaded Cane (30)	
Burial Blade (45)	
Blade of Mercy (30)	
Kirkhammer (55)	
Ludwig's Holy Blade (55)	
Reiterpallasch (35)	
Chikage (40)	
Rifle Spear (40)	
Stake Driver (45)	
Tonitrus (37)	
Logarius' Wheel (55)	
Beast Claw (45)	
Beasthunter Saif (40)	
Beast Cutter (40)	
Church Pick (40)	
Holy Moon. Sword (40)	
Simon's Bowblade (30)	
Rakuyo (45)	
Boom Hammer (45)	
Whirligig Saw (30)	
Bloodletter (40)	
Amygdalan Arm (40)	
Kos Parasite (40)	
Beast Claw (Rune) (25)	

Transformed R2 Attacks

Weapon (Stamina use)	Duration (based on 69 frames max)
Saw Cleaver (38)	
Saw Spear (35)	
Hunter Axe (50)	
Threaded Cane (32)	
Burial Blade (40)	
Blade of Mercy (45)	
Kirkhammer (40)	
Ludwig's Holy Blade (50)	
Reiterpallasch (0)	
Chikage (55)	
Rifle Spear (45)	
Stake Driver (55)	
Tonitrus (37)	
Logarius' Wheel (40)	
Beast Claw (50)	
Beasthunter Saif (35)	
Beast Cutter (50)	
Church Pick (45)	
Holy Moon. Sword (50)	
Simon's Bowblade (60)	
Rakuyo (23)	
Boom Hammer (80)	
Whirligig Saw (55)	
Bloodletter (45)	
Amygdalan Arm (45)	
Kos Parasite (56)	
Beast Claw (Rune) (30)	

Stamina Usage

While speed is an important factor to consider when choosing a weapon, its stamina usage can be equally, or even more important. R1 and R2 attacks are the bread and butter of a weapon, so we've included the cost in stamina for these in parenthesis after each weapon's name. If you're using a character with low stamina, weapons such as the Threaded Cane, Rifle Spear, Blade of Mercy, and Reiterpallasch are all great options. Weapons of this sort usually have short range; the Rifle Spear and Threaded Cane are exceptions to this, but their start-up durations are comparably longer.

Both the standard and Beast's Embrace rune movesets of the Beast Claw are low in stamina use – but you'll need to attack almost constantly to take advantage of its damage increase with Beasthood, which means this weapon actually works better for high stamina builds. Other weapons which work best for high stamina builds are strength weapons, such as the Amygdalan Arm, Bloodletter and Logarius' Wheel; their swings are slow and stamina costs are high, but their damage output per hit is tremendous. Either extreme is not always ideal, so you may instead want to use weapons with more general stamina costs. Weapons like these tend to be for characters balanced in the middle of things, so you'll still have quite a few options if you're not interested in investing heavily into only a few stats. The Saw Cleaver, Saw Spear, Church Pick, Whirligig Saw and Hunter Axe all use reasonable amounts of stamina and swing at a generally good speed for good damage, especially in their transformed modes, which will afford you better range.

Transformation Attacks

Normal Transformation Attacks: The quickest normal mode transformation attacks you can use belong to the Beasthunter Saif and Chikage, followed closely by the Saw Cleaver and Saw Spear. They're all good, but the Chikage deals the most damage; beware though, this weapon drains health while transformed. The most powerful transformation attacks are either slow to use, such as the Holy Moonlight Sword or Burial Blade's, or in the Bloodletter's specific case, dangerous. The Bloodletter's transformation attack inflicts self damage, but hits hard with massive impact to make up for this.

Transformed Transformation Attacks: The transformation attacks of the transformed Saw Spear and Saw Cleaver are quite similar, even sharing the same recovery times. Comparing the two, the Saw Spear hits first, but deals less damage than the Saw Cleaver, so it's up to you to decide which is more valuable. The threaded cane's transformation attack shares the same recovery speed as these weapons and strikes even faster, but for less damage. Many transformed mode transformation attacks swing in wide horizontal arcs which are great for crowds; the fastest weapon for this is the Beasthunter Saif, and it deals solid damage to boot.

Normal Transformation Attacks

Weapon (Stamina use)	Duration (based on 66 frames max)
Saw Cleaver (23+)	
Saw Spear (23+)	
Hunter Axe (30+)	
Threaded Cane (25+)	
Burial Blade (25+)	
Blade of Mercy (15+)	
Kirkhammer (40+)	
Ludw. Holy Blade (40+)	
Reiterpallasch (0+)	
Chikage (35+)	
Rifle Spear (0+)	
Stake Driver (15+)	
Tonitrus (40+)	
Logarius' Wheel (30+)	
Beast Claw (–)	(transformation)
Beasthunter Saif (30+)	
Beast Cutter (45+)	
Church Pick (30+)	
Holy Moon. Sword (40+)	
Simon's Bowblade (35+)	
Rakuyo (36+)	
Boom Hammer (30+)	
Whirligig Saw (25+)	
Bloodletter (30+)	
Amygdalan Arm (30+)	
Kos Parasite (28+)	
Beast Claw (Rune) (30+)	

Transformed Transformation Attacks

Weapon (Stamina use)	Duration (based on 74 frames max)
Saw Cleaver (30+)	
Saw Spear (30+)	
Hunter Axe (30+)	
Threaded Cane (25+)	
Burial Blade (20+)	
Blade of Mercy (15+)	
Kirkhammer (20+)	
Ludw. Holy Blade (30+)	
Reiterpallasch (23+)	
Chikage (20+)	
Rifle Spear (25+)	
Stake Driver (20+)	
Tonitrus (–)	N/A
Logarius' Wheel (0+)	
Beast Claw (25+)	
Beasthunter Saif (30+)	
Beast Cutter (50+)	
Church Pick (35+)	
Holy Moon. Sword (60+)	
Simon's Bowblade (35+)	
Rakuyo (50+)	
Boom Hammer (–)	N/A
Whirligig Saw (35+)	
Bloodletter (30+)	
Amygdalan Arm (50+)	
Kos Parasite (40+)	
Beast Claw (Rune) (30+)	

Charged R2 Attacks

Normal Charged R2 Attacks: Landing charged attacks can be tricky, especially if you intend to stagger, so speed is an important factor here. The Saw Cleaver, Saw Spear, Beast Cutter and Blade of Mercy will finish charging well before other attacks; the Blade of Mercy is the fastest, but also has the least range, so hitting your targets may be difficult. The Rakuyo may not be as swift, but its charged R2 is a powerful thrust with solid forward momentum. For high damage, the strongest charged attacks you can use belong to the Hunter Axe, Amygdalan Arm and Holy Moonlight Sword. The Holy Moonlight Sword's will deal the most damage of this bunch, and it has surprisingly good speed for an attack of this caliber!

Transformed Charged R2 Attacks: Quite a few weapons cannot use charged R2s when transformed, so you may want to pick your weapon based on this factor. The Saw Cleaver and Saw Spear's charged R2s are the quickest of all weapons. The Cleaver hits first but takes longer to recover, while the spear hits later and recovers faster, so you'll need to decide which is more important. What the tables won't show is the amazing forward momentum of the Rifle Spear's charged R2, so don't let the long bar scare you off. The Holy Moonlight Sword's charged R2 takes a while, but it if you want spectacular damage it can't be beat.

Normal Charged R2 Attacks

Weapon (Stamina use)	Duration (based on 92 frames max)
Saw Cleaver (50)	
Saw Spear (50)	
Hunter Axe (75)	
Threaded Cane (45)	
Burial Blade (65)	
Blade of Mercy (50)	
Kirkhammer (75)	
Ludwig's Holy Blade (75)	
Reiterpallasch (50)	
Chikage (60)	
Rifle Spear (55)	
Stake Driver (65)	
Tonitrus (55)	
Logarius' Wheel (65)	
Beast Claw (50)	
Beasthunter Saif (60)	
Beast Cutter (70)	
Church Pick (55)	
Holy Moon. Sword (60)	
Simon's Bowblade (20)	
Rakuyo (60)	
Boom Hammer (70)	
Whirligig Saw (45)	
Bloodletter (60)	
Amygdalan Arm (60)	
Kos Parasite (50)	
Beast Claw (Rune) (40)	

Transformed Charged R2 Attacks

Weapon (Stamina use)	Duration (based on 100 frames max)
Saw Cleaver (50)	
Saw Spear (50)	
Hunter Axe (100)	
Threaded Cane (–)	N/A
Burial Blade (100)	
Blade of Mercy (–)	N/A
Kirkhammer (80)	
Ludwig's Holy Blade (75)	
Reiterpallasch (–)	N/A
Chikage (60)	
Rifle Spear (60)	
Stake Driver (150)	
Tonitrus (55)	
Logarius' Wheel (20+20)	
Beast Claw (70)	
Beasthunter Saif (50)	
Beast Cutter (–)	N/A
Church Pick (70)	
Holy Moon. Sword (75)	
Simon's Bowblade (90)	
Rakuyo (–)	N/A
Boom Hammer (120)	
Whirligig Saw (80)	
Bloodletter (70)	
Amygdalan Arm (70+20)	
Kos Parasite (–)	N/A
Beast Claw (Rune) (–)	N/A

Weapon Regain

When you take damage, you have a limited window of time to recover lost health. This is indicated by an orange bar which appears where your total health was previously. To recover lost health, you'll simply need attack to an enemy. You can utilize this system on enemies even after they have been killed, but only during their death animations. There are two terms for this system, which can be used interchangeably: regain and rally.

The numbers beside each weapon in the table correspond to how much health its attacks will recover with their full attack rating, both when un-upgraded and fully upgraded. The amount of health you will receive relies closely, but not exactly, on the specific damage multiplier of the attack.

The Hunter Axe will net you the highest amount of health recovered per hit across all upgrade levels. At higher levels, the Kirkhammer rivals this weapon, and its normal mode will be able to regain health faster due to its quick swing speeds. The Whirligig Saw regains equally as high, but where it shines is with the rapid shreds of the transformed mode, all of which count towards the regain system! Don't let the small numbers for weapons like the Blade of Mercy fool you – you'll be able to hit twice as fast as heavier weapons and regain similar or even greater amounts. Be aware however; ranged attacks such as gunfire won't count towards the regain system.

Weapon Regain

Weapon	Base Regain / Fully Upgraded Regain (based on 125 HP max)
Saw Cleaver	
Saw Spear	
Hunter Axe	
Threaded Cane	
Burial Blade	
Blade of Mercy	
Kirkhammer	
Ludwig's Holy Blade	
Reiterpallasch	
Chikage	
Rifle Spear	
Stake Driver	
Tonitrus	
Logarius' Wheel	
Beasthunter Saif	
Beast Cutter	
Church Pick	
Holy Moon. Sword	
Simon's Bowblade	
Rakuyo	
Boom Hammer	
Whirligig Saw	
Bloodletter	
Amygdalan Arm	
Kos Parasite	
Beast Claw (Rune)	
Fist of Gratia	
Bare Fists	

Saw Cleaver

The Saw Cleaver is a very balanced, easy-to-use weapon. It only requires 8 strength and 7 skill, meaning that characters of any origin can use it without leveling up at all. It receives even bonuses from strength and skill, though it does benefit more from strength. The Saw Cleaver's normal mode deals 20% extra damage to enemies weak against serrated weapons, making it very useful against a number of strong foes. The cleaver doesn't have any special thrusting attacks, so beware when facing enemies with high physical defense. If the cleaver is your main weapon, you may want to consider using items like Molotov Cocktails against certain enemies, such as Brainsuckers.

> One of the trick weapons of the workshop, commonly used in the hunting business. This saw, effective at drawing the blood of beasts, transforms into a long cleaver that makes use of centrifugal force. The saw, with its set of blood-letting teeth, has become a symbol of the hunt, and only grows in effectiveness the more grotesquely transformed the beast.

Gem Advice

As you see in the "Damage from Upgrades" table, the Saw Cleaver does have Arcane scaling. This does not affect your physical damage, though, so it is completely unused unless you put an elemental gem into your weapon. If you want to make an elemental version of this weapon, you'll need to slot a gem such as Fire or Odd Arcane. Doing so will convert all of your weapon's physical damage to the element that you used, and strength and skill will no longer benefit you.

Instead, your arcane stat will be used to increase the cleaver's damage. Since the Saw Cleaver is already quite specialized for killing beasts, fire is a good element to choose. Most beasts are already weak against fire, and the serrated bonus will apply to that damage as well! Remember the bonus applies in normal mode only.

Acquisition

Type	Obtained from	Reference	Bath Messenger Requirements
Normal	One of three potential starting weapons / Shop	p665	None
Uncanny	Drops in Pthumeru Root Chalice Dungeons	–	Acquire Weapon
Lost	Drops in Central Pthumeru Root Chalice Dungeons	–	Acquire Weapon

Available Gem Slots

Weapon Type	Weapon Level		
	1	3	6
Normal	Radial	Radial	Waning
Uncanny	Radial	Radial	Triangular
Lost	Radial	Triangular	Waning

Average Physical Attack Increase (Strength)

Stat Range	Damage per Point	Estimated Attack Gained
9 to 25	2.94	50
26 to 50	1.52	38
50 to 99	0.33	16

Average Physical Attack Increase (Skill)

Stat Range	Damage per Point	Estimated Attack Gained
8 to 25	1.89	34
26 to 50	1.00	25
50 to 99	0.22	11

Damage from Upgrades

Weapon Level	Base	Scaling			
0	90	D	E	D
1	99	D	E	D
2	108	D	E	D
3	117	D	E	D
4	126	D	E	D
5	135	D	D	D
6	144	D	D	D
7	153	D	D	D
8	162	C	D	D
9	171	C	D	D
10	180	C	D	C

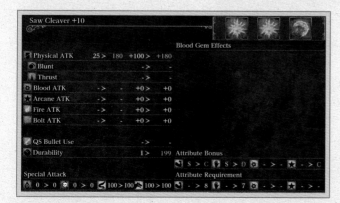

Normal Mode Tactics

The attacks in this mode have higher damage multipliers and cost less stamina; normal mode's attacks also benefit from the 20% boost in attack power against foes weak to serrated weapons. They are also slightly faster than transformed mode attacks. The Saw Cleaver is widely considered to be one of the best weapons in the game. Its quick Transform attack is both powerful and also raises your beast meter a large amount when coupled with Beast Blood Pellets. Keep in mind, the meter is smaller if you have low Beasthood or high Insight. Initiating with an R1 attack and following up with multiple L1 transformation attacks can max your beast meter rather quickly. Once the meter is raised, simple chains of R1 attacks can lead to a lot of damage.

Normal Mode Attacks Properties

Attack	Dmg ×	Type	Stamina	Impact	Note
R1	1.00		20	Light	quick and efficient
↳ R1 (2nd)	1.02		20	Light	
↳ R1 (3rd)	1.04		20	Light	
↳ R1 (4th)	1.06		20	Light	
↳ R1 (5th)	1.09		20	Light	multiplier resets following this attack
R1 (backstep)	0.95		15 (+10)	Light	
R1 (rolling)	0.95		17 (+10)	Light	fast start-up
R1 (frontstep)	0.95		17 (+10)	Light	fast start-up
R1 (sidestep)	1.00	Physical	17 (+10)	Light	better damage than R1 (frontstep) for the same cost
R1 (dash)	1.09		30 (+X)	Normal	
R2	1.20		35	Normal	
R2 (charged)	1.90		50	Normal	continuously hold the button to execute
R2 (backstep)	1.10		25 (+10)	Normal	
R2 (dash)	1.25		45 (+X)	Normal	
R2 (forward leap)	1.40		50	Normal	tap forward on the stick just as you press R2 to execute
Transform Attack	1.30		23 (+X)	Heavy	press L1 while performing another action to execute; forced Guard Break

Normal Mode Key Attacks

The R1 chain is the quickest way to deal damage, and its damage modifiers increase as the chain progresses. If you can execute five consecutive R1s safely, do so. The rolling and frontstep R1s have the quickest start-up of all the cleaver's attacks; they're useful when you need to strike quickly and are difficult to interrupt. Be cautious, though, as other players will be able to interrupt them if you use them predictably after rolling; if your opponent is expecting these attacks, a double forward roll or frontstep can get you through the bullets and into the enemy's face.

A fully-charged R2 attack is slow to perform but can stagger the enemy when you connect from behind; you can then follow up with a rear visceral attack. A more damaging option if you have an upgraded weapon is to perform a second charged R2 on the staggered enemy. This is dependent on your stats and weapon level, so experiment to see which works best. Normal R2s are slow and don't combo, which reduces their usefulness a bit.

The normal mode transformation attack is this weapon's key attack; it has a naturally heavy impact and is still reasonably fast. These features make it ideal for combos. ⬆ + ◎ > L1 is a great opener against light enemies, such as Huntsmen, and standard foes, such as Church Servants. You can frontstep in and immediately cause the enemy to flinch. This can then be followed up with additional L1s for a damaging combo.

Normal Mode R1

Normal Mode R2

Normal Mode Transform Attack

Transformed Mode Tactics

The Saw Cleaver's transformed mode is all about additional range. You sacrifice speed and damage and have higher stamina costs. You also lose the serrated bonus in this mode, but it can be worth it if you need to keep away from an enemy or when you need the range to strike an enemy's weak point. Even when transformed, the Saw Cleaver is a one-handed weapon; you can still use your gun, torch, or shield in this mode.

Transformed Mode Attacks Properties

Attack	Dmg ×	Type	Stamina	Impact	Note
R1	0.97		24	Light	hits high; useful for striking weak points
↳ R1 (2nd)	1.00		24	Light	
↳ R1 (3rd)	1.02		24	Light	multiplier resets following this attack
R1 (backstep)	0.95		15 (+10)	Light	
R1 (rolling)	0.95		20 (+10)	Light	fast start-up
R1 (frontstep)	1.00		20 (+10)	Light	fast start-up
R1 (sidestep)	1.00		20 (+10)	Light	
R1 (dash)	1.15	Physical	30 (+X)	Normal	better multiplier and range than Normal R1 (dash)
R2	1.25		38	Normal	good against groups of enemies
↳ R2 (2nd)	1.27		38	Normal	good against groups of enemies
R2 (charged)	1.70		50	Normal	continuously hold the button to execute
R2 (charged follow-up)	1.27		50	Massive	tap R2 after performing an R2 (charged); great impact
R2 (backstep)	1.10		27 (+10)	Normal	
R2 (dash)	1.20		45 (+X)	Normal	good against groups of weak enemies
R2 (forward leap)	1.30		50	Normal	tap forward on the stick just as you press R2 to execute
Transform Attack	1.30		30 (+X)	Normal	press L1 while performing another action to execute; forced Guard Break

Transformed Mode Key Attacks

The R1 chain is a series of vertical slashes that are good for narrow corridors or hitting specific enemy weak points, like the heads of Church Giants and Vicar Amelia. It also strikes low to the ground, making it useful for killing Carrion Crows and Wandering Nightmares. The transformed mode dashing R1 is one of the few transformed attacks with better damage than its normal counterpart, and it has better range, too.

The R2 chain is primarily horizontal, making it a good choice for fighting crowds. The fully-charged R2 can stagger enemies when used from behind, and the range of the charged R2 is very useful when sneaking up on a dangerous foe. Also, you can completely control the direction of the charged R2 until it executes when not locked-on to an enemy. Use this to surprise other players that are trying to roll behind you. If you press R2 again immediately following a charged R2, you can perform a special attack with massive impact. It can knockdown even large foes, so remember this when fighting bosses in co-op play! The follow-up R2 is often a better choice in terms of damage than a visceral attack on a staggered enemy, as well.

The transformation attack is once again useful; this version has less range and deals less armor damage, but it still works in combos against some enemies. The main issue is that its impact is less than that of the normal mode transformation attack. You'll notice this when breaking an enemy's super armor; the enemy won't flinch or stumble as much as they would against the normal mode version. This can allow some enemies to recover before you can continue your combo. Sometimes, it's better to roll away and reset the situation.

Transformed Mode R1

Transformed Mode R2

Transformed Mode Transform Attack

Saw Spear

The Saw Spear is very similar to the Saw Cleaver, but the spear puts more emphasis on skill. It only requires 7 strength and 8 skill, so it's another weapon that most characters will be able to use. The transformed mode is a one-handed weapon, so you can still use your off-hand weapon when transformed. The Saw Spear has both normal physical attacks and thrusting attacks; the thrusting attacks, in particular, are powerful and have good range. The thrust damage type is effective against some enemies with otherwise strong physical defense. Both of the Saw Spear's modes deal an extra 20% damage to enemies weak against serrated weapons.

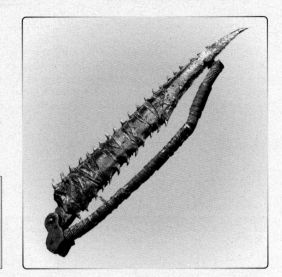

> One of the trick weapons of the workshop, commonly used by those who dedicate themselves to the hunt. This saw, effective at drawing the blood of beasts, transforms into a medium-range spear. The saw, with its set of blood-letting teeth, has become a symbol of the hunt, and only grows in effectiveness the more grotesquely transformed the beast.

Gem Advice

As with the Saw Cleaver, the Saw Spear does have Arcane scaling but it doesn't affect your physical damage, so it is completely unused unless you put an elemental gem into your weapon. Inserting a Fire or Odd Arcane gem will convert all of your weapon's physical damage to the element that you used. Your arcane stat will then be used to increase the spear's damage.

Adding a Fire gem is a good option. Most beasts are already weak against fire, and the serrated bonus will apply to that damage as well! You can also add Adept (Thrust) gems get more out of its thrust attacks in transformed mode, and its useful charged attacks make Striking gems an option worth considering.

Acquisition

Type	Obtained from	Reference	Bath Messenger Requirements
Normal	Central Yharnam	p43	Saw Hunter Badge
Uncanny	Drops in Central Pthumerian Root Chalice Dungeons	–	Acquire Weapon
Lost	Drops in Sinister/Lower Pthumerian Root Chalice Dungeons	–	Acquire Weapon

Available Gem Slots

Weapon Type	Weapon Level		
	1	3	6
Normal	Radial	Radial	Waning
Uncanny	Radial	Radial	Triangular
Lost	Radial	Triangular	Waning

Average Physical Attack Increase (Strength)

Stat Range	Damage per Point	Estimated Attack Gained
8 to 25	2.17	39
26 to 50	1.20	30
50 to 99	0.27	13

Average Physical Attack Increase (Skill)

Stat Range	Damage per Point	Estimated Attack Gained
9 to 25	2.94	50
26 to 50	1.52	38
50 to 99	0.33	16

Damage from Upgrades

Weapon Level	Base	Scaling		
0	85	D	D	D
1	93	D	D	D
2	101	D	D	D
3	109	D	D	D
4	117	D	D	D
5	125	D	D	D
6	133	D	C	D
7	141	D	C	C
8	149	D	C	C
9	157	D	C	C
10	170	D	C	C

Normal Mode Tactics

The Saw Spear's normal mode closely resembles that of the Saw Cleaver. When compared to transform mode, the attacks are all slightly faster and cost less stamina. They are also weaker, though. If you are able to strike an enemy multiple times at close range, normal mode is better.

Normal Mode Attacks Properties

Attack	Dmg ×	Type	Stamina	Impact	Note
R1	1.00		20	Light	faster than Transformed R1 chain
↳ R1 (2nd)	1.02		20	Light	
↳ R1 (3rd)	1.04		20	Light	
↳ R1 (4th)	1.06		20	Light	
↳ R1 (5th)	1.09		20	Light	very efficient damage; use when possible
R1 (backstep)	0.95		15 (+10)	Light	
R1 (rolling)	0.95		17 (+10)	Light	fast start-up
R1 (frontstep)	0.95		17 (+10)	Light	fast start-up
R1 (sidestep)	1.00	Physical	17 (+10)	Light	better damage than R1 (frontstep / rolling)
R1 (dash)	1.09		30 (+X)	Normal	
R2	1.20		35	Normal	
R2 (charged)	1.90		50	Normal	continuously hold the button to execute
R2 (backstep)	1.10		25 (+10)	Normal	
R2 (dash)	1.43		45 (+X)	Normal	
R2 (forward Drops in Ceap)	1.40		50	Normal	tap forward on the stick Root Chalice Dungeons as you press R2 to execute
Transform Attack	1.30		23 (+X)	Normal	press L1 while performing another action to execute; forced Guard Break

Normal Mode Key Attacks

The Saw Spear R1 attacks are nearly identical to the Saw Cleaver's R1 attacks. The R1 chain is the fastest way to deal damage, and its damage modifiers increase during combos. The rolling and frontstep R1s have the quickest start-up of all the Saw Spear's attacks; they can be useful when you need to strike quickly, and they are hard to interrupt. Take note that the sidestep R1 has a higher damage multiplier than the rolling or frontstep R1s even though it costs the same amount of stamina.

A fully-charged R2 attack is slow to perform, but can stagger the enemy when you connect from behind; you can then follow up with a rear visceral attack or another charged R2. It also has the highest damage modifier of any attack on this weapon, making it particularly good against enemies with high defense. If you have to fight with single strikes, a dashing R2 is reasonably powerful and quick, though it does cost a lot of stamina.

The transformation attack is a good combo tool. It executes quickly and has a decent impact; breaking an enemy's super armor with this technique forces them to stumble more than a normal R1. The long reach and good damage of the transformed R1 and R2 attacks are good natural follow-ups if the enemy is pushed back by this attack.

Normal Mode R1

Normal Mode R2

Normal Mode Transform Attack

Transformed Mode Tactics

The Saw Spear is great in transformed mode. A look at the tables will show you that the damage multipliers are good, but what the numbers don't show you is the range and versatility of the moveset. If you need to hit groups or move around and hit hard with single strikes, transformed mode is much better than normal mode.

Transformed Mode Attacks Properties

Attack	Dmg ×	Type	Stamina	Impact	Note
R1	1.09	Physical	25	Light	good damage modifier and range. but slower than Normal R1 chain
↳ R1 (2nd)	1.11	Physical	25	Light	hits high; good for striking enemy weak points
↳ R1 (3rd)	1.09	Physical	25	Light	
↳ R1 (4th)	1.11	Physical	25	Light	
R1 (backstep)	0.92	Thrust	30 (+10)	Light	fast with good range
R1 (rolling)	1.09	Physical	23 (+10)	Light	fast startup
R1 (frontstep)	1.09	Physical	23 (+10)	Light	fast startup
R1 (sidestep)	1.09	Physical	23 (+10)	Light	
R1 (dash)	0.89	Thrust	35 (+X)	Light	
R2	1.34	Thrust	35	Normal	very good damage modifier and range; key attack
R2 (charged)	1.75	Thrust	50	Normal	continuously hold the button to execute; can aim manually when unlocked
R2 (charged follow-up)	1.55	Physical	50	Heavy	tap R2 after performing an R2 (charged)
R2 (backstep)	1.19	Physical	25 (+10)	Normal	better damage and armor break than R1 (backstep)
R2 (dash)	1.19	Physical	45 (+X)	Normal	hits high; good for striking enemy weak points
R2 (forward leap)	1.34	Thrust	50	Normal	tap forward on the stick just as you press R2 to execute
Transform Attack	1.24	Physical	30 (+X)	Light	press L1 while performing another action to execute; forced Guard Break

Transformed Mode Key Attacks

The first R1 attack hits in a sweeping arc from the right of your character to the left and is excellent against a crowd. The second strikes overhead, making it useful for striking enemy weak points. The third R1 sweeps horizontally from left to right. Do not underestimate the value of these attacks. They have a good combination of speed, power, and range. Just be careful in narrow spaces; the first attack in particular tends to be stopped by walls. You can often get around this restriction by standing on the left side of a corridor to leave free room to swing on the right.

A better option is to simply use the R2 in these situations; it's a straight thrust that won't hit the walls. It also has a fantastic damage modifier and deals thrust damage rather than normal physical damage. You'll often see this attack deal more damage than you would expect against foes with high defenses, such as Brainsuckers. This is the Saw Spear's key attack. When used while not locked-on, you can control the direction of the attack until the last second. The charged R2 shares this property and has an even higher multiplier, but it does take more time and stamina to execute. When used from behind, it can stagger an opponent.

Also note that the R2, both charged and uncharged, can actually be aimed upwards if you are not locked on. The follow-up R2 has a heavy impact that blows small enemies away and causes even large foes to stumble. Master manually aiming the R2 attacks of this weapon, and you'll be a great asset to any Chalice Dungeon expedition! The dashing R2 is another excellent attack; it hits high enough to strike the heads of tall foes, like Vicar Amelia.

Transformed Mode R1

Transformed Mode R2

Transformed Mode Transform Attack

Hunter Axe

The Hunter Axe requires 9 strength and 8 skill to use, and its damage increases a lot more from strength than skill. If you want to focus on strength, this should be your starter weapon. Despite the axe's bladed edge, a lot of its attacks deal blunt damage. Another key feature of the axe is that it costs a lot of stamina to swing around; plan to increase your endurance along with your strength if you choose this weapon. The axe is very good at causing enemies to flinch and stumble, and it tears through enemy super armor quickly as well.

> One of the trick weapons of the workshop, commonly used on the hunt. Retains the qualities of an axe, but offers a wider palette of attacks by transforming. Boasts a heavy blunt attack, leading to high rally potential. No matter their pasts, beasts are no more than beasts. Some choose this axe to play the part of executioner.

Gem Advice

The Hunter Axe can be turned into an elemental weapon by equipping it with elemental gems, but this might not be the best choice since it has low arcane scaling. Physical damage boosts, like Tempering, work very well for the Hunter Axe. If you choose to specialize in the axe's transformed mode, many of your attacks will benefit from the Adept (Blunt) effect– most notably the very useful R2 and L2 attacks.

Another option is to utilize the Radiant gem effect to lower the stamina costs of your attacks. The Hunter Axe uses a lot of stamina per swing, so this might be worth a gem slot or even two. This is especially true if you haven't put many points into endurance, though users of stamina-boosting Runes might find the benefits of Radiant gems less attractive than the allure of increased damage.

Acquisition

Type	Obtained from	Reference	Bath Messenger Requirements
Normal	One of three potential starting weapons / Shop	p665	Saw Hunter Axe
Uncanny	Drops in Hintertomb Root Chalice Dungeons	–	Acquire Weapon
Lost	Drops in Ailing Loran Root Chalice Dungeons	–	Acquire Weapon

Available Gem Slots

Weapon Type	Weapon Level		
	1	3	6
Normal	Radial	Radial	Triangular
Uncanny	Radial	Radial	Waning
Lost	Radial	Triangular	Waning

Average Physical Attack Increase (Strength)

Stat Range	Damage per Point	Estimated Attack Gained
10 to 25	3.63	58
26 to 50	1.76	44
50 to 99	0.41	20

Average Physical Attack Increase (Skill)

Stat Range	Damage per Point	Estimated Attack Gained
9 to 25	1.82	31
26 to 50	0.96	24
50 to 99	0.22	11

Damage from Upgrades

Weapon Level	Base	Scaling			
0	98	D	E	D	
1	107	D	E	D	
2	116	D	E	D	
3	125	D	E	D	
4	134	D	E	D	
5	143	C	E	D	
6	152	C	E	D	
7	161	C	E	D	
8	170	C	D	D	
9	179	C	D	D	
10	196	B	D	C	

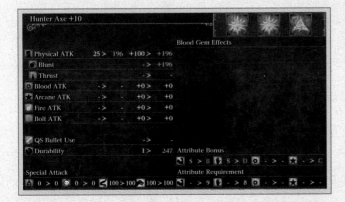

Normal Mode Tactics

In tight spaces, the normal mode axe can be swung freely while the transformed version of the axe will bounce off of walls. Additionally, even though normal mode swings are expensive compared to other weapons, normal mode costs less stamina per attack than transformed mode. If stamina or space is a concern, use the normal mode.

Normal Mode Attacks Properties

Attack	Dmg ×	Type	Stamina	Impact	Note
R1	1.00	Physical	25	Light	too slow to combo against some enemies
↳ R1 (2nd)	1.00	Physical	25	Light	
↳ R1 (3rd)	1.10	Physical	25	Light	
↳ R1 (4th)	1.20	Blunt	25	Light	
R1 (backstep)	0.95	Physical	15 (+10)	Light	fast start-up
R1 (rolling)	0.95	Physical	15 (+10)	Light	fast start-up
R1 (frontstep)	0.95	Physical	15 (+10)	Light	
R1 (sidestep)	0.95	Physical	15 (+10)	Light	
R1 (dash)	1.10	Physical	35 (+X)	Light	
R2	1.35	Blunt	45	Normal	causes many enemies to stumble easily
R2 (charged)	2.00	Blunt	75	Massive	continuously hold the button to execute
R2 (backstep)	1.30	Blunt	35 (+10)	Normal	
R2 (dash)	1.45	Physical	60 (+X)	Normal	better damage than a normal R2
R2 (forward leap)	1.40	Blunt	60	Normal	tap forward on the stick just as you press R2 to execute
Transform Attack	1.10	Physical	30 (+X)	Normal	press L1 while performing another action to execute; forced Guard Break

Normal Mode Key Attacks

The Hunter Axe R1 chain can be too slow to combo against quick enemies, but it rips through enemy super armor very quickly. It can help you set up large stumbles with other attacks. You always have to be mindful of your stamina usage, though; it's very easy to exhaust yourself with attacks. If that happens, you'll be left defenseless. Play it safe with one or two hits, and then back away and recover your stamina.

The normal mode R2 attack of the axe has good impact and super armor damage; it can cause even some medium-sized enemies to stumble in a single strike, making it an effective tool against enemies like the Huntsman's Minions. Single, well-timed R2 attacks are often more useful than R1 chains with the axe. The charged R2 has a massive impact that can knock down small and medium foes and stumble even large ones. It can also stagger enemies. Be warned, though, that it is slow to execute.

If the enemy is agile or aggressive, you may have difficulty performing a normal R2. In those cases, the backstep and dashing R2 attacks can be reliable. Wait just within the enemy's range to bait an attack, backstep out of range so the attack misses, and then either execute the backstep R2 as a counterattack or dash and perform a dashing R2. Remember that you can dash while locked-on, but you need to run forward to do so. For use against other players, refer to the Training Manual for info on the hidden dash technique p20.

Normal Mode R1

Normal Mode R2

Normal Mode Transform Attack

Transformed Mode Tactics

The Hunter Axe is much more useful in its transformed state. It has better range, better damage, and is even better at causing enemies to stumble. It does require a lot of stamina to use in this mode, but it's worth it. If you aren't in a narrow space, transformed mode will almost always produce better results.

Transformed Mode Attacks Properties

Attack	Dmg ×	Type	Stamina	Impact	Note
R1	1.05	Blunt	27	Light	sweeping arc is good against crowds
↳R1 (2nd)	1.15	Blunt	32	Light	hits high; useful for striking enemy weak points
↳R1 (3rd)	1.05	Physical	27	Light	
↳R1 (4th)	1.15	Blunt	32	Light	
↳R1 (5th)	1.20	Blunt	32	Light	
R1 (backstep)	1.00	Physical	15 (+10)	Light	
R1 (rolling)	0.95	Physical	15 (+10)	Light	fast start-up
R1 (frontstep)	0.95	Physical	15 (+10)	Light	fast start-up
R1 (sidestep)	0.95	Physical	15 (+10)	Light	
R1 (dash)	1.15	Physical	35 (+X)	Light	good damage; useful for hit-and-run tactics
R2	1.37	Blunt	50	Normal	hits high; useful for striking enemy weak points
R2 (charged)	1.30	Blunt	100	Massive	continuously hold the button to execute
R2 (backstep)	1.10	Physical	30 (+10)	Normal	
R2 (dash)	1.50	Blunt	60 (+X)	Normal	hits high; useful for striking enemy weak points
R2 (forward leap)	1.45	Blunt	60	Normal	tap forward on the stick just as you press R2 to execute
L2	1.25	Blunt	45	Normal	great range; good against crowds
↳L2 (2nd)	1.25	Blunt	45	Normal	great range; good against crowds
↳L2 (3rd)	1.35	Blunt	50	Heavy	hits high; useful for striking enemy weak points
Transform Attack	1.20	Blunt	30 (+X)	Normal	press L1 while performing another action to execute; forced Guard Break

Transformed Mode Key Attacks

The uncharged R2 is an overhead chop that can strike the heads of tall enemies and is quite useful, but it is overshadowed by the incredible charged version of the R2. The charged R2 is a double spin with great range, great power, and the ability to hit twice. Furthermore, the second hit has a massive impact that knocks down light and medium enemies and causes large foes to stumble. This is one of the best attacks in Bloodborne and is the main reason to use the Hunter Axe. The first hit of the charged R2 does more damage than the second, but the second hit has the heavy impact.

Against normal enemies that try to approach you in melee, begin charging the R2 as the enemy approaches. You want to time it so that they just enter range as your attack releases; they'll take a lot of damage and be knocked back, leaving you safe to repeat the tactic until the enemy is dead. If you manage to land this attack on an enemy that can be staggered from behind, the first hit will stagger them, and the second hit will deal double its normal damage. Against larger, more aggressive foes, you'll need another tactic; that's where the L2 chain comes in.

The L2 combo has very good range and breaks down enemy super armor very quickly. The first two swings of the combo are great against crowds, and the third hit strikes high. Once again, the downside is that the full chain consumes a large amount of stamina. The transformed axe's R1 chain is also useful, particularly when you are low on stamina, but the charged R2 and the L2 chain are your primary assets.

Transformed Mode R1

Transformed Mode R2

Transformed Mode Transform Attack

Threaded Cane

The Threaded Cane requires 7 strength and 9 skill to use. Among the starter weapons, the cane should be the weapon of choice for hunters focusing on skill. Increasing skill raises the damage of the Threaded Cane very quickly. At first glance, this weapon appears weak, but this is misleading. The normal mode deals 20% bonus damage against enemies weak to righteous weapons, and the transformed mode deals 20% bonus damage against foes weak against serrated weapons. This is the only weapon that receives a bonus against both types. Additionally, the Threaded Cane's quickness and low stamina consumption allow for very long combos.

> One of the trick weapons of the workshop, commonly used by hunters on their duties. Sufficiently deadly as a rigid bladed cane, but also serves as a whip when its blade is split into many. Concealing the weapon inside the cane and flogging the beasts with the whip is partly an act of ceremony, an attempt to demonstrate to oneself that the bloodlust of the hunt will never encroach upon the soul.

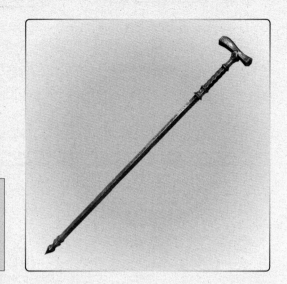

Gem Advice

The Threaded Cane is a very quick weapon in its normal mode and a very long-range weapon once transformed; this leads to a variety of options for gemming. Murky or Dirty gems combine well with the quick attacks of normal mode, and Striking can be useful if you use the cane for charged attacks against staggered foes. On the other hand, the range of the whip once transformed makes the Threaded Cane a safe weapon to use in conjunction with Fool or Poorman effects.

Still another option is the use of elemental gems. The Threaded Cane has good arcane scaling and low strength and skill requirements, so a pure arcane build could put this weapon to use with elemental gems. Since the cane has serrated bonus attack in transformed mode, adding something such as a Beasthunter effect could be done to convert this into a specialty beast-killer.

Acquisition

Type	Obtained from	Reference	Bath Messenger Requirements
Normal	One of three potential starting weapons / Shop	p665	Saw Hunter Badge
Uncanny	Drops in Central Pthumeru Root Chalice Dungeons	–	Acquire Weapon
Lost	Drops in Great Isz Root Chalice Dungeons	–	Acquire Weapon

Available Gem Slots

Weapon Type	Weapon Level		
	1	3	6
Normal	Radial	Radial	Triangular
Uncanny	Radial	Radial	Waning
Lost	Radial	Triangular	Waning

Average Physical Attack Increase (Strength)

Stat Range	Damage per Point	Estimated Attack Gained
8 to 25	1.17	21
26 to 50	0.64	16
50 to 99	0.14	7

Average Physical Attack Increase (Skill)

Stat Range	Damage per Point	Estimated Attack Gained
10 to 25	4.00	64
26 to 50	1.96	49
50 to 99	0.43	21

Damage from Upgrades

Weapon Level	Base	Scaling		
0	78	E	C	D
1	85	E	C	D
2	92	E	B	D
3	99	E	B	D
4	106	E	B	D
5	113	E	B	D
6	120	E	B	C
7	127	E	B	C
8	134	E	B	C
9	141	E	A	C
10	156	E	A	B

Normal Mode Tactics

When fighting against enemies weak to righteous weapons, you'll definitely want to use normal mode for the 20% damage bonus. Normal mode is also useful when you need thrust-type attacks. This can't be underestimated, as the normal mode Threaded Cane has some very quick thrusts that are perfect against certain enemies. Normal mode is also preferable in narrow corridors so that you don't hit the walls.

Normal Mode Attacks Properties

Attack	Dmg ×	Type	Stamina	Impact	Note
R1	1.00	Physical	17	Light	
↳ R1 (2nd)	1.02	Physical	17	Light	
↳ R1 (3rd)	1.04	Physical	17	Light	stamina-efficient damage
R1 (backstep)	1.05	Physical	10 (+10)	Light	moves forward; useful for counters
R1 (rolling)	1.05	Physical	20 (+10)	Light	quick start-up
R1 (frontstep)	1.05	Physical	20 (+10)	Light	quick start-up
R1 (sidestep)	1.05	Physical	20 (+10)	Light	
R1 (dash)	1.20	Physical	30 (+X)	Light	
R2	1.35	Thrust	30	Normal	
R2 (charged)	1.90	Thrust	45	Normal	continuously hold the button to execute
R2 (backstep)	1.20	Thrust	25 (+10)	Normal	
R2 (dash)	1.45	Thrust	45 (+X)	Normal	
R2 (forward leap)	1.40	Thrust	50	Normal	tap forward on the stick just as you press R2 to execute
Transform Attack	1.28	Physical	25 (+X)	Light	press L1 while performing another action to execute; forced Guard Break

Normal Mode Key Attacks

The uncharged R2 is a thrust attack, and it's quite a fast one. It's crucial against foes who are weak against thrusts, like Brainsuckers, but it's also useful against other foes as well due to being nearly as quick as an R1 while having better impact. The charged R2 has a high attack multiplier, which makes it good against enemies with high defense. This is important, since the low attack power of the Threaded Cane means that it struggles against enemies with high defense.

Landing a charged R2 from behind can stagger an enemy and allow for a rear visceral attack. A more advanced technique is to perform a second charged R2 instead of the visceral attack. This doesn't work for all weapons; some are too slow, and others have special R2 follow-ups that prevent it. It does work for the cane, though, and it works very well. When using an upgraded cane, it does more damage than the visceral attack would. The speed and low stamina consumption of the cane's charged R2 make it ideal for this tactic.

Another advanced technique is to perform a charged R2, use the visceral attack, move forward and perform another charged R2 while the enemy is trying to stand. This doesn't work on every enemy, but it's usually fatal on enemies that it does work on, like Huntsman's Minions. You can even combine it with the double charged R2 technique to ensure your attack is lethal; you won't need this normally, but it's something to remember for New Game+.

Normal Mode R1

Normal Mode R2

Normal Mode Transform Attack

Transformed Mode Tactics

If you are fighting enemies weak against serrated weapons, you will definitely want to transform your cane and take advantage of its 20% bonus damage. Beyond that, the transformed cane has very impressive reach. Against any opponent that you want to keep at a distance, or any quick enemy, this mode works well. It can also be used to hit the heads of tall enemies. One note of caution, though – the Threaded Cane can and will bounce off of obstacles in this mode.

Transformed Mode Attacks Properties

Attack	Dmg ×	Type	Stamina	Impact	Note
R1	1.02	Physical	17	Light	useful for counters
↳ R1 (2nd)	1.05	Physical	17	Light	
↳ R1 (3rd)	1.07	Physical	17	Light	
R1 (backstep)	1.07	Thrust	17 (+10)	Light	useful for counters
R1 (rolling)	0.96	Physical	15 (+10)	Light	
R1 (frontstep)	0.96	Physical	15 (+10)	Light	
R1 (sidestep)	0.96	Physical	15 (+10)	Light	
R1 (dash)	1.18	Physical	25 (+X)	Light	
R2	1.34	Physical	32	Normal	useful for counters
↳ R2 (2nd)	1.34	Physical	32	Normal	
R2 (backstep)	1.28	Thrust	25 (+10)	Normal	fantastic range; useful for counters
R2 (dash)	1.39	Physical	40 (+X)	Normal	hits high
R2 (forward leap)	1.39	Physical	50	Normal	tap forward on the stick just as you press R2 to execute
Transform Attack	1.28	Thrust	25 (+X)	Light	press L1 while performing another action to execute; forced Guard Break

Transformed Mode Key Attacks

The normal R1 chain for transformed mode has deceptive range. Normal enemies can't really handle this very well; you can simply step backwards as they try to attack to make them miss and then attack from outside of their range. Huntsmen wielding swords and axes are easy prey with this technique. Do be cautious of enemies with long attack ranges, such as pitchfork-wielders, though.

The real beauty of this tactic is that it makes scoring counter hits very easy. Counter hits do additional damage, and stacking the serrated damage bonus along with the bonus for landing a counter hit can let you deal serious damage – all while being safely out of range! You can use the R2 chain for this purpose as well; it hits quite hard when used as a proper counter. The backstep R2 also works for this tactic; it has amazing range and can easily catch your enemies off-guard. Be cautious of enemies with long-range attacks, though.

The dashing R2 is another extremely useful move for the transformed cane. At first glance, it doesn't seem particularly special, but it hits very high, so it is great at striking the heads of large enemies. Just be aware that it hits slightly to the right of your character, so you may need to dash to the enemy's left side when using it. You can run in after an enemy attack, land a hit on the enemy weak point, and escape with stamina to spare.

Transformed Mode R1

Transformed Mode R2

Transformed Mode Transform Attack

Burial Blade

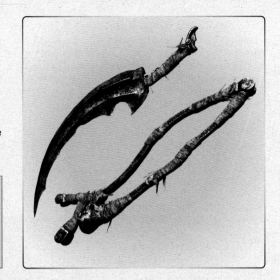

The Burial Blade requires 10 strength and 12 skill to use. Its physical damage increases mainly with skill; strength has a minimal effect. The Burial Blade also deals a small amount of arcane damage, which scales with your character's arcane stat. For characters with high skill who also want to use magic, the Burial Blade can be a powerful weapon. This is a very tricky weapon. In terms of speed and power, it's balanced, but its damage modifiers are a bit odd. The damage modifiers for dashing, rolling, and quickstepping attacks are all higher than average; the Burial Blade is designed around the concept of mobility and sneaky single strikes.

> Trick weapon wielded by Gehrman, the first hunter. A masterpiece that defined the entire array of weapons crafted at the workshop. Its blade is forged with siderite, said to have fallen from the heavens. Gehrman surely saw the hunt as a dirge of farewell, wishing only that his prey might rest in peace, never again to awaken to another harrowing nightmare.

Gem Advice

The Burial Blade can't be buffed with Fire Paper or other buff items, so equipping it with an elemental gem does not convert its physical damage to the elemental. As a result, it is not a good candidate for elemental gem effects. Since it does two types of damage from the beginning, consider using the Nourishing gem effect instead of the Tempering effect, as Tempering will only increase your physical damage, but not your arcane damage.

The Burial Blade is well-suited to single attacks, particularly rolling and quickstepping attacks. If you are using invincibility frames to dodge enemy attacks and then attacking with rolling attacks, you will land a lot of counterhits. The Finestrike gem effect synergizes perfectly with this playstyle. Maximum rank Finestrike effects are rivaled in power only by the best Poorman effects but are much safer to use, as your HP does not need to be low.

Acquisition

Type	Obtained from	Reference	Bath Messenger Requirements
Normal	Shop	p665	Old Hunter Badge
Uncanny	Drops in Lower Loran Root Chalice Dungeons	–	Acquire Weapon
Lost	Drops in Great Pthumeru Ihyll Root Chalice Dungeons	–	Acquire Weapon

Damage from Upgrades

Weapon Level	Base		Scaling		
	🗡	⭐	🔥	🔽	⭐
0	80	30	E	C	D
1	88	33	E	C	D
2	96	36	E	C	D
3	104	39	E	C	D
4	112	42	E	C	D
5	120	45	E	B	C
6	128	48	E	B	C
7	136	51	E	B	C
8	144	54	E	B	C
9	152	57	E	B	B
10	160	60	D	B	B

Available Gem Slots

Weapon Type	Weapon Level		
	1	3	6
Normal	Radial	Waning	Radial
Uncanny	Radial	Triangular	Radial
Lost	Radial	Triangular	Waning

Average Physical Attack Increase (Strength)

Stat Range	Damage per Point	Estimated Attack Gained
11 to 25	1.53	23
26 to 50	0.68	17
50 to 99	0.14	7

Average Physical Attack Increase (Skill)

Stat Range	Damage per Point	Estimated Attack Gained
13 to 25	3.69	48
26 to 50	1.68	42
50 to 99	0.37	18

Average Arcane Attack Increase (Arcane)

Stat Range	Damage per Point	Estimated Attack Gained
8 to 25	1.11	20
26 to 50	0.60	15
50 to 99	0.12	6

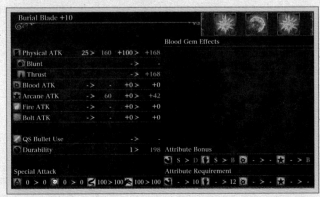

Normal Mode Tactics

The Burial Blade's normal mode is slightly faster than the transformed mode and uses less stamina, but it also has lower damage modifiers. As a result, it's more suited to long strings of attacks when compared to transformed mode. It's also useful in confined spaces where the transformed version would strike obstacles.

Normal Mode Attacks Properties

Attack	Dmg ×	Type	Stamina	Impact	Note
R1	1.00	Physical / Arcane	23	Light	
↳ R1 (2nd)	1.02	Physical / Arcane	23	Light	
↳ R1 (3rd)	1.05	Physical / Arcane	23	Light	
↳ R1 (4th)	1.05	Physical / Arcane	23	Light	
↳ R1 (5th)	1.05	Physical / Arcane	23	Light	
R1 (backstep)	1.05	Thrust / Arcane	12 (+10)	Light	powerful; low stamina cost; thrust damage type
R1 (rolling)	1.15	Physical / Arcane	15 (+10)	Light	powerful; low stamina cost
R1 (frontstep)	1.15	Physical / Arcane	15 (+10)	Light	powerful; low stamina cost
R1 (sidestep)	1.10	Physical / Arcane	15 (+10)	Light	powerful; low stamina cost
R1 (dash)	1.20	Physical / Arcane	20 (+X)	Light	
R2	1.22	Physical / Arcane	45	Normal	
R2 (charged)	1.70	Physical / Arcane	65	Normal	continuously hold the button to execute
R2 (backstep)	1.28	Physical / Arcane	28 (+10)	Normal	
R2 (dash)	1.32	Physical / Arcane	25 (+X)	Normal	useful for hit-and-run tactics; key attack
R2 (forward leap)	1.40	Physical / Arcane	60	Normal	tap forward on the stick just as you press R2 to execute
Transform Attack	1.60	Physical / Arcane	25 (+X)	Light	press L1 while performing another action to execute; forced Guard Break

Normal Mode Key Attacks

The Burial Blade's normal mode rolling and frontstep R1s are some of the best quick attacks in the game. These moves tend to be fast for all weapons, but they also tend to have multipliers less than 1.0. For the Burial Blade, they're even more powerful than normal R1 attacks.

The dashing R2 is a very strong attack for this weapon. It's considerably more powerful than a normal R2. The trick is hitting with it; it has a narrow hit box, so you need to aim properly if you use it while not locked-on. Against large opponents, this is not a big problem, but if you are having trouble hitting the enemy consistently, just use the dashing R1 instead, as it has a wider hit box. The transformation attack has a good damage multiplier, but it doesn't combo particularly well.

On the topic of combos – while the Burial Blade isn't specialized in normal R1s, they still aren't bad. If you can hit your opponent with multiple R1 attacks in combination, you should do so. There's no need to rely only on the rolling, quick-stepping, and dashing attacks; if you're safe to stand still and perform combos, do it! This advice is common to all of the weapons, but it's especially important to remember for weapons with specialized attacks, like the Burial Blade. It's very easy to over-rely on them and make things harder than they need to be. You may choose this weapon for its mobile strikes, but don't forget about your other options.

Normal Mode R1

Normal Mode R2

Normal Mode Transform Attack

Transformed Mode Tactics

The transformed mode of the Burial Blade has better range and damage multipliers at the expense of more stamina usage. Walls and obstacles can stop most of the transformed mode attacks if you hit them, so make sure you have plenty of space in which to use it. It does have some attacks that work well in narrow hallways, though, so this isn't a major concern.

Transformed Mode Attacks Properties

Attack	Dmg ×	Type	Stamina	Impact	Note
R1	1.10		28	Light	
↳ R1 (2nd)	1.10		28	Light	
↳ R1 (3rd)	1.12		28	Light	
↳ R1 (4th)	1.15		28	Light	
R1 (backstep)	1.15		12 (+10)	Light	powerful; low stamina cost
R1 (rolling)	1.20		12 (+10)	Light	powerful; low stamina cost
R1 (frontstep)	1.20		12 (+10)	Light	powerful; low stamina cost
R1 (sidestep)	1.20		18 (+10)	Light	due to extra stamina cost; frontstepping and rolling attacks are better
R1 (dash)	1.27		18 (+X)	Light	strikes horizontally
R2	1.45	Physical / Arcane	40	Normal	quick surprise attack
R2 (charged)	1.90		100	Heavy	continuously hold the button to execute
R2 (backstep)	1.45		28 (+10)	Normal	
R2 (dash)	1.50		25 (+X)	Normal	useful for hit-and-run tactics; key attack
R2 (forward leap)	1.45		60	Normal	tap forward on the stick just as you press R2 to execute
L2	1.40		50	Normal	good super armor damage; hits high
↳ L2 (2nd)	1.25		40	Normal	good super armor damage; hits high
↳ L2 (3rd)	1.50		50	Normal	good super armor damage; horizontal sweep
↳ L2 (4th)	1.50		50	Normal	good super armor damage; horizontal sweep
Transform Attack	1.10		20 (+X)	Light	press L1 while performing another action to execute; forced Guard Break

Transformed Mode Key Attacks

The charged R2 is one of the key techniques of the transformed Burial Blade. It is the weapon's hardest-hitting attack and has really impressive range. If you release R2 before the charge is finished, you'll perform the normal R2 as usual. The normal R2 is a quick horizontal swipe that you can use to catch the enemy off-guard. Against a human opponent, it's a guessing game for them whether you will fully charge the R2 or let it go early.

The L2 chain of the transformed Burial Blade is also quite good. It strikes vertically, so it's safe to use in narrow spaces. It's also great for hitting enemy weak points, like the head of Vicar Amelia. Each hit does good super armor damage, as well, making it a useful attack against bosses and strong enemies.

The dashing, rolling, and quickstepping attacks of transformed mode are all very good, just as with normal mode. In transformed mode, though, they hit even harder and have better range! The dashing R2 is fast, powerful, consumes only a small amount of stamina, and can be used while remaining highly mobile. It has a narrow hit box, so it is easy to miss your target when not locked-on. If you are having trouble with it, you can either use the dashing R1 instead or use the dashing R2 while locked-on, though you'll need to be moving forward toward the enemy in order to engage your dash. Check p20 for tips on how to conceal your dash from other players in PvP.

Transformed Mode R1

Transformed Mode R2

Transformed Mode Transform Attack

Blade of Mercy

The Blade of Mercy requires 7 strength and 12 skill to use. It receives large physical attack power increases for each point of skill that your character has, and it gains a boost to its arcane attack power for each point of the arcane stat. This is a quick weapon specialized in attacking after dodging and rolling. Its normal attacks deal little damage, but they are fast and consume little stamina. Choose this weapon if you want to focus on staying mobile. Similar to the Burial Blade, though, enemies with high arcane defense will be resistant to your attacks when you use the Blade of Mercy.

A special trick weapon passed down amongst hunters of hunters. One of the oldest weapons of the workshop. Splits into two when activated. The weapon's warped blades are forged with siderite, a rare mineral of the heavens. Most effective in swift attacks, such as after quick-stepping.

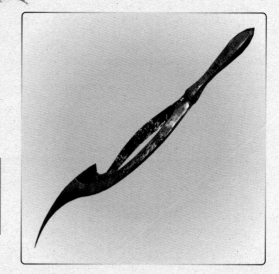

Gem Advice

The Blade of Mercy can't be buffed with Fire Paper or other buff items, so equipping it with an elemental gem does not convert its physical damage to the elemental. As a result, it is not a good candidate for elemental gem effects. Since it does two types of damage from the beginning, consider using the Nourishing gem effect instead of the Tempering effect, as Tempering will only increase your physical damage, but not your arcane damage.

Another key feature of the Blade of Mercy is its speed, especially in transformed mode. You can take advantage of this by equipping Murky or Dirty gems to use poison effects. The rapid attacks of the Blade of Mercy can build up poison very quickly, particularly with strong gems. This is one of the best weapons to use with poison; give it a try!

Acquisition

Type	Obtained from	Reference	Bath Messenger Requirements
Normal	Shop	p665	Crow Hunter Badge
Uncanny	Drops in Lower Loran Root Chalice Dungeons	–	Acquire Weapon
Lost	Drops in Great Pthumeru Ihyll Root Chalice Dungeons	–	Acquire Weapon

Damage from Upgrades

Weapon Level	Base		Scaling	
	🗡	⭐	✋	⭐
0	60	30	C	D
1	66	33	B	D
2	72	36	B	D
3	78	39	B	D
4	84	42	B	D
5	90	45	A	C
6	96	48	A	C
7	102	51	A	C
8	108	54	A	C
9	114	57	A	B
10	120	60	S	B

Available Gem Slots

Weapon Type	Weapon Level		
	1	3	6
Normal	Radial	Triangular	Radial
Uncanny	Radial	Waning	Radial
Lost	Radial	Triangular	Waning

Average Physical Attack Increase (Skill)

Stat Range	Damage per Point	Estimated Attack Gained
12 to 25	4.00	56
26 to 50	1.84	46
50 to 99	0.41	20

Average Arcane Attack Increase (Arcane)

Stat Range	Damage per Point	Estimated Attack Gained
8 to 25	1.00	18
26 to 50	0.60	15
50 to 99	0.12	6

Normal Mode Tactics

In normal mode, the focus is on powerful attacks after rolling and quickstepping. If you need to hit and run, this mode is better. You can roll in, strike, and then quickstep away. The attacks are all very quick, so this is a good weapon and mode to use against enemies that are aggressive or evasive.

Normal Mode Attacks Properties

Attack	Dmg ×	Type	Stamina	Impact	Note
R1	1.00	Physical / Arcane	15	Light	
↳ R1 (2nd)	1.02	Physical / Arcane	15	Light	
↳ R1 (3rd)	1.04	Physical / Arcane	15	Light	
R1 (backstep)	1.50	Physical / Arcane	15 (+10)	Light	very solid damage multiplier
R1 (rolling)	1.50	Physical / Arcane	15 (+10)	Light	very solid damage multiplier
R1 (frontstep)	1.50	Physical / Arcane	15 (+10)	Light	very solid damage multiplier
R1 (sidestep)	1.50	Physical / Arcane	15 (+10)	Light	very solid damage multiplier
R1 (dash)	1.40	Thrust / Arcane	20 (+X)	Light	thrust damage type; good against specific foes
R2	1.25	Physical / Arcane	30	Normal	
R2 (charged)	2.00	Physical / Arcane	50	Normal	continuously hold the button to execute
R2 (backstep)	1.80	Thrust / Arcane	25 (+10)	Normal	thrust damage type; good against specific foes
R2 (dash)	1.80	Physical / Arcane	25 (+X)	Normal	
R2 (forward leap)	1.50	Physical / Arcane	45	Normal	tap forward on the stick just as you press R2 to execute
Transform Attack	1.20	Physical / Arcane	15 (+X)	Normal	press L1 while performing another action to execute; forced Guard Break

Normal Mode Key Attacks

The damage multipliers for the rolling, backstep, frontstep, and sidestep R1s are all very high, and they consume very little stamina. This is precisely why this weapon is so good for hit and run tactics. The backstep R2 also has a very high damage multiplier, but, more importantly, it is a thrusting attack. If your R1s aren't doing much against an enemy's physical defenses, this might be an option for you. The transformation attack is another interesting move; it has almost double the range of your normal attacks.

The charged R2 is one of the quicker charged attacks in the game. This adds to the hit-and-run style of the Blade of Mercy, as you can dodge behind enemies' attacks and quickly execute charged R2s to stagger them. This is an advanced technique, but try fighting enemies without locking-on; this lets you roll behind them and immediately turn to land your charged attack rather than waiting for the lock-on autocorrect. It's much faster, but you'll need to get used to handling the camera manually.

One of the biggest tricks to rolling behind an enemy and landing the charged R2 is to not spend time adjusting your camera. Dodge behind the enemy and immediately begin charging your R2 while aiming your character toward the enemy. It's difficult to get used to at first, but have faith in your aim and trust yourself to know where the enemy is rather than making sure that you can see it. The time you save by performing this technique "blind" will allow you to stagger enemies much more reliably. Also, remember to check if performing a second charge attack does more damage for you than a Visceral Attack would!

Normal Mode R1

Normal Mode R2

Normal Mode Transform Attack

5

Transformed Mode Tactics

In its transformed "dual daggers" mode, the Blade of Mercy loses a bit of its hit-and-run power but gains incredible sustained damage. Use this mode against stationary targets, such as staggered bosses. It can also work well in co-op when another player has the enemy's attention, but always beware of enemy area-of-effect attacks.

Transformed Mode Attacks Properties

Attack	Dmg ×	Type	Stamina	Impact	Note
R1	0.90	Physical / Arcane	11	Light	
↳ R1 (2nd)	0.90	Physical / Arcane	11	Light	
↳ R1 (3rd)	0.90	Physical / Arcane	11	Light	
↳ R1 (4th)	1.25	Physical / Arcane	18	Light	key breakpoint; always try to reach this attack if possible
↳ R1 (5th)	1.10	Thrust / Arcane	13	Light	thrust damage type; good against specific foes
↳ R1 (6th)	1.12	Physical / Arcane	14	Light	
↳ R1 (7th)	1.18	Physical / Arcane	16	Light	
↳ R1 (8th)	1.18	Physical / Arcane	16	Light	thrust damage type; good against specific foes
R1 (backstep)	1.40	Physical / Arcane	15 (+10)	Light	
R1 (rolling)	1.40	Thrust / Arcane	15 (+10)	Light	thrust damage type; good against specific foes
R1 (frontstep)	1.40	Thrust / Arcane	15 (+10)	Light	thrust damage type; good against specific foes
R1 (sidestep)	1.40	Physical / Arcane	15 (+10)	Light	thrust damage type; good against specific foes
R1 (dash)	1.40	Thrust / Arcane	22 (+X)	Light	thrust damage type; good against specific foes
R2	1.50	Physical / Arcane	45	Normal	steps forward
↳ R2 (2nd)	1.60	Physical / Arcane	50	Normal	steps forward
R2 (backstep)	1.70	Physical / Arcane	25 (+10)	Normal	
R2 (dash)	1.70	Physical / Arcane	28 (+X)	Normal	key attack; good damage; can hit to the sides as well as the front
R2 (forward leap)	1.50	Thrust / Arcane	45	Normal	tap forward on the stick just as you press R2 to execute
L2	1.50	Physical / Arcane	45	Normal	steps backward
Transform Attack	1.30	Physical / Arcane	15 (+X)	Normal	press L1 while performing another action to execute; forced Guard Break

Transformed Mode Key Attacks

The R1 attack chain is one of the stars here. The damage ramps up until you reach your eighth attack before resetting. The multipliers don't look impressive, but the speed of the strikes causes the damage to pile up quickly. Since they also have low stamina costs, you can attack rapidly without resting, too. If you fit your Blade of Mercy with Murky or Dirty gems, you can build up poison on your foe very quickly.

The R1 chain is not, however, good against a crowd of enemies. It has low range and doesn't have sweeping arcs. The dashing R2, on the other hand, is a perfect tool for dealing with crowds. It has a lower damage multiplier than the normal mode R1, but it has a better hit box. It hits on the sides around your character as well as in front. Between the great hit box and the naturally high damage modifier, it's a very good move. It's especially helpful in Chalice Dungeons, where you often fight large groups of weak enemies.

The L2 attack is another interesting tool. It hits the space just in front of your character and then propels you backwards. This can be used as a combo finisher to help you escape from possible counterattacks. The range isn't great, but it can help you get out of a difficult situation while still doing damage. If your R2 carries you into a crowd, an L2 can get you back out. Another example: if you are in the middle of an R1 chain and a boss begins an area-of-effect attack, you can use the L2 followed by a backstep to deal damage and escape from harm. The Blade of Mercy in general requires a lot of technique and good judgment, and knowing when to use the L2 is an important piece of the puzzle.

Transformed Mode R1

Transformed Mode R2

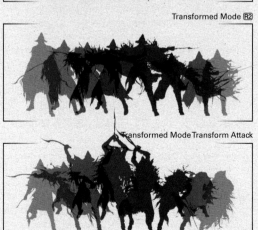

Transformed Mode Transform Attack

Kirkhammer

The Kirkhammer requires 16 strength and 10 skill to use, and its damage increases a lot more from strength than skill. It has the highest base physical damage of any weapon, though other weapons can surpass it at high stat levels due to scaling. The real beauty of the Kirkhammer, though, is its versatility. The normal moveset has a variety of fast attacks that work well against quick, evasive foes, and the transformed mode can produce massive hits capable of penetrating even the strongest defenses. Additionally, normal mode receives a massive 50% damage bonus against enemies weak to righteous weapons. There are a few enemies that have this weakness; the most notable are the Bloodlickers and the Lost Children of Antiquity.

> A trick weapon typically used by Healing Church hunters. On the one side, an easily-handled silver sword. On the other, a giant obtuse stone weapon, characterised by a blunt strike and extreme force of impact. Trick hunter weapons forged in the Healing Church workshop, said to be hidden somewhere in the Grand Cathedral, were made to the tenets of a rival school of craftsmanship.

Acquisition

Type	Obtained from	Reference	Bath Messenger Requirements
Normal	Shop	p665	Sword Hunter Badge
Uncanny	Drops in Lower Pthumeru Root Chalice Dungeons	–	Acquire Weapon
Lost	Drops in Great Isz Root Chalice Dungeons	–	Acquire Weapon

Available Gem Slots

Weapon Type	Weapon Level		
	1	3	6
Normal	Radial	Triangular	Radial
Uncanny	Radial	Waning	Radial
Lost	Radial	Triangular	Waning

Average Physical Attack Increase (Strength)

Stat Range	Damage per Point	Estimated Attack Gained
17 to 25	6.33	57
26 to 50	2.92	73
50 to 99	0.65	32

Average Physical Attack Increase (Skill)

Stat Range	Damage per Point	Estimated Attack Gained
11 to 25	1.80	27
26 to 50	0.88	22
50 to 99	0.18	9

Damage from Upgrades

Weapon Level	Base	Scaling		
0	105	C	E	D
1	115	C	E	D
2	125	B	E	D
3	135	B	E	D
4	145	B	E	D
5	155	B	E	C
6	165	B	E	C
7	175	A	E	C
8	185	A	E	B
9	195	A	E	B
10	210	A	E	B

Gem Advice

The Kirkhammer can be gemmed in several interesting ways. Adept (Blunt) is very powerful for its transformed mode. Tempering gems will benefit both modes. Radiant gems also work well for offsetting the high stamina costs of the Kirkhammer's attacks.

Another strategy is to make a fire-elemental Kirkhammer by using either a Fire or Odd Fire gem effect. All of its physical damage will be converted to fire, and it has decent arcane scaling to boost the fire damage, as well. But the real gimmicks begin when you hit the enemy with an Oil Urn... it will double the damage of the next hit from your Kirkhammer. This can be used to annihilate enemies that are weak to fire using leaping R2 and charged R2 attacks. Just beware if you see another player carrying a hammer and throwing Oil Urns around in PvP!

Kirkhammer +10

Blood Gem Effects

Physical ATK	25 > 210	+100 >	+270	
Blunt		->	+270	
Thrust		->	+270	
Blood ATK	->	-	+0 >	+0
Arcane ATK	->	-	+0 >	+0
Fire ATK	->	-	+0 >	+0
Bolt ATK			+0 >	+0

QS Bullet Use   ->

Durability   1 >   242   Attribute Bonus   S > A S > E - > - - > B

Special Attack   Attribute Requirement
0 > 0   0 > 0   100 > 100   100 > 100   - > 16   - > 10   - > -   - > -

Normal Mode Tactics

The normal mode of the Kirkhammer functions as a light, agile one-handed sword. At first glance, the low damage multipliers may make this mode seem weak, but the speed and low stamina cost of its attacks should not be ignored. Quick opponents can be handled easily thanks to the speed and reach of the sword mode. It's good against enemies with little or no super armor, but normal mode will struggle to cause large enemies to flinch or stumble.

Normal Mode Attacks Properties

Attack	Dmg ×	Type	Stamina	Impact	Note
R1	0.70	Physical	16	Light	
↳ R1 (2nd)	0.71	Physical	16	Light	
↳ R1 (3rd)	0.72	Physical	16	Light	
↳ R1 (4th)	0.74	Thrust	16	Light	can miss against some enemies
↳ R1 (5th)	0.76	Physical	16	Light	
R1 (backstep)	0.67	Physical	10 (+10)	Light	effective lead-in to the R1 chain
R1 (rolling)	0.67	Physical	10 (+10)	Light	strikes to the right of your character
R1 (frontstep)	0.67	Physical	10 (+10)	Light	strikes to the right of your character
R1 (sidestep)	0.67	Physical	10 (+10)	Light	long step forward; very easy to use
R1 (dash)	0.80	Physical	30 (+X)	Light	
R2	1.00	Thrust	55	Normal	
R2 (charged)	1.20	Thrust	75	Normal	continuously hold the button to execute
R2 (backstep)	0.85	Thrust	30 (+10)	Normal	cheap alternative to the uncharged R2
R2 (dash)	0.95	Thrust	50 (+X)	Normal	
R2 (forward leap)	1.20	Thrust	50	Normal	tap forward on the stick just as you press R2 to execute
Transform Attack	1.05	Blunt	40 (+X)	Heavy	press L1 while performing another action to execute; forced Guard Break

Normal Mode Key Attacks

The R1 chain is fast but weak. Each individual hit doesn't do much damage, and the attacks don't deal much super armor damage, either. Despite these limitations, the sweeping strikes and forward momentum of the chain make it very easy to use against a variety of enemies. Foes with no super armor can usually be killed in one combo. It also works well with the poison effects of Murky and Dirty gems.

The uncharged R2 is a surprisingly good attack. It has a 1.0 multiplier, meaning it strikes with the full attack rating of your Kirkhammer. On top of that, it's fast, has good reach, and is a thrusting attack. If you are disappointed in the damage of the R1 attacks, try it out. The downside is the high stamina cost; at 55 stamina, it will deplete your stamina very quickly. The relatively high damage and thrusting-type make this a key attack.

The charged R2 and the jumping R2 have the same damage multiplier, but the jumping R2 costs less stamina. You may have an easier time hitting the enemy with the charged R2 due to its range and the simplicity of the command, and it also has the ability to stagger foes from behind. Both attacks deal the same amount of super armor damage. They're quite similar, so judge which is better for you based on preference and the situation.

Normal Mode R1

Normal Mode R2

Normal Mode Transform Attack

Transformed Mode Tactics

The transformed mode is the polar opposite of normal mode. It's slow with tremendously powerful strikes. It consumes a lot of stamina, but it does a lot of super armor damage and has moves with great impact. Against enemies with high defense, the blunt trauma caused by the transformed Kirkhammer is a godsend.

Transformed Mode Attacks Properties

Attack	Dmg ×	Type	Stamina	Impact	Note
R1	1.00		30	Normal	also produces a 0.6x damage shockwave
↳ R1 (2nd)	1.00		30	Normal	also produces a 0.6x damage shockwave
R1 (backstep)	0.45		10 (+10)	Normal	
R1 (rolling)	0.85		30 (+10)	Normal	also produces a 0.6x damage shockwave
R1 (frontstep)	0.85		30 (+10)	Normal	also produces a 0.6x damage shockwave
R1 (sidestep)	0.85		30 (+10)	Normal	also produces a 0.6x damage shockwave
R1 (dash)	0.55		25 (+X)	Normal	
R2	1.25		40	Heavy	also produces a 0.75x damage shockwave
R2 (charged)	2.30		72	Massive	continuously hold the button to execute; also produces a 0.9x damage shockwave
R2 (charged follow-up)	1.40	Blunt	50 (+80)	Massive	excellent follow-up against staggered foes
R2 (backstep)	1.00		25 (+10)	Heavy	
R2 (dash)	1.05		40 (+X)	Heavy	
R2 (forward leap)	1.20		50	Heavy	tap forward on the stick just as you press R2 to execute; also produces a 0.75x damage shockwave
L2	1.15		32	Normal	
↳ L2 (2nd)	1.05		28	Normal	
↳ L2 (3rd)	1.45		38	Normal	also produces a 0.75x damage shockwave
Transform Attack	1.05		20 (+X)	Heavy	press L1 while performing another action to execute; forced Guard Break; also produces a 0.75x damage shockwave

Transformed Mode Key Attacks

The R1 chain of the hammer mode does solid blunt damage. Though it uses stamina quickly, it also causes enemies to flinch and stumble easily. Each hit also produces a small shockwave near the hammer. The shockwaves are .6 multiplier attacks and will strike any number of nearby enemies. If you just miss your target with the hammer, the shockwave will still connect.

This is a very useful feature for the Kirkhammer when fighting a crowd of enemies with no super armor; the main target of your assault will take the brunt of the damage, but nearby enemies will be stumbled by the shockwaves. This will prevent them from retaliating at close range. Note that the enemy will either be hit by the hammer or the shockwave, but not both. The R1 chain isn't the only technique that produces a shockwave; the normal R2 has a stronger one, and the charged R2's shockwaves are stronger still.

On the topic of the charged R2, the special follow-up R2 is often more powerful against a staggered opponent than a visceral attack would be. One strong tactic is to use a charged R2 to stagger the enemy, execute the follow-up R2, and then perform a jumping R2 as the enemy attempts to stand. This takes a huge amount of stamina, and you need to be patient when executing the jumping R2. If you don't wait for your character to fully recover from the follow-up R2, you'll do a normal uncharged R2 instead of the jumping R2. Despite the stat and execution hurdles, this is a devastating combo.

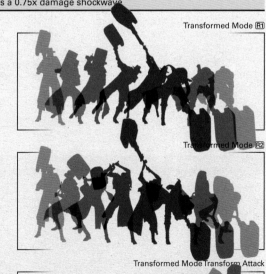

Transformed Mode R1

Transformed Mode R2

Transformed Mode Transform Attack

Ludwig's Holy Blade

Ludwig's Holy Blade requires 16 strength and 12 skill to use. It has slightly lower base damage than the Kirkhammer but better scaling. At high stat levels, the Holy Blade is numerically superior to the Kirkhammer. The Holy Blade is a beast of a weapon, if you'll pardon the pun. It scales well, has great normal mode attacks, has an incredible transformed moveset, and even receives 50% bonus damage versus enemies weak against righteous weapons — in both of its modes! Make no mistake; for high-level characters, this weapon is a strong contender for the best in Bloodborne.

> A trick weapon typically used by Healing Church hunters. It is said that the silver sword was employed by Ludwig, the first hunter of the church. When transformed, it combines with its sheath to form a greatsword. The Healing Church workshop began with Ludwig, and departed from old Gehrman's techniques to provide hunters with the means to hunt more terrifying beasts, and perhaps things still worse.

Gem Advice

Ludwig's Holy Blade really works well with a lot of gems. It has fantastic arcane scaling, which means that it works well with elemental gems; the fire elemental / Oil Urn trick from the Kirkhammer works here, too. It also has great physical damage if you choose not to use an elemental gem; Tempering will affect all of its attacks, while the transformed R1 attacks go well with Adept (Blunt). Adept (Thrust) can be used with the powerful R2 attacks.

The Holy Blade also has fantastic charge attacks that benefit a lot from Striking gem effects. Its range is good enough that Finestrike is also a really good option. You can even use Murky or Dirty gems in combination with the normal mode's quick attacks. This is a weapon for high-level characters, but it is extremely versatile for those who can use it.

Acquisition

Type	Obtained from	Reference	Bath Messenger Requirements
Normal	Shop	p665	Radiant Sword Hunter Badge
Uncanny	Drops in Cursed and Defiled Root Chalice Dungeons	–	Acquire Weapon
Lost	Drops in Great Isz Root Chalice Dungeons	–	Acquire Weapon

Available Gem Slots

Weapon Type	Weapon Level		
	1	3	6
Normal	Radial	Radial	Waning
Uncanny	Radial	Radial	Triangular
Lost	Radial	Triangular	Waning

Average Physical Attack Increase (Strength)

Stat Range	Damage per Point	Estimated Attack Gained
17 to 25	4.78	43
26 to 50	2.24	56
50 to 99	0.49	24

Average Physical Attack Increase (Skill)

Stat Range	Damage per Point	Estimated Attack Gained
13 to 25	4.77	62
26 to 50	2.24	56
50 to 99	0.49	24

Damage from Upgrades

Weapon Level	Base	Scaling		
0	100	D	D	D
1	110	D	D	D
2	120	C	D	C
3	130	C	D	C
4	140	C	C	C
5	150	B	C	B
6	160	B	C	B
7	170	B	B	B
8	180	B	B	B
9	190	B	B	B
10	200	B	B	A

Normal Mode Tactics

The normal mode of Ludwig's Holy Blade is literally identical to that of the Kirkhammer. The damage done only differs due to the different base attack power and scaling of the two weapons. While the multipliers are exactly the same, the Kirkhammer will fare better at lower stats while the Holy Blade will shine at high stat totals.

Normal Mode Attacks Properties

Attack	Dmg ×	Type	Stamina	Impact	Note
R1	0.70	Physical	16	Light	
↳ R1 (2nd)	0.71	Physical	16	Light	
↳ R1 (3rd)	0.72	Physical	16	Light	
↳ R1 (4th)	0.74	Thrust	16	Light	can miss against some enemies
↳ R1 (5th)	0.76	Physical	16	Light	
R1 (backstep)	0.67	Physical	10 (+10)	Light	effective lead-in to the R1 chain
R1 (rolling)	0.67	Physical	10 (+10)	Light	strikes to the right of your character
R1 (frontstep)	0.67	Physical	10 (+10)	Light	strikes to the right of your character
R1 (sidestep)	0.67	Physical	10 (+10)	Light	long step forward; very easy to use
R1 (dash)	0.80	Physical	30 (+X)	Light	
R2	1.00	Thrust	55	Normal	
R2 (charged)	1.20	Thrust	75	Normal	continuously hold the button to execute
R2 (backstep)	0.85	Thrust	30 (+10)	Normal	cheap alternative to the uncharged R2
R2 (dash)	0.95	Thrust	50 (+X)	Normal	
R2 (forward leap)	1.20	Thrust	50	Heavy	tap forward on the stick just as you press R2 to execute
Transform Attack	1.05	Blunt	40	Heavy	press L1 while performing another action to execute; forced Guard Break

Normal Mode Key Attacks

As mentioned in the Kirkhammer section, the normal mode of Ludwig's Holy Blade is fast but weak. One thing to consider about the R1 chain is that the fourth attack is a thrust. This has a couple of interesting implications. First, it's good damage against enemies that are weak against thrusts. Second, it can miss quite easily against some enemies, particularly large humanoid foes. If you fight without locking-on to the enemy, you'll need to aim that particular attack very carefully.

The uncharged R2 is still quite good, but some other alternatives are the backstep R2 and the dashing R2. They are both thrust attacks as well. The backstep R2 does significantly less damage than the normal R2, but it also costs less stamina, even when you include the cost of the backstep! The dashing R2 does a bit less damage than the normal R2 but has a similar cost. The advantage is that it can be used when running in from out of the enemy's range and combos into an R1 chain well.

The transformation attack does good super armor damage and has a solid impact. These features combine to make it a great combo finisher. Land a few R1s against an enemy with high super armor, and then perform the transformation attack to land a big stumble. This gives you time to either continue your assault or regain stamina for your next move, and your weapon will be transformed into greatsword mode.

Normal Mode R1

Normal Mode R2

Normal Mode Transform Attack

5

Transformed Mode Tactics

Ludwig's Holy Blade's transformed mode changes the sword and its sheath into a massive greatsword. The greatsword has excellent damage and range. Many of its attacks do blunt damage rather than normal physical damage, but it has some thrusts, too. It tears through super armor quickly. It does cost more stamina than normal mode, and it's slower, too. A bigger concern is that attacks in this mode can rebound off of obstacles if it isn't used carefully.

Transformed Mode Attacks Properties

Attack	Dmg ×	Type	Stamina	Impact	Note
R1	1.00	Blunt	36	Normal	be careful not to strike walls; often rebounds off of obstacles
↳ R1 (2nd)	1.00	Blunt	36	Normal	be careful not to strike walls; often rebounds off of obstacles
↳ R1 (3rd)	1.06	Blunt	36	Normal	
R1 (backstep)	0.56	Blunt	10 (+10)	Normal	special "push" attack
R1 (rolling)	0.90	Blunt	30 (+10)	Normal	be careful not to strike walls; often rebounds off of obstacles
R1 (frontstep)	0.90	Blunt	30 (+10)	Normal	be careful not to strike walls; often rebounds off of obstacles
R1 (sidestep)	0.90	Blunt	30 (+10)	Normal	be careful not to strike walls; often rebounds off of obstacles
R1 (dash)	1.01	Blunt	30 (+X)	Normal	be careful not to strike walls; often rebounds off of obstacles
R2	1.25	Thrust	50	Heavy	
R2 (charged)	2.20	Thrust	75	Heavy	continuously hold the button to execute; extremely powerful
R2 (charged follow-up)	1.56	Blunt	50	Massive	excellent follow-up against staggered foes
R2 (backstep)	1.06	Blunt	25 (+10)	Heavy	
R2 (dash)	1.14	Blunt	40 (+X)	Heavy	great for hit-and-run
R2 (forward leap)	1.20	Blunt	50	Heavy	tap forward on the stick just as you press R2 to execute; key attack due to its range
L2	1.15	Blunt	38	Normal	
↳ L2 (2nd)	1.15	Blunt	38	Normal	
↳ L2 (3rd)	1.18	Blunt	38	Normal	
↳ L2 (4th)	1.13	Thrust	38	Heavy	thrusting attack; can miss easily
Transform Attack	1.26	Blunt	30 (+X)	Heavy	press L1 while performing another action to execute; forced Guard Break

Transformed Mode Key Attacks

The first two hits of the R1 chain are very good against crowds, as are the rolling, frontstep, and sidestep R1s. The backstep R1 is a push attack with some odd properties. It doesn't have a heavy impact, but it can stagger light enemies as if it did. It does very little damage, but it also costs little stamina and can lead into an R1 chain combo. Don't rely on the R1 attacks too much in narrow hallways; they are likely to hit the walls rather than your target.

The uncharged R2 is a very hard-hitting thrust attack. The charged R2 takes that to the extreme, and it can (of course) stagger enemies when used from behind. The follow-up R2 can be used in place of a visceral attack for more damage once your weapon is sufficiently upgraded. The jumping R2 is another great attack; due to the weapon's large size, it has very good range. It doesn't do quite as much damage as the normal R2, but can be useful when you want to get closer to the enemy. Use it as an enemy approaches you; due to its range, many enemies can't react to it properly.

The L2 chain is a series of vertical strikes that are perfect for hitting the heads of tall enemies. They also work well in narrow spaces. The entire chain does good super armor damage and has good impact, too. It's also quick enough to hit mobile enemies. This is useful in Chalice Dungeons when another player has the enemy's attention; attack from the side and go for the stumble!

Transformed Mode R1

Transformed Mode R2

Transformed Mode Transform Attack

Reiterpallasch

The Reiterpallasch requires 8 strength, 12 skill, and 10 bloodtinge. The physical damage scales primarily with skill, and the gun damage scales only with bloodtinge. Don't attempt to use the Reiterpallasch without the required amount of bloodtinge; though the damage of its melee attacks will not be affected, you will rebound off of enemies when you strike them. This weapon is suited for characters with high skill and is unique in that it can operate as a gun in your right hand while transformed. Unlike the Rifle Spear, the Reiterpallasch's transformed mode is one-handed, meaning that you can wield a second gun in your off-hand! This leads to some unique strategies revolving around Reiterpallasch gun-interrupts and follow-ups using a sidearm with Bone Marrow Ash.

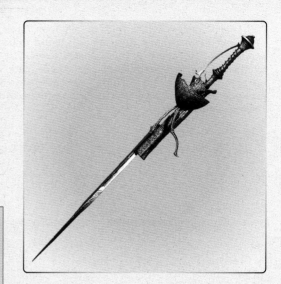

> Weapon wielded by the knights of Cainhurst. Combines an elegant knight's sword with the peculiar firearm wielded by the Cainhurst order. The old nobles, long-time imbibers of blood, are no strangers to the sanguine plague, and the disposal of beasts was a discrete task left to their servants, or knights, as they were called for the sake of appearances.

Gem Advice

The Reiterpallasch is completely unique in that you can actually use it to shoot elemental bullets. Slotting it with an elemental gem will convert all of the weapon's physical attack into elemental attack, and the elemental damage will even apply to the bullets it can fire! Another option is to stack Bloodtinge effects; with enough of them, the Reiterpallasch is the strongest pistol in the game. The downsides are that it takes your precious gem slots to do so and it cannot be buffed with Bone Marrow Ash.

If you instead opt to focus on a melee-oriented Reiterpallasch, Murky and Dirty gems work well with its quick attacks. Many of its attacks are thrusts, so it can also benefit from the Adept (Thrust) effect. In the end, how you gem this weapon should be based on how it fits into your playstyle.

Acquisition

Type	Obtained from	Reference	Bath Messenger Requirements
Normal	Shop	p665	Cainhurst Badge
Uncanny	Drops in Cursed and Defiled Root Chalice Dungeons	–	Acquire Weapon
Lost	Drops in Great Pthumeru Ihyll Root Chalice Dungeons	–	Acquire Weapon

Damage from Upgrades

Weapon Level	Base		Scaling			
0	75	75	E	C	E	D
1	82	82	E	C	E	D
2	89	89	E	B	E	D
3	96	96	E	B	E	D
4	103	103	E	B	E	D
5	110	110	E	B	D	D
6	117	117	E	B	D	C
7	124	124	E	A	D	C
8	131	131	E	A	D	C
9	138	138	E	A	D	C
10	150	150	E	A	D	B

Available Gem Slots

Weapon Type	Weapon Level		
	1	3	6
Normal	Radial	Triangular	Radial
Uncanny	Radial	Waning	Radial
Lost	Radial	Triangular	Waning

Average Physical Attack Increase (Strength)

Stat Range	Damage per Point	Estimated Attack Gained
9 to 25	0.82	14
26 to 50	0.44	11
50 to 99	0.08	4

Average Physical Attack Increase (Skill)

Stat Range	Damage per Point	Estimated Attack Gained
13 to 25	4.54	59
26 to 50	2.08	52
50 to 99	0.47	23

Average Blood Attack Increase (Bloodtinge)

Stat Range	Damage per Point	Estimated Attack Gained
11 to 25	1.87	28
26 to 50	0.84	21
50 to 99	0.18	9

Reiterpallasch +10

Blood Gem Effects

Physical ATK	25 > 150	+100 >	+180
Blunt		->	
Thrust		->	+180
Blood ATK	-> 150	+0 >	+59
Arcane ATK	-> -	+0 >	+0
Fire ATK	-> -	+0 >	+0
Bolt ATK	-> -	+0 >	+0
QS Bullet Use		->	1
Durability	1 >	149	

Attribute Bonus
S > E | S > A | -> D | -> B

Special Attack
0 > 0 | 0 > 0 | 100 > 100 | 100 > 100 | -> 8 | -> 12 | -> 10 | -> -

Normal Mode Tactics

For standard melee combat, you'll usually want to use the Reit-erpallasch's normal mode. The damage is higher, and you have a larger variety of attacks at your disposal. Unless you want to interrupt the enemy with a surprised shot or attack from a distance, normal mode is generally better. Enemies with strong thrust defense are an exception, as the transformed R1 chain is not thrust-type damage.

Normal Mode Attacks Properties

Attack	Dmg ×	Type	Stamina	Impact	Note
R1	1.00	Thrust	18	Light	thrust damage type; good against specific foes
↳ R1 (2nd)	1.05	Physical	18	Light	
↳ R1 (3rd)	1.02	Thrust	18	Light	thrust damage type; good against specific foes
↳ R1 (4th)	1.07	Physical	18	Light	
R1 (backstep)	0.95	Physical	15 (+10)	Light	
R1 (rolling)	0.95	Physical	15 (+10)	Light	
R1 (frontstep)	0.95	Physical	15 (+10)	Light	
R1 (sidestep)	0.95	Physical	15 (+10)	Light	long step forward; very easy to use
R1 (dash)	1.10	Physical	25 (+X)	Light	
R2	1.25	Physical	35	Normal	
R2 (charged)	1.90	Thrust	50	Heavy	continuously hold the button to execute; thrust damage type
R2 (backstep)	1.15	Thrust	30 (+10)	Normal	thrust damage type; good against specific foes
R2 (dash)	1.20	Thrust	30 (+X)	Normal	thrust damage type; good against specific foes
R2 (forward leap)	1.50	Thrust	50	Normal	tap forward on the stick just as you press R2 to execute
Transform Attack	1.00	Blood	0 (+X)	Light	press L1 while performing another action to execute; shoots a bullet; uses Blood Atk value

Normal Mode Key Attacks

The R1 chain, while not exceptionally powerful, uses a thrust as every other attack and is very quick. Enemies with no super armor that are weak to thrust attacks can be killed easily with this chain. Specifically, Braineaters can do nothing once you start this sequence. The first hit of the R1 chain is a very quick thrust that you can use by itself against aggressive enemies that give you little time to attack.

The normal R2 has a horizontal sweep, while the charged R2 is a straight-forward thrust. As with many weapons, a second charged R2 is often more powerful than a visceral attack. This does depend on your stats and upgrade level, so check to see which is better for you. Also remember that visceral attacks can give you other benefits through the use of Runes. From a damage perspective, though, a follow-up charged R2 is usually stronger.

The backstep and dashing R2 attacks are both strong thrusts. The dashing R2 in particular is good for hit-and-run tactics. Another notable move is the sidestep R1; it doesn't deal a lot of damage and doesn't have a special damage type, but it's fast, covers a lot of ground, and is easy to use. Sometimes, the best attacks don't do the most damage but instead are the easiest to hit with; missing a powerful attack does far less damage than connecting with a weaker one!

Normal Mode R1

Normal Mode R2

Normal Mode Transform Attack

Transformed Mode Tactics

In transformed mode, you can press R2 to fire a bullet from your Reiterpallasch. Compared to normal guns, it is very weak at first, but it can be the most powerful pistol in the game when stacked with gems! The main use of transformed mode, though, is to interrupt enemy attacks. Using Bone Marrow Ash does not affect your Reiterpallasch's shots; the effect is only applied to your left hand weapon. This is actually a benefit; you can use Bone Ash, interrupt an enemy with the Reiterpallasch's shot, and then fire your sidearm to take advantage of the double damage for attacking a staggered foe with the Bone Ash bonus.

Transformed Mode Attacks Properties

Attack	Dmg ×	Type	Stamina	Impact	Note
R1	0.75	Physical	16	Light	
↳ R1 (2nd)	0.90	Physical	16	Light	
↳ R1 (3rd)	0.95	Physical	16	Light	
R1 (backstep)	0.95	Physical	16 (+10)	Light	
R1 (rolling)	0.95	Thrust	16 (+10)	Light	thrust damage type; good against specific foes
R1 (frontstep)	0.95	Thrust	16 (+10)	Light	thrust damage type; good against specific foes
R1 (sidestep)	0.95	Thrust	16 (+10)	Light	thrust damage type; good against specific foes
R1 (dash)	1.15	Physical	25 (+X)	Light	
R2	1.00	Blood	0	Light	shoots bullet; uses Blood Atk value; key attack
R2 (forward leap)	1.40	Phys	50	Normal	tap forward on the stick just as you press R2 to execute
Transform Attack	1.10	Thrust	23 (+X)	Light	press L1 while performing another action to execute; forced Guard Break

Transformed Mode Key Attacks

The main reason why you would use the Reiterpallasch is the transformed mode R2. It's simply a gun shot. It does scale with bloodtinge, but the damage increase is quite low. On the other hand, if you use all of your gem slots to increase its blood damage, it can be quite strong. Even without that, you can use the R2 to interrupt enemy attacks. In PvP, it can surprise an opponent who is unfamiliar with the Reiterpallasch. If you have something other than a pistol as your sidearm, they may not expect for you to interrupt their attack.

As alluded to previously, using Bone Marrow Ash on a sidearm and then interrupting an attack with your transformed R2 leads to some very interesting situations. If you are using a Flamesprayer, for example, hitting an enemy with an Oil Urn will double the damage of the first hit. This can be double again by hitting a staggered enemy. So throw an Oil Urn, use Bone Marrow Ash on your Flamesprayer, interrupt the enemy with the transformed R2 of the Reiterpallasch, and then use the Flamesprayer while the enemy is down. You can easily deal thousands of points of damage with this technique.

This tactic obviously requires a lot of set-up, but it's worth it when you eradicate a boss in a matter of seconds. A less execution-intensive strategy that relies more upon the strength stat than the arcane stat is to simply use the Cannon with Bone Marrow Ash. This requires high strength (which doesn't benefit the Reiterpallasch much) but is effective without the need to use an Oil Urn. It does take effort to use these techniques, but having the ability to deal over 4000 damage just by interrupting a single attack is worth it.

Transformed Mode R1

Transformed Mode R2

Transformed Mode Transform Attack

Chikage

The Chikage requires 10 strength, 14 skill, and 12 bloodtinge. The normal mode scales with strength and skill, though it gains much more attack power from skill than strength. Normal mode does not scale with bloodtinge at all. Transformed mode scales only with bloodtinge. Even though the damage of transformed mode is unaffected by strength and skill, you must still meet the strength and skill requirements or your attacks will rebound off of the enemy. With normal mode, you must still meet the bloodtinge requirement even though bloodtinge does not affect the damage. The Chikage is different from all other weapons; not only do the different modes scale with different stats, but the transformed mode also has a negative effect that drains your health. This is balanced by the fact that it can also inflict rapid poisoning on the enemy, tearing off huge chunks of health quickly. This is a high-risk, high-reward weapon.

> Foreign-made weapon wielded by the royal guards who protect Annalise, Queen of the Vilebloods at Cainhurst Castle. When the intricate, rippled engraving that spans the Chikage's blade is imbrued with blood, the sword sings in scarlet hues. However, the rite eats away at the wielder's very essence.

Acquisition

Type	Obtained from	Reference	Bath Messenger Requirements
Normal	Shop	p665	Cainhurst Badge
Uncanny	Drops in Defiled and Cursed Root Chalice Dungeons	–	Acquire Weapon
Lost	Drops in Great Pthumeru Ihyll Root Chalice Dungeons	–	Acquire Weapon

Available Gem Slots

Weapon Type	Weapon Level		
	1	3	6
Normal	Radial	Radial	Triangular
Uncanny	Radial	Radial	Waning
Lost	Radial	Radial	Circular

Average Physical Attack Increase (Strength)

Stat Range	Damage per Point	Estimated Attack Gained
11 to 25	1.40	21
26 to 50	0.64	16
50 to 99	0.14	7

Average Physical Attack Increase (Skill)

Stat Range	Damage per Point	Estimated Attack Gained
15 to 25	3.64	40
26 to 50	1.64	41
50 to 99	0.37	18

Average Blood Attack Increase (Bloodtinge)

Stat Range	Damage per Point	Estimated Attack Gained
13 to 25	6.08	79
26 to 50	2.84	71
50 to 99	0.61	30

Damage from Upgrades

Weapon Level	Base		Scaling			
0	92	92	E	D	C	D
1	101	101	E	D	B	D
2	110	110	E	D	B	D
3	119	119	E	D	B	D
4	128	128	E	D	B	D
5	137	137	E	C	A	D
6	146	146	E	C	A	D
7	155	155	E	C	A	D
8	164	164	E	C	A	D
9	173	173	E	C	A	D
10	184	184	E	B	S	D

Gem Advice

The Chikage is a very unusual weapon, and it can be very difficult to find the correct gems for it. Its physical damage can't be converted to elemental damage, so those gems aren't a good choice. Physical damage increases, like Tempering, only affect normal mode, and blood damage increases, like the Bloodtinge effect, only affect transformed mode. Nourishing gems are better, since they benefit both modes. Fool and Poorman can be difficult to use in transformed mode due to transformed Chikage's health drain.

There are effects that do work well for Chikage, though. The Pulsing effect can be used to offset the HP loss of transformed mode. Dirty gems are another very strong choice. Chikage has a natural Rapid Poison effect in transformed mode, so boosting it with the Dirty effect can be a strong strategy. Consider using a mix of Pulsing and Dirty gem effects.

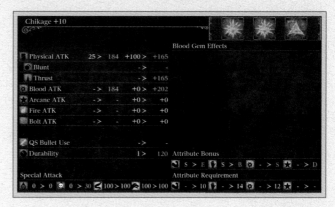

Normal Mode Tactics

If you have a build that focuses on skill but not bloodtinge, you will almost always want to use normal mode. If you have high skill and bloodtinge, you'll rely on this mode whenever the health drain from transformed mode is a problem. Generally speaking, any time you aren't using the rapid poison effect of the transformed mode, normal will be better for you. You can't use your sidearm in transformed mode, either, so you'll need to stick to normal when you want to use a gun, torch, or the shield.

Normal Mode Attacks Properties

Attack	Dmg ×	Type	Stamina	Impact	Note
R1	1.00	Physical	23	Light	
↳ R1 (2nd)	1.00	Physical	23	Light	
↳ R1 (3rd)	1.05	Physical	23	Light	
↳ R1 (4th)	1.10	Physical	23	Light	
↳ R1 (5th)	1.10	Physical	23	Light	
R1 (backstep)	1.00	Physical	20 (+10)	Light	horizontal sweep; useful against weak groups of enemies
R1 (rolling)	1.05	Physical	20 (+10)	Light	
R1 (frontstep)	1.05	Physical	20 (+10)	Light	
R1 (sidestep)	1.10	Physical	20 (+10)	Light	good range; easy to use
R1 (dash)	1.10	Physical	30 (+X)	Light	horizontal sweep; useful against weak groups of enemies
R2	1.27	Thrust	40	Normal	
R2 (charged)	1.85	Thrust	60	Heavy	continuously hold the button to execute
R2 (backstep)	1.25	Physical	40 (+10)	Normal	better than backstep R1 against single foes
R2 (dash)	1.17	Thrust	50 (+X)	Normal	quick forward thrust; useful surprise attack
R2 (forward leap)	1.45	Physical	50	Normal	tap forward on the stick just as you press R2 to execute
Transform Attack	1.42	Physical	35 (+X)	Normal	press L1 while performing another action to execute; forced Guard Break

Normal Mode Key Attacks

The sidestep R1 is strong; normally, sidestep attacks have lower multipliers. The dashing R1 is also powerful, and it hits in front of your character in a horizontal sweep. This is a great opening attack against a crowd of enemies. The backstep R1, while slightly weaker, has a similar sweep. The normal R1 chain doesn't have the same arc; it's more of a vertical series of slashes.

The charged R2 has a good multiplier and can stagger enemies when used from behind, but it charges rather slowly. It does do thrusting-type damage, though, as does the normal, uncharged R2. Since the Chikage has pretty good range, the backstep R2 can be an effective counter attack after dodging an enemy strike.

The normal mode dashing R2 attack is a quick, straight thrust that can catch other players off-guard in PvP. Remember to disguise your dash so that your opponent doesn't guess what you're up to! On the other hand, always be ready for this attack if you're fighting against someone wielding the Chikage. Overall, the normal mode of the Chikage isn't particularly remarkable, but it is well-balanced.

Normal Mode R1

Normal Mode R2

Normal Mode Transform Attack

Transformed Mode Tactics

The Chikage's transformed mode is for those who like to live on the edge. Every second, you will lose a percentage of your maximum health, but your attacks will cause rapid poison to build up in your prey. Once the poison builds up enough, the enemy will suddenly lose a chunk of health. Most difficult bosses are nearly immune to rapid poison, but the Wet Nurse and a few others are not. There are several tough normal enemies that are weak to rapid poisoning as well, such as the Loran Silverbeasts and Bloodlickers.

Transformed Mode Attacks Properties

Attack	Dmg ×	Type	Stamina	Impact	Note
R1	0.95	Physical	25	Light	scales with bloodtinge; knocks down dogs despite light impact
↳ R1 (2nd)	0.98	Physical	25	Light	scales with bloodtinge
↳ R1 (3rd)	1.00	Physical	25	Light	scales with bloodtinge
↳ R1 (4th)	1.02	Physical	25	Light	scales with bloodtinge
↳ R1 (5th)	1.07	Physical	25	Light	scales with bloodtinge
R1 (backstep)	1.02	Physical	25 (+10)	Light	scales with bloodtinge
R1 (rolling)	1.00	Physical	25 (+10)	Light	scales with bloodtinge
R1 (frontstep)	1.00	Physical	25 (+10)	Light	scales with bloodtinge
R1 (sidestep)	1.04	Physical	25 (+10)	Light	scales with bloodtinge
R1 (dash)	1.17	Physical	40 (+X)	Light	scales with bloodtinge
R2	1.50	Physical	55	Normal	scales with bloodtinge
R2 (charged)	2.25	Physical	60	Massive	continuously hold the button to execute; scales with bloodtinge
R2 (charged follow-up)	1.92	Physical	50	Massive	scales with bloodtinge
R2 (backstep)	1.29	Physical	50 (+10)	Heavy	hits high; useful for hitting enemy weak points; scales with bloodtinge
R2 (dash)	1.15	Thrust	60	Normal	scales with bloodtinge
R2 (forward leap)	1.47	Physical	60	Normal	tap forward on the stick just as you press R2 to execute; scales with bloodtinge
L2	1.15	Thrust	55	Normal	scales with bloodtinge
↳ L2 (2nd)	1.27	Physical	55	Normal	scales with bloodtinge
Transform Attack	0.95	Physical	20 (+X)	Normal	press L1 while performing another action to execute; forced Guard Break; scales with bloodtinge

Transformed Mode Key Attacks

The most important attacks of the transformed Chikage, by far, are its R1 attacks. Quick, consecutive strikes build up rapid poisoning. Even for enemies that are weak against rapid poison, you'll often need to connect with seven quick attacks or more in order to inflict the status. These quick attacks will enable you to do so.

If you focus on R1 attacks for rapid poisoning, there are some other things you can do to make things easier. First, adding rapid poison effect gems to your weapon can reduce the number of hits needed to cause the effect. Second, increasing your endurance so that you have enough stamina for long attack chains will ensure that you can hit the enemy until the poison strikes. Third, including HP recovery gems can offset the constant damage of transformed mode. If you want to use this weapon for the poison property, these preparations combined with rapid R1 attacks are very effective.

Outside of the poison effect, the transformed Chikage has another interesting trick— the charged R2 of transformed mode drains your health as you charge it. You can use this effect to quickly and safely drain your own health if you want to activate a near-death gem effect; this strategy works even if you don't have the proper stats for this weapon! The Chikage is a weapon that has many tactical uses; whether or not you benefit depends quite a bit on your strategic gem choices.

Transformed Mode R1

Transformed Mode R2

Transformed Mode Transform Attack

Rifle Spear

The Rifle Spear requires 10 strength, 11 skill, and 9 bloodtinge. The physical damage scales primarily with skill, and the gun damage scales only with bloodtinge. Despite the description stating that the Rifle Spear "lacks any notable functions," it's actually one of the best weapons in Bloodborne. It has a series of very long range attacks that are quick and deal great damage. Many of them are thrust-type, but it has normal physical strikes as well. The gun component starts off weak and should not be relied upon heavily unless you dedicate your gem slots to boosting blood attack.

A trick weapon crafted by the workshop heretics, the Powder Kegs. A prototype weapon serving as a simple firearm and spear, possibly created in imitation of a lost Cainhurst weapon. Lacks any notable functions, saving that it is the only trick weapon with an attached gun.

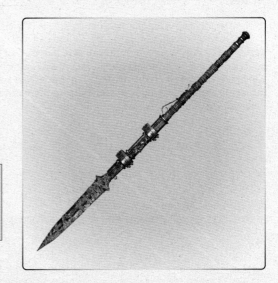

Gem Advice

Out of all the weapons, the Rifle Spear is the one that benefits the most from the Striking gem effect. The transformed charged R2 is probably the best attack in all of Bloodborne, so increasing its power via the Striking effect is a very good idea. If you want something that benefits all of your attacks, consider Tempering instead. The spear's range also makes it ideal for Finestrike, and its thrusting attacks work well with Adept (Thrust). The range also works well with Fool and Poorman effects, as the Rifle Spear tends to be a safe weapon that lets you control your HP.

It's not recommended, but stacking Bloodtinge effects can turn the Rifle Spear into the strongest blunderbuss. The problem is that blunderbuss attacks are most useful at close range, whereas the spear is best from a distance. It's hard to justify giving up those gem slots for Bloodtinge.

Acquisition

Type	Obtained from	Reference	Bath Messenger Requirements
Normal	Old Yharnam	p61	Powder Keg Hunter Badge
Uncanny	Drops in Lower Pthumeru Root Chalice Dungeons	–	Acquire Weapon
Lost	Drops in Ailing Loran Root Chalice Dungeons	–	Acquire Weapon

Damage from Upgrades

Weapon Level	Base		Scaling			
0	85	85	E	D	D	D
1	93	93	E	D	D	D
2	101	101	E	D	D	D
3	109	109	E	C	D	D
4	117	117	E	C	D	D
5	125	125	E	C	D	D
6	133	133	E	C	D	D
7	141	141	E	C	C	D
8	149	149	E	B	C	D
9	157	157	E	B	C	D
10	170	170	D	B	B	C

Available Gem Slots

Weapon Type	Weapon Level		
	1	3	6
Normal	Radial	Triangular	Radial
Uncanny	Radial	Waning	Radial
Lost	Radial	Triangular	Waning

Average Physical Attack Increase (Strength)

Stat Range	Damage per Point	Estimated Attack Gained
11 to 25	1.53	23
26 to 50	0.68	17
50 to 99	0.16	8

Average Physical Attack Increase (Skill)

Stat Range	Damage per Point	Estimated Attack Gained
12 to 25	3.57	50
26 to 50	1.64	41
50 to 99	0.37	18

Average Blood Attack Increase (Bloodtinge)

Stat Range	Damage per Point	Estimated Attack Gained
10 to 25	3.19	51
26 to 50	1.52	38
50 to 99	0.35	17

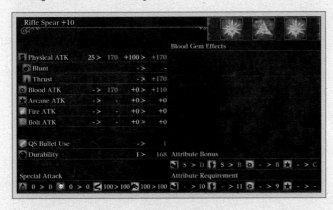

Normal Mode Tactics

Normal mode useful for quick, thrusting pokes. The Rifle Spear is used in one hand in normal mode, so you can still use your sidearm. The downside of normal mode is that many of its attacks rebound off of objects very easily, so it can be harder to use in tight spaces than the transformed mode. That said, the thrust attacks are unlikely to rebound unless there is something between you and your target.

Normal Mode Attacks Properties

Attack	Dmg ×	Type	Stamina	Impact	Note
R1	0.95	Thrust	18	Light	great range and speed
↳ R1 (2nd)	1.00	Thrust	18	Light	
↳ R1 (3rd)	1.05	Thrust	18	Light	
↳ R1 (4th)	1.10	Thrust	18	Light	
R1 (backstep)	0.90	Thrust	20 (+10)	Light	great for counter-hits
R1 (rolling)	0.85	Physical	18 (+10)	Light	
R1 (frontstep)	0.85	Physical	18 (+10)	Light	
R1 (sidestep)	0.85	Physical	18 (+10)	Light	
R1 (dash)	0.85	Thrust	25 (+X)	Light	
R2	1.35	Thrust	40	Normal	great for counters
R2 (charged)	1.95	Thrust	55	Heavy	continuously hold the button to execute; good choice after gun interrupt
R2 (backstep)	1.20	Physical	35 (+10)	Normal	great for counters
R2 (dash)	1.15	Physical	45 (+X)	Normal	
R2 (forward leap)	1.60	Thrust	50	Normal	tap forward on the stick just as you press R2 to execute
Transform Attack	Special	Special	0 (+X)	Special	press L1 while performing another action to execute; shoots a bullet; uses Blood Atk value

Normal Mode Key Attacks

The normal R1 chain is fast, has long range, and deals thrust damage. On top of that, it consumes very little stamina. Against enemies with no super armor, you can usually just press R1 until the enemy dies. It's really difficult for that sort of enemy to even get close to you. If enemies do get close, you'll generally want to quickstep away; make them come to you.

The backstep R1, backstep R2, and normal R2 attacks are all extremely useful for landing counter hits. The Rifle Spear's range makes it the ideal weapon for this; backstep once or twice to make sure the enemy's attack will miss, then attack! You'll deal extra damage. If you can just walk out of range, counter with a normal R2. If you need to backstep, decide whether to use backstep R1 or backstep R2 based on the enemy's defense. The backstep R2 is more powerful, but the backstep R1 is a thrust-type attack.

If you interrupt an enemy with a gunshot, the charged R2 usually deals more damage than a visceral attack would. You'll need to start charging the attack as soon as you interrupt the enemy. Be careful; if you're too slow the enemy may evade the attack. If you think you'll be too slow with your charge, a forward-jumping R2 is another option; the Rifle Spear's range makes this very reliable, and the damage is good.

Normal Mode R1

Normal Mode R2

Normal Mode Transform Attack

Transformed Mode Tactics

Transformed mode swaps the quick thrusts of normal mode for sweeping slashes that are good against crowds. It also doesn't rebound off of obstacles and walls. You do give up the rapid long range pokes, but in exchange you gain a very long-range, powerful charge attack. You give up access to your off-hand weapon, as the transformed Rifle Spear is held in two hands, but you also gain a blunderbuss attack that can be useful in a few situations.

Transformed Mode Attacks Properties

Attack	Dmg×	Type	Stamina	Impact	Note
R1	0.95	Physical	20	Light	
↳ R1 (2nd)	1.00	Physical	20	Light	sweeping arc; good for crowds
↳ R1 (3rd)	1.05	Physical	18	Light	
↳ R1 (4th)	1.10	Physical	18	Light	
R1 (backstep)	0.90	Thrust	25 (+10)	Light	great for counters
R1 (rolling)	0.90	Thrust	22 (+10)	Light	
R1 (frontstep)	0.90	Thrust	22 (+10)	Light	
R1 (sidestep)	0.90	Thrust	22 (+10)	Light	great for counters
R1 (dash)	0.90	Thrust	25 (+X)	Light	
R2	1.76	Thrust	45	Normal	
R2 (charged)	2.45	Thrust	60	Heavy	continuously hold the button to execute; key attack
R2 (backstep)	1.35	Physical	45 (+10)	Normal	great for counters
R2 (forward leap)	1.60	Physical	50	Normal	tap forward on the stick just as you press R2 to execute
L2	Special	Special	0	Special	fire a blunderbuss-style shot
Transform Attack	1.30	Physical	25 (+X)	Normal	press L1 while performing another action to execute; forced Guard Break

Transformed Mode Key Attacks

Make no mistake; the charged R2 is the star of this show. It's powerful, but the main draw for this attack is its range. Your character takes several quick steps before lunging forward for a deadly thrust. You can start the attack from far outside an enemy's range while it approaches, and it will be ready just as the enemy reaches you. Most of the enemies in the game fall for this. Only foes with very long-range attacks or a ton of super armor can do anything about it.

Beyond that, the charged R2 can stagger enemies if you hit them from behind. The distance that it travels means that this can hit enemies after attacks that would otherwise have carried them too far away. The direction of your thrust is only fixed after the attack is fully charged, so even evasive enemies will have trouble escaping. The only real downside to the attack is that it charges slowly.

If you don't fully charge it, the normal R2 deals less damage. More importantly, it doesn't travel as far as the charged R2. Normally, you'll want to stick to the charged R2. The R1 chain has sweeping attacks that are great against crowds, and the L2 will let you fire a blunderbuss-style scattershot. The L2 can be very powerful at close range if you equip gems to boost blood attack. The dashing R1 is another great way to surprise your opponent; it's fast and has excellent range.

Transformed Mode R1

Transformed Mode R2

Transformed Mode Transform Attack

Stake Driver

The Stake Driver requires 18 strength and 9 skill to use; it scales with strength and skill, but, between the two, it gains more attack power from strength. It has a combination of normal physical attacks, blunt attacks, and thrusting attacks depending on which mode you use. The key characteristic of this weapon is its explosive transformed charged R2 attack. It takes a long time to charge, but it has (by far) the highest damage multiplier in the game. Striking a staggered opponent or an enemy's weak spot with this attack is devastating, but the long charge time makes it challenging to use.

A trick weapon fashioned by the workshop heretics, the Powder Kegs. Favoured by the retired hunter Djura. The stake driver, with its queerly complex design, violently drives thick stakes into the flesh of foes. The stake driver allows for high-damage critical attacks, but is difficult to use and leaves its wielder wide open, but none of this should bother a mere Powder Keg.

Gem Advice

The Stake Driver can be converted into an elemental weapon, but its arcane scaling isn't high. Instead, it's better to focus on boosting its physical attack via Tempering gem effects. Probably the most noticeable trait of the Stake Driver is its transformed mode charged R2. It charges slowly but is capable of delivering a devastating hit. The Striking gem effect can be used to boost it, as it is a charge attack. That's obvious, but this next tip isn't— the Adept (Blunt) effect will boost it as well! The large explosion is counted as a blunt attack.

Secondary, but important, characteristics of the Stake Driver are its speed and low stamina costs. These traits combine to make it excellent for poison effects. Slot Murky or Dirty gems into your Stake Driver and reap the rewards! With these options, you can choose rather to focus on single, big hits or rapid attacks with this weapon.

Acquisition

Type	Obtained from	Reference	Bath Messenger Requirements
Normal	Shop	p665	Powder Keg Hunter Badge
Uncanny	Drops in Lower Hintertomb Root Chalice Dungeons	–	Acquire Weapon
Lost	Drops in Lower Loran Root Chalice Dungeons	–	Acquire Weapon

Available Gem Slots

Weapon Type	Weapon Level		
	1	3	6
Normal	Radial	Triangular	Radial
Uncanny	Radial	Waning	Radial
Lost	Radial	Triangular	Waning

Average Physical Attack Increase (Strength)

Stat Range	Damage per Point	Estimated Attack Gained
19 to 25	3.14	22
26 to 50	1.40	35
50 to 99	0.33	16

Average Physical Attack Increase (Skill)

Stat Range	Damage per Point	Estimated Attack Gained
10 to 25	2.69	43
26 to 50	1.32	33
50 to 99	0.29	14

Damage from Upgrades

Weapon Level	Base	Scaling		
0	85	D	D	D
1	93	D	D	D
2	101	D	D	D
3	109	D	D	D
4	117	D	D	D
5	125	D	D	D
6	133	D	D	D
7	141	D	D	C
8	149	C	D	C
9	157	C	D	C
10	170	C	C	C

Normal Mode Tactics

Normal mode attacks are generally stronger, though they tend to be normal physical attacks, but there are some thrusting attacks mixed in. This mode has more horizontal attacks, making it better for crowds. Usually, though, you should look for an opportunity to enter transformed mode.

Normal Mode Attacks Properties

Attack	Dmg ×	Type	Stamina	Impact	Note
R1	1.00	Physical	19	Light	horizontal sweep; good for crowds
↳ R1 (2nd)	1.02	Physical	19	Light	horizontal sweep; good for crowds
↳ R1 (3rd)	1.04	Physical	19	Light	horizontal sweep; good for crowds
↳ R1 (4th)	1.07	Thrust	19	Light	thrust; good against specific foes
↳ R1 (5th)	1.10	Physical	19	Light	horizontal sweep; good for crowds
R1 (backstep)	0.95	Thrust	15 (+10)	Light	thrust; good against specific foes
R1 (rolling)	0.95	Physical	15 (+10)	Light	
R1 (frontstep)	0.95	Physical	15 (+10)	Light	
R1 (sidestep)	1.05	Physical	15 (+10)	Light	
R1 (dash)	1.10	Physical	30 (+X)	Light	horizontal sweep; good for crowds
R2	1.35	Physical	45	Normal	
R2 (charged)	1.90	Physical	65	Heavy	continuously hold the button to execute
R2 (backstep)	0.95	Physical	30 (+10)	Normal	
R2 (dash)	1.25	Physical	45 (+X)	Normal	
R2 (forward leap)	1.50	Thrust	50	Normal	tap forward on the stick just as you press R2 to execute
Transform Attack	1.10	Physical	15 (+X)	Normal	press L1 while performing another action to execute; forced Guard Break

Normal Mode Key Attacks

The first three attacks of the Stake Driver R1 chain can be useful for hitting multiple enemies at once. The fourth attack is a thrust. These attacks are quick, so using a buff item like Fire Paper can add a lot of damage to long attack strings. These attacks are very stamina-efficient; this is one of the best attack sequences in the game to use buff items with. This also holds true for the transformed R1 chain.

Normal Mode R1

The dashing R1 is another attack that can strike multiple enemies; you can use it as an opener against weak crowds. The dashing R2 has a narrower hit box, but it also has more power. Consider using it against tougher opponents when fighting one-on-one. The normal charged R2 doesn't take as long to prepare as the transformed R2, but it also does far less damage. It can stagger enemies from behind, though, so it's good for that purpose.

Normal Mode R2

The transformation attack isn't particularly powerful, but you will probably use it often; this is a good way to prepare your Stake Driver's big attack in the middle of a fight. It's fairly quick, so you shouldn't have much difficulty switching modes. It's also worth noting that buffs like Bolt Paper persist through mode changes, so you can go from using it with normal R1 attacks to transformed R1 attacks without interruption.

Normal Mode Transform Attack

Transformed Mode Tactics

The Stake Driver's transformed mode swaps the sweeping physical attacks of normal mode for quick jabs. These jabs cost very little stamina and can be used rapidly. More importantly, transformed mode gains an extremely powerful charged attack. Be warned, though, that use of R2 attacks while in transformed mode will automatically return the weapon to normal mode. The only exception is the jumping R2, which can be used normally.

Transformed Mode Attacks Properties

Attack	Dmg ×	Type	Stamina	Impact	Note
R1	0.97	Physical	15	Light	thrust; good against specific foes
↳ R1 (2nd)	1.00	Physical	15	Light	thrust; good against specific foes
↳ R1 (3rd)	1.02	Physical	15	Light	thrust; good against specific foes
↳ R1 (4th)	1.04	Physical	15	Light	thrust; good against specific foes
R1 (backstep)	0.90	Physical	15 (+10)	Light	
R1 (rolling)	0.90	Physical	15 (+10)	Light	
R1 (frontstep)	0.90	Physical	15 (+10)	Light	
R1 (sidestep)	1.00	Physical	15 (+10)	Light	
R1 (dash)	1.10	Physical	30 (+X)	Normal	
R2	1.37	Blunt	55	Heavy	returns weapon to Normal mode
R2 (charged)	3.55	Blunt	150	Massive	continuously hold the button to execute; returns weapon to normal mode
R2 (forward leap)	1.30	Blunt	50	Normal	tap forward on the stick just as you press R2 to execute
Transform Attack	1.00	Physical	20 (+X)	Light	press L1 while performing another action to execute; forced Guard Break

Transformed Mode Key Attacks

The charged R2 is amazingly powerful, and it hits a small area in front of your character. The issue is that it is very slow, so it's difficult to use. You can begin preparing it as an enemy approaches from out of range; if your timing is correct, the explosion will trigger just as the enemy reaches you. The force of the blast is massive enough to knock down most enemies.

An even more powerful use of this attack is against staggered enemies; they take double damage from attacks, so a fully charged transformed R2 from the Stake Driver will eradicate a staggered opponent. The problem is that the enemy will certainly have time to stand back up and resume attacking before the charge finishes.

You can get around this limitation in multiplayer, though! Let another player interrupt the enemy with a gunshot or land a charged R2 with a different weapon to cause a stagger, and the unleash the charged R2 from your Stake Driver! You'll find that your transformed Stake Driver will synergize well if your partner is using a quick weapon like the Blade of Mercy to stagger enemies or a Hunter Pistol for interrupts. Just remember to budget for plenty of stamina if you intend to rely on this weapon, or you'll often find yourself unable to attack or roll; read about negative stamina on p19.

Transformed Mode R1

Transformed Mode R2

Transformed Mode Transform Attack

Tonitrus

Tonitrus requires 12 strength and 8 skill to use. Its physical attack increases more with strength than skill, and it gains a slight boost to its bolt attack power for each point of the arcane stat. Tonitrus is a unique trick weapon, indeed. It's the only weapon in your arsenal that can deal bolt damage without the use of Bolt Paper or a gem. It also does blunt damage; there are only a few enemies that are notably weak against blunt attacks, but it's useful to have Tonitrus when you face one. The transformed mode further augments the bolt damage, but it only lasts for seven seconds.

A unique trick weapon contrived by Archibald, the infamous eccentric of the Healing Church workshop. Striking this peculiar iron morning star flail like a match generates the same blue sparks that blanket a darkbeast. Unfortunately, for reasons untold, the hunters of Archibald's time did not fully take to the device.

Gem Advice

Tonitrus cannot be turned into a purely elemental weapon via gems, but it can still benefit quite a bit from Bolt and Odd Bolt effects thanks to the bolt damage boost of its transformation. Alternatively, you can use Nourishing gem effects to boost both its physical and elemental damage.

The other key feature of Tonitrus is that all of its attacks deal blunt damage. There's no reason to use a Tempering gem with this weapon for physical damage; just stick to the larger bonus that you can get from equivalent level Adept (Blunt) effects. Remember that some Fool and Poorman effects only work for physical damage, while others work for all damage; hunt out the effects that work for all damage to use with Tonitrus. You'll be able to amplify both your blunt damage and your bolt damage at the same time.

Acquisition

Type	Obtained from	Reference	Bath Messenger Requirements
Normal	Yahar'gul (Evening)	p84	Spark Hunter Badge
Uncanny	Drops in Ailing Loran Root Chalice Dungeons	–	Acquire Weapon
Lost	Drops in Lower Loran Root Chalice Dungeons	–	Acquire Weapon

Damage from Upgrades

Weapon Level	Base		Scaling		
0	80	40	D	E	D
1	88	44	D	E	D
2	96	48	D	E	D
3	104	52	D	E	D
4	112	56	D	E	D
5	120	60	C	E	D
6	128	64	C	E	D
7	136	68	C	E	D
8	144	72	C	E	D
9	152	76	C	E	D
10	160	80	B	E	D

Available Gem Slots

Weapon Type	Weapon Level		
	1	3	6
Normal	Radial	Radial	Waning
Uncanny	Radial	Radial	Triangular
Lost	Radial	Triangular	Waning

Average Physical Attack Increase (Strength)

Stat Range	Damage per Point	Estimated Attack Gained
13 to 25	3.15	41
26 to 50	1.44	36
50 to 99	0.33	16

Average Physical Attack Increase (Skill)

Stat Range	Damage per Point	Estimated Attack Gained
9 to 25	1.12	19
26 to 50	0.56	14
50 to 99	0.12	6

Average Bolt Attack Increase (Arcane)

Stat Range	Damage per Point	Estimated Attack Gained
9 to 25	1.06	18
26 to 50	0.56	14
50 to 99	0.12	6

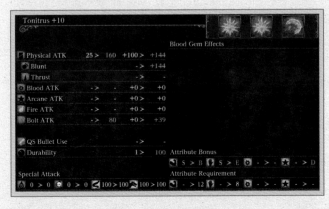

Tactics

Tonitrus is reasonably quick, and its split-damage type attacks do great damage against foes with low defense. Its stamina costs are also reasonable. You'll only encounter problems when facing enemies that resist blunt or bolt attacks. The Tonitrus doesn't have any thrust attacks, and it can't be buffed with Fire Paper to cover fire weaknesses either.

Normal Mode Attacks Properties

Attack	Dmg ×	Type	Stamina	Impact	Note
R1	1.00		23	Light	
↳ R1 (2nd)	1.02		23	Light	
↳ R1 (3rd)	1.04		23	Light	
↳ R1 (4th)	1.06		23	Light	
↳ R1 (5th)	1.08		23	Light	
R1 (backstep)	0.95		20 (+10)	Light	
R1 (rolling)	0.90		20 (+10)	Light	
R1 (frontstep)	0.90	Blunt / Bolt	20+ (10)	Light	
R1 (sidestep)	0.90		20 (+10)	Light	
R1 (dash)	1.05		20 (+X)	Normal	
R2	1.20		37	Normal	
R2 (charged)	1.90		55	Heavy	
R2 (backstep)	1.20		30 (+10)	Normal	
R2 (dash)	1.15		30 (+X)	Heavy	
R2 (forward leap)	1.50		50	Normal	tap forward on the stick just as you press R2 to execute
Transform Attack	1.08		40 (+X)	Light	press L1 while performing another action to execute; forced Guard Break

Normal Mode Key Attacks

With Tonitrus, the R1 chain is by far the most important attack. The weapon overall doesn't have a fancy moveset, so hammering away with the blunt R1 string is generally the best option. This isn't a weapon you choose for range, tricky thrusts that sneak past the enemy's defenses, or anything of the sort; this is a hefty, metallic mace covered in blue sparks of death. Mash R1 and bash your enemies' skulls in!

One odd point is that, for such a heavy looking weapon, most of its attacks don't have a lot of impact. If you need to deliver a bigger stumble when breaking an enemy's super armor, the dashing R2 is pretty good. The charged R2 also has a heavy impact, and it charges a lot quicker than you might imagine. It's great for rolling behind an enemy and striking for a stagger, and it can even be performed a second time before the enemy recovers in most cases.

The last attack of real note is the transformation attack; it coats the weapon in crackling blue pulses that increase your bolt damage. The attack itself, though, is weak for the stamina cost. It also has a light impact and isn't particularly fast; additionally, it cannot combo into itself. ⬆ + L1 > L1 won't work with this weapon; you'll need to use something like ⬆ + L1 > R1 > L1. In the end, it isn't really worth it. It's better to transform Tonitrus before engaging and in-between your assaults.

Transformed Mode Key Attacks

Tonitrus' transformed mode does not follow the same rules as other weapons. Instead, transformation is a seven second buff that has the following effects:

Base Bolt Damage +40	Bolt Scaling Up by 40%	Bolt Damage ×1.7

Activating this mode gives a huge boost to your bolt damage, without affecting your physical attack. In practice, you'll normally see a large overall damage increase when using the transformed Tonitrus; the added bolt damage outweighs the reduced physical damage. Tonitrus is most valuable early in the main game;

Normal Mode R1

Normal Mode R2

Normal Mode Transform Attack

once you begin scouring the Chalice Dungeons for treasures, you're likely to find Bolt gems that can be used to make other bolt-elemental weapons. Tonitrus may then find its role in your arsenal somewhat diminished.

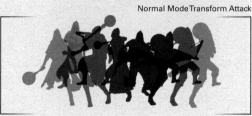

Logarius' Wheel

Logarius' Wheel requires 20 strength, 12 skill, and 10 arcane to use. Its strength scaling is immense; each point of strength that you add greatly improves this weapon's physical attack power. It also has moderate arcane scaling. This is a very powerful weapon in either mode. It requires a high stat investment but is a valuable tool for those able to use it. Both modes deal an additional 30% bonus damage to enemies that are weak against righteous weapons, as well.

> Weapon wielded by martyr Logarius' band of executioners. Used to slaughter the Vilebloods in Cainhurst. Bathed in pools of their blood, and forever steeped in their ire. Transform to release the power of the wheel and manifest their lingering rage in a show of utter brilliance.

Gem Advice

Logarius Wheel cannot be turned into a purely elemental weapon via gems, but it can still benefit quite a bit from Arcane and Odd Arcane effects thanks to the arcane damage boost of its transformed L2 attacks. Alternatively, you can use Nourishing gem effects to boost both its physical and elemental damage.

Radiant gems are exceptionally useful due to Logarius' Wheel's high stamina costs and the need to use the Regain system in transformed mode. Alternatively, Pulsing gems can offset the penalty associated with the transformed L2 and make you a little less reliant on Regain. Both Murky and Dirty gems work exceptionally well with the Logarius' Wheel due to the multi-hit R2 attacks of transformed mode; this is a recommended weapon if you want a build that focuses on inflicting poison. The combination of physical and arcane damage combined with poison covers a lot of situations.

Acquisition

Type	Obtained from	Reference	Bath Messenger Requirements
Normal	Shop	p665	Wheel Hunter Badge
Uncanny	Drops in Great Pthumeru Ihyll Root Chalice Dungeons	–	Acquire Weapon
Lost	Drops in Great Pthumeru Ihyll Root Chalice Dungeons	–	Acquire Weapon

Damage from Upgrades

Weapon Level	Base ⚔	Base ★	Scaling 🌊	Scaling ★
0	100	25	C	D
1	110	27	B	D
2	120	29	B	D
3	130	31	B	D
4	140	33	B	D
5	150	35	A	D
6	160	37	A	D
7	170	39	A	D
8	180	41	A	C
9	190	43	A	C
10	200	50	S	C

Available Gem Slots

Weapon Type	Weapon Level 1	Weapon Level 3	Weapon Level 6
Normal	Radial	Radial	Waning
Uncanny	Radial	Radial	Triangular
Lost	Radial	Triangular	Waning

Average Physical Attack Increase (Strength)

Stat Range	Damage per Point	Estimated Attack Gained
20 to 25	6.40	32
26 to 50	3.12	78
50 to 99	0.65	32

Note: this table represents growth with a +10 weapon

Average Arcane Attack Increase (Arcane)

Stat Range	Damage per Point	Estimated Attack Gained
10 to 25	0.87	13
26 to 50	0.44	11
50 to 99	0.10	5

Note: this table represents growth with a +10 weapon

Tactics

In normal mode, you'll have high physical damage and great impact on your attacks with this weapon. It also tears through enemy super armor very quickly. If your enemy has low arcane defense, you can change to transformed mode for an increase in arcane power. The multi-hit attacks of transformed mode are also amazing with certain gems.

Normal Mode Attacks Properties

Attack	Dmg ×	Type	Stamina	Impact	Note
R1	1.00		30	Normal	
↳ R1 (2nd)	1.00		30	Normal	
↳ R1 (3rd)	1.00		40	Normal	
R1 (backstep)	0.80		25	Normal	
R1 (rolling)	0.80		25	Normal	
R1 (frontstep)	0.80		25	Normal	
R1 (sidestep)	0.85	Blunt /	25	Normal	
R1 (dash)	1.05	Arcane	35	Normal	
R2	1.15		50	Heavy	
R2 (charged)	1.60		60	Massive	continuously hold the button to execute
R2 (backstep)	1.05		45	Heavy	
R2 (dash)	1.15		55	Normal	
R2 (forward leap)	1.30		50	Heavy	tap forward on the stick just as you press R2 to execute
Transform Attack	special		30	Normal	press L1 while performing another action to execute; forced Guard Break; multi-hit attack

Normal Mode Key Attacks

The charged R2 has incredible impact; it is very useful for breaking an enemy's super armor. The damage multiplier is also quite good. Unfortunately, it knocks most enemies too far away to follow-up with a leaping R2, and it's a bit too slow to chain. If you want a combo of hits, stick to the R1 chain instead.

The transformed R2 attacks hit multiple times quickly. This makes them extremely powerful for poisoning the enemy when used with Murky or Dirty gem effects. Transformed mode also synergizes well with the Lethal effect to Regain more HP when attacking. When combined with the Lead Elixir to prevent stumbling, this weapon can be a real powerhouse!

The normal transformation attack also hits multiple times, so it benefits from these effects, as well. The transformation attack that leads back to normal mode is really interesting; it's a large area of effect attack. It isn't particularly powerful, but it hits in a sphere around your character. You can use this when weak enemies are trying to surround you, which happens quite frequently in Chalice Dungeons.

Transformed Mode Key Attacks

In transformed mode, Logarius' Wheel's basic damage properties change. The physical damage is reduced, and the arcane damage is augmented. Using the L2 button, you can further augment the Arcane damage. Pressing L2 turns the wheel and increases your arcane power but also inflicts a constant health down effect on your character. Rapidly pressing L2 will heighten the effect.

Normal Mode R1

Normal Mode R2

Normal Mode Transform Attack

Wheel Turns	1 Turn	2 Turns	3 Turns	4 Turns
Arcane Multiplier	×1.1	×1.2	×1.3	×1.4
HP Drain (per 0.1 sec)	-0.1% HP	-0.2% HP	-0.3% HP	-0.4% HP

The health drain from this effect is subject to the Regain system, meaning that you can recover the damage as it occurs by attacking! This is why the transformed R2 is so good, and it's also the reason why Lethal gems synergize well with Logarius' Wheel.

The L2 effect lasts for 20 seconds. If you press L2 again during that time, you can refresh the effect, but there's a catch; you can't maintain a "4 turn" effect by turning the wheel only once. It will overwrite itself.

For example, if you turn the wheel 4 times, you have a multiplier of ×1.4. Ten seconds later, you decide to press L2 to refresh the effect, and you press it twice in a row for 2 turns. Your multiplier is now ×1.2. Even though there was time remaining on your ×1.4, it was replaced by the ×1.2.

You can use this to your advantage, though; sometimes, you might want to slow the HP drain down without stopping it. A single L2 will do the job! If you want to cancel the effect early, you can do so by either returning to normal mode or changing to a different weapon.

Beast Claw

The Beast Claw is a crafty weapon with a special gimmick. It requires 14 strength and 12 skill to use. The claw receives even bonuses from strength and skill, though it does benefit slightly more from strength. The Beast Claw is buffable and has fast attacks, so it works well with Fire Paper, Bolt Paper, and Empty Phantasm Shell. In transform mode, Beast Transformation is automatically activated without the use of Beast Blood Pellets. Rapid attacks will cause your damage to skyrocket; to really take advantage of this feature, you should raise your Beasthood as much as possible.

> Beastly weapon wielded by Irreverent Izzy. Crafted by chiselling the long bones of an undead darkbeast and fastening them to the weapon. The bones are still alive, and when unleashed, grant its wielder a spurt of beastly power. As flesh is flayed and blood is sprayed, the beast within awakens, and in time, the wielder of this weapon surges with both strength and feverish reverie.

Gem Advice

The Beast Claw can be converted into an elemental weapon, but this isn't a great idea. In the first place, the Beast Claw has low arcane scaling, so elemental damage will be low. More importantly, the main feature of this weapon is its ability to increase damage via Beast Transformation, but elemental damage is not increased at all. This is a waste of the Beast Claw's main ability!

Instead, consider slotting Radiant gem effects to lower your stamina costs. Since this weapon requires constant attacks to reach its maximum potential, lower stamina costs are fantastic. Physical damage increases, such as Tempering, are also useful. The damage bonus from such gems will be multiplied by the effects of Beast Transformation. Since you already need to avoid being hit to make good use of the Beast Claw, a Poorman gem effect is a perfect choice for highly-skilled players.

Acquisition

Type	Obtained from	Reference	Bath Messenger Requirements
Normal	Ailing Loran Chalice Dungeon	p447	Acquire weapon
Uncanny	Drops in Ailing Loran Root Chalice Dungeon	–	Acquire weapon
Lost	Drops in Lower Loran Root Chalice Dungeon	–	Acquire weapon

Available Gem Slots

Weapon Type	Weapon Level		
	1	3	6
Normal	Radial	Radial	Waning
Uncanny	Radial	Radial	Triangular
Lost	Radial	Triangular	Waning

Average Physical Attack Increase (Strength)

Stat Range	Damage per Point	Estimated Attack Gained
15 to 25	2.64	29
26 to 50	1.28	32
50 to 99	0.27	13

Average Physical Attack Increase (Skill)

Stat Range	Damage per Point	Estimated Attack Gained
13 to 25	1.54	20
26 to 50	0.72	18
50 to 99	0.16	8

Damage from Upgrades

Weapon Level	Base	Scaling			
0	75	D	E	D
1	82	D	E	D
2	89	D	E	D
3	96	D	E	D
4	103	D	E	D
5	110	D	D	D
6	117	D	D	D
7	124	D	D	D
8	131	C	D	D
9	138	C	D	D
10	150	C	D	D

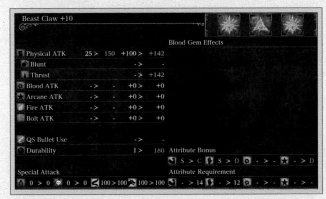

Beast Claw +10

Blood Gem Effects

Physical ATK	25 >	150	+100 > +142
Blunt		->	-
Thrust		->	+142
Blood ATK	->	-	+0 > +0
Arcane ATK	->	-	+0 > +0
Fire ATK	->	-	+0 > +0
Bolt ATK	->	-	+0 > +0
QS Bullet Use		->	-
Durability		1 >	180

Attribute Bonus
S < C S > D -> -> D

Special Attack

Attribute Requirement
0 > 0   0 > 0   100 > 100   100 > 100   -> 14   -> 12   -> -

5

Normal Mode Tactics

Normal mode attacks are more powerful than transformed attacks, but your Beast Transformation is not automatically activated in this state. Use normal mode when you aren't able to attack aggressively; you won't be building the Beast gauge, so you might as well do as much damage as possible with your single strikes. Alternatively, once your Beast gauge is already high from using transformed mode, you can swap back to normal mode to take advantage of the higher damage attacks!

Normal Mode Attacks Properties

Attack	Dmg ×	Type	Stamina	Impact	Note
R1	1.00		15	Light	
↳ R1 (2nd)	1.02		15	Light	
↳ R1 (3rd)	1.04		15	Light	
↳ R1 (4th)	1.06		15	Light	
↳ R1 (5th)	1.08		15	Light	damage multiplier resets following this attack
R1 (backstep)	0.95		15 (+10)	Light	
R1 (rolling)	0.95		15 (+10)	Light	
R1 (frontstep)	0.95	Physical	15 (+10)	Light	
R1 (sidestep)	0.95		15 (+10)	Light	
R1 (dash)	1.00		20 (+X)	Light	
R2	1.25		35	Normal	
R2 (charged)	1.80		50	Heavy	continuously hold the button to execute
R2 (backstep)	1.20		25 (+10)	Light	
R2 (dash)	1.25		40 (+X)	Normal	
R2 (forward leap)	1.50		50	Normal	tap forward on the stick just as you press R2 to execute

Normal Mode Key Attacks

The R1 chain is the most useful attack series for normal mode. It's quick and powerful, and you can deal a ton of damage very quickly if your Beast gauge is nearly full. The damage multiplier ramps up to its maximum on the fifth hit of the combo, so look for chances to land all five hits. The sidestep, frontstep, and rolling R1 attacks

Normal Mode R1

Normal Mode R2

are all thrusts; they work great against foes with low thrust defense, such as the Celestial Emissaries.

The charged R2 is reasonably quick and deals very solid damage. It can, of course, stagger many enemies when used from behind, and it's even fast enough to perform a second time against some foes while they are staggered. The dashing R2 is another thrust attack, and it has good power. You can use it to close the distance and quickly kill those pesky Brainsuckers.

There's no transformation attack for this mode, but it doesn't actually matter much. You'll normally want to transform before engaging the enemy so that you can build your meter up early in the battle; if you want to transform in the middle of the fight, either pick a moment while the enemy is recovering or retreat to a safe location.

Transformed Mode Tactics

Transformed mode should be used when you want to activate your Beast Transformation and fill your Beast gauge. Start the battle in this mode, and then shift to normal mode once the gauge is high enough for you. Even better, you can actually change to another weapon after filling the gauge if you like—essentially, you'll be using the transformed Beast Claw as a free Beast Blood Pellet!

Transformed Mode Attacks Properties

Attack	Dmg ×	Type	Stamina	Impact	Note
R1	0.95		14	Light	
↳ R1 (2nd)	1.00		20	Light	
R1 (backstep)	0.90		15 (+10)	Light	
R1 (rolling)	0.90		15 (+10)	Light	
R1 (frontstep)	0.90		15 (+10)	Light	
R1 (sidestep)	1.05		15 (+10)	Light	higher damage but same cost compared to rolling attacks
R1 (dash)	0.90		20 (+X)	Light	
R2	1.35	Physical	50	Normal	good for building Beast gauge
R2 (charged)	1.90		70	Massive	continuously hold the button to execute; creates a 1.05 damage shockwave
R2 (backstep)	1.15		40 (+10)	Light	wide hit box; useful
R2 (dash)	1.10		40 (+X)	Light	
R2 (forward leap)	1.40		50	Light	tap forward on the stick just as you press R2 to execute
L2	1.20		40	Light	good for building Beast gauge
Transform Attack	1.25		25 (+X)	Light	press L1 while performing another action to execute; forced Guard Break

Transformed Mode Key Attacks

Use of the transformed Beast Claw revolves 100% around the filling of the Beast gauge. Primarily, you'll want to focus on using R2 and L2 attacks. They all give a huge boost to the Beast gauge; use these attacks as often as you can without risking getting hit. Remember that you will take additional damage when your Beast gauge is filled! Even worse, getting knocked down will cost valuable time, and your gauge will deplete.

The R1 attack chain doesn't fill it very quickly, but it is safer and can be used to maintain the gauge in low stamina situations. One of the biggest challenges for using Beast Transformation is stamina management, so this is very helpful.

On the topic of stamina management, a really nice feature of the Beast Claw is that you can use the transformed mode with the Blood of Arianna for increased stamina regeneration while in a Beast Transformed state! Normally, you can't use either of those items together with Beast Blood Pellets. In this way, you can use a stamina-boosting effect, the Beast Transformation effect, and even add a weapon buff on top!

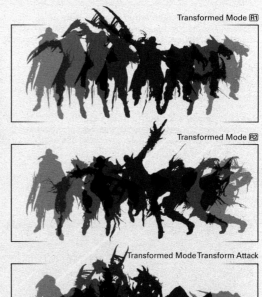

Transformed Mode R1

Transformed Mode R2

Transformed Mode Transform Attack

Beast Claw (Beast's Embrace Rune) OH

With the Beast's Embrace rune equipped, the Beast Claw's alternate moveset becomes accessible. This is still the same weapon, so its stat requirements and scaling remain the same; you'll need 14 strength and 12 skill to use it. Attacks are a bit slower with this new moveset, but still quite fast. You can also still buff this weapon, which will deal a whole lot of damage in combination with a highly filled Beasthood gauge. Both modes will automatically activate Beast Transformation while the rune is equipped. So, although attacks are a bit slower, the normal mode will also deal more damage as your meter builds. The Beast's Embrace rune will already add a good chunk to your Beasthood meter, but you can add more still by equipping Beast runes. Just be sure to keep your insight low, as this will subtract from your Beasthood.

> Beastly Weapon wielded by Irreverent Izzy. Crafted by chiselling the long bones of an undead darkbeast and fastening them to the weapon. The bones are still alive, and when unleashed, grant its wielder a spurt of beastly power. As flesh is flayed and blood is sprayed, the beast within awakens, and in time, the wielder of this weapon surges with both strength and feverish reverie.

Acquisition

Type	Obtained from	Reference	Bath Messenger Requirements
Normal	Ailing Loran Chalice Dungeon	p447	Acquire weapon
Uncanny	Drops in Ailing Loran Root Chalice Dungeon	–	Acquire weapon
Lost	Drops in Lower Loran Root Chalice Dungeon	–	Acquire weapon

Available Gem Slots

Weapon Type	Weapon Level		
	1	3	6
Normal	Radial	Triangular	Radial
Uncanny	Radial	Waning	Radial
Lost	Radial	Triangular	Waning

Average Physical Attack Increase (Strength)

Stat Range	Damage per Point	Estimated Attack Gained
14 to 25	2.64	29
26 to 50	1.28	32
50 to 99	0.27	13

Note: this table represents growth with a +10 weapon

Average Physical Attack Increase (Skill)

Stat Range	Damage per Point	Estimated Attack Gained
12 to 25	1.54	20
26 to 50	0.72	18
50 to 99	0.16	8

Note: this table represents growth with a +10 weapon

Damage from Upgrades

Weapon Level	Base	Scaling		
0	75	D	E	D
1	82	D	E	D
2	89	D	E	D
3	96	D	E	D
4	103	D	E	D
5	110	D	D	D
6	117	D	D	D
7	124	D	D	D
8	164	C	D	D
9	131	C	D	D
10	150	C	D	D

Gem Advice

You can convert the Beast Claw into a purely elemental weapon with gems, but doing so is a waste of potential damage and precious slots. Elemental scaling is low, so you're not going to see good returns from this stat, and Beasthood will only affect physical types of damage, not elemental ones. Gems that increase your physical damage will be multiplied by Beast Transformation, which is a huge incentive to slot them.

The vast majority of this weapon's attacks are physical, so Tempering effects will do much to increase your damage output. Its stat screen may show that it can deal thrust damage, but that only applies to a single attack, so it's not very useful. You're going to need to use a lot of attacks to fill your Beast gauge, and use plenty of stamina to do so; Radiant gems will help wonderfully in this area. The higher your Beast gauge, the more damage you'll take, so you're going to want to keep your health full, or at least high at all times. Poorman's gems synergize well with this, so consider slotting these to the Beast Claw.

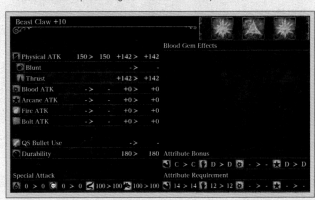

Normal Mode Tactics

Normal mode attacks are weaker than the transform mode, and some attacks are actually slower. This is not to say that this mode is bad, but you'll usually want to go for whatever is optimal. One of the main reasons you'd probably want to use this mode is so you can hold a firearm, which isn't possible in the transform mode. The other reason would be for its more traditional way of staggering enemies. Other than that, you'll probably want to switch to transformed mode.

Normal Mode Attacks Properties

Attack	Dmg ×	Type	Stamina	Impact	Note
R1	1.00	Physical	15	Light	
↳ R1 (2nd)	1.00	Physical	15	Light	
↳ R1 (3rd)	1.00	Physical	15	Normal	
↳ R1 (4th)	1.10	Physical	15	Normal	
R1 (backstep)	0.95	Physical	12 (+10)	Light	
R1 (rolling)	0.90	Physical	12 (+10)	Light	
R1 (frontstep)	0.90	Physical	12 (+10)	Light	
R1 (sidestep)	0.90	Physical	12 (+10)	Light	
R1 (dash)	1.05	Physical	20	Normal	
R2	1.20	Physical	25	Normal	good for building Beast gauge
R2 (charged)	1.40	Physical	40	Massive	continuously hold the button to execute; good for building Beast gauge
R2 (backstep)	1.15	Physical	20 (+10)	Normal	
R2 (dash)	1.25	Thrust	30 (+X)	Normal	
R2 (forward leap)	1.30	Physical	35	Normal	tap forward on the stick just as you press R2 to execute; good for building Beast gauge
Transform Attack	0.60	Physical	25 (+X)	Normal	press L1 while performing another action to execute; forced Guard Break; good for building Beast gauge
Transform Attack (2nd hit)	1.20	Physical	0	Normal	second hit

Normal Mode Key Attacks

The R1 chain isn't as fast as the transform mode's, but they are still fast in their own right. Rolling and quickstep R1s deal less damage than they do without the rune, but cost less stamina to use. In addition, they transition very smoothly into the R1 chain, which will allow you to hit aggressive enemies with high super armor more than once before needing to dodge.

In a sea of physical attacks, you do have at least one thrust type attack at your disposal; this would be the dashing R2. It's not ideal for every situation since you'll need the proper spacing to use it, but it's still an option if physical attacks aren't exactly cutting it. The standard R2 doesn't have good enough range to justify how stationary it is. That being the case, you may find more use in the leaping R2 for strong single hits.

The charged R2 deals good damage with massive impact. This can stagger enemies from behind, but it has limited range, so you'll need to be close, especially after the start-up. If you aren't using this for staggering opponents, you can dish out more damage with the transformation attack. Transformation attacks have more application than just hitting enemies while switching modes. These will fill your Beasthood gauge much quicker than any other move, and while they don't combo quickly between modes, they're fast enough to stun lock weaker enemies.

Normal Mode R1

Normal Mode R2

Normal Mode Transform Attack

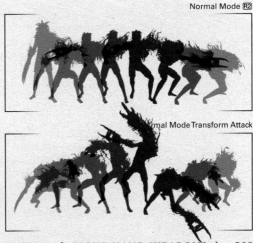

Transformed Mode Tactics

The Beast Claw is an amazing weapon when transformed. Attacks are faster, or about equally as fast those in the normal mode. There's also a lot of variety, but you won't be able to use a shield, torch or left hand firearm, since this mode uses both hands.

Transformed Mode Attacks Properties

Attack	Dmg ×	Type	Stamina	Impact	Note
R1	1.00		18	Light	
↳ R1 (2nd)	1.00		18	Light	
↳ R1 (3rd)	1.00		18	Light	
↳ R1 (4th)	1.05		18	Normal	
↳ R1 (5th)	1.10		18	Normal	
R1 (backstep)	0.60		5 (+10)	Light	
R1 (backstep) (2nd hit)	0.95		13	Light	second hit
R1 (rolling)	0.95		13 (+10)	Light	
R1 (frontstep)	0.95		13 (+10)	Light	
R1 (sidestep)	0.95		13 (+10)	Light	
R1 (dash)	0.60		5 (+X)	Light	
R1 (dash) (2nd hit)	1.05		20	Normal	second hit
R2	1.20	Physical	30	Normal	good for building Beast gauge
↳ R2 (2nd)	1.30		40	Normal	good for building Beast gauge
↳ R2 (3rd)	1.40		50	Massive	good for building Beast gauge
R2 (backstep)	1.20		15 (+10)	Normal	
R2 (dash)	0.60		5 (+X)	Normal	
R2 (dash) (2nd hit)	1.25		30	Heavy	second hit
R2 (forward leap)	0.60		0	Light	tap forward on the stick just as you press R2 to execute; can change direction during startup
R2 (forward leap) (2nd hit)	1.40		50	Normal	second hit
L2	0.30		50	Light	low damage but great for momentarily stunning groups; good for building Beast gauge
L2 (2nd hit)	0.10		0	Normal	second hit; can stagger opponenets; builds Beast gauge
Transform Attack	1.25		30 (+X)	Normal	press L1 while performing another action to execute; forced Guard Break

Transformed Mode Key Attacks

The R1 chain is faster and longer than the normal mode's. This extra speed costs more stamina, but a look at the tables will show this isn't much of an increase. The backstep R1 will hit twice; it uses the same amount of stamina as a single R1, but will deal more overall damage. For quick, single hits, you can use quick-step and rolling R1s. These attacks are all much better than they are without the Beast's Embrace rune, dealing more damage for less stamina.

This mode doesn't have a charge attack, but it does have a R2 chain in its stead. This chain is very powerful, and its modifier increases with every hit until the third. It is also very slow, so it's really only useful against enemies with little super armor. The leaping R2 is an interesting attack, both visually and mechanically. It will briefly send your character into the air, before crashing down some distance ahead. During the period where you are airborne, you can actually change your desired direction, which you can use as a fake out. Much more interestingly, if this attack connects with an enemy from behind, it can stagger!

The L2 is a beastly roar with a wide area of affect. As an attack, it deals very little damage, but that isn't its purpose. You can use this to build up Beasthood by hitting multiple enemies. The roar has two hitboxes centered on your character; the smaller one will build up large amounts of Beasthood, while the larger adds a more minimal amount. You'll want to use this in the middle of crowds and the closer the better – if you can avoid taking damage. It will shove away weaker enemies, but with stronger foes, you'll want to use it carefully; don't go intentionally running into groups of enemies!

Transformed Mode R1

Transformed Mode R2

Transformed Mode Transform Attack

Beasthunter Saif (OH)

Unlike most trick weapons, the Beasthunter Saif does not begin in its folded state – the weapon will instead close when activated. Using it requires 9 strength and 11 skill, the latter of which it scales best with, so skill-focused hunters will find this weapon to be a decent option. Despite what its name might imply, the Beasthunter Saif does not provide any additional damage bonus against beasts, as it lacks a serrated blade. This weapon deals primarily in physical damage, with a few thrust and blunt attacks thrown into the mix. However, these attacks can be slow and are not always optimal for handling enemies with specific weaknesses; it's recommended you carry a secondary option such as a thrust or blunt type weapon, or Molotovs.

> A trick weapon used by the old hunters. A second blade is found inside the curve of the main one. In its initial form, the saif can be wielded like a long curved sword, but when transformed, its blade is contracted, allowing for quick, repeated stabs. Although this trick weapon weapon allows for adaptive combat, it was later replaced by saws and similar weapons that were more effective at disposing of beasts.

Gem Advice

You can convert the Beasthunter Saif into an elemental weapon, but doing so would be a waste of your gem slots; this weapon scales little with arcane, meaning elemental damage will be low in turn. The Beasthunter Saifn outputs almost exclusively physical damage so slotting tempering gems will greatly increase your damage dealt.

One of the main advantages of the Beasthunter Saif's transformed mode is its speed. Since you'll be bombarding enemies with rapid attacks, you can build up heavy amounts of poison by slotting Murky or Dirty bloodgems to it. Consider slotting stamina cost reducing Radiant gems instead; this can mitigate the high stamina consumption of the normal mode and allow for longer combos when transformed.

Acquisition

Type	Obtained from	Reference	Bath Messenger Requirements
Normal	Hunter's Nightmare	p171	–
Uncanny	Chalice Dungeon treasures/ Chalice Dungeon rare shop	p668	Acquire Weapon
Lost		p668	Acquire Weapon

Available Gem Slots

Weapon Type	Weapon Level		
	1	3	6
Normal	Radial	Radial	Waning
Uncanny	Radial	Radial	Triangular
Lost	Radial	Triangular	Waning

Average Physical Attack Increase (Strength)

Stat Range	Damage per Point	Estimated Attack Gained
9 to 25	1.56	25
26 to 50	0.72	18
50 to 99	0.18	9

Note: this table represents growth with a +10 weapon

Average Physical Attack Increase (Skill)

Stat Range	Damage per Point	Estimated Attack Gained
11 to 25	3.79	53
26 to 50	1.76	44
50 to 99	0.39	19

Note: this table represents growth with a +10 weapon

Damage from Upgrades

Weapon Level	Base	Scaling			
0	90	E	D	D	
1	99	E	D	D	
2	108	E	D	D	
3	117	E	D	D	
4	126	E	D	D	
5	135	E	C	D	
6	144	E	C	D	
7	153	E	C	D	
8	162	E	C	D	
9	171	E	B	D	
10	180	D	B	C	

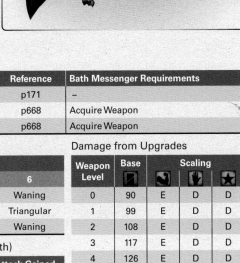

Normal Mode Tactics

This mode exchanges the transform's high speed and low stamina consumption for better range and damage. The vast majority of its attacks are horizontal sweeps, making it incredibly useful for crowd control, though less than favorable for hitting larger enemy weak points. In case that you find yourself surrounded, this mode will serve quite well.

Normal Mode Attacks Properties

Attack	Dmg ×	Type	Stamina	Impact	Note
R1	1.10	Physical	30	Normal	sweeping arc is good against crowds
↳R1 (2nd)	1.12	Physical	30	Normal	
↳R1 (3rd)	1.14	Physical	30	Normal	
↳R1 (4th)	1.16	Physical	30	Normal	
R1 (backstep)	1.00	Physical	25 (+10)	Normal	
R1 (rolling)	1.00	Physical	25 (+10)	Normal	fast startup after roll
R1 (frontstep)	1.00	Physical	25 (+10)	Normal	useful for hit-and-run tactics
R1 (sidestep)	1.00	Physical	25 (+10)	Normal	useful for hit-and-run tactics
R1 (dash)	1.20	Physical	40 (+X)	Normal	
R2	1.45	Physical	40	Heavy	
R2 (charged)	1.80	Blunt	60	Massive	continuously hold the button to execute; very good damage modifier
R2 (backstep)	1.30	Blunt	35 (+10)	Heavy	good damage; blunt damage typel good against specific foes
R2 (dash)	1.50	Physical	50 (+X)	Heavy	good against crowds
R2 (forward leap)	1.50	Physical	50	Normal	tap forward on the stick just as you press R2 to execute
Transform Attack	1.15	Physical	30(+X)	Light	press L1 while performing another action to execute; forced Guard Break

Normal Mode Key Attacks

Large horizontal arcs make up the entirety of the R1 swings. These attacks are good for handling large groups of weak enemies and catching dodging targets. For enemies with high super armor that require single hits, quickstep R1s will prove incredibly useful for jumping in and out of their range. Watch carefully and hang back to regenerate your stamina when necessary; this tactic will consume large amounts of it.

The standard R2's reach is only slightly better than that of the normal R1 and consumes more stamina. Even so, this can make quite the difference, especially owing to this attack's greater damage modifier. Speaking of high damage modifiers, the charged R2 has the highest across both modes. It can stagger from behind, and though the start-up is slow, the attack itself is quick with massive impact.

The charged R2 is one of the two blunt attacks you can use during this mode. The other is the backstep R2, which is faster and more reliable for dealing this type of damage. A great addition for a hit-and-run play style is the transformation attack; this will send your character back and away from harm, while dealing a decent amount of damage.

Normal Mode R1

Normal Mode R2

Normal Mode Transform Attack

Transformed Mode Tactics

In its transformed mode, the Beasthunter Saif emphasizes speed and close range combat. Due to its short range, this mode is really only useful for tackling single or clustered targets directly ahead. What makes this mode unique is the initial forward momentum on opening attacks; this paired with its low stamina consumption makes it a fantastic weapon for a hit-and-run playstyle.

Transformed Mode Attacks Properties

Attack	Dmg ×	Type	Stamina	Impact	Note
R1	0.95	Physical	20	Light	
↳ R1 (2nd)	0.98	Physical	20	Light	
↳ R1 (3rd)	1.00	Physical	20	Light	
R1 (backstep)	1.00	Physical	20 (+10)	Light	
R1 (rolling)	0.95	Physical	20 (+10)	Light	
R1 (frontstep)	0.95	Physical	20 (+10)	Light	useful for hit-and-run tactics
R1 (sidestep)	0.95	Physical	20 (+10)	Light	useful for hit-and-run tactics
R1 (dash)	1.10	Physical	30 (+X)	Light	
R2	1.30	Thrust	35	Normal	thrust damage type; good against specific foes
R2 (charged)	1.60	Thrust/Blunt	50	Massive	continuously hold the button to execute
R2 (backstep)	1.25	Physical	30 (+10)	Normal	
R2 (dash)	1.40	Physical	45 (+X)	Normal	
R2 (forward leap)	1.40	Blunt	50	Normal	tap forward on the stick just as you press R2 to execute
Transform Attack	1.10	Physical	30 (+X)	Normal	press L1 while performing another action to execute; forced Guard Break

Transformed Mode Key Attacks

The opening R1 of the transformed mode has great forward momentum, allowing you to get in close before enemies can attack. Though the normal R1 chain reduces more enemy super armor per hit, this mode's R1 chain is faster at breaking super armor with its rapid hit succession. Combine these two strategies, and you can lock weaker enemies into an R1 chain before they can react, ending encounters about as quickly as they start; the quickstep R1s are great for this as well.

The R2 and charged R2 are this weapon's only thrust attacks. Against enemies with high physical defenses that are weak to thrust damage, you're better off using the standard R2, since the charged version will take too long. The standard R2 has decent forward momentum – keep a distance away from enemies and hit them with an R2 during their recoveries.

When used from behind, the charged R2 can stagger enemies, however, its range is low and can leave you open during the start-up and recovery if you miss. This attack is unique in that it deals both thrust and blunt damage; when it does hit, make it count by equipping both thrust and blunt damage-increasing gems.

Transformed Mode R1

Transformed Mode R2

Transformed Mode Transform Attack

Beast Cutter (OH)

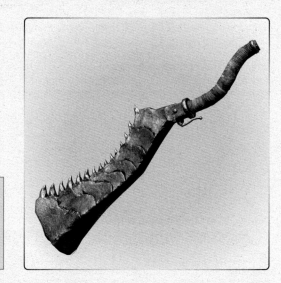

The Beast Cutter requires 11 strength and 9 skill to use. This weapon is quite similar in function to the Threaded Cane, but serves instead as a strong alternative for strength-focused characters. This weapon excels wonderfully in its versatility, but even more so with its impeccable range when transformed. Blunt damage is the Beast Cutter's forte. However, this is the only type of damage it inflicts. If you are using this as your main weapon, you'll want to carry a secondary option, unless you plan to brute force your way through things. It also receives a 20% damage bonus when used against enemies weak to serration in both modes!

> A trick weapon wielded by the old hunters. This thick iron cleaver slices through the roughest of beast hides, and when transformed, the blade splits into sections, allowing one to lash it in the fashion of a heavy whip. This crude weapon relies on brute force and is regrettably inelegant, suggesting that the hunts of the earliest hunters made for horrific affairs, painted in sanguine blacks and reds.

Gem Advice

The most apparent of options is to use Adept (blunt) effect gems. Since every one of the Beast Cutter's attacks is blunt type, this will greatly boost your overall damage. Considering that the transform mode drains large amounts of stamina per swing, another good option would be to slot Radiant gems to this weapon.

The Beast Cutter's extended range when transformed will allow you to easily counterhit enemies from a distance. This makes for a viable tactic, only further enhanced by Finestrike's particular bonus. Additionally, as this weapon scales best with strength, you may want to consider slotting it with Heavy gems. Lastly, Striking gems should also be taken into consideration; these can be used to bolster the normal mode's already powerful charged R2 for massive damage.

Acquisition

Type	Obtained from	Reference	Bath Messenger Requirements
Normal	Hunter's Nightmare	p166	–
Uncanny	Chalice Dungeon treasures/ Chalice Dungeon rare shop	p668	Acquire Weapon
Lost		p668	Acquire Weapon

Available Gem Slots

Weapon Type	Weapon Level		
	1	3	6
Normal	Radial	Radial	Triangular
Uncanny	Radial	Radial	Waning
Lost	Radial	Triangular	Waning

Average Physical Attack Increase (Strength)

Stat Range	Damage per Point	Estimated Attack Gained
11 to 25	3.21	45
26 to 50	1.56	39
50 to 99	0.33	16

Note: this table represents growth with a +10 weapon

Average Physical Attack Increase (Skill)

Stat Range	Damage per Point	Estimated Attack Gained
9 to 25	1.71	24
26 to 50	0.76	19
50 to 99	0.18	9

Note: this table represents growth with a +10 weapon

Damage from Upgrades

Weapon Level	Base	Scaling			
0	92	D	E	E	
1	101	D	E	E	
2	110	D	E	D	
3	119	E	C	D	
4	128	E	C	D	
5	137	E	B	C	
6	146	E	B	C	
7	155	E	B	C	
8	164	C	E	D	
9	173	C	E	D	
10	184	C	D	D	

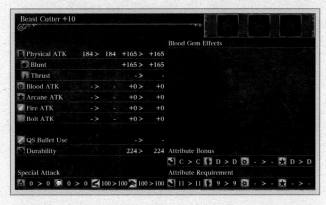

Normal Mode Tactics

The Beast Cutter's normal mode acts like a club with a basic, solid moveset. In this mode it relies primarily on quick, close-range hits; likewise, tackling single or a few closely grouped enemies is what it does best. In comparison to the transform mode, it is overall faster and less demanding of your stamina.

Normal Mode Attacks Properties

Attack	Dmg ×	Type	Stamina	Impact	Note
R1	1.00		25	Light	
↳ R1 (2nd)	1.02		25	Light	
↳ R1 (3rd)	1.04		25	Light	
↳ R1 (4th)	1.06		25	Light	
↳ R1 (5th)	1.08		25	Light	
R1 (backstep)	0.95		20 (+10)	Light	
R1 (rolling)	0.95		20 (+10)	Light	
R1 (frontstep)	0.95		20 (+10)	Light	
R1 (sidestep)	0.95	Blunt	20 (+10)	Light	
R1 (dash)	1.10		35 (+X)	Normal	
R2	1.20		40	Normal	
R2 (charged)	1.90		70	Heavy	continuously hold the button to execute
R2 (backstep)	1.10		35 (+10)	Normal	good forward momentum
R2 (dash)	1.30		50	Heavy	
R2 (forward leap)	1.40		55	Heavy	tap forward on the stick just as you press R2 to execute
Transform Attack	1.40		45 (+X)	Heavy	press L1 while performing another action to execute; forced Guard Break

Normal Mode Key Attacks

The Beast Cutter's R1 chain is the quickest way to dish out some solid damage. This chain has a decent damage multiplier and swings from a variety of different angles. After the initial overhead swing, the rest will move in a diagonal or horizontal manner. Though this weapon is not recommended for handling groups of enemies, this string can be useful for fending off approaching enemies mid-combo. Quickstep R1s deal slightly less damage than the weapon's attack rating, but are quick with good forward momentum.

The charged R2 is without a doubt this weapon's strongest attack. Charging this is slow, but with a damage multiplier of 1.90 it's well worth the wait. It can stagger when it connects with an enemy from behind, at which point you can follow through with a visceral attack or second charged R2. For a wide single strike you can use the standard R2; its forward momentum is great for hitting approaching enemies.

No other attack breaks enemy super armor as easily as the jumping R2. Performing this attack will expend a lot of stamina, but deals good damage and it can even cause some stronger enemies to stumble heavily and instantly upon impact. Using this attack twice in a row is usually a bad idea. Most enemies will recover from the first and hit you during the start-up of the second, so it's better to escape and regain your stamina.

Normal Mode R1

Normal Mode R2

Normal Mode Transform Attack

Transformed Mode Tactics

The Beast Cutter is a devastating weapon when used in transformed mode. In stark contrast to normal mode, attacks can reach exceptionally far and have great impact. The only drawbacks are its heavier stamina usage and slower swing speeds. Despite these shortcomings, the increased range and impact are what make this mode great.

Transformed Mode Attacks Properties

Attack	Dmg ×	Type	Stamina	Impact	Note
R1	0.95		30	Normal	sweeping arc is good against crowds
↳ R1 (2nd)	0.98		30	Normal	sweeping arc is good against crowds
R1 (backstep)	0.90		30 (+10)	Normal	sweeping arc is good against crowds
R1 (rolling)	1.00		30 (+10)	Normal	
R1 (frontstep)	1.00		30 (+10)	Normal	
R1 (sidestep)	1.00		30 (+10)	Normal	
R1 (dash)	1.10	Blunt	35 (+X)	Normal	similar to the normal mode R1
R2	1.30		50	Heavy	key attack; great range and damage
↳ R2 (2nd)	1.50		65	Massive	massive impact makes up for slow recovery
R2 (backstep)	1.20		40 (+10)	Heavy	great range; little forward momentum
R2 (dash)	1.35		55 (+X)	Heavy	great range; good against crowds
R2 (forward leap)	1.40		55	Heavy	tap forward on the stick just as you press R2 to execute
Transform Attack	1.50		50 (+X)	Normal	press L1 while performing another action to execute; forced Guard Break

Transformed Mode Key Attacks

The R1 chain swings in wide arcs ahead of your character and covers a decent amount of distance. The R1 chain has a damage multiplier lower than the weapon's attacking rating and consumes more stamina than the normal mode; however, its specialty lies in crowd control. These attacks are also useful for fighting in tight spaces; though they can rebound off walls or obstacles, they won't unless you're directly facing one.

If you need to use close range attacks without transforming to normal mode, rolling and quickstep R1s have you covered. Although these attacks are more stamina-intensive than their normal mode counterparts, they receive the full attack rating of the weapon. Take note that the dashing R1 uses the exact same damage multiplier and amount of stamina as the normal mode version.

The R2 is one of this weapon's best attacks by a long shot. Not only does this attack have incredible range, but it also utterly shreds through enemy super armor, causing even some of the largest of foes to stumble. In addition, the follow-up R2 has heavy impact and will allow you to flatten foes from a distance. A great tactic you can use is to ready this attack as an enemy approaches the tip of your range and hit them before they can react. With the correct timing and spacing, you can afford yourself relative safety during attacks.

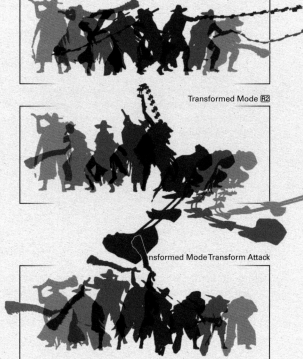

Transformed Mode R1

Transformed Mode R2

Transformed Mode Transform Attack

Church Pick (OH)

To use the Church Pick, you'll need to have 14 skill and 9 strength, though all character origins will meet the strength requirement by default. If you plan to use this as your main weapon, don't bother investing in strength since it scales low with this stat. Instead, focus on leveling your skill to receive better damage bonuses. As its description states, this is a highly practical weapon. It has both physical and thrusting attacks, the latter of which make up the entirety of transform mode's moveset. The Church Pick's thrusting attacks have an interesting property; they deal an extra 20% of damage to both enemies weak to righteous and serrated weapons! It can even be buffed with elemental items, and with these things combined, the Church Pick will absolutely destroy some enemies.

> One of the old trick weapons of the Healing Church, a hunting weapon formed from one of the giant picks that appear in old beast tales. The Church Pick initially serves as a large sword, but when transformed, functions as an extended war pick. In spite of its origins, it is a highly practical weapon.

Gem Advice

You can turn the Church Pick into a purely elemental weapon with gems. It doesn't scale too well with arcane though, so it probably isn't in your best interest to do this. You might instead want to focus on bolstering its main damage type with Adept (thrust) effects. Tempering gems work well too, but Adept (thrust) effects will give you the larger bonus in damage.

The Church Pick's rolling and quick-step R1s are great for single hits in both modes. These attacks are often necessary for tackling more aggressive enemies with high super armor. You'll most likely be landing a lot of counter hits using them, so you can make the single hit approach much less of a chore with the Finestrike effect. There aren't too many enemies weak to righteous damage, so you'll probably want to ignore Kinhunter gems and instead use your slots for the Beasthunter effect.

Acquisition

Type	Obtained from	Reference	Bath Messenger Requirements
Normal	Defeat Yahar'gul Hunter in Hunter's Nightmare	p172	–
Uncanny	Chalice Dungeon treasures/	p668	Acquire Weapon
Lost	Chalice Dungeon rare shop	p668	Acquire Weapon

Available Gem Slots

Weapon Type	Weapon Level		
	1	3	6
Normal	Radial	Radial	Triangular
Uncanny	Radial	Radial	Waning
Lost	Radial	Triangular	Waning

Average Physical Attack Increase (Strength)

Stat Range	Damage per Point	Estimated Attack Gained
9 to 25	2.13	32
26 to 50	0.96	24
50 to 99	0.22	11

Note: this table represents growth with a +10 weapon

Average Physical Attack Increase (Skill)

Stat Range	Damage per Point	Estimated Attack Gained
14 to 25	3.73	41
26 to 50	1.72	43
50 to 99	0.37	18

Note: this table represents growth with a +10 weapon

Damage from Upgrades

Weapon Level	Base	Scaling		
0	88	E	D	D
1	96	E	D	D
2	104	E	D	D
3	112	E	C	D
4	120	E	D	D
5	128	D	B	D
6	136	D	B	C
7	144	D	B	C
8	152	D	B	C
9	160	D	B	C
10	176	D	B	C

Normal Mode Tactics

The Church Pick's normal mode is quick, and will allow you to be nimble as well. Where this mode suffers is in its low reach, as you'll need to be right up against enemies to hit them. Stamina use isn't too bad though, so you can maneuver around quite a bit before attacking. If thrust attacks won't cut it against enemies with higher defenses, use this mode.

Normal Mode Attacks Properties

Attack	Dmg ×	Type	Stamina	Impact	Note
R1	0.95	Thrust	20	Light	
↳ R1 (2nd)	0.98	Physical	20	Light	
↳ R1 (3rd)	1.02	Physical	20	Light	
↳ R1 (4th)	1.06	Thrust	20	Light	
R1 (backstep)	0.95	Physical	20 (+10)	Light	forward momentum and sweeping arc are good against crowds
R1 (rolling)	0.95	Thrust	20 (+10)	Light	
R1 (frontstep)	0.95	Thrust	20 (+10)	Light	
R1 (sidestep)	0.95	Thrust	20 (+10)	Light	
R1 (dash)	1.05	Physical	30 (+X)	Normal	
R2	1.30	Thrust	40	Normal	better range than most attacks in this mode
R2 (charged)	1.70	Physical	55	Heavy	continuously hold the button to execute
R2 (backstep)	1.25	Physical	35 (+10)	Heavy	
R2 (dash)	1.40	Physical	50 (+X)	Heavy	
R2 (forward leap)	1.45	Physical	50	Heavy	tap forward on the stick just as you press R2 to execute
Transform Attack	1.20	Physical	30 (+X)	Heavy	press L1 while performing another action to execute; forced Guard Break

Normal Mode Key Attacks

The Church Pick's normal mode R1 chain opens with a thrust, and after two physical attacks, ends with another. If you have the stamina you can continue the combo, but it will repeat the sequence from the second hit onwards. It can be useful for dealing quick thrust damage, but you'll generally want to use the transform mode for these types of attacks. The R1 chain will stun lock enemies with next to no super armor with ease, but won't be as successful against more aggressive enemies with high super armor.

For these types of foes, you can use rolling and quickstep R1 attacks. Their range is quite short, however, so you'll most likely be dodging closely around your target to be able to attack. Since you'll be utilizing invincibility frames a lot more for these attacks, you'll also be landing a lot of counter hits. The standard R2 has better range and damage than most attacks in this mode, but requires precise aim if you're playing without using lock-on.

Thrust attacks are not ideal for all situations, of course, so the backstep R1 is worth keeping in mind. Despite this mode's usually short range, the forward momentum and horizontal swing of this attack make it quite useful for hitting multiple enemies. The transformation attack is another good option, especially when you need horizontal reach. The leaping R2 will deal physical damage as well with heavy impact, and has one of this mode's better damage multipliers.

Normal Mode R1

Normal Mode R2

Normal Mode Transform Attack

Transformed Mode Tactics

The Church Pick is an amazing weapon in transformed mode. Though it would appear to have no apparent thrust attacks, all of the moves in this mode will deal this damage type. Many attacks have similar damage multipliers and stamina costs to those in the normal mode, so you'll mainly be trading its higher speed for better range.

Transformed Mode Attacks Properties

Attack	Dmg ×	Type	Stamina	Impact	Note
R1	1.05		25	Light	hits high; useful for striking enemy weak points
↳ R1 (2nd)	1.00		25	Light	sweeping arc is good against crowds
↳ R1 (3rd)	1.00		25	Light	sweeping arc is good against crowds
↳ R1 (4th)	1.20		25	Normal	hits high; useful for striking enemy weak points
R1 (backstep)	0.95		20 (+10)	Light	
R1 (rolling)	1.00		20 (+10)	Light	
R1 (frontstep)	1.00		20 (+10)	Light	
R1 (sidestep)	1.00		20 (+10)	Light	forward momentum and sweeping arc are good against crowds
R1 (dash)	1.00	Thrust	35 (+X)	Normal	
R2	1.40		45	Normal	
R2 (charged)	1.90		70	Massive	continuously hold the button to execute
R2 (charged follow-up)	2.10		60	Massive	
R2 (backstep)	1.30		40 (+10)	Normal	
R2 (dash)	1.40		50 (+X)	Heavy	
R2 (forward leap)	1.50		50	Heavy	tap forward on the stick just as you press R2 to execute
L2	0.50		20	Normal	quick startup; short range
Transform Attack	1.35		35 (+X)	Normal	press L1 while performing another action to execute; forced Guard Break

Transformed Mode Key Attacks

The first R1 swings vertically overhead from your back to your front, and can be useful for striking weak spots on larger enemies. The subsequent two hits swing in wide horizontal arcs, which are great for crowd situations. These two attacks will also reach quite far around your character, and can fend off enemies trying to sneak up from behind. The last attack of the chain before it repeats is similar to the opening hit in speed and function, but deals much better damage.

Rolling and quickstep R1s cost the same amount they do in normal mode, but receive the Church Pick's full attack rating. They are also somewhat slower, but can still be better if you're going for single, solid hits. These attacks generally strike immediately ahead, but this is not the case for the sidestep R1, so keep this in mind when engaging multiple enemies. Another sweeping attack you can use is the backstep R1. The main thing its wider attacks have in common, including those in the R1 chain, is a prerequisite action. If you need something more immediate for controlling crowds, use the R2.

Fully charging the R2 will instead result in an overhead attack with a multiplier almost doubling your damage. This move can stagger when it connects with an enemy from behind, which you can then follow up with a rear visceral attack. An even better option is to use the follow-up R2; this can stagger as well, and has the highest damage multiplier of any the Church Pick's attacks. These attacks combined will do a horrendously large amount of damage, while taking a heavy toll on your stamina. Worry not though, since the amount of time it takes for most enemies to recover from this will give you plenty of time to distance yourself for regenerating stamina.

Transformed Mode R1

Transformed Mode R2

Transformed Mode Transform Attack

Holy Moonlight Sword OH

The Holy Moonlight Sword is a tremendously powerful weapon. It requires 16 strength, 12 skill and 14 arcane of its wielder. This weapon has comparatively lower base physical damage than Ludwig's Holy Blade and the Kirkhammer, but trumps both in overall damage by having the highest base arcane attack of any weapon in the game! Speaking of arcane, its transform mode can launch arcane waves outward, so it also doubles as a ranged weapon. In addition, it receives a good increase of scaling damage with high arcane levels and a 20% damage bonus against enemies weak to righteous weapons. In conjunction with its arcane damage, The Holy Moonlight Sword has very few physical or thrust attacks; its primary focus is instead on blunt damage. Without a doubt, this is an absolutely amazing weapon for strength and arcane specialized hunters.

> An arcane sword discovered long ago by Ludwig. When blue moonlight dances around the sword, and it channels the abyssal cosmos, its great blade will hurl a shadowy lightwave. The Holy Moonlight Sword is synonymous with Ludwig, the Holy Blade, but few ever set eyes on the on the great blade, and whatever guidance it has to offer, it seems to be of a very private, elusive sort.

Acquisition

Type	Obtained from	Reference	Bath Messenger Requirements
Normal	Speak to or attack Ludwig's head after killing him in Hunter's Nightmare	p652	–
Uncanny	Chalice Dungeon treasures/ Chalice Dungeon rare shop	p668	Acquire Weapon
Lost		p668	Acquire Weapon

Available Gem Slots

Weapon Type	Weapon Level		
	1	3	6
Normal	Radial	Triangular	Radial
Uncanny	Radial	Waning	Radial
Lost	Radial	Triangular	Waning

Average Physical Attack Increase (Strength)

Stat Range	Damage per Point	Estimated Attack Gained
16 to 25	4.22	38
26 to 50	2.04	51
50 to 99	0.43	21

Note: this table represents growth with a +10 weapon

Average Physical Attack Increase (Skill)

Stat Range	Damage per Point	Estimated Attack Gained
12 to 25	3.23	42
26 to 50	1.48	37
50 to 99	0.35	17

Note: this table represents growth with a +10 weapon

Average Arcane Attack Increase (Arcane)

Stat Range	Damage per Point	Estimated Attack Gained
14 to 25	1.89	34
26 to 50	1.40	35
50 to 99	0.31	15

Note: this table represents growth with a +10 weapon

Damage from Upgrades

Weapon Level	Base		Scaling		
	🗡	★	✊	✋	★
0	90	30	D	D	C
1	99	33	D	D	C
2	108	36	C	D	B
3	117	39	C	D	B
4	126	42	C	D	B
5	135	45	B	D	B
6	144	48	B	D	B
7	153	51	B	D	A
8	162	54	B	C	A
9	171	57	B	C	A
10	180	60	B	C	A

Gem Advice

Fire Paper and other buff items won't work on the Holy Moonlight Sword, so equipping it with an elemental gem to convert its damage is entirely pointless. Instead, you'll want to increase both of its inherent damage types. For this purpose, the use of Nourishing gems will benefit you greatly.

Though these won't increase your arcane damage, Adept (blunt) gems can be useful as this weapon's moveset is comprised of mainly blunt attacks. On that note, you may instead want to increase the damage of the few thrust attacks this weapon has for more versatility. Even players with high endurance may still want to offset the high stamina costs of the transform mode's attacks with Radiant Gems. This may take up valuable slot space, but will afford more aggressive players the stamina needed to maneuver as necessary.

Holy Moonlight Sword +10

Blood Gem Effects

Physical ATK	180 > 180	+252 >	+252
Blunt		+252 >	+252
Thrust		+252 >	+252
Blood ATK	- > -	+0 >	+0
Arcane ATK	100 > 100	+100 >	+100
Fire ATK	- > -	+0 >	+0
Bolt ATK	- > -	+0 >	+0
QS Bullet Use		1 >	1
Durability		250 >	250

Attribute Bonus
B > B C > C - > - A > A

Special Attack
0 > 0 0 > 0 100 > 100 100 > 100

Attribute Requirement
16 > 16 12 > 12 - > - 14 > 14

Normal Mode Tactics

The Holy Moonlight Sword's normal mode uses a moveset typical of a greatsword. Many of its attacks swing in wide horizontal arcs making it a good tool for crowd control. A large portion of attacks in this mode are blunt, though it also contains this weapon's only two thrust attacks, which are strong and very useful. What this mode lacks in its presentation, it makes up for in practical ability.

Normal Mode Attacks Properties

Attack	Dmg ×	Arc Dmg ×	Type	Stamina	Impact	Note
R1	1.00	0.50	Blunt / Arcane	25	Normal	be careful not to strike walls; often rebounds against obstacles
↳ R1 (2nd)	1.02	0.51	Blunt / Arcane	25	Normal	be careful not to strike walls; often rebounds against obstacles
↳ R1 (3rd)	1.06	0.53	Blunt / Arcane	25	Normal	
R1 (backstep)	0.90	0.45	Blunt / Arcane	20 (+10)	Normal	
R1 (rolling)	0.90	0.45	Blunt / Arcane	20 (+10)	Normal	be careful not to strike walls; often rebounds against obstacles
R1 (frontstep)	0.90	0.45	Blunt / Arcane	20 (+10)	Normal	
R1 (sidestep)	0.90	0.45	Blunt / Arcane	20 (+10)	Normal	
R1 (dash)	1.10	0.55	Blunt / Arcane	35 (+X)	Normal	
R2	1.30	0.65	Thrust / Arcane	40	Normal	key attack; quick and strong;
R2 (charged)	1.80	0.90	Thrust / Arcane	60	Heavy	continuously hold the button to execute
R2 (charged follow-up)	2.00	1.00	Blunt/ Arcane	65	Massive	exellent follow-up against staggered enemies
R2 (backstep)	1.20	0.60	Blunt/ Arcane	35 (+10)	Normal	
R2 (dash)	1.40	0.70	Physical / Arcane	50 (+X)	Heavy	
R2 (forward leap)	1.30	0.65	Blunt / Arcane	40	Heavy	tap forward on the stick just as you press R2 to execute
Transform Attack	1.20	1.00	Blunt / Arcane	40 (+X)	Heavy	press L1 while performing another action to execute; forced Guard Break

Normal Mode Key Attacks

The Holy Moonlight Sword's normal R1 chain, rolling R1 and quickstep R1s are useful for managing crowds. Their use is heavily limited in cramped or narrow spaces, however, since the swings tend to rebound off walls and objects. The R1 chain is a series of back and forth swings. Though quite basic, this is exactly what makes them so effective, as the broad strokes will not miss too easily.

The normal R2 is one of the best attacks available in this mode. It's a thrust attack, which is useful against enemies weak to this damage type, but where it really shines is in its speed. When used repeatedly, this attack is only somewhat slower than the R1 chain, but will easily stumble most normal enemies with each strike. The main downside is that it consumes large amounts of stamina when used this way; however, this will usually kill the average enemy before it can react. The dashing R2 is another strong attack with heavy impact. It has good forward momentum and a solid damage multiplier, making it good for hit-and-run tactics.

The charged R2 is this weapon's only other thrusting attack. When it connects with an enemy's rear, it can cause them to stagger. This attack steps forward while using the full extent of the blade. Much like with the Rifle Spear, this can make sneak attacks much easier to execute, since you'll be less likely to gain their attention by getting too close. When you've staggered an enemy, you can follow through with a rear visceral attack or the follow-up R2. In combination with the initial charged R2, the follow-up will almost always break an enemy's super armor, inflicting massive damage and impact.

Normal Mode R1

Normal Mode R2

Normal Mode Transform Attack

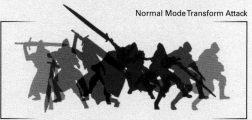

Transformed Mode Tactics

While this mode retains the overall range and physical damage of the normal mode, its arcane damage is what makes it shine. Most attacks receive roughly a 40% increase in arcane damage. R2 attacks can send out projectile waves of arcane, with each costing a single bullet to use. Once you've run dry of bullets it will function as a normal greatsword, and the arcane multiplier will lessen. Stamina usage in this mode rivals that of the Kirkhammer, so you'll need to be careful to not run out while fighting.

Transformed Mode Attacks Properties

Attack	Dmg ×	Arc Dmg ×	Type	Stamina	Impact	Note
R1	1.00	0.70	Blunt / Arcane	35	Normal	
↳ R1 (2nd)	1.02	0.72	Blunt / Arcane	35	Normal	
↳ R1 (3rd)	1.06	0.75	Blunt / Arcane	35	Normal	be careful not to strike walls; often rebounds against obstacles
↳ R1 (4th)	1.06	0.75	Blunt / Arcane	35	Normal	be careful not to strike walls; often rebounds against obstacles
R1 (backstep)	0.90	0.63	Blunt / Arcane	30 (+10)	Normal	
R1 (rolling)	0.90	0.63	Blunt / Arcane	30 (+10)	Normal	be careful not to strike walls; often rebounds against obstacles
R1 (frontstep)	0.90	0.63	Blunt / Arcane	30 (+10)	Normal	
R1 (sidestep)	0.90	0.63	Blunt / Arcane	30 (+10)	Normal	
R1 (dash)	1.10	0.77	Blunt / Arcane	45 (+X)	Normal	
R2	1.20	0.84	Blunt / Arcane	50	Heavy	uses a bullet: launches 4× arcane damage lightwave
R2 (charged)	1.40	0.98	Blunt / Arcane	75	Normal	uses a bullet: launches 5.60× arcane damage lightwave
R2 (charged follow-up)	1.40	0.98	Blunt / Arcane	75	Heavy	uses a bullet: launches 5.60× arcane damage lightwave
R2 (backstep)	1.20	0.84	Blunt / Arcane	45 (+10)	Heavy	uses a bullet: launches 3.6× arcane damage lightwave
R2 (dash)	1.20	0.84	Blunt / Arcane	60 (+X)	Heavy	luses a bullet: launches 4.40× arcane damage lightwave
R2 (forward leap)	1.30	0.91	Blunt / Arcane	60	Heavy	uses a bullet: launches 4.80× arcane damage lightwave
L2	1.50	1.05	Physical / Arcane	80	Massive	strong knockback; uses a bullet: 3× arcange damage
Transform Attack	1.30	1.30	Blunt / Arcane	60 (+X)	Massive	press L1 while performing another action to execute; forced Guard Break

Transformed Mode Key Attacks

The first two attacks of the R1 chain strike in a vertical manner. The first is an overhead, yet it lacks the range to strike most enemy weak points. Any attacks past these first two will swing horizontally, which is useful against groups or enemies that approach you mid-combo. Though this requires more stamina, the dashing R1's multiplier is higher than the peak point of the R1 chain. This can be handy against enemies with higher values of super armor that require a single hit approach.

Aside from when plunging, each of the R2 attacks in this mode will launch an arcane wave a good distance ahead. These projectiles will deal decent damage by themselves if you plan to use them for ranged combat. However, these attacks are especially devastating in combination with the blade at close range. That being the case, if you have at least two bullets and stagger an enemy from behind with a charged R2, instead of using a rear visceral attack, you can use the follow-up R2 for even greater damage and massive impact.

The L2 is one of the Holy Moonlight Sword's best attacks. It can launch even the larger foes far backward with massive impact, regardless of whether or not it has broken their super armor. This is especially useful against closely grouped enemies or for knocking opponents off cliffs and ledges. Be warned however, that the use of this move requires a significant amount of stamina and a single bullet.

Transformed Mode R1

Transformed Mode R2

Transformed Mode Transform Attack

Simon's Bowblade OH

Simon's Bow Blade requires 8 strength, 15 skill and 9 bloodtinge to use. Investments in strength will have no effect on its damage, so this definitely isn't weapon for characters highly invested in this stat. Its physical attack scales with skill, while bow shots scale with bloodtinge. Both of these stats receive high scaling bonuses, especially at high levels of upgrade. The Bowblade is a superb weapon in both modes, but it's most attractive feature is its long range attacks. If you haven't considered upgrading bloodtinge before, this weapon might just change that. The transform mode is incredibly useful; though it requires both hands, so you won't be able to use a firearm. Shots from the bow use bullets, but they won't interrupt enemy attacks. They're still very useful though, so equipping the Formless Odeon rune to increase the amount of bullets you can hold is a good idea.

> Choice weapon of Simon, one of the first Healing Church Hunters. Simon despised firearms, and so the Church workshop had this specially fashioned to his liking. The large curved blade serves as a bow when transformed. But aside from a few close friends, Simon was scoffed at for his choice of arms, for who would dare face the beasts with a measly bow?

Acquisition

Type	Obtained from	Reference	Bath Messenger Requirements
Normal	Complete Simon, Seeker of Secret's quest or kill him.	p651	–
Uncanny	Chalice Dungeon treasures/ Chalice Dungeon rare shop	p668	Acquire Weapon
Lost		p668	Acquire Weapon

Available Gem Slots

Weapon Type	Weapon Level		
	1	3	6
Normal	Radial	Triangular	Radial
Uncanny	Radial	Waning	Radial
Lost	Radial	Triangular	Waning

Average Physical Attack Increase (Skill)

Stat Range	Damage per Point	Estimated Attack Gained
15 to 25	3.53	53
26 to 50	2.44	61
50 to 99	0.55	27

Average Blood Attack Increase (Bloodtinge)

Stat Range	Damage per Point	Estimated Attack Gained
9 to 25	5.00	80
26 to 50	2.48	62
50 to 99	0.53	26

Damage from Upgrades

Weapon Level	Base		Scaling		
0	80	80	C	C	D
1	88	88	B	B	D
2	96	96	B	B	D
3	104	104	B	B	D
4	112	112	B	B	D
5	120	120	A	A	D
6	128	128	A	A	D
7	136	136	A	A	D
8	144	144	A	A	C
9	152	152	A	A	C
10	160	160	S	S	C

Gem Advice

Although you can't buff this weapon with items, or turn it into a completely elemental weapon with gems, you'll still have a number of options before you. Tempering effects work well for increasing your physical damage, while Nourishing gems will increase both of this weapon's damage types. Similarly, Bloodtinge and Odd Bloodtinge gems will increase shot damage. You won't always have a full supply of bullets, though, so focusing on both damage types might be the better choice.

Attacks in normal mode can build up large amounts of poison if slotted with stronger Murky and Dirty gems. You may land a lot of counter-hits using the Bowblade's ranged attacks, so Finestrike is another strong option. While both of the Bowblade's charge attacks will benefit from Striking gems, it has more interesting implications on the transform mode version. The shot from this attack deals solid damage, and the Striking effect can greatly boost it, allowing you to deal amazing damage from a distance.

Normal Mode Tactics

The Bowblade's normal mode attacks are fluid and combo into each other nicely. Attacks are also quick, which is good against evasive enemies that can be hard to hit with ranged attacks. Its stamina use is quite balanced, so you won't need to worry about running out too much.

Normal Mode Attacks Properties

Attack	Dmg ×	Type	Stamina	Impact	Note
R1	1.00	Physical	20	Light	
↳ R1 (2nd)	1.02	Physical	20	Light	
↳ R1 (3rd)	1.04	Physical	20	Light	
↳ R1 (4th)	1.08	Thrust	20	Light	thrust damage type; good against specific foes
R1 (backstep)	1.05	Thrust	15 (+10)	Light	thrust damage type; good against specific foes
R1 (rolling)	1.05	Physical	15 (+10)	Light	
R1 (frontstep)	1.05	Physical	15 (+10)	Light	
R1 (sidestep)	1.05	Physical	15 (+10)	Light	
R1 (dash)	1.10	Physical	25 (+X)	Light	
R2	1.30	Physical	40	Normal	
R2 (charged)	0.80	Physical	20	Normal	continuously hold the button to execute; thrust damage type
R2 (charged) (2nd hit)	1.70	Physical	40	Normal	second hit
R2 (backstep)	1.35	Physical	35 (+10)	Normal	
R2 (dash)	1.30	Physical	45 (+X)	Normal	
R2 (forward leap)	1.20	Physical	40	Light	tap forward on the stick just as you press R2 to execute
Transform Attack	0.85	Blood	35 (+X)	Normal	press L1 while performing another action to execute; shoots an arrow; uses a bullet; uses Blood Atk value

Normal Mode Key Attacks

The R1 chain uses a good combination of speed and damage. It even ends with a thrust attack, which is useful against enemies weak to this type. Backstep R1 is a more useful and accessible thrust attack, and worth keeping in mind. Rolling and quickstep R1s are excellent for dealing with foes requiring a more single hit approach, and they transition smoothly into the R1 chain too. These attacks usually score lower than most of a weapon's attack ratings, so the Bowblade is unusually efficient in this area.

The standard R2 steps forward while slashing in a wide horizontal arc. This has a very solid damage multiplier and works great against multiple enemies. The charged R2 hits twice and deals a lot of damage. The second hit alone has the highest multiplier of any of the Bowblade's attacks and can ever stagger enemies from behind.

The transformation attack is a great lead-in to the Bowblade's transform mode. It will send you a good amount back while letting an arrow loose. You can gain even more distance by using this as a follow-up to a backward quickstep, which you'll usually want when switching to the transform mode. Just make sure you have at least one bullet, or you'll use the transform mode's L2 attack, which probably isn't very useful for this purpose.

Normal Mode R1

Normal Mode R2

Normal Mode Transform Attack

Transformed Mode Tactics

Simon's Blowblade is a powerful ranged weapon when transformed. Arrow shots travel long distances, so you can deal some good damage without putting yourself in harm's way. Each shot takes a bullet to use, which isn't too demanding but can add up rather quickly. You'll still have a few melee attacks when you run out of bullets, but these are inferior compared to the normal mode, so it's better to switch back when this happens.

Transformed Mode Attacks Properties

Attack	Dmg ×	Type	Stamina	Impact	Note
R1	0.85	Blood	30	Light	shoots an arrow; uses a bullet; uses Blood Atk value
R2	1.05	Blood	60	Normal	shoots an arrow; uses a bullet; uses Blood Atk value
R2 (charged)	1.40	Blood	90	Heavy	shoots an arrow; uses a bullet; uses Blood Atk value; can stagger from long distances
R2 (forward leap)	1.20	Physical	40	Normal	tap forward on the stick just as you press R2 to execute
L2	0.70	Physical	15	Light	quick startup; all arrow attacks will perform this when empty on bullets
Transform Attack	1.35	Thrust	35	Normal	press L1 while performing another action to execute; forced Guard Break

Transformed Mode Key Attacks

There's little variety to the transform mode moveset. Your main method of attack, so long as you keep a steady supply of bullets, is arrow shots. The R1 shoots quickly, but in turn deals relatively low damage. This attack is best used for chipping away at enemy health, or finishing them off. The Standard R2 is slower than the the the R1, but it deals much better damage. It uses twice the amount of stamina, though, but this won't be much of an issue if you're fighting from afar.

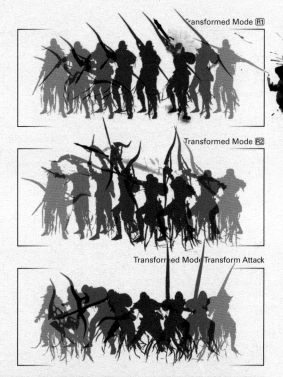

Transformed Mode R1

Transformed Mode R2

Transformed Mode Transform Attack

A fully charged R2 travels just as far as other shots, but can stagger foes from behind, even at long distances! Obviously, if you can't reach your target, you won't be able to follow through with a rear visceral attack, so this attack works much better as a support tool; try coordinating with ally players online. While enemies are distracted by an ally hunter, you can fish to stagger from a safe distance, which they can in turn follow up with a rear visceral attack. Another great use of this attack is for staggering fleeing targets, which may come in handy for handling more defensive players.

If you run out of bullets, you won't be completely defenseless – just incredibly limited. Attacks which would otherwise shoot arrows will perform the same attack as the L2. Its hits fast, but deals low damage and doesn't repeat quickly, so don't rely on it. The leaping R2 is quite literally a bow attack. Your character will jump forward and lunge with the bow; this does better damage than the L2, but you can deal more with a quickstep and transformation attack. This will cost only slightly more stamina, the damage is worth it.

Rakuyo (OH)

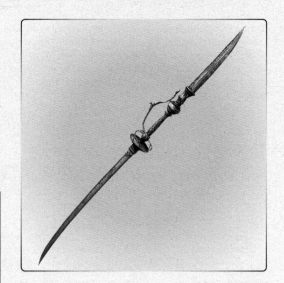

As its description states, the Rakuyo demands great dexterity. To wield this trick sword, you will need to have 10 strength and 20 skill. This weapon receives no scaling bonuses from strength – it's a skill weapon, and it scales highly with this stat. Increasing its damage is very straightforward since you'll only need to invest in one stat, and this will free you to pursue other attributes. Attacks are on par with the speed of the Chikage and use a similar amount of stamina; if the Chikage is a bit too risky for your tastes, this is a great alternative. The Rakuyo uses a mixture of normal physical and thrust attacks across both modes. If you look at the tables, you'll notice there are less thrust attacks overall, but they're usually good enough to warrant their use.

> Hunter weapon wielded by Lady Maria of the Astral Clocktower. A trick sword originated in the same counter as the Cainhurst Chikage, only this sword feeds not off blood, but instead demands great dexterity. Lady Maria was fond of this aspect of the Rakuyo, as she frowned upon blood blades, despite being a distant relative of the queen. One day, she abandoned her beloved Rakuyo, casting it into a dark well, when she could stomach it no longer.

Gem Advice

You can make the Rakuyo a purely elemental weapon with the use of gems, but its arcane scaling is low, so it's not the most effective use of slots. Considering that the majority the Rakuyo's attacks are normal physical type, Tempering effects will do well to increase its damage. If you want more use out of its thrusting attacks, you can slot Adept (blunt) effect gems.

A lot of really good attacks will use a lot of stamina; two noteworthy examples are the transformed R2 and L2 chains. Radiant gems will do well to combat their heavy stamina consumption, so consider these if you're willing to use slots for something other than damage. Some thrusting attacks have good forward momentum in addition to range; these attacks (among others) will land you a lot of easy counter hits, so Finestrike might be a good use of a gem slot.

Acquisition

Type	Obtained from	Reference	Bath Messenger Requirements
Normal	Defeat the Giant Fishman hanging from the ceiling in the cave below the well in the Fishing Hamlet	p192	–
Uncanny	Chalice Dungeon treasures/ Chalice Dungeon rare shop	p668	Acquire Weapon
Lost		p668	Acquire Weapon

Available Gem Slots

Weapon Type	Weapon Level		
	1	3	6
Normal	Radial	Radial	Triangular
Uncanny	Radial	Radial	Waning
Lost	Radial	Triangular	Waning

Average Physical Attack Increase (Skill)

Stat Range	Damage per Point	Estimated Attack Gained
20 to 25	5.00	25
26 to 50	2.28	57
50 to 99	0.51	25

Note: this table represents growth with a +10 weapon

Damage from Upgrades

Weapon Level	Base 🗡	Scaling ✋	Scaling ⭐
0	82	C	D
1	90	C	D
2	98	B	D
3	106	B	D
4	114	B	D
5	122	B	D
6	130	B	D
7	138	A	D
8	146	A	D
9	154	A	D
10	164	A	C

Normal Mode Tactics

There's less variety to the moveset for this mode, but you'll be able to use left hand weapons, which isn't something you can do while the Rakuyo is transformed. You can also stagger foes from behind with this mode. You're most likely going to have high investments in skill if you're using this weapon to begin with, so rear visceral attacks are going to deal more damage too.

Normal Mode Attacks Properties

Attack	Dmg ×	Type	Stamina	Impact	Note
R1	1.00	Physical	23	Light	
↳ R1 (2nd)	0.90	Thrust	16	Light	stamina efficient damage; thrust is good against specific foes
↳ R1 (3rd)	1.00	Physical	23	Light	
↳ R1 (4th)	1.15	Thrust	23	Light	thrust; good against specific foes
↳ R1 (5th)	1.00	Physical	23	Light	
R1 (backstep)	0.90	Physical	16 (+10)	Light	good against crowds
R1 (rolling)	0.90	Physical	16 (+10)	Light	
R1 (frontstep)	0.90	Physical	16 (+10)	Light	
R1 (sidestep)	0.90	Physical	16(+10)	Light	
R1 (dash)	1.10	Physical	33 (+X)	Light	
R2	1.35	Physical	45	Normal	
R2 (charged)	1.70	Thrust	60	Heavy	continuously hold the button to execute; thrust is good against specific foes
R2 (backstep)	1.25	Thrust	40 (+10)	Normal	thrust; good against specific foes
R2 (dash)	1.40	Thrust	54 (+X)	Normal	thrust; good against specific foes
R2 (forward leap)	1.40	Physical	54	Normal	
Transform Attack	1.30	Physical	36 (+X)	Normal	press L1 while performing another action to execute; forced Guard Break

Normal Mode Key Attacks

The R1 chain is a rapid alternation between normal physical and thrust type attacks. It may not be as fast as the transform mode R1 chain, but it can be somewhat useful for handling enemies weak to thrust attacks. Once the chain has finished, it will repeat, starting from the fourth attack onward. The fourth hit deals better thrust damage than the second, so this is an optimal looping point for dealing this type of damage.

Rolling and quickstep attacks are good for single strikes, and they don't cost much stamina for their type. They have good forward momentum, but the way the blade is swung offers you low range, so you may miss more evasive targets using these. The backstep R1 is much better in this regard, and it swings horizontally, allowing you to hit multiple enemies with ease. The backstep R2 costs a reasonable amount of stamina for its damage, and has good forward range since it's a thrust attack. If you're using this move for dodging attacks, you can get easily additional damage with counter hits.

The fully charged R2 is a high damage thrust with good forward momentum. These things together make for an attack with amazing reach, so it's well worth the price you'll pay in stamina to use it. It's best to begin the charge a bit before your target is within reach, so that you hit them before they can begin an attack. It can also be used to stagger enemies from behind. If an enemy is unaware of your presence, you can use this attack to stagger them without getting too close, alerting them of your presence.

Normal Mode R1

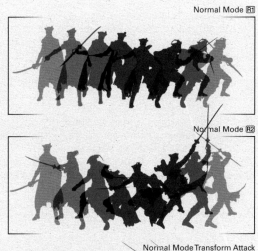

Normal Mode R2

Normal Mode Transform Attack

5

Transformed Mode Tactics

Stamina cost and damage is quite comparable between both modes. The main difference for this mode is in its speed; transforming the Rakuyo will snap the knife off of the hilt end of the weapon, which will then be used alongside sword swings, or for quickly alternating between hits.

Transformed Mode Attacks Properties

Attack	Dmg ×	Type	Stamina	Impact	Note
R1	1.00	Physical	23	Light	
↳ R1 (2nd)	1.00	Physical	16	Light	stamina efficient damage
↳ R1 (3rd)	1.20	Physical	30	Light	
↳ R1 (4th)	1.10	Physical	23	Light	
L2 (follow-up)	1.60	Physical	60 (+X)	Normal	follow-up to any part of the R1 combo
R1 (backstep)	0.90	Physical	16 (+10)	Light	
R1 (rolling)	0.90	Physical	16 (+10)	Light	
R1 (frontstep)	0.90	Physical	16 (+10)	Light	
R1 (sidestep)	0.90	Physical	16 (+10)	Light	
R1 (dash)	1.10	Physical	33 (+X)	Light	
R2	0.90	Thrust	23	Light	thrust; good against specific foes
↳ R2 (2nd)	0.95	Thrust	23	Light	thrust; good against specific foes
L2 (follow-up)	1.20	Thrust	40	Normal	Follow-up to any part of the R2 combo
R2 (backstep)	1.25	Thrust	40 (+10)	Normal	great for counters; thrust is good against specific foes
R2 (dash)	1.40	Thrust	55 (+X)	Normal	thrust; good against specific foes
R2 (forward leap)	1.40	Physical	55	Normal	
L2	0.95	Physical	30	Normal	360 degree spin is good against crowds
L2 (2nd hit)	1.00	Physical	30	Normal	second hit; 360 degree spin is good against crowds
↳ L2 (2nd)	1.05	Physical	30	Normal	360 degree spin is good against crowds
↳ L2 (2nd) (2nd hit)	1.10	Physical	30	Normal	second hit; 360 degree spin is good against crowds
Transform Attack	1.50	Thrust	50 (+X)	Normal	press L1 while performing another action to execute; forced Guard Break; thrust is good against specific foes

Transformed Mode Key Attacks

The R1 chain handles crowds quite well, despite not having the reach you'd usually expect of attacks used in this way. This chain only deals normal physical damage and performs much faster after the first hit. If your opponent isn't weak to thrust damage, you can dish out damage more quickly with this than you would using the normal mode's R1 chain. If you press L2 at any point during the chain, you'll use a unique combination attack. It uses a lot of stamina to perform, but it will deal good damage while removing more enemy super armor than any other single hit.

The backstep, rolling and quickstep R1s provide the same amount of stamina for damage as the normal mode, but will allow you to perform another action much earlier. These can be handy for single strikes, and they flow into the R1 chain quite well as a bonus. This mode doesn't have a charging attack, but it makes up for this by giving you an R2 chain instead. Both attacks of this chain score lower than the weapon's overall attack rating, but they're perfect for consistently dealing thrust damage. Like with the R1 chain, you can press L2 for a special combo attack; in this case, you'll perform another thrust, but with higher damage.

The dashing and backstep R2s are strong thrusting attacks as well. The dashing R2 deals out the better damage of the two, but you'll need proper spacing to use it. The backstep R2 may deal less damage, but benefits from its own distance control, since backstepping is a prerequisite. Used on its own, the L2 leads into a chain as well. Each time you press L2, your character will spin, slashing twice horizontally. These attacks are immensely useful for crowds, since they hit all the way around you multiple times. Performing both parts of this chain will use a whole lot of stamina, but provide a great deal of damage in return.

Transformed Mode R1

Transformed Mode R2

Transformed Mode Transform Attack

Boom Hammer (OH)

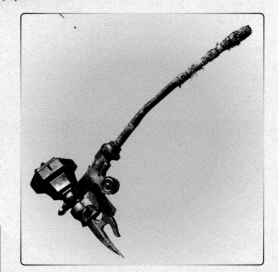

The Boom Hammer requires 14 strength and 8 skill to use. Its physical attack scales highest with strength, and receives very solid numbers up until level 50, at which point it begins to drop off. This is most certainly not a weapon for skill-oriented characters, as investments in this stat return poorly overall, even at higher levels of upgrade.

The Boom Hammer and Tonitrus are quite similar in a few ways. For example, it is the only right hand weapon in the game that deals fire damage without the use of a Fire Paper or gems. Additionally, all of its attacks are blunt. However, it does not deal elemental damage in its normal mode. Transforming the Boom Hammer will ignite the tip, adding fire damage and explosive effects to some attacks. Keep in mind though, that the weapon will reset to the normal mode after every attack.

> A trick weapon used by the old hunters, and crafted by the workshop heretic, the Powder Kegs. A giant hammer equipped with a miniature furnace. When ignited and fired, it emits a volley of flame that explodes furiously upon impact. Crush the beasts, then burn them – the brute simplicity of the Boom Hammer was favoured by hunters with an acute distaste for beasts

Gem Advice

Due the transform mode's innate fire elemental ability, gems will not turn the Boom Hammer into a completely elemental weapon. You might consider using Tempering gems, but these will only increase the physical damage of this weapon. Instead, think about slotting Nourishing gems to increase both of this weapon's damage types.

If you look at the tables, you may notice that all of the Boom Hammer's attacks deal blunt damage. This is a key feature that can be greatly enhanced by equipping Adept (blunt) effect gems. Again, don't bother with the Tempering gems; you'll receive a larger bonus from more specialized gems. When transformed, the Boom Hammer's attacks will eat through stamina, so you may want to balance this out with Radiant gems.

Acquisition

Type	Obtained from	Reference	Bath Messenger Requirements
Normal	Hunter's Nightmare	p168	–
Uncanny	Chalice Dungeon treasures/	p668	Acquire Weapon
Lost	Chalice Dungeon rare shop	p668	Acquire Weapon

Damage from Upgrades

Weapon Level	Base		Scaling		
0	90	60	B	E	D
1	99	66	C	E	D
2	108	72	B	E	D
3	117	78	B	E	D
4	126	84	B	E	D
5	135	90	B	E	D
6	144	96	B	E	D
7	153	102	B	E	C
8	162	108	B	E	C
9	171	114	A	E	C
10	180	120	A	E	C

Available Gem Slots

Weapon Type	Weapon Level		
	1	3	6
Normal	Radial	Waning	Radial
Uncanny	Radial	Triangular	Radial
Lost	Radial	Triangular	Waning

Note: this table represents growth with a +10 weapon

Average Physical Attack Increase (Strength)

Stat Range	Damage per Point	Estimated Attack Gained
14 to 25	5.89	53
26 to 50	2.28	57
50 to 99	0.49	24

Note: this table represents growth with a +10 weapon

Average Physical Attack Increase (Skill)

Stat Range	Damage per Point	Estimated Attack Gained
8 to 25	1.24	21
26 to 50	0.60	15
50 to 99	0.14	7

Note: this table represents growth with a +10 weapon

Average Fire Attack Increase (Arcane)

Stat Range	Damage per Point	Estimated Attack Gained
6 to 25	3.89	35
26 to 50	1.08	27
50 to 99	0.22	11

Note: this table represents growth with a +10 weapon

Tactics

Attacks in normal mode use a reasonable amount of stamina. In stark contrast, transformed attacks will use around double the stamina and chain slower into normal mode attacks after each reset. This may all seem unreasonable, but this transform mode is focused on single, high damage strikes. For the most effective use of this weapon, make a habit out of keeping it transformed at all times, both in and outside of combat to ensure the first hit always counts!

Normal Mode Attacks Properties

Attack	Dmg ×	Type	Stamina	Impact	Note
R1	1.00	Blunt	25	Normal	sweeping arc is good for crowds; transform = 40 stamina, & 1× fire damage
↳ R1 (2nd)	1.02	Blunt	25	Normal	sweeping arc is good for crowds
↳ R1 (3rd)	1.04	Blunt	25	Normal	sweeping arc is good for crowds
R1 (backstep)	0.90	Blunt	20 (+10)	Normal	transform = 30 (+10) stamina & 1× fire damage
R1 (rolling)	0.90	Blunt	20 (+10)	Normal	transform = 30 (+10) stamina & 1× fire damage
R1 (frontstep)	0.90	Blunt	20 (+10)	Normal	transform = 30 (+10) stamina & 1× fire damage
R1 (sidestep)	0.90	Blunt	20 (+10)	Normal	transform = 30 (+10) stamina & 1× fire damage
R1 (dash)	1.10	Blunt	35 (+X)	Normal	transform = 50 (+X) stamina & 1.10× fire damage
R2	1.35	Blunt	45	Heavy	sweeping arc is good for crowds; transform = 60 stamina, 1.30× fire & 1.30× blunt damage
R2 (charged)	1.90	Blunt	70	Massive	continuously hold R2 to execute; transform = 90 stamina, 1.80× fire & 1.80× blunt damage
R2 (backstep)	1.20	Blunt	40 (+10)	Heavy	transform = 50 (+10) stamina & 1.20× fire damage
R2 (dash)	1.45	Blunt	55 (+X)	Heavy	transform = 70 (+X) stamina & 1.45× fire damage
R2 (forward leap)	1.50	Blunt	50	Heavy	tap the stick forward as you pres R2 to execute; transform = 75 stamina & 1.50× fire damage
Transform Attack	0.80	Blunt / Fire	25 (+X)	Normal	press L1 while performing another action to execute; forced Guard Break; also deals 0.80× fire damage

Normal Mode Key Attacks

The Boom Hammer's normal R1 chain is slow, but will stun-lock most enemies with normal impact. This chain swings back and forth horizontally, which is useful against crowds. Another good feature of these attacks is that they won't rebound off walls and obstacles. This is true for the entirety of this weapon's moveset, but is especially important for wide attacks such as these.

In most cases, the leaping R2 will cause enemies to instantly stumble with its heavy impact. It also deals more damage for less stamina than the dashing R1. This attack works as a great combo tool for the Boom Hammer's slower swing speeds. Quickstep backward during any combo and follow up with a leaping R2; this will usually break high enemy super armor.

The damage multiplier for the charged R2 is almost double the weapon's overall attack. The time it takes to charge is not that bad and it can stagger foes from behind. Since you're most likely to have low investments in skill with this weapon, a second charge attack will deal more damage than a rear visceral attack. This will almost always send enemies falling forward with massive impact, giving ample time for you to retreat and recover stamina.

Transformed Mode Key Attacks

Aside from being almost imperceptibly slower, The Boom Hammer's moveset remains ultimately the same in this mode. Instead, attacks receive enhancements from fire damage. A high damage combo you can use against enemies with low super armor is a back and forth between the L1 and R1 attacks. Doing so basically keeps the Boom Hammer ignited constantly, which will allow you to deal constant fire damage.

The most notably improved attack in this mode is the charged R2. This attack gains a medium area of effect explosion, and for the amount of damage this

Normal Mode R1

Normal Mode R2

Normal Mode Transform Attack

generates, the charge time is still very good. Don't forget, this can also be used to hit enemies from behind cover! A similar attack is the leaping R2, though the explosion has a smaller radius.

Whirligig Saw  (OH)

The Whirligig Saw requires 18 strength and 12 dexterity to use. Though it requires a high investment in strength, this will not be wasted, as it scales exceptionally well with this stat. It even receives an S rating when fully upgraded! Many attacks in normal mode offset the Whirligig Saw's scaling by having low damage multipliers. The real star of the show is the transform mode, which rapidly shreds with some attacks. In addition, this mode deals a 20% damage increase against enemies weak to serration. Both modes utilize the game's regain system very well. All things considered, the Whirligig Saw should feel comfortable to anyone familiar with Logarius' Wheel.

A trick weapon crafted by the workshop heretics, the Powder Kegs, and weapon of choice for the old hunter Valtr, the Beast Eater. This weapon pummels beasts in its mace form, but its true strength lies in its attached mechanical saws. These discs, lined with serrated teeth, spin rapidly, thrashing the flesh of beasts into fine shreds.

Gem Advice

The Whirligig Saw scales quite well with arcane, making it a good candidate for damage conversion with the use of elemental effect gems. Since the transform mode deals extra damage against enemies weak to serration, you may want to convert its damage to fire, another common weaknesses among beasts.

Adept (blunt) effect gems can be used to boost the damage of most the normal mode's attacks. This is a good option considering their generally low damage multipliers. You may also want to take advantage of the faster swing speeds of the normal mode, and rapid shredding of the transformed mode by slotting Dirty and Murky gems. These attacks will build up poison very quickly, making the Whirligig Saw one of the best weapons you can use for this purpose.

Acquisition

Type	Obtained from	Reference	Bath Messenger Requirements
Normal	Hunter's Nightmare	p171	–
Uncanny	Chalice Dungeon treasures/ Chalice Dungeon rare shop	p668	Acquire Weapon
Lost		p668	Acquire Weapon

Available Gem Slots

Weapon Type	Weapon Level		
	1	3	6
Normal	Radial	Radial	Triangular
Uncanny	Radial	Radial	Waning
Lost	Radial	Triangular	Waning

Average Physical Attack Increase (Strength)

Stat Range	Damage per Point	Estimated Attack Gained
18 to 25	6.29	44
26 to 50	2.92	73
50 to 99	0.65	32

Note: this table represents growth with a +10 weapon

Average Physical Attack Increase (Skill)

Stat Range	Damage per Point	Estimated Attack Gained
12 to 25	1.77	23
26 to 50	0.80	20
50 to 99	0.16	8

Note: this table represents growth with a +10 weapon

Damage from Upgrades

Weapon Level	Base	Scaling		
0	92	B	E	D
1	104	B	E	D
2	113	B	E	C
3	122	B	E	C
4	131	A	E	C
5	140	A	E	C
6	149	A	E	B
7	158	A	E	B
8	167	A	E	B
9	197	A	E	B
10	190	S	D	B

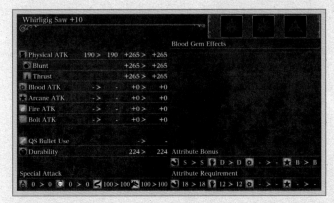

5

Normal Mode Tactics

For the most part, damage multipliers for normal mode attacks score lower than the weapon's overall attack rating. Attacks are mainly blunt, but there are a few thrust attacks at your disposal. You may want to use this mode for its speed and comparatively lower stamina costs, especially when handling more evasive enemies.

Normal Mode Attacks Properties

Attack	Dmg ×	Type	Stamina	Impact	Note
R1	0.75	Blunt	18	Light	
↳ R1 (2nd)	0.78	Blunt	18	Light	
↳ R1 (3rd)	0.81	Blunt	18	Light	
↳ R1 (4th)	0.85	Thrust	18	Light	thrust damage; good against specific foes
R1 (backstep)	0.70	Thrust	12 (+10)	Light	thrust damage; good against specific foes
R1 (rolling)	0.70	Blunt	12 (+10)	Light	
R1 (frontstep)	0.70	Blunt	12 (+10)	Light	
R1 (sidestep)	0.70	Blunt	12 (+10)	Light	long step forward
R1 (dash)	0.85	Thrust	28 (+X)	Normal	thrust damage; good against specific foes
R2	1.05	Blunt	30	Normal	
R2 (charged)	1.30	Blunt	45	Heavy	continuously hold the button to execute
R2 (backstep)	1.00	Blunt	25(+10)	Heavy	
R2 (dash)	1.15	Blunt	40 (+X)	Normal	
R2 (forward leap)	1.20	Blunt	50	Heavy	
Transform Attack	1.15	Physical	35 (+X)	Normal	press L1 while performing another action to execute; forced Guard Break

Normal Mode Key Attacks

The R1 chain is a series of fast blows and, while not exactly rapid, their speed will somewhat make up for the low damage multipliers. Blunt attacks receive higher rates of health regain, which synergizes well with the speed of these attacks and more aggressive play. The fourth hit of this chain is thrust type, though its usefulness can be quite limited due it to being so late in the chain.

The backstep R1 makes for a better and more useful thrust attack. Its damage multiplier low, but it uses much less stamina than the dashing R1 thrust. Backsteps won't put much distance between you and the range of most enemy attacks, if at all. They also require specific timing to properly utilize the invincibility frames, so in some cases the dashing R1's higher stamina may be worth it. The normal R2 has much better damage than most attacks, but you're better off just using the transform mode R1s for faster swing speeds and similar damage.

A charged R2 will deal much more damage than other attacks, but it's really only useful for setting up rear visceral attacks. Instead, consider using the leaping R2. This is a great alternative; it uses slightly more stamina, but deals a fairly similar amount of damage without the long charge. It's also great for breaking enemy super armor, which it does with high impact.

Normal Mode R1

Normal Mode R2

Normal Mode Transform Attack

Transformed Mode Tactics

The Whirligig Saw's transform mode uses a large array of physical attacks, which is a good balance to all of the blunt and thrust attacks of the normal mode. This mode is overall slower and consumes more stamina, but deals more damage per hit. It also gains a 20% attack bonus against enemies weak to serrated weapons. This mode is similar to Logarius' Wheel with its shredding attacks; players utilizing the regain system will benefit greatly from using this mode.

Transformed Mode Attacks Properties

Attack	Dmg ×	Type	Stamina	Impact	Note
R1	1.00	Physical	30	Normal	
↳ R1 (2nd)	1.03	Physical	30	Normal	
↳ R1 (3rd)	1.12	Physical	30	Normal	
↳ R1 (4th)	1.15	Physical	30	Normal	high damage; also produces two 0.30× shreds
R1 (backstep)	1.00	Physical	25 (+10)	Normal	
R1 (rolling)	0.95	Physical	25 (+10)	Normal	
R1 (frontstep)	0.95	Physical	25 (+10)	Normal	
R1 (sidestep)	0.95	Physical	25 (+10)	Normal	
R1 (dash)	1.08	Physical	40 (+X)	Normal	
R2	1.30	Physical	55	Heavy	
R2 (charged)	1.80	Blunt	80	Massive	continuously hold the button to execute; also produces three 0.30× shreds
R2 (backstep)	1.20	Blunt	25 (+10)	Normal	also produces two 0.30× shreds
R2 (dash)	1.40	Physical	65 (+X)	Heavy	
R2 (forward leap)	1.50	Physical	65	Heavy	tap forward on the stick as you pres R2; also produces two 0.30× shreds
L2	0.80	Physical	25	Light	continuously hold the button to execute
L2 (held 1)	0.60	Physical	10	Light	
L2 (held 2)	0.30	Physical	0	Light	
L2 (held 3)	0.60	Physical	10	Heavy	
Transform Attack	1.05	Blunt	25 (+X)	Light	press L1 while performing another action; also produces two 0.30× shreds

Transformed Mode Key Attacks

The R1 chain has a good damage multiplier and peaks at the fourth hit with a small area of effect grinding attack. If you manage to pull off the whole thing, it will deal a great amount of damage. Otherwise, you can use the first R1 for prodding back enemies. Quickstep R1s are very useful for this purpose as well. Single hits are almost a necessity for some enemies, and for these instances you can use a backward quickstep R1. This gives good forward momentum which is only complimented by the forward jab.

A fully charged R2 will take a lot longer than most other weapons' equivalent attacks to perform, but it is very powerful and creates a small, continuous grinding area of effect. If you feel that an enemy is getting too close during the long charge, releasing it early is not a bad idea. Doing so will result in a standard R2, but with its start-up out of the way during the charge, the swing will be near instant! This can also work as a strong fake out against players online. Another two grinding attacks are the leaping and backstep R2s; the leaping R2 deals more damage, but the backstep R2 uses less than half the amount of stamina to perform.

Holding L2 causes your character to hold the blade outward while it spins. This chips away stamina quickly while active and cancels upon release. You can still slowly move around while doing this, which will allow you to walk into enemies with the blade. Enemies with next to no super armor will be stun locked, unable to attack; Foes with high super armor values will appear to flinch, but can still attack, so don't get too greedy! Tapping L2 also works as a forward jab, though the damage multiplier for a single hit isn't that good by itself.

Transformed Mode R1

Transformed Mode R2

Transformed Mode Transform Attack

5

Bloodletter (OH)

The Bloodletter requires 14 strength, 6 skill and 16 bloodtinge to use. It receives no attribute bonus rating with skill, but it has an excellent one in strength, and an even better one with bloodtinge. In fact, it scales better with bloodtinge than the Chikage at similar levels. There's a lot of incentive to invest your points into this stat with this weapon, and you'll want to for effective use of its transformed mode. Its normal mode is unaffected by this stat though, and scales separately with strength. Though the normal mode has short range, it offers both thrust and blunt attacks, which can be useful against enemies with otherwise high defenses. So you may want split your stat investments evenly between strength and bloodtinge to balance the uses of both modes. Otherwise, you can dump your points into one stat for higher damage. It arguably has the superior moveset while transformed, so in this case, you might want to focus on bloodtinge.

> The demented hunter weapon brandished by Brador, the Healing Church assassin. The Bloodletter assumes its true and terrifying form after it draws upon blood from the inner reaches of one's body and soul. This is the only effective means of expelling tainted blood, or so Brador, isolated in his cell, continued to believe.

Gem Advice

The Bloodletter cannot be converted into a purely elemental weapon with gems, so don't waste your slots on this. Adept (blunt) effects will increase the damage of the normal mode, while Odd Bloodtinge and Bloodtinge gems increase the damage of the transformed mode. You'll get a larger bonus using gems like these, since their effects are more specifically focused. You can use this to balance the damage between both modes if you're focusing more on one stat than the other. If you want to increase the damage types of both modes at once, equip Nourishing gems to this weapon.

The transformed mode has good range, especially with its rolling and quickstep attacks. You'll most likely be landing a lot of counter hits using these moves, and the Finestrike gem will only enhance them. Stamina costs for both modes are quite reasonable for the amount of damage they deal, but can add up very quickly, especially if you're dodging around your targets, which is almost necessary for using the normal mode. If you're finding yourself running low on stamina, try slotting Radiant gems to this weapon.

Acquisition

Type	Obtained from	Reference	Bath Messenger Requirements
Normal	Kill Brador, Church Assassin's physical body in the Underground Cells of Hunter's Nightmare	p653	–
Uncanny	Chalice Dungeon treasures/ Chalice Dungeon rare shop	p668	Acquire Weapon
Lost		p668	Acquire Weapon

Available Gem Slots

Weapon Type	Weapon Level		
	1	3	6
Normal	Radial	Radial	Triangular
Uncanny	Radial	Radial	Waning
Lost	Radial	Radial	Circular

Average Physical Attack Increase (Strength)

Stat Range	Damage per Point	Estimated Attack Gained
14 to 25	5.45	60
26 to 50	2.52	63
50 to 99	0.55	27

Average Blood Attack Increase (Bloodtinge)

Stat Range	Damage per Point	Estimated Attack Gained
16 to 25	5.54	72
26 to 50	2.80	70
50 to 99	0.59	29

Damage from Upgrades

Weapon Level	Base		Scaling		
	🗡	❄	🦴	❄	★
0	90	90	C	B	D
1	99	99	C	B	D
2	108	108	B	B	D
3	117	117	B	B	D
4	126	126	B	A	D
5	135	135	B	A	D
6	120	144	B	A	D
7	134	153	A	A	D
8	149	162	A	A	D
9	164	171	A	A	D
10	180	180	A	S	C

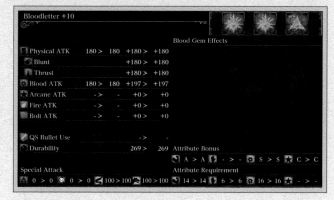

Bloodletter +10

Blood Gem Effects

Physical ATK	180 >	180	+180 >	+180
Blunt			+180 >	+180
Thrust			+180 >	+180
Blood ATK	180 >	180	+197 >	+197
Arcane ATK	->	-	+0 >	+0
Fire ATK	->	-	+0 >	+0
Bolt ATK	->	-	+0 >	+0
QS Bullet Use		->		
Durability	269 >	269		

Attribute Bonus
🦴 A > A ⚡ - > - ❄ S > S ★ C > C

Special Attack
⚔ 0 > 0 ⚙ 0 > 0 🔥 100 > 100 ⚡ 100 > 100

Attribute Requirement
💪 14 > 14 🏃 6 > 6 ❄ 16 > 16 ★ - > -

Normal Mode Tactics

The Bloodletter's normal mode has shorter range than the transformed, but deals primarily physical types of damage. Not all enemies are weak to blood damage, so you'll want to use this mode for those that aren't. Another reason you may want to use this mode is because it only requires your right hand, which will allow you to use a firearm for interrupts.

Normal Mode Attacks Properties

Attack	Dmg ×	Type	Stamina	Impact	Note
R1	1.00	Blunt	23	Light	
↳ R1 (2nd)	1.00	Blunt	23	Light	
↳ R1 (3rd)	1.00	Blunt	23	Light	
↳ R1 (4th)	1.10	Thrust	23	Light	
R1 (backstep)	0.95	Blunt	15 (+10)	Normal	
R1 (rolling)	0.95	Blunt	18 (+10)	Light	
R1 (frontstep)	0.95	Blunt	18 (+10)	Light	
R1 (sidestep)	0.95	Blunt	18 (+10)	Light	
R1 (dash)	1.10	Thrust	30 (+X)	Normal	
R2	1.50	Thrust	40	Normal	
R2 (charged)	1.90	Blunt	60	Heavy	continuously hold the button to execute
R2 (backstep)	1.40	Blunt	30(+10)	Heavy	
R2 (dash)	1.50	Blunt	40 (+X)	Heavy	
R2 (forward leap)	1.40	Blunt	40	Heavy	tap forward on the stick just as you press R2 to execute
Transform Attack	1.30	Blood	30 (+X)	Massive	press L1 while performing another action to execute; forced Guard Break; scales with bloodtinge; inflicts 20% damage to user

Normal Mode Key Attacks

The Bloodletter's normal mode R1 chain has low range, so it's best used against single enemies. The chain isn't very fast, but it hits at a consistent rate, so you usually won't have to worry about enemies escaping between strikes. You'll need to get in close, so enemies with high super armor may require you to dodge around them quite a bit. For this purpose, you have the rolling and quickstep R1s, but keep in mind these attacks can miss when used against smaller enemies. If you're having a hard time sticking close to your target while dodging its attacks, you can back off and use a leaping R2 for a powerful single strike. This attack deals far better damage and has good forward momentum; however, you'll need to keep an eye on your stamina usage.

The standard R2 is another thrust attack you can use, and a good one at that. It's not very fast due to the start-up, but it has a solid damage multiplier that can make handling enemies with high defenses less of a chore. Fully charging the R2 won't deal thrust damage, but it has an even higher damage multiplier. Additionally, this attack can stagger enemies from behind. You can follow this up with a rear visceral attack, but you're likely to have low investments in skill if you're using this weapon, so its damage will be low. Instead, consider using another charged R2 for better damage.

Transforming from this mode requires plunging the Bloodletter deep into your chest. This will remove 20% of your maximum health, which can kill you if used haphazardly. It's better you use the transformation attack for switching modes. By doing so, you can recover a portion of health lost performing this attack with the regain system, while sending enemies flying back with massive impact.

Normal Mode R1

Normal Mode R2

Normal Mode Transform Attack

Transformed Mode Tactics

The Bloodletter is an amazing weapon while transformed. All of its attacks in this mode deal blood attack, which rely solely on your bloodtinge stat for damage. Compared to the normal mode, it has far better range and uses only slightly more stamina. Keep in mind that blood attacks will knock back dog enemies, which can be useful if you're trying to combo them.

Transformed Mode Attacks Properties

Attack	Dmg ×	Type	Stamina	Impact	Note
R1	1.05		25	Normal	sweeping arc is good for crowds; scales with bloodtinge
↳ R1 (2nd)	1.05		25	Normal	sweeping arc is good for crowds; scales with bloodtinge
↳ R1 (3rd)	1.05		25	Normal	hits high; useful for striking enemy weak points; scales with bloodtinge
↳ R1 (4th)	1.10		25	Normal	hits high; useful for striking enemy weak points; scales with bloodtinge
↳ R1 (5th)	1.10		25	Normal	hits high; useful for striking enemy weak points; scales with bloodtinge
R1 (backstep)	1.00		17 (+10)	Normal	scales with bloodtinge
R1 (rolling)	1.00		17 (+10)	Normal	scales with bloodtinge
R1 (frontstep)	1.00		17 (+10)	Normal	scales with bloodtinge
R1 (sidestep)	1.00		17 (+10)	Normal	scales with bloodtinge
R1 (dash)	1.15	Blood	30 (+X)	Normal	scales with bloodtinge
R2	1.50		45	Normal	scales with bloodtinge
R2 (charged)	2.00		70	Massive	continuously hold the button to execute; scales with bloodtinge
R2 (charged) (2nd hit)	1.50		0	Massive	scales with bloodtinge
R2 (backstep)	1.40		40 (+10)	Normal	scales with bloodtinge
R2 (dash)	1.40		50	Heavy	scales with bloodtinge
R2 (forward leap)	1.40		40	Heavy	tap forward on the stick just as you press R2 to execute; scales with bloodtinge
L2	0.00		0	Heavy	scales with bloodtinge; inflicts heavy self frenzy buildup
L2 (2nd hit)	2.00		90	Heavy	scales with bloodtinge
Transform Attack	1.20		30 (+X)	Heavy	press L1 while performing another action to execute; forced Guard Break; scales with bloodtinge

Transformed Mode Key Attacks

The first two hits of the R1 chain swing in wide horizontal arcs, making them great for crowds. The following three swing overhead, which can be used to reach taller enemy weak spots. They aren't always reliable for this purpose though, since your target may move out of position before you can use them. A more powerful and reliable attack for this function is the leaping R2, but it will cost you more stamina to use.

Rolling and quickstep R1s have solid forward momentum range, making them good for hit-and-run tactics. To add to this, they deal more damage than their normal mode counterparts and for less slightly stamina. The standard R2 is another attack with good forward range, and it has a strong damage modifier to boot. Fully charging the R2 takes a while, but deals a massive amount of damage in a small area of effect. It can also stagger enemies if it connects with their backs, and you can then follow up with a rear visceral attack or second charged R2.

The L2 is a powerful area of effect attack that tears through most enemy defenses and super armor. It's just as strong as the charged R2 and executes much faster. On the other hand, it will use a larger amount of stamina and inflicts heavy frenzy build-up upon your character. The safest way to use this attack is to wear something that will lower your frenzy gauge, like the Ashen Hunter attire, while keeping your insight low. By combining these things, you can possibly use this attack twice for massive damage, and still have time to use a sedative. The transformation attack doesn't inflict self-damage like the normal mode does, so don't worry about that when using it.

Transformed Mode R1

Transformed Mode Transform Attack

Amygdalan Arm (OH)

The Amygdalan Arm requires a hefty 17 strength to use. So while all characters by default meet the minimal skill requirement of 9 for this weapon, an investment in strength is necessary to wield it. Accordingly, this weapon scales best with strength, and receives excellent ratings at higher levels of upgrade. The normal moveset of this weapon is most effective against singular foes, whereas the transformed moveset is best applied against groups of enemies. The dual nature of this weapon makes it fairly adaptable between situations. In addition, this weapon inflicts a solid amount of arcane damage in both modes and scales moderately well with the stat. This is a valuable option for hunters focusing on strength and arcane.

The arm of a small Amygdala Great One. Strictly speaking, the Amygdalan Arm is no trick weapon of any soft, but certain madmen wield them like clubs. Starts as a large, tough blunt weapon formed of bone, but when extended, the hand quivers as if it were still alive.

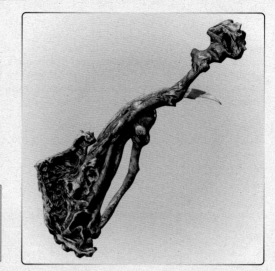

Acquisition

Type	Obtained from	Reference	Bath Messenger Requirements
Normal	Hunter's Nightmare	p168	–
Uncanny	Chalice Dungeon treasures/	p668	Acquire Weapon
Lost	Chalice Dungeon rare shop	p668	Acquire Weapon

Available Gem Slots

Weapon Type	Weapon Level		
	1	3	6
Normal	Radial	Radial	Triangular
Uncanny	Radial	Radial	Waning
Lost	Radial	Triangular	Waning

Average Physical Attack Increase (Strength)

Stat Range	Damage per Point	Estimated Attack Gained
17 to 25	4.25	34
26 to 50	2.04	51
50 to 99	0.43	21

Note: this table represents growth with a +10 weapon

Average Physical Attack Increase (Skill)

Stat Range	Damage per Point	Estimated Attack Gained
9 to 25	1.13	18
26 to 50	0.56	14
50 to 99	0.12	6

Note: this table represents growth with a +10 weapon

Average Arcane Attack Increase (Arcane)

Stat Range	Damage per Point	Estimated Attack Gained
6 to 25	1.26	24
26 to 50	0.68	17
50 to 99	0.16	8

Note: this table represents growth with a +10 weapon

Damage from Upgrades

Weapon Level	Base		Scaling		
0	80	40	C	E	D
1	88	44	C	E	D
2	96	48	B	E	D
3	104	52	B	E	D
4	112	56	B	E	D
5	120	60	B	E	D
6	128	64	B	E	C
7	136	68	B	E	C
8	144	72	A	E	C
9	152	76	A	E	C
10	184	80	A	E	C

Gem Advice

Equipping an elemental gem will not convert the Amygdalan Arm's physical damage to elemental, nor can it be buffed with the use of items. Tempering gems can be used to increase the damage of blunt attacks, but they won't affect your arcane damage. Instead, consider using Nourishing gems; these are a much better use of your slots and will increase your damage overall.

If you are without Nourishing gems, Arcane and Odd Arcane gems with physical attack increasing secondary effects can be used to supplement its already good arcane damage. Radiant gems are another good use of your slots, as they will offset its above average stamina usage. Also note that the Amygdalan Arm has two powerful charging attacks that can be greatly improved with Striking gems.

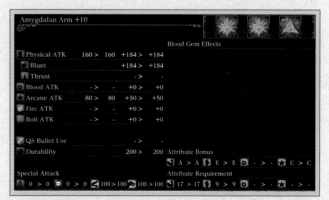

Normal Mode Tactics

The Amygdalan Arm's normal mode is very straightforward. The majority of its attacks are short, heavy swings aimed immediately ahead of your character. This mode is best suited for close combat with single foes; however, the windups are slow, which limits its use against more evasive targets. This mode deals almost exclusively blunt damage, making it useful against enemies weak to this particular type.

Normal Mode Attacks Properties

Attack	Dmg ×	Arc Dmg ×	Type	Stamina	Impact	Note
R1	1.00	1.00	Blunt / Arcane	25	Normal	
↳ R1 (2nd)	1.00	1.00	Blunt / Arcane	25	Normal	
↳ R1 (3rd)	1.10	1.10	Blunt / Arcane	25	Normal	
↳ R1 (4th)	1.20	1.20	Blunt / Arcane	25	Normal	
R1 (backstep)	0.95	0.95	Blunt / Arcane	20 (+10)	Normal	
R1 (rolling)	0.95	0.95	Blunt / Arcane	15 (+10)	Normal	
R1 (frontstep)	0.95	0.95	Blunt / Arcane	15 (+10)	Normal	quick start-up
R1 (sidestep)	0.95	0.95	Blunt / Arcane	15 (+10)	Normal	
R1 (dash)	1.10	1.10	Blunt / Arcane	35 (+X)	Heavy	
R2	1.30	1.30	Blunt / Arcane	40	Heavy	
R2 (charged)	1.80	1.80	Blunt / Arcane	60	Massive	continuously hold the button to execute
R2 (follow-up)	1.80	1.80	Blunt / Arcane	50	Massive	
R2 (backstep)	1.35	1.35	Blunt / Arcane	35 (+10)	Normal	
R2 (dash)	1.40	1.40	Blunt / Arcane	50 (+X)	Heavy	
R2 (forward leap)	1.40	1.40	Blunt / Arcane	50	Heavy	tap forward on the stick just as you press R2 to execute
Transform Attack	1.15	1.15	Physical / Arcane	30 (+X)	Heavy	press L1 while performing another action to execute; forced Guard Break

Normal Mode Key Attacks

While lacking in speed and range, each hit will remove a solid amount of enemy super armor; you can use this to lock most normal enemies into the Amygdalan Arm's R1 chain. However, this is not recommended against sturdier enemies, who will strike back before their super armor's breaking point. In these instances, swift, single blows such as quickstep R1s will suffice.

The charged R2 is especially powerful, but takes a long time to fully charge. An upside to the long charge is that it gives plenty of time for you to change its direction. This attack can stagger enemies from behind, opening them up for a rear visceral attack, but you may instead want to use its powerful follow up R2. Both attacks have massive impact, giving ample time for the follow up while enemies are grounded from the first – just be sure to conserve your stamina to use it.

The dashing R2 has a good damage multiplier and decent swing speed. The main drawback to this attack is in its long recovery; this won't be much of an issue against most enemies thanks to its high super armor reduction and impact. Take note, the transformation attack is one of this mode's more useful tools; it has good speed and heavy impact, making it ripe for longer combos.

Normal Mode R1

Normal Mode R2

Normal Mode Transform Attack

Transformed Mode Tactics

The Amygdalan Arm's transform mode is quite superior to its normal mode. It has far better reach and uses a similar amount of stamina with each attack. In fact, it will suit most situations much better due to its wider variety of moves. If you are fighting crowds or enemies resistant to blunt damage, transformed mode is the way to go.

Transformed Mode Attacks Properties

Attack	Dmg ×	Arc Dmg ×	Type	Stamina	Impact	Note
R1	0.95	0.95	Physical / Arcane	25	Normal	sweeping arc is good against crowds
↳ R1 (2nd)	1.00	1.00	Physical / Arcane	25	Normal	sweeping arc is good against crowds
↳ R1 (3rd)	1.05	1.05	Physical / Arcane	25	Normal	
↳ R1 (4th)	1.15	1.15	Physical / Arcane	25	Normal	
R1 (backstep)	0.90	0.90	Physical / Arcane	20 (+10)	Normal	
R1 (rolling)	0.90	0.90	Physical / Arcane	20 (+10)	Normal	
R1 (frontstep)	0.90	0.90	Physical / Arcane	20 (+10)	Normal	
R1 (sidestep)	0.90	0.90	Physical / Arcane	20 (+10)	Normal	
R1 (dash)	1.10	1.10	Physical / Arcane	45 (+X)	Normal	
R2	1.20	1.20	Physical / Arcane	45	Heavy	
R2 (2nd hit)	0.80	0.80	Physical / Arcane	10	Light	second hit; can be canceled; stand still to execute
R2 (charged)	1.70	1.70	Blunt /Arcane	70	Massive	surprise attack; continuously hold the button to execute
R2 (charged) (2nd hit)	0.80	0.80	Physical / Arcane	10	Light	second hit; can be canceled; stand still to execute
R2 (charged) (3rd hit)	0.85	0.85	Physical / Arcane	10	Light	third hit; can be canceled; stand still to execute
R2 (backstep)	1.20	1.20	Physical / Arcane	30 (+10)	Heavy	good range. though little forward momentum
R2 (dash)	1.30	1.30	Physical / Arcane	50 (+X)	Heavy	
R2 (forward leap)	1.40	1.40	Blunt / Arcane	50	Heavy	tap forward on the stick just as you press R2 to execute
Transform Attack	1.50	1.50	Blunt / Arcane	50	Massive	press L1 while performing another action to execute; forced Guard Break

Transformed Mode Key Attacks

The first two swings of the R1 chain hit in wide horizontal arcs that are exceptionally good for handling multiple enemies. In this situation, however, you'll want to back out rather than continue, since the following two swings move vertically. One of best features of these of attacks is that, despite their wide range, they can be swung freely without the repercussion of bouncing off walls.

The R2 of this weapon is odd one, but that is precisely its strength! If you perform no other actions, including movement, a second surprise hit will execute after the initial slash; if the first hit doesn't break your target's super armor, this additional one will usually do the trick. Another easy way to break super armor is by using the leaping R2. When facing enemies with high amounts of super armor, use this as a follow up attack to ensure they are stumbled during your recovery.

The charged R2 uses the same gimmick as the standard R2, but is by far the dirtiest move this mode has to offer. On top of dealing high damage, the massive impact of this attack will send enemies straight to the ground. If you stand idle after, your character will perform two delayed slashes made for hitting enemies as they recover. This deals a lot of damage and can cause enemies to stumble more than once. For even better damage, immediately follow the charged R2 with a massive impact transformation attack.

Transformed Mode R1

Transformed Mode R2

Transformed Mode Transform Attack

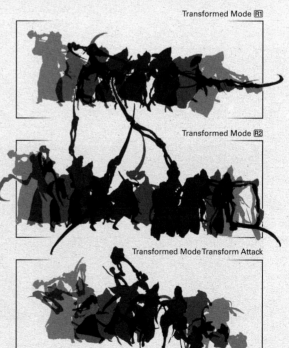

Kos Parasite (Milkweed Rune) OH

The Kos parasite has no requirements other than 20 arcane. It's a big investment, but this is a weapon intended for characters heavily focused on this stat and aiming to take advantage of its impressive scaling. When equipped, nothing will appear to change. This would lead many to assume that the weapon is useless; but this is far from the truth. The true power of the Kos Parasite is revealed when used in combination with the Milkweed Rune. The Kos Parasite is an arcane weapon in the purest of senses. All of its attacks deal solely in this damage type. On top of its already excellent scaling, its damage multipliers are usually close to, or even double the weapon's attack rating! Even so, you may have trouble dealing sufficient damage to enemies with high arcane defenses, or players using the Loch Shield, so this weapon is not ideal for all situations.

When the carcass of Kos washed up on the coast, its insides were teeming with tiny parasites, unlike any found in humans. The atypical weapon can only be clasped tight and swung, but a Kos Parasite is said to stimulate phantasms inhabiting a lumen-wood.

Gem Advice

The Kos Parasite is already an elemental weapon, so it can't be buffed with items or converted to another damage type with gems. Don't bother with Tempering gems as these will have little effect. Instead, think about increasing your arcane damage with Arcane and Odd Arcane gems.

The Kos Parasite uses a lot of stamina while transformed; especially if you are using evasive attacks, such as quickstep R1s. A way you can lessen this is by slotting radiant gems. If you often find yourself using the projectile vomit attack, you may want to consider slotting Murky gems to increase your poison build-up. Since this will add build-up to all of your attacks, you can poison.

Acquisition

Type	Obtained from	Reference	Bath Messenger Requirements
Normal	Defeat the Orphan of Kos in the Fishing Hamlet	p199	–
Uncanny	Chalice Dungeon treasures/ Chalice Dungeon rare shop	p668	Acquire Weapon
Lost		p668	Acquire Weapon

Available Gem Slots

Weapon Type	Weapon Level		
	1	3	6
Normal	Radial	Waning	Radial
Uncanny	Radial	Triangular	Waning
Lost	Radial	Triangular	Waning

Average Arcane Attack Increase (Arcane)

Stat Range	Damage per Point	Estimated Attack Gained
20 to 25	5.40	27
26 to 50	1.32	33
50 to 99	0.31	15

Note: this table represents growth with a +10 weapon

Damage from Upgrades

Weapon Level	Base ★	Scaling ★
0	30	D
1	33	D
2	36	D
3	39	D
4	42	D
5	45	D
6	48	D
7	51	D
8	54	D
9	57	D
10	60	C

Normal Mode Tactics

Attacks are slow in normal mode, and chain into each other at an equally sluggish pace. It's useful against enemies with low to no super armor, but can otherwise leave you open during attacks. Take note that its stamina use is much more reasonable in comparison to the transform mode. This only highlighted by the similar damage output between them.

Normal Mode Attacks Properties

Attack	Dmg ×	Type	Stamina	Impact	Note
R1	2.00		24	Normal	
↳ R1 (2nd)	2.10		24	Normal	
↳ R1 (3rd)	2.20		24	Normal	
R1 (backstep)	1.50		18 (+10)	Normal	projectile vomits forward; inflicts poison buildup
R1 (rolling)	1.00		0 (+10)	Normal	
R1 (rolling) (2nd hit)	1.70		18	Normal	second hit
R1 (frontstep)	1.00		0 (+10)	Normal	
R1 (frontstep) (2nd hit)	1.70		18	Normal	second hit
R1 (sidestep)	1.00		0 (+10)	Normal	
R1 (sidestep) (2nd hit)	1.70	Arcane	18	Normal	second hit
R1 (dash)	2.10		28 (+X)	Normal	
R2	2.35		40	Normal	
R2 (charged)	1.00		0	Normal	continuously hold the button to execute
R2 (charged) (2nd hit)	2.70		50	Heavy	
R2 (backstep)	2.20		32 (+10)	Heavy	
R2 (dash)	1.00		0 (+X)	Normal	
R2 (dash) (2nd hit)	2.35		44	Heavy	
R2 (forward leap)	2.45		50	Normal	tap forward on the stick just as you pres R2 to execute
Transform Attack	2.20		28 (+X)	Heavy	press L1 while performing another action to execute; forced Guard Break

Normal Mode Key Attacks

The Kos Parasite's R1 chain is slow with low reach. The first two hits swing horizontally, but aren't particularly wide or good against crowds. Really, you'll want to use the rolling and quickstep R1s for damage. These will send a wriggling tentacle a solid span forward, which hits multiple times. These attacks are useful for evasive play, which may be necessary against enemies with high super armor.

The backstep R1 will cause your character to projectile vomit forward. It will do relatively low damage on impact, but its main purpose is to poison enemies. This can be a bit impractical to use as it will usually land at the origin point of your backstep. However, by unlocking and angling the camera upwards, you can increase the distance your vomit travels!

A fully charged R2 takes a while to perform, but can stagger opponents from behind. It has pretty good range, so you can use it for sneaking up on enemies. On the other hand, its second hit can miss if you're not close enough, so you don't want to stand too far from your target.

Normal Mode R1

Normal Mode R2

Normal Mode Transform Attack

Transformed Mode Tactics

The Kos Parasite's attacks are much better in transform mode. While still quite slow, they receive a good increase in reach. One of the main downsides to using this mode is in its stamina to use. It lacks a charged R2, so you'll need to use the normal mode for to use rear visceral attacks. It also requires the use of both hands, so frontal visceral attacks are out the question as well.

Transformed Mode Attacks Properties

Attack	Dmg ×	Type	Stamina	Impact	Note
R1	2.10		28	Normal	
↳R1 (2nd)	2.10		28	Normal	
↳R1 (3rd)	2.35		28	Heavy	
R1 (backstep)	1.50		18 (+10)	Normal	projectile vomits forward; inflicts poison buildup
R1 (rolling)	2.05		22 (+10)	Normal	quick surprise attack
R1 (frontstep)	2.05		22 (+10)	Normal	
R1 (sidestep)	2.05		22 (+10)	Normal	
R1 (dash)	2.20		32 (+X)	Normal	
R2	2.50		56	Heavy	
R2 (backstep)	2.40	Arcane	44 (+10)	Heavy	
R2 (dash)	1.10		0 (+X)	Normal	good range and damage
R2 (dash) (2nd hit)	2.50		60	Heavy	second hit
R2 (forward leap)	2.50		56	Heavy	tap forward on the stick just as you pres R2 to execute
L2	0.90		100	Light	large area of affect attack; uses 2 bullets
L2 (2nd hit)	1.10		0	Light	second hit
L2 (3rd hit)	1.10		0	Light	third hit
L2 (4th hit)	3.20		0	Heavy	fourth hit
Transform Attack	2.00		24	Light	press L1 while performing another action to execute; forced Guard Break; shoots 15 projectiles

Transformed Mode Key Attacks

The R1 chain is much more useful this time around. The ranges of these attacks are increased in this mode, and the third hit finishes off with heavy impact. Rolling and quickstep R1s also see improvements in reach, but use more stamina and do less damage. You can still use the backstep R1 to vomit on enemies, but it costs a lot more stamina, so you're better off using this attack in normal mode.

The R2 is one of the best attacks you can use in this mode. On top of having great range, it strikes with high damage and massive impact. Although this consumes a lot of stamina, you can use its length to even further distance yourself for hit-and-run tactics. An even better attack you can use is the dashing R2; it has similar reach, does better damage, but requires more stamina. Since you need some space to get the dash going, it works best as an opening attack.

A single use of the L2 will do slightly more damage than a full R1 chain. This attack is a large, multi hit area of effect explosion that consumes two bullets when used. The start-up is slow, so you'll need to careful about when you use it, especially against foes with high super armor since they may continue attacks through the initial hits. Another thing to keep in mind is your bullet count. Without enough bullets, this attack will attempt and fail which can leave you wide open for a period of time.

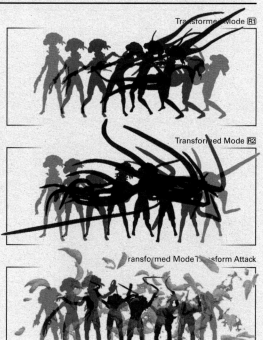

Transformed Mode R1

Transformed Mode R2

Transformed Mode Transform Attack

Left Hand Weapons

Hunter Pistol

Pistol made at the workshop, for hunters stalking beasts. Hunter firearms are specially crafted to employ Quicksilver Bullets fused with the wielder's own blood, boosting damage against beasts. The pistol is a quicker draw than the blunderbuss, allowing for speedier responses to attacks.

Required Stats

Strength	Skill	Bloodtinge
7	9	5

Basic Info

Found	Unlock in Shop	Circle Slot
One of two potential starting weapons	Saw Hunter Badge	Yes

Damage from Upgrades

Weapon Level	Base	Scaling
0	70	D
1	79	D
2	88	D
3	97	C
4	107	C
5	115	B
6	124	B
7	133	B
8	142	B
9	151	B
10	160	A

The Hunter Pistol is better than blunderbuss-type weapons at interrupting enemy attacks. It also deals better damage from range. Compared to the chief pistol alternative, the Evelyn, the Hunter Pistol has higher base damage but lower scaling. If your character has less than 20 bloodtinge, the Hunter Pistol is stronger than the Evelyn. At 21 points, they are equal in power. If your bloodtinge is 22 or higher, Evelyn is a better choice.

Hunter Pistol

Hunter Blunderbuss

Hunter Blunderbuss

A blunderbuss created at the workshop for the hunters' line of work. Hunter firearms are specially crafted to employ Quicksilver Bullets fused with the wielder's own blood, boosting damage against beasts. The impact of this highly-effective weapon counters beasts' swift movements, and its wide spread is nigh-on guaranteed to hit the mark.

Required Stats

Strength	Skill	Bloodtinge
7	9	5

Basic Info

Found	Unlock in Shop	Circle Slot
One of two potential starting weapons	Saw Hunter Badge	Yes

Damage from Upgrades

Weapon Level	Base	Scaling
0	20	D
1	22	C
2	25	C
3	27	B
4	30	B
5	32	B
6	35	B
7	37	A
8	40	A
9	42	A
10	45	A

Blunderbuss-type firearms do more damage than pistols when close to the target and less when farther away. The bullets spread out, making it easier to hit quick enemies. Blunderbuss shots also have a stronger impact than bullets fired from pistols. If you have 27 bloodtinge or less, Ludwig's Rifle is stronger than the Hunter Blunderbuss. From 28 to 32 bloodtinge their damage is the same, and from 33 bloodtinge onward the Hunter Blunderbuss is stronger.

Repeating Pistol

Ludwig's Rifle

Repeating Pistol

Repeating pistol typically used by Healing Church hunters. Crafted with mostly metal parts exhibiting a complex design, the repeating pistol fires two shots at once, making it a ravenous consumer of Quicksilver Bullets. Should be used sparingly compared to its workshop counterpart, as the trump card in one's arsenal.

Required Stats

Strength	Skill	Bloodtinge
10	11	8

Basic Info

Found	Unlock in Shop	Circle Slot
N / A	Sword Hunter Badge	Yes

The Repeating Pistol always does more damage than the Hunter Pistol and Evelyn, but it takes two bullets per shot. Its damage is comparable to that of the Hunter Blunderbuss, but it works from much farther away. The main drawback is the ammo consumption; this weapon is a worthy choice for using Bone Marrow Ash when you want to defeat an strong enemy from range.

Damage from Upgrades

Weapon Level	Base	Scaling
0	90	D
1	101	D
2	112	C
3	123	C
4	134	C
5	145	B
6	156	B
7	167	B
8	178	B
9	189	B
10	200	B

Ludwig's Rifle

A rifle typically used by Healing Church hunters. It is said that this rifle was employed by Ludwig, the first hunter of the Church. Its long, heavy barrel makes up in range for what it lacks in reload speed. Ludwig's Rifle exhibits several departures from the workshop's design, suggesting that the Church anticipated much larger inhuman beasts.

Required Stats

Strength	Skill	Bloodtinge
9	10	9

Basic Info

Found	Unlock in Shop	Circle Slot
N / A	Radiant Sword Hunter Badge	Yes

Ludwig's Rifle functions similarly to the Hunter Blunderbuss, but it has a longer range. The bullet spread reaches much farther and hits a very wide area, but the damage still doesn't match that of a pistol from range. If you have 27 bloodtinge or less, Ludwig's Rifle is stronger than the Hunter Blunderbuss. From 28 to 32 bloodtinge their damage is the same, and from 33 bloodtinge onward the Hunter Blunderbuss is stronger. If you want to shoot a spread-shot pattern from far away, though, this is the weapon for you.

Damage from Upgrades

Weapon Level	Base	Scaling
0	20	E
1	23	E
2	27	E
3	30	E
4	34	D
5	37	D
6	41	D
7	44	D
8	48	D
9	51	D
10	55	D

Evelyn

Special pistol used by Cainhurst knights. The Evelyn uses Quicksilver Bullets, just as any workshop firearm, but the Cainhurst variant relies more on blood-tinge. Lovingly named after a woman and graced with an intricate design, Evelyns were adored by Cainhurst knights.

Required Stats

Strength	Skill	Bloodtinge
9	11	18

Basic Info

Found	Unlock in Shop	Circle Slot
Cainhurst Castle [p109]	Cainhurst Badge	Yes

The Evelyn is almost identical to the Hunter Pistol. It's useful for ranged attacks and interrupting enemies. The Hunter Pistol has higher base damage but lower scaling. If your character has less than 20 bloodtinge, the Hunter Pistol is stronger than the Evelyn. At 21 points, they are equal in power. If your bloodtinge is 22 or higher, Evelyn is a better choice. The Repeating Pistol is stronger than both, but costs two bullets per shot.

Damage from Upgrades

Weapon Level	Base	Scaling
0	60	B
1	68	B
2	76	B
3	84	A
4	92	A
5	100	A
6	108	A
7	116	S
8	124	S
9	132	S
10	140	S

Cannon

Large prototype firearms fashioned by the workshop heretics, the Powder Kegs. Use of this weapon is equivalent to toting a mounted cannon, complete with its ridiculous weight, staggering kick, and lavish use of Quicksilver Bullets, into battle. Such a monstrosity was doomed from the start, and indeed its development was cut short. Yet, against impossibly gigantic foes, it might be just the thing.

Required Stats

Strength	Skill
30	13

Basic Info

Found	Unlock in Shop	Circle Slot
Forbidden Woods [p95]	Find Cannon to Unlock	No

The Cannon is capable of the strongest attacks in Bloodborne, but it consumes 12 Quicksilver Bullets per shot and has high stat requirements. If you are using a high strength character, this weapon is the ultimate perk. It does excellent damage, even from range, and it can be strengthened even further by using Bone Marrow Ash or attacking staggered enemies to deal double damage. This weapon is an absolute boss-killer; if you are struggling with an enemy, this weapon can be your last hope. Remember to make some Blood Bullets before firing each shot!

Damage from Upgrades

Weapon Level	Base	Scaling
0	200	E
1	240	E
2	280	E
3	320	E
4	360	E
5	400	E
6	440	E
7	480	D
8	520	D
9	560	D
10	600	D

Evelyn

Cannon

5

Flamesprayer

A special weapon used by certain members of the Healing Church. Spits searing flames by using blood-imbued Quicksilver Bullets as a special medium. Not the most efficient weapon by any stretch, but sometimes a sea of flame is just what the doctor ordered. Besides, the beasts of Yharnam can always use a good cleansing.

Required Stats

Skill	Arcane
10	8

Basic Info

Found	Unlock in Shop	Circle Slot
Gift from Gilbert [p635]	Radiant Sword Hunter Badge	No

Damage from Upgrades

Weapon Level	Base	Scaling ★
0	45	D
1	50	D
2	55	D
3	60	D
4	65	D
5	70	D
6	75	D
7	80	C
8	85	C
9	90	B
10	95	B

To use the Flamesprayer, you hold down L2 instead of pressing it, and a continuous stream of fire comes out. The fire covers a wide area in front of your character and can hit an enemy three times per bullet consumed. The damage scales with your arcane stat rather than bloodtinge. The damage is fire elemental, so hitting an enemy with an Oil Urn will roughly double the damage, but it only works on the first hit. Using Bone Marrow Ash will increase the damage for one Quicksilver Bullet (roughly three hits). Hitting an opponent who is staggered (either through interrupting an attack with gunfire or via a charged attack from behind) will deal double damage on the first hit only.

By combining the use of Oil Urns and Bone Marrow Ash and staggering the enemy, you can quickly deal thousands of points of damage with this weapon for the cost of two or three bullets. Thanks to this synergy, the Flamesprayer can be as powerful as the Cannon; it requires more effort to setup, but costs less bullets. Even without the stagger or the Oil Urn, using Bone Marrow Ash on the Flamesprayer can deal a lot of damage to enemies weak against fire or decimate a group of weak foes.

Flamesprayer

Rosmarinus

Rosmarinus

A special weapon used by the Choir, high-ranking members of the Healing Church. Sprays a cloud of sacred mist created by using blood-imbued Quicksilver Bullets as a special medium. Arias are heard wherever sacred mist is seen, proving that the mist is a heavenly blessing. "Oh, fair maiden, why is it that you weep?"

Required Stats

Skill	Arcane
8	8

Basic Info

Found	Unlock in Shop	Circle Slot
N/A	Cosmic Eye Watcher Badge	No

Damage from Upgrades

Weapon Level	Base ★	Scaling ★
0	30	B
1	35	B
2	40	B
3	45	B
4	50	A
5	55	A
6	60	A
7	65	A
8	70	S
9	75	S
10	80	S

The Rosmarinus functions just like the Flamesprayer, but it deals arcane damage instead of fire damage. As a result, its damage cannot be increased with the use of Oil Urns. On the other hand, it scales better with your arcane stat. Rosmarinus is good versus enemies that are weak against arcane damage. You can still use Bone Marrow Ash and staggers to boost the damage of the Rosmarinus, and it can provide a huge boost of damage for characters with a high arcane stat.

Hunter's Torch

A torch formed by wrapping a pine resin-drenched cloth around the end of a long stick. Once used in Old Yharnam. Designed to incinerate beasts and victims touched by the scourge. Its fire damage is highly effective against beasts.

Damage from Upgrades

Weapon Level	Base	Scaling
0	50	B
1	55	B
2	60	B
3	65	B
4	70	B
5	75	B
6	80	B
7	85	B
8	90	B
9	95	B
10	100	B

Required Stats

Strength
6

Basic Info

Found	Unlock in Shop	Circle Slot
Old Yharnam [p59]	Find Hunter's Torch to Unlock	No

Hunter's Torch

The Hunter's Torch serves as a light source in dark areas, but it can also be used to attack enemies. It deals fire damage; striking an enemy after hitting them with an Oil Urn will roughly double the damage of the hit. The damage scales with your arcane stat, and it can be helpful against enemies that are weak against fire if you don't have a stronger source of fire damage. Some enemies, such as beast patients, fear flame and will be less aggressive if you are using a Hunter's Torch.

Torch

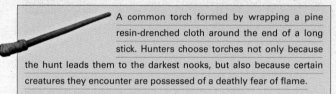

A common torch formed by wrapping a pine resin-drenched cloth around the end of a long stick. Hunters choose torches not only because the hunt leads them to the darkest nooks, but also because certain creatures they encounter are possessed of a deathly fear of flame.

Required Stats

Strength
6

Basic Info

Found	Unlock in Shop	Circle Slot
Central Yharnam [p37]	No Badge	No

The Torch is strictly inferior to the Hunter's Torch. It cannot be upgraded. It can be used to strike an enemy for fire damage, but the amount that it deals is very low. It should only be used as a light source and to scare enemies that fear flame. Replace it once you find the Hunter's Torch.

Torch

Wooden Shield

A crude wooden shield used by the masses who have arisen to join the hunt. Hunters do not normally employ shields, ineffectual against the strength of the beasts as they tend to be. Shields are nice, but not if they engender passivity.

Required Stats

Strength	Skill
8	8

Basic Info

Found	Unlock in Shop	Circle Slot
Cathedral Ward [p53]	No Badge	No

Simply put, the shield will not protect you from much at all. You can block attacks by holding L2, but each attack will still damage you. Each hit will also reduce your stamina; once your stamina hits zero, your guard will be broken and the enemy will hit be able to hit you. Worse still, you'll take additional damage if you are struck by the enemy while your guard is broken. To defend yourself in Bloodborne, learn to use the invincibility frames of your rolls and quicksteps!

Wooden Shield

Piercing Rifle  OH

A rifle engineered by the Oto Workshop, the precursor to the workshop of the heretical Powder Kegs. Designed for hunting on narrow streets, this rifle has been optimized to perforation wounds, but is unfit for reliably countering attacks.

Required Stats

Strength	Skill	Bloodtinge
9	10	9

Basic Info

Found	Unlock in Shop	Circle Slot
N/A	Firing Hammer Badge	Yes

The Piercing Rifle has higher base damage than most standard firearms, and great scaling to boot. The Evelyn's higher scaling will still beat in overall damage by a slight amount, but you won't need to invest nearly as many points into bloodtinge to be able to this weapon. This is good if you want to distribute your stats more evenly, but you'll still want to weigh your options since its recovery period is pretty drawn out. Its name is derived from its ability to pierce through enemies, which will allow you hit multiple targets in a line, making this especially useful against funneled crowds. As its description states, this weapon isn't particularly good for countering attacks, but it's still very possible.

Damage from Upgrades

Weapon Level	Base	Scaling
0	80	D
1	88	D
2	96	D
3	104	C
4	112	C
5	120	B
6	128	B
7	136	B
8	144	A
9	152	A
10	160	A

Piercing Rifle

Gatling Gun

Gatling Gun OH

This is a highly-customised, portable version of the stationary gatling gun operated by the old hunter Djura in Old Yharnam. It was the weapon of choice of the youngest of Djura's three companions. The Gatling Gun boasts exceptional rapid-firing functionality, but is considered a cumbersome weapon, due to its excessive weight and insatiable consumption of Quicksilver Bullets.

Required Stats

Strength	Skill
28	12

Basic Info

Found	Unlock in Shop	Circle Slot
Hunter's Nightmare [p168]	Find Gatling Gun to Unlock	Yes

The Gatling Gun takes a moment to start up, but fires rapidly once it does. It consumes Quicksilver Bullets quickly, but this isn't quite as bad as it seems, since you'll fire multiple shots per bullet. When you hit your target, only every few shots will actually deal damage. You can still move around while firing bullets, but only at walking speed. If you need to avoid something, it's better you roll or quickstep out of the way, rather than run or dash, since you'll otherwise need to wait for the weapon to be completely lowered. You can use Bone Marrow Ash on the Gatling Gun, but this won't affect its damage, so it's a waste of the item.

Damage from Upgrades

Weapon Level	Base	Scaling
0	80	E
1	90	E
2	100	E
3	110	E
4	120	E
5	130	E
6	140	B
7	150	D
8	160	D
9	170	D
10	180	D

Church Cannon  OH

An oversized weapon used by the Healing Church. A type of cannon that fires with a curved trajectory and creates an explosion upon impact. Originaly designed for use by brawny men with deteriorated brains, not just for any ordinary hunter. But the men lacked the wits to effective operate firearms, and the weapon was quietly ushered into permanent storage.

Damage from Upgrades

Weapon Level	Base	Scaling
0	160	E
1	192	E
2	224	E
3	256	E
4	288	D
5	320	D
6	352	D
7	384	D
8	416	D
9	448	D
10	480	D

Required Stats

Strength	Skill
27	16

Basic Info

Found	Unlock in Shop	Circle Slot
Hunter's Nightmare [p173]	Find Church Cannon to Unlock	No

The Church Cannon is quite similar to the Cannon, but with some key differences. Shots do not travel straight ahead a set distance before exploding. Instead, they launch in a curved trajectory and explode upon impact. You'll use 10 Quicksilver bullets for each shot, which is less than the Cannon, but you'll also deal less damage. This is still really good, since you'll be able to fire twice without equipping the Formless Oedon Rune. Though with this rune in combination with blood bullets, you can even shoot three times!

You can actually send shots much further than the Cannon's by aiming your camera upwards while firing. This isn't very practical to do in the middle of combat, however. Shots can fly over the heads of enemies and past them, and you won't be able to see if they've moved out of position. These things aside, it can still work as a handy pre-emptive attack from outside of an enemy's field of vision.

Fist of Gratia OH

A chunk of iron fitted with finger holes. The hulking hunter woman Simple Gratia, ever hopeless when handling hunter firearms, preferred to knock the lights out of beasts with this hunk of iron, which incidentally caused heavy stagger. Gratia was a fearsome hunter, and to onlookers, her unrelenting pummelling appeared oddly heroic. No wonder this weapon later assumed her name.

Damage from Upgrades

Weapon Level	Base	Scaling
0	60	D
1	67	C
2	74	C
3	81	B
4	88	B
5	95	B
6	102	B
7	109	A
8	116	A
9	123	A
10	140	A

Required Stats

Strength	Skill	Bloodtinge
7	8	5

Basic Info

Found	Unlock in Shop	Circle Slot
Hunter's Nightmare [p172]	Find Fist of Gratia to Unlock	No

The Fist of Gratia's main purpose isn't dealing great damage – it's to strip off massive amounts of enemy super armor in quick blows. Two hits alone from the Fist are generally enough to break the super armor of some of the sturdiest of foes. It works well with just about any weapon for this reason, but it compliments slower, heavier weapons best. These are usually weapons focused on strength, and the Fist of Gratia scales highly with this stat, which is another reason you'll want to pair them. If an enemy has too much super armor for you to continually stun, you can punch them with the Fist of Gratia. In combination with any super armor damage you've already dealt, it will usually cause your target to stumble instantly.

Loch Shield OH

An artisanal shield crafted with blue glass. Originally used to safeguard the leader presiding over a sacred Healing Church ceremony, and later supplied to tomb prospectors, in particular those exploring the labyrinth of Isz. The blue is fashioned after a lake, and the shield greatly reduces all forms of non-physical damage.

Required Stats

Strength	Skill
11	8

Basic Info

Found	Unlock in Shop	Circle Slot
Research Hall [p185]	Find Loch Shield to Unlock	No

Similar to the Wooden Shield, the Loch Shield does little to defend you from physical attacks. The Loch Shield's true purpose is to defend you from all other types of non-physical damage, which it does a tremendous job at. Holding L2 will bring the shield up to block attacks, but it will take off stamina while absorbing hits. Try to keep the shield up only when necessary, since you'll recover stamina by a much slower amount while defending. If you're not careful and run out of stamina while holding L2, your guard will be broken and you'll receive additional damage.

Healing Items

The following items are used primarily for healing yourself. Some restore HP while others remove status ailments. Some of them also offer other special benefits. Note that you can't have all of these at the same time; you'll need to make some difficult choices.

Blood Vial

Once a patient has had their blood ministered, a unique but common treatment in Yharnam, successive infusions recall the first, and are all the more invigorating for it. No surprise that most Yharnamites are heavy users of blood.

This standard healing item will heal 40% of your HP. It is permanently mapped to the ▲ button, so it doesn't need to be assigned to a spot in your quick inventory. You can hold up to 20 by default, but this number can be increased by equipping Communion runes; see p602 for more information. You can store up to 600 Blood Vials in the Hunter's Dream

Shop	○	◐	☾	○	NG+
Normal	180	360	540	720	900
Dungeon	–	690	1700	3500	5200
Rare Dungeon	–	860	2100	4300	6400

Iosefka's Blood Vial

Blood vial acquired from Iosefka's clinic. This refined blood, highly invigorating, restores a larger amount of HP. The product of a slow and careful refinement process, this rare blood vial appears to be a clinic original.

You can receive this item as a gift from the clinic doctor, Iosefka. Speak with her through the door early in the game to receive it. If you use it, you can speak to her again to get another one. After you defeat Gascoigne, an imposter will take over the clinic and turn Iosefka into a Celestial Emissary. Killing the "Iosefka" Emissary will give you one final vial. See p645 for more info on this quest.

When used, Iosefka's Blood Vial restores 70% of your HP. You can only hold one at a time, and it can't be stored. This precious vial gives you one large, extra heal. Make careful use of it, as after Iosefka is gone you'll not see many more until New Game+! Rest in peace, Iosefka.

Blood of Arianna

Blood taken from Arianna, Cathedral Ward woman of pleasure. The sweet blood of Arianna restores HP, and temporarily speeds stamina recovery. A member of the old Healing Church would know that her blood is similar indeed, to precisely what was once forbidden.

In order to acquire the Blood of Arianna, you must first rescue her from the Cathedral Ward and send her to Oedon Chapel. See p639 for the quest details. Speak to her in Oedon Chapel, and she'll offer you a vial of her blood. She won't give you one if you already have it or if you have the Blood of Adella; you have to choose which you want to use. You also cannot store this item.

The Blood of Arianna heals 25% of your HP and increases your stamina regeneration by a considerable amount! It only lasts for a few seconds, but it's very powerful when used tactically. If you use it just before staggering a boss, for example, you'll be able to do more damage while the boss is helpless. You can combine this with a weapon buff, like Bolt Paper, to squeeze out even more damage. It can also be very powerful in PvP. Sweet Arianna brings pleasure, indeed.

Iosefka will appear in the clinic after you've visited the Hunter's Dream for the first time.

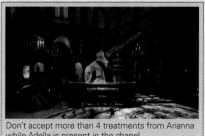

Don't accept more than 4 treatments from Arianna while Adella is present in the chapel.

Some areas have dangerous poison swamps.

Blood of Adella

Blood taken from Adella, the nun of the Healing Church. Restores an amount of HP, then continues to gradually restore HP for a short time. The Healing Church nuns are chosen for their merit as vessels of blood, and groomed as Blood Saints. The mere chance of being treated with their blood lends legitimacy to the Healing Church and communion.

In order to obtain the Blood of Adella, you must first rescue Adella from the Unseen Village and send her to Oedon Chapel. See p641 for more details. At Oedon Chapel, she will give you her blood. You can only hold one, though, and she won't give it to you if you have the Blood of Arianna. This item cannot be stored.

The Blood of Adella is a very useful defensive item. It heals you for 25% of your HP, and then it continues to gradually heal you for a few seconds. Of course this can help a lot in boss battles, but there are other really interesting situational uses, too. Chikage wielders can use this to offset the damage from transformed mode, for example. Another tactic is to use the Blood of Adella as a Blood Bullet generator; you can shoot all your Blood Bullets and create more several times while the Blood of Adella continues to heal you!

Antidote

Small medicinal tablets that counteract poison. Used to treat ashen blood, the baffling sickness that ravaged Old Yharnam long ago. These tablets only provide short-term relief. The ashen blood ailment eventually triggered the spread of the beastly scourge.

Antidotes remove poison build-up and heal the slow poisoning status. Whenever you are venturing into poisonous swamps or fighting enemies like the Blood-starved Beast, keep some equipped to your quick items and ready-to-use. You can hold 10 at one time, and you can keep 99 in storage. Always stock up!

Shop	○	◑	☾	○	NG+	Required Badge
Normal	300	600	1300	2300	2800	Sword Hunter Badge [p596]
Dungeon	–	870	1900	3300	4000	--
Rare Dungeon	–	1080	2300	4100	5000	--

Sedative

Liquid medicine concocted at Byrgenwerth. Calms the nerves. Those who delve into the arcane fall all-too-easily into madness, and thick human blood serves to calm the frayed nerves of these inquisitive minds. Naturally, this often leads to a reliance on blood ministration.

Sedatives reduce your Frenzy build-up. Once Frenzy builds up fully, you'll suffer 70% of your maximum HP in damage, which will often result in death. Worse still, Frenzy can continue to build up even after you escape from the source. Often, you'll need to use more than one Sedative over the course of a fight with enemies such as Winter Lanterns. You won't be able to buy them until late in the game, so save the Sedatives you find and make sure they're in your quick inventory slots when you need them!

Shop	○	◑	☾	○	NG+	Required Badge
Normal	600	1200	2600	4600	5600	Cosmic Eye Watcher Badge [p596]
Dungeon	1	1	1	1	1	Cosmic Eye Watcher Badge [p596]
Rare Dungeon	–	1300	2800	5000	6100	--

Blood of Adeline OH

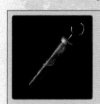
Blood taken from Adeline, patient of the research hall. Restores HP, then continues to rejuvenate HP for some time. Adeline was originally one of the Blood Saints who received treatment by the Church to cultivate worthy blood. Adeline's was one of the few cases that turned out favourably.

The Blood of Adeline will instantly restore 50% of your total HP upon use, and your HP will continue to regenerate gradually for 10 seconds after that. To acquire this blood you'll need to go to the Research Hall and give some Brain Fluid to Adeline in the Floor 1 Laboratory. For more information on this, refer to p654. Like other specialty blood items, you can only hold one of these at a time, and further requests will be denied until you have used the one you're holding. After giving the third Brain Fluid to Adeline you will be unable to receive any more of her blood, so if you're going for the Milkweed Rune, make sure to get a vial of her blood first or you'll have to wait until NG+.

Use an antidote before your poison meter fills up to avoid taking any damage.

Attack Items

The following items are used primarily for causing damage to the enemy. Some of them do have other uses, but the main purpose for Attack Items is to kill beasts, hunters, and anything else that gets in your way! These tend to be most helpful in the early parts of the game, but they also have tactical uses later.

Molotov Cocktail

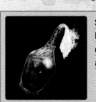

Since the tragedy that struck Old Yharnam, fire has become a staple in beast hunts, and is thought to cleanse impurity. Certain types of beasts have an abnormal fear of flame.

Damage Scaling	Strength D	Arcane A

When locked-on, Molotov Cocktails are thrown toward the enemy in a forward arc. When not locked-on, the Molotov will move in the direction your character is facing. The camera's orientation can also effect the height of the throw; you can use this to throw them over walls and other obstacles. For extra precision, you can use the Monocular for manual aim. Molotovs do 20 Armor Damage, so they can be used to setup a combo from a distance. You can hold 10 at one time.

When a Molotov strikes an enemy or a solid object, it explodes, causing fire damage. This fire damage is strongly influenced by your character's arcane stat. Molotov Cocktails are very useful against enemies that are weak against fire, such as Brainsuckers. They can be boosted by Oil Urns and do extra damage on counter-hits. They also receive a double damage bonus against staggered foes.

Early in the game, Molotov Cocktails are useful for defeating tough enemies like Scourge Beasts and the Cleric Beast. They have an area-of-effect, so they're great against enemy groups, too. They decrease in usefulness later in the game, but players with a high arcane stat can still use them to good effect against certain foes. The damage bonuses from Oil Urns and staggering an enemy stack, so with a high arcane stat it's possible to deal over 2000 damage with a single Molotov against an enemy with a fire weakness.

Shop	○	◗	☾	●	NG+	Required Badge
Normal	180	380	860	1600	2000	–
Dungeon	–	550	1200	2300	2900	–
Rare Dungeon	–	680	1500	2800	3600	–

Rope Molotov Cocktail

Since the tragedy that struck Old Yharnam, fire has become a staple in beast hunts, and is thought to cleanse impurity. Certain types of beasts have an abnormal fear of flame.

Damage Scaling	Strength D	Arcane A

In terms of damage, the Rope Molotov is identical to the normal Molotov; the difference is how it is thrown. Instead of tossing the Rope Molotov into the air, your character will drop it on the ground directly behind you. At first, this may seem like a negative as it can't be aimed, but Rope Molotovs are very useful. Do note, though, that locking-on to the target you want to hit doesn't work; these are much better when used unlocked. Rope Molotov damage is increased in the same ways normal Molotov damage is, so Oil Urns are still a good support item.

Many enemies and bosses will chase you very aggressively, and a Rope Molotov can be used to deal damage while running away. This applies in fights against other players, as well; if you are being chased, a Rope Molotov can send a strong message: "Back off, or die in a fire!" It creates a small area of effect, so you don't even need a direct hit. If you hit an enemy with an Oil Urn and then fake a retreat, you can catch them off guard with a burst of damage.

Rope Molotovs are also great when you are being surrounded; keep facing the biggest threat, and use one of these if another enemy approaches from behind. Another special feature of Rope Molotovs is that they are much faster to use than normal Molotovs. If, for example, a boss like Vicar Amelia is staggered, you can turn your back and spam Rope Molotovs very quickly. The key to using Rope Molotovs in general is to play without locking-on. You can hold 10 in your inventory.

Shop	○	◗	☾	●	NG+	Required Badge
Normal	190	400	900	1700	2100	Powder Keg Hunter Badge [p595]
Dungeon	–	580	1300	2400	3000	–
Rare Dungeon	–	720	1600	3000	3700	–

Throwing knives are effective from a distance against groups of weaker enemies.

Throwing Knife

Throwing knife with a finely-serrated blade. One of the old hunter Henryk's favourite weapons.

Damage Scaling	Strength D	Skill A

When you are locked-on, Throwing Knives are flung toward the target; when you aren't locked on, you can aim them manually. Your character's facing determines the direction and the camera position controls the height. You can also use the Monocular if you want to aim with greater precision, and can have up to 20 in your inventory at once.

Throwing Knives deal physical damage that scales with your strength and skill; they can deal counter-hit damage, and it's actually pretty easy to do thanks to their range. Some enemies take additional damage if you hit a specific weak point, like the heads of the Church Giants. Be careful, though; if you are too far away, the damage drops off.

Throwing Knives are useful in a variety of situations. You can use them to get one enemy's attention without alerting other nearby foes; this is great if you want to take it slow and fight one-on-one battles. Against powerful enemies that don't flinch easily, Throwing Knives can be used to setup a combo; they deal 20 Armor Damage per hit, so you can hit with a couple of knives before engaging to make sure the enemy will flinch or stumble. They also make a nice ranged weapon when you want to save your bullets. If you are faced with a swarm of weak enemies, you can use Throwing Knives to keep them at bay.

Shop	○	◗	☾	●	NG+	Required Badge
Normal	100	200	450	800	1000	Saw Hunter Badge [p595]
Dungeon	–	290	700	1200	1500	–
Rare Dungeon	–	360	800	1400	1800	–

Poison Knife

Often used for self-defence by special doctors in the Healing Church. They say that hunters traditionally avoid the use of poison, likely because the poison is too slow to act in the heat of the hunt.

Damage Scaling	Strength D	Skill

Poison Knives are very similar to Throwing Knives in how they are used. Their physical damage scales with strength and skill, and, while they are weaker than normal Throwing Knives, they cause poison to build up in the enemy. When enough poison builds up, the enemy begins to take damage over time from the Slow Poisoning status. You can hold up to 20 in your inventory. Each Poison Knife inflicts poison build-up on the target, but the amount is reduced by the enemy's poison resistance; some enemies need to be hit with more knives than others. When poisoned, the enemy will take damage over time. Once again, this can be reduced by the enemy's poison resistance; some enemies will take very little damage. Note that only the physical portion of the knives' damage scales; the poison damage is unaffected by your stats.

Against some strong enemies, these knives are a life-saver. Once an enemy is poisoned, you are free to dodge or run away without attacking while it dies. In co-op with another player, coordinating knife usage can be very useful; by throwing Poison Knives together, you can poison an enemy much more quickly. This can also be useful to in conjunction with a weapon slotted with Murky Gems; the combination will help you build up the poison effect both from range and in melee. In PvP, successfully poisoning another player will put pressure on them to use an Antidote or heal. This creates an opening for you to finish them off; keep up the pressure!

Shop	○	◗	☾	●	NG+	Required Badge
Normal	300	600	1300	2300	2800	Cosmic Eye Watcher Badge [p596]
Dungeon	–	870	1900	3300	4000	–
Rare Dungeon	–	1080	2300	4100	5000	–

5

Delayed Molotov `OH`

A special hunter tool crafted by the old Oto Workshop. These molotovs wedge into the ground when thrown, and explode on a timed delay. A shame that such a complex gadget must be sacrificed with each use of this inefficient hunter tool. Nevertheless, delayed molotovs are cherished by the minority of hunters who prefer the tricksier kill. This creation is one of the earliest-known roots of the Powder Kegs.

Damage Scaling	Strength D	Arcane A

Delayed Molotovs have the same damage scaling as normal Molotovs, inflict the same amount of damage when they hit, and deal fire damage. This means they also work well with arcane builds, but that is where their similarities end. When throwing a Delayed Molotov you will perform an underarm toss and the device will land a short distance in front of your character; you cannot increase this range regardless of how you angle your camera. Also unlike normal Molotovs, these do not explode on contact. Instead, once it makes contact with a surface a short two-second fuse is triggered, and only when that has expired will the device explode.

The fact that you always know exactly where they will go and don't have to worry about lining up a throw can work in your favor,

however. If you're locked onto an enemy and backing away from it, you can throw a Delayed Molotov so that the enemy walks into it and not have to worry about a normal Molotov getting thrown over them as the close in. It's worth remembering, however, that while these devices will stick to any normal surface, they will not stick to enemies. Their ability to stick to any surface does make them ideal for setting traps. Any time you know another player or enemy is about to round a corner or come through a doorway, you can attach one of these devices nearby to give them a nasty surprise.

Shop	○	◑	☾	●	NG+	Required Badge
Normal	270	570	1300	2400	3000	Firing Hammer Badge

They may be inefficient, but they get the job done.

Delayed Rope Molotov `OH`

A special hunter tool crafted by the old Oto Workshop. These molotovs wedge into the ground when thrown behind one's back, and explode on a timed delay. A shame that such a complex gadget must be sacrificed with each use of this inefficient hunter tool. Nevertheless, delayed molotovs are cherished by the minority of hunters who prefer the tricksier kill. This creation is one of the earliest-known roots of the Powder Kegs.

Damage Scaling	Strength D	Arcane A

Damage wise, the Rope version of the Delayed Molotov is exactly the same as the normal one, but their usage is quite different. Like traditional Rope Molotovs, instead of throwing them in front of you, these are dropped behind your character, only now when they hit the ground you have a short 1.5 second timer before the explosion. With normal Rope Molotovs you never really want to be locked on to your target, but because you now have a timer to work with, you can lock on, start moving away, drop one behind you, and then keep backing up past the explosion's radius safely. This new tactical avenue allows you to create a guessing game for any other player you are facing; by mixing up throwing normal Molotovs, Delayed Molotovs and Rope Molotovs while moving around it will be difficult for opponents to pin you down.

Where as normal Delayed Molotovs excel for setting traps where you are already in position and looking to ambush players coming after you, Delayed Rope Molotovs are better used as a means of deterring them from chasing you. Any time you round a corner or go through a doorway with a player close behind you, drop one of these once you're out of their sight; unsuspecting players that follow quickly behind you and get caught in the blast, and even if a player does realize what you're doing, they'll have to wait for the explosion, which gives you time to set up your next move.

Shop	○	◑	☾	●	NG+	Required Badge
Normal	290	600	1400	2600	3200	Firing Hammer Badge

Rope Molotovs are ideal for those with a short fuse...

Support Items

These items don't deal damage directly to your enemies, and they don't heal you, either. Don't let that fool you, though; there are countless situations in which Support Items are the difference between a difficult battle and an easy win. If you aren't using these items, you are playing Bloodborne the hard way.

Beast Blood Pellet

Large medicinal pellets, supposedly formed of coagulated beast blood. Banned by the Healing Church due to their unclear origin. Grants a spurt of beasthood. Ripping apart the flesh of one's enemies and being rained upon by their splattering blood invigorates one's sense of beasthood, feeding strength and euphoric feeling alike.

These pellets temporarily awaken your inner beast and increase your attack power for 60 seconds. While under their influence, each successive hit will build up your beast gauge. Your physical attack power will increase depending on how much you fill your beast gauge, but be warned that your defense will fall as well. There are six levels of attack bonus; check out the table.

Points in Beast Gauge	1 – 24	25 – 49	50 – 99	100 – 199	200 – 299	300 –
Physical Attack Power UP	1.2	1.3	1.4	1.5	1.6	1.7
Defense Power DOWN	0.8	0.7	0.6	0.5	0.4	0.2

Note that the maximum level you can reach is limited by your character's Beasthood stat. Equipping certain attire will increase it and having high Insight decreases it. If you want to maximize your Beasthood, you'll want to keep 0 Insight. Consider equipping the Ashen Hunter Garb – it has the highest Beasthood of any attire.

Having a high maximum doesn't help much if you can't fill your gauge, though. Attacks fill the gauge, but it automatically depletes over time. R1 attacks don't fill the gauge much; R2 attacks are generally better for this purpose. Multi-hit attacks also do well.

The best weapon in the game for filling the meter when using Beast Blood Pellets is Logarius' Wheel; the transformed mode's R2 attack fills the gauge very rapidly. The downside is that Beasthood only benefits physical attack power, while the Logarius' Wheel deals a lot of arcane damage. You can actually swap to another weapon after filling the gauge, though! You won't lose your Beasthood for swapping weapons if you used a pellet. Choose your favorite physical weapon and have it equipped in a quick-change slot.

You might think to use the Beast Claw in combination with the Beast Blood Pellets, but there is no benefit in doing so. The transformed state that enables you to increase your beast gauge does not stack with the pellets' effect. It is, however, worth using Radiant Gems to reduce the stamina costs of your attacks. The Anti-Clockwise Metamorphosis Rune to increase your stamina also helps. This will enable you to keep attacking and get as much damage out of your beast-state as possible. The Beast Runes also augment your transformed state.

Use these pellets whenever you want to do more damage and don't expect to be hit much; co-op with an NPC or another player is a perfect time to try them out. Let the other player get the boss's attention, and then let loose! The more you can attack, the better. Unleash the beast!

Shop	○	◓	☾	◑	NG+	Required Badge
Insight	2	2	2	2	2	Cosmic Eye Watcher Badge [p596]

Transformation attacks, R2 strikes and other heavy swings will fill your meter faster.

The transformed R2 attacks of Logarius' Wheel will fill your meter very quickly.

5

Blue Elixir

Dubious liquid medicine used in strange experiments conducted by high ministers of the Healing Church. A type of anesthetic that numbs the brain. Hunters, able to retain consciousness by force of will, make use of a secondary effect of the medicine, which dilutes their presence while standing still.

Drinking a Blue Elixir will render your character partially transparent for 30 seconds. During this time, it is harder for most enemies to see you. What this means is that you can get closer to them before they notice you and attack. Note that this only applies to your visual presence; the enemy can still hear you! If you run, fight, or do anything that makes a lot of sound, the enemy can still find you.

Blue Elixirs are very powerful against ranged enemies; they're usually far enough away that they can't hear you, so using an elixir will allow you to cover dangerous open ground quickly and sneak up on them. Huntsmen using rifles and Lost Giant Children are two examples. They also work against Wandering Nightmares, which is fantastic since they tend to run away as soon as they see you. Nightmare Frontier is one area where Blue Elixirs truly shine; they'll keep you hidden from the Lost Giant Children and let you capture Bloodstone Shards from the Wandering Nightmares. You'll find four in the Forbidden Woods; it's worth saving them for Nightmare Frontier!

Don't underestimate the effect of the elixirs in PvP; if you intend to hide, it can really help. If you stand in the right spot and use a Blue Elixir, your enemy might just walk right by...

Shop	○	◗	☾	○	NG+	Required Badge
Insight	2	2	2	2	2	Cosmic Eye Watcher Badge [p596]

Lead Elixir

A heavy, syrupy liquid medicine. Temporarily shifts weight to make deflection of attacks easier, but must be used with care, as it also slows movement with no change to defense. Its recipe for this mysterious concoction is unknown, but some postulate that it materializes only within the most desperate nightmares.

Drinking a Lead Elixir slows down your walking and running speeds, but it gives you a small amount of super armor. This means that you can take a light hit or two without flinching. Large hits will still cause you to flinch or stumble, and multiple consecutive hits will also break your super armor. You can, however, still roll and quickstep while this elixir is in effect. It lasts for 30 seconds, and you can only hold three at a time. The best use of this elixir is for users of slow, hard-hitting weapons. You can trade hits with a light enemy and break their super armor with your heavy weapon. As long as the enemy attack is weak, you can even get your health back via the regain system. This elixir can be especially useful for a heavy weapon user against light weapon users in PvP. Just beware the decreased movement speed; you won't be able to run away if something goes wrong, and you won't be able to catch your opponent if they flee.

Shop	○	◗	☾	○	NG+	Required Badge
Insight	2	2	2	2	2	Reach Blood Moon time

Lead Elixirs can also reduce the effects of knockdown attacks, causing you only to flinch or stumble instead.

Oil Urn

When this urn hits its mark, the target is drenched in oil, and made extremely flammable. Fire is commonplace on the hunt, and oil urns accentuate its effect. Sometimes, when hunters burn beasts, they appear intoxicated by the euphoria of purification.

When locked-on, Oil Urns are thrown toward the enemy in a forward arc. When not locked-on, the urn will move in the direction your character is facing. The camera's orientation can also effect the height of the throw; you can use this to throw them over walls and other obstacles. For extra precision, you can use the Monocular for manual aim. You can have a maximum of 10 in your inventory at once.

When an enemy is hit with an Oil Urn, it will take roughly double damage from the next fire-elemental attack that hits it. Used in conjunction with with the Flamesprayer or Molotovs, you can set up some extremely damaging combos. Fire damage from a weapon gem can be multiplied as well, but note that it doesn't work well with visceral attacks; the first hit of a visceral attack is extremely weak, and it will be the hit that is multiplied.

Shop	○	◗	☾	○	NG+	Required Badge
Normal	360	680	1360	2400	3000	Powder Keg Hunter Badge [p595]
Dungeon	–	960	2000	3500	4400	–
Rare Dungeon	–	1200	2400	4300	5400	–

Oil urns are most effective against stationary targets.

Pungent Blood Cocktail

Mature blood cocktail that releases a pungent odor when thrown that attracts blood-thirsty beasts. A precious tool in sadly short supply. In Yharnam, they produce more blood than alcohol, as the former is the more intoxicating.

When locked-on, Pungent Blood Cocktails are thrown toward the enemy in a forward arc. When not locked-on, the cocktail will move in the direction your character is facing. The camera's orientation can also effect the height of the throw; you can use this to throw them over walls and other obstacles. For extra precision, you can use the Monocular for manual aim. You can hold up to 10 at one time.

Pungent Blood Cocktails attract certain enemies, and they do so to the extent that the enemy will completely ignore you during its effect. It only last for a few seconds, but it's usually enough for you to either perform a deadly R1 combo or a charged R2 for a stagger. The best part is that these cocktails work on some of the strongest enemies in the game, including the Beast Claw wielding Hunter in Yahar'gul, Unseen Village (Blood Moon).

Shop	○	◑	☾	●	NG+	Required Badge
Normal	1000	2000	5000	10000	15000	Saw Hunter Badge [p595]
Insight	1	1	1	1	1	–
Rare Dungeon	–	3600	9000	18000	27000	–

Numbing Mist

Throw to create a mist cloud that numbs a hunter's life essence and prevents restoration of HP. Said to be used by the blood hunters of Cainhurst, its recipe is a secret closely guarded by the line of nobles inhabiting the castle.

Numbing Mist blocks healing effects. This is most useful in PvP; if you can hit an enemy player with this, they'll be unable to restore their HP using Blood Vials! It lasts an entire minute, too, so this is a very powerful item to use, whether early in a fight or after you've already done some damage. On the other hand, you obviously need to be careful not to get hit with one of these yourself.

This item also works against computer-controlled opponents; the most important of which are enemy Hunters and Vicar Amelia. You'll find six of them in the Cathedral Ward; use them wisely, since you'll need to acquire the Cainhurst Badge to be able to buy them. You can only hold 10 in your inventory. This is a valuable item, and you should think carefully about where and when you use it... and don't miss!

Shop	○	◑	☾	●	NG+	Required Badge
Insight	2	2	2	2	2	Cainhurst Badge [p596]

Pebble

Small pebbles found throughout Yharnam. Can be thrown at foes. Quite thrilling.

When locked-on, Pebbles are thrown toward the enemy in a forward arc. When not locked-on, the cocktail will move in the direction your character is facing. The camera's orientation can also effect the height of the throw; you can use this to throw them over walls and other obstacles. For extra precision, you can use the Monocular for manual aim. Don't underestimate this rock star! Throughout your journey, you'll constantly encounter large groups of foes, and they'll often patrol around. Sneak up behind the group slowly, and lock-on to one of the enemies in the back of the group. Then, throw a Pebble. This will get that enemy's attention without alerting his allies. In this fashion, you can fight the enemy one-on-one, rather than in large groups.

This trick doesn't work with gunfire; the sound of the shot alerts other enemies. Throwing Knives can be used for it, but they are better served as a source of ranged damage. Besides, you can hold 20 of these Pebbles; that's 20 enemies that you don't have to fight in a group! Just be mindful not to hit a gun-wielding enemy with a Pebble. They won't run to you; they'll just start shooting. Aim for a melee-only enemy, and then retreat back to safe location for an easy one-on-one fight. Thrilling, indeed!

Shop	○	◑	☾	●	NG+	Required Badge
Normal	10	10	10	10	10	–
Dungeon	–	2	2	2	2	–
Rare Dungeon	–	20	20	20	20	–

Pungent Blood Cocktails can buy you time to escape if you're out of healing items.

Numbing Mist will block the healing abilities of human players and NPCs alike.

5

Fire Paper

Coarse paper that applies fire to weapons when rubbed. A hunter tool found in the Healing Church workshop. Since the tragedy that struck Old Yharnam, fire has become a staple in the beast hunts, and is thought to cleanse impurity. Certain types of beasts have an abnormal fear of flame.

In general, Fire Paper is most useful against beast-type enemies.

When used, Fire Paper sets your weapon on fire. In addition to looking really cool, this adds 80 points of fire damage to every attack that you do. This is a flat 80 points; it doesn't matter how fast or slow, or strong or weak your attack is. Every attack gets 80 additional points of fire damage. This means that weapons that attack quickly and cost little stamina gain more benefit from Fire Paper than slow, stamina-expensive weapons do.

The Reiterpallasch is one good choice; it has fast, low-stamina attacks. More interestingly, the bullets it fires in transformed mode benefit from the paper! As a result, you can actually shoot fire damage bullets. The Threaded Cane and the Stake Driver are also good choices, as are the normal modes of the Kirkhammer and Ludwig's Holy Blade. You cannot use Fire Paper with the following weapons: Burial Blade, Blade of Mercy, Chikage, Rifle Spear, Tonitrus, and Logarius' Wheel. Weapons with elemental gems also cannot be used. Use Fire Paper on your weapon when you fight a tough enemy with low fire defense. Also take note that Oil Urns can boost the damage of Fire Paper, but each Oil Urn only works for one hit. This isn't a great use of Oil Urns; instead consider using Arianna's Blood for a stamina recovery boost. This will help you get the most out of your Fire Paper. Fire Paper's effect lasts for one minute, and you can hold 10 at once.

Shop	○	◐	☾	○	NG+	Required Badge
Normal	720	1720	4200	8400	12600	Radiant Sword Hunter Badge [p596]
Dungeon	1	1	1	1	1	Radiant Sword Hunter Badge [p596]
Rare Dungeon	–	3000	7500	15000	23000	–

If you suspect an ambush, try springing it from a safe distance with a pebble...

...because you never know what might be hiding in the shadows and smoke.

Bolt Paper

Coarse paper that applies bolt to weapons when rubbed. Invented by Archibald, the infamous eccentric of the Healing Church workshop. Artificially recreates the blue sparks that are said to surround darkbeasts. Unlike the other strange weapons created by Archibald, this one was favored by many hunters, in particular those who had even once laid eyes on a darkbeast.

Bolt Paper acts exactly the same as Fire Paper, with the only difference being that you'll get an increase of 80 bolt damage rather than fire. Weapons that are capable of doing a lot of hits in a short period of time will once again see the best increase in overall damage, because the additional damage will be applied to more hits.

You cannot use Bolt Paper with the following weapons: Burial Blade, Blade of Mercy, Chikage, Rifle Spear, Tonitrus, and Logarius' Wheel. Weapons with elemental gems also cannot be used.

Use Bolt Paper on your weapon when you fight a tough enemy with low bolt defense. Bolt Paper's effect lasts for one minute, and you can hold 10 at once. If you want to cancel the effect early for any reason, just quick swap to your other weapon and back. This cancels the effect, and is most useful when you want to rebuff your weapon; this gives you more control over when the effect fades. You don't want to run out of juice in the middle of a tough fight!

Shop	○	◐	☾	○	NG+	Required Badge
Normal	900	2100	5000	9600	14000	Spark Hunter Badge [p595]
Insight	1	1	1	1	1	Spark Hunter Badge [p595]
Rare Dungeon	–	3800	9000	17000	25000	–

Bolt Paper can give you an edge against enemies that take less damage from fire.

Bone Marrow Ash will also change the visual effects of ranged weapons and their fire, so if you're invaded by someone with a glowing Cannon, beware.

Shaman Bone Blades can turn even the most powerful enemies against each other.

Bone Marrow Ash

Additional medium that strengthens Quicksilver Bullets. According to the workshop, this is a special bone marrow ash collected from Hemwick Charnel Lane. Invaluable to hunters with weak bloodtinge who require the use of stronger firearms.

Bone Marrow Ash greatly increases the power of your next Quicksilver Bullet shot. It can only be used on your left-hand weapon; it won't apply to the shots fired by Reiterpallasch or the Rifle Spear. For weapons that hit multiple times per Quicksilver Bullet, like the Flamesprayer, the bonus is applied to all of the hits for the first bullet. Using Bone Marrow Ash on a strong weapon, like the Cannon or the Repeating Pistol, can result in very high damage. The most damaging single-hit attack in the game is done by using Bone Marrow Ash on a Cannon and shooting a staggered enemy; it can deal well over 4000 damage. Similar damage can be done with a Flamesprayer, Bone Marrow Ash, and an Oil Urn.

The main purpose of Bone Marrow Ash is to turn your sidearm into a damaging ranged weapon; guns are normally better-suited to interrupting enemy attacks than dealing serious damage. Bone Marrow changes that. You can only hold 10 at once, and it is worth staying fully-stocked at all times. For dangerous enemies such as Winter Lanterns, a couple of Bone Marrow Ash shots from a pistol or the Cannon from range will make your life a whole lot easier. This is invaluable to all hunters, whether they have weak bloodtinge or not!

Shop	○	◗	☾	●	NG+	Required Badge
Normal	320	740	1800	3600	5600	Radiant Sword Hunter Badge [p596]
Rare Dungeon	–	1300	3200	6500	10000	–

Shaman Bone Blade

A blade of bone coated with gruesome spinal fluid. Used by old labyrinth watchers, in particular, those presiding over rituals. When a victim is cut by this blade, the green spinal fluid temporarily numbs the senses, disturbing the target's gross motor skills. The blade, never intended for battle, must cut deep to be effective, and breaks.

When you use a Shaman Bone Blade, your character will perform a very short-ranged stab. If this stab hits a target, it will inflict confusion for a few seconds. While confused, the enemy will attack other enemies in their line of sight; even better, other foes will attack the confused enemy, as well! You can only hold three at a time; you have to be very careful when and where you use them, and you have to try not to miss! It works on most enemies, including some bosses. You can use it on ranged opponents, such as the Giant Lost Children, to have them attack other enemies from a distance. Another option is to use a Shaman Bone Blade on a strong enemy that is surrounded by weaker ones to make them gang up on the strong one – especially useful in dungeons.

The biggest challenge is actually hitting an enemy with the blade. There are three other items that can help a lot – Blue Elixirs, Lead Elixirs, and Pungent Blood Cocktails. If you are trying to confuse a ranged enemy into attacking its allies, use a Blue Elixir to get close with your Shaman Bone Blade. If you are trying to confuse a melee foe, the Lead Elixir can help you land the hit without being interrupted. You can also use Blood Cocktails to lure beasts away from their masters, hit them with a Shaman Bone Blade, and watch as they literally bite the hand that feeds!

Shop	○	◗	☾	●	NG+	Required Badge
Insight	1	1	1	1	1	Acquire Lower Pthumeru Chalice

Bold Hunter's Mark

Dangling, upside-down rune etched in the mind of a hunter. This reminder allows one to envision the rune with clarity. Allows a hunter to awaken again without losing Blood Echoes, a trick that seems nearly too good to be true.

Using a Bold Hunter's Mark will return you to the last Lamp that you rested it. You won't lose any Blood Echoes, either. This is really useful when you've died once and are having trouble getting back to your Blood Echoes, since dying again would make them disappear forever. It's also useful when you just want a shortcut back to the Hunter's Dream. The item takes around three seconds to use, so if you want to use it to escape combat you'll need to time it carefully.

Shop	○	◗	☾	●	NG+	Required Badge
Normal	400	800	1200	1200	1200	Sword Hunter Badge [p596]
Dungeon	–	1200	1700	1700	1700	–
Rare Dungeon	–	1400	2100	2100	2100	–

Shining Coins

Various coins that are particularly luminous. There are very few uses for spare change during the hunt, but these will serve as guides through the darkness. Or, one could save them until morning, if it ever comes.

When you use a Shining Coin, your character will drop it on the ground. The coin will sparkle faintly; the main use is to guide other players in co-op. If you get separated, having a coin trail to follow will let you regroup; just be warned that invading players can follow them as well! Even in single player, it's helpful to mark the paths you've taken in a labyrinth. Some of the later Chalice Dungeons are very large, so knowing where you've already been can save you some time. You can carry 99 of them at once, and they aren't expensive. Use them to keep from getting lost.

Shop	○	◖	☾	◗	NG+	Required Badge
Normal	20	20	20	20	20	Radiant Sword Hunter Badge [p596]
Dungeon	–	40	40	40	40	–
Rare Dungeon	–	100	100	100	100	–

Use the Monocular to target enemies' heads or other weak points with thrown weapons or gunfire.

Hand Lantern

Small portable lantern. This hunting accessory provides light while leaving both hands free to hold weapons. The torch, however, provides a stronger source of light.

Using the Hand Lantern will cause you to emit light until you use it again. The Torch is certainly brighter, but using the Hand Lantern ironically keeps your hands free to use other weapons. This item is reusable; you only need one. Anytime you are in the dark, you can use it for a little extra light.

Shop	○	◖	☾	◗	NG+	Required Badge
Normal	2000	2000	2000	2000	2000	Sword Hunter Badge [p596]

Monocular

Monocular used to view things up close. Not a hunter's tool, but a simple antique, to be used as one sees fit.

The Monocular can be found on the Yharnam Path in the Cathedral Ward (p51). There's only one, and it's infinitely reusable. Looking through the Monocular zooms the camera and places a crosshair on the screen. You can use this to aim firearms and items. Firearms can only be used from a short distance away, but this can let you aim at a specific weak point on an enemy. Items, on the other hand, can often be used from farther away; specifically, Throwing Knives and Poison Knives can be thrown from quite some distance. They'll do less physical damage from long range, but this doesn't matter much in the case of Poison Knives. You can't run while using the Monocular, but you can quickstep. To exit the Monocular view, you need to activate the item a second time, making it difficult to juggle back and forth between zooming in and using Throwing Knives. The best use of the Monocular is to examine the scenery for lore clues and beautiful vistas.

Tiny Music Box

A small music box received from a young Yharnam girl. Plays a song shared by her mother and father. Inside the lid is a small scrap of paper, perhaps an old message. Two names can be made out, however faintly. Viola and Gascoigne.

To get the Tiny Music Box, you need to speak to the Little Girl in Central Yharnam before fighting Gascoigne. Agree to search for her mother, and she'll give you the Tiny Music Box. See p642 for more details on this quest. The Tiny Music Box can be used during the Gascoigne boss fight to stun Gascoigne one time. It's best saved for his final form; check p328 for information on the fight. Rest in peace, Gascoigne...

Hunter's Mark

Dangling, upside-down rune etched in one's mind. Symbol of a hunter. By focusing all of one's thoughts on this rune, a hunter loses all Blood Echoes, but awakens fresh, as if it were all just a bad dream.

You begin the game with this item and can use it an unlimited number of times. It removes all of your Blood Echoes and sends you back to the last Lamp that you rested at. This is usually a fate worse than death, as you'll never be able to retrieve your Blood Echoes, whereas you have the opportunity to recover them if you simply die. It's better to use a Bold Hunter's Mark. An exception to this would be the times when you don't have many Blood Echoes and you just want a shortcut back to the Hunter's Dream; that's the only situation in which you are likely to use this. But the rune is etched into your very mind, and it will never leave you. You are a hunter, and a hunter must hunt.

Multiplayer Items

These items are strictly for use in online play. They control summoning, invading, and being summoned, as well as in-game messaging features. If you are playing offline, these items won't affect you.

Vileblood Register

Red-leather record of the Vilebloods loyal to the covenant of Annalise, Queen of the Vilebloods, as Cainhurst Castle. A record of the Vilebloods, blood-lusting hunters who seek blood dregs of their prey, kept throughout the ages.

When playing online, you can use this item to check the covenant standings of the Vilebloods. This is essentially a leaderboard system for Vileblood invasions. This is found as a treasure in Cainhurst Castle; check p109 for more details on finding this item.

Beckoning Bell

Great old bell discovered in the underground labyrinth. Its ring resonates across worlds, and the first hunter used it as a special signal to call hunters from other worlds to cross the gap and cooperate. A human must use Insight to ring this uncanny bell, but the benefits of cross-world cooperation are many.

By spending one point of Insight, you can ring this bell and attempt to summon allies. Having other players with you makes things easier, but this can only be done online. Also note that bosses will have additional health for every allied player that is with you when you enter the boss room; they'll have 50% additional health if you have one ally with you, and the boss's health will actually be double the normal value if you have two allies. You need to enter the Hunter's Dream with at least one point of Insight to acquire this item; a messenger will give it to you as a gift.

Small Resonant Bell

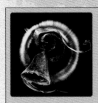

Small bell discovered in the old underground labyrinth. Its ring resonates across worlds, and the first hunter used it as a special signal to call hunters from other worlds to cross the gap and cooperate. This bell resonates with its counterpart, the Beckoning Bell. Ring to help hunters in other worlds.

By ringing this bell, you'll indicate that you wish to assist another hunter in their world. The game will perform matchmaking, and then you'll join another player's game as a guest. Help them defeat the area boss, and you'll be rewarded and sent back to your own world. This bell can be purchased from the Insight Shop for one point of Insight after you have acquired the Beckoning Bell. You need to gather 10 points of Insight before the Insight Shop will open, though!

Sinister Resonant Bell

A blood-stained bell discovered in the old underground labyrinth. One of the resonating bells that cross the gaps of worlds, but this one knells for misfortune and malice. The Sinister Bell is an object of dark thoughts. Ring it to become the enemy of a hunter in another world.

The Sinister Resonant Bell acts as the counterpoint to the Small Resonant Bell. When you ring it, rather than offering help to players in other worlds, you're signifying hostile intent and will join their game as an invader once a connection has been established. Once you ring the bell it will continuously look for someone to invade as long as you're in an area where invasion is possible. To acquire this bell you'll first need to have picked up the Beckoning Bell, after which you'll be able to purchase it from the Insight shop for 1 point of Insight.

Silencing Blank

Hunters are linked by the resonance of bells with special encoded timbres. This inaudible burst disrupts such resonance. Fire to end cooperation, and prevent further cooperation. Firing this does not disrupt the resonance of a sinister bell.

Using this item will allow you to send summoned allies back to their worlds. Be warned that this does not work on invading players – only friendly players will be sent home! You need to enter the Hunter's Dream with at least one point of Insight to acquire this item; a messenger will give it to you as a gift.

Notebook

Messengers are inhabitants of the dream who revere the brave hunters. Use them to send messages to other worlds. Leave notes with messengers, read the notes left by messengers in other worlds, and rate notes to participate in the formation of a shared inter-plane intelligence.

The Notebook will allow you to read and rate other player's messages as well as compose notes of your own. Perhaps you will warn hunters that follow of the perils ahead? Or maybe you intend to deceive them and lead them to an early demise? Don't worry; we won't judge. You receive the Notebook as a gift from the messengers in the Hunter's Dream; see p31 for more details.

5

Vermin OH

A centipede-like creature discovered on successful hunts by League hunters. Vermin, found hidden within filth, are only seen by League confederates, and are the root of man's impurity. The League has assumed the task of finding and crushing all vermin. Perhaps there is some mercy in the madness. Those who wish to see vermin can, and those who choose to are provided with boundless purpose.

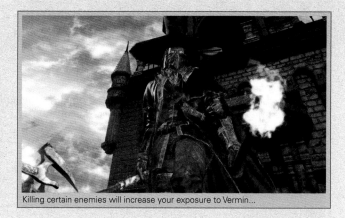

Killing certain enemies will increase your exposure to Vermin...

To obtain these insects you'll need to have the Impurity Oath Caryll Rune equipped to signify you are a member of the League, and then either complete a successful co-op session, or kill a boss while having a League NPC Summoned. There are also a couple of especially strong Old Hunters in the Hunter's Nightmare that will drop one once upon their death. While they do not give you any Blood Echoes or Insight, each one you use will raise your standing within the League, and for using five you can talk to Valtr and be recognized as the master of the League. You shouldn't stop there, however, because you can keep using more and check your standing within the League Staff to see who within the League is the best at dealing with filth. For more information on Valtr, please refer to the Hunter's Appendices chapter.

League Staff OH

Hides a directory listing the names of League confederates. The League staff is the sign of a confederate. A directory within the hilt lists the names of fellow confederates. Members of the League brandish this staff to indicate themselves to fellow members of the League. There shall be no sympathy for those engaged in the bloody mission of the League. No matter that an oath must be taken to uphold the illusion.

While playing online you can use the League Staff to check the ranking (determined by the number of Vermin they have used) of all confederates within the League. To acquire it you will need to talk to Valtr in the Forbidden Woods and join the League, and then after using one Vermin, talk to him again and he will give you the League Staff. Check p650 if you wish to find out more about Valtr.

Valtr is watching...Crush but a single Vermin to receive his approval and the League Staff.

Old Hunter Bell OH

One of the resonating bells that cross the gaps of worlds. This bell is cracked and stained with the blood of beasts. A human must expend Insight to ring this uncanny bell. The old hunters, who have long passed from the dream but cannot forget the feeling of the hunt, rely upon messengers to relay their thoughts. Ring the bell at their side, and they are certain to give a listen. For the night of the hunt is long, and unchanging.

After acquiring at least one point of Insight, if you return to the Hunter's Dream you'll be able to find the Old Hunter Bell at the top of the stairs just outside the Workshop, near where you acquire the Notebook. Once you have this item you'll be able to see the small glowing red pillars of light that indicate the point at which you can call upon the aid of Old Hunters. Attempting to summon an Old Hunter also requires a point of Insight, so if you do not have any you will be unable to summon them. The Old Hunters can be powerful allies and provide valuable assistance against tough enemies and even bosses, but remember that any summon points in an area will disappear once the boss of that area is defeated. For a list of the allies you can summon with this bell check p656.

The Old Hunter Bell is a welcome new addition.

Blood Echo Items

Blood Echo Items give you Blood Echoes to use as currency or experience when you use them. Whether you use them immediately for the boost they can give you or save them for the future is up to you; it is a good idea to keep a few around for weapon repairs, but in general you should use most of your stock after clearing an area. This will help you level up quickly.

Save your blood echo items for when you really need them, such as after repeated deaths or when you need just a few more echoes to afford a new piece of equipment.

Coldblood Dew

Hunters sustained by the dream gain strength from Blood Echoes. They imbibe the blood with thoughts of reverence, indeed gratitude, for their victims.

Rank	1	2	3
Echoes Granted	350	500	1000

Thick Coldblood

A strong will produces thick blood. Doubtless, the product of obsession, a potent source of human strength.

Rank	4	5	6
Echoes Granted	1200	1500	1800

Frenzied Coldblood

This manifestation of madness comes from a mind teetering on the very brink, but has a sane mind ever produced anything of true significance?

Rank	7	8	9
Echoes Granted	2000	3000	5000

Kin Coldblood

Coldblood of inhuman kin of the cosmos, brethren of the Great Ones. Dare not to delve into the world beyond humanity, the eldritch Truth touched upon long ago at Byrgenwerth.

Rank	10	11	12
Echoes Granted	8000	10000	20000

Great One Coldblood

Relic containing the Blood Echoes of a Great One. Use to gain cosmically nightmarish Blood Echoes. Like a true revelation, this uncanny relic defies understanding.

Echoes Granted	40000

Old Great One Coldblood

Relic containing the Blood Echoes of an old Great One. Use to gain cosmically nightmarish Blood Echoes. Like a true revelation, this uncanny relic defies understanding.

Echoes Granted	50000

Revered Great One Coldblood

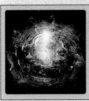

Relic containing the Blood Echoes of a revered Great One. Use to gain cosmically nightmarish Blood Echoes. Like a true revelation, this uncanny relic defies understanding.

Echoes Granted	100000

5

Arcane Items

The following items can only be used if you meet a certain arcane stat requirement. The requirement differs for each weapon. Additionally, these items can be reused over and over, but they cost Quicksilver Bullets each time. If you have an arcane build that uses elemental weapons, access to these items is a nice bonus.

Old Hunter Bone

The bone of an old hunter whose name is lost. It is said that he was an apprentice to old Gehrman, and a practitioner of the art of Quickening, a technique particular to the first hunters. It is most appropriate that hunters, carriers of the torch who are sustained by the dream, would tease an old art from his remains.

The Old Hunter Bone is found in the Healing Church Workshop [p71]. You need 15 points of arcane stat to use it, and it costs four bullets per use. It increases the speed of your rolling and quicksteps.

This does not increase the number of invincibility frames in your roll. It does, however, allow you to recover from a roll much more quickly; this means you can start another roll sooner. In that way, the Old Hunter Bone can actually provide you with more invincibility.

For example, let's say you roll three times without the Old Hunter Bone, and three times with its effect. The percentage of time that you spent invincible would be higher for when you used the Old Hunter Bone because there were less recovery frames in-between your rolls.

This also lets you recover more quickly and begin charging an R2 attack sooner. You can use this with a fast weapon, like the Saw Cleaver, to perform backstabs more reliably! If you combine this with the Oedon Writhe Rune, you can even regenerate some of the ammo you spend to use the Old Hunter Bone! Remember to make Blood Bullets often when using the Old Hunter Bone.

The Tiny Tonitrus is especially effective against multiple enemies.

Tiny Tonitrus

Tonitrus is a unique weapon crafted by Archibald, the infamous eccentric of the Healing Church workshop. This is a similar morning star mace that utilizes Quicksilver Bullets. When struck into the ground, it recreates the blue sparks that are said to surround the darkbeasts. Like Archibald's masterpiece, this too is a superb conductor of the powerful blue sparks.

Tiny Tonitrus requires 25 points of the arcane to use and costs 6 bullets each time you use it. It deals bolt damage and scales with an S rating in arcane. It fires a linear series of lightning bolts directly in front of you. This lightning can climb some small objects and will travel a fixed distance before stopping. You can find the Tiny Tonitrus in the Holding Cells area within Yahar'gul, Unseen Village (Blood Moon), which is on p132. The damage is pure bolt, so enemies weak against that element will take more damage than usual from Tiny Tonitrus. The best use of this item involves luring your foes into a narrow corridor or onto a narrow walkway; as they line up you can fire your spell and hit them all!

Since it has an S rating, the damage actually continues to increase noticeably all the way to 99 points of arcane. This can't be increased by gem effects such as Fool or Odd Bolt, however.

Empty Phantasm Shell

Empty invertebrate shell that is said to be a familiar of a Great One. The Healing Church has discovered a great variety of invertebrates, or phantasms, as they are called. Shells with slime still harbour arcane power, and can be rubbed on weapons to imbue them with their strength.

The Empty Phantasm Shell requires 15 arcane to be used and consumes three bullets with each use. It adds 80 points of arcane damage to each attack while it persists, and it lasts for one minute. To find it you'll need to venture up to the upper floors of the College Building in Byrgenwerth, which are on p127.

The main point here is that it adds exactly 80 points of damage to each individual attack. No matter how strong or weak your attack is, it adds 80 points. No more, and no less. This means that weapons that attack quickly and cost little stamina gain more benefit from Empty Phantasm Shell than slow, stamina-expensive weapons do.

The Reiterpallasch is one good choice; it has fast, low-stamina attacks. More interestingly, the bullets it fires in transformed mode benefit! As a result, you can actually shoot arcane damage bullets. The Threaded Cane and the Stake Driver are also good choices, as are the normal modes of the Kirkhammer and Ludwig's Holy Blade. You cannot use Empty Phantasm Shell with the following weapons: Burial Blade, Blade of Mercy, Chikage, Rifle Spear, Tonitrus, and Logarius' Wheel. Weapons with elemental gems also cannot be used.

Augur of Ebrietas

One of the secret rites of the Choir, high-ranking members of the Healing Church. Use spirits, the invertebrates known to be augurs of the Great Ones, to partially summon abandoned Ebrietas. One of the few rites that allow one to directly utilize the power of the Great Ones, and evidence that the Choir had approached the eldritch Truth.

Arcane Stat	Damage
18	299
25	336
50	483
99	660

Augur of Ebrietas requires 18 points in arcane to use; it summons forth giant tentacles from your hand that deal arcane damage. It only costs one bullet per use, and has an S rating in arcane scaling. Augur of Ebrietas also knocks down most enemies. Only the tip damages enemies; just the tip. This attack has a very long recovery. Augur of Ebrietas is found on the first floor of the Nightmare Lecture Building [p115].

The primary use of this spell is to knock down enemies, and it can be used to interrupt or stagger in the same manner as gunshots and charged attacks, respectively. You can use it to knock enemies into environmental hazards, like fires or pools of poison, or you can use it to let a co-op partner position themselves behind the enemy.

Augur of Ebrietas will send most human-sized enemies flying or knock them down.

A Call Beyond

One of the secret rites of the Choir. Long ago, the Healing Church used phantasms to reach a lofty plane of darkness, but failed to make contact with the outer reaches of the cosmos. The rite failed to achieve its intended purpose, but instead created a small exploding star, now a powerful part of the Choir's arsenal. At times, failure is the mother of invention.

Arcane Stat	Damage
40	264
50	321
99	494

A Call Beyond can be the most damaging magic item in the game with careful use. It is found in the Upper Cathedral Ward [p143], requires 40 points of arcane to use, and has S scaling in arcane. It consumes seven bullets per cast. When used, A Call Beyond creates a scattering of magical stars that fly away from your character. Each one that hits the enemy deals a chunk of pure arcane damage.

At first, this spell seems very hard to control, but most of the shots do actually home-in on your lock-on target. They travel along a very wide, arcing path, though, and they'll disappear if they hit an obstacle on the way. For this reason, it's best to use this spell in wide open spaces. Low ceilings will also interfere with your shots, so make sure you have vertical clearance as well.

Fortunately, most boss rooms have a wide open space where you can use this. You'll need to experiment to find the best distance to use it from. Generally, casting it from near maximum lock-on range produces the best results. It's also better against large enemies; once again, bosses are often good targets. It does take time to cast, though, so you may have an easier time using it in co-op.

The table shows how much arcane attack power each hit of A Call Beyond has. The trick is to connect with as many hits as possible for maximum damage! Hitting with up to six hits is not uncommon, so, while the number in the table is reduced by the enemy's arcane defense, single-target damage numbers higher than 2500 are possible with 99 points of arcane.

A Call Beyond has some homing capability, and is most effective at longer range.

Choir Bell

Special hunter tool of the Choir, high-ranking members of the church. Fashioned after a bell that projects an arcane sound across planes of existence. The sound of this smaller, silver version of the bell does not cross planes, but grants vigor and healing to all cooperators.

Arcane Stat	Healing
20	440
25	513
50	880
99	1200

The Choir Bell requires 20 points of arcane to cast and uses seven Quicksilver Bullets, but it may be the most powerful magic item in the game; it heals you and all nearby members of your team in co-op! It scales with an S in arcane and thus heals more HP when you have a higher arcane stat. It's found in the Chapel Rafters of Nightmare of Mensis [p157]. If you want to play the role of a dedicated healer in combat, use Runes that increase or replenish your Quicksilver Bullets, such as Formless Oedon and Oedon Writhe. Additionally, remember to make good use of Blood Bullets. Make Blood Bullets each time just before using the Choir Bell, and its effective cost will be three bullets! This lets you heal your entire team for only a few bullets, which you can then regenerate using Runes.

Beast Roar

One of the forbidden hunter tools made by Irreverent Izzy. Borrow the strength of the terrible undead darkbeasts, if only for a moment, to blast surrounding foes back with the force of a roaring beast. The indescribable sound is broadcast with the caster's own vocal cords, which begs the question, what terrible things lurk deep within the frames of men?

The Beast Roar can be found in the Forbidden Woods [p93]. This interesting item requires 15 points of arcane to use and costs two Quicksilver Bullets. It does no damage, but can knock down the enemy. In fact, it can knock down several enemies! It hits in a large sphere around your character. Beast Roar can be resisted by enemies with more than 20 points of super armor. In order to knock down such foes, you need to break their super armor with Beast Roar, but it only deals 20 points of super armor damage. You'll need to hit the enemy with other attacks to reduce their super armor to 20 or below before using Beast Roar.

As an example, using Beast Roar once by itself against a Huntsman's Minion will not cause a knockdown. If you hit the minion with a Saw Cleaver R1 first and then use Beast Roar, the minion will be knocked down. While Beast Roar can be used against big enemies, it really works best against small ones that have no super armor. Enemies knocked down by Beast Roar can collide with and knock down other enemies, too. Do note that they will have a short period of invincibility while they are down, though. This magic item is extremely deadly when used on narrow walkways and rafters. Pay attention to your surroundings at all times!

Use the Executioner Gloves at closer range while the enemy is unable to dodge.

The Beast Roar is most effective against lighter enemies with low super armor.

Executioner's Glove

One of the secret treasures hidden at Cainhurst. The gloves of an executioner from a faraway land. Passed from executioner father to executioner son, these gloves can be used to summon wrathful spirits of the past by smearing them with blood. It is said that the nobles found immeasurable delight in the dances of these vengeful specters.

Arcane Stat	Damage
20	116.5
25	146.75
50	298
99	430

Found in Cainhurst Castle [p110], the Executioner's Glove requires 20 points of arcane stat to use, and it costs three bullets. As with most of the spells, it scales with an S in arcane. In the table, you'll find the attack power values at various important break points of the arcane stat. Remember that this is before enemy defense is considered; the enemy would have to have zero arcane defense to hit these numbers.

Among all of the magic items, the Executioner's Glove might be the most straight-forward; it's a damage spell that fires three arcane skulls forward toward the enemy. In close range, all three can hit; farther away, usually only one will connect. This can be tricky to dodge by rolling sideways – it's better to dodge forward through the skulls using invincibility frames if you encounter this attack. The numbers shown in the table are per hit; you could deal up to three times those amounts if all of the skulls hit the enemy.

Messenger's Gift

A strange gift from the messengers, inhabitants of the dream who revere the brave hunters. Use to envelop oneself in a black nightmarish mist, then transform into a messenger. The illusion is a parlor trick, and any large movement will break the spell. To preserve the guise, proceed very slowly.

You can find the Messenger's Gift at the end of the Swampy Gorge in Nightmare Frontier [p123], and using it requires only a single bullet with an arcane stat of 10. It does no damage, doesn't heal you, and has no scaling. All it does is turn you into a message!

Well, it makes you look like one... as long as you don't make any large movements. If you try to run, roll, attack, or use an item, the effect will break. This spell is entirely for fooling other players online. Whether you are an invader setting up an ambush or a normal hunter hiding from the Vilebloods, this is the best camouflage you'll find in this nightmare.

The best way to use this message is to find an environmental effect, such as the clouds of smoke in Old Yharnam, and hide there. Behind tall grass, trees, and other objects are other potential hiding spots. Blind corners near stairs also work. The main point is to never rely solely on the disguise; use its low height to keep out of sight! Then again, sometimes there's refuge in audacity... hide yourself in the most visible location and pray! Be warned that alert players will not fall for this trick, but it can be useful when you are on the run. You never know when the other player's concentration might lapse and allow you a chance to disguise yourself.

Blackskye Eye OH

Soft eye blessed by a phantasm. They were discovered through Byrgenwerth's contact with the arcane, but in the end revealed nothing. Deep within the eye lies a vast stretch of dark sky that rumbles with an endless meteor storm. The slightest rub of the tiny orb, and the rock will tumble and soar.

Arcane Stat	Damage
16	237
25	276
50	396
99	540

To acquire the Blacksky Eye you will first need to give two Brain Fluids to Adeline in the Research Hall to get the Balcony Key. Once you have the key, go out onto the Balcony and you'll find this item on a corpse sitting in a chair among the lumenflowers. For more information on Adeline, please refer to p654.

With a requirement of only 16 arcane, you do not need to invest a lot to be able to use this attack, and it has a lot of qualities that can help fill gaps in your existing arsenal. Even with the minimum stat requirement it deals good damage, easily out-damaging most firearms unless they have been significantly upgraded, while still only using 1QS Bullet per shot. The S rank scaling it has also gives it decent damage growth should you invest more points into arcane. If you're locked on to an enemy that is either directly below or above you, this attack will compensate and still hit them, just like with firearms.

It also has slightly more range than firearms, so if you're facing another player in PvP that likes to keep you away with guns, you can use this to out-range them. While you can move during the initial part of the casting animation where your character puts their fingers to their temple, once the projectile actually starts to fire you'll be locked in place and unable to move for a short period of time. The extra range this attack provides can help offset the animation lock,

The Blackskye Eye will see to many a slain foe.

The Blackskye Eye is ideal for Arcane builds.

because if you're using it at maximum range, it's highly unlikely that another player could reach you before you can move again.

You can use it to knock down small enemies such as any of the Dog varieties. You cannot, however, interrupt an opponent with it. Another major benefit is the fact that it is practically silent, so it is an excellent alternative to a Pebble if you're looking to pull individual enemies out of groups. You can also use it to stealthily kill enemies without alerting others nearby to your presence.

Madaras Whistle OH

Whistle of the Madaras twins, denizens of the Forbidden Woods. The twins grew up alongside a poisonous snake, and developed a silent, inhuman kinship. The poisonous snake grew uncontrollably, raised on a healthy diet of beast entrails. Even after their deaths, it is said to respond to the call of the twins' whistle from within the Nightmare.

Bloodtinge Stat	Damage
18	444.5
25	541.5
50	1000
99	1400

The Madaras Whistle is held by one of the twins in the Forbidden Woods, so to get it you need to get him to appear and kill him for it. To do that you will first need to speak to Valtr in the Woods and Join the League to get the Impurity Caryll Rune, then after equipping that rune you will need to acquire a Vermin. Vermin can be acquired by partaking in a

Kill the Madaras Twin for his whistle.

successful co-op session, summoning a fellow Confederate of the League and killing a boss with them, or by killing one of the stronger Old Hunters in the Hunter's Nightmare. Once you have a Vermin, use it, and then return to the Woods and speak with Valtr again to

5

become recognized as a full member of the League. If you now leave the area via the Lamp and come straight back again, you'll find Younger Twin Madaras standing nearby with his back to you; kill him and he'll drop the Whistle for you.

Although the Whistle requires 18 bloodtinge, and uses bloodtinge for scaling, it still deals arcane Damage, so it's a great way for players with bloodtinge builds to inflict a lot of arcane damage. Upon blowing the whistle, a portal to the Nightmare opens beneath you, and shortly after that the head of a giant snake will come bursting up through it. The time between blowing the Whistle and the snake appearing is extremely small, and if you're not careful it's very easy to get hit by the snake yourself. This attack also has quite a small area of effect (not much bigger than the radius around your character), but up until the point that the snake starts to withdraw into the portal the attack is considered active, so make sure you don't move back into the area prematurely.

After blowing the Whistle you can avoid the snake by either walking in a straight line without stopping or changing directions, or alternatively you can Quickstep in any direction to be less predictable. The small radius and inherent danger for the user are offset by the speed and sheer amount of damage it's possible to inflict with this

Death from below...

attack. Anytime you're near a boss and only have a second or so to act, you can use this attack to inflict a large amount of damage quickly, and still have to evade as needed. Similarly it can be very good against aggressive enemies that relentlessly pursue you. Enemy Hunters often fall into this category, so you can wait for them to get close, blow the Whistle, and then Quickstep backwards away from them and watch as they get hit while trying to follow.

Accursed Brew OH

Skull of a local from the violated fishing village. The inside of the skull was forcibly searched for eyes, as evidenced by innumerable scratches and indentations. No wonder the skull became stewed in curses. They who offer baneful chants. Weep with them, as one in trance.

Arcane Stat	Damage
30	500
50	660
99	900

The Accursed Brew is held by the Fisher Priest near the entrance to the Fishing Hamlet [p190], but before he'll hand it over to you he must first recognize you as an ally. To accomplish this you'll need the Milkweed Caryll Rune, which you can get by giving three Brain Fluids to Adeline in the Research Hall. For more information on this, please refer to p654. Once you have the rune, equip it so that you take on the appearance of a Lumenwood, and then speak to the Fishing Hamlet Priest; after the conversation he will willingly hand over the Accursed Brew.

This item has quite a high requirement of 30 arcane, so using it will require a significant investment and it's only really recommended for full arcane builds. You will need 2 QS Bullets to use this attack, and once initiated, a skull will materialize in your character's hand, and then be thrown a short distance before exploding. The distance it travels before exploding is about half of your normal lock-on range, so you'll need to be quite close to your target when using it. As well as exploding automatically after traveling a short distance, the skull will also blow up upon contact with any surface or enemy. Because the skull is thrown straight it's much easier to hit targets than with other thrown weapons such as Molotovs. The large radius means that even should you not land a direct hit, you're still likely to hit your target.

The actual radius of the explosion is slightly smaller than it appears, so always take that into consideration when using it without locking

Equip the Milkweed Rune and the Fisher Priest will bear a gift.

The Accursed Brew is another welcome boon to those adept in the Arcane arts.

on to a target. With the correct spacing, however, this attack can be extremely effective at clearing corners that enemies are either hiding behind or are about to come around. Because the skull will detonate in mid-air, you can throw it past the corner of a wall or doorframe and have it blow up just on the other side, hitting any enemies that think they're safe behind the wall. It's also very effective against groups of enemies, since it's extremely easy to hit all of them with a single attack, and the relatively high damage to small QS Bullet ratio allows you to inflict a lot of damage with minimal resource usage.

Fortification Materials

These are some of most important items in the game when it comes to upgrading your character and attack power – do not underestimate the difference an upgraded weapon makes. It's actually worth planning your route through the game according to where you can find good supplies of Blood Stones, and make frequent trips back to the Hunter's Dream to use them.

Blood Stone Shard

A solid shard that forms in coldblood. After death, a substance in the blood hardens, and that which does not crystalize is called a blood stone. At the workshop, these bloodstones are embedded in weapons to fortify them.

Blood Stone Shards are used in fortifying your weapon up to +3, so they're one of the most important items you should aim to acquire in the early stages of the game. Some areas such as the Cathedral Ward have an abundance of them that you can pick up, with the Yharnam Path area being especially lucrative. Some enemies, such as the Large Huntsmen and Scourge Beasts in Central Yharnam, also have a chance to drop these items when killed, as do bosses in level 1 Chalice Dungeons. If you're looking to stock up on some of this item early in the game, you may want to spend some time hunting those enemies. Acquiring the Radiant Sword Hunter Badge [p596] will unlock them for purchase from the Bath Messenger for 2000 Blood Echoes, and once you advance time to night you'll also be able to purchase them from the Insight Trade for 1 Insight. Once you've unlocked them in the shops, it's worth using your Insight points to get them, so that you can conserve Blood Echoes for other things. If you find a weapon you want to use, it's worth using three Blood Stone Shards on it as soon as possible, because doing so unlocks a Blood Gem slot. With the addition of Blood Gems your weapon can gain incredible attack power boosts, so these first few upgrades using basic Blood Stone Shards are actually the most important of all.

Blood Rock

A solid shard that forms in coldblood. After death, a substance in the blood hardens, and that which does not crystalize is called a blood stone. This is no mere chunk, it is nearly a boulder. Few blood stones of such size have ever been discovered, even considering the combined experience of all the hunters.

Only two Blood Rocks can be picked up in the main game: one in the Nightmare of Mensis, and the other in the Fishing Hamlet; three others can also be acquired by opening large sarcophagus chests in each type of the depth 5 root Chalice Dungeons. Once you've picked those up, you're only other options are to try and get one to drop from depth 5 Chalice Dungeon bosses or, after defeating Mergo's Wet Nurse in the main game, you can also acquire them through Insight Trade for 60 Insight per Rock. Use this material on the weapon you use most often, and ideally on a weapon that benefits greatly from maximum attack power.

Twin Blood Stone Shards

A solid shard that forms in coldblood. After death, a substance in the blood hardens, and that which does not crystalize is called a blood stone. At the workshop, these bloodstones are embedded in weapons to fortify them.

Twin Blood Stone Shards are the material you'll need to fortify weapons up to +6, which you should start working towards after getting through the first couple of areas in the game. The earliest point you can reliably pick up some of these items is in Hemwick Charnel Lane, and then you'll be able to find an abundance of them in the Forbidden Woods. If you obtain the Cosmic Eye Watcher Badge [p596] this item will be added to the Bath Messenger's shop inventory at a cost of 10,000 Blood Echoes each, and once you've progressed far enough to advance the time to Blood Moon, you'll also be able to get them from the Insight Trade for 2 Insight. The Large Huntsmen and Church Giants in the Forbidden Woods have a good chance to drop them when killed, but you may also want to seek out the Lost Children of Antiquity in Forsaken Cainhurst Castle (or Kidnappers, especially those found in Chalice Dungeons), as they have higher drop rates. Alternatively, if you're venturing into depth 2-3 Chalice Dungeons, you may also get one of these as a drop from the bosses you defeat there. You'll be able to buy them from the Insight shop before you can get them from the Bath Messengers.

Blood Stone Chunk

A solid shard that forms in coldblood. After death, a substance in the blood hardens, and that which does not crystalize is called a blood stone. A chunk will never appear in the blood of an ordinary human. Seek deadlier foes if bloodstone chunks are needed.

You can never buy these highly coveted items from the Bath Messenger, but after defeating The One Reborn, you will be able to acquire them through Insight Trade at a cost of 20 each. When it comes to picking them up, the best area in the game is Yahar'gul Unseen Village (Blood Moon), but you'll also be able to find quite a few in the Nightmare of Mensis. The best enemies to hunt in order to get them are either the Church Giant on the Lecture Building 2F, or the Scourge Beasts in the Upper Cathedral Ward. Both of those enemies have the same drop rate, but since there are more Scourge Beasts, it's much more effective to go after them. Bosses in depth 3-4 Chalice Dungeons have the highest chance to drop this item, but since the drop rate is still quite low, however, you should do everything you can to increase your Discovery stat before going after them.

Gem Items

There are few precious and unique items you can acquire that will create preset Blood Gems when used. These can give you access to useful gem effects early in the game, and some are Droplet-shaped, which means they will work on any weapon type.

Red Jeweled Brooch

A woman's bright-red brooch, engraved with the name Viola. Perhaps this jewel is a gift from a hunter. Use to change into a droplet blood gem that fortifies any weapon. With the proper workshop tool, various weapons can be fortified.

You can pick this brooch up from the corpse of a woman in the Tomb of Oedon [p44], just after defeating Father Gascoigne. The woman's resting place is no mere coincidence; though the actual circumstances of her death remain a mystery. You can either use this item to obtain the Red Blood Gem, or give it to the Young Girl in Central Yharnam to confirm her mother's death. For more on this, see p642.

Gold Pendant

Pendant of Vicar Amelia. Use to change into a blood gem, which fortifies weapons. This pendant, passed down among vicars who head the Healing Church, is a reminder of the cautionary adage, words that will open the gates of Byrgenwerth.

You'll acquire this item by defeating Vicar Amelia in the Cathedral Ward [p55]. If you use it, you'll obtain the Gold Blood Gem, a radial gem that increases your attack power against beasts. There is no reason to keep this pendant, so you should use it to acquire the gem.

Tear Stone

Silver-shining tear stone. Use to change into a droplet blood gem that fortifies any weapon. A doll sheds neither blood nor tears, and thus its nature remains unknown. Whoever thinks this is precious must be troubled by severe naiveté.

You'll be given this item by the Doll if you talk to her after handing over the Small Hair Ornament. Its true significance is unknown, but there isn't any reason not to use it to acquire the Tear Blood Gem, which grants some very useful HP recovery. For more on her quest, please refer to p635.

Key Items

The items covered in this section are all very important either to progressing through the game or to reaching some of Bloodborne's more secret areas and rewards. Most of these items cannot be carried over to New Game +.

The Oedon Tomb Key opens the gate blocking the way to the Cathedral Ward.

Oedon Tomb Key

Key to the gate that blocks the Tomb of Oedon. Beyond the tomb, Oedon Chapel can be found in the center of the Cathedral Ward. Only today the church is abandoned, and some say that the residents of Oedon have all gone mad.

This key unlocks the gate blocking your way to the Cathedral Ward from the Central Yharnam sewers. It is held by Father Gascoigne and he won't give it up without a fight, so you'll have to defeat him in order to access the Cathedral Ward [p44].

Lunarium Key

Key to the lunarium facing the lake on the second floor of Byrgenwerth College. In his final years, Master Willem was fond of the lookout, and the rocking chair that he kept there for meditation. In the end, it is said, he left his secret with the lake.

You'll find this key lying on the corner of a shelf on the third floor of Byrgenwerth [p127] as you explore the observatory. It opens the door to the terrace on the second floor, allowing access to Provost Willem and the Moonside Lake.

You'll find the Lunarium Key on a lab table in the attic of Byrgenwerth.

Lecture Theatre Key

Key to the Lecture Theatre in the Lecture Building. Today, the two-story Lecture Building is adrift in the nightmare, but once it was a place of reflection, where scholars learned of history and archaeology. Perhaps it still is, as the students in the lecture theatre appear to await the return of their professor.

This key can be found on the professor's desk in the unlocked hall of the Lecture Building [p115], accessed via the first floor. It unlocks the other lecture theater across the hall and grants access to the adjoining laboratories.

Upper Cathedral Key

The key to the Upper Cathedral Ward seal. The upper echelons of the Healing Church are formed by the School of Mensis, based in the Unseen Village, and the Choir occupying the Upper Cathedral Ward. This key brings one a step closer to the Choir.

This key opens the locked door on the top floor of the Healing Church Workshop next to the treasure chest containing the Radiant Sword Hunter Badge. It can be found in the hands of a dead Choir member in the Holding Cells of Yahar'gul, Unseen Village (Blood Moon) (p132).

Orphanage Key

Key to the Orphanage, birthplace of the Choir. The Orphanage, shadowed by the Grand Cathedral, was a place of scholarship and experimentation, where young orphans became potent unseen thinkers for the Healing Church. The Choir, that would later split from the Healing Church, was a creation of the Orphanage.

You'll receive this key after killing one of the Brainsuckers behind a one-way door on the second floor of the Orphanage [p142]. It opens the building's front entrance on the first floor, providing both a shortcut back outside and access to an outdoor staircase leading to the area's boss.

To reach the Upper Cathedral Key, you'll need to drop through a broken railing in the area above.

The Orphanage Key is held by a Brainsucker on the other side of a locked door on the second floor.

Iron Door Key

Of the three great bridges that link the two cathedral cradles, this key opens the iron door that leads to the midlevel bridge. There are no thieves in the nightmare. Then, why lock a door? Be warned, there must be a very, very good reason.

You'll find this key on a corpse near the lower-most mirror during the second phase of the boss fight with Micolash [p155]. It unlocks a small side door in the library where the first phase of the battle occurs, but take heed of the warning – there is indeed an extremely good reason why this door is locked, and you'd be wise to bring a few Sedatives with you if you plan to open it.

Enter Iosefka's Clinic through the Forbidden Woods to acquire the Cainhurst Summons.

Don't forget to pick up the Unopened Summons from the desk to the right of Cainhurst's thrones.

Hunter Chief Emblem

A cloth emblem that belonged to the captain of the Church hunters long ago. Opens the main gate that leads to the round plaza of the Great Cathedral. The main gate is shut tight on nights of the hunt, and could only be opened from the other side with this emblem. In other words, the captain's return, and this emblem, determined the end of the hunt.

This cloth talisman will become available for purchase at the shop in the Hunter's Dream when you obtain the Sword Hunter Badge. You won't be able to get very far into the Cathedral Ward without the emblem, so you'll need to defeat the Cleric Beast and obtain the badge before you can access the Grand Cathedral or any of the connecting areas.

Cainhurst Summons

An old blood-stained summons, inviting an honoured guest to the forsaken Castle Cainhurst. Rather bafflingly, it is addressed to you. Do not hesitate; the stagecoach leaves from Hemwick crossing.

Found on the operating table where you first awake in Iosefka's Clinic after sneaking in through the Forbidden Woods [p102], having this item in your possession will trigger the appearance of a phantom stagecoach as you approach the large obelisk at Hemwick Crossing in Hemwick Charnel Lane [p78]. The stagecoach will take you to Cainhurst Castle, home of the vampiric aristocrats known as the Vilebloods.

Buy
Key Items

Hunter Chief Emblem
Key to the gate to the Grand Cathedral's round pla

The Hunter Chief Emblem will appear in the Bath Messengers' shop lineup when you obtain the Sword Hunter Badge.

Unopened Summons

An old, sealed summons. Like the first of its kind, it is an invitation to Cainhurst, but for whom is not known, as it lacks an addressee.

The Unopened Summons lies on a small desk to the right of Queen Annalise's throne in Cainhurst Castle [p113]. Giving it to Alfred will allow him to travel to Cainhurst, at which point he will slaughter the Queen and enable you to collect her flesh for offering at the Altar of Despair.

Small Hair Ornament

A small, very ordinary hair ornament. Although it has been lost for quite some time, one can still see signs of the care with which this tasteful ornament was once kept. Its colour would stand out most brilliantly against a head of greyish hair.

You'll find the Small Hair Ornament on a shelf in the Abandoned Old Workshop after making a very careful series of drops from the scaffolding above [p71]. Giving this item to the doll in the Hunter's Dream will allow you to obtain the Tear Stone, which can be used to create a Blood Gem with a powerful health regeneration effect.

Ring of Betrothal

The inhuman beings known as the Great Ones imbued this ring of betrothal with some special meaning. In the age of the Great Ones, wedlock was a blood contract, only permitted to those slated to bear a special child.

You'll find this ring in a large treasure chest on the second level of the Pthumerian Ihyll Chalice Dungeon. It can be offered to Queen Annalise in Cainhurst Castle for some extra dialogue, but serves no other purpose.

Queenly Flesh

What remains of Annalise, blood queen of Cainhurst. This pinkish lump of flesh remains warm, as if cursed. All hail the undying queen of blood!

You'll be able to obtain Queen Annalise's remains by examining her throne in Cainhurst Castle [p1136 after she has been killed by Alfred, or you've killed her yourself and reloaded the area. Offering this item to the Altar of Despair after defeating Ebrietas in the Upper Cathedral Ward will revive the queen.

Tonsil Stone

A latticed, deformed rock, or perhaps a meteorite. Appears useless, but possesses some odd gravitational force that prevents its riddance. A dubious soul once said: "Step lightly round to the right of the great cathedral, and seek an ancient, shrouded church... The gift of the godhead will grant you strength..."

You can receive the Tonsil Stone by talking to any residential NPC after entering the Forbidden Woods, the easiest one to reach, however, is in a house along the Village Outskirts in the Forbidden Woods [p93]. Having this item in your possession allows you to survive being grabbed by the False God at the entrance of Yahar'gul; its grab will instead teleport you to the first floor of the Lecture Building.

Yharnam Stone

A sacred heirloom left by Yharnam, Pthumerian Queen. The Queen lies dead, but her horrific consciousness is only asleep, and stirs in unsettling motions.

A trophy item obtained after defeating Queen Yharnam at the bottom of Pthumerian Ihyll, the Yharnam Stone serves no purpose other than as a testament to your victory...

The Small Hair Ornament is hidden in a cabinet in the Abandoned Old Workshop.

Short Ritual Root Chalice

One of the root chalices that breaks various seals in the Old Labyrinth. The glass chalice, when full, is used in a short ritual to quickly create and join a Chalice Dungeon (not for use in a ritual using standard materials). Short rituals are conducted at a makeshift altar.

You'll acquire the Short Ritual Root Chalice after defeating the Pthumerian Elder on the third level of the Lower Hintertomb. This chalice is an important online item required for using the Makeshift Altar in the Hunter's Dream, which allows for drop-in matchmaking in the Chalice Dungeons.

Messenger Top Hat

Hat that messengers are oddly fond of. A nice top hat rounds out any Yharnam gentleman. The inhabitants of the stump appear to have an interest in adornment. Why not let them be happy, and revel as babes?

The Messenger Top Hat is located on a broken beam in the lower section of the Healing Church Workshop and several careful drops from upper platforms are required in order to reach it [p71]. Giving it to the Stump Messengers in the Hunter's Dream will change their appearance.

Worn Messenger Top Hat

Hat that messengers are oddly fond of. For some reason, they prefer rumpled top hats to new ones. The inhabitants of the stump appear to have an interest in adornment. Why not let them be happy, and revel as babes?

The Worn Messenger Top Hat is a DLC item and will be added to your inventory at the beginning of them game when activated. Giving it to your messengers will alter their appearance.

You can obtain the Queenly Flesh by either helping Alfred reach Cainhurst or killing Queen Annalise yourself.

Black Messenger Hat

Hat that messengers are oddly fond of. Symbol of the preventative hunters of the Healing Church. The inhabitants of the stump appear to have an interest in adornment. Why not let them be happy, and revel as babes?

This item can be given to the Stump Messengers in the Hunter's Dream to change their appearance. You'll find it on a rooftop just outside the Oedon Chapel in the Cathedral Ward, accessed via a ladder behind the gate at the top of the nearby stairs [p53].

Once you've obtained an accessory for your messengers, examine the stump in the Hunter's Dream...

Yharnam Messenger Hat

Hat that messengers are oddly fond of. Commonly called a Yharnam hat. The inhabitants of the stump appear to have an interest in adornment. Why not let them be happy, and revel as babes?

The Yharnam Messenger Hat is a DLC item obtained at the start of the game when activated. Giving it to the Stump Messengers in the Hunter's Dream will change their appearance.

White Messenger Ribbon

White ribbon that messengers are oddly fond of. A ribbon made of fine lace that shines remarkably, more suited to pretty young girls than silly old messengers.

You'll receive this item at the house near the fountain in Central Yharnam upon conclusion of Gascoigne's daughter's quest [p39]. Giving it to the Stump Messengers in the Hunter's Dream will change their appearance accordingly.

Messenger Head Bandage

Accessory adored by naïve messengers imitating the bandages of scourge victims, unaware of their meaning. The inhabitants of the stump appear to have an interest in adornment. Why not let them be happy, and revel as babes?

This item can be given to the Stump Messengers in the Hunter's Dream to change their appearance. It is obtained as DLC and will be added to your inventory at the beginning of the game when activated.

Red Messenger Ribbon

Red ribbon that messengers are oddly fond of. The thick, pungent red was drawn from the organs of some unfortunate victim. A strange choice indeed, but perhaps for the messengers wearing this accessory constitutes a form of mourning.

This ribbon can be obtained from the Maneater Boar in the Central Yharnam sewers during Gascoigne's daughter's quest [p44]. You can either keep it to give to your messengers or return it to the girl's older sister in their house near the fountain in Central Yharnam.

Bloody Messenger Head Bandage

Accessory adored by naïve messengers imitating the bandages of scourge victims, unaware of their meaning. The spatters of blood give it a particularly nice touch. The inhabitants of the stump appear to have an interest in adornment. Why not let them be happy, and revel as babes?

Giving this item to the Stump Messengers in the Hunter's Dream will change their appearance. In order to obtain it, you'll need to carefully cross the rafters in the Old Yharnam church and drop to the scaffolding on the far side [p63].

Messenger Urn Dance

Accessory adored by naïve messengers. The messengers wear the urns, filled with incense that wards off beasts, on their heads upside-down, suggesting a predilection to the dark. The inhabitants of the stump appear to have an interest in adornment. Why not let them be happy, and revel as babes?

This item is found in the hands of a corpse on the upper level of the Oedon Chapel [p68]. To reach it, you'll need to ride the elevator to the Healing Church Workshop and step off just before it reaches the top, then follow the rooftops back into the chapel. Giving it to your messengers in the Hunter's Dream will comically alter their appearance.

Underground Cell Key OH

Key to the cell below the Grand Cathedral. Hunters are held within the underground cell, so that things better left unseen, and knowledge better left unknown, will decay quietly in the fallow darkness.

In a darkened room you will find the key.

This key will unlock the majority of the cells in the Underground Cell [p173] area towards the end of the Hunter's Nightmare, with the only exception being the Inner Chamber Cell. By opening those cells you'll be able to take on a fearsome Hunter and claim the Church Pick weapon from him, as well as free the tormented, Yamamura the Wanderer to get his Attire set. To acquire it you will need to make your way up to the Rafters of the Research Hall and activate the mechanism there to raise the staircases. Only then will you be able to reach Floor 3 – West Side [p185], where the key resides.

Balcony Key  OH

Key to the balcony on the first floor of the Research Hall. Lady Maria of the Astral Clocktower gave this to the patient, Adeline. Maria had hoped Adeline would find comfort in the faint breeze that carried the scent of flowers from the outside, but Adeline couldn't fathom her intentions.

Give two Brain Fluids to the Adeline to receive the Balcony Key.

To obtain this key you'll first need to offer a helping hand to Adeline in the Floor 1 Laboratory room of the Research Hall [p179]. You will need to give her two of the Brain Fluids that she wants, which will mean exploring some of the Research Hall to find them; the first can be found on a staircase landing between Floor 3 and 4 [p183], and the second one is on a beam in the Upper Rafters [p184]. For more information on Adeline's quest, please refer to p654.

Astral Clocktower Key  OH

Key to the Astral Clocktower at the top of the Grand Cathedral. The caretaker of the tower's numerous patients, known to them only as Lady Maria, made her home behind the giant star-interpreting clock.

Defeat the Living Failures for the key to the Astral Clocktower.

You'll automatically receive this key upon defeating the Living Failures boss towards the end of the Research Hall [p186]. Once you have it you'll be able to open the door to the Astral Clocktower that the boss was guarding.

5

Underground Cell Inner Chamber Key OH

Key to the inner chamber of the cell below the Grand Cathedral. The innermost chamber of the underground cell holds a lone madman. He wears a beast hide, and rings a bell that emits no sound. Unending death awaits those who can hear the soundless bell.

To open the final cell in the Underground Cell area you'll need to travel all the way to the Lighthouse Hut in the Fishing Hamlet [p194]. When you reach that area you'll find Simon on the ground just inside the hut, and if you speak with him twice he will drop this key along with his Bowblade. If you have never spoken with Simon, the key will be sitting on the floor near the lamp. Once you get inside the cell you'll be able to speak with and kill Brador if you wish, but make sure you get all of his Attire first, because you'll be unable to once he's dead.

Follow the Seeker of Secrets and he will trust you with this key.

Laurence's Skull OH

Skull of Laurence, first vicar of the Healing Church. In reality he became the first cleric beast, and his human skull only exists within the Nightmare. The skull is a symbol of Laurence's past, and what he failed to protect. He is destined to seek his skull, but even if he found it, it could never restore his memories.

Laurence's Skull is located on a hidden altar beneath the surgery altar in the Recovery Room; the same altar that acts as an elevator leading to the Research Hall [p173]. To reach it you will either need to enter the Recovery Room via the Balcony you can access from the 1st Floor Balcony in the Research Hall, or to access it earlier, walk onto the altar so that it goes up, and then run off before it gets too high. Once you have the skull, bring it to the Nightmare Grand Cathedral in the Hunter's Nightmare to face off against Laurence, the First Vicar.

Return Laurence's Skull to it's owner to do battle with him.

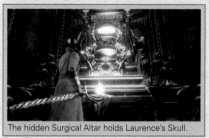

The hidden Surgical Altar holds Laurence's Skull.

Eye Pendant OH

An eye pendant which unlocks the surgery altar. There are two cathedrals in the Hunter's Dream. One lies past the River of Blood, and another contains the private research hall of the Healing Church. Only chosen members of the Healing Church, or their lamentable patients, can enter the research hall, using this eye. Grant eyes to the surgery altar skull.

The Eye Pendant is sitting on an altar at the back of the Nightmare Grand Cathedral in the Hunter's Nightmare [p167]. It is required to activate the surgery altar in the Recovery Room.

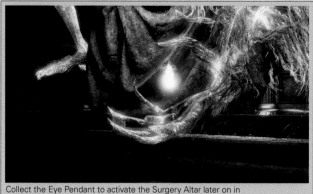

Collect the Eye Pendant to activate the Surgery Altar later on in the Recovery Room.

Celestial Dial OH

A celestial dial that functions with the giant Astral Clock in the Grand Cathedral. When the dial is held up towards the Astral Clock, the clock will come to life, and reveal a secret to its curious interloper.

After defeating Lady Maria of the Astral Clocktower, The Celestial Dial will appear on the floor near the entrance of the room you fight her in [p187]. Once you have it, walk over to the opposite end of the room to activate the mechanism and open the path to the Fishing Hamlet.

The Celestial Dial will open the path to the Fishing Hamlet.

Eye of a Blood-drunk Hunter OH

The eye of a blood-drunk hunter. Its pupil is collapsed and turned to mush, indicating the onset of the scourge of beasts. A hunter who goes drunk with blood is said to be taken by the Nightmare, destined to wander forever, engaged in an endless hunt. It is a fate that no hunter can escape.

You will need to acquire this item before you can enter the Hunter's Nightmare area, so getting it should be a high priority. To make it appear you will need to first progress through the main game until you have defeated Vicar Amelia in the Grand Cathedral and inspected the altar at the back of the room to advance time to Night. At that time you can return to the Hunter's Dream and you'll find this item at the base of the stairs, exactly where the Messengers gave you their gifts at the start of the game.

The Eye of a Blood-drunk Hunter will set you on the Old Hunter's path...

Brain Fluid OH

Greyish amoeba-shaped brain fluid. Wobbles and bounces. Extracted from a patient whose head expanded until that was all that they were. Once, a young girl had an older brother who was determined to become a doctor, and so she wilfully became his patient. In the end, this led to their encounter with the Eldritch Truth, for which they considered themselves blessed.

In the early days of the Healing Church, the Great Ones were linked to the ocean, and so the cerebral patients would imbibe water, and listen for the howl of the sea.

Brain fluid writhed inside the head, the initial makings of internal eyes.

We fail to realise our own latent potential, until the moment it is lost, and we sense its absence. Ironically, this is the very nature of insight, like the moment one licks one's own blood, only to be startled by its sweetness.

You can obtain three Brain Fluids in total, each of which can be given to Adeline for a different reward. Since they all come with slightly different descriptions, they're also worth obtaining for the lore insight they provide. The first Brain Fluid is found on a staircase landing between Floor 3 and 4 [p183], and to reach the second one you will need to go to the Upper Rafters [p184]. The third one can only be obtained from Adeline herself after having given her the first two. For more details on this, please refer to [p654].

Adeline craves Brain Fluid.

Each Brain Fluid tells a story.

Insight Items

Consuming one of these items increases your Insight. High levels of Insight decrease your Beasthood and make you more vulnerable to Frenzy, but Insight is a useful currency. You can use it to summon other players, or you can shop with it in the Insight Shop.

Madman's Knowledge

Skull of a madman touched by the wisdom of the Great Ones. Making contact with eldritch wisdom is a blessing, for even if it drives one mad, it allows one to serve a grander purpose, for posterity.

Insight Gained	1

Great One's Wisdom

Fragments of the lost wisdom of the Great Ones, beings that might be described as gods. At Byrgenwerth, Master Willem had an epiphany: "We are thinking on the basest of planes. What we need, are more eyes."

Insight Gained	2

...and your messengers will equip the headwear of your choice.

There are four umbilical cords in total, each obtained in different ways and places.

One Third of Umbilical Cord

One of the heirlooms used to contact the Great Ones, originating in the child of the Vilebloods. Long ago, in an encounter with the Great Ones, a contract was established, establishing the hunters and the Hunter's Dream. A great relic, also known as the Cord of the Eye. Every infant Great One has this precursor to the umbilical cord.

Every Great One loses its child, and then yearns for a surrogate. The Third Umbilical Cord precipitated the encounter with the pale moon, which beckoned the hunters and conceived the hunter's dream.

Every Great One loses its child, and then yearns for a surrogate, and Oedon, the formless Great One, is no different. To think, it was corrupted blood that began this eldritch liaison.

Every Great One loses its child, and then yearns for a surrogate. Provost Willem sought the Cord in order to elevate his being and thoughts to those of a Great One, by lining his brain with eyes.

Every Great One loses its child, and then yearns for a surrogate. This Cord granted the Mensis audience with Mergo, but resulted in the stillbirth of their brains.

Use to gain Insight and, so they say, eyes on the inside, although no one remembers what that truly entails.

Insight Gained	3

There are four versions of this item, and each one has a different description. In order to get the final ending, you must use at least three of the four before speaking with Gehrman by the big tree in the Hunter's Dream at the end of the game.

You can get One Third of Umbilical Cord from both Arianna's and Imposter Iosefka's quests, which you can read about on p639 and p646 respectively. Another can be picked up in the Healing Church Workshop (p71), and the final one is gained by defeating Mergo's Wet-nurse (p354). Remember: if you want to fight the true final boss, you need to acquire and use three of these in one playthrough.

Blood Dreg

The Vilebloods of Cainhurst, blood-lusting hunters, see these frightful things in coldblood. They often appear in the blood of echo fiends, that is to say, the blood of hunters. Queen Annalise partakes in these blood dregs offerings, so that she may one day bear the Child of Blood, the next Vileblood heir.

Insight Gained	1

Blood Dregs are vile things, coveted by Annalise, Vileblood Queen Annalise. To get them, equip the Corruption Caryll Rune and kill other hunters. You can find Annalise at the top of Cainhurst Castle, and, after kneeling before her, agree to give her these in exchange for her respect. You can also use them to gain one point of Insight, which is a good idea once you've already gotten the Deep Respect gesture from Annalise.

Badges

Badges are proof of your achievements and can be shown to the bath messengers in the Hunter's Dream to expand the shop inventory. You'll sometimes find these valuable relics on the bodies of the fallen, but you may also receive them from other hunters. Obtaining certain badges will add extremely useful and important items to the shop's lineup, so it's worth going out of your way to find them.

Saw Hunter Badge

Badge crafted long ago at the Workshop. Attests to one's prowess as a hunter of beasts. The Workshop is gone, and no group recognizes this meaningless badge, except the messengers in the bath, who understand its profundity. Certain things can only be entrusted with a hunter in possession of this badge, or so they believe.

Shop Items Unlocked	Hunter Axe, Threaded Cane, Saw Spear, Hunter Blunderbuss, Hunter Pistol, Throwing Knife, Pungent Blood Cocktail

You'll find this badge on a corpse beside the Maneater Boar in the Central Yharnam sewers [p44]. In addition to unlocking the basic hunter weapons at the shop, this badge will make Throwing Knives and Beast Blood Cocktails available for sale, providing you with a backup source of ranged attacks and an extremely helpful means of distracting beast-type enemies and hostile hunters.

Powder Keg Hunter Badge

Badge crafted by the Powder Kegs, the heretics of the Workshop. The Powder Kegs adoration of complex design and big booms culminated in weapon designs that contrast with those traditionally of the Workshop. The late Powder Kegs, bless their souls, had a motto: "If a weapon ain't got kick, it just ain't worth it."

Shop Items Unlocked	Rope Molotov Cocktail, Oil Urn, Rifle Spear, Stake Driver

This badge is obtained from Djura in Old Yharnam, but there are a couple of ways you can obtain it from him. If you go up his tower straight away and fight him, you'll automatically receive the badge upon his defeat. You can also come into Old Yharnam from the back by going through Yahar'gul, Unseen Village (Evening), and if you climb his tower without being seen he'll be friendly and you can talk to him; agree to not harm the beasts and he'll hand of the badge willingly. For full details on Djura, please refer to p648.

Old Hunter Badge

This hunter's badge, crafted in Gehrman's time, has no practical purpose, except perhaps to assist in romanticizing about the past. The badge was a special privilege for the hunters of the past, and should not be dishonored. It should be left in peace, unless one is truly prepared to assume the will of those gone before.

Shop Items Unlocked	Burial Blade, Gehrman's Hunter Cap, Gehrman's Hunter Garb, Gehrman's Hunter Trousers

You'll receive this badge after defeating Gehrman in the Hunter's Dream; you cannot obtains it early by attacking him prior to the final sequence of events at the base. To fight Gehrman, you must refuse his offer to behead you and end the nightmare; check [p160] for more information.

Crow Hunter Badge

Badge of a hunter of hunters, who hunts those who have become intoxicated by their bloodlust. The badge of the hunter of hunters is quietly passed down from generation to generation, usually to an outsider from the hinterlands. To be entrusted with this cursed badge, one must be strong, resilient to the seduction of blood, and gracious when taking a comrade's life.

Shop Items Unlocked	Blade of Mercy, Beak Mask, Crowfeather Garb, Crowfeather Manchettes, Crowfeather Trousers

This badge is held by Eileen and can be obtained either by killing her at any point during the hunt or completing her quest. For more information on her quest, check p636. It will add her attire, and more importantly her weapon, to the shop inventory.

Spark Hunter Badge

Badge crafted in secret by Archibald, the infamous eccentric of the Healing Church, for his friends. Archibald was fascinated by the blue sparks that emanate from the hides of the darkbeasts, and dedicated his life to its artificial reproduction, in a style of inquiry that, incidentally, closely followed the methodology of Byrgenwerth.

Shop Items Unlocked	Tonitrus, Bolt Paper
Insight Shop Items Unlocked	Bolt Paper

You'll receive this badge after defeating Darkbeast Paarl in the Unseen Village of Yahar'gul. Paarl is a tough foe if you fight him early in the game; check p334 for tips on the battle. If you are just after Tonitrus, you can pick one up from a corpse at the opposite end of Yahar'gul; there's no need to fight Paarl for it. The Spark Hunter Badge does give you access to Bolt Paper, though, which is quite useful, and you'll need to defeat Paarl to collect the Powder Keg Hunter Badge, as well.

5

Sword Hunter Badge

One of the badges crafted by the Healing Church. The silver sword is a symbol of a Church hunter. Ludwig was the first of many Healing Church hunters to come, many of whom were clerics. As it was, clerics transformed into the most hideous beasts.

Shop Items Unlocked	Kirkhammer, Repeating Pistol, Antidote, Bold Hunter's Mark, Hand Lantern, Hunter Chief Emblem

You'll acquire the Sword Hunter Badge after defeating the Cleric Beast in Central Yharnam; the strategy can be found on p326. It adds several useful items to the shop, including Antidotes; they will come in very handy in Old Yharnam, so you might want to face Cleric Beast before you challenge the old city.

Radiant Sword Hunter Badge

One of the badges crafted by the Healing Church. The radiant sword indicates the heirs to the will of Ludwig. These hunters, also known as Holy Blades, are what remains of an ancient line of heroes that date back to a very early age of honour and chivalry.

Shop Items Unlocked	Ludwig's Holy Blade, Ludwig's Rifle, Flamesprayer, Fire Paper, Bone Marrow Ash, Shining Coins, Bloodstone Shard, Tomb Prospector Hood, Tomb Prospector Garb, Tomb Prospector Gloves, Tomb Prospector Trousers
Insight Shop Items Unlocked	Fire Paper

This badge can be found in a treasure chest on the top floor of the Healing Church Workshop; it's just outside the door to the Upper Cathedral Ward [p69]. The Radiant Sword Hunter Badge is one of the most important badges to collect; obtaining it adds Bloodstone Shards to the shop's inventory, which will allow you to upgrade weapons easily. It also unlocks Fire Paper and Bone Marrow Ash; these are very useful support items.

Wheel Hunter Badge

Martyr Logarius led a band of executioners, and this badge was crafted at their dedicated workshop. The wheel symbolizes righteous destiny. Their workshop was a secretive enclave of mystical beliefs and heady fanaticism which served as the backbone of the Executioners' unique brand of justice.

Shop Items Unlocked	Logarius' Wheel, Gold Ardeo

The Wheel Hunter Badge is held by Alfred, the Church hunter encountered at the shrine leading to Old Yharnam, and can be obtained by giving him the Unopened Summons; see p644 for more information on his quest. Killing him in any location other than where you first meet him will also get you the badge, but you'll miss out on his quest.

Cosmic Eye Watcher Badge

Badge of a member of the Choir, elites of the Healing Church. The eye signifies the very cosmos. The Choir stumbled upon an epiphany, very suddenly and quite by accident. Here we stand, feet planted in the earth, but might the cosmos be very near us, only just above our heads?

Shop Items Unlocked	Rosmarinus, Poison Knife, Sedative, Twin Bloodstone Shards
Insight Shop Items Unlocked	Sedatives, Beast Blood Pellets

You'll find this badge on a corpse in the Orphanage of the Upper Cathedral Ward p142. Although you won't be able to reach it until very late, picking it up allows you to purchase Twin Bloodstone Shards from the shop. This will allow you to experiment with a wider variety of weapons. The Sedatives it unlocks are also useful, as any hunter who has stared down a Winter Lantern should know!

Cainhurst Badge

Badge of the royal guards of Cainhurst, loyal guardians of the Vileblood Queen Annalise. The Vilebloods are hunters of blood, and hunt prey as they search for blood dregs. The hunter who joins them is faced with a decision: to merely borrow their strength, or to become one of them, heart and soul.

Shop Items Unlocked	Reiterpallasch, Chikage, Evelyn, Cainhurst Helmet, Cainhurst Armor, Cainhurst Gauntlets, Cainhurst Leggings
Insight Shop Items Unlocked	Numbing Mist

To obtain the Cainhurst Badge, you must speak with Queen Annalise of Cainhurst Castle and swear an oath to the Vilebloods. To learn more about the Vileblood quest, check out the section on Annalise on p647. Acquiring this badge allows you to purchase the Vileblood weapons and armor and adds Numbing Mist to the Insight shop's inventory.

Firing Hammer Badge OH

Badge crafted by the Oto Workshop, precursor to the workshop of the heretical Powder Kegs. The Powder Kegs were driven by singular ideas, and crafted strange weapons of great intricacy. It is clear that the philosophy of the Powder Kegs was already established at this time.

Shop Items Unlocked	Delayed Molotov, Rope Delayed Molotov, Piercing rifle

This badge is held by the Bestial Hunter in the Hunter's Nightmare (p26). In order to obtain it you'll need to defeat him first. Although the badge does not add many items to your shop lineup, if you're a Trophy hunter or a completionist it's still quite important, because it's the only way you can gain access to the Piercing Rifle.

Caryll Runes

Caryll Runes are special items that you can attach to your character at the workshop in the Hunter's Dream. You can use up to four at one time, and they provide a variety of very helpful effects. Use them tactically depending on the environments you plan to explore and the enemies you expect to face.

Rune Workshop Tool

Before you can make use of Runes, you'll need the Rune Workshop Tool. This is found in Hemwick after defeating the Witch of Hemwick. Check out p605 for more on this tool, and refer to p79 to find it in the Hemwick area guide. After you have the tool, approach the Memory Altar in the Workshop and press ⊗ to equip Runes in your memory slots.

You have three normal Memory Slots four basic runes, and a fourth "Oath Memory" slot. The basic runes are for use with normal Caryll Runes, and the Oath Memory slot is for Oath Runes only. Some runes have up to three different ranks, with higher ranked runes having more powerful effects. Try to collect the most powerful versions!

After finding the Rune Workshop Tool, examine the Memory Altar in the Hunter's Dream to equip runes.

You'll find a Clockwise Metamorphosis rune in the Nightmare Frontier just beneath Patches' perch.

Caryll Runes

This section lists every possible Caryll Rune, along with the different ranks and their effects. You'll also find some guidance on where they can be found.

Moon

A secret symbol left by Caryll, runesmith of Byrgenwerth. A transcription of "moon," as spoken by the Great Ones inhabiting the nightmare. Gain more Blood Echoes. The Great Ones that inhabit the nightmare are sympathetic in spirit, and often answer when called upon.

Moon Runes grant more Blood Echoes from defeating enemies. If you want to level up or purchase a lot of consumable items from the shop, these Runes are very helpful. They don't grant any bonuses in combat, however, so only use Moon Runes when you don't need the boost that other Runes can give.

Effect	Acquired from
Echoes from defeated foes up +10%	Yahar'gul [p83]
Echoes from defeated foes up +20%	Nightmare of Mensis [p155]
Echoes from defeated foes up +30%	Brain of Mensis [p293]

Eye

A secret symbol left by Caryll, runesmith of Byrgenwerth. A transcription of "eye," as spoken by left-behind Great Ones. Allows one to make additional discoveries. Eyes symbolize the truth Master Willem sought in his research. Disillusioned by the limits of human intellect, Master Willem looked to beings from higher planes for guidance, and sought to line his brain with eyes in order to elevate his thoughts.

Eye Runes increase your Discovery stat. This will allow you to find more items from defeated foes. If you find yourself running out of Blood Vials and Quicksilver Bullets in long Chalice Dungeons, Eye Runes can help you stock up when scavenging from the corpses of your enemies. They don't grant any bonuses in combat, however, so only use Eye Runes when you don't need the boost that other Runes can give.

Effect	Acquired from
Increased Discovery (Level 1)	Nightmare of Mensis [p155]
Increased Discovery (Level 2)	Provost Willem [p640]
Increased Discovery (Level 3)	Depth 5 Isz Root Dungeon Treasure

5

Clockwise Metamorphosis

A secret symbol left by Caryll, runesmith of Byrgenwerth. The twisted cross means "metamorphosis." Rotated clockwise, this rune boosts HP. The discovery of blood made their dream of evolution a reality. Metamorphosis, and the excesses and deviation that followed, were only the beginning.

Clockwise Metamorphosis increases your maximum HP. If you can't decide what Rune you want to use, this is an excellent generic choice. It'll help keep you alive! Max HP increases are extremely valuable in Bloodborne, as the Regain mechanic is only useful when you are able to take damage without dying. If the enemy kills you in one or two hits, you won't have the chance to Regain health at all!

Effect	Acquired from
Max HP + 5%	Forbidden Woods [p99]
Max HP +10%	Nightmare Frontier [p122]
Max HP + 15%	Depth 5 Pthumeru Root Dungeon Treasure

To acquire the level 3 Blood Rapture Rune, you'll need to meet up with Eileen at the Grand Cathedral during the Blood Moon after helping her defeat Henryk. Eileen's final opponent will drop the rune when defeated.

Anti-Clockwise Metamorphosis

A secret symbol left by Caryll, runesmith of Byrgenwerth. The twisted cross means "metamorphosis." Rotated anti-clockwise, this rune boosts stamina. The discovery of blood made their dream of evolution a reality. Metamorphosis, and the excesses and deviation that followed, were only the beginning.

Anti-Clockwise Metamorphosis boosts your maximum stamina. Whereas Clockwise Metamorphosis can be viewed as the default defensive Rune, this is the default offensive Rune. Having more stamina allows you to execute longer attack strings without retreating, and it's more useful for users of weapons with high-stamina costs. If you like weapons such as the Hunter Axe and Logarius' Wheel, for example, Anti-Clockwise Metamorphosis can be a huge boon!

Effect	Acquired from
Max Stamina + 10%	Forbidden Woods [p99]
Max Stamina + 15%	Patches the Spider [p649]
Max Stamina + 20%	Depth 5 Loran Root Dungeon Treasure

Clawmark

A Caryll rune that transcribes inhuman sounds. The "Clawmark" is an impulse to seek the warmth of blood like a beast. It strengthens visceral attacks, one of the darker hunter techniques. Although the difference is subtle, Runesmith Caryll describes the "Beast" as a horrific and unwelcome instinct deep within the hearts of men, while "Clawmark" is an alluring invitation to accept this very nature.

The Clawmark Rune increases the damage of your Visceral attacks. Given that staggered foes already take double damage from other attacks, it isn't always particularly useful. The main benefits of Visceral attacks are the knockback that they can cause and the invincibility frames that they give you. In a crowd of foes, they are a lot safer than performing a normal attack as a follow-up. If you are using other Runes to augment your Visceral attacks, Clawmark could be a helpful bonus.

Visceral attacks do good damage if your weapon isn't upgraded much or if your stats are still low. Once you have a maxed out weapon and appropriate stats, they tend to under-perform. They are, however, affected by damage multipliers like the Fool and Poorman gem effects, so using a Clawmark Rune can give them respectable damage with the correct gem effects. If you just want to deal a lot of damage but don't want to give up the Rune slots, consider using other attacks to follow up on a stagger instead.

Effect	Acquired from
Visceral attack power + 10%	Drop from Yahar'gul Hunter (Beast Claw) [p317]
Visceral attack power + 20%	Gilbert's Quest [p635]
Visceral attack power + 30%	Depth 5 Loran Root Dungeon Treasure

Blood Rapture

A Caryll rune that transcribes inhuman sounds. The "Blood Rapture" is the raw euphoria of the warmth of blood. Restores HP with visceral attacks, one of the darker hunter techniques. This rune resonates with servants of the Queen, carrier of the Child of Blood, who yearn for their Queen's blood with little hope of requitement. For them, they find solace in "Blood Rapture," that serves as a surrogate for their desires.

With Blood Rapture, your Visceral attacks will restore some of your HP. This is a good alternate form of healing if you like to use interrupts often. The amount healed is a fixed value, not a percentage; this means that Blood Rapture synergizes better with high defense than high maximum HP. You can use Blood Rapture as a tool to maintain the Fool effect, but note that the healing from Blood Rapture occurs after the damage for the Visceral attack is calculated; you won't get the Fool damage bonus on your Visceral attack if you start it with less than full HP.

Effect	Acquired from
Visceral attacks restore 200 HP	Defeat Shadows of Yharnam Boss [p338]
Visceral attacks restore 250 HP	Depth 4 Pthumeru Root Dungeon Treasure
Visceral attacks restore 300 HP	Eileen the Crow's Quest [p636]

Obtaining the Heir Rune is very important if you fight other hunters often.

You'll find a better Oedon Writhe in Iosefka's Clinic.

Oedon Writhe

A Caryll rune that transcribes inhuman sounds. "Writhe" sees a subtle mucous in the warmth of blood, and acknowledges visceral attacks as one of the darker hunter techniques. Visceral attacks restore Quicksilver Bullets. Human or no, the oozing blood is a medium of the highest grade, and the essence of the formless Great One, Oedon. Both Oedon, and Oedon's inadvertent worshippers, surreptitiously seek the precious blood.

Rear Visceral attacks can also trigger this effect, so staggering enemies from behind can lead to bullet restoration as well; that works well if you are using a weapon with a fast charged R2, like the Saw Cleaver. When combined with a powerful, high ammo consumption firearm like the Cannon, you can alternate between Rear Visceral attacks on weak foes and Cannon blasts on strong ones. All told, this is probably the most useful Rune that affects Visceral attacks. It can be used in combination with the others, though, to make Visceral attacks a viable tactic in many fights. Just beware that they won't benefit you as much against foes that can't be staggered easily.

Effect	Acquired from
Visceral attacks restore 1 Quicksilver Bullet	Adella's Quest [p641]
Visceral attacks restore 2 Quicksilver Bullets	Imposter Iosefka [p646]
Visceral attacks restore 3 Quicksilver Bullets	Depth 5 Pthumeru Root Dungeon Treasure

Heir

A secret symbol left by Caryll, runesmith of Byrgenwerth. The "Heir" sees sentimentality in the warmth of blood, acknowledging this as one of the darker hunter techniques. More Blood Echoes gained from visceral attacks. Perhaps the "Heir" is a hunter who bears the echoing will of those around him.

The Heir Rune gives you additional Blood Echoes when you kill enemies with Visceral attacks. As with the Moon Rune, this is helpful if you want to level up or purchase a lot of consumable items from the shop. Heir Runes don't grant any bonuses in combat, however, so only use them when you don't need the boost that other Runes can give.

Effect	Acquired from
More Blood Echoes from Visceral attacks (Level 1)	Eileen's Quest [p636]
More Blood Echoes from Visceral attacks (Level 2)	Yahar'gul [p131]
More Blood Echoes from Visceral attacks (Level 3)	Depth 5 Pthumeru Root Dungeon Treasure

Arcane Lake

A secret symbol left by Caryll, runesmith of Byrgenwerth. This transcription of the Great Ones' inhuman voices ripples like a watery reflection. This rune means "Lake," and those branded by it enjoy augmented defense. Great volumes of water serve as a bulwark guarding sleep, and an augur of the eldritch Truth. Overcome this hindrance, and seek what is yours.

The Arcane Lake effect reduces the damage you take from arcane attacks. When you are facing enemies that deal arcane damage, this is very useful; the rest of the time, it does absolutely nothing to benefit you. That said, there are some extremely dangerous arcane attacks throughout the game. Some of the most notable ones are listed here.

Enemy	Bestiary
Ebrietas, Daughter of the Cosmos	p350
Martyr Logarius	p342
Celestial Emissary	p348
Witch of Hemwick	p332
The One Reborn	p346
Amygdala	p340
Rom, the Vacuous Spider	p344
Gehrman, the First Hunter	p356

Effect	Acquired from
Arcane Damage Reduction +5%	Yahar'gul [p136]
Arcane Damage Reduction +7%	Byrgenwerth [p127]
Arcane Damage Reduction +10%	Depth 5 Isz Root Dungeon Treasure

5

Fading Lake

A secret symbol left by Caryll, runesmith of Byrgenwerth. This transcription of the Great Ones' inhuman voices ripples like a watery reflection. This rune means "Lake," and those branded by it enjoy augmented defense. Great volumes of water serve as a bulwark guarding sleep, and an augur of the eldritch Truth. Overcome this hindrance, and seek what is yours.

Fading Lake reduces the damage you take from fire attacks. Once again, it's only useful against certain foes, but it can be the difference between life and death in those situations. Enemies with notably dangerous fire attacks are listed here.

Effect	Acquired from
Fire Damage Reduction +5%	Nightmare Frontier [p119]
Fire Damage Reduction +7%	Depth 4 Loran Root Dungeon Treasure
Fire Damage Reduction +10%	Depth 5 Loran Root Dungeon Treasure

Enemy	Bestiary
Shadow of Yharnam	p338
Pthumerian Elder	p388
Keeper of the Old Lords	p378
Watchdog of the Old Lords	p376

Dissipating Lake

A secret symbol left by Caryll, runesmith of Byrgenwerth. This transcription of the Great Ones' inhuman voices ripples like a watery reflection. This rune means "Lake," and those branded by it enjoy augmented defense. Great volumes of water serve as a bulwark guarding sleep, and an augur of the eldritch Truth. Overcome this hindrance, and seek what is yours.

Arcane Lake reduces arcane damage, and Fading Lake reduces fire damage; you're a very sharp person (you're reading this, after all!), so you probably guessed what's coming next. Dissipating Lake reduces bolt damage.

Effect	Acquired from
Bolt Damage Reduction +5%	Forbidden Woods [p100]
Bolt Damage Reduction +7%	Depth 4 Loran Root Dungeon Treasure
Bolt Damage Reduction +10%	Depth 5 Loran Root Dungeon Treasure

Lake

A secret symbol left by Caryll, runesmith of Byrgenwerth. This transcription of the Great Ones' inhuman voices ripples like a watery reflection. This rune means "Lake," and those branded by it enjoy augmented defense. Great volumes of water serve as a bulwark guarding sleep, and an augur of the eldritch Truth. Overcome this hindrance, and seek what is yours.

The Lake Rune increases your physical defense. The vast majority of enemy attacks in the game deal physical damage, so this is very useful. Stacking physical damage reduction can help a lot if you like to rely on the Regain system to regenerate your health, too. Just be extra careful of enemies with special attacks and those that buff their weapons with elemental damage; physical defense won't help you against them.

Effect	Acquired from
Physical Damage Reduction +5%	Hemwick Charnel Lane [p79]
Physical Damage Reduction +7%	Depth 4 Pthumeru Root Dungeon Treasure
Physical Damage Reduction +10%	Depth 5 Pthumeru Root Dungeon Treasure

Great Lake

A secret symbol left by Caryll, runesmith of Byrgenwerth. This transcription of the Great Ones' inhuman voices ripples like a watery reflection. This rune means "Lake," and those branded by it enjoy augmented defense. Great volumes of water serve as a bulwark guarding sleep, and an augur of the eldritch Truth. Overcome this hindrance, and seek what is yours.

Great Lake reduces the damage you take from all damage types. Against enemy attacks that deal more than one type of damage, Great Lake is very useful. It can simultaneously reduce both types of damage. In the main game, there aren't that many enemies that fall into this category. In PvP, other players who wield weapons like the Burial Blade, Blade of Mercy, Tonitrus, or Logarius' Wheel will find their attacks to be less effective against you. Usually, though, it's better to use one of the more specific Lake Runes.

Effect	Acquired from
All Damage Reduction +3%	Depth 3 Hintertomb Root Dungeon Treasure
All Damage Reduction +4%	Upper Cathedral Ward [p140]
All Damage Reduction +5%	Depth 5 Isz Root Dungeon Treasure

Clear Deep Sea

A secret symbol left by Caryll, runesmith of Byrgenwerth. This transcription of the Great Ones' inhuman voices depicts downreaching currents. This rune means "Deep Sea," and grants augmented resistance. Great volumes of water serve as a bulwark guarding sleep, and an augur of the eldritch Truth. Overcome this hindrance, and seek what is yours.

Clear Deep Sea adds Slow Poison resistance. It's useful any time you are up against that status. Within the main game, Nightmare Frontier is where you'll find it most useful. Slow Poison also shows up in Chalice Dungeons fairly frequently, and other players will be eager to use it against you as well.

Effect	Acquired from
Slow Poison Resistance +100	Forbidden Woods [p99]
Slow Poison Resistance +200	Nightmare Frontier [p123]
Slow Poison Resistance +300	Depth 5 Loran Root Dungeon Treasure

The only Stunning Deep Sea rune not acquired in the dungeons is found on a ledge overlooking one of the poison swamps in the Nightmare Frontier.

Stunning Deep Sea

A secret symbol left by Caryll, runesmith of Byrgenwerth. This transcription of the Great Ones' inhuman voices depicts downreaching currents. This rune means "Deep Sea," and grants augmented resistance. Great volumes of water serve as a bulwark guarding sleep, and an augur of the eldritch Truth. Overcome this hindrance, and seek what is yours.

Stunning Deep Sea protects you from Rapid Poison. This is mostly helpful against other players, as the damage is applied instantly once the gauge is filled. If you anticipate enemies wielding Chikage or Dirty gems, prepare by equipping Stunning Deep Sea into your Memory Slots.

Effect	Acquired from
Rapid Poison Resistance +100	Depth 3 Hintertomb Root Dungeon Treasure
Rapid Poison Resistance +200	Nightmare Frontier [p122]
Rapid Poison Resistance +300	Depth 5 Loran Root Dungeon Treasure

The level 2 Great Deep Sea rune is hidden in the caverns at the bottom of the Nightmare Frontier in the last poison swamp before the boss area.

Deep Sea

A secret symbol left by Caryll, runesmith of Byrgenwerth. This transcription of the Great Ones' inhuman voices depicts downreaching currents. This rune means "Deep Sea," and grants augmented resistance. Great volumes of water serve as a bulwark guarding sleep, and an augur of the eldritch Truth. Overcome this hindrance, and seek what is yours.

Deep Sea adds Frenzy resistance. There are only a few sources of Frenzy in all of Bloodborne, but they are very dangerous. Of particular note are the Winter Lanterns. Their ability to inflict Frenzy is truly terrifying; having a Deep Sea Rune equipped can save you from death (or heavy reliance on Sedatives)!

Effect	Acquired from
Frenzy Resistance +100	Depth 3 Hintertomb Root Dungeon Treasure
Frenzy Resistance +200	Forbidden Woods [p99]
Frenzy Resistance +300	Depth 5 Isz Root Dungeon Treasure

Great Deep Sea

A secret symbol left by Caryll, runesmith of Byrgenwerth. This transcription of the Great Ones' inhuman voices depicts downreaching currents. This rune means "Deep Sea," and grants augmented resistance. Great volumes of water serve as a bulwark guarding sleep, and an augur of the eldritch Truth. Overcome this hindrance, and seek what is yours.

Great Deep Sea increases all of your status resistances. This is overall the best Deep Sea Rune for PvP, since it protects against both Slow and Rapid Poisoning. In terms of the main campaign, though, you'll generally do better to use whichever Rune is best suited to the area you are exploring.

Effect	Acquired from
All Status Resistance +50	Depth 3 Hintertomb Root Dungeon Treasure
All Status Resistance +100	Nightmare Frontier [p125]
All Status Resistance +150	Depth 5 Isz Root Dungeon Treasure

Beast

A secret symbol left by Caryll, runesmith of Byr-genwerth. A transcription of the roar of a labyrinth beast, the bearer of the "Beast" rune has accentu-ated transformation effects. "Beast" is one of the early Caryll Runes, as well as one of the first to be deemed forbidden. The discovery of blood en-tailed the discovery of undesirable beasts.

This Rune directly increases your Beasthood stat. As a result, you'll have a higher maximum attack boost while in the Beast Transfor-mation state. This is only helpful when you are using Beast Blood Pellets or the transformed mode of the Beast Claw. Furthermore, it isn't that difficult to maintain high Beasthood without this Rune. You can equip armor with high beasthood, and maintaining low levels of Insight will also help. Check p13 in the Training Manual for more information on Beasthood and Beast Transformation.

Effect	Acquired from
Beasthood +20	Beast-possessed Soul in Healing Church Workshop [p275]
Beasthood +50	Afflicted Beggar [p643]
Beasthood +100	Depth 5 Loran Root Dungeon Treasure

Communion

A secret symbol left by Caryll, runesmith of Byr-genwerth. Several runes relate to "blood," includ-ing "Communion," which raises the maximum number of blood vials one may carry. This rune represents the Healing Church and its ministers. Blood ministration is, of course, the pursuit of communion.

The Communion Runes increase the number of Blood Vials you can hold. This is very helpful, particularly if you have difficulty making use of the Regain system. By default, each of your Blood Vials heals you for about 40% of your maximum health, but this effect can be increased using the Radiance Oath Rune; Communion and Radiance work very well together. If you often use Blood Bullets or simply don't like Regain, this can help. Having the extra vials can also be very useful to keep yourself topped-off if you like to rely on the Fool gem effect. On the other hand, if you keep the Pulsing effect on your weapons this Rune may be unnecessary.

Effect	Acquired from
Maximum Blood Vials +1	Healing Church Workshop [p68]
Maximum Blood Vials +2	Lecture Building 2F [p145]
Maximum Blood Vials +3	Iosefka's Clinic [p103]
Maximum Blood Vials +4	Celestial Emissary [p348]
Maximum Blood Vials +5	Depth 5 Pthumeru Root Dungeon Treasure

Formless Oedon

A secret symbol left by Caryll, runesmith of Byr-genwerth. The Great One Oedon, lacking form, exists only in voice, and is symbolized by this rune. Those branded by it enjoy a larger supply of Quicksilver Bullets. Human or no, the oozing blood is a medium of the highest grade, and the essence of the formless Great One, Oedon. Both Oedon, and Oedon's inadvertent worshippers, surreptitiously seek the precious blood.

Formless Oedon increases your maximum number of Quicksilver Bullets. Quicksilver Bullets are very useful resource for you, so this synergizes with a number of tactics. If you like to use high-con-sumption firearms like the Cannon, or to a lesser extent the Repeat-ing Pistol, this Rune can help you squeeze in extra shots, especially if you use Blood Bullets, too. If you like to interrupt the enemy with gunshots, this can give you more chances to succeed. It also works well with spells. They tend to consume a lot of bullets, so having a higher maximum means you get more casts. Combine this with the Oedon Writhe Rune, and spell usage will become a lot more viable.

Effect	Acquired from
Maximum Quicksilver Bullets +1	Young Girl's Quest [p642]
Maximum Quicksilver Bullets +2	Depth 3 Pthumeru Root Dungeon Treasure
Maximum Quicksilver Bullets +3	Chapel Samaritan [p637]
Maximum Quicksilver Bullets +4	Healing Church Workshop [p68]
Maximum Quicksilver Bullets +5	Depth 5 Pthumeru Root Dungeon Treasure

Guidance OH

A Caryll rune discovered by the old hunter Lud-wig along with the Holy Moonlight Sword. Boosts amount of life recovered by rallying. When Lud-wig closed his eyes, he saw darkness, or perhaps nothingness, and that is where he discovered the tiny beings of light. Ludwig was certain that these playful dancing sprites offered "guidance," and emptied Ludwig of his fears, at least in the midst of a hunt.

Effect	Acquired from
Boosts rally potential +10%	Research Hall [p184]
Boosts rally potential +20%	Hunter's Nightmare [p172]
Boosts rally potential +30%	Depth 5 Root Dungeons

Rally potential governs how much health you recover with each swing of your weapon as part of the Regain system, and by equip-ping one of these Guidance runes you will be able to increase that amount. Getting more health back with each attack will allow you to replenish your health quicker after getting hit, which in turn will allow you to be more aggressive when fighting enemies. Since the increase is applied to each hit you land, faster weapons or ones with attacks that hit multiple times get the most benefit from these runes.

Oath Runes

The following Runes are special and can only be placed in your character's Oath Memory Slot. They each provide a powerful, unique effect, but their main function is actually to identify your faction in multiplayer. For more details on the multiplayer system, check out p25. Be careful when selecting one of the following Runes, or you might find yourself fighting for the wrong faction!

Radiance

A secret symbol left by Caryll, runesmith of Byrgenwerth. The rune for "Radiance," adopted by the sworn executioners under Logarius' command. The executioners despise the impure Vilebloods, and no matter what the circumstances, would never cooperate with the bloodthirsty hunters who serve the queen, Annalise.

The Radiance Oath effect increases the amount of HP your Blood Vials heal. This has a very obvious synergy with the Communion Rune. Just remember not to heal too early, lest you waste the effect! This Oath Rune will mark you as a Hunter of Vilebloods. It can be acquired from Alfred's quest, which you can read about on p644.

The Radiance rune can be found on Alfred's body at the altar where you first met him once his quest is complete.

Corruption

A secret symbol left by Caryll, runesmith of Byrgenwerth. Several runes contain a nuance of "Blood," including the rune of "Corruption," associated with the oath of the corrupt. Pledgers of this oath are Cainhurst Vilebloods, hunters of blood who find dregs for their Queen in cold-blood, particularly in that of hunters. Yet the corrupt are heretics in the eyes of the Church, and thus subject to the wrath of the Executioners.

The Corruption Oath effect provides you with a small amount of continuous healing when you are low on health. This effect can save you, of course, but it can also work against you. If you like to use the Poorman effect on your weapons, be warned that the healing from Corruption can ruin the effect. This Rune will be mark you as a Vileblood. It can be acquired from Annalise's quest [p647].

You'll receive the Corruption rune upon taking the Vileblood oath.

Hunter

A secret symbol left by Caryll, runesmith of Byrgenwerth. This red-smudged rune means "Hunter," and was adopted by the hunter of hunters oath. These watchmen admonish those who have become intoxicated with blood. Be they men or beasts, anyone who has antagonized the pledgers of the "Hunter" oath surely has an issue with blood.

The Hunter Oath increases your stamina regeneration rate; it synergizes with practically everything. If you use weapons that cost a lot of stamina to swing about, such as the Hunter Axe, this Oath can help you maintain enough stamina for defensive rolls... or more massive axe swings! It also works well with Beast Transformation; better stamina regeneration means more consecutive attacks, which it turn increases your damage multiplier from the Beast gauge. Utilizing this Rune marks you as a Hunter of Hunters. It can be acquired from Eileen's quest [p636].

Eileen will give you the Hunter rune if you help her defeat Henryk and come to her aid at the Grand Cathedral.

5

Impurity OH

A Caryll rune that transcribes inhuman sounds. This rune, discovered inside the forbidden beast eater, came to symbolise "Impurity," and the oath of the League. Confederates of the League cooperate with hunters from other worlds, and hunt to discover vermin. Vermin writhe within filth, and are the root of man's impurity. Crush all vermin without hesitation.

To obtain the Impurity rune you'll need to travel to the Forbidden Woods Lamp and enter the small windmill building nearby, where Valtr, Master of the League now resides. Once there, speak with him and agree to join the League to receive the rune. Equipping the rune has the added benefit of giving you an extra 2% HP during any co-op session, but the main reason to equip it is so that you're identified as a Confederate of the League during co-op. For more information on Valtr, please refer to p650.

Equip the Impurity Rune to show your loyalty to the League...

... and fellow Confederates will come to your aid.

Beast's Embrace OH

After repeated experiments in controlling the scourge of beasts, the gentle "Embrace" rune was discovered. When its implementation failed, the "Embrace" became a forbidden rune, but this knowledge became a foundation of the Healing Church. Those who swear this oath take on a ghastly form, and enjoy accentuated transformation effects, especially while wielding a beast weapon.

While the increase to your Beasthood provided by this rune is only relatively small, it does have other rather more unique properties. Equipping the rune will cause your character model to undergo a slight transformation and take on a more beastly appearance, including a large fur mane. Additionally, if you have this rune equipped at the same time as the Beast Claw weapon, the moveset of the weapon will change, and you'll gain access to entirely new attacks. To acquire this rune you will first need to get Laurence's Skull from the hidden altar in the Recovery Room (p173), and then take it to the Nightmare Grand Cathedral in the Hunter's Nightmare so that you can face Laurence, the First Vicar (p363). Upon defeating him you will automatically get the rune.

Defeat Laurence, the First Vicar for the Beast's Embrace Rune.

Embrace the Beast within when you equip this rune.

Milkweed **OH**

A Caryll Rune envisioned by Adeline, patient of the research hall. A transcription of the inhuman, sticky whispers that reveal the nature of a celestial attendant. Those who take this oath become a lumenwood that peers towards the sky, feeding phantasms in its luscious bed. Phantasms guide us, and lead to further discoveries.

Equipping this rune will cause your character to take on the unique appearance of a lumenwood, overwriting your existing character's facial features and head attire. Once you're in this state you'll be able to tap into the hidden powers of the otherwise unimpressive Kos Parasite weapon, unlocking its full potential. As an added benefit you'll also gain a small increase to item discovery. Obtaining this rune will mean aiding Adeline in the Research Hall, because only once you have given her three of the Brain Fluids she wants will she hand the rune over to you. For information on how to do this, please refer to p654.

The Milkweed Rune will be Adeline's final gift to you.

Warning! There may be side effects to equipping the Milkweed Rune.

Tools

Blood Gem Workshop Tool

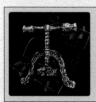

A misplaced workshop tool from the Hunter's Dream. The hunter who retrieves this can fortify weapons by kneading blood gems into them. Blood gems add properties to weapons when used to fortify them, as blood defines an organism.

The Blood Gem Workshop Tool is accessible after you defeat Father Gascoigne at the Tomb of Oedon, and can be found in a treasure chest in front of the stairway leading to the Oedon Chapel (p45). Once you've obtained this important item, you'll be able to attach Blood Gems to your weapons and benefit from their effects.

Rune Workshop Tool

Runesmith Caryll, student of Byrgenwerth, transcribed the inhuman utterings of the Great Ones into what are now called Caryll Runes. The hunter who retrieves this workshop tool can etch Caryll Runes into the mind to attain their wondrous strength. Provost Willem would have been proud of Caryll's runes, as they do not rely upon blood in any measure.

This workshop tool can be found on a corpse in the Witch's Abode after defeating the Witch of Hemwick (p79). It allows you to equip Caryll Runes, many of which have extremely useful and powerful effects, so it's well worth a side trip as soon as you have access to Hemwick Charnel Lane.

Workshop Haze Extractor

A misplaced workshop tool from the Hunter's Dream. The hunter who retrieves this can extract arcane haze from ritual materials. But alas, spent materials are lost.

You'll find the Workshop Haze Extractor in a treasure chest on the second level of the Lower Pthumerian Labyrinth (p436). As its name implies, this tool is used for extracting Arcane Haze from ritual materials for use in creating more advanced Chalice Dungeons. You'll need this item in order to access deeper reaches of the labyrinths and to add the optional Sinister Bell objective to certain Root Chalice areas, so be sure to pick it up as soon as you can.

Blood Gems

Gems are very important items that allow you to customize your weapons. Each gem has a rating, and higher rated gems have more powerful effects. To get the most powerful gems, you'll need to explore the Chalice Dungeons.

Basics

In order to attach gems to your weapons, you'll need three things. First, you'll need a gem. Second, you'll need a weapon that can equip a gem; this means you'll need to upgrade your weapon to unlock gem slots. Finally, you'll need the Blood Gem Workshop Tool. It can be obtained just before entering Oedon Chapel (p45). With those elements in place, you can attach gems to your weapon by approaching the workbench in the Hunter's Dream and selecting "Blood Gem Fortification."

Gem Shapes and Alternate Weapons

Right-hand weapons can have up to three gem slots, and some left-hand weapons have one slot. There are different slot shapes, though; not every gem will fit every slot. The slot types are: Radial, Triangular, Waning, and Circle. Your gem's shape needs to match the slot you want to use it in. If you find a really great gem but the shape doesn't properly match your weapon, don't give up hope. There are actually two alternate versions of every right-hand weapon – the Lost and Uncanny versions. They're identical to normal weapons except that they have different slot configurations. These alternate weapons can be found in Chalice Dungeons; check the weapon page for your favorite weapon for more information on where you can find the Lost and Uncanny versions. There is also an exceedingly rare fifth type of gem shape – Droplet gems. These are "almighty" gems; they can fit in any type of gem slot!

Using one of the unique gem items such as the Tear Stone will grant you a blood gem with predetermined effects.

Unique Gems

Most Blood Gems are randomly generated when they appear, but there are some preset gems, and even a rare few that you create by using unique items you may acquire. These few unique gems are covered here.

Red Blood Gem

A blood gem that fortifies weapons and adds various properties. Droplet blood gems are special gems that adapt to various weapons and shapes. Created from a bright-red brooch, this blood gem strengthens the effect of rallying. A quintessential hunter skill, rallying symbolizes the battle-worn hunter who Is often the only thing standing after a bloodbath.

This unique, Droplet-shaped Blood Gem is acquired by using the Red Brooch, found on a woman's corpse in the Tomb of Oedon. It raises your physical attack by 2.7% and boosts rally potential by 1.8%, making it similar to a below average Lethal gem that can still be useful in the first half of the game.

Gold Blood Gem

A blood gem that fortifies weapons and adds various properties. Most radial blood gems have effects that bear upon physical attacks, and this golden radial blood gem, kept for generations within the Church, strengthens attacks against those afflicted intensely by beasthood. When the clerics began transforming into unspeakable beasts, the Church needed something to retaliate with.

This gem is acquired by defeating Vicar Amelia and then using the Gold Pendant she drops. It's a Radial gem that grants a decent boost to attack strength against beasts. The Saw Cleaver and Saw Spear are good candidates for fortifying with this gem, because they both have Radial slots and their serrated damage bonus already makes them your ideal beast-killers.

Tear Blood Gem

A blood gem that fortifies weapons and adds various properties. Droplet blood gems are special gems that adapt to various weapons and shapes. Created from a shining silver doll tear, this blood gem is a quiet but unfaltering friend that continually restores HP, the life essence of a hunter. Perhaps the doll's creator had wished for just such a friend, albeit in vain.

You can obtain this gem by giving the Doll the Small Hair Ornament and then talking to her. She'll give you the Tear Stone, which produces this gem when you use it. It's a very useful gem, and worth equipping to your sidearm if it has a gem slot, at least until late in the game when you begin to find powerful Circle-shaped Blood Gems.

Positive Effects and Cursed Gems

Gems are, to a certain extent, random. Behind the scenes, each gem has a budget of points. Every positive effect that is added to a gem takes points from the budget, and every negative effect adds points back. What this means is that gems with negative effects can also have stronger positive effects. These are known as "Cursed" gems; they're powerful but have a downside. For example, let's consider a gem with a rating of 10 with an Odd Bloodtinge effect. Let's say the effect is "Blood Attack + 50." If it also had a negative Kinhunter effect of "Attack versus beasts down by 8.1%," the positive Odd Bloodtinge could go higher; it might be something like "Blood Attack +62.6." If you put that gem on a Hunter Pistol, its attacks would be more powerful in general, but it would do less damage against beasts.

Don't worry too much about the exact values, here; it's just an example. The key point to remember is that Cursed gems have negative effects and often have stronger positive effects to compensate. If you see something like a Cursed Dense effect (weapon durability down), it might actually be a blessing in disguise!

The other important point is that not all gems are created equal. For example, a 20-rated Adept (Blunt) gem won't help you at all if you're using a Blade of Mercy, as it has no blunt attacks. Think carefully about which gems you choose, and don't hesitate to test them out on a variety of enemies!

Ratings

Gems can have up to three effects, and each gem has a rating that determines the strength of its effects. Higher-rated gems are stronger than lower-rated gems. The weakest gems have a rating of one, and the strongest gems have a rating of 20. You'll pick up some gems in the course of the main game, but if you want the most powerful gems you'll need to spend time in the Chalice Dungeons. Chalice Dungeons with a high Ritual Level are difficult, but they also have the best gems.

The following table shows how high the Ritual Level needs to be for you to reach each gem rating. This just shows the general tendencies of the system and should not be taken as a hard-and-fast rule.

Gem Ratings by Ritual Level

Gem Rating	Ritual Level				
	1	2	3	4	5
20	–	–	–	–	Chalice Boss
19	–	–	–	–	Floor Boss
18	–	–	–	–	Treasure
17	–	–	–	–	Normal Foes
16	–	–	–	Chalice Boss	Normal Foes
15	–	–	–	Floor Boss	Normal Foes
14	–	–	–	Treasure	–
13	–	–	–	Normal Foes	–
12	–	–	Chalice Boss	Normal Foes	–
11	–	–	Floor Boss	Normal Foes	–
10	–	Chalice Boss	Treasure	–	–
9	–	Floor Boss	Normal Foes	–	–
8	Chalice Boss	Treasure	Normal Foes	–	–
7	Floor Boss	Normal Foes	Normal Foes	–	–
6	Treasure	Normal Foes	–	–	–
5	Normal Foes	Normal Foes	–	–	–
4	Normal Foes	–	–	–	–
3	Normal Foes	–	–	–	–
2	–	–	–	–	–
1	–	–	–	–	–

Chalice Boss: These gems drop from the overall dungeon boss.
Floor Boss: These gems drop from a boss on the first two floors of the dungeon.
Treasure: These gems are found as treasure at the end of side areas within the dungeon.
Normal Foes: These gems drop from non-boss enemies.

Gem Effect Stacking

You can equip the same effect on a weapon multiple times, and the effects will stack. In fact, this is often the best way to use gems. You can make a weapon for use against beasts that stacks the Hunter effect multiple times, for example. You might be tempted to stack the gem effects of your left- and right- hand weapons, but this won't work in most cases. Effects generally only apply to the weapon you put them on rather than your character overall; an Odd Bloodtinge effect on your Saw Cleaver won't increase the damage of your Hunter Pistol, even if you hold them at the same time.

This even applies to effects like Fool that increase your damage at full HP. Sorry! You were clever to think of it, but it doesn't work. One major exception is the Pulsing effect that enables passive HP regeneration; it stacks! This makes it an amazing effect for a left-hand weapon...

Buffable and Non-buffable Weapons

There are two types of weapons in Bloodborne: weapons that can be buffed (strengthened) with Fire Paper, Bolt Paper, or Empty Phantasm Shell, and those that cannot. Usually, weapons that can be buffed only deal physical damage; the lone exception is the Reiterpallasch. Weapons that cannot be buffed always have more than one damage type.

This is an important distinction because some gems work differently depending on the type of weapon in which they are placed. Don't worry too much about it; the gem effects list will explain how each gem works for both types when there is a difference. Refer to the following lists when you need a reminder about which category a weapon is in.

> **Buffable Weapons**
> Saw Cleaver, Saw Spear, Hunter Axe, Threaded Cane, Kirkhammer, Ludwig's Holy Blade, Stake Driver, Beast Claw, Reiterpallasch
>
> **Non-buffable Weapons**
> Burial Blade, Blade of Mercy, Chikage, Rifle Spear, Tonitrus, Logarius' Wheel

Gem Effects

This section lists every possible gem effect along with the range of values that it can have. You'll also find some guidance on how to use the different types of effects, but don't let these tips interfere with your own creativity! Making your own custom weapons is an exciting part of Bloodborne, and a lot of the choices are based on the gems you find and your personal playstyle.

Odd Bloodtinge

This effect adds a set amount of blood attack to your weapon. The possible values range from +1 blood attack to +93.8 blood attack. This effect only works on weapons that already have blood attack naturally; most of the guns fall into this category. You can use Odd Bloodtinge to make weapons like the Hunter Pistol powerful even with a low bloodtinge stat.

Among the right-hand weapons, the Chikage can also be used with the Odd Bloodtinge effect; its transformed mode does only blood-type damage and is the only mode that will benefit from this effect. Reiterpallasch and the Rifle Spear can also use Odd Bloodtinge, but the bonus damage is only applied to their gun attacks.

Most enemies aren't really weak against blood attacks. The usefulness of blood attacks is that they are often usable from range. There are a few enemies with low blood defense, though; they're prime targets for the Chikage's transformed mode or firearms with Bone Marrow Ash.

Odd Arcane

This effect adds a set amount of arcane attack to your weapon. The possible values range from +1 arcane attack to +93.8 arcane attack. For non-buffable weapons, like the Tonitrus, they will receive the bonus arcane damage provided by the gem effect.

For buffable weapons, like Ludwig's Holy Blade, it's more complicated. All of the weapon's base physical attack is converted to arcane attack, and the weapon will use arcane scaling instead of scaling with strength and skill. It also receives the bonus arcane damage from the gem effect. Applying this gem effect to a buffable weapon will prevent it from receiving the effects of Fire Paper, Bolt Paper, and Empty Phantasm Shell.

With Odd Arcane, left-handed firearms can add arcane attack to their bullets while retaining the normal blood attack. The Reiterpallasch can also shoot arcane-elemental bullets when using this gem effect, but it will lose its blood attack value.

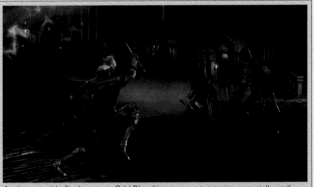
As they provide flat bonuses, Odd Bloodtinge gems synergize especially well with the Chikage's transformed mode when your character's level is low.

Notably High Arcane Defense

Enemy	Page
Wandering Nightmare	p671
Celestial Child	p247
Brainsucker	p273
Parasite Larva	p242
Giant Lost Child	p282

Gems that convert your weapon's entire damage type to arcane are particularly useful in the Forbidden Woods.

Arcane damage can be very useful in Chalice Dungeons; a lot of common foes there are weak to arcane. On the other hand, there are also a number of bosses in the main game scenario that are resistant to arcane.

Notably High Arcane Defense

Enemy	Page
Parasite Larva	p242
Small Celestial Emissary	p241
Brainsucker	p273
Martyr Logarius	p342
Scholar	p245
The One Reborn	p346
Ebrietas, Daughter of the Cosmos	p350
Celestial Emissary	p348
Micolash, Host of the Nightmare	p352
Loran Cleric	p304
Labyrinth Rat	p233
Large Nightmare Apostle	p289
Labyrinth Madman	p299
Yharnam, Pthumerian Queen	p392
Undead Giant	p374

Notably Low Arcane Defense

Enemy	Page
Bell Ringer (Black Robe)	p287
Carrion Crow	p231
Rotted Corpse	p233
Maneater Boar	p270
Large Huntsman	p231
Church Giant	p271
Abhorrent Beast	p386
Huntsman's Minion	p267
Snake Ball	p241
Large Snake Ball	p279
Loran Silverbeast	p281
Garden of Eyes	p285
Fluorescent Flower	p286
Cramped Casket	p288
Skeletal Puppet	p249

Notably Low Arcane Defense

Enemy	Page
Mergo's Attendant	p248
Mergo's Chief Attendant	p290
Mergo's Wet Nurse	p354
Moon Presence	p358
Gel	p253
Keeper's Hunting Dog	p305
Gravekeeper Scorpion	p252
Watcher's Gravedigger	p254
Keeper of the Old Lords	p378
Labyrinth Watcher	p250
Labyrinth Warrior	p302
Merciless Watcher	p296
Pthumerian Descendant	p382
Pthumerian Elder	p388
Darkbeast Paarl	p334
Bloodletting Beast	p390

Odd Fire

This effect adds a set amount of fire attack to your weapon. The possible values range from +1 fire attack to +93.8 fire attack. For non-buffable weapons, like the Logarius' Wheel, they will receive the bonus fire damage provided by the gem effect.

For buffable weapons, like the Kirkhammer, it's more complicated. All of the weapon's base physical attack is converted to fire attack, and the weapon will use arcane scaling instead of scaling with strength and skill. It also receives the bonus fire damage from the gem effect. Applying this gem effect to a buffable weapon will prevent it from receiving the effects of Fire Paper, Bolt Paper, and Empty Phantasm Shell.

Also note that Oil Urns will increase the damage dealt to enemies by this effect, though each Oil Urn will only increase the damage for one hit. Still, you can do a surprising burst of damage by stacking multiple Odd Fire effects on a hard-hitting weapon and using an Oil Urn. Always be on-guard if another player throws an Oil Urn at you in PvP, particularly if they are carrying something massive like a Kirkhammer!

With Odd Fire, left-handed firearms can add fire attack to their bullets while retaining the normal blood attack. The Reiterpallasch can also shoot fire-elemental bullets when using this gem effect, but it will lose its blood attack value.

As you can see from the tables, there are tons of enemies in Bloodborne that are weak against fire attacks and very few that resist fire damage. These facts, combined with the availability of Oil Urns, make fire a very important element in any hunter's arsenal.

Notably High Fire Defense

Enemy	Page
Executioner	p269
Church Giant	p271
Keeper's Hunting Dog	p305
Watchdog of the Old Lord	p355

Notably Low Fire Defense

Enemy	Page
Scourge Beast	p266
Brainsucker	p273
Rabid Dog	p230
Cleric Beast	p326
Maneater Boar	p270
Father Gascoigne	p328
Father Gascoigne (Beast)	p328
Beast Patient (Male)	p236
Wandering Nightmare	p671
Blood-starved Beast	p330
Vicar Amelia	p336
Abhorrent Beast	p386
Beast-possessed Soul	p275
Witch of Hemwick	p332

Notably Low Fire Defense

Enemy	Page
Darkbeast Paarl	p334
Snake Parasite	p240
Small Celestial Emissary	p241
Scholar	p245
Loran Silverbeast	p281
Fluorescent Flower	p286
Lost Child of Antiquity	p244
Bloodlicker	p280
Cramped Casket	p288
The One Reborn	p346
Ebrietas, Daughter of the Cosmos	p350
Celestial Emissary	p348
Large Nightmare Apostle	p289
Skeletal Puppet	p249
Mergo's Attendant	p248
Mergo's Chief Attendant	p290
Mergo's Wet Nurse	p354
Moon Presence	p358
Loran Cleric	p304
Gel	p253
Gravekeeper Scorpion	p252
Ashen Blood Beast Patient (Female)	p237
Merciless Watcher	p296
Pthumerian Descendant	p382
Pthumerian Elder	p388
Bloodletting Beast	p390

5

Odd Bolt

This effect adds a set amount of bolt attack to your weapon. The possible values range from +1 bolt attack to +93.8 bolt attack. For non-buffable weapons, like the Blade of Mercy, they will receive the bonus bolt damage provided by the gem effect.

For buffable weapons, like the Saw Spear, it's more complicated. All of the weapon's base physical attack is converted to bolt attack, and the weapon will use arcane scaling instead of scaling with strength and skill. It also receives the bonus bolt damage from the gem effect. Applying this gem effect to a buffable weapon will prevent it from receiving the effects of Fire Paper, Bolt Paper, and Empty Phantasm Shell.

With Odd Bolt, left-handed firearms can add bolt attack to their bullets while retaining the normal blood attack. The Reiterpallasch can also shoot bolt-elemental bullets when using this gem effect, but it will lose its blood attack value. There are several enemies that are weak against bolt attacks, and among them are many difficult foes. Of particular note are the Celestial Emissaries and Ebrietas.

Notably High Bolt Defense

Enemy	Page
Church Giant	p271
Abhorrent Beast	p386
Darkbeast Paarl	p334
Parasite Larva	p242
Loran Cleric	p304

Notably Low Bolt Defense

Enemy	Page
Brainsucker	p273
Executioner	p269
Wandering Nightmare	p671
Snake Parasite	p240
Small Celestial Emissary	p241
Scholar	p245
Giant Lost Child	p282

Notably Low Bolt Defense

Enemy	Page
Crawler	p246
Large Crawler	p283
Children of Rom	p344
Fluorescent Flower	p286
Rom, the Vacuous Spider	p344
Lost Child of Antiquity	p244
Forsaken Castle Spirit	p242
Cramped Casket	p288
Ebrietas, Daughter of the Cosmos	p350
Celestial Emissary	p348
Mergo's Attendant	p248
Mergo's Chief Attendant	p290
Giant Lost Child	p282
Mergo's Wet Nurse	p354
Moon Presence	p358
Gel	p253
Gravekeeper Scorpion	p252
Labyrinth Madman	p299
Evil Labyrinth Spirit	p298
Undead Giant	p374

Odd Tempering

This effect adds a set amount of physical attack to your weapon. The possible values range from +0.6 physical attack to +56.3 physical attack. All right-hand weapons, with the notable exception of the transformed mode of Chikage, deal physical-type damage, so this goes well with anything. Interestingly enough, this gem also adds to blood attack, so it works for Chikage's transformed mode and firearms, as well!

Adept

There are two types of Adept effect— blunt and thrust. Adept (Blunt) only increases the damage of blunt attacks, and Adept (Thrust) only increases the damage of thrust attacks. Unfortunately, it's often difficult to tell the damage type of your attack, as this information is not displayed in-game. Your weapon stat screen will show you if your weapon has blunt or thrust attacks, but won't tell you which attacks have those properties. Luckily, you can find the damage types listed in each weapon's attack table starting on p481! This effect can range from a +0.4% increase all the way up to a +33.8% increase; it can be quite powerful. This is especially true if you have a weapon with a powerful thrust, such as the transformed charged R2 of Ludwig's Holy Blade. When used against enemies with low thrust defense, like Brainsuckers, it can be incredibly damaging.

Note that blunt and thrust do not apply to elemental damage; only your physical and blood attacks can benefit from this effect. The Adept effect doesn't mix well with elemental effects! Specifically, fire, arcane, and bolt do not benefit. Oddly enough, blood attacks do benefit; your transformed Chikage's dashing R2 will indeed receive the bonus from an Adept (Thrust) effect!

Notably Low Blunt Defense

Enemy	Page
Executioner	p269
Huntsman's Minion	p267
Mergo's Chief Attendant	p290
Gravekeeper Scorpion	p252
Merciless Watcher	p296

Notably Low Thrust Defense

Enemy	Page
Brainsucker	p273
Small Celestial Emissary	p241
Scholar	p245
Crawler	p246
Large Crawler	p283
Ebrietas, Daughter of the Cosmos	p350
Celestial Emissary	p348
Mergo's Attendant	p248
Mergo's Chief Attendant	p290
Gel	p253
Labyrinth Warrior	p302
Cramped Casket	p288
Undead Giant	p374

Weapons modified to inflict only fire damage are extremely effective against beasts, especially after using an Oil Urn.

Bloodtinge gems provide percentage increases to blood damage, so they're most effective with strong weapon scaling and a high bloodtinge stat.

Bloodtinge

The Bloodtinge effect increases your blood attack by a percentage ranging from +0.4% to +33.8%. Firearms are prime candidates for this effect. Reiterpallasch and the Rifle Spear do benefit from the Bloodtinge effect. This only works for their gunshots, but if you are able to stack three +33.8% Bloodtinge effects on them and have a high bloodtinge stat, their shots surpass most normal firearms when not using Bone Marrow Ash. It also works with Chikage, but it only affects the transformed mode attacks; if you specialize in the transformed Chikage it could be worth it, but you may be better off with a Tempering effect instead. Test it out to figure out what works best for your playstyle.

Arcane

The Arcane effect increases your arcane attack by a percentage ranging from +0.3% to +28.1%. Logarius' Wheel, the Burial Blade, and the Blade of Mercy will receive the bonus arcane damage provided by the gem effect.

Tonitrus, Chikage, and the Rifle Spear are special cases; they cannot benefit from this gem. If you would like for them to have arcane attack, you'll need to use the Odd Arcane effect instead.

For buffable weapons, like Ludwig's Holy Blade, it's more complicated. All of the weapon's base physical attack is converted to arcane attack, and the weapon will use arcane scaling instead of scaling with strength and skill. It then receives the bonus arcane damage from the gem effect. Applying this gem effect to a buffable weapon will prevent it from receiving the effects of Fire Paper, Bolt Paper, and Empty Phantasm Shell. Left-handed firearms cannot use the Arcane effect. The Reiterpallasch can, and this enables it to shoot arcane-elemental bullets when using this gem effect. It will lose its blood attack value, though.

Fire

The Fire effect increases your fire attack by a percentage ranging from +0.3% to +28.1%. Non-buffable weapons cannot benefit from this gem. If you would like for them to have fire attack, you'll need to use the Odd Fire effect instead.

For buffable weapons, like Ludwig's Holy Blade, it's more complicated. All of the weapon's base physical attack is converted to fire attack, and the weapon will use arcane scaling instead of scaling with strength and skill. It then receives the bonus fire damage from the gem effect. Applying this gem effect to a buffable weapon will prevent it from receiving the effects of Fire Paper, Bolt Paper, and Empty Phantasm Shell. Left-handed firearms cannot use the Fire effect. The Reiterpallasch can, and this enables it to shoot fire-elemental bullets when using this gem effect. It will lose its blood attack value, though.

The Bolt effect increases your bolt attack by a percentage ranging from +0.3% to +28.1%. Tonitrus will receive the bonus bolt damage provided by the gem effect, but all other non-buffable weapons cannot benefit from this gem. If you would like for them to have bolt attack, you'll need to use the Odd Bolt effect instead.

For buffable weapons, like Ludwig's Holy Blade, it's more complicated. All of the weapon's base physical attack is converted to bolt attack, and the weapon will use arcane scaling instead of scaling with strength and skill. It then receives the bonus bolt damage from the gem effect. Applying this gem effect to a buffable weapon will prevent it from receiving the effects of Fire Paper, Bolt Paper, and Empty Phantasm Shell. Left-handed firearms cannot use the Bolt effect. The Reiterpallasch can, and this enables it to shoot bolt-elemental bullets when using this gem effect. It will lose its blood attack value, however.

Tempering

This effect increases your physical attack by a percentage. The possible values range from +0.3% to +28.1%. All right-hand weapons, with the notable exception of the transformed mode of Chikage, deal physical-type damage, so this goes well with anything. Interestingly enough, this gem also adds to blood attack, so it works for Chikage's transformed mode and firearms, as well!

Gems that change your weapon's damage type to bolt can be very helpful against the powerful enemies in Yahar'gul when the Blood Moon is out.

Split-damage weapons like the Tonitrus benefit most from Nourishing gems, which boost their attack power evenly.

Nourishing

Nourishing increases all of a weapon's attack power by a percentage. The values can be from +0.3% to +24.4%. This boost applies to all of a weapon's damage types. At first glance, this seems like a weaker effect than Tempering, since the maximum Nourishing effect (24.4%) is less than the maximum Tempering effect (28.1%). The key is to use the Nourishing effect with a weapon like Logarius' Wheel that has multiple damage types; all of the attack powers will receive the boost! In the case of the Logarius' Wheel, its physical attack and its arcane will both be increased.

The Nourishing effect can apply to every weapon that has a gem slot, but it's best used for those that have more than one damage type; specifically: Tonitrus, Logarius' Wheel, Burial Blade, and the Blade of Mercy. It can be used for firearms as well, but the Bloodtinge effect is better for those.

Notably, there is a negative version of this effect. The values range from -0.3% to -24.4%. This a terrible effect in almost every situation and should be avoided.

Heavy

The Heavy effect adds strength scaling to a weapon. The effect values can be from +0.3 to +28.1. This can be used on any right-hand weapon, but it only influences the weapon's physical attack. Blood attack is completely ignored, so this will not affect the shot power of Reiterpallasch and the Rifle Spear. It's also useless for Chikage's transformed mode.

This effect is best used to tailor a weapon to your stats. If you have high strength, the Heavy effect will offer some benefit. That said, this only affects physical damage and Tempering is often better.

Tempering gems provide an unconditional damage boost that doesn't depend on your current HP, so you'll always benefit from their effects.

Heavy gems are best suited to weapons that already have high strength scaling such as Ludwig's Holy Blade or the Kirkhammer, and are most effective for characters focused heavily on strength.

Sharp

The Sharp effect adds skill scaling to a weapon. The effect values can be from +0.3 to +28.1. This can be used on any right-hand weapon, but it only influences the weapon's physical attack. Blood attack is completely ignored, so this will not affect the shot power of Reiterpallasch and the Rifle Spear. It's also useless for Chikage's transformed mode.

This effect is best used to tailor a weapon to your stats. If you have high skill, the Sharp effect will offer some benefit. That said, this only affects physical damage and Tempering is often better.

Warm

The Warm effect adds bloodtinge scaling to a weapon. The effect values can be from +0.3 to +28.1. This only works for weapons that naturally have blood attack, and it only increases blood attack. It will increase the power of left-hand weapons, Chikage's transformed mode, and the gunshots of Reiterpallasch and the Rifle Spear. If you have high bloodtinge, the Warm effect will offer some benefit. That said, the Bloodtinge effect is usually better.

Beasthunter

This gem effect increases your damage against beasts. The value ranges from +0.4% to +33.8%. The effect stacks multiplicatively; having three max Beasthunter effects on your weapon will give you a stunning 139% increase to your damage against beasts. Obviously, this is a huge boon against beast-type enemies. The limitation is that it only works against beasts; this isn't really a great effect for your main weapon, but if you want to keep a weapon dedicated strictly to killing beasts this effect will work very well. This can appear as a negative effect with values ranging from -0.4% to -33.8%. There are a lot of enemies that count as beasts, so this isn't great, but if you may be able to tolerate the negative version of this effect if the gem comes with something else that you really want. Just be prepared to deal with beasts in another way; items, a co-op partner, or a backup weapon are all possible options.

Beasts

Enemy	Page
Scourge Beast	p266
Carrion Crow	p230
Rabid Dog (Gray)	p231
Cleric Beast	p326
Labyrinth Rat	p233
Maneater Boar	p270
Large Huntsman	p231
Father Gascoigne (Beast)	p328
Beast Patient (Male)	p236
Ashen Blood Beast Patient (Female)	p237
Blood-starved Beast	p330
Vicar Amelia	p336
Abhorrent Beast	p386
Beast-possessed Soul	p275
Hunting Dog	p238
Darkbeast Paarl	p334
Loran Silverbeast	p281
Keeper's Hunting Dog	p305
Labyrinth Madman	p299
Watchdog of the Old Lord	p376
Bloodletting Beast	p390

Cold

The Cold effect adds between +0.3 and +28.1 arcane scaling to a weapon. Weapons that naturally have arcane attack (Logarius' Wheel, Burial Blade, and Blade of Mercy) can use this. It can also be used with buffable weapons, but they must first be equipped with either an Arcane effect or an Odd Arcane effect; since those effects convert their physical attack to arcane, the Cold effect will then function properly. If you have high a arcane stat, the Cold effect will offer some benefit. That said, the Arcane effect is usually better.

Cold gems provide a boost to the arcane damage of weapons like Logarius' Wheel, but you're better off using Arcane gems if you have access to them.

Kinhunter

This gem effect increases your damage against kin. The value ranges from +0.4% to +33.8%. The effect stacks multiplicatively; having three max Kinhunter effects on your weapon will give you a stunning 139% increase to your damage against kin. Obviously, this is a huge boon against kin-type enemies. The limitation is that it only works against kin; this isn't really a great effect for your main weapon, but if you want to keep a weapon dedicated strictly to killing kin this effect will work very well. This can appear as a negative effect with values ranging from -0.4% to -33.8%. There are less kin enemies than beasts, so you may be able to tolerate the negative version of this effect if the gem comes with something else that you really want. Just be prepared to deal with kin in another way; items, a co-op partner, or a backup weapon are all possible options. There are very few enemies in the game fall in to the Kin category.

Kin

Enemy	Page
Celestial Child	p247
Small Celestial Emissary	p241
Fluorescent Flower	p286
Ebrietas, Daughter of the Cosmos	p350
Celestial Emissary	p348

Very few enemies are classified as Kin, severely limiting the usefulness of Kinhunter gems except in certain situations and against specific bosses.

Murky

The Murky gem effect gives you the ability to inflict Slow Poison build-up on the enemy. At low levels you'll likely kill the enemy before inflicting the status, but at high levels it can be very effective. The range goes from +0.2 to +18.7. The effect can be applied to any right-hand weapon, but note that the gun attacks of Reiterpallasch and the Rifle Spear cannot inflict poison.

Poison build-up is the same per hit, regardless of the damage that your attack does, so for this reason it works best with fast weapons and weapons with multi-hit attacks. The Blade of Mercy can build up poison very quickly with its rapid transformed mode R1 attacks and has very low stamina consumption. Logarius' Wheel's transformed mode R2 hits several times and also works well with the Murky effect. Some tough enemies are actually easy to poison, and it's also very useful in co-op; you can coordinate gems so that multiple players are causing build-up. Since bosses receive a major health boost during cooperative play, the damage from poison is even more valuable and can really add up over a lengthy battle

Enemies weak to Slow Poison Build-up

Enemy	Page
Abhorrent Beast	p386
Kidnapper	p276
Giant Lost Child	p282
Fluorescent Flower	p286
Parasite Larva	p242
Labyrinth Warrior	p302

Dirty

The Dirty gem effect gives you the ability to inflict Rapid Poison build-up on the enemy. At low levels, the build-up is too slow; you'll kill the enemy before inflicting the status. At high levels, though, it can be very effective. The range goes from +0.2 to +18.7. The effect can be applied to any right-hand weapon, but note that the gun attacks of Reiterpallasch and the Rifle Spear cannot inflict poison. Poison build-up is the same per hit, regardless of the damage that your attack does. For this reason, poison works best with fast weapons and weapons with multi-hit attacks. The Blade of Mercy can build up poison very quickly with its rapid transformed mode R1 attacks and has very low stamina consumption. Logarius' Wheel's transformed mode R2 hits several times and also works well with the Dirty effect.

The Chikage is another weapon that you may be drawn to when using the Dirty effect; it has a natural Rapid Poison effect in its transformed mode. This is a good match, and the transformed Chikage, when loaded with three max Dirty effects, can do more Rapid Poison build-up in a single hit than any other weapon in the game. Despite that, the Blade of Mercy is an equally worthy weapon for your Dirty effects for fighting normally; the attack speed and low stamina costs are enough to make up for the lower build-up per hit. In PvP, on the other hand, it may be difficult to land large combos on the enemy, so dealing a lot of build-up in one attack is extremely useful.

Enemies weak to Fast Poison Build-up

Enemy	Page
Kidnapper	p286
Parasite Larva	p242
Loran Silverbeast	p281
Giant Lost Child	p282
Crawler	p246
Large Crawler	p283
Fluorescent Flower	p286
Bloodlicker	p280

Finestrike

The Finestrike effect increases your damage when you land a counterhit. Your attack power will be increased between +0.4% and +37.5% depending on the power of the effect. To get the bonus, you have to land a counterhit, which means that you need to strike the enemy as it attacks or just after. It's harder to pull off than a normal attack, but the damage bonus is extremely high.

Of all the weapons, this effect works best with the Rifle Spear; the combination of speed and range makes it easy to land counterhits. The power is also quite good, so the boost from the Finestrike effect is also high. Particularly in co-op, where the enemy is not focused on you exclusively, you can get a very nice bonus from stacking Finestrike.

In PvP, it may be difficult to land counterhits, but it will certainly surprise other players if you hit them with a weapon dedicated to Finestrike effects. A risky tactic that will work against some players is to use a large weapon loaded with Finestrike effects in conjunction with a Lead Elixir. If they try to interrupt your attack, it will fail and they'll eat a massive counter hit. This is suicide against a good player, though; they'll recognize your gimmick immediately and hit you hard from range or with charge attacks that break your temporary super armor.

Radiant

This effect reduces the stamina cost of your attacks; the value ranges from a 0.1% decrease in cost to a 9.4% decrease! If you are using a stamina hog like the Hunter Axe or the Kirkhammer, this effect may be even more valuable than a damage increase. On the other hand, a light weapon like the Blade of Mercy is already stamina-efficient, so the Radiant effect might be overkill.

Also be warned that this effect has a negative version that increases costs. You can have you costs increased from 0.1% all the way up to 9.4%. This is pretty terrible, but if your gem has another really good effect, you might be able to live with it. If you're using a light weapon, the increased cost might not bother you as much as it otherwise would, and you could always use the Anti-Clockwise Metamorphosis Caryll Rune to increase your max stamina. Just be sure that the other effect is worth it!

Striking

Striking increases the damage of your charge attacks; these are the moves that require you to hold R2 until they execute. The possible increases range from +0.4% to +37.5%. This only influences the physical damage, though; elemental attack power is not increased by the Striking effect.

In some ways, this is similar to Finestrike; the damage increase that comes from this effect is massive, but it requires skillful play to gain the benefit. For weapons like the Hunter Axe, Ludwig's Holy Blade, and the Rifle Spear that have amazing charged R2 attacks, this effect can really shine. Just remember that when you are using R1 or uncharged R2 attacks, you won't see any damage increase at all! This is an amazing effect for advanced players.

Remember that some weapons have faster charge attacks than others. The Saw Cleaver, for example, isn't as powerful as some other weapons, but its charged R2 comes out very quickly. You can reliably strike an enemy with it and can even perform a second

charged attack while an enemy is staggered from your first one to deal incredible damage. When combined with this gem effect, the damage is frankly ridiculous. Non-buffable weapons are generally not recommended for this effect. They have split damage types, and only the physical portion of their attacks will be increased by Striking. Check the table at the start of this chapter for a reminder about charged attack speeds.

Pulsing

The Pulsing effect will restore a few points of your HP each second; yes, it's as powerful as it sounds. The effect ranges from +0.5 HP per second to +5.6 HP per second. This effect will stack if you have it on your left-hand weapon and your right-hand weapon. This is a passive, defensive effect. It won't help your damage output, it can keep you alive. There are tons of special situations in which you might use it, as well. In a poison swamp, you can use this to limit how often you need to heal the poison damage. If you use the transformed Chikage, this can help to offset the health drain. If you're running low on your stock of Blood Vials, you can use this to heal so that you can save up.

Having this on a back-up firearm is very good. You can use your main firearm for damage and only swap when you need the HP regain. The challenge is that you'll need to find this effect on either a Circle gem or a Droplet gem. You can actually get a moderately strong one in the main game from the Doll's sidequest; check p635 for the details. This can also appear as a negative effect with values ranging from -0.5 HP per second to -26.3 HP per second. This is one of the worst negative effects possible, and you should avoid it if you can.

Though it doesn't see the same damage increase as purely physical weapons, the Burial Blade's swift charge attacks and powerful knockdown effects make it a strong candidate for Striking gems nonetheless.

Combining Striking and Radiant effects on a weapon can have devastating effects, particularly on large weapons such as Ludwig's Holy Blade.

Lethal

You might expect a gem effect named "Lethal" to increase your attack power, but it does not. Instead, it improves the amount of health you can Regain after taking damage. It increases the HP you Regain per hit by a percentage. The percentage can vary from +0.2% to +18.8%. If you have an aggressive playstyle, this can work out pretty well as you will be able to Regain more HP while attacking. It synergizes very well with Lead Elixirs. Lead Elixirs grant you super armor so you can take a hit or two without flinching; this means that you can keep swinging your weapon. With a heavy weapon, you can get hit, keep swinging, make the enemy flinch, and possibly even Regain all the health you lost thanks to the Lethal effect.

Lethal gems stack excellently with the Guidance Caryll Rune, allowing you to aggressively trade blows with most enemies with little regard for your own wellbeing.

Dense

The Dense effect slows the rate that your weapon loses durability; this makes it harder for your weapon to break. The values can range from 0.4 to 37.5. This is not a particularly useful effect. As long as you repair your equipment whenever you return to the Hunter's Dream, you shouldn't have problems with it breaking.

The Dense effect can also appear on Cursed gems as a negative effect; the values range from -2 to -187.5. Of all the negative effects, this one is the most manageable. Different weapons have different natural durability ratings, though; this effect is easier to deal with on high durability weapons like the Logarius' Wheel. Be warned; low durability weapons like Tonitrus, Chikage, and Reiterpallasch will break very quickly when under a Cursed Dense effect.

Fool

There are two versions of the Fool effect; one raises your physical attack, and the other one raises all of your attack power regardless of element. The requirement, though, is that you must be at full health.

Fool (physical) can range from +0.4% to +35.6%. For most weapons, this is the better choice; it gives a huge boost in attack power. In fact, it's only slightly less powerful than Striking or Finestrike, but the condition is easier to fulfill. This is an excellent effect, and it does apply to the gunshots of Reiterpallasch and the Rifle Spear. Fool (all) can range from +0.3% to +30%. For Tonitrus, Logarius' Wheel, Burial Blade, and Blade of Mercy, this is the better effect as it increases both the physical and elemental attack powers of those weapons.

Both forms of this gem are pretty bad for Chikage; in normal mode, they're fine, but transformed mode doesn't work well at all. The

health drain from the transformed Chikage ruins the Fool effect. Combining the Fool effect with the Pulsing effect is a very good idea; the HP regeneration from Pulsing will keep your HP full for use with Fool. You don't even have to have the Pulsing effect on your main weapon; it can go on a firearm.

Poorman

There are two versions of the Poorman effect; one raises your physical attack, and the other one raises all of your attack power regardless of element. The requirement, though, is that you must have low HP; specifically, you must be below 30% of your maximum HP. This is far riskier to use then the Fool effect. Poorman (physical) can range from +0.4% to +37.5%. For most weapons, this is the better choice; it gives a huge boost in attack power. In fact, it's as powerful as Striking or Finestrike, but the condition is obviously risky to maintain. This is an excellent effect, and it does apply to the gunshots of Reiterpallasch and the Rifle Spear. Poorman (all) can range from +0.3% to +31.9%. For Tonitrus, Logarius' Wheel, Burial Blade, and Blade of Mercy, this is the better effect as it increases both the physical and elemental attack powers of those weapons.

Both forms of this gem are pretty bad for Chikage; in normal mode, they're fine, but transformed mode doesn't work well at all. The health drain from the transformed Chikage ruins the makes it difficult to maintain the Poorman effect unless you balance it with a Pulsing effect.

On the other hand, Chikage is an excellent, safe way to activate the Poorman effect without putting yourself in danger; just equip Chikage and use transform mode until the Poorman effect appears, and then immediately swap to normal mode. You can then change to whichever weapon you would like to use.

There are two main approaches to the use of this gem effect; either stack HP so that you can survive a light hit even in Poorman mode or completely ignore HP and focus on dodging everything. If you choose to stack HP, a high vitality stat is required, and you should use Clockwise Metamorphosis Runes for the additional HP. Ignoring HP altogether and trying to dodge everything is honestly a pretty bad idea in Bloodborne; there are no reliable shields, and the game's Regain mechanic is based entirely around the assumption that you will get hit. Enemies have a variety of fast, nearly impossible to dodge low-damage attacks that normally wouldn't bother you... but they'll be fatal if you don't increase your max HP and instead focus on the Poorman effect.

That said, if you have the patience and the skill, ignoring HP frees up stat points and Rune slots to pump damage. If you like life on the edge, don't touch your vitality at all and keep yourself poor, man!

An interesting style of play is to carry two weapons with Poorman and Fool effects separately, and swapping weapons depending on your damage taken mid-combat.

5

Attire

In this section we present all of the many attire oprions Bloodborne provides for the more fashion-conscious player. Their effects on your defense aren't always dramatic, but the confidence they instill can't be underestimated; looking good can kill.

Crown of Illusions

One of the precious secrets of Cainhurst. The old king's crown is said to reveal illusions, and expose a mirage that hides a secret. And so Logarius donned the crown of his own volition, determined to prevent a single soul from stumbling upon the vile secret. What visions did he see, sitting serenely upon his new throne?

WHERE TO FIND Defeat Martyr Logarius [p113]

Basic Stats	Buy	Sell											
Crown of Illusions	–	35000	40	30	20	70	50	30	20	7	7	4	4
(no chest piece)	–	–	–	–	–	–	–	–	–	–	–	–	–
(no arms piece)	–	–	–	–	–	–	–	–	–	–	–	–	–
(no legs piece)	–	–	–	–	–	–	–	–	–	–	–	–	–

Mensis Cage

The School of Mensis controls the Unseen Village. The hexagonal iron cage suggests their strange ways. The cage is a device that restrains the will of the self, allowing one to see the profane world for what it is. It also serves as an antenna that facilitates contact with the Great Ones of the dream. But to an observer, the iron cage appears to be precisely what delivered them to their harrowing nightmare.

WHERE TO FIND Defeat Micolash, Host of the Nightmare [p352]

Basic Stats	Buy	Sell											
Mensis Cage	–	6000	60	20	10	30	40	20	10	8	13	2	5
(no chest piece)	–	–	–	–	–	–	–	–	–	–	–	–	–
(no arms piece)	–	–	–	–	–	–	–	–	–	–	–	–	–
(no legs piece)	–	–	–	–	–	–	–	–	–	–	–	–	–

Arianna's Attire

A finely tailored bordeaux dress. Worn by the nobles of the old bloodline that traces back to the forsaken Castle Cainhurst. The shoes are worn by Arianna, woman of the night in the Cathedral Ward. Innocent and cute, in contrast with its owner.

WHERE TO FIND Dress: Forsaken Cainhurst [p107], Shoes: Kill Arianna [p639]

Basic Stats	Buy	Sell											
(no head piece)	–	–	–	–	–	–	–	–	–	–	–	–	–
Noble Dress	–	1200	50	60	40	130	60	40	70	23	31	27	38
(no arms piece)	–	–	–	–	–	–	–	–	–	–	–	–	–
Arianna's Shoes	–	2000	40	50	40	50	40	40	50	14	18	16	22

Ashen Hunter Attire

Attire of the retired hunter Djura. Painted with ash in a ceremony to ward off blood. The worn wolf cap was his trademark. Djura is known through his contact with the Powder Kegs, the heretics of the workshop. He is said to have been both uncommonly kind and dreadfully foolish. Djura felt defeated by the state of Old Yharnam, and renounced his hunter's vows.

SHOP Insight Shop | **UNLOCK CONDITION** Defeat or befriend Retired Hunter Djura [p648]

Basic Stats

	Buy	Sell											
Gray Wolf Cap	1	700	50	40	40	50	20	50	30	9	12	19	37
Ashen Hunter Garb	3	2100	100	110	80	110	70	50	70	25	45	60	70
Ashen Hunter Gloves	1	700	40	60	50	40	50	40	50	13	24	28	32
Ashen Hunter Trousers	1	700	60	50	50	60	50	50	50	15	26	30	37

Black Church Attire (Male)

Attire of Healing Church hunters. The Holy Shawl, symbol of the Healing Church, flutters proudly on the backs of the garb. The white surgical gloves intricate embroidery weaves a spell that protects their wearer. The Church engages in the hunt in a medical capacity. When a cancer is discovered, one must pinpoint its location, reach in, and wrench it from the host's bosom. Most Healing Church hunters are elementary doctors who understand the importance of early prevention of the scourge, achieved by disposing of victims, and even potential victims, before signs of sickness manifest themselves. Their black attire is synonymous with fear, and that peculiar Yharnam madness.

WHERE TO FIND Cathedral Ward [p52]

Basic Stats

	Buy	Sell											
Black Church Hat (Male)	–	210	40	40	40	50	60	50	50	20	19	2	13
Black Church Garb (Male)	–	420	90	90	110	110	110	100	110	60	58	9	40
Surgical Long Gloves	–	210	40	40	50	70	50	50	50	32	31	4	22
Black Church Trousers	–	210	50	50	60	70	60	60	60	34	33	5	23

Black Church Attire (Female)

Attire of Healing Church hunters. The Holy Shawl, symbol of the Healing Church, flutters proudly on the backs of the garb. The white surgical gloves intricate embroidery weaves a spell that protects their wearer. The Church engages in the hunt in a medical capacity. When a cancer is discovered, one must pinpoint its location, reach in, and wrench it from the host's bosom. Most Healing Church hunters are elementary doctors who understand the importance of early prevention of the scourge, achieved by disposing of victims, and even potential victims, before signs of sickness manifest themselves. Their black attire is synonymous with fear, and that peculiar Yharnam madness.

WHERE TO FIND Cathedral Ward [p52]

Basic Stats

	Buy	Sell											
Black Church Hat (Female)	–	210	40	40	40	50	60	50	50	20	19	2	13
Black Church Garb (Female)	–	420	90	90	110	110	110	100	110	60	58	9	40
Surgical Long Gloves	–	210	40	40	50	70	50	50	50	32	31	4	22
Black Church Dress	–	210	50	50	60	70	60	60	60	34	33	5	23

Bone Ash Attire

Armor made of bone ash, worn by the oldest keepers. The keepers, who mind the slumbering Great Ones, gained eternal life, preserved in ashen form in a ceremony of flame that cremated body and soul. Now, their frail armor is white and sinewy, a window into an arcane lost art. The long, pointed hat is a symbol of the old keepers and is considered evidence of their companionship, forged in a certain sin.

SHOP Insight Shop | **UNLOCK CONDITION** Defeat Keeper of the Old Lords [p378]

Basic Stats	👁 Buy	Sell	⬛	🌑	🔺	✴	⭐	〰	♫	💀	▽	🌀
Bone Ash Mask	2	7500	60	30	40	20	20	60	60	11	9	14	8
Bone Ash Armor	4	15000	110	80	100	40	40	140	140	33	29	41	25
Bone Ash Gauntlets	2	7500	60	30	50	30	40	70	70	17	15	22	13
Bone Ash Leggings	2	7500	60	40	50	50	40	80	70	19	17	24	15

Cainhurst Armor

Silver armor worn by the royal guards who protect Annalise, Queen of the Vilebloods at Cainhurst Castle. This paper-thin silver armor is said to deflect blood of ill-intent, and is what allows the royal guards to capture prey for their beloved Queen, so that one day, she may bear a Child of Blood.

SHOP Bath Messengers | **UNLOCK CONDITION** Cainhurst Badge [p596]

Basic Stats	🩸 Buy	Sell	⬛	🌑	🔺	✴	⭐	〰	♫	💀	▽	🌀
Cainhurst Helmet	27000	18900	60	40	40	60	20	40	10	12	13	8	7
Cainhurst Armor	44000	30800	120	70	110	120	40	80	30	36	40	26	22
Cainhurst Gauntlets	21000	14700	60	30	50	70	40	40	30	19	21	13	11
Cainhurst Leggings	21000	14700	60	40	60	70	40	40	40	21	23	15	13

Charred Hunter Attire

One of the staple articles of hunter attire, fashioned at the workshop. A product of the scourge of the beast that once plagued Old Yharnam and culminated in the town's fiery cleansing. Designed to be highly resistant to fire. Wearers of this attire hunted down victims of the scourge who survived the raging flames and stench of singed blood.

WHERE TO FIND Old Yharnam [p61]

Basic Stats	🩸 Buy	Sell	⬛	🌑	🔺	✴	⭐	〰	♫	💀	▽	🌀
(no head piece)	–	–	–	–	–	–	–	–	–	–	–	–	–
Charred Hunter Garb	–	1080	110	100	70	100	40	140	60	29	37	45	58
Charred Hunter Gloves	–	540	60	40	40	50	40	70	40	15	20	24	30
Charred Hunter Trousers	–	540	60	60	50	60	40	80	40	17	21	27	33

Choir Attire

Attire of the Choir, high-ranking members of the Healing Church. Members of the Choir are both the highest-ranking clerics of the Healing Church, and scholars who continue the work that began at Byrgenwerth. Together with the left behind Great One, they look to the skies, in search of astral signs, that may lead them to the rediscovery of true greatness. The eye covering indicates their debt to the teachings of Master Willem, even though their paths diverged.

WHERE TO FIND Upper Cathedral Ward [p141]

Basic Stats	Buy	Sell	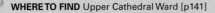										
Blindfold Cap	–	600	30	40	40	40	70	50	50	15	13	4	13
Choir Garb	–	1200	80	80	80	80	150	110	110	46	38	16	38
Choir Gloves	–	600	40	40	40	40	70	60	70	24	20	8	20
Choir Trousers	–	600	50	50	50	60	80	60	60	26	22	9	22

Crowfeather Attire

Attire worn by Eileen the Crow, Hunter of Hunters, known in particular for her crowfeather cape. The wood-carved beak contains incense to mask scents of blood and beast. Hunters of Hunters dress as crows to suggest sky burial. The first Hunter of Hunters came from a foreign land, and gave the dead a virtuous native funeral ritual, rather than impose a blasphemous Yharnam burial service upon them, with the hope that former compatriots might be returned to the skies, and find rest in a hunter's dream.

SHOP Bath Messengers | **UNLOCK CONDITION** Acquire Crow Hunter Badge [p595]

Basic Stats	Buy	Sell	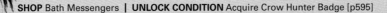										
Beak Mask	10000	6300	50	40	40	60	30	40	30	8	10	40	2
Crowfeather Garb	18000	12600	100	110	80	120	70	80	70	29	37	46	21
Crowfeather Manchettes	8000	5600	40	60	50	70	50	50	50	15	20	25	11
Crowfeather Trousers	8000	5600	50	70	50	70	40	50	50	17	21	27	12

Executioner Attire

Attire worn by the band of executioners commanded by the martyr Logarius. The conical gold helmet, symbol of the executioners, represents luminosity, ambition, and an un-flagging resolve to face impurity, staring it down with stern, golden spirit. Later became the basis for all Church attire, especially with its heavy draping of Holy Shawl. The brass rivets of the gauntlets are unique to the executioners, and reflect their adoration of hand-to-hand combat. As the great Logarius once said, "Acts of goodness are not always wise, and acts of evil are not always foolish, but regardless, we shall always strive to be good."

SHOP Bath Messengers | **UNLOCK CONDITION** Wheel Hunter Badge [p596]

WHERE TO FIND Forsaken Cainhurst Castle [p108]

Basic Stats	Buy	Sell	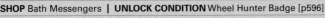										
Gold Ardeo	60000	6000	50	40	60	40	40	40	70	12	15	13	16
Executioner Garb	–	1800	90	120	110	100	110	90	100	53	45	17	45
Executioner Gauntlets	–	900	40	60	40	50	60	50	50	26	24	9	24
Executioner Trousers	–	900	50	70	50	60	60	60	50	30	26	10	26

5

Foreign Attire (Male)

Clothing worn upon awakening to the nightmare of blood and beasts. The hood suggests that its wearer had to stay out of sight, and travel by cover of darkness. The bandage looks terribly worn and unsanitary. A faint memory recalls blood ministration, involving the transfusion of unknown blood. Not long after, the nightmare began. Not typical clothing for Yharnam, perhaps it is of foreign origin. It is said, after all, the traveler came to Yharnam from afar. Without memory, who will ever know?

WHERE TO FIND Default Attire

Basic Stats

	Buy	Sell	▭	◐	△	☀	★	🍃	♫	☠	▽	◎
Black Hood	–	150	20	30	20	30	20	30	30	8	6	8	4
Foreign Garb (Male)	–	300	60	60	40	50	40	60	60	27	19	27	16
Sullied Bandage	–	150	30	40	30	30	40	40	40	14	10	14	8
Foreign Trousers	–	150	40	50	40	40	50	50	50	16	11	16	9

Foreign Attire (Female)

Clothing worn upon awakening to the nightmare of blood and beasts. The hood suggests that its wearer had to stay out of sight, and travel by cover of darkness. The bandage looks terribly worn and unsanitary. A faint memory recalls blood ministration, involving the transfusion of unknown blood. Not long after, the nightmare began. Not typical clothing for Yharnam, perhaps it is of foreign origin. It is said, after all, the traveler came to Yharnam from afar. Without memory, who will ever know?

WHERE TO FIND Default Attire

Basic Stats

	Buy	Sell	▭	◐	△	☀	★	🍃	♫	☠	▽	◎
Black Hood	–	150	20	30	20	30	20	30	30	8	6	8	4
Foreign Garb (Female)	–	300	60	60	40	50	40	60	60	27	19	27	16
Sullied Bandage	–	150	30	40	30	30	40	40	40	14	10	14	8
Foreign Trousers	–	150	40	50	40	40	50	50	50	16	11	16	9

Gascoigne's Attire

Hunter attire worn by Father Gascoigne. Similar to hunter garb created at the workshop, only these are tainted by a pungent beastly stench that eats away at Gascoigne. The dingy scarf is a Holy Shawl and symbol of the Healing Church, from which Gascoigne would eventually part ways. "Father" is a title used for clerics in a foreign land, and there is no such rank in the Healing Church.

SHOP Insight Shop | **UNLOCK CONDITION** Defeat Father Gascoigne [p328]

Basic Stats

	Buy	Sell	▭	◐	△	☀	★	🍃	♫	☠	▽	◎
Gascoigne's Cap	1	700	40	40	30	40	50	50	50	17	13	7	15
Gascoigne's Garb	3	2100	90	110	100	80	110	110	100	52	40	23	45
Gascoigne's Gloves	1	700	40	60	60	50	60	60	40	28	21	12	24
Gascoigne's Trousers	1	700	50	60	60	50	60	60	50	31	23	14	26

Gehrman's Hunter Attire

Hunter attire of Gehrman, the first hunter. Created before the workshop existed by making adjustments to everyday clothing, and later became the basis for all hunter's garb. The hunter's emphasis on engaging beasts with speed, and therefore of selecting lightweight attire, no doubt traces back to Gehrman's own combat style.

SHOP Bath Messengers | **UNLOCK CONDITION** Old Hunter Badge [p595]

Basic Stats	♠ Buy	♠ Sell	■	◐	▲	☀	★	∿	♫	☠	▽	◎	
Gehrman's Hunter Cap	7000	4900	40	40	40	50	30	40	30	11	12	17	15
Gehrman's Hunter Garb	17000	11900	100	80	80	100	50	80	70	33	37	52	46
(no arms piece)	–	–	–	–	–	–	–	–	–	–	–	–	–
Gehrman's Hunter Trousers	7000	4900	50	50	50	60	50	50	50	19	21	29	27

Graveguard Attire

Clothing of Dores, graveguard of the Forbidden Woods. The pale countenance of the mask mimics the labyrinth Watchers. Countless bloodied ritual tools hang from the back of the robe. Manchettes and kilt are covered in the blood of untidy rituals. Willem kept two loyal servants back at Byrgenwerth. When they were sent into the labyrinth, they encountered the eldritch Truth, and went mad. One became the password gatekeeper, while Dores became a graveguard of the forest. Both remained loyal, even in madness.

WHERE TO FIND Forbidden Woods [p99]

Basic Stats	♠ Buy	♠ Sell	■	◐	▲	☀	★	∿	♫	☠	▽	◎	
Graveguard Mask	–	2800	40	40	50	40	50	40	50	16	16	32	13
Graveguard Robe	–	5600	80	80	90	80	100	80	110	50	49	49	40
Graveguard Manchettes	–	2800	40	50	50	50	60	50	60	27	26	26	22
Graveguard Kilt	–	2800	50	50	60	50	60	60	60	29	28	28	23

Henryk's Hunter Attire

Hunter's attire worn by Henryk, the old hunter. The taciturn old hunter Henryk was once partners with Father Gascoigne, and though they were a fierce and gallant duo, their partnership led to Henryk's tragically long life. Henryk's unique yellow garb is resistant to bolt and will be of great help to any hunter who has inherited the onus of the hunt.

SHOP Insight Shop | **UNLOCK CONDITION** Defeat Henryk [p315]

Basic Stats	👁 Buy	♠ Sell	■	◐	▲	☀	★	∿	♫	☠	▽	◎	
Henryk's Hunter Cap	1	700	50	50	40	40	20	30	60	7	14	15	20
Henryk's Hunter Garb	3	2100	100	100	80	80	70	100	150	21	41	45	60
Henryk's Hunter Gloves	1	700	50	40	50	40	50	60	70	11	22	23	32
Henryk's Hunter Trousers	1	700	50	60	60	50	50	60	80	12	24	25	34

5

Heroine Doll Attire

Discarded doll clothing, likely a spare for dress-up. A deep love for the doll can be surmised by the fine craftsmanship of this article, and the care with which it was kept. It borderlines on mania, and exudes a slight warmth.

WHERE TO FIND Healing Church Workshop [p71]

Basic Stats	Buy	Sell	■	◐	◭	✴	★	🪶	♫	💀	▽	◎
Doll Hat	–	7000	10	10	10	20	20	30	20	14	10	13	10
Doll Clothes	–	14000	30	30	30	40	40	50	40	42	31	38	31
Doll Gloves	–	7000	30	30	30	40	40	50	40	22	16	20	16
Doll Skirt	–	7000	40	40	40	50	50	60	50	24	18	22	18

Hunter Attire

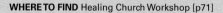

One of the standard articles of hunter attire fashioned at the workshop, accompanied with a short cape to wipe away blood. A fine piece of hunter attire that provides stable defense to anyone facing Yharnam's beastly threat. Recognizable by its withered feathers, the cap is fashioned after one of the old hunters. This attire allows one to stalk beasts unannounced, by cover of night.

WHERE TO FIND Central Yharnam [p39]

Basic Stats	Buy	Sell	■	◐	◭	✴	★	🪶	♫	💀	▽	◎
Hunter Hat	–	240	50	50	40	50	20	50	30	5	11	14	16
Hunter Garb (Cape)	–	480	110	110	80	110	40	110	70	17	33	48	44
Hunter Gloves	–	240	50	50	50	50	40	60	50	9	17	27	25
Hunter Trousers	–	240	60	60	50	60	50	60	50	10	19	30	27

Hunter Attire (City)

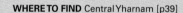

One of the standard articles of hunter attire fashioned at the workshop. A fine piece of hunter attire that provides stable defense to anyone facing Yharnam's beastly threat. Hat worn by hunters who admire formality. Some hunters place an emphasis on form, as seen by the use of the threaded cane. For them, formality, beauty, and justice are the very essence of our humanity, and precisely what keeps hunters from becoming something else.

WHERE TO FIND Cathedral Ward [p49]

Basic Stats	Buy	Sell	■	◐	◭	✴	★	🪶	♫	💀	▽	◎
Top Hat	–	420	30	70	40	20	20	30	40	14	13	10	8
Hunter Garb	–	420	110	100	80	110	40	110	70	17	33	56	58
Hunter Gloves	–	240	50	50	50	50	40	60	50	9	17	27	25
Hunter Trousers	–	240	60	60	50	60	50	60	50	10	19	30	27

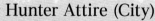
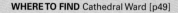

Knight's Attire (Male)

Adornment prized by the knights of Cainhurst. The wig resembles a ponytail of silver hair. The garb is a regal piece graced by intricate goldwork, the gloves graced with goldwork on red fabric. The trousers are made with the finest leather. The Cainhurst way is a mix of nostalgia and bombast. They take great pride even in the blood-stained corpses of beasts that they leave behind, confident that they will stand as examples of decadent art.

WHERE TO FIND Forsaken Cainhurst Castle [p110]

Basic Stats	Buy	Sell											
Knight's Wig (Male)	–	12600	30	40	40	60	40	30	50	8	14	13	12
Knight's Garb (Male)	–	25200	90	70	80	140	40	50	80	26	43	40	36
Knight's Gloves (Male)	–	10500	40	50	50	70	40	40	50	13	22	21	19
Knight's Trousers	–	10500	50	50	60	70	50	50	50	15	24	23	21

Knight's Attire (Female)

Adornment prized by the knights of Cainhurst. The wig resembles a ponytail of silver hair. The garb is a regal piece graced by intricate goldwork, the gloves graced with goldwork on red fabric. The dress is made with the finest leather. The Cainhurst way is a mix of nostalgia and bombast. They take great pride even in the blood-stained corpses of beasts that they leave behind, confident that they will stand as examples of decadent art.

WHERE TO FIND Forsaken Cainhurst Castle [p110]

Basic Stats	Buy	Sell											
Knight's Wig (Female)	–	12600	30	40	40	60	40	30	50	8	14	13	12
Knight's Garb (Female)	–	25200	90	70	80	140	40	50	80	26	43	40	36
Knight's Gloves (Female)	–	10500	40	50	50	70	40	40	50	13	22	21	19
Knight's Dress	–	10500	50	50	60	70	50	50	50	15	24	23	21

Madman Attire

Most tomb prospectors, members of the Healing Church chosen to explore the old labyrinth, are unable to withstand the weight of the old knowledge, and go mad. This attire is worn by those lost souls. Truth oft resembles madness, inaccessible to the dull of mind. Those who go mad are merely thoughtful souls who failed to reach any conclusions. The appendages draped across them are said to be a kind of protective charm, or at least, that is what these lost souls believe with all their hearts.

SHOP Insight Shop | **UNLOCK CONDITION** Defeat Forgotten Madman & Madman's Escort [p384]

Basic Stats	Buy	Sell											
Madman Hood	1	3000	40	30	40	40	60	50	50	18	17	1	9
Madman Garb	3	6000	80	70	80	80	120	110	110	59	52	4	29
Madman Manchettes	1	3000	40	40	50	40	60	60	60	29	27	1	15
Madman Leggings	1	3000	50	50	60	50	70	40	60	33	29	2	17

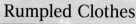

Rumpled Clothes

Common Yharnam cap. Well-worn, the hat losing its shape and the clothes damp with sweat.

WHERE TO FIND Healing Church Workshop [p71]

Basic Stats	⚒ Buy	⚒ Sell	▭	◐	▲	✦	★	🍃	♫	☠	▽	🌀
Rumpled Yharnam Hat	–	30	20	20	20	10	20	60	30	8	11	13	8
Sweaty Clothes	–	60	60	50	50	40	40	100	60	27	35	38	27
(no arms piece)	–	–	–	–	–	–	–	–	–	–	–	–	–
(no legs piece)	–	–	–	–	–	–	–	–	–	–	–	–	–

Student Attire

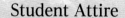

Uniform of the students of Byrgenwerth, a bygone institute learning. This alternative lacks the thick cape. The Healing Church has its roots in Byrgenwerth, and naturally borrows heavily from its uniform design. The focus not on knowledge, or thought, but on pure pretension would surely bring Master Willem to despair, if only he knew.

WHERE TO FIND Lecture Building 1F [p115]

Basic Stats	⚒ Buy	⚒ Sell	▭	◐	▲	✦	★	🍃	♫	☠	▽	🌀
(no head piece)	–	–	–	–	–	–	–	–	–	–	–	–	–
Student Uniform	–	8640	70	60	60	90	140	60	70	42	31	35	45
(no arms piece)	–	–	–	–	–	–	–	–	–	–	–	–	–
Student Trousers	–	4800	50	50	50	60	70	50	50	24	18	19	19

Student Attire (Coat)

Uniform of the students of Byrgenwerth, a bygone institute of learning. The uniform features a thick cape. The Healing Church has its roots in Byrgenwerth, and naturally borrows heavily from its uniform design. The focus not on knowledge, or thought, but on pure pretension would surely bring Master Willem to despair, if only he knew.

WHERE TO FIND Byrgenwerth [p127]

Basic Stats	⚒ Buy	⚒ Sell	▭	◐	▲	✦	★	🍃	♫	☠	▽	🌀
(no head piece)	–	–	–	–	–	–	–	–	–	–	–	–	–
Student Uniform (Coat)	–	11200	70	70	70	100	140	60	70	42	31	35	35
(no arms piece)	–	–	–	–	–	–	–	–	–	–	–	–	–
Student Trousers	–	4800	50	50	50	60	70	50	50	24	18	19	19

Tomb Prospector Attire

Attire of tomb prospectors who explore the old labyrinth on behalf of the Healing Church. The Healing Church traces its roots to Byrgenwerth, and is therefore aware of the ruins' true importance. They contain much more than mere hunter trinkets, indeed, they hide the very secrets of the old Great Ones, sought after by those with the insight to imagine greatness.

SHOP Bath Messengers | **UNLOCK CONDITION** Radiant Sword Hunter Badge [p596]

Basic Stats	Buy	Sell	⬛	🌑	▲	☀	★	🍃	🎵	☠	▽	@	
Tomb Prospector Hood	6000	3600	40	40	50	50	60	50	50	18	16	4	15
Tomb Prospector Garb	18000	10800	90	90	100	90	120	100	110	55	57	13	45
Tomb Prospector Gloves	6000	3600	40	40	60	50	60	60	60	29	27	6	24
Tomb Prospector Trousers	6000	3600	50	60	60	60	70	60	50	31	29	8	26

White Church Attire (Male)

Attire of special Church doctors. These doctors are superiors to the black preventative hunters, and specialists in experimentally backed blood ministration and the scourge of the beast. They believe that medicine is not a means of treatment but rather a method for research, and that some knowledge can only be obtained by exposing oneself to sickness.

WHERE TO FIND Forbidden Woods [p93]

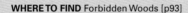

Basic Stats	Buy	Sell	⬛	🌑	▲	☀	★	🍃	🎵	☠	▽	@	
White Church Hat (Male)	–	240	30	40	40	60	60	60	60	21	18	3	12
White Church Garb (Male)	–	480	80	80	110	120	110	100	110	63	55	11	36
Surgical Long Gloves	–	210	40	40	50	70	50	50	50	32	31	4	22
White Church Trousers	–	240	50	40	50	80	70	60	60	36	31	7	21

White Church Attire (Female)

Attire of special Church doctors. These doctors are superiors to the black preventative hunters, and specialists in experimentally backed blood ministration and the scourge of the beast. They believe that medicine is not a means of treatment but rather a method for research, and that some knowledge can only be obtained by exposing oneself to sickness.

WHERE TO FIND Forbidden Woods [p93]

Basic Stats	Buy	Sell	⬛	🌑	▲	☀	★	🍃	🎵	☠	▽	@	
White Church Hat (Female)	–	240	30	40	40	60	60	60	60	21	18	3	12
White Church Garb (Female)	–	480	80	80	110	120	110	100	110	63	55	11	36
Surgical Long Gloves	–	210	40	40	50	70	50	50	50	32	31	4	22
White Church Dress	–	240	50	40	50	80	70	60	60	36	31	7	21

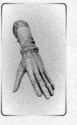

5

Yahar'gul Black Attire

Black attire worn by hunters of the Unseen Village. The hunters of Yahar'gul answer to the village's founders, the School of Mensis. Hunters in name only, these kidnappers wear their black hoods low to shadow their eyes. Removing the hood reveals something reminiscent of a warrior of a previous age. They blend into the night wearing this attire. This headwear is made of metal, a rarity for hunter garb, and has high defense, but only against physical attacks.

WHERE TO FIND Yahar'gul, Unseen Village (Evening) [p85]

Basic Stats

	Buy	Sell	▢	◯	△	✳	★	🪶	♪	☠	▽	◉
Black Hooded Iron Helm	–	900	60	40	10	20	20	30	20	13	12	12	8
Iron Yahar'gul Helm*	–	810	60	40	10	20	20	30	10	5	7	9	12
Yahar'gul Black Garb	–	1800	110	90	90	80	60	40	60	45	37	41	37
Yahar'gul Black Gloves	–	900	50	60	60	50	40	40	40	24	20	22	20
Yahar'gul Black Trousers	–	900	60	60	60	60	40	40	40	26	21	24	21

*Found in Yahar'gul, Unseen Village (Blood Moon) [p130].

Yharnam Hunter Attire (Male)

Ludwig, the first hunter of the Healing Church, once recruited Yharnamites to serve as hunters. This hunter's attire was made for new recruits, and has excellent straightforward defense. But not nearly enough to allow an ordinary man to stand any real chance against the beasts.

SHOP Bath Messengers | **UNLOCK CONDITION** Buy from Bath Messengers [p666]

Basic Stats

	Buy	Sell	▢	◯	△	✳	★	🪶	♪	☠	▽	◉
Yharnam Hunter Cap (Male)	500	250	50	40	40	40	50	50	50	16	13	14	16
Yharnam Hunter Garb (Male)	1000	500	110	80	90	90	80	100	90	48	40	41	48
Yharnam Hunter Gloves	500	250	40	50	60	40	50	60	50	25	22	22	25
Yharnam Hunter Trousers	500	250	50	60	60	50	50	60	60	27	23	24	27

Yharnam Hunter Attire (Female)

Ludwig, the first hunter of the Healing Church, once recruited Yharnamites to serve as hunters. This hunter's attire was made for new recruits, and has excellent straightforward defense. But not nearly enough to allow an ordinary woman to stand any real chance against the beasts.

SHOP Bath Messengers | **UNLOCK CONDITION** Buy from Bath Messengers [p666]

Basic Stats

	Buy	Sell	▢	◯	△	✳	★	🪶	♪	☠	▽	◉
Yharnam Hunter Cap (Female)	500	250	50	40	40	40	50	50	50	16	13	14	16
Yharnam Hunter Garb (Female)	1000	500	110	80	90	90	80	100	90	48	40	41	48
Yharnam Hunter Gloves	500	250	40	50	60	40	50	60	50	25	22	22	25
Yharnam Hunter Trousers	500	250	50	60	60	50	50	60	60	27	23	24	27

Brador's Attire `OH`

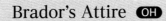

The bloodied hide of a horrible cleric beast, pulled over the back. Without the attached beast hide, this foreign garb wouldn't raise anyone's eyebrows. The scalp is of a horrible cleric beast, indicating that hunter Brador, a Healing Church assassin, had killed a compatriot. Afterward, he wore his ally's own scalp, and hid himself away, deep below in a cell. The Church provided him with a single, soundless bell of death, to ensure their secrets would be kept. Brador donned a compatriot's beastly scalp and hide while still moist with blood. Most of the blood stains on this hide were from that day.

WHERE TO FIND One piece is acquired from killing each phantom of Brador [p653]

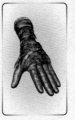

Basic Stats

	Buy	Sell											
Brador's Testimony	–	4800	50	60	50	50	20	20	30	18	10	6	56
Beast Hide Garb	–	7200	120	120	70	80	60	40	50	38	31	20	66
Bloodied Arm Bands	–	3600	30	40	30	40	40	30	40	10	14	14	36
Bloodied Trousers	–	3600	40	50	40	50	50	40	50	11	16	16	46

Butcher's Attire `OH`

Attire of the Madaras twins, denizens of the Forbidden Woods, likely belonging to the older of the two. Both the twins became hunters, and brought back and dissected their beast prey, in order to support the villagers in their forbidden research. The twins grew up in silent kinship with a poisonous snake. Eventually they learned human ways, and became hunters. When they discovered vermin even in their beloved snake, the younger brother is said to have murdered the older.

WHERE TO FIND Hunter's Nightmare [p171]

Basic Stats

	Buy	Sell											
Butcher Mask	–	1500	50	30	50	30	40	30	50	20	19	11	9
Butcher Garb	–	3000	100	60	100	60	90	70	110	53	59	33	29
Butcher Gloves	–	1500	60	40	60	40	50	40	60	27	31	17	15
Butcher Trousers	–	1500	60	40	60	50	50	50	60	32	34	19	17

Constable's Attire `OH`

Once upon a time, a troupe of foreign constables chased a beast all the way to Yharnam, and this is what they wore. The constables became victims of the beast, except for one survivor, who in turn devoured the creature whole, all by himself. This fable is a favourite among Yharnamites, who are partial to any stories of pompous, intolerant foreigners who suffer for their ignorance. It makes the blood taste that much sweeter. The iron helm resembles an upside-down bucket. A single hole allows one to peek out with a single eye, which is probably all that its original owner had. The Master's Iron Helm is passed down among masters of the League. Valtr had in fact lost the ability to see vermin long ago.

WHERE TO FIND Hunter's Nightmare [p170], Helm: Defeat Valtr, Master of the League [p650] | **UNLOCK CONDITION** Master's Iron Helm: Complete Valtr, Master of the League's Questline [p650]

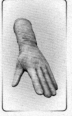

Basic Stats

	Buy	Sell											
One-eyed Iron Helm	–	7500	60	20	50	50	20	30	0	6	10	13	23
Constable's Garb	–	10000	90	100	70	80	100	110	120	44	35	23	52
Constable's Gloves	–	5000	60	60	50	50	50	60	60	23	17	12	31
Constable's Trousers	–	5000	60	60	50	50	50	60	70	25	18	14	35
Master's Iron Helm	–	15000	60	20	50	50	20	30	0	6	10	13	23

5

Decorative Old Hunter Attire (OH)

The old hunter top hat is warped by blood stains. In the old days, when hunters were ten a penny, this was part of their standard garb. The garb is decorated with brass trinkets. The gauntlets are made of brass to protect their weapon-bearing hands. At the time, some hunters believed that certain metals would ward off beast blood. On a night of the hunt, it is no wonder that people would resort to superstition.

WHERE TO FIND Hunter's Nightmare [p164/p166], Garb & Trousers: Research Hall [p180]

Basic Stats	Buy	Sell	▢	☾	⬓	✳	★	🍃	♫	☠	▽	◎
Old Hunter Top Hat	–	1100	30	60	40	30	30	20	40	8	5	17	13
Decorative Old Hunter Garb	–	2200	110	70	80	110	60	120	50	36	23	38	48
Old Hunter Gloves	–	1000	60	50	50	60	50	70	40	19	10	23	29
Decorative Old Hunter Trousers	–	1100	70	50	50	70	40	70	40	19	13	20	29

Enlarged Head (OH)

An enlarged head of a patient of the Cathedral, with a cavity that just happens to fit a human head, although one would be mad to try it on. But if you do, listen carefully, for the sticky sound. Drip, drop. As water, seeping up from the depths, slowly, steadily.

WHERE TO FIND Research Hall [p183]

Basic Stats	Buy	Sell	▢	☾	⬓	✳	★	🍃	♫	☠	▽	◎
Enlarged Head	–	10	20	60	0	20	50	20	20	6	6	1	0

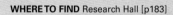

Harrowed Attire (OH)

Certain Church hunters obfuscate their identities and slip into the nooks and crannies of the city. This is the garb that allows these harrowed individuals to go unnoticed. These hunters are keen to early signs of the scourge, serving as a first line of defence against its outbreak. Or perhaps, when the time is ripe, they find signs of the scourge where there are none. It just goes to show, the corner beggar is not always who he seems.

WHERE TO FIND Fishing Hamlet [p192]

Basic Stats	Buy	Sell	▢	☾	⬓	✳	★	🍃	♫	☠	▽	◎
Harrowed Hood	–	50	60	40	50	40	60	50	50	20	19	2	18
Harrowed Garb	–	1000	120	80	90	90	110	90	110	56	58	9	44
Harrowed Gloves	–	500	60	40	40	60	50	40	50	35	31	4	25
Harrowed Trousers	–	500	70	50	50	60	60	50	60	38	33	5	27

Maria's Hunter Attire OH

Among the first hunters, all students of Gehrman, was the lady hunter Maria. This was her hunter's attire, crafted in Cainhurst. Maria is distantly related to the undead queen, but had great admiration for Gehrman, unaware of his curious mania.

WHERE TO FIND UNLOCK CONDITION: Defeat Lady Maria of the Astral Clocktower [p187/p368]

Basic Stats

	Buy	Sell	◻	◐	◢	✴	★	✑	♫	☠	▽	◎
Maria Hunter Cap	3	21000	40	40	40	70	30	40	50	6	17	10	4
Maria Hunter Garb	5	42000	80	70	80	150	70	60	80	20	51	30	16
Maria Hunter Gloves	3	21000	50	50	50	70	50	50	50	10	27	15	8
Maria Hunter Trousers	3	21000	50	50	60	80	50	50	50	11	30	17	9

Old Hunter Attire OH

The old hunter cap has a wide brim that hides their sharp gaze. In the old days, when hunters were ten a penny, this was part of their standard garb. The old hunter gauntlets were made of brass to protect their weapon-bearing hands. The trousers protected countless hunters from the beasts in an older age. A widespread belief of the period was that "beast blood crept up the right leg," and this led to the double-wrapped belt. At the time, some hunters believed that certain metals would ward off beast blood. On a night of the hunt, it is no wonder that some resort to superstition. One day, the hunters disappeared, and Yharnamites began to whisper of the hunters' sin. Drunk with blood, chasing after beasts, they would pass on to the Nightmare, every last one of them.

WHERE TO FIND Hunter's Nightmare [p164/p167]

Basic Stats

	Buy	Sell	◻	◐	◢	✴	★	✑	♫	☠	▽	◎
Old Hunter Cap	–	1000	50	30	40	50	30	60	20	11	5	13	19
Old Hunter Garb	–	2000	100	70	80	100	70	120	50	36	19	44	48
Old Hunter Gloves	–	1000	60	50	50	60	50	70	40	19	10	23	29
Old Hunter Trousers	–	1000	60	50	60	60	50	70	40	20	11	25	33

Yamamura's Hunter Attire OH

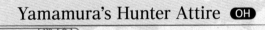

Garb of a distant Eastern land, worn by Yamamura the Wanderer. The standard hunter's hat and staff were given to him when he became a hunter and confederate of the League. The old hunter arm bands wound tightly to prevent infection with the scourge. Of course, the idea that the scourge was infectious was pure hearsay. This Eastern warrior pursued a beast for honourable revenge, then became a hunter of the League. But when he stared straight into impurity, it drove him mad.

WHERE TO FIND Defeat Yamamura the Wanderer [p172/p655]

Basic Stats

	Buy	Sell	◻	◐	◢	✴	★	✑	♫	☠	▽	◎
Yamamura Hunter Hat	–	4000	50	30	40	50	30	60	20	5	11	19	13
Khaki Haori	–	19200	80	60	70	90	80	130	70	37	34	25	18
Old Hunter Arm Bands	–	4000	40	40	40	50	60	90	50	19	17	12	11
Wine Hakama	–	9600	40	40	50	50	60	90	50	21	19	19	15

5

Chapter 6

Hunter's Appendices

This chapter's title might suggest that some of its contents are mere footnotes in the grand scheme of Bloodborne, but that's certainly not the case. Learning about the diverse and mysterious characters Yharnam is home to is one of the game's true joys, and this is the place to come if you want their full stories. It's also home to full shop lists, a trophy guide and a very special interview with Bloodborne's director, Hidetaka Miyazaki.

NPCs

The term "NPC" stands for "Non–Player Character" and refers to any characters not under your direct control. You'll meet many NPCs in Yharnam and the surrounding regions as you proceed through the game, each with different goals and intentions – some will be friends and others foes, but your own choices are what will ultimately determine how they interact with you. Interactions with NPCs in the Old Hunters areas are not affected by the time of day in Yharnam; they are solely dependent upon your progression through those areas and can be completed after gaining access to the Hunter's Nightmare without further advancing through the main story.

In this chapter you'll find detailed information on the various NPCs with whom you'll cross paths during the hunt, as well as step–by–step breakdowns of how to complete their quests and receive all possible rewards.

Event Flow

This chart outlines the overall flow of NPC interactions throughout the game and provides an overview of how to complete every available quest in a single game cycle. While this is the recommended path of progression, it is by no means means the only one available; you may choose to complete particular events in a different order depending upon your priorities.

Central Yharnam | Gilbert's House | ○ ☁ ☾ ●
Speak with Gilbert.

▼

Hunter's Dream | Workshop | ○ ☁ ☾ ●
Speak with Gehrman.

▼

Central Yharnam | Iosefka's Clinic | ○ ☁ ☾ ●
Speak with Iosefka.

▼

Central Yharnam | Gilbert's House | ○ ☁ ☾ ●
Speak with Gilbert after defeating the Cleric Beast.

▼

Central Yharnam | Drydock Rafters | ○ ☁ ☾ ●
Speak with Eileen.

▼

Central Yharnam | Canal Residence | ○ ☁ ☾ ●
Speak with the Young Girl and agree to look for her mother, then defeat Father Gascoigne and pick up the Red Jeweled Brooch.

▼

Cathedral Ward | Oedon Chapel | ○ ● ☾ ●
Speak with the Blind Samaritan.

▼

Central Yharnam | Iosefka's Clinic | ○ ● ☾ ●
Speak with Impostor Iosefka.

▼

Central Yharnam | Gilbert's House | ○ ● ☾ ●
Speak with Gilbert.

Central Yharnam | Canal Bridge | ○ ● ☾ ●
Speak to the Lonely Old Woman and send her to the Oedon Chapel.

▼

Central Yharnam | Canal Residence | ○ ● ☾ ●
Reload your save file, speak with the Young Girl and refuse to give her the brooch, then send her to the Oedon Chapel.

▼

Central Yharnam | Boar Tunnel | ○ ● ☾ ●
Reload your save file, defeat the Maneater Boar in the sewers and retrieve the Red Messenger Ribbon.

▼

Cathedral Ward | Outside Oedon Chapel | ○ ● ☾ ●
Speak with Eileen after defeating Vicar Amelia (but before examining the skull) and listen to the warning about Henryk. If Eileen doesn't appear here, reload your save file.

▼

Cathedral Ward | Lower Chapel | ○ ● ☾ ●
Speak with Alfred and agree to cooperate.

▼

Central Yharnam | Tomb of Oedon | ○ ● ☾ ●
Defeat Henryk and speak with Eileen.

▼

Cathedral Ward | Foggy Alley | ○ ● ☾ ●
After defeating Vicar Amelia but before examining the nearby skull, speak to Arianna and send her to the Oedon Chapel.

▼

Cathedral Ward | Foggy Alley | ○ ● ☾ ●
After speaking to Arianna, immediately cross the street and tell the Bigoted Old Man about the clinic.

▼

Yahar'gul, Unseen Village | Storeroom | ○ ● ☾ ●
Before examining the skull in the Grand Cathedral, infiltrate Yahar'gul. Speak to Adella while wearing Healing Church clothing and send her to the Oedon Chapel. From this point on, do not accept more than four vials of blood from Arianna.

▼

Old Yharnam | Djura's Tower | ○ ● ☾ ●
After defeating Darkbeast Paarl, access Djura's tower via the Graveyard of the Darkbeast. Speak to Djura and select, "Spare the beasts of Old Yharnam," then leave the area without attacking any enemies.

▼

Cathedral Ward | Grand Cathedral

Examine the skull in the Grand Cathedral to advance the time to night.

▼

Cathedral Ward | Forbidden Woods Route

Speak to Alfred and ask about Byrgenwerth.

▼

Forbidden Woods | Village Outskirts

Speak to Patches in the residence near the kennels and obtain the Tonsil Stone.

▼

Forbidden Woods | Windmill Balconies

Speak to the Afflicted Beggar and send him to the clinic.

▼

Central Yharnam | Iosefka's Clinic

Sneak into the clinic through the Forbidden Woods and kill the Celestial Emissaries, then trigger Impostor Iosefka's warning dialogue without turning her hostile. Pick up the Cainhurst Summons and leave the clinic through the rear exit without opening the front door.

▼

Central Yharnam | Gilbert's House

From the rear of the clinic, open the gates leading back to the main entrance and visit Gilbert. Exhaust his dialogue, reload your save file and exhaust his dialogue again.

▼

Cathedral Ward | Oedon Chapel

Speak to each of the refugees in the Oedon Chapel to collect the various quest rewards available at this point.

▼

Hemwick Charnel Lane | Hemwick Crossing

Approach the large obelisk to trigger a cutscene, then enter the carriage to travel to Cainhurst Castle.

▼

Cainhurst Castle | Throne Room

Speak to Queen Annalise and swear an oath to the Vilebloods to obtain her quest rewards, then pick up the Unopened Summons from the desk. Kill an NPC hunter or another player to obtain a Blood Dreg, then return to Annalise and trade it for the remaining reward.

▼

Cathedral Ward | Forbidden Woods Route

Give Alfred the Unopened Summons.

▼

Cainhurst Castle | Throne Room

Exhaust Alfred's dialogue and collect the Queenly Flesh from the throne.

▼

Lecture Building 1F | Patches' Lab

Speak to Patches through the door.

▼

Nightmare Frontier | Lower Caves

Approach the area marked with Shining Coins to trigger the event with Patches.

▼

Byrgenwerth | Lunarium

Talk to Provost Willem and, optionally, kill him. Jump into the lake and defeat Rom, the Vacuous Spider; then approach the Pthumerian Bride to advance the time of day to Blood Moon.

▼

Central Yharnam | Iosefka's Clinic

Enter the clinic and kill Impostor Iosefka to obtain the One Third Umbilical Cord.

▼

Central Yharnam | Gilbert's House

Proceed to Gilbert's house and defeat the nearby Beast Patient.

▼

Central Yharnam | Canal Residence

Give the Red Messenger Ribbon to the Older Sister, then reload your save file and collect the White Messenger Ribbon from the corpse at the bottom of the ladder.

▼

Cathedral Ward | Oedon Chapel

Speak with each of the refugees and exhaust their dialogue. To prevent the Lonely Old Woman's death, do NOT tell her, "I have my share of woes" after she returns from her first search for items.

▼

Cathedral Ward | Grand Cathedral

Speak with Eileen outside the cathedral and exhaust her dialogue.

▼

Cathedral Ward | Grand Cathedral

Defeat the Bloody Crow of Cainhurst inside the cathedral, then return to Eileen and exhaust her dialogue again.

▼

Lecture Building 2F | Patches' Lab

Retrieve the Upper Cathedral Ward Key from Yahar'gul and defeat The One Reborn, then confront Patches face-to-face in the lab. Choose either option when prompted and exhaust the remainder of his dialogue to receive the quest rewards.

▼

Cathedral Ward | Oedon Chapel

Speak to Arianna after defeating The One Reborn.

▼

Upper Cathedral Ward | Altar of Despair

Defeat Ebrietas and offer the Queenly Flesh at the Altar of Despair to revive Annalise.

▼

Cathedral Ward | Lower Chapel

Search Alfred's body for the remaining quest reward.

▼

Cathedral Ward | Oedon Chapel

Speak with Arianna in the abandoned room below the Oedon Chapel library after defeating Micolash, then kill the pink Celestial Child and collect the One Third Umbilical Cord.

▼

Hunter's Nightmare | Chapel Tunnel

Speak with Simon, Seeker of Secrets. Express your interest in nightmares.

▼

6

Hunter's Nightmare | Underground Corpse Pile | ○ ● ☾ ●

Speak to Ludwig, the Holy Blade (Head) after his defeat while wearing Black Church Garb, White Church Garb, Choir Garb, Executioner Garb, Tomb Prospector Garb or Gascoigne's Garb and answer "No".

▼

Hunter's Nightmare | Underground Corpse Pile | ○ ● ☾ ●

Return to Ludwig, the Holy Blade (Head)'s location and speak to Simon, Seeker of Secrets.

▼

Research Hall | Research Hall Entrance | ○ ● ☾ ●

Speak with Simon, Seeker of Secrets.

▼

Research Hall | Floor 1 - Laboratory | ○ ● ☾ ●

Speak with Adelina, Research Hall Patient after acquiring Brain Fluid x1 and grant her request.

▼

Hunter's Nightmare | Underground Cells | ○ ● ☾ ●

After acquiring the Underground Cell Key, enter Yamamura the Wanderer's cell. Mercy kill him, as he cannot be saved.

▼

Fishing Hamlet | Lighthouse Hut | ○ ● ☾ ●

Speak to Simon, Seeker of Secrets.

▼

Research Hall | Floor 1 - Laboratory | ○ ● ☾ ●

Speak to Adelina, Research Hall Patient with another Brain Fluid on hand, and grant her next request.

▼

Fishing Hamlet | Flooded Village - Overlook | ○ ● ☾ ●

Defeat Brador, Church Assassin as he invades.

▼

Fishing Hamlet | Flooded Village - Stilts | ○ ● ☾ ●

Defeat Brador, Church Assassin as he invades a second time.

▼

Fishing Hamlet | Access Tunnel | ○ ● ☾ ●

Defeat Brador, Church Assassin as he invades a third time.

▼

Hunter's Nightmare | Underground Cells | ○ ● ☾ ●

Defeat Brador, Church Assassin as he invades a final time. Access Brador's cell, listen to his final monologue and eliminate him.

▼

Research Hall | Floor 1 - Laboratory | ○ ● ☾ ●

Speak to Adelina, Research Hall Patient in her new position behind the laboratory door. Kill her, then speak to her with the newfound Brain Fluid to fulfill her final request.

▼

Fishing Hamlet | Hamlet Causeway | ○ ● ☾ ●

Speak to the Fishing Hamlet Priest with the Milkweed Caryll Rune equipped to receive the Accursed Brew.

▼

Hunter's Dream | Foot of the Great Tree | ○ ● ☾ ●

Speak to Gehrman after defeating Mergo's Wet Nurse to initiate the game's final sequence of events.

Gehrman, the First Hunter

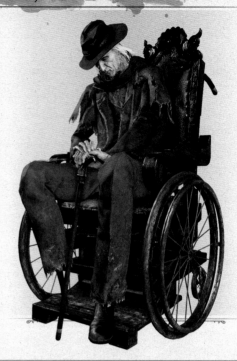

For combat information on Gehrman, please see p356.

Gehrman is a kindly old man whom you'll first meet upon awakening in the Hunter's Dream. He is the workshop's founder and the very first hunter, though due to his advanced age he now serves only as an advisor; as such, he has a wealth of experience and will provide you with his wisdom and guidance throughout your exploration of Yharnam. You'll usually find him in the workshop building but he'll occasionally be absent, in which case he'll sometimes leave you a message with a hint or suggestion about where you should go next. Attacking him when he is in the workshop will cause him to temporarily disappear but will have no other effects, so you don't need to worry about accidentally turning him hostile. At the end of the game Gehrman will move to the base of the tree adjoining the workshop, at which point you can speak to him to initiate the game's final boss sequences and closing events. In order to obtain the Old Hunter Badge from him, you must select "Refuse" when prompted with a choice during his dialogue; attacking him before initiating the conversation will proceed with the event as though you had selected "Refuse."

Event Items

Item	Requirement
Old Hunter Badge	Clear the first boss battle in the game's final sequence of events.

Interactions

Hunter's Dream | Workshop | ○ ● ☾ ●

Speak to him each time you visit the Hunter's Dream to receive additional dialogue. His dialogue will update after you defeat bosses and when the time of day advances; he'll also sometimes be absent but will leave messages on the ground in his usual location.

▼

Hunter's Dream | Foot of the Great Tree | ○ ● ☾ ●*

Enter the field of flowers beyond the iron gate and speak to him at the foot of the large tree to initiate the game's final sequence of events.

*after defeating Mergo's Wet Nurse

Doll

A soulless automaton residing in the Hunter's Dream, the doll's purpose is to care for new hunters and embolden their flesh with the power of blood echoes. Due to her lack of human emotion, it can be difficult to tell what she's thinking; she isn't one for frivolous conversation, but will occasionally share profound musings when you speak to her over the course of the game. Her aloof and sometimes coy disposition tends to give the impression that she knows more than she's willing to divulge, but in reality she is quite naive and her knowledge of the world outside the dream comes only from the stories shared with her by past hunters.

Event Items

Item	Requirement
Tear Stone	Give her the Small Hair Ornament from the Abandoned Workshop.

Hunter's Dream | Vicinity of the Workshop | ○ ◑ ☾ ●

Throughout the game, you can speak to the doll to level up using your accumulated Blood Echoes. Even if you kill her, you can still level up by examining her body. She will move around the general vicinity of the workshop and can sometimes be found next the tombstone to the left of the building's rear entrance.

▼

Hunter's Dream | Vicinity of the Workshop | ○ ◑ ☾ ●

When you acquire the Small Hair Ornament from the Abandoned Workshop, give it to her and she'll reward you with a Tear Stone.

▼

Hunter's Dream | Front Steps | ○ ◑ ☾ ●*

Once you've defeated Mergo's Wet Nurse, the doll will be waiting at the foot of the workshop steps and will instruct you to speak with Gehrman. You can continue to level up at this point and she will still accept the Small Hair Ornament.

*after defeating Mergo's Wet Nurse

Interactions

Hunter's Dream | Front Steps | ○ ◑ ☾ ◉

The first time you enter the Hunter's Dream, the doll will be lying beside the steps leading to the workshop entrance. When you return with at least one point of insight, she will be active and able to engage in conversation with you.

▼

Basic Information

	Hunter's Dream	300	0	Item Drops	None	40	40	40	40	80	75	90	999	999	—	—

Gilbert

Gilbert is a foreigner to Yharnam afflicted with the Scourge who traveled to the city in search of a cure. This being the case, he sympathizes with your situation from the start and does his best to help you in spite of his worsening condition; by the time you first meet him he's already incapacitated with no hope of survival, and can only provide you with information. However, if you visit him regularly he'll also entrust you with his Flamesprayer, a powerful weapon that can prove extremely useful in a wide variety of situations. Sadly, as Gilbert himself resignedly admits, there is no way to save him; when you return to his house during the Blood Moon you'll find him transformed into a beast, leaving you with only the unenviable task of ending his suffering.

Event Items

Item	Requirement
Flamesprayer	Speak to him in the evening after entering the Oedon Chapel for the first time.
"Clawmark" Rune	After fulfilling the requirements outlined in the "Interactions" table, return to his house when the Blood Moon is out and defeat the nearby Beast Patient.

Interactions

Central Yharnam | Gilbert's House | ○ ◑ ☾ ◉

Speak to him and exhaust his dialogue.

▼

Central Yharnam | Gilbert's House | ○ ◑ ☾ ◉*

Speak to him and exhaust his dialogue.

*when the Cleric Beast has been defeated

Central Yharnam | Gilbert's House | ○ ● ☾ ◉

Speak to him after entering the Oedon Chapel for the first time and exhaust his dialogue.

▼

Central Yharnam | Gilbert's House | ○ ◑ ☾ ◉

Speak to him and exhaust his dialogue, then reload the area and speak to him again.

▼

Central Yharnam | Gilbert's House | ○ ◑ ☾ ●

Speak to him and exhaust his dialogue, then reload the area and speak to him again.

6

Eileen the Crow

Eileen is an assassin whose sworn duty is to dispose of other hunters that have been corrupted by their lust for blood. Like the player, she hails from outside Yharnam and is a foreigner to the region, but her presence in the city is driven by an entirely different set of motives; she makes a point of keeping a low profile and operating in the shadows, and you may never meet her in the first place if you don't go out of your way to explore. You can start her quest either on the Dry Dock – Rafters in Central Yharnam or to the left of the Oedon Chapel's front entrance in the Cathedral Ward, and your choices after that point will determine her fate. Helping Eileen defeat Henryk in the Tomb of Oedon is the tipping point of her quest – failure to do so before entering the Forbidden Woods for the first time will result in her becoming your enemy, and will prevent you from receiving any of the successive rewards other than the Crow Hunter Badge.

Equipment Central Yharnam, Cathedral Ward

Right Hand 1	Blade of Mercy +4	Head	Beak Mask
Right Hand 2	Bare Fists	Body	Crowfeather Garb
Left Hand 1	Hunter Pistol +4	Hands	Crowfeather Manchettes
Left Hand 2	Bare Fists	Feet	Crowfeather Trousers

Equipment Grand Cathedral

Right Hand 1	Blade of Mercy +10	Head	Beak Mask
Right Hand 2	Bare Fists	Body	Crowfeather Garb
Left Hand 1	Hunter Pistol +10	Hands	Crowfeather Manchettes
Left Hand 2	Bare Fists	Feet	Crowfeather Trousers

Strategy

Should Eileen become your enemy at any point, you'll have a tricky battle on your hands. She's very agile and will usually use her Blade of Mercy in its transformed mode, making her attacks quick and hard to predict; she'll also occasionally attempt to interrupt you and will perform a visceral attack if she's successful. She'll sometimes toss a Throwing Knife at you if you're out of range of her pistol, so it's important not to let your guard down even if she's far away. Interrupting her swift swings can be difficult but is the most effective means of defeating her; she's very good at dodging, so it's a good idea to lure her into a narrow space where she can't evade your attacks. She tends to walk straight into charged R2 thrust attacks from weapons with long reach, but transformation attacks and slower R1 combos may not be fast enough to hit her before she quicksteps out of the way.

Event Items

Item	Requirement
Bold Hunter's Mark ×4 "Shake Off Cape" Gesture	Exhaust Eileen's opening dialogue in Central Yharnam or the Cathedral Ward.
"Shhh!" Gesture	Speak to Eileen outside the Oedon Chapel and listen to her warning about Henryk.
"Approval" Gesture	Speak to Eileen after defeating Henryk.
"Wait" Gesture	Speak to Eileen before entering the Grand Cathedral to fight the Bloody Crow of Cainhurst.
Crow Hunter Badge	Kill Eileen at any point or speak to her after defeating the Bloody Crow of Cainhurst.
"Hunter" Rune	Speak to Eileen after defeating the Bloody Crow of Cainhurst.

Interactions

Central Yharnam | Dry Dock

Speak to her twice at the Dry Dock in Central Yharnam to begin her quest and receive the initial rewards. If you miss her in this location, you can still trigger her opening dialogue outside the Oedon Chapel.

Cathedral Ward | Oedon Chapel

If you didn't start her quest in Central Yharnam, you can do so outside the Oedon Chapel instead. Failure to trigger her initial dialogue before entering the Forbidden Woods will instantly end her quest and permanently remove her from the game.

Cathedral Ward | Oedon Chapel

Speak to Eileen outside the Oedon Chapel immediately after opening both gates to the Cathedral Ward plaza and reloading the area. She'll tell you about Henryk, her current assassination target, and teach you a gesture. Defeating further bosses before speaking to Eileen in this spot may prevent her from appearing.

Central Yharnam | Tomb of Oedon

If you head straight to Father Gascoigne's boss area after Eileen warns you about Henryk, he will attack you immediately and Eileen will arrive partway through the battle to assist you. If you reload the game after receiving Eileen's warning, she will already be fighting Henryk when you arrive.

Central Yharnam | Tomb of Oedon

Help Eileen defeat Henryk to obtain the Heir rune, and speak to her before entering the Forbidden Woods to learn a gesture and advance her quest along the "good" path.

If you do not defeat Henryk before entering the Forbidden Woods, Eileen's quest will advance along the "bad" path.

Cathedral Ward | Grand Cathedral |

If you helped Eileen defeat Henryk, you'll find her wounded outside the Grand Cathedral. Speak to her to learn a gesture, then proceed into the cathedral and defeat the Bloody Crow of Cainhurst to obtain the Bloody Rapture rune.

If you didn't help Eileen defeat Henryk, she will be waiting inside the Grand Cathedral and will attack you on sight; defeating her yields the Crow Hunter Badge and ends her quest.

Cathedral Ward | Grand Cathedral |

Speak to Eileen outside the Grand Cathedral after defeating the Bloody Crow of Cainhurst to conclude her quest and receive the final set of rewards.

Basic Information

Central Yharnam/Cathedral Ward	■ 1261	⚚ 2318	Item Drops											
			Crow Hunter Badge ×1 [100%]	220	253	202	284	177	202	185	134	153	—	—

Chapel Samaritan

The Blind Samaritan is a well–meaning Yharnamite doing his best to save his fellow townsfolk from the Scourge. You'll meet him in the Oedon Chapel after crossing through the Central Yharnam sewers, at which point he'll inform you that the chapel is safe from beasts and ask you to share this information with any refugees you meet. There are a total of six NPCs who can be sent to the Oedon Chapel, but only four are required for completing the quest: the Lonely Old Woman, Arianna, Woman of the Night, the Bigoted Old man and Adella, Nun of the Healing Church. It is also possible to send the Afflicted Beggar and the Young Girl to the chapel; however, sending the beggar will result in the deaths of the other refugees, and the Young Girl will be killed en route.

6

Interactions

Cathedral Ward | Oedon Chapel |

Talk to him for the first time and you'll be able to inform refugees about the Oedon Chapel.

Cathedral Ward | Oedon Chapel |

Speak to him after sending the Lonely Old Woman in the residence outside the Central Yharnam drydock to Oedon Chapel.

Cathedral Ward | Oedon Chapel |

Speak to him after sending Arianna from her residence on the Cathedral Ward side street to the Oedon Chapel.

Cathedral Ward | Oedon Chapel |

Speak to him after sending the Bigoted Old Man living across the street from Arianna to the Oedon Chapel.

Event Items

Item	Requirement
"Triumph" Gesture	Send at least one refugee to the Oedon Chapel.

Cathedral Ward | Oedon Chapel |

Speak to him after infiltrating Yahar'gul, rescuing Adella and sending her to the Oedon Chapel.

Cathedral Ward | Oedon Chapel |

Quest is successfully completed if all four of the above NPCs safely reach the Oedon Chapel before the Blood Moon.

Quest is failed if any of the above NPCs die for any reason or do not safely reach the chapel before the Blood Moon.

Cathedral Ward | Oedon Chapel |

Sending the Afflicted Beggar to the Oedon Chapel will result in the successive deaths of any other refugees present, including the Blind Samaritan.

Basic Information

Cathedral Ward	■ 211	⚚ 202	Item Drops											
			Formless Oedon ×1 [100%]	77	77	77	77	120	75	90	200	180	—	—

Lonely Old Woman

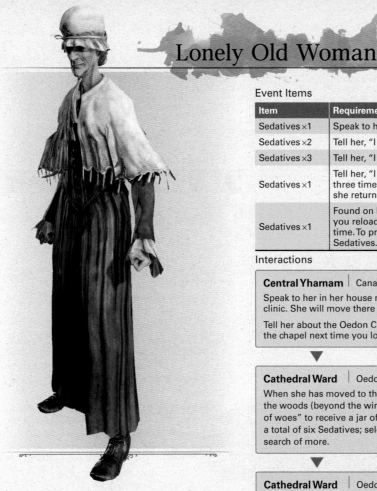

Event Items

Item	Requirement
Sedatives ×1	Speak to her after nightfall and tell her, "I have my share of woes."
Sedatives ×2	Tell her, "I have my share of woes" a second time.
Sedatives ×3	Tell her, "I have my share of woes" a third time.
Sedatives ×1	Tell her, "I have my share of woes" after receiving Sedatives from her three times, then reload the area twice and speak to her again when she returns.
Sedatives ×1	Found on her corpse outside the Oedon Chapel's side entrance when you reload the area after telling her, "I have my share of woes" a fifth time. To prevent her death, don't send her on a second search for Sedatives.

Interactions

Central Yharnam | Canal Bridge
Speak to her in her house near the Central Yharnam drydock and tell her about the clinic. She will move there when you reload the area, ending her quest.

Tell her about the Oedon Chapel instead of the clinic and she will take up residence in the chapel next time you load a new area.

▼

Cathedral Ward | Oedon Chapel
When she has moved to the chapel, speak with her after reaching the second half of the woods (beyond the windmill) and choose the dialogue option, "I have my share of woes" to receive a jar of Sedatives. You can repeat this process two more times for a total of six Sedatives; selecting the option a fourth time will trigger her to leave in search of more.

▼

Cathedral Ward | Oedon Chapel
After receiving all six Sedatives initially available from her, tell her, "I have my share of woes" a fourth time and reload the area. Read the letter on her chair and reload the area two more times, then speak to her to receive another jar of Sedatives.

▼

Cathedral Ward | Oedon Chapel
After she brings back the seventh jar of Sedatives, speak to her again and select, "I have my share of woes," then reload the area. You'll find her lying dead outside the chapel near the well, clutching one last jar of Sedatives. Skipping this step or answering, "No" to the prompt will prevent her death, in which case she will remain at the chapel with the other refugees.

This grouchy old woman lives near the Dry Dock in Central Yharnam. Like most other Yharnamites, she distrusts outsiders and will make a show of belligerence when you first meet her, but will nevertheless ask you if you know of any safe places where she can take refuge during the coming night's hunt. Telling her about the clinic will result in her becoming a victim of the impostor doctor's experiments; informing her of the Oedon Chapel will cause her to move there and enable further interactions with her as the night progresses, culminating in her going mad and (ironically) becoming much more personable in the process.

Basic Information

Central Yharnam/Cathedral Ward	■ 457	⚓ 118	Item Drops Sedatives ×1 [100%]	60	50	50	40	40	100	60	69	83	—	—

Arianna, Woman of the Night

A prostitute residing in one of the Cathedral Ward's darker corners, Arianna is a living testament to the old adage, "Beauty is only skin deep." Her elegant appearance belies a personality as blunt as a bludgeon, and her very blood bears striking similarities to that which was once forbidden by the Healing Church. You can speak to her at her home in the Cathedral Ward as soon as you reach the area, but she won't be seeking sanctuary until after you defeat one of the three bosses accessible from this part of Yharnam. Return to her after defeating the Witch of Hemwick, the Blood-starved Beast or Vicar Amelia to inform her of a safe (or not-so-safe) haven; you'll need to send her to the Oedon Chapel in order to access the remainder of her questline. Beware that once Adella arrives at the chapel, she will become jealous of Arianna and kill her after you receive blood from her five times in Adella's presence. If Arianna survives to the end of the game, she'll move to the abandoned room below the Oedon Chapel Library after you defeat Micolash in the Nightmare of Mensis; killing the nearby Celestial Child will get you a One Third Umbilical Cord, but will cause Arianna to die as well.

Event Items

Item	Requirement
Blood of Arianna (Unlimited)	Speak with her during the evening or nighttime when not already carrying a vial of her or Adella's blood.
One Third Umbilical Cord	Kill the pink Celestial Child after completing her quest.

Interactions

Cathedral Ward | Foggy Alley

Speak to her after defeating the Witch of Hemwick, the Blood-starved Beast or Vicar Amelia and tell her about the clinic, causing her to move there and ending her quest.

Speak to her after defeating one of the abovementioned bosses and direct her to the Oedon Chapel to enable further interactions with her when she arrives there.

▼

Cathedral Ward | Oedon Chapel

Speak with her in the Oedon Chapel to receive a vial of her unique blood. You can return for another vial after using the first one and reloading the area.

▼

Cathedral Ward | Oedon Chapel

If you receive five vials of Arianna's blood while Adella the Nun is present in the chapel, Adella will murder Arianna next time you reload the area, failing her quest.

▼

Cathedral Ward | Oedon Chapel

When the Blood Moon comes out, Arianna will become afflicted with a mysterious condition and will be unable to provide any more blood.

▼

Cathedral Ward | Oedon Chapel

After defeating The One Reborn, Arianna's condition will worsen.

▼

Cathedral Ward | Oedon Chapel

After defeating Micolash in the Nightmare of Mensis, Arianna will be missing from the chapel and you'll find a trail of blood leading to the rear door. Climb down the ladder from the basement library and you'll find her in the abandoned room below. The pink Celestial Child will drop an all-important One Third Umbilical Cord when killed, but killing it will instantly result in Arianna's death.

Basic Information

	■	✦	Item Drops										
Cathedral Ward	481	103	Arianna's Shoes ×1 [100%]	88	106	78	173	97	78	116	79	97	—	—

Bigoted Old Man

The Bigoted Old Man lives across the street from Arianna in the Foggy Alley of the Cathedral Ward. He's just an ordinary citizen of Yharnam, complete with the endemic suspicious streak, and wants nothing to do with you until he overhears you direct his neighbor Arianna to a place of refuge. At this point he'll challenge you to convince him that he should follow her; he'll make a show of rejecting anything you say no matter how many times you say it, but when he thinks you're not looking, he'll sneak off to the location opposite the one you suggest. If he ends up in the chapel, he'll remain there for the rest of the game and occasionally offer a few new lines of dialogue, but won't provide any other rewards.

Event Items

Item	Requirement
–	–

Interactions

Cathedral Ward | Foggy Alley

Speak to him after telling Arianna about one of the two refuges and you'll be able to inform him of them as well. Note that you can access his dialogue prompt multiple times before leaving the area, and he will move to the OPPOSITE location of the one you last selected (for example, if you tell him to go to the clinic, he'll go to the chapel instead). If he ends up at the clinic, he'll disappear from the game and his quest will end.

▼

Cathedral Ward | Oedon Chapel

If you send him to the chapel, he will remain there for the rest of the game and complain about you or occasionally one of the other refugees. Apart from a few new lines of dialogue as the night progresses, he will not offer you any items or other rewards.

Basic Information

Cathedral Ward	573	118	Item Drops: Pungent Blood Cocktail ×3 [100%]	124	115	115	106	106	196	133	96	115	–	–

Provost Willem

Provost Willem is the head of Byrgenwerth, an academic institute from which the Healing Church originated. He and his students pioneered research on the old blood discovered in the subterranean labyrinths beneath the city of Yharnam, aiming to advance the evolution of humankind and achieve higher planes of thought. Despite Willem's central role in the foundation of the Healing Church and particularly the Choir, their paths ultimately diverged and Byrgenwerth was abandoned by all but a few loyal scholars; now, at the end of his days and barely even able to speak, he can only sit in his favorite chair and await the arrival of one who can unlock lake's secret.

Event Items

Item	Requirement
–	–

Interactions

Byrgenwerth | Lunarium

You'll find him on the outdoor balcony, incapacitated and unable to speak. Attempting to talk to him will earn you some insight and a hint as to what to do next, but he has no other role in the game. He will drop a useful rune when killed, so you have nothing to lose and everything to gain by putting him out of his misery.

Basic Information

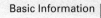

Byrgenwerth	1011	2545	Item Drops: Eye ×1 [100%]	91	91	91	91	70	70	70	999	999	–	–

Adella, Nun of the Healing Church

Adella is a Healing Church nun whose outward modesty hides a jealous and unstable disposition. You'll meet her in the Storeroom of Yahar'gul during your first trip to the village, but she'll be too scared to speak with you unless you're wearing Healing Church clothing. To earn her trust, you must equip one of the following pieces of "Body" attire before initiating conversation: Black Church Garb, White Church Garb, Choir Garb, Executioner Garb, Tomb Prospector Garb or Gascoigne's Garb. Doing so will allow you to inform her of one of the refuge locations, at which point you should send her to the Oedon Chapel; she will take up residence there and begin offering her blood, but will kill Arianna out of jealousy if you show a preference for the prostitute's blood instead. Adella will go insane when the Blood Moon comes out, after which time she will no longer be able to provide you with any further blood.

Event Items

Item	Requirement
Madman's Knowledge	Speak to her in Yahar'gul while wearing Healing Church clothes.
"Church Bow (Female)" Gesture	Speak to her in the Oedon Chapel for the first time.
Blood of Adella (Unlimited)	Speak to her after loading the area when not already carrying a vial of her or Arianna's blood.

Interactions

Yahar'gul, Unseen Village | Storeroom | ○ ● ☾ ◐

Speak to her while wearing Healing Church clothing and tell her about the clinic. She'll move there and disappear from the game, ending her quest.

Speak to her while wearing Healing Church clothing and tell her about the Oedon Chapel. She'll take up residence there next time you load the area, allowing further interactions with her.

Speak to her while wearing Healing Church clothing, but tell her about neither the clinic nor the chapel. She'll return to the Cathedral Ward and disappear from the game, ending her quest.

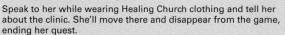

Cathedral Ward | Oedon Chapel | ○ ● ☾ ◐

When Adella moves to the Oedon Chapel, she'll provide you with a vial of her unique blood. You can continue to receive this item from her each time you reload the area if you aren't already carrying a vial of her or Arianna's blood.

▼

Cathedral Ward | Oedon Chapel | ○ ● ☾ ◐

Adella will murder Arianna if you receive the prostitute's blood a total of five times while both women present in the Oedon Chapel.

▼

Cathedral Ward | Oedon Chapel | ○ ◐ ☾ ●

During the Blood Moon, Adella will go insane and will no longer be able to provide you with her blood. No further conversation with her is possible at this point.

Basic Information

Yahar'gul/Cathedral Ward	■ 513	⚶ 256	Item Drops											
			Oedon Writhe ×1 [100%]	203	211	228	244	269	236	236	180	184	—	—

Young Girl & Older Sister

These sweet and innocent Yharnam girls are the daughters of Viola and Gascoigne. Their father left on the hunt and their mother departed shortly thereafter to search for him, leaving the girls alone amid increasing danger and uncertain prospects of survival. Their parents have not yet returned and, in her desperation, the younger daughter turns to you to locate them; sadly, you'll have to be the bearer of bad news regardless of how you decide to intervene, and your choices will have little effect on the outcome other than to determine the means of her demise. One way or another, her journey begins and ends in Central Yharnam; you can reach her home through the Canals by climbing a series of ladders back towards the Plaza. In order to complete her quest to the fullest possible extent and receive the final rewards, you'll need to withhold the news of her mother's death and direct her to the Oedon Chapel, which will result in her being killed and devoured by the Maneater Boar in the central sewers; from this point onward, the boar will drop her bloodied hair ribbon when defeated. Afterward, her older sister will return home and inquire as to her whereabouts, at which point you may either keep the bloody ribbon or hand it over to conclude the quest and reunite Gascoigne's family once again.

Event Items

Item	Requirement
Tiny Music Box	Agree to search for the girls' mother.
Red Messenger Ribbon	Send the younger daughter to the Oedon Chapel and defeat the Maneater Boar in the sewers.
White Messenger Ribbon	Return the Red Messenger ribbon to the older sister.

Interactions

Central Yharnam | Canal Residence |

Speak to the younger daughter at the house near the Plaza in Central Yharnam and agree to search for her mother – she'll give you the Tiny Music Box and tell you about her mother's brooch.

▼

Central Yharnam | Canal Residence |

Give her the Red Jeweled Brooch to immediately end her quest.

Do not give her the Red Jeweled Brooch and you'll be able to send her to the Oedon Chapel or Iosefka's Clinic instead if you've learned about them.

▼

Central Yharnam | Canal Residence |

If you tell her about Iosefka's Clinic, she'll move there when you reload the area and will become a victim of Impostor Iosefka's experiments, ending her quest.

If you tell her about the Oedon Chapel she'll attempt to make her way there, but will be eaten by the Maneater Boar in the Central Yharnam Boar Tunnel along the way. You must reload the area in order to trigger her departure.

If you don't tell her about either location before nightfall, her quest will automatically advance and you'll no longer be able to do so. You can still give her the brooch at this point, but reloading the area after speaking to her will end the quest regardless of your choice.

▼

Central Yharnam | Canal (Boar Tunnel) |

After she has left for the Oedon Chapel, defeat the Maneater Boar in the Boar Tunnel and retrieve the Red Messenger Ribbon.

▼

Central Yharnam | Canal Residence |

If you sent her to the chapel and she was eaten by the Maneater Boar, her older sister will appear in their house during the Blood Moon – return there and give her the Red Messenger Ribbon.

▼

Central Yharnam | Canal Residence |

Speak to the older sister and reload the area, then retrieve the White Messenger Ribbon from the corpse at the bottom of the nearby ladder to conclude the quest.

Afflicted Beggar

Please check the Abhorrent Beast on p386 for strategy-related information on the Afflicted Beggar.

The Afflicted Beggar is a Scourge victim first encountered consuming the dead bodies of three Yharnamites on the Windmill Balconies in the Forbidden Woods. While he makes great effort to appear normal, in reality he is barely clinging to his humanity and will reveal his true form if you attack him three times at any point in his quest. Challenging him early on can result in an extremely tough battle, but you can completely avoid the fight by sending him to the clinic; doing so will indeed cure him of his beasthood, enabling you to effortlessly obtain the rune he carries. Telling him about the Oedon Chapel will cause him to take up residence outside and begin preying upon any other refugees present there; when none remain, he will take his leave without a word and will be gone for the rest of the current game cycle. He will slaughter his first victim immediately after moving to the chapel, and will kill another refugee each time you defeat a boss.

Event Items

Item	Requirement
Pungent Blood Cocktail ×2	Speak to him in the Forbidden Woods and tell him about the clinic or the chapel.
Beast Blood Pellet ×3	Speak to him after he kills the Bigoted Old Man.
Beast Blood Pellet ×2	Speak to him after he kills the Lonely Old Woman.
Beast Blood Pellet ×2	Speak to him after he kills Adella.
Beast Blood Pellet ×3	Speak to him after he kills the Blind Samaritan.
Beast Blood Pellet ×2	Speak to him after he kills Arianna.

Interactions

Forbidden Woods | Windmill Balconies

Speak to him on the Windmill Balconies and tell him about the clinic. He will move there and disappear from the game, ending his quest.

Speak to him on the windmill roof and tell him about the Oedon Chapel. He will move there and immediately begin killing any other NPCs present.

Attack him three times on the Windmill Balconies and he will t ransform into the Abhorrent Beast. Defeat him to end his quest and prevent him from harming any other refugees.

▼

Cathedral Ward | Outside Oedon Chapel

Speak to him after he has killed his first victim to receive a few Beast Blood Pellets.

▼

Cathedral Ward | Outside Oedon Chapel

Speak to him after he has killed his second victim to receive a few Beast Blood Pellets.

▼

Cathedral Ward | Outside Oedon Chapel

Speak to him after he has killed his third victim to receive a few Beast Blood Pellets.

▼

Cathedral Ward | Outside Oedon Chapel

Speak to him after he has killed his fourth victim to receive a few Beast Blood Pellets.

▼

Cathedral Ward | Outside Oedon Chapel

Speak to him after he has killed his fifth and final victim to receive a few Beast Blood Pellets. When you reload the area after all occupants of the chapel are dead, he will permanently disappear from the game.

Basic Information

Location			Item Drops												
Forbidden Woods/ Cathedral Ward	1123	3911	Beast ×1 [100%]	97	97	97	106	68	78	68	102	98	—	—

Alfred, Hunter of Vilebloods

Alfred is a member of the Executioners, an order of hunters affiliated with the Healing Church. He is on a mission to assassinate the Vileblood queen and free the Executioners' former leader, Logarius, from eternal stewardship of the castle's seal. You'll first meet Alfred at the small shrine beside the Lower Oedon Chapel, the building whose central altar hides the route to Old Yharnam. Agreeing to cooperate with him enables you to summon him outside the Church of the Good Chalice, where he will assist you during the battle with the Blood-starved Beast, as well as behind the shortcut gate near Gilbert's House if you haven't already fought the Cleric Beast. You'll find him waiting atop the stairway to the Forbidden Woods after nightfall, at which point you may give him the Unopened Summons found on the desk near Annalise's throne; doing so will allow him to travel to Cainhurst Castle, where he will finish what his master started and slaughter the queen. With his mission finally fulfilled, Alfred will thank you for your assistance and leave Cainhurst; when you return to the Cathedral Ward, you'll find him mysteriously dead at the altar where you first met him.

Strategy

If you make Alfred your enemy before he moves to Cainhurst, he'll fight you with his Kirkhammer and Ludwig's Rifle. While he can be a tough opponent early on, his slow transformed swings are easy to interrupt and create many opportunities for you to perform visceral attacks. His rifle has longer range than the Hunter Blunderbuss but a lower rate of fire, so you can quickstep forward when he fires and hit him with R1 combos before he recovers. Should you turn him hostile at Cainhurst Castle, you'll have a much tougher fight on your hands – he'll be equipped Logarius' Wheel and will continually drink Lead Elixirs, which will cause your attacks to bounce off of him. His swings with the wheel are a little more difficult to predict, but interrupts are still the most effective way to deal with him; thrusting charge attacks from weapons such as Ludwig's Holy Blade or the Rifle Spear are also very effective.

Event Items

Item	Requirement
Fire Paper ×3 "Pray" Gesture	Speak to him at the Lower Chapel and agree to cooperate.
Wheel Hunter Badge "Church Bow (Male)" Gesture	Speak to him outside the Forbidden Woods and give him the Unopened Summons from the desk in the Cainhurst Castle throne room.
"Roar" Gesture	Exhaust his dialogue in the throne room of Cainhurst Castle.
"Radiance" Rune	Found on his body at the shrine where you first met him after he completes his mission and leaves Cainhurst.

Equipment Cathedral Ward

Right Hand 1	Bare Fists	Head	Nothing
Right Hand 2	Kirkhammer +5	Body	Executioner Garb
Left Hand 1	Bare Fists	Hands	Executioner Gauntlets
Left Hand 2	Ludwig's Rifle +5	Feet	Executioner Trousers

Equipment Cainhurst Castle

Right Hand 1	Logarius' Wheel +1	Head	Gold Ardeo
Right Hand 2	Bare Fists	Body	Executioner Garb
Left Hand 1	Ludwig's Rifle +10	Hands	Executioner Gauntlets
Left Hand 2	Bare Fists	Feet	Executioner Trousers

Interactions

Cathedral Ward | Lower Chapel

To begin his quest and receive the initial rewards, speak to him at the small altar outside the lower chapel and agree to cooperate.

▼

Old Yharnam | Church of the Good Chalice

After completing the previous step, you'll be able to summon him outside the Old Yharnam boss room to help you defeat the Blood-starved Beast.

▼

Cathedral Ward | Forbidden Woods Route

He'll move to this location after nightfall. Give him the Unopened Summons and he will reward you with the Wheel Hunter Badge and a gesture; next time you load an area he will move to Cainhurst Castle and kill Queen Annalise.

▼

Cainhurst Castle | Throne Room

Exhaust his dialogue to receive the final reward.

Cathedral Ward ▼ | Lower Chapel

Found dead in his starting location at the altar outside the lower chapel; at this point his quest is complete and no further interactions are possible.

Basic Information

Location			Item Drops											
Cathedral Ward/Old Yharnam/ Cainhurst Castle	1716	1605	Fire Paper ×3 [100%]	170	230	188	166	213	187	187	174	160	—	—

Iosefka

Iosefka is an earnest, kindhearted doctor of the Healing Church who oversees the clinic in Central Yharnam. She cares deeply for her patients' well-being and strictly forbids you from reentry into the facility for fear of exposing them to the Scourge, but is still willing to provide you with her valuable experimental blood vials. Visiting Iosefka frequently will cause her to open up to you a bit, but she'll still deny you entry into the clinic; you can continue to receive a new Iosefka's Blood Vial from her each time you return until evening, at which point Iosefka will be replaced by an impostor who won't offer you any more vials. Beware that attacking the clinic door three times will cause her to leave permanently, preventing you from being able to receive any more blood from her.

Event Items

Item	Requirement
Iosefka's Blood Vial (Unlimited)	Speak to her for the first time and receive one, then reload the area after using it and speak to her again to receive another. She'll continue giving you vials until she is replaced by the impostor in the evening.

Equipment

Right Hand 1	Bare Fists		Head	Nothing
Right Hand 2	Bare Fists		Body	White Church Garb
Left Hand 1	Bare Fists		Hands	Surgical Long Gloves
Left Hand 2	Bare Fists		Feet	Nothing

Interactions

Central Yharnam | Iosefka's Clinic | ○ � ◐ ○ ●
She will appear behind the door of the operating room where you first awoke once you have died or warped to the Hunter's Dream; exhaust her dialogue to receive the initial reward.

▼

Central Yharnam | Iosefka's Clinic | ○ ◐ ○ ●
Reload the area and speak to her after using the Iosefka's Blood Vial to receive another one; can be done three times.

▼

Central Yharnam | Iosefka's Clinic | ○ ◐ ○ ●
The fourth time you return for another Iosefka's Blood Vial, her dialogue will change slightly. From this point until evening, you can continue to receive an unlimited number of vials from her after using the previous one and reloading the area.

▼

Central Yharnam | Iosefka's Clinic | ○ ● ○ ○
Disappears from the game and is replaced by the impostor; at this point you can no longer receive free Iosefka's Blood Vials.

Basic Information

			Item Drops											
Central Yharnam	584	1896	None		160	152	196	247	213	196	205	173	165	—	—

Impostor Iosefka

the clinic with full knowledge that they'll become her test subjects, or confront her in the second floor operating room to dispense swift and arbitrary justice. In order to claim the most valuable item she holds, however, you'll need to retreat from the clinic and let her live until the Blood Moon is out; at this point you'll find her collapsed in the operating room and can obtain her One Third Umbilical Cord by killing her.

Strategy

If you choose to fight the impostor before the Blood Moon is out, you'll have a very tough duel on your hands – she has a tremendous amount of health and is very agile, and the tight spaces in the clinic make it extremely difficult to evade her attacks once she switches her Threaded Cane to whip mode. At first she'll walk slowly toward you while using basic melee attacks and occasionally casting Augur of Ebrietas, but when you reduce her health to 50% she'll transform her weapon and begin throwing Numbing Mist, using Blood Vials and casting A Call Beyond. Interrupts are effective during the first part of the fight but are much less so during the second; the best strategy is to lure her into a more open area such as the first floor hallway where you have more room to evade her attacks, then keep the pressure on her with R1 combos to prevent her from recovering her health.

Event Items

Item	Requirement
Lead Elixir ×2	Speak to her after sending the Young Girl to the clinic.
Numbing Mist ×2	Speak to her after sending the Lonely Old Woman to the clinic.
Numbing Mist ×2	Speak to her after sending Arianna to the clinic.
Numbing Mist ×2	Speak to her after sending the Bigoted Old Man to the clinic.
Numbing Mist ×2	Speak to her after sending Adella to the clinic.
Beast Blood Pellet ×2	Speak to her after sending the Afflicted Beggar to the clinic.
Blue Elixir ×3	Received instead of the above rewards every time you send a refugee to the clinic after becoming her accomplice.
One Third Umbilical Cord	Kill her during the Blood Moon when she has gone insane.

Equipment

Right Hand 1	Threaded Cane +7		Head	Nothing
Right Hand 2	Bare Fists		Body	White Church Garb
Left Hand 1	Repeating Pistol +7		Hands	Surgical Long Gloves
Left Hand 2	Bare Fists		Feet	Nothing

An impostor who replaces the real Iosefka in the evening after you enter the Oedon Chapel for the first time. Though her origins and affiliation are a mystery, she's a fanatical mad doctor in the classic sense – she'll initially ask you to send refugees to the clinic on the pretense of providing them with medical treatment, but after sneaking in through the rear entrance accessed vis the Forbidden Woods, you'll discover her true intentions and force her hand. At this point you may continue on as her willing accomplice and resume sending victims to

Interactions

Central Yharnam | Iosefka's Clinic | ○ ● ☾ ◐
She will take the real Iosefka's place starting in the evening after you enter the Cathedral Ward; speaking to her for the first time will open the clinic as a destination for refugees.

▼

Central Yharnam | Iosefka's Clinic | ○ ● ☾ ◐
Speak to her after sending the Young Girl from the Canal Residence to the clinic.

▼

Central Yharnam | Iosefka's Clinic | ○ ● ☾ ◐
Speak to her after sending the Lonely Old Woman from the residence near the drydock to the clinic.

▼

Central Yharnam | Iosefka's Clinic | ○ ● ☾ ◐
Speak to her after sending Arianna to the clinic.

Central Yharnam | Iosefka's Clinic | ○ ● ☾ ◐
Speak to her after sending the Bigoted Old Man living across the street from Arianna to the clinic.

▼

Central Yharnam | Iosefka's Clinic | ○ ● ☾ ◐
Speak to her after infiltrating Yahar'gul and sending Adella, the kidnapped nun, to the clinic.

▼

Central Yharnam | Iosefka's Clinic | ○ ● ☾ ◐
Speak to her after sending the Afflicted Beggar in the Forbidden Woods to the clinic.

▼

Central Yharnam | Iosefka's Clinic | ○ ● ☾ ●
Enter the clinic through the Forbidden Woods and proceed to the upstairs operating room to turn her hostile; doing so will halt her quest's progression, and killing her at this point will prevent you from obtaining the One Third Umbilical Cord she possesses.

Basic Information

			Item Drops											
Central Yharnam	1789	3200	Oedon Writhe ×1 [100%] One Third of Umbilical Cord [100%]*	160	152	196	247	213	196	205	199	185	—	—

*Blood Moon only

Vileblood Queen Annalise

Annalise is the queen and sole survivor of the Vilebloods, vampiric aristocrats born from forbidden blood who once lived in Cainhurst Castle. With the exception of Queen Annalise herself, the Vilebloods were murdered during a genocidal invasion by Logarius and his band of Executioners; Logarius then sealed the queen in an illusory prison and assumed the role of its warden, repelling any who ventured into the castle and threatened to break the seal. After freeing Logarius from his fate, you can either honor his wishes by finishing what he started, or swear an oath to the Vilebloods and take up arms against the Healing Church. If you wish to complete Alfred's quest, you'll need to guide him to Cainhurst and allow him to kill Queen Annalise, but you may restore her to life afterward by offering her remains at the Altar of Despair in the Upper Cathedral Ward. You can also kill the queen yourself by attacking her 50 times, which will allow you to collect her flesh the next time you reload the area.

Event Items

Item	Requirement
Cainhurst Badge "Corruption" Rune "Respect" Gesture	Swear an oath to the Vilebloods.
"Deep Respect" Gesture	Offer one or more Blood Dregs to Queen Annalise after joining the Vilebloods.

Interactions

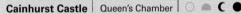

Cainhurst Castle | Queen's Chamber |

You'll first meet her in the throne room of Cainhurst Castle after defeating Martyr Logarius and approaching the wall behind his throne with the Crown of Illusions equipped. In order to obtain the items she holds, you must swear an oath to the Vilebloods.

▼

Cainhurst Castle | Queen's Chamber |

Offer Queen Annalise at least one Blood Dreg to receive an additional gesture. You can obtain these items by defeating NPC hunters and townsfolk, or by killing other players while online.

▼

Cainhurst Castle | Queen's Chamber |

At any point after obtaining the Ring of Betrothal, you can offer it to the queen for a few lines of additional dialogue, though she will steadfastly rebuff your advances.

▼

Cainhurst Castle | Queen's Chamber |

If you have given Alfred the Unopened Summons from the desk near Annalise's throne, he will move to the throne room and kill her; once he has done so, examine her throne to obtain the Queenly Flesh.

▼

Cainhurst Castle | Queen's Chamber |

After defeating Ebrietas, Daughter of the Cosmos, trade the Queenly Flesh to the Altar of Despair to revive Queen Annalise. She will reappear on her throne at Cainhurst Castle, allowing you to resume offering her Blood Dregs.

6

Basic Information

Special Weakness: Righteous

			Item Drops		97	88	88	88	88	88	97	72	78	—	—
Cainhurst Castle	573	4200	None												

Retired Hunter Djura

Djura is a retired hunter holed up in a tower in Old Yharnam. He is notable for having been both uncommonly kind and dreadfully foolish during his active days, a fact still reflected in his devotion to protecting the once-human beasts of the ruined district. When you first enter the area he will warn you away and will fire upon you with an emplaced gatling gun; you may choose to scale the tower and confront him or leave him alone and proceed on to the boss. If you leave Djura alone and return to Old Yharnam through Yahar'gul after defeating Darkbeast Paarl, you can sneak up to the tower using the ladder shortcut and climb to the top without Djura or his friend spotting you. If you approach Djura in this manner he will not be hostile and will readily explain his circumstances to you, at which point you'll have to decide whether he is friend or foe; if you comply with his wishes and promise to leave the beasts of Old Yharnam alone, you'll earn his friendship and the rewards from his quest. Bear in mind that although you'll still get the badge from defeating him in combat, you can only obtain the gesture by befriending him.

Strategy

If you decide that Djura is your enemy, you're in for a heated battle in a small and dangerous arena. He uses a Hunter Blunderbuss and the Stake Driver, an unusual weapon with short reach but very high attack speed, and will throw Molotovs at you as well. In addition to his swift attacks and the wide spread from his scattergun, Djura will also attempt to interrupt your swings and will sometimes follow through with a visceral attack if he succeeds; he's an aggressive opponent and will use the limited space atop the tower to his full advantage, pressuring you into backing toward the edges at every opportunity. By interrupting one of his attacks with his back to the edge, however, you can turn Djura's advantage against him and throw him from the tower with a visceral attack, killing him in the process.

Event Items

Item	Requirement
Powder Keg Hunter Badge "Brush Off Dust" Gesture	Enter Old Yharnam through the Graveyard of the Dark-beast and climb Djura's tower without him seeing you, then speak to him when he approaches you.

Equipment

Right Hand 1	Stake Driver +4		Head	Gray Wolf Cap
Right Hand 2	Bare Fists		Body	Ashen Hunter Garb
Left Hand 1	Hunter Blunderbuss +4		Hands	Ashen Hunter Gloves
Left Hand 2	Bare Fists		Feet	Ashen Hunter Trousers

Interactions

Old Yharnam | Djura's Tower | ○ ◗ ☾ ●

When you first enter Old Yharnam, he will threaten you from afar and will open fire from his tower with an emplaced gatling gun if you proceed into the area.

Old Yharnam | Djura's Tower | ○ ◗ ☾ ●

If you head directly to the tower and kill him, he'll drop his badge and his quest will end.

Old Yharnam | Djura's Tower | ○ ◗ ☾ ●

If you leave him alone and continue on to defeat the Blood-starved Beast, you can come back later and befriend him.

Old Yharnam | Djura's Tower | ○ ◗ ☾ ●

Leave him alone during your first trip to Old Yharnam and defeat Darkbeast Paarl first, then enter the area through the Graveyard of the Darkbeast and climb the tower without Djura detecting you until you reach the top. He will dismount the gatling gun and approach, but will not be hostile and can be engaged in conversation.

Old Yharnam | Djura's Tower | ○ ◗ ☾ ●

Speaking to him and selecting, "Spare the beasts of Old Yharnam" will earn his respect, at which point he will hand you the quest rewards and will remain friendly toward you.

Old Yharnam | Djura's Tower | ○ ◗ ☾ ●

If at any point after earning his trust you attack any of the enemies in Old Yharnam, he will immediately turn hostile again with no chance of reconciliation.

Basic Information

			Item Drops											
Old Yharnam	1261	875	Powder Keg Hunter Badge ×1 [100%]	228	237	202	237	177	176	185	127	172	—	—

Patches the Spider

A familiar face with an unfamiliar body, Patches will make his presence known once you've entered the Forbidden Woods, from which point he will take every possible opportunity to force the Tonsil Stone upon you and lure you into the clutches of his illegitimate god, Amygdala. The first place you're likely to encounter him is at the house near the kennels and the portcullis in the Forbidden Woods; with the Tonsil Stone in your hands, you'll be able to access the Lecture Building and the Nightmare Frontier, allowing you to complete Patches' quest and receive the associated rewards. He'll later appear in the Chalice Dungeons as a merchant, assisting you during your explorations by providing much-needed and accordingly overpriced items.

Event Items

Item	Requirement
Tonsil Stone	Speak to him in any of the occupied residences of Yharnam after entering the Forbidden Woods.
"Beg for Life" Gesture "Anti-Clockwise Metamorphosis" Rune	Confront him in the Lecture Building after defeating Amygdala and speak to him face-to-face.

Interactions

Central Yharnam
Cathedral Ward
Forbidden Woods
Hemwick Charnel Lane | Residence of any generic NPC | ○ ◒ ☾ ●

When you enter the Forbidden Woods, he will take over various residences in and around Yharnam; speak to him in any of these locations to receive the Tonsil Stone.

▼

Cathedral Ward | Entrance of Yahar'gul | ○ ◒ ☾ ●

Allow the False God clinging to the wall above the entrance to grab you. With the Tonsil Stone in your possession, you'll be brought to the Lecture Building rather than killed.

▼

Lecture Building 1F | Patches' Lab | ○ ◒ ☾ ●

Speak to him and proceed through the Lecture Hall to the Nightmare Frontier.

▼

Nightmare Frontier | Lower Caves | ○ ◒ ☾ ●

Approach his position to initiate an event in which he shoves you off the cliff.

▼

Lecture Building 2F | Patches' Lab | ○ ◒ ☾ ●

Enter his hideout through the floor hatch behind the Church Giant and speak to him to receive a gesture. Speak to him again and select either dialogue prompt, then speak to him a final time to receive a rune.

6

Basic Information

Location	■	✦	Item Drops											
Lecture Building 1F	455	5453	Great One's Wisdom ×1 [100%]	75	75	75	75	66	50	55	200	270	—	—

Valtr, Master of the League OH

Valtr is the sole survivor of a trio of constables who once chased a beast from a neighboring region all the way to Yharnam. His two comrades were slain by the beast, but he in turn dispatched the creature and devoured its entire corpse by himself. This led Valtr to discover the "Impurity" rune, which allows its bearer to see Vermin – the root of man's impurity. Valtr resolved to expunge all Vermin in the name of ultimate purification and formed the League of Confederates to further this all but unattainable goal. The endless march of time has slowly eroded his strength, and in his advancing age he now seeks a candidate worthy enough to take his place as Master of the League.

Strategy

Should you decide to attack Valtr in the Forbidden Woods, know that you'll have a tough fight on your hands – especially if you do so during your first visit to the area. He has a great deal of HP and wields the Whirligig Saw, a trick weapon whose individual attacks in its transformed mode can inflict multiple hits and deal tremendous amounts of damage very quickly. Valtr isn't the most agile of opponents, but will still attempt to dodge your gunshots and thrown weapons with quicksteps; he will also occasionally fire a burst at you with his Hunter Blunderbuss, especially if you back out of range of his melee attacks. His slow swings provide good opportunities to interrupt him, however, and if you have the Beast Roar or another means of knocking him backward, you can use it to send him flying off the upper floor of the shortcut elevator to his death.

Equipment

Right Hand 1	Whirligig Saw +6	Head	One-Eyed Iron Helm
Right Hand 2	Bare Fists	Body	Constable's Garb
Left Hand 1	Hunter Blunderbuss +6	Hands	Constable's Gloves
Left Hand 2	Bare Fists	Feet	Constable's Trousers

Event Items

Item	Requirement
"Impurity" Rune	Agree to join the League.
League Staff "League Oath" Gesture	Speak to Valtr after crushing one Vermin.
Upgraded "League Oath" Gesture	Complete Valtr's quest through Step 4.
Master's One-Eyed Iron Helm	Complete Valtr's quest through Step 5.
One-Eyed Iron Helm	Kill Valtr at any time before completing Step 5.

Interactions

Forbidden Woods | Small Windmill |
Speak to him the first time and agree to join the League. He will give you the "Impurity" Caryll Rune, allowing you to obtain Vermin. "Valtr, Master of the League" becomes available as a summoned NPC at this point.

▼

Forbidden Woods | Small Windmill |
Speak to him after crushing one Vermin to receive the League Staff and the "League Oath" gesture.

▼

Forbidden Woods | Small Windmill |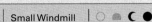
Speak to him after crushing a total of two Vermin for a few additional lines of dialogue.

▼

Forbidden Woods | Small Windmill |
Speak to him and exhaust his dialogue after crushing a total of five Vermin to receive the upgraded "League Oath" gesture.

▼

Forbidden Woods | Small Windmill |
Change areas and return to the Forbidden Woods after completing Step 4. Enter the Small Windmill and collect the Master's One-Eyed Iron Helm from the spot where Valtr was standing. From this point onward, "Valtr, Beast Eater" will replace "Valtr, Master of the League" in all of his summon locations.

Basic Information

			Item Drops											
Forbidden Woods	3617	7277	One-Eyed Iron Helm [100%]	244	220	202	211	203	237	230	140	128	—	—

Simon, Seeker of Secrets OH

A mysterious figure encountered in the Hunter's Nightmare. Although his outward appearance suggests a destitute beggar, his presence in the nightmare and his apparent preoccupation with secrets betray some manner of hidden agenda. In order to reach his initial location, you'll need to loop back through the Chapel Tunnel from the River of Blood; depending upon your actions he may or may not appear at the Underground Corpse Pile after defeating Ludwig, but as long as you speak to express your interest in nightmares to him before clearing that boss battle, you'll find him on the floor of the Lighthouse Hut in the Fishing Hamlet.

Strategy

Simon doesn't use standard firearms, wielding instead the Fists of Gratia and Simon's Bowblade. The Bowblade becomes a completely different type of ranged weapon in its transformed mode, however, and he will alternate between peppering you with ranged attacks and striking up close with the blade's sword form. His attacks are relatively weak compared to other NPCs and ordinary R1 combos are effective; he can be interrupted when using close-range attacks but attempting to do so while his weapon is in bow mode will almost always result in the two of you trading shots, which can prevent you from being able to follow through with a visceral attack in time. While he has relatively low health compared to other enemy Hunters in the Hunter's Nightmare, he can still put up a respectable fight if you attempt to kill him early in the game.

Equipment

Right Hand 1	Bare Fists		Head	Harrowed Hood
Right Hand 2	Simon's Bowblade +8		Body	Harrowed Garb
Left Hand 1	Bare Fists		Hands	Harrowed Gloves
Left Hand 2	Fists of Gratia +8		Feet	Harrowed Trousers

Event Items

Item	Requirement
Holy Moonlight Sword	Speak to Simon before defeating Ludwig. Tell Simon that you're interested in the nightmare. Defeat Ludwig and speak to him while wearing Healing Church attire, then reload the area and speak with Simon to receive the sword. It can still be obtained directly from Ludwig if you do not complete Step 2 of the Seeker's quest.
Simon's Bowblade Underground Cell Inner Chamber Key	Complete Simon's quest through Step 3 or kill him at any point before then to obtain the Bowblade. You will receive the key from him if he survives to this point; otherwise you'll find it on a corpse in the same room.

Interactions

Hunter's Nightmare | Nightmare Chapel | ○ ◖ ☾ C ●

Circle back through the hall behind the locked door in the Nightmare Chapel to find him. Tell him you're interested in the nightmare to advance his quest.

▼

Hunter's Nightmare | Underground Corpse Pile | ○ ◖ ☾ C ●

Defeat Ludwig, then speak to his head while equipped Healing Church attire in your body slot and answer "no." Reload the area to find Simon standing next to Ludwig's head; speak to him and he will give you the Holy Moonlight Sword. This step will be automatically skipped if you don't speak to the Seeker before defeating Ludwig, or if you tell Ludwig "yes" or speak to him when not wearing Church attire.

▼

Research Hall | Research Hall Entrance | ○ ◖ ☾ C ●

If you answered "No" to Ludwig while wearing Church attire and received the Holy Moonlight Sword from Simon, he will be waiting at the Research Hall Lamp when you arrive. He will offer a few additional lines of dialogue, but no new rewards. If you handled Step 2 in any other way, the Seeker will not be present in this location and the quest will skip to Step 4.

▼

Fishing Hamlet | Lighthouse Hut | ○ ◖ ☾ C ●

Defeat Maria and make your way to the Lighthouse Hut. Simon will be inside lying on the ground directly to the right of the entrance; speak to him to obtain Simon's Bowblade and the Underground Cell Inner Chamber Key. If Simon has already been killed or if you did not start his quest before this point, the key will instead be located on a corpse near the Lamp.

Basic Information

	■	⚔	Item Drops											
Hunter's Nightmare	2925	8547	Simon's Bowblade [100%]	276	194	211	228	252	211	244	214	206	—	—
Research Hall	2925	8547	Simon's Bowblade [100%]	276	194	211	228	252	211	244	214	206	—	—
Fishing Hamlet	1896	2137	Simon's Bowblade [100%]	276	194	211	228	252	211	244	222	214	—	—

Ludwig, the Holy Blade (Head) OH

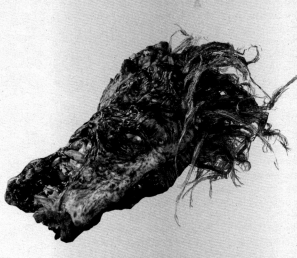

The first hunter of the Healing Church and founder of their workshop. Though Ludwig dedicated his life to the good of his fellow hunters, he ultimately became victim to the curse of blood and beasts, eventually becoming trapped in the nightmare like so many after him. Though completely transformed when you first encounter him, deep down Ludwig still retains his pride as a hunter and will rediscover his guiding light for one last hunt, partially regaining his humanity mid-battle. If you are wearing Healing Church attire when you speak to him after his defeat, he will implore you to validate his sacrifices and enable him to finally rest in peace; whether you choose to tell him a merciful lie or the bitter truth is your decision alone.

Event Items

Item	Requirement
Holy Moonlight Sword	To obtain the sword without killing him, speak to him while wearing Healing Church attire and answer, "Yes;" otherwise, receive it from the Seeker of Secrets or simply attack Ludwig and he will drop it.

Interactions

Hunter's Nightmare | Underground Corpse Pile |

After being defeated in battle, Ludwig's head will remain on the ground to the left of the stairs leading to the exit. If you speak to him while wearing non-Church attire he'll offer a few lines of dialogue, then fall silent; in this case you'll need to finish him in order to obtain the Holy Moonlight Sword. If you're wearing a Healing Church garment in your body slot, Ludwig's dialogue will change and he'll offer you a yes/no prompt; answer yes and he'll give you the sword immediately. If you answer "no" and reload the area, the Seeker of Secrets will show up and finish Ludwig; at this point you can obtain the sword by speaking to the Seeker.

Basic Information				Item Drops												
Special Weakness: Serration	■	♠														
Hunter's Nightmare	—	0	Holy Moonlight Sword]100%]	140	140	140	140	252	119	168	999	999	—	—		

Brador, Church Assassin

An assassin of the Healing Church tasked with protecting the secrets hidden beyond the Hunter's Nightmare, Brador has been willingly locked away in the deepest cell of the Research Hall's prison for so long that his eccentric manner could be the result of eroding sanity or merely old age. He has seen many a comrade fall to the scourge of beasts and has freed at least one by his own hand, donning the bloodied hide as a testament and sequestering himself in the nightmare away from prying eyes. Although your progress into the Fishing Hamlet will eventually brand you his target, Brador is loath to claim another victim and will initially offer you a sincere warning to stay away. He will invade you in a total of four locations throughout the Fishing Hamlet and the Hunter's Nightmare, and will invade repeatedly in the same spots each time you return until you open his cell and kill him.

Strategy

Brador will not attempt to defend himself when you enter his cell and any attack will kill him. For the invading version of Brador, please see p325 of the Bestiary chapter.

Equipment

Right Hand 1	Bloodletter +9	Head	Brador's Testimony
Right Hand 2	Bare Fists	Body	Beast Hide Garb
Left Hand 1	Ludwig's Rifle +9	Hands	Bloodied Armbands
Left Hand 2	Bare Fists	Feet	Bloodied Trousers

Event Items

Item	Requirement
Bloodied Armband	Defeat Brador's phantom at the location specified in Step 2.
Beast Hide Garb	Defeat Brador's phantom at the location specified in Step 3.
Bloodied Trousers	Defeat Brador's phantom at the location specified in Step 4.
Brador's Testimony	Defeat Brador's phantom at the location specified in Step 5.
Bloodletter	Put an end to Brador once and for all by killing him in his cell.

Interactions

Hunter's Nightmare | Underground Cells

Speak to him through the door of his cell and answer either "I hear the bell" or "I hear nothing." Your choice here has no effect on the quest other than eliciting different responses from Brador.

▼

Fishing Hamlet | Flooded Village – Overlook

Brador will invade at the far end of the first bridge past the Lighthouse Hut; defeat him and you will receive the Bloodied Armbands.

▼

Fishing Hamlet | Flooded Village – Stilts

Brador will invade at Position A when you exit through the scaffolding under the building; defeat him and you will receive the Beast Hide Garb.

▼

Fishing Hamlet | Access Tunnel

Brador will invade at the dead end branch of the cave leading back to the well; defeat him and you will receive the Bloodied Trousers.

▼

Fishing Hamlet | Underground Cells

After you have obtained the key to his cell [p651], Brador will invade at the top of the connecting stairwell when you return to the Underground Cells. Defeat him and you will receive Brador's Testimony.

▼

Hunter's Nightmare | Underground Cells

Kill Brador in his cell and he will drop the Bloodletter. Eliminating him here will also put an end to his constant invasions.

Basic Information

				Item Drops											
Research Hall	■ —	✦ 0	Bloodletter [100%]	221	245	177	202	159	123	159	187	181	—	—

6

Adeline, Research Hall Patient

Event Items

Item	Requirement
Blood of Adeline	Give Adeline one Brain Fluid. The order in which you give them to her has no effect on the quest, but if you are already carrying another special blood vial (such as Arianna's or Adella's) you won't be able to receive blood from her. If you speak to Adeline again after changing areas with no other special blood vials in your inventory, you can continue to receive vials of her blood until you complete her quest.
Balcony Key	Give Adeline the second Brain Fluid.
"Milkweed" Rune	Give Adeline the third and final Brain Fluid.

Interactions

Research Hall	Floor 1 Laboratory	

Speak to Adeline in the first floor laboratory and listen to her request for Brain Fluid.

Research Hall	Floor 1 Laboratory	

Obtain Brain Fluid from one of two NPC patients in the Research Hall: one in the Upper Rafters, and the other is on a landing between floors 3 and 4 next to a Church Doctor enemy Hunter armed with a Threaded Cane and a Repeating Pistol. Both of these patients are the "Head Only" type and must be attacked in order to obtain the Brain Fluid; which one you obtain and hand in first makes no difference. Adeline will offer you a vial of her blood and will continue to do so each time you return when not in possession of a unique blood vial.

Research Hall	Floor 1 Laboratory	

Give Adeline the other Brain Fluid obtainable from the NPC patients in the Research Hall. Note that you must leave the Research Hall and return at least three times after handing in the first Brain Fluid in order to advance to this step.

Research Hall	Floor 1 Laboratory	

After handing in the second Brain Fluid, leave and return to the Research Hall no fewer than three times. On your third return trip, Adeline will have transformed into the "Head Only" patient type and will be located immediately to the left of the entrance to the lab where you originally met her, behind the open door. Exhaust her dialogue, then attack her only once to receive the third Brain Fluid. She will immediately revive; at this point, give her the third Brain Fluid to complete her quest and obtain the Milkweed rune.

Adeline is a hapless but kindly patient of the Research Hall and a former Blood Saint of the Healing Church. You'll encounter her after entering the Floor 1 Laboratory via the connecting elevator, at which point she'll implore you to bring her Brain Fluid and offer her blood in return. Do so and she'll make good on her word; do so again and she'll show her gratitude by handing over the Balcony Key, giving you access to the Blacksky Eye. Giving her a third Brain Fluid (her own, no less) will, bizarrely, enable her to achieve an epiphany and free her from a terrible burden; at this point she will share her discovery with you and fade away in peaceful contentment.

Basic Information

			Item Drops	
Research Hall	458	610	Balcony Key ×1 [100%]	99 99 99 99 108 89 89 120 180 — —

Yamamura the Wanderer 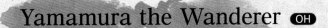 OH

A transient warrior from an Eastern land who became a hunter after arriving in Yharnam. Yamamura's mission began with the goal of honorable revenge and ended in tragedy – he eventually fell in with the League of Confederates, but was unprepared for the revelations that awaited among their ranks and ultimately lost his sanity when faced with the abject impurity of mankind. You'll find him locked in a cell immediately to the left of the stairwell connecting the Underground Corpse Pile to the Underground Cells, repeating a prayer out loud while banging his head on the wall. When you obtain the Underground Cell Key you can enter Yamamura's cell and release him from his suffering with a swift coup de grâce to obtain his equipment and access him as a summoned ally for several boss fights.

Event Items

Item	Requirement
Yamamura Hunter Hat Khaki Haori Old Hunter Arm Bands Wine Hakama	Kill him in his cell and end his suffering.

Interactions

Hunter's Nightmare | Underground Cells | ○ ◐ ☾ ●

Use the Underground Cell Key [p185] to access his cell and kill him to receive his equipment. Bringing a merciful end to his torment also enables you to summon his spirit to assist you with several boss fights.

Basic Information

			Item Drops											
Hunter's Nightmare	■ —	2826	Yamamura's Hunter Attire	152	133	151	178	187	279	160	147	140	—	—

Fishing Hamlet Priest OH

A priest of the Fishing Hamlet and survivor of a raid by the hunters long ago. The raid left many of the hamlet's residents and their guardian Great One, Kos, dead; in retribution, the remaining villagers laid a curse of blood upon the hunters and their descendants. Although he normally wanders around the hamlet outskirts muttering baneful chants and will not acknowledge your presence, speaking to him with the Milkweed rune equipped will enable him to identify you as a kindred spirit, at which point he will reward you with the Accursed Brew and go back to wandering around. Note that while the priest has a standard HP value, he is technically invincible and cannot be killed or turned hostile.

Event Items

Item	Requirement
Accursed Brew	Speak to him while equipped with the "Milkweed" Oath Rune.

Interactions

Fishing Halmet | Hamlet Causeway | ○ ◐ ☾ ●

Speak to him with the "Milkweed" rune equipped. He will recognize you as an ally and bestow upon you the Accursed Brew.

Basic Information

			Item Drops											
Fishing Hamlet	■ 2541	0	None	97	97	97	97	142	124	435	200	180	—	—

6

Summoned NPCs (OH)

There's also a number of NPCs that can be summoned in both the normal game areas and in Chalice Dungeons to aid you during the hunt, particularly during boss fights. The conditions for summoning these allies vary; the Old Hunter Bell is a universal requirement for calling any of them, but you must also equip the "Impurity" rune in order to summon League Confederates. In certain cases you must begin or complete specific quests before summoning a particular character, such as Henryk and Valtr; in others you will lose your opportunity to summon the NPCs in question if you've already killed them, such as the younger Madaras twin. In the tables below, you'll find detailed information on where each of these new allies can be summoned and what prerequisites must be met before you can do so.

Normal Game Areas (OH)

Old Hunter Henriett (OH)

Equipment

Right Hand 1	Kirkhammer +3/+8
Right Hand 2	Bare Fists
Left Hand 1	Hunter's Torch +3/+8
Left Hand 2	Repeating Pistol +3/+8
Items	Molotov Cocktail
Head	Top Hat
Body	Hunter Garb
Hands	Hunter Gloves
Feet	Hunter Trousers

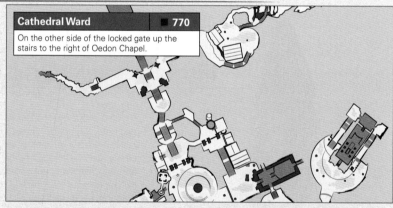

Cathedral Ward   ■ 770

On the other side of the locked gate up the stairs to the right of Oedon Chapel.

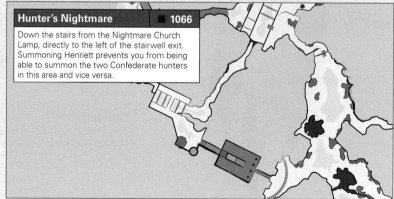

Hunter's Nightmare   ■ 1066

Down the stairs from the Nightmare Church Lamp, directly to the left of the stairwell exit. Summoning Henriett prevents you from being able to summon the two Confederate hunters in this area and vice versa.

Yamamura the Wanderer OH

Equipment

Right Hand 1	Chikage +6/+4/+7
Right Hand 2	Bare Fists
Left Hand 1	Piercing Rifle +6/+4/+7
Left Hand 2	Bare Fists
Items	Throwing Knife
Head	Yamamura Hunter Hat
Body	Khaki Haori
Hands	Old Hunter Arm Bands
Feet	Wine Hakama

Research Hall ■ 835

In plain view immediately to the right of the boss room entrance. In order to summon him you must first kill him in the Underground Cells area and equip the "Impurity" rune.

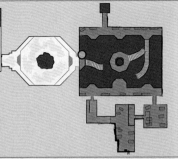

Yahar'gul, Unseen Village ■ 796

In plain sight along the path to the Graveyard of the Darkbeast after dropping from the cave exit. In order to summon Yamamura for this fight, you must first kill him in the Hunter's Nightmare and equip the "Impurity" rune. Additionally, you can summon either Yamamura or Antal to assist you in battle against Darkbeast Paarl, but not both simultaneously.

Yahar'gul Unseen Village (Blood Moon) ■ 960

Behind a carriage on the left side of the road a short distance before the boss room. Note that you must be equipped with the "Impurity" rune in order to summon Yamamura and he will not be available until you've killed him in the Hunter's Nightmare. You can summon either Yamamura or Antal to assist you during the battle with The One Reborn, but both hunters cannot be summoned simultaneously.

6

Defector Antal OH

Equipment

Right Hand 1	Church Pick +4/+7
Right Hand 2	Bare Fists
Left Hand 1	Flamesprayer +4/+7
Left Hand 2	Bare Fists
Items	Throwing Knife
Head	Black Hooded Iron Helm
Body	Yahar'gul Black Garb
Hands	Yahar'gul Black Gloves
Feet	Yahar'gul Black Trousers

Yahar'gul, Unseen Village ■ 847

When you drop down onto the narrow fenced path leading to Darkbeast Paarl, take a right to reach this summon point. You can only summon either Antal or Yamamura to assist you, not both simultaneously.

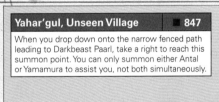

Yahar'gul Unseen Village (Blood Moon) ■ 1099

Behind the overturned carriage just outside the boss room.

Younger Madaras Twin OH

Equipment

Right Hand 1	Hunter Axe +4/+6/+9
Right Hand 2	Bare Fists
Left Hand 1	Hunter Blunderbuss +4/+6/+9
Left Hand 2	Bare Fists
Items	Fire Paper
Head	Butcher Mask
Body	Butcher Garb
Hands	Butcher Gloves
Feet	Butcher Trousers

Forbidden Woods — 676

In the corner of the small gated area opposite the boss room, to the left of the corpse in front of the giant tombstone holding the "Clockwise Metamorphosis" rune. You cannot summon him if you have already killed him outside the Small Windmill or are not wearing the "Impurity" rune.

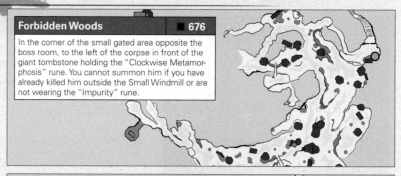

Byrgenwerth — 858

Near the Byrgenwerth Lamp in an alcove between two trees. He will only appear if you are wearing the "Impurity" rune and have not already killed him outside the Small Windmill.

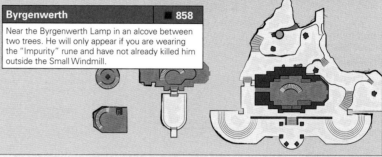

Hunter's Nightmare — 904

At the end of the semi-hidden path in the Bloody Plaza where the first Nightmare Executioner approaches from. The summon point will only be there if you haven't already killed him in the Forbidden Woods, are wearing the "Impurity" rune, and have not summoned Old Hunter Henriett.

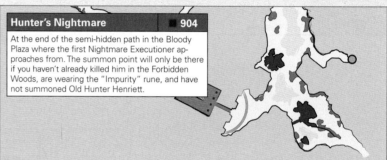

Old Hunter Henryk OH

Equipment

Right Hand 1	Saw Cleaver +4/+6
Right Hand 2	Bare Fists
Left Hand 1	Hunter Pistol +4/+6
Left Hand 2	Bare Fists
Items	Throwing Knife
Head	Henryk's Hunter Cap
Body	Henryk's Hunter Garb
Hands	Henryk's Hunter Gloves
Feet	Henryk's Hunter Trousers

Forbidden Woods — 900

Along the wall at the intersection leading to the boss area. He will not appear unless you have defeated him at the Tomb of Oedon and are wearing the "Impurity" rune.

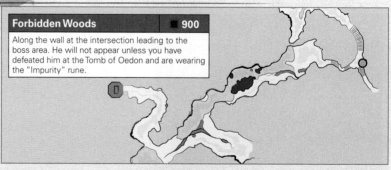

Byrgenwerth — 1015

On the second floor, between two couches near the treasure chest. You won't be able to summon him unless you have defeated him at the Tomb of Oedon and are equipped with the "Impurity" rune.

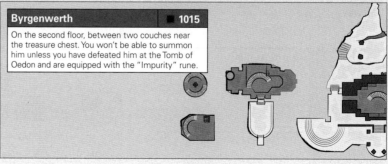

Mensis Scholar Damian OH

Equipment

Right Hand 1	Threaded Cane +6/+8/+10
Right Hand 2	Bare Fists
Left Hand 1	Loch Shield
Left Hand 2	Bare Fists
Items	Augur of Ebrietas, Blacksky Eye, Choir Bell
Head	Mensis Cage
Body	Student Uniform
Hands	Nothing
Feet	Student Trousers

Byrgenwerth ■ 746

In plain view outside the boss room. Bear in mind that summoning him will prevent you from being able to summon Henryk or the younger Madaras twin, but his habit of spamming the Choir Bell makes him well worth the tradeoff.

Upper Cathedral Ward ■ 923

In plain view in the hallway connecting the elevator to the Altar of Despair.

Great Isz, Layer 3 ■ 1499

To the right of the stairs leading down to the boss room. Summoning Damian will prevent you from being able to summon Waller or Gremia, but his ability to use the Choir Bell with reckless abandon is a considerable asset.

Valtr, Master of the League/Beast Eater* OH

Equipment

Right Hand 1	Whirligig Saw +8/+9
Right Hand 2	Bare Fists
Left Hand 1	Hunter Blunderbuss +8/+9
Left Hand 2	Bare Fists
Items	None
Head	One-Eyed Iron Helm
Body	Constable's Garb
Hands	Constable's Gloves
Feet	Constable's Trousers

Hunter's Nightmare – Mouth of the River ■ 1186 ■ 1695

Along the right wall directly opposite the Eye Collector as you approach the boss room, slightly obscured behind the terrain. In order to summon him, you must be equipped with the "Impurity" rune and you may not enlist his aid if you have already summoned Henriett.

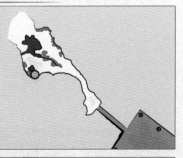

Hunter's Nightmare – Grand Cathedral ■ 1031 ■ 1474

In plain sight just inside the door of the Grand Cathedral.

*Note: When you summon Valtr, he will appear wearing his helmet and will be identified as "Valtr, Master of the League" until you have completed his quest and obtained the Master's One-Eyed Iron Helm. From this point onward he will be summoned as "Valtr, Beast Eater" and will appear without his helmet. He is stronger as "Beast Eater," so it's worth completing his quest before summoning him for these fights.

Madman Wallar OH

Equipment

Right Hand 1	Amygdalan Arm +7/+7/+10/+10
Right Hand 2	Bare Fists
Left Hand 1	Ludwig's Rifle +7/+7/+10/+10
Left Hand 2	Bare Fists
Items	–
Head	Madman Hood
Body	Madman Garb
Hands	Madman Manchettes
Feet	Madman Leggings

Lower Pthumerian [Layer 3]　■ 978

The path to the right from the first Lamp on this floor will take you to the top level of the large garden area. On the right-hand corner of this platform nearest to the path that you took to get here is where you can summon Old Hunter Madman Wallar.

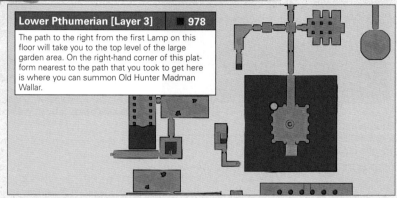

Lower Pthumerian [Layer 4]　■ 978

Take the left door just before going straight ahead towards the boss room. In the next room with the Merciless Watcher guarding a chest containing a Sage's Wrist is the summon point where you can call Madman Wallar.

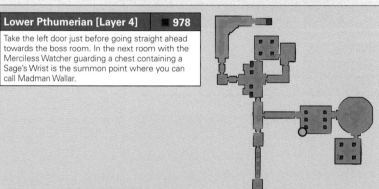

Cursed Pthumerian Defilement [Layer 3]　■ 882

Madman Wallar can be summoned in the ladder pit room with the locked exit gate facing you as you enter. Just look to your left to spot the summon point. Both Madman Wallar and Queen Killer can be summoned to take on Amygdala together.

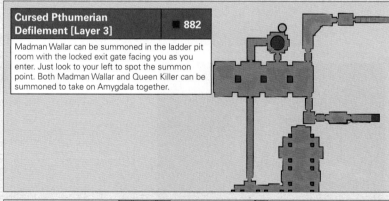

Great Pthumeru Ihyll [Layer 3]　■ 1234

Once you've made your exit from the first tunnel, you can summon Madman Wallar from behind the large tombstone directly ahead. You won't be able to enlist the help of Prospector Olek and Queen Killer at the same time, but Madman Wallar can still be summoned regardless of who you choose, so be sure to summon him if you need the extra help.

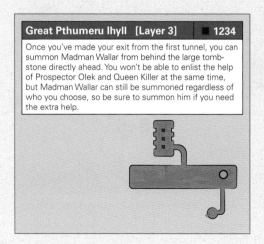

Great Isz [Layer 3]　■ 1055

This summoning point can be found in the room below the one containing the shop that sells the Sinister Isz Root Chalice. If you enter via the long corridor with the boulder trap, it will be in the corner to the right. Make sure after summoning him that you exit via the shortcut gate you can open in this room so he doesn't get crushed by the boulder!

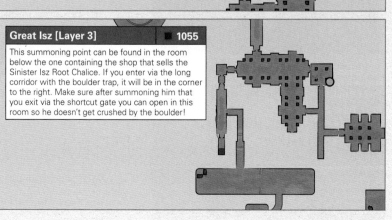

Tomb Prospector Olek OH

Equipment

Right Hand 1	Kirkhammer +2/+3/+7/+7/+10/+10
Right Hand 2	Bare Fists
Left Hand 1	Hunter's Torch +2/+3/+7/+7/+10/+10
Left Hand 2	Repeating Pistol +2/+3/+7/+7/+10/+10
Items	Molotov Cocktail
Head	Tomb Prospector Hood
Body	Tomb Prospector Garb
Hands	Tomb Prospector Gloves
Feet	Tomb Prospector Trousers

Central Pthumerian [Layer 3] ■ 746

To the right of the exit gate to the boss room on this floor is a large, dark room. The summon point you're looking for is in the far right-hand corner from where you enter.

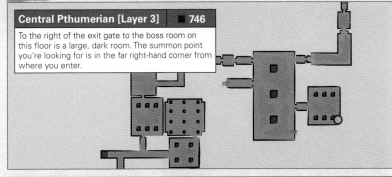

Lower Pthumerian [Layer 3] ■ 941

You can summon Prospector Olek just to the left of the entrance that leads to the boss room for assistance against Rom, the Vacuous Spider.

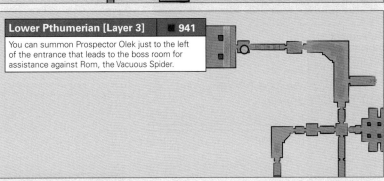

Lower Pthumerian [Layer 4] ■ 941

Take the path to the left, just before the entrance door to the boss room on this floor and when you reach the room with the ladder, do not go up it just yet. In the top right corner from where you entered this room you see the glow where you can summon Prospector Olek to assist you.

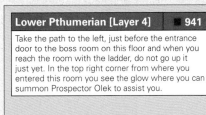
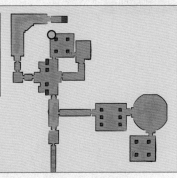

Cursed Pthumerian Defilement [Layer 2] ■ 1020

A little to the left of where you enter the large stone elevator room, you can summon Prospector Olek. His aid will be much appreciated against the Cursed Watchdog of the Old Lords boss. Summoning Olek will remove your ability to summon Queen Killer and vice versa.

Pthumerian Labyrinth [Layer 3] ■ 656

In the left corner of the locked exit gate room that leads to the boss, just as you enter.

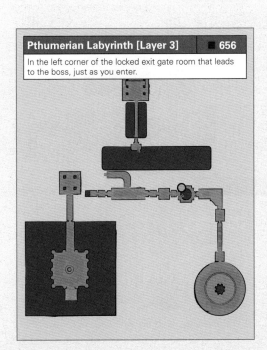

Great Pthumeru Ihyll [Layer 3] ■ 1261

Prospetor Olek can be summoned in the ladder well room with the locked exit door. Look to your left as you enter. Summoning him will forbid you from summoning Queen Killer on this floor.

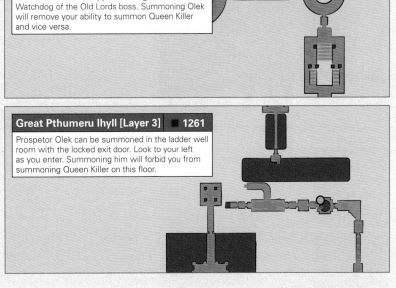

6

Queen Killer OH

Equipment

Right Hand 1	Logarius' Wheel
Right Hand 2	Bare Fists
Left Hand 1	Cannon +10/+10/+10
Left Hand 2	Bare Fists
Items	Rope Molotov
Head	Gold Ardeo
Body	–
Hands	–
Feet	–

Cursed Pthumerian Defilement [Layer 2] ■ 882

Just before you open the door to the boss room you can find the summon point for Old Hunter Queen Killer to your left. If you have summoned Prospector Olek on this floor you will not be able to summon Queen Killer and vice versa.

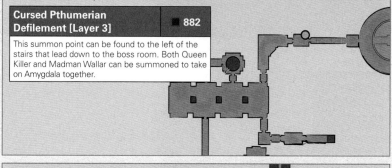

Cursed Pthumerian Defilement [Layer 3] ■ 882

This summon point can be found to the left of the stairs that lead down to the boss room. Both Queen Killer and Madman Wallar can be summoned to take on Amygdala together.

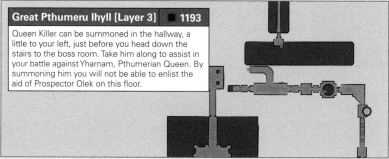

Great Pthumeru Ihyll [Layer 3] ■ 1193

Queen Killer can be summoned in the hallway, a little to your left, just before you head down the stairs to the boss room. Take him along to assist in your battle against Yharnam, Pthumerian Queen. By summoning him you will not be able to enlist the aid of Prospector Olek on this floor.

Beastclaw Jozef OH

Equipment

Right Hand 1	Beast Claw +10/+10
Right Hand 2	Bare Fists
Left Hand 1	–
Left Hand 2	Bare Fists
Items	–
Head	Tomb Prospector Hood
Body	Charred Hunter Garb
Hands	Charred Hunter Gloves
Feet	Charred Hunter Trousers

Ailing Loran [Layer 3] ■ 912

Shortly after passing the lamp on this floor you'll come to a crossroads room; take the path on the right and follow it round. The summon point is in the small room you enter in the top right corner. He will prove a useful ally against the Abhorrent Beast. Summoning him will not allow you to summon Old Hunter Vitus on this floor.

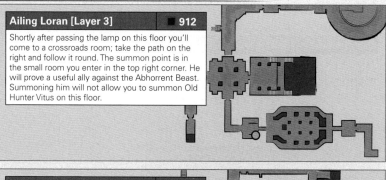

Lower Loran [Layer 3] ■ 1020

At the bottom of the spiral staircase room you can summon Beastclaw Jozef. Summoning him will not allow you to summon Old Hunter Vitus on this floor.

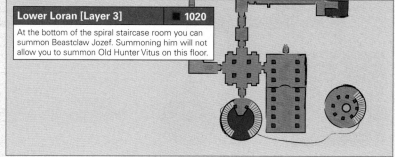

Old Hunter Vitus (OH)

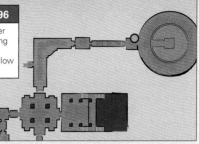

Ailing Loran [Layer 3]   ▪ 996

Before entering the boss room, look in the corner to the left and you'll find this summon point. Bring him along to make your fight against the Loran Darkbeast smoother. Summoning him will not allow you to summon Beastclaw Jozef.

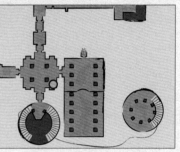

Lower Loran [Layer 3]   ▪ 1068

After entering the room with the locked gate leading to the boss chamber, head to the left to find the summon point. Bring him along to make your fight against the Loran Darkbeast easier. Summoning him will not allow you to summon Beastclaw Jozef on this floor.

Equipment

Right Hand 1	Beast Cutter +10/+10
Right Hand 2	Bare Fists
Left Hand 1	Hunter Pistol +10/+10
Left Hand 2	Bare Fists
Items	Fire Paper
Head	Old Hunter Cap
Body	Old Hunter Garb
Hands	Old Hunter Gloves
Feet	Old Hunter Trousers

Mensis Scholar Damian (OH)

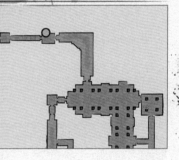

Great Isz [Layer 3]   ▪ 1049

The summoning point for Damian on this floor is just to the right of the stairs you take down to fight Ebrietas, Daughter of the Cosmos. Summoning him will not allow you to summon Madman Wallar and Sir Gremia on this floor.

Equipment

Right Hand 1	Threaded Cane +10
Right Hand 2	Bare Fists
Left Hand 1	Loch Shield
Left Hand 2	Bare Fists
Items	Augur of Ebrietas

Head	Mensis Cage
Body	Student Uniform
Hands	–
Feet	Student Trousers

Tomb Prospector Sir Gremia (OH)

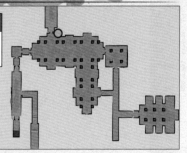

Great Isz [Layer 3]   ▪ 1042

The summon point for Tomb Prospector Sir Gremia can be found behind a rundown old carriage, just to the right of the entrance to the boss room.

Equipment

Right Hand 1	Ludwig's Holy Blade +10
Right Hand 2	Bare Fists
Left Hand 1	Hunter's Torch +10
Left Hand 2	Rosmarinus +10
Items	Augur of Ebrietas

Head	Tomb Prospector Hood
Body	Tomb Prospector Garb
Hands	Tomb Prospector Gloves
Feet	Tomb Prospector Trousers

6

Shops

Scavenging the corpses of fallen foes can provide an important source of basic items like Blood Vials and Quicksilver Bullets, but when you need larger quantities or more specialized supplies, you'll probably find yourself visiting a shop. The two shops you'll be visiting most frequently are located in the Hunter's Dream and can be accessed from the beginning of the game, though you'll need to save up at least one point of insight in order to access the Insight Shop. You'll also occasionally encounter merchants in the Chalice Dungeons who will sell a smaller selection of basic items, as well as certain Holy Chalices depending upon the areas in which you meet them. Shop inventories will expand to include new merchandise when you acquire badges or other items, defeat certain enemies, or when the time of day advances, so be sure to check back frequently and browse the latest offerings when you obtain a new badge or clear a major story event.

Bath Messengers

The Bath Messengers are the most straightforward of the game's merchants; they can be found in the lower bath in the Hunter's Dream from the beginning of the game, and offer you the options to buy and sell items. Their inventory will expand every time you obtain certain key items, such as badges or chalices, and will carry over to subsequent game cycles. This means you'll always be able to obtain particular items from them once you've fulfilled the associated requirement. Collecting a new weapon in the Old Hunters areas will also unlock that weapon for purchase in the Bath Messengers shop. Owning a new weapon will also unlock its Uncanny and Lost variant for purchase in any Chalice Dungeon Bath Messengers shop. Purchasing these variants there will in turn make them available back in the regular Hunter's Nightmare shop.

Consumables

Item		Requirement	○	◗	☾	●	NG+
	Blood Vial	None	180	360	540	720	900
	Quicksilver Bullets	None	160	240	320	400	500
	Antidote	Sword Hunter Badge	300	600	1300	2300	2800
	Sedative	Cosmic Eye Watcher Badge	600	1200	2600	4600	5600
	Molotov Cocktail	None	180	380	860	1600	2000
	Rope Molotov Cocktail	Powder Keg Hunter Badge	190	400	900	1700	2100
	Delayed Molotov	Firing Hammer Badge	270	570	1300	2400	3000
	Delayed Rope Molotov	Firing Hammer Badge	290	600	1400	2600	3200
	Oil Urn	Powder Keg Hunter Badge	360	680	1360	2400	3000
	Pungent Blood Cocktail	Saw Hunter's Badge	1000	2000	5000	10000	15000
	Throwing Knife	Saw Hunter's Badge	100	200	450	800	1000

Consumables

Item		Requirement	○	◗	☾	●	NG+
	Poison Knife	Cosmic Eye Watcher Badge	300	600	1300	2300	2800
	Pebble	None	10	10	10	10	10
	Fire Paper	Radiant Sword Hunter Badge	720	1720	4200	8400	12600
	Bolt Paper	Spark Hunter Badge	900	2100	5000	9600	14000
	Bone Marrow Ash	Radiant Sword Hunter Badge	320	740	1800	3600	5600
	Bold Hunter's Mark	Sword Hunter Badge	400	800	1200	1200	1200
	Shining Coins	Radiant Sword Hunter Badge	20	20	20	20	20
	Hand Lantern	Sword Hunter Badge	2000	2000	2000	2000	2000

Key Items

Item		Requirement	Price
	Hunter Chief Emblem	Sword Hunter Badge	10000

Right Hand Weapons

Item	Requirement/Root Chalice	Price
Saw Cleaver	Saw Hunter's Badge Uncanny: Pthumeru Lost: Central Pthumeru	1000
Saw Spear	Saw Hunter's Badge Uncanny: Central Pthumeru Lost: Sinister/Lower Pthumeru	1000
Hunter Axe	Saw Hunter's Badge Uncanny: Hintertomb Lost: Ailing Loran	1100
Beasthunter Saif	Hunter's Nightmare Uncanny/Lost: Purchase in any Chalice Dungeon shop	16000
Threaded Cane	Saw Hunter's Badge Uncanny: Central Pthumeru Lost: Great Isz	1200
Beast Cutter	Hunter's Nightmare Uncanny/Lost: Purchase in any Chalice Dungeon shop	20000
Burial Blade	Old Hunter Badge Uncanny: Lower Loran Lost: Great Pthumeru Ihyll	60000
Blade of Mercy	Crow Hunter Badge Uncanny: Lower Loran Lost: Great Pthumeru Ihyll	40000
Church Pick	Defeat Yahar'gul Hunter [p323] Uncanny/Lost: Purchase in any Chalice Dungeon shop	16000
Kirkhammer	Sword Hunter Badge Uncanny: Lower Pthumeru Lost: Great Isz	3000
Ludwig's Holy Blade	Radiant Sword Hunter Badge Uncanny: Cursed and Defiled Lost: Great Isz	20000
Holy Moonlight Sword	Defeat Ludwig [p652] Uncanny/Lost: Purchase in any Chalice Dungeon shop	80000
Simon's Bowblade	See Simon's quest [p651] Uncanny/Lost: Purchase in any Chalice Dungeon shop	24000
Reiterpallasch	Cainhurst Badge Uncanny: Cursed and Defiled Lost: Great Pthumeru Ihyll	18000
Chikage	Cainhurst Badge Uncanny: Cursed and Defiled Lost: Great Pthumeru Ihyll	50000
Rakuyo	Defeat the Giant Fishman [p192] Uncanny/Lost: Purchase in any Chalice Dungeon shop	50000
Rifle Spear	Powder Keg Hunter Badge Uncanny: Lower Pthumeru Lost: Ailing Loran	4000
Stake Driver	Powder Keg Hunter Badge Uncanny: Lower Hintertomb Lost: Lower Loran	8000
Boom Hammer	Hunter's Nightmare Uncanny/Lost: Purchase in any Chalice Dungeon shop	28000
Whirligig Saw	Hunter's Nightmare Uncanny/Lost: Purchase in any Chalice Dungeon shop	30000
Tonitrus	Spark Hunter Badge Uncanny: Ailing Loran Lost: Lower Loran	26000
Logarius' Wheel	Wheel Hunter Badge Uncanny: Great Pthumeru Ihyll Lost: Great Pthumeru Ihyll	13000
Bloodletter	Kill Brador's physical body [p653] Uncanny/Lost: Purchase in any Chalice Dungeon shop	44000
Amygdalan Arm	Hunter's Nightmare Uncanny/Lost: Purchase in any Chalice Dungeon shop	66000
Beast Claw	Ailing Loran Chalice Dungeon Layer 2 Uncanny: Ailing Loran Lost: Lower Loran	34000
Kos Parasite	Defeat Orphan Kos [p371] Uncanny/Lost: Purchase in any Chalice Dungeon shop	60000

Left Hand Weapons

Item	Requirement	Price
Hunter Pistol	Saw Hunter's Badge	1600
Hunter Blunderbuss	Saw Hunter's Badge	1700
Repeating Pistol	Sword Hunter Badge	3000
Ludwig's Rifle	Radiant Sword Hunter Badge	10000
Piercing Rifle	Firing Hammer Badge	20000
Evelyn	Cainhurst Badge	16000
Cannon	Obtain one elsewhere	18000
Gatling Gun	Kill Djura's Disciple	30000
Church Cannon	Underneath the Surgical Altar	40000
Flamesprayer	Radiant Sword Hunter Badge	8000
Rosmarinus	Cosmic Eye Watcher Badge	60000
Fist of Gratia	Collect in the Cell Block	10000
Hunter's Torch	Obtain one elsewhere	2000
Loch Shield	Raise stairs in Research Hall first in order to reach.	70000

Materials

Item	Requirement	Price
Bloodstone Shard	Radiant Sword Hunter Badge	2000
Twin Bloodstone Shard	Cosmic Eye Watcher Badge	10000
Ritual Blood (1)	Pthumeru Chalice	2500
Ritual Blood (2)	Defiled Chalice	6000
Ritual Blood (3)	Great Pthumeru Ihyll Chalice	12000
Ritual Blood (4)	Yharnam Stone	24000
Ritual Blood (5)	Available in NG+	48000
Tomb Mold (1)	Sinister Hintertomb Chalice	2000
Tomb Mold (2)	Defiled Chalice	5000
Tomb Mold (3)	Great Pthumeru Ihyll Chalice	10000
Tomb Mold (4)	Yharnam Stone	20000
Tomb Mold (5)	Available in NG+	40000

6

Attire

Item		Requirement	Price
	Yharnam Hunter Cap	None	500
	Yharnam Hunter Garb	None	1000
	Yharnam Hunter Gloves	None	500
	Yharnam Hunter Trousers	None	500
	Tomb Prospector Hood	Radiant Sword Hunter Badge	6000
	Tomb Prospector Garb	Radiant Sword Hunter Badge	18000
	Tomb Prospector Gloves	Radiant Sword Hunter Badge	6000
	Tomb Prospector Trousers	Radiant Sword Hunter Badge	6000
	Gold Ardeo	Wheel Hunter Badge	60000
	Cainhurst Helmet	Cainhurst Badge	27000

Attire

Item		Requirement	Price
	Cainhurst Armor	Cainhurst Badge	44000
	Cainhurst Gauntlets	Cainhurst Badge	21000
	Cainhurst Leggings	Cainhurst Badge	21000
	Beak Mask	Crow Hunter Badge	10000
	Crowfeather Garb	Crow Hunter Badge	18000
	Crowfeather Manchettes	Crow Hunter Badge	8000
	Crowfeather Trousers	Crow Hunter Badge	8000
	Gehrman's Hunter Cap	Old Hunter Badge	7000
	Gehrman's Hunter Garb	Old Hunter Badge	17000
	Gehrman's Hunter Trousers	Old Hunter Badge	7000

Insight Shop

The Insight Shop can be found in the upper bath outside the middle door of the base building in the Hunter's Dream, and as its name implies, uses Insight as its currency rather than blood echoes. In order for the merchant messengers to appear, you'll need to have at least one point of Insight. Once they're open they will remain so, even if your insight drops to zero. Their inventory includes many items not sold by the Bath Messengers and will expand as you obtain badges, explore Chalice Dungeons and defeat certain enemies.

Consumables

Item		Requirement	Price
	Beast Blood Pellet	Cosmic Eye Watcher Badge	2
	Blue Elixir	Cosmic Eye Watcher Badge	2
	Lead Elixir	Blood Moon	2
	Pungent Blood Cocktail	None	1
	Numbing Mist	Cainhurst Badge	2
	Fire Paper	Radiant Sword Hunter Badge	1
	Bolt Paper	Spark Hunter Badge	1
	Shaman Bone Blade	Complete Lower Pthumerian Labyrinth	1
	Sedatives	Cosmic Eye Watcher Badge	1
	Small Resonant Bell	Beckoning Bell	1
	Sinister Resonant Bell	Beckoning Bell	1

Materials

Item		Requirement	Price
	Blood Stone Shard	Nighttime	1
	Twin Blood Stone Shards	Blood Moon	2
	Blood Stone Chunk	Defeat The One Reborn	30
	Coldblood Flowerbud	Obtain the Loran Chalice	2
	Bloodshot Eyeball	Defeat the Witch of Hemwick	2
	Living String	Defeat the Brain of Mensis	10
	Pearl Slug	Obtain the Isz Chalice	3
	Red Jelly	Clear Pthumeru Ihyll Dungeon	5
	Short Ritual Root Chalice	Complete the Pthumerian Labyrinth	10
	Coldblood Flower Bulb	Available in NG+	4
	Blooming Coldblood Flower	Available in NG+	8
	Sage's Wrist	Available in NG+	1
	Sage's Hair	Available in NG+	2
	Inflicted Organ	Available in NG+	2
	Yellow Backbone	Available in NG+	3
	Bastard of Loran	Available in NG+	7

Attire

Item	Requirement	Price
Henryk's Hunter Cap	Defeat Henryk	1
Henryk's Hunter Garb	Defeat Henryk	3
Henryk's Hunter Gloves	Defeat Henryk	1
Henryk's Hunter Trousers	Defeat Henryk	1
Maria Hunter Cap	Defeat Lady Maria of the Astral Clocktower	3
Maria Hunter Garb	Defeat Lady Maria of the Astral Clocktower	5
Maria Hunter Gloves	Defeat Lady Maria of the Astral Clocktower	3
Maria Hunter Trousers	Defeat Lady Maria of the Astral Clocktower	3
Gascoigne's Cap	Defeat Gascoigne	1
Gascoigne's Garb	Defeat Gascoigne	3
Gascoigne's Gloves	Defeat Gascoigne	1
Gascoigne's Trousers	Defeat Gascoigne	1

Attire

Item	Requirement	Price
Gray Wolf Cap	Defeat or befriend Djura	1
Ashen Hunter Garb	Defeat or befriend Djura	3
Ashen Hunter Gloves	Defeat or befriend Djura	1
Ashen Hunter Trousers	Defeat or befriend Djura	1
Bone Ash Mask	Defeat the Keeper of the Old Lords	2
Bone Ash Armor	Defeat the Keeper of the Old Lords	4
Bone Ash Gauntlets	Defeat the Keeper of the Old Lords	2
Bone Ash Leggings	Defeat the Keeper of the Old Lords	2
Madman Hood	Defeat the Forgotten Madman & Madman's Escort	1
Madman Garb	Defeat the Forgotten Madman & Madman's Escort	3
Madman Manchettes	Defeat the Forgotten Madman & Madman's Escort	1
Madman Leggings	Defeat the Forgotten Madman & Madman's Escort	1

Dungeon Shop (Common)

As you explore Chalice Dungeons, you'll occasionally encounter a messenger bath similar to the ones found in the Hunter's Dream. You can purchase basic consumable items from these shops and, depending upon the dungeons in which you encounter them, they'll also sell certain Holy Chalices as well. Acquiring any weapon that's new in The Old Hunters will also unlock its Uncanny and Lost variant in any Chalice Dungeon Bath Messengers shop. Purchasing these variants will then make them available back in the regular Hunter's Nightmare shop.

Chalices

Item	Requirement	Price
Sinister Lower Pthumeru Root Chalice	Lower Pthumerian Labyrinth [L1]	9000
Sinister Hintertomb Root Chalice	Lower Hintertombs [L3]	10000
Sinister Pthumeru Ihyll Root Chalice	Great Pthumeu Ihyll [L3]	16000
Sinister Lower Loran Root Chalice	Lower Loran [L3]	18000
Sinister Isz Root Chalice	Isz Gravestone [L3]	20000

Consumables

Name	Requirement	🌑	🌙	⚪	NG+
Blood Vial	None	690	1700	3500	5200
Quicksilver Bullets	None	600	1500	3000	4500
Molotov Cocktail	None	550	1200	2300	2900
Rope Molotov Cocktail	None	580	1300	2400	3000
Oil Urn	None	960	2000	3500	4400
Throwing Knife	None	290	700	1200	1500
Poison Knife	None	870	1900	3300	4000
Antidote	None	870	1900	3300	4000
Bold Hunter's Mark	None	1200	1700	1700	1700
Pebble	None	2	2	2	2
Shining Coins	None	40	40	40	40

Right Hand Weapons

Item		Requirement	Price
	Uncanny/Lost Beasthunter Saif		16000
	Uncanny/Lost Beast Cutter		20000
	Uncanny/Lost Church Pick		16000
	Uncanny/Lost Holy Moonlight Sword	Acquire the standard version of this weapon	80000
	Uncanny/Lost Simon's Bowblade		24000
	Uncanny/Lost Rakuyo		50000

Right Hand Weapons

Item		Requirement	Price
	Uncanny/Lost Boom Hammer		28000
	Uncanny/Lost Whirligig Saw		30000
	Uncanny/Lost Bloodletter	Acquire the standard version of this weapon	44000
	Uncanny/Lost Amygdalan Arm		66000
	Uncanny/Lost Kos Parasite		60000

Dungeon Shop (Rare)

After confronting Patches face-to-face in the Lecture Building and completing his quest, he'll appear in the Chalice Dungeons on extremely rare occasion to sell you items at drastically inflated prices. You'll find him hanging upside-down from the ceiling, so watch carefully above you as you explore to avoid missing him.

Right Hand Weapons

Item		Requirement	Price
	Uncanny/Lost Beasthunter Saif		16000
	Uncanny/Lost Beast Cutter		20000
	Uncanny/Lost Church Pick		16000
	Uncanny/Lost Holy Moonlight Sword		80000
	Uncanny/Lost Simon's Bowblade		24000
	Uncanny/Lost Rakuyo	Acquire the standard version of this weapon	50000
	Uncanny/Lost Boom Hammer		28000
	Uncanny/Lost Whirligig Saw		30000
	Uncanny/Lost Bloodletter		44000
	Uncanny/Lost Amygdalan Arm		66000
	Uncanny/Lost Kos Parasite		60000

Consumables

Item		◗	☾	●	NG+
	Blood Vial	860	2100	4300	6400
	Quicksilver Bullets	750	1800	3700	5600
	Molotov Cocktail	680	1500	2800	3600
	Rope Molotov Cocktail	720	1600	3000	3700
	Oil Urn	1200	2400	4300	5400
	Throwing Knife	360	800	1400	1800
	Poison Knife	1080	2300	4100	5000
	Antidote	1080	2300	4100	5000
	Sedative	1300	2800	5000	6100
	Bold Hunter's Mark	1400	2100	2100	2100
	Pebble	20	20	20	20
	Shining Coins	100	100	100	100
	Fire paper	3000	7500	15000	23000
	Bolt Paper	3800	9000	17000	25000
	Bone Marrow Ash	1300	3200	6500	10000
	Pungent Blood Cocktail	3600	9000	18000	27000

Insight

Insight is inhuman knowledge and represents your awareness of the nightmare's effects. In addition to its use as a currency at the insight shop and during multiplayer, acquiring more insight provides certain benefits but also poses a few risks. High levels of Insight will decrease your Beasthood stat, and while that does mean that you will fill the Beast Gauge faster, you won't be able to reach the later damage modifiers that come with a bigger gauge. Your Frenzy resistance is also heavily dependent on how much Insight you have, and the more you have the more susceptible you will be to getting Frenzied. Some enemies and aspects of the environment will also change at particular insight thresholds, such as the Church Servants in the Cathedral Ward gaining powered-up weapons and new attacks; with extremely high insight you'll also become able to see things during the day which would otherwise only be visible when the Blood Moon is out.

Encountering or defeating bosses, meeting various characters and witnessingcertain events will often cause you to gain a few points of insight; these conditions can only be fulfilled once per playthrough, with the exception that Chalice Dungeon bosses can be defeated repeatedly for insight bonuses if you recreate the dungeons in which they appear. Simply encountering bosses in recreated dungeons won't yield repeated insight rewards, though, and you won't gain insight from seeing dungeon bosses you've already met in the main game. Moving to a new cycle will reset all encounters and allow you to obtain insight from them again, and successful on-line interactions such as invasions or cooperative play will generally reward you with a point of insight as well. Below, you'll find tables summarizing the points at which insight is rewarded, the amounts you'll receive in each case, and the minimum amount required for various changes to take place.

The Oedon Chapel doesn't look at all suspicious with little Insight...

...but with 40 or more Insight the Truth is revealed.

Chalice Dungeon Insight Events

Trigger Condition	Insight
Defeat the Brainsucker (boss version)	2
Defeat the Maneater Boar (Eyeballs) (boss version)	2
First encounter with the Keeper of the Old Lords	1
Defeat the Keeper of the Old Lords	2
Defeat the Loran Silverbeast (boss version)	2
Defeat the Undead Giant (boss version)	2
Defeat the Merciless Watcher (boss version)	2
Defeat the Beast-possessed Soul (boss version)	2
First encounter with Blood-starved Beast	1
Defeat the Blood-starved Beast	2
First encounter with Pthumerian Descendant or Elder	1
Defeat the Pthumerian Descendant or Elder	2
First encounter with Watchdog of the Old Lords	1
Defeat the Watchdog of the Old Lords	2
Defeat the Abhorrent Beast (boss version)	2
First encounter with Rom, the Vacuous Spider	2
Defeat Rom, the Vacuous Spider	2
First encounter with Ebrietas, Daughter of the Cosmos	3
Defeat Ebrietas, Daughter of the Cosmos	3
First encounter with Yharnam, Pthumerian Bride	1
Defeat the Yharnam, Pthumerian Bride	3
First encounter with Darkbeast Paarl	1
Defeat Darkbeast Paarl	3
First encounter with Bloodletting Beast (either variant)	1
Defeat the Bloodletting Beast (either variant)	3
First encounter with Amygdala	3
Defeat Amygdala	3

6

Main Game Insight Events

NPC/Location	Trigger Condition	Insight Awarded
Central Yharnam	First encounter with the Cleric Beast	1
Central Yharnam	Defeat the Cleric Beast	3
Central Yharnam	First encounter with Father Gascoigne	1
Central Yharnam	First encounter with Father Gascoigne (Beast)	1
Central Yharnam	Defeat Father Gascoigne	2
Impostor Iosefka	Each time she rewards you with an item before becoming her accomplice	1
Impostor Iosefka	Each time she rewards you with an item after you become her accomplice	2
Old Yharnam	First encounter with the Blood-starved Beast	1
Old Yharnam	Defeat the Blood-starved Beast	2
Abandoned Old Workshop	Enter the Old Abandoned Workshop for the first time	2
Cathedral Ward	First encounter with Vicar Amelia	1
Cathedral Ward	Defeat Vicar Amelia	3
Hemwick Charnel Lane	First encounter with the Witch of Hemwick	1
Hemwick Charnel Lane	Defeat the Witch of Hemwick	2
Yahar'gul (Evening)	Arrive in Yahar'gul after being taken by a Kidnapper in the Cathedral Ward	1
Yahar'gul (Evening)	First encounter with Darkbeast Paarl	1
Yahar'gul (Evening)	Defeat Darkbeast Paarl	3
Central Yharnam	Enter Iosefka's Clinic through the rear entrance via the Forbidden Woods	1
Forbidden Woods	Defeat the Shadows of Yharnam	2
Cathedral Ward	Let the False God grab you while in possession of the Tonsil Stone to enter the Lecture Building	2
Nightmare Frontier	Arrive in the Nightmare Frontier via the Lecture Building 1F	2
Nightmare Frontier	First encounter with Amygdala	3
Nightmare Frontier	Defeat Amygdala	3
Forsaken Cainhurst Castle	Ride the carriage from Hemwick to Cainhurst Castle	2
Forsaken Cainhurst Castle	First encounter with Martyr Logarius	1
Forsaken Cainhurst Castle	Defeat Martyr Logarius	3
Forsaken Cainhurst Castle	Enter the Queen's Chambers	2
Queen Annalise	Attack her 50 times, reload the area and approach her remains	3
Provost Willem	Speak to him twice and trigger him to point at the lake	2
Byrgenwerth	First encounter with Rom, the Vacuous Spider	2
Byrgenwerth	Defeat Rom, the Vacuous Spider	2
Upper Cathedral Ward	Defeat the Celestial Emissary	2
Upper Cathedral Ward	First encounter with Ebrietas, Daughter of the Cosmos	3
Upper Cathedral Ward	Defeat Ebrietas, Daughter of the Cosmos	3
Yahar'gul (Blood Moon)	First encounter with The One Reborn	1
Yahar'gul (Blood Moon)	Defeat The One Reborn	3
Lecture Building	Enter the locked lab via the second floor and meet Patches the Spider face-to-face	2
Nightmare of Mensis	Enter the Nightmare of Mensis via the Lecture Building 2F	3
Nightmare of Mensis	First encounter with Micolash, Host of the Nightmare	1
Nightmare of Mensis	Defeat Micolash, Host of the Nightmare	2
Oedon Chapel	Approach Arianna's baby after she moves to the room under the chapel	3
Nightmare of Mensis	First encounter with Mergo's Wet Nurse	3
Nightmare of Mensis	Defeat Mergo's Wet Nurse	3
Hunter's Dream	First encounter with Gehrman, the First Hunter	1
Hunter's Dream	Defeat Gehrman, the First Hunter	3
Hunter's Dream	First encounter with the Moon Presence	5
Hunter's Dream	Defeat the Moon Presence	5
Hunter's Nightmare	Be thrown by Amygdala and arrive in the Hunter's Nightmare	2
Research Hall	Enter the Research Hall for the first time	2
Fishing Hamlet	Arrive at the Fishing Hamlet for the first time	4
Hunter's Nightmare	Ludwig, the Holy Blade defeated	3
Hunter's Nightmare	Laurence, the First Vicar defeated	3
Research Hall	Living Failures defeated	2
Research Hall	Lady Maria of the Astral Clocktower defeated	3
Fishing Hamlet	Orphan of Kos defeated	5
Hunter's Nightmare	First encounter with Ludwig, the Accursed	1
Hunter's Nightmare	First encounter with Laurence, the First Vicar	1
Research Hall	First encounter with Living Failures	2
Research Hall	First encounter with Lady Maria of the Astral Clocktower	1
Fishing Hamlet	First encounter with Orphan of Kos	5
Research Hall	Obtain the Milkweed Rune from Adeline	2

Required Insight	Area	Change
1	Hunter's Dream	Doll activates and allows you to channel blood echoes
10	Hunter's Dream	Insight shop opens
15	Cathedral Ward	Church Servants gain weapon auras and new attacks
15	Hemwick Charnel Lane	Mad Ones appear in Hemwick at night
40	Cathedral Ward	False God is visible even when the Blood Moon isn't out
40	Yahar'gul, Unseen Village	Amygdala is visible even when the Blood Moon isn't out
40	Dream Refuge	Hunter's Dream music changes even when the Blood Moon isn't out
60	–	Auditory hallucinations–a baby's crying voice can be heard in all areas except the Hunter's Dream and Chalice Dungeons

Special Enemies

Wandering Nightmare

A peculiar enemy that appears in many areas, but sometimes only under specific conditions. These creatures do not attack at all, but will instead flee the moment they spot you, and disappear if you fail to finish them quickly enough. Wandering Nightmares (outside Chalice Dungeons) are guaranteed to drop Bloodstones the first time you defeat them, but killing them repeatedly will yield no further loot. While harmless on their own, they are often positioned to lead you into ambushes or other dangerous situations if you pursue them blindly, so be sure to examine your surroundings carefully before approaching them.

In earlier areas, a single Molotov will kill them, and is often the best way to hit one if it runs out of reach. Throwing Knives are also well-suited to this task, but physical attacks will inflict little damage and repeated blows are necessary to get the job done. If you see a Wandering Nightmare before it sees you, examine the surrounding area carefully and check for possible ambushes in the direction you intend to chase it. If you're spotted before you have a chance to react, don't panic or run after it carelessly – these enemies will reappear the next time you enter the area, so you can always come back for it later if it gets away.

Basic Information

Area			Item Drops											
Cathedral Ward	47	18	Blood Stone Shard ×3, Twin Bloodstone Shards	660	561	660	330	160	160	160	10	90	—	—
Old Yharnam	46	11	Bloodstone Shard ×3	645	548	645	323	160	160	160	10	90		
Healing Church Workshop	49	14	Twin Bloodstone Shards ×2	660	561	660	330	160	160	160	10	90		
Hemwick Charnel Lane	58	33	Twin Bloodstone Shards ×2	675	574	675	338	160	160	160	10	90		
Yahar'gul (Evening)	68	46	Twin Bloodstone Shards ×3	720	612	720	360	160	160	160	10	90		
Forbidden Woods	69	47	Twin Bloodstone Shards ×3	735	625	735	368	160	160	160	10	90		
Forsaken Cainhurst Castle	153	70	Bloodstone Chunk ×2	795	676	795	398	160	160	160	10	90		
Nightmare Frontier	69	54	Bloodstone Shard ×2	750	638	750	375	160	160	160	10	90		
Nightmare Frontier	78	56	Bloodstone Shard ×2	765	650	765	383	160	160	160	10	90		
Yahar'gul (Blood Moon)	155	69	Bloodstone Chunk ×2, Twin Bloodstone Shards ×3	810	689	810	405	160	160	160	10	90		
Upper Cathedral Ward	49	14	Bloodstone Chunk ×2	660	561	660	330	160	160	160	10	90		
Nightmare of Mensis	206	85	Bloodstone Chunk ×3	855	727	855	428	160	160	160	10	90		
Chalice Dungeon Base Level	47	14	Random gem based on area ×1	660	561	660	330	160	160	160	10	90		
Hunter's Nightmare	186	27	Bloodstone Chunk ×2 [100%]	825	701	825	412	220	220	220	10	90		
Research Hall	206	87	Bloodstone Chunk ×2 [100%]	855	726	855	427	228	228	228	10	90		
Fishing Hamlet	214	40	Bloodstone Chunk ×3 [100%]	900	765	900	450	240	240	240	10	90		

Preset Chalice Dungeons: Pthumerian Labyrinth, Hintertomb, Lower Hintertomb, Lower Pthumerian Labyrinth, Cursed Pthumerian Defilement, Ailing Loran, Isz Gravestone, Pthumeru Ihyll

Large Wandering Nightmare

Large Wandering Nightmares behave in much the same way as the smaller version: they will flee as soon as they spot you and disappear if not killed soon afterward. However, if you do manage to corner them, they will fight back with slap attacks that will knock you down if they connect, potentially allowing them to escape if you aren't able to finish them off as soon as you recover. Like their smaller kin, they are guaranteed to drop Bloodstones the first time you defeat them, but will drop nothing if killed repeatedly.

Molotovs are still the best way to eliminate them before they see you, or afterward, if you aren't able to catch up with them in time. Throwing Knives offer a more accurate means of hitting them if they do escape; otherwise you'll have to chase them into a wall or an obstacle in order to close the distance. Their slap attacks aren't too dangerous but can immobilize you long enough for them to escape, so plan your approach carefully and try to chase them into an enclosed area, where they can't get too far away from you if they knock you down.

Basic Information			Item Drops												
Nightmare Frontier	97	648	Twin Bloodstone Shards ×3	750	638	750	375	200	200	200	70	90	—		
Nightmare Frontier	110	676	Bloodstone Chunk ×2, Twin Bloodstone Shards ×3	765	650	765	383	200	200	200	70	90			
Chalice Dungeon Base Level	67	107	Random gem based on area ×1	660	561	660	330	200	200	200	70	90			

Preset Chalice Dungeons: Lower Loran

Hole Digger

medium distance, it will projectile vomit multiple times and at close range, it will spew an arc onto the floor ahead of it. The latter attack will leave lingering pools of acidic vomit which can make it hard to approach, especially in the tight tunnels they usually inhabit. One of the most unique things about the Hole Digger is its grotesque ability to reposition its head. It has a fast grab attack used directly ahead at close range; when this connects, the Hole Digger will swallow you, inflicting moderate amounts of Frenzy buildup and damage, before spitting you out.

Strategy

Hole Diggers are a solitary sort, so you usually won't have too much trouble handling them. As previously stated, the Hole Digger is slow, and though its feeler attacks travel far, you can still stand well outside of its range to bombard it with projectile attacks. Molotovs work exceptionally well for handling these enemies; likewise, Fire Paper or Bolt Paper will boost your damage exponentially. Even at close range, you can attack the Hole Digger with relative safety by simply positioning yourself to either of its sides. Never approach the Hole Digger from its current front-side, as this is where all of its attacks are initiated. It turns slowly, so much so that you can even reposition yourself to the opposite side of it before it can react. Standing at its current backside isn't a bad idea either; though it can reposition its head to face you, this process leaves it quite vulnerable, opening it to all manners of attack.

The Hole Digger is a rare specimen indeed, encountered only within the chalice dungeons – and even then its infrequent appearances make it hard to confirm its existence. It's quite slow, and would appear to have low range at first glance, but don't be fooled; its feelers can stretch surprisingly far and they hit hard. Despite their generally slow attack speeds, some of their close and medium range attacks are quick, which may catch you off guard – especially its leap. From a

Basic Information			Item Drops												
Chalice Dungeon Depth 1	211	98		145	103	62	103	78	78	78	120	90	—		
Chalice Dungeon Depth 2	307	98		151	108	65	108	78	78	78	120	90			
Chalice Dungeon Depth 3	812	98	Heavy gem based on dungeon ×1 [8%], Blood Vial ×3 [8%], Blood Vial ×2 [20%], Lead Elixir ×1 [2%]	188	134	80	134	78	78	78	120	90			
Chalice Dungeon Depth 4	1369	98		204	146	87	146	78	78	78	120	90			
Chalice Dungeon Depth 5	1465	98		207	148	89	148	78	78	78	120	90			
Depth 5 (Great Pthumeru Ihyll)	1617	98		210	150	90	150	78	78	78	120	90			

Gestures

Gestures are activated by pressing on the left side of the touch-pad and selecting the one you want from the list, or by holding ⊗ and performing a gesture with the controller. You'll have a decent selection from the start of the game, and can acquire more from various places and characters as you progress. If you want to get the full set, check out the table here for all of their locations and requirements.

Gesture Name	Acquired By
Point Forward	Obtained by default at the start of the game.
Hunter's Salutation	Obtained by default at the start of the game.
Conviction	Obtained by default at the start of the game.
Joy	Obtained by default at the start of the game.
Sit Down	Obtained by default at the start of the game.
Wave	Obtained by default at the start of the game.
Hunter's Rally	Obtained by default at the start of the game.
Shake off Cape	Speak with Eileen the Crow (p636) for the first time (can be done in either Central Yharnam or Cathedral Ward).
Pray	Speak with Alfred, the Vileblood Hunter (p644) for the first time and agree to cooperate with him.
Church Bow (Male)	Obtain the Unopened Summons from the Iosefka's Clinic and give it to Alfred, the Vileblood Hunter at his new location on the Forbidden Woods Route in the Cathedral Ward.
Curtsy	Speak with Arianna, Woman of the Night (p639) in the Foggy Alley of Cathedral Ward and tell her about Oedon Chapel to get her to relocate there. Speak with her again in the chapel to receive the gesture.
Church Bow (Female)	Speak with Adella, Nun of the Healing Church (p641) in the Storeroom area of Yahar'gul, Unseen Village (Evening) while wearing one of the church related garbs and tell her about the Oedon Chapel. Speak with her again after she moves there to get the gesture.
Shh!	Speak with Eileen the Crow (p636) outside the Oedon Chapel in the Cathedral ward and listen to her warning about Henryk.
Approval	Speak with Eileen the Crow (p636) again after defeating Henryk.
Wait	During the Blood Moon, speak with Eileen the Crow (p636) at the top of the Grand Cathedral Stairs before entering to face the Hunter inside.
Triumph	Speak with the Chapel Samaritan (p637) in the Cathedral Ward's Oedon Chapel after having sent someone there.
Roar	Speak with Alfred, Hunter of Vilebloods (p644) after he has killed Vileblood Queen Annalise in Forsaken Cainhurst Castle.
Beg for Life	After reaching Lecture Building 2F, go down the ladder to Patches' Lab and speak to Patches the Spider.
Brush off Dust	Defeat Darkbeast Paarl in Yahar'gul, Unseen Village (Evening) so that you can enter Old Yharnam from the back, and then climb up Djura's (p648) tower and talk to him.
Respect	Kneel before Vileblood Queen Annalise (p647) in Forsaken Cainhurst Castle and join the Vilebloods.
Deep Respect	After joining the Vilebloods, offer one or more Blood Dregs to Vileblood Queen Annalise and she'll give you this gesture.
Make Contact	Step out onto the Orphanage Balcony in the Upper Cathedral Ward and inspect the charred body there.

League Oath (Confederate) OH

Before you can obtain this Gesture you must go to the Forbidden Woods and enter the small windmill near the lamp so that you can speak with Valtr and become a member of the League. After joining, equip the Impurity Oath Caryll Rune, and then you will need to either complete a successful co-op session with another player, or summon one of the League NPCs and defeat a boss with them to obtain a Vermin. Use the Vermin, and then return to Valtr in the Woods and he will reward you with the League Staff and this Gesture. To find out more about Valtr and the League, please refer to p650.

League Oath (Master) OH

There is no way to obtain this Gesture independent of the Confederate version, so you will have to acquire that one first before you can get this version. After using five Vermin, speak with Valtr again and he will recognize you as the worthy successor that he has been searching for and you will be recognized as the Master of the League. Once that has taken place, the Confederate version of the Gesture will automatically change to this one that has a slightly different animation. For full details on Valtr refer to p650.

Trophy Guide

In this section we'll show you how to unlock every Trophy that Bloodborne has to offer. Some you will get naturally as you try to uncover the source of the nightmare, but due to the nature of the endings, at least three playthroughs will be required to get them all. There are many different paths through the game, as you can see in the Progression Guide starting on p201 (which you can refer to if you need help working out what order to do things in). The essential information about how to reach each area is also included here, to help make this a one-stop guide to collecting all Trophies.

Progression Trophies

This group of Trophies consists of the ones that you'll get for killing all of the non-optional bosses – the ones blocking your path to completing the game.

Father Gascoigne

Rank	🏆 Bronze
Description	Defeat the beast that once was Father Gascoigne.

Area [p44] | Strategy [p328]

To make it out of Central Yharnam and continue your quest to seek the Paleblood you'll need to defeat Father Gascoigne. He can be found in the Tomb of Oedon area of Central Yharnam, which you can reach by going along the Canals and across the Lower Bridge; defeat him to unlock this Trophy.

Vicar Amelia

Rank	🏆 Bronze
Description	Defeat the beast that once was Vicar Amelia.

Area [p55] | Strategy [p336]

The prayer that Vicar Amelia is offering within the Grand Cathedral will not save her from the hunt this night. Before you can vanquish the beast and unlock this Trophy, you must first open the way to the Grand Cathedral. The quickest way to reach Amelia is to kill the Cleric Beast in Central Yharnam to get the Sword Hunter Badge, which will allow you to purchase the Hunter Chief Emblem from the Bath Messenger in the Hunter's Dream. With this item in hand you can approach the Plaza Gate and open it to reach the back half of the Cathedral Ward. Alternatively, go to the Lower Chapel in the Cathedral Ward to access Old Yharnam, and after completing that area, enter the now-open door in the Oedon Chapel and go through the Healing Church Workshop. At the end of that area you can drop down to the back half of the Cathedral Ward and reach the stairs that will take you the Grand Cathedral.

Shadows of Yharnam

Rank	🏆 Bronze
Description	Defeat the Shadows of Yharnam.

Area [p101] | Strategy [p338]

After defeating Vicar Amelia, you can inspect the altar at the back of the Grand Cathedral to get the password that will let you access the Forbidden Woods. Battle your way through that area and you'll find the mysterious Shadows of Yharnam defending the path to Byrgenwerth with their lives; put an end to them to unlock this Trophy.

Rom, the Vacuous Spider

Rank	🏆 Bronze
Description	Defeat Great One: Rom, the Vacuous Spider.

Area [p127] | Strategy [p344]

To acquire this Trophy you'll need to face and defeat Rom, the Vacuous Spider, one of the Great Ones. To reach him, enter the Byrgenwerth College Building, and after making your way out onto the Lunarium, dive into his hiding place within the Moonside Lake.

The One Reborn

Rank	🏆 Bronze
Description	Defeat the One Reborn.

Area [p137] | Strategy [p346]

The One Reborn can be found near the End of The Road in Yahar'gul, Unseen Village (Blood Moon). To reach that area you'll need to go through the suspicious door at the end of the Main Hallway of Lecture Building 2F. This Trophy will unlock as soon as you've defeated him.

Micolash, Host of the Nightmare

Rank	🏆 Bronze
Description	Defeat Micolash, Host of the Nightmare.

Area [p154] | Strategy [p352]

Shortly after crossing the Vertical Lift Bridge in the Nightmare of Mensis, you'll encounter Micolash, Host of the Nightmare; killing him will not only end his dream, but also unlock this Trophy.

Mergo's Wet Nurse

Rank	🏆 Bronze
Description	Defeat Great One: Mergo's Wet Nurse.

Area [p159] | Strategy [p354]

Defeating Mergo's Wet Nurse will put an end to the child's suffering and unlock this Trophy. To reach it you'll need to fight your way up to Mergo's Loft: Rooftops, in the Nightmare of Mensis, and then take the elevator up at the end of the path.

Ludwig, the Holy Blade OH

Rank	🏆 Bronze
Description	Defeat the beast that was once Ludwig, the Holy Blade.

Area [p172] | Strategy [p360]

Ludwig can be a very difficult fight, so it's recommended that you go to the Forbidden Woods and speak with Valtr to join the League and get the Impurity Caryll Rune. With that rune equipped you'll be able to summon Valtr and Younger Twin Madaras to aid you in the boss fight, making it much easier. They will provide a much stronger assistance against Ludwig than Old Hunter Henriett, who can be summoned behind the Nightmare Church. After defeating him, either cleave his remaining head or wear Church Garb and speak to it (answering yes to his question) to receive the Holy Moonlight Sword, which you'll need for the Old Hunter's Essence Trophy.

Living Failures OH

Rank	🏆 Bronze
Description	Defeat the failed attempts to become Great Ones.

Area [p186] | Strategy [p366]

To reach the Living Failures you'll need to make your way to the very top of the Research Hall and activate the staircase mechanism to move the stairs. Only then will you be able to access the door to this boss. If you have killed Yamamura in his cell – thus freeing him from captivity – you will be able to summon him outside the entrance to the boss area, and he can assist you greatly in this battle.

Lady Maria of the Astral Clocktower OH

Rank	🏆 Bronze
Description	Defeat Lady Maria of the Astral Clocktower.

Area [p187] | Strategy [p368]

You'll be able to face Lady Maria straight after beating the Living Failures, and she is a powerful and relentless foe. Make sure to bring a left-handed firearm that is good for interrupts, as they'll offer one of the best ways of damaging her. If you have more than one 'Clawmark' Caryll Rune, it's worth stacking them on your character at the Memory Altar in the Hunter's Dream to increase your Visceral Attack damage after an Interrupt.

Orphan of Kos OH

Rank	🏆 Silver
Description	Defeat Great One: Orphan of Kos.

Area [p199] | Strategy [p371]

Be prepared, plan ahead, and prepare to die... This will be one of the hardest Trophies to earn across both the main game and the Old Hunters. Be patient and learn Kos's patterns. Eventually you will know when to evade, and when to interrupt – bring a very powerful weapon to take full advantage of each opening. 'Orphan of Kos' is a Trophy hard won; only the best hunters will manage it.

Laurence, the First Vicar OH

Rank	🏆 Bronze
Description	Defeat the beast that was once Laurence, the First Vicar.

Area [p167] | Strategy [p363]

Before you can face Laurence in battle you must first find his skull, which is well hidden on a secret altar beneath the surgery altar in the Recovery Room. To access the hidden altar you will need to step onto the surgery altar so that it starts to go up, and then quickly run off it so that you land back in the room. Once the elevator comes to a stop the hidden altar will be revealed and you'll be able to recover Laurence's Skull. With the skull in hand you'll be able to initiate the battle with Laurence by returning it to him in the Nightmare Grand Cathedral (which of course is in the Hunter's Nightmare). The mighty Valtr can once again aid you in this battle if you have joined the League and have the Impurity rune equipped – you'll find his summon sign just inside the Cathedral.

End the suffering of the Living Failures and you will be rewarded with this Trophy.

Win your duel with Lady Maria and the Trophy will be yours.

This Trophy will be one of the hardest you will earn in Bloodborne. Are you ready?

Exploration Trophies

To unlock these Trophies you'll need to stray from the safety of the main path and explore all of the optional side areas within the game to find the hidden bosses within them. While you can attempt them in any order you wish, a recommended route through them is provided in the Hunting Grounds Chapter.

Cleric Beast

Rank	🏆 Bronze
Description	Defeat Cleric Beast.

Area [p41] | Strategy [p326]

The Cleric Beast can be found at the end of the Great Bridge in Central Yharna, and is the first boss that you're likely to encounter. While it is technically optional, defeating it will open up some useful features, as well as earn you this Trophy.

Blood-starved Beast

Rank	🏆 Bronze
Description	Defeat Blood-starved Beast.

Area [p64] | Strategy [p330]

To defeat the Blood-starved beast you'll need to take a trip down to Old Yharnam, which you can do almost immediately after entering the Cathedral Ward. Not only will killing it unlock this Trophy, but you'll also get the Chalice of Pthumeru Trophy for acquiring the Holy Chalice that it drops.

If you want to reach the path that leads to Hemwick Charnel Lane where the witch resides, you'll need to first make it to the back of the Cathedral Ward. The quickest way is to defeat the Cleric Beast to get the Sword Hunter Badge, which unlocks the Hunter Chief Emblem in the Bath Messenger, and use that to get past the Plaza Gate in the Cathedral Ward. Alternatively, you can complete Old Yharnam to open up the Healing Church Workshop, and then go through that area to reach the ledge at the end; drop down from the ledge to land in the back half of the Cathedral Ward. Once you reach Hemwick, go through the area and kill the Witch at the end to unlock the Trophy.

The Witch of Hemwick

Rank	🏆 Bronze
Description	Defeat The Witch of Hemwick.

Area [p79] | Strategy [p332]

If you want to reach the path that leads to Hemwick Charnel Lane where the witch resides, you'll need to first make it to the back of the Cathedral Ward. The quickest way is to defeat the Cleric Beast to get the Sword Hunter Badge, which unlocks the Hunter Chief Emblem in the Bath Messenger, and use that to get past the Plaza Gate in the Cathedral Ward. Alternatively, you can complete Old Yharnam to open up the Healing Church Workshop, and then go through that area to reach the ledge at the end; drop down from the ledge to land in the back half of the Cathedral Ward. Once you reach Hemwick, go through the area and kill the Witch at the end to unlock the Trophy.

Cleric Beast will likely be the first Trophy you will unlock.

Darkbeast Paarl

Rank	🏆 Bronze
Description	Defeat Darkbeast Paarl.

Area [p83] | Strategy [p334]

Before you can kill Darkbeast Paarl and unlock this Trophy you'll need to find your way to him, and that means getting into Yahar'gul, Unseen Village. If you want to face this beast as early as possible, you'll need to first defeat the Blood-starved Beast at the end of Old Yharnam so that the Kidnappers begin to appear in various areas (see p80 for their exact locations). Let yourself get killed by one of these Kidnappers and they'll take you to Yahar'gul, Unseen Village (Evening), and then work your way through the area to face Paarl. Alternatively, you can wait until you reach the area later in the game once the Blood Moon is out; the area will be more difficult at that time, but the fight with Paarl will be much easier due to your increased level.

Amygdala

Rank	🏆 Bronze
Description	Defeat Great One: Amygdala.

Area [p125] | Strategy [p340]

Amygdala can be found at the end of the Nightmare Frontier, an area you'll need to go through the Lecture Building to reach. You can access the 1st floor of the Lecture Building by getting the Tonsil Stone and letting the False God's attack hit you in the room at the end of the Cliffs in the Cathedral Ward. To reach the 2nd floor, you can just progress through the game normally and examine the mummy at the end of Yahar'gul, Unseen Village (Blood Moon). Defeating this boss will also unlock the Chalice of Ailing Loran Trophy for acquiring the Holy Chalice that it drops.

Slay 'Darkbeast Paarl' during either visits to Yahar'gul, Unseen Village to score this Trophy.

Martyr Logarius

Rank	Bronze
Description	Defeat Martyr Logarius.

Area [p113] | Strategy [p342]

After making your way to Forsaken Cainhurst Castle (see the Cainhurst Trophy), continue through the area and you'll come face-to-face with Martyr Logarius at the end. He's an extremely challenging foe, so be sure to check his strategy section to find out his weaknesses.

Celestial Emissary

Rank	Bronze
Description	Defeat Great One: Celestial Emissary.

Area [p143] | Strategy [p348]

The Celestial Emissary can be found in the Lumenflower Garden area of the Upper Cathedral Ward and you'll unlock the Trophy as soon as you defeat it.

Ebrietas, Daughter of the Cosmos

Rank	Bronze
Description	Defeat Great One: Ebrietas, Daughter of the Cosmos.

Area [p143] | Strategy [p350]

Upon defeating the Celestial Emissary in the Upper Cathedral Ward you'll be able to see an ornate stained-glass window near the Lumenflower Garden Lamp. If you break through that window you can access a hidden part of the area. Make your way along the walkways and down the elevator at the end to reach the Altar of Despair, where you'll find Ebrietas. Defeating her not only unlocks this Trophy, but also the Chalice of Isz Trophy, for getting the Holy Chalice she drops.

Defeat Ebrietas, Daughter of the Cosmos, in the Upper Cathedral Ward to obtain her trophy.

Deny the 'Celestial Emissary' and all his allies their independence day if you wish to unlock this Trophy.

Cainhurst

Rank	Silver
Description	Gain entry to Cainhurst, the lost and ruined castle.

Area [p104] | Strategy –

This Trophy will unlock as soon as you enter the Cainhurst Castle Grounds; to get there you will first need to fulfill a couple of requirements. The first thing to obtain is the Cainhurst Summons, which can be found in the 2nd Floor Operating Room within Iosefka's Clinic. To reach that area, enter the Forbidden Woods and progress far enough to access the Subterranean Cave. At the back of the Cave is a ladder that you can climb to reach a small graveyard, from which there's a path leading into the Clinic. With the summons in your possession, head to Hemwick Charnel Lane (after killing the Witch of Hemwick) and inspect the Obelisk in the middle of the Execution Grounds to trigger the Cainhurst Carriage event. Board the carriage and you'll have the trophy in no time at all.

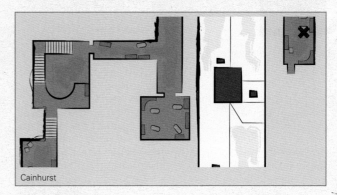

Cainhurst

The Choir

Rank	Silver
Description	Gain entry to the realm of the Choir, the high stratum of the Healing Church.

Area [p138] | Strategy –

To unlock this Trophy you'll need to travel to the Upper Cathedral Ward. To get the key you need to open the door in the Healing Church Workshop, take a trip into Yahar'gul, Unseen Village (Blood Moon). The Upper Cathedral Key can be found in the Holding Cells area of Yahar'gul, and to reach it you'll need to drop down onto the ledge outside from above, so that you can get into the cell. Once you have the key, make your way up the tower in the Healing Church Workshop and open the door to access this area.

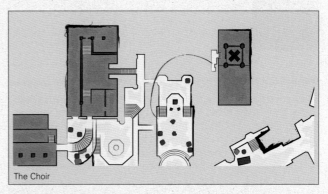

The Choir

6

Defeat the 'Yharnam, Pthumerian Queen' at the end of the Great Pthumeru Ihyll Chalice Dungeon to unlock the trophy of her namesake.

Chalice Dungeon Trophies

There are only a few Trophies relating to the Chalice Dungeons, and unlocking them will not only require you to explore different areas of the main game, but also work your way through all of the dungeons themselves.

Chalice of Pthumeru

Rank	Bronze
Description	Acquire the Chalice of Pthumeru that seals the catacombs form a web deep below Yharnam.

Area [p64] | Strategy [p330]

To unlock this Trophy you'll need to obtain the Pthumeru Chalice, which you'll be awarded for defeating the Blood-starved Beast at the end of Old Yharnam.

Chalice of Ailing Loran

Rank	Bronze
Description	Acquire the Chalice of Ailing Loran that seals the tragic land lost to the sands.

Area [p125] | Strategy [p340]

You can obtain the Lower Loran Chalice to unlock this Trophy by defeating Amygdala at the end of the Nightmare Frontier. See the Amygdala trophy for details on getting to the Nightmare Frontier.

Chalice of Isz

Rank	Bronze
Description	Acquire the Great Chalice of Isz that seals the home of the cosmic kin.

Area [p143] | Strategy [p350]

The Great Isz Chalice that you need to unlock this Trophy can be obtained by defeating Ebrietas, Daughter of the Cosmos. You'll find Ebrietas within the Altar of Despair section of the Upper Cathedral Ward.

Yharnam, Pthumerian Queen

Rank	Gold
Description	Defeat Yharnam, Blood Queen of the Old Labyrinth.

Area [p468] | Strategy [p392]

Reaching Yharnam, Pthumerian Queen is no easy task – you'll need to fight your way through nearly all of the fixed Chalice Dungeons to accomplish it. She is located on the final floor of the Pthumeru Ihyll Dungeon, a Depth 5 Dungeon, so it's highly recommended that you take her on in co-op with other Hunters.

The Source of the Dream

Rank	Silver
Description	Discover the abandoned old workshop, the source of the hunter's dream.

Area [p71] | Strategy –

Discovering the source of the dream requires a trip into the Healing Church Workshop, so you won't be able to unlock this Trophy until you have completed Old Yharnam. Once you've finished that area, the door in the Odeon Chapel of Cathedral Ward will open and you can enter the Healing Church Workshop. Make your way around to wooden bridge at the top of the tower's lower section, and then use the ledges there to drop down to where the door is that leads to the Abandoned Old Workshop; the Trophy will unlock as soon as you enter the area.

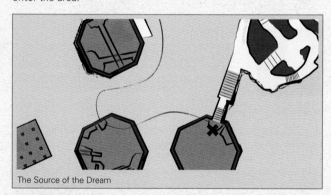

The Source of the Dream

Nightmare Lecture Building

Rank	Silver
Description	Gain entry into the Byrgenwerth lecture building, that drifts within the realm of nightmare.

Area [p114] | Strategy –

There are a couple of ways you can unlock this Trophy. It's possible to unlock it late in the game through normal progress – examining the mummy in the room beyond the boss of Yahar'gul, Unseen Village (Blood Moon) will take you to the 2nd floor of this building. Unlocking it earlier requires the Tonsil Stone, which can be obtained by entering the Forbidden Woods so that Spider-man Patches takes over the residential NPCs; he'll give you the stone if you talk to any of them. Once you have the stone, return to the Cathedral Ward and go to the room at the end of the cliffs; approach the door at the other end of the room to trigger the False God's attack and let it hit you. Without the stone the attack would kill you, but with it you'll be transported to the 1st floor of the Lecture Building and unlock the Trophy.

Completionist Trophies

These Trophies are for hunters who like to collect every item, acquire all weapons, and generally make themselves as strong and well-rounded as possible.

Blood Gem Contact

Rank		Bronze
Description		Acquire a blood gem that imbues hunter weapons with special strength.

Area [p51] | Strategy –

To unlock this Trophy you simply need to acquire a Blood Gem of any strength. While you may be lucky enough to have one drop from an enemy, the first guaranteed place you can unlock this Trophy is by getting the Tempering Blood Gemstone from the chest at the end of the Yharnam Path in the Cathedral Ward.

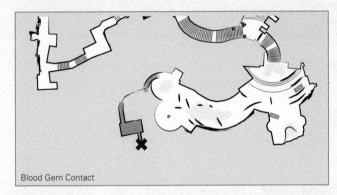

Blood Gem Contact

Rune Contact

Rank		Bronze
Description		Acquire a Caryll Rune that endows hunters with special strength.

Area [p68] | Strategy –

Similar to the Blood Gem Contact Trophy, picking up any level of Caryll Rune will unlock this Trophy. The first place that you can get a Rune will depend on the order you tackle the areas in, but the first ones will generally be either a Communion Caryll Rune just before the Tower Bridge in the Healing Church Workshop, or a Lake one that you can find at the end of the Castle Bluff in Hemwick Charnel Lane.

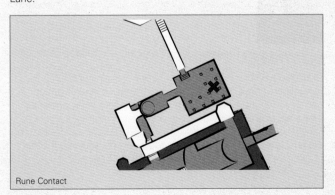

Rune Contact

Rune Master

Rank		Silver
Description		Acquire an extremely precious Caryll Rune.

Area [p68] | Strategy –

If you went to the Healing Church Workshop to get the Communion Caryll Rune, you can follow the hidden path in the elevator shaft there to reach a chest containing a Formless Oedon Caryll Rune. Acquiring that Rune that will unlock this Trophy.

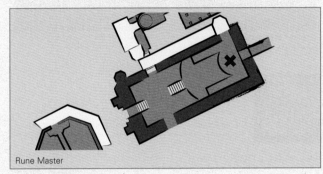

Rune Master

Blood Gem Master

Rank		Silver
Description		Acquire an extremely precious blood gem.

Area – | Strategy –

To unlock this Trophy you will need to get a Blood Gem that has a rating of 15 or higher, and the easiest way to get one is to venture into the Chalice Dungeons. The floor bosses of Depth 4 Dungeons can drop Gems of a high enough level, or you can find them from chests/random enemy drops in Depth 5 labyrinths.

Descend the stairs behind the Church Giant (Wrecking Ball) and open the chest at the dead end to obtain the Blood Gem Contract trophy.

You can either get off the elevator at the secret exit or jump down to it from above.

6

Collecting the Blood Rock here in the Nightmare Mensis will allow you to max your weapon to +10 for the 'Weapon Master', completionist Trophy.

Weapon Master

Rank	Silver
Description	Acquire a weapon of the highest level.

Area [p157 & p198] | Strategy –

Getting a weapon to +9 is a relatively easy task with the myriad of ways to get Shards, Twin Shards and Chunks, but to reach the fabled heights of +10 you will need a Blood Rock, and they are in extremely short supply. The first guaranteed one that you can find is by going through the Crumbled Wall on the Middle Bridge in Nightmare of Mensis, and then dropping down to the small room below. Outside of that one, the Breeding Pit below the Fishing Hamlet provides you with an alternate option, otherwise you'll need to try your luck by venturing into Depth 5 randomly generated Root Chalice Dungeons.

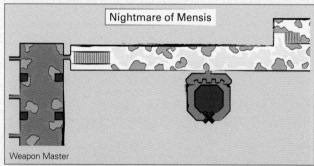
Weapon Master

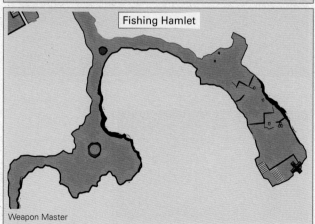
Weapon Master

Hunter's Craft

Rank	Gold
Description	Acquire all special hunter tools.

Area – | Strategy –

To become a true master hunter you must by familiar with all of the tools that have been passed down from hunter to hunter through the generations. The effects of the different tools may vary, but they each offer something unique that can aid you in your quest; acquire all of the tools available to unlock this Trophy.

Hunter's Tools Locations

Name	Location	Page
Old Hunter Bone	In the Abandoned Old Workshop area of the Healing Church Workshop.	p71
Beast Roar	In a small shack near the end of the Village Outskirts in the Forbidden Woods.	p93
Augur of Ebrietas	In the small room you can reach by going through Lecture Theater 2 in Lecture Building 1F.	p115
Messenger's Gift	At the end of the Swampy Gorge in Nightmare Frontier.	p123
Executioner's Glove	In the Secluded Reading Room area of Forsaken Cainhurst Castle.	p110
Empty Phantasm Shell	On the College: Upper Floors of Byrgenwerth.	p127
Tiny Tonitrus	In the Holding Cells area of Yahar'gul, Unseen Village (Blood Moon).	p132
A Call Beyond	On the Grand Cathedral Walkways in the Upper Cathedral Ward.	p143
Choir Bell	In the Chapel Rafters area of Nightmare of Mensis.	p157

Hunter's Essence

Rank	Gold
Description	Acquire all hunter weapons.

Area – | Strategy –

Acquiring a true hunter's essence takes mastery of the many different weapons available to you. To get started on that path (and to unlock this Trophy), you'll need to obtain all of them. For details on just how to accomplish this mammoth task, consult the tables on the following page.

Old Hunter's Essence OH

Rank	Gold
Description	Acquire all old hunter weapons.

Area – | Strategy –

Obtaining a normal Hunter's Essence is no longer considered the pinnacle of what it means to be a true hunter; to reach that lofty goal you'll need to delve deep into the nightmare to experience all that it has to offer – only then can you tap into the Old Hunter's Essence. Unlocking this Trophy will require you to fully explore each of the new areas to find all of the hidden weapons, and defeat some of the toughest foes the game has to offer.

Collect the Boom Hammer on the lower floor of the Nightmare House.

Underneath the hidden Surgical Altar you will find the powerful Church Cannon.

Name	Acquisition info	Page
Beast Cutter	On the way up the stairs to the Nightmare Grand Cathedral, you will see two protruding platforms either side of the stairway. Turn onto the left platform, and then drop off the edge to the level below to reach the Beast Cutter on the corpse in front of you.	p166
Boom Hammer	On the ground floor of the Nightmare Residence by the dead man in the wheelchair.	p168
Piercing Rifle	Kill the Bestial Hunter in the Hunter's Nightmare for the Firing Hammer Badge, which will allow you to purchase this firearm from the shop in the Hunter's Dream for 20000 Blood Echoes.	p168
Gatling Gun	Follow the River of Blood into the Beast Cave and kill Djura's Disciple to acquire the Gatling Gun.	p168
Amygdalan Arm	In the same area where you acquired the Gatling Gun, slay the Blood-starved Beast and his allies before collecting this weapon at the back of his lair.	p168
Beasthunter Saif	Take the ladder upwards that leads to the Bloody Plaza, then take a left and drop down. Kill the Old Hunter that will attempt to ambush you here then grab this weapon on the nearby overlook.	p171
Whirligig Saw	You will see this before you can reach it on a large, raised, tombstone just before you ascend the ladder to the Bloody Plaza. Head through the Nightmare Church with the Lamp, then drop down into the Corpse Ravine and fight your way through the crows and Old Hunter to reach this weapon.	p171
Holy Moonlight Sword	After defeating Ludwig, the Accursed, wear any Church Garb and talk to his surviving head to collect this very powerful blade. Alternately, cleave his head with your weapon to acquire it.	p652
Fist of Gratia	Approach the Underground Cells from where you fought Ludwig, the Accursed in the Underground Corpse Pile. This weapon can be found in the third cell to your right on the prostrated corpse in corner.	p172
Church Cannon	Enter the Recovery Room, and then raise the surgery altar to reveal the hidden altar beneath. Pull the nearby lever and step onto the elevator to be taken down to another secret room, where you'll find this weapon in a chest.	p173
Loch Shield	After raising the staircases with the mechanism at the top of the Research Hall, make your way back down to the Floor 3. Once there you can drop off the ledge outside the Laboratory onto a landing. From that landing follow the stairs down to a small platform, where you'll find this shield on a corpse.	p185
Church Pick	Use the Underground Cell Key on the cell door to your left in the Underground Cells. It will be the fourth door to your left from where you enter this area via the Underground Corpse Pile, or the second on your right if you are coming down the stairs from the elevator to the Research Hall area. Kill the Hunter lurking here and loot this weapon from his cold, dead hands.	p172
Rakuyo	Climb down the ladder situated at the well in the Fishing Hamlet. At the bottom there are two Giant Fishmen in a large cavern, and the one hanging off the ceiling is holding this weapon. Kill him to take it, but be prepared – one of these enemies is lethal; two will provide a sizable challenge.	p192
Simon's Bowblade	If you follow the quest of Simon, Seeker of Secrets, you'll find him on the floor of the Lighthouse Hut in the Fishing Hamlet, and he will give you his weapon as he expires with his final breath. Alternatively you can kill him at any point before that if you wish to get the weapon earlier, and you'll still find the Underground Cell Inner Chamber Key in the Lighthouse Hut when you get there.	p651
Bloodletter	Take the Underground Cell Inner Chamber Key that The Seeker of Secrets gave you with his last words and head back to the Underground Corpse Pile. Make your way back to the Underground Cells, and then go through the open gate and down the stairs to reach the cell door. Upon entering the cell you'll find Brador sat inside; kill him to get this weapon. Remember to kill him in all of the places first, however, or you won't be able to get his attire.	p653
Kos Parasite	Kill the Orphan of Kos. Refer to the boss strategies section for advice on slaying this monster, as this boss will prove more than a substantial challenge. Upon his demise, he will yield you the Kos Parasite weapon.	p199

6

Right Hand Weapons

Name	Acquisition info	Page
Saw Cleaver	Can be selected as one of the starting weapons you get from the Messengers during your first trip to the Hunter's Dream, or can be purchased from the Bath Messengers for 1000 Blood Echoes after obtaining the Saw Hunter's Badge.	p481
Saw Spear	On a corpse hanging in the Dry Dock - Rafters section of Central Yharnam, or can be purchased from the Bath Messenger for 100 Blood Echoes after obtaining the Saw Hunter's Badge.	p484
Hunter Axe	Can be selected as one of the starting weapons you get from the Messengers during your first trip to the Hunter's Dream, or can be purchased from the Bath Messengers for 1100 Blood Echoes after obtaining the Saw Hunter's Badge.	p487
Threaded Cane	Can be selected as one of the starting weapons you get from the Messengers during your first trip to the Hunter's Dream, or can be purchased from the Bath Messengers for 1100 Blood Echoes after obtaining the Saw Hunter's Badge.	p490
Blade of Mercy	Purchase from the Bath Messenger for 40,000 Blood Echoes after obtaining the Crow Hunter Badge.	p496
Kirkhammer	Purchase from the Bath Messenger for 3000 Blood Echoes after obtaining the Sword Hunter Badge.	p499
Ludwig's Holy Blade	Purchase from the Bath Messenger for 20,000 Blood Echoes after obtaining the Radiant Sword Hunter Badge.	p502
Reiterpallasch	Can be found in the Entrance Hall of Forsaken Cainhurst Castle (p107), or purchased from the Bath Messenger for 18,000 Blood Echoes after obtaining the Cainhurst Badge.	p505
Chikage	Purchase from the Bath Messenger for 50,000 Blood Echoes after obtaining the Cainhurst Badge	p508
Rifle Spear	Can be found in the Storage Area of Old Yharnam (p61), or purchased from the Bath Messenger for 4000 Blood Echoes after obtaining the Powder Key Hunter Badge.	p511
Stake Driver	Purchase from the Bath Messenger for 8000 Blood Echoes after obtaining the Powder Keg Hunter Badge.	p514
Tonitrus	Can be found at the end of Main Street - West in Yahar'gul, Unseen Village (p84), or purchased from the Bath Messenger for 26,000 Blood Echoes after obtaining the Spark Hunter Badge.	p517
Logarius' Wheel	Purchase from the Bath Messenger for 13,000 Blood Echoes after obtaining the Wheel Hunter Badge.	p519
Beast Claw	Can first be obtained from a chest on Level 2 of the Ailing Loran Chalice Dungeon.	p521
Burial Blade	Purchase from the Bath Messenger for 60,000 Blood Echoes after obtaining the Old Hunter Badge.	p493

Left Hand Weapons

Name	Acquisition info	Page
Hunter Pistol	Can be selected as one of the starting weapons you get from the Messengers during your first trip to the Hunter's Dream, or can be purchased from the Bath Messengers for 1600 Blood Echoes after obtaining the Saw Hunter's Badge.	p559
Hunter Blunderbuss	Can be selected as one of the starting weapons you get from the Messengers during your first trip to the Hunter's Dream, or can be purchased from the Bath Messengers for 1700 Blood Echoes after obtaining the Saw Hunter's Badge.	p559
Repeating Pistol	Purchase from the Bath Messenger for 3000 Blood Echoes after obtaining the Sword Hunter Badge.	p560
Ludwig's Rifle	Purchase from the Bath Messenger for 10,000 Blood Echoes after obtaining the Radiant Sword Hunter Badge.	p560
Evelyn	Can be found in the Library 1F section of Forsaken Cainhurst Castle (p109), or purchased from the Bath Messenger for 16,000 Blood Echoes after obtaining the Cainhurst Badge.	p561
Cannon	Can be found in the Windmill Cogs area of the Forbidden Woods.	p561
Flamesprayer	Given as a gift by Gilbert if you speak with him after kill Father Gascoigne (p35), or can be purchased from the Bath Messenger for 8000 Blood Echoes after obtaining the Radiant Sword Hunter Badge.	p562
Rosmarinus	Purchase from the Bath Messenger for 60,000 Blood Echoes after obtaining the Cosmic Eye Watcher Badge.	p562
Hunter's Torch	Can be found in the Rooftops area of Old Yharnam.	p563

Miscellaneous Trophies

This final selection of Trophies is where you'll find the ones that do not quite fit into one of the previous categories, and they are all related to the different endings that you can get in the game. If you wish to see all of them and eventually go on to unlock the Platinum Trophy, you will need to complete the game at least three times.

Yharnam Sunrise

Rank		Gold
Description		You lived through the hunt, and saw another day.

Area [p160] | **Strategy –**

To unlock this Trophy you will need to choose 'Submit your life" during the final conversation with Gehrman below the Great Tree in the Hunter's Dream.

Honoring Wishes

Rank		Gold
Description		Captivated by the moon presence, you pledge to watch over the hunter's dream.

Area [p160] | **Strategy [p356]**

If you 'Refuse' Gehrman's offer when you talk to him, you'll then have to fight him to complete the game, after which this Trophy will unlock.

Childhood's Beginning

Rank		Gold
Description		You became an infant Great One, lifting humanity to its next childhood.

Area [p160] | **Strategy [p358]**

In order to unlock this Trophy you'll need to acquire and use three One Third of Umbilical items before you start the final conversation with Gehrman at the Great Tree. During the conversation you will need to 'Refuse' his offer again so that you can fight him, after which you will face the Moon Presence, and only after defeating that foe will the ending commence and the Trophy unlock.

Impostor Iosefka holds one of the umbilical cords you'll need to earn this trophy, but it can only be obtained from her while the Blood Moon is out.

Collect all three parts of this umbilical cord to unlock the true ending and the related hidden, 'Childhood's Beginning' Trophy.

Arianna must move to the Oedon Chapel and survive until the end of the game in order for you to obtain her umbilical cord.

Bloodborne

Rank		Platinum
Description		All trophies acquired. Hats off!

Area – | **Strategy –**

After fighting your way through the Chalice Dungeons, collecting every weapon, and seeing all that the game has to offer on your journey to unlock the other Trophies, when all of it is finally done and that last Trophy unlocks, the coveted Bloodborne Platinum Trophy will also be yours.

You'll receive the final umbilical cord after defeating Mergo's Wet Nurse.

One Third of Umbilical Cord Locations

Area	Location	Page	Info
Healing Church Workshop	Abandoned Old Workshop	p71	After entering the Workshop you'll find the item sitting on the altar.
Cathedral Ward	Oedon Chapel	p48	Fulfill certain conditions within Arianna's quest. (p639).
Iosefka's Clinic	3rd Floor Operating Room	p102	Enter the room during the Blood Moon when Iosefka (Imposter) is still alive and kill her.
Nightmare of Mensis	Mergo's Loft: Rooftop	p159	Defeat Mergo's Wet Nurse.

6

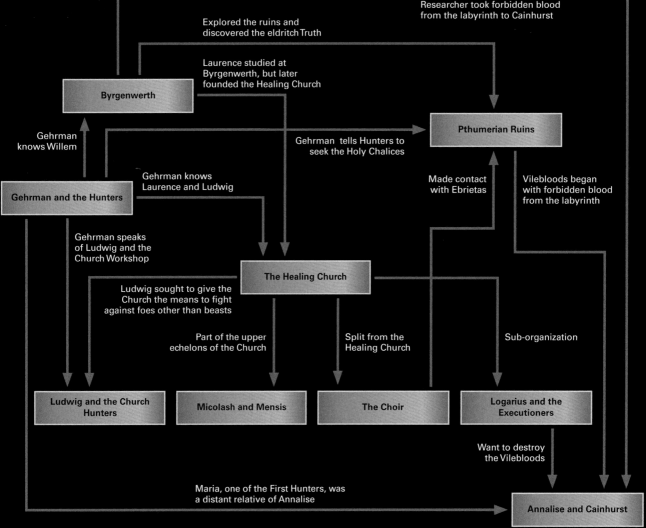

Byrgenwerth Lore

Provost Willem

Byrgenwerth is an old place of learning (1) that now lies abandoned. In its day, Byrgenwerth was home to scholars, and the school was headed by Provost Willem. The students learned of history and archaeology (2). One day, the scholars of Byrgenwerth had an encounter with the eldritch Truth (3) in the tombs below Yharnam (4).

This encounter led to an inquiry into the cosmos from within the old labyrinth (5). Master Willem and his students began to study about the Great Ones, beings who may be called "gods (6)." Expeditions were sent into the labyrinth, but some of the investigators went mad upon encountering the eldritch Truth (7). Medicine made from blood was developed at Byrgenwerth to stave off madness, but its use led to a dependence on blood ministration (8).

Provost Willem had an epiphany – humans need more eyes to become like the Great Ones (6). He even sought a Third Umbilical Cord to line his brain with eyes (9). Disillusioned by the limits of human intellect (10), Willem valued knowledge (11) and wished to elevate his thoughts to that of a Great One (9).

The scholars of Byrgenwerth also played a role in the Kos incident. The skulls of locals in the fishing village were forcibly searched for internal eyes (12). Even now, the accursed villagers mill about in the Nightmare while muttering their hatred of Byrgenwerth (13). The corpse of Kos was also found to be filled with small, inhuman parasites (14).

Laurence and Willem had a disagreement, and Laurence left Byrgenwerth (15). Laurence went on to become the first vicar of the Healing Church (16), and the scholars of the Church continue the work began at Byrgenwerth (17). Willem had admonished Laurence to "fear the old blood" as Laurence took his leave (15); this cautionary adage is still handed down among the vicars who head the Healing Church (18).

Runesmith Caryll is another famous student of Byrgenwerth; Caryll focused on transcribing the words of the Great Ones as runes (19). Unlike the path taken by the Healing Church, this method of transcending humanity does not rely on blood (19).

Though the school is now long-abandoned and access is restricted by the Healing Church (20), Master Willem can still be found there overlooking the lake that hides Vacuous Rom (21).

Laurence, the First Vicar

1 Alfred Dialogue
2 Lecture Theatre Key
3 Kin Coldblood
4 Alfred Dialogue
5 Augur of Ebrietas
6 Great One's Wisdom
7 Graveguard Set
8 Sedative
9 Third Umbilical Cord
10 Eye Rune
11 Student Uniform
12 Accursed Brew
13 Fishing Hamlet Priest Dialogue
14 Kos Parasite
15 Laurence and Willem Dialogue
16 Laurence's Skull
17 Choir Set
18 Gold Pendant
19 Rune Workshop Tool
20 Alfred Dialogue
21 Lunarium Key

Associates

| Gehrman, the First Hunter | | Laurence, First Vicar of the Healing Church |

Gehrman begs for Master Willem to free him from the Dream

Laurence disagrees with Willem over the use of blood ministration

Provost Willem, head of Byrgenwerth

| Vacuous Rom | | Fishing Hamlet |

Willem guides Hunters to Rom in the Moonside Lake

The Fishing Villagers mutter their hatred of Byrgenwerth

Byrgenwerth Lore | References

1 | Alfred Dialogue

Byrgenwerth is an old place of learning.

2 | Lecture Theatre Key

Key to the Lecture Theatre in the Lecture Building. Today, the two-story Lecture Building is adrift in the nightmare, but once it was a place of reflection, where scholars learned of history and archaeology. Perhaps it still is, as the students in the lecture theatre appear to await the return of their professor.

3 | Kin Coldblood

Coldblood of inhuman kin of the cosmos, brethren of the Great Ones. Use to gain unspeakable Blood Echoes. Dare not to delve into the world beyond humanity, the eldritch Truth touched upon long ago at Byrgenwerth.

4 | Alfred Dialogue

Well, once a group of young Byrgenwerth scholars discovered a holy medium deep within the tomb.

5 | Augur of Ebrietas

Remnant of the eldritch Truth encountered at Byrgenwerth. Use phantasms, the invertebrates known to be augurs of the Great Ones, to partially summon abandoned Ebrietas. The initial encounter marked the start of an inquiry into the cosmos from within the old labyrinth, and led to the establishment of the Choir.

6 | Great One's Wisdom

Fragments of the lost wisdom of the Great Ones, beings that might be described as gods. Use to gain Insight. At Byrgenwerth, Master Willem had an epiphany: "We are thinking on the basest of planes. What we need, are more eyes."

7 | Graveguard Set

Robe of Dores, graveguard of the Forbidden Woods. Countless bloodied ritual tools hang from its back. Willem kept two loyal servants back at Byrgenwerth. When they were sent into the labyrinth, they encountered the eldritch Truth, and went mad. One became the password gatekeeper, while Dores became a graveguard of the forest. Both remained loyal, even in madness.

8 | Sedative

Liquid medicine concocted at Byrgenwerth. Calms the nerves. Those who delve into the arcane fall all-too-easily to madness, and thick human blood serves to calm the frayed nerves of these inquisitive minds. Naturally, this often leads to a reliance on blood ministration.

9 | Third Umbilical Cord

A great relic, also known as the Cord of the Eye. Every infant Great One has this precursor to the umbilical cord. Provost Willem sought the Cord in order to elevate his being and thoughts to those of a Great One, by lining his brain with eyes. The only choice, he knew, if man were to ever match Their greatness.

A secret symbol left by Caryll, runesmith of Byrgenwerth. A transcription of "eye," as spoken by left-behind Great Ones. Allows one to make additional discoveries. Eyes symbolize the truth Master Willem sought in his research. Disillusioned by the limits of human intellect, Master Willem looked to beings from higher planes for guidance, and sought to line his brain with eyes in order to elevate his thoughts.

11 | Student Uniform

Uniform of the students of Byrgenwerth, a bygone institute of learning. This alternative lacks the thick cape. This Healing Church has its roots in Byrgenwerth, and naturally borrows heavily from its uniform design. The focus not on knowledge, or thought, but on pure pretension would surely bring Master Willem to despair, if only he knew.

12 | Accursed Brew

Skull of a local from the violated fishing village. The inside of the skull was forcibly searched for eyes, as evidenced by innumerable scratches and indentations. No wonder the skull became stewed in curses. They who offer baneful chants. Weep with them, as one in trance.

13 | Fishing Hamlet Priest Dialogue

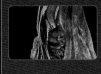
Byrgenwerth... Byrgenwerth... Blasphemous murderers... Blood-crazed fiends... Atonement for the wretches... By the wrath of Mother Kos...

14 | Kos Parasite

When the carcass of Kos washed up on the coast, its insides were teeming with tiny parasites, unlike any found in humans. This atypical weapon can only be clasped tight and swung, but a Kos Parasite is said to stimulate phantasms inhabiting a lumenwood.

15 | Laurence and Willem Dialogue

LAURENCE: Master Willem, I've come to bid you farewell. **WILLEM:** Oh, I know, I know. **WILLEM:** You think now, to betray me. **LAURENCE:** No, but you will never listen. **LAURENCE:** I tell you, I will not forget our adage. **WILLEM:** ...The blood makes us human, makes us more than human, makes us human no more. **WILLEM:** ...We are born of the blood, made men by the blood, undone by the blood. **WILLEM:** Our eyes are yet to open... **WILLEM & LAURENCE:** Fear the old blood. **WILLEM:** By the gods, fear it, Laurence. **LAURENCE:** I must take my leave.

Skull of Laurence, first vicar of the Healing Church. In reality he became the first cleric beast, and his human skull only exists within the Nightmare. The skull is a symbol of Laurence's past, and what he failed to protect. He is destined to seek his skull, but even if he found it, it could never restore his memories.

17 | Choir Set

Attire of the Choir, high-ranking members of the Healing Church. Members of the Choir are both the highest-ranking clerics of the Healing Church, and scholars who continue the work that began at Byrgenwerth. Together with the left behind Great One, they look to the skies, in search of astral signs, that may lead them to the rediscovery of true greatness.

18 | Gold Pendant

Pendant of Vicar Amelia. Use to change into a blood gem, which fortifies weapons. This pendant, passed down among the vicars who head the Healing Church, is a reminder of the cautionary adage. To reveal the adage, touch the altar skull.

19 | Rune Workshop

Runesmith Caryll, student of Byrgenwerth, transcribed the inhuman utterings of the Great Ones into what are now called Caryll Runes. The hunter who retrieves this workshop tool can etch Caryll Runes into the mind to attain their wondrous strength. Provost Willem would have been proud of Caryll's runes, as they do not rely upon blood in any measure.

20 | Alfred Dialogue

But today, the college lies deep within a tangled wood, abandoned and decrepit. And furthermore, the Healing Church has declared Byrgenwerth forbidden ground.

21 | Lunarium Key

Key to the lunarium facing the lake on the second floor of Byrgenwerth College. In his final years, Master Willem was fond of the lookout, and the rocking chair that he kept there for meditation. In the end, it is said, he left his secret with the lake.

Healing Church Lore

The Healing Church has its roots in Byrgenwerth (1). Researchers there encountered a remnant of the eldritch Truth and began exploring the labyrinths below Yharnam (2). Investigations led to further encounters with the eldritch Truth (3), Great Ones that might be described as gods (4). Humans, however, were incapable of understanding the wisdom of the Great Ones, and some of the investigators went mad (3).

Master Willem concluded that the only choice for humans to match the greatness of the Great Ones was to seek more eyes (4/5); he went so far as to seek the Third Umbilical Cord of an infant Great One in order to line his brain with eyes (5). He did not believe in the usage of direct blood ministration, and admonished Laurence to "Fear the Old Blood (6)." Laurence did not accept Willem's opinion (6), and his departure led to the foundation of a Healing Church (7); indeed, Laurence became the first vicar of the church (7).

The Healing Church is known as the source of blood healing (8). They performed experimental treatments on patients in their research hall to cultivate worthy blood (9). The Church chooses nuns for their merits as vessels of blood and grooms them to become Blood Saints (10). The efficacy of this blood as a treatment for disease is a source of power for the Church, as it lends legitimacy to their teachings (10). Deep within the Grand Cathedral of the Healing Church is a holy medium (11) — the source of eldritch blood. In reality, this is the left-behind Great One, Ebrietas. Blood ministration is the pursuit of communion (12); in other words, the Church is seeking to refine blood to be like that of the Great Ones. To that end, the Church often sends tomb prospectors to explore the labyrinth, but most go mad (13).

Within the higher ranks of the Healing Church, there are two main groups: the School of Mensis and the Choir (14). The formation of the Choir began with investigations in the labyrinth (2). Its roots lie in the Orphanage near the Grand Cathedral (15). The Orphanage was a place of scholarship and experimentation, and the Choir arose from these activities (15). The Choir members are both the highest ranking clerics of the Church and scholars who continue the research began at Byrgenwerth (16). Members of the Choir cover their eyes to indicate their debt to the teachings of Master Willem (17).

Martyr Logarius

The Choir claims that the land of Isz lies in contact with the cosmos, and that allows the Great Ones to function on transcendental planes (18). The Great Isz Chalice was the first holy chalice brought back to the surface since the days of Byrgenwerth, and it allowed the Choir to have audience with Ebrietas (19). They believe that the cosmos are just above their heads (20), and so, they search for astral signs with the left behind Great One, Ebrietas (16). They once used phantasms to attempt to make contact with the outer reaches of the cosmos, but failed to do so (21). The Choir eventually split from the Healing Church (14).

The other major division within the Healing Church is the School of Mensis (14). The School of Mensis founded Yahar'gul, the Unseen Village (22). The "hunters" of Yahar'gul are in reality mere kidnappers (22). The Church also has special "hunters" pretending to be beggars on the street (23). No one is safe; even the nuns of the Healing Church find themselves to be targets of Mensis' hunt (24/10).

The School of Mensis is performing a ritual that requires a special newborn (25). This ritual is hidden by the spider of Byrgenwerth, Vacuous Rom (26). Micolash, the host of the Nightmare of Mensis, knows of Rom. Indeed, he wishes for Kos to grant eyes to Mensis as she did for Rom (27). Kos, however, is dead (28/29).

Mensis was granted audience with Mergo thanks to a Third Cord, but the encounter resulted in the stillbirth of their brains (30). Instead of Kos, the Great One that is beckoned by a baby's cry atop the Nightmare Mensis is Mergo's Wet Nurse (31); in place of Mergo's actual mother, the Wet Nurse is the one who gives sustenance.

The Great Ones that inhabit the nightmare are sympathetic in nature and often answer when called upon (32). The Great Ones are not, however, all benevolent; some are quite rotten and evil (33). Mensis retrieved an immense brain from within the Nightmare, but it was filled with evil eyes on the inside (33).

Great Ones can impact human thoughts and actions without the humans' knowledge, as evidenced by the "inadvertent" worshippers of Oedon (34). In the end, it is difficult to say to what extent the dark rituals of Mensis are performed by their own will and to what extent it is the influence of a Great One. The same can be said of their desire to summon the long-dead Kos. It is only known that one result of their ghastly rituals was The One Reborn (35).

The Healing Church has a storied history with many legendary figures. Among the most impactful was the first Church Hunter, Ludwig (36). Ludwig's Healing Church workshop began to deviate from Gehrman's techniques to prepare for battles with more terrifying beasts (37). Laurence, the first vicar of the Church, became the first Cleric Beast (7); perhaps Ludwig sought the means to defeat future Cleric Beasts? In his endeavors, Ludwig was guided by a shining light (38), the Holy Moonlight Sword (39). Unfortunately, he was eventually claimed by the Hunter's Nightmare and became a horrifying beast (40). Despite his sad fate, the Holy Blades, possessors of the Radiant Sword Hunter Badge, have inherited his will, and they exist as the remnant of his ancient line of heroes (41).

Another of the first Healing Church hunters was a man named Simon (42). Unlike most hunters, he disliked guns, and the Church workshop created a bow specifically for him (42). Many of his comrades scoffed at Simon's preference (42). Indeed, throughout the ages, there have been many unique weapons – some favored, and some not.

Tonitrus is one such weapon. It was created by Archibald, who is known as an infamous eccentric from the Healing Church workshop (43). The hunters of his day did not really take to the use of Tonitrus (43). On the other hand, he also invented Bolt Paper, which is widely used by many hunters (44). Archibald was fascinated by the sparks of the undead darkbeasts and dedicated his life to their reproduction (45); curiously, his methodology was very similar to that of Byrgenwerth (45).

Ebrietas

Not all of the notable figures associated with the Church were quite so scientific. The Martyr Logarius and his band of Executioners believed in their righteous destiny and operated a secretive, fanatical workshop steeped in mysticism (46). Logarius' Executioners adored hand-to-hand combat (47) and used large wheels to slaughter the Vilebloods of Cainhurst (48). The Executioners' clothing, and the Holy Shawl in particular, became the basis for all Church attire (49).

Logarius thought that the Vilebloods of Cainhurst were fiendish creatures and that their blood threatens the purity of the Church's communion (50). He led his band of Executioners to Cainhurst, but they were unable to destroy the ruler of the Vilebloods (51). According to Executioner Alfred, "Logarius became a blessed anchor, guarding us from evil (51)." Logarius donned the Crown of Illusions to prevent anyone from discovering the secret of the Vilebloods (52).

The Healing Church has many secrets and works quite hard to keep them. The Healing Church assassin Brador killed a former compatriot who became a cleric beast (53). Ever since that day, he has worn his ally's scalp as a hat and secluded himself beneath the Cathedral in the Hunter's Nightmare. The Church gave him a soundless bell. Those who can hear the bell are those who know the Church's secrets. They are marked for death, and Brador will pursue them eternally. Brador believes that he can be purified if he is able to expel the tainted blood from his body (53).

Among the secrets guarded by Brador is the Church's research on human subjects. High ministers of the Healing Church have concocted odd medicines that numb the brain for use in their strange experiments (55). In the early days of the Healing Church, cerebral patients would imbibe water; within, the brain fluid would writhe and churn — the initial makings of internal eyes (56).

1	Student Uniform	29	Kos Parasite
2	Augur of Ebrietas	30	Third Umbilical Cord
3	Graveguard Robe	31	Mergo's Wet Nurse
4	Great One's Wisdom	32	Moon Rune
5	Third Umbilical Cord	33	Living String
6	Willem and Laurence Dialogue	34	Formless Oedon Rune
7	Laurence's Skull	35	The One Reborn
8	Alfred Dialogue	36	Sword Hunter Badge
9	Blood of Adeline	37	Ludwig's Holy Blade
10	Blood of Adella	38	Ludwig Dialogue
11	Alfred Dialogue	39	Holy Moonlight Sword
12	Communion	40	Ludwig
13	Madman Garb	41	Radiant Sword Hunter Badge
14	Upper Cathedral Ward Key	42	Simon's Bowblade
15	Orphanage Key	43	Tonitrus
16	Choir Garb	44	Bolt Paper
17	Blindfold Cap	45	Spark Hunter Badge
18	Isz Root Chalice	46	Wheel Hunter Badge
19	Great Isz Chalice	47	Executioner Gauntlets
20	Cosmic Eye Watcher Badge	48	Logarius Wheel
21	A Call Beyond	49	Executioner Garb
22	Yahar'gul Black Garb	50	Alfred Dialogue
23	Harrowed Garb	51	Alfred Dialogue
24	Adella Dialogue	52	Crown of Illusions
25	Lore Note	53	Brador's Testimony
26	Lore Note	54	Bloodletter
27	Micolash Dialogue	55	Blue Elixir
28	Fish Villager Dialogue	56	Brain Fluid

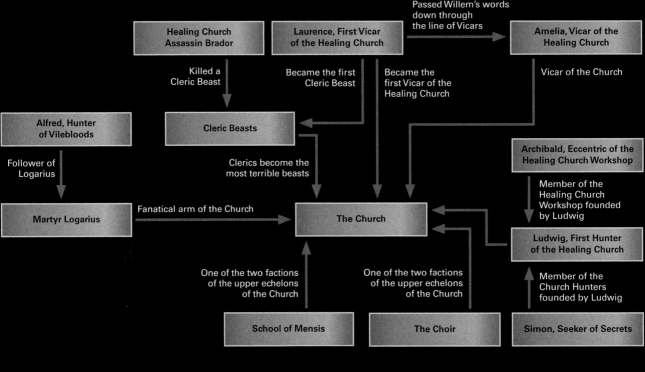

Healing Church Lore | References

1 | Student Uniform

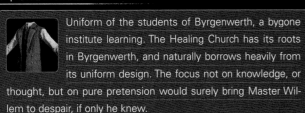

Uniform of the students of Byrgenwerth, a bygone institute learning. The Healing Church has its roots in Byrgenwerth, and naturally borrows heavily from its uniform design. The focus not on knowledge, or thought, but on pure pretension would surely bring Master Willem to despair, if only he knew.

2 | Augur of Ebrietas

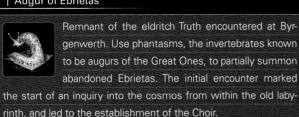

Remnant of the eldritch Truth encountered at Byrgenwerth. Use phantasms, the invertebrates known to be augurs of the Great Ones, to partially summon abandoned Ebrietas. The initial encounter marked the start of an inquiry into the cosmos from within the old labyrinth, and led to the establishment of the Choir.

3 | Graveguard Robe

Robe of Dores, graveguard of the Forbidden Woods. Countless bloodied ritual tools hang from its back. Willem kept two loyal servants back at Byrgenwerth. When they were sent into the labyrinth, they encountered the eldritch Truth, and went mad. One became the password gatekeeper, while Dores became a graveguard of the forest. Both remained loyal, even in madness.

4 | Great One's Wisdom

Fragments of the lost wisdom of the Great Ones, beings that might be described as gods. Use to gain Insight. At Byrgenwerth, Master Willem had an epiphany: "We are thinking on the basest of planes. What we need, are more eyes."

5 | Third Umbilical Cord

A great relic, also known as the Cord of the Eye. Every infant Great One has this precursor to the umbilical cord. Provost Willem sought the Cord in order to elevate his being and thoughts to those of a Great One, by lining his brain with eyes. The only choice, he knew, if man were to ever match Their greatness.

6 | Laurence and Willem Dialogue

LAURENCE: Master Willem, I've come to bid you farewell. **WILLEM:** Oh, I know, I know. **WILLEM:** You think now, to betray me. **LAURENCE:** No, but you will never listen. **LAURENCE:** I tell you, I will not forget our adage. **WILLEM:** ...The blood makes us human, makes us more than human, makes us human no more. **WILLEM:** ...We are born of the blood, made men by the blood, undone by the blood. **WILLEM:** Our eyes are yet to open... **WILLEM & LAURENCE:** Fear the old blood. **WILLEM:** By the gods, fear it, Laurence. **LAURENCE:** I must take my leave.

7 | Laurence's Skull

Skull of Laurence, first vicar of the Healing Church. In reality he became the first cleric beast, and his human skull only exists within the Nightmare. The skull is a symbol of Laurence's past, and what he failed to protect. He is destined to seek his skull, but even if he found it, it could never restore his memories.

8 | Alfred Dialogue

As you know, the Healing Church is the fountainhead of blood healing.

9 | Blood of Adeline

Blood taken from Adeline, patient of the research hall. Adeline was originally one of the Blood Saints who received treatment by the Church to cultivate worthy blood. Adeline's was one of the few cases that turned out favorably.

10 | Blood of Adella

Blood taken from Adella, nun of the Healing Church. The Healing Church nuns are chosen for their merit as vessels for blood, and groomed as Blood Saints. The mere chance of being treated with their blood lends legitimacy to the Healing Church and communion.

11 | Alfred Dialogue

But I have heard that the holy medium of blood healing is venerated in the main cathedral.

12 | Communion

A secret symbol left by Caryll, runesmith of Byrgenwerth. Several runes relate to "Blood," including "Communion," which raises the maximum number of blood vials one may carry. This rune represents the Healing Church and its ministers. Blood ministration is, of course, the pursuit of communion.

13 | Madman Garb

Most tomb prospectors, members of the Healing Church chosen to explore the old labyrinth, are unable to withstand the weight of the old knowledge, and go mad. This attire is worn by those lost souls. Truth oft resembles madness, inaccessible to the dull of mind. Those who go mad are merely thoughtful souls who failed to reach any conclusions.

14 | Upper Cathedral Ward Key

The key to the Upper Cathedral Ward seal. The upper echelons of the Healing Church are formed by the School of Mensis, based in the Unseen Village, and the Choir occupying the Upper Cathedral Ward. This key brings one a step closer to the Choir.

15 | Orphanage Key

Key to the Orphanage, birthplace of the Choir. The Orphanage, shadowed by the Grand Cathedral, was a place of scholarship and experimentation, where young orphans became potent unseen thinkers for the Healing Church. The Choir, that would later split the Healing Church, was a creation of the Orphanage.

16 | Choir Garb

Attire of the Choir, high-ranking members of the Healing Church. Members of the Choir are both the highest-ranking clerics of the Healing Church, and scholars who continue the work that began at Byrgenwerth. Together with the left behind Great One, they look to the skies, in search of astral signs, that may lead them to the rediscovery of true greatness.

17 | Blindfold Cap

Attire of the Choir, high-ranking members of the Healing Church. Members of the Choir are both the highest-ranking clerics of the Healing Church, and scholars who continue the work that began at Byrgenwerth. The eye covering indicates their debt to the teachings of Master Willem, even though their paths diverged.

18 | Isz Root Chalice

According to the Choir, the land of Isz lies in contact with the cosmos, which allowed the Great Ones to function on transcendental planes of thought.

19 | Great Isz Chalice

The Great Isz Chalice became the cornerstone of the Choir, the elite delegation of the Healing Church. It was also the first Great Chalice brought back to the surface since the time of Byrgenwerth, and allowed the Choir to have audience with Ebrietas.

20 | Cosmic Eye Watcher Badge

Badge of a member of the Choir, elites of the Healing Church. The eye signifies the very cosmos. The Choir stumbled upon an epiphany, very suddenly and quite by accident. Here we stand, feet planted in the earth, but might the cosmos be very near us, only just above our heads?

21 | A Call Beyond

One of the secret rites of the Choir. Long ago, the Healing Church used phantasms to reach a lofty plane of darkness, but failed to make contact with the outer reaches of the cosmos. The rite failed to achieve its intended purpose, but instead created a small exploding star, now a powerful part of the Choir's arsenal. At times, failure is the mother of invention.

22 | Yahar'gul Black Garb

Thick black pullover worn by hunters of the Unseen Village. The hunters of Yahar'gul answer to the village's founders, the School of Mensis. Hunters in name only, these kidnappers blend into the night wearing this attire. Designed primarily to defend from physical attacks, the binding of thick rope serves both to protect its wearer, and restrain his foes.

23 | Harrowed Garb

Certain Church hunters obfuscate their identities and slip into the nooks and crannies of the city. This is the garb that allows these harrowed individuals to go unnoticed. These hunters are keen to early signs of the scourge, serving as a first line of defence against its outbreak. Or perhaps, when the time is ripe, they find signs of the scourge where there are none. It just goes to show, the corner beggar is not always who he seems.

24 | Adella Dialogue

I was seized on the street by a hulking brute in the Cathedral Ward and locked up here. There were many others, but they've been taken away... And I've heard moans, echoing in the distance, ever since...

25 | Lore Note

Nightmarish rituals crave a newborn. Find one, and silence its harrowing cry.

26 | Lore Note

The spider hides all manner of rituals, certain to reveal nothing, for true enlightenment need not be shared.

27 | Micolash Dialogue

Ahh, Kos, or some say Kosm... Do you hear our prayers? As you once did for the vacuous Rom, Grant us eyes, grant us eyes.

28 | Fish Villager Dialogue

Mother is dead, her baby, taken.

29 | Kos Parasite

When the carcass of Kos washed up on the coast, its insides were teeming with tiny parasites, unlike any found in humans. This atypical weapon can only be clasped tight and swung, but a Kos Parasite is said to stimulate phantasms inhabiting a lumenwood.

30 | Third Umbilical Cord

A great relic, also known as the Cord of the Eye. Every infant Great One has this precursor to the umbilical cord. Every Great One loses its child, and then yearns for a surrogate. This Cord granted Mensis audience with Mergo, but resulted in the stillbirth of their brains. Use to gain Insight and, so they say, eyes on the inside, although no one remembers what that truly entails.

31 | Mergo's Wet Nurse

32 | Moon Rune

A secret symbol left by Caryll, runesmith of Byrgenwerth. A transcription of "Moon," as spoken by the Great Ones inhabiting the nightmare. The Great Ones that inhabit the nightmare are sympathetic in spirit, and often answer when called upon.

33 | Living String

Special material used in a Holy Chalice ritual. The immense brain that Mensis retrieved from the nightmare was indeed lined with eyes on the inside, but they were of an evil sort, and the brain itself was terribly rotten. But even still, it was a legitimate Great One, and left a relic. A living relic, at that, which is a precious thing indeed.

34 | Formless Oedon Rune

A secret symbol left by Caryll, runesmith of Byrgenwerth. The Great One Oedon, lacking forms, exists only in voice, and is symbolized by this rune. Human or no, the oozing blood is a medium of the highest grade, and the essence of the formless Great One, Oedon. Both Oedon, and his inadvertent worshippers, surreptitiously seek the precious blood.

35 | The One Reborn

36 | Sword Hunter Badge

One of the badges crafted by the Healing Church. The silver sword is a symbol of a Church hunter. Ludwig was the first of many Healing Church hunters to come, many of whom were clerics. As it was, clerics transformed into the most hideous beasts.

37 | Ludwig's Holy Blade

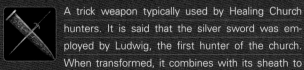

A trick weapon typically used by Healing Church hunters. It is said that the silver sword was employed by Ludwig, the first hunter of the church. When transformed, it combines with its sheath to form a greatsword. The Healing Church workshop began with Ludwig, and departed from old Gehrman's techniques to provide hunters with the means to hunt more terrifying beasts, and perhaps things still worse.

38 | Ludwig Dialogue

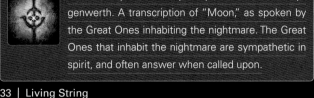

Good hunter, have you seen the thread of light? "Just a hair, a fleeting thing, yet I clung to it, steeped as I was in the stench of blood and beasts." "I never wanted to know what it really was. Really, I didn't."

39 | Holy Moonlight Sword

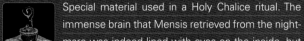

An arcane sword discovered long ago by Ludwig. When blue moonlight dances around the sword, and it channels the abyssal cosmos, its great blade will hurl a shadowy lightwave. The Holy Moonlight Sword is synonymous with Ludwig, the Holy Blade, but few have ever set eyes on the great blade, and whatever guidance it has to offer, it seems to be of a very private, elusive sort.

40 | Ludwig

41 | Radiant Sword Hunter Badge

One of the badges crafted by the Healing Church. The radiant sword indicates the heirs to the will of Ludwig. These hunters, also known as Holy Blades, are what remains of an ancient line of heroes that date back to a very early age of honor and chivalry.

42 | Simon's Bowblade

Choice weapon of Simon, one of the first Healing Church hunters. Simon despised firearms, and so the Church workshop had this specially fashioned to his liking. The large curved blade serves as a bow when transformed. But aside from a few close friends, Simon was scoffed at for his choice of arms, for who would dare face the beasts with a measly bow?

43 | Tonitrus

A unique trick weapon contrived by Archibald, the infamous eccentric of the Healing Church workshop. Striking this peculiar iron morning star flail like a match generates the same blue sparks that blanket a darkbeast. Unfortunately, for reasons untold, the hunters of Archibald's time did not fully take to the device.

44 | Bolt Paper

Coarse paper that applies bolt to weapons when rubbed. Invented by Archibald, the infamous eccentric of the Healing Church workshop. Artificially recreates the blue sparks that are said to surround darkbeasts. Unlike the other strange weapons created by Archibald, this one was favored by many hunters, in particular those who had even once laid eyes on a darkbeast.

45 | Spark Hunter Badge

Badge crafted in secret by Archibald, the infamous eccentric of the Healing Church, for his friends. Archibald was fascinated by the blue sparks that emanate from the hides of the darkbeasts, and dedicated his life to its artificial reproduction, in a style of inquiry that, incidentally, closely followed the methodology of Byrgenwerth.

46 | Wheel Hunter Badge

Martyr Logarius led a band of Executioners, and this badge was crafted at their dedicated workshop. The wheel symbolizes righteous destiny. Their workshop was a secretive enclave of mystical beliefs and heady fanaticism which served as the backbone of the Executioners' unique brand of justice.

47 | Executioner Gauntlets

Gauntlets worn by the band of Executioners commanded by the martyr Logarius. The brass rivets are unique to the executioners, and reflect their adoration of hand-to-hand combat. As the great Logarius once said, "Acts of goodness are not always wise, and acts of evil are not always foolish, but regardless, we shall always strive to be good."

48 | Logarius Wheel

Weapon wielded by martyr Logarius' band of executioners. Used to slaughter the Vilebloods in Cainhurst. Bathed in pools of their blood, and forever steeped in their ire. Transform to release the power of the wheel and manifest their lingering rage in a show of utter brilliance.

49 | Executioner Garb

Attire worn by the band of executioners commanded by the martyr Logarius. Later became the basis for all Church attire, with its heavy draping of Holy Shawl. As the great Logarius once said, "Acts of goodness are not always wise, and acts of evil are not always foolish, but regardless, we shall always strive to be good."

50 | Alfred Dialogue

Once, a scholar betrayed his fellows at Byrgenwerth... ...and brought forbidden blood back with him to Cainhurst Castle. It was there that the first of the inhuman Vilebloods was born. The Vilebloods are fiendish creatures who threaten the purity of the Church's blood healing.

51 | Alfred Dialogue

In his time, Master Logarius led his executioners into Cainhurst Castle to cleanse it of the Vilebloods. But all did not go well, and Master Logarius became a blessed anchor, guarding us from evil. ...Tragic, tragic times...

52 | Crown of Illusions

One of the precious secrets of Cainhurst. The old king's crown is said to reveal illusions, and expose a mirage that hides a secret. And so Logarius donned the crown of his own volition, determined to prevent a single soul from stumbling upon the vile secret. What visions did he see, sitting serenely upon his new throne?

53 | Brador's Testimony

The scalp of a horrible cleric beast, indicating that hunter Brador, a Healing Church assassin, had killed a compatriot. Afterward, he wore his ally's own scalp, and hid himself away, deep below in a cell. The Church provided him with a single, soundless bell of death, to ensure their secrets would be kept.

54 | Bloodletter

The demented hunter weapon brandished by Brador, the Healing Church assassin. The Bloodletter assumes its true and terrifying form after it draws upon blood from the inner reaches of one's body and soul. This is the only effective means of expelling tainted blood, or so Brador, isolated in his cell, continued to beleive.

55 | Blue Elixir

Dubious liquid medicine used in strange experiments conducted by high ministers of the Healing Church. A type of anesthetic that numbs the brain. Hunters, able to retain consciousness by force of will, make use of a secondary effect of the medicine, which dilutes their presence while standing still.

56 | Brain Fluid

In the early days of the Healing Church, the Great Ones were linked to the ocean, and so the cerebral patients would imbibe water, and listen for the howl of the sea. Brain fluid writhed inside the head, the initial makings of internal eyes.

The Hunters Lore

Gehrman was the First Hunter (1) and an acquaintance of Laurence (2) and Willem (3). He fought beasts with speed and agility, and his style became the basis for later hunters (4). His weapon is forged from siderite, a rare mineral which is said to have fallen from the heavens (1). The only other hunter known to use a siderite weapon is Eileen the Crow (5).

The first hunters were Gehrman's apprentices (6). These hunters were practitioners of the art of Quickening (7), and among them was the Lady Hunter Maria, who admired Gehrman greatly (6). Gehrman has a peculiar mania, and Maria was specifically unaware of this (6). Interestingly, the Doll's clothing is described as a product of borderline mania , and the Doll has a special dialogue when Maria is defeated by the player (9).

A precursor to an umbilical cord from an infant Great One led to the encounter with the pale moon (10). The pale moon called out to the hunters and created the Hunter's Dream as it sought a surrogate child (10). Hunters who dream need not fear death (11/12). Today, old Gehrman's purpose is to remain

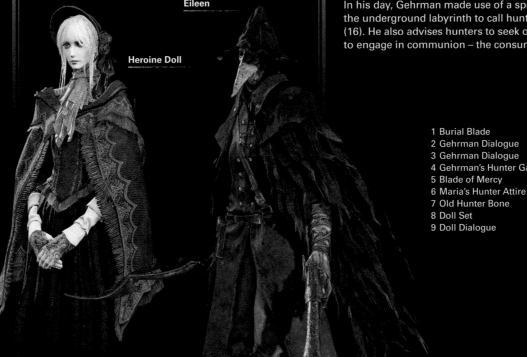

Gehrman

in the Hunter's Dream (13), where he is waiting for Laurence to accomplish some task (2). He seems unaware of Laurence's fate (14). Gehrman's fitful murmurs betray that he is not necessarily in the Dream by his own will (3).

Gehrman generally serves only as an adviser to hunters (13), but on some nights, he joins the hunt himself (15). He sees it as a dirge of farewell, and wishes only that his prey will not awaken to further nightmares (1).

In his day, Gehrman made use of a special bell discovered in the underground labyrinth to call hunters from other worlds (16). He also advises hunters to seek out the Holy Chalices and to engage in communion – the consumption of blood (17).

Eileen

Heroine Doll

1 Burial Blade	10 Third Umbilical Cord
2 Gehrman Dialogue	11 Eileen Dialogue
3 Gehrman Dialogue	12 Eileen Dialogue
4 Gehrman's Hunter Garb	13 Doll Dialogue
5 Blade of Mercy	14 Laurence's Skull
6 Maria's Hunter Attire	15 Gehrman Dialogue
7 Old Hunter Bone	16 Beckoning Bell
8 Doll Set	17 Gehrman Dialogue
9 Doll Dialogue	

Hunters sustained by the dream imbibe the blood of their victims (18). Hunters are healed and strengthened by blood (18), but it is also intoxicating (19). The hunters of hunters, such as Eileen, seek out and eliminate those who have become addled by blood (20). Hunters who go drunk with blood are said to be taken by the Nightmare, destined to hunt forever (21); the hunters of hunters seek to prevent this so that their former compatriots might find rest in a hunter's dream (22).

In the old days, hunters were much more common (23). Old Hunters tended to believe in superstitions, such as the idea that certain metals would ward off the blood of beasts (24) or that beast blood would creep up their right legs (25). One day, the hunters vanished from Yharnam (26). All that remained were rumors of the hunters' sin; drunk with blood they all passed on to the Nightmare (26).

That's the legend, at least. In truth, some of the Old Hunters, such as Djura, still stalk the streets of Yharnam. Djura was a hunter who had contact with the Powder Kegs (27). It is said that the state of Old Yharnam drove him to renounce his hunter's vows (27); in reality, he understood that the beasts of Yharnam are actually humans taken by the scourge (28).

A sickness known as "ashen blood" ravaged Old Yharnam, and that epidemic triggered the spread of the beastly scourge (29). A collapsed, mushy pupil is an indicator of the onset of the scourge (21). Djura and his companions have seen their share of tragedy; the youngest of his three companions was taken by the Nightmare (30), while another still remains faithfully by his side in Old Yharnam to help him protect the beastly residents.

Lady Maria

Djura

The Hunters | Connections

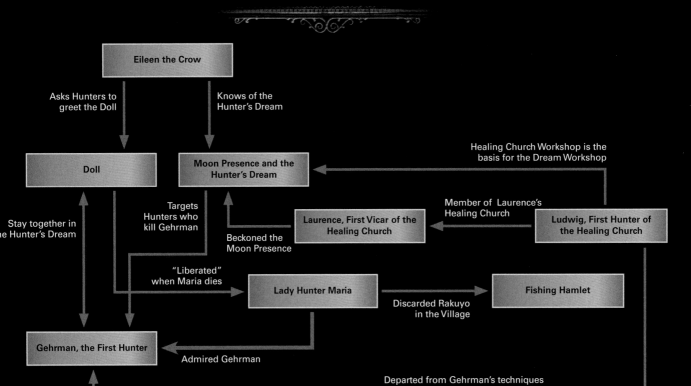

Eileen the Crow

Asks Hunters to greet the Doll

Knows of the Hunter's Dream

Doll

Moon Presence and the Hunter's Dream

Healing Church Workshop is the basis for the Dream Workshop

Stay together in the Hunter's Dream

Targets Hunters who kill Gehrman

Beckoned the Moon Presence

Laurence, First Vicar of the Healing Church

Member of Laurence's Healing Church

Ludwig, First Hunter of the Healing Church

"Liberated" when Maria dies

Lady Hunter Maria

Discarded Rakuyo in the Village

Fishing Hamlet

Gehrman, the First Hunter

Admired Gehrman

Departed from Gehrman's techniques

Gehrman tells new hunters tales of Ludwig and the Healing Church Workshop (31). The techniques of hunters began at that point to deviate from Gehrman's original style (32). Ludwig was the first Healing Church hunter (32), and recruited Yharnamites to serve as hunters (33). There have been numerous Healing Church hunters through the years, many of them clerics – unfortunately, clerics transform into the most hideous beasts (34). The Healing Church workshop's deviations from Gehrman's methods were made to help hunters hunt such beasts (35).

The Hunters Lore | References

1 | Burial Blade

Trick weapon wielded by Gehrman, the first hunter. A masterpiece that defined the entire array of weapons crafted at the workshop. Its blade is forged with siderite, said to have fallen from the heavens. Gehrman surely saw the hunt as a dirge of farewell, wishing only that his prey might rest in peace, never again to awaken to another harrowing nightmare.

2 | Gehrman Dialogue

Oh, Laurence... what's taking you so long... I've grown too old for this, of little use now, I'm afraid...

3 | Gehrman Dialogue

...Oh, Laurence... Master Willem... Somebody, help me... Unshackle me, please, anybody...

4 | Gehrman's Hunter Garb

Hunter attire of Gehrman, the first hunter. Created before the workshop existed by making adjustments to everyday clothing, and later became the basis for all hunter's garb. The hunter's emphasis on engaging beasts with speed, and therefore of selecting lightweight attire, no doubt traces back to Gehrman's own combat style.

5 | Blade of Mercy

A special trick weapon passed down among hunters of hunters. One of the oldest weapons of the workshop. Splits into two when activated. The weapon's warped blades are forged with siderite, a rare mineral of the heavens. Most effective in swift attacks, such as after quick-stepping.

6 | Maria's Hunter Attire

Among the first hunters, all students of Gehrman, was the lady hunter Maria. This was her hunter's garb, crafted in Cainhurst. Maria is distantly related to the undead queen, but had great admiration for Gehrman, unaware of his curious mania.

7 | Old Hunter Bone

The bone of an old hunter whose name is lost. It is said that he was an apprentice to old Gehrman, and a practitioner of the art of Quickening, a technique particular to the first hunters. It is most appropriate that hunters, carriers of the torch who are sustained by the dream, would tease an old art from his remains.

8 | Doll Set

Discarded doll clothing, likely a spare for dress-up. A deep love for the doll can be surmised by the fine craftsmanship of this article, and the care with which it was kept. It borderlines on mania, and exudes a slight warmth.

9 | Doll Dialogue

Good hunter. This may sound strange, but... Have I somehow changed? Moments ago, from some place, perhaps deep within, I sensed a liberation from heavy shackles. Not that I would know... How passing strange...

10 | Third Umbilical Cord

A great relic, also known as the Cord of the Eye. Every infant Great One has this precursor to the umbilical cord. Every Great One loses its child, and then yearns for a surrogate. The Third Umbilical Cord precipitated the encounter with the pale moon, which beckoned the hunters and conceived the Hunter's Dream. Use to gain Insight and, so they say, eyes on the inside, although no one remembers what that truly entails.

11 | Eileen Dialogue

You still dream, I should think?

12 | Eileen Dialogue

No more dreams for me. This is my last chance. What a fool I am. I'll have to tread carefully.

13 | Doll Dialogue

Did you speak with Gehrman? He was a hunter long, long ago, but now serves only to advise them. He is obscure, unseen in the dreaming world. Still, he stays here, in this dream... ...such is his purpose...

14 | Laurence's Skull

Skull of Laurence, first vicar of the Healing Church. In reality he became the first cleric beast, and his human skull only exists within the Nightmare. The skull is a symbol of Laurence's past, and what he failed to protect. He is destined to seek his skull, but even if he found it, it could never restore his memories.

15 | Gehrman Dialogue

It always comes down to the hunters' helper to clean up after these sorts of messes. Tonight, Gehrman joins the hunt...

16 | Beckoning Bell

Great old bell discovered in the underground labyrinth. Its ring resonates across worlds, and the first hunter used it as a special signal to call hunters from other worlds to cross the gap and cooperate. A human must use Insight to ring this uncanny bell, but the benefits of cross-world cooperation are many.

17 | Gehrman Dialogue

If the beasts loom large, and threaten to crush your spirits, seek a Holy Chalice. As every hunter before you has. A Holy Chalice will reveal the tomb of the gods, ...where hunters partake in communion...

18 | Coldblood Dew

Droplet of coldblood containing Blood Echoes. Use to gain Blood Echoes. Hunters sustained by the dream gain strength from Blood Echoes. They imbibe the blood with thoughts of reverence, indeed gratitude, for their victims.

19 | Pungent Blood Cocktail

Mature blood cocktail that releases a pungent odor when thrown that attracts blood-thirsty beasts. A precious tool in sadly short supply. In Yharnam, they produce more blood than alcohol, as the former is the more intoxicating.

20 | Crow Hunter Badge

Badge of a Hunter of Hunters, who hunts those who have become addled with blood. The badge of the Hunter of Hunters is quietly passed down from generation to generation, usually to an outsider from the hinterlands. To be entrusted with this cursed badge, one must be strong, resilient to the seduction of blood, and gracious when taking a comrade's life.

21 | Eye of a Blood-drunk Hunter

The eye of a blood-drunk hunter. Its pupil is collapsed and turned to mush, indicating the onset of the scourge of the beasts. A hunter who goes drunk with blood is said to be taken by the Nightmare, destined to wander forever, engaged in an endless hunt. It is a fate that no hunter can escape.

22 | Crowfeather Garb

Attire worn by Eileen the Crow, Hunter of Hunters, known in particular for her crowfeather cape. Hunters of Hunters dress as crows to suggest sky burial. The first Hunter of Hunters came from a foreign land, and gave the dead a virtuous native funeral ritual, rather than impose a blasphemous Yharnam burial service upon them, with the hope that former compatriots might be returned to the skies, and find rest in a hunter's dream.

23 | Old Hunter Cap

Old hunter cap with a wide brim that hides their sharp gaze. In the old days, when hunters were ten a penny, this was part of their standard garb.

24 | Old Hunter Gloves

Old hunter gauntlets made of brass to protect their weapon-bearing hands. At the time, some hunters believed that certain metals would ward off beast blood. On a night of the hunt, it is no wonder that some resort to superstition.

25 | Old Hunter Trousers

Old hunter trousers that protected countless hunters from the beasts in an older age. A widespread belief of the period was that "beast blood crept up the right leg," and this led to the double-wrapped belt.

26 | Old Hunter Garb

Old hunter garb. One day, the hunters disappeared, and Yharnamites began to whisper of the hunters' sin. Drunk with blood, chasing after beasts, they would pass on to the Nightmare, every last one of them.

27 | Grey Wolf Cap

Attire of the retired hunter Djura. This worn wolf cap was his trademark. Djura is known through his contact with the Powder Kegs, the heretics of the workshop. He is said to have been both uncommonly kind and dreadfully foolish. Djura felt defeated by the state of Old Yharnam, and renounced his hunter's vows.

28 | Djura Dialogue

I no longer dream, but I was once a hunter, too. There's nothing more horrific than a hunt. In case you've failed to realize... The things you hunt, they're not beasts. They're people. One day, you will see...

29 | Antidote

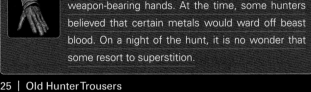

Small medicinal tablets that counteract poison. Used to treat ashen blood, the baffling sickness that ravaged Old Yharnam long ago. These tablets only provide short-term relief. The ashen blood ailment eventually triggered the spread of the beastly scourge.

30 | Gatling Gun

This is a highly-customized, portable version of the stationary gatling gun operated by the old hunter Djura in Old Yharnam. It was the weapon of choice of the youngest of Djura's three companions. The Gatling Gun boasts exceptional rapid-firing functionality, but is considered a cumbersome weapon, due to its excessive weight and insatiable consumption of Quicksilver Bullets. NOTE: This weapon is found in the Hunter's Nightmare...

31 | Gehrman Dialogue

The Healing Church, and the Blood Ministers who belong to it... Were once guardians of the hunters, in the times of the hunter... Ludwig.

32 | Ludwig's Holy Blade

A trick weapon typically used by Healing Church hunters. It is said that the silver sword was employed by Ludwig, the first hunter of the church. When transformed, it combines with its sheath to form a greatsword. The Healing Church workshop began with Ludwig, and departed from old Gehrman's techniques to provide hunters with the means to hunt more terrifying beasts, and perhaps things still worse.

33 | Yharnam Hunter Garb

Ludwig, the first hunter of the Healing Church, once recruited Yharnamites to serve as hunters. This hunter's attire was made for new recruits, and has excellent straightforward defense. But not nearly enough to allow an ordinary man to stand any real chance against beasts.

34 | Sword Hunter Badge

One of the badges crafted by the Healing Church. The silver sword is a symbol of a Church hunter. Ludwig was the first of many Healing Church hunters to come, many of whom were clerics. As it was, clerics transformed into the most hideous beasts.

35 | Ludwig's Rifle

A rifle typically used by Healing Church hunters. It is said that this rifle was employed by Ludwig, the first hunter of the Church. Its long, heavy barrel makes up in range for what it lacks in reload speed. The Healing Church workshop began with Ludwig, and departed from old Gehrman's techniques to provide hunters with the means to hunt more terrifying beasts, and perhaps thing still worse.

Yharnamites Lore

Modern day Yharnam is a city of madness (1); it is said to be a cursed city (2) of intoxicating blood (3) and wild beasts. The populace tends to be quite intolerant of outsiders (4/5/6/7). The "pebble"-filled streets (8) are home to some very odd characters indeed, not the least of whom is Father Gascoigne.

Gascoigne is a hunter who wears a dingy Holy Shawl (9) and a wide-brimmed hat; he was once a member of the Healing Church, but he eventually parted ways with the church (for reasons unknown) (9). In the past, Gascoigne was a partner to Old Hunter Henryk (10). He is also a husband to Viola (11/12) and the father of two young girls (12/13). He acts as an executioner to the beasts of Yharnam (14).

Father Gascoigne's story is a tragic tale. His wife's corpse can be found at Oedon Tomb near where Gascoigne is chopping up corpses (6). Gascoigne's garments are tainted by a pungent beastly stench that eats away at him (16). The blood has gotten to him (17). He has been struggling to distinguish beasts from humans (18/19), though a special song that he shared with his wife can help him remember (20). As Eileen observes, though, he is falling apart (21), and he eventually becomes a beast himself. Perhaps awareness of his own inner beast is what led him to see normal humans as beasts.

But his story grows darker still. With both he and his wife dead, the hunters of Yharnam are left with a very difficult choice regarding his orphaned daughters. Informing the younger daughter of her mother's death drives her into despair, but withholding that information and instructing her to seek shelter at Oedon Chapel results in her gory demise (22). Hunters who send her to Iosefka's Clinic leave her at the mercy of the fake doctor's devious experiments (23). If the hunters ignore her plight, she eventually wanders off into the night alone.

Later in the night, her older sister professes to be searching for her (13). If a hunter returns the younger sister's ribbon as proof of her demise (24), the older sister at first seems distraught but can already be heard admiring the ribbon as the hunter walks away (25). The blood moon has a powerful effect on humans; it blurs the very line between man and beast (26). Madness abounds in the late hours of the hunt.

Gascoigne

Gascoigne's former partner, Old Hunter Henryk, is still stalking the streets of Yharnam, as well. Eileen warns hunters to stay away from Henryk, as he is one of the blood-drunk hunters that she is tracking (27). Henryk's partnership with Father Gascoigne helped him to survive and lead a long life (10), but he has outlived both Gascoigne and Viola.

In Oedon Chapel, another odd character can be found — the Chapel Samaritan. The Chapel Samaritan has a very odd and suspicious way of speaking but really wants to help people and make friends (28/29). The incense of Oedon Chapel wards off beasts, though it also masks the smell of approaching hunters (30/31). This incense allows for Oedon Chapel to functions as a sanctuary for Yharnam's refugees.

Arianna, lady of the night, is one such refugee. She finds herself running low on incense before the night is over, and asks hunters to find a safe place for her (32). In Oedon Chapel, she offers her blood as thanks (33). Her blood is very similar to blood forbidden by the old Healing Church (34), and her clothing is reminiscent of the nobles of Cainhurst (35). Arianna is distrusted by some other Yharnamites (36). Her blood does seem to be quite special; it is possible for her to give birth to a kin baby under the blood moon (37).

Adella, nun of the Healing Church, is another refugee that can be directed to take shelter in Oedon Chapel. Pious lady that she is, she respects members of the Healing Church (38/39). She appears to have quite a jealous streak (40), however, as she will kill Arianna if hunters prefer Arianna's blood to her own (41).

Arianna, Adella, and the other refugees of Yharnam can alternatively take refuge in Iosefka's clinic. There are however, two different people claiming to be "Iosefka." In the afternoon, the real Iosefka is in her clinic and will provide hunters with carefully refined blood (42/43). After the hunt has reached Cathedral Ward, though, she is replaced by an imposter. In addition to having different voices, the two can be distinguished by their armaments; the original Iosefka does not carry weapons, but the fake does (44).

The fake Iosefka is performing human experiments; she seems to believe that she is successfully preventing humans from falling to the beastly scourge (45/46). She claims that humans must find a way to surpass our own stupidity (47). This is quite similar to the desire of Micolash, who wishes for eyes from Kos to be cleansed of beastly idiocy (48). Indeed, as her experiments progress, it seems that she does begin to develop inner eyes (49/50). When she dies, she leaves a Cord of the Eye, as well.

Old Hunter Henryk   Impostor Iosefka

Arianna

1 Black Church Garb	26 Lore Note
2 Gilbert Dialogue	27 Eileen Dialogue
3 Pungent Blood Cocktail	28 Chapel Samaritan Dialogue
4 Gilbert Dialogue	29 Chapel Samaritan Dialogue
5 Gilbert Dialogue	30 Chapel Samaritan Dialogue
6 Yharnamite Dialogue	31 Chapel Samaritan Dialogue
7 Constable Garb	32 Arianna Dialogue
8 Pebble	33 Arianna Dialogue
9 Gascoigne's Garb	34 Blood of Arianna
10 Henryk's Hunter Garb	35 Noble Dress
11 Red Jewelled Brooch	36 Bigoted Man Dialogue
12 Tiny Music Box	37 Arianna Baby
13 Older Sister Dialogue	38 Adella Dialogue
14 Hunter Axe	39 Adella Dialogue
15 Location of the	40 Adella Jealous
Red Jewelled Brooch	41 Arianna Dead
16 Gascoigne's Hat	42 Iosefka Dialogue
17 Gascoigne Dialogue	43 Iosefka's Blood Vial
18 Gascoigne Dialogue	44 Iosefka Hand Comparison
19 Gascoigne Dialogue	45 Iosefka Dialogue
20 Little Girl Dialogue	46 Iosefka Dialogue
21 Eileen Dialogue	47 Iosefka Dialogue
22 Red Messenger Ribbon	48 Micolash Dialogue
23 White Messenger Ribbon	49 Iosefka Dialogue
24 Older Sister Dialogue	50 Brain Fluid
25 Older Sister Dialogue	

Yharnamites Lore | References

1 | Black Church Garb

Attire of Healing Church hunters. Most Healing Church hunters are elementary doctors who understand the importance of early prevention of the scourge, achieved by disposing of victims, and even potential victims, before signs of sickness manifest themselves. Their black attire is synonymous with fear, and that peculiar Yharnam madness.

2 | Gilbert Dialogue

This town is cursed. Whatever your reasons might be, you should plan a swift exit. Whatever can be gained from this place, it will do more harm than good...

3 | Pungent Blood Cocktail

Mature blood cocktail that releases a pungent odor when thrown that attracts blood-thirsty beasts. A precious tool in sadly short supply. In Yharnam, they produce more blood than alcohol, as the former is the more intoxicating.

4 | Gilbert Dialogue

You must have had a fine time of it. Yharnam has a special way of treating guests.

5 | Gilbert Dialogue

Yharnamites don't share much with outsiders.

6 | Yharnamite Dialogue

Lousy offcomer. Who'd open their door on a night of the hunt! Away with you. Now!

7 | Constable Garb

Once upon a time, a troupe of foreign constables chased a beast all the way to Yharnam, and this is what they wore. The constables became victims of the beast, except for one survivor, who in turn devoured the creature whole, all by himself. This fable is a favorite among Yharnamites, who are partial to any stories of pompous, intolerant foreigners who suffer for their ignorance. It makes the blood taste that much sweeter.

8 | Pebble

Small pebbles found throughout Yharnam. Can be thrown at foes. Quite thrilling.

9 | Gascoigne's Garb

Hunter attire worn by Father Gascoigne. The dingy scarf is a Holy Shawl and symbol of the Healing Church, from which Gascoigne would eventually part ways. "Father" is a title used for clerics in a foreign land, and there is no such rank in the Healing Church.

10 | Henryk's Hunter Garb

Hunter's attire worn by Henryk, the old hunter. The taciturn old hunter Henryk was once partners with Father Gascoigne, and though they were a fierce and gallant duo, their partnership led to Henryk's tragically long life.

11 | Red Jewelled Brooch

A woman's bright-red brooch, engraved with the name Viola. Perhaps the jewel is a gift from a hunter.

12 | Tiny Music Box

A small music box received from a young Yharnam girl. Plays a song shared by her mother and father. Inside the lid is a small scrap of paper, perhaps an old message. Two names can be made out, however faintly. Viola and Gascoigne.

13 | Older Sister Dialogue

Oh, you haven't by any chance... seen my little sister, have you? I told her to look after the house, but she's run off somewhere. She's still quite small, and wears a big white ribbon. Have you seen her out there anywhere?

14 | Hunter Axe

One of the trick weapons of the workshop, commonly used on the hunt. No matter their pasts, beasts are no more than beasts. Some choose this axe to play the part of executioner.

15 | Location of the Red Jewelled Brooch

16 | Gascoigne's Hat

Hunter attire worn by Father Gascoigne. Similar to hunter garb created at the workshop, only these are tainted by a pungent beastly stench that eats away at Gascoigne. "Father" is a title used for clerics in a foreign land, and there is no such rank in the Healing Church.

17 | Gascoigne Dialogue

The sweet blood, oh, it sings to me. It's enough to make a man sick...

18 | Gascoigne Dialogue

...Beasts all over the shop... ...You'll be one of them, sooner or later...

19 | Gascoigne Dialogue

Too proud to show your true face, eh?

20 | Little Girl Dialogue

Oh, I mustn't forget. If you find my mum, give her this music box. ...It plays one of daddy's favorite songs. And when daddy forgets us we play it for him so he remembers. Mum's so silly, running off without it!

21 | Eileen Dialogue

You must've killed Gascoigne as well, then? He was falling apart, I'm sure it had to be done. But try to keep your hands clean.

22 | Red Messenger Ribbon

Red ribbon that messengers are oddly fond of. The thick, pungent red was drawn from the organs of some unfortunate victim. A strange choice indeed, but perhaps for the messengers wearing this accessory constitutes a form of mourning.

23 | White Messenger Ribbon

White ribbon that messengers are oddly fond of. A ribbon made of fine lace that shines remarkably, more suited to pretty young girls than silly old messengers.

24 | Older Sister Dialogue

Oh, how did this happen... Why would she ever go outside?

25 | Older Sister Dialogue

What a perfect ribbon... And now it's mine... I can't wait to try it on...

26 | Lore Note

When the red moon hangs low, the line between man and beast is blurred. And when the Great Ones descend, a womb will be blessed with child.

27 | Eileen Dialogue

Henryk, an old hunter, has gone mad. And he's my mark.. Don't go near the tomb below Oedon Chapel in the Cathedral Ward. I have business there first...

28 | Chapel Samaritan Dialogue

When the night of the hunt passes, s'pose, we could be friends, maybe? Now, I know I hardly deserve it, but... Well, I had to just, ask, you know?

29 | Chapel Samaritan Dialogue

I just wanted to help... people...

30 | Chapel Samaritan Dialogue

...Hmm? Oh... you must be... a hunter. Very sorry, the incense must've masked your scent.

31 | Chapel Samaritan Dialogue

But if you spot anyone with their wits about 'em... Tell 'em about this here Oedon Chapel. They'll be safe here. The incense wards off the beasts.

32 | Arianna Dialogue

Oh, thank goodness. You're a hunter, right? Might you know of a safe place? The night is long, and I've very little of the incense left...

33 | Arianna Dialogue

I'd like to tender my thanks, but I haven't much to offer... All I can give is my blood. But... would you even take a whore's blood?

34 | Blood of Arianna

Blood taken from Arianna, Cathedral Ward woman of pleasure. The sweet blood of Arianna restores HP, and temporarily speeds stamina recovery. A member of the old Healing Church would know that her blood is similar indeed, to precisely what was once forbidden.

35 | Noble Dress

A finely tailored bordeaux dress. Worn by the nobles of the old bloodline that traces back to the forsaken Castle Cainhurst.

36 | Bigoted Man Dialogue

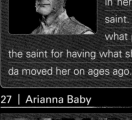

Beware the lady of the night. I can see it in her eyes. She deeply resents the young saint. She hears people whisper. She knows what people think of her. Yes, she despises the saint for having what she doesn't. Bloody wench, they shoulda moved her on ages ago.

27 | Arianna Baby

38 | Adella Dialogue

Ahh, by your garb... the Healing Church... You've come to save me... Ahh! Thank you, dear saint!

39 | Adella Dialogue

The town is in disarray, but there are still people here. Together, we await the help of the Healing Church.

40 | Adella Jealous

41 | Arianna Dead

42 | Iosefka Dialogue

I'll do what I can, of course. Perhaps this will help you, if only in some small way. This night is long, but morning always comes.

43 | Iosefka's Blood Vial

Blood vial acquired from Iosefka's clinic. This refined blood, highly invigorating, restores a larger amount of HP. The product of a slow and careful refinement process, this rare blood vial appears to be a clinic original.

44 | Iosefka Hand Comparison

45 | Iosefka Dialogue

The treatment is going well, stabilized, for the most part. Fascinating, really...

46 | Iosefka Dialogue

Things need not change... You'll do the rescuing, and I'll do the saving...

47 | Iosefka Dialogue

There aren't many humans left, I know, but find me every last one you can. We must find a way. To surpass our own stupidity. You're one of the bright ones. Don't you see how much this means?

48 | Micolash Dialogue

Grant us eyes, grant us eyes. Plant eyes on our brains, to cleanse our beastly idiocy.

49 | Iosefka Dialogue

God, I'm nauseous... Have you felt this? It's progressing, I can see things... I knew it, I'm different. I'm no beast... I... Oh... God, it feels awful... but, it proves that I'm chosen... Don't you see? How they writhe, writhe inside my head... It's... rather... rapturous...

50 | Brain Fluid

In the early days of the Healing Church, the Great Ones were linked to the ocean, and so the cerebral patients would imbibe water, and listen for the howl of the sea. Brain fluid writhed inside the head, the initial makings of internal eyes.

Drained of Blood
An Interview with Hidetaka Miyazaki

The following pages present an interview with Bloodborne's director, Hidetaka Miyazaki alongside carefully selected pieces of the game's concept artwork.

Future Press: First off, congratulations on your new role as company president.

Mr. Miyazaki: Well, thank you very much.

In relation to that, would you say that assuming the role of president has reduced the amount of time you're directly involved with game design? Most people would assume that's the case. How would you say your time is divided now between company-president duties and game development duties?

Well, to be honest, I'm probably shirking a lot of my presidential duties, or you could say that everyone around me is humoring me on that front (laughs). In terms of percentages, though, I'd say it's around 20 per cent. Out of your typical five-day workweek, I'd need to devote a little over a day that kind of work. Still, it's not as if I was able to devote 100 per cent of my time to directorial duties even before. Once I knew that we'd build the current company structure, I had the director-level staff plan a new production workflow, one that helps support my work when I'm running short on time, so I wouldn't say that I'm devoting less time to game design now.

Regarding the process of creating Bloodborne, could you tell us what the development process had in common with, for example, Demon's Souls or Dark Souls, or how it's been different?

I wouldn't say it's been that different, but there are two points in particular that come to mind. The first one, which I touched on a little bit just now, is that the director-level staff in the company are now all participating in a unified production workflow. As for what I'm leaving to them in particular, one thing we need from the start of the project is the ability to express our concepts and aims in words. When I'm doing all of that by myself, I tend to verbalize the bare minimum necessary...or, to put it in a bad way, I tended to procrastinate a lot (laughs). I couldn't get away with that here. I think a lot of good came out of that arrangement. Verbalizing it and bringing it out to other people made me notice a lot I wouldn't have otherwise.

The chalice dungeons, one of the biggest elements we added to this game, are something that came out precisely because I got other people involved in the operation. The other point is the environment that the title and its production team were working within. This marked a major change. With Demon's Souls, of course – and while we worked on Dark Souls, too – the expectations around us were still pretty low. All around us, there was always the idea that "there's no way that something like this will sell."

That's no longer the case with Bloodborne, so it's become notably easier to make. We're feeling more pressure at the same time, but even with that, I think it's the kind of environment that makes a game developer happy. We really owe a lot to the gamers who gave so much praise to our previous titles. It's all thanks to them.

As you worked on Demon's Souls and Dark Souls, was there anything you envisioned for the game but weren't able to make happen? Were you able to make any of those things happen in Bloodborne based on your past experience?

There are a lot of things, both big and small. If I were to bring up a few of these easier-to-understand details... I could bring up how armor parameters are now based on percentages, or how the effects of items are now based on giving bonuses to your stats.

One problem we had with Demon's Souls was that once you reached a high enough level, the whole idea of armor began to lose meaning to some extent. In Demon's Souls, armor parameters were based on static values that you weren't able to power up at all. As players grew stronger, the percentage of their total defensive ability derived from armor grew smaller and smaller. The importance of your armor equipment declined gradually as time went on, and eventually, once you were high-level enough, armor was little more than decoration. You'd start thinking "This isn't very different from going around naked."

So, in order to fix that, we implemented an armor upgrade system in Dark Souls. We had it so you could boost your armor's stats, ensuring that even as your character got stronger, the percentage of their defense governed by armor wouldn't go down, ensuring that it remained important. I think this did have at least some effect, but there were some problems with the formula we used, and it was an extremely difficult thing to fine-tune. We only had so many resources we could devote to the balancing process, so it wound up being a bit of a problem.

So we considered those experiences and based Bloodborne's armor on percentage reductions. As the player grows, the percentage that armor plays in your character's overall defense doesn't go down, armor remains an important aspect of the game, and it was much easier for us to fine-tune as well. Your inventory of items works much the same way. For items like Molotov Cocktails which had a static attack stat, you'd rely on them a great deal at first; they'd help give you another option during battle. By the endgame, though, they wouldn't be much use at all, and that's a problem we wanted to tackle.

An easy-to-understand example of this an item like Throwing Knives, I think. Items are one of the things that contribute to the role-playing experience, so we figured it'd be more fun if the game offered enough leeway that you could do things like create a character who relied on Throwing Knives for their offense. For Bloodborne, taking recovery items – which are pretty much essential to the game – and making them their own category makes it easier, I think, for players to express more personality with the items they use. It's nothing flashy, maybe, but it's one element that I hope turns out well.

Making these changes must require a fine-tuning process, acquiring an idea that this or that change is the right decision to make. How do you decide what way to adjust the game's balance? Do you have people test the game and make adjustments based on their reactions?

Good question. For this game, I participated in the balancing process for things like the basic feel of the game and its foundational elements. For other detailed aspects beyond that, especially when it comes to competitive multiplayer and post-ending repeat play, my strategy was to leave that to the balance team. Either way, though, I keep a close eye on our test-play runs and our feedback.

For the former in particular, to put it in an extreme way, if it's not any fun to play, I think that immediately discounts it, and that applies no matter what your concept or your aim is. I remember devoting a pretty long time to repeated test-play sessions, even asking SCE to get involved. However, that doesn't mean we're simply accepting

all the feedback we receive at face value. We focus on aspects that make players feel stressed out, out of place, or bored. For that kind of feedback, we listened carefully and went to see what we can do about it. That doesn't mean, though, that we necessarily implement the suggested solution as-is.

Once we know what needs improvement and figure out how to solve that, we try to find a solution that follows our concept and aims… One that adheres to the overall world-view of the game. If we didn't do that, the game would feel like this big patchwork mess.

We imagine you'll be releasing patches for the game after it goes on sale?

…That's a hard question to answer, but yes, I imagine so. I'm sure users would much prefer it if we released something free of imperfections from the get-go, and that's a perfectly reasonable expectation to have, but realistically speaking, I think patches are a necessary thing. To put it simply, it's important for balance, particularly with competitive multiplayer.

Will you gauge gamer reactions as you work on that?

Certainly, yes. I think our game-balance team will be working alongside SCE to handle whatever issues arise. Myself, I'll just try to be careful not to butt in too much on their work. I mean, it's not that I don't like watching gamers post gameplay videos or give their takes on the game, but at the same time, I don't think I could assess every single one of them, even if I tried.

So with that in mind, if I started insisting on changes based on this one video I happened to watch, that'll wind up twisting the balance in unexpected directions. The concept and aims I brought into this project are important to me, of course, but – as hard as it can be each time – I try to maintain a polite distance from the balancing process. Back when I worked on Armored Core, we usually had some free time after development wrapped up, I would often be the one directly fine-tuning the parameters and so on afterward. Going as far as that nowadays, though, would be pretty tough.

You mentioned the chalice dungeons earlier. Were those inspired by Rogue or NetHack or some of the other roguelikes you've played, or...

The idea for chalice dungeons actually came from kind of a different place. First, I think that with the sort of games we make, difficult games where the fun lies in the strategy you tackle them with, it's hard to beat the surprise factor you get when you play it for the first time.

That period when you're groping around for a way to get past new and unknown difficulties, then sharing your experience with everyone and chatting about this and that. That kind of fun naturally doesn't last forever, but we were wondering if there was some way we could keep that going, even if it was just in a virtual kind of way. That was what first led to the chalice dungeon idea.

As a result, the chalice dungeons are a completely separate system in the game. The way that each dungeon has different elements used to generate it in order to keep things fresh, and the way that you can keep a dungeon in place after generating it in order to share it with others, are both ideas that extend out from that original concept. I think there are a lot of role-playing games out there where the structure of the dungeon changes every time you play, but that approach doesn't let you share the dungeon and strategize about it with others.

For a game like this one, based on the idea of learning about your environment and taking advantage of it to overcome obstacles, making them sharable was a necessity. Working on the chalice

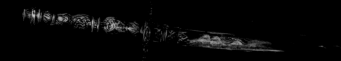

Some people say the Wooden Shield gets more and more important the more times you play through the game.

dungeons in this game, though, has kindled an interest in so-called procedural games in me; to see where that kind of approach might lead. Chalice dungeons are not strictly procedural in nature, though.

Adding chalice dungeons to this game, we feel, reduces the emphasis the game places on repeat play. Was this entirely in order to reduce the hurdles to getting through the game? Or did you want the dungeons to provide the core "replay value" to the game this time?

That's a bit of a surprise to hear, actually. Speaking for us, we had no intention to downplay post-ending repeat play. That concept is still front and center in this game. Bloodborne features multiple endings, and there are a couple of options if you want to see them all: play through the game again, or create a different character and start at level one. I think you're free to choose whatever approach you like, and that stance on our part hasn't changed since Demon's Souls. Repeated play in this game offers a lot of incentive, as well as a

lot of this series' trademark challenge and fun too, I think. This game has the Wooden Shield – the only shield in the game – and it doesn't seem like a very reliable piece of equipment, but some people say that it gets more and more important the more times you play through the game with it. The game's battle system relies on the idea that you're going to take some hits now and then, which is what I think leads to ideas like that. But, anyway, that just serves to demonstrate that we're in no way downplaying repeat runs through the game.

I think that, with Demon's Souls and Dark Souls, the games made a point of not revealing the full story to you, keeping it an enigma and leaving some of it to gamers' imaginations.

That's true, yes.

So the world of Bloodborne has the Hunter's Dream, and then several areas referred to as nightmares. There's a world that serves as the game's "reality" as well, right?

Ah, so you're asking if areas like Yharnam are meant to be reality? Well, that has some implications within the story. Yharnam at night, with the Hunters and all, truly is a nightmare-like world, but is it actually a nightmare? Or was it? That kind of thing. I think different gamers will have different interpretations of that, especially depending on which ending they reach. That's something deliberate on our part. This might be going off-topic a bit, but I like reading about how gamers interpret or think about the story and world of my games. So I don't want to rob them of that space for open interpretation. That, after all, is part of the fun I get to have after development (laughs). Still, this can often be a delicate thing, and I'm not exactly an expert at it either, so I can't be confident yet about whether it'll go well or not. Apologies in advance if it doesn't, then.

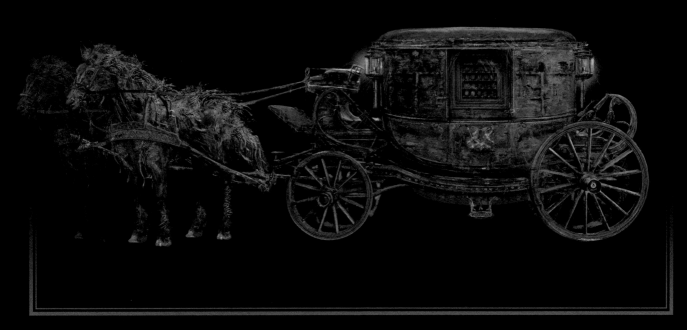

Whether it's Willem or the Choir or the School of Mensis, each has a certain background philosophy that drives them.

We think creating this story where you're working inside of dreams allows you a lot of creative freedom. You can do things you normally couldn't do in reality. But if you go too far with that, it may all just get too crazy and players wouldn't find it fun. How do you manage that kind of balance, between reality and dreams?

I think you're absolutely right. It'd be no fun if you could just do whatever you wanted in dreams. So in this game, the setting of Yharnam is essentially based in reality. It's so dark and dismal that it's entirely possible to interpret it as an actual nightmare in the end, but this isn't some kind of dream world where anything you can picture will come to life. I think that Bloodborne has aspects of both Gothic and Cthulhu-style horror, but it's the former that's depicted from the start and provides a guide for the game's visual feel. That's because Gothic horror is based more in the world of reality.

Of course, that doesn't mean it's real – it's a world of grotesque, scary horror. And here, you have a world like that which is gradually being eroded away by Cthulhu-style horror. That kind of image.

That's interesting... To get a bit more into the story, everyone at Future Press really liked the character Iosefka.

Oh, I'm glad to hear that. I think you're probably referring to the non-fake one, but the doctor at the clinic is a character that I really like, both the real one and the fake one. Some people in Yharnam are just completely beyond help, but she, or the two of them, are different.

Did she really transform into a beast? Or is there any hope of her being alive somewhere?

Hmm... To be honest with you, I don't think there's any chance of that for her. In the latter part of the game, if you go inside Iosefka's clinic, I think you'll run into something that suggests as much.

Did you have a reason for not creating a story path where she survived?

That... Well, what should I say? Let's just say that I tried to make one, but the rest of the studio was against it (laughs). That's not too removed from the truth, and it also has the side effect of keeping me safe from them!
Things like that happened during the development of Dark Souls, too. I remember that figuring out what to do with Sif, the Great Grey Wolf was a huge hassle. But regardless, and sorry to repeat myself, but I'm glad to hear that you like her. At the same time, I hope you'll provide just as much support to her fake as well!
That's a character I like a great deal too, but during development, I'd say to the team "She's one of the heroines of this game" and nobody would believe me, which left me a bit crestfallen. That's one of the underlying themes of the game... Or, you could say that I have a thing for the "scholarly investigator" character trope. You have Sage Freke in Demon's Souls and Master Willem in this game, and the fake Iosefka kind of descends from there. But, perhaps because I'm not that good at characterization, none of those characters ever seem to get very popular. It makes me feel a little sorry for the fake Iosefka, if she follows that same route.

Everyone at Future Press liked Willem, too.

Really? Well, that's great to hear.

You have these kind of trademark characters, investigators seeking the truth that stay from the path a little. People like Freke and Logan. Willem was also one of their favorite characters in this game, but in general, he doesn't speak to the player. Instead, all of his dialogue is in flashback form.

Yeah, Willem is certainly that way.

What was the reason for that?

Well, not to go back to my old crutch of being not so great at characterization, but if we had him speaking directly to you about all the supreme truths of the world or whatnot, it would've wound up really hackneyed. In a general way, I wanted the text we wrote to be as protective as possible of his dignity, his way of thinking. That was the approach I took. Really, whether it comes to Willem or the Choir or the School of Mensis, each of them has a certain background philosophy that drives them.
At the start of development, we had this forum where I'd write whatever came to mind on a daily basis and the rest of the team could browse through it. I'd write about things like the meaning of the mind's eye and its limitations upon people, or discussions about blood and beast transformations, and a really large amount of other meaningless stuff like that. Most of which really never made it into

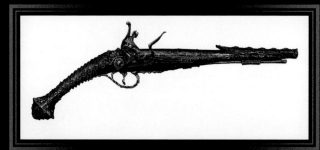

> Generally, every other game I make
> is inscrutable and interpretive, then the
> next one is easier to understand.

the game (laughs). Of course, the theme with this game was not to tell too much story, just like before, so I think our approach turned out well enough.

The doll was another character that really stoked our curiosities. Making a gesture toward her and seeing her react was something that struck us as oddly soothing.

Thank you very much.

Whose idea was that? It's a really good one.

I think that idea sprang out from my assorted ramblings on the forum, but it was [Masaru] Yamamura, one of the designers, who actually implemented it. That was a pretty busy period during development, I think, but he managed to make the time to do it and tell me "Hey, Miyazaki, check out this thing I made". I gave him the OK for that immediately, of course. That was all thanks to his efforts. Ever since the Demon's Souls days, I've always have problems coming up with heroines for our games, but I really like that doll, including her design. Hopefully the gamers who play it will think the same way.

One unique aspect of your games is that the truths behind them are rarely revealed in-game.

Well, that's not necessarily something I aim for, but I do try to leave room open for people's imaginations.

Right, there's enough room left open for people to let their imaginations run wild. In this game, the hero is motivated to set off following a hastily-written note telling you to "seek pale-

blood to transcend the hunt". The term "paleblood" is hardly used at all afterwards, though.**

Right. I had considered making that a little easier to understand... but we wound up going with that. I think there are two different ways you could interpret "paleblood" here. One is the color of the sky after you defeat the Vacuous Spider and the Mensis secret ritual is revealed. The sky there is a very pale blue, like a body drained of blood. I think there's also a message placed in Yahar'gul, Unseen Village that calls back to that. This is before the ritual is revealed, so when you're kidnapped and go to Yahar'gul, you don't know what it could mean yet. Then, after the ritual, you could look at it again and it'll dawn on you... That was my intention, anyway, but I have to admit, that's probably a bit tough to pick up on (laughs). But either way, this leads to the interpretation that "seek paleblood" refers to uncovering that ritual and putting a stop to it.

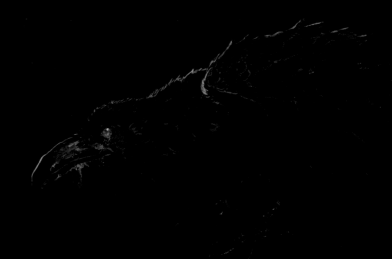

Was it not referring to the blood of the Great Ones?

Right, that's another interpretation. "Paleblood" is another name for the monster that comes from the moon under certain conditions. I think there's another message in the lecture building that hints at this, but I don't want to go into too much more detail here. This is someplace where I want to leave room open for the imagination – both my own and the imaginations of gamers.

The scene after you defeat Amelia also leaves a lot to the imagination…

That's meant to give you a look into the memory of Laurence, who appears in the cut-scene as well. His skull served as the start of the Healing Church itself, but it's taken the form of a twisted beast. There's a lot you can imagine from that.
Masaaki Yamagiwa, Producer at SCE JAPAN Studio: I sure can't (laughs).
Oh, that's all right. The gamers definitely will. I'm trusting on that. Of course, I'm sure we may get some criticism that gamers aren't given enough explanation, and I'll gladly accept that if so. But I think the fun of imagining things for yourself is one of the core tenets I follow. I like trying to focus on the fun of exploring this really dark place, then attempting to shine a light upon it. If that winds up simply being too hard to understand, then that's just another sign that I'm stretching it a bit, I think.
However, if you don't mind me going off topic a bit, but I kind of have a virtual pendulum in my mind. Generally, every other game I make is inscrutable and interpretive, then the next one is easier to understand. Armored Core 4 was my first game as a director. That was really hard to understand, but then my next one, For Answer, was a lot more approachable. Then Demon's Souls was inscrutable, Dark Souls more approachable, and now we have Bloodborne. Of course, generally speaking they're all on the hard-to-understand side, so I bet some would say "They're all the same!" to that (laughs). But Armored Core 4, the first one… That one's especially hard to follow.

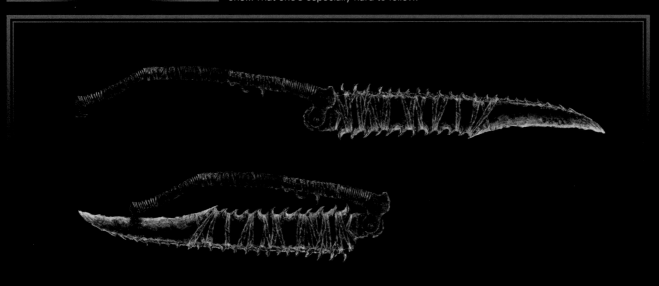

were involved in. **Have you ever created a dark world for a game, then see it have an impact on your personal life or those of your team?**

Mmm, I think I'm safe on that at least (laughs). But it's certainly true that this game is a lot drearier than my previous ones. I think it's because, whenever I'm crafting a fantasy story, I always wind up mixing in some of the other things I look up to.
It's these things that provide the creative energy I use, after all. The beauty of a heartfelt prayer, for example. That's the kind of thing that provides inspiration to me. So the things you see in Bloodborne – the dismalness, the lack of salvation, the insanity and so on – I suppose I look up to those, too, in my own way. There's something beautiful in there that I feel.

> It's these things that provide
>
> the creative energy I use...

Masaaki Yamagiwa: I had no idea what was going on at all. Oh, yeah, just put it out like that (laughs)! But it's true. A lot of the studio would have agreed with you back then. Someone posted up a story summary on this video site, and one of the team members from back then said "I finally understand the story after watching that. It's actually kind of interesting, isn't it?" And I still remember the very mixed feelings I had, hearing that. I mean, it shows there's such a thing as too much, you know?

You discussed shining a light on a dark story earlier. With this game, there's a scene with a baby crying inside of a nightmare. Some of our writers with children mentioned that scene really struck them emotionally. It projected a much more morbid image that we could've predicted from previous games you

This is meant partly as a joke, but that baby is Mergo, right? Could you talk a little about Mergo? We thought it'd be better if Gwynevere was the wet nurse instead…

I don't know where that came from (laughs). But in the world of Bloodborne, babies that are treated as "special" in one way or the other are offered as lures to the Great Ones. The Great Ones have all lost their children because of their positions, and as a result, they're attracted to these special babies. The babies are one way of calling them. This story setup was something I came up with pretty readily in my mind. When it comes to living creatures, the stronger or more advanced you are, the fewer offspring you produce in your life. Even with human beings, the birth rates in more advanced countries are lower, right? Looking back, I wonder if facts like that were at the root of the idea.

Here are some questions from the fans. What's your favorite weapon?

Weapon? That's a tough one, but one I'd give right off is the threaded cane. I think it's the hardest of your initial weapons to use, but I like the design, that little touch of class it has. That's why they're priced a little higher. We're secretly playing favorites (laughs).

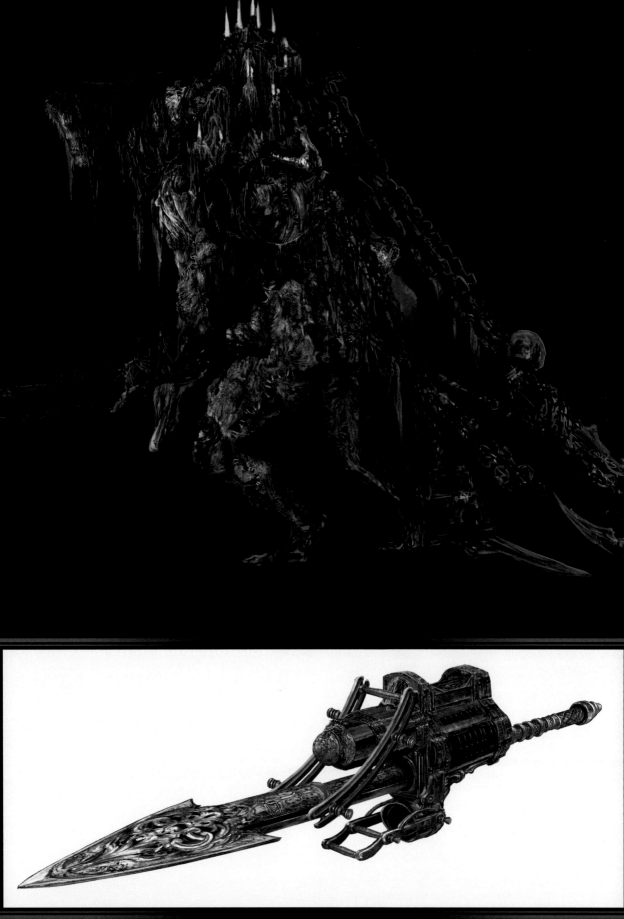

And your favorite boss?

That's another hard one. Hmm... Which would it be for this game? Maybe this is cheating a little, but if you ignore gameplay for a moment, it's Rom, the Vacuous Spider. From the design and atmosphere to that kind of plaintive air she has, I really like her. There are some oddly cute aspects to her moves and modeling.

Another question from the community. A lot of foes in this game are nightmare-like in appearance. Are any of them based off scary experiences that you yourself have ever had? Or more generally, where do you get ideas for their designs?

I, personally, have never had any really scary or paranormal experiences. I don't have any occult powers, and I definitely haven't seen any ghosts. Maybe that's part of why I "look up to" things like that, like I talked about before. I suppose I'm a little jealous of people who are scared of the dark. So the inspiration for ideas comes from somewhere a little different. For this game, for example, one theme was the "inner clash" going on within the beast-type foes.
The urge to transform into a beast is in conflict with the basic sense of humanity we all have. That humanity serves as a kind of shackle, keeping the transformation in its place. The stronger the shackle keeping that urge to transform in place is, the larger the recoil once that shackle is finally broken. The results cause you to transform into a larger creature, or a more twisted one. The struggle between these two urges is one concept here. You see that pretty clearly with the beast characters designed early on – especially the Cleric Beast, which serves as their icon of sorts. That connects with the idea that the cleric is really the most fearsome beast of them all.

Humanity serves as a kind of shackle, keeping the transformation in its place.

How did you think about and fine-tune the balance in the PvE and PvP fighting?

This has been the case since the Demon's Souls days, but the first thing I focus on is strategy. Whether or not a battle feels or good, or is fun, lies at the core of this. Things like PvP balance get considered once that core is in place. Of course, when I say that, I don't mean that we don't see PvP balance as important. I didn't do any PvP balancing work for this project, but this approach is something that I think is shared among the entire balancing team.

The health-regain system reminds us of the system you see in some fighting games where damage is permanent after the second hit. Were games like that in your mind when this system was conceived?

No, not exactly. The regain system was something we came up with to encourage the sense that you're fighting a life-and-death struggle, one of the themes supporting this game's battle system. It changes the concept of your defense to something more proactive, and it invites you to take a more fatalistic approach to fighting, encouraging that to-the-death feel. That was both the inspiration for, and the aim of, the regain system.

The original concept called for something like a "post-attack guard". If you attack after receiving damage, you regain the damage you would have avoided if you had defended. You're taking a more proactive tactic with the attack, even though it's still after the fact. It opens up more room for on-the-fly decisions and strategies, and again, it hopefully leads to a more life-or-death approach. That was the idea, or the hope, which led to that system. The life-or-death aspect of fighting is one of the core themes of this game, and the regain system is one of the most important elements that supports this.

There's a character in the game called Patches the Spider. Is that an upgrade, or a downgrade for him? Did someone on the team have something against him?

That's not an "upgrade", exactly (laughs). There are a lot of other spider-men in the game apart from Patches, but all the others have long since gone insane. Patches, despite being exposed to enough of the world's mysteries to be transformed into a monster, has still retained his sanity and is still continuing with his research. Thinking about it that way, he's a pretty rare existence in this world. As his creator, I can't help but feel a sense of pride that he's made it this far.

We still have lots of wonderful memories from our last visit here. The only regret was that we weren't able to check out From's legendary president's office. What's inside there, anyway?

Legendary president's office? What's that? I've never heard of it (laughs). If you're talking about the office [former From president Naotoshi] Jin had, I'm afraid that's already been packed up. That, and I'd better not talk about what that office used to look like anyway. I

wouldn't want anyone getting mad at me, after all. As for my own office, well, that's not something I can really show to other people. It's just a huge mess. There's all kinds of games, videos, board games, manga, reference books, figures, and so forth all over the place. It's crazy. Even if I told you "Go ahead, check it out," I think Mr. Kokura over in the PR department would probably put a stop to it. (laughs)

Now it's even more of a mystery (laughs).

It's probably best that it remains a mystery to some extent. I think everyone on the team would agree with me there (laughs).

Here's another community question. A lot of the names for items, lands, and NPCs are very creative. How do you choose them?

I do occasionally get hints and suggestions from everyone on the team, as well as Frognation, the company that's handled the English versions of our games since Demon's Souls. But in the end, I choose all the names. That's always been the case for the titles I've directed. Names are an incredibly important part of any world you want to depict, of course, but even more than that, I just love coming up with them. I'm a bit of a naming nerd, I guess. It's always fun for me. I consider things like word origins, how it sounds in expressions, regional considerations, the whole thing. The single exception here is the titles of my games. I'm really terrible at that, and really, I never had a good experience with it (laughs).

Two final questions for you. What kind of things have you been into lately? Things you've liked, things you do often, games you've played, movies you've watched, books you like?

Hmm, that's tough. I read a ton of different books all the time, so I'll try to stick with answers relevant to our discussion (laughs). But... This isn't any particular title, but I've been getting a little sentimental lately, so sometimes I've been rereading things, or looking back and playing older games again. It's a fresh experience, since my emotional makeup is a lot different now than it was when I was younger. I still cherish a lot of works, too, and it's fun to gauge those differences. That's been a favorite pastime of mine lately. It's like I'm being amazed, just blown away at how deep really good creative works can be. But that's what's fun about them. I also work to keep abreast of the new releases in each media genre, of course, but that's kind of more an extension of my workaholic ways, and I tend to get distracted a lot from it (laughs).

Names are an incredibly important part of any world, but even more than that, I just love coming up with them.

You've created Demon's Souls, Dark Souls, and now Bloodborne. When you make these games, what kind of elements do you think serve to best support them? Also, when you make games like these, tell us what you find personally fun about the development process.

This is something I say all the time, but it all comes down to a sense of achievement. I think the essence of games lies in attaching meaning and value to the actions you take. Demon's Souls, Dark Souls and Bloodborne all have one thing in common, and that's how it places that meaning and value on the sense of achievement you can earn from playing.

That's how the battles and exploration elements work, and it applies to the world setting and story as well. You defeat powerful enemies, discover hidden locations and shortcuts, gain an understanding of the game's structure, and use the window you're given to imagine the game's world and story. My intention here is that every aspect of game design either creates or enhances the joy, or the sense of achievement, you feel as a result of these actions. That, and as for what I find fun about it... That's a difficult question. To be honest, I can't get enough of the game-director role because it's kind of like being the total overall designer for a game. If I had to give one aspect in particular, though, it'd be the map design.

Outside of the chalice dungeons, I personally laid out all of the maps in Bloodborne, something I like doing a lot. That connects to the sense of achievement I talked about, too. Adding flow and meaning to the map structure helps provide a sort of joy to the player, the fun of drawing up a map of the land in your mind. That adds value to player actions. Along those lines, it's a really game-like design, I think. I really like that kind of thing.

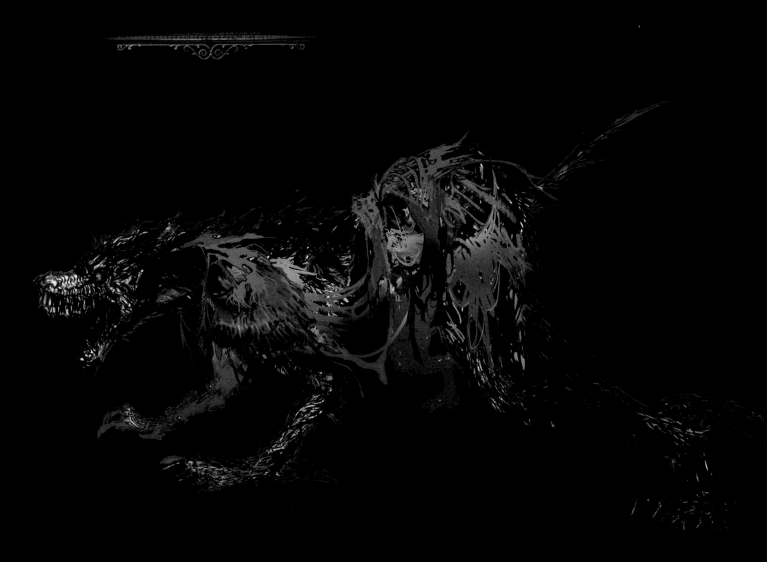

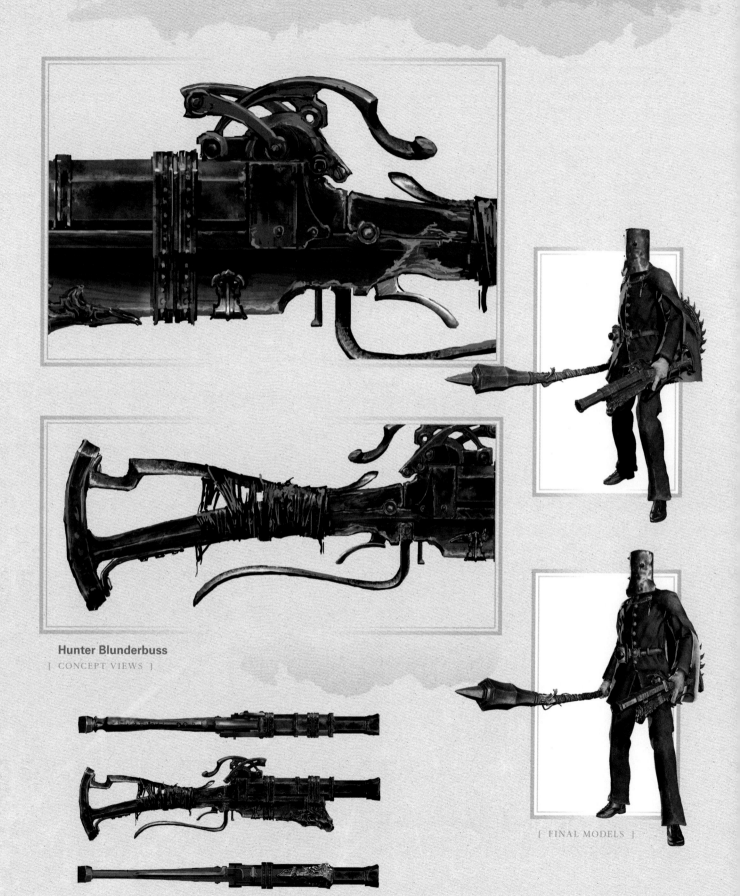

Hunter Blunderbuss

[CONCEPT VIEWS]

[FINAL MODELS]

Valtr, Master of the League
[CONCEPT ARTWORK]

Yharnam Hunter
[CONCEPT ARTWORK]

Yharnam Hunter Attire
[FINAL PIECES]

Burial Blade
[CONCEPT ARTWORK]

Foreign Attire
[ATTIRE CONCEPT ARTWORK]

Cainhurst Noble
[CONCEPT ARTWORK]

Cainhurst Attire
[FINAL PIECES]

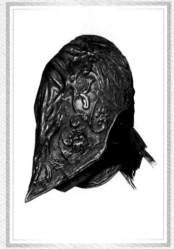

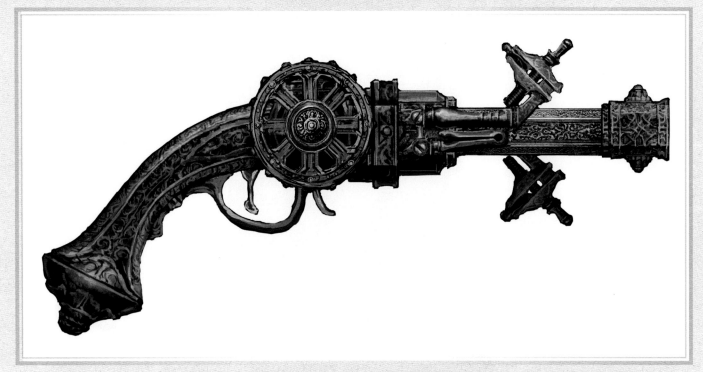

Repeating Pistol
[CONCEPT ARTWORK]

Reiterpallasch
[CONCEPT VIEWS]

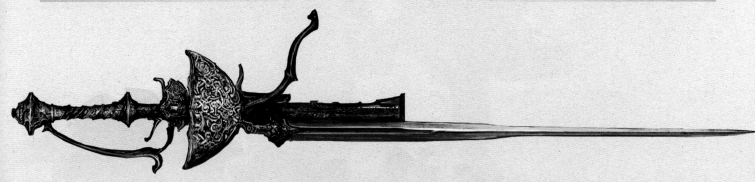

Lady Maria
of the Astral Clocktower
[CONCEPT ARTWORK]

Ludwig's Rifle
[CONCEPT VIEWS]

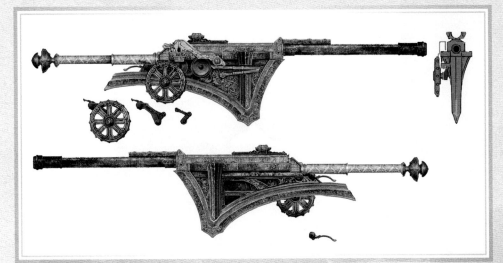

Rakuyo
[FINAL MODEL]

Maria's Attire
[FINAL PIECES]

Father Gascoigne
[CONCEPT ARTWORK]

Hunter Pistol
[CONCEPT VIEWS]

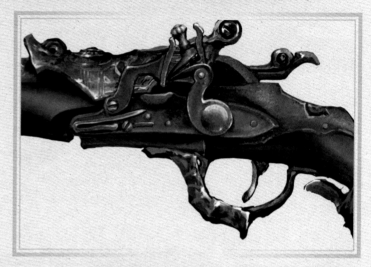

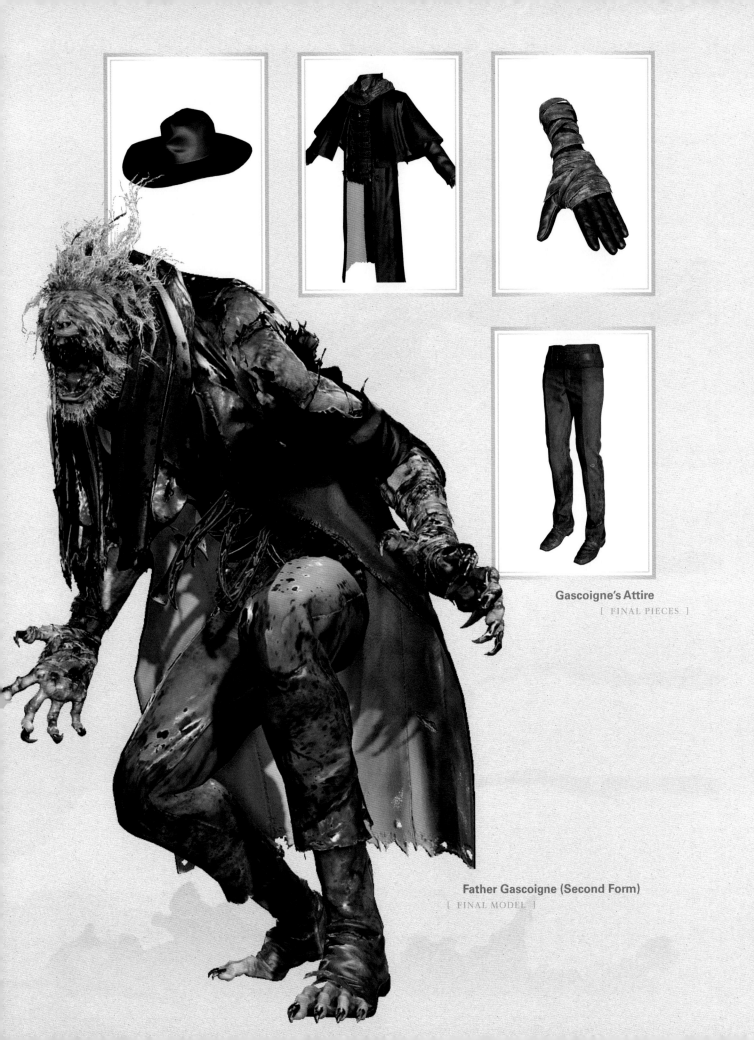

Gascoigne's Attire
[FINAL PIECES]

Father Gascoigne (Second Form)
[FINAL MODEL]

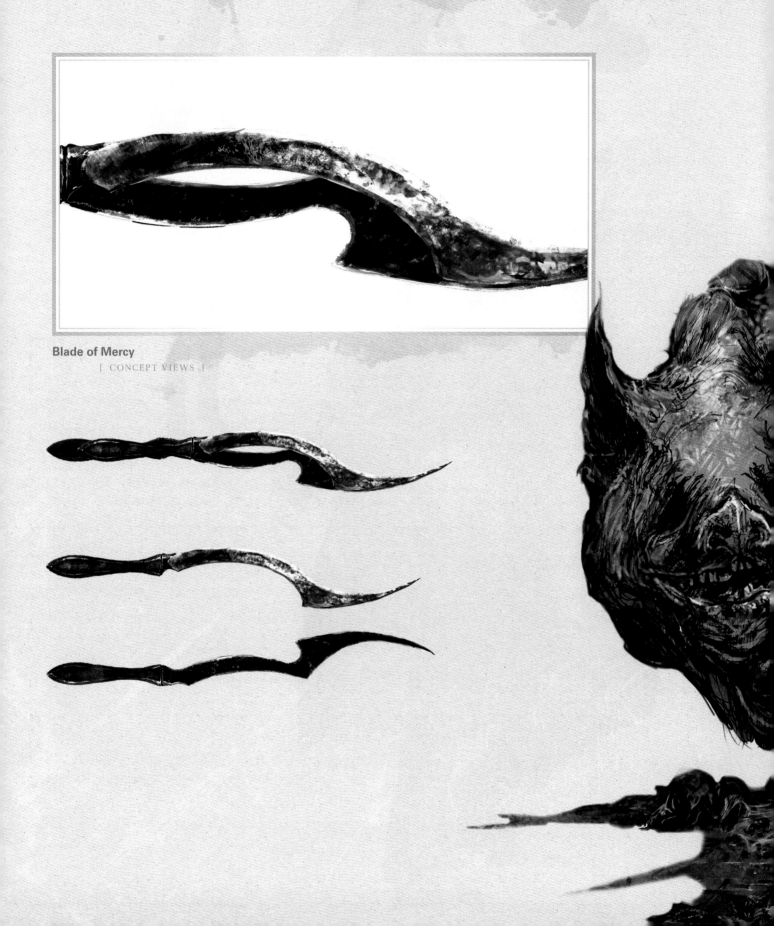

Blade of Mercy
[CONCEPT VIEWS]

Graveguard Attire
[FINAL PIECES]

Maneater Boar
[CONCEPT ARTWORK]

The Witch of Hemwick
[CONCEPT ARTWORK]

Logarius' Wheel
[CONCEPT ARTWORKS]

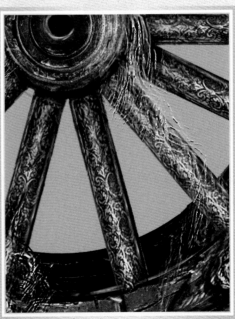

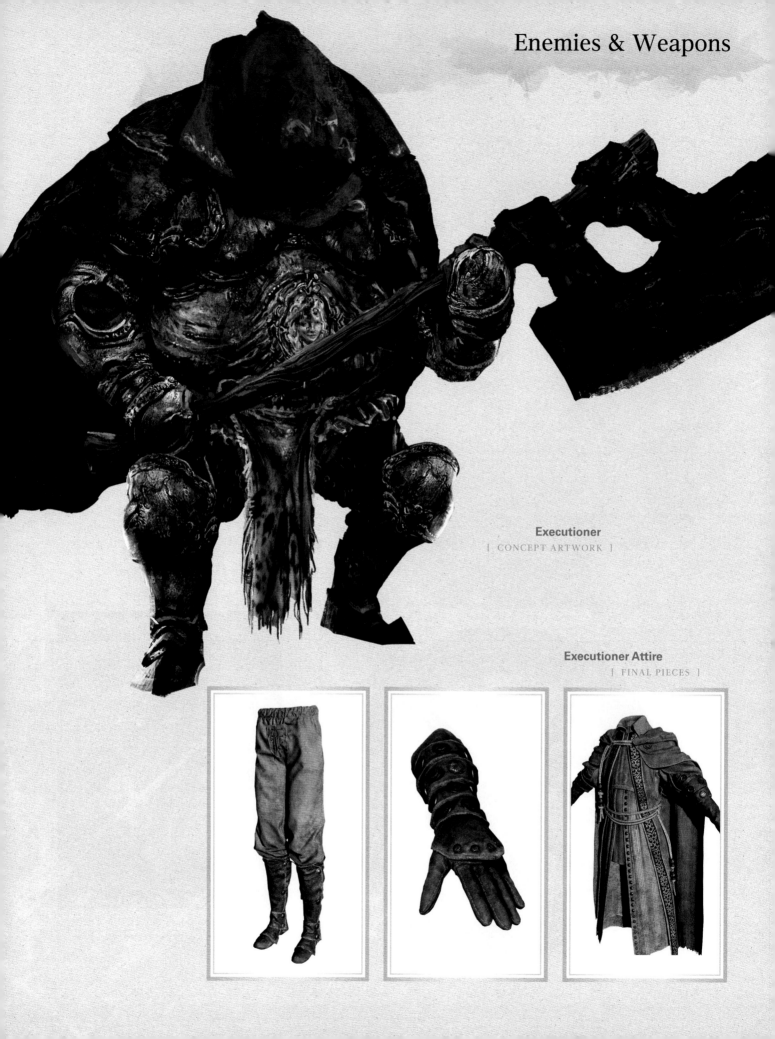

Executioner
[CONCEPT ARTWORK]

Executioner Attire
[FINAL PIECES]

Cannon
[CONCEPT VIEWS]

Alfred, Hunter of Vilebloods
[FINAL MODEL]

Rosmarinus
[CONCEPT ARTWORK]

Rifle Spear
[CONCEPT VIEWS]

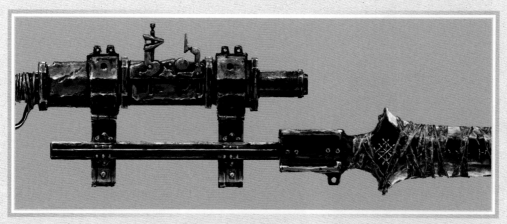

Saw Cleaver

[CONCEPT ARTWORKS]

Cleric Beast

[FINAL MODEL]

Cleric Beast
[CONCEPT ARTWORK]

Enemies & Weapons

Old Hunter
[CONCEPT ARTWORK]

Lore Index

This index lists all of the important topics you may want to research in order to piece Bloodborne's story together. Under each entry you'll find a list of items with page references, and following those will lead you to relevant lore text, all of which is taken straight from the game and collected in this book.

Index

If you're looking for the quickest way to find a particular item, this is the place to come. Everything is arranged alphabetically, and the pages linked to are the most relevant ones for the item or topic. All weapon names are also displayed in bold so that they stand out and are even easier to find. In cases where an item can be bought, a second red link will lead to the shop page you'll find it on. If an item would benefit from a link to a map position, a blue page is used in addition to its normal reference page.

6

Bloodborne

OFFICIAL COMPLETE GUIDE

FUTUREPRESS 25th Anniversary Edition

Created and published by
Future Press Verlag & Marketing GmbH
Mansteinstr. 52, 20253 Hamburg, Germany

Managing Directors	Frank Glaser
	Jörg Kraut
Editor-in-chief	Wil Murray
Senior Author	Bruce Byrne
Authors	Anwar Hassan
	Franz von Eisenheim
	Grant (Glance)
	Jenn Fern
	Lucas Hofstatter
	Marcus Sanders (ENB)
	Mike "LobosJr" Villalobos
Illustrator	Wil Murray
Assets Translator	Hirofumi Yamada
Layout	Sven Kanth
Coordinator	Ryan Payton
Stay in touch	future-press.com
	support@future-press.com
Social media	/futurepress

Credits and Thanks

© 2024 Sony Interactive Entertainment Inc. Bloodborne is a
trademark of Sony Interactive Entertainment.

© 2024 Future Press Verlag und Marketing GmbH. All rights
reserved, including the right of reproduction in whole or in part
in any form.

All other copyrights or trademarks are the property of their
respective owners and are used under license.
ISBN-13: 978-3-86-993133-3

Limits of Liability and Disclaimer of Warranty: THE AUTHOR AND
PUBLISHER MAKE NO WARRANTY OF ANY KIND, EXPRESSED
OR IMPLIED, WITH REGARD TO THESE PROGRAMS OR THE
DOCUMENTATION CONTAINED IN THIS BOOK. THE AUTHOR
AND PUBLISHER SPECIFICALLY DISCLAIM ANY WARRANTIES OF
MERCHANTABILITY OR FITNESS FOR A PARTICULAR PURPOSE.
THE AUTHOR AND PUBLISHER SHALL NOT BE LIABLE IN ANY
EVENT FOR INCIDENTAL OR CONSEQUENTIAL DAMAGES IN
CONNECTION WITH, OR ARISING OUT OF, THE FURNISHING,
PERFORMANCE, OR USE OF THESE PROGRAMS.

A sincere *THANK YOU*
to everyone at FromSoftware and Sony Interactive
Entertainment who helped us to make this book a reality.
You all have our eternal gratitude.

We would like to thank the following people in particular
for their untiring support throughout this project:

FromSoftware, Inc.	Hidetaka Miyazaki
	Yasunori Ogura
SIE JAPAN Studio	Masaaki Yamagiwa
SIE Japan Asia	Yasuhiro Kitao

Special Thanks to the following people who accompanied
and helped us during production:

SIE Europe	Anna Healy, Chris Brown, Claire Coopland, David Evans, Judy Ward, Jun Yoshino, Matthew Johnson, Mika Yokoo, Tegan Curry
SIE America	Aaron Michael McFarland, Aram Jabbari, Benn Ayinde, Brian Dunn, Dais Kawaguchi, JM Garcia, Jon Regala, Keema Moorer, Kumi Yuasa, Matt Owca, Sebastian Casallas, Tsubasa Inaba
8-4, Ltd.	Hiroko Minamoto, John Ricciardi, Justin Epperson, Mark MacDonald

Thanks to our friends & families

Jonathan Gagné, Joseph Shook, Leuca Hache, Ryan Payton,
David Waybright, Annette Byrne, Kathleen & Patrick Murray,
Ulrike, Jim & Caitlin Murray, Grit, Jil & Emmie Preuss, Katja,
Lea & Alex Glaser